PEARSON   ALWAYS LEARNING

Charles D. Miller • Vern E. Heeren • John Hornsby

Mathematical Ideas
with Appendices

Northern Virginia Community College
Second Custom Edition

Taken from:
Mathematical Ideas, Twelfth Edition
by Charles D. Miller, Vern E. Heeren, John Hornsby with Margaret L. Morrow
and Jill Van Newenhizen

Mathematical Ideas, Eleventh Edition
by Charles D. Miller, Vern E. Heeren, and John Hornsby

Mathematical Ideas, Eighth Edition
by Charles D. Miller, Vern E. Heeren, and E. John Hornsby, Jr.

Mathematical Ideas, Sixth Edition
by Charles D. Miller, Vern E. Heeren, and E. John Hornsby, Jr.

Go! Technology in Action, Complete, Fourth Edition
by Alan Evans, Kendall Martin, and Mary Anne Poatsy

ISBN 10: 1-256-34567-9
ISBN 13: 978-1-256-34567-1

CONTENTS

1 THE ART OF PROBLEM SOLVING 1

2 THE BASIC CONCEPTS OF SET THEORY 43

3 INTRODUCTION TO LOGIC 83

6 THE REAL NUMBERS AND THEIR REPRESENTATIONS 221

7 THE BASIC CONCEPTS OF ALGEBRA 283

8   GRAPHS, FUNCTIONS, AND SYSTEMS OF EQUATIONS AND INEQUALITIES 361

15 GRAPH THEORY 791

Additional Appendices

Taken from: *Mathematical Ideas*, Eighth Edition by Charles D. Miller,
        Vern E. Heeren, and E. John Hornsby, Jr.

        Mathematical Ideas, Sixth Edition by Charles D. Miller,
        Vern E. Heeren, and E. John Hornsby, Jr.

        Go! Complete, Technology in Action, Fourth Edition by Alan Evans,
        Kendall Martin, and Mary Anne Poatsy

PREFACE

After eleven editions and over four decades, *Mathematical Ideas* continues to be one of the most popular textbooks in liberal arts mathematics education. We are proud to present the twelfth edition of a text that offers non-physical science students a practical coverage that connects mathematics to the world around them. It is a flexible book that has evolved alongside changing trends but remains steadfast to its original objectives.

This edition continues to feature a theme that was introduced in the previous edition. Movies and television have become entrenched in our society and appeal to a broad range of interests. Every chapter opener contains reference to a popular movie, television show, or event, including discussion of a scene that deals with the mathematics covered in the chapter. The margin notes, long a popular hallmark of the book, include similar references. These references are indicated with a clapboard icon ▣. Many of the chapter openers and margin notes have been revised for this edition. We hope that users will enjoy visiting Hollywood while learning mathematics.

Mathematical Ideas is written with a variety of students in mind. It is well suited for several courses, including those geared toward the aforementioned liberal arts audience and survey courses in mathematics, finite mathematics, and mathematics for prospective and in-service elementary and middle-school teachers. Ample topics are included for a two-term course, yet the variety of topics and flexibility of sequence makes the text suitable for shorter courses as well. Our main objectives continue to be comprehensive coverage, appropriate organization, clear exposition, an abundance of examples, and well-planned exercise sets with numerous applications.

NEW TO THIS EDITION

- Movie and television references have been updated throughout the book.

- Pointers have been added to Examples. They guide students and provide on-the-spot reminders and warnings to avoid common pitfalls.

- Every chapter now includes an Extension, a mini-section that delves deeper into a related topic.

- Enhancing the already well-respected exercise sets, over 1000 exercises are new or modified.

- Graphing calculator screens have been redesigned and now show the output in Math-Print format (available on some TI-84 calculators).

- Figure and table references within the text are set using the same typeface as the figure or table, making it easier for students to identify and connect them.

- The text has been streamlined to make it easier for students to recognize key content.

- A completely new set of videos has been developed to support student learning outside the classroom. They are useful for online or hybrid courses, as well as student self-study, and are available on DVD and in MyMathLab.

OVERVIEW OF CHAPTERS

- **Chapter 1 (The Art of Problem Solving)** introduces the student to inductive reasoning, pattern recognition, and problem-solving techniques. We continue to provide exercises based on the monthly Calendar from *Mathematics Teacher* and have added new ones throughout this edition, beginning in Section 1.4. At the request of reviewers, Section 1.2 now includes coverage of arithmetic and geometric sequences.

- **Chapter 2 (The Basic Concepts of Set Theory)** includes updated exercises on surveys and a revised discussion of the work of Georg Cantor. (*Note:* Instructors should feel free to cover Chapter 3 before Chapter 2 if they desire.)

- **Chapter 3 (Introduction to Logic)** introduces the fundamental concepts of inductive and deductive logic. There is a new chapter opener from *Shrek the Third*. We have included additional exercises from the work of Raymond Smullyan and expanded the coverage of logical fallacies. The logic problems and Sudoku puzzles from the previous edition have been replaced with new ones.

- **Chapter 4 (Numeration Systems)** covers various types of numeration systems, as well as modular number systems. At reviewer request, we have expanded the former single section on historical numeration systems into two sections. Section 4.1 now includes full coverage of Roman numerals, and Section 4.2 discusses the Hindu-Arabic, Babylonian, Mayan, and Greek systems.

- **Chapter 5 (Number Theory)** presents an introduction to topics such as prime and composite numbers and the Fibonacci sequence. A new chapter opener appears in this edition. The former Section 5.1 was split into two sections. The new Section 5.2 (*Large Prime Numbers*) includes discussion of the ever-changing search for large primes.

- **Chapter 6 (The Real Numbers and Their Representations)** introduces some of the basic concepts of real numbers, their various forms of representation, and operations of arithmetic with them. The chapter opener is new. Most of the exercises involving real-life data have been updated, and several new ones have been included.

- **Chapter 7 (The Basic Concepts of Algebra)** can be used to present the basics of algebra (linear and quadratic equations, applications, exponents, polynomials, and factoring) to students for the first time, or as a review of previous courses. There is a new chapter opener, and applications have been updated in this chapter as well.

- **Chapter 8 (Graphs, Functions, and Systems of Equations and Inequalities)** is the second of our two algebra chapters, and continues with graphs, equations, and applications of linear, quadratic, exponential, and logarithmic functions and models. Systems of equations are covered, and in this edition we have split the former Section 8.7 into two sections, the second of which covers applications of systems. Many exercises in this chapter include updated data.

- **Chapter 9 (Geometry)** covers elementary plane geometry, transformational geometry, constructions, non-Euclidean geometry, and chaos and fractals. The new chapter opener comes from *The Simpsons,* which for two decades has provided many mathematics-education moments. At reviewer request, the order of former Sections 9.3 and 9.4 has been reversed, so that *The Geometry of Triangles: Congruence, Similarity, and the Pythagorean Theorem* now precedes *Perimeter, Area, and Circumference.*

  (*Note:* The former Chapter 10, *Trigonometry*, is now included in this edition as Chapter 14.)

- **Chapter 10 (Counting Methods)** focuses on elementary counting techniques, in preparation for the chapter to follow. We have included a completely new chapter opener on the coin toss in Super Bowl XLIV, added problems from *Mathematics Teacher*, and included a discussion of "unwanted ordering." The Extension on Magic Squares, formerly in Chapter 5, is now part of this chapter.

- **Chapter 11 (Probability)** covers the basics of probability, odds, and expected value. In this edition, we include problems from *Mathematics Teacher* for the first time.

- **Chapter 12 (Statistics)** is an introduction to statistics that focuses on the measures of central tendency, dispersion, and position and discusses the normal distribution, regression, and correlation. The new chapter opener provides a real life example of Simpson's paradox, and examples and exercises include updated data.

- **Chapter 13 (Personal Financial Management)** provides the student with the basics of the mathematics of finance as applied to inflation, consumer debt, and house buying. We include a section on investing, with emphasis on stocks, bonds, and mutual funds. Examples and exercises have been updated to reflect current interest rates and investment returns. A new Extension, *Ponzi Schemes and Other Investment Frauds*, has been added to this edition.

- **Chapter 14 (Trigonometry)** was formerly Chapter 10. It provides an introduction to some basic concepts of plane trigonometry, including angles in standard position, right angle trigonometry, and the laws of sines and cosines.

- **Chapter 15 (Graph Theory)** covers the basic concepts of graph theory and its applications. We have reformatted much of the discussion for easier reading.

- **Chapter 16 (Voting and Apportionment)** deals with issues in voting methods and apportionment of votes, topics which have become increasingly popular in liberal arts mathematics courses. A new chapter opener features the 2008 movie *Swing Vote*, and we have revised and streamlined exposition (particularly in Section 16.3) for readability. A new Extension, *Two Additional Apportionment Methods*, is now included.

COURSE OUTLINE CONSIDERATIONS

Chapters in the text are, in most cases, independent and may be covered in the order chosen by the instructor. The few exceptions are as follows:

- Chapter 6 contains some material dependent on the ideas found in Chapter 5.

- Chapter 6 should be covered before Chapter 7 if student background so dictates.

- Chapters 7 and 8 form an algebraic "package" and should be covered in sequential order.

- A thorough coverage of Chapter 11 depends on knowledge of Chapter 10 material, although probability can be covered without teaching extensive counting methods by avoiding the more difficult exercises.

- The latter part of Chapter 12, on inferential statistics, depends on an understanding of probability (Chapter 11).

- Chapter 14 requires some basic equation-solving ability.

FEATURES OF THE TWELFTH EDITION

ENHANCED Chapter Openers In keeping with the Hollywood theme, chapter openers address a scene or situation from a popular movie or a television series or event. Many are new to this edition. Some openers illustrate the correct use of mathematics, while others address how mathematics is misused. In the latter case, we subscribe to the premise that we can all learn from the mistakes of others. Some openers include a problem statement that the reader is asked to solve. We hope that you enjoy reading these chapter openers as much as we have enjoyed preparing them.

ENHANCED **Varied Exercise Sets** We continue to present a variety of exercises that integrate drill, conceptual, and applied problems and have included over 1000 new or modified exercises to this edition. The text contains a wealth of exercises to provide students with opportunities to practice, apply, connect, and extend the mathematical skills they are learning. We have updated the exercises that focus on real-life data and have retained their titles for easy identification. Several chapters are enriched with new applications, particularly Chapters 6, 7, 8, 11, 12, and 13. We continue to use graphs, tables, and charts when appropriate. Many of the graphs use a style similar to that seen by students in today's print and electronic media.

ENHANCED **Margin Notes** This popular feature is a hallmark of this text and has been retained and updated where appropriate. These notes are interspersed throughout the text and deal with various subjects such as lives of mathematicians, historical vignettes, philatelic and numismatic reproductions, anecdotes on mathematics textbooks of the past, newspaper and magazine articles, and current research in mathematics. Several new Hollywood-related margin notes have also been added.

ENHANCED **Extensions** These mini-sections delve deeper into related topics and include their own exercise sets. New Extensions have been written for chapters that previously did not have this feature.

Collaborative Investigations The importance of cooperative learning is addressed in this end-of-chapter feature.

Problem-Solving Hints Special paragraphs labeled "Problem-Solving Hint" relate the discussion of problem-solving strategies to techniques that have been presented earlier.

ENHANCED **Optional Graphing Technology** We continue to provide sample graphing calculator screens to show how technology can be used to support results found analytically. These screens have been re-designed and now show the output in MathPrint format. It is not essential, however, that a student have a graphing calculator to study from this text. *The technology component is optional.*

Art Program The text continues to feature a full-color design. Color is used for instructional emphasis in text discussions, examples, graphs, and figures. Many new photos have been incorporated to provide visual appeal.

For Further Thought These entries encourage students to share amongst themselves their reasoning processes to gain a deeper understanding of key mathematical concepts.

Example Titles The numerous, carefully selected examples that illustrate concepts and skills are titled so that students can see at a glance the topic under consideration.

UPDATED **Emphasis on Real Data in the Form of Graphs, Charts, and Tables** We continue to use up-to-date information from magazines, newspapers, and the Internet to create real applications that are relevant and meaningful.

Chapter Tests Each chapter concludes with a chapter test so that students can check their mastery of the material.

SUPPLEMENTS

STUDENT SUPPLEMENTS

Student's Solutions Manual
ISBN-10: 0-321-69384-1; ISBN-13: 978-0-321-69384-6

- This manual by Carrie Green provides solutions to the odd-numbered exercises in the exercise sets, the Extensions, and the Appendix exercises, as well as solutions for all the Chapter Test exercises.

Video Resources on DVD with Optional Captioning
ISBN-10: 0-321-71649-3; ISBN-13: 978-0-321-71649-1

- This completely new set of videos was developed by Sue Glascoe of Mesa Community College. Making use of newer teaching technologies, the videos clearly cover important definitions, procedures, and concepts by working through examples and exercises from the textbook. They are ideal for online and hybrid courses, as well as supplemental instruction for traditional courses. Optional subtitles are available.

INSTRUCTOR SUPPLEMENTS

Annotated Instructor's Edition
ISBN-10: 0-321-69406-6; ISBN-13: 978-0-321-69406-5

- This special edition of the text provides answers next to the text exercises for quick reference, when space is available. Longer answers, indicated by an icon ⊡ after the exercise, can be found in the back of the book.

Instructor's Solutions Manual
ISBN-10: 0-321-69405-8; ISBN-13: 978-0-321-69405-8

- This manual by Carrie Green contains solutions to all end-of-section exercises, Extension, Chapter Test, and Appendix exercises.

ENHANCED ### Insider's Guide with Math Goes to Hollywood Teaching Notes
ISBN-10: 0-321-71643-4; ISBN-13: 978-0-321-71643-9

- This updated guide now includes detailed *Math Goes to Hollywood* teaching notes to help instructors integrate the movies from the text into their courses. The new movie notes include the name of the movie, clip segment times, related mathematical topics, correlation to the text, summary of mathematical content, and discussion questions.

- The *Insider's Guide* includes resources to help faculty with course preparation and classroom management. It provides helpful teaching tips correlated to each section of the text, as well as general teaching advice.

Instructor's Testing Manual (online only)
- This manual contains four tests for each chapter of the text. Answer keys are included.

TestGen® (online only)
- TestGen enables instructors to build, edit, print, and administer tests using a computerized bank of questions developed to cover all text objectives.

PowerPoint Lecture Presentation (online only)
- These fully editable lecture slides include definitions, key concepts, and examples for use in a lecture setting and are available for each section of the text.

Online supplements can be found in MyMathLab or downloaded from www.pearsonhighered.com/irc.

MEDIA SUPPLEMENTS

MyMathLab

MyMathLab® Online Course

MyMathLab® is a text-specific, easily customizable online course that integrates interactive multimedia instruction with textbook content. MyMathLab gives instructors the tools they need to deliver all or a portion of their course online, whether their students are in a lab setting or working from home.

- **Interactive homework exercises**, correlated to the textbook at the objective level, are algorithmically generated for unlimited practice and mastery. Most exercises are free-response and provide guided solutions, sample problems, and tutorial learning aids for extra help.

- **Personalized Study Plan,** generated when students complete a test or quiz, indicates which topics have been mastered and links to tutorial exercises for topics students have not mastered. The Study Plan can be customized so that the topics available match course contents or so that students' homework results determine mastery.

- **Multimedia learning aids**, such as video lectures and podcasts, animations, and a complete multimedia textbook, help students independently improve their understanding and performance. Instructors can assign these multimedia learning aids as homework to help students grasp the concepts.

- **Homework and Test Manager** allows instructors to assign homework, quizzes, and tests that are automatically graded. They can select just the right mix of questions from the MyMathLab exercise bank, instructor-created custom exercises, and/or Test-Gen® test items.

- **Gradebook,** designed specifically for mathematics and statistics, automatically tracks students' results, lets instructors stay on top of student performance, and gives them control over how to calculate final grades. They can also add offline (paper-and-pencil) grades to the gradebook.

- **MathXL Exercise Builder** allows instructors to create static and algorithmic exercises for their online assignments. They can use the library of sample exercises as an easy starting point, or they can edit any course-related exercise.

- **Pearson Tutor Center** (www.pearsontutorservices.com) access is automatically included with MyMathLab. The Tutor Center is staffed by qualified math instructors who provide textbook-specific tutoring for students via toll-free phone, fax, email, and interactive Web sessions.

- **Specific features for *Mathematical Ideas*** include
  - Completely new concept review videos
  - Interactive mathematics and societal timeline

Students using MyMathLab® do their assignments in the Flash®-based MathXL Player, which is compatible with almost any browser (Firefox®, Safari™, or Internet Explorer®) on almost any platform (Macintosh® or Windows®). MyMathLab is powered by CourseCompass™, Pearson Education's online teaching and learning environment, and by MathXL®, our online homework, tutorial, and assessment system. MyMathLab is available to qualified adopters. For more information, visit www.mymathlab.com or contact your Pearson representative.

Math XL

MathXL® Online Course

MathXL® is an online homework, tutorial, and assessment system that accompanies Pearson's textbooks in mathematics or statistics.

- **Interactive homework exercises**, correlated to the textbook at the objective level, are algorithmically generated for unlimited practice and mastery. Most exercises are free-response and provide guided solutions, sample problems, and learning aids for extra help.

- **Personalized Study Plan,** generated when students complete a test or quiz or homework, indicates which topics have been mastered and links to tutorial exercises for topics students have not mastered. Instructors can customize the available topics in the study plan to match their course concepts.

- **Multimedia learning aids**, such as video lectures and animations, help students independently improve their understanding and performance. These are assignable as homework, to further encourage their use.

- **Gradebook,** designed specifically for mathematics and statistics, automatically tracks students' results, lets instructors stay informed of student performance, and gives them control over how to calculate final grades.

- **MathXL Exercise Builder** allows instructors to create static and algorithmic exercises for their online assignments. They can use the library of sample exercises as an easy starting point or the Exercise Builder to edit any of the course-related exercises.

- **Homework and Test Manager** lets instructors create online homework, quizzes, and tests that are automatically graded. They can select just the right mix of questions from the MathXL exercise bank, instructor-created custom exercises, and/or TestGen test items.

The new, Flash®-based MathXL Player is compatible with almost any browser (Firefox®, Safari™, or Internet Explorer®) on almost any platform (Macintosh® or Windows®). MathXL is available to qualified adopters. For more information, visit our website at www.mathxl.com, or contact your Pearson representative.

ACKNOWLEDGMENTS

We wish to thank the following reviewers for their helpful comments and suggestions for this and previous editions of the text. (Reviewers of the twelfth edition are noted with an asterisk.)

H. Achepohl, *College of DuPage*

Shahrokh Ahmadi, *Northern Virginia Community College*

Richard Andrews, *Florida A&M University*

Cindy Anfinson, *Palomar College*

*Erika Asano, *University of South Florida, St. Petersburg*

Elaine Barber, *Germanna Community College*

Anna Baumgartner, *Carthage College*

James E. Beamer, *Northeastern State University*

Elliot Benjamin, *Unity College*

Jaime Bestard, *Barry University*

Joyce Blair, *Belmont University*

Gus Brar, *Delaware County Community College*

Roger L. Brown, *Davenport College*

Douglas Burke, *Malcolm X College*

John Busovicki, *Indiana University of Pennsylvania*

Ann Cascarelle, *St. Petersburg Junior College*

Kenneth Chapman, *St. Petersburg Junior College*

Gordon M. Clarke, *University of the Incarnate Word*

M. Marsha Cupitt, *Durham Technical Community College*

James Curry, *American River College*

Rosemary Danaher, *Sacred Heart University*

Ken Davis, *Mesa State College*

Nancy Davis, *Brunswick Community College*

George DeRise, *Thomas Nelson Community College*

Catherine Dermott, *Hudson Valley Community College*

Greg Dietrich, *Florida Community College at Jacksonville*

*Vincent Dimiceli, *Oral Roberts University*

Diana C. Dwan, *Yavapai College*

Laura Dyer, *Belleville Area College*

Jan Eardley, *Barat College*

Joe Eitel, *Folsom College*

Azin Enshai, *American River College*

Gayle Farmer, *Northeastern State University*

Michael Farndale, *Waldorf College*

Gordon Feathers, *Passaic County Community College*

Thomas Flohr, *New River Community College*

Bill Fulton, *Black Hawk College—East*

Anne Gardner, *Wenatchee Valley College*

*Justin M. Gash, *Franklin College*

Donald Goral, *Northern Virginia Community College*

Glen Granzow, *Idaho State University*

Larry Green, *Lake Tahoe Community College*

Arthur D. Grissinger, *Lock Haven University*

Don Hancock, *Pepperdine University*

Denis Hanson, *University of Regina*

Marilyn Hasty, *Southern Illinois University*

Shelby L. Hawthorne, *Thomas Nelson Community College*

Jeff Heiking, *St. Petersburg Junior College*

Laura Hillerbrand, *Broward Community College*

*Corinne Irwin, *University of Texas at Austin*

Jacqueline Jensen, *Sam Houston State University*

Emanuel Jinich, *Endicott College*

Frank Juric, *Brevard Community College-Palm Bay*

Karla Karstens, *University of Vermont*

*Najam Khaja, *Centennial College*

Hilary Kight, *Wesleyan College*

Barbara J. Kniepkamp, *Southern Illinois University at Edwardsville*

Suda Kunyosying, *Shepherd College*

Yu-Ju Kuo, *Indiana University of Pennsylvania*

*Stephane Lafortune, *College of Charleston*

Pam Lamb, *J. Sargeant Reynolds Community College*

John Lattanzio, *Indiana University of Pennsylvania*

John W. Legge, *Pikeville College*

*Dawn Locklear, *Crown College*

*Bin Lu, *California State University, Sacramento*

Leo Lusk, *Gulf Coast Community College*

Sherrie Lutsch, *Northwest Indian College*

Rhonda Macleod, *Florida State University*

Andrew Markoe, *Rider University*

Darlene Marnich, *Point Park College*

Victoria Martinez, *Okaloosa Walton Community College*

Chris Mason, *Community College of Vermont*

Mark Maxwell, *Maryville University*

Carol McCarron, *Harrisburg Area Community College*

Delois McCormick, *Germanna Community College*

Daisy McCoy, *Lyndon State College*

Cynthia McGinnis, *Okaloosa Walton Community College*

Vena McGrath, *Davenport College*

Robert Moyer, *Fort Valley State University*

Shai Neumann, *Brevard Community College*

Barbara Nienstedt, *Gloucester County College*

Chaitanya Nigam, *Gateway Community-Technical College*

Vladimir Nikiforov, *University of Memphis*

*Vicky Ohlson, *Trenholm State Technical College*

Jean Okumura, *Windward Community College*

*Stan Perrine, *Charleston Southern University*

Bob Phillips, *Mesabi Range Community College*

Kathy Pinchback, *University of Memphis*

Priscilla Putman, *New Jersey City University*

Scott C. Radtke, *Davenport College*

*Doraiswamy Ramachandran, *California State University, Sacramento*

John Reily, *Montclair State University*

Beth Reynolds, *Mater Dei College*

Shirley I. Robertson, *High Point University*

Andrew M. Rockett, *CW Post Campus of Long Island University*

Kathleen Rodak, *St. Mary's College of Ave Maria University*

*Cynthia Roemer, *Union County College*

*Lisa Rombes, *Washtenaw Community College*

Abby Roscum, *Marshalltown Community College*

D. Schraeder, *McLennan Community College*

Wilfred Schulte, *Cosumnes River College*

Melinda Schulteis, *Concordia University*

Gary D. Shaffer, *Allegany College of Maryland*

Doug Shaw, *University of North Iowa*

Jane Sinibaldi, *York College of Pennsylvania*

*Nancy Skocik, *California University of Pennsylvania*

Larry Smith, *Peninsula College*

Marguerite Smith, *Merced College*

Charlene D. Snow, *Lower Columbia College*

H. Jeannette Stephens, *Whatcom Community College*

Suzanne J. Stock, *Oakton Community College*

*Dawn M. Strickland, *Winthrop University*

Dian Thom, *McKendree College*

Claude C. Thompson, *Hollins University*

Mark Tom, *College of the Sequoias*

Ida Umphers, *University of Arkansas at Little Rock*

Karen Villarreal, *University of New Orleans*

*Dr. Karen Walters, *Northern Virginia Community College*

Wayne Wanamaker, *Central Florida Community College*

David Wasilewski, *Luzerne County Community College*

William Watkins, *California State University, Northridge*

*Alice Williamson, *Sussex County Community College*

Susan Williford, *Columbia State Community College*

Tom Witten, *Southwest Virginia Community College*

Fred Worth, *Henderson State University*

Rob Wylie, *Carl Albert State College*

Henry Wyzinski, *Indiana University Northwest*

A project of this magnitude cannot be accomplished without the help of many other dedicated individuals. Marnie Greenhut served as acquisitions editor for this edition. Carol Merrigan provided excellent production supervision. Anne Kelly, Greg Tobin, Tracy Patruno, Roxanne McCarley, Elle Driska, and Christine O'Brien of Pearson Addison-Wesley gave us their unwavering support.

Beth Anderson continued to provide outstanding photo research. Terry McGinnis gave her usual excellent behind-the-scenes guidance. Thanks go to Dr. Margaret L. Morrow of Plattsburgh State University and Dr. Jill Van Newenhizen of Lake Forest College, who wrote the material on graph theory and voting/apportionment, respectively. Chris Heeren and Paul Lorczak did an outstanding job of accuracy- and answer-checking. Mike McCraith of Cuyahoga Community College joined the cast with the addition of new movie cards. And finally, we thank our loyal users over these many editions for making this book one of the most successful in its market.

Vern E. Heeren

John Hornsby

THE ART OF PROBLEM SOLVING

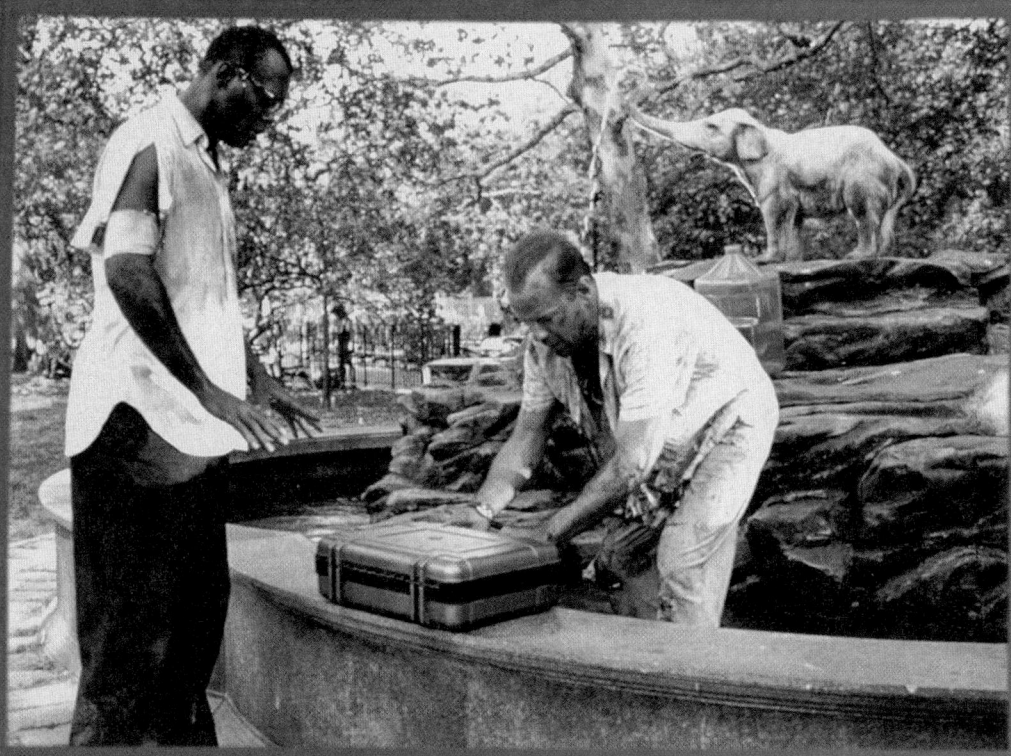

The 1995 movie *Die Hard: With a Vengeance* stars Bruce Willis as New York Detective John McClane. In this film, McClane is tormented by villain Simon Gruber (Jeremy Irons), who plants bombs around the city and poses riddles and puzzles for disarming them. In one situation, Simon gives McClane and store owner Zeus Carver (Samuel L. Jackson) the following riddle by telephone to solve in 5 minutes.

> *On the fountain there should be two jugs. Do you see them? A 5-gallon and a 3-gallon. Fill one of the jugs with exactly 4 gallons of water, and place it on the scale, and the timer will stop. You must be precise. One ounce more or less will result in detonation.*

McClane and Carver were able to solve the riddle and defuse the bomb. Can you solve it? The answer is on page 2.

1

1.1 SOLVING PROBLEMS BY INDUCTIVE REASONING

Characteristics of Inductive and Deductive Reasoning • Pitfalls of Inductive Reasoning

Solution to the Chapter Opener Problem This is one way to do it: With both jugs empty, fill the 3-gallon jug and pour its contents into the 5-gallon jug. Then fill the 3-gallon jug again, and pour it into the 5-gallon jug until the latter is filled. There is now (3 + 3) − 5 = 1 gallon in the 3-gallon jug. Empty the 5-gallon jug, and pour the 1 gallon of water from the 3-gallon jug into the 5-gallon jug. Finally, fill the 3-gallon jug and pour all of it into the 5-gallon jug, resulting in 1 + 3 = 4 gallons in the 5-gallon jug.

(*Note*: There is another way to solve this problem. See if you can discover the alternative solution.)

Characteristics of Inductive and Deductive Reasoning

The development of mathematics can be traced to the Egyptian and Babylonian cultures (3000 B.C.–A.D. 260) as a necessity for problem solving. To solve a problem or perform an operation, a cookbook-like recipe was given, and it was performed repeatedly to solve similar problems.

By observing that a specific method worked for a certain type of problem, the Babylonians and the Egyptians concluded that the same method would work for any similar type of problem. Such a conclusion is called a *conjecture*. A **conjecture** is an educated guess based on repeated observations of a particular process or pattern. The method of reasoning we have just described is called *inductive reasoning*.

Inductive Reasoning

Inductive reasoning is characterized by drawing a general conclusion (making a conjecture) from repeated observations of specific examples. The conjecture may or may not be true.

In testing a conjecture obtained by inductive reasoning, it takes only one example that does not work to prove the conjecture false. Such an example is called a **counterexample.**

Inductive reasoning provides a powerful method of drawing conclusions, but there is no assurance that the observed conjecture will always be true. For this reason, mathematicians are reluctant to accept a conjecture as an absolute truth until it is formally proved using methods of *deductive reasoning*. Deductive reasoning characterized the development and approach of Greek mathematics, as seen in the works of Euclid, Pythagoras, Archimedes, and others. During the classical Greek period (600 B.C.–A.D. 450), general concepts were applied to specific problems, resulting in a structured, logical development of mathematics.

Deductive Reasoning

Deductive reasoning is characterized by applying general principles to specific examples.

We now look at examples of these two types of reasoning. In this chapter, we often refer to the **natural,** or **counting, numbers:**

$$1, 2, 3, \ldots \quad \text{Natural (counting) numbers}$$

↑
Ellipsis points

The three dots (*ellipsis points*) indicate that the numbers continue indefinitely in the pattern that has been established. The most probable rule for continuing this pattern is "add 1 to the previous number," and this is indeed the rule that we follow.

Now consider the following list of natural numbers:

$$2, 9, 16, 23, 30.$$

What is the next number of this list? What is the pattern? After studying the numbers, we might see that $2 + 7 = 9$, and $9 + 7 = 16$. Do we add 16 and 7 to get 23?

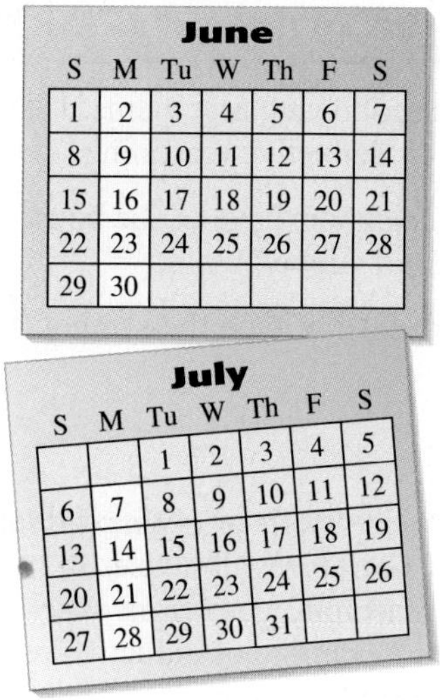

June

S	M	Tu	W	Th	F	S
1	2	3	4	5	6	7
8	9	10	11	12	13	14
15	16	17	18	19	20	21
22	23	24	25	26	27	28
29	30					

July

S	M	Tu	W	Th	F	S
		1	2	3	4	5
6	7	8	9	10	11	12
13	14	15	16	17	18	19
20	21	22	23	24	25	26
27	28	29	30	31		

Figure 1

Do we add 23 and 7 to get 30? Yes. It seems that any number in the given list can be found by adding 7 to the preceding number, so the next number in the list would be $30 + 7 = 37$.

We set out to find the "next number" by reasoning from observation of the numbers in the list. We may have jumped from these observations to the general statement that any number in the list is 7 more than the preceding number. This is an example of *inductive reasoning*.

By using inductive reasoning, we concluded that 37 was the next number. Suppose the person making up the list has another answer in mind. The list of numbers

$$2, 9, 16, 23, 30$$

actually gives the dates of Mondays in June if June 1 falls on a Sunday. The next Monday after June 30 is July 7. With this pattern, the list continues as

$$2, 9, 16, 23, 30, 7, 14, 21, 28, \ldots.$$

See the calendar in **Figure 1**. The correct answer would then be 7. The process used to obtain the rule "add 7" in the preceding list reveals a main flaw of inductive reasoning. *We can never be sure that what is true in a specific case will be true in general. Inductive reasoning does not guarantee a true result, but it does provide a means of making a conjecture.*

We now review some basic notation. Throughout this book, we use *exponents* to represent repeated multiplication.

$$\text{Base} \rightarrow 4^3 = 4 \cdot 4 \cdot 4 = 64 \quad \text{4 is used as a factor 3 times.}$$

$$\uparrow$$
$$\text{Exponent}$$

Exponential Expression

If a is a number and n is a counting number $(1, 2, 3, \ldots)$, then the exponential expression a^n is defined as follows.

$$a^n = \underbrace{a \cdot a \cdot a \cdot \ldots \cdot a}_{n \text{ factors of } a}$$

The number a is the **base** and n is the **exponent.**

With deductive reasoning, we use general statements and apply them to specific situations. For example, consider the **Pythagorean theorem:**

In any right triangle, the sum of the squares of the legs (shorter sides) is equal to the square of the hypotenuse (longest side).

Thus, if we know that the lengths of the shorter sides are 3 inches and 4 inches, we can find the length of the longest side. Let h represent the length of the longest side.

$$3^2 + 4^2 = h^2 \quad \text{Pythagorean theorem}$$
$$9 + 16 = h^2 \quad 3^2 = 3 \cdot 3 = 9; 4^2 = 4 \cdot 4 = 16$$
$$25 = h^2 \quad \text{Add.}$$
$$5 = h \quad \text{The positive square root of 25 is 5.}$$

Thus, the longest side measures 5 inches. We used the general rule (the Pythagorean theorem) and applied it to the specific situation.

Reasoning through a problem usually requires certain *premises*. A **premise** can be an assumption, law, rule, widely held idea, or observation. Then reason inductively or deductively from the premises to obtain a **conclusion.** The premises and conclusion make up a **logical argument.**

▮▮ **EXAMPLE 1** Identifying Premises and Conclusions

Identify each premise and the conclusion in each of the following arguments. Then tell whether each argument is an example of inductive or deductive reasoning.

(a) Our house is made of adobe. Both of my next-door neighbors have adobe houses. Therefore, all houses in our neighborhood are made of adobe.

(b) All keyboards have the symbol @. I have a keyboard. I can type the symbol @.

(c) Today is Tuesday. Tomorrow will be Wednesday.

SOLUTION

(a) The premises are "Our house is made of adobe" and "Both of my next-door neighbors have adobe houses." The conclusion is "Therefore, all houses in our neighborhood are made of adobe." Because the reasoning goes from specific examples to a general statement, the argument is an example of inductive reasoning (although it may very well have a false conclusion).

(b) Here, the premises are "All keyboards have the symbol @" and "I have a keyboard." The conclusion is "I can type the symbol @." This reasoning goes from general to specific, so deductive reasoning was used.

(c) There is only one premise here, "Today is Tuesday." The conclusion is "Tomorrow will be Wednesday." The fact that Wednesday immediately follows Tuesday is being used, even though this fact is not explicitly stated. Because the conclusion comes from general facts that apply to this special case, deductive reasoning was used. ▮▮▮

The earlier calendar example illustrated how inductive reasoning may, at times, lead to false conclusions. However, in many cases, inductive reasoning does provide correct results if we look for the most *probable* answer.

▮▮ **EXAMPLE 2** Predicting the Next Number in a Sequence

Use inductive reasoning to determine the *probable* next number in each list below.

(a) 5, 9, 13, 17, 21, 25, 29   **(b)** 1, 1, 2, 3, 5, 8, 13, 21   **(c)** 2, 4, 8, 16, 32

SOLUTION

(a) Each number in the list is obtained by adding 4 to the previous number. The probable next number is $29 + 4 = 33$. (This is an example of an *arithmetic sequence*.)

(b) Beginning with the third number in the list, 2, each number is obtained by adding the two previous numbers in the list. That is,

$$1 + 1 = 2, \quad 1 + 2 = 3, \quad 2 + 3 = 5,$$

and so on. The probable next number in the list is $13 + 21 = 34$. (These are the first few terms of the famous *Fibonacci sequence*.)

(c) It appears here that to obtain each number after the first, we must double the previous number. Therefore, the most probable next number is $32 \times 2 = 64$. (This is an example of a *geometric sequence*.) ▮▮▮

In the 2003 movie *A Wrinkle in Time*, young Charles Wallace, played by David Dorfman, is challenged to identify a particular sequence of numbers. He correctly identifies it as the **Fibonacci sequence.**

Inductive reasoning often can be used to predict an answer in a list of similarly constructed computation exercises, as shown in the next example.

EXAMPLE 3   Predicting the Product of Two Numbers

Consider the list of equations. Predict the next multiplication fact in the list.

$$37 \times 3 = 111$$
$$37 \times 6 = 222$$
$$37 \times 9 = 333$$
$$37 \times 12 = 444$$

SOLUTION

The left side of each equation has two factors, the first 37 and the second a multiple of 3, beginning with 3. Each product (answer) consists of three digits, all the same, beginning with 111 for 37×3. Thus, the next multiplication fact would be

$$37 \times 15 = 555, \quad \text{which is indeed true.} \qquad ▮▮▮$$

Table 1

Number of Points	Number of Regions
1	1
2	2
3	4
4	8
5	16

Pitfalls of Inductive Reasoning

There are pitfalls associated with inductive reasoning. A classic example involves the maximum number of regions formed when chords are constructed in a circle. When two points on a circle are joined with a line segment, a *chord* is formed.

Locate a single point on a circle. Because no chords are formed, a single interior region is formed. See **Figure 2(a)**. Locate two points and draw a chord. Two interior regions are formed, as shown in **Figure 2(b)**. Continue this pattern. Locate three points, and draw all possible chords. Four interior regions are formed, as shown in **Figure 2(c)**. Four points yield 8 regions and five points yield 16 regions. See **Figures 2(d) and 2(e)**.

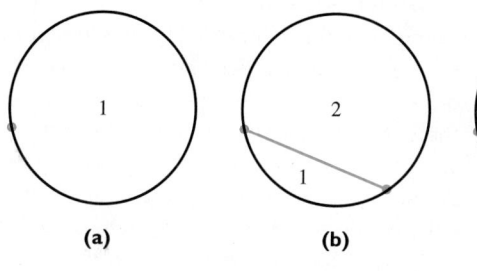
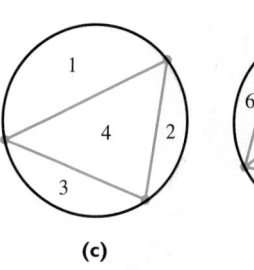
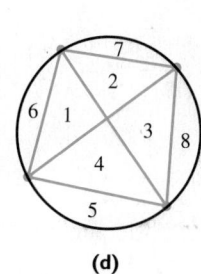
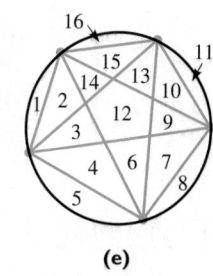

(a)   (b)   (c)   (d)   (e)

Figure 2

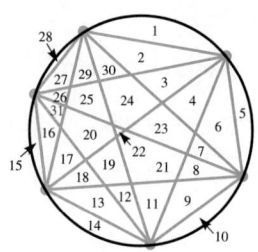

Figure 3

The results of the preceding observations are summarized in **Table 1** in the margin. The pattern formed in the column headed "Number of Regions" is the same one we saw in **Example 2(c)**, where we predicted that the next number would be 64. It seems here that for each additional point on the circle, the number of regions doubles. A reasonable inductive conjecture would be that for six points, 32 regions would be formed. But as **Figure 3** indicates, there are *only 31 regions*. The pattern of doubling ends when the sixth point is considered. Adding a seventh point would yield 57 regions. The numbers obtained here are

$$1, 2, 4, 8, 16, 31, 57.$$

For n points on the circle, the number of regions is given by the formula

$$\frac{n^4 - 6n^3 + 23n^2 - 18n + 24}{24}. \; *$$

---

*For more information on this and other similar patterns, see "Counting Pizza Pieces and Other Combinatorial Problems," by Eugene Maier, in the January 1988 issue of *Mathematics Teacher*, pp. 22–26.

We can use a graphing calculator to construct a table of values that indicates the number of regions for various numbers of points. Using X rather than *n*, we can define Y_1 using the expression given on the previous page. (see **Figure 4(a)**). Then, creating a table of values, as in **Figure 4(b)**, we see how many regions (indicated by Y_1) there are for any number of points (X).

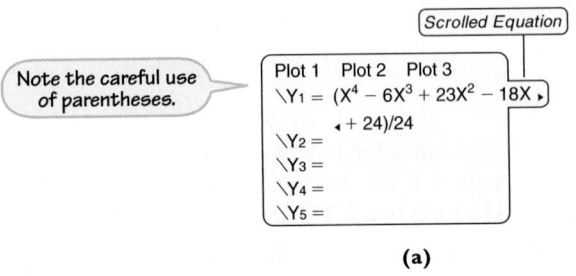

(a)   (b)

Figure 4

For Further Thought

Inductive Reasoning Anecdote

The following anecdote concerning inductive reasoning appears in the first volume of the *In Mathematical Circles* series by Howard Eves.

A scientist had two large jars before him on the laboratory table. The jar on his left contained 100 fleas; the jar on his right was empty. The scientist carefully lifted a flea from the jar on the left, placed the flea on the table between the two jars, stepped back, and in a loud voice said, "Jump." The flea jumped and was put in the jar on the right. A second flea was carefully lifted from the jar on the left and placed on the table

between the two jars. Again the scientist stepped back and in a loud voice said, "Jump." The flea jumped and was put in the jar on the right. In the same manner, the scientist treated each of the 100 fleas in the jar on the left, and each flea jumped as ordered.

The two jars were then interchanged and the experiment continued with a slight difference. This time the scientist carefully lifted a flea from the jar on the left, yanked off its hind legs, placed the flea on the table between the jars, stepped back, and in a loud voice said, "Jump." The flea did not jump, and was put in the jar on the right. A second flea was carefully lifted from the jar on the left, its hind legs yanked off, and then placed on the table between the two jars. Again the scientist stepped back and in a loud voice said, "Jump." The flea did not jump, and was put in the jar on the right. In this manner, the scientist treated each of the 100 fleas in the jar on the left, and in no case did a flea jump when ordered. The scientist recorded the following induction:

"A flea, if its hind legs are yanked off, cannot hear."

For Group or Individual Investigation

Discuss or research examples from advertising that lead consumers to draw incorrect conclusions.

1.1 EXERCISES

In Exercises 1–12, determine whether the reasoning is an example of deductive or inductive reasoning.

1. If the mechanic says that it will take seven days to repair your car, then it will actually take ten days. The mechanic says, "I figure it'll take a week to fix it, ma'am." Then you can expect it to be ready ten days from now.

2. If you take your vitamins, you'll feel a lot better. You take your vitamins. Therefore, you'll feel a lot better.

3. It has rained every day for the past six days, and it is raining today as well. So it will also rain tomorrow.

4. Carrie's first three children were boys. If she has another baby, it will be a boy.

5. Finley had 85 baseball cards. His mom gave him 20 more for his birthday. Therefore, he now has 105 of them.

6. If the same number is subtracted from both sides of a true equation, the new equation is also true. I know that $9 + 18 = 27$. Therefore, $(9 + 18) - 13 = 27 - 13$.

7. If you build it, they will come. You build it. Therefore, they will come.

8. All men are mortal. Socrates is a man. Therefore, Socrates is mortal.

9. It is a fact that every student who ever attended Delgado University was accepted into graduate school. Because I am attending Delgado, I can expect to be accepted to graduate school, too.

10. For the past 97 years, a rare plant has bloomed in Columbia each summer, alternating between yellow and green flowers. Last summer, it bloomed with green flowers, so this summer it will bloom with yellow flowers.

11. In the sequence 5, 10, 15, 20, 25, . . . , the most probable next number is 30.

12. Lady Gaga's last four single releases have reached the Top Ten in the pop charts, so her current release will also reach the Top Ten.

13. Discuss the differences between inductive and deductive reasoning. Give an example of each.

14. Give an example of faulty inductive reasoning.

Determine the most probable next term in each of the following lists of numbers.

15. 6, 9, 12, 15, 18

16. 13, 18, 23, 28, 33

17. 3, 12, 48, 192, 768

18. 32, 16, 8, 4, 2

19. 3, 6, 9, 15, 24, 39

20. $\dfrac{1}{3}, \dfrac{3}{5}, \dfrac{5}{7}, \dfrac{7}{9}, \dfrac{9}{11}$

21. $\dfrac{1}{2}, \dfrac{3}{4}, \dfrac{5}{6}, \dfrac{7}{8}, \dfrac{9}{10}$

22. 1, 4, 9, 16, 25

23. 1, 8, 27, 64, 125

24. 2, 6, 12, 20, 30, 42

25. 4, 7, 12, 19, 28, 39

26. $-1, 2, -3, 4, -5, 6$

27. 5, 3, 5, 5, 3, 5, 5, 5, 3, 5, 5, 5, 5, 3, 5, 5, 5, 5

28. 8, 2, 8, 2, 2, 8, 2, 2, 2, 8, 2, 2, 2, 2, 8, 2, 2, 2, 2

29. Construct a list of numbers similar to those in **Exercise 15** such that the most probable next number in the list is 60.

30. Construct a list of numbers similar to those in **Exercise 26** such that the most probable next number in the list is 9.

Use the list of equations and inductive reasoning to predict the next equation, and then verify your conjecture.

31.
$(9 \times 9) + 7 = 88$
$(98 \times 9) + 6 = 888$
$(987 \times 9) + 5 = 8888$
$(9876 \times 9) + 4 = 88{,}888$

32.
$(1 \times 9) + 2 = 11$
$(12 \times 9) + 3 = 111$
$(123 \times 9) + 4 = 1111$
$(1234 \times 9) + 5 = 11{,}111$

33.
$3367 \times 3 = 10{,}101$
$3367 \times 6 = 20{,}202$
$3367 \times 9 = 30{,}303$
$3367 \times 12 = 40{,}404$

34.
$15873 \times 7 = 111{,}111$
$15873 \times 14 = 222{,}222$
$15873 \times 21 = 333{,}333$
$15873 \times 28 = 444{,}444$

35.
$34 \times 34 = 1156$
$334 \times 334 = 111{,}556$
$3334 \times 3334 = 11{,}115{,}556$

36.
$11 \times 11 = 121$
$111 \times 111 = 12{,}321$
$1111 \times 1111 = 1{,}234{,}321$

37.
$$3 = \frac{3(2)}{2}$$
$$3 + 6 = \frac{6(3)}{2}$$
$$3 + 6 + 9 = \frac{9(4)}{2}$$
$$3 + 6 + 9 + 12 = \frac{12(5)}{2}$$

38.
$$2 = 4 - 2$$
$$2 + 4 = 8 - 2$$
$$2 + 4 + 8 = 16 - 2$$
$$2 + 4 + 8 + 16 = 32 - 2$$

39.
$$5(6) = 6(6 - 1)$$
$$5(6) + 5(36) = 6(36 - 1)$$
$$5(6) + 5(36) + 5(216) = 6(216 - 1)$$
$$5(6) + 5(36) + 5(216) + 5(1296) = 6(1296 - 1)$$

40.
$$3 = \frac{3(3-1)}{2}$$
$$3 + 9 = \frac{3(9-1)}{2}$$
$$3 + 9 + 27 = \frac{3(27-1)}{2}$$
$$3 + 9 + 27 + 81 = \frac{3(81-1)}{2}$$

41.
$$\frac{1}{2} = 1 - \frac{1}{2}$$
$$\frac{1}{2} + \frac{1}{4} = 1 - \frac{1}{4}$$
$$\frac{1}{2} + \frac{1}{4} + \frac{1}{8} = 1 - \frac{1}{8}$$
$$\frac{1}{2} + \frac{1}{4} + \frac{1}{8} + \frac{1}{16} = 1 - \frac{1}{16}$$

42.
$$\frac{1}{1 \cdot 2} = \frac{1}{2}$$
$$\frac{1}{1 \cdot 2} + \frac{1}{2 \cdot 3} = \frac{2}{3}$$
$$\frac{1}{1 \cdot 2} + \frac{1}{2 \cdot 3} + \frac{1}{3 \cdot 4} = \frac{3}{4}$$
$$\frac{1}{1 \cdot 2} + \frac{1}{2 \cdot 3} + \frac{1}{3 \cdot 4} + \frac{1}{4 \cdot 5} = \frac{4}{5}$$

A story is often told about how the great mathematician Carl Friedrich Gauss (1777–1855) at a very young age was told by his teacher to find the sum of the first 100 counting numbers. While his classmates toiled at the problem, Carl simply wrote down a single number and handed it in to his teacher. His answer was correct. When asked how he did it, the young Carl explained that he observed that there were 50 pairs of numbers that each added up to 101. (See below.) So the sum of all the numbers must be 50 × 101 = 5050.

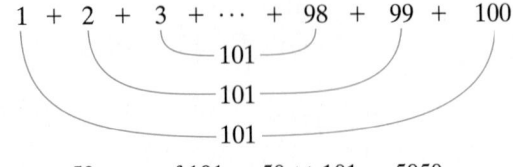

$$1 + 2 + 3 + \cdots + 98 + 99 + 100$$
101
101
101
$$50 \text{ sums of } 101 = 50 \times 101 = 5050$$

Use the method of Gauss to find each sum.

43. $1 + 2 + 3 + \cdots + 200$

44. $1 + 2 + 3 + \cdots + 400$

45. $1 + 2 + 3 + \cdots + 800$

46. $1 + 2 + 3 + \cdots + 2000$

47. Modify the procedure of Gauss to find the sum $1 + 2 + 3 + \cdots + 175$.

48. Explain in your own words how the procedure of Gauss can be modified to find the sum $1 + 2 + 3 + \cdots + n$, where *n* is an odd natural number. (When an odd natural number is divided by 2, it leaves a remainder of 1.)

49. Modify the procedure of Gauss to find the sum $2 + 4 + 6 + \cdots + 100$.

50. Use the result of **Exercise 49** to find the sum $4 + 8 + 12 + \cdots + 200$.

51. What is the most probable next number in this list?

$$12, 1, 1, 1, 2, 1, 3$$

(*Hint:* Think about a clock with chimes.)

52. What is the next term in this list?

$$\text{O, T, T, F, F, S, S, E, N, T}$$

(*Hint:* Think about words and their relationship to numbers.)

53. (a) Choose any three-digit number with all different digits. Now reverse the digits, and subtract the smaller from the larger. Record your result. Choose another three-digit number and repeat this process. Do this as many times as it takes for you to see a pattern in the different results you obtain. (*Hint:* What is the middle digit? What is the sum of the first and third digits?)

(b) Write an explanation of this pattern.

54. Choose any number, and follow these steps.

(a) Multiply by 2.
(b) Add 6.
(c) Divide by 2.
(d) Subtract the number you started with.
(e) Record your result.

Repeat the process, except in Step (b), add 8. Record your final result. Repeat the process once more, except in Step (b), add 10. Record your final result.

(f) Observe what you have done. Then use inductive reasoning to explain how to predict the final result.

55. Complete the following.

$$142,857 \times 1 = \underline{\qquad}$$
$$142,857 \times 2 = \underline{\qquad}$$
$$142,857 \times 3 = \underline{\qquad}$$
$$142,857 \times 4 = \underline{\qquad}$$
$$142,857 \times 5 = \underline{\qquad}$$
$$142,857 \times 6 = \underline{\qquad}$$

What pattern exists in the successive answers? Now multiply 142,857 by 7 to obtain an interesting result.

56. Refer to **Figures 2(b)–(e)** and **Figure 3**. Instead of counting interior regions of the circle, count the chords formed. Use inductive reasoning to predict the number of chords that would be formed if seven points were used.

1.2 AN APPLICATION OF INDUCTIVE REASONING: NUMBER PATTERNS

Number Sequences • Successive Differences • Number Patterns and Sum Formulas • Figurate Numbers

Number Sequences

An ordered list of numbers such as

$$3, 9, 15, 21, 27, \ldots$$

is called a *sequence.* A **number sequence** is a list of numbers having a first number, a second number, a third number, and so on, called the **terms** of the sequence.

The sequence that begins

$$5, 9, 13, 17, 21, \ldots$$

is an *arithmetic sequence,* or *arithmetic progression.* In an **arithmetic sequence,** each term after the first is obtained by adding the same number, called the **common difference.** To find the common difference, choose any term after the first and subtract from it the preceding term. If we choose $9 - 5$ (the second term minus the first term), for example, we see that the common difference is 4. To find the term following 21, we add 4 to get $21 + 4 = 25$.

Similarly, the sequence that begins

$$2, 4, 8, 16, 32, \ldots$$

is a *geometric sequence,* or *geometric progression.* In a **geometric sequence,** each term after the first is obtained by multiplying by the same number, called the **common ratio.** To find the common ratio, choose any term after the first and divide it by the preceding term. If we choose $\frac{4}{2}$ (the second term divided by the first term), for example, we see that the common ratio is 2. To find the term following 32, we multiply by 2 to get $32 \cdot 2 = 64$.

▌▌ **EXAMPLE 1** Identifying Arithmetic and Geometric Sequences

For each sequence, determine if it is an *arithmetic sequence,* a *geometric sequence,* or *neither.* If it is either arithmetic or geometric, give the next term in the sequence.

(a) $5, 10, 15, 20, 25, \ldots$ **(b)** $3, 12, 48, 192, 768, \ldots$ **(c)** $1, 4, 9, 16, 25, \ldots$

SOLUTION

(a) If we choose *any* term after the first term, and subtract the preceding term, we find that the common difference is 5.

$$10 - 5 = 5 \quad\quad 15 - 10 = 5 \quad\quad 20 - 15 = 5 \quad\quad 25 - 20 = 5$$

Therefore, this is an arithmetic sequence. The next term in the sequence is

$$25 + 5 = 30.$$

(b) If any term after the first is multiplied by 4, the following term is obtained.

$$\frac{12}{3} = 4 \quad\quad \frac{48}{12} = 4 \quad\quad \frac{192}{48} = 4 \quad\quad \frac{768}{192} = 4$$

Therefore, this is a geometric sequence. The next term in the sequence is

$$768 \cdot 4 = 3072.$$

(c) While there is a pattern here (the terms are the squares of the first five counting numbers), there is neither a common difference nor a common ratio. (Verify this) This is neither an arithmetic nor a geometric sequence. ▌▌▌

Successive Differences

Some sequences may provide more difficulty in making a conjecture about the next term. Often the **method of successive differences** may be applied in such cases. Consider the sequence

$$2, 6, 22, 56, 114, \ldots.$$

Because the next term is not obvious, subtract the first term from the second term, the second from the third, the third from the fourth, and so on.

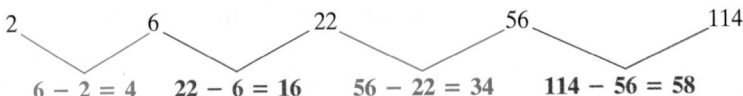

Now repeat the process with the sequence 4, 16, 34, 58 and continue repeating until the difference is a constant value, as shown in line (4).

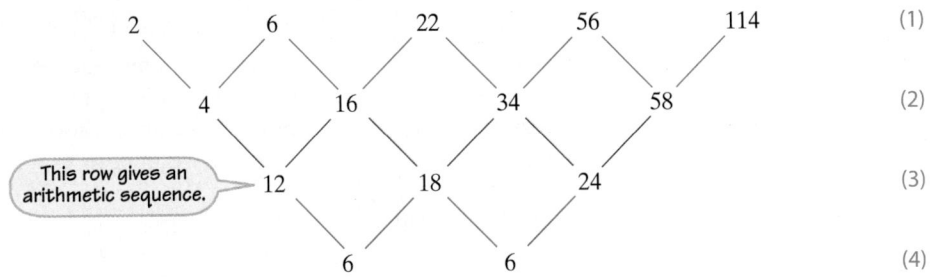

Once a line of constant values is obtained, simply work "backward" by adding until the desired term of the given sequence is obtained. Thus, for this pattern to continue, another 6 should appear in line (4), meaning that the next term in line (3) would have to be $24 + 6 = 30$. The next term in line (2) would be $58 + 30 = 88$. Finally, the next term in the given sequence would be $114 + 88 = \mathbf{202}$.

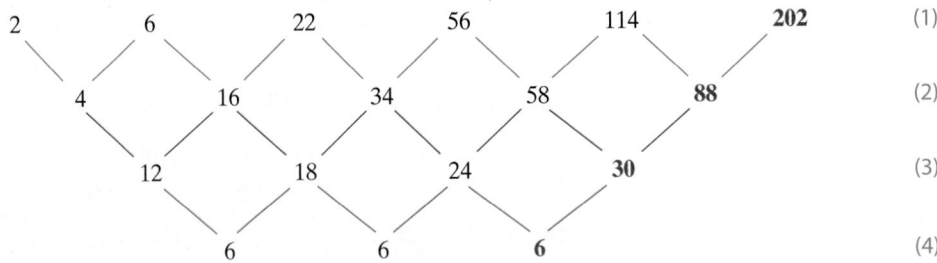

▌▌ **EXAMPLE 2** Using Successive Differences

Determine the next number in each sequence.

(a) $14, 22, 32, 44, \ldots$ **(b)** $5, 15, 37, 77, 141, \ldots$

SOLUTION

(a) Use the method of successive differences to obtain the following.

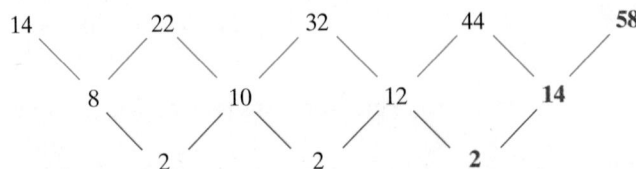

Once the row of 2s was obtained and extended, we were able to get $12 + 2 = 14$, and $44 + 14 = 58$, as shown above. The next number in the sequence is **58**.

(b) Proceeding as before, obtain the following diagram.

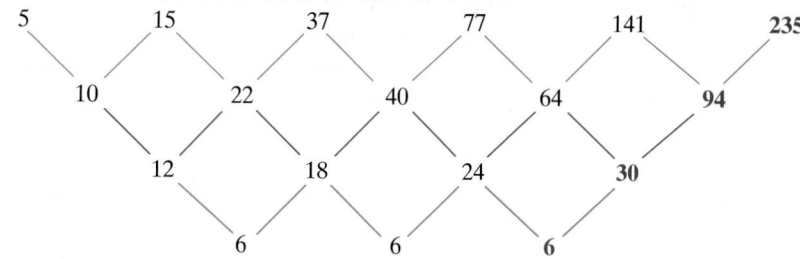

The numbers in the "diagonal" at the far right were obtained by adding: $24 + 6 = 30$, $64 + 30 = 94$, and $141 + 94 = 235$. The next number in the sequence is **235**. ▋▋▋

The method of successive differences will not always work. For example, try it on the Fibonacci sequence in **Example 2(b)** of **Section 1.1** and see what happens.

Number Patterns and Sum Formulas

Mathematics features a seemingly endless variety of number patterns. Observe the following pattern.

$$1 = 1^2$$
$$1 + 3 = 2^2$$
$$1 + 3 + 5 = 3^2$$
$$1 + 3 + 5 + 7 = 4^2$$
$$1 + 3 + 5 + 7 + 9 = 5^2$$

In each case, the left side of the equation is the indicated sum of consecutive odd counting numbers beginning with 1, and the right side is the square of the number of terms on the left side. Inductive reasoning would suggest that the next line in this pattern is as follows.

$$1 + 3 + 5 + 7 + 9 + 11 = 6^2$$

Evaluating each side shows that each side simplifies to 36.

We cannot conclude that this pattern will continue indefinitely, because observation of a finite number of examples does *not* guarantee that the pattern will continue. However, mathematicians have proved that this pattern does indeed continue indefinitely, using a method of proof called **mathematical induction.** (See any standard college algebra text.)

Any even counting number may be written in the form $2k$, where k is a counting number. It follows that the kth odd counting number is written $2k - 1$. For example, the **third** odd counting number, 5, can be written

$$2(3) - 1.$$

Using these ideas, we can write the result obtained above as follows.

> **Sum of the First _n_ Odd Counting Numbers**
>
> If n is any counting number, then the following is true.
>
> $$1 + 3 + 5 + \cdots + (2n - 1) = n^2$$

▌▌ **EXAMPLE 3** Predicting the Next Equation in a List

In each of the following, several equations are given illustrating a suspected number pattern. Determine what the next equation would be, and verify that it is indeed a true statement.

(a)
$$1^2 = 1^3$$
$$(1 + 2)^2 = 1^3 + 2^3$$
$$(1 + 2 + 3)^2 = 1^3 + 2^3 + 3^3$$
$$(1 + 2 + 3 + 4)^2 = 1^3 + 2^3 + 3^3 + 4^3$$

(b)
$$1 = 1^3$$
$$3 + 5 = 2^3$$
$$7 + 9 + 11 = 3^3$$
$$13 + 15 + 17 + 19 = 4^3$$

(c)
$$1 = \frac{1 \cdot 2}{2}$$
$$1 + 2 = \frac{2 \cdot 3}{2}$$
$$1 + 2 + 3 = \frac{3 \cdot 4}{2}$$
$$1 + 2 + 3 + 4 = \frac{4 \cdot 5}{2}$$

(d)
$$12{,}345{,}679 \times 9 = 111{,}111{,}111$$
$$12{,}345{,}679 \times 18 = 222{,}222{,}222$$
$$12{,}345{,}679 \times 27 = 333{,}333{,}333$$
$$12{,}345{,}679 \times 36 = 444{,}444{,}444$$

SOLUTION

(a) The left side of each equation is the square of the sum of the first n counting numbers, while the right side is the sum of their cubes. The next equation in the pattern would be

$$(1 + 2 + 3 + 4 + 5)^2 = 1^3 + 2^3 + 3^3 + 4^3 + 5^3.$$

Each side simplifies to 225, so the pattern is true for this equation.

(b) The left sides of the equations contain the sum of odd counting numbers, starting with the first (1) in the first equation, the second and third (3 and 5) in the second equation, the fourth, fifth, and sixth (7, 9, and 11) in the third equation, and so on. The right side contains the cube (third power) of the number of terms on the left side in each case. Following this pattern, the next equation would be

$$21 + 23 + 25 + 27 + 29 = 5^3,$$

which can be verified by computation.

(c) The left side of each equation gives the indicated sum of the first n counting numbers, and the right side is always of the form

$$\frac{n(n + 1)}{2}.$$

For the pattern to continue, the next equation would be

$$1 + 2 + 3 + 4 + 5 = \frac{5 \cdot 6}{2}.$$

Because each side simplifies to 15, the pattern is true for this equation.

(d) In each case, the first factor on the left is 12,345,679 and the second factor is a multiple of 9 (that is, 9, 18, 27, 36). The right side consists of a nine-digit number, all digits of which are the same (that is, 1, 2, 3, 4). For the pattern to continue, the next equation would be as follows.

$$12{,}345{,}679 \times 45 = 555{,}555{,}555$$

Verify that this is a true statement.

▌▌▌

The patterns established in **Examples 3(a) and 3(c)** can be written as follows.

Special Sum Formulas

For any counting number n, the following are true.

$$(1 + 2 + 3 + \cdots + n)^2 = 1^3 + 2^3 + 3^3 + \cdots + n^3$$

and

$$1 + 2 + 3 + \cdots + n = \frac{n(n + 1)}{2}$$

We can provide a general deductive argument showing how the second equation is obtained.

Let S represent the sum $1 + 2 + 3 + \cdots + n$. This sum can also be written as $S = n + (n - 1) + (n - 2) + \cdots + 1$. Write these two equations as follows.

$$
\begin{aligned}
S &= 1 & + 2 & \quad + 3 & + \cdots + n \\
S &= n & + (n - 1) & + (n - 2) & + \cdots + 1 \\
\hline
2S &= (n + 1) + (n + 1) + (n + 1) + \cdots + (n + 1) & & \text{Add the corresponding sides.}
\end{aligned}
$$

$2S = n(n + 1)$ There are n terms of $n + 1$.

$S = \dfrac{n(n + 1)}{2}$ Divide both sides by 2.

Figurate Numbers

Pythagoras and his Pythagorean brotherhood studied numbers of geometric arrangements of points, such as **triangular numbers, square numbers,** and **pentagonal numbers. Figure 5** illustrates the first few of each of these types of numbers.

The **figurate numbers** possess numerous interesting patterns. Every square number greater than 1 is the sum of two consecutive triangular numbers. (For example, $9 = 3 + 6$ and $25 = 10 + 15$.)

In the 1959 Disney animation *Donald in Mathmagic Land*, Donald Duck travels back in time to meet the Greek mathematician **Pythagoras** (c. 540 B.C.), who with his fellow mathematicians formed the Pythagorean brotherhood. The brotherhood devoted its time to the study of mathematics and music.
© Disney Enterprises, Inc.

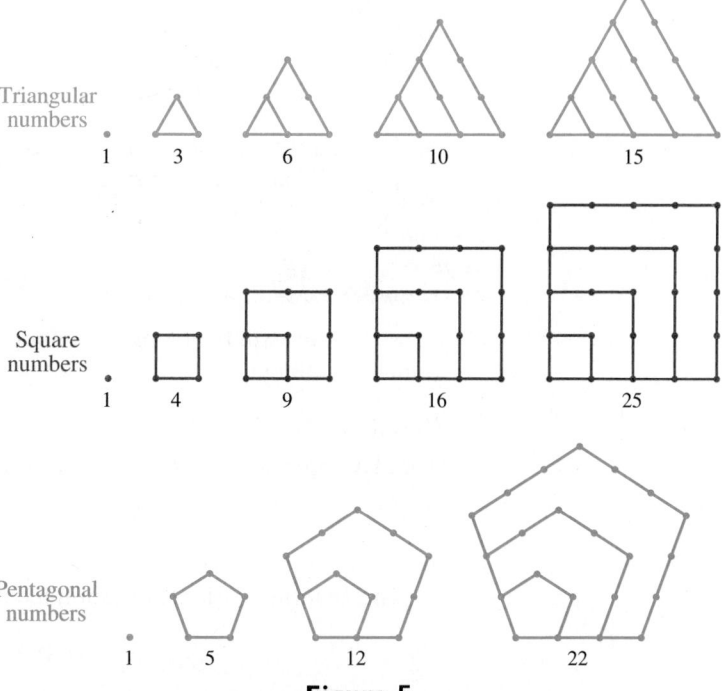

Triangular numbers   1   3   6   10   15

Square numbers   1   4   9   16   25

Pentagonal numbers   1   5   12   22

Figure 5

Every pentagonal number can be represented as the sum of a square number and a triangular number. (For example, $5 = 4 + 1$ and $12 = 9 + 3$.) Many other such relationships exist.

In the expression T_n, n is called a **subscript.** T_n is read **"T sub n,"** and it represents the triangular number in the nth position in the sequence. For example,

$$T_1 = 1, \quad T_2 = 3, \quad T_3 = 6, \quad \text{and} \quad T_4 = 10.$$

S_n and P_n represent the nth square and pentagonal numbers, respectively.

Formulas for Triangular, Square, and Pentagonal Numbers

For any natural number n, the following are true.

The nth triangular number is given by $\quad T_n = \dfrac{n(n + 1)}{2}$.

The nth square number is given by $\quad S_n = n^2$.

The nth pentagonal number is given by $\quad P_n = \dfrac{n(3n - 1)}{2}$.

▮▮ **EXAMPLE 4** Using the Formulas for Figurate Numbers

Use the formulas to find each of the following.

(a) seventh triangular number

(b) twelfth square number

(c) sixth pentagonal number

SOLUTION

(a) $T_7 = \dfrac{n(n + 1)}{2} = \dfrac{7(7 + 1)}{2} = \dfrac{7(8)}{2} = \dfrac{56}{2} = 28$ Formula for a triangular number, $n = 7$

(b) $S_{12} = n^2 = 12^2 = 144$ Formula for a square number, $n = 12$

$12^2 = 12 \cdot 12$

Inside the brackets, multiply first and then subtract.

(c) $P_6 = \dfrac{n(3n - 1)}{2} = \dfrac{6[3(6) - 1]}{2} = \dfrac{6(18 - 1)}{2} = \dfrac{6(17)}{2} = 51$ ▮▮▮

▮▮ **EXAMPLE 5** Illustrating a Figurate Number Relationship

Show that the sixth pentagonal number is equal to the sum of 6 and 3 times the fifth triangular number.

SOLUTION

From **Example 4(c),** $P_6 = 51$. The fifth triangular number is 15. Thus,

$$51 = 6 + 3(15) = 6 + 45 = 51. \qquad\qquad ▮▮▮$$

The general relationship examined in **Example 5** can be written as follows.

$$P_n = n + 3 \cdot T_{n-1} \quad (n \geq 2)$$

■■ **EXAMPLE 6** Predicting the Value of a Pentagonal Number

The first five pentagonal numbers are 1, 5, 12, 22, 35. Use the method of successive differences to predict the sixth pentagonal number.

SOLUTION

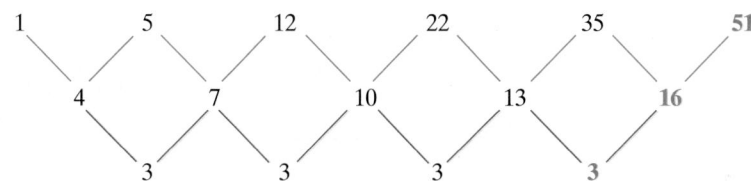

After the second line of successive differences, we work backward to find that the sixth pentagonal number is **51**, which was also found in **Example 4(c).** ■■■

For Further Thought

Kaprekar Constants

Take any three-digit number whose digits are not all the same. Arrange the digits in decreasing order, and then arrange them in increasing order. Now subtract. Repeat the process, using a 0 if necessary in the event that the difference consists of only two digits. For example, suppose that we choose a number whose digits are 1, 4, and 8, such as 841.

$$\begin{array}{r} 841 \\ -148 \\ \hline 693 \end{array} \qquad \begin{array}{r} 963 \\ -369 \\ \hline 594 \end{array} \qquad \begin{array}{r} 954 \\ -459 \\ \hline 495 \end{array}$$

Notice that we have obtained the number 495, and the process will lead to 495 again.

The number 495 is called a **Kaprekar constant.** The number 495 will eventually always be generated if this process is applied to such a three-digit number.

For Group or Individual Investigation

1. Apply the process of Kaprekar to a two-digit number, in which the digits are not the same. (Interpret 9 as 09 if necessary.) Compare the results. What seems to be true?

2. Repeat the process for four digits, comparing results after several steps. What conjecture can be made for this situation?

1.2 EXERCISES

For each sequence, determine if it is an arithmetic *sequence, a* geometric *sequence, or* neither. *If it is either arithmetic or geometric, give the next term in the sequence.*

1. 6, 16, 26, 36, 46, . . .

2. 8, 16, 24, 32, 40, . . .

3. 5, 15, 45, 135, 405, . . .

4. 2, 12, 72, 432, 2592, . . .

5. 1, 8, 27, 81, 243, . . .

6. 2, 8, 18, 32, 50, . . .

7. 256, 128, 64, 32, 16, . . .

8. 4096, 1024, 256, 64, 16, . . .

9. 1, 3, 4, 7, 11, . . .

10. 0, 1, 1, 2, 3, . . .

11. 12, 14, 16, 18, 20, . . .

12. 10, 50, 90, 130, 170, . . .

Use the method of successive differences to determine the next number in each sequence.

13. 1, 4, 11, 22, 37, 56, . . .

14. 3, 14, 31, 54, 83, 118, . . .

15. 6, 20, 50, 102, 182, 296, . . .

16. 1, 11, 35, 79, 149, 251, . . .

17. 0, 12, 72, 240, 600, 1260, 2352, ...

18. 2, 57, 220, 575, 1230, 2317, ...

19. 5, 34, 243, 1022, 3121, 7770, 16799, ...

20. 3, 19, 165, 771, 2503, 6483, 14409, ...

21. Refer to **Figures 2 and 3** in **Section 1.1.** The method of successive differences can be applied to the sequence of interior regions,

$$1, 2, 4, 8, 16, 31,$$

to find the number of regions determined by seven points on the circle. What is the next term in this sequence? How many regions would be determined by eight points? Verify this using the formula given at the end of that section.

22. Suppose that the expression $n^2 + 3n + 1$ determines the nth term in a sequence. That is, to find the first term, let $n = 1$. To find the second term, let $n = 2$, and so on.

  (a) Find the first four terms of the sequence.

  (b) Use the method of successive differences to predict the fifth term of the sequence.

  (c) Find the fifth term by letting $n = 5$ in the expression $n^2 + 3n + 1$. Does your result agree with the one you found in part (b)?

In Exercises 23–32, several equations are given illustrating a suspected number pattern. Determine what the next equation would be, and verify that it is indeed a true statement.

23. $(1 \times 9) - 1 = 8$
$(21 \times 9) - 1 = 188$
$(321 \times 9) - 1 = 2888$

24. $(1 \times 8) + 1 = 9$
$(12 \times 8) + 2 = 98$
$(123 \times 8) + 3 = 987$

25. $999{,}999 \times 2 = 1{,}999{,}998$
$999{,}999 \times 3 = 2{,}999{,}997$

26. $101 \times 101 = 10{,}201$
$10{,}101 \times 10{,}101 = 102{,}030{,}201$

27. $3^2 - 1^2 = 2^3$
$6^2 - 3^2 = 3^3$
$10^2 - 6^2 = 4^3$
$15^2 - 10^2 = 5^3$

28. $1 = 1^2$
$1 + 2 + 1 = 2^2$
$1 + 2 + 3 + 2 + 1 = 3^2$
$1 + 2 + 3 + 4 + 3 + 2 + 1 = 4^2$

29. $2^2 - 1^2 = 2 + 1$
$3^2 - 2^2 = 3 + 2$
$4^2 - 3^2 = 4 + 3$

30. $1^2 + 1 = 2^2 - 2$
$2^2 + 2 = 3^2 - 3$
$3^2 + 3 = 4^2 - 4$

31. $1 = 1 \times 1$
$1 + 5 = 2 \times 3$
$1 + 5 + 9 = 3 \times 5$

32. $1 + 2 = 3$
$4 + 5 + 6 = 7 + 8$
$9 + 10 + 11 + 12 = 13 + 14 + 15$

Use the formula $S = \dfrac{n(n+1)}{2}$ to find each sum.

33. $1 + 2 + 3 + \cdots + 300$

34. $1 + 2 + 3 + \cdots + 500$

35. $1 + 2 + 3 + \cdots + 675$

36. $1 + 2 + 3 + \cdots + 825$

Use the formula $S = n^2$ to find each sum. (Hint: To find n, add 1 to the last term and divide by 2.)

37. $1 + 3 + 5 + \cdots + 101$

38. $1 + 3 + 5 + \cdots + 49$

39. $1 + 3 + 5 + \cdots + 999$

40. $1 + 3 + 5 + \cdots + 301$

41. Use the formula for finding the sum

$$1 + 2 + 3 + \cdots + n$$

to discover a formula for finding the sum

$$2 + 4 + 6 + \cdots + 2n.$$

42. State in your own words the following formula discussed in this section.

$$(1 + 2 + 3 + \cdots + n)^2 = 1^3 + 2^3 + 3^3 + \cdots + n^3$$

43. Explain how the following diagram geometrically illustrates the formula $1 + 3 + 5 + 7 + 9 = 5^2$.

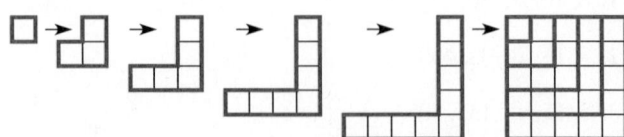

44. Explain how the following diagram geometrically illustrates the formula $1 + 2 + 3 + 4 = \dfrac{4 \times 5}{2}$.

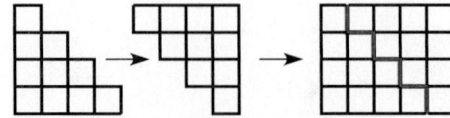

45. Use patterns to complete the table below.

Figurate Number	1st	2nd	3rd	4th	5th	6th	7th	8th
Triangular	1	3	6	10	15	21		
Square	1	4	9	16	25			
Pentagonal	1	5	12	22				
Hexagonal	1	6	15					
Heptagonal	1	7						
Octagonal	1							

46. The first five triangular, square, and pentagonal numbers may be obtained using sums of terms of sequences, as shown below.

Triangular	Square	Pentagonal
$1 = 1$	$1 = 1$	$1 = 1$
$3 = 1 + 2$	$4 = 1 + 3$	$5 = 1 + 4$
$6 = 1 + 2 + 3$	$9 = 1 + 3 + 5$	$12 = 1 + 4 + 7$
$10 = 1 + 2 + 3 + 4$	$16 = 1 + 3 + 5 + 7$	$22 = 1 + 4 + 7 + 10$
$15 = 1 + 2 + 3 + 4 + 5$	$25 = 1 + 3 + 5 + 7 + 9$	$35 = 1 + 4 + 7 + 10 + 13$

Notice the successive differences of the added terms on the right sides of the equations. The next type of figurate number is the **hexagonal** number. (A hexagon has six sides.) Use the patterns above to predict the first five hexagonal numbers.

47. Eight times any triangular number, plus 1, is a square number. Show that this is true for the first four triangular numbers.

48. Divide the first triangular number by 3 and record the remainder. Divide the second triangular number by 3 and record the remainder. Repeat this procedure several more times. Do you notice a pattern?

49. Repeat **Exercise 48,** but instead use square numbers and divide by 4. What pattern is determined?

50. Exercises 48 and 49 are specific cases of the following: When the numbers in the sequence of n-agonal numbers are divided by n, the sequence of remainders obtained is a repeating sequence. Verify this for $n = 5$ and $n = 6$.

51. Every square number can be written as the sum of two triangular numbers. For example, $16 = 6 + 10$. This can be represented geometrically by dividing a square array of dots with a line as shown.

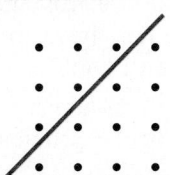

The triangular arrangement above the line represents 6, the one below the line represents 10, and the whole arrangement represents 16. Show how the square numbers 25 and 36 may likewise be geometrically represented as the sum of two triangular numbers.

52. A fraction is in **lowest terms** if the greatest common factor of its numerator and its denominator is 1. For example, $\frac{3}{8}$ is in lowest terms, but $\frac{4}{12}$ is not.

(a) For $n = 2$ to $n = 8$, form the fractions

$$\frac{n\text{th square number}}{(n + 1)\text{st square number}}.$$

(b) Repeat part (a) with triangular numbers.

(c) Use inductive reasoning to make a conjecture based on your results from parts (a) and (b), observing whether the fractions are in lowest terms.

*In addition to the formulas for T_n, S_n, and P_n, the following formulas are true for **hexagonal** numbers (H), **heptagonal** numbers (Hp), and **octagonal** numbers (O):*

$$\text{H}_n = \frac{n(4n - 2)}{2}, \quad \text{Hp}_n = \frac{n(5n - 3)}{2}, \quad \text{O}_n = \frac{n(6n - 4)}{2}.$$

Use these formulas to find each of the following.

53. the sixteenth square number

54. the eleventh triangular number

55. the ninth pentagonal number

56. the seventh hexagonal number

57. the tenth heptagonal number

58. the twelfth octagonal number

59. Observe the formulas given for H_n, Hp_n, and O_n, and use patterns and inductive reasoning to predict the formula for N_n, the nth **nonagonal** number. (A nonagon has nine sides.) Then use the fact that the sixth nonagonal number is 111 to further confirm your conjecture.

60. Use the result of **Exercise 59** to find the tenth nonagonal number.

Use inductive reasoning to answer each question.

61. If you add two consecutive triangular numbers, what kind of figurate number do you get?

62. If you add the squares of two consecutive triangular numbers, what kind of figurate number do you get?

63. Square a triangular number. Square the next triangular number. Subtract the smaller result from the larger. What kind of number do you get?

64. Choose a value of n greater than or equal to 2. Find T_{n-1}, multiply it by 3, and add n. What kind of figurate number do you get?

In an arithmetic sequence, the nth term a_n is given by the formula

$$a_n = a_1 + (n - 1)d,$$

where a_1 is the first term and d is the common difference. Similarly, in a geometric sequence, the nth term is given by

$$a_n = a_1 \cdot r^{n-1}.$$

Here r is the common ratio. Use these formulas to determine the indicated term in the given sequence.

65. The eleventh term of $2, 6, 10, 14, \ldots$

66. The sixteenth term of $5, 15, 25, 35, \ldots$

67. The 21st term of $19, 39, 59, 79, \ldots$

68. The 36th term of $8, 38, 68, 98, \ldots$

69. The 101st term of $\frac{1}{2}, 1, \frac{3}{2}, 2, \ldots$

70. The 151st term of $0.75, 1.50, 2.25, 3.00, \ldots$

71. The eleventh term of $2, 4, 8, 16, \ldots$

72. The ninth term of $1, 4, 16, 64, \ldots$

73. The 12th term of $1, \frac{1}{2}, \frac{1}{4}, \frac{1}{8}, \ldots$

74. The 10th term of $1, \frac{1}{3}, \frac{1}{9}, \frac{1}{27}, \ldots$

75. The 8th term of $40, 10, \frac{5}{2}, \frac{5}{8}, \ldots$

76. The 9th term of $10, 2, \frac{2}{5}, \frac{2}{25}, \ldots$

1.3 STRATEGIES FOR PROBLEM SOLVING

A General Problem-Solving Method • Using a Table or Chart • Working Backward • Using Trial and Error • Guessing and Checking • Considering a Similar, Simpler Problem • Drawing a Sketch • Using Common Sense

A General Problem-Solving Method

In the first two sections of this chapter we stressed the importance of pattern recognition and the use of inductive reasoning in solving problems. Probably the most famous study of problem-solving techniques was developed by George Polya (1888–1985), among whose many publications was the modern classic *How to Solve It*. In this book, Polya proposed a four-step method for problem solving.

George Polya, author of the classic *How to Solve It*, died at the age of 97 on September 7, 1985. A native of Budapest, Hungary, he was once asked why there were so many good mathematicians to come out of Hungary at the turn of the century. He theorized that it was because mathematics is the cheapest science. It does not require any expensive equipment, only pencil and paper. He authored or coauthored more than 250 papers in many languages, wrote a number of books, and was a brilliant lecturer and teacher. Yet, interestingly enough, he never learned to drive a car.

Polya's Four-Step Method for Problem Solving

Step 1 **Understand the problem.** You cannot solve a problem if you do not understand what you are asked to find. The problem must be read and analyzed carefully. You may need to read it several times. After you have done so, ask yourself, "What must I find?"

Step 2 **Devise a plan.** There are many ways to attack a problem. Decide what plan is appropriate for the particular problem you are solving.

Step 3 **Carry out the plan.** Once you know how to approach the problem, carry out your plan. You may run into "dead ends" and unforeseen roadblocks, but be persistent.

Step 4 **Look back and check.** Check your answer to see that it is reasonable. Does it satisfy the conditions of the problem? Have you answered all the questions the problem asks? Can you solve the problem a different way and come up with the same answer?

In Step 2 of Polya's problem-solving method, we are told to devise a plan. Here are some hints and strategies that may prove useful.

PROBLEM-SOLVING HINTS

Make a table or a chart.	If a formula applies, use it.
Look for a pattern.	Work backward.
Solve a similar, simpler problem.	Guess and check.
Draw a sketch.	Use trial and error.
Use inductive reasoning.	Use common sense.
Write an equation and solve it.	Look for a "catch" if an answer seems too obvious or impossible.

Fibonacci (1170–1250) discovered the sequence named after him in a problem on rabbits. Fibonacci (son of Bonaccio) is one of several names for Leonardo of Pisa. His father managed a warehouse in present-day Bougie (or Bejaia), in Algeria. Thus it was that Leonardo Pisano studied with a Moorish teacher and learned the "Indian" numbers that the Moors and other Moslems brought with them in their westward drive.

   Fibonacci wrote books on algebra, geometry, and trigonometry.

Using a Table or Chart

▮▮ **EXAMPLE 1** Solving Fibonacci's Rabbit Problem

A man put a pair of rabbits in a cage. During the first month the rabbits produced no offspring but each month thereafter produced one new pair of rabbits. If each new pair thus produced reproduces in the same manner, how many pairs of rabbits will there be at the end of 1 year? (This problem is a famous one in the history of mathematics and first appeared in *Liber Abaci*, a book written by the Italian mathematician Leonardo Pisano (also known as Fibonacci) in the year 1202.)

SOLUTION

Step 1 **Understand the problem.** We can reword the problem as follows:

> *How many pairs of rabbits will the man have at the end of one year if he starts with one pair, and they reproduce this way: During the first month of life, each pair produces no new rabbits, but each month thereafter each pair produces one new pair?*

Step 2 **Devise a plan.** Because there is a definite pattern to how the rabbits will reproduce, we can construct **Table 2.**

Table 2

Month	Number of Pairs at Start	Number of New Pairs Produced	Number of Pairs at End of Month
1st			
2nd			
3rd			
4th			
5th			
6th			
7th			
8th			
9th			
10th			
11th			
12th			

The answer will go here.

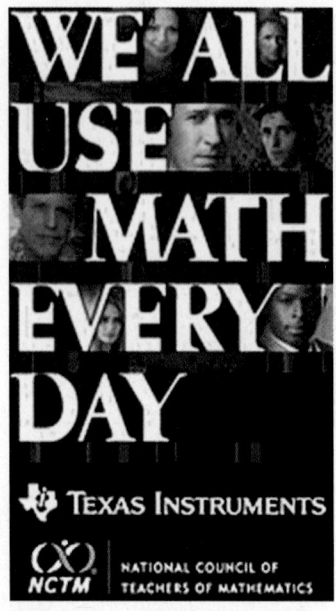

Step 3 **Carry out the plan.** At the start of the first month, there is only one pair of rabbits. No new pairs are produced during the first month, so there is $1 + 0 = 1$ pair present at the end of the first month. This pattern continues. In the table, we add the number in the first column of numbers to the number in the second column to get the number in the third.

Month	Number of Pairs at Start	+	Number of New Pairs Produced	=	Number of Pairs at End of Month	
1st	1		0		1	$1 + 0 = 1$
2nd	1		1		2	$1 + 1 = 2$
3rd	2		1		3	$2 + 1 = 3$
4th	3		2		5	•
5th	5		3		8	•
6th	8		5		13	•
7th	13		8		21	•
8th	21		13		34	•
9th	34		21		55	•
10th	55		34		89	•
11th	89		55		144	•
12th	144		89		**233**	$144 + 89 = 233$

> The answer is the final entry.

There will be **233** pairs of rabbits at the end of one year.

Step 4 **Look back and check.** Go back and make sure that we have interpreted the problem correctly. Double-check the arithmetic. We have answered the question posed by the problem, so the problem is solved. ▮▮▮

Working Backward

▮▮ **EXAMPLE 2** Determining a Wager at the Track

Ronnie Virgets goes to the racetrack with his buddies on a weekly basis. One week he tripled his money, but then lost $12. He took his money back the next week, doubled it, but then lost $40. The following week he tried again, taking his money back with him. He quadrupled it, and then played well enough to take that much home, a total of $224. How much did he start with the first week?

SOLUTION

This problem asks us to find Ronnie's starting amount. Since we know his final amount, the method of working backward can be applied.

Because his final amount was $224 and this represents four times the amount he started with on the third week, we *divide* $224 by 4 to find that he started the third week with $56. Before he lost $40 the second week, he had this $56 plus the $40 he lost, giving him $96. This represented double what he started with, so he started with $96 *divided by* 2, or $48, the second week. Repeating this process once more for the first week, before his $12 loss he had

$$\$48 + \$12 = \$60,$$

which represents triple what he started with. Therefore, he started with

$$\$60 \div 3 = \$20. \quad \text{Answer}$$

To check, observe the following equations that depict winnings and losses.

First week: $(3 \times \$20) - \$12 = \$60 - \$12 = \$48$

Second week: $(2 \times \$48) - \$40 = \$96 - \$40 = \$56$

Third week: $(4 \times \$56) = \$224$ His final amount ▮▮▮

Augustus De Morgan was an English mathematician and philosopher, who served as professor at the University of London. He wrote numerous books, one of which was *A Budget of Paradoxes*. His work in set theory and logic led to laws that bear his name and are covered in other chapters. He died in the same year as Charles Babbage.

Using Trial and Error

Recall that $5^2 = 5 \cdot 5 = 25$. That is, 5 squared is 25. Thus, 25 is called a **perfect square.**

$$1, \quad 4, \quad 9, \quad 16, \quad 25, \quad 36, \quad \text{and so on}$$ Perfect squares

▐▐ **EXAMPLE 3** Finding Augustus De Morgan's Birth Year

The mathematician Augustus De Morgan lived in the nineteenth century. He made the following statement: "I was x years old in the year x^2." In what year was he born?

SOLUTION

We must find the year of De Morgan's birth. The problem tells us that he lived in the nineteenth century, which is another way of saying that he lived during the 1800s. One year of his life was a perfect square, so we must find a number between 1800 and 1900 that is a perfect square. Use trial and error.

$$42^2 = 42 \cdot 42 = 1764$$
$$43^2 = 43 \cdot 43 = 1849 \quad \longleftarrow \boxed{\text{1849 is between 1800 and 1900.}}$$
$$44^2 = 44 \cdot 44 = 1936$$

The only natural number whose square is between 1800 and 1900 is 43, since $43^2 = 1849$. Therefore, De Morgan was 43 years old in 1849. The final step in solving the problem is to subtract 43 from 1849 to find the year of his birth.

$$1849 - 43 = 1806 \quad \longleftarrow \boxed{\text{He was born in 1806.}}$$

Although the following check may seem unorthodox, it works: Look up De Morgan's birth date in a book dealing with mathematics history, such as *An Introduction to the History of Mathematics*, Sixth Edition, by Howard W. Eves.   ▐▐▐

Guessing and Checking

As mentioned above, $5^2 = 25$. The inverse (opposite) of squaring a number is called taking the **square root.** We indicate the positive square root using a **radical symbol** $\sqrt{}$. Thus, $\sqrt{25} = 5$. Also,

$$\sqrt{4} = 2, \quad \sqrt{9} = 3, \quad \sqrt{16} = 4, \quad \text{and so on.}$$ Square roots

The next problem deals with a square root and dates back to Hindu mathematics, circa 850.

▐▐ **EXAMPLE 4** Finding the Number of Camels

One-fourth of a herd of camels was seen in the forest; twice the square root of that herd had gone to the mountain slopes; and 3 times 5 camels remained on the riverbank. What is the numerical measure of that herd of camels?

SOLUTION

The numerical measure of a herd of camels must be a counting number. Because the problem mentions "one-fourth of a herd" and "the square root of that herd," the number of camels must be both a multiple of 4 and a perfect square, so that only whole numbers are used. The least counting number that satisfies both conditions is 4. We write an equation where x represents the numerical measure of the herd, and then substitute 4 for x to see if it is a solution.

One-fourth of the herd	+	Twice the square root of that herd	+	3 times 5 camels	=	The numerical measure of the herd.

$$\frac{1}{4}x \quad + \quad 2\sqrt{x} \quad + \quad 3 \cdot 5 \quad = \quad x$$

$$\frac{1}{4}(4) + 2\sqrt{4} + 3 \cdot 5 = 4 \qquad \text{Let } x = 4.$$

$$1 + 4 + 15 \stackrel{?}{=} 4 \qquad \sqrt{4} = 2$$

$$20 \neq 4$$

Because 4 is not the solution, try **16**, the next perfect square that is a multiple of 4.

$$\frac{1}{4}(16) + 2\sqrt{16} + 3 \cdot 5 = 16 \qquad \text{Let } x = 16.$$

$$4 + 8 + 15 \stackrel{?}{=} 16 \qquad \sqrt{16} = 4$$

$$27 \neq 16$$

Because 16 is not a solution, try **36**.

$$\frac{1}{4}(36) + 2\sqrt{36} + 3 \cdot 5 = 36 \qquad \text{Let } x = 36.$$

$$9 + 12 + 15 \stackrel{?}{=} 36 \qquad \sqrt{36} = 6$$

$$36 = 36$$

Thus, 36 is the numerical measure of the herd. *Check*: "One-fourth of 36, plus twice the square root of 36, plus 3 times 5" gives 9 plus 12 plus 15, which equals 36. ▮▮▮

Considering a Similar, Simpler Problem

▮▮ **EXAMPLE 5** Finding the Units Digit of a Power

The 1952 film *Hans Christian Andersen* features Danny Kaye as the Danish writer of fairy tales. In a scene outside a schoolhouse, he sings a song to an inchworm: "Inchworm, inchworm, measuring the marigolds, you and your arithmetic, you'll probably go far." Following the scene, students in the schoolhouse are heard singing arithmetic facts:

Two and two are four,
Four and four are eight,
Eight and eight are sixteen,
Sixteen and sixteen are thirty-two.

Their answers are all **powers of 2.**

The digit farthest to the right in a counting number is called the *ones* or *units* digit, because it tells how many ones are contained in the number when grouping by tens is considered. What is the ones (or units) digit in 2^{4000}?

SOLUTION

Recall that 2^{4000} means that 2 is used as a factor 4000 times.

$$2^{4000} = \underbrace{2 \times 2 \times 2 \times \ldots \times 2}_{4000 \text{ factors}}$$

To answer the question, we examine some smaller powers of 2 and then look for a pattern. We start with the exponent 1 and look at the first twelve powers of 2.

$2^1 = 2$	$2^5 = 32$	$2^9 = 512$
$2^2 = 4$	$2^6 = 64$	$2^{10} = 1024$
$2^3 = 8$	$2^7 = 128$	$2^{11} = 2048$
$2^4 = 16$	$2^8 = 256$	$2^{12} = 4096$

Notice that in any one of the four rows above, the ones digit is the same all the way across the row. The final row, which contains the exponents 4, 8, and 12, has the ones digit 6. Each of these exponents is divisible by 4, and because 4000 is divisible by 4, we can use inductive reasoning to predict that the units digit in 2^{4000} is **6**.

(*Note*: The units digit for any other power can be found if we divide the exponent by 4 and consider the remainder. Then compare the result to the list of powers above. For example, to find the units digit of 2^{543}, divide 543 by 4 to get a quotient of 135 and a remainder of **3**. The units digit is the same as that of 2^3, which is **8**.) ▮▮▮

Drawing a Sketch

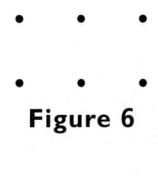

Figure 6

■■ **EXAMPLE 6** Connecting the Dots

An array of nine dots is arranged in a 3×3 square, as shown in **Figure 6**. Is it possible to join the dots with exactly four straight line segments if you are not allowed to pick up your pencil from the paper and may not trace over a segment that has already been drawn? If so, show how.

SOLUTION

Figure 7 shows three attempts. In each case, something is wrong. In the first sketch, one dot is not joined. In the second, the figure cannot be drawn without picking up your pencil from the paper or tracing over a line that has already been drawn. In the third figure, all dots have been joined, but you have used five line segments as well as retraced over the figure.

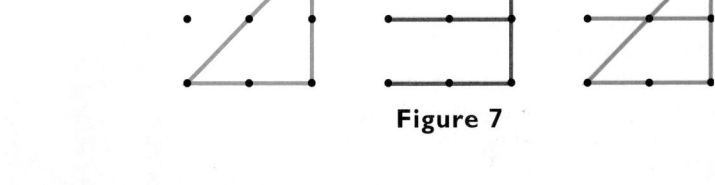

Figure 7

The conditions of the problem can be satisfied, as shown in **Figure 8**. We "went outside of the box," which was not prohibited by the conditions of the problem. This is an example of creative thinking—we used a strategy that often is not considered at first. ■■■

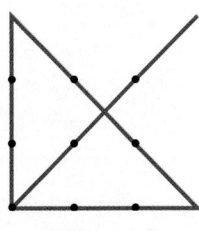

Figure 8

Using Common Sense

PROBLEM-SOLVING HINTS Some problems involve a "catch." They seem too easy or perhaps impossible at first because we tend to overlook an obvious situation. Look carefully at the use of language in such problems. And, of course, never forget to use common sense.

In *Die Hard: With a Vengeance* (see the **Chapter Opener**), Simon taunts McClane with a riddle that has its origins in Egyptian mathematics.

As I was going to St. Ives,
I met a man with seven wives.
Every wife had seven sacks,
Every sack had seven cats,
Every cat had seven kittens.
Kittens, cats, sacks, and wives,
How many were going to St. Ives?

"My phone number is 555 and the answer. Call me in 30 seconds or die."

By calling 555-0001, he was able to contact Simon. Do you see why 1 is the answer to this riddle? (Use **common sense**.)

■■ **EXAMPLE 7** Determining Coin Denominations

Two currently minted United States coins together have a total value of $1.05. One is not a dollar. What are the two coins?

SOLUTION

Our initial reaction might be, "The only way to have two such coins with a total of $1.05 is to have a nickel and a dollar, but the problem says that one of them is not a dollar." This statement is indeed true. What we must realize here is that the one that is not a dollar is the nickel, and the *other* coin is a dollar! So the two coins are a dollar and a nickel. ■■■

1.3 EXERCISES

One of the most popular features in the journal Mathematics Teacher, *published by the National Council of Teachers of Mathematics, is the monthly calendar. It provides an interesting, unusual, or challenging problem for each day of the month. Problems are contributed by the editors of the journal, teachers, and students, and the contributors are cited in each issue. Some of these exercises are problems chosen from these calendars over the past years, with the day, month, and year for the problem indicated. The authors want to thank the many contributors for permission to use these problems.*

Use the various problem-solving strategies to solve each problem. In many cases there is more than one possible approach, so be creative.

1. *Class Members* A classroom contains an equal number of boys and girls. If 8 girls leave, twice as many boys as girls remain. What was the original number of students present? (May 24, 2008)

2. *Give Me a Digit* Given a two-digit number, make a three-digit number by putting a 6 as the right-most digit. Then add 6 to the resulting three-digit number and remove the right-most digit to obtain another two digit number. If the result is 76, what is the original two-digit number? (October 18, 2009)

3. *Missing Digit* Look for a pattern and find the missing digit x.

$$
\begin{array}{cccc}
3 & 2 & 4 & 8 \\
7 & 2 & 1 & 3 \\
8 & 4 & x & 5 \\
4 & 3 & 6 & 9
\end{array}
$$

(February 14, 2009)

4. *Abundancy* An integer $n > 1$ is **abundant** if the sum of its proper divisors (positive integer divisors smaller than n) is greater than n. Find the smallest abundant integer. (November 27, 2009)

5. *Cross-Country Competition* The schools in an athletic conference compete in a cross-country meet to which each school sends three participants. Erin, Katelyn, and Iliana are the three representatives from one school.

Erin finished the race in the middle position; Katelyn finished after Erin, in the 19th position; and Iliana finished 28th. How many schools took part in the race? (May 27, 2008)

6. *Gone Fishing* Four friends go fishing one day and bring home a total of 11 fish. If each person caught at least 1 fish, then which of the following *must* be true?
   A. One person caught exactly 2 fish.
   B. One person caught exactly 3 fish.
   C. One person caught fewer than 3 fish.
   D. One person caught more than 3 fish.
   E. Two people each caught more than 1 fish.
   (May 24, 2008)

7. *Cutting a Square in Half* In how many ways can a single straight line cut a square in half? (October 2, 2008)

8. *You Lie!* Max, Sam, and Brett were playing basketball. One of them broke a window, and the other two saw him break it. Max said, "I am innocent." Sam said, "Max and I are both innocent." Brett said, "Max and Sam are both innocent." If only one of them is telling the truth, who broke the window? (September 21, 2008)

9. *Bookworm Snack* A 26-volume encyclopedia (one for each letter) is placed on a bookshelf in alphabetical order from left to right. Each volume is 2 inches thick, including the front and back covers. Each cover is $\frac{1}{4}$ inch thick. A bookworm eats straight through the encyclopedia, beginning inside the front cover of volume A and ending after eating through the back cover of volume Z. How many inches of book did the bookworm eat? (November 12, 2008)

10. *Pick a Card, Any Card* Three face cards from an ordinary deck of playing cards lie facedown in a horizontal row and are arranged such that immediately to the right of a king is a queen or two queens, immediately to the left of a queen is a queen or two queens, immediately to the left of a heart is a spade or two spades, and immediately to the right of a spade is a spade or two spades. Name the three cards in order. (April 23, 2008)

11. ***Catwoman's Cats*** If you ask Batman's nemesis, Catwoman, how many cats she has, she answers with a riddle: "Five-sixths of my cats plus seven." How many cats does Catwoman have? (April 20, 2003)

12. ***Pencil Collection*** Bob gave four-fifths of his pencils to Barbara, then he gave two-thirds of the remaining pencils to Bonnie. If he ended up with ten pencils for himself, with how many did he start? (October 12, 2003)

13. ***Adding Gasoline*** The gasoline gauge on a van initially read $\frac{1}{8}$ full. When 15 gallons were added to the tank, the gauge read $\frac{3}{4}$ full. How many more gallons are needed to fill the tank? (November 25, 2004)

14. ***Gasoline Tank Capacity*** When 6 gallons of gasoline are put into a car's tank, the indicator goes from $\frac{1}{4}$ of a tank to $\frac{5}{8}$. What is the total capacity of the gasoline tank? (February 21, 2004)

15. ***Number Pattern*** What is the relationship between the rows of numbers?

$$18, \quad 38, \quad 24, \quad 46, \quad 42$$
$$8, \quad 24, \quad 8, \quad 24, \quad 8$$

(May 26, 2005)

16. ***Unknown Number*** The number in an unshaded square is obtained by adding the numbers connected with it from the row above. (The 11 is one such number.) What is the value of x? (December 22, 2008)

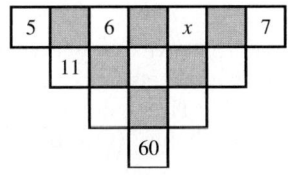

17. ***Locking Boxes*** You and I each have one lock and a corresponding key. I want to mail you a box with a ring in it, but any box that is not locked will be emptied before it reaches its recipient. How can I safely send you the ring? (Note that you and I each have keys to our own lock but not to the other lock.) (May 4, 2004)

18. ***Woodchuck Chucking Wood*** Nine woodchucks can chuck eight pieces of wood in 3 hours. How much wood can a woodchuck chuck in 1 hour? (May 24, 2004)

19. ***Number in a Sequence*** In the sequence 16, 80, 48, 64, A, B, C, D, each term beyond the second term is the arithmetic mean (average) of the two previous terms. What is the value of D? (April 26, 2004)

20. ***Unknown Number*** Cindy was asked by her teacher to subtract 3 from a certain number and then divide the result by 9. Instead, she subtracted 9 and then divided the result by 3, giving an answer of 43. What would her answer have been if she had worked the problem correctly? (September 3, 2004)

21. ***Labeling Boxes*** You are working in a store that has been very careless with the stock. Three boxes of socks are each incorrectly labeled. The labels say *red socks, green socks*, and *red and green socks*. How can you relabel the boxes correctly by taking only one sock out of one box, without looking inside the boxes? (October 22, 2001)

22. ***Vertical Symmetry in States' Names*** (If a vertical line is drawn through the center of a figure and the left and right sides are reflections of each other across this line, the figure is said to have vertical symmetry.) When spelled with all capital letters, each letter in HAWAII has vertical symmetry. Find the name of a state whose letters all have vertical and horizontal symmetry. (September 11, 2001)

23. ***Sum of Hidden Dots on Dice*** Three dice with faces numbered 1 through 6 are stacked as shown. Seven of the eighteen faces are visible, leaving eleven faces hidden on the back, on the bottom, and between dice. The total number of dots not visible in this view is _____.

A. 21
B. 22
C. 31
D. 41
E. 53

(September 17, 2001)

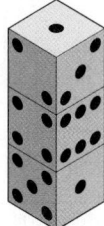

24. ***Mr. Green's Age*** At his birthday party, Mr. Green would not directly tell how old he was. He said, "If you add the year of my birth to this year, subtract the year of my tenth birthday and the year of my fiftieth birthday, and then add my present age, the result is eighty." How old was Mr. Green? (December 14, 1997)

25. ***Unfolding and Folding a Box*** An unfolded box is shown below.

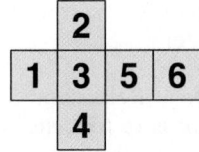

Which figure shows the box folded up? (November 7, 2001)

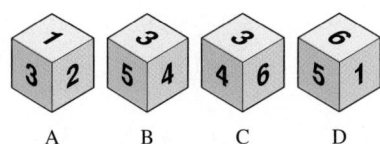

A   B   C   D

26. ***Age of the Bus Driver*** Today is your first day driving a city bus. When you leave downtown, you have twenty-three passengers. At the first stop, three people exit and five people get on the bus. At the second stop, eleven people exit and eight people get on the bus. At the third stop, five people exit and ten people get on. How old is the bus driver? (April 1, 2002)

27. *Matching Triangles and Squares* How can you connect each square with the triangle that has the same number? Lines cannot cross, enter a square or triangle, or go outside the diagram. (October 15, 1999)

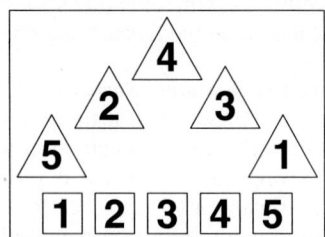

28. *Squared Rectangle* A **squared rectangle,** shown here, is a rectangle whose interior can be completely divided into two or more squares. The number written inside a square is the length of a side of that square. Compute the area of this squared rectangle. (September 22, 2009)

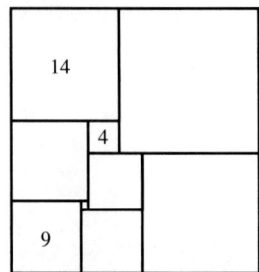

29. *Forming Perfect Square Sums* How must one place the integers from 1 to 15 in each of the spaces below in such a way that no number is repeated and the sum of the numbers in any two consecutive spaces is a perfect square? (November 11, 2001)

30. *How Old?* Pat and Chris have the same birthday. Pat is twice as old as Chris was when Pat was as old as Chris is now. If Pat is now 24 years old, how old is Chris? (December 3, 2001)

31. *Difference Triangle* Balls numbered 1 through 6 are arranged in a **difference triangle.** Note that in any row, the difference between the larger and the smaller of two successive balls is the number of the ball that appears below them. Arrange balls numbered 1 through 10 in a difference triangle. (May 6, 1998)

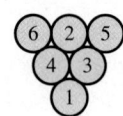

32. *Clock Face* By drawing two straight lines, divide the face of a clock into three regions such that the numbers in the regions have the same total. (October 28, 1998)

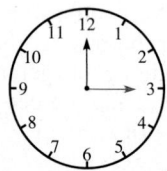

33. *Alphametric* If a, b, and c are digits for which

$$\begin{array}{cccc} & 7 & a & 2 \\ - & 4 & 8 & b \\ \hline & c & 7 & 3, \end{array}$$

then $a + b + c =$ _____.

A. 14 **B.** 15 **C.** 16 **D.** 17 **E.** 18

(September 22, 1999)

34. *Perfect Square* Only one of these numbers is a perfect square. Which one is it? (October 8, 1997)

329476 389372 964328
326047 724203

35. *Sleeping on the Way to Grandma's House* While traveling to his grandmother's for Christmas, George fell asleep halfway through the journey. When he awoke, he still had to travel half the distance that he had traveled while sleeping. For what part of the entire journey had he been asleep? (December 25, 1998)

36. *Counting Puzzle (Rectangles)* How many rectangles of any size are in the figure shown? (September 10, 2001)

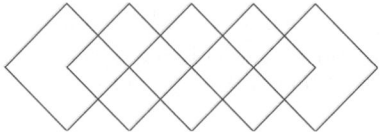

37. *Buckets of Water* You have brought two unmarked buckets to a stream. The buckets hold 7 gallons and 3 gallons of water, respectively. How can you obtain exactly 5 gallons of water to take home? (October 19, 1997)

38. *Multiples of 9* The first two of three consecutive multiples of 9 sum to 2511. What are the numbers? (January 4, 2010)

39. *Counting Puzzle (Rectangles)* How many rectangles are in the figure? (March 27, 1997)

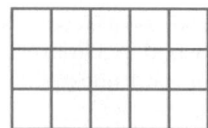

40. *Digit Puzzle* Place each of the digits 1, 2, 3, 4, 5, 6, 7, and 8 in separate boxes so that boxes that share common corners do not contain successive digits. (November 29, 1997)

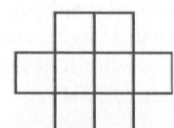

41. Palindromic Number (*Note:* A **palindromic number** is a number whose digits read the same left to right as right to left. For example, 383, 12321, and 9876789 are palindromic.) The odometer of the family car read 15951 when the driver noticed that the number was palindromic. "Curious," said the driver to herself. "It will be a long time before that happens again." But 2 hours later, the odometer showed a new palindromic number. (*Author's note:* Assume it was the next possible one.) How fast was the car driving in those 2 hours? (December 26, 1998)

42. How Much Is That Doggie in the Window? A man wishes to sell a puppy for $11. A customer who wants to buy it has only foreign currency. The exchange rate for the foreign currency is as follows: 11 round coins = $15, 11 square coins = $16, 11 triangular coins = $17. How many of each coin should the customer pay? (April 20, 2008)

43. Final Digits of a Power of 7 What are the final two digits of 7^{1997}? (November 29, 1997)

44. Consecutive Whole Numbers The sum of nine consecutive whole numbers is 123,456,789,987,654,321. What is the difference between the largest and smallest of these numbers? (October 4, 2008)

45. Summing the Digits When $10^{50} - 50$ is expressed as a single whole number, what is the sum of its digits? (April 7, 2008)

46. Units Digit of a Power of 3 If you raise 3 to the 324th power, what is the units digit of the result?

47. Units Digit of a Power of 7 What is the units digit in 7^{491}?

48. Frog Climbing up a Well A frog is at the bottom of a 20-foot well. Each day it crawls up 4 feet, but each night it slips back 3 feet. After how many days will the frog reach the top of the well?

49. Going Postal Joanie wants to mail a package that requires $1.53 in postage. If she has only 5-cent and 8-cent stamps, what is the smallest number of stamps she could use that would total exactly $1.53? (August 20, 2008)

50. Money Spent at a Bazaar Christine O'Brien bought a book for $10 and then spent half her remaining money on a train ticket. She then bought lunch for $4 and spent half her remaining money at a bazaar. She left the bazaar with $8. How much money did she start with?

51. Matching Socks A drawer contains 20 black socks and 20 white socks. If the light is off and you reach into the drawer to get your socks, what is the minimum number of socks you must pull out in order to be sure that you have a matching pair?

52. Counting Puzzle (Squares) How many squares are in the figure?

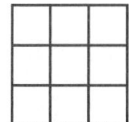

53. Counting Puzzle (Triangles) How many triangles are in the figure?

54. Fun with Fractions A strip of paper is $\frac{2}{3}$ meter long. Can a strip exactly $\frac{1}{2}$ meter long be made without the use of a ruler? If so, how? (September 8, 2008)

55. Perfect Number A **perfect number** is a counting number that is equal to the sum of all its counting number divisors except itself. For example, 28 is a perfect number because its divisors other than itself are 1, 2, 4, 7, and 14, and $1 + 2 + 4 + 7 + 14 = 28$. What is the least perfect number?

56. Naming Children Becky's mother has three daughters. She named her first daughter Penny and her second daughter Nichole. What did she name her third daughter?

57. Growth of a Lily Pad A lily pad grows so that each day it doubles its size. On the twentieth day of its life, it completely covers a pond. On what day was the pond half covered?

58. Interesting Property of a Sentence Comment on an interesting property of this sentence: "A man, a plan, a canal, Panama." (*Hint:* See **Exercise 41.**)

59. High School Graduation Year of Author One of the authors of this book graduated from high school in the year that satisfies these conditions: (1) The sum of the digits is 23; (2) The hundreds digit is 3 more than the tens digit; (3) No digit is an 8. In what year did he graduate?

60. Analyzing Units A day is divided into 24 hours. Each hour has 60 minutes, and each minute has 60 seconds. In another system of measurement, each day has 20 naps and each nap has 40 winks. How many seconds are in a wink? (November 10, 2008)

61. Adam and Eve's Assets Eve said to Adam, "If you give me one dollar, then we will have the same amount of money." Adam then replied, "Eve, if you give me one dollar, I will have double the amount of money you are left with." How much does each have?

62. Missing Digits Puzzle In the addition problem below, some digits are missing as indicated by the blanks. If the problem is done correctly, what is the sum of the missing digits?

$$
\begin{array}{r}
\_\ 3\ 5 \\
8\ \_\ 6 \\
+\ 1\ 4\ \_ \\
\hline
\_\ 4\ 0\ 8
\end{array}
$$

63. Missing Digits Puzzle Fill in the blanks so that the multiplication problem below uses all digits 0, 1, 2, 3, ..., 9 exactly once, and is correctly worked.

$$
\begin{array}{r}
\_\ 0\ 2 \\
\times\quad\ 3\ \_ \\
\hline
\_\ 5,\ \_\ \_\ \_
\end{array}
$$

64. Magic Square A **magic square** is a square array of numbers that has the property that the sum of the numbers in any row, column, or diagonal is the same. Fill in the square below so that it becomes a magic square, and all digits 1, 2, 3, ..., 9 are used exactly once.

6		8
	5	
		4

65. Magic Square Refer to **Exercise 64.** Complete the magic square below so that all counting numbers 1, 2, 3, . . . , 16 are used exactly once, and the sum in each row, column, or diagonal is 34.

6			9
	15		14
11		10	
16		13	

66. Decimal Digit What is the 100th digit in the decimal representation for $\frac{1}{7}$?

67. Pitches in a Baseball Game What is the minimum number of pitches that a baseball player who pitches a complete game can make in a regulation 9-inning baseball game?

68. Weighing Coins You have eight coins. Seven are genuine and one is a fake, which weighs a little less than the other seven. You have a balance scale, which you may use only three times. Tell how to locate the bad coin in three weighings. (Then show how to detect the bad coin in only *two* weighings.)

69. Geometry Puzzle When the diagram shown is folded to form a cube, what letter is opposite the face marked Z?

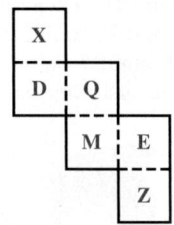

70. Number Pattern If the pattern below continues, where would the number 289 appear?

$$
\begin{array}{ccccc}
 & & 1 & & \\
 & 3 & & 5 & \\
7 & & 9 & & 11
\end{array}
$$

(November 11, 2008)

71. Geometry Puzzle Draw the following figure without picking up your pencil from the paper and without tracing over a line you have already drawn.

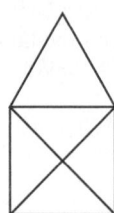

72. Geometry Puzzle Repeat **Exercise 71** for this figure.

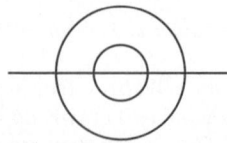

73. Paying for a Mint Brian Altobello has an unlimited number of cents (pennies), nickels, and dimes. In how many different ways can he pay 15¢ for a chocolate mint? (For example, one way is 1 dime and 5 pennies.)

74. Books on a Shelf Volumes 1 and 2 of *The Complete Works of Wally Smart* are standing in numerical order from left to right on your bookshelf. Volume 1 has 450 pages and Volume 2 has 475 pages. Excluding the covers, how many pages are between page 1 of Volume 1 and page 475 of Volume 2?

75. *Area and Perimeter* Triangle ABC has sides 10, 24, and 26 cm long. A rectangle that has an area equal to that of the triangle is 3 cm wide. Find the perimeter of the rectangle. (November 13, 2008)

76. *Teenager's Age* A teenager's age increased by 2 gives a perfect square. Her age decreased by 10 gives the square root of that perfect square. She is 5 years older than her brother. How old is her brother?

77. *Ages* James, Dan, Jessica, and Cathy form a pair of married couples. Their ages are 36, 31, 30, and 29. Jessica is married to the oldest person in the group. James is older than Jessica but younger than Cathy. Who is married to whom, and what are their ages?

78. *Making Change* In how many different ways can you make change for a half dollar using currently minted U.S. coins, if cents (pennies) are not allowed?

79. *Days in a Month* Some months have 30 days and some have 31 days. How many months have 28 days?

80. *Dirt in a Hole* How much dirt is there in a cubical hole, 6 feet on each side?

81. *Final Digit* What is the last digit of $49,327^{1783}$? (April 11, 2009)

82. *Missing Digit* Find the missing digit, x, in the product given by

$$(172195)(572167) = 985242x6565.$$

(May 3, 2009)

83. *Geometry Puzzle* What is the maximum number of small squares in which we may place crosses ($\times$) and not have any row, column, or diagonal completely filled with crosses? Illustrate your answer.

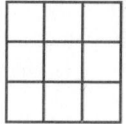

84. *Making Change* Webster has some pennies, dimes, and quarters in his pocket. When Josefa asks him for change for a dollar, Webster discovers that he cannot make the change exactly. What is the largest possible total value of the coins in his pocket? (October 5, 2009)

85. *Fibonacci Property* Refer to **Example 1**, and observe the sequence of numbers in color. Choose any four successive terms. Multiply the first one chosen by the fourth. Then multiply the two middle terms. Repeat this process. What do you notice when the two products are compared?

1.4 CALCULATING, ESTIMATING, AND READING GRAPHS

Calculation • Estimation • Interpretation of Graphs

Calculation

The search for easier ways to calculate and compute has culminated in the development of hand-held calculators and computers. For the general population, a calculator that performs the operations of arithmetic and a few other functions is sufficient. These are known as **four-function calculators.** Students who take higher mathematics courses (engineers, for example) usually need the added power of **scientific calculators. Graphing calculators,** which actually plot graphs on small screens, are also available. *Always refer to your owner's manual if you need assistance in performing an operation with your calculator. If you need further help, ask your instructor or another student who is using the same model.*

Current models of calculators differ from earlier versions in that they can display both the information the user inputs and the result generated on the same screen. In this way, the user can verify that the information entered into the calculator is correct. Although it is not necessary to have a graphing calculator to study the material presented in this text, we occasionally include graphing calculator screens to support results obtained or to provide supplemental information.*

The photograph shows the **Sharp EL-2139 HB,** a typical four-function calculator.

Since the introduction of hand-held calculators in the early 1970s, the methods of everyday arithmetic have been drastically altered. One of the first consumer models available was the Texas Instruments SR-10, which sold for nearly $150 in 1973. It could perform the four operations of arithmetic and take square roots, but could do very little more.

---

*Because they are the most popular models of graphing calculators, we include screens similar to those generated by TI-83 Plus and TI-84 Plus models from Texas Instruments.

The popular **TI-84 Plus** graphing calculator is shown here.

The screens that follow illustrate some common entries and operations.

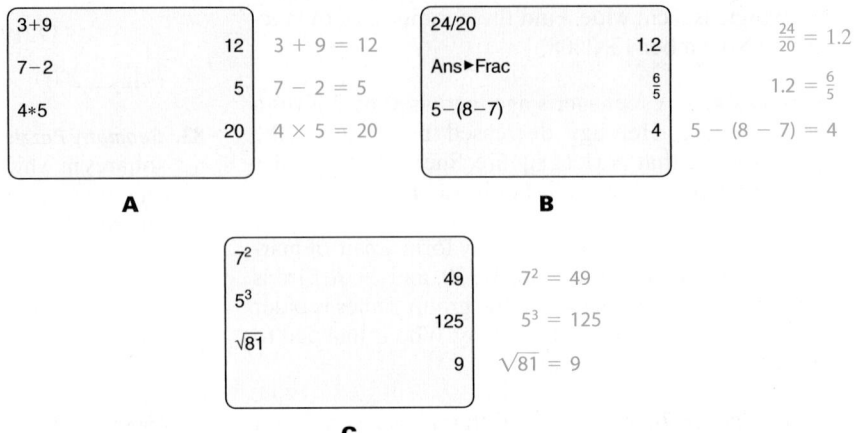

Screen A illustrates how two numbers can be added, subtracted, or multiplied. Screen B shows how two numbers can be divided, how the decimal quotient (stored in the memory cell Ans) can be converted into a fraction, and how parentheses can be used in a computation. Screen C shows how a number can be squared, how it can be cubed, and how its square root can be taken.

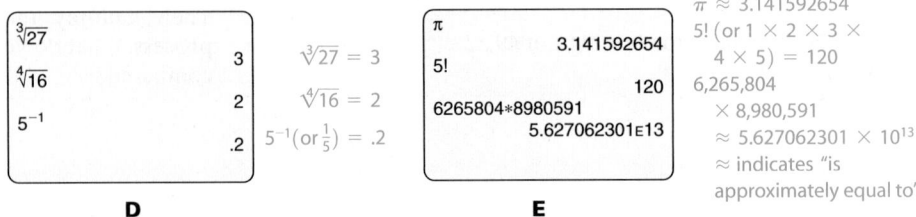

Screen D shows how other roots (cube root and fourth root) can be found, and how the reciprocal of a number can be found using −1 as an exponent. Screen E shows how π can be accessed with its own special key, how a **factorial** (as indicated by !) can be found and how a result might be displayed in **scientific notation**. (The "E13" following 5.627062301 means that this number is multiplied by 10^{13}. This answer is still only an approximation, because the product 6,265,804 × 8,980,591 contains more digits than the calculator can display.)

Estimation

Although calculators can make life easier when it comes to computations, many times we need only estimate an answer to a problem, and in these cases a calculator may not be necessary or appropriate.

EXAMPLE 1 Estimating an Appropriate Number of Birdhouses

A birdhouse for swallows can accommodate up to 8 nests. How many birdhouses would be necessary to accommodate 58 nests?

SOLUTION

If we divide 58 by 8 either by hand or with a calculator, we get 7.25. Can this possibly be the desired number? Of course not, because we cannot consider fractions of birdhouses. Do we need 7 or 8 birdhouses? To provide nesting space for the nests left over after the 7 birdhouses (as indicated by the decimal fraction), we should plan to use 8 birdhouses. In this problem, we must round our answer *up* to the next counting number. ▮▮▮

▌▌ **EXAMPLE 2**   Approximating Average Number of Yards per Carry

In 2009, Cedric Benson carried the football 301 times for 1251 yards (*Source:* www.nfl.com). Approximate his average number of yards per carry that year.

SOLUTION

Because we are are asked only to find Cedric's approximate average, we can say that he carried about 300 times for about 1200 yards, and his average was about $\frac{1200}{300} = 4$ yards per carry. (A calculator shows that his average to the nearest tenth was 4.2 yards per carry. Verify this.)   ▐▐▐

▌▌ **EXAMPLE 3**   Comparing Proportions of Workers by Age Groups

In a recent year, there were approximately 127,000 males in the 25 – 29-year age bracket working on farms. This represented part of the total of 238,000 farm workers in that age bracket. Of the 331,000 farm workers in the 40 – 44-year age bracket, 160,000 were males. Without using a calculator, determine which age bracket had a larger proportion of males.

SOLUTION

Think in terms of thousands instead of dealing with all the zeros. First, we analyze the age bracket 25 – 29 years. Because there were a total of 238 thousand workers, of which 127 thousand were males, there were

$$238 - 127 = 111 \text{ thousand female workers.}$$ More than half were males.

In the 40 – 44-year age bracket, of the 331 thousand workers, there were 160 thousand males, giving

$$331 - 160 = 171 \text{ thousand female workers.}$$ Fewer than half were males.

The 25 – 29-year age bracket had the larger proportion of males.   ▐▐▐

Interpretation of Graphs

In a **circle graph,** or **pie chart,** a circle is used to indicate the total of all the data categories represented. The circle is divided into sectors, or wedges (like pieces of a pie), whose sizes show the relative magnitudes of the categories. The sum of all the fractional parts must be 1 (for 1 whole circle).

▌▌ **EXAMPLE 4**   Interpreting Information in a Circle Graph

Use the circle graph in **Figure 9** to determine how much of the amount spent for a $3.50 gallon of gasoline in California goes to refinery margin and to crude oil cost.

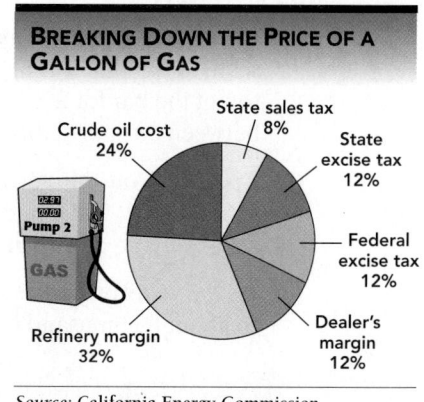

Source: California Energy Commission.

Figure 9

SOLUTION

The sectors in the circle graph in **Figure 9** are sized to match how the price is divided. For example, the greatest portion of the price (32%) goes to the refinery, while the least portion (8%) goes for state sales tax. As expected, the percents total 100%. The price of gasoline is $3.50 per gallon.

$$\text{Refinery margin: } \$3.50 \times \underbrace{0.32}_{32\% \text{ converted to a decimal}} = \$1.12$$

$$\text{Crude oil cost: } \$3.50 \times \underbrace{0.24}_{24\% \text{ converted to a decimal}} = \$0.84$$ ▮▮▮

A **bar graph** is used to show comparisons. It consists of a series of bars (or simulations of bars) arranged either vertically or horizontally. In a bar graph, values from two categories are paired with each other (for example, years with sales).

▮▮ **EXAMPLE 5** Interpreting Information in a Bar Graph

The bar graph in **Figure 10** shows U.S. sales of motor scooters, which have gained popularity due to their fuel efficiency. The graph compares sales in thousands.

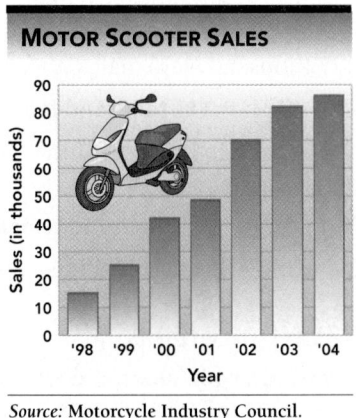

Source: Motorcycle Industry Council.

Figure 10

(a) Estimate sales in 2000 and 2004.

(b) In what years were sales greater than 50 thousand?

(c) Describe the change in sales as the years progressed.

SOLUTION

(a) Locate the top of the bar for 2000, and move horizontally across to the vertical scale to see that it is about 40. Sales in 2000 were about 40 thousand. Follow the top of the bar for 2004 across to the vertical scale to see that it lies about halfway between 80 and 90 thousand, so sales in 2004 were about 85,000.

(b) Locate 50 on the vertical scale and follow the line across to the right. Three years—2002, 2003, and 2004—have bars that extend above the line for 50, so sales were greater than 50 thousand in those years.

(c) As the years progressed, sales increased steadily, from about 15 thousand in 1998 to about 85 thousand in 2004. ▮▮▮

A **line graph** is used to show changes or trends in data over time. To form a line graph, we connect a series of points representing data with line segments.

▮▮ **EXAMPLE 6** Interpreting Information in a Line Graph

Current projections indicate that funding for Medicare will not cover its costs unless the program changes. The line graph in **Figure 11** shows Medicare funds in billions of dollars for the years 2004 through 2013.

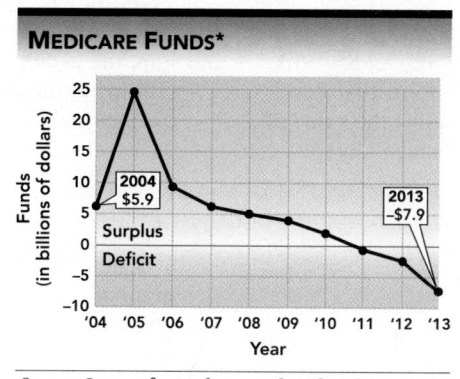

MEDICARE FUNDS*

Source: Centers for Medicare and Medicaid Services.
*Projected

Figure 11

(a) Estimate the funds in the years 2005 and 2006. About how much did the funding decrease from 2005 to 2006?

(b) Which is the only period in which Medicare funds increased? What is the projected trend from 2005 to 2013?

(c) In which year is it projected that funds will first show a deficit?

SOLUTION

(a) At the bottom of the graph, locate 2005, and read up to find that the point has a height of about 25 (billion dollars). Similarly, the point for 2006 has height about 10 (billion dollars). The funding *decreased* by about

$$25 - 10 = 15 \text{ billion dollars.} \quad \text{2005 amount} - \text{2006 amount}$$

(b) The graph *rises* from 2004 to 2005, so funds increased between these two years. The graph *falls* during 2005 to 2013, so funds will decrease.

(c) From 2004 to 2010, the graph is always above 0, but in 2011, it falls slightly below 0 for the first time, indicating a deficit. ▮▮▮

1.4 EXERCISES

Perform the indicated operations and give as many digits in your answer as shown on your calculator display. (The number of displayed digits may vary depending on the model used.)

1. $39.7 + (8.2 - 4.1)$

2. $2.8 \times (3.2 - 1.1)$

3. $\sqrt{5.56440921}$

4. $\sqrt{37.38711025}$

5. $\sqrt[3]{418.508992}$

6. $\sqrt[3]{700.227072}$

7. 2.67^2

8. 3.49^3

9. 5.76^5

10. 1.48^6

11. $\dfrac{14.32 - 8.1}{2 \times 3.11}$

12. $\dfrac{12.3 + 18.276}{3 \times 1.04}$

13. $\sqrt[5]{1.35}$

14. $\sqrt[6]{3.21}$

15. $\dfrac{\pi}{\sqrt{2}}$

16. $\dfrac{2\pi}{\sqrt{3}}$

17. $\sqrt[4]{\dfrac{2143}{22}}$

18. $\dfrac{12,345,679 \times 72}{\sqrt[3]{27}}$

19. $\dfrac{\sqrt{2}}{\sqrt[3]{6}}$

20. $\dfrac{\sqrt[3]{12}}{\sqrt{3}}$

21. Choose any number consisting of five digits. Multiply it by 9 on your calculator. Now add the digits in the answer. If the sum is more than 9, add the digits of this sum, and repeat until the sum is less than 10. Your answer will always be 9. Repeat the exercise with a number consisting of six digits. Does the same result hold?

22. Use your calculator to *square* the following two-digit numbers ending in 5: 15, 25, 35, 45, 55, 65, 75, 85. Write down your results, and examine the pattern that develops. Then use inductive reasoning to predict the value of 95^2. Write an explanation of how you can mentally square a two-digit number ending in 5.

Perform each calculation and observe the answers. Then fill in the blank with the appropriate response.

23. $\boxed{\frac{-3}{-8}}$; $\boxed{\frac{-5}{-4}}$; $\boxed{\frac{-2.1}{-4.3}}$

    Dividing a negative number by another negative number gives a _____ product.
    (negative/positive)

24. $\boxed{5 \cdot -4}$; $\boxed{-3 \cdot 8}$; $\boxed{2.1 \cdot -4.3}$

    Multiplying a negative number by a positive number gives a _____ product.
    (negative/positive)

25. $\boxed{5.6^0}$; $\boxed{\pi^0}$; $\boxed{2^0}$; $\boxed{120^0}$

    Raising a nonzero number to the power 0 gives a result of _____.

26. $\boxed{1^2}$; $\boxed{1^3}$; $\boxed{1^{-3}}$; $\boxed{1^0}$

    Raising 1 to any power gives a result of _____.

27. $\boxed{\frac{1}{7}}$; $\boxed{\frac{1}{-9}}$; $\boxed{\frac{1}{3}}$; $\boxed{\frac{1}{-8}}$

    The sign of the reciprocal of a number is _____ the sign of the number.
    (the same as/different from)

28. $\boxed{5 \div 0}$; $\boxed{9 \div 0}$; $\boxed{0 \div 0}$

    Dividing a number by 0 gives a(n) _____ on a calculator.

29. $\boxed{0 \div 8}$; $\boxed{0 \div -2}$; $\boxed{0 \div \pi}$

    Zero divided by a nonzero number gives a quotient of _____.

30. $\boxed{\sqrt{-3}}$; $\boxed{\sqrt{-4}}$; $\boxed{\sqrt{-10}}$

    Taking the square root of a negative number gives a(n) _____ on a calculator.

31. $\boxed{-3 \cdot -4 \cdot -5}$; $\boxed{-3 \cdot -4 \cdot -5 \cdot -6 \cdot -7}$;

    $\boxed{-3 \cdot -4 \cdot -5 \cdot -6 \cdot -7 \cdot -8 \cdot -9}$

    Multiplying an *odd* number of negative numbers gives a _____ product.
    (positive/negative)

32. $\boxed{-3 \cdot -4}$; $\boxed{-3 \cdot -4 \cdot -5 \cdot -6}$;

    $\boxed{-3 \cdot -4 \cdot -5 \cdot -6 \cdot -7 \cdot -8}$

    Multiplying an *even* number of negative numbers gives a _____ product.
    (positive/negative)

33. Find the decimal representation of $\frac{1}{6}$ on your calculator. Following the decimal point will be a 1 and a string of 6s. The final digit will be a 7 if your calculator *rounds off* or a 6 if it *truncates*. Which kind of calculator do you have?

34. Choose any three-digit number and enter the digits into a calculator. Then enter them again to get a six-digit number. Divide this six-digit number by 7. Divide the result by 13. Divide the result by 11. What is interesting about your answer? Explain why this happens.

35. Choose any digit except 0. Multiply it by 429. Now multiply the result by 259. What is interesting about your answer? Explain why this happens.

36. Choose two natural numbers. Add 1 to the second and divide by the first to get a third. Add 1 to the third and divide by the second to get a fourth. Add 1 to the fourth and divide by the third to get a fifth. Continue this process until you discover a pattern. What is the pattern?

Give an appropriate counting number answer to each question in Exercises 37–40. (Find the least counting number that will work.)

37. **Pages to Store Trading Cards** A plastic page designed to hold trading cards will hold up to 9 cards. How many pages will be needed to store 563 cards?

38. **Drawers for DVDs** A sliding drawer designed to hold DVD cases has 20 compartments. If Chris wants to house his collection of 408 Disney DVDs, how many such drawers will he need?

39. **Containers for African Violets** A gardener wants to fertilize 800 African violets. Each container of fertilizer will supply up to 60 plants. How many containers will she need to do the job?

40. *Fifth-Grade Teachers Needed* False River Academy has 155 fifth-grade students. The principal, Butch LeBeau, has decided that each fifth-grade teacher should have a maximum of 24 students. How many fifth-grade teachers does he need?

In Exercises 41–46, use estimation to determine the choice closest to the correct answer.

41. *Price per Acre of Land* To build a "millennium clock" on Mount Washington in Nevada that would tick once each year, chime once each century, and last at least 10,000 years, the nonprofit Long Now Foundation purchased 80 acres of land for $140,000. Which one of the following is the closest estimate to the price per acre?

A. $1000   **B.** $2000   **C.** $4000   **D.** $11,200

42. *Time of a Round-Trip* The distance from Seattle, Washington, to Springfield, Missouri, is 2009 miles. About how many hours would a roundtrip from Seattle to Springfield and back take a bus that averages 50 miles per hour for the entire trip?

A. 60   **B.** 70   **C.** 80   **D.** 90

43. *People per Square Mile* Buffalo County in Nebraska has a population of 40,249 and covers 968 square miles. About how many people per square mile live in Buffalo County?

A. 40   **B.** 400   **C.** 4000   **D.** 40,000

44. *Revolutions of Mercury* The planet Mercury takes 88.0 Earth days to revolve around the sun once. Pluto takes 90,824.2 days to do the same. When Pluto has revolved around the sun once, about how many times will Mercury have revolved around the sun?

A. 100,000   **B.** 10,000   **C.** 1000   **D.** 100

45. *Reception Average* In 2009, Brandon Marshall of the Denver Broncos caught 101 passes for 1120 yards. His approximate number of yards gained per catch was _____.

A. $\dfrac{1}{11}$ **B.** 110   **C.** 1.1   **D.** 11

46. *Area of the Sistine Chapel* The Sistine Chapel in Vatican City measures 40.5 meters by 13.5 meters.

Which is the closest approximation to its area?

A. 110 meters   **B.** 55 meters
C. 110 square meters   **D.** 600 square meters

Immigration *The circle graph below shows the approximate percent of immigrants admitted into the United States during the 1990s. Use the graph to answer the questions in Exercises 47–50.*

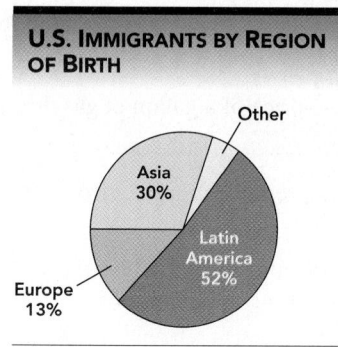

U.S. IMMIGRANTS BY REGION OF BIRTH

Other
Asia 30%
Latin America 52%
Europe 13%

Source: U.S. Bureau of the Census.

47. What percent of the immigrants were from the "Other" group of countries?

48. What percent of the immigrants were not from Asia?

49. In a group of 2,000,000 immigrants, how many would you expect to be from Europe?

50. In a group of 4,000,000 immigrants, how many more would there be from Latin America than all the other regions combined?

Milk Production *The bar graph shows total U.S. milk production in billions of pounds for the years 2001 through 2007. Use the bar graph to work Exercises 51–54.*

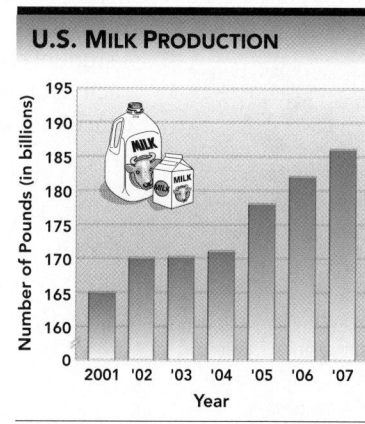

U.S. MILK PRODUCTION

Source: U.S. Department of Agriculture.

51. In what years was U.S. milk production greater than 175 billion pounds?

52. In what two years was U.S. milk production about the same?

53. Estimate U.S. milk production in 2001 and 2007.

54. Describe the change in U.S. milk production from 2001 to 2007.

Gasoline Prices The line graph shows the average price, adjusted for inflation, that Americans have paid for a gallon of gasoline for selected years since 1970. Use the line graph to work Exercises 55–58.

55. Over which 5-year period did the greatest increase in the price of a gallon of gas occur? About how much was this increase?

56. Estimate the price of a gallon of gas during 1985, 1990, 1995, and 2000.

57. Describe the trend in gas prices from 1980 to 1995.

58. During which year(s) did a gallon of gas cost approximately $1.50?

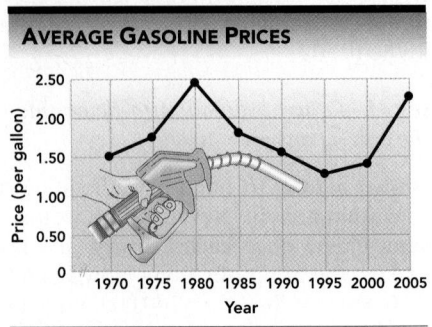

AVERAGE GASOLINE PRICES

Source: Energy Information Administration.

EXTENSION Using Writing to Learn about Mathematics

Journals • Learning Logs • Reports on Articles • Term Papers

Research has indicated that the ability to express mathematical observations in writing can serve as a positive force in one's continued development as a mathematics student. The implementation of writing in the mathematics class can use several approaches.

Journals One way of using writing in mathematics is to keep a journal in which you spend a few minutes explaining what happened in class that day. The journal entries may be general or specific, depending on the topic covered, the degree to which you understand the topic, your interest level at the time, and so on. Journal entries are usually written in informal language and are often an effective means of communicating to yourself, your classmates, and your instructor what feelings, perceptions, and concerns you are having at the time.

Learning Logs Although journal entries are for the most part unstructured writings in which the student's thoughts are allowed to roam freely, entries in learning logs are typically more structured. An instructor may pose a specific question for a student to answer in a learning log. In this text, we intersperse writing exercises in each exercise set that are appropriate for answering in a learning log. For example, consider **Exercise 13** in the exercise set for the opening section in this chapter.

Discuss the differences between inductive and deductive reasoning. Give an example of each.

Here is a possible response to this exercise.

Mathematical writing takes many forms. One of the most famous author/mathematicians was **Charles Dodgson** (1832–1898), who used the pen name **Lewis Carroll.**

Dodgson was a mathematics lecturer at Oxford University in England. Queen Victoria told Dodgson how much she enjoyed *Alice's Adventures in Wonderland* and how much she wanted to read his next book; he is said to have sent her *Symbolic Logic,* his most famous mathematical work.

The *Alice* books made Carroll famous. Late in life, however, Dodgson shunned attention and denied that he and Carroll were the same person, even though he gave away hundreds of signed copies to children and children's hospitals.

Deductive reasoning occurs when you go from general ideas to specific ones. For example, I know that I can multiply both sides of $\frac{1}{2}x = 6$ by 2 to get $x = 12$, because I can multiply both sides of any equation by whatever I want (except 0). Inductive reasoning goes the other way. If I have a general conclusion from specific observations, that's inductive reasoning. Example – in the numbers 4, 8, 12, 16, and so on, I can conclude that the next number is 20, since I always add 4 to get the next number.

Reports on Articles   The motto "Publish or perish" has long been around, implying that a scholar in pursuit of an academic position must publish in a journal in his or her field. There are numerous journals that publish papers in mathematics research and/or mathematics education. In Activity 3, we suggest some articles that have appeared within the last few years. A report on such an article can help you understand what mathematicians do and what ideas mathematics teachers use to convey concepts to their students.

Term Papers   Professors in mathematics survey courses are, in increasing numbers, requiring short term papers of their students. In this way, you can become aware of the plethora of books and articles on mathematics and mathematicians, many written specifically for the layperson. In Activities 5 and 6, we provide a list of possible term paper topics.

EXTENSION ACTIVITIES

Rather than include a typical exercise set, we list some suggested activities in which writing can be used to enhance awareness and learning of mathematics.

Activity 1   Keep a journal. After each class, write for a few minutes on your perceptions about the class, the topics covered, or whatever you feel is appropriate.

Activity 2   Keep a learning log, answering at least one writing exercise from each exercise set covered in your class syllabus. Ask your teacher for suggestions of other types of specific writing assignments.

Activity 3   The National Council of Teachers of Mathematics publishes journals in mathematics education: *Teaching Children Mathematics* and *Mathematics Teacher* are two that can be found online or in the periodicals section of most college and university libraries. We have chosen several recent articles in each of these journals. Write a short report on one of these articles according to guidelines specified by your instructor.

From *Mathematics Teacher*
2004

Devaney, Robert L. "Fractal Patterns and Chaos Games." November 2004, p. 228.

Francis, Richard L. "New Worlds to Conquer." October 2004, p. 166.

Hansen, Will. "War and Pieces." September 2004, p. 70.

Mahoney, John F. "How Many Votes Are Needed to Be Elected President?" October 2004, p. 154.

2005

Clausen, Mary C. "Did You 'Code'?" November 2005, p. 260.

Comstock, Jocelyne M., Sean P. Madden, and James P. Downing. "Paper Moon: Simulating a Total Solar Eclipse." December 2005/January 2006, p. 312.

Parker, Dennis. "Partitioning the Interior of a Circle with Chords." September 2005, p. 120.

Quinn, Jennifer J., and Arthur T. Benjamin. "Revisiting Fibonacci and Related Sequences." December 2005/January 2006, p. 357.

2006

Cline, Kelly S. "Classroom Voting in Mathematics." September 2006, p. 100.

Gordon, Sheldon P. "Placement Tests: The Shaky Bridge Connecting School and College Mathematics." October 2006, p. 174.

Johnson, Iris DeLoach. "Grandfather Tang Goes to High School." March 2006, p. 522.

Wong, Michael. "The Human Body's Built-In Range Finder: The Thumb Method of Indirect Distance Measurement." May 2006, p. 622.

From *Teaching Children Mathematics*

2004

Anthony, Glenda J., and Margaret A. Walshaw. "Zero: A 'None' Number?" August 2004, p. 38.

Buschman, Larry. "Teaching Problem Solving in Mathematics." February 2004, p. 302.

Joram, Elana, Christina Hartman, and Paul R. Trafton. " 'As People Get Older, They Get Taller': An Integrated Unit on Measurement, Linear Relationships, and Data Analysis." March 2004, p. 344.

Mann, Rebecca L. "Balancing Act: The Truth Behind the Equals Sign." September 2004, p. 65.

2005

Flores, Alfinio, Erin E. Turner, and Renee C. Bachman. "Posing Problems to Develop Conceptual Understanding: Two Teachers Make Sense of Division of Fractions." October 2005, p. 17.

Hansen, Laurie E. "ABCs of Early Mathematics Experiences." November 2005, p. 208.

Sherrill, Carl M. "Math Riddles: Helping Children Connect Words and Numbers." March 2005, p. 368.

Thompson, Tony, and Stephen Sproule. "Calculators for Students with Special Needs." March 2005, p. 391.

2006

Barnes, Mary Kathleen. "How Many Days 'til My Birthday? Helping Kindergarten Students Understand Calendar Connections and Concepts." February 2006, p. 290.

Cassel, Darlinda, Anne Reynolds, and Eileen Lillard. "A Mathematical Exploration of Grandpa's Quilt." March 2006, p. 340.

de Groot, Cornelis, and Timothy Whalen. "Longing for Division." April 2006, p. 410.

Nugent, Christina M. "How Many Blades of Grass Are on a Football Field?" February 2006, p. 282.

Activity 4 One of the most popular mathematical films of all time is *Donald in Mathmagic Land*, a 1959 Disney short that is available on DVD. Spend an entertaining half-hour watching this film, and write a report on it according to the guidelines of your instructor.

Activity 5 Write a report according to the guidelines of your instructor on one of the following mathematicians, philosophers, and scientists.

© Disney Enterprises, Inc.

Abel, N.	Cardano, G.	Gauss, C.	Noether, E.
Agnesi, M. G.	Copernicus, N.	Hilbert, D.	Pascal, B.
Agnesi, M. T.	De Morgan, A.	Kepler, J.	Plato
Al-Khowârizmi	Descartes, R.	Kronecker, L.	Polya, G.
Apollonius	Euler, L.	Lagrange, J.	Pythagoras
Archimedes	Fermat, P.	Leibniz, G.	Ramanujan, S.
Aristotle	Fibonacci	L'Hôspital, G.	Riemann, G.
Babbage, C.	(Leonardo	Lobachevsky, N.	Russell, B.
Bernoulli, Jakob	of Pisa)	Mandelbrot, B.	Somerville, M.
Bernoulli,	Galileo (Galileo	Napier, J.	Tartaglia, N.
Johann	Galilei)	Nash, J.	Whitehead, A.
Cantor, G.	Galois, E.	Newton, I.	Wiles, A.

Activity 6 Write a term paper on one of the following topics in mathematics according to the guidelines of your instructor.

Babylonian mathematics
Egyptian mathematics
The origin of zero
Plimpton 322
The Rhind papyrus
Origins of the Pythagorean theorem
The regular (Platonic) solids
The Pythagorean brotherhood
The Golden Ratio (Golden Section)
The three famous construction problems of the Greeks
The history of the approximations of π
Euclid and his "Elements"
Early Chinese mathematics
Early Hindu mathematics
Origin of the word *algebra*
Magic squares
Figurate numbers
The Fibonacci sequence
The Cardano/Tartaglia controversy
Historical methods of computation (logarithms, the abacus, Napier's rods, the slide rule, etc.)

Pascal's triangle
The origins of probability theory
Women in mathematics
Mathematical paradoxes
Unsolved problems in mathematics
The four-color theorem
The proof of Fermat's Last Theorem
The search for large primes
Fractal geometry
The co-inventors of calculus
The role of the computer in the study of mathematics
Mathematics and music
Police mathematics
The origins of complex numbers
Goldbach's conjecture
The use of the Internet in mathematics education
The development of graphing calculators
Mathematics education reform movement
Multicultural mathematics
The Riemann Hypothesis

Activity 7 Investigate a computer program that focuses on teaching children elementary mathematics, and write a critical review of it as if you were writing for a journal that contains software reviews of educational material. Be sure to address the higher-level thinking skills in addition to drill and practice.

Activity 8 The following Web sites provide a fascinating list of mathematics-related topics. Go to one of them, choose a topic that interests you, and report on it, according to the guidelines of your instructor.

www.mathworld.wolfram.com

www.world.std.com/~reinhold/mathmovies.html

www.maths.surrey.ac.uk/hosted-sites/R.Knott/

http://dir.yahoo.com/Science/Mathematics/

www.cut-the-knot.com/

www.ics.uci.edu/~eppstein/recmath.html

Activity 9 A theme of mathematics-related scenes in movies and television is found throughout this book. Prepare a report on one or more such scenes, and determine whether the mathematics involved is correct or incorrect. If correct, show why. If incorrect, find the correct answer. See www.math.harvard.edu/~knill/mathmovies/ and www.mathclassgoestohollywood.com.

Activity 10 The longest running animated television series is *The Simpsons*, having begun in 1989. The Web site www.simpsonsmath.com explores the occurrence of mathematics in the episodes on a season-by-season basis. Watch several episodes and elaborate on the mathematics found in them.

COLLABORATIVE INVESTIGATION

Discovering Patterns in Pascal's Triangle

One fascinating array of numbers, **Pascal's triangle,** consists of rows of numbers, each of which contains one more entry than the one before. The first six rows are shown here.

To discover some of its patterns, divide the class into groups of four students each. Within each group designate one student as A, one as B, one as C, and one as D. Then perform the following activities in order.

1. Discuss among group members some of the properties of the triangle that are obvious from observing the first six rows shown.

2. It is fairly obvious that each row begins and ends with 1. Discover a method whereby the other entries in a row can be determined from the entries in the row immediately above it. (*Hint*: In the fifth row, 6 = 3 + 3.) Then, as a group, find the next three rows of the triangle, and have each member prepare his or her own copy of the entire first nine rows for later reference.

3. Now each student in the group will investigate a particular property of the triangle. In some cases, a calculator will be helpful. All students should begin working at the same time. (A discussion follows.)

Student A: Find the sum of the entries in each row. Notice the pattern that emerges. Now write the tenth row of the triangle.

Student B: Investigate the successive differences in the diagonals from upper left to lower right. For example, in the diagonal that begins $1, 2, 3, 4, \ldots$, the successive differences are all 1; in the diagonal that begins $1, 3, 6, \ldots$, the successive differences are 2, 3, 4, and so on. Do this up through the diagonal that begins $1, 6, 21, \ldots$.

Student C: Find the values of the first five powers of the number 11, starting with 11^0 (recall $11^0 = 1$).

Student D: Arrange these nine rows of the triangle with all rows "flush left," and then draw lightly dashed arrows as shown:

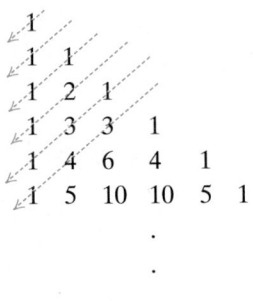

and so on. Then add along the diagonals. Write these sums in order from left to right.

4. After all students have concluded their individual investigations in Item 3, return to a group discussion.

   (a) Have student A report the result found in Item 3, and then make a prediction concerning the sum of the entries in the tenth row.

   (b) Have student B report the successive differences discovered in the diagonals. Then have all students in the group investigate the successive differences in the diagonal that begins $1, 7, 28 \ldots$. (It may be necessary to write a few more rows of the triangle.)

   (c) Have student C report the relationship between the powers of 11 found, and then determine the value of 11^5. Why does the pattern not continue here?

   (d) Have student D report the sequence of numbers found. Then, as a group, predict what the next sum will be by observing the pattern in the sequence. Confirm your prediction by actual computation.

5. Choose a representative from each group to report to the entire class the observations made throughout this investigation.

6. Find a reference to Pascal's triangle on the Internet and prepare a report.

CHAPTER 1 TEST

In Exercises 1 and 2, decide whether the reasoning involved is an example of inductive or deductive reasoning.

1. Carol Britz is a sales representative for a publishing company. For the past 16 years, she has exceeded her annual sales goal, primarily by selling mathematics textbooks. Therefore, she will also exceed her annual sales goal this year.

2. For all natural numbers n, n^2 is also a natural number. 176 is a natural number. Therefore, 176^2 is a natural number.

3. **Magic Hexagon** (A **magic hexagon** has all entries in the columns and diagonals adding up to the same sum.) Find the constant sum for the magic hexagon, and fill in the numbers so that every column or diagonal has that sum. (From *Mathematics Teacher* monthly calendar, November 20, 2007.)

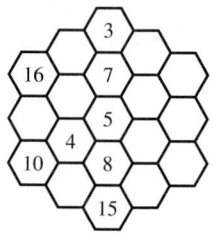

4. Use the list of equations and inductive reasoning to predict the next equation, and then verify your conjecture.

$$65,359,477,124,183 \times 17 = 1,111,111,111,111,111$$
$$65,359,477,124,183 \times 34 = 2,222,222,222,222,222$$
$$65,359,477,124,183 \times 51 = 3,333,333,333,333,333$$

5. Use the method of successive differences to find the next term in the sequence

$$3, 11, 31, 69, 131, 223, \ldots.$$

6. Find the sum $1 + 2 + 3 + \cdots + 250$.

7. Consider the following equations, where the left side of each is an octagonal number.

$$1 = 1$$
$$8 = 1 + 7$$
$$21 = 1 + 7 + 13$$
$$40 = 1 + 7 + 13 + 19$$

Use the pattern established on the right sides to predict the next octagonal number. What is the next equation in the list?

8. Use the result of **Exercise 7** and the method of successive differences to find the first eight octagonal numbers. Then divide each by 4 and record the remainder. What is the pattern obtained?

9. Describe the pattern used to obtain the terms of the Fibonacci sequence

$$1, 1, 2, 3, 5, 8, 13, 21, \ldots.$$

Use problem-solving strategies to solve each problem, taken from the date indicated in the monthly calendar of Mathematics Teacher.

10. **Building a Fraction** Each of the four digits 2, 4, 6, and 9 is placed in one of the boxes to form a fraction. The numerator and the denominator are both two-digit whole numbers. What is the smallest value of all the common fractions that can be formed? Express your answer as a common fraction. (November 17, 2004)

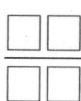

11. **Units Digit of a Power of 9** What is the units digit (ones digit) in the decimal representation of 9^{1997}? (January 27, 1997)

12. **Counting Puzzle (Triangles)** How many triangles are in this figure? (January 6, 2000)

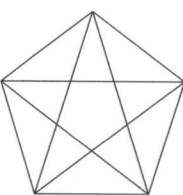

13. **Make Them Equal** Consider the following:

$$1\ 2\ 3\ 4\ 5\ 6\ 7\ 8\ 9\ 0 = 100.$$

Leaving all the numerals in the order given, insert addition and subtraction signs into the expression to make the equation true. (March 23, 2008)

14. **Shrinkage** Dr. Small is 36 inches tall, and Ms. Tall is 96 inches tall. If Dr. Small shrinks 2 inches per year and Ms. Tall grows $\frac{2}{3}$ of an inch per year, how tall will Ms. Tall be when Dr. Small disappears altogether? (November 2, 2007)

15. **Units Digit of a Sum** Find the units digit (ones digit) of the decimal numeral representing the number $11^{11} + 14^{14} + 16^{16}$. (February 14, 1994)

16. Based on your knowledge of elementary arithmetic, describe the pattern that can be observed when the following operations are performed:

$$9 \times 1, \quad 9 \times 2, \quad 9 \times 3, \ldots, 9 \times 9.$$

(*Hint:* Add the digits in the answers. What do you notice?)

Use your calculator to evaluate each of the following. Give as many decimal places as the calculator displays.

17. $\sqrt{98.16}$

18. 3.25^3

19. *Basketball Scoring Results* During the 2008–09 NCAA women's basketball season, Destini Hughes of LSU made 28 of her 96 field goal attempts. This means that for every 10 attempts, she made approximately _____ of them.

    A. 4   **B.** 3   **C.** 2   **D.** 1

20. *Unemployment Rate* The line graph shows the overall unemployment rate in the U.S. civilian labor force for the years 1998 through 2005.

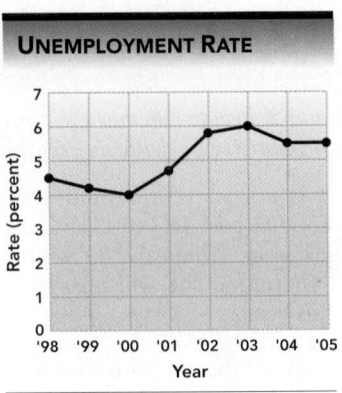

Source: U.S. Department of Labor.

(a) Between which pairs of consecutive years did the unemployment rate decrease?

(b) What was the general trend in the unemployment rate between 2000 and 2003?

(c) Estimate the overall unemployment rate in 2003 and 2004. About how much did the unemployment rate decline between 2003 and 2004?

THE BASIC CONCEPTS OF SET THEORY

2

In the movie *I.Q.*, Meg Ryan plays Catherine Boyd, Alfred Einstein's brilliant niece, who is attracted to blue-collar worker Ed Walters (Tim Robbins). Ed pretends to be a physicist.

ED: I think your uncle wants us to dance.

CATHERINE: Oh, now, don't be irrelevant, Ed. You can't get from there to here.

ED: Why not?

CATHERINE: Now don't tell me that a famous and brilliant scientist such as yourself doesn't know about Zeno's paradox.

ED: Remind me.

CATHERINE: You can't get from there to here because you always have to cover half the remaining distance, like from me to you. I have to cover half of it. Then, see, I still have half of that remaining, so I cover half that . . . and since there are infinite halves left, I can't ever get there.

ED (taking her in his arms and starting to dance): So how did that happen?

CATHERINE: I don't know.

43

Prior to the twentieth century, some ideas in *set theory* were considered *paradoxes* (wrong opinions). *Zeno's paradox,* as described by Catherine and seen in **Exercises 51 and 52** of the **Extension,** has been around in several forms for thousands of years.

2.1 SYMBOLS AND TERMINOLOGY

Designating Sets • Sets of Numbers and Cardinality • Finite and Infinite Sets • Equality of Sets

The basic ideas of set theory were developed by the German mathematician **Georg Cantor** (1845–1918) in about 1875. Cantor created a new field of theory and at the same time continued the long debate over infinity that began in ancient times. He developed counting by one-to-one correspondence to determine how many objects are contained in a set. Infinite sets differ from finite sets by not obeying the familiar law that the whole is greater than any of its parts.

Designating Sets

A **set** is a collection of objects. The objects belonging to the set are called the **elements,** or **members,** of the set. Sets are designated using the following three methods: (1) *word description,* (2) the *listing method,* and (3) *set-builder notation.*

The set of even counting numbers less than 10	Word description
$\{2, 4, 6, 8\}$	Listing method
$\{x \mid x \text{ is an even counting number less than 10}\}$	Set-builder notation

The set-builder notation above is read "the set of all x such that x is an even counting number less than 10." Set-builder notation uses the algebraic idea of a *variable.* (Any symbol would do, but just as in other algebraic applications, the letter x is a common choice.)

Variable representing
an element in general
↓
$$\{x \mid x \text{ is an even counting number less than 10}\}$$
↑
Criteria by which an element
qualifies for membership in the set

Sets are commonly given names (usually capital letters), such as E for the set of all letters of the English alphabet.

$$E = \{a, b, c, d, e, f, g, h, i, j, k, l, m, n, o, p, q, r, s, t, u, v, w, x, y, z\}$$

The listing notation can often be shortened by establishing the pattern of elements included and using ellipsis points to indicate a continuation of the pattern.

$$E = \{a, b, c, d, \dots, x, y, z\}, \quad \text{or} \quad E = \{a, b, c, d, e, \dots, z\}.$$

The set containing no elements is called the **empty set,** or **null set.** The symbol $\emptyset$ is used to denote the empty set, so $\emptyset$ and $\{\ \}$ have the same meaning. We do *not* denote the empty set with the symbol $\{\emptyset\}$ because this notation represents a set with one element (that element being the empty set).

▍▍ EXAMPLE 1 Listing Elements of Sets

Give a complete listing of all the elements of each set.

(a) the set of counting numbers between six and thirteen

(b) $\{5, 6, 7, \dots, 13\}$

(c) $\{x \mid x \text{ is a counting number between 6 and 7}\}$

SOLUTION

(a) This set can be denoted $\{7, 8, 9, 10, 11, 12\}$. (Notice that the word *between* excludes the endpoint values.)

(b) This set begins with the element 5, then 6, then 7, and so on, with each element obtained by adding 1 to the previous element in the list. This pattern stops at 13, so a complete listing is $\{5, 6, 7, 8, 9, 10, 11, 12, 13\}$.

(c) There are no counting numbers between 6 and 7, so this is the empty set $\{\ \}$, or $\emptyset$. ▐▐▐

For a set to be useful, it must be well defined. For example, the preceding set E of the letters of the English alphabet is well defined. Given the letter q, we know that q is an element of E. Given the Greek letter θ (theta), we know that it is not an element of set E.

However, given the set C of all good singers, and a particular singer, Raeanna, it may not be possible to say whether

Raeanna is an element of C or   Raeanna is *not* an element of C.

The problem is the word "good"; how good is good? Because we cannot necessarily decide whether a given singer belongs to set C, set C is not well defined.

The letter q is an element of set E, where E is the set of all the letters of the English alphabet. To show this, the symbol $\in$ is used.

$$q \in E \qquad \text{This is read "q is an element of set } E.\text{"}$$

The letter θ is not an element of E. To show this, $\in$ with a slash mark is used.

$$\theta \notin E \qquad \text{This is read "}\theta\text{ is not an element of set } E.\text{"}$$

▐▐ **EXAMPLE 2** Applying the Symbol $\in$

Decide whether each statement is *true* or *false*.

(a) $3 \in \{1, 2, 5, 9, 13\}$ **(b)** $0 \in \{0, 1, 2, 3\}$ **(c)** $\dfrac{1}{5} \notin \left\{\dfrac{1}{3}, \dfrac{1}{4}, \dfrac{1}{6}\right\}$

SOLUTION

(a) Because 3 is *not* an element of the set $\{1, 2, 5, 9, 13\}$, the statement is *false*.

(b) Because 0 is indeed an element of the set $\{0, 1, 2, 3\}$, the statement is *true*.

(c) This statement says that $\frac{1}{5}$ is not an element of the set $\left\{\frac{1}{3}, \frac{1}{4}, \frac{1}{6}\right\}$, which is *true*.   ▐▐▐

Sets of Numbers and Cardinality

Important categories of numbers are summarized below.

Sets of Numbers

Natural or Counting numbers $\{1, 2, 3, 4, \dots\}$

Whole numbers $\{0, 1, 2, 3, 4, \dots\}$

Integers $\{\dots, -3, -2, -1, 0, 1, 2, 3, \dots\}$

Rational numbers $\left\{\dfrac{p}{q} \,\middle|\, p \text{ and } q \text{ are integers, and } q \neq 0\right\}$

(*Examples:* $\frac{3}{5}$, $-\frac{7}{9}$, 5, 0. Any rational number may be written as a terminating decimal number, such as 0.25, or a repeating decimal number, such as 0.666 ....)

Real numbers $\{x \,|\, x \text{ is a number that can be expressed as a decimal}\}$

Irrational numbers $\{x \,|\, x \text{ is a real number and } x \text{ cannot be expressed as a quotient of integers}\}$

(*Examples:* $\sqrt{2}$, $\sqrt[3]{4}$, π. Decimal representations of irrational numbers are neither terminating nor repeating.)

The number of elements in a set is called the **cardinal number,** or **cardinality,** of the set. The symbol

$$n(A), \quad \text{which is read } \textbf{\textit{``n of A,''}}$$

represents the cardinal number of set A. If elements are repeated in a set listing, they should not be counted more than once when determining the cardinal number of the set.

EXAMPLE 3 Finding Cardinal Numbers

Find the cardinal number of each set.

(a) $K = \{2, 4, 8, 16\}$ **(b)** $M = \{0\}$ **(c)** $B = \{1, 1, 2, 2, 3\}$

(d) $R = \{4, 5, \ldots, 12, 13\}$ **(e)** $\emptyset$

SOLUTION

(a) Set K contains four elements, so the cardinal number of set K is 4, and $n(K) = 4$.

(b) Set M contains only one element, 0, so $n(M) = 1$.

(c) If elements are repeated in a set listing, they should not be counted more than once when determining the cardinal number of the set. Set B has only three *distinct* elements, so $n(B) = 3$.

(d) Although only four elements are listed, the ellipsis points indicate that there are other elements in the set. Counting them all, we find that there are ten elements, so $n(R) = 10$.

(e) The empty set, $\emptyset$, contains no elements, so $n(\emptyset) = 0$.   ■■■

A close-up of a camera lens shows the **infinity symbol, ∞,** defined in this case as any distance greater than 1000 times the focal length of a lens.

The sign was invented by the mathematician John Wallis in 1655. Wallis used 1/∞ to represent an infinitely small quantity.

Finite and Infinite Sets

If the cardinal number of a set is a particular whole number (0 or a counting number), as in all parts of **Example 3,** we call that set a **finite set.** Given enough time, we could finish counting all the elements of any finite set and arrive at its cardinal number.

Some sets, however, are so large that we could never finish the counting process. The counting numbers themselves are such a set. Whenever a set is so large that its cardinal number is not found among the whole numbers, we call that set an **infinite set.**

EXAMPLE 4 Designating an Infinite Set

Designate all odd counting numbers by the three common methods of set notation.

SOLUTION

The set of all odd counting numbers   Word description

$\{1, 3, 5, 7, 9, \ldots\}$ Listing method

$\{x \mid x \text{ is an odd counting number}\}$ Set-builder notation   ■■■

Equality of Sets

Set Equality

Set A is **equal** to set B provided the following two conditions are met:

1. Every element of A is an element of B, and

2. Every element of B is an element of A.

Two sets are equal if they contain exactly the same elements, regardless of order.

$$\{a, b, c, d\} = \{a, c, d, b\} \quad \text{Both sets contain exactly the same elements.}$$

Repetition of elements in a set listing does not add new elements.

$$\{1, 0, 1, 2, 3, 3\} = \{0, 1, 2, 3\} \quad \text{Both sets contain exactly the same elements.}$$

▮▮ **EXAMPLE 5** Determining Whether Two Sets Are Equal

Are $\{-4, 3, 2, 5\}$ and $\{-4, 0, 3, 2, 5\}$ equal sets?

SOLUTION

Every element of the first set is an element of the second. However, 0 is an element of the second and not of the first. The sets do not contain exactly the same elements, so they are not equal.

$$\{-4, 3, 2, 5\} \neq \{-4, 0, 3, 2, 5\} \qquad \text{▮▮▮}$$

▮▮ **EXAMPLE 6** Determining Whether Two Sets Are Equal

Decide whether each statement is *true* or *false*.

(a) $\{3\} = \{x \,|\, x \text{ is a counting number between 1 and 5}\}$

(b) $\{x \,|\, x \text{ is a negative natural number}\} = \{y \,|\, y \text{ is a number that is both rational and irrational}\}$

SOLUTION

(a) The set on the right contains *all* counting numbers between 1 and 5, namely 2, 3, and 4, while the set on the left contains *only* the number 3. Because the sets do not contain exactly the same elements, they are not equal. The statement is *false*.

(b) All natural numbers are positive, so the set on the left is ∅. By definition, if a number is rational, it cannot be irrational, so the set on the right is also ∅. Because each set is the empty set, the sets are equal. The statement is *true*. ▮▮▮

2.1 EXERCISES

Match each set in Column I with the appropriate description in Column II.

I

1. $\{1, 3, 5, 7, 9\}$

2. $\{x \,|\, x \text{ is an even integer greater than 4 and less than 6}\}$

3. $\{\ldots, -4, -3, -2, -1\}$

4. $\{\ldots, -5, -3, -1, 1, 3, 5, \ldots\}$

5. $\{2, 4, 8, 16, 32\}$

6. $\{\ldots, -4, -2, 0, 2, 4, \ldots\}$

7. $\{2, 4, 6, 8, 10\}$

8. $\{2, 4, 6, 8\}$

II

A. the set of all even integers

B. the set of the five least positive integer powers of 2

C. the set of even positive integers less than 10

D. the set of all odd integers

E. the set of all negative integers

F. the set of odd positive integers less than 10

G. ∅

H. the set of the five least positive integer multiples of 2

List all the elements of each set. Use set notation and the listing method to describe the set.

9. the set of all counting numbers less than or equal to 6

10. the set of all whole numbers greater than 8 and less than 18

11. the set of all whole numbers not greater than 4

12. the set of all counting numbers between 4 and 14

13. $\{6, 7, 8, \ldots, 14\}$

14. $\{3, 6, 9, 12, \ldots, 30\}$

15. $\{-15, -13, -11, \ldots, -1\}$

16. $\{-4, -3, -2, \ldots, 4\}$

17. $\{2, 4, 8, \ldots, 256\}$

18. $\{90, 87, 84, \ldots, 69\}$

19. $\{x \mid x$ is an even whole number less than 11$\}$

20. $\{x \mid x$ is an odd integer between -8 and 7$\}$

Denote each set by the listing method. There may be more than one correct answer.

21. the set of all counting numbers greater than 20

22. the set of all integers between -200 and 500

23. the set of Great Lakes

24. the set of U.S. presidents who served after Richard Nixon and before Barack Obama

25. $\{x \mid x$ is a positive multiple of 5$\}$

26. $\{x \mid x$ is a negative multiple of 6$\}$

27. $\{x \mid x$ is the reciprocal of a natural number$\}$

28. $\{x \mid x$ is a positive integer power of 4$\}$

Denote each set by set-builder notation, using x as the variable. There may be more than one correct answer.

29. the set of all rational numbers

30. the set of all even natural numbers

31. $\{1, 3, 5, \ldots, 75\}$

32. $\{35, 40, 45, \ldots, 95\}$

Give a word description for each set. There may be more than one correct answer.

33. $\{-9, -8, -7, \ldots, 7, 8, 9\}$

34. $\left\{ 1, \dfrac{1}{2}, \dfrac{1}{3}, \dfrac{1}{4}, \ldots \right\}$

35. $\{$Alabama, Alaska, Arizona, $\ldots$, Wisconsin, Wyoming$\}$

36. $\{$Alaska, California, Hawaii, Oregon, Washington$\}$

Identify each set as finite *or* infinite.

37. $\{2, 4, 6, \ldots, 932\}$ 38. $\{6, 12, 18\}$

39. $\left\{ \dfrac{1}{2}, \dfrac{2}{3}, \dfrac{3}{4}, \ldots \right\}$

40. $\{ \ldots, -100, -80, -60, -40, \ldots \}$

41. $\{x \mid x$ is a natural number greater than 50$\}$

42. $\{x \mid x$ is a natural number less than 50$\}$

43. $\{x \mid x$ is a rational number$\}$

44. $\{x \mid x$ is a rational number between 0 and 1$\}$

Find $n(A)$ for each set.

45. $A = \{0, 1, 2, 3, 4, 5, 6, 7\}$

46. $A = \{-3, -1, 1, 3, 5, 7, 9\}$

47. $A = \{2, 4, 6, \ldots, 1000\}$

48. $A = \{0, 1, 2, 3, \ldots, 3000\}$

49. $A = \{a, b, c, \ldots, z\}$

50. $A = \{x \mid x$ is a vowel in the English alphabet$\}$

51. $A =$ the set of integers between -20 and 20

52. $A =$ the set of sanctioned U.S. senate seats

53. $A = \left\{ \dfrac{1}{3}, \dfrac{2}{4}, \dfrac{3}{5}, \dfrac{4}{6}, \ldots, \dfrac{27}{29}, \dfrac{28}{30} \right\}$

54. $A = \left\{ \dfrac{1}{2}, -\dfrac{1}{2}, \dfrac{1}{3}, -\dfrac{1}{3}, \ldots, \dfrac{1}{10}, -\dfrac{1}{10} \right\}$

55. Although x is a consonant, why can we write "x is a vowel in the English alphabet" in **Exercise 50?**

56. Explain how **Exercise 53** can be answered without actually listing and then counting all the elements.

Identify each set as well defined *or* not well defined.

57. $\{x \mid x$ is a real number$\}$

58. $\{x \mid x$ is a good athlete$\}$

59. $\{x \mid x$ is a difficult course$\}$

60. $\{x \mid x$ is a counting number less than 2$\}$

Fill each blank with either ∈ or ∉ to make each statement true.

61. 5 _____ {2, 4, 5, 7}

62. −4 _____ {4, 7, 8, 12}

63. −12 _____ {3, 8, 12, 18}

64. 0 _____ {−2, 0, 5, 9}

65. {3} _____ {2, 3, 4, 6}

66. {6} _____ {5 + 1, 6 + 1}

67. 8 _____ {11 − 2, 10 − 2, 9 − 2, 8 − 2}

68. The statement 3 ∈ {9 − 6, 8 − 6, 7 − 6} is true even though the *symbol* 3 does not appear in the set. Explain.

Write true *or* false *for each statement.*

69. 3 ∈ {2, 5, 6, 8}

70. 6 ∈ {−2, 5, 8, 9}

71. b ∈ {h, c, d, a, b}

72. m ∈ {l, m, n, o, p}

73. 9 ∉ {6, 3, 4, 8}

74. 2 ∉ {7, 6, 5, 4}

75. {k, c, r, a} = {k, c, a, r}

76. {e, h, a, n} = {a, h, e, n}

77. {5, 8, 9} = {5, 8, 9, 0}

78. {3, 7, 12, 14} = {3, 7, 12, 14, 0}

79. {4} ∈ {{3}, {4}, {5}}

80. 4 ∈ {{3}, {4}, {5}}

81. {x | x is a natural number less than 3} = {1, 2}

82. {x | x is a natural number greater than 10} = {11, 12, 13, ...}

Write true *or* false *for each statement.*

> Let A = {2, 4, 6, 8, 10, 12}, B = {2, 4, 8, 10},
> and C = {4, 10, 12}.

83. 4 ∈ A

84. 8 ∈ B

85. 4 ∉ C

86. 8 ∉ B

87. Every element of C is also an element of A.

88. Every element of C is also an element of B.

89. The human mind likes to create collections. Why do you suppose this is so? In your explanation, use one or more particular "collections," mathematical or otherwise.

90. Explain the difference between a well-defined set and a not well-defined set. Give examples and use terms introduced in this section.

*Two sets are **equal** if they contain identical elements. However, two sets are **equivalent** if they contain the same number of elements (but not necessarily the same elements). For each condition, give an example or explain why it is impossible.*

91. two sets that are neither equal nor equivalent

92. two sets that are equal but not equivalent

93. two sets that are equivalent but not equal

94. two sets that are both equal and equivalent

95. *Overpaid Actors* A *Forbes* magazine survey of a recent five-year period considered 100 featured Hollywood actors. The table shows the "worst" ten actors, in terms of how much their films returned per dollar that the actor earned.

MOST OVERPAID ACTORS

Rank	Actor	Return per Dollar to Actor
1.	Will Ferrell	$3.29
2.	Ewan McGregor	$3.75
3.	Billy Bob Thornton	$4.00
4.	Eddie Murphy	$4.43
5.	Ice Cube	$4.77
6.	Tom Cruise	$7.18
7.	Drew Barrymore	$7.43
8.	Leonardo DiCaprio	$7.52
9.	Samuel L. Jackson	$8.59
10.	Jim Carrey	$8.62

Source: Forbes.com

(a) List the set of actors with a return of at least $7.40.

(b) List the set of actors with a return of at most $3.75.

96. *Burning Calories* Candice Cotton likes cotton candy, each serving of which contains 220 calories. To burn off unwanted calories, Candice participates in her favorite activities, shown below, in increments of 1 hour and never repeats a given activity on a given day.

Activity	Symbol	Calories Burned per Hour
Volleyball	v	160
Golf	g	260
Canoeing	c	340
Swimming	s	410
Running	r	680

(a) On Monday, Candice has time for no more than two hours of activities. List all possible sets of activities that would burn off at least the number of calories obtained from three cotton candies.

(b) Assume that Candice can afford up to three hours of time for activities on Wednesday. List all sets of activities that would burn off at least the number of calories in five cotton candies.

(c) Candice can spend up to four hours in activities on Saturday. List all sets of activities that would burn off at least the number of calories in seven cotton candies.

2.2 VENN DIAGRAMS AND SUBSETS

Venn Diagrams • Complement of a Set • Subsets of a Set • Proper Subsets • Counting Subsets

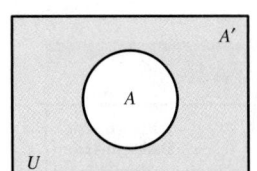

The entire region bounded by the rectangle represents the universal set U, while the portion bounded by the circle represents set A.

Figure 1

Venn Diagrams

In the statement of a problem, there is either a stated or implied **universe of discourse.** The universe of discourse includes all things under discussion at a given time. For example, in studying reactions to a proposal that a certain campus raise the minimum age of individuals to whom beer may be sold, the universe of discourse might be all the students at the school, the nearby members of the public, the board of trustees of the school, or perhaps all these groups of people.

In set theory, the universe of discourse is called the **universal set,** typically designated by the letter **U.** The universal set might change from problem to problem.

Also in set theory, we commonly use **Venn diagrams,** developed by the logician John Venn (1834–1923). In these diagrams, the universal set is represented by a rectangle, and other sets of interest within the universal set are depicted by circular regions (sometimes ovals or other shapes). See **Figure 1.**

Complement of a Set

The colored region inside U and outside the circle in **Figure 1** is labeled A' (read "**A prime**"). This set, called the *complement* of A, contains all elements that are contained in U but not contained in A.

> **The Complement of a Set**
>
> For any set A within the universal set U, the **complement** of A, written A', is the set of elements of U that are not elements of A. That is,
>
> $$A' = \{x \mid x \in U \text{ and } x \notin A\}.$$

▮▮ **EXAMPLE 1** Finding Complements

Find each set.

Let $U = \{a, b, c, d, e, f, g, h\}$, $M = \{a, b, e, f\}$, and $N = \{b, d, e, g, h\}$.

(a) M' **(b)** N'

SOLUTION

(a) Set M' contains all the elements of set U that are *not* in set M. Because set M contains a, b, e, and f, these elements will be disqualified from belonging to set M'.

$$M' = \{c, d, g, h\}$$

(b) Set N' contains all the elements of U that are not in set N, so $N' = \{a, c, f\}$. ▮▮▮

Consider the complement of the universal set, U'. The set U' is found by selecting all the elements of U that do not belong to U. There are no such elements, so there can be no elements in set U'. This means that for any universal set U,

$$U' = \emptyset.$$

Now consider the complement of the empty set, $\emptyset'$. Because $\emptyset' = \{x \mid x \in U \text{ and } x \notin \emptyset\}$ and set $\emptyset$ contains no elements, every member of the universal set U satisfies this description. Therefore, for any universal set U,

$$\emptyset' = U.$$

Subsets of a Set

Suppose that we are given the universal set $U = \{1, 2, 3, 4, 5\}$, while $A = \{1, 2, 3\}$. Every element of set A is also an element of set U. Because of this, set A is called a *subset* of set U, written

$$A \subseteq U.$$

("A is not a subset of set U" would be written $A \nsubseteq U$.)

A Venn diagram showing that set M is a subset of set N is shown in **Figure 2**.

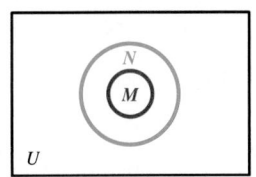

Figure 2

Subset of a Set

Set A is a **subset** of set B if every element of A is also an element of B. In symbols, this is written $A \subseteq B.$

▮▮ **EXAMPLE 2** Determining Whether One Set is a Subset of Another

Write $\subseteq$ or $\nsubseteq$ in each blank to make a true statement.

(a) $\{3, 4, 5, 6\}$ _____ $\{3, 4, 5, 6, 8\}$ **(b)** $\{1, 2, 6\}$ _____ $\{2, 4, 6, 8\}$

(c) $\{5, 6, 7, 8\}$ _____ $\{5, 6, 7, 8\}$

SOLUTION

(a) Because every element of $\{3, 4, 5, 6\}$ is also an element of $\{3, 4, 5, 6, 8\}$, the first set is a subset of the second, so $\subseteq$ goes in the blank.

$$\{3, 4, 5, 6\} \subseteq \{3, 4, 5, 6, 8\}$$

(b) $\{1, 2, 6\} \nsubseteq \{2, 4, 6, 8\}$ 1 does not belong to $\{2, 4, 6, 8\}$.

(c) $\{5, 6, 7, 8\} \subseteq \{5, 6, 7, 8\}$ ▮▮▮

As **Example 2(c)** suggests, every set is a subset of itself.

$$B \subseteq B, \quad \text{for any set } B.$$

The statement of set equality in **Section 2.1** can be formally presented.

Set Equality (Alternative definition)

Suppose A and B are sets. Then $A = B$ if $A \subseteq B$ and $B \subseteq A$ are both true.

Proper Subsets

Suppose that we are given the following sets.

$$B = \{5, 6, 7, 8\} \quad \text{and} \quad A = \{6, 7\}$$

A is a subset of B, but A is not all of B. There is at least one element in B that is not in A. (Actually, in this case there are two such elements, 5 and 8.) In this situation, A is called a *proper subset* of B. To indicate that A is a proper subset of B, write

$$A \subset B.$$

Notice the similarity of the subset symbols, $\subset$ and $\subseteq$, to the inequality symbols from algebra, $<$ and $\leq$.

Proper Subset of a Set

Set A is a **proper subset** of set B if $A \subseteq B$ and $A \neq B$. In symbols, this is written $A \subset B.$

▮▮ **EXAMPLE 3**   Determining Subset and Proper Subset Relationships

Decide whether $\subset$, $\subseteq$, or both could be placed in each blank to make a true statement.

(a) $\{5, 6, 7\}$ _____ $\{5, 6, 7, 8\}$ **(b)** $\{a, b, c\}$ _____ $\{a, b, c\}$

SOLUTION

(a) Every element of $\{5, 6, 7\}$ is contained in $\{5, 6, 7, 8\}$, so $\subseteq$ could be placed in the blank. Also, the element 8 belongs to $\{5, 6, 7, 8\}$ but not to $\{5, 6, 7\}$, making $\{5, 6, 7\}$ a proper subset of $\{5, 6, 7, 8\}$. Place $\subset$ in the blank.

(b) The set $\{a, b, c\}$ is a subset of $\{a, b, c\}$. Because the two sets are equal, $\{a, b, c\}$ is not a proper subset of $\{a, b, c\}$. Only $\subseteq$ may be placed in the blank.   ▮▮▮

Set A is a subset of set B if every element of set A is also an element of set B. This definition can be reworded by saying that set A is a subset of set B if there are no elements of A that are not also elements of B. This second form of the definition shows that the empty set is a subset of any set.

$$\emptyset \subseteq B, \quad \text{for any set } B.$$

This is true because it is not possible to find any elements of $\emptyset$ that are not also in B. (There are no elements in $\emptyset$.) The empty set $\emptyset$ is a proper subset of every set except itself.

$$\emptyset \subset B \quad \text{if } B \text{ is any set other than } \emptyset.$$

Every set (except $\emptyset$) has at least two subsets, $\emptyset$ and the set itself.

▮▮ **EXAMPLE 4**   Listing All Subsets of a Set

Find all possible subsets of each set.

(a) $\{7, 8\}$ **(b)** $\{a, b, c\}$

SOLUTION

(a) By trial and error, the set $\{7, 8\}$ has four subsets: $\emptyset, \{7\}, \{8\}, \{7, 8\}$.

(b) Here, trial and error leads to eight subsets for $\{a, b, c\}$:

$$\emptyset, \{a\}, \{b\}, \{c\}, \{a, b\}, \{a, c\}, \{b, c\}, \{a, b, c\}.$$ ▮▮▮

Counting Subsets

In **Example 4,** the subsets of $\{7, 8\}$ and the subsets of $\{a, b, c\}$ were found by trial and error. An alternative method involves drawing a **tree diagram**, a systematic way of listing all the subsets of a given set. See **Figure 3**.

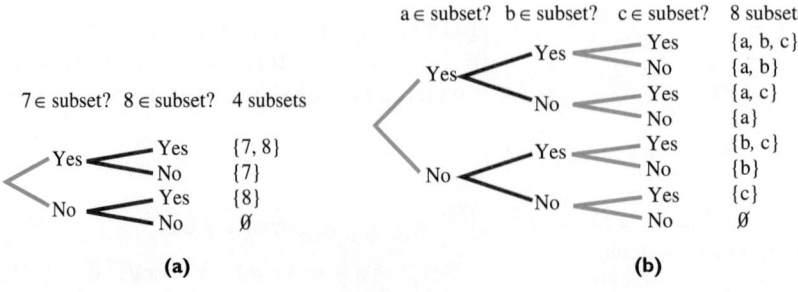

(a)   **(b)**

Figure 3

Powers of 2

$2^0 = 1$

$2^1 = 2$

$2^2 = 2 \cdot 2 = 4$

$2^3 = 2 \cdot 2 \cdot 2 = 8$

$2^4 = 2 \cdot 2 \cdot 2 \cdot 2 = 16$

$2^5 = 32$

$2^6 = 64$

$2^7 = 128$

$2^8 = 256$

$2^9 = 512$

$2^{10} = 1024$

$2^{11} = 2048$

$2^{12} = 4096$

$2^{15} = 32{,}768$

$2^{20} = 1{,}048{,}576$

$2^{25} = 33{,}554{,}432$

$2^{30} = 1{,}073{,}741{,}824$

In **Example 4,** we determined the number of subsets of a given set by making a list of all such subsets and then counting them. The tree diagram method also produced a list of all possible subsets. To obtain a formula for finding the number of subsets, we use inductive reasoning. That is, we observe particular cases to try to discover a general pattern.

Begin with the set containing the least number of elements possible—the empty set. This set, $\emptyset$, has only one subset, $\emptyset$ itself. Next, a set with one element has only two subsets, itself and $\emptyset$. These facts, together with those obtained in **Example 4** for sets with two and three elements, are summarized here.

Number of elements	0	1	2	3
Number of subsets	1	2	4	8

This chart suggests that as the number of elements of the set increases by one, the number of subsets doubles. If so, then the number of subsets in each case might be a power of 2. Since every number in the second row of the chart is indeed a power of 2, add this information to the chart.

Number of elements	0	1	2	3
Number of subsets	$1 = 2^0$	$2 = 2^1$	$4 = 2^2$	$8 = 2^3$

This chart shows that the number of elements in each case is the same as the exponent on the base 2. Inductive reasoning gives the following generalization.

Number of Subsets

The number of subsets of a set with n elements is $\mathbf{2^n}$.

Because the value 2^n includes the set itself, we must subtract 1 from this value to obtain the number of proper subsets of a set containing n elements.

Number of Proper Subsets

The number of proper subsets of a set with n elements is $\mathbf{2^n - 1}$.

As shown in **Chapter 1,** although inductive reasoning is a good way of *discovering* principles or arriving at a *conjecture,* it does not provide a proof that the conjecture is true in general. The two formulas above are true, by observation, for $n = 0, 1, 2,$ or 3. (For a general proof, see **Exercise 69** at the end of this section.)

▮▮ **EXAMPLE 5** Finding the Numbers of Subsets and Proper Subsets

Find the number of subsets and the number of proper subsets of each set.

(a) $\{3, 4, 5, 6, 7\}$ **(b)** $\{1, 2, 3, 4, 5, 9, 12, 14\}$

SOLUTION

(a) This set has 5 elements and $2^5 = 2 \cdot 2 \cdot 2 \cdot 2 \cdot 2 = 32$ subsets. Of these, $2^5 - 1 = 32 - 1 = 31$ are proper subsets.

(b) This set has 8 elements. There are $2^8 = 256$ subsets and 255 proper subsets.   ▮▮▮

2.2 EXERCISES

Match each set or sets in Column I with the appropriate description in Column II.

I

1. $\{p\}, \{q\}, \{p, q\}, \emptyset$

2. $\{p\}, \{q\}, \emptyset$

3. $\{a, b\}$

4. $\emptyset$

II

A. the proper subsets of $\{p, q\}$

B. the complement of $\{c, d\}$, if $U = \{a, b, c, d\}$

C. the complement of U

D. the subsets of $\{p, q\}$

Insert $\subseteq$ or $\not\subseteq$ in each blank so that the resulting statement is true.

5. $\{-2, 0, 2\}$ _____ $\{-2, -1, 1, 2\}$

6. $\{M, W, F\}$ _____ $\{S, M, T, W, Th\}$

7. $\{2, 5\}$ _____ $\{0, 1, 5, 3, 7, 2\}$

8. $\{a, n, d\}$ _____ $\{r, a, n, d, y\}$

9. $\emptyset$ _____ $\{a, b, c, d, e\}$

10. $\emptyset$ _____ $\emptyset$

11. $\{-5, 2, 9\}$ _____ $\{x \mid x \text{ is an odd integer}\}$

12. $\left\{1, 2, \dfrac{9}{3}\right\}$ _____ the set of rational numbers

Decide whether $\subset$, $\subseteq$, both, or neither can be placed in each blank to make the statement true.

13. $\{P, Q, R\}$ _____ $\{P, Q, R, S\}$

14. $\{red, blue, yellow\}$ _____ $\{yellow, blue, red\}$

15. $\{9, 1, 7, 3, 5\}$ _____ $\{1, 3, 5, 7, 9\}$

16. $\{S, M, T, W, Th\}$ _____ $\{W, E, E, K\}$

17. $\emptyset$ _____ $\{0\}$

18. $\emptyset$ _____ $\emptyset$

19. $\{0, 1, 2, 3\}$ _____ $\{1, 2, 3, 4\}$

20. $\left\{\dfrac{5}{6}, \dfrac{9}{8}\right\}$ _____ $\left\{\dfrac{6}{5}, \dfrac{8}{9}\right\}$

For Exercises 21–40, tell whether each statement is true *or* false. *U is the universal set.*

Let $U = \{a, b, c, d, e, f, g\}$, $A = \{a, e\}$,
$B = \{a, b, e, f, g\}$, $C = \{b, f, g\}$, and $D = \{d, e\}$.

21. $A \subset U$

22. $C \not\subseteq U$

23. $D \subseteq B$

24. $D \not\subseteq A$

25. $A \subset B$

26. $B \subseteq C$

27. $\emptyset \not\subseteq A$

28. $\emptyset \subseteq D$

29. $\emptyset \subseteq \emptyset$

30. $D \subset B$

31. $D \not\subseteq B$

32. $A \not\subseteq B$

33. There are exactly 6 subsets of C.

34. There are exactly 31 subsets of B.

35. There are exactly 3 proper subsets of A.

36. There are exactly 4 subsets of D.

37. There is exactly 1 subset of $\emptyset$.

38. There are exactly 128 proper subsets of U.

39. The Venn diagram below correctly represents the relationship among sets A, D, and U.

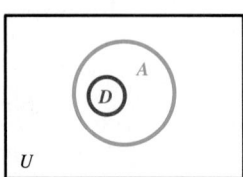

40. The Venn diagram below correctly represents the relationship among sets B, C, and U.

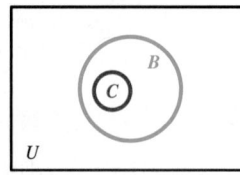

Find **(a)** *the number of subsets and* **(b)** *the number of proper subsets of each set.*

41. $\{a, b, c, d, e, f\}$

42. the set of days of the week

43. $\{x \mid x \text{ is an odd integer between } -4 \text{ and } 6\}$

44. $\{x \mid x \text{ is an odd whole number less than } 4\}$

Let $U = \{1, 2, 3, 4, 5, 6, 7, 8, 9, 10\}$ and find the complement of each set.

45. $\{1, 2, 3, 4, 6, 8\}$

46. $\{2, 5, 9, 10\}$

47. $\{1, 3, 4, 5, 6, 7, 8, 9, 10\}$

48. $\{1, 2, 3, 4, 5, 6, 7, 8, 9\}$

49. U

50. $\emptyset$

Vacationing in California Terry McGinnis is planning a trip with her two sons to California. In weighing her options concerning whether to fly or drive from their home in Iowa, she has listed the following characteristics.

Fly to California	Drive to California
Higher cost	Lower cost
Educational	Educational
More time to see the sights in California	Less time to see the sights in California
Cannot visit relatives along the way	Can visit relatives along the way

Refer to these characteristics in Exercises 51–56.

51. Find the smallest universal set *U* that contains all listed characteristics of both options.

Let F represent the set of characteristics of the flying option and let D represent the set of characteristics of the driving option. Use the universal set from **Exercise 51.**

52. Give the set *F′*.   **53.** Give the set *D′*.

Find the set of elements common to both sets in Exercises 54–56.

54. *F* and *D*   **55.** *F′* and *D′*

56. *F* and *D′*

Meeting in a Hospitality Suite Amie Carobrese, Bruce Collin, Corey Chapman, Dwayne Coy, and Eric Cobbe plan to meet at the hospitality suite after the CEO makes his speech at the January sales meeting of their publishing company. Denoting these five people by A, B, C, D, and E, list all the possible sets of this group in which the given number of them can gather.

57. five people   **58.** four people

59. three people   **60.** two people

61. one person   **62.** no people

63. Find the total number of ways that members of this group can gather in the suite. (*Hint:* Find the total number of sets in your answers to **Exercises 57–62.**)

64. How does your answer in **Exercise 63** compare with the number of subsets of a set of five elements? Interpret the answer to **Exercise 63** in terms of subsets.

65. The twenty-five members of the mathematics club must send a delegation to a meeting for student groups at their school. The delegation can include as many members of the club as desired, but at least one member must attend. How many different delegations are possible? (*Mathematics Teacher* calendar problem)

66. In **Exercise 65,** suppose ten of the club members say they do not want to be part of the delegation. Now how many delegations are possible?

67. *Selecting Bills* Suppose you have the bills shown here.

(a) If you must select at least one bill, and you may select up to all of the bills, how many different sums of money could you make?

(b) In part (a), remove the condition "you must select at least one bill." How many sums are possible?

68. *Selecting Coins* The photo shows a group of obsolete U.S. coins, consisting of one each of the penny, nickel, dime, quarter, and half dollar. Repeat **Exercise 65,** replacing "bill(s)" with "coin(s)."

69. In discovering the expression (2^n) for finding the number of subsets of a set with *n* elements, we observed that for the first few values of *n*, increasing the number of elements by one doubles the number of subsets. Here, you can prove the formula in general by showing that the same is true for any value of *n*. Assume set *A* has *n* elements and *s* subsets. Now add one additional element, say *e*, to the set *A*. (We now have a new set, say *B*, with *n* + 1 elements.) Divide the subsets of *B* into those that do not contain *e* and those that do.

(a) How many subsets of *B* do not contain *e*? (*Hint:* Each of these is a subset of the original set *A*.)

(b) How many subsets of *B* do contain *e*? (*Hint:* Each of these would be a subset of the original set *A*, with the element *e* inserted.)

(c) What is the total number of subsets of *B*?

(d) What do you conclude?

70. Explain why ∅ is both a subset and an element of {∅}.

▌ ▌ ▌ ▌ ▌ ▌ ▌ ▌ ██ **2.3 SET OPERATIONS AND CARTESIAN PRODUCTS**

Intersection of Sets • Union of Sets • Difference of Sets • Ordered Pairs
• Cartesian Product of Sets • Venn Diagrams • De Morgan's Laws

Intersection of Sets

Two candidates, Aimee Berger and Darien Estes, are running for a seat on the city council. A voter deciding for whom she should vote recalled the campaign promises, each given a code letter, made by the candidates.

Honest Aimee Berger	Determined Darien Estes
Spend less money, m	Spend less money, m
Emphasize traffic law enforcement, t	Crack down on crooked politicians, p
Increase service to suburban areas, s	Increase service to the city, c

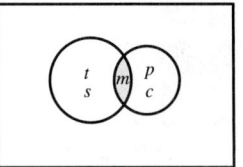

Figure 4

The only promise common to both candidates is promise m, to spend less money. Suppose we take each candidate's promises to be a set. The promises of Berger give the set $\{m, t, s\}$, while the promises of Estes give $\{m, p, c\}$. The common element m belongs to the *intersection* of the two sets, as shown in color in the Venn diagram in **Figure 4**.

$$\{m, t, s\} \cap \{m, p, c\} = \{m\} \quad \cap \text{ represents set intersection.}$$

The intersection of two sets is itself a set.

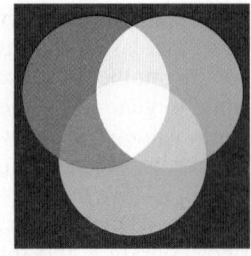

$A \cap B$

Figure 5

Intersection of Sets

The **intersection** of sets A and B, written $A \cap B$, is the set of elements common to both A and B.

$$A \cap B = \{x \mid x \in A \text{ and } x \in B\}$$

Form the intersection of sets A and B by taking all the elements included in both sets, as shown in color in **Figure 5**.

▌▌ **EXAMPLE 1** Finding Intersections

Find each intersection.

(a) $\{3, 4, 5, 6, 7\} \cap \{4, 6, 8, 10\}$ **(b)** $\{9, 14, 25, 30\} \cap \{10, 17, 19, 38, 52\}$

(c) $\{5, 9, 11\} \cap \emptyset$

SOLUTION

(a) The elements common to both sets are 4 and 6.

$$\{3, 4, 5, 6, 7\} \cap \{4, 6, 8, 10\} = \{4, 6\}$$

(b) These two sets have no elements in common.

$$\{9, 14, 25, 30\} \cap \{10, 17, 19, 38, 52\} = \emptyset$$

(c) There are no elements in $\emptyset$, so there can be no elements belonging to both $\{5, 9, 11\}$ and $\emptyset$.

$$\{5, 9, 11\} \cap \emptyset = \emptyset$$

▌▌▌

White light can be viewed as the intersection of the three primary colors.

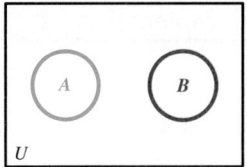

Disjoint sets

Figure 6

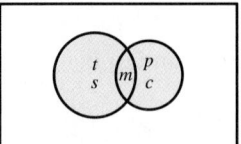

Figure 7

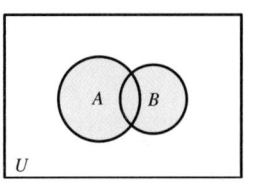

$A \cup B$

Figure 8

Examples 1(b) and 1(c) show two sets that have no elements in common. Sets with no elements in common are called **disjoint sets.** (See **Figure 6.**) A set of dogs and a set of cats would be disjoint sets.

$$\text{Sets } A \text{ and } B \text{ are disjoint if } A \cap B = \emptyset.$$

Union of Sets

Referring again to the lists of campaign promises, suppose a pollster wants to summarize the types of promises made by the candidates. The pollster would need to study *all* the promises made by *either* candidate, or the set $\{m, t, s, p, c\}$. This set is the *union* of the sets of promises, as shown in color in the Venn diagram in **Figure 7**.

> Be careful not to confuse this symbol with the universal set U.

$$\{m, t, s\} \cup \{m, p, c\} = \{m, t, s, p, c\} \qquad \cup \text{ denotes set union.}$$

Again, the union of two sets is a set.

Union of Sets

The **union** of sets A and B, written $A \cup B$, is the set of all elements belonging to either A or B.

$$A \cup B = \{x \mid x \in A \text{ or } x \in B\}$$

Form the union of sets A and B by taking all the elements of set A and then including the elements of set B that are not already listed. See **Figure 8.**

▮▮ **EXAMPLE 2** Finding Unions

Find each union.

(a) $\{2, 4, 6\} \cup \{4, 6, 8, 10, 12\}$

(b) $\{a, b, d, f, g, h\} \cup \{c, f, g, h, k\}$

(c) $\{3, 4, 5\} \cup \emptyset$

SOLUTION

(a) Start by listing all the elements from the first set, 2, 4, and 6. Then list all the elements from the second set that are not in the first set, 8, 10, and 12. The union is made up of *all* these elements.

$$\{2, 4, 6\} \cup \{4, 6, 8, 10, 12\} = \{2, 4, 6, 8, 10, 12\}$$

(b) $\{a, b, d, f, g, h\} \cup \{c, f, g, h, k\} = \{a, b, c, d, f, g, h, k\}$

(c) Because there are no elements in $\emptyset$, the union of $\{3, 4, 5\}$ and $\emptyset$ contains only the elements 3, 4, and 5.

$$\{3, 4, 5\} \cup \emptyset = \{3, 4, 5\} \qquad\qquad ▮▮▮$$

Recall from the previous section that A' represents the *complement* of set A. *Set A' is formed by taking all the elements of the universal set U that are not in set A.*

▌▌ **EXAMPLE 3** | Finding Intersections and Unions of Complements

Find each set. Let

$$U = \{1, 2, 3, 4, 5, 6, 9\}, \ A = \{1, 2, 3, 4\}, \ B = \{2, 4, 6\}, \ \text{and} \ C = \{1, 3, 6, 9\}.$$

(a) $A' \cap B$ **(b)** $B' \cup C'$ **(c)** $A \cap (B \cup C')$ **(d)** $(A' \cup C') \cap B'$

SOLUTION

(a) First identify the elements of set A', the elements of U that are not in set A.

$$A' = \{5, 6, 9\}$$

Now, find $A' \cap B$, the set of elements belonging both to A' and to B.

$$A' \cap B = \{5, 6, 9\} \cap \{2, 4, 6\} = \{6\}$$

(b) $B' \cup C' = \{1, 3, 5, 9\} \cup \{2, 4, 5\} = \{1, 2, 3, 4, 5, 9\}$

(c) First find the set inside the parentheses.

$$B \cup C' = \{2, 4, 6\} \cup \{2, 4, 5\} = \{2, 4, 5, 6\}$$

Now, find the intersection of this set with A.

$$\begin{aligned} A \cap (B \cup C') &= A \cap \{2, 4, 5, 6\} \\ &= \{1, 2, 3, 4\} \cap \{2, 4, 5, 6\} \\ &= \{2, 4\} \end{aligned}$$

(d) $A' = \{5, 6, 9\}$ and $C' = \{2, 4, 5\}$, so

$$A' \cup C' = \{5, 6, 9\} \cup \{2, 4, 5\} = \{2, 4, 5, 6, 9\}.$$

$B' = \{1, 3, 5, 9\}$, so

$$(A' \cup C') \cap B' = \{2, 4, 5, 6, 9\} \cap \{1, 3, 5, 9\} = \{5, 9\}. \qquad ▌▌▌$$

For Further Thought

Comparing Properties

The arithmetic operations of addition and multiplication, when applied to numbers, have some familiar properties. If a, b, and c are *real numbers*, then the **commutative property of addition** says that the order of the numbers being added makes no difference:

$$a + b = b + a.$$

(Is there a **commutative property of multiplication?**) The **associative property of addition** says that when three numbers are added, the grouping used makes no difference:

$$(a + b) + c = a + (b + c).$$

(Is there an **associative property of multiplication?**) The number 0 is called the **identity element for addition** since adding it to any number does not change that number:

$$a + 0 = a.$$

(What is the **identity element for multiplication?**) Finally, the **distributive property of multiplication over addition** says that

$$a(b + c) = ab + ac.$$

(Is there a distributive property of addition over multiplication?)

For Group or Individual Investigation

Now consider the operations of union and intersection, applied to sets. By recalling definitions, or by trying examples, answer the following questions.

1. Is set union commutative?   Set intersection?

2. Is set union associative?   Set intersection?

3. Is there an identity element for set union? If so, what is it? How about set intersection?

4. Is set intersection distributive over set union? Is set union distributive over set intersection?

▌▌ **EXAMPLE 4** Describing Sets in Words

Describe each set in words.

(a) $A \cap (B \cup C')$ **(b)** $(A' \cup C') \cap B'$

SOLUTION

(a) This set might be described as "the set of all elements that are in A, and also are in B or not in C."

(b) One possibility is "the set of all elements that are not in A or not in C, and also are not in B." ▌▌▌

Difference of Sets

Suppose that $A = \{1, 2, 3, \ldots, 10\}$ and $B = \{2, 4, 6, 8, 10\}$. If the elements of B are excluded (or taken away) from A, the set $C = \{1, 3, 5, 7, 9\}$ is obtained. C is called the *difference* of sets A and B.

Difference of Sets

The **difference** of sets A and B, written $A - B$, is the set of all elements belonging to set A and not to set B.

$$A - B = \{x \mid x \in A \text{ and } x \notin B\}$$

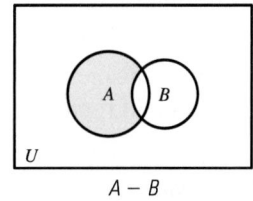

$A - B$

Figure 9

Because $x \notin B$ has the same meaning as $x \in B'$ the set difference $A - B$ can also be described as

$$\{x \mid x \in A \text{ and } x \in B'\}, \quad \text{or} \quad A \cap B'.$$

Figure 9 illustrates the idea of set difference. The region in color represents $A - B$.

▌▌ **EXAMPLE 5** Finding Set Differences

Find each set.

$$\text{Let} \quad U = \{1, 2, 3, 4, 5, 6, 7\}, \quad A = \{1, 2, 3, 4, 5, 6\},$$
$$B = \{2, 3, 6\}, \quad \text{and} \quad C = \{3, 5, 7\}.$$

(a) $A - B$ **(b)** $B - A$ **(c)** $(A - B) \cup C'$

SOLUTION

(a) Begin with set A and exclude any elements found also in set B.

$$A - B = \{1, 2, 3, 4, 5, 6\} - \{2, 3, 6\} = \{1, 4, 5\}$$

(b) To be in $B - A$, an element must be in set B and not in set A. But all elements of B are also in A. Thus, $B - A = \emptyset$.

(c) From part (a), $A - B = \{1, 4, 5\}$. Also, $C' = \{1, 2, 4, 6\}$.

$$(A - B) \cup C' = \{1, 2, 4, 5, 6\}$$ ▌▌▌

The results in **Examples 5(a) and 5(b)** illustrate that, in general,

$$A - B \neq B - A.$$

Ordered Pairs

When writing a set that contains several elements, the order in which the elements appear is not relevant. For example,

$$\{1, 5\} = \{5, 1\}.$$

However, there are many instances in mathematics where, when two objects are paired, the order in which the objects are written is important. This leads to the idea of the *ordered pair*. When writing ordered pairs, use parentheses rather than braces, which are reserved for writing sets.

Ordered Pairs

In the **ordered pair** (a, b), a is called the **first component** and b is called the **second component.** In general, $(a, b) \neq (b, a)$.

Two ordered pairs (a, b) and (c, d) are **equal** provided that their first components are equal and their second components are equal.

$$(a, b) = (c, d) \quad \textit{if and only if} \quad a = c \textit{ and } b = d.$$

▮▮ **EXAMPLE 6** Determining Equality of Sets and of Ordered Pairs

Decide whether each statement is *true* or *false*.

(a) $(3, 4) = (5 - 2, 1 + 3)$ **(b)** $\{3, 4\} \neq \{4, 3\}$ **(c)** $(7, 4) = (4, 7)$

SOLUTION

(a) Because $3 = 5 - 2$ and $4 = 1 + 3$, the first components are equal and the second components are equal. The statement is *true*.

(b) Because these are sets and not ordered pairs, the order in which the elements are listed is not important. Because these sets are equal, the statement is *false*.

(c) The ordered pairs $(7, 4)$ and $(4, 7)$ are not equal because they do not satisfy the requirements for equality of ordered pairs. The statement is *false*.   ▮▮▮

Cartesian Product of Sets

A set may contain ordered pairs as elements. If A and B are sets, then each element of A can be paired with each element of B, and the results can be written as ordered pairs. The set of all such ordered pairs is called the *Cartesian product* of A and B, written $A \times B$ and read **"A cross B."** The name comes from that of the French mathematician René Descartes.

Cartesian Product of Sets

The **Cartesian product** of sets A and B is defined as follows.

$$A \times B = \{(a, b) \mid a \in A \text{ and } b \in B\}$$

▮▮ **EXAMPLE 7** Finding Cartesian Products

Let $A = \{1, 5, 9\}$ and $B = \{6, 7\}$. Find each set.

(a) $A \times B$ **(b)** $B \times A$

SOLUTION

(a) Pair each element of A with each element of B. Write the results as ordered pairs, with the element of A written first and the element of B written second. Write as a set.

$$A \times B = \{(1, 6), (1, 7), (5, 6), (5, 7), (9, 6), (9, 7)\}$$

(b) Because B is listed first, this set will consist of ordered pairs that have their components interchanged when compared to those in part (a).

$$B \times A = \{(6, 1), (7, 1), (6, 5), (7, 5), (6, 9), (7, 9)\} \qquad ▮▮▮$$

The order in which the ordered pairs themselves are listed is not important. For example, another way to write $B \times A$ in **Example 7(b)** would be

$$\{(6, 1), (6, 5), (6, 9), (7, 1), (7, 5), (7, 9)\}.$$

▮▮ **EXAMPLE 8** Finding the Cartesian Product of a Set with Itself

Let $A = \{1, 2, 3, 4, 5, 6\}$. Find $A \times A$.

SOLUTION

Pair 1 with each element in the set, 2 with each element, and so on.

$$\begin{aligned}
A \times A = \{ &(1, 1), (1, 2), (1, 3), (1, 4), (1, 5), (1, 6), \\
&(2, 1), (2, 2), (2, 3), (2, 4), (2, 5), (2, 6), \\
&(3, 1), (3, 2), (3, 3), (3, 4), (3, 5), (3, 6), \\
&(4, 1), (4, 2), (4, 3), (4, 4), (4, 5), (4, 6), \\
&(5, 1), (5, 2), (5, 3), (5, 4), (5, 5), (5, 6), \\
&(6, 1), (6, 2), (6, 3), (6, 4), (6, 5), (6, 6)\} \qquad ▮▮▮
\end{aligned}$$

The **Cartesian product** in **Example 8** represents all possible results that are obtained when two distinguishable dice are rolled. This Cartesian product is important when studying certain problems in counting techniques and probability.

From **Example 7** it can be seen that, in general,

$$A \times B \neq B \times A,$$

because they do not contain exactly the same ordered pairs. However, each set contains the same number of elements, six. Furthermore, $n(A) = 3$, $n(B) = 2$, and $n(A \times B) = n(B \times A) = 6$. Because $3 \cdot 2 = 6$, one might conclude that the cardinal number of the Cartesian product of two sets is equal to the product of the cardinal numbers of the sets. In general, this conclusion is correct.

Cardinal Number of a Cartesian Product

If $n(A) = a$ and $n(B) = b$, then the following is true.

$$n(A \times B) = n(B \times A) = n(A) \cdot n(B) = n(B) \cdot n(A) = ab = ba$$

▮▮ **EXAMPLE 9** Finding Cardinal Numbers of Cartesian Products

Find $n(A \times B)$ and $n(B \times A)$ from the given information.

(a) $A = \{a, b, c, d, e, f, g\}$ and $B = \{2, 4, 6\}$ **(b)** $n(A) = 24$ and $n(B) = 5$

SOLUTION

(a) Because $n(A) = 7$ and $n(B) = 3$, $n(A \times B)$ and $n(B \times A)$ both equal $7 \cdot 3$, or 21.

(b) $n(A \times B) = n(B \times A) = 24 \cdot 5 = 5 \cdot 24 = 120$ ▮▮▮

An **operation** is a rule or procedure by which one or more objects are used to obtain another object. The most common operations on sets are summarized in the box on the next page.

Set Operations

Let A and B be any sets, with U the universal set.

The **complement** of A, written A', is

$$A' = \{x \mid x \in U \text{ and } x \notin A\}.$$

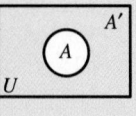

The **intersection** of A and B is

$$A \cap B = \{x \mid x \in A \text{ and } x \in B\}.$$

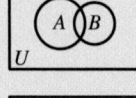

The **union** of A and B is

$$A \cup B = \{x \mid x \in A \text{ or } x \in B\}.$$

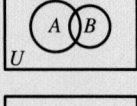

The **difference** of A and B is

$$A - B = \{x \mid x \in A \text{ and } x \notin B\}.$$

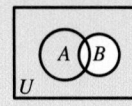

The **Cartesian product** of A and B is

$$A \times B = \{(x, y) \mid x \in A \text{ and } y \in B\}.$$

Venn Diagrams

With a single set, we can use a Venn diagram as in **Figure 10**. The universal set U is divided into two regions, one representing set A and the other representing set A'.

Two sets A and B within the universal set suggest a Venn diagram as in **Figure 11**. Region 1 includes those elements outside of both set A and set B. Region 2 includes the elements belonging to A but not to B. Region 3 includes those elements belonging to both A and B. How would you describe the elements of region 4?

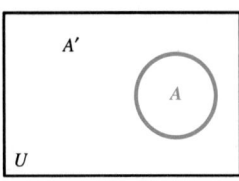

Figure 10

EXAMPLE 10 Shading Venn Diagrams to Represent Sets

Draw a Venn diagram similar to **Figure 11** and shade the region or regions representing each set.

(a) $A' \cap B$ **(b)** $A' \cup B'$

SOLUTION

(a) Refer to **Figure 11**. Set A' contains all the elements outside of set A—in other words, the elements in regions 1 and 4. Set B is made up of the elements in regions 3 and 4. The intersection of sets A' and B is made up of the elements in the region common to (1 and 4) and (3 and 4), which is region 4. Thus, $A' \cap B$ is represented by region 4, shown in color in **Figure 12**. This region can also be described as $B - A$.

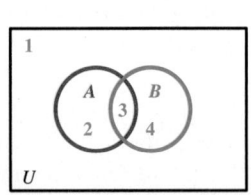

Numbering is arbitrary. The numbers indicate four regions, not cardinal numbers or elements.

Figure 11

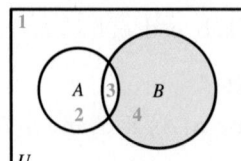 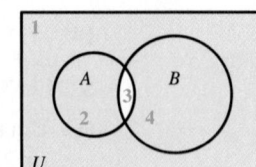

Figure 12   **Figure 13**

(b) Again, set A' is represented by regions 1 and 4, while B' is made up of regions 1 and 2. The union of A' and B', the set $A' \cup B'$, is made up of the elements belonging to the union of regions 1, 2, and 4, which are in color in **Figure 13**. ▮▮▮

EXAMPLE 11   Locating Elements in a Venn Diagram

Place the elements of the sets in their proper locations in a Venn diagram.

Let $U = \{q, r, s, t, u, v, w, x, y, z\}$, $A = \{r, s, t, u, v\}$,   and $B = \{t, v, x\}$.

SOLUTION

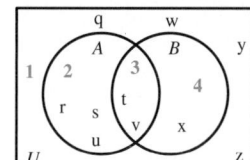

Because $A \cap B = \{t, v\}$, elements t and v are placed in region 3 in **Figure 14**. The remaining elements of A, that is r, s, and u, go in region 2. The figure shows the proper placement of all other elements.

Figure 14   ■■■

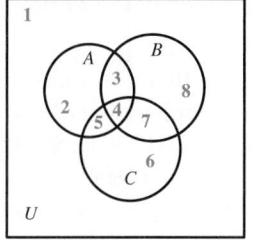

Numbering is arbitrary. The numbers indicate regions, not cardinal numbers or elements.

Figure 15

To include three sets A, B, and C within a universal set, draw a Venn diagram as in **Figure 15**, where again an arbitrary numbering of the regions is shown.

EXAMPLE 12   Shading a Set in a Venn Diagram

Shade the set $(A' \cap B') \cap C$ in a Venn diagram similar to the one in **Figure 15**.

SOLUTION

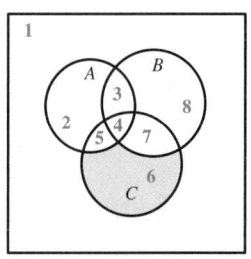

$(A' \cap B') \cap C$

Figure 16

Work first inside the parentheses. As shown in **Figure 16**, set A' is made up of the regions outside set A, or regions 1, 6, 7, and 8. Set B' is made up of regions 1, 2, 5, and 6. The intersection of these sets is given by the overlap of regions 1, 6, 7, 8 and 1, 2, 5, 6, or regions 1 and 6.

For the final Venn diagram, find the intersection of regions 1 and 6 with set C. As seen in **Figure 16**, set C is made up of regions 4, 5, 6, and 7. The overlap of regions 1, 6 and 4, 5, 6, 7 is region 6, the region in color in **Figure 16**.   ■■■

EXAMPLE 13   Verifying a Statement Using a Venn Diagram

Is the statement $(A \cap B)' = A' \cup B'$ true for every choice of sets A and B?

SOLUTION

To help decide, use the regions labeled in **Figure 11**. Set $A \cap B$ is made up of region 3, so that $(A \cap B)'$ is made up of regions 1, 2, and 4. These regions are in color in **Figure 17(a)**.

To find a Venn diagram for set $A' \cup B'$, first check that A' is made up of regions 1 and 4, while set B' includes regions 1 and 2. Finally, $A' \cup B'$ is made up of regions 1 and 4, or 1 and 2, that is, regions 1, 2, and 4. These regions are in color in **Figure 17(b)**.

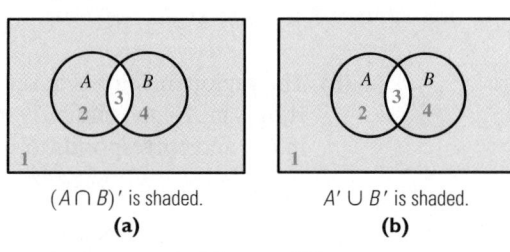

| $(A \cap B)'$ is shaded. | $A' \cup B'$ is shaded. |
| (a) | (b) |

Figure 17

The fact that the same regions are in color in both Venn diagrams suggests that

$$(A \cap B)' = A' \cup B'.$$

■■■

De Morgan's Laws

The result of **Example 13** can be stated in words.

> *The complement of the intersection of two sets is equal to the union of the complements of the two sets.*

As a result, it is natural to ask ourselves whether it is also true that the complement of the *union* of two sets is equal to the *intersection* of the complements of the two sets (where the words "intersection" and "union" are substituted for each other). This was investigated by the British logician Augustus De Morgan (1806–1871) and was found to be true. (See the margin note on **page 21.**) DeMorgan's two laws for sets follow.

De Morgan's Laws for Sets

For any sets A and B,

$$(A \cap B)' = A' \cup B' \quad \text{and} \quad (A \cup B)' = A' \cap B'.$$

The Venn diagrams in **Figure 17** strongly suggest the truth of the first of De Morgan's laws. They provide a *conjecture*. Actual proofs of De Morgan's laws would require methods used in more advanced courses on set theory.

▮▮ **EXAMPLE 14** Describing Regions in Venn Diagrams Using Symbols

For the Venn diagrams, write a symbolic description of the region in color, using A, B, C, $\cap$, $\cup$, $-$, and $'$ as necessary.

(a)
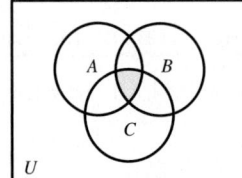

(b)
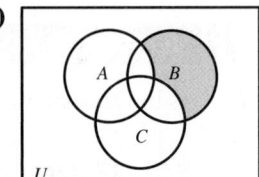

(c) Refer to the figure in part (b) and give two additional ways of describing the region in color.

SOLUTION

(a) The region in color belongs to all three sets, A and B and C. Therefore, the region corresponds to

$$A \cap B \cap C.$$

(b) The region in color is in set B and is not in A and is not in C. Because it is not in A, it is in A', and similarly it is in C'. The region is, therefore, in B and in A' and in C', and corresponds to

$$B \cap A' \cap C'.$$

(c) The region in color includes all of B, except for the regions belonging to either A or C. This suggests the idea of set difference. The region may be described as

$$B - (A \cup C), \quad \text{or equivalently,} \quad B \cap (A \cup C)'. \qquad ▮▮▮$$

2.3 EXERCISES

Match each term in Group I with the appropriate description A–F in Group II. Assume that A and B are sets.

I

1. the intersection of A and B

2. the union of A and B

3. the difference of A and B

4. the complement of A

5. the Cartesian product of A and B

6. the difference of B and A

II

A. the set of elements in A that are not in B

B. the set of elements common to both A and B

C. the set of elements in the universal set that are not in A

D. the set of elements in B that are not in A

E. the set of ordered pairs such that each first element is from A and each second element is from B, with every element of A paired with every element of B

F. the set of elements that are in A or in B or in both A and B

Perform the indicated operations, and designate each answer using the listing method.

Let $U = \{a, b, c, d, e, f, g\}$, $X = \{a, c, e, g\}$,
      $Y = \{a, b, c\}$,   *and* $Z = \{b, c, d, e, f\}$.

7. $X \cap Y$ **8.** $X \cup Y$ **9.** $Y \cup Z$

10. $Y \cap Z$ **11.** $X \cup U$ **12.** $Y \cap U$

13. X' **14.** Y'

15. $X' \cap Y'$ **16.** $X' \cap Z$

17. $X \cup (Y \cap Z)$ **18.** $Y \cap (X \cup Z)$

19. $(Y \cap Z') \cup X$ **20.** $(X' \cup Y') \cup Z$

21. $(Z \cup X')' \cap Y$ **22.** $(Y \cap X')' \cup Z'$

23. $X - Y$ **24.** $Y - X$

25. $X \cap (X - Y)$ **26.** $Y \cup (Y - X)$

27. $X' - Y$ **28.** $Y' - X$

29. $(X \cap Y') \cup (Y \cap X')$ **30.** $(X \cap Y') \cap (Y \cap X')$

Describe each set in words.

31. $A \cup (B' \cap C')$ **32.** $(A \cap B') \cup (B \cap A')$

33. $(C - B) \cup A$ **34.** $B \cap (A' - C)$

35. $(A - C) \cup (B - C)$ **36.** $(A' \cap B') \cup C'$

Adverse Effects of Alcohol and Tobacco *The table lists some common adverse effects of prolonged tobacco and alcohol use.*

Tobacco	Alcohol
Emphysema, e	Liver damage, l
Heart damage, h	Brain damage, b
Cancer, c	Heart damage, h

Let T be the set of listed effects of tobacco and A be the set of listed effects of alcohol. Find each set.

37. the smallest possible universal set U that includes all the effects listed

38. A' **39.** T' **40.** $T \cap A$

41. $T \cup A$ **42.** $T \cap A'$

Describe in words each set in Exercises 43–48.

Let $U =$ the set of all tax returns,
   $A =$ the set of all tax returns with itemized deductions,
   $B =$ the set of all tax returns showing business income,
   $C =$ the set of all tax returns filed in 2009,
   $D =$ the set of all tax returns selected for audit.

43. $B \cup C$ **44.** $A \cap D$ **45.** $C - A$

46. $D \cup A'$ **47.** $(A \cup B) - D$ **48.** $(C \cap A) \cap B'$

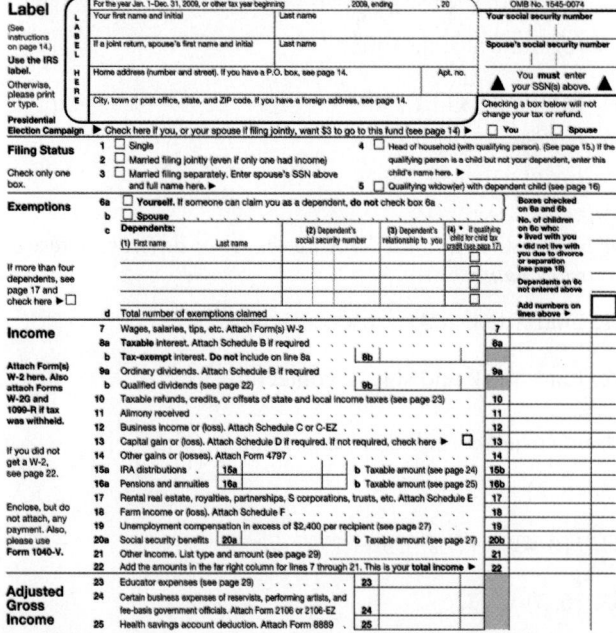

Assuming that A and B represent any two sets, identify each statement as either always true *or* not always true.

49. $A \subseteq (A \cup B)$

50. $A \subseteq (A \cap B)$

51. $(A \cap B) \subseteq A$

52. $(A \cup B) \subseteq A$

53. $n(A \cup B) = n(A) + n(B)$

54. $n(A \cup B) = n(A) + n(B) - n(A \cap B)$

For Exercises 55–60, use your results in parts (a) and (b) to answer part (c).

Let $U = \{1, 2, 3, 4, 5\}$, $X = \{1, 3, 5\}$, $Y = \{1, 2, 3\}$,
and $Z = \{3, 4, 5\}$.

55. (a) Find $X \cup Y$.
(b) Find $Y \cup X$.
(c) State a conjecture.

56. (a) Find $X \cap Y$.
(b) Find $Y \cap X$.
(c) State a conjecture.

57. (a) Find $X \cup (Y \cup Z)$.
(b) Find $(X \cup Y) \cup Z$.
(c) State a conjecture.

58. (a) Find $X \cap (Y \cap Z)$.
(b) Find $(X \cap Y) \cap Z$.
(c) State a conjecture.

59. (a) Find $(X \cup Y)'$.
(b) Find $X' \cap Y'$.
(c) State a conjecture.

60. (a) Find $(X \cap Y)'$.
(b) Find $X' \cup Y'$.
(c) State a conjecture.

In Exercises 61 and 62, let X be the set of different letters in your last name.

61. Find $X \cup \emptyset$ and state a conjecture.

62. Find $X \cap \emptyset$ and state a conjecture.

Decide whether each statement is true or false.

63. $(3, 2) = (5 - 2, 1 + 1)$

64. $(10, 4) = (7 + 3, 5 - 1)$

65. $(6, 3) = (3, 6)$

66. $(2, 13) = (13, 2)$

67. $\{6, 3\} = \{3, 6\}$

68. $\{2, 13\} = \{13, 2\}$

69. $\{(1, 2), (3, 4)\} = \{(3, 4), (1, 2)\}$

70. $\{(5, 9), (4, 8), (4, 2)\} = \{(4, 8), (5, 9), (4, 2)\}$

Find A × B and B × A, for A and B defined as follows.

71. $A = \{2, 8, 12\}$, $B = \{4, 9\}$

72. $A = \{3, 6, 9, 12\}$, $B = \{6, 8\}$

73. $A = \{d, o, g\}$, $B = \{p, i, g\}$

74. $A = \{b, l, u, e\}$, $B = \{r, e, d\}$

For the sets specified in Exercises 75–78, use the given information to find n(A × B) and n(B × A).

75. the sets in **Exercise 71**

76. the sets in **Exercise 73**

77. $n(A) = 35$ and $n(B) = 6$

78. $n(A) = 13$ and $n(B) = 5$

Find the cardinal number specified.

79. If $n(A \times B) = 72$ and $n(A) = 12$, find $n(B)$.

80. If $n(A \times B) = 300$ and $n(B) = 30$, find $n(A)$.

Place the elements of these sets in the proper locations in the given Venn diagram.

81. Let $U = \{a, b, c, d, e, f, g\}$,
$A = \{b, d, f, g\}$,
$B = \{a, b, d, e, g\}$.

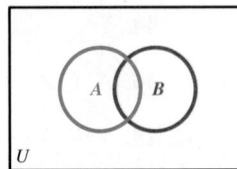

82. Let $U = \{5, 6, 7, 8, 9, 10, 11, 12, 13\}$,
$M = \{5, 8, 10, 11\}$,
$N = \{5, 6, 7, 9, 10\}$.

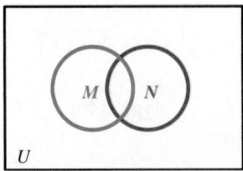

Use a Venn diagram similar to the one shown below to shade each set.

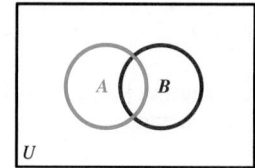

83. $B \cap A'$ **84.** $A \cup B$

85. $A' \cup B$ **86.** $A' \cap B'$

87. $B' \cup A$ **88.** $A' \cup A$

89. $B' \cap B$ **90.** $A \cap B'$

91. $B' \cup (A' \cap B')$ **92.** $(A \cap B) \cup B$

93. U' **94.** $\emptyset'$

In Exercises 95 and 96, place the elements of the sets in the proper location in a Venn diagram similar to the one shown below.

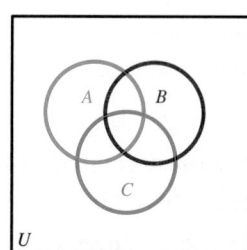

95. Let $U = \{m, n, o, p, q, r, s, t, u, v, w\}$,
   $A = \{m, n, p, q, r, t\}$,
   $B = \{m, o, p, q, s, u\}$,
   $C = \{m, o, p, r, s, t, u, v\}$.

96. Let $U = \{1, 2, 3, 4, 5, 6, 7, 8, 9\}$,
   $A = \{1, 3, 5, 7\}$,
   $B = \{1, 3, 4, 6, 8\}$,
   $C = \{1, 4, 5, 6, 7, 9\}$.

Use a Venn diagram to shade each set.

97. $(A \cap B) \cap C$ **98.** $(A \cap C') \cup B$

99. $(A \cap B) \cup C'$ **100.** $(A' \cap B) \cap C$

101. $(A' \cap B') \cap C$ **102.** $(A \cup B) \cup C$

103. $(A \cap B') \cup C$ **104.** $(A \cap C') \cap B$

105. $(A \cap B') \cap C'$ **106.** $(A' \cap B') \cup C$

107. $(A' \cap B') \cup C'$ **108.** $(A \cap B)' \cup C$

Write a symbolic description of each shaded area. Use the symbols A, B, C, ∩, ∪, −, and ' as necessary. More than one answer may be possible.

109. 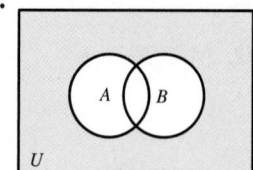   **110.**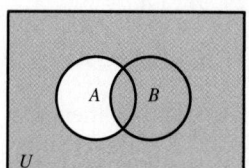

111. 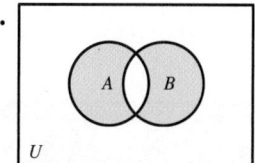   **112.**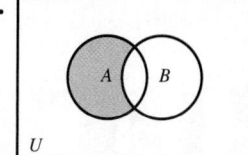

113.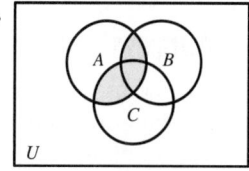

114.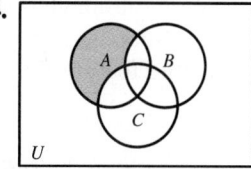

115.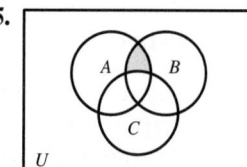

116.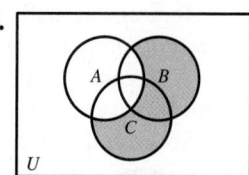

Suppose A and B are sets. Describe the conditions under which each statement would be true.

117. $A = A - B$ **118.** $A = B - A$

119. $A = A - \emptyset$ **120.** $A = \emptyset - A$

121. $A \cup \emptyset = \emptyset$ **122.** $A \cap \emptyset = \emptyset$

123. $A \cap \emptyset = A$ **124.** $A \cup \emptyset = A$

125. $A \cup A = \emptyset$ **126.** $A \cap A = \emptyset$

127. $A \cup B = A$ **128.** $A \cap B = B$

For Exercises 129–135, draw two appropriate Venn diagrams to decide whether the given statement is always true or not always true.

129. $A \cap A' = \emptyset$

130. $A \cup A' = U$

131. $(A \cap B) \subseteq A$

132. $(A \cup B) \subseteq A$

133. If $A \subseteq B$, then $A \cup B = A$.

134. If $A \subseteq B$, then $A \cap B = B$.

135. $(A \cup B)' = A' \cap B'$
(De Morgan's second law)

136. If A and B are sets, is it necessarily true that $n(A - B) = n(A) - n(B)$?

137. If $Q = \{x \,|\, x \text{ is a rational number}\}$ and $H = \{x \,|\, x \text{ is an irrational number}\}$, describe each set.
(a) $Q \cup H$
(b) $Q \cap H$

2.4 SURVEYS AND CARDINAL NUMBERS

Surveys • Cardinal Number Formula • Tables

Surveys

Problems involving sets of people (or objects) sometimes require analyzing known information about certain subsets to obtain cardinal numbers of other subsets. In this section, we apply three problem-solving techniques to such problems: Venn diagrams, cardinal number formulas, and tables. The "known information" is quite often (although not always) obtained by conducting a survey.

Suppose a group of students on a college campus is asked to compare some animated feature films, and the following information is produced.

34 like *Up*	12 like *Up* and *Mr. Fox*
29 like *The Princess and the Frog*	10 like *Princess* and *Mr. Fox*
26 like *Fantastic Mr. Fox*	4 like all three films
16 like *Up* and *Princess*	5 like none of these films.

To determine the total number of students surveyed, we cannot just add the eight numbers above because there is some overlap. For example, in **Figure 18**, the 34 students who like *Up* should not be positioned in region *b* but should be distributed among regions *b*, *c*, *d*, and *e*, in a way that is consistent with all of the given data. (Region *b* actually contains those students who like *Up* but do not like *The Princess and the Frog* and do not like *Fantastic Mr. Fox*.)

Because, at the start, we do not know how to distribute the 34 who like *Up*, we look first for some more manageable data. The smallest total listed, the 4 students who like all three films, can be placed in region *d* (the intersection of the three sets). The 5 who like none of the three must go into region *a*. Then, the 16 who like *Up* and *Princess* must go into regions *d* and *e*. Because region *d* already contains 4 students, we must place

$$16 - 4 = 12 \quad \text{in region } e.$$

Because 12 like *Up* and *Mr. Fox* (regions *c* and *d*), we place

$$12 - 4 = 8 \quad \text{in region } c.$$

Now that regions *c*, *d*, and *e* contain 8, 4, and 12 students, respectively, we must place

$$34 - 8 - 4 - 12 = 10 \quad \text{in region } b.$$

By similar reasoning, all regions are assigned their correct numbers. See **Figure 19** on the next page.

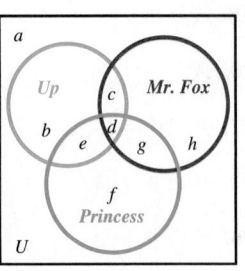

Figure 18

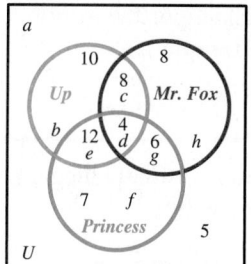

Figure 19

‖‖ EXAMPLE 1 Analyzing a Survey

Using the survey data on student preferences for animated feature films, as summarized in **Figure 19**, answer each question.

(a) How many students like *Fantastic Mr. Fox* only?

(b) How many students like exactly two films?

(c) How many students were surveyed?

SOLUTION

(a) A student who likes *Mr. Fox* only does not like *Up* and does not like *Princess*. These students are inside the regions for *Mr. Fox* and outside the regions for *Up* and *Princess*. Region *h* is the appropriate region in **Figure 19**, and we see that eight students like *Fantastic Mr. Fox* only.

(b) The students in regions *c*, *e*, and *g* like exactly two films. The total number of such students is

$$8 + 12 + 6 = 26.$$

(c) Each student surveyed has been placed in exactly one region of **Figure 19**, so the total number surveyed is the sum of the numbers in all eight regions:

$$5 + 10 + 8 + 4 + 12 + 7 + 6 + 8 = 60.$$ ███

Cardinal Number Formula

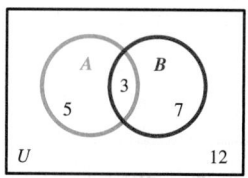

Figure 20

If the numbers shown in **Figure 20** are the cardinal numbers of the individual regions, then

$$n(A) = 5 + 3 = 8, \quad n(B) = 3 + 7 = 10, \quad n(A \cap B) = 3,$$

and $$n(A \cup B) = 5 + 3 + 7 = 15.$$

Notice that $n(A \cup B) = n(A) + n(B) - n(A \cap B)$ because $15 = 8 + 10 - 3$. This relationship is true for any two sets A and B.

Cardinal Number Formula

For any two sets A and B, the following is true.

$$n(A \cup B) = n(A) + n(B) - n(A \cap B)$$

This formula can be rearranged to find any one of its four terms when the others are known.

‖‖ EXAMPLE 2 Applying the Cardinal Number Formula

Find $n(A)$ if $n(A \cup B) = 22$, $n(A \cap B) = 8$, and $n(B) = 12$.

SOLUTION

We solve the cardinal number formula for $n(A)$.

$$n(A) = n(A \cup B) - n(B) + n(A \cap B)$$
$$= 22 - 12 + 8$$
$$= 18$$ ███

Sometimes, even when information is presented as in **Example 2**, it is more convenient to fit that information into a Venn diagram as in **Example 1.**

▮▮ **EXAMPLE 3** Analyzing Data in a Report

Scott Heeren, who leads a group of software engineers who investigate illegal activities on social networking sites, reported the following information.

T = the set of group members following patterns on Twitter

F = the set of group members following patterns on Facebook

L = the set of group members following patterns on LinkedIn

$$n(T) = 13 \qquad n(T \cap F) = 9 \qquad n(T \cap F \cap L) = 5$$
$$n(F) = 16 \qquad n(F \cap L) = 10 \qquad n(T' \cap F' \cap L') = 3$$
$$n(L) = 13 \qquad n(T \cap L) = 6$$

How many engineers are in Scott's group?

SOLUTION

The data supplied by Scott are reflected in **Figure 21.** The sum of the numbers in the diagram gives the total number of engineers in the group.

$$3 + 3 + 1 + 2 + 5 + 5 + 4 + 2 = 25 \qquad ▮▮▮$$

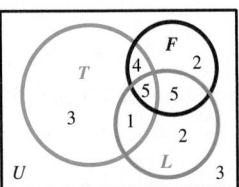

Figure 21

Tables

Sometimes information appears in a table rather than a Venn diagram, but the basic ideas of union and intersection still apply.

▮▮ **EXAMPLE 4** Analyzing Data in a Table

Melanie Cutler, the officer in charge of the cafeteria on a military base, wanted to know if the beverage that enlisted men and women preferred with lunch depended on their ages. On a given day, Melanie categorized her lunch patrons according to age and preferred beverage, recording the results in a table.

		Beverage			
		Cola (C)	Iced Tea (I)	Sweet Tea (S)	Totals
	18–25 (Y)	45	10	35	90
Age	26–33 (M)	20	25	30	75
	Over 33 (O)	5	30	20	55
	Totals	70	65	85	220

Using the letters in the table, find the number of people in each set.

(a) $Y \cap C$ **(b)** $O' \cup I$

SOLUTION

(a) The set Y includes all personnel represented across the top row of the table (90 in all), while C includes the 70 down the left column. The intersection of these two sets is just the upper left entry, 45 people.

(b) The set O' excludes the bottom row, so it includes the first and second rows. The set I includes the middle column only. The union of the two sets represents

$$45 + 10 + 35 + 20 + 25 + 30 + 30 = 195 \text{ people.} \qquad ▮▮▮$$

2.4 EXERCISES

Use the numerals representing cardinalities in the Venn diagrams to give the cardinality of each set specified.

1.

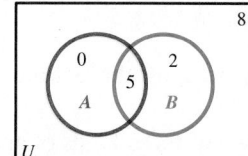

(a) $A \cap B$ (b) $A \cup B$
(c) $A \cap B'$ (d) $A' \cap B$
(e) $A' \cap B'$

2.

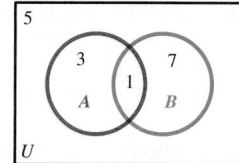

(a) $A \cap B$ (b) $A \cup B$
(c) $A \cap B'$ (d) $A' \cap B$
(e) $A' \cap B'$

3.

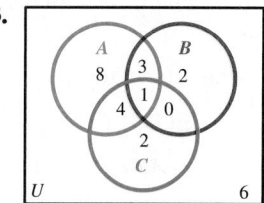

(a) $A \cap B \cap C$ (b) $A \cap B \cap C'$
(c) $A \cap B' \cap C$ (d) $A' \cap B \cap C$
(e) $A' \cap B' \cap C$ (f) $A \cap B' \cap C'$
(g) $A' \cap B \cap C'$ (h) $A' \cap B' \cap C'$

4.

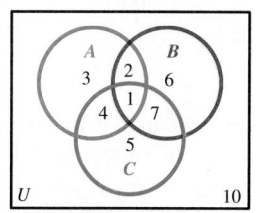

(a) $A \cap B \cap C$ (b) $A \cap B \cap C'$
(c) $A \cap B' \cap C$ (d) $A' \cap B \cap C$
(e) $A' \cap B' \cap C$ (f) $A \cap B' \cap C'$
(g) $A' \cap B \cap C'$ (h) $A' \cap B' \cap C'$

In Exercises 5–10, make use of an appropriate formula.

5. Find the value of $n(A \cup B)$ if $n(A) = 12, n(B) = 14$, and $n(A \cap B) = 5$.

6. Find the value of $n(A \cup B)$ if $n(A) = 16, n(B) = 28$, and $n(A \cap B) = 5$.

7. Find the value of $n(A \cap B)$ if $n(A) = 20, n(B) = 12$, and $n(A \cup B) = 25$.

8. Find the value of $n(A \cap B)$ if $n(A) = 20, n(B) = 24$, and $n(A \cup B) = 30$.

9. Find the value of $n(A)$ if $n(B) = 35$, $n(A \cap B) = 15$, and $n(A \cup B) = 55$.

10. Find the value of $n(B)$ if $n(A) = 20, n(A \cap B) = 6$, and $n(A \cup B) = 30$.

Draw an appropriate Venn diagram and use the given information to fill in the number of elements in each region.

11. $n(A) = 19$, $n(B) = 13$, $n(A \cup B) = 25$, $n(A') = 11$

12. $n(U) = 43$, $n(A) = 25$, $n(A \cap B) = 5$, $n(B') = 30$

13. $n(A') = 25$, $n(B) = 28$, $n(A' \cup B') = 40$, $n(A \cap B) = 10$

14. $n(A \cup B) = 15$, $n(A \cap B) = 8$, $n(A) = 13$, $n(A' \cup B') = 11$

15. $n(A) = 57$, $n(A \cap B) = 35$, $n(A \cup B) = 81$, $n(A \cap B \cap C) = 15$, $n(A \cap C) = 21$, $n(B \cap C) = 25$, $n(C) = 49$, $n(B') = 52$

16. $n(A) = 24$, $n(B) = 24$, $n(C) = 26$, $n(A \cap B) = 10$, $n(B \cap C) = 8$, $n(A \cap C) = 15$, $n(A \cap B \cap C) = 6$, $n(U) = 50$

17. $n(A) = 15$, $n(A \cap B \cap C) = 5$, $n(A \cap C) = 13$, $n(A \cap B') = 9$, $n(B \cap C) = 8$, $n(A' \cap B' \cap C') = 21$, $n(B \cap C') = 3$, $n(B \cup C) = 32$

18. $n(A \cap B) = 21$, $n(A \cap B \cap C) = 6$, $n(A \cap C) = 26$, $n(B \cap C) = 7$, $n(A \cap C') = 20$, $n(B \cap C') = 25$, $n(C) = 40$, $n(A' \cap B' \cap C') = 2$

Use Venn diagrams to work each problem.

19. *Writing and Producing Music* Joe Long worked on 9 music projects last year.

Joe Long, Bob Gaudio, Tommy DeVito, and Frankie Valli
The Four Seasons

He wrote and produced 3 projects.
He wrote a total of 5 projects.
He produced a total of 7 projects.

(a) How many projects did he write but not produce?
(b) How many projects did he produce but not write?

20. *Compact Disc Collection* Gitti Lindner is a fan of the music of Paul Simon and Art Garfunkel. In her collection of 25 compact discs, she has the following:

> 5 on which both Simon and Garfunkel sing
> 7 on which Simon sings
> 8 on which Garfunkel sings
> 15 on which neither Simon nor Garfunkel sings.

(a) How many of her compact discs feature only Paul Simon?

(b) How many of her compact discs feature only Art Garfunkel?

(c) How many feature at least one of these two artists?

(d) How many feature at most one of these two artists?

21. *Fan Response to Singers* Julie Davis, a pop culture analyst, wanted to evaluate the relative appeal of different singers. She interviewed 65 fans and determined the following:

> 37 like Jazmine Sullivan
> 36 like Carrie Underwood
> 31 like Brad Paisley
> 14 like Jazmine and Carrie
> 21 like Jazmine and Brad
> 14 like Carrie and Brad
> 8 like all three singers.

How many of these fans like:

(a) exactly two of these singers?

(b) exactly one of these singers?

(c) none of these singers?

(d) Jazmine, but neither Carrie nor Brad?

(e) Brad and exactly one of the other two?

22. *Financial Aid for Students* At the University of Louisiana, half of the 48 mathematics majors were receiving federal financial aid as follows:

> 5 had Pell Grants
> 14 participated in the College Work Study Program
> 4 had TOPS scholarships
> 2 had TOPS scholarships and participated in Work Study.

Those with Pell Grants had no other federal aid.

How many of the 48 math majors had:

(a) no federal aid?

(b) more than one of these three forms of aid?

(c) federal aid other than these three forms?

(d) a TOPS scholarship or Work Study?

(e) exactly one of these three forms of aid?

23. *Cooking Habits* Eric Dangerfield interviewed 140 people in a suburban shopping center to find out some of their cooking habits. He obtained the results given at the top of the next column.

> 58 use microwave ovens
> 63 use electric ranges
> 58 use gas ranges
> 19 use microwave ovens and electric ranges
> 17 use microwave ovens and gas ranges
> 4 use both gas and electric ranges
> 1 uses all three

(a) How many use exactly two of these kinds of appliances?

(b) How many use at least two of these kinds of appliances?

24. *Non-Mainline Religious Beliefs* 140 U.S. adults were surveyed.

Let $A =$ the set of respondents who believe in astrology,
$R =$ the set of respondents who believe in reincarnation,
$Y =$ the set of respondents who believe in the spirituality of yoga.

The survey revealed the following information:

$$n(A) = 35 \qquad n(R \cap Y) = 8$$
$$n(R) = 36 \qquad n(A \cap Y) = 10$$
$$n(Y) = 32 \qquad n(A \cap R \cap Y) = 6$$
$$n(A \cap R) = 19$$

How many of the respondents believe in:

(a) astrology, but not reincarnation?

(b) at least one of these three things?

(c) reincarnation but neither of the others?

(d) exactly two of these three things?

(e) none of the three?

25. *Survey on Attitudes Toward Religion* Researchers interviewed a number of people and recorded the following data. Of all the respondents:

> 240 think Hollywood is unfriendly toward religion
> 160 think the media are unfriendly toward religion
> 181 think scientists are unfriendly toward religion
> 145 think both Hollywood and the media are unfriendly toward religion
> 122 think both scientists and the media are unfriendly toward religion
> 80 think exactly two of these groups are unfriendly toward religion
> 110 think all three groups are unfriendly toward religion
> 219 think none of these three groups is unfriendly toward religion.

How many respondents:

(a) were surveyed?

(b) think exactly one of these three groups is unfriendly toward religion?

26. Student Goals Carol Britz, who sells college textbooks, interviewed freshmen on a community college campus to find out the main goals of today's students.

Let W = the set of those who want to be wealthy,
F = the set of those who want to raise a family,
E = the set of those who want to become experts in their fields.

Carol's findings are summarized here.

$n(W) = 160$	$n(E \cap F) = 90$
$n(F) = 140$	$n(W \cap F \cap E) = 80$
$n(E) = 130$	$n(E') = 95$
$n(W \cap F) = 95$	$n[(W \cup F \cup E)'] = 10$

Find the total number of students interviewed.

27. Hospital Patient Symptoms Jesse Fisher conducted a survey among 75 patients admitted to the cardiac unit of a Santa Fe hospital during a two-week period.

Let B = the set of patients with high blood pressure,
C = the set of patients with high cholesterol levels,
S = the set of patients who smoke cigarettes.

Jesse's data are as follows.

$n(B) = 47$	$n(B \cap S) = 33$
$n(C) = 46$	$n(B \cap C) = 31$
$n(S) = 52$	$n(B \cap C \cap S) = 21$

$$n[(B \cap C) \cup (B \cap S) \cup (C \cap S)] = 51$$

Find the number of these patients who:

(a) had either high blood pressure or high cholesterol levels, but not both

(b) had fewer than two of the indications listed

(c) were smokers but had neither high blood pressure nor high cholesterol levels

(d) did not have exactly two of the indications listed.

28. Song Themes It was once said that country-western songs emphasize three basic themes: love, prison, and trucks. A survey of the local country-western radio station produced the following data.

12 songs about a truck driver who is in love while in prison
13 about a prisoner in love
28 about a person in love
18 about a truck driver in love
3 about a truck driver in prison who is not in love
2 about people in prison who are not in love and do not drive trucks
8 about people who are out of prison, are not in love, and do not drive trucks
16 about truck drivers who are not in prison

(a) How many songs were surveyed?

Find the number of songs about:

(b) truck drivers   **(c)** prisoners

(d) truck drivers in prison

(e) people not in prison

(f) people not in love.

29. Use the figure below to find the numbers of the regions belonging to each set.

(a) $A \cap B \cap C \cap D$

(b) $A \cup B \cup C \cup D$

(c) $(A \cap B) \cup (C \cap D)$

(d) $(A' \cap B') \cap (C \cup D)$

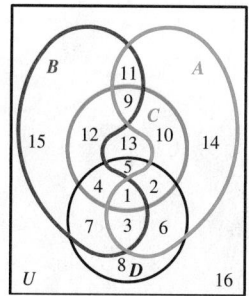

30. Sports Viewing A survey of 130 TV viewers was taken.

52 watch football
56 watch basketball
62 watch tennis
60 watch golf
21 watch football and basketball
19 watch football and tennis
22 watch basketball and tennis
27 watch football and golf
30 watch basketball and golf
21 watch tennis and golf
3 watch football, basketball, and tennis
15 watch football, basketball, and golf
10 watch football, tennis, and golf
10 watch basketball, tennis, and golf
3 watch all four of these sports
5 don't watch any of these four sports

Use a Venn diagram to answer each question.

(a) How many of these viewers watch football, basketball, and tennis, but not golf?

(b) How many watch exactly one of these four sports?

(c) How many watch exactly two of these four sports?

Solve each problem.

31. *Basketball Positions* Donna DePaulis runs a basketball program in California. On the first day of the season, 60 young women showed up and were categorized by age level and by preferred basketball position, as shown in the following table.

		Position			
		Guard (*G*)	Forward (*F*)	Center (*N*)	Totals
Age	Junior High (*J*)	9	6	4	19
	Senior High (*S*)	12	5	9	26
	College (*C*)	5	8	2	15
	Totals	26	19	15	60

Using the set labels (letters) in the table, find the number of players in each of the following sets.

(a) $J \cap G$ **(b)** $S \cap N$ **(c)** $N \cup (S \cap F)$

(d) $S' \cap (G \cup N)$ **(e)** $(S \cap N') \cup (C \cap G')$

(f) $N' \cap (S' \cap C')$

32. *Army Housing* A study of U.S. Army housing trends categorized personnel as commissioned officers (*C*), warrant officers (*W*), or enlisted (*E*), and categorized their living facilities as on-base (*B*), rented off-base (*R*), or owned off-base (*O*). One survey yielded the following data.

		Facilities			
		B	*R*	*O*	Totals
Personnel	*C*	12	29	54	95
	W	4	5	6	15
	E	374	71	285	730
	Totals	390	105	345	840

Find the number of personnel in each of the following sets.

(a) $W \cap O$ **(b)** $C \cup B$

(c) $R' \cup W'$ **(d)** $(C \cup W) \cap (B \cup R)$

(e) $(C \cap B) \cup (E \cap O)$ **(f)** $B \cap (W \cup R)'$

33. Could the information of **Example 4** have been presented in a Venn diagram similar to those in **Examples 1 and 3**? If so, construct such a diagram. Otherwise, explain the essential difference of **Example 4**.

34. Explain how a cardinal number formula can be derived for the case where *three* sets occur. Specifically, give a formula relating $n(A \cup B \cup C)$ to

$$n(A), \ n(B), \ n(C), \ n(A \cap B), \ n(A \cap C),$$
$$n(B \cap C), \ \text{and} \ n(A \cap B \cap C).$$

Illustrate with a Venn diagram.

EXTENSION Infinite Sets and Their Cardinalities

One-to-One Correspondence and Equivalent Sets • The Cardinal Number $\aleph_0$
• Infinite Sets • Sets That Are Not Countable

One-to-One Correspondence and Equivalent Sets
Georg Cantor, profiled on **page 44,** met with much resistance in the late 1800s when he first developed modern set theory because of his ideas on infinite sets. The results discussed here, however, are commonly accepted today. Recall the following from **Section 2.1.**

1. The cardinal number of a set is the number of elements it contains.

2. Two sets are *equivalent* if their cardinal numbers are equal.

3. A set is *infinite* if its cardinal number is "too large" to be found among the whole numbers.

We can easily establish the equivalence of two finite sets by counting their elements and comparing their cardinal numbers. But the elements of an infinite set cannot be counted in the same sense. Cantor addressed this difficulty using the idea of a **one-to-one correspondence** between sets. The sets $A = \{1, 2, 3\}$ and $B = \{3, 6, 9\}$, for example, can be placed in such correspondence as follows (among other ways):

$$\{1, \quad 2, \quad 3\}$$
$$\updownarrow \quad \updownarrow \quad \updownarrow$$
$$\{3, \quad 6, \quad 9\}.$$

This correspondence is "one-to-one" because each element of each set is paired with exactly one element of the other set. The equivalence of A and B is denoted **$A \sim B$**.

On the other hand, the sets $C = \{1, 8, 12\}$ and $D = \{6, 11\}$ are *not* equivalent. Any correspondence between them, such as

$$\{1, \quad 8, \quad 12\}$$
$$\updownarrow \quad \searrow \quad \nearrow$$
$$\{6, \quad 11\}$$

is not one-to-one. (Two different elements from C must be paired with a single element of D.)

Cantor extended this idea that one-to-one correspondence establishes equivalence to his study of infinite sets.

The Cardinal Number $\aleph_0$

The most basic infinite set is the set of counting numbers, $\{1, 2, 3, 4, 5, \ldots\}$. The counting numbers are said to have the infinite cardinal number $\aleph_0$ (the first Hebrew letter, aleph, with a zero subscript, read "aleph-null"). Think of $\aleph_0$ as being the "smallest" infinite cardinal number. To the question "How many counting numbers are there?", we answer "There are $\aleph_0$ of them."

Now, any set that can be placed in a one-to-one correspondence with the counting numbers will have the same cardinal number, or $\aleph_0$. There are many such sets.

██ EXAMPLE 1 Showing that $\{0, 1, 2, 3, \ldots\}$ Has Cardinal Number $\aleph_0$

Verify that the set of whole numbers $\{0, 1, 2, 3, \ldots\}$ has cardinal number $\aleph_0$.

SOLUTION

We know that $\aleph_0$ is the cardinal number of the set of counting numbers (by definition). To show that another set, such as the whole numbers, also has $\aleph_0$ as its cardinal number, we must show that set to be equivalent to the set of counting numbers. Equivalence is established by a one-to-one correspondence between the two sets.

$$\{1, \quad 2, \quad 3, \quad 4, \quad 5, \quad 6, \ldots, \quad n, \quad \ldots\} \text{ Counting numbers}$$
$$\updownarrow \ \updownarrow \ \updownarrow \ \updownarrow \ \updownarrow \ \updownarrow \qquad \updownarrow \qquad \updownarrow$$
$$\{0, \quad 1, \quad 2, \quad 3, \quad 4, \quad 5, \ldots, \quad n-1, \quad \ldots\} \text{ Whole numbers}$$

The pairing of the counting number n with the whole number $n - 1$ continues indefinitely, with neither set containing any element not used up in the pairing process. Even though the set of whole numbers has an additional element (the number 0) compared to the set of counting numbers, the correspondence proves that both sets have the same cardinal number, $\aleph_0$. ███

The result in **Example 1** shows that intuition is a poor guide for dealing with infinite sets. Because the sets of counting numbers and whole numbers can be placed in a one-to-one correspondence, the two sets have the same cardinal number.

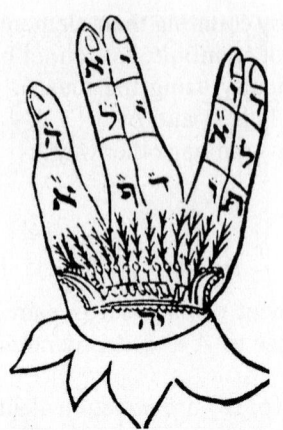

Aleph and other letters of the **Hebrew alphabet** are shown on a Kabbalistic diagram representing one of the ten emanations of God during Creation. Kabbalah, the ultramystical tradition within Judaism, arose in the fifth century and peaked in the sixteenth century in both Palestine and Poland.

Kabbalists believed that the Bible held mysteries that could be discovered in permutations, combinations, and anagrams of its very letters. Each letter in the aleph-bet has a numerical value (aleph = 1), and thus a numeration system exists. The letter Y stands for 10, so 15 should be YH (10 + 5). However, YH is a form of the Holy Name, so instead TW (9 + 6) is the symbol.

Infinite Sets The set $\{5, 6, 7\}$ is a proper subset of the set $\{5, 6, 7, 8\}$, and there is no way to place these two sets in a one-to-one correspondence. However, the set of counting numbers is a proper subset of the set of whole numbers, and **Example 1** showed that these two sets *can* be placed in a one-to-one correspondence. This important property is used in the formal definition of an infinite set.

> **Infinite Set**
>
> A set is **infinite** if it can be placed in a one-to-one correspondence with a proper subset of itself.

▌ **EXAMPLE 2** Showing that $\{\ldots, -3, -2, -1, 0, 1, 2, 3, \ldots\}$ Has Cardinal Number $\aleph_0$

Verify that the set of integers $\{\ldots, -3, -2, -1, 0, 1, 2, 3, \ldots\}$ has cardinal number $\aleph_0$.

SOLUTION

A one-to-one correspondence can be set up between the set of integers and the set of counting numbers.

$$\{1, \quad 2, \quad 3, \quad 4, \quad 5, \quad 6, \quad 7, \quad \ldots, \quad 2n, \quad 2n+1, \quad \ldots\}$$
$$\updownarrow \; \updownarrow \; \updownarrow \; \updownarrow \; \updownarrow \; \updownarrow \; \updownarrow \qquad \updownarrow \qquad \updownarrow$$
$$\{0, \quad 1, \quad -1, \quad 2, \quad -2, \quad 3, \quad -3, \quad \ldots, \quad n, \quad -n, \quad \ldots\}$$

Because of this one-to-one correspondence, the cardinal number of the set of integers is the same as the cardinal number of the set of counting numbers, $\aleph_0$. ▌▌▌

The one-to-one correspondence of **Example 2** proves that the set of integers is infinite—it was placed in one-to-one correspondence with a proper subset of itself.

As shown by **Example 2,** there are just as many integers as there are counting numbers. This result is not at all intuitive, and the next result is even less so. There is an infinite number of fractions between any two counting numbers. For example, there is an infinite set of fractions $\left\{\frac{1}{2}, \frac{3}{4}, \frac{7}{8}, \frac{15}{16}, \frac{31}{32}, \ldots\right\}$ between the counting numbers 0 and 1. This should imply that there are "more" fractions than counting numbers. However, there are just as many fractions as counting numbers.

▌ **EXAMPLE 3** Showing that the Set of Rational Numbers Has Cardinal Number $\aleph_0$

Verify that the cardinal number of the set of rational numbers is $\aleph_0$.

SOLUTION

First show that a one-to-one correspondence may be set up between the set of non-negative rational numbers and the counting numbers. This is done by the following ingenious scheme, devised by Georg Cantor.

Look at **Figure 22** on the next page. The nonnegative rational numbers whose denominators are 1 are written in the first row. Those whose denominators are 2 are written in the second row, and so on. Every nonnegative rational number appears in this list sooner or later. For example, $\frac{327}{189}$ is in row 189 and column 327.

Figure 22

To set up a one-to-one correspondence between the set of nonnegative rationals and the set of counting numbers, follow the path drawn in **Figure 22**. Let $\frac{0}{1}$ correspond to 1, let $\frac{1}{1}$ correspond to 2, $\frac{2}{1}$ to 3, $\frac{1}{2}$ to 4 $\left(\text{skip } \frac{2}{2}, \text{ since } \frac{2}{2} = \frac{1}{1}\right)$, $\frac{1}{3}$ to 5, $\frac{1}{4}$ to 6, and so on. The numbers under the colored disks are omitted because they can be reduced to lower terms, and were thus included earlier in the listing.

This procedure sets up a one-to-one correspondence between the set of nonnegative rationals and the counting numbers, showing that both of these sets have the same cardinal number, $\aleph_0$. Now by using the method of **Example 2** (i.e., letting each negative number follow its corresponding positive number), we can extend this correspondence to include negative rational numbers as well. Thus, the set of all rational numbers has cardinal number $\aleph_0$. ▬▬▬

A set is called **countable** if it is finite or if it has cardinal number $\aleph_0$. All the infinite sets of numbers discussed so far—the counting numbers, the whole numbers, the integers, and the rational numbers—are countable.

Sets That Are Not Countable

▋▋ **EXAMPLE 4**   Showing that the Set of Real Numbers Does Not Have Cardinal Number $\aleph_0$

Verify that the set of all real numbers does not have cardinal number $\aleph_0$.

SOLUTION

There are two possibilities:

1. The set of real numbers has cardinal number $\aleph_0$.

2. The set of real numbers does not have cardinal number $\aleph_0$.

If we assume that the first statement is true, then a one-to-one correspondence can be set up between the set of real numbers and the set of counting numbers.

In a later chapter, we show that every real number can be written as a decimal number (or simply "decimal"). Thus, in the one-to-one correspondence we are assuming, some decimal corresponds to the counting number 1, some decimal corresponds to 2, and so on. Suppose the correspondence begins as follows:

$$1 \leftrightarrow 0.68458429006\ldots$$
$$2 \leftrightarrow 0.13479201038\ldots$$
$$3 \leftrightarrow 0.37291568341\ldots$$
$$4 \leftrightarrow 0.935223671611\ldots$$
and so on.

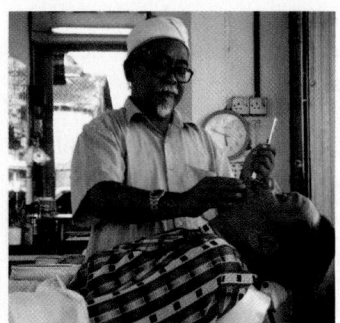

The Barber Paradox is a version of a paradox of set theory that Bertrand Russell proposed in the early twentieth century.

1. The men in a village are of two types: men who do not shave themselves and men who do.
2. The village barber shaves all men who do not shave themselves and he shaves only those men.

But who shaves the barber?
The barber cannot shave himself. If he did, he would fall into the category of men who shave themselves. However, (2) above states that the barber does not shave such men.

So the barber does not shave himself. But then he falls into the category of men who do not shave themselves. According to (2), the barber shaves all of these men; hence, the barber shaves himself, too.

We find that the barber cannot shave himself, yet the barber does shave himself—a paradox.

Zeno's paradox of the Tortoise and Achilles was given in its original form by Zeno of Elea.

In the original story, the Tortoise is able to convince Achilles (the Greek hero of Homer's *The Illiad*) that in a race, given a small head start, the Tortoise is always able to defeat Achilles. (See the **Chapter Opener** and **Exercises 51 and 52** in this **Extension**.) The resolution of this paradox is discussed on the Web site www.mathacademy.com.

Assuming the existence of a one-to-one correspondence between the counting numbers and the real numbers means that every decimal is in the list above. Let's construct a new decimal K as follows. The first decimal in the above list has 6 as its first digit. Let K start as $K = 0.4\ldots$. We picked 4 because $4 \neq 6$. (We could have used any other digit except 6.) Because the second digit of the second decimal in the list is 3, we let $K = 0.45\ldots$ (because $5 \neq 3$). The third digit of the third decimal is 2, so let $K = 0.457\ldots$ (because $7 \neq 2$). The fourth digit of the fourth decimal is 2, so let $K = 0.4573\ldots$ (because $3 \neq 2$). Continue defining K in this way.

Is K in the list that we assumed to contain all decimals? The first decimal in the list differs from K in at least the first position (K starts with 4, and the first decimal in the list starts with 6). The second decimal in the list differs from K in at least the second position, and the nth decimal in the list differs from K in at least the nth position. Every decimal in the list differs from K in at least one position, so that K cannot possibly be in the list. In summary:

> We assume every decimal is in the list above.
> The decimal K is not in the list.

Because these statements cannot both be true, the original assumption has led to a contradiction. This forces the acceptance of the only possible alternative to the original assumption: It is not possible to set up a one-to-one correspondence between the set of reals and the set of counting numbers. The cardinal number of the set of reals is not equal to $\aleph_0$.   ▌▌▌

The set of counting numbers is a proper subset of the set of real numbers. Because of this, it would seem reasonable to say that the cardinal number of the set of reals, commonly written c, is greater than $\aleph_0$. (The letter c here represents *continuum*.) Other, even larger, infinite cardinal numbers can be constructed. For example, the set of all subsets of the set of real numbers has a cardinal number larger than c. Continuing this process of finding cardinal numbers of sets of subsets, more and more, larger and larger infinite cardinal numbers are produced.

The six most important infinite sets of numbers were listed in **Section 2.1.** All of them have been dealt with in this **Extension,** except the irrational numbers. The irrationals have decimal representations, so they are all included among the real numbers. Because the irrationals are a subset of the reals, you might guess that the irrationals have cardinal number $\aleph_0$, just like the rationals. However, because the union of the rationals and the irrationals is all the reals, that would imply that the cardinality of the union of two disjoint countable sets is c. But **Example 2** showed that this is not the case. A better guess is that the cardinal number of the irrationals is c (the same as that of the reals). This is, in fact, true.

Cardinal Numbers of Infinite Number Sets

Infinite Set	Cardinal Number
Natural or counting numbers	$\aleph_0$
Whole numbers	$\aleph_0$
Integers	$\aleph_0$
Rational numbers	$\aleph_0$
Irrational numbers	c
Real numbers	c

EXTENSION EXERCISES

Match each set in Column I with the set in Column II that has the same cardinality. Give the cardinal number.

I	II
1. $\{6\}$	**A.** $\{x\,|\,x$ is a rational number$\}$
2. $\{-16, 14, 3\}$	**B.** $\{26\}$
3. $\{x\,|\,x$ is a natural number$\}$	**C.** $\{x\,|\,x$ is an irrational number$\}$
4. $\{x\,|\,x$ is a real number$\}$	**D.** $\{x, y, z\}$
5. $\{x\,|\,x$ is an integer between 5 and 6$\}$	**E.** $\{x\,|\,x$ is a real number that satisfies $x^2 = 25\}$
6. $\{x\,|\,x$ is an integer that satisfies $x^2 = 100\}$	**F.** $\{x\,|\,x$ is an integer that is both even and odd$\}$

Place each pair of sets into a one-to-one correspondence, if possible.

7. $\{I, II, III\}$ and $\{x, y, z\}$

8. $\{a, b, c, d\}$ and $\{2, 4, 6\}$

9. $\{a, d, d, i, t, i, o, n\}$ and $\{a, n, s, w, e, r\}$

10. $\{$Obama, Clinton, Bush$\}$ and $\{$Michelle, Hillary, Laura$\}$

Give the cardinal number of each set.

11. $\{a, b, c, d, \ldots, k\}$

12. $\{9, 12, 15, \ldots, 36\}$

13. $\emptyset$

14. $\{0\}$

15. $\{300, 400, 500, \ldots\}$

16. $\{-35, -28, -21, \ldots, 56\}$

17. $\left\{-\dfrac{1}{4}, -\dfrac{1}{8}, -\dfrac{1}{12}, \ldots\right\}$

18. $\{x\,|\,x$ is an even integer$\}$

19. $\{x\,|\,x$ is an odd counting number$\}$

20. $\{b, a, 1, 1, a, d\}$

21. $\{$Jan, Feb, Mar, $\ldots$, Dec$\}$

22. $\{$Alabama, Alaska, Arizona, $\ldots$, Wisconsin, Wyoming$\}$

23. Lew Lefton has revised the old song "100 Bottles of Beer on the Wall" to illustrate a property of infinite cardinal numbers.

Fill in the blank in the first verse of Lefton's composition:

$\aleph_0$ bottles of beer on the wall, $\aleph_0$ bottles of beer, take one down and pass it around, _____ bottles of beer on the wall.
(*Source:* http://people.math.gatech.edu/~llefton)

$$\aleph_0 - 1 = ?$$

24. Two one-to-one correspondences are considered "different" if some elements are paired differently in one than in the other.

$$\begin{matrix} \{a, & b, & c\} \\ \updownarrow & \updownarrow & \updownarrow \\ \{a, & b, & c\} \end{matrix} \quad \text{and} \quad \begin{matrix} \{a, & b, & c\} \\ \updownarrow & \updownarrow & \updownarrow \\ \{c, & b, & a\} \end{matrix} \quad \text{are different,}$$

while $\quad \begin{matrix} \{a, & b, & c\} \\ \updownarrow & \updownarrow & \updownarrow \\ \{c, & a, & b\} \end{matrix} \quad \text{and} \quad \begin{matrix} \{b, & c, & a\} \\ \updownarrow & \updownarrow & \updownarrow \\ \{a, & b, & c\} \end{matrix} \quad \text{are not.}$

(a) How many *different* correspondences can be set up between the two sets $\{$Jamie Foxx, Mike Myers, Madonna$\}$ and $\{$Austin Powers, Ray Charles, Eva Peron$\}$?

(b) Which one of these correspondences pairs each person with the appropriate famous movie role?

Determine whether each pair of sets is equal, equivalent, both, *or* neither.

25. $\{u, v, w\}, \{v, u, w\}$ 　　**26.** $\{48, 6\}, \{4, 86\}$

27. $\{X, Y, Z\}, \{x, y, z\}$

28. $\{$top$\}, \{$pot$\}$

29. $\{x\,|\,x$ is a positive real number$\}$, $\{x\,|\,x$ is a negative real number$\}$

30. $\{x\,|\,x$ is a positive rational number$\}$, $\{x\,|\,x$ is a negative real number$\}$

Show that each set has cardinal number $\aleph_0$ by setting up a one-to-one correspondence between the given set and the set of counting numbers.

31. the set of positive even integers

32. $\{-10, -20, -30, -40, \ldots\}$

33. $\{1,000,000,\ 2,000,000,\ 3,000,000,\dots\}$

34. the set of odd integers

35. $\{2, 4, 8, 16, 32, \dots\}$
(*Hint*: $4 = 2^2$, $8 = 2^3$, $16 = 2^4$, and so on)

36. $\{-17, -22, -27, -32, \dots\}$

In Exercises 37–40, identify the given statement as always true *or* not always true. *If not always true,* give a counterexample.

37. If A and B are infinite sets, then A is equivalent to B.

38. If set A is an infinite set and set B can be put in a one-to-one correspondence with a proper subset of A, then B must be infinite.

39. If A is an infinite set and A is not equivalent to the set of counting numbers, then $n(A) = c$.

40. If A and B are both countably infinite sets, then $n(A \cup B) = \aleph_0$.

Exercises 41 and 42 are geometric applications of the concept of infinity.

41. The set of real numbers can be represented by an infinite line, extending indefinitely in both directions. Each point on the line corresponds to a unique real number, and each real number corresponds to a unique point on the line.

(a) Use the figure below, where the line segment between 0 and 1 has been bent into a semicircle and positioned above the line, to prove that

$\{x \mid x$ is a real number between 0 and 1$\}$ *is equivalent to* $\{x \mid x$ is a real number$\}$.

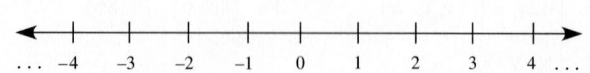

(b) What fact does part (a) establish about the set of real numbers?

42. Show that the two vertical line segments shown here both have the same number of points.

Show that each set can be placed in a one-to-one correspondence with a proper subset of itself to prove that the set is infinite.

43. $\{3, 6, 9, 12, \dots\}$

44. $\{4, 7, 10, 13, 16, \dots\}$

45. $\left\{\dfrac{3}{4}, \dfrac{3}{8}, \dfrac{3}{12}, \dfrac{3}{16}, \dots\right\}$

46. $\left\{1, \dfrac{4}{3}, \dfrac{5}{3}, 2, \dots\right\}$

47. $\left\{\dfrac{1}{9}, \dfrac{1}{18}, \dfrac{1}{27}, \dfrac{1}{36}, \dots\right\}$

48. $\{-3, -5, -9, -17, \dots\}$

49. Describe the distinction between *equal* and *equivalent* sets.

50. Explain how the correspondence suggested in **Example 4** shows that the set of real numbers between 0 and 1 is not countable.

The Paradoxes of Zeno The **Chapter Opener** discussed the scene in the movie I.Q. *that deals with Zeno's paradox. Zeno was born about 496 B.C. in southern Italy. Two forms of his paradox are given below. What is your explanation for the following two examples of Zeno's paradoxes?*

51. Achilles, if he starts out behind a tortoise, can never overtake the tortoise even if he runs faster.

Suppose Tortoise has a head start of one meter and goes one-tenth as fast as Achilles. When Achilles reaches the point where Tortoise started, Tortoise is then one-tenth meter ahead. When Achilles reaches *that* point, Tortoise is one-hundredth meter ahead. And so on. Achilles gets closer but can never catch up.

52. Motion itself cannot occur.

You cannot travel one meter until after you have first gone a half meter. But you cannot go a half meter until after you have first gone a quarter meter. And so on. Even the tiniest motion cannot occur because a tinier motion would have to occur first.

COLLABORATIVE INVESTIGATION

Surveying the Members of Your Class

This group activity is designed to determine the number of students present in your class without actually counting the members one by one. This will be accomplished by having each member of the class determine one particular set in which he or she belongs, and then finding the sum of the cardinal numbers of the subsets.

For this activity, we designate three sets: X, Y, and Z.

$X = \{$students in the class registered with the Republican party$\}$

$Y = \{$students in the class 24 years of age or younger$\}$

$Z = \{$students who have never been married$\}$

Each student in the class will belong to one of the sets X, X', one of the sets Y, Y', and one of the sets Z, Z'. (The complement of a set consists of all elements in the universe (class) that are not in the set.)

As an example, suppose that a student is a 23-year-old divorced Democrat. The student belongs to the sets X', Y, and Z'. The set to which the student belongs is

$$X' \cap Y \cap Z'.$$

In the Venn diagram that follows, the eight subsets are identified by lowercase letters (a)–(h).

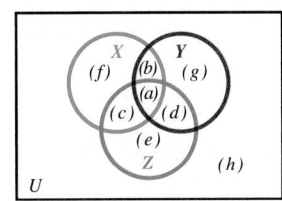

The final column in the following table will be completed when a survey is made. Each student should now determine to which set he or she belongs. (The student described earlier belongs to (g).)

Region	Description in Terms of Set Notation	Number of Class Members in the Set
(a)	$X \cap Y \cap Z$	
(b)	$X \cap Y \cap Z'$	
(c)	$X \cap Y' \cap Z$	
(d)	$X' \cap Y \cap Z$	
(e)	$X' \cap Y' \cap Z$	
(f)	$X \cap Y' \cap Z'$	
(g)	$X' \cap Y \cap Z'$	
(h)	$X' \cap Y' \cap Z'$	

The instructor will now poll the class to see how many members are in each set. *Remember that each class member will belong to one and only one set.*

After the survey is made, find the sum of the numbers in the final column. They should add up to *exactly* the number of students present. Count the class members individually to verify this.

Topics for Discussion

1. Suppose that the final column entries do not add up to the total number of class members. What might have gone wrong?

2. Why can't a class member be a member of more than one of the eight subsets listed?

CHAPTER 2 TEST

In Exercises 1–14, let

$U = \{a, b, c, d, e, f, g, h\}$, $A = \{a, b, c, d\}$,

$B = \{b, e, a, d\}$, *and* $C = \{a, e\}$.

Find each set.

1. $A \cup C$

2. $B \cap A$

3. B'

4. $A - (B \cap C')$

Identify each statement as true *or* false.

5. $b \in A$

6. $C \subseteq A$

7. $B \subset (A \cup C)$

8. $c \notin C$

9. $n[(A \cup B) - C] = 4$

10. $\emptyset \subset C$

11. $A \cap B'$ is equivalent to $B \cap A'$

12. $(A \cup B)' = A' \cap B'$

Find each of the following.

13. $n(A \times C)$

14. the number of proper subsets of A

Give a word description for each set.

15. $\{-3, -1, 1, 3, 5, 7, 9\}$

16. $\{$January, February, March, . . . , December$\}$

Express each set in set-builder notation.

17. $\{-1, -2, -3, -4, \ldots\}$

18. $\{24, 32, 40, 48, \ldots, 88\}$

Place $\subset$, $\subseteq$, both, or neither in each blank to make a true statement.

19. $\emptyset$ _____ $\{x \mid x$ is a counting number between 20 and 21$\}$

20. $\{4, 9, 16\}$ _____ $\{4, 5, 6, 7, 8, 9, 10\}$

Shade each set in an appropriate Venn diagram.

21. $X \cup Y'$ **22.** $X' \cap Y'$

23. $(X \cup Y) - Z$

24. $[(X \cap Y) \cup (Y \cap Z) \cup (X \cap Z)] - (X \cap Y \cap Z)$

Facts About Inventions *The table lists ten inventions, together with other pertinent data.*

Invention	Date	Inventor	Nation
Adding machine	1642	Pascal	France
Barometer	1643	Torricelli	Italy
Electric razor	1917	Schick	U.S.
Fiber optics	1955	Kapany	England
Geiger counter	1913	Geiger	Germany
Pendulum clock	1657	Huygens	Holland
Radar	1940	Watson-Watt	Scotland
Telegraph	1837	Morse	U.S.
Thermometer	1593	Galileo	Italy
Zipper	1891	Judson	U.S.

Let $U =$ the set of all ten inventions,
      $A =$ the set of items invented in the United States,
and $T =$ the set of items invented in the twentieth century.

List the elements of each set.

25. $A \cap T$

26. $(A \cup T)'$

27. $A - T'$

28. State De Morgan's laws for sets in words rather than symbols.

29. The numerals in the Venn diagram indicate the number of elements in each particular subset.

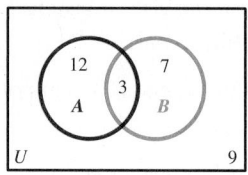

Determine the number of elements in each set.

(a) $A \cup B$ **(b)** $A \cap B'$ **(c)** $(A \cap B)'$

30. ***Financial Aid to College Students***   Three major sources of financial aid are government grants, private scholarships, and the colleges themselves. Susan Brilling, Financial Aid Director of a small private Southern college, surveyed the records of 100 sophomores and found the following:

     49 receive government grants
     55 receive private scholarships
     43 receive aid from the college
     23 receive government grants and private scholarships
     18 receive government grants and aid from the college
     28 receive private scholarships and aid from the college
     8 receive help from all three sources.

How many of the students in the survey:

(a) have government grants only?

(b) have private scholarships but not government grants?

(c) receive financial aid from only one of these sources?

(d) receive aid from exactly two of these sources?

(e) receive no financial aid from any of these sources?

(f) receive no aid from the college or from the government?

INTRODUCTION TO LOGIC

In the 2007 movie *Shrek the Third*, Shrek searches for the rightful heir to the throne of the Kingdom of Far Far Away, while Prince Charming schemes to gain the throne for himself. The Prince, knowing that Pinocchio's nose grows if he lies, questions Pinocchio.

PRINCE CHARMING: So tell me puppet, where is Shrek?

PINOCCHIO: Well, I don't know where he's not.

PRINCE CHARMING: You're telling me you don't know where Shrek is?

PINOCCHIO: It wouldn't be inaccurate to assume that I couldn't exactly not say that is or isn't almost partially incorrect.

PRINCE CHARMING: So you do know where he is!

PINOCCHIO: On the contrary, I'm possibly more or less not definitely rejecting the idea that in no way, with any amount of uncertainty, that I undeniably do or do not know where he shouldn't probably be. If that indeed wasn't where he isn't. Even if he wasn't not where I knew he was, it could mean. . . .

Unable to contain his frustration with Pinocchio's roundabout answer, one of the Three Little Pigs blurts out that Shrek has gone to search for the rightful heir. The pig was unable to follow Pinocchio's logic, or lack of it. In this chapter, we examine the basics of the study of logic.

3.1 STATEMENTS AND QUANTIFIERS

Statements • Negations • Symbols • Quantifiers • Quantifiers and Number Sets

Statements

This section introduces the study of **symbolic logic,** which uses letters to represent statements, and symbols for words such as *and, or, not.* Logic is used in the study of the **truth value** (that is, the truth or falsity) of statements with multiple parts. The truth value of such statements depends on their components.

Many kinds of sentences occur in ordinary language, including factual statements, opinions, commands, and questions. Symbolic logic discusses only the type that involves facts. A **statement** is a declarative sentence that is either true or false, but not both simultaneously.

Gottfried Leibniz (1646–1716) was a wide-ranging philosopher and a universalist who tried to patch up Catholic–Protestant conflicts. He promoted cultural exchange between Europe and the East. Chinese ideograms led him to search for a universal symbolism. He was an early inventor of **symbolic logic.**

Electronic mail provides a means of communication. ⎱ Statements
$12 + 6 = 13$ ⎰ Each is either true or false.

Access the file.
Did the Saints win the Super Bowl? ⎱ Not statements
Tim Lincecum is a better baseball player than Cliff Lee. ⎰ Each cannot be identified as being either true or false.
This sentence is false.

Of the sentences that are not statements, the first is a command, and the second is a question. The third is an opinion. "This sentence is false" is a paradox: If we assume it is true, then it is false, and if we assume it is false, then it is true.

A **compound statement** may be formed by combining two or more statements. The statements making up a compound statement are called **component statements.** Various **logical connectives,** or simply **connectives,** such as *and, or, not,* and *if . . . then,* can be used in forming compound statements. (While a statement such as "Today is not Tuesday" does not consist of two component statements, for convenience it is considered compound, because its truth value is determined by noting the truth value of a different statement, "Today is Tuesday.")

▮▮ **EXAMPLE 1** Deciding Whether a Statement Is Compound

Decide whether each statement is compound. If so, identify the connective.

(a) Lord Byron wrote sonnets, and the poem exhibits iambic pentameter.

(b) You can pay me now, or you can pay me later.

(c) If he said it, then it must be true.

(d) My pistol was made by Smith and Wesson.

SOLUTION

(a) This statement is compound, because it is made up of the component statements "Lord Byron wrote sonnets" and "the poem exhibits iambic pentameter." The connective is *and.*

(b) The connective here is *or.* The statement is compound.

(c) The connective here is *if . . . then,* discussed in more detail in **Section 3.3.** The statement is compound.

(d) While the word "and" is used in this statement, it is not used as a *logical* connective. It is part of the name of the manufacturer. The statement is not compound. ▌▌▌

Negations

The sentence "Anthony Mansella has a red truck" is a statement. The **negation** of this statement is "Anthony Mansella does not have a red truck." ***The negation of a true statement is false, and the negation of a false statement is true.***

▌▌ **EXAMPLE 2** Forming Negations

Form the negation of each statement.

(a) That city has a mayor.   (b) The moon is not a planet.

SOLUTION

(a) To negate this statement, we introduce *not* into the sentence: "That city does not have a mayor."

(b) The negation is "The moon is a planet." ▌▌▌

One way to detect incorrect negations is to check truth values. ***A negation must have the opposite truth value from the original statement.***

The next example uses some of the inequality symbols in **Table 1**. In the case of an inequality involving a variable, the negation must have the opposite truth value for *any* replacement of the variable.

```
TEST  LOGIC
1: =
2: ≠
3: >
4: ≥
5: <
6: ≤
```

The TEST menu of the TI-83/84 Plus calculator allows the user to test the truth or falsity of statements involving =, ≠, >, ≥, <, and ≤. If a statement is true, it returns a 1. If it is false, it returns a 0.

Table 1

Symbolism	Meaning	Examples	
$a < b$	a is less than b	$4 < 9$	$\frac{1}{2} < \frac{3}{4}$
$a > b$	a is greater than b	$6 > 2$	$-5 > -11$
$a \leq b$	a is less than or equal to b	$8 \leq 10$	$3 \leq 3$
$a \geq b$	a is greater than or equal to b	$-2 \geq -3$	$-5 \geq -5$

▌▌ **EXAMPLE 3** Negating Inequalities

```
4<9
              1
4>9
              0
```

$4 < 9$ is true, as indicated by the 1.
$4 > 9$ is false, as indicated by the 0.

Give a negation of each inequality. Do *not* use a slash symbol.

(a) $x < 9$ (b) $7x + 11y \geq 77$

SOLUTION

(a) The negation of "x is less than 9" is "x is *not* less than 9." Because we cannot use "not," which would require writing $x \not< 9$, phrase the negation as "x is greater than or equal to 9," or

$$x \geq 9.$$

(b) The negation, with no slash, is

$$7x + 11y < 77.$$

▌▌▌

```
TEST  LOGIC
1: and
2: or
3: xor
4: not(
```

The LOGIC menu of the TI-83/84 Plus calculator allows the user to test truth or falsity of statements involving *and, or, exclusive or* (see **Exercise 77** in **Section 3.2**), and *not*.

Symbols

The study of logic uses symbols. Statements are represented with letters, such as p, q, or r. Several symbols for connectives are shown in **Table 2**.

Table 2

Connective	Symbol	Type of Statement
and	$\wedge$	Conjunction
or	$\vee$	Disjunction
not	$\sim$	Negation

The symbol $\sim$ represents the connective *not*. If p represents the statement "Barack Obama was president in 2009" then $\sim p$ represents "Barack Obama was not president in 2009."

▌▌ **EXAMPLE 4** Translating from Symbols to Words

Let p represent "It is 70° today," and let q represent "It is Tuesday." Write each symbolic statement in words.

(a) $p \vee q$ **(b)** $\sim p \wedge q$ **(c)** $\sim(p \vee q)$ **(d)** $\sim(p \wedge q)$

SOLUTION

(a) From the table, $\vee$ symbolizes *or*. Thus, $p \vee q$ represents

It is 70° today or it is Tuesday.

(b) It is not 70° today and it is Tuesday.

(c) It is not the case that it is 70° today or it is Tuesday.

(d) It is not the case that it is 70° today and it is Tuesday.   ▌▌▌

The statement in **Example 4(c)** usually is translated as **"Neither p nor q."**

Quantifiers

Quantifiers are used to indicate *how many* cases of a particular situation exist. The words **all, each, every,** and **no(ne)** are called **universal quantifiers,** while words and phrases such as **some, there exists,** and **(for) at least one** are called **existential quantifiers.** *Be careful when forming the negation of a statement involving quantifiers.*

The negation of a statement must be false if the given statement is true and must be true if the given statement is false, in all possible cases. Consider this statement.

All girls in the group are named Mary.

Many people would write the negation of this statement as "No girls in the group are named Mary" or "All girls in the group are not named Mary." But neither of these is correct. To see why, look at the three groups below.

Group I: Mary Jane Payne, Mary Meyer, Mary O'Hara
Group II: Mary Johnson, Lisa Pollak, Margaret Watson
Group III: Donna Garbarino, Paula Story, Rhonda Alessi, Kim Falgout

These groups contain all possibilities that need to be considered. In Group I, *all* girls are named Mary. In Group II, *some* girls are named Mary (and some are not). In Group III, *no* girls are named Mary. Look at the truth values in **Table 3** on the next page, and keep in mind that "some" means "at least one (and possibly all)."

Aristotle, the first to systematize the logic we use in everyday life, appears above in a detail from the painting *The School of Athens*, by Raphael. He is shown debating a point with his teacher **Plato.**

Table 3 Truth Value as Applied to:

	Group I	Group II	Group III
(1) All girls in the group are named Mary. **(Given)**	T	F	F
(2) No girls in the group are named Mary. **(Possible negation)**	F	F	T
(3) All girls in the group are not named Mary. **(Possible negation)**	F	F	T
(4) Some girls in the group are not named Mary. **(Possible negation)**	F	T	T

Negation (for Group III, statements (2)/(3) and (4))

The negation of the given statement (1) must have opposite truth values in *all* cases. It can be seen that statements (2) and (3) do not satisfy this condition (for Group II), but statement (4) does. It may be concluded that the correct negation for "All girls in the group are named Mary" is "Some girls in the group are not named Mary." Other ways of stating the negation include the following.

> Not all girls in the group are named Mary.
>
> It is not the case that all girls in the group are named Mary.
>
> At least one girl in the group is not named Mary.

Table 4 shows how to find the negation of a statement involving quantifiers.

Table 4 Negations of Quantified Statements

Statement	Negation
All do.	Some do not. (Equivalently: Not all do.)
Some do.	None do. (Equivalently: All do not.)

The negation of the negation of a statement is simply the statement itself. For instance, the negations of the statements in the Negation column are simply the corresponding original statements in the Statement column. As an example, the negation of "Some do not" is "All do."

■■ **EXAMPLE 5** Forming Negations of Quantified Statements

Form the negation of each statement.

(a) Some cats have fleas.   **(b)** Some cats do not have fleas.

(c) No cats have fleas.

SOLUTION

(a) Because *some* means "at least one," the statement "Some cats have fleas" is really the same as "At least one cat has fleas." The negation of this is

"No cat has fleas."

(b) The statement "Some cats do not have fleas" claims that at least one cat, somewhere, does not have fleas. The negation of this is

"All cats have fleas."

(c) The negation is   "Some cats have fleas."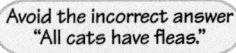

Avoid the incorrect answer "All cats have fleas."

■■■

Quantifiers and Number Sets

Earlier we introduced sets of numbers.

Sets of Numbers

Natural or Counting numbers $\{1, 2, 3, 4, \ldots\}$

Whole numbers $\{0, 1, 2, 3, 4, \ldots\}$

Integers $\{\ldots, -3, -2, -1, 0, 1, 2, 3, \ldots\}$

Rational numbers $\left\{\frac{p}{q} \,\middle|\, p \text{ and } q \text{ are integers, and } q \neq 0\right\}$

(*Examples:* $\frac{3}{5}$, $-\frac{7}{9}$, 5, 0. Any rational number may be expressed as a terminating decimal number, such as 0.25, or a repeating decimal number, such as 0.666 . . . .)

Real numbers $\{x \,|\, x \text{ is a number that can be written as a decimal}\}$

Irrational numbers $\{x \,|\, x \text{ is a real number and } x \text{ cannot be written as a quotient of integers}\}$

(*Examples:* $\sqrt{2}$, $\sqrt[3]{4}$, π. Decimal representations of irrational numbers are neither terminating nor repeating.)

▮▮ **EXAMPLE 6** Deciding Whether Quantified Statements Are True or False

Decide whether each statement involving a quantifier is *true* or *false*.

(a) There exists a whole number that is not a natural number.

(b) Every integer is a natural number.

(c) Every natural number is a rational number.

(d) There exists an irrational number that is not real.

SOLUTION

(a) Because there is such a whole number (it is 0), this statement is true.

(b) This statement is false, because we can find at least one integer that is not a natural number. For example, −1 is an integer but is not a natural number.

(c) Because every natural number can be written as a fraction with denominator 1, this statement is true.

(d) In order to be an irrational number, a number must first be real. Because we cannot give an irrational number that is not real, this statement is false. (Had we been able to find at least one, the statement would have then been true.) ▮▮▮

3.1 EXERCISES

Decide whether each is a statement or is not a statement.

1. February 2, 2009, was a Monday.

2. The ZIP code for Oscar, LA, is 70762.

3. Listen, my children, and you shall hear of the midnight ride of Paul Revere.

4. Yield to oncoming traffic.

5. $5 + 9 \neq 14$ and $4 - 1 = 12$

6. $5 + 9 \neq 12$ or $4 - 2 = 5$

7. Some numbers are positive.

8. Millard Fillmore was president of the United States in 1851.

9. Accidents are the main cause of deaths of children under the age of 7.

10. *The Dark Knight* was the top-grossing movie of 2008.

11. Where are you going tomorrow?

12. Behave yourself and sit down.

13. Kevin "Catfish" McCarthy once took a prolonged continuous shower for 340 hours, 40 minutes.

14. One gallon of milk weighs more than 3 pounds.

Decide whether each statement is compound.

15. I read the *Detroit Free Press*, and I read the *Sacramento Bee*.

16. My brother got married in Copenhagen.

17. Tomorrow is Saturday.

18. Mamie Zwettler is younger than 18 years of age, and so is her friend Emma Lister.

19. Jay Beckenstein's wife loves Ben and Jerry's ice cream.

20. The sign on the back of the car read "Canada or bust!"

21. If Lorri Morgan sells her quota, then Michelle Cook will be happy.

22. If Bobby is a politician, then Mitch is a crook.

Write a negation for each statement.

23. Her aunt's name is Hermione.

24. The flowers are to be watered.

25. Every dog has its day.

26. No rain fell in southern California today.

27. Some books are longer than this book.

28. All students present will get another chance.

29. No computer repairman can play blackjack.

30. Some people have all the luck.

31. Everybody loves somebody sometime.

32. Everyone loves a winner.

Give a negation of each inequality. Do not use a slash symbol.

33. $x > 12$

34. $x < -6$

35. $x \geq 5$

36. $x \leq 19$

37. Try to negate the sentence "The exact number of words in this sentence is ten" and see what happens. Explain the problem that arises.

38. Explain why the negation of "$x > 5$" is not "$x < 5$."

Let p represent the statement "She has green eyes" and let q represent the statement "He is 60 years old." Translate each symbolic compound statement into words.

39. $\sim p$

40. $\sim q$

41. $p \wedge q$

42. $p \vee q$

43. $\sim p \vee q$

44. $p \wedge \sim q$

45. $\sim p \vee \sim q$

46. $\sim p \wedge \sim q$

47. $\sim(\sim p \wedge q)$

48. $\sim(p \vee \sim q)$

Let p represent the statement "Chris collects DVDs" and let q represent the statement "Josh is an art major." Convert each compound statement into symbols.

49. Chris collects DVDs and Josh is not an art major.

50. Chris does not collect DVDs or Josh is not an art major.

51. Chris does not collect DVDs or Josh is an art major.

52. Josh is an art major and Chris does not collect DVDs.

53. Neither Chris collects DVDs nor Josh is an art major.

54. Either Josh is an art major or Chris collects DVDs, and it is not the case that both Josh is an art major and Chris collects DVDs.

55. Incorrect use of quantifiers often is heard in everyday language. Suppose you hear that a local electronics chain is having a 40% off sale, and the radio advertisement states "All items are not available in all stores." Do you think that, literally translated, the ad really means what it says? What do you think is really meant? Explain your answer.

56. Repeat **Exercise 55** for the following: "All people don't have the time to devote to maintaining their vehicles properly."

Refer to the groups of art labeled A, B, *and* C, *and identify by letter the group or groups that are satisfied by the given statements involving quantifiers.*

A

B

C

57. All pictures have frames.

58. No picture has a frame.

59. At least one picture does not have a frame.

60. Not every picture has a frame.

61. At least one picture has a frame.

62. No picture does not have a frame.

63. All pictures do not have frames.

64. Not every picture does not have a frame.

Decide whether each statement in Exercises 65–74 involving a quantifier is true *or* false.

65. Every whole number is an integer.

66. Every natural number is an integer.

67. There exists a rational number that is not an integer.

68. There exists an integer that is not a natural number.

69. All rational numbers are real numbers.

70. All irrational numbers are real numbers.

71. Some rational numbers are not integers.

72. Some whole numbers are not rational numbers.

73. Each whole number is a positive number.

74. Each rational number is a positive number.

75. Explain the difference between the following statements.

> All students did not pass the test.
> Not all students passed the test.

76. The statement "For some real number x, $x^2 \geq 0$" is true. However, your friend does not understand why, because he claims that $x^2 \geq 0$ is true for *all* real numbers x (and not *some*). How would you explain his misconception to him?

77. Write the following statement using "every": There is no one here who has not done that at one time or another.

78. Only one of these statements is true. Which one is it?
A. For some real number x, $x \not< 0$.
B. For all real numbers x, $x^3 > 0$.
C. For all real numbers x less than 0, x^2 is also less than 0.
D. For some real number x, $x^2 < 0$.

3.2 TRUTH TABLES AND EQUIVALENT STATEMENTS

Conjunctions • Disjunctions • Negations • Mathematical Statements • Truth Tables • Alternative Method for Constructing Truth Tables • Equivalent Statements and De Morgan's Laws

Conjunctions

Truth values of component statements are used to find truth values of compound statements. To begin, we must decide on truth values of the **conjunction p and q,** symbolized $p \wedge q$. Here, the connective *and* implies the idea of "both." The following statement is true, because each component statement is true.

Monday immediately follows Sunday and March immediately follows February.

True

On the other hand, the following statement is false, even though part of the statement (Monday immediately follows Sunday) is true.

Monday immediately follows Sunday and March immediately follows January.

False

For the conjunction $p \wedge q$ to be true, both p and q must be true. This result is summarized by a table, called a **truth table,** which shows all four of the possible combinations of truth values for the conjunction p *and* q.

Truth Table for the Conjunction p and q

p and *q*

p	q	$p \wedge q$
T	T	T
T	F	F
F	T	F
F	F	F

▮▮ **EXAMPLE 1** Finding the Truth Value of a Conjunction

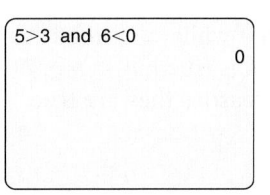

The calculator returns a "0" for 5 > 3 *and* 6 < 0, indicating that the statement is false.

Let p represent "$5 > 3$" and let q represent "$6 < 0$." Find the truth value of $p \wedge q$.

SOLUTION

Here p is true and q is false. Looking in the second row of the conjunction truth table shows that $p \wedge q$ is false.   ▮▮▮

In some cases, the logical connective *but* is used in compound statements.

He wants to go to the mountains but she wants to go to the beach.

Here, *but* is used in place of *and* to give a different emphasis to the statement. We consider this statement as we would consider the conjunction using the word *and*. The truth table for the conjunction, given above, would apply.

Disjunctions

In ordinary language, the word *or* can be ambiguous. The expression "this or that" can mean either "this or that or both," or "this or that but not both." For example, consider the following statement.

I will paint the wall or I will paint the ceiling.

This statement probably means: "I will paint the wall or I will paint the ceiling or I will paint both." On the other hand, consider the following statement.

I will drive the Lexus or the BMW to the store.

It probably means "I will drive the Lexus, or I will drive the BMW, but I will not drive both."

The symbol $\vee$ represents the first *or* described. That is,

$p \vee q$ means   "p or q or both."   Disjunction

With this meaning of *or*, $p \vee q$ is called the **inclusive disjunction,** or just the **disjunction** of p and q. In everyday language, the disjunction implies the idea of "either." For example, consider the following disjunction.

I have a quarter or I have a dime.

It is true whenever I have either a quarter, a dime, or both. The only way this disjunction could be false would be if I had neither coin. *The disjunction $p \vee q$ is false only if both component statements are false.*

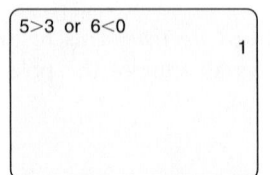

The calculator returns a "1" for $5 > 3$ *or* $6 < 0$, indicating that the statement is true.

Truth Table for the Disjunction   *p* or *q*

p or *q*

p	*q*	*p* $\vee$ *q*
T	T	T
T	F	T
F	T	T
F	F	F

■■ **EXAMPLE 2** Finding the Truth Value of a Disjunction

Table 5

Statement	Reason That It Is True
$8 \geq 8$	$8 = 8$
$3 \geq 1$	$3 > 1$
$-5 \leq -3$	$-5 < -3$
$-4 \leq -4$	$-4 = -4$

Let p represent "$5 > 3$" and let q represent "$6 < 0$." Find the truth value of $p \vee q$.

SOLUTION

Here, as in **Example 1,** p is true and q is false. The second row of the disjunction truth table shows that $p \vee q$ is true.   ■■■

The symbol $\geq$ is read **"is greater than or equal to,"** while $\leq$ is read **"is less than or equal to."** If a and b are real numbers, then $a \leq b$ is true if $a < b$ or $a = b$. **Table 5** in the margin shows several statements and the reasons they are true.

Negations

The **negation** of a statement p, symbolized $\sim p$, must have the opposite truth value from the statement p itself. This leads to the truth table for the negation.

Truth Table for the Negation   not *p*

not *p*

p	$\sim p$
T	F
F	T

■■ **EXAMPLE 3** Finding the Truth Value of a Compound Statement

Suppose p is false, q is true, and r is false. What is the truth value of the compound statement $\sim p \wedge (q \vee \sim r)$?

SOLUTION

Here parentheses are used to group q and $\sim r$ together. Work first inside the parentheses. Because r is false, $\sim r$ will be true. Because $\sim r$ is true and q is true, find the truth value of $q \vee \sim r$ by looking in the first row of the *or* truth table. This row gives the result T.

Because p is false, $\sim p$ is true, and the final truth value of $\sim p \wedge (q \vee \sim r)$ is found in the top row of the *and* truth table. From the *and* truth table, when $\sim p$ is true, and $q \vee \sim r$ is true, the statement

$$\sim p \wedge (q \vee \sim r) \quad \text{is true.}$$

We can use a short-cut symbolic method that involves replacing the statements with their truth values, letting T represent a true statement and F represent a false statement.

$$\sim p \wedge (q \vee \sim r)$$
$$\sim F \wedge (T \vee \sim F) \quad \text{Work within parentheses first.}$$
$$T \wedge (T \vee T) \quad \sim F \text{ gives T.}$$
$$T \wedge T \quad \quad T \vee T \text{ gives T.}$$

The compound statement is true. → T   T ∧ T gives T.   ▌▌▌

Mathematical Statements

We can use truth tables to determine the truth values of compound mathematical statements.

EXAMPLE 4 Deciding Whether a Compound Mathematical Statement Is True or False

Let p represent the statement $3 > 2$, q represent $5 < 4$, and r represent $3 < 8$. Decide whether each statement is *true* or *false*.

(a) $\sim p \wedge \sim q$ **(b)** $\sim(p \wedge q)$ **(c)** $(\sim p \wedge r) \vee (\sim q \wedge \sim p)$

SOLUTION

(a) Because p is true, $\sim p$ is false. By the *and* truth table, if one part of an "and" statement is false, the entire statement is false.

$$\sim p \wedge \sim q \quad \text{is false.}$$

(b) For $\sim(p \wedge q)$, first work within the parentheses. Because p is true and q is false, $p \wedge q$ is false by the *and* truth table. Next, apply the negation. The negation of a false statement is true.

$$\sim(p \wedge q) \quad \text{is true.}$$

(c) Here p is true, q is false, and r is true. This makes $\sim p$ false and $\sim q$ true. By the *and* truth table, $\sim p \wedge r$ is false, and $\sim q \wedge \sim p$ is also false. By the *or* truth table,

$$(\sim p \wedge r) \vee (\sim q \wedge \sim p) \quad \text{is false.}$$
$$\downarrow \quad \quad \quad \downarrow$$
$$F \quad \vee \quad F$$

(Alternatively, see **Example 8(b)**.)   ▌▌▌

When a quantifier is used with a conjunction or a disjunction, we must be careful in determining the truth value, as shown in the following example.

EXAMPLE 5 Deciding Whether a Quantified Mathematical Statement Is True or False

Decide whether each statement is *true* or *false*.

(a) For some real number x, $x < 5$ and $x > 2$.

(b) For every real number x, $x > 0$ or $x < 1$.

(c) For all real numbers x, $x^2 > 0$.

SOLUTION

(a) Replacing x with 3 (as an example) gives $3 < 5$ and $3 > 2$. Because both $3 < 5$ and $3 > 2$ are true statements, the given statement is true by the *and* truth table. (Remember: *Some* means "at least one.")

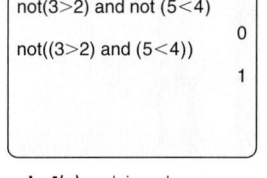

not(3>2) and not (5<4)   0

not((3>2) and (5<4))   1

Example 4(a) explains why

$$\sim(3 > 2) \wedge [\sim(5 < 4)]$$

is false. The calculator returns a 0. For a true statement such as

$$\sim[(3 > 2) \wedge (5 < 4)],$$

it returns a 1.

George Boole (1815–1864) grew up in poverty. His father, a London tradesman, gave him his first mathematics lessons and taught him to make optical instruments. Boole was largely self-educated. At 16 he worked in an elementary school and by age 20 had opened his own school. He studied mathematics in his spare time. He died of lung disease at age 49.

Boole's ideas have been used in the design of computers and telephone systems.

(b) No matter which real number might be tried as a replacement for *x*, at least one of the two statements

$$x > 0, \quad x < 1$$

will be true. Because an "or" statement is true if one or both component statements are true, the entire statement as given is true.

(c) Because the quantifier is a universal quantifier, we need only find one case in which the inequality is false to make the entire statement false. Can we find a real number whose square is not positive (that is, not greater than 0)? Yes, we can—0 is the *only* real number whose square is not positive. This statement is false. ■■■

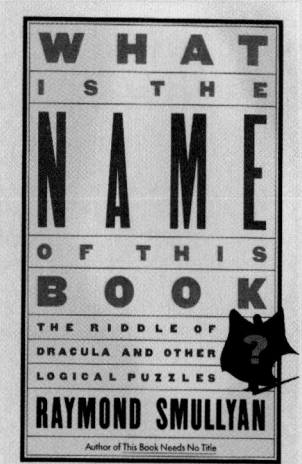

For Further Thought

Whose Picture Am I Looking At?

Raymond Smullyan is one of today's foremost writers of logic puzzles. This professor of mathematics and philosophy is now retired from Indiana University and has written several books on recreational logic, including *What Is the Name of This Book?*, *The Lady or the Tiger?*, and *Alice in Puzzleland*. The first of these includes the following puzzle, which has been around for many years.

For Group or Individual Investigation

A man is looking at a portrait. Someone asked him, "Whose picture are you looking at?" He replied: "Brothers and sisters, I have none, but this man's father is my father's son. ("This man's father" means, of course, the father of the man in the picture.)

Whose picture was the man looking at? (The answer is on **page 96.**)

p	*q*	Compound Statement
T	T	
T	F	
F	T	
F	F	

Truth Tables

In the preceding examples, the truth value for a given statement was found by going back to the basic truth tables. In the long run, it is easier to first create a complete truth table for the given statement itself. Then final truth values can be read directly from this table.

In this book we use the standard format shown in the margin for listing the possible truth values in compound statements involving two component statements.

EXAMPLE 6 Constructing a Truth Table

Consider the statement $(\sim p \wedge q) \vee \sim q$.

(a) Construct a truth table.

(b) Suppose both *p* and *q* are true. Find the truth value of the compound statement.

SOLUTION

(a) Begin by listing all possible combinations of truth values for *p* and *q*, as above. Then list the truth values of $\sim p$, which are the opposite of those of *p*, as shown in the table in the margin.

p	*q*	$\sim p$
T	T	F
T	F	F
F	T	T
F	F	T

Use only the "~p" column and the "q" column, along with the *and* truth table, to find the truth values of ~p ∧ q. List them in a separate column.

p	q	~p	~p ∧ q
T	T	F	F
T	F	F	F
F	T	T	T
F	F	T	F

Next include a column for ~q.

p	q	~p	~p ∧ q	~q
T	T	F	F	F
T	F	F	F	T
F	T	T	T	F
F	F	T	F	T

Finally, make a column for the entire compound statement. To find the truth values, use *or* to combine ~p ∧ q with ~q.

p	q	~p	~p ∧ q	~q	(~p ∧ q) ∨ ~q
T	T	F	F	F	F
T	F	F	F	T	T
F	T	T	T	F	T
F	F	T	F	T	T

(b) Look in the first row of the final truth table above, where both *p* and *q* have truth value T. Read across the row to find that the compound statement is false.   ▮▮▮

▮▮ **EXAMPLE 7**   Constructing a Truth Table

Construct the truth table for $p \wedge (\sim p \vee \sim q)$.

SOLUTION

Proceed as shown.

p	q	~p	~q	~p ∨ ~q	p ∧ (~p ∨ ~q)
T	T	F	F	F	F
T	F	F	T	T	T
F	T	T	F	T	F
F	F	T	T	T	F

If a compound statement involves three component statements *p*, *q*, and *r*, we will use the following standard format in setting up the truth table.

p	q	r	**Compound Statement**
T	T	T	
T	T	F	
T	F	T	
T	F	F	
F	T	T	
F	T	F	
F	F	T	
F	F	F	

Emilie, Marquise du Châtelet
(1706–1749) participated in the scientific activity of the generation after Newton and Leibniz. Educated in science, music, and literature, she was studying mathematics at the time (1733) she began a long intellectual relationship with the philosopher **François Voltaire** (1694–1778). She and Voltaire competed independently in 1738 for a prize offered by the French Academy on the subject of fire. Although du Châtelet did not win, her dissertation was published by the academy in 1744.

▮▮▮

EXAMPLE 8 Constructing a Truth Table

Consider the statement $(\sim p \wedge r) \vee (\sim q \wedge \sim p)$.

(a) Construct a truth table.

(b) Suppose p is true, q is false, and r is true. Find the truth value of this statement.

SOLUTION

(a) There are three component statements: p, q, and r. The truth table thus requires eight rows to list all possible combinations of truth values of p, q, and r. The final truth table can be found in much the same way as the ones earlier.

p	q	r	$\sim p$	$\sim p \wedge r$	$\sim q$	$\sim q \wedge \sim p$	$(\sim p \wedge r) \vee (\sim q \wedge \sim p)$
T	T	T	F	F	F	F	F
T	T	F	F	F	F	F	F
T	F	T	F	F	T	F	F
T	F	F	F	F	T	F	F
F	T	T	T	T	F	F	T
F	T	F	T	F	F	F	F
F	F	T	T	T	T	T	T
F	F	F	T	F	T	T	T

(b) By the third row of the truth table in part (a), the compound statement is false. (This is an alternative method for working part (c) of **Example 4.**) ▐▐▐

> **PROBLEM-SOLVING HINT** One strategy for problem solving is to notice a pattern and use inductive reasoning. This strategy is applied in the next example.

EXAMPLE 9 Using Inductive Reasoning

If n is a counting number, and a logical statement is composed of n component statements, how many rows will appear in the truth table for the compound statement?

SOLUTION

To answer this question, we examine some of the earlier truth tables in this section. The truth table for the negation has one statement and two rows. The truth tables for the conjunction and the disjunction have two component statements, and each has four rows. The truth table in **Example 8(a)** has three component statements and eight rows.

Summarizing these in **Table 6** (seen in the margin) reveals a pattern encountered earlier. Inductive reasoning leads us to the conjecture that if a logical statement is composed of n component statements, it will have 2^n rows. This can be proved using more advanced concepts. ▐▐▐

The result of **Example 9** is reminiscent of the formula for the number of subsets of a set having n elements.

> **Number of Rows in a Truth Table**
>
> A logical statement having n component statements will have 2^n rows in its truth table.

Answer to the problem of *Whose Picture Am I Looking At?*

Most people give the incorrect answer that the man is looking at his own picture. The correct answer is that the man is looking at a picture of his son.

Smullyan helps the reader to understand why this is correct. Because he has no siblings, "my father's son" must refer to the man himself, so the second part of the problem can be reworded "This man's father is myself." Thus, the man in the picture must be his own son.

Table 6

Number of Statements	Number of Rows
1	$2 = 2^1$
2	$4 = 2^2$
3	$8 = 2^3$

Alternative Method for Constructing Truth Tables

After making a reasonable number of truth tables, some people prefer the shortcut method shown in **Example 10,** which repeats **Examples 6 and 8.**

▮▮ EXAMPLE 10 Constructing Truth Tables

Construct the truth table for each compound statement.

(a) $(\sim p \land q) \lor \sim q$ **(b)** $(\sim p \land r) \lor (\sim q \land \sim p)$

SOLUTION

(a) Start by inserting truth values for $\sim p$ and for q. Then, use the *and* truth table to obtain the truth values for $\sim p \land q$.

p	q	(~p	∧	q)	∨	~q		p	q	(~p	∧	q)	∨	~q
T	T	F		T				T	T	F	F	T		
T	F	F		F				T	F	F	F	F		
F	T	T		T				F	T	T	T	T		
F	F	T		F				F	F	T	F	F		

Now disregard the two preliminary columns of truth values for $\sim p$ and for q, and insert truth values for $\sim q$. Finally, use the *or* truth table.

p	q	(~p ∧ q)	∨	~q		p	q	(~p ∧ q)	∨	~q
T	T	F		F		T	T	F	F	F
T	F	F		T		T	F	F	T	T
F	T	T		F		F	T	T	T	F
F	F	F		T		F	F	F	T	T

These steps can be summarized as follows.

p	q	(~p	∧	q)	∨	~q
T	T	F	F	T	F	F
T	F	F	F	F	T	T
F	T	T	T	T	T	F
F	F	T	F	F	T	T
		①	②	①	④	③

> The circled numbers indicate the order in which the various columns of the truth table were found.

(b) Work as follows.

p	q	r	(~p	∧	r)	∨	(~q	∧	~p)
T	T	T	F	F	T	F	F	F	F
T	T	F	F	F	F	F	F	F	F
T	F	T	F	F	T	F	T	F	F
T	F	F	F	F	F	F	T	F	F
F	T	T	T	T	T	T	F	F	T
F	T	F	T	F	F	F	F	F	T
F	F	T	T	T	T	T	T	T	T
F	F	F	T	F	F	T	T	T	T
			①	②	①	⑤	③	④	③

> The circled numbers indicate the order.

▮▮▮

Equivalent Statements and De Morgan's Laws

Two statements are **equivalent** if they have the same truth value in *every* possible situation. The columns of the two truth tables that were the last to be completed will be the same for equivalent statements.

▐▌ **EXAMPLE 11** Deciding Whether Two Statements Are Equivalent

Are the following two statements equivalent?

$$\sim p \wedge \sim q \quad \text{and} \quad \sim(p \vee q)$$

SOLUTION

Construct a truth table for each statement.

p	q	$\sim p \wedge \sim q$
T	T	F
T	F	F
F	T	F
F	F	T

p	q	$\sim(p \vee q)$
T	T	F
T	F	F
F	T	F
F	F	T

Because the truth values are the same in all cases, as shown in the columns in color, the statements $\sim p \wedge \sim q$ and $\sim(p \vee q)$ are equivalent. Equivalence is written with a three-bar symbol, $\equiv$.

$$\sim p \wedge \sim q \equiv \sim(p \vee q) \qquad\qquad ▐▌▐$$

In the same way, the statements $\sim p \vee \sim q$ and $\sim(p \wedge q)$ are equivalent. We call these equivalences *De Morgan's laws*.

De Morgan's Laws for Logical Statements

For any statements p and q, the following equivalences are valid.

$$\sim(p \vee q) \equiv \sim p \wedge \sim q \quad \text{and} \quad \sim(p \wedge q) \equiv \sim p \vee \sim q$$

(Compare the logic statements of De Morgan's laws with the set versions on **page 64.**) De Morgan's laws can be used to find the negations of certain compound statements.

▐▌ **EXAMPLE 12** Applying De Morgan's Laws

Find a negation of each statement by applying De Morgan's laws.

(a) I got an A or I got a B. **(b)** She won't try and he will succeed.

(c) $\sim p \vee (q \wedge \sim p)$

SOLUTION

(a) If p represents "I got an A" and q represents "I got a B," then the compound statement is symbolized $p \vee q$. The negation of $p \vee q$ is $\sim(p \vee q)$. By one of De Morgan's laws, this is equivalent to

$$\sim p \wedge \sim q,$$

or, in words,   **I didn't get an A and I didn't get a B.**

This negation is reasonable—the original statement says that I got either an A or a B. The negation says that I didn't get *either* grade.

(b) From one of De Morgan's laws, $\sim(p \wedge q) \equiv \sim p \vee \sim q$, so the negation becomes

She will try or he won't succeed.

(c) Negate both component statements and change $\vee$ to $\wedge$.

$$\sim[\sim p \vee (q \wedge \sim p)] \equiv p \wedge \sim(q \wedge \sim p)$$

Now apply De Morgan's law again.

$$p \land \sim(q \land \sim p) \equiv p \land (\sim q \lor \sim(\sim p))$$
$$\equiv p \land (\sim q \lor p)$$

A truth table will show that the statements

$$\sim p \lor (q \land \sim p) \quad \text{and} \quad p \land (\sim q \lor p) \quad \text{are negations of each other.} \quad \blacksquare\blacksquare\blacksquare$$

3.2 EXERCISES

Use the concepts introduced in this section to answer Exercises 1–6.

1. If q is false, what must be the truth value of the statement $(p \land \sim q) \land q$?

2. If q is true, what must be the truth value of the statement $q \lor (q \land \sim p)$?

3. If the statement $p \land q$ is true, and p is true, then q must be _____.

4. If the statement $p \lor q$ is false, and p is false, then q must be _____.

5. If $\sim(p \lor q)$ is true, what must be the truth values of the component statements?

6. If $\sim(p \land q)$ is false, what must be the truth values of the component statements?

Let p represent a false statement and let q represent a true statement. Find the truth value of the given compound statement.

7. $\sim p$

8. $\sim q$

9. $p \lor q$

10. $p \land q$

11. $p \lor \sim q$

12. $\sim p \land q$

13. $\sim p \lor \sim q$

14. $p \land \sim q$

15. $\sim(p \land \sim q)$

16. $\sim(\sim p \lor \sim q)$

17. $\sim[\sim p \land (\sim q \lor p)]$

18. $\sim[(\sim p \land \sim q) \lor \sim q]$

19. Is the statement $6 \geq 2$ a conjunction or a disjunction? Why?

20. Why is the statement $8 \geq 3$ true? Why is $5 \geq 5$ true?

Let p represent a true statement, and q and r represent false statements. Find the truth value of the given compound statement.

21. $(p \land r) \lor \sim q$

22. $(q \lor \sim r) \land p$

23. $p \land (q \lor r)$

24. $(\sim p \land q) \lor \sim r$

25. $\sim(p \land q) \land (r \lor \sim q)$

26. $(\sim r \land \sim q) \lor (\sim r \land q)$

27. $\sim[(\sim p \land q) \lor r]$

28. $\sim[r \lor (\sim q \land \sim p)]$

29. $\sim[\sim q \lor (r \land \sim p)]$

30. What is the only possible case in which the statement $(p \land \sim q) \land \sim r$ is true?

Let p represent the statement $16 < 8$, let q represent the statement $5 \not> 4$, and let r represent the statement $17 \leq 17$. Find the truth value of the given compound statement.

31. $p \land r$

32. $p \lor \sim q$

33. $\sim q \lor \sim r$

34. $\sim p \land \sim r$

35. $(p \land q) \lor r$

36. $\sim p \lor (\sim r \lor \sim q)$

37. $(\sim r \land q) \lor \sim p$

38. $\sim(p \lor \sim q) \lor \sim r$

Give the number of rows in the truth table for each compound statement.

39. $p \lor \sim r$

40. $p \land (r \land \sim s)$

41. $(\sim p \land q) \lor (\sim r \lor \sim s) \land r$

42. $[(p \lor q) \land (r \land s)] \land (t \lor \sim p)$

43. $[(\sim p \land \sim q) \land (\sim r \land s \land \sim t)] \land (\sim u \lor \sim v)$

44. $[(\sim p \land \sim q) \lor (\sim r \lor \sim s)]$
$\lor [(\sim m \land \sim n) \land (u \land \sim v)]$

45. If the truth table for a certain compound statement has 128 rows, how many distinct component statements does it have?

46. Is it possible for the truth table of a compound statement to have exactly 54 rows? Why or why not?

Construct a truth table for each compound statement.

47. $\sim p \land q$

48. $\sim p \lor \sim q$

49. $\sim(p \land q)$

50. $p \lor \sim q$

51. $(q \lor \sim p) \lor \sim q$

52. $(p \land \sim q) \land p$

53. $\sim q \wedge (\sim p \vee q)$　　**54.** $\sim p \vee (\sim q \wedge \sim p)$

55. $(p \vee \sim q) \wedge (p \wedge q)$

56. $(\sim p \wedge \sim q) \vee (\sim p \vee q)$

57. $(\sim p \wedge q) \wedge r$

58. $r \vee (p \wedge \sim q)$

59. $(\sim p \wedge \sim q) \vee (\sim r \vee \sim p)$

60. $(\sim r \vee \sim p) \wedge (\sim p \vee \sim q)$

61. $\sim(\sim p \wedge \sim q) \vee (\sim r \vee \sim s)$

62. $(\sim r \vee s) \wedge (\sim p \wedge q)$

Use one of De Morgan's laws to write the negation of each statement.

63. You can pay me now or you can pay me later.

64. I am not going or she is going.

65. It is summer and there is no snow.

66. $\frac{1}{2}$ is a positive number and -9 is less than zero.

67. I said yes but she said no.

68. Dan La Chapelle tried to sell the software, but he was unable to do so.

69. $6 - 1 = 5$ and $9 + 13 \neq 7$

70. $8 < 10$ or $5 \neq 2$

71. Prancer or Vixen will lead Santa's reindeer sleigh next Christmas.

72. The lawyer and the client appeared in court.

Identify each statement as true *or* false.

73. For every real number x,　$x < 14$ or $x > 6$.

74. For every real number x,　$x > 9$ or $x < 9$.

75. There exists an integer n such that $n > 0$ and $n < 0$.

76. For some integer n,　$n \geq 3$ and $n \leq 3$.

77. Complete the truth table for *exclusive disjunction*. The symbol $\underline{\vee}$ represents "one or the other is true, but not both."

p	q	$p \underline{\vee} q$
T	T	
T	F	
F	T	
F	F	

Exclusive disjunction

78. Attorneys sometimes use the phrase "and/or." This phrase corresponds to which usage of the word *or*: inclusive or exclusive disjunction?

Decide whether each compound statement is true *or* false. *Remember that* $\underline{\vee}$ *is the* exclusive disjunction *of* **Exercise 77.**

79. $3 + 1 = 4 \underline{\vee} 2 + 5 = 7$

80. $3 + 1 = 4 \underline{\vee} 2 + 5 = 10$

81. $3 + 1 = 6 \underline{\vee} 2 + 5 = 7$

82. $3 + 1 = 12 \underline{\vee} 2 + 5 = 10$

83. In his book *The Lady or the Tiger and Other Logic Puzzles,* Raymond Smullyan proposes the following problem. It is taken from the classic Frank Stockton short story, in which a prisoner must make a choice between two doors: behind one is a beautiful lady, and behind the other is a hungry tiger.

What if each door has a sign, and the man knows that only one sign is true?

The sign on Door 1 reads:

IN THIS ROOM THERE IS A LADY AND IN THE OTHER ROOM THERE IS A TIGER.

The sign on Door 2 reads:

IN ONE OF THESE ROOMS THERE IS A LADY AND IN ONE OF THESE ROOMS THERE IS A TIGER.

With this information, the man is able to choose the correct door. Can you?

84. In Raymond Smullyan's books, he writes about an island in which certain inhabitants are called knights and others are called knaves. Knights always tell the truth, and knaves always lie. Every inhabitant is either a knight or a knave.

Three inhabitants—A, B, and C—were standing together in a garden. A stranger passed by and asked A, "Are you a knight or a knave?" A answered, but rather indistinctly, so the stranger could not make out what he said. The stranger then asked B, "What did A say?" B replied "A said that he is a knave." At this point, the third inhabitant, C, said, "Don't believe B; he is lying!"

The question is, what are B and C?

3.3 THE CONDITIONAL AND CIRCUITS

Conditionals • Negation of a Conditional • Circuits

Conditionals

"If you build it, he will come."
  —The Voice in the movie *Field of Dreams*

Ray Kinsella, an Iowa farmer in the movie *Field of Dreams*, hears a voice from the sky. No one else, including his wife Annie, can hear it. Ray interprets it as a promise that if he builds a baseball field in his cornfield, then the ghost of Shoeless Joe Jackson (a baseball star in the early days of the twentieth century) would come to play on it.

This promise came in the form of a conditional statement. A **conditional** statement is a compound statement that uses the connective *if . . . then*.

If I read for too long, *then* I get tired.
If looks could kill, *then* I would be dead.
If he doesn't get back soon, *then* you should go look for him.

> Conditional statements

In each of these conditional statements, the component coming after the word *if* gives a condition (but not necessarily the only condition) under which the statement coming after *then* will be true. For example, "If it is over 90°, then I'll go to the mountains" tells one possible condition under which I will go to the mountains—if the temperature is over 90°.

The conditional is written with an arrow, so "if p, then q" is symbolized as follows.

$$p \rightarrow q \quad \text{If } p, \text{then } q.$$

We read $p \rightarrow q$ as "**p implies q**" or "**if p, then q.**" In the conditional $p \rightarrow q$, the statement p is the **antecedent,** while q is the **consequent.**

The conditional connective may not always be explicitly stated. That is, it may be "hidden" in an everyday expression. For example, consider the following statement.

Big girls don't cry.

It can be written in *if . . . then* form as

If you're a big girl, *then* you don't cry.

As another example, consider this statement.

It is difficult to study when you are distracted.

It can be written

If you are distracted, *then* it is difficult to study.

In the quotation "If you build it, he will come" from the movie *Field of Dreams*, the word "then" is not stated but understood from the context of the statement. "You build it" is the antecedent, and "he will come" is the consequent.

The conditional truth table is a little harder to define than the tables in the previous section. To see how to define the conditional truth table, we analyze a statement made by a politician, Senator Laura Kennedy.

If I am elected, then taxes will go down.

There are four possible combinations of truth values for the two component statements. Let p represent "I am elected," and let q represent "Taxes will go down."

In his April 21, 1989, five-star review of *Field of Dreams*, the *Chicago Sun-Times* movie critic Roger Ebert gave an explanation of why the movie has become an American classic.

There is a speech in this movie about baseball that is so simple and true that it is heartbreaking. And the whole attitude toward the players reflects that attitude. Why do they come back from the great beyond and play in this cornfield? Not to make any kind of vast, earthshattering statement, but simply to hit a few and field a few, and remind us of a good and innocent time.

The photo above was taken in 2007 in Dyersville, Iowa, at the actual scene of the filming. The carving "Ray Loves Annie" in the bleacher seats can be seen in a quick shot during the movie. It has weathered over time.

$\sqrt[3]{250}$ $90°$ $(0, -3)$

θ $45.5 \div 2^{-1}$ ∞

$x = (4+8)-3$ $|a|$

$y = -x + 2$ $\frac{1}{4}$

10^2 $\geq$ $f(x) =$

The importance of **symbols** was emphasized by the American philosopher-logician **Charles Sanders Peirce** (1839–1914), who asserted the nature of humans as symbol-using or sign-using organisms. Symbolic notation is half of mathematics, Bertrand Russell once said.

As we analyze the four possibilities, it is helpful to think in terms of the following: "Did Senator Laura Kennedy lie?" If she lied, then the conditional statement is considered false. If she did not lie, then the conditional statement is considered true.

Possibility	Elected?	Taxes Go Down?	
1	Yes	Yes	p is T, q is T.
2	Yes	No	p is T, q is F.
3	No	Yes	p is F, q is T.
4	No	No	p is F, q is F.

The four possibilities are as follows.

1. In the first case assume that the senator was elected and taxes did go down (p is T, q is T). The senator told the truth, so place T in the first row of the truth table. (We do not claim that taxes went down *because* she was elected. It is possible that she had nothing to do with it at all.)

2. In the second case assume that the senator was elected and taxes did not go down (p is T, q is F). Then the senator did not tell the truth (that is, she lied). So we put F in the second row of the truth table.

3. In the third case assume that the senator was defeated, but taxes went down anyway (p is F, q is T). The senator did not lie. She only promised a tax reduction if she were elected. She said nothing about what would happen if she were not elected. In fact, her campaign promise gives no information about what would happen if she lost. Because we cannot say that the senator lied, place T in the third row of the truth table. (See the margin note.)

4. In the last case assume that the senator was defeated and taxes did not go down (p is F, q is F). We cannot blame her, because she only promised to reduce taxes if elected. Thus, T goes in the last row of the truth table.

You Lie! (or Do You?) Granted, the T for Case 3 is less obvious than the F for Case 2. However, the laws of symbolic logic permit only one of two truth values. Since no lie can be established in Case 3, we give the senator the benefit of the doubt. Likewise, *any* conditional statement is declared to be true whenever its antecedent is false.

The completed truth table for the conditional is defined as follows.

Truth Table for the Conditional   If p, then q

If p, then q

p	q	$p \rightarrow q$
T	T	T
T	F	F
F	T	T
F	F	T

The use of the conditional connective in no way implies a cause-and-effect relationship. Any two statements may have an arrow placed between them to create a compound statement. Consider this example.

If I pass mathematics, then the sun will rise the next day.

It is true, because the consequent is true. (See the special characteristics following **Example 1** on the next page.) There is, however, no cause-and-effect connection between my passing mathematics and the rising of the sun. The sun will rise no matter what grade I get.

▮▮ **EXAMPLE 1** Finding the Truth Value of a Conditional

Given that p, q, and r are all false, find the truth value of the statement.

$$(p \rightarrow {\sim}q) \rightarrow ({\sim}r \rightarrow q)$$

SOLUTION

Using the short-cut method explained in **Example 3** of the previous section, we can replace p, q, and r with F (since each is false) and proceed as before, using the negation and conditional truth tables as necessary.

$$
\begin{array}{ccc}
(p \rightarrow {\sim}q) & \rightarrow & ({\sim}r \rightarrow q) \\
(F \rightarrow {\sim}F) & \rightarrow & ({\sim}F \rightarrow F) \\
(F \rightarrow T) & \rightarrow & (T \rightarrow F) \qquad \text{Use the negation truth table.}\\
T & \rightarrow & F \qquad\qquad \text{Use the conditional truth table.}\\
& \mathbf{F} &
\end{array}
$$

The statement $(p \rightarrow {\sim}q) \rightarrow ({\sim}r \rightarrow q)$ is false when p, q, and r are all false. ▮▮▮

Special Characteristics of Conditional Statements
1. $p \rightarrow q$ is false only when the antecedent is *true* and the consequent is *false*.
2. If the antecedent is *false*, then $p \rightarrow q$ is automatically *true*.
3. If the consequent is *true*, then $p \rightarrow q$ is automatically *true*.

▮▮ **EXAMPLE 2** Determining Whether a Conditional Is True or False

Write *true* or *false* for each statement. Here T represents a true statement, and F represents a false statement.

(a) $T \rightarrow (7 = 3)$ **(b)** $(8 < 2) \rightarrow F$ **(c)** $(4 \neq 3 + 1) \rightarrow T$

SOLUTION

(a) Because the antecedent is true, while the consequent, $7 = 3$, is false, the given statement is false by the first point mentioned above.

(b) The antecedent is false, so the given statement is true by the second observation.

(c) The consequent is true, making the statement true by the third characteristic of conditional statements. ▮▮▮

▮▮ **EXAMPLE 3** Constructing Truth Tables

Construct a truth table for each statement.

(a) $({\sim}p \rightarrow {\sim}q) \rightarrow ({\sim}p \wedge q)$ **(b)** $(p \rightarrow q) \rightarrow ({\sim}p \vee q)$

SOLUTION

(a) Insert the truth values of ${\sim}p$ and ${\sim}q$. Find the truth values of ${\sim}p \rightarrow {\sim}q$.

p	q	${\sim}p$	${\sim}q$	${\sim}p \rightarrow {\sim}q$
T	T	F	F	T
T	F	F	T	T
F	T	T	F	F
F	F	T	T	T

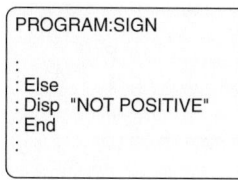

```
PROGRAM:SIGN
: Input A
: If A>0
: Then
: Disp "POSITIVE"
:
:
```

```
PROGRAM:SIGN
:
: Else
: Disp "NOT POSITIVE"
: End
:
```

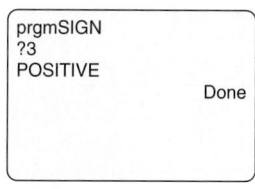

```
prgmSIGN
?3
POSITIVE
                Done
```

```
prgmSIGN
?-5
NOT POSITIVE
                Done
```

Conditional statements are useful in writing programs. The short program in the first two screens determines whether a number is positive. Notice the lines that begin with *If* and *Then*.

Next use $\sim p$ and q to find the truth values of $\sim p \wedge q$.

p	q	$\sim p$	$\sim q$	$\sim p \rightarrow \sim q$	$\sim p \wedge q$
T	T	F	F	T	F
T	F	F	T	T	F
F	T	T	F	F	T
F	F	T	T	T	F

Now find the truth values of $(\sim p \rightarrow \sim q) \rightarrow (\sim p \wedge q)$.

p	q	$\sim p$	$\sim q$	$\sim p \rightarrow \sim q$	$\sim p \wedge q$	$(\sim p \rightarrow \sim q) \rightarrow (\sim p \wedge q)$
T	T	F	F	T	F	F
T	F	F	T	T	F	F
F	T	T	F	F	T	T
F	F	T	T	T	F	F

(b) For $(p \rightarrow q) \rightarrow (\sim p \vee q)$, go through steps similar to the ones above.

p	q	$p \rightarrow q$	$\sim p$	$\sim p \vee q$	$(p \rightarrow q) \rightarrow (\sim p \vee q)$
T	T	T	F	T	T
T	F	F	F	F	T
F	T	T	T	T	T
F	F	T	T	T	T

▐▐▐

As the truth table in **Example 3(b)** shows, the statement

$$(p \rightarrow q) \rightarrow (\sim p \vee q)$$

is always true, no matter what the truth values of the components. Such a statement is called a **tautology.** Several other examples of tautologies (as can be checked by forming truth tables) are

$$p \vee \sim p, \quad p \rightarrow p, \quad \text{and} \quad (\sim p \vee \sim q) \rightarrow \sim (p \wedge q). \quad \text{Tautologies}$$

The truth tables in **Example 3** also could have been found by the alternative method shown in **Section 3.2.**

Negation of a Conditional

Suppose that someone makes the following conditional statement.

"If it rains, then I take my umbrella."

When will the person have lied to you? The only case in which you would have been misled is when it rains *and* the person does *not* take the umbrella. Letting p represent "it rains" and q represent "I take my umbrella," you might suspect that the symbolic statement

$$p \wedge \sim q$$

is a candidate for the negation of $p \rightarrow q$. This would imply that

$$\sim (p \rightarrow q) \equiv p \wedge \sim q.$$

This is indeed the case, as the following truth table indicates.

p	q	$p \rightarrow q$	$\sim (p \rightarrow q)$	$\sim q$	$p \wedge \sim q$
T	T	T	F	F	F
T	F	F	T	T	T
F	T	T	F	F	F
F	F	T	F	T	F

↑ ≡ ↑

In the 1959 Disney short film *Donald in Mathmagicland,* Donald Duck, dressed as Alice from Lewis Carroll's *Through the Looking Glass,* is attacked by a "none-too-friendly group of chess pieces." Logic and **chess** have been paired for centuries. Most scholars agree that chess dates back at least 1500 years, coming from Northern India and Afghanistan following trade routes through Persia.

Good chess players rely on memory, imagination, determination, and inspiration. They are pattern thinkers that use long-established sets of consequences and probabilities.

In the end, logic does not necessarily dictate the final outcome of any chess game, for if it did, humans would not stand a chance when playing faceless, number-crunching computers.
© Disney Enterprises, Inc.

Sources: www.imdb.com, Walter A. Smart.

> **Negation of $p \rightarrow q$**
>
> The negation of $p \rightarrow q$ is $p \wedge \sim q$.

Because

$$\sim(p \rightarrow q) \equiv p \wedge \sim q,$$

by negating each expression we have

$$\sim[\sim(p \rightarrow q)] \equiv \sim(p \wedge \sim q).$$

The left side of the above equivalence is $p \rightarrow q$, and one of De Morgan's laws can be applied to the right side.

$$p \rightarrow q \equiv \sim p \vee \sim(\sim q)$$
$$p \rightarrow q \equiv \sim p \vee q$$

This final row indicates that a conditional may be written as a disjunction.

> **Writing a Conditional as a Disjunction**
>
> $p \rightarrow q$ is equivalent to $\sim p \vee q$.

▌▌ EXAMPLE 4 Determining Negations

Determine the negation of each statement.

(a) If you build it, he will come.   **(b)** All dogs have fleas.

Do not try to negate a conditional with another conditional.

SOLUTION

(a) If b represents "you build it" and q represents "he will come," then the given statement can be symbolized by $b \rightarrow q$. The negation of $b \rightarrow q$, as shown earlier, is $b \wedge \sim q$, so the negation of the statement is

> You build it and he will not come.

(b) First, we must restate the given statement in *if . . . then* form.

> If it is a dog, then it has fleas.

Based on our earlier discussion, the negation is

> It is a dog and it does not have fleas.   ▮▮▮

As seen in **Example 4,** the negation of a conditional statement is written as a conjunction.

▌▌ EXAMPLE 5 Determining Statements Equivalent to Conditionals

Write each conditional as an equivalent statement without using *if . . . then*.

(a) If the Indians win the pennant, then Johnny will go to the World Series.

(b) If it's Borden's, it's got to be good.

SOLUTION

(a) Because the conditional $p \rightarrow q$ is equivalent to $\sim p \vee q$, let p represent "The Indians win the pennant" and q represent "Johnny will go to the World Series." Restate the conditional as

> The Indians do not win the pennant or Johnny will go to the World Series.

(b) If p represents "it's Borden's" and if q represents "it's got to be good," the conditional may be restated as

It's not Borden's or it's got to be good. ▪▪▪

Circuits

One of the first nonmathematical applications of symbolic logic was seen in the master's thesis of Claude Shannon in 1937. Shannon showed how logic could be used to design electrical circuits. His work was immediately used by computer designers. Then in the developmental stage, computers could be simplified and built for less money using the ideas of Shannon.

To see how Shannon's ideas work, look at the electrical switch shown in **Figure 1.** We assume that current will flow through this switch when it is closed and not when it is open.

Figure 2 shows two switches connected in *series.* In such a circuit, current will flow only when both switches are closed. Note how closely a series circuit corresponds to the conjunction $p \wedge q$. We know that $p \wedge q$ is true only when both p and q are true.

A circuit corresponding to the disjunction $p \vee q$ can be found by drawing a *parallel* circuit, as in **Figure 3.** Here, current flows if either p or q is closed or if both p and q are closed.

The circuit in **Figure 4** corresponds to the statement $(p \vee q) \wedge \sim q$, which is a compound statement involving both a conjunction and a disjunction.

Simplifying an electrical circuit depends on the idea of equivalent statements from **Section 3.2.** Recall that two statements are equivalent if they have the same truth table final column. The symbol ≡ is used to indicate that the two statements are equivalent. Some equivalent statements are shown in the following box.

Figure 1

Series circuit

Figure 2

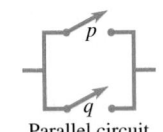

Parallel circuit

Figure 3

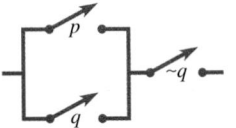

Figure 4

Equivalent Statements Used to Simplify Circuits

$$p \vee (q \wedge r) \equiv (p \vee q) \wedge (p \vee r) \qquad p \vee p \equiv p$$
$$p \wedge (q \vee r) \equiv (p \wedge q) \vee (p \wedge r) \qquad p \wedge p \equiv p$$
$$p \rightarrow q \equiv \sim q \rightarrow \sim p \qquad \sim(p \wedge q) \equiv \sim p \vee \sim q$$
$$p \rightarrow q \equiv \sim p \vee q \qquad \sim(p \vee q) \equiv \sim p \wedge \sim q$$

If T represents any true statement and F represents any false statement, then

$$p \vee \mathrm{T} \equiv \mathrm{T} \qquad p \vee \sim p \equiv \mathrm{T}$$
$$p \wedge \mathrm{F} \equiv \mathrm{F} \qquad p \wedge \sim p \equiv \mathrm{F}.$$

Circuits can be used as models of compound statements, with a closed switch corresponding to T, while an open switch corresponds to F.

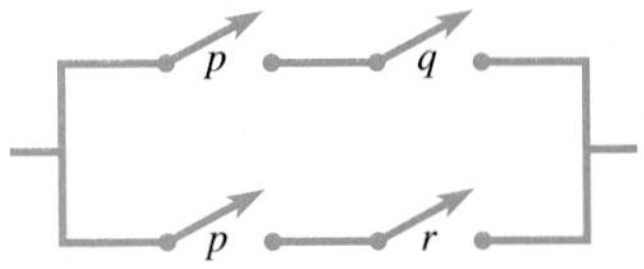

▌▌ **EXAMPLE 6** Simplifying a Circuit

Simplify the circuit of **Figure 5.**

SOLUTION

At the top of **Figure 5,** p and q are connected in series, and at the bottom, p and r are connected in series. These are interpreted as the compound statements $p \wedge q$ and $p \wedge r$, respectively. These two conjunctions are connected in parallel, as indicated by the figure treated as a whole.

Write the disjunction of the two conjunctions.

$$(p \wedge q) \vee (p \wedge r)$$

Figure 5

Figure 6

(Think of the two switches labeled "p" as being controlled by the same lever.) By one of the pairs of equivalent statements in the preceding box,

$$(p \wedge q) \vee (p \wedge r) \equiv p \wedge (q \vee r),$$

which has the circuit of **Figure 6.** This circuit is logically equivalent to the one in **Figure 5,** and yet it contains only three switches instead of four—which might well lead to a large savings in manufacturing costs. ▮▮▮

▮▮ **EXAMPLE 7** Drawing a Circuit for a Conditional Statement

Draw a circuit for $p \to (q \wedge \sim r)$.

SOLUTION

From the list of equivalent statements in the box, $p \to q$ is equivalent to $\sim p \vee q$. This equivalence gives $p \to (q \wedge \sim r) \equiv \sim p \vee (q \wedge \sim r)$, which has the circuit diagram in **Figure 7.** ▮▮▮

Figure 7

3.3 EXERCISES

Rewrite each statement using the if . . . then *connective. Rearrange the wording or add words as necessary.*

1. You can believe it if you see it on the Internet.

2. It must be alive if it is breathing.

3. Every integer divisible by 10 is divisible by 5.

4. All perfect square integers have units digit 0, 1, 4, 5, 6, or 9.

5. All Marines love boot camp.

6. Every picture tells a story.

7. No pandas live in Idaho.

8. No guinea pigs are scholars.

9. An opium eater cannot have self-command.

10. Running Bear loves Little White Dove.

Decide whether each statement is true *or* false.

11. If the antecedent of a conditional statement is false, the conditional statement is true.

12. If the consequent of a conditional statement is true, the conditional statement is true.

13. If q is true, then $(p \wedge q) \to q$ is true.

14. If p is true, then $\sim p \to (q \vee r)$ is true.

15. The negation of "If pigs fly, I'll believe it" is "If pigs don't fly, I won't believe it."

16. The statements "If it flies, then it's a bird" and "It does not fly or it's a bird" are logically equivalent.

17. Given that $\sim p$ is true and q is false, the conditional $p \to q$ is true.

18. Given that $\sim p$ is false and q is false, the conditional $p \to q$ is true.

19. Explain why the statement "If $3 = 5$, then $4 = 6$" is true.

20. In a few sentences, explain how to determine the truth value of a conditional statement.

Tell whether each conditional is true (T) *or* false (F).

21. $T \to (7 < 3)$ **22.** $F \to (4 \neq 8)$

23. $F \to (5 \neq 5)$ **24.** $(8 \geq 8) \to F$

25. $(5^2 \neq 25) \rightarrow (8 - 8 = 16)$

26. $(5 = 12 - 7) \rightarrow (9 > 0)$

Let s represent "She has a bird for a pet," let p represent "he trains dogs," and let m represent "they raise alpacas." Express each compound statement in words.

27. $\sim m \rightarrow p$

28. $p \rightarrow \sim m$

29. $s \rightarrow (m \wedge p)$

30. $(s \wedge p) \rightarrow m$

31. $\sim p \rightarrow (\sim m \vee s)$

32. $(\sim s \vee \sim m) \rightarrow \sim p$

Let b represent "I ride my bike," let s represent "it snows," and let p represent "the play is cancelled." Write each compound statement in symbols.

33. If I ride my bike, then the play is cancelled.

34. If it snows, then I ride my bike.

35. If the play is cancelled, then it does not snow.

36. If I do not ride my bike, then it does not snow.

37. The play is cancelled, and if it snows then I do not ride my bike.

38. I ride my bike, or if the play is cancelled then it snows.

39. It snows if the play is cancelled.

40. I'll ride my bike if it doesn't snow.

Find the truth value of each statement. Assume that p and r are false, and q is true.

41. $\sim r \rightarrow q$

42. $\sim p \rightarrow \sim r$

43. $q \rightarrow p$

44. $\sim r \rightarrow p$

45. $p \rightarrow q$

46. $\sim q \rightarrow r$

47. $\sim p \rightarrow (q \wedge r)$

48. $(\sim r \vee p) \rightarrow p$

49. $\sim q \rightarrow (p \wedge r)$

50. $(\sim p \wedge \sim q) \rightarrow (p \wedge \sim r)$

51. $(p \rightarrow \sim q) \rightarrow (\sim p \wedge \sim r)$

52. $(p \rightarrow \sim q) \wedge (p \rightarrow r)$

53. Explain why, if we know that p is true, we also know that

$$[r \vee (p \vee s)] \rightarrow (p \vee q)$$

is true, even if we are not given the truth values of q, r, and s.

54. Construct a true statement involving a conditional, a conjunction, a disjunction, and a negation (not necessarily in that order), that consists of component statements p, q, and r, with all of these component statements false.

Construct a truth table for each statement. Identify any tautologies.

55. $\sim q \rightarrow p$

56. $p \rightarrow \sim q$

57. $(\sim p \rightarrow q) \rightarrow p$

58. $(\sim q \rightarrow \sim p) \rightarrow \sim q$

59. $(p \vee q) \rightarrow (q \vee p)$

60. $(p \wedge q) \rightarrow (p \vee q)$

61. $(\sim p \rightarrow \sim q) \rightarrow (p \wedge q)$

62. $r \rightarrow (p \wedge \sim q)$

63. $[(r \vee p) \wedge \sim q] \rightarrow p$

64. $[(r \wedge p) \wedge (p \wedge q)] \rightarrow p$

65. $(\sim r \rightarrow s) \vee (p \rightarrow \sim q)$

66. $(\sim p \wedge \sim q) \rightarrow (s \rightarrow r)$

67. What is the minimum number of Fs that must appear in the final column of a truth table for us to be assured that the statement is not a tautology?

68. If all truth values in the final column of a truth table are F, how can we easily transform the statement into a tautology?

Write the negation of each statement. Remember that the negation of $p \rightarrow q$ is $p \wedge \sim q$.

69. If that is an authentic Rolex watch, I'll be surprised.

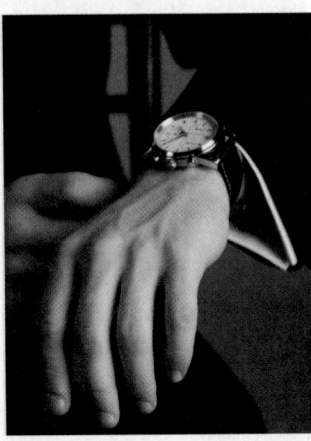

70. If Minnie Ripperton reaches that note, she will shatter glass.

71. If the English measures are not converted to metric measures, then the spacecraft will crash on the surface of Saturn.

72. If you say "I do," then you'll be happy for the rest of your life.

73. "If you want to be happy for the rest of your life, never make a pretty woman your wife." *Jimmy Soul*

74. "If loving you is wrong, I don't want to be right." *Luther Ingram*

Write each statement as an equivalent statement that does not use the if . . . then *connective. Remember that*

$$p \rightarrow q \quad \text{is equivalent to} \quad {\sim}p \vee q.$$

75. If you give your plants tender, loving care, they flourish.

76. If the check is in the mail, I will buy you lunch.

77. If she doesn't, he will.

78. If I say "black," she says "white."

79. All residents of Pensacola are residents of Florida.

80. All women were once girls.

Use truth tables to decide which of the pairs of statements are equivalent.

81. $p \rightarrow q$; $\ {\sim}p \vee q$ **82.** ${\sim}(p \rightarrow q)$; $\ p \wedge {\sim}q$

83. $p \rightarrow q$; $\ {\sim}q \rightarrow {\sim}p$ **84.** $q \rightarrow p$; $\ {\sim}p \rightarrow {\sim}q$

85. $p \wedge {\sim}q$; $\ {\sim}q \rightarrow {\sim}p$ **86.** $p \rightarrow q$; $\ q \rightarrow p$

87. $p \rightarrow {\sim}q$; $\ {\sim}p \vee {\sim}q$ **88.** ${\sim}p \wedge q$; $\ {\sim}p \rightarrow q$

89. $q \rightarrow {\sim}p$; $\ p \rightarrow {\sim}q$ **90.** ${\sim}p \rightarrow q$; $\ p \vee q$

Write a logical statement representing each of the following circuits. Simplify each circuit when possible.

91.

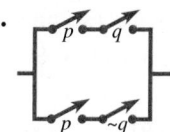

92.

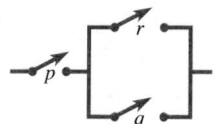

93.

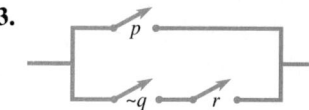

94.

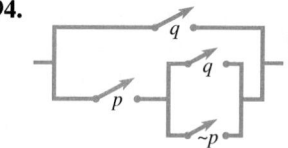

95.

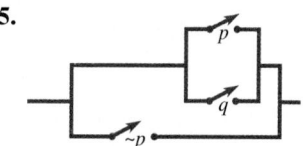

96.

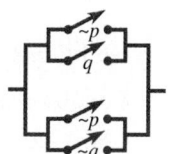

Draw circuits representing the following statements as they are given. Simplify if possible.

97. $p \wedge (q \vee {\sim}p)$ **98.** $({\sim}p \wedge {\sim}q) \wedge {\sim}r$

99. $(p \vee q) \wedge ({\sim}p \wedge {\sim}q)$

100. $({\sim}q \wedge {\sim}p) \vee ({\sim}p \vee q)$

101. $[(p \vee q) \wedge r] \wedge {\sim}p$

102. $[({\sim}p \wedge {\sim}r) \vee {\sim}q] \wedge ({\sim}p \wedge r)$

103. ${\sim}q \rightarrow ({\sim}p \rightarrow q)$ **104.** ${\sim}p \rightarrow ({\sim}p \vee {\sim}q)$

105. Refer to **Figures 5 and 6** in **Example 6.** Suppose the cost of the use of one switch for an hour is $0.06. By using the circuit in **Figure 6** rather than the circuit in **Figure 5,** what is the savings for a year of 365 days, assuming that the circuit is in continuous use?

106. Explain why the circuit shown will always have exactly one open switch. What does this circuit simplify to?

3.4 THE CONDITIONAL AND RELATED STATEMENTS

Converse, Inverse, and Contrapositive • Alternative Forms of "If p, then q"
• Biconditionals • Summary of Truth Tables

Converse, Inverse, and Contrapositive

Many mathematical properties and theorems are stated in *if . . . then* form. Any conditional statement $p \rightarrow q$ is made up of an antecedent p and a consequent q. If they are interchanged, negated, or both, a new conditional statement is formed. Suppose that we begin with a conditional statement.

If you stay, then I go.   Conditional Statement

By interchanging the antecedent ("you stay") and the consequent ("I go"), we obtain a new conditional statement.

If I go, then you stay.   Converse

This new conditional is called the **converse** of the given conditional statement.

By negating both the antecedent and the consequent, we obtain the **inverse** of the given conditional statement.

If you do not stay, then I do not go.   Inverse

If the antecedent and the consequent are both interchanged *and* negated, the **contrapositive** of the given conditional statement is formed.

If I do not go, then you do not stay.   Contrapositive

These three related statements for the conditional $p \rightarrow q$ are summarized below. (***The inverse is the contrapositive of the converse.***)

Alfred North Whitehead (1861–1947) and Bertrand Russell worked together on *Principia Mathematica*. During that time, Whitehead was teaching mathematics at Cambridge University and had written *Universal Algebra*. In 1910 he went to the University of London, exploring not only the philosophical basis of science but also the "aims of education" (as he called one of his books). It was as a philosopher that he was invited to Harvard University in 1924. Whitehead died at the age of 86 in Cambridge, Massachusetts.

Related Conditional Statements

Conditional Statement	$p \rightarrow q$	(If p, then q.)
Converse	$q \rightarrow p$	(If q, then p.)
Inverse	$\sim p \rightarrow \sim q$	(If not p, then not q.)
Contrapositive	$\sim q \rightarrow \sim p$	(If not q, then not p.)

EXAMPLE 1 Determining Related Conditional Statements

Determine each of the following, given the conditional statement

If I live in Orlando, then I live in Florida.

(a) the converse   **(b)** the inverse   **(c)** the contrapositive

SOLUTION

(a) Let p represent "I live in Orlando" and q represent "I live in Florida." Then the given statement may be written $p \rightarrow q$. The converse, $q \rightarrow p$, is

If I live in Florida, then I live in Orlando.

Notice that for this statement, the converse is not necessarily true, even though the given statement is true.

(b) The inverse of $p \rightarrow q$ is $\sim p \rightarrow \sim q$. Thus, the inverse is

If I don't live in Orlando, then I don't live in Florida.

Again, this is not necessarily true.

Bertrand Russell (1872–1970) was a student of Whitehead's before they wrote the *Principia*. Like his teacher, Russell turned toward philosophy. His works include a critique of Leibniz, analyses of mind and of matter, and a history of Western thought.

Russell became a public figure because of his involvement in social issues. Deeply aware of human loneliness, he was "passionately desirous of finding ways of diminishing this tragic isolation." During World War I he was an antiwar crusader, and he was imprisoned briefly. Again in the 1960s he championed peace. He wrote many books on social issues, winning the Nobel Prize for Literature in 1950.

(c) The contrapositive, $\sim q \rightarrow \sim p$, is

If I don't live in Florida, then I don't live in Orlando.

The contrapositive, like the given conditional statement, is true. ▐▐▐

Example 1 shows that the converse and inverse of a true statement need not be true. They *can* be true, but they need not be. The relationships between the related conditionals are shown in the truth table that follows.

		Conditional	Converse	Inverse	Contrapositive
p	q	$p \rightarrow q$	$q \rightarrow p$	$\sim p \rightarrow \sim q$	$\sim q \rightarrow \sim p$
T	T	T	T	T	T
T	F	F	T	T	F
F	T	T	F	F	T
F	F	T	T	T	T

Equivalent (Conditional and Contrapositive); *Equivalent* (Converse and Inverse)

As this truth table shows,

1. *A conditional statement and its contrapositive always have the same truth values,* making it possible to replace any statement with its contrapositive without affecting the logical meaning.

2. *The converse and inverse always have the same truth values.*

Equivalences

A conditional statement and its contrapositive are equivalent. Also, the converse and the inverse are equivalent.

▐▐ **EXAMPLE 2** Determining Related Conditional Statements

For the conditional statement $\sim p \rightarrow q$, write each of the following.

(a) the converse   **(b)** the inverse   **(c)** the contrapositive

SOLUTION

(a) The converse of $\sim p \rightarrow q$ is $q \rightarrow \sim p$.

(b) The inverse is $\sim(\sim p) \rightarrow \sim q$, which simplifies to $p \rightarrow \sim q$.

(c) The contrapositive is $\sim q \rightarrow \sim(\sim p)$, which simplifies to $\sim q \rightarrow p$. ▐▐▐

Alternative Forms of "If p, then q"

The conditional statement "if p, then q" can be stated in several other ways in English. Consider this statement.

If you go to the outlet mall, then you will find a place to park.

It can also be written as follows.

Going to the outlet mall is *sufficient* for finding a place to park.

According to this statement, going to the outlet mall is enough to guarantee finding a place to park. Going to other places, such as schools or office buildings, *might* also guarantee a place to park, but at least we *know* that going to the outlet mall does. Thus, $p \rightarrow q$ can be written "p is sufficient for q." Knowing that p has occurred is sufficient to guarantee that q will also occur.

On the other hand, consider this statement, which has a different meaning.

Having the set on is necessary for watching television. (∗)

Here, we are saying that one condition that is necessary for watching television is that the set be turned on. This may not be enough. The set might be broken, for example. The statement labeled (∗) could be written as

If you watch television, then the set was turned on.

As this example suggests, $p \rightarrow q$ is the same as "q is necessary for p." In other words, if q doesn't happen, then neither will p. Notice how this idea is closely related to the idea of equivalence between a conditional statement and its contrapositive.

Common Translations of $p \rightarrow q$

The conditional $p \rightarrow q$ can be translated in any of the following ways, none of which depends on the truth or falsity of $p \rightarrow q$.

If p, then q.	p is sufficient for q.
If p, q.	q is necessary for p.
p implies q.	All p are q.
p only if q.	q if p.

Example: If you live in Dubuque, then you live in Iowa. _{Statement}

You live in Iowa if you live in Dubuque.
You live in Dubuque only if you live in Iowa.
Living in Iowa is necessary for living in Dubuque.   Common
Living in Dubuque is sufficient for living in Iowa.   translations
All residents of Dubuque are residents of Iowa.
Being a resident of Dubuque implies residency in Iowa.

▮▮ **EXAMPLE 3** Rewording Conditional Statements

Write each statement in the form "if p, then q."

(a) You'll be sorry if I go.   **(b)** Today is Tuesday only if yesterday was Monday.

(c) All nurses wear white shoes.

SOLUTION

(a) If I go, then you'll be sorry.

(b) If today is Tuesday, then yesterday was Monday.

(c) If you are a nurse, then you wear white shoes.   ▮▮▮

▮▮ **EXAMPLE 4** Translating from Words to Symbols

Let p represent "A triangle is equilateral," and let q represent "A triangle has three sides of equal length." Write each of the following in symbols.

(a) A triangle is equilateral if it has three sides of equal length.

(b) A triangle is equilateral only if it has three sides of equal length.

SOLUTION

(a) $q \rightarrow p$ **(b)** $p \rightarrow q$ ▮▮▮

Principia Mathematica, the title chosen by Whitehead and Russell, was a deliberate reference to *Philosophiae naturalis principia mathematica,* or "mathematical principles of the philosophy of nature," Isaac Newton's epochal work of 1687. Newton's *Principia* pictured a kind of "clockwork universe" that ran via his Law of Gravitation. Newton independently invented the calculus, unaware that Leibniz had published his own formulation of it earlier.

Biconditionals

The compound statement **p if and only if q** (often abbreviated **p iff q**) is called a **biconditional.** It is symbolized $p \leftrightarrow q$, and is interpreted as the conjunction of the two conditionals $p \to q$ and $q \to p$. Using symbols, this conjunction is written $(q \to p) \land (p \to q)$ so that, by definition,

$$p \leftrightarrow q \equiv (q \to p) \land (p \to q). \quad \text{Biconditional}$$

The truth table for the biconditional $p \leftrightarrow q$ can be determined using this definition.

Truth Table for the Biconditional   p if and only if q

p if and only if *q*

p	q	$p \leftrightarrow q$
T	T	T
T	F	F
F	T	F
F	F	T

A biconditional is true when both component statements have the same truth value. It is false when they have different truth values.

▮▮ **EXAMPLE 5** Determining Whether Biconditionals Are True or False

Determine whether each biconditional statement is *true* or *false.*

(a) $6 + 8 = 14$ if and only if $11 + 5 = 16$

(b) $6 = 5$ if and only if $12 \neq 12$

(c) $5 + 2 = 10$ if and only if $17 + 19 = 36$

SOLUTION

(a) Both $6 + 8 = 14$ and $11 + 5 = 16$ are true. By the truth table for the biconditional, this biconditional is true.

(b) Both component statements are false, so by the last line of the truth table for the biconditional, this biconditional statement is true.

(c) Because the first component ($5 + 2 = 10$) is false, and the second is true, this biconditional statement is false.   ▮▮▮

Summary of Truth Tables

Truth tables have been derived for several important types of compound statements.

Summary of Basic Truth Tables

1. $\sim p$, the **negation** of p, has truth value opposite that of p.

2. $p \land q$, the **conjunction,** is true only when both p and q are true.

3. $p \lor q$, the **disjunction,** is false only when both p and q are false.

4. $p \to q$, the **conditional,** is false only when p is true and q is false.

5. $p \leftrightarrow q$, the **biconditional,** is true only when both p and q have the same truth value.

3.4 EXERCISES

*For each given conditional statement (or statement that can be written as a conditional), write (**a**) the converse, (**b**) the inverse, and (**c**) the contrapositive in if . . . then form. In some of the exercises, it may be helpful to first restate the given statement in if . . . then form.*

1. If beauty were a minute, then you would be an hour.

2. If you lead, then I will follow.

3. If it ain't broke, don't fix it.

4. If I had a nickel for each time that happened, I would be rich.

5. Walking in front of a moving car is dangerous to your health.

6. Milk contains calcium.

7. Birds of a feather flock together.

8. A rolling stone gathers no moss.

9. If you build it, he will come.

10. Where there's smoke, there's fire.

11. $p \rightarrow \sim q$

12. $\sim p \rightarrow q$

13. $\sim p \rightarrow \sim q$

14. $\sim q \rightarrow \sim p$

15. $p \rightarrow (q \vee r)$ (*Hint:* Use one of De Morgan's laws as necessary.)

16. $(r \vee \sim q) \rightarrow p$ (*Hint:* Use one of De Morgan's laws as necessary.)

17. Discuss the equivalences that exist among a given conditional statement, its converse, its inverse, and its contrapositive.

18. State the contrapositive of "If the square of a natural number is even, then the natural number is even." The two statements must have the same truth value. Use several examples and inductive reasoning to decide whether both are true or both are false.

Write each statement in the form "if p, then q."

19. If it is muddy, I'll wear my galoshes.

20. If I finish studying, I'll go to the party.

21. "19 is positive" implies that 19 + 1 is positive.

22. "Today is Wednesday" implies that yesterday was Tuesday.

23. All integers are rational numbers.

24. All whole numbers are integers.

25. Doing logic puzzles is sufficient for driving me crazy.

26. Being in Kalamazoo is sufficient for being in Michigan.

27. A day's growth of beard is necessary for Jeff Marsalis to shave.

28. Being an environmentalist is necessary for being elected.

29. I can go from Boardwalk to Baltic Avenue only if I pass GO.

30. The principal will hire more teachers only if the school board approves.

31. No whole numbers are not integers.

32. No integers are irrational numbers.

33. The Nationals will win the pennant when their pitching improves.

34. Sarah will be a liberal when pigs fly.

35. A rectangle is a parallelogram with a right angle.

36. A parallelogram is a four-sided figure with opposite sides parallel.

37. A triangle with two perpendicular sides is a right triangle.

38. A square is a rectangle with two adjacent sides equal.

39. The square of a two-digit number whose units digit is 5 will end in 25.

40. An integer whose units digit is 0 or 5 is divisible by 5.

41. One of the following statements is not equivalent to all the others. Which one is it?
    A. *r* only if *s*.   **B.** *r* implies *s*.
    C. If *r*, then *s*.   **D.** *r* is necessary for *s*.

42. Many students have difficulty interpreting *necessary* and *sufficient*. Use the statement "Being in Vancouver is sufficient for being in North America" to explain why "*p* is sufficient for *q*" translates as "if *p*, then *q*."

43. Use the statement "To be an integer, it is necessary that a number be rational" to explain why "*p* is necessary for *q*" translates as "if *q*, then *p*."

44. Explain why the statement "A week has eight days if and only if October has forty days" is true.

Identify each statement as true *or* false.

45. $6 = 9 - 3$ if and only if $8 + 2 = 10$.

46. $3 + 1 \neq 7$ if and only if $8 \neq 8$.

47. $8 + 7 \neq 15$ if and only if $3 \times 5 \neq 8$.

48. $6 \times 2 = 18$ if and only if $9 + 7 \neq 16$.

49. George H. W. Bush was president if and only if George W. Bush was not president.

50. Burger King sells Big Macs if and only if Apple manufactures Ipods.

Two statements that can both be true about the same object are **consistent.** *For example,* "It is green" *and* "It weighs 60 pounds" *are consistent statements. Statements that cannot both be true about the same object are called* **contrary.** "It is a Nissan" *and* "It is a Mazda" *are contrary. In Exercises 51–56, label each pair of statements as either* contrary *or* consistent.

51. Michael Jackson is alive. Michael Jackson is dead.

52. Barack Obama is a Democrat. Barack Obama is a Republican.

53. That animal has four legs. That same animal is a cat.

54. That book is nonfiction. That book costs more than $150.

55. This number is a whole number. This same number is irrational.

56. This number is positive. This same number is a natural number.

57. This number is an integer. This same number is a rational number.

58. This number is a whole number. This same number is a negative number.

59. Make up two statements that are consistent.

60. Make up two statements that are contrary.

3.5 ANALYZING ARGUMENTS WITH EULER DIAGRAMS

Logical Arguments • Arguments with Universal Quantifiers • Arguments with Existential Quantifiers

Leonhard Euler (1707–1783) won the Academy prize and edged out du Châtelet and Voltaire. That was a minor achievement, as was the invention of "Euler circles" (which antedated Venn diagrams). Euler was the most prolific mathematician of his generation despite blindness that forced him to dictate from memory.

Logical Arguments

With inductive reasoning we observe patterns to solve problems. Now we study how deductive reasoning may be used to determine whether logical arguments are valid or invalid.

A logical argument is made up of **premises** (assumptions, laws, rules, widely held ideas, or observations) and a **conclusion.** Recall that *deductive* reasoning involves drawing specific conclusions from given general premises. When reasoning from the premises of an argument to obtain a conclusion, we want the argument to be valid.

> **Valid and Invalid Arguments**
>
> An argument is **valid** if the fact that all the premises are true forces the conclusion to be true. An argument that is not valid is **invalid.** It is called a **fallacy.**

"Valid" and "true" do not have the same meaning—an argument can be valid even though the conclusion is false. **(See Example 4.)**

Arguments with Universal Quantifiers

Several techniques can be used to check whether an argument is valid. One such technique is based on **Euler diagrams.**

Leonhard Euler (pronounced "Oiler") was one of the greatest mathematicians who ever lived. He is immortalized in mathematics history with the important irrational number e, named in his honor. This number appears throughout mathematics, and is discussed in **Chapters 6 and 8.**

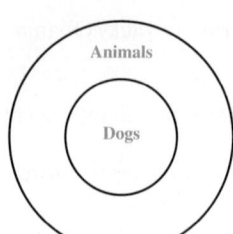

Figure 8

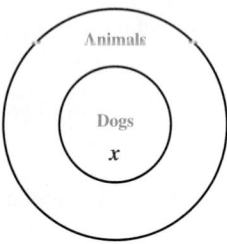

x represents Dotty.

Figure 9

▌▌ EXAMPLE 1 Using an Euler Diagram to Determine Validity

Is the following argument valid?

> All dogs are animals.
> Dotty is a dog.
> _____
> Dotty is an animal.

SOLUTION

To begin, draw regions to represent the first premise. Because all dogs are animals, the region for "dogs" goes inside the region for "animals," as in **Figure 8**.

The second premise, "Dotty is a dog," suggests that "Dotty" would go inside the region representing "dogs." Let *x* represent "Dotty." **Figure 9** shows that "Dotty" is also inside the region for "animals." If both premises are true, the conclusion that Dotty is an animal must be true also. The argument is valid. ■■■

▌▌ EXAMPLE 2 Using an Euler Diagram to Determine Validity

Is the following argument valid?

> All rainy days are cloudy.
> Today is not cloudy.
> _____
> Today is not rainy.

SOLUTION

In **Figure 10**, the region for "rainy days" is drawn entirely inside the region for "cloudy days." Since "Today is *not* cloudy," place an *x* for "today" *outside* the region for "cloudy days." See **Figure 11**. Placing the *x* outside the region for "cloudy days" forces it also to be outside the region for "rainy days." Thus, if the two premises are true, then it is also true that today is not rainy. The argument is valid.

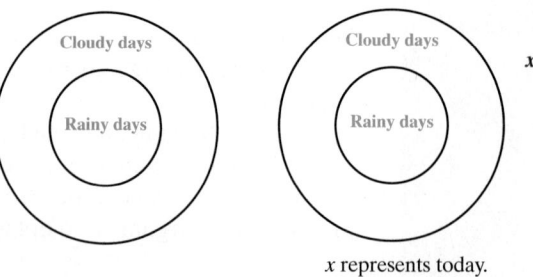

Figure 10   **Figure 11**

x represents today.

■■■

▌▌ EXAMPLE 3 Using an Euler Diagram to Determine Validity

Is the following argument valid?

> All magnolia trees have green leaves.
> That plant has green leaves.
> _____
> That plant is a magnolia tree.

SOLUTION

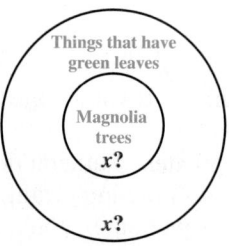

Figure 12

The region for "magnolia trees" goes entirely inside the region for "things that have green leaves." See **Figure 12.** The *x* that represents "that plant" must go inside the region for "things that have green leaves," but can go either inside or outside the region for "magnolia trees." Even if the premises are true, we are not forced to accept the conclusion as true. This argument is invalid. It is a fallacy. ■■■

▌▌ EXAMPLE 4 Using an Euler Diagram to Determine Validity

Is the following argument valid?

All expensive things are desirable.
All desirable things make you feel good.
All things that make you feel good make you live longer.

All expensive things make you live longer.

SOLUTION

A diagram for the argument is given in **Figure 13.**
  If each premise is true, then the conclusion
must be true because the region for "expensive
things" lies completely within the region for
"things that make you live longer." Thus, the argument is valid. (This argument is an example of the
fact that a *valid* argument need *not* have a true
conclusion.)

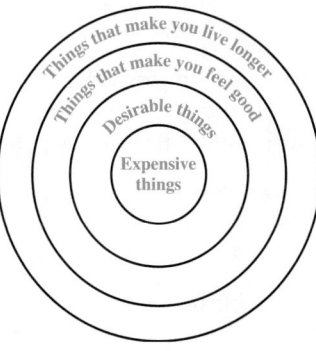

Figure 13   ▮▮▮

Arguments with Existential Quantifiers

▌▌ EXAMPLE 5 Using an Euler Diagram to Determine Validity

Is the following argument valid?

Some students go to the beach for Spring Break.
I am a student.

I go to the beach for Spring Break.

SOLUTION

The first premise is sketched in **Figure 14,** where some (but not necessarily *all*)
students go to the beach. There are two possibilities for *I*, as shown in **Figure 15.**
One possibility is that *I* go to the beach. The other is that *I* don't. Since the truth of the
premises does not force the conclusion to be true, the argument is invalid.   ▮▮▮

Figure 14

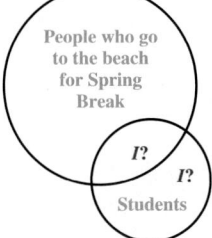

Figure 15

For Further Thought (cont.)

3. **Loaded Question and Complex Claims** This fallacy involves one person asking a question or making a statement that is constructed in such a way as to obtain an answer in which the responder agrees to something with which he does not actually agree.

Teenager Beth to her father: I hope you enjoyed embarrassing me in front of my friends.

If Beth gets the expected response "No, I didn't enjoy it," the answer allows Beth to interpret that while her father didn't enjoy it, he did indeed embarrass her.

4. *Post Hoc* **Reasoning** An argument that is based on the false belief that if event A preceded event B, then A must have caused B is called *post hoc* reasoning.

Johnny: I wore my Hawaiian shirt while watching all three playoff games, and my team won all three games. So I am going to wear that shirt every time I watch them.

The fact that Johnny put the same shirt on before each game has nothing to do with the outcomes of the games.

5. **Red Herring** (also called *Smoke Screen,* or *Wild Goose Chase*) This fallacy involves introducing an irrelevant topic to divert attention away from the original topic, allowing the person making the argument to seemingly prevail.

(From the movie *Field of Dreams,* in a scene where Annie and Beulah are arguing at a town meeting about the banning of books)

Beulah: I say smut and filth like this has no place in our schools. . . . The so-called novels of Terence Mann endorse promiscuity, godlessness, the mongrelization of the races, and disrespect to high-ranking officers of the United States army. And that is why school boards across the country have been banning his books since 1969.
Annie: Excuse me, madam. Terence Mann was a warm and gentle voice of reason in a time of great madness. He coined the phrase "Make love, not war." . . . He was talking about peace, and love, and understanding . . .
Beulah: Oh yeah, well your husband plowed under his corn and built a baseball field . . . the weirdo. . . .
Annie: Now there's an intelligent response.

While most of the people in the audience agreed that Annie's husband Ray was doing strange things, those things had nothing to do with banning books.

6. **Shifting the Burden of Proof** A person making a claim usually is required to support that claim. In this fallacy, if the claim is difficult to support, that person turns the burden of proof of that claim over to someone else.

Employee: You accuse me of embezzling money? That's ridiculous.
Employer: Well, until you can prove otherwise, you will just have to accept it as true.

If money has been disappearing, it is up to the employer to prove that this employee is guilty. The burden of proof is on the employer, but he is insinuating that the employee must prove that he is not the one taking the money.

7. **Straw Man** This fallacy involves creating a false image (like a scarecrow, or straw man) of someone else's position in an argument.

Dan Quayle: I have as much experience in the Congress as Jack Kennedy did when he sought the presidency.
Lloyd Bentsen: Senator, I served with Jack Kennedy. I knew Jack Kennedy. Jack Kennedy was a friend of mine. And Senator, you're no Jack Kennedy.
Dan Quayle: That was really uncalled for, Senator.
Lloyd Bentsen: You're the one that was making the comparison, Senator.

While this was the defining moment of the 1988 vice-presidential debate, Bentsen expertly used the straw man fallacy. Quayle did not compare himself or his accomplishments to those of Kennedy, but merely stated that he had spent as much time in Congress as Kennedy had when the latter ran for president.

For Group or Individual Investigation

Use the Internet to investigate the following additional logical fallacies.

Appeal to Authority	Appeal to Common	Common Practice
Two Wrongs	Belief	Wishful Thinking
Appeal to Fear	Indirect Consequences	Appeal to Pity
Appeal to Prejudice	Appeal to Loyalty	Appeal to Vanity
Guilt by Association	Appeal to Spite	Hasty Generalization
	Slippery Slope	

3.5 EXERCISES

Decide whether each argument is valid *or* invalid.

1. All amusement parks have thrill rides.
   Universal Orlando is an amusement park.

   Universal Orlando has thrill rides.

2. All disc jockeys play music.
   Phlash Phelps is a disc jockey.

   Phlash Phelps plays music.

3. All politicians lie, cheat, and steal.
   That man lies, cheats, and steals.

   That man is a politician.

4. All Southerners speak with an accent.
   Bill Leonard speaks with an accent.

   Bill Leonard is a Southerner.

5. All dogs love to bury bones.
   Puddles does not love to bury bones.

   Puddles is not a dog.

6. All vice-presidents use cell phones.
   Bob DeBiasio does not use a cell phone.

   Bob DeBiasio is not a vice-president.

7. All residents of Minnesota know how to live in freezing temperatures.
   Jessica Rockswold knows how to live in freezing temperatures.

   Jessica Rockswold lives in Minnesota.

8. All people who apply for a loan must pay for a title search.
   Kurt Massey paid for a title search.

   Kurt Massey applied for a loan.

9. Some dinosaurs were plant eaters.
   Danny was a plant eater.

   Danny was a dinosaur.

10. Some philosophers are absent minded.
    Nicole Mallon is a philosopher.

    Nicole Mallon is absent minded.

11. Some nurses wear blue uniforms.
    Dee Boyle is a nurse.

    Dee Boyle wears a blue uniform.

12. Some trucks have sound systems.
    Some trucks have gun racks.

    Some trucks with sound systems have gun racks.

13. Refer to **Example 3.** If the second premise and the conclusion were interchanged, would the argument then be valid?

14. Refer to **Example 4.** Give a different conclusion than the one given there so that the argument is still valid.

Construct a valid argument based on the Euler diagram shown.

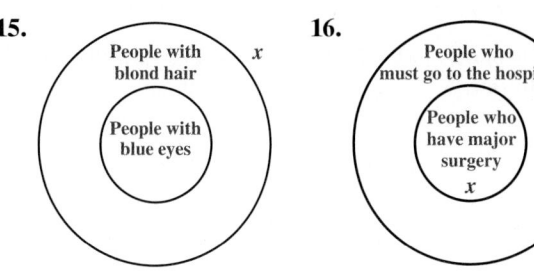

15.   *x* represents Natalie Graham

16.   *x* represents Mark Robinson

As mentioned in the text, an argument can have a true conclusion yet be invalid. In these exercises, each argument has a true conclusion. Identify each argument as valid *or* invalid.

17. All birds fly.
    All planes fly.

    A bird is not a plane.

18. All cars have tires.
    All tires are rubber.

    All cars have rubber.

19. All chickens have beaks.
    All hens are chickens.

    All hens have beaks.

20. All chickens have beaks.
    All birds have beaks.

    All chickens are birds.

21. Little Rock is northeast of Texarkana.
    Little Rock is northeast of Austin.

    Texarkana is northeast of Austin.

22. Veracruz is south of Tampico.
    Tampico is south of Monterrey.

    Veracruz is south of Monterrey.

23. No whole numbers are negative.
    −3 is negative.

    −3 is not a whole number.

24. A scalene triangle has a longest side.
    A scalene triangle has a largest angle.

    The largest angle in a scalene triangle is opposite the longest side.

In Exercises 25–30, the premises marked A, B, *and* C *are followed by several possible conclusions. Take each conclusion in turn, and check whether the resulting argument is valid or invalid.*

A. *All people who drive contribute to air pollution.*

B. *All people who contribute to air pollution make life a little worse.*

C. *Some people who live in a suburb make life a little worse.*

25. Some people who live in a suburb contribute to air pollution.

26. Some people who live in a suburb drive.

27. Suburban residents never drive.

28. Some people who contribute to air pollution live in a suburb.

29. Some people who make life a little worse live in a suburb.

30. All people who drive make life a little worse.

EXTENSION Logic Problems and Sudoku

How to Solve Logic Problems • How to Solve Sudoku

Logic problems, which are based on deductive reasoning, appear in periodicals such as *Original Logic Problems, World-Class Logic Problems,* and *England's Best Logic Problems* (all PennyPress), and *Logic Puzzles* (Dell). The following explanation on solving such problems appeared in the February 2010 issue of *Original Logic Problems.*

How to Solve Logic Problems Solving logic problems is entertaining and challenging. All the information you need to solve a logic problem is given in the introduction and clues, and in illustrations, when provided. If you've never solved a logic problem before, our sample should help you get started. Fill in the Sample Solving Chart as you follow our explanation. We use a "•" to signify "Yes" and an "X" to signify "No."

Sample Logic Problem

Five couples were married last week, each on a different weekday. From the information provided, determine the woman (one is Cathy) and man (one is Paul) who make up each couple, as well as the day on which each couple was married.

1. Anne was married on Monday, but not to Wally.
2. Stan's wedding was on Wednesday. Rob was married on Friday, but not to Ida.
3. Vern (who married Fran) was married the day after Eve.

Sample Solving Chart:	PAUL	ROB	STAN	VERN	WALLY	MONDAY	TUESDAY	WEDNESDAY	THURSDAY	FRIDAY
ANNE										
CATHY										
EVE										
FRAN										
IDA										
MONDAY										
TUESDAY										
WEDNESDAY										
THURSDAY										
FRIDAY										

1	PAUL	ROB	STAN	VERN	WALLY	MONDAY	TUESDAY	WEDNESDAY	THURSDAY	FRIDAY
ANNE		×	×		×	•	×	×	×	×
CATHY						×				
EVE						×				
FRAN						×				
IDA		×				×				×
MONDAY		×	×							
TUESDAY		×	×							
WEDNESDAY	×	×	•	×	×					
THURSDAY										
FRIDAY	×	•	×	×	×					

Explanation

Anne was married Mon. (1), so put a "•" at the intersection of Anne and Mon. Put "X"s in all the other days in Anne's row and all the other names in the Mon. column. (Whenever you establish a relationship, as we did here, be sure to place "X"s at the intersections of all relationships that become impossible as a result.) Anne wasn't married to Wally (1), so put an "X" at the intersection of Anne and Wally. Stan's wedding was Wed. (2), so put a "•" at the intersection of Stan and Wed. (Don't forget the "X"s.) Stan didn't marry Anne, who was married Mon., so put an "X" at the intersection of Anne and Stan. Rob was married Fri., but not to Ida (2), so put a "•" at the intersection of Rob and Fri., and "X"s at the intersections of Rob and Ida and Ida and Fri. Rob also didn't marry Anne, who was married Mon., so put an "X" at the intersection of Anne and Rob. Now your chart should look like **chart 1.**

Vern married Fran (3), so put a "•" at the intersection of Vern and Fran. This leaves Anne's only possible husband as Paul, so put a "•" at the intersection of Anne and Paul and Paul and Mon. Vern and Fran's wedding was the day after Eve's (3), which wasn't Mon. [Anne], so Vern's wasn't Tue. It must have been Thu. [see chart], so Eve's was Wed. (3). Put "•"s at the intersections of Vern and Thu., Fran and Thu., and Eve and Wed. Now your chart should look like **chart 2.**

2	PAUL	ROB	STAN	VERN	WALLY	MONDAY	TUESDAY	WEDNESDAY	THURSDAY	FRIDAY
ANNE	•	×	×	×	×	•	×	×	×	×
CATHY	×			×		×		×	×	
EVE	×			×		×	×	•	×	×
FRAN	×	×	×	•	×	×	×	×	•	×
IDA	×	×		×		×		×	×	×
MONDAY	•	×	×	×	×					
TUESDAY	×	×	×	×	×					
WEDNESDAY	×	×	•	×	×					
THURSDAY	×	×	×	•	×					
FRIDAY	×	•	×	×	×					

3	PAUL	ROB	STAN	VERN	WALLY	MONDAY	TUESDAY	WEDNESDAY	THURSDAY	FRIDAY
ANNE	•	×	×	×	×	•	×	×	×	×
CATHY	×	•	×	×	×	×	×	×	×	•
EVE	×	×	•	×	×	×	×	•	×	×
FRAN	×	×	×	•	×	×	×	×	•	×
IDA	×	×	×	×	•	×	•	×	×	×
MONDAY	•	×	×	×	×					
TUESDAY	×	×	×	×	×					
WEDNESDAY	×	×	•	×	×					
THURSDAY	×	×	×	•	×					
FRIDAY	×	•	×	×	×					

The chart shows that Cathy was married Fri., Ida was married Tue., and Wally was married Tue. Ida married Wally, and Cathy's wedding was Fri., so she married Rob. After this information is filled in, Eve could only have married Stan. You've completed the puzzle, and your chart should now look like **chart 3.**

In summary: Anne and Paul, Mon.; Cathy and Rob, Fri.; Eve and Stan, Wed.; Fran and Vern, Thu.; Ida and Wally, Tue.

In some problems, it may be necessary to make a logical guess based on facts you've established. When you do, always look for clues or other facts that disprove it. If you find that your guess is incorrect, eliminate it as a possibility.

How to Solve Sudoku

Sudoku is a simple game that has gained great popularity in the United States during the past few years. It is believed that the game originated as Number Place in the United States over 25 years ago, but gained in popularity only after it became a sensation in Japan, where it was renamed Sudoku, meaning "single number." (*Source: Sudoku #13*, 2005, Platinum Magazine Group.)

There is only one rule in Sudoku: **"Fill in the grid so that every row, every column, and every 3 × 3 box contains the digits 1 through 9."** This involves scanning the given digits, marking up the grid, and analyzing. Here is a sample Sudoku.

		7	3	2				
8	4		1			9		
					8	2	1	
		9		8	7			5
2	8		4		1		6	3
1			5	6		9		
5	3	8						9
	9				2		1	4
			7	5	6			

Given Form

9	1	7	3	2	8	4	5	6
8	4	2	1	5	6	3	9	7
6	5	3	7	4	9	8	2	1
3	6	9	2	8	7	1	4	5
2	8	5	4	9	1	7	6	3
1	7	4	5	6	3	9	8	2
5	3	8	6	1	4	2	7	9
7	9	6	8	3	2	5	1	4
4	2	1	9	7	5	6	3	8

Solved Form

You can find Sudoku puzzles and solving strategies online at www.sudoku.org.uk and at www.pennydellsudokusolver.com.

EXTENSION EXERCISES

Follow the guidelines to solve each logic problem, which appeared in the February 2010 issue of Original Logic Problems, *published by PennyPress.*

1. *Breath Taking* As part of a weekly tradition, Drew and four of his friends met for lunch at Aristotle's Grill. Each person enjoyed a different lunch special, but when it came time for the post-meal conversation, the five quickly realized that they were all in need of a mint or two. Luckily, each person had a container of mints on his or her person. No two friends had the same brand of mint (one is Inti-mints), and no two friends had mints with the same flavor. A few seconds later they were all ready to talk, but they agreed that next week, they'll be a little more careful about what they order for lunch! From the information provided, can you determine the meal enjoyed by each friend, as well as the brand and flavor of mint each person used afterward?

(a) The friend who had garlic shrimp ate a couple of orange-flavored mints (which weren't Fresh Air mints). The person who ordered the spanakopita isn't the one who had wintergreen-flavored TKO mints.

(b) The friend who ate French onion soup followed it with a few Liplickers mints. Nash (who didn't have the spearmint-flavored mints) didn't order garlic shrimp.

(c) Neither Nash nor Xerxes is the one who ate a tuna-salad sandwich. The friend who had a buffalo-chicken sandwich isn't the one who freshened his or her breath with spearmint-flavored mints.

(d) One friend had a couple of cinnamon-flavored Deltoids mints. The Liplickers mints were vanilla-flavored.

(e) Ilse (who ate a buffalo-chicken sandwich) didn't have wintergreen-flavored mints. Neither Uma nor Xerxes is the friend who had a couple of Fresh Air mints.

2. *Kings of Hearts* Although the exact origins of the holiday are murky, the tradition of Valentine's Day probably harkens back to the Middle Ages, when it was better known as the feast of Saint Valentine. Couples exchanged gifts on this February holiday even back then, and no one gave more expensive and elaborate valentines than the royalty of that time. One Valentine's Day, each of four kings, each whom ruled a different small kingdom, gave his queen a different valuable gift. It just goes to show that love (or at least the idea of it) stands the test of time! From the information provided, can you determine the king and queen of each kingdom, as well as the gift each king gave his wife for the feast of Saint Valentine?

(a) King Jacobus didn't give his queen a platinum crown.

(b) Neither the jeweled scepter nor the platinum crown was the gift given to Queen Meyla (who was married to either King Kevrick or King Vermond).

(c) Queen Dejah (who was married to either King Fedris or King Jacobus) wasn't the ruler of Undervale.

(d) King Kevrick wasn't the ruler of the Dalelands.

(e) Neither the platinum crown nor the set of velvet robes was the gift given by King Vermond.

(f) The queen of Undervale (who was married to either King Fedris or King Jacobus) was given a golden throne by her husband.

(g) Queen Tilnara wasn't given a jeweled scepter by her husband. Queen Aasta ruled Hightop.

		QUEEN				KINGDOM				GIFT			
		AASTA	DEJAH	MEYLA	TILNARA	DALELANDS	HIGHTOP	SHADOW COAST	UNDERVALE	GOLDEN THRONE	JEWELED SCEPTER	PLATINUM CROWN	VELVET ROBES
KING	FEDRIS												
	JACOBUS												
	KEVRICK												
	VERMOND												
GIFT	GOLDEN THRONE												
	JEWELED SCEPTER												
	PLATINUM CROWN												
	VELVET ROBES												
KINGDOM	DALELANDS												
	HIGHTOP												
	SHADOW COAST												
	UNDERVALE												

3. New Year's Revelations Lucy and four of her friends met at the Golden Panda for dinner one evening in January. Much to their surprise, they had wandered in to the restaurant during a celebration of the Chinese New Year. Luckily for the five, this meant a discount on their meals and a free session with the mysterious medium Madame Wau Pei. The five friends had their fortunes told, one at a time. Each person told the mystic the date and year of his or her birth and learned that, according to Chinese astrology, each friend's birth year is designated by a different animal. Also, each of the five was told that he or she has a different lucky element. Before leaving the restaurant, the five friends compared their predictions, noticing that all of them had a long journey in their future—the trip back home! From the information provided, determine the order in which the five friends had their fortunes told, the year in which each person was born, and each person's lucky element.

(a) Toni was the third person to get her fortune told. The person whose lucky element is wood was the last person to see the fortune-teller.

(b) Earl (whose lucky element is fire) had his fortune told immediately before the person who was born in the Year of the Rooster. The fourth person to visit the fortune-teller was born in the Year of the Dragon.

(c) The person born in the Year of the Ox had his or her fortune told at some point before the one whose lucky element is metal. Ivana was born in the Year of the Horse.

(d) The person whose lucky element is water (who was born in the Year of the Cow) wasn't the first person to have his or her fortune told.

(e) The person whose lucky element is earth had his or her fortune told exactly two after Philip.

		FRIEND					YEAR				ELEMENT				
		EARL	IVANA	LUCY	PHILIP	TONI	COW	DRAGON	HORSE	OX	ROOSTER	EARTH	FIRE	METAL	WATER	WOOD
ORDER	FIRST															
	SECOND															
	THIRD															
	FOURTH															
	FIFTH															
ELEMENT	EARTH															
	FIRE															
	METAL															
	WATER															
	WOOD															
YEAR	COW															
	DRAGON															
	HORSE															
	OX															
	ROOSTER															

4. Barn Again For as long as I can remember, I've dreamed of owning my own bed-and-breakfast, and it looks like my dream is about to come true! We'd like our inn to be distinctive, so my husband and I have decided to purchase a barn and convert it into unique living quarters. We viewed five barns recently, each of which had once served a different purpose. My husband and I visited each barn with a different contractor, each of whom gave us a different estimate ($50,000, $60,000, $70,000, $80,000, or $100,000) for the conversion. Each barn has a different feature that makes it appealing (one has a functioning hoist), but we still haven't decided which one to buy—we're starting to go a little haywire! From the information provided, determine the contractor who visited each barn with us and the special feature of each structure, as well as the estimate given for the renovation of each barn.

(a) The apple barn (which has distinctive octagonal windows) will cost exactly $20,000 less to convert than the barn we visited with a Bill's Building representative. The estimate for renovating the hay barn is higher than the estimate for converting the potato barn.

(b) The barn we visited with the person from AB Contracting (which isn't the barn that has fabulous heavy beams) will cost more to renovate than the barn we viewed with the contractor from Pine Valley but exactly $10,000 less to convert than the horse barn.

(c) The estimates for converting the apple barn and the barn with lovely board-and-batten siding are the lowest and highest estimates, in some order.

(d) The barn we visited with the contractor from Dekker Ltd. will cost exactly $20,000 more to renovate than the barn with insulation worth preserving.

(e) The old dairy barn will cost more to renovate than the one we visited with the representative from Vander Estates.

		BARN					FEATURE					ESTIMATE				
		APPLE	DAIRY	HAY	HORSE	POTATO	BEAMS	HOIST	INSULATION	SIDING	WINDOWS	$50,000	$60,000	$70,000	$80,000	$100,000
CONTRACTOR	AB CONTRACTING															
	BILL'S BUILDING															
	DEKKER LTD.															
	PINE VALLEY															
	VANDER ESTATES															
ESTIMATE	$50,000															
	$60,000															
	$70,000															
	$80,000															
	$100,000															
FEATURE	BEAMS															
	HOIST															
	INSULATION															
	SIDING															
	WINDOWS															

Solve each Sudoku, which appeared in Dell Original Sudoku, *March 2010, Penny Publications. (They are categorized according to difficulty level.)*

5. Easy

	4		1	6	8			5
		9		5			2	8
	6		9					4
		4	7		9			
	3	8		4		2	9	
			2		3	8		
2					1		6	
9	7			2		5		
4			6	9	5		7	

6. Easy

2		3			8	1	4	
	7		6	2	4			
	8			3				7
8	4	7	2				6	
			8		6			
	1				9	4	8	2
7				6			2	
			9	5	7		1	
	6	9	3			5		4

7. Medium

8	3		6					1
	1			4			5	6
		6			8			
		7	1				3	8
		1		2		4		
5	4				6	1		
			5			7		
9	8			7			1	
6					1		2	3

8. Medium

			4	5		6		
4	5					3		9
	6	1			3			8
5	8				1		6	
		9		3		2		
	4		9				1	7
8			1			7	3	
1		5					9	2
		6		7	2			

9. Hard

	1			2				4
4		9			1		7	
		8				9		
	3		6				2	
7				3				9
	9				8		5	
		2				4		
	8		2			6		5
9				8			3	

10. Hard

	2			9		6	7	
	5	6						
			6		4			5
	6	9						1
			3	6	9			
8						9	4	
1			4		7			
						4	2	
	4	8		2			3	

3.6 ANALYZING ARGUMENTS WITH TRUTH TABLES

Truth Tables (Two Premises) • Valid and Invalid Argument Forms • Truth Tables (More Than Two Premises) • Arguments of Lewis Carroll

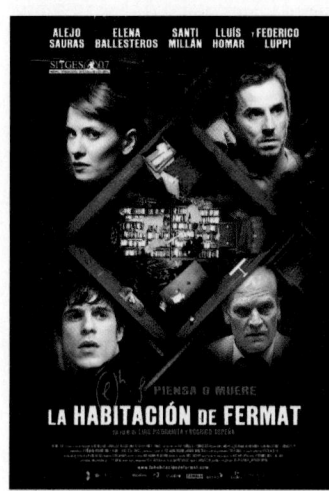

In the 2007 Spanish film *La Habitacion de Fermat (Fermat's Room)*, four mathematicians are invited to dinner, only to discover that the room in which they are meeting is designed to eventually crush them as walls creep in closer and closer. The only way for them to delay the inevitable is to answer enigmas, questions, puzzles, problems, and riddles that they are receiving on a cell phone.

One of the enigmas deals with a hermetically sealed room that contains a single light bulb. There are three switches outside the room, and only one of the switches controls the bulb. You are allowed to push any or all of the buttons as many times as you wish before you enter the room, but once you enter you cannot return to the switches outside. How can you determine which one controls the bulb? (The answer is on **page 126**.)

Truth Tables (Two Premises)

In **Section 3.5** we used Euler diagrams to test the validity of arguments. While Euler diagrams often work well for simple arguments, difficulties can develop with more complex ones, because Euler diagrams require a sketch showing every possible case. In complex arguments, it is hard to be sure that all cases have been considered.

In deciding whether to use Euler diagrams to test the validity of an argument, look for quantifiers such as "all," "some," or "no." These words often indicate arguments best tested by Euler diagrams. If these words are absent, it may be better to use truth tables to test the validity of an argument.

As an example of this method, consider the following argument:

> If the floor is dirty, then I must mop it.
> The floor is dirty.
> _____
> I must mop it.

To test the validity of this argument, we begin by identifying the *component* statements found in the argument. They are "the floor is dirty" and "I must mop it." We assign the letters p and q to represent these statements:

$$p \text{ represents "the floor is dirty";}$$
$$q \text{ represents "I must mop it."}$$

Now we write the two premises and the conclusion in symbols.

> Premise 1: $p \rightarrow q$
> Premise 2: p
> _____
> Conclusion: q

To decide if this argument is valid, we must determine whether the conjunction of both premises implies the conclusion for all possible cases of truth values for p and q. Therefore, write the conjunction of the premises as the antecedent of a conditional statement, and the conclusion as the consequent.

$$[(p \rightarrow q) \quad \wedge \quad p] \quad \rightarrow \quad q$$

premise   and   premise   implies   conclusion

Finally, construct the truth table for this conditional statement, as shown below.

p	q	$p \rightarrow q$	$(p \rightarrow q) \wedge p$	$[(p \rightarrow q) \wedge p] \rightarrow q$
T	T	T	T	T
T	F	F	F	T
F	T	T	F	T
F	F	T	F	T

Because the final column, shown in color, indicates that the conditional statement that represents the argument is true for all possible truth values of p and q, the statement is a tautology. Thus, the argument is valid.

Answer to the Light Bulb question on **page 125.**

Label the switches 1, 2, and 3. Turn switch 1 on and leave it on for several minutes. Then turn switch 1 off, turn switch 2 on, and then immediately enter the room. If the bulb is on, then you know that switch 2 controls it. If the bulb is off, touch it to see if it is still warm. If it is, then switch 1 controls it. If the bulb is not warm, then switch 3 controls it.

The pattern of the argument in the floor-mopping example

$$p \rightarrow q$$
$$\underline{p}$$
$$q$$

is called **modus ponens,** or the *law of detachment.*

To test the validity of an argument using a truth table, follow the steps in the box.

Testing the Validity of an Argument with a Truth Table

Step 1 Assign a letter to represent each component statement in the argument.

Step 2 Express each premise and the conclusion symbolically.

Step 3 Form the symbolic statement of the entire argument by writing the *conjunction* of *all* the premises as the antecedent of a conditional statement, and the conclusion of the argument as the consequent.

Step 4 Complete the truth table for the conditional statement formed in Step 3. If it is a tautology, then the argument is valid; otherwise, it is invalid.

▮▮ **EXAMPLE 1** Using a Truth Table to Determine Validity

Determine whether the argument is *valid* or *invalid*.

If my check arrives in time, I'll register for the fall semester.
I've registered for the fall semester.

My check arrived in time.

SOLUTION

Let p represent "my check arrives (arrived) in time" and let q represent "I'll register (I've registered) for the fall semester." The argument can be written as follows.

$$p \rightarrow q$$
$$\underline{q}$$
$$p$$

To test for validity, construct a truth table for the statement $[(p \rightarrow q) \wedge q] \rightarrow p$.

p	q	$p \rightarrow q$	$(p \rightarrow q) \wedge q$	$[(p \rightarrow q) \wedge q] \rightarrow p$
T	T	T	T	T
T	F	F	F	T
F	T	T	T	**F**
F	F	T	F	T

The third row of the final column of the truth table shows F, and this is enough to conclude that the argument is invalid. ▮▮▮

If a conditional and its converse were logically equivalent, then an argument of the type found in **Example 1** would be valid. Because a conditional and its converse are *not* equivalent, the argument is an example of what is sometimes called the **fallacy of the converse.**

▮▮ **EXAMPLE 2** Using a Truth Table to Determine Validity

Determine whether the argument is *valid* or *invalid*.

If a man could be in two places at one time, I'd be with you.
I am not with you.

A man can't be in two places at one time.

SOLUTION

If p represents "a man could be in two places at one time" and q represents "I'd be with you," the argument is written as follows.

$$p \to q$$
$$\underline{\sim q}$$
$$\sim p$$

The symbolic statement of the entire argument is as follows.

$$[(p \to q) \land \sim q] \to \sim p$$

The truth table for this argument indicates a tautology, and the argument is valid.

p	q	$p \to q$	$\sim q$	$(p \to q) \land \sim q$	$\sim p$	$[(p \to q) \land \sim q] \to \sim p$
T	T	T	F	F	F	T
T	F	F	T	F	F	T
F	T	T	F	F	T	T
F	F	T	T	T	T	T

The pattern of reasoning of this example is called **modus tollens,** or the *law of contraposition,* or *indirect reasoning.*   ■■■

With reasoning similar to that used to name the fallacy of the converse, the fallacy

$$p \to q$$
$$\underline{\sim p}$$
$$\sim q$$

is called the **fallacy of the inverse.** An example of such a fallacy is "If it rains, I get wet. It doesn't rain. Therefore, I don't get wet."

■ EXAMPLE 3 ▏Using a Truth Table to Determine Validity

Determine whether the argument is *valid* or *invalid.*

> I'll buy a car or I'll take a vacation.
> I won't buy a car.
> ——————————————
> I'll take a vacation.

SOLUTION

If p represents "I'll buy a car" and q represents "I'll take a vacation," the argument is symbolized as follows.

$$p \lor q$$
$$\underline{\sim p}$$
$$q$$

We must set up a truth table for the statement $[(p \lor q) \land \sim p] \to q$.

p	q	$p \lor q$	$\sim p$	$(p \lor q) \land \sim p$	$[(p \lor q) \land \sim p] \to q$
T	T	T	F	F	T
T	F	T	F	F	T
F	T	T	T	T	T
F	F	F	T	F	T

The statement is a tautology and the argument is valid. Any argument of this form is valid by the law of **disjunctive syllogism.**   ■■■

▌▌ **EXAMPLE 4** Using a Truth Table to Determine Validity

Determine whether the argument is *valid* or *invalid*.

> If it squeaks, then I use WD-40.
> If I use WD-40, then I must go to the hardware store.
> If it squeaks, then I must go to the hardware store.

SOLUTION

Let p represent "it squeaks," let q represent "I use WD-40," and let r represent "I must go to the hardware store." The argument takes on the following general form.

$$p \rightarrow q$$
$$q \rightarrow r$$
$$p \rightarrow r$$

Make a truth table for this statement, which requires eight rows.

$$[(p \rightarrow q) \wedge (q \rightarrow r)] \rightarrow (p \rightarrow r)$$

p	q	r	$p \rightarrow q$	$q \rightarrow r$	$p \rightarrow r$	$(p \rightarrow q) \wedge (q \rightarrow r)$	$[(p \rightarrow q) \wedge (q \rightarrow r)] \rightarrow (p \rightarrow r)$
T	T	T	T	T	T	T	T
T	T	F	T	F	F	F	T
T	F	T	F	T	T	F	T
T	F	F	F	T	F	F	T
F	T	T	T	T	T	T	T
F	T	F	T	F	T	F	T
F	F	T	T	T	T	T	T
F	F	F	T	T	T	T	T

This argument is valid because the final statement is a tautology. This pattern of argument is called **reasoning by transitivity,** or the *law of hypothetical syllogism.* ▌▌▌

Valid and Invalid Argument Forms

A summary of the valid and invalid forms of argument presented so far in this section follows.

In a scene near the beginning of the 1974 film *Monty Python and the Holy Grail*, an amazing application of **poor logic** leads to the apparent demise of a supposed witch. Some peasants have forced a young woman to wear a nose made of wood. The convoluted argument they make is this: Witches and wood are both burned, and because witches are made of wood, and wood floats, and ducks also float, if she weighs the same as a duck, then she is made of wood and, therefore, is a witch!

Valid Argument Forms

Modus Ponens	Modus Tollens	Disjunctive Syllogism	Reasoning by Transitivity
$p \rightarrow q$ p	$p \rightarrow q$ $\sim q$	$p \vee q$ $\sim p$	$p \rightarrow q$ $q \rightarrow r$
q	$\sim p$	q	$p \rightarrow r$

Invalid Argument Forms (Fallacies)

Fallacy of the Converse	Fallacy of the Inverse
$p \rightarrow q$ q	$p \rightarrow q$ $\sim p$
p	$\sim q$

Truth Tables (More Than Two Premises)

When an argument contains more than two premises, it is necessary to determine the truth values of the conjunction of *all* of them. ***If at least one premise in a conjunction of several premises is false, then the entire conjunction is false.***

| **EXAMPLE 5** Using a Truth Table to Determine Validity

Determine whether the argument is *valid* or *invalid*.

If Eddie goes to town, then Mabel stays at home. If Mabel does not stay at home, then Rita will cook. Rita will not cook. Therefore, Eddie does not go to town.

SOLUTION

In an argument written in this manner, the premises are given first, and the conclusion is the statement that follows the word "Therefore." Let p represent "Eddie goes to town," let q represent "Mabel stays at home," and let r represent "Rita will cook."

$$p \rightarrow q$$
$$\sim q \rightarrow r$$
$$\underline{\sim r}$$
$$\sim p$$

To test validity, set up a truth table for this statement.

$$[(p \rightarrow q) \land (\sim q \rightarrow r) \land \sim r] \rightarrow \sim p$$

p	q	r	$p \rightarrow q$	$\sim q$	$\sim q \rightarrow r$	$\sim r$	$(p \rightarrow q) \land (\sim q \rightarrow r) \land \sim r$	$\sim p$	$[(p \rightarrow q) \land (\sim q \rightarrow r) \land \sim r] \rightarrow \sim p$
T	T	T	T	F	T	F	F	F	T
T	T	F	T	F	T	T	T	F	**F**
T	F	T	F	T	T	F	F	F	T
T	F	F	F	T	F	T	F	F	T
F	T	T	T	F	T	F	F	T	T
F	T	F	T	F	T	T	T	T	T
F	F	T	T	T	T	F	F	T	T
F	F	F	T	T	F	T	F	T	T

Because the final column does not contain all Ts, the statement is not a tautology. The argument is invalid.   ■■■

Arguments of Lewis Carroll

Consider the following verse, which has been around for many years.

> *For want of a nail, the shoe was lost. For want of a shoe, the horse was lost. For want of a horse, the rider was lost. For want of a rider, the battle was lost. For want of a battle, the war was lost.*
> *Therefore, for want of a nail, the war was lost.*

Each line of the verse may be written as an *if . . . then* statement. For example, the first line may be restated as "if a nail is lost, then the shoe is lost." The conclusion, "for want of a nail, the war was lost," follows from the premises, because repeated use of the law of transitivity applies. Arguments such as the one used by Lewis Carroll in the next example often take on a similar form.

▮▮ **EXAMPLE 6** Supplying a Conclusion to Assure Validity

Supply a conclusion that yields a valid argument for the following premises.

Babies are illogical.

Nobody is despised who can manage a crocodile.

Illogical persons are despised.

SOLUTION

First, write each premise in the form *if . . . then. . . .*

If you are a baby, then you are illogical.

If you can manage a crocodile, then you are not despised.

If you are illogical, then you are despised.

Let *p* be "you are a baby," let *q* be "you are logical," let *r* be "you can manage a crocodile," and let *s* be "you are despised." The statements can be written symbolically.

$$p \rightarrow \sim q$$
$$r \rightarrow \sim s$$
$$\sim q \rightarrow s$$

Begin with any letter that appears only once. Here *p* appears only once. Using the contrapositive of $r \rightarrow \sim s$, which is $s \rightarrow \sim r$, rearrange the statements as follows.

$$p \rightarrow \sim q$$
$$\sim q \rightarrow s$$
$$s \rightarrow \sim r$$

From the three statements, repeated use of reasoning by transitivity gives the conclusion

$$p \rightarrow \sim r, \quad \text{which leads to a valid argument.}$$

In words, the conclusion is "If you are a baby, then you cannot manage a crocodile," or, as Lewis Carroll would have written it, "Babies cannot manage crocodiles." ▮▮▮

Alice in the Forest of Forgetfulness

When Alice entered the Forest of Forgetfulness, she often forgot what day of the week it was. She encountered a Lion and a Unicorn, two strange creatures. The Lion lies on Mondays, Tuesdays, and Wednesdays and tells the truth on the other days of the week. The Unicorn, on the other hand, lies on Thursdays, Fridays, and Saturdays, but tells the truth on the other days of the week.

One day Alice met the Lion and the Unicorn resting under a tree. They made the following statements:

Lion: Yesterday was one of my lying days.
Unicorn: Yesterday was one of my lying days, too.

From these two statements, Alice was able to deduce the day of the week. What day was it? (The answer is on **page 133**.)

(Adapted from a problem in Raymond Smullyan's *What Is the Name of This Book?*)

3.6 EXERCISES

Each argument is either valid by one of the forms of valid arguments discussed in this section, or it is a fallacy by one of the forms of invalid arguments discussed. (See the summary boxes.) Decide whether the argument is valid *or a* fallacy, *and give the form that applies.*

1. If James Taylor comes to town, then I will go to the concert.
If I go to the concert, then I'll call in sick for work.

If James Taylor comes to town, then I'll call in sick for work.

2. If you use binoculars, then you get a glimpse of the space shuttle.
If you get a glimpse of the space shuttle, then you'll be amazed.

If you use binoculars, then you'll be amazed.

3. If Julie Nhem works hard enough, she will get a promotion.
Julie Nhem works hard enough.

She gets a promotion.

4. If Andrew Noble sells his quota, he'll get a bonus.
Andrew Noble sells his quota.

He gets a bonus.

5. If he doesn't have to get up at 3:00 A.M., he's ecstatic.
He's ecstatic.

He doesn't have to get up at 3:00 A.M.

6. If she buys another pair of shoes, her closet will overflow.
Her closet will overflow.

She buys another pair of shoes.

7. If Mariano Rivera pitches, the Yankees win.
The Yankees do not win.

Mariano Rivera does not pitch.

8. If Nelson Dida plays, the opponent gets shut out.
The opponent does not get shut out.

Nelson Dida does not play.

9. "If we evolved a race of Isaac Newtons, that would not be progress." (quote from Aldous Huxley)
We have not evolved a race of Isaac Newtons.

That is progress.

10. "If I have seen farther than others, it is because I stood on the shoulders of giants." (quote from Sir Isaac Newton)
I have not seen farther than others.

I have not stood on the shoulders of giants.

11. She uses e-commerce or she pays by credit card.
She does not pay by credit card.

She uses e-commerce.

12. Mia kicks or Drew passes.
Drew does not pass.

Mia kicks.

Use a truth table to determine whether the argument is valid *or* invalid.

13. $p \lor q$
p

$\sim q$

14. $p \land \sim q$
p

$\sim q$

15. $\sim p \to \sim q$
q

p

16. $p \lor \sim q$
p

$\sim q$

17. $p \to q$
$q \to p$

$p \land q$

18. $\sim p \to q$
p

$\sim q$

19. $p \to \sim q$
q

$\sim p$

20. $p \to \sim q$
$\sim p$

$\sim q$

21. $(p \land q) \lor (p \lor q)$
q

p

22. $(p \to q) \land (q \to p)$
p

$p \lor q$

23. $(\sim p \lor q) \land (\sim p \to q)$
p

$\sim q$

24. $(r \land p) \to (r \lor q)$
$q \land p$

$r \lor p$

25. $(\sim p \land r) \to (p \lor q)$
$\sim r \to p$

$q \to r$

26. $(p \to \sim q) \lor (q \to \sim r)$
$p \lor \sim r$

$r \to p$

27. Earlier we showed how to analyze arguments using Euler diagrams. Refer to **Example 4** in this section, restate each premise and the conclusion using a quantifier, and then draw an Euler diagram to illustrate the relationship.

28. Explain in a few sentences how to determine the statement for which a truth table will be constructed so that the arguments that follow in **Exercises 29–38** can be analyzed for validity.

Determine whether each argument is valid *or* invalid.

29. Joey loves to watch movies. If Terry likes to jog, then Joey does not love to watch movies. If Terry does not like to jog, then Carrie drives a school bus. Therefore, Carrie drives a school bus.

30. If Hurricane Gustave hit that grove of trees, then the trees are devastated. People plant trees when disasters strike and the trees are not devastated. Therefore, if people plant trees when disasters strike, then Hurricane Gustave did not hit that grove of trees.

31. If the social networking craze continues, then downloading music will remain popular. American Girl dolls are favorites or downloading music will remain popular. American Girl dolls are not favorites. Therefore, the social networking craze does not continue.

32. Carrie Underwood sings or Joe Jonas is not a teen idol. If Joe Jonas is not a teen idol, then Jennifer Hudson does not win a Grammy. Jennifer Hudson wins a Grammy. Therefore, Carrie Underwood does not sing.

33. The Dolphins will be in the playoffs if and only if Chad leads the league in passing. Tony coaches the Dolphins or Chad leads the league in passing. Tony does not coach the Dolphins. Therefore, the Dolphins will not be in the playoffs.

34. If I've got you under my skin, then you are deep in the heart of me. If you are deep in the heart of me, then you are not really a part of me. You are deep in the heart of me or you are really a part of me. Therefore, if I've got you under my skin, then you are really a part of me.

35. If Dr. Hardy is a department chairman, then he lives in Atlanta. He lives in Atlanta and his first name is Larry. Therefore, if his first name is not Larry, then he is not a department chairman.

36. If I were your woman and you were my man, then I'd never stop loving you. I've stopped loving you. Therefore, I am not your woman or you are not my man.

37. All men are created equal. All people who are created equal are women. Therefore, all men are women.

38. All men are mortal. Socrates is a man. Therefore, Socrates is mortal.

39. Suppose that you ask a stranger for the time and you get the following response:

> "If I tell you the time, then we'll start chatting. If we start chatting, then you'll want to meet me at a truck stop. If we meet at a truck stop, then we'll discuss my family. If we discuss my family, then you'll find out that my daughter is available for marriage. If you find out that she is available for marriage, then you'll want to marry her. If you want to marry her, then my life will be miserable since I don't want my daughter married to some fool who can't afford a $10 watch."

Use reasoning by transitivity to draw a valid conclusion.

40. Molly Riggs made the following observation: "If I want to determine whether an argument leading to the statement

$$[(p \rightarrow q) \land {\sim}q] \rightarrow {\sim}p$$

is valid, I only need to consider the lines of the truth table which lead to T for the column headed $(p \rightarrow q) \land {\sim}q$." Molly was very perceptive. Can you explain why her observation was correct?

In the arguments used by Lewis Carroll, it is helpful to restate a premise in if . . . then form in order to more easily identify a valid conclusion. The following premises come from Lewis Carroll. Write each premise in if . . . then form.

41. All my poultry are ducks.

42. None of your sons can do logic.

43. Guinea pigs are hopelessly ignorant of music.

44. No teetotalers are pawnbrokers.

45. No teachable kitten has green eyes.

46. Opium-eaters have no self-command.

47. I have not filed any of them that I can read.

48. All of them written on blue paper are filed.

Exercises 49–54 involve premises from Lewis Carroll. Write each premise in symbols, and then in the final part, give a conclusion that yields a valid argument.

49. Let p be "it is a duck," q be "it is my poultry," r be "one is an officer," and s be "one is willing to waltz."

  (a) No ducks are willing to waltz.

  (b) No officers ever decline to waltz.

  (c) All my poultry are ducks.

  (d) Give a conclusion that yields a valid argument.

50. Let p be "one is able to do logic," q be "one is fit to serve on a jury," r be "one is sane," and s be "he is your son."

  (a) Everyone who is sane can do logic.

  (b) No lunatics are fit to serve on a jury.

  (c) None of your sons can do logic.

  (d) Give a conclusion that yields a valid argument.

51. Let p be "one is honest," q be "one is a pawnbroker," r be "one is a promise-breaker," s be "one is trustworthy," t be "one is very communicative," and u be "one is a wine-drinker."

  (a) Promise-breakers are untrustworthy.

  (b) Wine-drinkers are very communicative.

  (c) A person who keeps a promise is honest.

  (d) No teetotalers are pawnbrokers. (*Hint:* Assume "teetotaler" is the opposite of "wine-drinker.")

  (e) One can always trust a very communicative person.

  (f) Give a conclusion that yields a valid argument.

52. Let p be "it is a guinea pig," q be "it is hopelessly ignorant of music," r be "it keeps silent while the *Moonlight Sonata* is being played," and s be "it appreciates Beethoven."

  (a) Nobody who really appreciates Beethoven fails to keep silent while the *Moonlight Sonata* is being played.

  (b) Guinea pigs are hopelessly ignorant of music.

  (c) No one who is hopelessly ignorant of music ever keeps silent while the *Moonlight Sonata* is being played.

  (d) Give a conclusion that yields a valid argument.

53. Let *p* be "it begins with 'Dear Sir'," *q* be "it is crossed," *r* be "it is dated," *s* be "it is filed," *t* be "it is in black ink," *u* be "it is in the third person," *v* be "I can read it," *w* be "it is on blue paper," *x* be "it is on one sheet," and *y* be "it is written by Brown."

(a) All the dated letters are written on blue paper.

(b) None of them are in black ink, except those that are written in the third person.

(c) I have not filed any of them that I can read.

(d) None of them that are written on one sheet are undated.

(e) All of them that are not crossed are in black ink.

(f) All of them written by Brown begin with "Dear Sir."

(g) All of them written on blue paper are filed.

(h) None of them written on more than one sheet are crossed.

(i) None of them that begin with "Dear Sir" are written in the third person.

(j) Give a conclusion that yields a valid argument.

54. Let *p* be "he is going to a party," *q* be "he brushes his hair," *r* be "he has self-command," *s* be "he looks fascinating," *t* be "he is an opium-eater," *u* be "he is tidy," and *v* be "he wears white kid gloves."

(a) No one who is going to a party ever fails to brush his hair.

(b) No one looks fascinating if he is untidy.

(c) Opium-eaters have no self-command.

(d) Everyone who has brushed his hair looks fascinating.

(e) No one wears white kid gloves unless he is going to a party. (*Hint:* "*a* unless *b*" ≡ ∼*b* → *a*.)

(f) A man is always untidy if he has no self-command.

(g) Give a conclusion that yields a valid argument.

Answer to Alice in the Forest of Forgetfulness problem on **page 130:**

The only days the Lion can say, "I lied yesterday" are Mondays and Thursdays. The only days the Unicorn can say "I lied yesterday" are Thursdays and Sundays. Therefore the only day they can both say that is Thursday.

COLLABORATIVE INVESTIGATION

Logic Problems and Sudoku Revisited

Logic problems and Sudoku were first discussed in the **Extension** on **pages 120–124.** The problems here require more time and reasoning skills than the ones appearing in the **Extension.** They are taken from *Original Logic Problems*, February 2010, and *Dell Original Sudoku*, March 2010.

The class may wish to divide up into groups and see which group can solve these problems fastest.

EXERCISES

Note: As an exception to our usual style, answers to these Collaborative Investigation Exercises are given in the back of the book.

1. **Out to Launch**   The National Space Association has scheduled five rockets for launch early next year. Each rocket (including the *Penchant*) will take off in a different month (January through May) on a different date (the 1st through the 5th). Each rocket will launch from a different site (including the San Simeon Launch Center) and engage in a different mission. For fans of the space program, next year will be a real blast! From the information provided, determine the month and date of the launch of the rocket from each launch site, as well as each rocket's mission.

(a) The date of the May launch is numbered exactly two lower than the date of the Willard Island launch. None of the rockets will launch on February 1. The mission to test a new propulsion system won't be launching in January.

(b) The *Liberty* and the rocket that will blast off in April will launch from Cape Carnival and Willard Island in some order. Neither the rocket on a mission to measure magnetic fields (which won't launch on the 1st of a month) nor the Willard Island rocket will blast off on the 3rd of a month.

(c) The *Bravura* will launch the month after the rocket that will blast off on the 4th of a month (which will launch later than the rocket that will land on the moon). The *Liberty* won't blast off on the 2nd of a month.

(d) The rocket that will launch from Cape Carnival won't be testing a new propulsion system. The *Twilight*'s mission (which isn't the mission to repair a satellite) won't begin on the 5th of a month.

(e) The rocket on a mission to investigate strange radiation will launch at some point earlier in the year than the *Liberty* (which won't be repairing a satellite) but at some point later in the year than the vessel that will blast off from the Vandyke Facility.

(f) The rocket that will blast off from Eddings Air Force Base will launch on a lower-numbered date than the one that will launch in March (which won't be testing a new propulsion system), which will blast off on a lower-numbered date than the *Falconer*.

2. ***Super Challenger Puzzle*** To solve the following Super Challenger puzzle, place a number into every box so that each row across, each column down, each small 16-box square (there are 16 of these), and each of the two diagonals contains each number from 1 to 16. No number may appear more than once in any one row or column, in either diagonal, or within any small 16-box square.

CHAPTER 3 TEST

Write a negation for each statement.

1. $6 - 3 = 3$

2. All men are created equal.

3. Some members of the class went on the field trip.

4. If that's the way you feel, then I will accept it.

5. She applied and got a student loan.

Let p represent "You will love me" and let q represent "I will love you." Write each statement in symbols.

6. If you won't love me, then I will love you.

7. I will love you if you will love me.

8. I won't love you if and only if you won't love me.

Using the same statements as for Exercises 6–8, write each of the following in words.

9. $\sim p \wedge q$

10. $\sim(p \vee \sim q)$

In each of the following, assume that p is true and that q and r are false. Find the truth value of each statement.

11. $\sim q \wedge \sim r$

12. $r \vee (p \wedge \sim q)$

13. $r \rightarrow (s \vee r)$ (The truth value of the statement *s* is unknown.)

14. $p \leftrightarrow (p \rightarrow q)$

15. Explain in your own words why, if *p* is a statement, the biconditional $p \leftrightarrow \sim p$ must be false.

16. State the necessary conditions for each of the following.
   (a) a conditional statement to be false
   (b) a conjunction to be true
   (c) a disjunction to be false

Construct a truth table for each of the following.

17. $p \wedge (\sim p \vee q)$

18. $\sim(p \wedge q) \rightarrow (\sim p \vee \sim q)$

Decide whether each statement is true *or* false.

19. Some negative integers are whole numbers.

20. All irrational numbers are real numbers.

Write each conditional statement in if . . . then *form.*

21. All integers are rational numbers.

22. Being a rhombus is sufficient for a polygon to be a quadrilateral.

23. Being divisible by 2 is necessary for a number to be divisible by 4.

24. She digs dinosaur bones only if she is a paleontologist.

For each statement, write (**a**) *the converse,* (**b**) *the inverse, and* (**c**) *the contrapositive.*

25. If a picture paints a thousand words, the graph will help me understand it.

26. $\sim p \rightarrow (q \wedge r)$ (Use one of De Morgan's laws as necessary.)

27. Use an Euler diagram to determine whether the argument is *valid* or *invalid*.

All members of that athletic club save money.
Don O'Neal is a member of that athletic club.

Don O'Neal saves money.

28. Match each argument in parts (a)–(d) in the next column with the law that justifies its validity, or the fallacy of which it is an example, in choices A–F.

A. Modus ponens
B. Modus tollens
C. Reasoning by transitivity
D. Disjunctive syllogism
E. Fallacy of the converse
F. Fallacy of the inverse

(a) If he eats liver, then he'll eat anything.
He eats liver.

He'll eat anything.

(b) If you use your seat belt, you will be safer.
You don't use your seat belt.

You won't be safer.

(c) If I hear *Mr. Bojangles*, I think of her.
If I think of her, I smile.

If I hear *Mr. Bojangles*, I smile.

(d) She sings or she dances.
She does not sing.

She dances.

Use a truth table to determine whether each argument is valid *or* invalid.

29. If I write a check, it will bounce. If the bank guarantees it, then it does not bounce. The bank guarantees it. Therefore, I don't write a check.

30. $\sim p \rightarrow \sim q$
$\dfrac{q \rightarrow p}{p \vee q}$

NUMERATION SYSTEMS

Bud Abbott and Lou Costello were probably the best-known comedy team in the United States during the 1940s and 1950s.

In their 1941 film *In the Navy*, Seaman Pomeroy Watson (Costello) tries to convince Smokey Adams (Abbott) that he can feed seven sailors with a tray of twenty-eight doughnuts so that the sailors will each get thirteen doughnuts. In an amazing misuse of place value and arithmetic algorithms, he shows how 7 divided into 28 is 13. He then multiplies 13 by 7 to get 28, and finally adds 13 seven times to get 28. It is a routine that must be seen to be believed.

While Costello's methods were done for laughs, there are algorithms that are unfamiliar to most students that do indeed yield correct answers. Some of them will be discussed in this chapter.

4.1 HISTORICAL NUMERATION SYSTEMS

Basics of Numeration • Ancient Egyptian Numeration • Ancient Roman Numeration • Classical Chinese Numeration

Symbols designed to represent objects or ideas are among the oldest inventions of humans. These Indian symbols in Arizona are several hundred years old.

Basics of Numeration

The various ways of symbolizing and working with the counting numbers are called **numeration systems.** The symbols representing the numbers are called **numerals.**

Numeration systems have developed over many millennia of human history. Ancient documents provide insight into methods used by the early Sumerian peoples, the Egyptians, the Babylonians, the Greeks, the Romans, the Chinese, the Hindus, and the Mayan people, as well as others.

Keeping accounts by matching may have developed as humans established permanent settlements and began to grow crops and raise livestock. People might have kept track of the number of sheep in a flock by matching pebbles with the sheep, for example. The pebbles could then be kept as a record of the number of sheep.

A more efficient method is to keep a **tally stick.** With a tally stick, one notch or **tally** is made on a stick for each sheep. Tally marks provide a crude and inefficient numeration system. For example, the numeral for the number thirteen might be

|||||||||||||, ← 13 tally marks

which requires the recording of 13 symbols, and later interpretation requires careful counting of symbols.

Even today, tally marks are used, especially when keeping track of things that occur one or a few at a time, over space or time. To facilitate the counting of the tally, we often use a sort of "grouping" technique as we go.

卌 卌 ||| ← Numeral (tally) for 13

A long evolution of numeration systems throughout recorded history would take us from tally marks to our own modern system, the **Hindu-Arabic system,** which utilizes the set of symbols

$$\{1, 2, 3, 4, 5, 6, 7, 8, 9, 0\}.$$

That system is discussed in some detail in **Sections 4.2–4.4.**

Ancient Egyptian Numeration

Tally sticks like this one were used by the English in about 1400 A.D. to keep track of financial transactions. Each notch stands for one pound sterling.

An essential feature of all more advanced numeration systems is **grouping,** which allows for less repetition of symbols and makes numerals easier to interpret. Most historical systems, including our own, have used groups of ten, indicating that people commonly learn to count by using their fingers. The size of the groupings (again, usually ten) is called the **base** of the number system.

The ancient Egyptian system is an example of a **simple grouping system.** It utilized ten as its base, and its various symbols are shown in **Table 1** on the next page. The symbol for 1 (|) is repeated, in a tally scheme, for 2, 3, and so on up to 9. A new symbol is introduced for 10 (∩), and that symbol is repeated for 20, 30, and so on, up to 90. This pattern enabled the Egyptians to express numbers up to 9,999,999 with just the seven symbols shown in the table.

The numbers denoted by the seven Egyptian symbols are all *powers* of the base ten.

$$10^0 = 1, \quad 10^1 = 10, \quad 10^2 = 100, \quad 10^3 = 1000, \quad 10^4 = 10{,}000,$$
$$10^5 = 100{,}000, \quad 10^6 = 1{,}000{,}000$$

These expressions, called *exponential expressions,* were first defined in **Section 1.1.** In the expression 10^4, for example, 10 is the *base* and 4 is the *exponent.* Recall that the exponent indicates the number of repeated factors of the base to be multiplied.

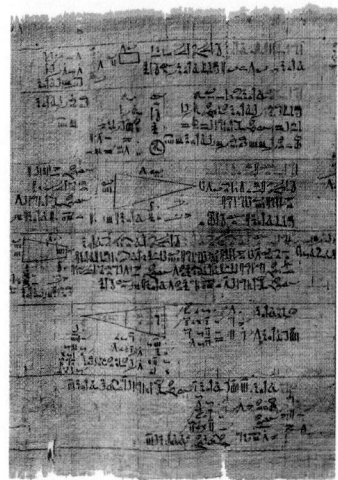

Much of our knowledge of **Egyptian mathematics** comes from the **Rhind papyrus,** from about 3800 years ago. A small portion of this papyrus, showing methods for finding the area of a triangle, is reproduced here.

Table 1	Early Egyptian Symbols	
Number	**Symbol**	**Description**
1	|	Stroke
10	∩	Heel bone
100	𝟡	Scroll
1000	𝄇	Lotus flower
10,000	⌠	Pointing finger
100,000	☟	Burbot fish
1,000,000	𝕏	Astonished person

▮▮ **EXAMPLE 1** Interpreting an Egyptian Numeral

Write the number below in Hindu-Arabic form.

☟☟ 𝄇𝄇𝄇𝄇𝄇 𝟡𝟡𝟡𝟡 ∩∩∩∩∩|||
                              ∩∩∩∩||||

SOLUTION

Refer to **Table 1** for the values of the Egyptian symbols. Each ☟ represents 100,000. Therefore, two ☟s represent 2 · 100,000, or 200,000. Proceed as shown.

two	☟	2 · 100,000 = 200,000
five	𝄇	5 · 1000 = 5000
four	𝟡	4 · 100 = 400
nine	∩	9 · 10 = 90
seven	|	7 · 1 = 7

205,497 ← Answer   ▮▮▮

▮▮ **EXAMPLE 2** Creating an Egyptian Numeral

Write 376,248 in Egyptian form.

SOLUTION

3   7   6,   2   4   8
↓   ↓   ↓   ↓   ↓   ↓

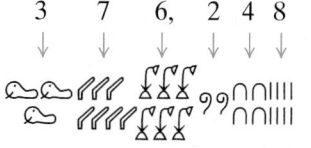

Refer to **Table 1** as needed.   ▮▮▮

An Egyptian tomb painting shows scribes tallying the count of a grain harvest. **Egyptian mathematics** was oriented more to practicality than was Greek or Babylonian mathematics, although the Egyptians did have a formula for finding the volume of a certain portion of a pyramid.

The position or order of the symbols makes no difference in a simple grouping system. Each of the numerals 𝟡𝟡∩∩∩||||, ||||∩∩∩𝟡𝟡, and ||∩∩𝟡𝟡∩|| would be interpreted as 234. In **Examples 1 and 2,** like symbols are grouped together and groups of greater-valued symbols are positioned to the left.

A simple grouping system is well suited to addition and subtraction.

       𝄇𝄇   𝟡𝟡   ∩∩∩ ||
    + 𝄇   𝟡𝟡𝟡   ∩ |||||

We use a + sign for convenience and draw a line under the numbers being added, although the Egyptians did not do this.

Sum: 𝄇𝄇𝄇 𝟡𝟡𝟡 ∩∩ ||||
              𝟡𝟡   ∩∩ ||||

Two |s plus six |s is equal to eight |s, and so on.

Sometimes regrouping, or "carrying," is needed.

Archaeological investigation has provided much of what we know about the numeration systems of ancient peoples.

Subtraction is done in much the same way, as shown in the next example.

EXAMPLE 3 Subtracting Egyptian Numerals

Work each subtraction problem.

(a)
999 ∩∩ IIII
99 ∩∩ III
−999 ∩ IIII

(b)
99∩∩∩∩ II
−9 ∩∩ IIII

SOLUTION

(a)

999 ∩∩ IIII
99 ∩∩ III
−999 ∩ IIII
Difference: 99 ∩∩∩ III

As with addition, work from right to left and subtract.

(b) To subtract four Is from two Is, "borrow" one heel bone, which is equivalent to ten Is. Finish the problem after writing ten additional Is on the right.

Regrouped: 99 ∩∩∩ IIIIIII / IIIIII   one ∩ = ten Is

− 9 ∩∩ IIII
Difference: 9 ∩ IIIIIIII

▮▮▮

A procedure such as those described above is called an **algorithm:** a rule or method for working a problem. The Egyptians used an interesting algorithm for multiplication that requires only an ability to add and to double numbers, as shown in **Example 4.** For convenience, this example uses our symbols rather than theirs.

EXAMPLE 4 Using the Egyptian Multiplication Algorithm

A rectangular room in an archaeological excavation measures 19 cubits by 70 cubits. (A cubit, based on the length of the forearm, from the elbow to the tip of the middle finger, was approximately 18 inches.) Find the area of the room.

SOLUTION

Multiply the width and length to find the area of a rectangle. Build two columns of numbers as shown at the top of the next page. Start the first column with 1, the second with 70. Each column is built downward by doubling the number above. Keep going until the first column contains numbers that can be added to equal 19. Then add the corresponding numbers from the second column.

$$\begin{array}{cc} \rightarrow & 1 & 70 & \leftarrow \\ \rightarrow & 2 & 140 & \leftarrow \\ & 4 & 280 \\ & 8 & 560 \\ \rightarrow & 16 & 1120 & \leftarrow \end{array}$$

$1 + 2 + 16 = 19$ $70 + 140 + 1120 = \mathbf{1330}$

Thus $19 \cdot 70 = \mathbf{1330}$, and the area of the given room is 1330 square cubits. ■■■

Ancient Roman Numeration

Roman numerals are still used today, mainly for decorative purposes, on clock faces, for heading numbers in outlines, chapter numbers in books, copyright dates of movies, and so on. The base is again 10, with distinct symbols for 1, 10, 100, and 1000. The Romans, however, deviated from pure simple grouping in several ways. For the symbols and some examples, see **Tables 2 and 3**, respectively.

Table 2 Roman Symbols

Number	Symbol
1	I
5	V
10	X
50	L
100	C
500	D
1000	M

Table 3 Selected Roman Numerals

Number	Numeral
6	VI
12	XII
19	XIX
30	XXX
49	XLIX
85	LXXXV
25,040	$\overline{\text{XXV}}$ XL
35,000	$\overline{\text{XXXV}}$
5,105,004	$\overline{\overline{\text{V}}}\,\overline{\text{CV}}\,\text{IV}$
7,000,000	$\overline{\overline{\text{VII}}}$

Special Features of the Roman System

1. In addition to symbols for 1, 10, 100, and 1000, "extra" symbols denote 5, 50, and 500. This allows less symbol repetition within a numeral. It is like a secondary base 5 grouping functioning within the base 10 simple grouping.

2. A *subtractive feature* was introduced, whereby a smaller-valued symbol, placed immediately to the left of one of larger value, meant to subtract. Thus IV = 4, while VI = 6. Only certain combinations were used in this way:
   (a) I preceded only V or X.
   (b) X preceded only L or C.
   (c) C preceded only D or M.

3. A *multiplicative feature,* rather than more symbols, allowed for larger numbers:
   (a) A bar over a numeral meant to multiply by 1000.
   (b) A double bar meant to multiply by 1000^2, that is, by 1,000,000.

Adding and subtracting with Roman numerals is very similar to the Egyptian method, except that the subtractive feature of the Roman system sometimes makes the processes more involved. With Roman numerals we cannot add IV and VII to get the sum VVIII by simply combining like symbols. (Even XIII would be incorrect.) The safest method is to rewrite IV as IIII, then add IIII and VII, getting VIIIII. We convert this to VVI, and then to XI by regrouping. Subtraction, which is similar, is shown in the following example.

EXAMPLE 5　Subtracting Roman Numerals

Thomas DiGiano, a Roman official, has 26 servants. If, on a given Saturday, he has excused 14 of them to attend a Lucky Lyres concert at the Forum, how many are still at home to serve the banquet?

SOLUTION

To find the answer, we subtract XIV from XXVI. Set up the problem in terms of simple grouping numerals (that is, XIV is rewritten as XIIII):

Problem:　XXVI　Problem restated without　　XXVI
　　　　　− XIV　subtractive notation:　　　− XIIII

Regrouped:　XXIIIIII
　　　　　− XIIII
　　　　　　XII　← Answer

Since four **I**s cannot be subtracted from one **I**, we have "borrowed" in the top numeral, writing XXVI as XXIIIIII. The subtraction can then be carried out. Thomas has 12 servants home for the banquet. ■■■

Computation, in early forms, was often aided by mechanical devices just as it is today. The Roman merchants, in particular, did their figuring on a counting board, or **counter,** on which lines or grooves represented 1s, 10s, 100s, etc., and on which the spaces between the lines represented 5s, 50s, 500s, and so on. Discs or beads (called *calculi,* the word for "pebbles") were positioned on the board to denote numbers, and *calculations* were carried out by moving the discs around and simplifying.

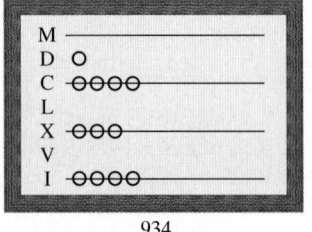

934

Figure 1

EXAMPLE 6　Adding on a Roman Counting Board

A Roman merchant wants to calculate the sum 934 + 286. Use counting boards to carry out the following steps.

(a) Represent the first number, 934.

(b) Represent the second number, 286, beside the first.

(c) Represent the sum, in simplified form.

SOLUTION

(a) See **Figure 1.**　　**(b)** See **Figure 2.**

(c) See **Figure 3.** The simplified answer is MCCXX, or 1220. In the process of simplification, five discs on the bottom line were replaced by a single disc in the V space. This made two Vs that were replaced by an additional disc on the X line. Five of those on the X line were then replaced by one in the L space, and this process continued until the disc on the M line finally appeared. ■■■

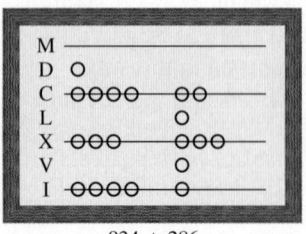

934 + 286

Figure 2

Classical Chinese Numeration

The preceding examples show that simple grouping, although an improvement over tallying, still requires considerable repetition of symbols. To denote 90, for example, the ancient Egyptian system must utilize nine ∩s: ∩∩∩∩∩∩∩∩∩. If an additional symbol (a "multiplier") was introduced to represent nine, say "9," then 90 could be denoted 9 ∩. All possible numbers of repetitions of powers of the base could be handled by introducing a separate multiplier symbol for each counting number less than the base.

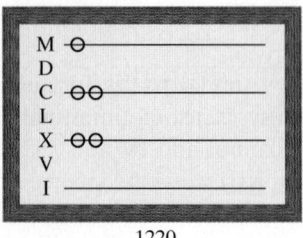

1220

Figure 3

Table 4 Chinese Symbols

Number	Symbol
1	一
2	二
3	三
4	四
5	五
6	六
7	七
8	八
9	九
10	十
100	百
1000	千
0	零

Just such a system was developed many years ago in China. We show the predominant Chinese version, which used the symbols shown in **Table 4**. We call this type of system a **multiplicative grouping system.** In general, a numeral in such a system would contain pairs of symbols, each pair containing a multiplier (with some counting number value less than the base) and then a power of the base. The Chinese numerals are read from top to bottom rather than from left to right.

If the Chinese system were *pure* multiplicative grouping, the number 2014 would be denoted as shown in **Figure 4**. But three special features of the system show that they had started to move beyond multiplicative grouping toward something more efficient.

二 2
·
千 1000
+
零 0
·
百 100
+
一 1
·
十 10
+
四 4
·
一 1

2014 in pure multiplicative grouping

Figure 4

Special Features of the Chinese System

1. A single symbol, rather than a pair, denotes the number of 1s. The multiplier (1, 2, 3, 4, . . . , or 9) is written, but the power of the base (10^0) is omitted. See **Figure 5** (and also **Examples 7(a), (b), and (c)**).
2. In the 10s pair, if the multiplier is 1 it is omitted. See **Figure 6** (and **Example 8(a)**).
3. When a particular power of the base is totally missing, the omission is denoted with the zero symbol. See **Figure 7** (and **Examples 7(b) and 8(b)**). If two or more consecutive powers are missing, just one zero symbol denotes the total omission. (See **Example 7(c)**.) The omission of 1s and 10s and any other powers occurring at the extreme bottom of a numeral need not be denoted at all. (See **Example 7(d)**.)

二 2
·
千 1000
+
零 0
·
百 100
+
一 1
·
十 10
+
四 4

2014 with feature 1

Figure 5

二 2
·
千 1000
+
零 0
·
百 100
+
十 10
+
四 4

2014 with features 1 and 2

Figure 6

二 2
·
千 1000
+
零 0
+
十 10
+
四 4

2014 with features 1, 2, and 3

Figure 7

Note that, for clarification in the following examples, we have emphasized the grouping into pairs by spacing and by colored braces. These features were *not* part of the actual numerals in practice.

EXAMPLE 7 Interpreting Chinese Numerals

Interpret each Chinese numeral.

(a) 三
千
一
百
六
十
四

(b) 七
百
零
三

(c) 五
千
零
九

(d) 四
千
二
百

SOLUTION

(a)
三 千 } $3 \cdot 1000 = 3000$
一 百 } $1 \cdot 100 = 100$
六 十 } $6 \cdot 10 = 60$
四 $4(\cdot 1) = 4$
Total: 3164

(b)
七 百 } $7 \cdot 100 = 700$
零 $0(\cdot 10) = 00$
三 $3(\cdot 1) = 3$
Total: 703

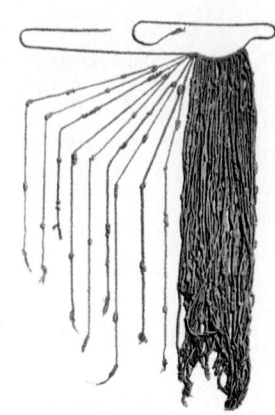

This illustration is of a **quipu.** In *Ethnomathematics: A Multicultural View of Mathematical Ideas,* Marcia Ascher writes:

A quipu is an assemblage of colored knotted cotton cords. Cotton cordage and cloth were of unparalleled importance in Inca culture. The colors of the cords, the way the cords are connected, the relative placement of the cords, the spaces between the cords, the types of knots on the individual cords, and the relative placement of the knots are all part of the logical-numerical recording.

(c) $5 \cdot 1000 = 5000$

$0(\cdot 100) = 000$

$0(\cdot 10) = 00$

$9(\cdot 1) = 9$

Total: 5009

(d) $4 \cdot 1000 = 4000$

$2 \cdot 100 = 200$

Total: 4200

EXAMPLE 8 Creating Chinese Numerals

Write a Chinese numeral for each number.

(a) 614   **(b)** 5090

SOLUTION

(a) The number 614 is made up of six 100s, one 10, and four 1s, as depicted at the right.

$6 \cdot 100:$

$(1 \cdot)10:$

$4(\cdot 1):$

(b) The number 5090 consists of five 1000s, no 100s, and nine 10s (no 1s).

$5 \cdot 1000:$

$0(\cdot 100):$

$9 \cdot 10:$

4.1 EXERCISES

Convert each Egyptian numeral to Hindu-Arabic form.

1. 𐤒𓏢𓏢𓏢𓏭𓏭𓏭|||||

2. 𓏭𓏭𓆼𓆼𓆼𓆼𓏭||

3. 𓃭𓃭𓃭𓃭 𓂝𓂝𓂝 ///𓆼𓆼𓆼𓏭𓏭|||||
      𓃭𓃭𓃭 𓂝𓂝𓂝 ///𓆼𓆼𓆼𓆼𓏭𓏭||||

4. 𓃭𓃭𓃭𓏢𓏢𓏢𓏢𓏢𓆼𓆼𓏭𓏭𓏭|

Convert each Hindu-Arabic numeral to Egyptian form.

5. 23,145

6. 427

7. 8,657,000

8. 306,090

Chapter 1 of the book of Numbers in the Bible describes a census of the draft-eligible men of Israel after Moses led them out of Egypt into the Desert of Sinai, about 1450 B.C. Write an Egyptian numeral for the number of available men from each tribe listed.

9. 59,300 from the tribe of Simeon

10. 46,500 from the tribe of Reuben

11. 74,600 from the tribe of Judah

12. 45,650 from the tribe of Gad

13. 62,700 from the tribe of Dan

14. 54,400 from the tribe of Issachar

Convert each Roman numeral to Hindu-Arabic form.

15. CLXXXII

16. MDXCVII

17. $\overline{\text{XIV}}$

18. $\overline{\overline{\text{V}}}\text{CXXID}$

Convert each Hindu-Arabic numeral to Roman form.

19. 2861

20. 749

21. 25,619

22. 6,402,524

Convert each Chinese numeral to Hindu-Arabic form.

23.

24.

25.

26.

Convert each Hindu-Arabic numeral to Chinese form.

27. 960   **28.** 63   **29.** 7012   **30.** 2416

Though Chinese art forms began before written history, their highest development was achieved during four particular dynasties. Write traditional Chinese numerals for the beginning and ending dates of each dynasty listed.

31. Ming (1368 to 1644)

32. Sung (960 to 1279)

33. T'ang (618 to 907)

34. Han (202 B.C. to A.D. 220)

Work each addition or subtraction problem, using regrouping as necessary. Convert each answer to Hindu-Arabic form.

35.

36.

37.

38.

39.

40.

41.

42.

Use the Egyptian algorithm to find each product.

43. 32 · 47

44. 29 · 75

45. 64 · 127

46. 52 · 131

In Exercises 47 and 48, convert all numbers to Egyptian numerals. Multiply using the Egyptian algorithm, and add using the Egyptian symbols. Give the final answer using a Hindu-Arabic numeral.

47. *Value of a Biblical Treasure* The book of Ezra in the Bible describes the return of the exiles to Jerusalem. When they rebuilt the temple, the King of Persia gave them the following items: thirty golden basins, a thousand silver basins, four hundred ten silver bowls, and thirty golden bowls. Find the total value of this treasure, if each gold basin is worth 3000 shekels, each silver basin is worth 500 shekels, each silver bowl is worth 50 shekels, and each golden bowl is worth 400 shekels.

48. *Total Bill for King Solomon* King Solomon told the King of Tyre (now Lebanon) that Solomon needed the best cedar for his temple, and that he would "pay you for your men whatever sum you fix." Find the total bill to Solomon if the King of Tyre used the following numbers of men: 5500 tree cutters at two shekels per week each, for a total of seven weeks; 4600 sawers of wood at three shekels per week each, for a total of 32 weeks; and 900 sailors at one shekel per week each, for a total of 16 weeks.

Explain why each step would be an improvement in the development of numeration systems.

49. progressing from carrying groups of pebbles to making tally marks on a stick

50. progressing from tallying to simple grouping

51. utilizing a subtractive technique within simple grouping, as the Romans did

52. progressing from simple grouping to multiplicative grouping

Recall that the ancient Egyptian system described in this section was simple grouping, used a base of ten, and contained seven distinct symbols. The largest number expressible in that system is 9,999,999. Identify the largest number expressible in each of the following simple grouping systems. (In Exercises 57–60, d can be any counting number.)

53. base ten, five distinct symbols

54. base ten, ten distinct symbols

55. base five, five distinct symbols

56. base five, ten distinct symbols

57. base ten, d distinct symbols

58. base five, d distinct symbols

59. base seven, d distinct symbols

60. base b, d distinct symbols (where b is any counting number 2 or greater)

61. The Chinese system presented in the text has symbols for 1 through 9, and also for 10, 100, and 1000. What is the greatest number expressible in that system?

62. The Chinese system did eventually adopt two additional symbols, for 10,000 and 100,000. What greatest number could then be expressed?

63. If the first (least-valued) six symbols of the Roman system are arranged from greatest value to least, left to right, what famous number is denoted?

64. The number in **Exercise 63** is denoted with six symbols as a Roman numeral. How many symbols would it require as
(a) a Chinese numeral?
(b) an Egyptian numeral?

4.2 MORE HISTORICAL NUMERATION SYSTEMS

Basics of Positional Numeration • Hindu-Arabic Numeration • Babylonian Numeration • Mayan Numeration • Greek Numeration

Basics of Positional Numeration

A simple grouping system relies on repetition of symbols to denote the number of each power of the base. A multiplicative grouping system uses multipliers in place of repetition, which is more efficient. The ultimate in efficiency is attained with a **positional system** in which only multipliers are used. The various powers of the base require no separate symbols, because the power associated with each multiplier can be understood by the position that the multiplier occupies in the numeral.

If the Chinese system had evolved into a positional system, then the numeral for 7482 could be written

rather than

.

In the positional version on the left, the lowest symbol is understood to represent two 1s (10^0), the next one up denotes eight 10s (10^1), then four 100s (10^2), and finally seven 1000s (10^3). Each symbol in a numeral now has both a *face value,* associated with that particular symbol (the multiplier value), and a *place value* (a power of the base), associated with the place, or position, occupied by the symbol.

Positional Numeration

In a positional numeral, each symbol (called a **digit**) conveys two things:

1. **face value**—the inherent value of the symbol
2. **place value**—the power of the base that is associated with the position that the digit occupies in the numeral.

Hindu-Arabic Numeration

The place values in a Hindu-Arabic numeral, from right to left, are 1, 10, 100, 1000, and so on. The three 4s in the number 46,424 all have the same face value but different place values. The first 4, on the left, denotes four 10,000s, the next one denotes four 100s, and the one on the right denotes four 1s. Place values (in base ten) are named as shown here.

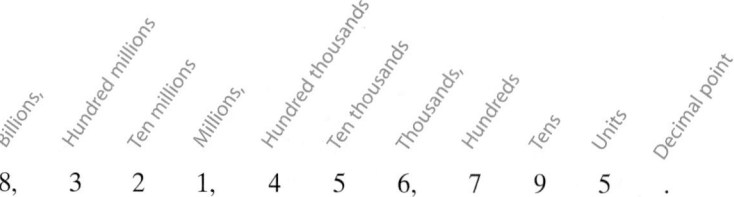

This numeral is read as eight billion, three hundred twenty-one million, four hundred fifty-six thousand, seven hundred ninety-five.

To work successfully, a positional system must have a symbol for zero to serve as a **placeholder** in case one or more powers of the base are not needed. Because of this requirement, some early numeration systems took a long time to evolve to a positional form, or never did. Although the traditional Chinese system does utilize a zero symbol, it never did incorporate all the features of a positional system, but remained essentially a multiplicative grouping system.

The one numeration system that did achieve the maximum efficiency of positional form is our own system, the **Hindu-Arabic** system. Its symbols have been traced to the Hindus of 200 B.C. They were picked up by the Arabs and eventually transmitted to Spain, where a late tenth-century version appeared like this:

$$I\,Z\,\chi\,y\,9\,b\,7\,8\,9.$$

The earliest stages of the system evolved under the influence of navigational, trade, engineering, and military requirements. And in early modern times, the advance of astronomy and other sciences led to a structure well suited to fast and accurate computation.

The purely positional form that the system finally assumed was introduced to the West by Leonardo Fibonacci of Pisa (1170–1250) early in the thirteenth century, but widespread acceptance of standardized symbols and form was not achieved until the invention of printing during the fifteenth century. Since that time, no better system of numeration has been devised, and the positional base ten Hindu-Arabic system is commonly used around the world today.

The Hindu-Arabic system and notation will be investigated further in **Sections 4.3 and 4.4**. The systems we consider next, the Babylonian and the Mayan, achieved the main ideas of positional numeration without fully developing those ideas.

Table 5	Babylonian Symbols
Number	**Symbol**
1	▼
10	‹

Babylonian Numeration

The Babylonians used a base of 60 in their system. Because of this, in theory they would then need distinct symbols for numbers from 1 through 59 (just as we have symbols for 1 through 9). However, the Babylonian method of writing on clay with wedge-shaped sticks gave rise to only *two* symbols, as shown in **Table 5**. The number 47 would be written

‹‹‹‹▼▼▼▼▼▼▼   or   ‹‹▼▼▼▼ ‹‹▼▼▼ .   The number 47

Since the Babylonian system had base 60, the "digit" on the right in a multi-digit number represented the number of 1s, with the second "digit" from the right giving the number of 60s. The third digit would give the number of 3600s (60 · 60 = 3600), and so on.

Special Features of the Babylonian System

1. Rather than using distinct symbols for each number less than the base (60), the Babylonians expressed face values in base 10 simple grouping, using only the two symbols

   ‹ for 10   and   ▼ for 1.

   The system is, therefore, base 10 simple grouping *within* base 60 positional.

2. The earliest Babylonian system lacked a place holder symbol (zero), so missing powers of the base were difficult to express. Blank spaces within a numeral would be open to misinterpretation.

EXAMPLE 1 Converting Babylonian Numerals to Hindu-Arabic

Convert each Babylonian numeral to Hindu-Arabic form.

(a) ⟨⟨⟨⟨⟨⟨▼▼▼   (b) ⟨⟨⟨▼▼▼▼ ⟨⟨ ▼▼▼▼⟨⟨▼▼   (c) ⟨⟨▼▼▼▼▼⟨▼⟨⟨⟨▼▼▼▼▼▼

SOLUTION

(a) Here we have five 10s and three 1s.

$$5 \cdot 10 = 50$$
$$3 \cdot 1 = \underline{3}$$
$$53 \leftarrow \text{Answer}$$

(b) This "two-digit" Babylonian number represents twenty-two 1s and fifty-eight 60s.

$$22 \cdot 1 = 22$$
$$58 \cdot 60 = \underline{3480}$$
$$3502 \leftarrow \text{Answer}$$

(c) Here we have a three-digit number.

$$36 \cdot 1 = 36$$
$$11 \cdot 60 = 660$$
$$25 \cdot 3600 = \underline{90{,}000}$$
$$90{,}696 \leftarrow \text{Answer}$$ ■■■

EXAMPLE 2 Converting Hindu-Arabic Numerals to Babylonian

Convert each Hindu-Arabic numeral to Babylonian form.

(a) 733   (b) 75,904   (c) 43,233

SOLUTION

(a) To write 733 in Babylonian, we will need some 60s and some 1s. Divide 60 into 733. The quotient is 12, with a remainder of 13. Thus we need twelve 60s and thirteen 1s.

⟨▼▼⟨▼▼▼ ← 733

(b) For 75,904, we need some 3600s, as well as some 60s and some 1s. Divide 75,904 by 3600. The answer is 21, with a remainder of 304. Divide 304 by 60. The quotient is 5, with a remainder of 4.

⟨⟨▼ ▼▼▼▼▼ ▼▼▼▼ ← 75,904

(c) Divide 43,233 by 3600. The answer is 12, with a remainder of 33. We need no 60s here. In a system such as ours we would use a 0 to show that no 60s are needed. Since the early Babylonians had no such symbol, they merely left a space.

⟨▼▼ ⟨⟨⟨▼▼▼ ← 43,233 ■■■

Example 2(c) illustrates the problem presented by the lack of a symbol for zero. In our system we know that 202 is not the same as 2002 or 20,002. The lack of a zero symbol was a major difficulty with the very early Babylonian system. A symbol for zero was introduced about 300 B.C.

Mayan Numeration

The Mayan Indians of Central America and Mexico also used what is basically a positional system. Like the Babylonians, the Mayans did not use base 10—they used base 20, with a twist. In a true base 20 system, the digits would represent 1s, 20s, $20 \cdot 20 = 400$s, $20 \cdot 400 = 8000$s, and so on. The Mayans used 1s, 20s, $18 \cdot 20 = 360$s, $20 \cdot 360 = 7200$s, and so on. It is possible that they multiplied 20 by 18 (instead of 20) since $18 \cdot 20$ is close to the number of days in a year, convenient for astronomy. The symbols of the Mayan system are shown in **Table 6**.

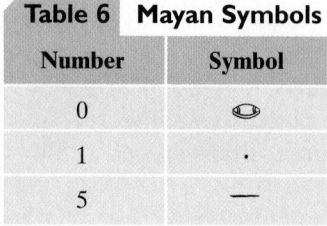

Table 6	Mayan Symbols
Number	**Symbol**
0	◉
1	·
5	—

The Mayans were one of the first civilizations to invent a placeholder. They had a zero symbol many hundreds of years before it reached western Europe. Mayan numerals are written from top to bottom, just as in the classical Chinese system.

> **Special Features of the Mayan System**
>
> 1. Rather than using distinct symbols for each number less than the base (20), the Mayans expressed face values in base 5 simple grouping, using only the two symbols — for 5 and · for 1. The system is, therefore, base 5 simple grouping *within* base 20 positional.
> 2. Place values in base 20 would normally be
> $$1, \quad 20, \quad 20^2 = 400, \quad 20^3 = 8000,$$
> $$20^4 = 160,000, \quad \text{and so on.}$$
> However, the Mayans multiplied by 18 rather than 20 in just one case, so the place values are
> $$1, \quad 20, \quad 20 \cdot 18 = 360, \quad 360 \cdot 20 = 7200,$$
> $$7200 \cdot 20 = 144,000, \quad \text{and so on.}$$

▌▌ EXAMPLE 3 Converting Mayan Numerals to Hindu-Arabic

Convert each Mayan numeral to Hindu-Arabic form.

(a)   **(b)**

SOLUTION

(a) The top group of symbols represents twelve 20s, while the bottom group represents nine 1s.

$$12 \cdot 20 = 240$$
$$9 \cdot 1 = \underline{9}$$
$$249 \leftarrow \text{Answer}$$

(b)
$$8 \cdot 360 = 2880$$
$$0 \cdot 20 = 0$$
$$15 \cdot 1 = \underline{15}$$
$$2895 \leftarrow \text{Answer}$$ ▮▮▮

▌▌ EXAMPLE 4 Converting Hindu-Arabic Numerals to Mayan

Convert each Hindu-Arabic numeral to Mayan form.

(a) 277   **(b)** 1238

SOLUTION

(a) The number 277 requires thirteen 20s (divide 277 by 20) and seventeen 1s.

$\leftarrow 277$

(b) Divide 1238 by 360. The quotient is 3, with remainder 158. Divide 158 by 20. The quotient is 7, with remainder 18. Thus we need three 360s, seven 20s, and eighteen 1s.

$\leftarrow 1238$ ▮▮▮

Table 7	Greek Symbols
Number	**Symbol**
1	α
2	β
3	γ
4	δ
5	ϵ
6	ς
7	ζ
8	η
9	θ
10	ι
20	κ
30	λ
40	μ
50	ν
60	ξ
70	o
80	π
90	φ
100	ρ
200	σ
300	τ
400	υ
500	ϕ
600	χ
700	ψ
800	ω
900	λ

Greek Numeration

The classical Greeks of Ionia assigned values to the 24 letters of their ordinary alphabet, together with three obsolete Phoenician letters (the digamma ς for 6, the koppa φ for 90, and the sampi λ for 900). See **Table 7**. This scheme, usually called a **ciphered system,** makes all counting numbers less than 1000 easily represented. It avoids repetitions of symbols but requires vast multiplication tables for 27 distinct symbols. Computation would be very burdensome. The base is 10, but the system is quite different than simple grouping, multiplicative grouping, or positional.

▮▮ **EXAMPLE 5** Converting Greek Numerals to Hindu-Arabic

Convert each Greek numeral to Hindu-Arabic form.

(a) $\lambda\alpha$ **(b)** $\tau\xi\epsilon$ **(c)** $\lambda\varphi\theta$ **(d)** $\chi\delta$

SOLUTION

(a) 31   **(b)** 365   **(c)** 999   **(d)** 604   ▮▮▮

For numbers larger than 999, the Greeks introduced two additional techniques.

Special Features of the Greek System

1. Multiples of 1000 (up to 9000) are indicated with a small stroke next to a units symbol. For example, 9000 would be denoted $\prime\theta$.
2. Multiples of 10,000 are indicated by the letter M (from the word *myriad*, meaning ten thousand) with the multiple (a units symbol) shown above the M. The number 50,000 would be denoted $\overset{\epsilon}{M}$.

▮▮ **EXAMPLE 6** Converting Hindu-Arabic Numerals to Greek

Convert each Hindu-Arabic numeral to Greek form.

(a) 3000   **(b)** 40,000   **(c)** 7694   **(d)** 88,888

SOLUTION

(a) $\prime\gamma$ **(b)** $\overset{\delta}{M}$ **(c)** $\prime\zeta\chi\varphi\delta$ **(d)** $\overset{\eta}{M}\prime\eta\omega\pi\eta$ ▮▮▮

4.2 EXERCISES

Identify each numeral in Exercises 1–20 as Babylonian, Mayan, or Greek. Give the equivalent in the Hindu-Arabic system.

1. ⬥

2. ⟨⟨▼▼

3. ⟨⟨⟨▼▼

4. ≣

5. $\sigma\lambda\delta$

6. $\omega o\beta$

7. ⬥

8. ⬥

9. ⟨⟨▼⟨⟨▼▼

10. ⟨▼▼▼⟨⟨⟨▼▼

11. ⟨⟨▼▼ ⟨⟨▼ ⟨⟨▼

12. ⟨⟨⟨▼▼▼ ⟨⟨ ▼▼ ⟨⟨⟨▼

13. ⬥

14. ⬥

15. ⬥

16. ⬥

17. ⟨⟨▼▼⟨⟨▼⟨▼▼▼▼

18. ⟨⟨ ▼▼ ⟨⟨ ⟨ ▼▼▼▼▼ ⟨⟨ ▼▼▼

19. $\overset{\alpha}{M}\prime\epsilon\rho\mu\theta$

20. $\overset{\eta}{M}\omega\eta$

Write each number as a Babylonian numeral.

21. 21   **22.** 32   **23.** 293

24. 412   **25.** 1514   **26.** 3280

27. 5190   **28.** 7842   **29.** 43,205

30. 90,180

Write each number as a Mayan numeral.

31. 12   **32.** 32   **33.** 151

34. 208   **35.** 4694   **36.** 4328

37. 64,712   **38.** 61,598

Write each number as a Greek numeral.

39. 39   **40.** 51   **41.** 92

42. 106   **43.** 412   **44.** 381

45. 2769   **46.** 9814   **47.** 54,726

48. 80,102

4.3 ARITHMETIC IN THE HINDU-ARABIC SYSTEM

Expanded Form • Historical Calculation Devices

Expanded Form

The historical development of numeration culminated in positional systems. The most successful of these is the Hindu-Arabic system, which has base ten and, therefore, has place values that are powers of 10.

We now review exponential expressions, or powers (defined in **Section 1.1**), because they are the basis of expanded form in a positional system.

EXAMPLE 1   Evaluating Powers

Find each power.

(a) 10^3 **(b)** 7^2 **(c)** 5^4

SOLUTION

(a) $10^3 = 10 \cdot 10 \cdot 10 = 1000$
(10^3 is read "10 cubed," or "10 to the third power.")

(b) $7^2 = 7 \cdot 7 = 49$
(7^2 is read "7 squared," or "7 to the second power.")

(c) $5^4 = 5 \cdot 5 \cdot 5 \cdot 5 = 625$
(5^4 is read "5 to the fourth power.")   ▮▮▮

To simplify work with exponents, it is agreed that

$$a^0 = 1, \quad \text{for any nonzero number } a.$$

Thus, $7^0 = 1, 52^0 = 1$, and so on. At the same time,

$$a^1 = a, \quad \text{for any number } a.$$

For example, $8^1 = 8$, and $25^1 = 25$. The exponent 1 is usually omitted.

By using exponents, numbers can be written in **expanded form** in which the value of the digit in each position is made clear. For example,

$$924 = 900 + 20 + 4$$
$$= (9 \cdot 100) + (2 \cdot 10) + (4 \cdot 1)$$
$$= (9 \cdot 10^2) + (2 \cdot 10^1) + (4 \cdot 10^0). \quad \text{100} = 10^2, 10 = 10^1, \text{and } 1 = 10^0$$

This Iranian stamp should remind us that counting on fingers (and toes) is an age-old practice. In fact, our word **digit,** referring to the numerals 0–9, comes from a Latin word for "finger" (or "toe"). Aristotle first noted the relationships between fingers and base ten in Greek numeration. Anthropologists go along with the notion. Some cultures, however, have used two, three, or four as number bases, for example, counting on the joints of the fingers or the spaces between them.

There is much evidence that early humans (in various cultures) used their fingers to represent numbers. As calculations became more complicated, finger reckoning, as illustrated above, became popular. The Romans became adept at this sort of calculating, carrying it to 10,000 or perhaps higher.

▌▌ **EXAMPLE 2** Writing Numbers in Expanded Form

Write each number in expanded form.

(a) 1906   **(b)** 46,424

SOLUTION

(a) $1906 = (1 \cdot 10^3) + (9 \cdot 10^2) + (0 \cdot 10^1) + (6 \cdot 10^0)$

Because $0 \cdot 10^1 = 0$, this term could be omitted, but the form is clearer with it included.

(b) $46{,}424 = (4 \cdot 10^4) + (6 \cdot 10^3) + (4 \cdot 10^2) + (2 \cdot 10^1) + (4 \cdot 10^0)$ ▌▌▌

▌▌ **EXAMPLE 3** Simplifying Expanded Numbers

Simplify each expansion.

(a) $(3 \cdot 10^5) + (2 \cdot 10^4) + (6 \cdot 10^3) + (8 \cdot 10^2) + (7 \cdot 10^1) + (9 \cdot 10^0)$

(b) $(2 \cdot 10^1) + (8 \cdot 10^0)$

SOLUTION

(a) $(3 \cdot 10^5) + (2 \cdot 10^4) + (6 \cdot 10^3) + (8 \cdot 10^2) + (7 \cdot 10^1) + (9 \cdot 10^0) = 326{,}879$

(b) $(2 \cdot 10^1) + (8 \cdot 10^0) = 28$ ▌▌▌

Expanded notation can be used to see why standard algorithms for addition and subtraction really work. The key idea behind these algorithms is based on the **distributive property.**

Distributive Property

For all real numbers a, b, and c,

$$(b \cdot a) + (c \cdot a) = (b + c) \cdot a.$$

For example, $(3 \cdot 10^4) + (2 \cdot 10^4) = (3 + 2) \cdot 10^4$
$$= 5 \cdot 10^4.$$

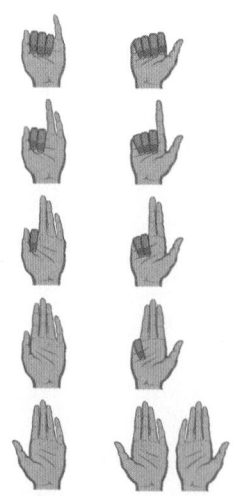

Finger Counting The first digits many people used for counting were their fingers. In Africa the Zulu used the method shown here to count to ten. They started on the left hand with palm up and fist closed. The Zulu finger positions for 1–5 are shown above on the left. The Zulu finger positions for 6–10 are shown on the right.

▌▌ **EXAMPLE 4** Adding Expanded Forms

Use expanded notation to add 23 and 64.

SOLUTION

$$23 = (2 \cdot 10^1) + (3 \cdot 10^0)$$
$$\underline{+\ 64 = (6 \cdot 10^1) + (4 \cdot 10^0)}$$
$$(8 \cdot 10^1) + (7 \cdot 10^0) = 87 \quad \text{Sum}$$ ▌▌▌

▌▌ **EXAMPLE 5** Subtracting Expanded Forms

Use expanded notation to subtract 254 from 695.

SOLUTION

$$695 = (6 \cdot 10^2) + (9 \cdot 10^1) + (5 \cdot 10^0)$$
$$\underline{-254 = (2 \cdot 10^2) + (5 \cdot 10^1) + (4 \cdot 10^0)}$$
$$(4 \cdot 10^2) + (4 \cdot 10^1) + (1 \cdot 10^0) = 441 \quad \text{Difference}$$ ▌▌▌

▌▌ EXAMPLE 6 Carrying in Expanded Form

Use expanded notation to add 75 and 48.

SOLUTION

$$
\begin{array}{r}
75 = (7 \cdot 10^1) + (5 \cdot 10^0) \\
+\ 48 = \underline{(4 \cdot 10^1) + (8 \cdot 10^0)} \\
(11 \cdot 10^1) + (13 \cdot 10^0)
\end{array}
$$

The units position (10^0) has room for only one digit, so we modify $13 \cdot 10^0$.

$$
\begin{aligned}
13 \cdot 10^0 &= (10 \cdot 10^0) + (3 \cdot 10^0) && \text{Distributive property} \\
&= (1 \cdot 10^1) + (3 \cdot 10^0) && 10 \cdot 10^0 = 1 \cdot 10^1
\end{aligned}
$$

The 1 from 13 moved to the left (carried) from the units position to the tens position.

$$
\overbrace{(11 \cdot 10^1) + \overbrace{(1 \cdot 10^1)}^{13 \cdot 10^0} + (3 \cdot 10^0)}
$$

$$
\begin{aligned}
&= (12 \cdot 10^1) + (3 \cdot 10^0) && \text{Distributive property} \\
&= (10 \cdot 10^1) + (2 \cdot 10^1) + (3 \cdot 10^0) && \text{Modify } 12 \cdot 10^1. \\
&= (1 \cdot 10^2) + (2 \cdot 10^1) + (3 \cdot 10^0) && 10 \cdot 10^1 = 1 \cdot 10^2 \\
&= 123 && \text{Sum} \qquad ▪▪▪
\end{aligned}
$$

▌▌ EXAMPLE 7 Borrowing in Expanded Form

Use expanded notation to subtract 186 from 364.

SOLUTION

$$
\begin{array}{r}
364 = (3 \cdot 10^2) + (6 \cdot 10^1) + (4 \cdot 10^0) \\
-186 = \underline{(1 \cdot 10^2) + (8 \cdot 10^1) + (6 \cdot 10^0)}
\end{array}
$$

We cannot subtract 6 from 4. The units position borrows from the tens position.

$$
(3 \cdot 10^2) + (6 \cdot 10^1) + (4 \cdot 10^0)
$$

$$
\begin{aligned}
&= (3 \cdot 10^2) + (5 \cdot 10^1) + (1 \cdot 10^1) + (4 \cdot 10^0) && \text{Distributive property} \\
&= (3 \cdot 10^2) + (5 \cdot 10^1) + (10 \cdot 10^0) + (4 \cdot 10^0) && 1 \cdot 10^1 = 10 \cdot 10^0 \\
&= (3 \cdot 10^2) + (5 \cdot 10^1) + (14 \cdot 10^0) && \text{Distributive property}
\end{aligned}
$$

We cannot take 8 from 5 in the tens position, so we borrow from the hundreds.

$$
(3 \cdot 10^2) + (5 \cdot 10^1) + (14 \cdot 10^0)
$$

$$
\begin{aligned}
&= (2 \cdot 10^2) + (1 \cdot 10^2) + (5 \cdot 10^1) + (14 \cdot 10^0) && \text{Distributive property} \\
&= (2 \cdot 10^2) + (10 \cdot 10^1) + (5 \cdot 10^1) + (14 \cdot 10^0) && 1 \cdot 10^2 = 10 \cdot 10^1 \\
&= (2 \cdot 10^2) + (15 \cdot 10^1) + (14 \cdot 10^0) && \text{Distributive property}
\end{aligned}
$$

Now we can complete the subtraction.

$$
\begin{array}{r}
(2 \cdot 10^2) + (15 \cdot 10^1) + (14 \cdot 10^0) \\
-\ (1 \cdot 10^2) + \ (8 \cdot 10^1) + \ (6 \cdot 10^0) \\
\hline
(1 \cdot 10^2) + \ (7 \cdot 10^1) + \ (8 \cdot 10^0) = 178 \qquad \text{Difference} \quad ▪▪▪
\end{array}
$$

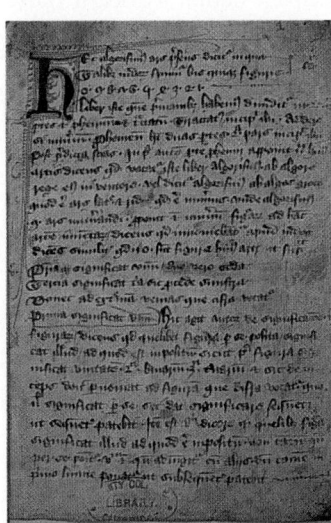

The **Carmen de Algorismo** (opening verses shown here) by Alexander de Villa Dei, thirteenth century, popularized the new art of "algorismus":

> . . . from these twice five figures 0 9 8 7 6 5 4 3 2 1 of the Indians we benefit . . .

The *Carmen* related that Algor, an Indian king, invented the art. But actually, "algorism" (or "algorithm") comes in a roundabout way from the name Muhammad ibn Musa al-Khorârizmi, an Arabian mathematician of the ninth century, whose arithmetic book was translated into Latin. Furthermore, this Muhammad's book on equations, *Hisab al-jabr w'almuqâbalah,* yielded the term "algebra" in a similar way.

Smart phones perform mathematical calculations and many other functions as well.

Examples 4–7 used expanded notation and the distributive property to clarify our usual addition and subtraction methods. In practice, our actual work for these four problems would appear as follows.

$$
\begin{array}{cccc}
& & 1 & 2\ 15 \\
23 & 695 & 75 & \cancel{3}\cancel{6}{}^1 4 \\
+\ 64 & -\ 254 & +\ 48 & -\ 1\ 8\ 6 \\
\hline
87 & 441 & 123 & 1\ 7\ 8
\end{array}
$$

The procedures seen in this section also work for positional systems with bases other than ten.

Historical Calculation Devices

Because our numeration system is based on powers of ten, it is often called the **decimal system,** from the Latin word *decem,* meaning ten.* Over the years, many methods have been devised for speeding calculations in the decimal system.

One of the oldest calculation methods is the **abacus,** a device made with a series of rods with sliding beads and a dividing bar. Reading from right to left, the rods have values of 1, 10, 100, 1000, and so on. The bead above the bar has five times the value of those below. Beads moved *toward* the bar are in the "active" position, and those toward the frame are ignored. In our illustrations of *abaci* (plural form of abacus), such as in **Figure 8**, the activated beads are shown in black.

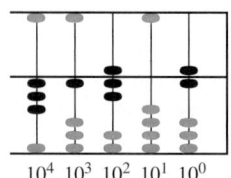

$$10^4 \ 10^3 \ 10^2 \ 10^1 \ 10^0$$

Figure 8

EXAMPLE 8 Reading an Abacus

The **speed and accuracy of the abacus** are well known, according to www.ucmasusa.com. In a contest held between a Japanese **soroban** (the Japanese version of the abacus) expert and a highly skilled desk-calculator operator, the abacus won on addition, subtraction, division, and combinations of these operations. The electronic calculator won only on multiplication.

What number is shown on the abacus in **Figure 8**?

SOLUTION

Find the number as follows.

> Beads above the bar have five times the value.

$$(3 \cdot 10{,}000) + (1 \cdot 1000) + [(1 \cdot 500) + (2 \cdot 100)] + 0 \cdot 10 + [(1 \cdot 5) + (1 \cdot 1)]$$
$$= 30{,}000 + 1000 + 500 + 200 + 0 + 5 + 1$$
$$= 31{,}706$$

■■■

As paper became more readily available, people gradually switched from devices like the abacus (though these still are commonly used in some areas) to paper-and-pencil methods of calculation. One early scheme, used in India and Persia, was the **lattice method,** which arranged products of single digits into a diagonalized lattice.

December was the tenth month in an old form of the calendar. It is interesting to note that *decem* became *dix* in the French language; a ten-dollar bill, called a "dixie," was in use in New Orleans before the Civil War. "Dixie Land" was a nickname for that city before Dixie came to refer to all the Southern states, as in Daniel D. Emmett's song, written in 1859.

EXAMPLE 9   Using the Lattice Method for Products

Find the product 38 · 794 by the lattice method.

SOLUTION

Step 1   Write the problem, with one number at the side and one across the top.

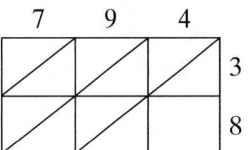

Step 2   Within the lattice, write the products of all pairs of digits from the top and side.

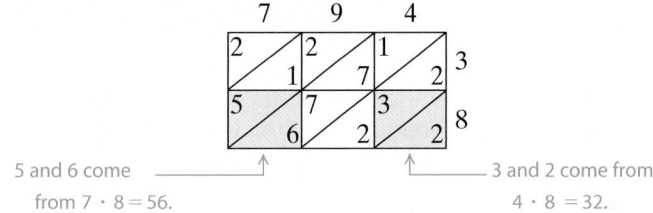

5 and 6 come from 7 · 8 = 56.

3 and 2 come from 4 · 8 = 32.

Step 3   Starting at the right of the lattice add diagonally, carrying as necessary.

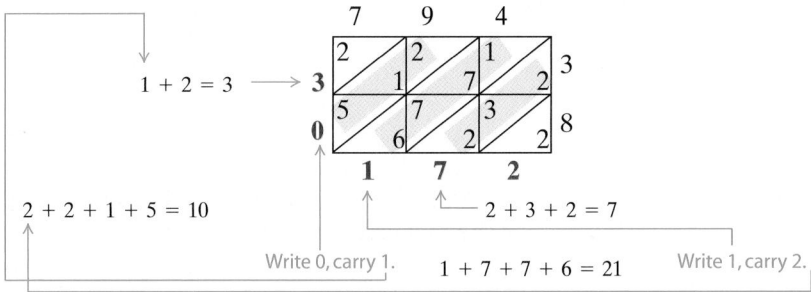

1 + 2 = 3

2 + 2 + 1 + 5 = 10

2 + 3 + 2 = 7

Write 0, carry 1.

1 + 7 + 7 + 6 = 21

Write 1, carry 2.

Step 4   Read the answer around the left side and bottom: 38 · 794 = **30,172**.   ███

The Scottish mathematician John Napier (1550–1617) introduced a significant calculating tool called **Napier's rods,** or **Napier's bones.** Napier's invention, based on the lattice method of multiplication, is widely acknowledged as a very early forerunner of modern computers. It consisted of a set of strips, several for each digit 0 through 9, on which multiples of each digit appeared in a sort of lattice column. See **Figure 9**.

An additional strip, called the *index,* could be laid beside any of the others to indicate the multiplier at each level. **Figure 10** shows how to multiply 2806 by 7. Select the rods for 2, 8, 0, and 6, placing them side by side. Then using the index, locate the level for a multiplier of 7. The resulting lattice gives the product, **19,642.**

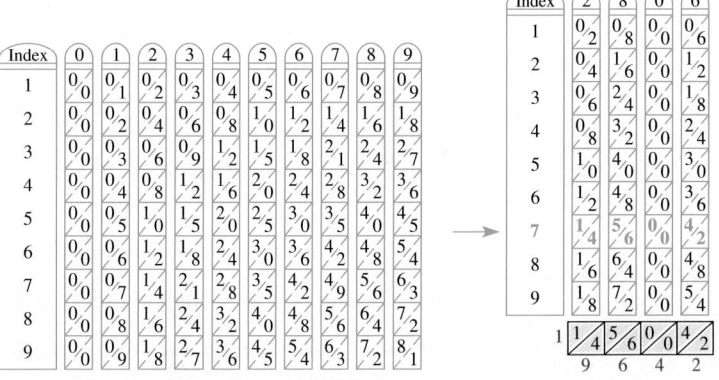

Figure 9

Figure 10

John Napier's most significant mathematical contribution, developed over a period of at least 20 years, was the concept of **logarithms,** which, among other things, allow multiplication and division to be accomplished with addition and subtraction. It was a great computational advantage given the state of mathematics at the time (1614).

Napier, a supporter of John Knox and James I, published a widely read anti-Catholic work that analyzed the Biblical book of Revelation. He concluded that the Pope was the Antichrist and that the Creator would end the world between 1688 and 1700. Napier was one of many who, over the years, have miscalculated the end of the world.

Napier's rods were an early step toward modern computers.

▌▌ EXAMPLE 10 Multiplying with Napier's Rods

Use Napier's rods to find the product of 723 and 4198.

SOLUTION

We line up the rods for 4, 1, 9, and 8 next to the index, as in **Figure 11**. The product 3 · 4198 is found as described in **Example 9** and written at the bottom of the figure. Then 2 · 4198 is found similarly and written below, shifted one place to the left. (Why?) Finally, the product 7 · 4198 is written shifted two places to the left.

  The final answer is found by addition.

$$723 \cdot 4198 = \mathbf{3{,}035{,}154}$$ ▌▌▌

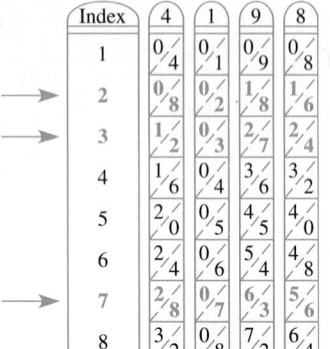

Figure 11

Another paper-and-pencil method of multiplication is the **Russian peasant method,** which is similar to the Egyptian method of doubling explained in **Section 4.1.** To multiply 37 and 42 by the Russian peasant method, make two columns headed by 37 and 42. Form the first column by dividing 37 by 2 again and again, ignoring any remainders. Stop when 1 is obtained. Form the second column by doubling each number down the column.

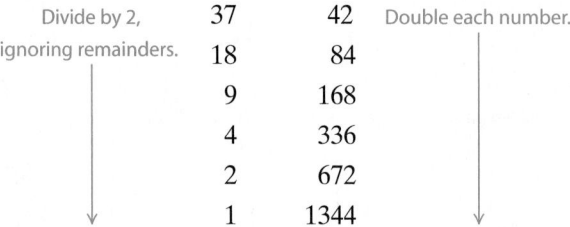

	Divide by 2, ignoring remainders.	37	42	Double each number.
		18	84	
		9	168	
		4	336	
		2	672	
		1	1344	

Now add up only the second column numbers that correspond to odd numbers in the first column. Omit those corresponding to even numbers in the first column.

	→	37	42	←	
		18	84		
Identify odd numbers.	→	9	168	←	Add these numbers.
		4	336		
		2	672		
	→	1	1344	←	

$$37 \cdot 42 = \mathbf{42} + \mathbf{168} + \mathbf{1344} = \mathbf{1554} \; \leftarrow \text{Answer}$$

Most people use standard algorithms for adding and subtracting, carrying or borrowing when appropriate, as illustrated following **Example 7.** An interesting alternative is the **nines complement method** for subtracting. To use this method, we first agree that the nines complement of a digit *n* is 9 − *n*. For example, the nines complement of 0 is 9, of 1 is 8, of 2 is 7, and so on, up to the nines complement of 9, which is 0.

  To carry out the nines complement method, complete the following steps:

Step 1 Align the digits as in the standard subtraction algorithm.

Step 2 Add leading zeros, if necessary, in the subtrahend so that both numbers have the same number of digits.

Step 3 Replace each digit in the subtrahend with its nines complement, and then add.

Step 4 Finally, delete the leading digit (1), and add 1 to the remaining part of the sum.

For a way to include a little magic with your calculations, check out http://digicc.com/fido.

▌▌ **EXAMPLE 11** Using the Nines Complement Method

Use the nines complement method to subtract $2803 - 647$.

SOLUTION

	Step 1	Step 2	Step 3	Step 4	
	2803	2803	2803	2155	
	− 647	− 0647	+ 9352	+ 1	
			12,155	2156	Difference

▌▌▌

For Further Thought

Calculating on the Abacus

The abacus has been (and still is) used to perform rapid calculations. Add 526 and 362 as shown.

Start with 526 on the abacus.

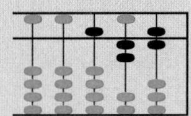

To add 362, start by "activating" an additional 2 on the 1s rod.

Next, activate an additional 6 on the 10s rod.

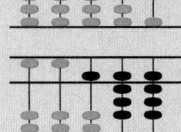

Finally, activate an additional 3 on the 100s rod.

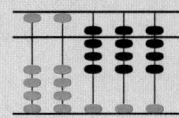

The sum, read from the abacus, is **888**.

For problems where carrying or borrowing is required, it takes a little more thought and skill.

For Group or Individual Investigation

1. Use an abacus to add: $13,728 + 61,455$. Explain each step of your procedure.

2. Use an abacus to subtract: $6512 - 4816$. Explain each step of your procedure.

4.3 EXERCISES

Write each number in expanded form.

1. 84   **2.** 352   **3.** 9446   **4.** 12,398

5. four thousand, nine hundred twenty-four

6. fifty-two thousand, one hundred eighteen

7. fourteen million, two hundred six thousand, forty

8. two hundred twelve million, eleven thousand, nine hundred sixteen

Simplify each expansion.

9. $(7 \cdot 10^1) + (5 \cdot 10^0)$

10. $(8 \cdot 10^2) + (2 \cdot 10^1) + (0 \cdot 10^0)$

11. $(4 \cdot 10^3) + (3 \cdot 10^2) + (8 \cdot 10^1) + (0 \cdot 10^0)$

12. $(5 \cdot 10^5) + (0 \cdot 10^4) + (3 \cdot 10^3) + (5 \cdot 10^2) + (6 \cdot 10^1) + (8 \cdot 10^0)$

13. $(7 \cdot 10^7) + (4 \cdot 10^5) + (1 \cdot 10^3) + (9 \cdot 10^0)$

14. $(3 \cdot 10^8) + (8 \cdot 10^6) + (2 \cdot 10^4) + (3 \cdot 10^0)$

In each of the following, add in expanded notation.

15. $37 + 42$ **16.** $582 + 613$

In each of the following, subtract in expanded notation.

17. $85 - 32$ **18.** $724 - 423$

Perform each addition using expanded notation.

19. $75 + 34$ **20.** $557 + 378$

21. $434 + 299$ **22.** $6755 + 4827$

Perform each subtraction using expanded notation.

23. $54 - 48$ **24.** $364 - 59$

25. $645 - 439$ **26.** $816 - 335$

Identify the number represented on each abacus.

27. 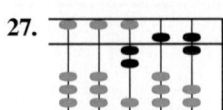 **28.**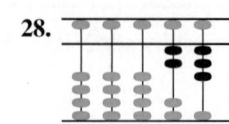

29. 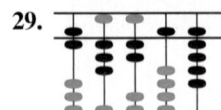 **30.**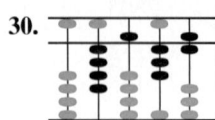

Sketch an abacus to show each number.

31. 38   **32.** 183   **33.** 2547   **34.** 70,163

Use the lattice method to find each product.

35. 65 · 29   **36.** 32 · 741

37. 525 · 73   **38.** 912 · 483

*Refer to **Example 10** where Napier's rods were used. Then complete Exercises 39 and 40.*

39. Find the product of 723 and 4198 by completing the lattice process shown here.

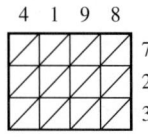

40. Explain how Napier's rods could have been used in **Example 10** to set up one complete lattice product rather than adding three individual (shifted) lattice products. Illustrate with a sketch.

*Use Napier's rods (**Figure 9**) to find each product.*

41. 8 · 62   **42.** 32 · 73

43. 26 · 8354   **44.** 526 · 4863

Perform each subtraction using the nines complement method.

45. 283 − 41   **46.** 536 − 425

47. 50,000 − 199   **48.** 40,002 − 4846

Use the Russian peasant method to find each product.

49. 5 · 92   **50.** 41 · 53

51. 62 · 529   **52.** 145 · 63

The Hindu-Arabic system is positional and uses ten as the base. Describe any advantages or disadvantages that may have resulted in each case.

53. Suppose the base had been larger, say twelve or twenty.

54. Suppose the base had been smaller, maybe eight or five.

4.4 CONVERSION BETWEEN NUMBER BASES

General Base Conversions • Computer Mathematics

General Base Conversions

In this section we consider bases other than ten, but we use the familiar Hindu-Arabic symbols. We indicate bases other than ten with a spelled-out subscript, as in the numeral 43_{five}. ***Whenever a number appears without a subscript, it is assumed that the intended base is ten.*** Be careful how you read (or verbalize) numerals here. The numeral 43_{five} is read "four three base five." (Do *not* read it as "forty-three," as that terminology implies base ten and names a totally different number.)

Table 8 gives powers of some numbers used as alternative bases.

Table 8   Selected Powers of Some Alternative Number Bases

	Fourth Power	Third Power	Second Power	First Power	Zero Power
Base two	16	8	4	2	1
Base five	625	125	25	5	1
Base seven	2401	343	49	7	1
Base eight	4096	512	64	8	1
Base sixteen	65,536	4096	256	16	1

Base Ten	Base Five	Base Ten	Base Five
0	0	16	31
1	1	17	32
2	2	18	33
3	3	19	34
4	4	20	40
5	10	21	41
6	11	22	42
7	12	23	43
8	13	24	44
9	14	25	100
10	20	26	101
11	21	27	102
12	22	28	103
13	23	29	104
14	24	30	110
15	30	31	111

Table 9 Base Five Numerals

For example, the base two row of **Table 8** indicates that

$$2^4 = 16, \quad 2^3 = 8, \quad 2^2 = 4, \quad 2^1 = 2, \quad \text{and} \quad 2^0 = 1.$$

We begin with the base five system, which requires just five distinct symbols, 0, 1, 2, 3, and 4. **Table 9** compares base five and decimal (base ten) numerals for the whole numbers 0 through 31. Notice that because only the symbols 0, 1, 2, 3, and 4 are used in base five, we must use two digits in base five when we get to 5_{ten}.

5_{ten} is expressed as one 5 and no 1s, that is as 10_{five}.

6_{ten} becomes 11_{five} (one 5 and one 1).

While base five uses fewer distinct symbols than base ten (an apparent advantage because there are few symbols to learn), it often requires more digits than base ten to denote the same number (a disadvantage because more symbols must be written).

You will find that in any base, if you denote the base "b," then the base itself will be 10_b, just as occurred in base five. For example,

$$7_{\text{ten}} = 10_{\text{seven}}, \quad 16_{\text{ten}} = 10_{\text{sixteen}}, \quad \text{and so on.}$$

EXAMPLE 1 Converting from Base Five to Base Ten

Convert 1342_{five} to decimal form.

SOLUTION

Referring to the powers of five in **Table 8**, we see that this number has one 125, three 25s, four 5s, and two 1s.

$$1342_{\text{five}} = (1 \cdot 125) + (3 \cdot 25) + (4 \cdot 5) + (2 \cdot 1)$$
$$= 125 + 75 + 20 + 2$$
$$= 222$$

A shortcut for converting from base five to decimal form, which is *particularly useful when you use a calculator,* can be derived as follows.

$$1342_{\text{five}} = (1 \cdot 5^3) + (3 \cdot 5^2) + (4 \cdot 5) + 2$$
$$= ((1 \cdot 5^2) + (3 \cdot 5) + 4) \cdot 5 + 2 \quad \text{Factor 5 out of the three quantities in parentheses.}$$
$$= (((1 \cdot 5) + 3) \cdot 5 + 4) \cdot 5 + 2 \quad \text{Factor 5 out of the two "inner" quantities.}$$

The inner parentheses around $1 \cdot 5$ are not needed because the product would be automatically done before the 3 is added. Therefore, we can write

$$1342_{\text{five}} = ((1 \cdot 5 + 3) \cdot 5 + 4) \cdot 5 + 2.$$

This series of products and sums is easily done as an uninterrupted sequence of operations on a calculator, with no intermediate results written down. The same method works for converting to base ten from any other base.

Calculator Shortcut for Base Conversion

To convert from another base to decimal form, follow these steps.

Step 1 Start with the first digit on the left and multiply by the base.

Step 2 Then add the next digit, multiply again by the base, and so on.

Step 3 Add the last digit on the right. ***Do not multiply it by the base.***

Exactly how you accomplish these steps depends on the type of calculator you use. With some models, only the digits, the multiplications, and the additions need to be entered, in order. With others, you may need to press the ▭ key following each addition of a digit. If you handle grouped expressions on your calculator by actually entering parentheses, then enter the expression just as illustrated above and in the following example. (The number of left parentheses to start with will be two fewer than the number of digits in the original numeral.)

▍▍ **EXAMPLE 2** Using the Calculator Shortcut

Use the calculator shortcut to convert 244314_{five} to decimal form.

SOLUTION

$$244314_{\text{five}} = ((((2 \cdot 5 + 4) \cdot 5 + 4) \cdot 5 + 3) \cdot 5 + 1) \cdot 5 + 4$$
$$= 9334 \quad \text{Note the four left parentheses for a six-digit numeral.}$$

▍▍ **EXAMPLE 3** Converting from Base Ten to Base Five

Convert 497 from decimal form to base five.

SOLUTION

The base five place values, starting from the right, are

$$1, \quad 5, \quad 25, \quad 125, \quad 625, \quad \text{and so on.}$$

Because 497 is between 125 and 625, it will require no 625s, but some 125s, as well as possibly some 25s, 5s, and 1s.

- Dividing 497 by 125 determines the proper number of 125s. The quotient is 3, with remainder 122. So we need three 125s.
- The remainder, 122, is divided by 25 (the next place value) to find the proper number of 25s. The quotient is 4, with remainder 22, so we need four 25s.
- Dividing 22 by 5 yields 4, with remainder 2. So we need four 5s.
- Dividing 2 by 1 yields 2 (with remainder 0), so we need two 1s.

Thus, 497 consists of three 125s, four 25s, four 5s, and two 1s, so $497 = 3442_{\text{five}}$. More concisely, this process can be written as follows.

$$497 \div 125 = 3 \qquad \text{Remainder 122}$$
$$122 \div 25 = 4 \qquad \text{Remainder 22}$$
$$22 \div 5 = 4 \qquad \text{Remainder 2}$$
$$2 \div 1 = 2 \qquad \text{Remainder 0}$$
$$497 = 3442_{\text{five}}$$

Check:
$$3442_{\text{five}} = (3 \cdot 125) + (4 \cdot 25) + (4 \cdot 5) + (2 \cdot 1)$$
$$= 375 + 100 + 20 + 2$$
$$= 497 \checkmark$$

The symbol here is the ancient Chinese "**yin-yang,**" in which the black and the white enfold each other, each containing a part of the other. A kind of duality is conveyed between destructive (yin) and beneficial (yang) aspects.

Leibniz (1646–1716) studied Chinese ideograms in search of a universal symbolic language and promoted East–West cultural contact.

Niels Bohr (1885–1962), famous Danish Nobel laureate in physics (atomic theory), adopted the yin-yang symbol in his coat of arms to depict his principle of *complementarity,* which he believed was fundamental to reality at the deepest levels. Bohr also pushed for East–West cooperation.

In its 1992 edition, *The World Book Dictionary* first judged "yin-yang" to have been used enough to become a permanent part of our ever changing language, assigning it the definition, "made up of opposites."

The calculator shortcut for converting from another base to decimal form involved repeated *multiplications* by the other base. (See **Example 2.**) A shortcut for converting from decimal form to another base makes use of repeated *divisions* by the other base. Just divide the original decimal numeral, and the resulting quotients in turn, by the desired base until the quotient 0 appears.

Woven fabric is a binary system of threads going lengthwise (warp threads— tan in the diagram above) and threads going crosswise (weft or woof). At any point in a fabric, either warp or weft is on top, and the variation creates the pattern.

Nineteenth-century looms for weaving operated using punched cards, "programmed" for pattern. The looms were set up with hooked needles, the hooks holding the warp. Where there were holes in cards, the needles moved, the warp lifted, and the weft passed under. Where no holes were, the warp did not lift, and the weft was on top. The system parallels the on–off system in calculators and computers. In fact, these looms were models in the development of modern calculating machinery.

Joseph Marie Jacquard (1752–1823) is credited with improving the mechanical loom so that mass production of fabric was feasible.

▍▍ **EXAMPLE 4**   Using a Shortcut to Convert from Base Ten

Repeat **Example 3** using the shortcut just described.

SOLUTION

Remainder

$$
\begin{array}{r|l}
5 & 497 \\
5 & 99 \quad \longleftarrow \quad 2 \\
5 & 19 \quad \longleftarrow \quad 4 \\
5 & 3 \quad \longleftarrow \quad 4 \\
& 0 \quad \longleftarrow \quad 3
\end{array}
$$

Read the answer from the remainder column, reading from the bottom up.

$$497 = 3442_{\text{five}}$$

To see why this shortcut works, notice the following:

- The first division shows that four hundred ninety-seven 1s are equivalent to ninety-nine 5s and two 1s. (The two 1s are set aside and account for the last digit of the answer.)
- The second division shows that ninety-nine 5s are equivalent to nineteen 25s and four 5s. (The four 5s account for the next digit of the answer.)
- The third division shows that nineteen 25s are equivalent to three 125s and four 25s. (The four 25s account for the next digit of the answer.)
- The fourth (and final) division shows that the three 125s are equivalent to no 625s and three 125s. The remainders, as they are obtained *from top to bottom*, give the number of 1s, then 5s, then 25s, then 125s.

The methods for converting between bases ten and five, including the shortcuts, can be adapted for conversions between base ten and any other base.

▍▍ **EXAMPLE 5**   Converting from Base Seven to Base Ten

Convert 6343_{seven} to decimal form, by expanding in powers, and by using the calculator shortcut.

SOLUTION

$$
\begin{aligned}
6343_{\text{seven}} &= (6 \cdot 7^3) + (3 \cdot 7^2) + (4 \cdot 7^1) + (3 \cdot 7^0) \\
&= (6 \cdot 343) + (3 \cdot 49) + (4 \cdot 7) + (3 \cdot 1) \\
&= 2236
\end{aligned}
$$

Calculator shortcut: $6343_{\text{seven}} = ((6 \cdot 7 + 3) \cdot 7 + 4) \cdot 7 + 3 = 2236.$ ▍▍▍

▍▍ **EXAMPLE 6**   Converting from Base Ten to Base Seven

Convert 7508 to base seven.

SOLUTION

Remainder

Divide 7508 by 7, then divide the resulting quotient by 7, until a quotient of 0 results.

$$
\begin{array}{r|l}
7 & 7508 \\
7 & 1072 \quad \longleftarrow \quad 4 \\
7 & 153 \quad \longleftarrow \quad 1 \\
7 & 21 \quad \longleftarrow \quad 6 \\
7 & 3 \quad \longleftarrow \quad 0 \\
& 0 \quad \longleftarrow \quad 3
\end{array}
$$

From the remainders, reading bottom to top, $7508 = 30614_{\text{seven}}.$ ▍▍▍

To handle conversions between arbitrary bases (where neither is ten), go from the given base to base ten and then to the desired base.

▮▮ **EXAMPLE 7** Converting between Two Bases Other Than Ten

Convert 3164_{seven} to base five.

SOLUTION

Convert to decimal form.

$$3164_{\text{seven}} = (3 \cdot 7^3) + (1 \cdot 7^2) + (6 \cdot 7^1) + (4 \cdot 7^0)$$
$$= (3 \cdot 343) + (1 \cdot 49) + (6 \cdot 7) + (4 \cdot 1)$$
$$= 1029 + 49 + 42 + 4$$
$$= 1124$$

Convert this decimal result to base five.

Remainder

$$
\begin{array}{r|l}
5 & 1124 \\
5 & 224 \quad\leftarrow\quad 4 \\
5 & 44 \quad\leftarrow\quad 4 \\
5 & 8 \quad\leftarrow\quad 4 \\
5 & 1 \quad\leftarrow\quad 3 \\
& 0 \quad\leftarrow\quad 1
\end{array}
$$

From the remainders, $3164_{\text{seven}} = 13444_{\text{five}}$. ▮▮▮

Computer Mathematics

There are three alternative base systems that are most useful in computer applications—**binary** (base two), **octal** (base eight), and **hexadecimal** (base sixteen).

Computers and handheld calculators use the binary system for their internal calculations because that system consists of only two symbols, 0 and 1. All numbers can then be represented by electronic "switches," where "on" indicates 1 and "off" indicates 0. The octal and hexadecimal systems have been used extensively by programmers who work with internal computer codes and for communication between the CPU (central processing unit) and a printer or other output device.

The binary system is extreme in that it has only two available symbols (0 and 1). Thus, representing numbers in binary form requires more digits than in any other base. **Table 10** shows the whole numbers up to 20 expressed in binary form.

▮▮ **EXAMPLE 8** Converting from Binary to Decimal

Convert 110101_{two} to decimal form, by expanding in powers, and by using the calculator shortcut.

SOLUTION

$$110101_{\text{two}} = (1 \cdot 2^5) + (1 \cdot 2^4) + (0 \cdot 2^3) + (1 \cdot 2^2) + (0 \cdot 2^1) + (1 \cdot 2^0)$$
$$= (1 \cdot 32) + (1 \cdot 16) + (0 \cdot 8) + (1 \cdot 4) + (0 \cdot 2) + (1 \cdot 1)$$
$$= 32 + 16 + 0 + 4 + 0 + 1$$
$$= 53$$

Calculator shortcut: $110101_{\text{two}} = ((((1 \cdot 2 + 1) \cdot 2 + 0) \cdot 2 + 1) \cdot 2 + 0) \cdot 2 + 1$
$$= 53$$

Note the four left parentheses for a six-digit numeral. ▮▮▮

Table 10 Base Two Numerals

Base Ten (decimal)	Base Two (binary)
0	0
1	1
2	10
3	11
4	100
5	101
6	110
7	111
8	1000
9	1001
10	1010
11	1011
12	1100
13	1101
14	1110
15	1111
16	10000
17	10001
18	10010
19	10011
20	10100

■ ■ EXAMPLE 9   Converting from Decimal to Octal

Trick or Tree? The octal number 31 is equal to the decimal number 25. This may be written as

31 OCT = 25 DEC

Does this mean that Halloween and Christmas fall on the same day of the year?

Convert 9583 to octal form.

SOLUTION

Divide repeatedly by 8, writing the remainders at the side.

Remainder

$$
\begin{array}{r|r}
8 & 9583 \\
8 & 1197 \quad\leftarrow\quad 7 \\
8 & 149 \quad\leftarrow\quad 5 \\
8 & 18 \quad\leftarrow\quad 5 \\
8 & 2 \quad\leftarrow\quad 2 \\
& 0 \quad\leftarrow\quad 2
\end{array}
$$

From the remainders, $9583 = 22557_{\text{eight}}.$ ■ ■ ■

The hexadecimal system, having base 16, which is greater than 10, presents a new problem. Because distinct symbols are needed for all whole numbers from 0 up to one less than the base, base sixteen requires more symbols than are normally used in our decimal system. Computer programmers commonly use the letters **A, B, C, D, E, and F** as hexadecimal digits for **the numbers ten through fifteen, respectively.**

■ ■ EXAMPLE 10   Converting from Hexadecimal to Decimal

Convert $\text{FA5}_{\text{sixteen}}$ to decimal form.

SOLUTION

$$
\begin{aligned}
\text{FA5}_{\text{sixteen}} &= (15 \cdot 16^2) + (10 \cdot 16^1) + (5 \cdot 16^0) \\
&= 3840 + 160 + 5 \\
&= 4005
\end{aligned}
$$

F and A represent 15 and 10, respectively.

■ ■ ■

■ ■ EXAMPLE 11   Converting from Decimal to Hexadecimal

Convert 748 from decimal form to hexadecimal form.

SOLUTION

Use repeated division by 16.

Remainder   Hexadecimal notation

$$
\begin{array}{r|r}
16 & 748 \\
16 & 46 \quad\leftarrow\quad 12 \quad\leftarrow\quad C \\
16 & 2 \quad\leftarrow\quad 14 \quad\leftarrow\quad E \\
& 0 \quad\leftarrow\quad 2 \quad\leftarrow\quad 2
\end{array}
$$

From the remainders at the right, $748 = 2\text{EC}_{\text{sixteen}}.$ ■ ■ ■

Converting Calculators A number of scientific calculators are available that will convert between decimal, binary, octal, and hexadecimal, and will also do calculations directly in all of these separate modes. Instant conversions can also be done with Microsoft EXCEL or online. For example, see www.easycalculation.com.

The decimal whole numbers 0 through 17 are shown in **Table 11** on the next page along with their equivalents in the common computer-oriented bases (two, eight, and sixteen). Conversions among binary, octal, and hexadecimal can generally be accomplished by the shortcuts illustrated in the remaining examples.

The binary system is the natural one for internal computer workings because of its compatibility with the two-state electronic switches. It is very cumbersome, however, for human use, because so many digits occur even in the numerals for relatively small numbers. The octal and hexadecimal systems are the choices of computer programmers mainly because of their close relationship with the binary system. *Both eight and sixteen are powers of two.*

Table 11 **Some Decimal Equivalents in the Common Computer-Oriented Bases**

Decimal (Base Ten)	Hexadecimal (Base Sixteen)	Octal (Base Eight)	Binary (Base Two)
0	0	0	0
1	1	1	1
2	2	2	10
3	3	3	11
4	4	4	100
5	5	5	101
6	6	6	110
7	7	7	111
8	8	10	1000
9	9	11	1001
10	A	12	1010
11	B	13	1011
12	C	14	1100
13	D	15	1101
14	E	16	1110
15	F	17	1111
16	10	20	10000
17	11	21	10001

Table 12

Octal	Binary
0	000
1	001
2	010
3	011
4	100
5	101
6	110
7	111

When conversions involve one base that is a power of the other, there is a quick conversion shortcut available. For example, because $8 = 2^3$, every octal digit (0 through 7) can be expressed as a 3-digit binary numeral. See **Table 12.**

▌▌ **EXAMPLE 12** Converting from Octal to Binary

Convert 473_{eight} to binary form.

SOLUTION

Replace each octal digit with its 3-digit binary equivalent. (Leading zeros can be omitted only when they occur in the left-most group.) Combine the equivalents into a single binary numeral.

$$\begin{array}{ccc} 4 & 7 & 3_{\text{eight}} \\ \downarrow & \downarrow & \downarrow \\ 100 & 111 & 011_{\text{two}} \end{array}$$
$$473_{\text{eight}} = 100111011_{\text{two}} \quad ▌▌▌$$

▌▌ **EXAMPLE 13** Converting from Binary to Octal

Convert 10011110_{two} to octal form.

SOLUTION

Start at the right and break the digits into groups of three. Then convert the groups to their octal equivalents.
Finally, $10011110_{\text{two}} = 236_{\text{eight}}.$

$$\begin{array}{ccc} 10 & 011 & 110_{\text{two}} \\ \downarrow & \downarrow & \downarrow \\ 2 & 3 & 6_{\text{eight}} \end{array}$$

▌▌▌

Because $16 = 2^4$, every hexadecimal digit can be equated to a 4-digit binary numeral (see **Table 13** below), and conversions between binary and hexadecimal forms can be done in a manner similar to that used in **Examples 12 and 13**.

▌▌ **EXAMPLE 14** Converting from Hexadecimal to Binary

Convert $8B4F_{\text{sixteen}}$ to binary form.

SOLUTION

Each hexadecimal digit yields a 4-digit binary equivalent.

8	B	4	F_{sixteen}
↓	↓	↓	↓
1000	1011	0100	1111_{two}

Combining these groups of digits, $8B4F_{\text{sixteen}} = 1000101101001111_{\text{two}}$.   ▮▮▮

Several games and tricks are based on the binary system. For example, **Table 14** can be used to find the age of a person 31 years old or younger. The person need only tell you the columns that contain his or her age. For example, suppose Kathy Apogee says that her age appears in columns B, C, and D. To find her age, add the numbers from the top row of these columns:

Kathy is $2 + 4 + 8 = 14$ years old.

Do you see how this trick works? (See **Exercises 69–72.**)

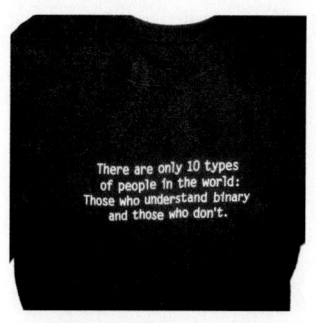

The following message was seen on the front of a T-shirt. "There are only 10 types of people in the world: Those who understand binary and those who don't." Do YOU understand this message?

Table 13

Hexadecimal	Binary
0	0000
1	0001
2	0010
3	0011
4	0100
5	0101
6	0110
7	0111
8	1000
9	1001
A	1010
B	1011
C	1100
D	1101
E	1110
F	1111

Table 14

A	B	C	D	E
1	2	4	8	16
3	3	5	9	17
5	6	6	10	18
7	7	7	11	19
9	10	12	12	20
11	11	13	13	21
13	14	14	14	22
15	15	15	15	23
17	18	20	24	24
19	19	21	25	25
21	22	22	26	26
23	23	23	27	27
25	26	28	28	28
27	27	29	29	29
29	30	30	30	30
31	31	31	31	31

4.4 EXERCISES

List the first twenty counting numbers in each base.

1. seven (Only digits 0 through 6 are used in base seven.)

2. eight (Only digits 0 through 7 are used.)

3. nine (Only digits 0 through 8 are used.)

4. sixteen (The digits 0, 1, 2, . . . , 9, A, B, C, D, E, F are used in base sixteen.)

Write (in the same base) the counting numbers just before and just after the given number. (Do not convert to base ten.)

5. 14_{five}

6. 555_{six}

7. $B6F_{\text{sixteen}}$

8. 10111_{two}

Determine the number of distinct symbols needed in each of the following positional systems.

9. base three

10. base seven

11. base eleven

12. base sixteen

Determine, in each base, the least and greatest four-digit numbers and their decimal equivalents.

13. three

14. sixteen

Convert each number to decimal form by expanding in powers and by using the calculator shortcut.

15. 24_{five}

16. 62_{seven}

17. 1011_{two}

18. 35_{eight}

19. $3BC_{\text{sixteen}}$

20. 34432_{five}

21. 2366_{seven}

22. 101101110_{two}

23. 70266_{eight}

24. $ABCD_{\text{sixteen}}$

25. 2023_{four}

26. 6185_{nine}

27. 41533_{six}

28. 88703_{nine}

Convert each number from decimal form to the given base.

29. 86 to base five

30. 65 to base seven

31. 19 to base two

32. 935 to base eight

33. 147 to base sixteen

34. 2730 to base sixteen

35. 36401 to base five

36. 70893 to base seven

37. 586 to base two

38. 12888 to base eight

39. 8407 to base three

40. 11028 to base four

41. 9346 to base six

42. 99999 to base nine

Make each conversion as indicated.

43. 43_{five} to base seven

44. 27_{eight} to base five

45. 6748_{nine} to base four

46. $C02_{\text{sixteen}}$ to base seven

Convert each number from octal form to binary form.

47. 367_{eight}

48. 2406_{eight}

Convert each number from binary form to octal form.

49. 100110111_{two}

50. 11010111101_{two}

Make each conversion as indicated.

51. DC_{sixteen} to binary

52. $F111_{\text{sixteen}}$ to binary

53. 101101_{two} to hexadecimal

54. $101111011101000_{\text{two}}$ to hexadecimal

Identify the greatest number from each list.

55. 42_{seven}, 37_{eight}, $1D_{\text{sixteen}}$

56. 1101110_{two}, 414_{five}, $6F_{\text{sixteen}}$

*There is a theory that twelve would be a better base than ten for general use. This is mainly because twelve has more divisors (1, 2, 3, 4, 6, 12) than ten (1, 2, 5, 10), which makes fractions easier in base twelve. The base twelve system is called the **duodecimal system**. In the decimal system we speak of a one, a ten, and a hundred (and so on); in the duodecimal system we say a one, a dozen (twelve), and a gross (twelve squared, or one hundred forty-four).*

57. Adam Goldstein's clients ordered 9 gross, 10 dozen, and 11 copies of *The Help* during 2010. How many copies was that in base ten?

58. Which amount is larger: 3 gross, 6 dozen or 2 gross, 19 dozen?

*One common method of converting symbols into binary digits for computer processing is called **ASCII** (American Standard Code of Information Interchange). The uppercase letters A through Z are assigned the numbers 65 through 90, so A has binary code 1000001 and Z has code 1011010. Lowercase letters a through z have codes 97 through 122 (that is, 1100001 through 1111010). ASCII codes, as well as other numerical computer output, normally appear without commas.*

Write the binary code for each letter.

59. C

60. X

61. k

62. q

Break each code into groups of seven digits and write as letters.

63. 1001000100010110011001010000

64. 100001110010001010101100001111001011

Translate each word into an ASCII string of binary digits. (Be sure to distinguish uppercase and lowercase letters.)

65. New

66. Orleans

67. Explain why the octal and hexadecimal systems are convenient for people who code for computers.

68. There are thirty-seven counting numbers whose base eight numerals contain two digits but whose base three numerals contain four digits. Find the least and greatest of these numbers.

Refer to **Table 14** *for Exercises 69–72.*

69. After observing the binary forms of the numbers 1–31, identify a common property of all **Table 14** numbers in each of the following columns.

(a) Column A

(b) Column B

(c) Column C

(d) Column D

(e) Column E

70. Explain how the "trick" of **Table 14** works.

71. How many columns would be needed for **Table 14** to include all ages up to 63?

72. How many columns would be needed for **Table 14** to include all ages up to 127?

In our decimal system, we distinguish odd and even numbers by looking at their ones (or units) digits. If the ones digit is even (0, 2, 4, 6, or 8), the number is even. If the ones digit is odd (1, 3, 5, 7, or 9), the number is odd. For Exercises 73–80, determine whether this same criterion works for numbers expressed in the given bases.

73. two   **74.** three   **75.** four   **76.** five

77. six   **78.** seven   **79.** eight   **80.** nine

81. Consider all even bases. If the above criterion works for all, explain why. If not, find a criterion that does work for all even bases.

82. Consider all odd bases. If the above criterion works for all, explain why. If not, find a criterion that does work for all odd bases.

Determine whether the given base five numeral represents one that is divisible by five.

83. 3204_{five} **84.** 200_{five}

85. 2310_{five} **86.** 342_{five}

*Recall that conversions between binary and octal are simplified because eight is a power of 2: $8 = 2^3$. (See **Examples 12 and 13**.) The same is true of conversions between binary and hexadecimal, because $16 = 2^4$. (See **Example 14**.) Direct conversion between octal and hexadecimal does not work the same way, because 16 is not a power of 8. Explain how to carry out each conversion without using base ten, and give an example.*

87. hexadecimal to octal   **88.** octal to hexadecimal

Devise a method (similar to the one for conversions between binary, octal, and hexadecimal) for converting between base three and base nine, and use it to carry out each conversion.

89. 6504_{nine} to base three

90. 81170_{nine} to base three

91. 212201221_{three} to base nine

92. 200121021_{three} to base nine

*The colors seen on a computer screen consist of combinations of the primary colors red (R), green (G), and blue (B). The intensity of each of the three ranges from 0 to 255. This allows $255^3 = 16{,}581{,}375$ distinct colors (at least theoretically), where a particular color's designation may require up to 9 digits. For example, the (R, G, B) designation for black is (0, 0, 0), white is (255, 255, 255), and gray is (128, 128, 128). But the colors are coded in **HTML** (HyperText Markup Language) in hexadecimal, so each primary color intensity then requires no more than two digits. ($255 = FF_{\text{sixteen}}$.) White is coded FFFFFF, and black is 000000. Give similar HTML codes for the following colors.*

93. gray   **94.** yellow (255, 255, 0)

95. hot pink (255, 105, 180)   **96.** the color (171, 205, 239)

EXTENSION Modular Systems

Clock Arithmetic • Modular Systems • Residues of Large Numbers

Clock Arithmetic The numeration systems already discussed in this chapter all begin with the infinite set of whole numbers (or perhaps natural numbers), then devise ways to represent them, and use them for counting, calculating, and so on. There are many applications, however, where it is useful somehow to "reduce" the infinite set of numbers to a finite set. For example, consider this question:

Suppose it is 8 o'clock right now. What time will it be 33 hours from now?

Figure 12

Considering hours only (no minutes or seconds), any such question should have its answer in the finite set

$$\{1, 2, 3, \ldots, 12\}.$$

But how is the answer found? One way is to use a 12-hour clock face, as in **Figure 12**, where 12 is replaced by 0 and the finite set for our 12-hour clock system is

$$\{0, 1, 2, 3, 4, 5, 6, 7, 8, 9, 10, 11\}.$$

Place the hour hand at 8. Then rotate it clockwise through a 33-hour arc. Wherever it stops is the answer. (Check that it is 5 o'clock.) **Example 1** shows another option, not using the clock face.

▮▮ **EXAMPLE 1** Computing a Sum in 12-Hour Clock Arithmetic

In 12-hour clock arithmetic, find the sum $8 + 33$.

SOLUTION

Use a calculator, and observe that

$$8 + 33 = 41 \quad \text{and} \quad \frac{41}{12} = 3.416666667.^*$$

We don't care about the whole number of trips around the clock face, so drop the 3. Then multiply by 12 (and round if necessary) to obtain the remainder.

$$3.416666667 - 3 = 0.416666667$$
$$12 \cdot 0.416666667 = 5 \quad \leftarrow \text{The remainder is the answer.}$$

In 12-hour clock arithmetic, $8 + 33 = 5$. Thus, we have found that

$$8 + 33 = 3 \cdot 12 + 5,$$

which you can check directly. ▮▮▮

Dividing any whole number by 12 will always yield a remainder in the set

$$\{0, 1, 2, 3, 4, 5, 6, 7, 8, 9, 10, 11\}.$$

Thus the answer to any 12-hour clock arithmetic problem will be in this finite set. Every whole number, no matter how large, is "equivalent" to exactly one of these 12 remainders.

▮▮ **EXAMPLE 2** Computing a Product in 12-Hour Clock Arithmetic

In 12-hour clock arithmetic, find the product $547 \cdot 11{,}873$.

SOLUTION

$$547 \cdot 11{,}873 = 6{,}494{,}531$$
$$\frac{6{,}494{,}531}{12} = 541{,}210.9167$$
$$12 \cdot 0.9167 = 11 \quad \leftarrow \text{The remainder is the answer.}$$

In 12-hour clock arithmetic, $547 \cdot 11{,}873 = 11$. ▮▮▮

Plagued by serious maritime mishaps linked to navigational difficulties, several European governments offered prizes for an effective method of determining longitude. The largest prize was 20,000 pounds (equivalent to several million dollars in today's currency) offered by the British Parliament in the Longitude Act of 1714. While famed scientists, academics, and politicians pursued an answer in the stars, **John Harrison,** a clock maker, set about to build a clock that could maintain accuracy at sea. This turned out to be the key, and Harrison's **Chronometer** eventually earned him the prize.

For a fascinating account of this drama and of Harrison's struggle to collect his prize money from the government, see the book *The Illustrated Longitude* by Dava Sobel and William J. H. Andrewes.

*The equals symbol, =, is used in computations in this section despite the fact that some of the quotients are actually approximations.

EXAMPLE 3 Applying a 7-day "Clock"

Suppose that today is Thursday, January 15, 2015. What will be the day of the week exactly one year from today?

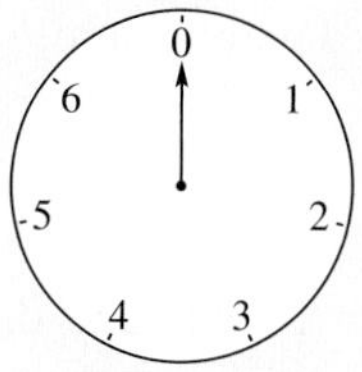

SOLUTION

Because 2015 is not divisible by 4, it is not a leap year so it has 365 days. In this case we need the remainder after 365 is divided by 7. We could rotate the "day hand" on the 7-day clock face in **Figure 13** or calculate as follows.

$$\frac{365}{7} = 52.14285714 \quad \text{and} \quad 52.14285714 - 52 = 0.14285714$$

$$7 \cdot 0.14285714 = 1$$

One year from today will be one day past Thursday—that is, Friday.   ■■■

In this 7-day clock system, every whole number, no matter how large, is equivalent to exactly one remainder in the set $\{0, 1, 2, 3, 4, 5, 6\}$.

Modular Systems The many applications of such systems, which reduce the infinite set of whole numbers to a finite subset, based on remainders, have prompted mathematicians to expand these ideas to **modular systems** in general. **Example 3** showed that, in the 7-day clock system, 365 and 1 are, in a sense, equivalent. More formally, we say that 365 and 1 are **congruent modulo** 7 (or **congruent mod** 7), which is written

$$365 \equiv 1 \,(\text{mod}\, 7) \quad \text{The sign} \equiv \text{indicates congruence.}$$

By observing 7-day clock hand movements, we also see that, for example,

$$8 \equiv 1 \,(\text{mod}\, 7), \quad 15 \equiv 1 \,(\text{mod}\, 7), \quad \text{and so on.}$$

In each case, the congruence is true because the difference of the two congruent numbers is a multiple of 7.

$$8 - 1 = 7 = 1 \cdot 7, \quad 15 - 1 = 14 = 2 \cdot 7, \quad 365 - 1 = 364 = 52 \cdot 7$$

Congruence Modulo n

The integers a and b are **congruent modulo n** (where n is a natural number greater than 1 called the **modulus**) if and only if the difference $a - b$ is divisible by n. Symbolically, this congruence is written as follows.

$$a \equiv b \,(\text{mod}\, n)$$

Because being divisible by n is the same as being a multiple of n, we can say that

$$a \equiv b \,(\text{mod}\, n) \quad \textbf{if and only if} \quad a - b = kn \quad \textbf{for some integer } k.$$

EXAMPLE 4 Checking the Truth of Modular Equations

Decide whether each statement is *true* or *false*.

(a) $16 \equiv 10 \,(\text{mod}\, 2)$ **(b)** $49 \equiv 32 \,(\text{mod}\, 5)$ **(c)** $30 \equiv 345 \,(\text{mod}\, 7)$

SOLUTION

(a) The difference $16 - 10 = 6$ is divisible by 2, so $16 \equiv 10 \,(\text{mod}\, 2)$ is *true*.

(b) The statement $49 \equiv 32 \,(\text{mod}\, 5)$ is *false*, because $49 - 32 = 17$, which is not divisible by 5.

(c) The statement $30 \equiv 345 \,(\text{mod}\, 7)$ is *true*, because $30 - 345 = -315$ is divisible by 7. (It doesn't matter if we find $30 - 345$ or $345 - 30$.)   ■■■

Figure 13

A **chess clock** or double clock is used to time chess, backgammon, and Scrabble games. Push one button, and that clock stops—the other begins simultaneously. When a player's allotted time for the game has expired, that player will lose if he or she has not made the required number of moves.

Emanuel Lasker achieved mastery in both mathematics and chess. He was best known as a World Chess Champion for 27 years, until 1921. Lasker also was famous in mathematical circles for his work concerning the theory of primary ideals, algebraic analogies of prime numbers. The **Lasker-Noether theorem** bears his name along with that of **Emmy Noether.** Noether extended Lasker's work. Her father had been Lasker's Ph.D. advisor.

There is another method of determining if two numbers, a and b, are congruent modulo n.

Criterion for Congruence

$a \equiv b \pmod{n}$ if and only if the same remainder is obtained when a and b are divided by n.

For example, we know that $27 \equiv 9 \pmod 6$ because $27 - 9 = 18$, which is divisible by 6. Now, if 27 is divided by 6, the quotient is 4 and the remainder is 3. Also, if 9 is divided by 6, the quotient is 1 and the remainder is 3. According to the criterion above, $27 \equiv 9 \pmod 6$ since both remainders are the same.

Addition, subtraction, and multiplication can be performed in any modular system. Because final answers should be whole numbers less than the modulus, we can first find an answer using ordinary arithmetic. Then, as long as the answer is nonnegative, simply divide it by the modulus and keep the remainder. This produces the least nonnegative integer that is congruent (modulo n) to the ordinary answer.

▮▮ **EXAMPLE 5** Performing Modular Arithmetic

Find each sum, difference, or product.

(a) $(50 + 34) \pmod 7$ **(b)** $(27 - 5) \pmod 6$ **(c)** $(8 \cdot 9) \pmod{10}$

SOLUTION

(a) First add 50 and 34 to get 84. Then divide 84 by 7. The remainder is 0, so we obtain $84 \equiv 0 \pmod 7$ and

$$(50 + 34) \equiv 0 \pmod 7.$$

(b) $27 - 5 = 22$. Divide 22 by 6, obtaining 4 as a remainder.

$$(27 - 5) \equiv 4 \pmod 6$$

(c) Since $8 \cdot 9 = 72$, and 72 leaves a remainder of 2 when divided by 10,

$$(8 \cdot 9) \equiv 2 \pmod{10}. \qquad ▮▮▮$$

PROBLEM-SOLVING HINT A modular system $(\bmod\, n)$ allows only a fixed set of remainder values, $0, 1, 2, \ldots, n - 1$. One practical approach to solving modular equations, at least when n is reasonably small, is to simply try all these integers. For each solution found in this way, others can be found by adding multiples of the modulus to it.

▮▮ **EXAMPLE 6** Solving Modular Equations

Solve each modular equation for whole number solutions.

(a) $(3 + x) \equiv 5 \pmod 7$ **(b)** $5x \equiv 4 \pmod 9$

(c) $6x \equiv 3 \pmod 8$ **(d)** $8x \equiv 8 \pmod 8$

SOLUTION

(a) Because dividing 5 by 7 yields remainder 5, the criterion for congruence is that the given equation is true only if dividing $3 + x$ by 7 also yields remainder 5. Try replacing x, in turn, by 0, 1, 2, 3, 4, 5, and 6.

$x = 0$: $(3 + 0) \equiv 5 \pmod 7$ is false.   The remainder is 3.

$x = 1$: $(3 + 1) \equiv 5 \pmod 7$ is false.   The remainder is 4.

$x = 2$: $(3 + 2) \equiv 5 \pmod 7$ is true.   The remainder is 5.

Try $x = 3, x = 4, x = 5$, and $x = 6$ to see that none work. Of the integers from 0 through 6, only 2 is a solution of the equation $(3 + x) \equiv 5 \pmod 7$.

Because 2 is a solution, find other solutions to this mod 7 equation by repeatedly adding 7.

$$2 + 7 = 9, \quad 9 + 7 = 16, \quad 16 + 7 = 23, \quad \text{and so on.}$$

The set of all nonnegative solutions of $(3 + x) \equiv 5 \pmod 7$ is

$$\{2, 9, 16, 23, 30, 37, \ldots\}.$$

(b) Dividing 4 by 9 yields remainder 4. Because the modulus is 9, check the remainders when $5x$ is divided by 9 for $x = 0, 1, 2, 3, 4, 5, 6, 7$, and 8.

$x = 0$: $5 \cdot 0 \equiv 4 \pmod 9$ is false.   The remainder is 0.

$x = 1$: $5 \cdot 1 \equiv 4 \pmod 9$ is false.   The remainder is 5.

Continue trying numbers. Only $x = 8$ works.

$$5 \cdot 8 = 40 \equiv 4 \pmod 9 \quad \text{The remainder is 4.}$$

The set of all nonnegative solutions to the equation $5x \equiv 4 \pmod 9$ is

$$\{8, 8 + 9, 8 + 9 + 9, 8 + 9 + 9 + 9, \ldots\}, \quad \text{or} \quad \{8, 17, 26, 35, 44, 53, \ldots\}.$$

(c) To solve $6x \equiv 3 \pmod 8$, try the numbers 0, 1, 2, 3, 4, 5, 6, and 7. None work. Therefore, the equation $6x \equiv 3 \pmod 8$ has no solutions. Write the set of all solutions as the empty set, $\emptyset$.

This result is reasonable because $6x$ will always be even, no matter which whole number is used for x. Because $6x$ is even and 3 is odd, the difference $6x - 3$ will be odd and therefore not divisible by 8.

(d) To solve $8x \equiv 8 \pmod 8$, try the numbers 0, 1, 2, 3, 4, 5, 6, and 7. *Any* replacement will work. The solution set is $\{0, 1, 2, 3, \ldots\}$, the set of all whole numbers. ■■■

Some problems can be solved by writing down two or more modular equations and finding their common solutions, as in the next example.

■■ **EXAMPLE 7**   Finding the Number of Discs in a CD Collection

Julio wants to arrange his CD collection in equal size stacks, but after trying stacks of 4, stacks of 5, and stacks of 6, he finds that there is always 1 disc left over. Assuming Julio owns more than one CD, what is the least possible number of discs in his collection?

SOLUTION

The given information leads to three modular equations,

$$x \equiv 1 \pmod 4, \quad x \equiv 1 \pmod 5, \quad \text{and} \quad x \equiv 1 \pmod 6.$$

For the first equation, try $x = 0, x = 1, x = 2$, and $x = 3$. The value 1 works, as it does for the other two equations as well. So the solution sets are, respectively,

$$\{1, 5, 9, 13, 17, 21, 25, 29, 33, 37, 41, 45, 49, 53, 57, \mathbf{61}, 65, 69, \ldots\},$$

$$\{1, 6, 11, 16, 21, 26, 31, 36, 41, 46, 51, 56, \mathbf{61}, 66, 71, 76, \ldots\},$$

and $\{1, 7, 13, 19, 25, 31, 37, 43, 49, 55, \mathbf{61}, \ldots\}.$

The least common solution greater than 1 is 61, so the least possible number of discs in the collection is 61. ■■■

▌▌ **EXAMPLE 8** Applying Congruences to a Construction Problem

Jeanne Bronson, a dry-wall contractor, is ordering materials to finish a 17-foot-by-45-foot room. The wallboard panels come in 4-foot widths. Show that, after uncut panels are applied, all four walls will require additional partial strips of the same width.

SOLUTION

The width of any partial strip needed will be the remainder when the wall length is divided by 4 (the panel width). In terms of congruence, we must show that $17 \equiv 45 \pmod{4}$. By the criterion for congruence, we see that this is true because both 17 and 45 give the same remainder (namely 1) when divided by 4. A 1-foot partial strip will be required for each wall. (In this case, Jeanne can use four 1-foot strips, cut from a single panel, so there will be no waste.) ▌▌▌

Residues of Large Numbers The basic concern in a modular system with modulus n is

Given any whole number a, no matter how large, find the number b in the set

$$\{0, 1, 2, 3, \ldots, n - 1\} \text{ such that } a \equiv b \pmod{n}.$$

This number b is the *remainder* when a is divided by n. It is called the **residue** of a, modulo n. To find this residue can be thought of as to "mod." To mod a very large number a, we should definitely make use of a calculator. In fact, many modern applications involve huge numbers and require powerful computers and sophisticated algorithms to complete the process. (For example, see **Extension Modern Cryptography** in **Chapter 5.**)

The process used earlier can be summarized.

Calculator Routine for Finding the Residue of a, Modulo n

In a modular system, the residue modulo n for a number a can be found by completing these three steps, in turn.

Step 1 Divide a by the modulus n.
Step 2 Subtract the integer part of the quotient to obtain only the fractional part.
Step 3 Multiply the fractional part of the quotient by n.

The final result is the residue modulo n.

▌▌ **EXAMPLE 9** Finding the Modular Residue of a Large Number

Find the residue of 846,238,527, modulo 23.

SOLUTION

$$\frac{846,238,527}{23} = 36,792,979.434783 \quad \text{(Your calculator may not display this many decimal places.)}$$

$$36,792,979.434783 - 36,792,979 = 0.434783$$

$$23 \cdot 0.434783 = 10 \quad \leftarrow \text{residue}$$

The residue is 10. ($846,238,527 = 36,792,979 \cdot 23 + 10$.) ▌▌▌

Suppose we want to calculate the product of 458,687 and 931,056, modulo 18. The calculator displays the answer in exponential form.

$$458,687 \cdot 931,056 = 4.270632835 \text{E}11$$

Step 1, dividing by 18, yields 2.372573797E10, and we can't tell what the integer part is for Step 2. To get around this difficulty, we can use the fact that, in general,

the residue of a product equals the product of the residues

and employ the maxim,

"mod before you multiply."

▌▌ **EXAMPLE 10** Finding the Residue of a Large Product

Find the residue of 458,687 · 931,056, modulo 18.

SOLUTION

$$\frac{458,687}{18} = 25,482.61111 \quad \text{and} \quad \frac{931,056}{18} = 51,725.33333$$

$$25,482.61111 - 25,482 = 0.61111 \quad \text{and} \quad 51,725.33333 - 51,725 = 0.33333$$

$$0.61111 \cdot 18 = 11 \quad \text{and} \quad 0.33333 \cdot 18 = 6$$

Now the product of the individual residues is 11 · 6 = 66. Since 66 is still not less than 18, simply mod again.

$$\frac{66}{18} = 3.666\ldots, \quad 3.666\ldots - 3 = 0.666\ldots, \quad \text{and} \quad 18 \cdot 0.666\ldots = 12$$

The residue, modulo 18, of 458,687 · 931,056 is 12. ▌▌▌

EXTENSION EXERCISES

Find each sum or product in 12-hour clock arithmetic.

1. 7 + 16

2. 3 + 21

3. 9 · 7

4. 7 · 11

Find each sum or product in 7-day clock arithmetic.

5. 6 + 42

6. 5 + 365

7. 4 · 28

8. 3 · 54

The military uses a 24-hour clock to avoid the problems of "A.M." and "P.M." For example, 1100 *hours is 11 A.M., while* 2100 *hours is 9 P.M.* (12 noon + 9 hours). *In these designations, the last two digits represent minutes, and the digits before that represent hours. Find each sum in the 24-hour clock system.*

9. 1400 + 500

10. 1300 + 1800

11. 0750 + 1630

12. 1545 + 0815

13. Explain how the following three statements can *all* be true. (*Hint:* Think of clocks.)

$$1145 + 1135 = 2280$$
$$1145 + 1135 = 1120$$
$$1145 + 1135 = 2320$$

Answer true *or* false *for each statement.*

14. 5 ≡ 19 (mod 3)

15. 35 ≡ 8 (mod 9)

16. 5445 ≡ 0 (mod 3)

17. 7021 ≡ 4202 (mod 6)

Work each modular arithmetic problem.

18. (12 + 7)(mod 4)

19. (62 + 95)(mod 9)

20. (35 − 22)(mod 5)

21. (82 − 45)(mod 3)

22. (5 · 8)(mod 3)

23. (32 · 21)(mod 8)

24. [4 · (13 + 6)] (mod 11)

25. [(10 + 7) · (5 + 3)] (mod 10)

26. The text described how to do arithmetic mod *n* when the ordinary answer comes out nonnegative. Explain what to do when the ordinary answer is negative.

Find all nonnegative solutions for each equation.

27. $x \equiv 3 \pmod 7$

28. $(2 + x) \equiv 7 \pmod 3$

29. $6x \equiv 2 \pmod 2$

30. $(5x - 3) \equiv 7 \pmod 4$

Solve each problem.

31. *Odometer Readings* For many years automobile odometers showed five whole number digits and a digit for tenths of a mile. For those odometers showing just five whole number digits, totals are recorded according to what modulus?

32. *Distance Traveled by a Car* If a car's five-digit whole number odometer shows a reading of 29,306, *in theory* how many miles might the car have traveled?

33. *Silver Spoon Collection* Cheryl Falkowski has a collection of silver spoons from all over the world. She finds that she can arrange her spoons in sets of 7 with 6 left over, sets of 8 with 1 left over, or sets of 15 with 3 left over. If Cheryl has fewer than 200 spoons, how many are there?

34. *Piles of Ticket Stubs* Steven Booth finds that whether he sorts his White Sox ticket stubs into piles of 10, piles of 15, or piles of 20, there are always 2 left over. What is the least number of stubs he could have (assuming he has more than 2)?

35. *Flight Attendant Schedules* Megan Carvolth and Michele Dorsey, flight attendants for two different airlines, are close friends and like to get together as often as possible. Megan flies a 21-day schedule (including days off), which then repeats, while Michele has a repeating 30-day schedule. Both of their routines include layovers in Chicago, New Orleans, and San Francisco. The table below shows which days of each of their individual schedules they are in these cities. (Assume the first day of a cycle is day number 1.)

	Days in Chicago	Days in New Orleans	Days in San Francisco
Megan	1, 2, 8	5, 12	6, 18, 19
Michele	23, 29, 30	5, 6, 17	8, 10, 15, 20, 25

If today is July 1 and both are starting their schedules today (day 1), list the days during July and August that they will be able to see each other in each of the three cities.

The following formula can be used to find the day of the week on which a given year begins.* Here y represents the year (which must be after 1582, when our current calendar began). First calculate

$$a = y + [\![(y - 1)/4]\!] - [\![(y - 1)/100]\!] + [\![(y - 1)/400]\!],$$

where, in general, $[\![x]\!]$ is the greatest integer less than or equal to x. (For example, $[\![9.2]\!] = 9$, and $[\![\pi]\!] = 3$.) After finding a, find the smallest nonnegative integer b such that

$$a \equiv b \pmod 7.$$

Then b gives the day of January 1, with b = 0 representing Sunday, b = 1 Monday, and so on.
Find the day of the week on which January 1 would occur in each year.

36. 1812   **37.** 1865

38. 2006   **39.** 2020

Some people believe that Friday the thirteenth is unlucky. The table* below shows the months that will have a Friday the thirteenth if the first day of the year is known. A year is a leap year if it is divisible by 4. The only exception to this rule is that a century year (1900, for example) is a leap year only when it is divisible by 400.

First Day of Year	Non-leap Year	Leap Year
Sunday	Jan., Oct.	Jan., April, July
Monday	April, July	Sept., Dec.
Tuesday	Sept., Dec.	June
Wednesday	June	March, Nov.
Thursday	Feb., March, Nov.	Feb., Aug.
Friday	August	May
Saturday	May	Oct.

Use the table to determine the months that have a Friday the thirteenth for each year.

40. 2011   **41.** 2012

42. 2013   **43.** 2200

44. Modular arithmetic can be used to create **residue designs.** For example, the designs (11, 3) and (65, 3) are shown here.

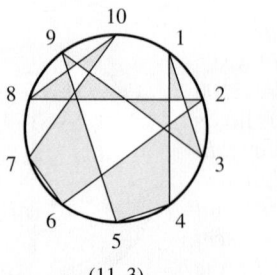 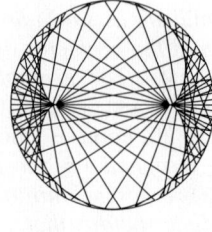

(11, 3)   (65, 3)

*Given in "An Aid to the Superstitious," by G. L. Ritter, S. R. Lowry, H. B. Woodruff, and T. L. Isenhour. *The Mathematics Teacher,* May 1977, pp. 456–457.

To see how such designs are created, construct a new design, (11, 5), by proceeding as follows.

(a) Draw a circle and divide the circumference into 10 equal parts. Label the division points as 1, 2, 3, ..., 10.

(b) Since $1 \cdot 5 \equiv 5 \pmod{11}$, connect 1 and 5. (We use 5 as a multiplier because we are making an (11, 5) design.)

(c) $2 \cdot 5 \equiv 10 \pmod{11}$
Therefore, connect 2 and _____.

(d) $3 \cdot 5 \equiv$ _____ $\pmod{11}$
Connect 3 and _____.

(e) $4 \cdot 5 \equiv$ _____ $\pmod{11}$
Connect 4 and _____.

(f) $5 \cdot 5 \equiv$ _____ $\pmod{11}$
Connect 5 and _____.

(g) $6 \cdot 5 \equiv$ _____ $\pmod{11}$
Connect 6 and _____.

(h) $7 \cdot 5 \equiv$ _____ $\pmod{11}$
Connect 7 and _____.

(i) $8 \cdot 5 \equiv$ _____ $\pmod{11}$
Connect 8 and _____.

(j) $9 \cdot 5 \equiv$ _____ $\pmod{11}$
Connect 9 and _____.

(k) $10 \cdot 5 \equiv$ _____ $\pmod{11}$
Connect 10 and _____.

(l) You might want to shade some of the regions you have found to make an interesting pattern. For more information, see "Residue Designs," by Phil Locke in *The Mathematics Teacher,* March 1972, pages 260–263.

Identification numbers are used in various ways for many kinds of different products.* Books, for example, are assigned International Standard Book Numbers (ISBNs).

For many years, 10-digit ISBNs have been used. In 2007 a conversion process to 13 digits was begun. The 10-digit ISBN for this book is

0-321-69381-7.

The first digit, 0, identifies the book as being published in an English-language country. The next digits, 321, identify the publisher, and 69381 identifies this particular book. The final 7 is a check digit designed to help detect an invalid ISBN. (Maybe a wrong digit was entered, or two digits were inadvertently transposed.)

In general, if the digits are denoted $x_1, x_2, x_3, \ldots, x_{10}$, then the check digit x_{10} is calculated using multipliers 1, 2, 3, 4, and so on up to 9, according to the formula at the top of the next column.

*For an interesting general discussion, see "The Mathematics of Identification Numbers," by Joseph A. Gallian in The College Mathematics Journal, *May 1991, p. 194.*

$$x_{10} = (1x_1 + 2x_2 + 3x_3 + 4x_4 + 5x_5 + 6x_6 + 7x_7 + 8x_8 + 9x_9) \pmod{11}$$

For the ISBN 0-321-69381-7,

$$\begin{aligned} x_{10} &= (1 \cdot 0 + 2 \cdot 3 + 3 \cdot 2 + 4 \cdot 1 + 5 \cdot 6 + 6 \cdot 9 \\ &\quad + 7 \cdot 3 + 8 \cdot 8 + 9 \cdot 1) \pmod{11} \\ &= 194 \pmod{11} \\ &= 7 \end{aligned}$$

(If a check "digit" is 10, the letter X is used instead of 10.)

When an order for this book is received, the ISBN is entered into a computer, and the check (final digit on the right) digit evaluated. If this result does not match the check digit on the order, the order will not be processed.

Does each ISBN have the correct check digit?

45. 0-275-98341-2   **46.** 0-374-29288-7

Find the appropriate check digit for each ISBN. (Note: The positions of hyphens (or spaces) may vary (or there may be none). This does not affect the determination of the check digit.)

47. *Man of the Century,* by Jonathan Kwitny, 0-8050-2688- _____

48. *1776,* by David McCullough, 0-7432-2671- _____

For a 13-digit ISBN, the check digit is found by the formula

$$x_{13} = 10 - (x_1 + 3x_2 + x_3 + 3x_4 + x_5 + 3x_6 + \cdots + x_{11} + 3x_{12}) \pmod{10}.$$

The multipliers alternate 1, 3, 1, 3, and so on. Does each of the following 13-digit ISBNs have the correct check digit?

49. 978-0-06-193979-1   **50.** 978-1-4391-6857-8

Find the appropriate check digit for each ISBN.

51. *The Christmas Sweater,* by Glenn Beck, 978-1-4165-9485- _____

52. *One to Nine, The Inner Life of Numbers,* by Andrew Hodges, 978-0-393-33723- _____

Find the modular residue of each product.

53. $9{,}512{,}673 \cdot 2{,}583{,}691 \pmod{6}$

54. $369{,}852{,}142 \cdot 789{,}654{,}031 \pmod{9}$

55. $14{,}501{,}302{,}706 \cdot 281{,}460{,}555 \pmod{19}$

56. $87{,}641{,}330 \cdot 21{,}376{,}486 \pmod{23}$

COLLABORATIVE INVESTIGATION

A Perpetual Calendar Algorithm

In this chapter we examined some alternative algorithms for arithmetic computations. Algorithms give us a specified method of carrying out a procedure that produces a desired result. The algorithm that follows allows us to find the day of the week on which a particular date occurred or will occur.

In applying the algorithm, you will need to know whether a particular year is a leap year. ***In general, if a year is divisible (evenly) by 4, it is a leap year. However, there are exceptions***. Century years, such as 1800 and 1900, are not leap years, despite the fact that they are divisible by 4. Furthermore, as an exception to the exception, a century year that is divisible by 400 (such as the year 2000) is a leap year.

In groups of three to five students, read the algorithm and then work the Topics for Discussion.

The Algorithm

This algorithm requires several *key numbers*. Key numbers for the month, day, and century are determined by the following tables.

Month	Key
January	1 (0 if a leap year)
February	4 (3 if a leap year)
March	4
April	0
May	2
June	5
July	0
August	3
September	6
October	1
November	4
December	6

Day	Key		Century	Key
Saturday	0		1700s	4
Sunday	1		1800s	2
Monday	2		1900s	0
Tuesday	3		2000s	6
Wednesday	4			
Thursday	5			
Friday	6			

The algorithm works as follows. We use **October 10, 1942,** as an example.

Step 1 **Obtain the following five numbers.** *Example*

1. The number formed by the last two digits of the year — 42
2. The number in Step 1, divided by 4, with the remainder ignored — 10
3. The month key (1 for October in our example) — 1
4. The day of the month (10 for October 10) — 10
5. The century key (0 for the 1900s) — 0

Step 2 **Add these five numbers.** 63

Step 3 **Divide the sum by 7, and retain the remainder.** ($\frac{63}{7} = 9$, with remainder 0)

Step 4 **Find this remainder in the day key table.** (The number 0 implies that October 10, 1942 was a Saturday.)

(This algorithm was provided to the authors by the late Dan Foley, of the University of New Orleans. We remember him as a good friend and excellent mathematician.)

Topics for Discussion

1. Have each person in the group determine the day of the week on which he or she was born.

2. Among the group members, discuss whether the following poem applies. (This is all in good fun, of course.)

   Monday's child is fair of face,
   Tuesday's child is full of grace.
   Wednesday's child is full of woe,
   Thursday's child has far to go.
   Friday's child is loving and giving,
   Saturday's child works hard for a living.
   But the child that is born on the Sabbath
   day is bonny and good, happy and gay.

3. Determine the day of the week on which the following important historical events occurred.
   (a) December 7, 1941 (the bombing of Pearl Harbor)
   (b) November 22, 1963 (the assassination of John F. Kennedy)
   (c) July 4, 1976 (the bicentennial of the United States)
   (d) January 1, 2000 (the "dreaded" Y2K day)
   (e) September 11, 2001 (the terrorist attacks on the United States)

CHAPTER 4 TEST

In each case, identify the numeration system, and give the Hindu-Arabic equivalent.

1. 𓂋 𓎼𓎼 𓎼𓎼𓎼 ∩∩∩ ‖ ‖

2. $\overline{\text{XCDLXXIV}}$

3.
三
百
人
十
五

4. ⟨⟨▼▼ ⟨▼▼⟨⟨
⟨⟨▼ ⟨▼▼⟨⟨

5.
⋰
◉
⋱

6. $\overset{\epsilon}{\text{M}}$,γφκδ

Perform each operation using the alternative algorithm specified.

7. 23 · 45 (Russian peasant or Egyptian method)

8. 246 · 97 (Lattice method)

9. 21,425 − 8198 (Nines complement method)

Convert each number to base ten.

10. 243_{five}

11. 100101_{two}

12. $\text{BEEF}_{\text{sixteen}}$

Convert as indicated.

13. 49 to binary

14. 2930 to base five

15. 10101110_{two} to octal

16. 7215_{eight} to hexadecimal

17. 5041_{six} to decimal

18. $\text{BAD}_{\text{sixteen}}$ to binary

Briefly explain each of the following.

19. the advantage of multiplicative grouping over simple grouping

20. the advantage of positional over multiplicative grouping

21. the advantage, in a positional numeration system, of a smaller base over a larger base

22. the advantage, in a positional numeration system, of a larger base over a smaller base

23. Explain a quick method to convert a base nine numeral to base three.

24. Illustrate your method from **Exercise 23** by converting 765_{nine} to base three.

4.5 | Clock Arithmetic and Modular Systems

Finite Systems and Clock Arithmetic • Modular Systems

Finite Systems and Clock Arithmetic   At the beginning of this chapter we described a "mathematical system" as

1. a set of elements along with
2. one or more operations for combining those elements, and
3. one or more relations for comparing those elements.

The numeration systems studied in the first three sections mainly involved the set of whole numbers. The operations were mostly addition and multiplication, and the relation was that of equality. Because the set of whole numbers is infinite, that system is an **infinite mathematical system.** In this section, we consider some **finite mathematical systems,** based on finite sets.

The **12-hour clock system** is based on an ordinary clock face, except that 12 is replaced by 0 so that the finite set of the system is {0, 1, 2, 3, 4, 5, 6, 7, 8, 9, 10, 11}. (We will need just one hand on our clock.) See Figure 5.

As an operation for this clock system, addition is defined as follows: add by moving the hour hand in a *clockwise* direction. For example, to add 5 and 2 on a clock, first move the hand to 5, as in Figure 6. Then, to add 2, move the hand 2 more hours in a clockwise direction. The hand stops at 7, so

$$5 + 2 = 7.$$

This result agrees with traditional addition. However, the sum of two numbers from the 12-hour clock system is not always what might be expected, as the following example shows.

FIGURE 5

Plus 2 hours

5 + 2 = 7

FIGURE 6

▥ EXAMPLE 1   Finding Clock Sums by Hand Rotations

Find each sum in 12-hour clock arithmetic.

(a) 8 + 9   **(b)** 11 + 3

SOLUTION

(a) Move the hand to 8, as in Figure 7. Then advance the hand clockwise through 9 more hours. It stops at 5, so 8 + 9 = 5.

(b) To find 11 + 3, proceed as shown in Figure 8. Check that 11 + 3 = 2.   ▥

Because there are infinitely many whole numbers, it is not possible to write a complete table of addition facts for that set. Such a table, to show the sum of every possible pair of whole numbers, would have infinite numbers of rows and columns, making it impossible to construct.

On the other hand, the 12-hour clock system uses only the whole numbers 0, 1, 2, 3, 4, 5, 6, 7, 8, 9, 10, and 11. In effect, the clock face serves to "reduce" the infinite set of whole numbers to the finite set {0, 1, 2, 3, 4, 5, 6, 7, 8, 9, 10, 11}. No matter how large a whole number results from additions (clockwise motions around the clock), the result is always equivalent, in this system, to one of the numbers 0 through 11. A table of all possible sums for this system requires only 12 rows and 12 columns. The 12-hour clock **addition table** is shown in Table 10 on the following page. The significance of the colored diagonal line will be discussed later.

Plus 9 hours

8 + 9 = 5

FIGURE 7

Plus 3 hours

11 + 3 = 2

FIGURE 8

EXAMPLE 2 Finding Clock Sums by Addition Table

Use the 12-hour clock addition table to find each sum.

(a) $7 + 11$ **(b)** $11 + 1$

SOLUTION

(a) Rather than following rotations around the clock face, we simply refer to the table. Find 7 on the left of the addition table and 11 across the top. The intersection of the row headed 7 and the column headed 11 gives the number 6. Thus, $7 + 11 = 6$.

(b) Also from the table, $11 + 1 = 0$.

Mathematical systems are characterized by the properties they possess, specifically, the properties of their operations and relations. Five properties that many of the most commonly applied systems have are the *closure, commutative, associative, identity,* and *inverse* properties. We can check whether the 12-hour clock system has these properties.

Plagued by serious maritime mishaps linked to navigational difficulties, several European governments offered prizes for an effective method of determining longitude. The largest prize was 20,000 pounds (equivalent to several million dollars in today's currency) offered by the British Parliament in the Longitude Act of 1714. While famed scientists, academics, and politicians pursued an answer in the stars, **John Harrison,** a clock maker, set about to build a clock that could maintain accuracy at sea. This turned out to be the key, and Harrison's **Chronometer** eventually earned him the prize.

For a fascinating account of this drama and of Harrison's struggle to collect his prize money from the government, see the book *The Illustrated Longitude* by Dava Sobel and William J. H. Andrewes.

TABLE 10 12-Hour Clock Addition

+	0	1	2	3	4	5	6	7	8	9	10	11
0	0	1	2	3	4	5	6	7	8	9	10	11
1	1	2	3	4	5	6	7	8	9	10	11	0
2	2	3	4	5	6	7	8	9	10	11	0	1
3	3	4	5	6	7	8	9	10	11	0	1	2
4	4	5	6	7	8	9	10	11	0	1	2	3
5	5	6	7	8	9	10	11	0	1	2	3	4
6	6	7	8	9	10	11	0	1	2	3	4	5
7	7	8	9	10	11	0	1	2	3	4	5	6
8	8	9	10	11	0	1	2	3	4	5	6	7
9	9	10	11	0	1	2	3	4	5	6	7	8
10	10	11	0	1	2	3	4	5	6	7	8	9
11	11	0	1	2	3	4	5	6	7	8	9	10

Table 10 shows that the sum of two numbers on a clock face is always a number on the clock face. That is, if a and b are any clock numbers in the set of the system, then $a + b$ is also in the set of the system. Therefore, the system has the **closure property.** (The set of the system is *closed* under clock addition.)

Notice also that in this system $9 + 6$ and $6 + 9$ both yield 3. And the answers, the two 3s, are located in positions that are mirror images of one another with respect to the diagonal line shown. Observe another case—the results for $5 + 8$ and $8 + 5$ are also located symmetrically with respect to the diagonal line, and both results are 1. The entries throughout the entire table occur in equal, diagonally symmetric, pairs. This means that for any clock numbers a and b, $a + b = b + a$. The system, therefore, has the **commutative property.**

The next question is: When any three elements are combined in a given order, say $a + b + c$, does it matter whether the first and second or the second and third are associated initially? In other words, is it true that, for any elements a, b, and c in the 12-hour clock system, $(a + b) + c = a + (b + c)$?

EXAMPLE 3 Checking the Associative Property for Clock Addition

Is 12-hour clock addition associative?

SOLUTION

It would take lots of work to prove that the required relationship *always* holds. But a few examples should either disprove it (by revealing a *counterexample*—a case where it fails to hold), or should make it at least plausible. Using the clock numbers 4, 5, and 9, we see that

$$(4 + 5) + 9 = 9 + 9 \qquad\qquad 4 + (5 + 9) = 4 + 2$$
$$= 6 \qquad\qquad\qquad\qquad\qquad = 6.$$

Thus, $(4 + 5) + 9 = 4 + (5 + 9)$. Try another example:

$$(7 + 6) + 3 = 1 + 3 \qquad\qquad 7 + (6 + 3) = 7 + 9$$
$$= 4 \qquad\qquad\qquad\qquad\qquad = 4.$$

So $(7 + 6) + 3 = 7 + (6 + 3)$. Any other examples checked also will work. The 12-hour clock system therefore has the **associative property.**

Our next question is whether the clock face contains some element (number) that, when combined with any element (in either order), produces that same element. Such an element (call it e) would satisfy $a + e = a$ and $e + a = a$ for any element a of the system. Notice in Table 10 that $4 + 0 = 0 + 4 = 4$, $6 + 0 = 0 + 6 = 6$, and so on. The number 0 is the required *identity element.* The system has the **identity property.**

Generally, if a finite system has an identity element e, it can be located easily in the operation table. Check the body of Table 10 for a column that is identical to the column at the left side of the table. Because the column under 0 meets this requirement, $a + 0 = a$ holds for all elements a in the system. Thus, 0 is *possibly* the identity. Now locate 0 at the left of the table. Because the corresponding row is identical to the row at the top of the table, $0 + a = a$ also holds for all elements a, which is the other requirement of an identity element. Hence, 0 is *indeed* the identity.

Our 12-hour clock system can be expanded to include operations besides addition. For example, subtraction can be performed on a 12-hour clock. Subtraction may be interpreted on the clock face by a movement in the *counterclockwise* direction. For example, to perform the subtraction $2 - 5$, begin at 2 and move 5 hours counterclockwise, ending at 9, as shown in Figure 9. Therefore, in this system,

$$2 - 5 = 9.$$

In our usual system, subtraction may be checked by addition, and this is also the case in clock arithmetic. To check that $2 - 5 = 9$, simply add $9 + 5$, either by using rotation on the clock face or consulting the addition table. In either case, the result is 2, verifying the accuracy of this subtraction.

The *additive inverse, $-a$,* of an element a in clock arithmetic is the element that satisfies this statement: $a + (-a) = 0$ and $(-a) + a = 0$. Such an element, if it exists, can be determined either on the clock face or by using the addition table, as shown in the next example.

Minus 5 hours

$2 - 5 = 9$

FIGURE 9

EXAMPLE 4 Finding Additive Inverses in Clock Arithmetic

Determine the additive inverse, if it exists, for each number in 12-hour clock arithmetic.

(a) 8   **(b)** 2

SOLUTION

(a) Use the clock face to solve the equation

$$8 + x = 0.$$
$$x = 4 \qquad \text{It is 4 hours from 8 to 0.}$$

The additive inverse of 8 is 4.

(b) Refer to the addition table to solve the equation

$$2 + x = 0.$$
$$x = 10 \qquad \text{The row headed 2 has 0 in the column headed 10.}$$

The additive inverse of 2 is 10.

A **chess clock** or double clock is used to time chess, backgammon, and Scrabble games. Push one button, and that clock stops—the other begins simultaneously. When a player's allotted time for the game has expired, that player will lose if he or she has not made the required number of moves.

Mathematics and chess both involve structured relationships and demand logical thinking. Emanuel Lasker achieved mastery in both fields. He was best known as a World Chess Champion for 27 years, until 1921. Lasker also was famous in mathematical circles for his work concerning the theory of primary ideals, algebraic analogies of prime numbers. An important result, the Lasker-Noether theorem, bears his name along with that of Emmy Noether. Noether extended Lasker's work. Her father had been Lasker's Ph.D. advisor.

The methods used in Example 4 may be used to verify that *every* element of the system has an additive inverse (also in the system). So the system has the **inverse property.**

A simpler way to verify the inverse property, if you have the table, is to make sure the identity element appears exactly once in each row, and that the pair of elements that produces it also produces it in the opposite order. (This last condition is automatically true if the commutative property holds for the system.) For example, note in Table 10 that row 3 contains one 0, under the 9, so $3 + 9 = 0$, and that row 9 contains 0, under the 3, so $9 + 3 = 0$ also. Therefore, 3 and 9 are inverses.

Table 11 lists all the elements and their additive inverses. Notice that one element, 6, is its own inverse for addition.

TABLE 11 Inverses for 12-Hour Clock Addition

Clock value a	0	1	2	3	4	5	6	7	8	9	10	11
Additive inverse $-a$	0	11	10	9	8	7	6	5	4	3	2	1

Using the additive inverse symbol, we can say that in clock arithmetic,

$$-5 = 7, \quad -11 = 1, \quad -10 = 2, \quad \text{and so on.}$$

We have now seen that the 12-hour clock system, with addition, has all five properties that we set out to check: closure, commutative, associative, identity, and inverse. Having discussed additive inverses, we can define subtraction formally. Notice that the definition is the same as for ordinary subtraction of whole numbers.

Subtraction on a Clock

If a and b are elements in clock arithmetic, then the **difference,** $a - b$, is defined as

$$a - b = a + (-b).$$

EXAMPLE 5 Finding Clock Differences

Find each difference.

(a) $8 - 5$ **(b)** $6 - 11$

SOLUTION

(a) $8 - 5 = 8 + (-5)$ Use the definition of subtraction.

$\qquad = 8 + 7$ The additive inverse of 5 is 7, from the table of inverses.

$\qquad = 3$

This result agrees with traditional arithmetic. Check by adding 5 and 3; the sum is 8.

(b) $6 - 11 = 6 + (-11)$

$\qquad = 6 + 1$ The additive inverse of 11 is 1.

$\qquad = 7$ ▪

Clock numbers can also be multiplied. For example,

$$5 \cdot 4 = 4 + 4 + 4 + 4 + 4 = 8. \quad \text{Add five 4s.}$$

EXAMPLE 6   Finding Clock Products

Find each product, using clock arithmetic.

(a) $6 \cdot 9$ **(b)** $3 \cdot 4$ **(c)** $6 \cdot 0$ **(d)** $0 \cdot 8$

SOLUTION

(a) $6 \cdot 9 = 9 + 9 + 9 + 9 + 9 + 9 = 6$ **(b)** $3 \cdot 4 = 4 + 4 + 4 = 0$

(c) $6 \cdot 0 = 0 + 0 + 0 + 0 + 0 + 0 = 0$ **(d)** $0 \cdot 8 = 0$ ▪

Some properties of the system of 12-hour clock numbers with the operation of multiplication will be investigated in Exercises 6–8.

Modular Systems   We now expand the ideas of clock arithmetic to **modular systems** in general. Recall that 12-hour clock arithmetic was set up so that answers were always whole numbers less than 12. For example, $8 + 6 = 2$. The traditional sum, $8 + 6 = 14$, reflects the fact that moving the clock hand forward 8 hours from 0, and then forward another 6 hours, amounts to moving it forward 14 hours total. But because the final position of the clock is at 2, we see that 14 and 2 are, in a sense, equivalent. More formally, we say that 14 and 2 are **congruent modulo** 12 (or **congruent mod** 12), which is written

$$14 \equiv 2 \text{ (mod 12)} \quad \text{The sign} \equiv \text{indicates congruence.}$$

By observing clock hand movements, you can also see that, for example,

$$26 \equiv 2 \text{ (mod 12)}, \qquad 38 \equiv 2 \text{ (mod 12)}, \qquad \text{and so on.}$$

In each case, the congruence is true because the difference of the two congruent numbers is a multiple of 12:

$$14 - 2 = 12 = 1 \cdot 12, \quad 26 - 2 = 24 = 2 \cdot 12, \quad 38 - 2 = 36 = 3 \cdot 12.$$

This suggests the following definition.

Congruence Modulo m

The integers a and b are **congruent modulo m** (where m is a natural number greater than 1 called the **modulus**) if and only if the difference $a - b$ is divisible by m. Symbolically, this congruence is written

$$a \equiv b \text{ (mod } m\text{).}$$

Because being divisible by m is the same as being a multiple of m, we can say that

$$a \equiv b \; (\text{mod } m) \text{ if and only if } a - b = km \text{ for some integer } k.$$

EXAMPLE 7   Checking the Truth of Modular Equations

Decide whether each statement is *true* or *false*.

(a) $16 \equiv 10 \; (\text{mod } 2)$ **(b)** $49 \equiv 32 \; (\text{mod } 5)$ **(c)** $30 \equiv 345 \; (\text{mod } 7)$

SOLUTION

(a) The difference $16 - 10 = 6$ is divisible by 2, so $16 \equiv 10 \; (\text{mod } 2)$ is true.

(b) The statement $49 \equiv 32 \; (\text{mod } 5)$ is false, because $49 - 32 = 17$, which is not divisible by 5.

(c) The statement $30 \equiv 345 \; (\text{mod } 7)$ is true, because $30 - 345 = -315$ is divisible by 7. (It doesn't matter if we find $30 - 345$ or $345 - 30$.)

There is another method of determining if two numbers, a and b, are congruent modulo m.

Criterion for Congruence

$a \equiv b \; (\text{mod } m)$ if and only if the same remainder is obtained when a and b are divided by m.

For example, we know that $27 \equiv 9 \; (\text{mod } 6)$ because $27 - 9 = 18$, which is divisible by 6. Now, if 27 is divided by 6, the quotient is 4 and the remainder is 3. Also, if 9 is divided by 6, the quotient is 1 and the remainder is 3. According to the criterion above, $27 \equiv 9 \; (\text{mod } 6)$ since both remainders are the same.

Addition, subtraction, and multiplication can be performed in any modular system just as with clock numbers. Because final answers should be whole numbers less than the modulus, we can first find an answer using ordinary arithmetic. Then, as long as the answer is nonnegative, simply divide it by the modulus and keep the remainder. This produces the smallest nonnegative integer that is congruent (modulo m) to the ordinary answer.

EXAMPLE 8   Performing Modular Arithmetic

Find each sum, difference, or product.

(a) $(9 + 14) \; (\text{mod } 3)$ **(b)** $(27 - 5) \; (\text{mod } 6)$ **(c)** $(50 + 34) \; (\text{mod } 7)$
(d) $(8 \cdot 9) \; (\text{mod } 10)$ **(e)** $(12 \cdot 10) \; (\text{mod } 5)$

SOLUTION

(a) First add 9 and 14 to get 23. Then divide 23 by 3. The remainder is 2, so we obtain $23 \equiv 2 \; (\text{mod } 3)$ and

$$(9 + 14) \equiv 2 \; (\text{mod } 3).$$

(b) $27 - 5 = 22$. Divide 22 by 6, obtaining 4 as a remainder:

$$(27 - 5) \equiv 4 \ (\text{mod } 6).$$

(c) $50 + 34 = 84$. When 84 is divided by 7, a remainder of 0 is found:

$$(50 + 34) \equiv 0 \ (\text{mod } 7).$$

(d) Since $8 \cdot 9 = 72$, and 72 leaves a remainder of 2 when divided by 10,

$$(8 \cdot 9) \equiv 2 \ (\text{mod } 10).$$

(e) $(12 \cdot 10) \ (\text{mod } 5) = 120 \equiv 0 \ (\text{mod } 5)$ ■

PROBLEM-SOLVING HINT Modular systems can often be applied to questions involving cyclical changes. For example, our method of dividing time into weeks causes the days to repeatedly cycle through the same pattern of seven. Suppose today is Sunday and we want to know what day of the week it will be 45 days from now. Because we don't care how many weeks will pass between now and then, we can discard the largest whole number of weeks in 45 days and keep the remainder. (We are finding the smallest nonnegative integer that is congruent to 45 modulo 7.) Dividing 45 by 7 leaves remainder 3, so the desired day of the week is 3 days past Sunday, or *Wednesday.*

EXAMPLE 9 Using Modular Methods to Find the Day of the Week

If today is Thursday, November 12, and *next* year is a leap year, what day of the week will it be one year from today?

SOLUTION

A modulo 7 system applies here, but we need to know the number of days between today and one year from today. Today's date, November 12, is unimportant except that it shows we are later in the year than the end of February and therefore the next year (starting today) will contain 366 days. (This would not be so if today were, say, January 12.) Now dividing 366 by 7 produces 52 with remainder 2. Two days past Thursday is our answer. That is, one year from today will be a Saturday. ■

PROBLEM-SOLVING HINT A modular system (mod m) allows only a fixed set of remainder values, $0, 1, 2, \ldots, m - 1$. One practical approach to solving modular equations, at least when m is reasonably small, is to simply try all these integers. For each solution found in this way, others can be found by adding multiples of the modulus to it.

> **EXAMPLE 10** **Solving Modular Equations**

Solve each modular equation for whole number solutions.

(a) $(3 + x) \equiv 5 \pmod 7$ **(b)** $5x \equiv 4 \pmod 9$
(c) $6x \equiv 3 \pmod 8$ **(d)** $8x \equiv 8 \pmod 8$

SOLUTION

(a) Because dividing 5 by 7 yields remainder 5, the criterion for congruence is that the given equation is true only if dividing $3 + x$ by 7 also yields remainder 5. Try replacing x, in turn, by 0, 1, 2, 3, 4, 5, and 6.

$x = 0$: $(3 + 0) \equiv 5 \pmod 7$ is false. The remainder is 3.

$x = 1$: $(3 + 1) \equiv 5 \pmod 7$ is false. The remainder is 4.

$x = 2$: $(3 + 2) \equiv 5 \pmod 7$ is true. The remainder is 5.

Try $x = 3$, $x = 4$, $x = 5$, and $x = 6$ to see that none work. Of the integers from 0 through 6, only 2 is a solution of the equation $(3 + x) \equiv 5 \pmod 7$.

Because 2 is a solution, find other solutions to this mod 7 equation by repeatedly adding 7:

$$2 + 7 = 9, \quad 9 + 7 = 16, \quad 16 + 7 = 23, \quad \text{and so on.}$$

The set of all nonnegative solutions of $(3 + x) \equiv 5 \pmod 7$ is

$$\{2, 9, 16, 23, 30, 37, \dots \}.$$

(b) Dividing 4 by 9 yields remainder 4. Because the modulus is 9, check the remainders when $5x$ is divided by 9 for $x = 0, 1, 2, 3, 4, 5, 6, 7$, and 8.

$5y = 4 (m 9)$

$x = 0$: $5 \cdot 0 \equiv 4 \pmod 9$ is false. The remainder is 0.

$x = 1$: $5 \cdot 1 \equiv 4 \pmod 9$ is false. The remainder is 5.

Continue trying numbers. Only $x = 8$ works:

$$5 \cdot 8 = 40 \equiv 4 \pmod 9. \quad \text{The remainder is 4.}$$

The set of all nonnegative solutions to the equation $5x \equiv 4 \pmod 9$ is

$$\{8, 8 + 9, 8 + 9 + 9, 8 + 9 + 9 + 9, \dots \} \quad \text{or} \quad \{8, 17, 26, 35, 44, 53, \dots \}.$$

(c) To solve $6x \equiv 3 \pmod 8$, try the numbers 0, 1, 2, 3, 4, 5, 6, and 7. None work. Therefore, the equation $6x \equiv 3 \pmod 8$ has no solutions. Write the set of all solutions as the empty set, $\emptyset$.

This result is reasonable because $6x$ will always be even, no matter which whole number is used for x. Because $6x$ is even and 3 is odd, the difference $6x - 3$ will be odd and therefore not divisible by 8.

(d) To solve $8x \equiv 8 \pmod 8$, trying the integers 0, 1, 2, 3, 4, 5, 6, and 7. *Any* replacement will work. The solution set is $\{0, 1, 2, 3, \dots \}$. ▨

Some problems can be solved by writing down two or more modular equations and finding their common solutions. The next example illustrates the process.

> **EXAMPLE 11**   **Finding the Number of Discs in a CD Collection**

Julio wants to arrange his CD collection in equal size stacks, but after trying stacks of 4, stacks of 5, and stacks of 6, he finds that there is always 1 disc left over. Assuming Julio owns more than one CD, what is the least possible number of discs in his collection?

SOLUTION

The given information leads to three modular equations,

$$x \equiv 1 \ (\text{mod } 4), \quad x \equiv 1 \ (\text{mod } 5), \quad \text{and} \quad x \equiv 1 \ (\text{mod } 6).$$

For the first equation, try $x = 0$, $x = 1$, $x = 2$, and $x = 3$. The value 1 works, as it does for the other two equations as well. So the solution sets are, respectively,

$$\{1, 5, 9, 13, 17, 21, 25, 29, 33, 37, 41, 45, 49, 53, 57, \mathbf{61}, 65, 69. \ldots \},$$
$$\{1, 6, 11, 16, 21, 26, 31, 36, 41, 46, 51, 56, \mathbf{61}, 66, 71, 76, \ldots \},$$
and $\qquad\qquad\quad \{1, 7, 13, 19, 25, 31, 37, 43, 49, 55, \mathbf{61}, \ldots \}.$

The least common solution greater than 1 is 61, so the least possible number of discs in the collection is 61. ◼

> **EXAMPLE 12**   **Applying Congruences to a Construction Problem**

A dry-wall contractor is ordering materials to finish a 17-foot-by-45-foot room. The wallboard panels come in 4-foot widths. Show that, after uncut panels are applied, all four walls will require additional partial strips of the same width.

SOLUTION

The width of any partial strip needed will be the remainder when the wall length is divided by 4 (the panel width). In terms of congruence, we must show that $17 \equiv 45$ (mod 4). By the criterion for congruence, we see that this is true because both 17 and 45 give the same remainder (namely 1) when divided by 4. A 1-foot partial strip will be required for each wall. (In this case four 1-foot strips can be cut from a single panel, so there will be no waste.) ◼

For Further Thought

A Card Trick

Many card "tricks" that have been around for years are really not illusions at all but are based on mathematical properties that allow anyone to do them with no special conjuring abilities. One of them is based on mod 14 arithmetic.

In this trick, suits play no role. Each card has a numerical value: 1 for ace, 2 for two, ..., 11 for jack, 12 for queen, and 13 for king. The deck is shuffled and given to a spectator, who is instructed to place the deck of cards face up on a table and is told to follow the procedure described: The top card is removed from the deck and laid on the table with its face up. (We shall call it the "starter" card.) The starter card will be at the bottom of a pile. In order to form a pile, note

(continued)

the value of the starter card, and then add cards on top of it while counting up to 13. For example, if the starter card is a six, pile up seven cards on top of it. If it is a jack, add two cards to it, and so on.

When the first pile is completed, it is picked up and placed face down. The next card from the deck becomes the starter card for the next pile, and the process is repeated. This continues until all cards are used or until there are not enough cards to complete the last pile. Any cards that are left over are put aside, face down, for later use. We will refer to these as "leftovers."

The performer then requests that a spectator choose three piles at random. The remaining piles are added to the leftovers. The spectator is then instructed to turn over any two top cards from the piles. The performer is then able to determine the value of the third top card.

The secret to the trick is that the performer adds the values of the two top cards that were turned over, and then adds 10 to this sum. The performer then counts off this number of cards from the leftovers. The number of cards remaining in the leftovers is the value of the remaining top card!

For Group Discussion or Individual Investigation

1. Obtain a deck of playing cards and perform the "trick" as described above. (As with many activities, you'll find that doing it is simpler than describing it.) Does it work?
2. Explain why this procedure works. (If you want to see how someone else explained it, using modulo 14 arithmetic, see "An Old Card Trick Revisited," by Barry C. Felps, in the December 1976 issue of the journal *The Mathematics Teacher*.)

4.5 EXERCISES

Find each difference on the 12-hour clock.

1. $8 - 3$ **2.** $4 - 9$ **3.** $2 - 8$ **4.** $0 - 3$

5. Complete the 12-hour clock multiplication table below. You can use repeated addition and the addition table (for example, $3 \cdot 7 = 7 + 7 + 7 = 2 + 7 = 9$) or use mod 12 multiplication techniques, as in Example 8, parts (d) and (e).

·	0	1	2	3	4	5	6	7	8	9	10	11
0	0	0	0	0	0	0	0	0	0	0	0	0
1	0	1	2	3	4	5	6	7	8	9	10	11
2	0	2	4	6	8	10		2	4		8	
3	0	3	6	9	0	3	6			3	6	
4	0	4	8			8		4			4	8
5	0	5	10	3	8		6	11	4			
6	0	6	0		0	6	0	6		6		6
7	0	7	2	9				1			10	
8	0	8	4	0				8	4		8	4
9	0	9			0		6		0			
10	0	10	8			2						2
11	0	11										1

By referring to your table in Exercise 5, determine which properties hold for the system of 12-hour clock numbers with the operation of multiplication.

6. closure   **7.** commutative

8. identity (If so, what is the identity element?)

A 5-hour clock system utilizes the set {0, 1, 2, 3, 4}, and relates to the clock face shown here.

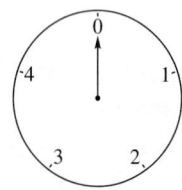

5-hour clock

9. Complete this 5-hour clock addition table.

+	0	1	2	3	4
0	0	1	2	3	4
1	1	2	3	4	
2	2	3	4		1
3	3	4			
4	4				3

Which properties are satisfied by the system of 5-hour clock numbers with the operation of addition?

10. closure

11. commutative

12. identity (If so, what is the identity element?)

13. inverse (If so, name the inverse of each element.)

14. Complete this 5-hour clock multiplication table.

·	0	1	2	3	4
0	0	0	0	0	0
1	0	1	2	3	4
2	0	2	4		
3	0	3			
4	0	4			

Determine which properties hold for the system of 5-hour clock numbers with the operation of multiplication.

15. closure   **16.** commutative

17. identity (If so, what is the identity element?)

In clock arithmetic, as in ordinary arithmetic, a − b = d is true if and only if b + d = a. Similarly, a ÷ b = q if and only if b · q = a.

Use the idea above and your 5-hour clock multiplication table of Exercise 14 to find each quotient on a 5-hour clock.

18. 1 ÷ 3   **19.** 3 ÷ 1

20. 2 ÷ 3   **21.** 3 ÷ 2

22. Is division commutative on a 5-hour clock? Explain.

23. Is there an answer for 4 ÷ 0 on a 5-hour clock? Find it or explain why not.

The military uses a 24-hour clock to avoid the problems of "A.M." and "P.M." For example, 1100 hours is 11 A.M., while 2100 hours is 9 P.M. (12 noon + 9 hours). In these designations, the last two digits represent minutes, and the digits before that represent hours. Find each sum in the 24-hour clock system.

24. 1400 + 500   **25.** 1300 + 1800

26. 0750 + 1630   **27.** 1545 + 0815

28. Explain how the following three statements can *all* be true. (*Hint:* Think of clocks.)

$$1145 + 1135 = 2280$$
$$1145 + 1135 = 1120$$
$$1145 + 1135 = 2320$$

Answer true *or* false *for each statement.*

29. $5 \equiv 19 \pmod 3$ **30.** $35 \equiv 8 \pmod 9$

31. $5445 \equiv 0 \pmod 3$ **32.** $7021 \equiv 4202 \pmod 6$

Work each modular arithmetic problem.

33. $(12 + 7)(\bmod 4)$ **34.** $(62 + 95)(\bmod 9)$

35. $(35 - 22)(\bmod 5)$ **36.** $(82 - 45)(\bmod 3)$

37. $(5 \cdot 8)(\bmod 3)$ **38.** $(32 \cdot 21)(\bmod 8)$

39. $[4 \cdot (13 + 6)](\bmod 11)$

40. $[(10 + 7) \cdot (5 + 3)](\bmod 10)$

41. The text described how to do arithmetic mod *m* when the ordinary answer comes out nonnegative. Explain what to do when the ordinary answer is negative.

Work each modular arithmetic problem.

42. $(3 - 27)(\bmod 5)$ **43.** $(16 - 60)(\bmod 7)$

44. $[(-8) \cdot 11](\bmod 3)$ **45.** $[2 \cdot (-23)](\bmod 5)$

In Exercises 46 and 47:
(a) *Complete the given addition table.*
(b) *Decide whether the closure, commutative, identity, and inverse properties are satisfied.*
(c) *If the inverse property is satisfied, give the inverse of each number.*

46. mod 4

+	0	1	2	3
0	0	1	2	3
1				
2				
3				

47. mod 7

+	0	1	2	3	4	5	6
0	0	1	2	3	4	5	6
1	1	2	3	4	5	6	
2							
3							
4							
5							
6							

In Exercises 48–51:
(a) *Complete the given multiplication table.*
(b) *Decide whether the closure, commutative, identity, and inverse properties are satisfied.*
(c) *Give the inverse of each nonzero number that has an inverse.*

48. mod 2

·	0	1
0	0	0
1	0	

49. mod 3

·	0	1	2
0	0	0	0
1	0	1	2
2	0	2	

50. mod 4

·	0	1	2	3
0	0	0	0	0
1	0	1	2	3
2	0	2		
3	0	3		

51. mod 9

·	0	1	2	3	4	5	6	7	8
0	0	0	0	0	0	0	0	0	0
1	0	1	2	3	4	5	6	7	8
2	0	2	4	6	8			5	
3	0	3	6	0		6		3	6
4	0	4	8		7		6		5
5	0	5	1		2		3	8	
6	0	6	3	0	6	3	0	6	3
7	0	7	5			8			2
8	0	8	7		4	3			1

52. Explain why a modular system containing the number 0 cannot satisfy the inverse property for multiplication.

Find all nonnegative solutions for each equation.

53. $x \equiv 3 \ (\bmod 7)$

54. $(2 + x) \equiv 7 \ (\bmod 3)$

55. $6x \equiv 2 \ (\bmod 2)$

56. $(5x - 3) \equiv 7 \ (\bmod 4)$

Solve each problem.

57. ***Odometer Readings*** For many years automobile odometers showed five whole number digits and a digit for tenths of a mile. For those odometers showing just five whole number digits, totals are recorded according to what modulus?

58. ***Distance Traveled by a Car*** If a car's five-digit whole number odometer shows a reading of 29,306, *in theory* how many miles might the car have traveled?

59. ***Determining Day of the Week*** Refer to Example 9 in the text. (Recall that *next* year is a leap year.) Assuming today was Thursday, January 12, answer the following questions.
  (a) How many days would the next year (starting today) contain?
  (b) What day of the week would occur one year from today?

60. ***Silver Spoon Collection*** Roxanna Parker has a collection of silver spoons from all over the world. She finds that she can arrange her spoons in sets of 7 with 6 left over, sets of 8 with 1 left over, or sets of 15 with 3 left over. If Roxanna has fewer than 200 spoons, how many are there?

61. *Piles of Ticket Stubs* Lawrence Rosenthal finds that whether he sorts his White Sox ticket stubs into piles of 10, piles of 15, or piles of 20, there are always 2 left over. What is the least number of stubs he could have (assuming he has more than 2)?

62. *Determining a Range of Dates* Assume again, as in Example 9, that *next* year is a leap year. If the next year (starting today) does *not* contain 366 days, what is the range of possible dates for today?

63. *Flight Attendant Schedules* Robin Strang and Kristyn Wasag, flight attendants for two different airlines, are close friends and like to get together as often as possible. Robin flies a 21-day schedule (including days off), which then repeats, while Kristyn has a repeating 30-day schedule. Both of their routines include layovers in Chicago, New Orleans, and San Francisco. The table below shows which days of each of their individual schedules they are in these cities. (Assume the first day of a cycle is day number 1.)

	Days in Chicago	Days in New Orleans	Days in San Francisco
Robin	1, 2, 8	5, 12	6, 18, 19
Kristyn	23, 29, 30	5, 6, 17	8, 10, 15, 20, 25

If today is July 1 and both are starting their schedules today (day 1), list the days during July and August that they will be able to see each other in each of the three cities.

The following formula can be used to find the day of the week on which a given year begins. *Here y represents the year (which must be after 1582, when our current calendar began). First calculate*

$$a = y + [(y - 1)/4] - [(y - 1)/100]$$
$$+ [(y - 1)/400],$$

where $[x]$ represents the greatest integer less than or equal to x. (For example, $[9.2] = 9$, and $[\pi] = 3$.) After finding a, find the smallest nonnegative integer b such that

$$a \equiv b \text{ (mod 7)}.$$

*Given in "An Aid to the Superstitious," by G. L. Ritter, S. R. Lowry, H. B. Woodruff, and T. L. Isenhour. *The Mathematics Teacher,* May 1977, pp. 456–457.

Then b gives the day of January 1, with $b = 0$ representing Sunday, $b = 1$ Monday, and so on.

Find the day of the week on which January 1 would occur in each year.

64. 1812   **65.** 1865

66. 2006   **67.** 2020

Some people believe that Friday the thirteenth is unlucky. The table below shows the months that will have a Friday the thirteenth if the first day of the year is known. A year is a leap year if it is divisible by 4. The only exception to this rule is that a century year (1900, for example) is a leap year only when it is divisible by 400.*

First Day of Year	Non-leap Year	Leap Year
Sunday	Jan., Oct.	Jan., April, July
Monday	April, July	Sept., Dec.
Tuesday	Sept., Dec.	June
Wednesday	June	March, Nov.
Thursday	Feb., March, Nov.	Feb., Aug.
Friday	August	May
Saturday	May	Oct.

Use the table to determine the months that have a Friday the thirteenth for each year.

68. 2007   **69.** 2008

70. 2009   **71.** 2200

72. Modular arithmetic can be used to create **residue designs.** For example, the designs (11, 3) and (65, 3) are shown here.

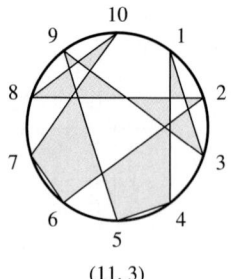 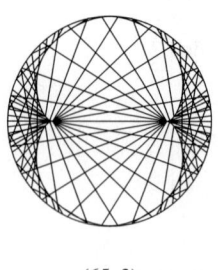

(11, 3)   (65, 3)

To see how such designs are created, construct a new design, (11, 5), by proceeding as follows.

  (a) Draw a circle and divide the circumference into 10 equal parts. Label the division points as 1, 2, 3, . . . , 10.

(b) Since $1 \cdot 5 \equiv 5 \pmod{11}$, connect 1 and 5. (We use 5 as a multiplier because we are making an (11, 5) design.)

(c) $2 \cdot 5 \equiv 10 \pmod{11}$

Therefore, connect 2 and _____.

(d) $3 \cdot 5 \equiv$ _____ $\pmod{11}$

Connect 3 and _____.

(e) $4 \cdot 5 \equiv$ _____ $\pmod{11}$

Connect 4 and _____.

(f) $5 \cdot 5 \equiv$ _____ $\pmod{11}$

Connect 5 and _____.

(g) $6 \cdot 5 \equiv$ _____ $\pmod{11}$

Connect 6 and _____.

(h) $7 \cdot 5 \equiv$ _____ $\pmod{11}$

Connect 7 and _____.

(i) $8 \cdot 5 \equiv$ _____ $\pmod{11}$

Connect 8 and _____.

(j) $9 \cdot 5 \equiv$ _____ $\pmod{11}$

Connect 9 and _____.

(k) $10 \cdot 5 \equiv$ _____ $\pmod{11}$

Connect 10 and _____.

(l) You might want to shade some of the regions you have found to make an interesting pattern. For more information, see "Residue Designs," by Phil Locke in *The Mathematics Teacher,* March 1972, pages 260–263.

Identification numbers are used in various ways for many kinds of different products.* Books, for example, are assigned International Standard Book Numbers (ISBNs). Each ISBN is a ten-digit number. It includes a check digit, which is determined on the basis of modular arithmetic. The ISBN for one version of this book is

0-321-36146-6.

*For an interesting general discussion, see "The Mathematics of Identification Numbers," by Joseph A. Gallian in *The College Mathematics Journal,* May 1991, p. 194.

The first digit, 0, identifies the book as being published in an English-speaking country. The next digits, 321, identify the publisher, while 36146 identifies this particular book. The final digit, 6, is a check digit. To find this check digit, start at the left and multiply the digits of the ISBN by 10, 9, 8, 7, 6, 5, 4, 3, and 2, respectively. Then add these products. For this book we get

$$(10 \cdot 0) + (9 \cdot 3) + (8 \cdot 2) + (7 \cdot 1) + (6 \cdot 3)$$
$$+ (5 \cdot 6) + (4 \cdot 1) + (3 \cdot 4) + (2 \cdot 6) = 126.$$

The check digit is the smallest number that must be added to this result to get a multiple of 11. Because $126 + 6 = 132$, a multiple of 11, the check digit is 6. (It is possible to have a check "digit" of 10; the letter X is used instead of 10.)

When an order for this book is received, the ISBN is entered into a computer, and the check digit evaluated. If this result does not match the check digit on the order, the order will not be processed. Does each ISBN have the correct check digit?

73. 0-275-98341-2

74. 0-374-29288-7

Find the appropriate check digit for each ISBN. (Note: The positions of hyphens (or spaces) may vary (or there may be none), but this does not affect the determination of the check digit.)

75. *Man of the Century,* by Jonathan Kwitny, 0-8050-2688- _____

76. *Winning,* by Jack Welch, 0-06-075394- _____

77. *1776,* by David McCullough, 0-7432-2671- _____

78. *The Da Vinci Code,* by Dan Brown, 0-385-50420- _____

4.6 Properties of Mathematical Systems

An Abstract System • Closure Property • Commutative Property • Associative Property • Identity Property • Inverse Property • Distributive Property

An Abstract System Clock arithmetic and modular systems, discussed in the previous section, were built upon ordinary numbers and involved familiar operations such as addition, subtraction, multiplication, and division. We begin this section by presenting a more abstract system, where the elements and the operations have no implied mathematical significance. This way, we can concentrate on investigating the properties of the system without preconceived notions of what they may be.

TABLE 12

☆	a	b	c	d
a	a	b	c	d
b	b	d	a	c
c	c	a	d	b
d	d	c	b	a

To begin, we introduce a finite mathematical system made up of the set of elements {a, b, c, d} and an operation we will write with the symbol ☆. We define the system in Table 12, an **operation table** that shows how operation ☆ combines any two elements from the set {a, b, c, d}. To use the table to find, say, c ☆ d, first locate c on the left, and d across the top. This row and column intersect at b, so that

$$c \ \☆\ d = b.$$

As with clock arithmetic, the important properties we shall look for in this system are the following: *closure, commutative, associative, identity,* and *inverse.*

Closure Property For this system to be closed under the operation ☆, the answer to any possible combination of elements from the system must be in the set {a, b, c, d}. A glance at Table 12 shows that the answers in the body of the table are all elements of this set. This means that the system is closed. If an element other than a, b, c, or d had appeared in the body of the table, or if any position in the body of the table had contained no entry, the system would not have been closed.

TABLE 13

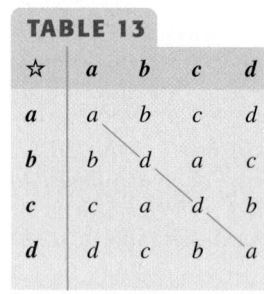

☆	a	b	c	d
a	a	b	c	d
b	b	d	a	c
c	c	a	d	b
d	d	c	b	a

←Commutative Property In order for the system to have the commutative property, it must be true that Γ ☆ Δ = Δ ☆ Γ, where Γ and Δ stand for any elements from the set {a, b, c, d}. For example,

$$c \ ☆ \ d = b \quad \text{and} \quad d \ ☆ \ c = b, \quad \text{so} \quad c \ ☆ \ d = d \ ☆ \ c.$$

To see that the same is true for *all* choices of Γ and Δ, observe that Table 13 is symmetric with respect to the diagonal line shown. This "diagonal line test" establishes that ☆ is a commutative operation for this system.

Associative Property The system is associative if (Γ ☆ Δ) ☆ Y = Γ ☆ (Δ ☆ Y), where Γ, Δ, and Y represent any elements from the set {a, b, c, d}. There is no quick way to check a table for the associative property, as there is for the commutative property. All we can do is try some examples. Using the table that defines operation ☆,

$$(a \ ☆ \ d) \ ☆ \ b = d \ ☆ \ b = c, \quad \text{and} \quad a \ ☆ \ (d \ ☆ \ b) = a \ ☆ \ c = c,$$

so that

$$(a \ ☆ \ d) \ ☆ \ b = a \ ☆ \ (d \ ☆ \ b).$$

In the same way,

$$b \ ☆ \ (c \ ☆ \ d) = (b \ ☆ \ c) \ ☆ \ d.$$

In both these examples, changing the location of parentheses did not change the answers. Because the two examples worked, we suspect that the system is associative. We cannot be sure of this, however, unless every possible choice of three letters from the set is checked. (Although we have not completely verified it here, this system does, in fact, satisfy the associative property.)

Identity Property For the identity property to hold, there must be an element Δ from the set of the system such that Δ ☆ X = X and X ☆ Δ = X, where X represents any element from the set {a, b, c, d}. We can see that a is such an element as follows. In Table 13, the column below a (at the top) is identical to the column at the left, and the row across from a (at the left) is identical to the row at the top. Therefore, a is in fact the identity element of the system. (It is shown in more advanced courses that if a system has an identity element, it has *only* one.)

Bernard Bolzano (1781–1848) was an early exponent of rigor and precision in mathematics. Many early results in such areas as calculus were produced by the masters in the field; these masters knew what they were doing and produced accurate results. However, their sloppy arguments caused trouble in the hands of the less gifted. The work of Bolzano and others helped put mathematics on a strong footing.

Inverse Property We found earlier that a is the identity element for the system using operation ☆. If there is an inverse in this system for, say, the element b, and if Δ represents the inverse of b, then

$$b ☆ \Delta = a \quad \text{and} \quad \Delta ☆ b = a \quad \text{(because } a \text{ is the identity element).}$$

Inspecting the table for operation ☆ shows that Δ can be replaced with c:

$$b ☆ c = a \quad \text{and} \quad c ☆ b = a.$$

So we see that c is the inverse of b.

We can inspect the table to see if every element of our system has an inverse in the system. We see (in Table 13) that the identity element a appears once in each row, and that, in each case, the pair of elements that produces a also produces it in the opposite order. Therefore, we conclude that the system satisfies the inverse property.

In summary, the mathematical system made up of the set $\{a, b, c, d\}$ and operation ☆ satisfies the closure, commutative, associative, identity, and inverse properties.

Potential Properties of a Single-Operation System

Here a, b, and c represent elements from the set of any system, and $\circ$ represents the operation of the system.

Closure The system is closed if for all elements a and b,

$$a \circ b$$

is in the set of the system.

Commutative The system has the commutative property if

$$a \circ b = b \circ a$$

for all elements a and b of the system.

Associative The system has the associative property if

$$(a \circ b) \circ c = a \circ (b \circ c)$$

for every choice of three elements a, b, and c of the system.

Identity The system has the identity property if there exists an identity element e (where e is in the set of the system) such that

$$a \circ e = a \quad \text{and} \quad e \circ a = a$$

for every element a of the system.

Inverse The system has the inverse property if, for every element a of the system, there is an element x in the system such that

$$a \circ x = e \quad \text{and} \quad x \circ a = e,$$

where e is the identity element of the system.

EXAMPLE 1 Identifying the Properties of a System

Table 14 on the next page defines a system consisting of the set $\{0, 1, 2, 3, 4, 5\}$ under an operation designated $\otimes$. Which properties above are satisfied by this system?

TABLE 14

⊗	0	1	2	3	4	5
0	0	0	0	0	0	0
1	0	1	2	3	4	5
2	0	2	4	0	2	4
3	0	3	0	3	0	3
4	0	4	2	0	4	2
5	0	5	4	3	2	1

SOLUTION

All the numbers in the body of the table come from the set $\{0, 1, 2, 3, 4, 5\}$, so the system is closed. If we draw a line from upper left to lower right, we could fold the table along this line and have the corresponding elements match; the system has the commutative property.

To check for the associative property, try some examples:

$$2 \otimes (3 \otimes 5) = 2 \otimes 3 = 0 \quad \text{and} \quad (2 \otimes 3) \otimes 5 = 0 \otimes 5 = 0,$$

so that $\qquad\qquad 2 \otimes (3 \otimes 5) = (2 \otimes 3) \otimes 5.$

Also, $\qquad\qquad 5 \otimes (4 \otimes 2) = (5 \otimes 4) \otimes 2.$

Any other examples that we might try would also work. The system has the associative property.

Because the column at the left of the operation table is repeated under 1 in the body of the table, 1 is a candidate for the identity element in the system. To be sure that 1 is the identity element here, check that the row corresponding to 1 at the left is identical with the row at the top of the table. Since it is, 1 is indeed the identity element.

To find inverse elements, look for the identity element, 1, in the rows of the table. The identity element appears in the second row, $1 \otimes 1 = 1$; and in the bottom row, $5 \otimes 5 = 1$; so 1 and 5 both are their own inverses. There is no identity element in the rows opposite the numbers 0, 2, 3, and 4, so none of these elements has an inverse.

In summary, the system made up of the set $\{0, 1, 2, 3, 4, 5\}$ under this operation $\otimes$ satisfies the closure, associative, commutative, and identity properties, but not the inverse property. ◼

TABLE 15

⊠	1	2	3	4	5	6
1	1	2	3	4	5	6
2	2	4	6	1	3	5
3	3	6	2	5	1	4
4	4	1	5	2	6	3
5	5	3	1	6	4	2
6	6	5	4	3	2	1

EXAMPLE 2 Identifying the Properties of a System

Table 15 defines a system consisting of the set of numbers $\{1, 2, 3, 4, 5, 6\}$ under an operation designated ⊠. Which properties are satisfied by this system?

SOLUTION

Notice here that 0 is not an element of this system. This is perfectly legitimate. Because we are defining the system, we can include (or exclude) whatever we wish. Check that the system satisfies the closure, commutative, associative, and identity properties, with identity element 1. Let us now check for inverses. The element 1 is its own inverse, because $1 \boxtimes 1 = 1$. In row 2, the identity element 1 appears under the number 4, so $2 \boxtimes 4 = 1$ (and $4 \boxtimes 2 = 1$), with 2 and 4 inverses of each other. Also, 3 and 5 are inverses of each other, and 6 is its own inverse. Because each number in the set of the system has an inverse, the system satisfies the inverse property. ◼

Distributive Property
When a mathematical system has two operations, rather than just one, we can look for the **distributive property.**

Distributive Property

Let ☆ and ∘ be two operations defined for elements in the same set. Then ☆ is distributive over ∘ if

$$a \; ☆ \; (b \circ c) = (a \; ☆ \; b) \circ (a \; ☆ \; c)$$

for every choice of elements a, b, and c from the set.

It is a well-known fact that multiplication is distributive over (or with respect to) addition on the set of real numbers. For example,

$$5 \cdot (8 + 3) = 5 \cdot 11 = 55 \quad \text{and} \quad 5 \cdot 8 + 5 \cdot 3 = 40 + 15 = 55,$$

so
$$5 \cdot (8 + 3) = 5 \cdot 8 + 5 \cdot 3.$$

EXAMPLE 3 Testing for the Distributive Property

Is addition distributive over multiplication on the set of whole numbers?

SOLUTION

To find out, replace ☆ with addition (+) and ∘ with multiplication (·) in the statement of the distributive property at the bottom of the previous page:

$$a + (b \cdot c) = (a + b) \cdot (a + c). \quad \text{Is this true in general?}$$

We need to find out whether this statement is true for *every* choice of three whole numbers that we might make. Try an example. If $a = 3$, $b = 4$, and $c = 5$,

$$a + (b \cdot c) = 3 + (4 \cdot 5) = 3 + 20 = 23,$$

while
$$(a + b) \cdot (a + c) = (3 + 4) \cdot (3 + 5) = 7 \cdot 8 = 56.$$

Since $23 \neq 56$, we have $3 + (4 \cdot 5) \neq (3 + 4) \cdot (3 + 5)$. This false result is a *counter-example* (an example showing that a general statement is false). This counterexample shows that addition is *not* distributive over multiplication on the whole numbers.

TABLE 16

☆	a	b	c	d	e
a	a	a	a	a	a
b	a	b	c	d	e
c	a	c	e	b	d
d	a	d	b	e	c
e	a	e	d	c	b

The final example illustrates how the distributive property may hold for an abstract finite system.

EXAMPLE 4 Testing for the Distributive Property

Suppose that the set $\{a, b, c, d, e\}$ has two operations ☆ and ∘ defined by Tables 16 and 17. The distributive property of ☆ with respect to ∘ holds in this system. Verify for the following case: $e \,☆\, (d \circ b) = (e \,☆\, d) \circ (e \,☆\, b)$.

SOLUTION

First evaluate the left side of the equation by using the tables.

$$e \,☆\, (d \circ b) = e \,☆\, e \quad \text{Use the } \circ \text{ table.}$$
$$= b \quad \text{Use the } ☆ \text{ table.}$$

TABLE 17

∘	a	b	c	d	e
a	a	b	c	d	e
b	b	c	d	e	a
c	c	d	e	a	b
d	d	e	a	b	c
e	e	a	b	c	d

Now, evaluate the right side of the equation.

$$(e \,☆\, d) \circ (e \,☆\, b) = c \circ e \quad \text{Use the } ☆ \text{ table twice.}$$
$$= b \quad \text{Use the } \circ \text{ table.}$$

Each time the final result is b; the distributive property is verified for this case.

4.6 EXERCISES

For each system in Exercises 1–10, decide which of the properties of single-operation systems are satisfied. If the identity property is satisfied, give the identity element. If the inverse property is satisfied, give the inverse of each element. If the identity property is satisfied but the inverse property is not, name the elements that have no inverses.

1. {1, 2}; operation ⊗

⊗	1	2
1	1	2
2	2	1

2. {1, 2, 3, 4}; operation ⊗

⊗	1	2	3	4
1	1	2	3	4
2	2	4	1	3
3	3	1	4	2
4	4	3	2	1

3. {1, 2, 3, 4, 5, 6, 7}; operation ⊠

⊠	1	2	3	4	5	6	7
1	1	2	3	4	5	6	7
2	2	4	6	0	2	4	6
3	3	6	1	4	7	2	5
4	4	0	4	0	4	0	4
5	5	2	7	4	1	6	3
6	6	4	2	0	6	4	2
7	7	6	5	4	3	2	1

4. {1, 2, 3, 4, 5}; operation ⊠

⊠	1	2	3	4	5
1	1	2	3	4	5
2	2	4	0	2	4
3	3	0	3	0	3
4	4	2	0	4	2
5	5	4	3	2	1

5. {1, 3, 5, 7, 9}; operation ☆

☆	1	3	5	7	9
1	1	3	5	7	9
3	3	9	5	1	7
5	5	5	5	5	5
7	7	1	5	9	3
9	9	7	5	3	1

6. {1, 3, 5, 7}; operation ☆

☆	1	3	5	7
1	1	3	5	7
3	3	1	7	5
5	5	7	1	3
7	7	5	3	1

7. {A, B, F}; operation *

*	A	B	F
A	B	F	A
B	F	A	B
F	A	B	F

8. {m, n, p}; operation J

J	m	n	p
m	n	p	n
n	p	m	n
p	n	n	m

9. {r, s, t, u}; operation Z

Z	r	s	t	u
r	u	t	r	s
s	t	u	s	r
t	r	s	t	u
u	s	r	u	t

10. {A, J, T, U}; operation #

#	A	J	T	U
A	A	J	T	U
J	J	T	U	A
T	T	U	A	J
U	U	A	J	T

The tables in the finite mathematical systems that we developed in this section can be obtained in a variety of ways. For example, let us begin with a square, as shown in the figure. Let the symbols a, b, c, and d be defined as shown in the figure.

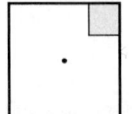

Let *a* represent zero rotation— leave the original square as is.

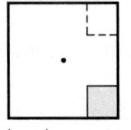

Let *b* represent rotation of 90° clockwise from original position.

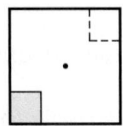

Let *c* represent rotation of 180° clockwise from original position.

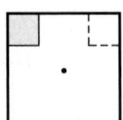

Let *d* represent rotation of 270° clockwise from original position.

Define an operation □ for these letters as follows. To evaluate b □ c, for example, first perform b by rotating the square 90°. (See the figure.) Then perform operation c by rotating the square an additional 180°. The net result is the same as if we had performed d only. Thus,

$$b \,\square\, c = d.$$

Start with *a*.   Perform *b*.   Start with *b*, and perform *c*.

Use this method to find each of the following.

11. $b \,\square\, d$ **12.** $b \,\square\, b$ **13.** $d \,\square\, b$ **14.** $a \,\square\, b$

Solve each problem.

15. Complete the table at the right for the system of square rotations described above.

□	a	b	c	d
a	a	b	c	d
b	b	c		a
c	c		a	
d	d	a		

16. Which of the properties from this section are satisfied by this system?

17. Define a universal set U as the set of counting numbers. Form a new set that contains all possible subsets of U. This new set of subsets together with the operation of set intersection forms a mathematical system. Which of the properties listed in this section are satisfied by this system?

18. Replace the word "intersection" with the word "union" in Exercise 17; then answer the same question.

19. Complete the table at the right so that the result is *not* the same as operation □ of Exercise 15, but so that the five properties listed in this section still hold.

	a	b	c	d
a				
b				
c				
d				

Try examples to help you decide whether each operation, when applied to the integers, satisfies the distributive property.

20. subtraction with respect to multiplication

21. addition with respect to subtraction

22. subtraction with respect to addition

Recall that Example 3 provided a counterexample for the general statement

$$a + (b \cdot c) = (a + b) \cdot (a + c).$$

Thus, addition is not *distributive with respect to multiplication. Now work Exercises 23–26.*

23. Decide if the statement above is true for each of the following sets of values.
   (a) $a = 2, b = -5, c = 4$
   (b) $a = -7, b = 5, c = 3$
   (c) $a = -8, b = 14, c = -5$
   (d) $a = 1, b = 6, c = -6$

24. Find another set of a, b, and c values that make the statement true.

25. Under what general conditions will the statement above be true?

26. Explain why, regardless of the results in Exercises 23–25, addition is still *not* distributive with respect to multiplication.

27. Give the conditions under which each equation would be true.
   (a) $a + (b - c) = (a + b) - (a + c)$
   (b) $a - (b + c) = (a - b) + (a - c)$

28. (a) Find values of a, b and c such that
$$a - (b \cdot c) = (a - b) \cdot (a - c).$$
   (b) Does this mean that subtraction is distributive with respect to multiplication? Explain.

Verify for the mathematical system of Example 4, defined by Tables 16 and 17, that the distributive property holds for each case.

29. $c \star (d \circ e) = (c \star d) \circ (c \star e)$

30. $a \star (a \circ b) = (a \star a) \circ (a \star b)$

31. $d \star (e \circ c) = (d \star e) \circ (d \star c)$

32. $b \star (b \circ b) = (b \star b) \circ (b \star b)$

Exercises 33 and 34 are for students who have studied sets.

33. Use Venn diagrams to show that the distributive property for union with respect to intersection holds for sets *A, B,* and *C.* That is,

$$A \cup (B \cap C) = (A \cup B) \cap (A \cup C).$$

34. Use Venn diagrams to show that *another* distributive property holds for sets *A, B,* and *C.* It is the distributive property of intersection with respect to union.

$$A \cap (B \cup C) = (A \cap B) \cup (A \cap C)$$

Exercises 35 and 36 are for students who have studied logic.

35. Use truth tables to show that the following distributive property holds:

$$p \vee (q \wedge r) \equiv (p \vee q) \wedge (p \vee r).$$

36. Use truth tables to show that *another* distributive property holds:

$$p \wedge (q \vee r) \equiv (p \wedge q) \vee (p \wedge r).$$

4.7 Groups

Groups • Symmetry Groups • Permutation Groups

Groups We have considered some mathematical systems, most of which have satisfied some or all of the closure, associative, commutative, identity, inverse, and distributive properties. Systems are commonly classified according to which properties they satisfy. One important category, when a single operation is considered, is the mathematical *group,* which we define here.

> **Group**
>
> A mathematical system is called a **group** if, under its operation, it satisfies the closure, associative, identity, and inverse properties.

Some sets of numbers, under certain operations, form groups. Others do not.

EXAMPLE 1 Checking the Group Properties

Does the set $\{-1, 1\}$ under the operation of multiplication form a group?

SOLUTION

Check the necessary four properties.

Closure The given system leads to the multiplication table below. All entries in the body of the table are either -1 or 1; the system is closed.

·	−1	1
−1	1	−1
1	−1	1

Niels Henrik Abel (1802–1829) of Norway was identified in childhood as a mathematical genius but never received in his lifetime the professional recognition his work deserved.

At 16, influenced by a perceptive teacher, he read the works of Newton, Euler, and Lagrange. One of Abel's achievements was the demonstration that a general formula for solving fifth-degree equations does not exist. The quadratic formula (for equations of degree 2) is well known, and formulas do exist for solving third- and fourth-degree equations. Abel's accomplishment ended a search that had lasted for years.

In the study of abstract algebra, groups that have the commutative property are referred to as **abelian groups** in honor of Abel. He died of tuberculosis at age 27.

Associative   Try some examples:

$$-1 \cdot (-1 \cdot 1) = -1 \cdot (-1) = 1$$

and $\qquad [-1 \cdot (-1)] \cdot 1 = 1 \cdot 1 = 1,$

so $\qquad -1 \cdot (-1 \cdot 1) = [-1 \cdot (-1)] \cdot 1.$

Also $\qquad 1 \cdot [(-1) \cdot 1] = 1 \cdot (-1) = -1$

and $\qquad [1 \cdot (-1)] \cdot 1 = -1 \cdot 1 = -1,$

so $\qquad 1 \cdot [(-1) \cdot 1] = [1 \cdot (-1)] \cdot 1.$

Any other examples likewise will work. This system satisfies the associative property.

Identity   The operation table for the system shows that the identity element is 1. (The column under 1 is identical to the column at the left, and the row to the right of 1 is identical to the row at the top.)

Inverse   Check in the table that -1 is its own inverse, because $-1 \cdot (-1) = 1$ (the identity element); also, 1 is its own inverse.

All four of the properties are satisfied, so the system is a group. ■

EXAMPLE 2   Checking the Group Properties

Does the set $\{-1, 1\}$ under the operation of addition form a group?

SOLUTION

The addition table below shows that closure is not satisfied, so there is no need to check further. The system is not a group.

+	−1	1
−1	−2	0
1	0	2

■

EXAMPLE 3   Checking the Group Properties

Does the set of integers $\{\ldots, -3, -2, -1, 0, 1, 2, 3, \ldots\}$ under the operation of addition form a group?

SOLUTION

Check the required properties.

Closure   The sum of any two integers is an integer; the system is closed.

Associative   Try some examples:

$$2 + (5 + 8) = 2 + 13 = 15$$

and $\qquad (2 + 5) + 8 = 7 + 8 = 15,$

so $\qquad 2 + (5 + 8) = (2 + 5) + 8.$

Also $\qquad -4 + (7 + 14) = -4 + 21 = 17$

and $\qquad (-4 + 7) + 14 = 3 + 14 = 17,$

so $\qquad -4 + (7 + 14) = (-4 + 7) + 14.$

Apparently, addition of integers is associative.

Amalie ("Emmy") Noether
(1882–1935) was an outstanding
mathematician in the field of
abstract algebra. She studied
and worked in Germany at a time
when it was very difficult for a
woman to do so. At the University
of Erlangen in 1900, Noether was
one of only two women. Although
she could attend classes,
professors could and did deny her
the right to take the exams for
their courses. Not until 1904 was
Noether allowed to officially
register. She completed her
doctorate four years later.

In 1916 Emmy Noether went to
Göttingen to work with David
Hilbert on the general theory of
relativity. But even with Hilbert's
backing and prestige, it was three
years before the faculty voted to
make Noether a *Privatdozent,* the
lowest rank in the faculty. In 1922
Noether was made an unofficial
professor (or assistant). She
received no pay for this post,
although she was given a small
stipend to lecture in algebra.

Noether's area of interest was
abstract algebra, particularly
structures called rings and ideals.
(Groups are structures, too, with
different properties.) One special
type of ring bears her name; she
was the first to study its properties.

Identity   We know that $a + 0 = a$ and $0 + a = a$ for any integer a. The identity element for addition of integers is 0.

Inverse   Given any integer a, its additive inverse, $-a$, is also an integer. For example, 5 and -5 are inverses. The system satisfies the inverse property.

Since all four properties are satisfied, this (infinite) system *is* a group. ■

Symmetry Groups   Groups can be built upon sets of objects other than numbers. An example is the group of **symmetries of a square**, which we now develop. First, cut out a small square, and label it as shown in Figure 10.

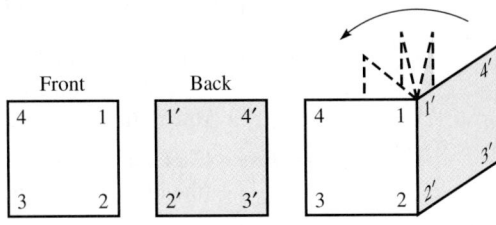

FIGURE 10

Make sure that 1 is in front of 1′, 2 is in front of 2′, 3 is in front of 3′, and 4 is in front of 4′. Let the letter M represent a clockwise rotation of 90° *about the center of the square* (marked with a dot in Figure 11). Let N represent a rotation of 180°, and so on. A list of the symmetries of a square is given in Figure 11.

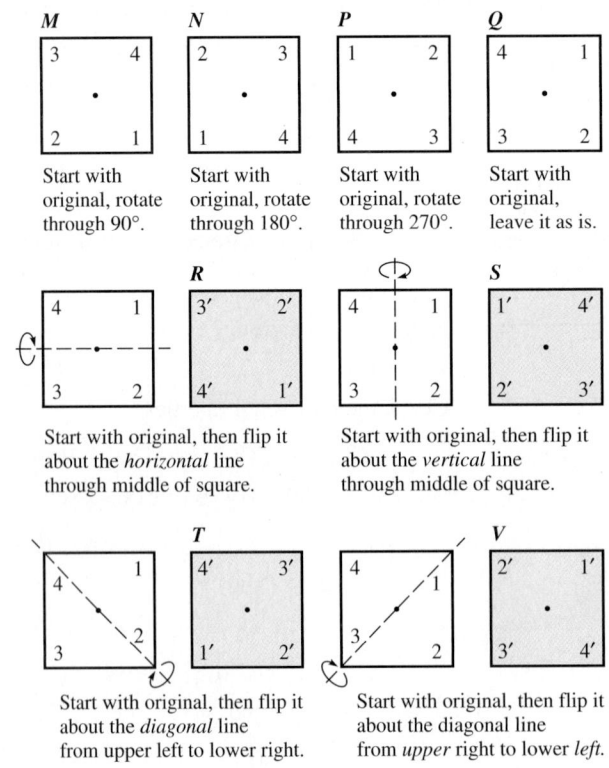

Symmetries of a square

FIGURE 11

Combine symmetries as follows: Let NP represent N followed by P. Performing N and then P is the same as performing just M, so that $NP = M$. See Figure 12.

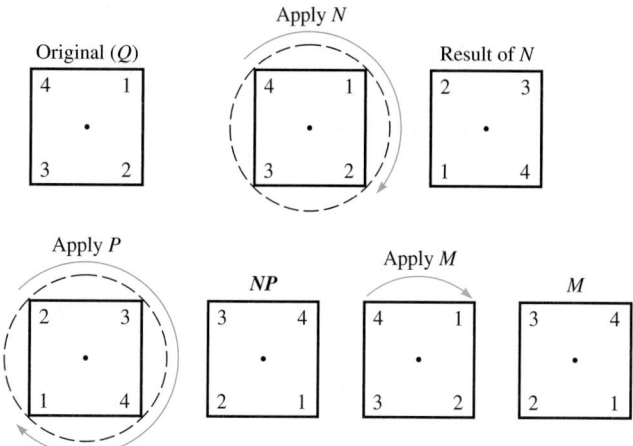

Think of N as advancing each corner two quarter turns clockwise. Thus 4 goes from upper left to lower right. To this result apply P, which advances each corner three quarter turns. Thus 2 goes from upper left to lower left. The result, NP, is the same as advancing each (original) corner one quarter turn, which M does. Thus $NP = M$.

FIGURE 12

EXAMPLE 4   Combining Symmetries of a Square

Find RT using the symmetries of Figure 11.

SOLUTION

First, perform R by flipping the square about a horizontal line through the middle. Then, perform T by flipping the result of R about a diagonal from upper left to lower right. The result of RT is the same as performing only M, so that $RT = M$.

The method in Example 4 can be used to complete Table 18 for combining the symmetries of a square.

TABLE 18

□	M	N	P	Q	R	S	T	V
M	N	P	Q	M	V	T	R	S
N	P	Q	M	N	S	R	V	T
P	Q	M	N	P	T	V	S	R
Q	M	N	P	Q	R	S	T	V
R	T	S	V	R	Q	N	M	P
S	V	R	T	S	N	Q	P	M
T	S	V	R	T	P	M	Q	N
V	R	T	S	V	M	P	N	Q

EXAMPLE 5   Verifying the Group Properties

Show that the system made up of the symmetries of a square is a group.

SOLUTION

For the system to be a group, it must satisfy the closure, associative, identity, and inverse properties.

Closure All the entries in the body of Table 18 come from the set $\{M, N, P, Q, R, S, T, V\}$. Thus, the system is closed.

Associative Try examples:

$$P(MT) = P(R) = T.$$

Also, $(PM)T = (Q)T = T,$

so that $P(MT) = (PM)T.$

Other similar examples also work. (See Exercises 25–28.) Thus, the system has the associative property.

Identity The column at the left in the table is repeated under Q. Check that Q is indeed the identity element.

Inverse In the first row, Q appears under P. Check that M and P are inverses of each other. In fact, every element in the system has an inverse. (See Exercises 29–34.)

Because all four properties are satisfied, the system is a group. ▪

EXAMPLE 6   Verifying that a System Has a Subgroup

TABLE 19

□	M	N	P	Q
M	N	P	Q	M
N	P	Q	M	N
P	Q	M	N	P
Q	M	N	P	Q

Form a mathematical system by using only the set $\{M, N, P, Q\}$ from the group of symmetries of a square. Is this new system a group?

SOLUTION

Table 19 for the elements $\{M, N, P, Q\}$ is just one corner of the table for the entire system. Verify that the system represented by this table satisfies all four properties and thus is a group. This new group is a *subgroup* of the original group of the symmetries of a square. ▪

Permutation Groups   A very useful example of a group comes from studying the arrangements, or permutations, of a list of numbers. Start with the symbols 1-2-3, in that order.

There are several ways in which the order could be changed—for example, 2-3-1. This rearrangement is written

1-2-3

2-3-1.

Replace 1 with 2, replace 2 with 3, and replace 3 with 1. In the same way,

$$1\text{-}2\text{-}3$$
$$3\text{-}1\text{-}2$$

means replace 1 with 3, 2 with 1, and 3 with 2, while

$$1\text{-}2\text{-}3$$
$$3\text{-}2\text{-}1$$

says to replace 1 with 3, leave the 2 unchanged, and replace 3 with 1. All possible rearrangements of the symbols 1-2-3 are listed below where, for convenience, a name has been given to each rearrangement.

A^*: 1-2-3	B^*: 1-2-3	C^*: 1-2-3	D^*: 1-2-3	E^*: 1-2-3	F^*: 1-2-3
2-3-1	2-1-3	1-2-3	1-3-2	3-1-2	3-2-1

Two rearrangements can be combined as with the symmetries of a square; for example, the symbol B^*F^* means to first apply B^* to 1-2-3 and then apply F^* to the result. Rearrangement B^* changes 1-2-3 into 2-1-3. Then apply F^* to this result: 1 becomes 3, 2 is unchanged, and 3 becomes 1. In summary:

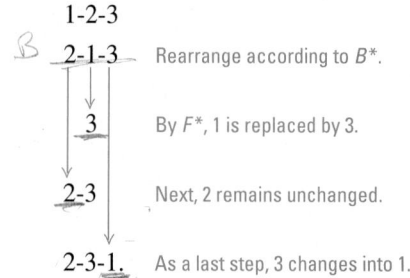

$$1\text{-}2\text{-}3$$
$$2\text{-}1\text{-}3 \qquad \text{Rearrange according to } B^*.$$
$$3 \qquad \text{By } F^*, 1 \text{ is replaced by } 3.$$
$$2\text{-}3 \qquad \text{Next, } 2 \text{ remains unchanged.}$$
$$2\text{-}3\text{-}1. \qquad \text{As a last step, } 3 \text{ changes into } 1.$$

The net result of B^*F^* is to change 1-2-3 into 2-3-1, which is exactly what A^* does to 1-2-3. Therefore,

$$B^*F^* = A^*.$$

EXAMPLE 7 Combining Rearrangements

Find D^*E^*.

SOLUTION

Use the procedure described above.

$$1\text{-}2\text{-}3$$
$$1\text{-}3\text{-}2 \qquad \text{Rearrange according to } D^*.$$
$$3 \qquad E^* \text{ replaces } 1 \text{ with } 3.$$
$$3 \quad 1 \qquad E^* \text{ replaces } 2 \text{ with } 1.$$
$$3\text{-}2\text{-}1 \qquad E^* \text{ replaces } 3 \text{ with } 2.$$

Elie-Joseph Cartan (1869–1951) did extensive work in **group theory.** His 1894 doctoral thesis completely categorized all finite groups known at the time. The classification of *all* finite groups took 150 years and culminated with the monster group (see page 215) constructed in 1980 by Robert Griess, Jr.

Throughout the last half of the twentieth century, physicists were able to apply the structure of some of these groups to improve their understanding of the basic particles of matter and their quantum interactions, thereby enabling them to formulate ever better theories of the fundamental forces of nature.

The result is that D^*E^* converts 1-2-3 into 3-2-1, as does F^*, so

$$D^*E^* = F^*.$$

As further examples, $A^*B^* = D^*$ and $F^*E^* = B^*$.

Once again, we see that we encountered a mathematical system: the set $\{A^*, B^*, C^*, D^*, E^*, F^*\}$ and the operation of the combination of two rearrangements. To see whether this system is a group, check the requirements.

Closure Combine any two rearrangements and the result is another rearrangement, so the system is closed.

Associative Try an example:

First $(B^*D^*)A^* = E^*A^* = C^*.$

Also $B^*(D^*A^*) = B^*B^* = C^*,$

so that $(B^*D^*)A^* = B^*(D^*A^*).$

Because other examples will work out similarly, the system is associative.

Identity The identity element is C^*. If x is any rearrangement, then we have $xC^* = C^*x = x$.

Inverse Does each rearrangement have an inverse rearrangement? Begin with the basic order 1-2-3 and then apply, say B^*, resulting in 2-1-3. The inverse of B^* must convert this 2-1-3 back into 1-2-3, by changing 2 into 1 and 1 into 2. But B^* itself will do this. Hence, $B^*B^* = C^*$ and B^* is its own inverse. By the same process, E^* and A^* are inverses of each other. Also, each of C^*, D^*, and F^* is its own inverse.

Because all four requirements are satisfied, the system is a group. Rearrangements are also referred to as *permutations,* so this group is sometimes called the **permutation group on three symbols.** The total number of different permutations of a given number of symbols can be determined by techniques described in the chapter on counting methods.

4.7 EXERCISES

What is wrong with the way in which each question is stated?

1. Do the integers form a group?

2. Does multiplication satisfy all of the group properties?

Decide whether each system is a group. If not a group, identify all properties that are not satisfied. (Recall that any system failing to satisfy the identity property automatically fails to satisfy the inverse property also.) For the finite systems, it may help to construct tables. For infinite systems, try some examples to help you decide.

3. $\{0\}$; multiplication

4. $\{0\}$; addition

5. $\{0, 1\}$; addition

6. $\{0\}$; subtraction

7. $\{-1, 1\}$; division

8. $\{0, 1\}$; multiplication

9. $\{-1, 0, 1\}$; multiplication

10. $\{-1, 0, 1\}$; addition

11. integers; subtraction

12. integers; multiplication

13. odd integers; multiplication

14. counting numbers; addition

15. rational numbers; addition

16. even integers; addition

17. prime numbers; addition

18. nonzero rational numbers; multiplication

19. Explain why a *finite* group based on the operation of ordinary addition of numbers cannot contain the element 1.

20. Explain why a group based on the operation of ordinary addition of numbers *must* contain the element 0.

Exercises 21–34 apply to the system of symmetries of a square presented in the text. Find each combination.

21. *RN*

22. *PR*

23. *TV*

24. *VP*

Verify each statement.

25. $N(TR) = (NT)R$

26. $V(PS) = (VP)S$

27. $T(VN) = (TV)N$

28. $S(MR) = (SM)R$

Find the inverse of each element.

29. *N* **30.** *Q* **31.** *R* **32.** *S* **33.** *T* **34.** *V*

*A group that also satisfies the commutative property is called a **commutative group** (or an **abelian group,** after Niels Henrik Abel). Determine whether each group is commutative.*

35. the group of symmetries of a square

36. the subgroup of Example 6

37. the integers under addition

38. the permutation group on three symbols

Give illustrations to support your answers for Exercises 39–42.

39. Produce a mathematical system with two operations which is a group under one operation but not a group under the other operation.

40. Explain what property is gained when the system of counting numbers is extended to the system of whole numbers.

41. Explain what property is gained when the system of whole numbers is extended to the system of integers.

42. Explain what property is gained when the system of integers is extended to the system of rational numbers.

Consider the following set of "actions" (A, B, C, and D) on three symbols (a, b, and c):

A:	a	b	c		B:	a	b	c		C:	a	b	c		D:	a	b	c
	a	b	c			c	b	a			a	$-b$	c			c	$-b$	a

(*continued*)

The resulting system is somewhat similar to the permutation group on three symbols discussed in the text, except that not all possible rearrangements of a, b, and c are included, and two of the actions involve sign changes. The operation of the system is the combination of actions as follows, for example, BD represents B followed by D:

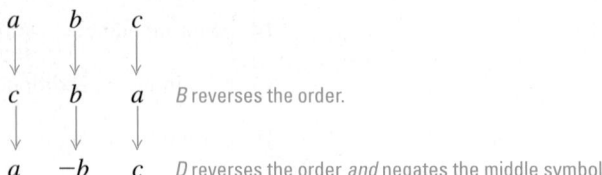

The net result, from beginning to end, is simply to negate the middle symbol, which is exactly what C does. Therefore, $BD = C.$

43. Verify, for yourself, the entries shown in the following operation table and fill in the missing entries.

	A	B	C	D
A	A	B	C	D
B	B	A		C
C	C		A	
D	D			A

44. (a) Is there an identity element in this system?
(b) If so, what is it?

45. (a) Is closure satisfied by this system?
(b) Explain.

46. (a) Is this system commutative?
(b) Explain.

47. (a) Is the distributive property satisfied in this system?
(b) Explain.

48. (a) Assuming the associative property is satisfied, is the system a group?
(b) Explain.

NUMBER THEORY

5

The 1997 movie *Contact*, based on the Carl Sagan novel of the same name, portrays Jodie Foster as scientist Ellie Arroway. After years of searching, Ellie makes contact with intelligent life in outer space. Her contact is verified after receiving radio signals that indicate **prime numbers**: 2, 3, 5, 7, 11, and so on. Her superiors are not convinced, asking why the aliens don't just speak English. Ellie's response:

> Well, maybe because 70% of the planet speaks other languages. Mathematics is the only true universal language, Senator. It's no coincidence that they're using primes . . . . Prime numbers—that would be integers that are divisible only by themselves and 1.

In this chapter, you will learn about those prime numbers, which are the building blocks of number theory, and, hence, of mathematics.

179

5.1 PRIME AND COMPOSITE NUMBERS

Primes, Composites, and Divisibility • The Fundamental Theorem of Arithmetic

Primes, Composites, and Divisibility

The famous German mathematician Carl Friedrich Gauss once remarked, "Mathematics is the Queen of Science, and number theory is the Queen of Mathematics." **Number theory** is the branch of mathematics devoted to the study of the properties of the **natural numbers,** also called the **counting numbers** or the **positive integers.**

$$N = \{1, 2, 3, \dots\}$$

A key concept of number theory is the idea of *divisibility*. One counting number is *divisible* by another if the operation of dividing the first by the second leaves a remainder 0.

> Do not confuse $b \mid a$ with b/a. The expression $b \mid a$ denotes the *statement* "b divides a." For example, $3 \mid 12$ is a true statement, while $5 \mid 14$ is a false statement. On the other hand, b/a denotes the *operation* "b divided by a." For example, $28/4$ yields the result 7.

Divisibility

The natural number a is **divisible** by the natural number b if there exists a natural number k such that $a = bk$. If b divides a, then we write $b \mid a$.

Notice that if b divides a, then the quotient a/b or $\frac{a}{b}$ is a natural number. For example, 4 divides 20 because there exists a natural number k such that

$$20 = 4k.$$

The value of k here is 5, because

$$20 = 4 \cdot 5.$$

> The ideas of **even** and **odd natural numbers** are based on the concept of divisibility. A natural number is even if it is divisible by 2 and odd if it is not. Every even number can be written in the form $2k$ (for some natural number k), while every odd number can be written in the form $2k - 1$. Another way to say the same thing: 2 divides every even number but fails to divide every odd number. (If a is even, then $2 \mid a$, whereas if a is odd, then $2 \nmid a$.)

The natural number 20 is not divisible by 7, since there is no natural number k satisfying $20 = 7k$. Alternatively, "20 divided by 7 gives quotient 2 with remainder 6" and since there is a nonzero remainder, divisibility does not hold. We write $7 \nmid 20$ to indicate that 7 does *not* divide 20.

If the natural number a is divisible by the natural number b, then b is a **factor** (or **divisor**) of a, and a is a **multiple** of b. For example, 5 is a factor of 30, and 30 is a multiple of 5. Also, 6 is a factor of 30, and 30 is a multiple of 6. The number 30 equals $6 \cdot 5$. This product $6 \cdot 5$ is called a **factorization** of 30. Other factorizations of 30 include

$$3 \cdot 10, \quad 2 \cdot 15, \quad 1 \cdot 30, \quad \text{and} \quad 2 \cdot 3 \cdot 5.$$

▋▋ EXAMPLE 1 Checking Divisibility

Decide whether the first number is divisible by the second.

(a) 45; 9 **(b)** 60; 7 **(c)** 19; 19 **(d)** 26; 1

SOLUTION

(a) Is there a natural number k that satisfies $45 = 9k$? The answer is yes, because $45 = 9 \cdot 5$, and 5 is a natural number. Therefore, 9 divides 45, written $9 \mid 45$.

(b) Because the quotient $60 \div 7$ is not a natural number, 60 is not divisible by 7, written $7 \nmid 60$.

(c) The quotient $19 \div 19$ is the natural number 1, so 19 is divisible by 19. (***In fact, any natural number is divisible by itself.***)

> For any natural number a, it is true that $a \mid a$, and also that $1 \mid a$.

(d) The quotient $26 \div 1$ is the natural number 26, so 26 is divisible by 1. (***In fact, any natural number is divisible by 1.***) ▋▋▋

EXAMPLE 2 Finding Factors

Find all the natural number factors of each number.

(a) 36   **(b)** 50   **(c)** 11

SOLUTION

(a) To find the factors of 36, try to divide 36 by 1, 2, 3, 4, 5, 6, and so on. This gives the following natural number factors of 36: 1, 2, 3, 4, 6, 9, 12, 18, and 36.

(b) The factors of 50 are 1, 2, 5, 10, 25, and 50.

(c) The only natural number factors of 11 are 11 and 1.   ▌▌▌

Prime and Composite Numbers

A natural number greater than 1 that has only itself and 1 as factors is called a **prime number.** A natural number greater than 1 that is not prime is called **composite.**

Mathematicians agree that the natural number 1 is neither prime nor composite.

Alternative Definition of a Prime Number

A **prime number** is a natural number that has *exactly* two different natural number factors (which clarifies that 1 is not a prime).

There is a systematic method for identifying prime numbers in a list of numbers: 2, 3, . . . , *n*. The method, known as the **Sieve of Eratosthenes,** is named after the Greek geographer, poet, astronomer, and mathematician (about 276–192 B.C.).

To construct such a sieve, list all the natural numbers from 2 through some given natural number *n*, such as 100. The number 2 is prime, but all other multiples of 2 (4, 6, 8, 10, and so on) are composite. Circle the prime 2, and cross out all other multiples of 2. The next number not crossed out and not circled is 3, the next prime. Circle the 3, and cross out all other multiples of 3 (6, 9, 12, 15, and so on) that are not already crossed out. Circle the next prime, 5, and cross out all other multiples of 5 not already crossed out. Continue this process for all primes less than or equal to the square root of the last number in the list. For this list, we may stop with 7, because the next prime, 11, is greater than the square root of 100, which is 10. At this stage, simply circle all remaining numbers that are not crossed out.

Table 1 shows the Sieve of Eratosthenes for 2, 3, 4, . . . , 100.

How to Use Up Lots of Chalk In 1903, the mathematician F. N. Cole presented before a meeting of the American Mathematical Society his discovery of a factorization of the number

$$2^{67} - 1.$$

He walked up to the chalkboard, raised 2 to the 67th power, and then subtracted 1. Then he moved over to another part of the board and multiplied out

193,707,721
× 761,838,257,287.

The two calculations agreed, and Cole received a standing ovation for a presentation that did not include a single word.

Table 1   Sieve of Eratosthenes

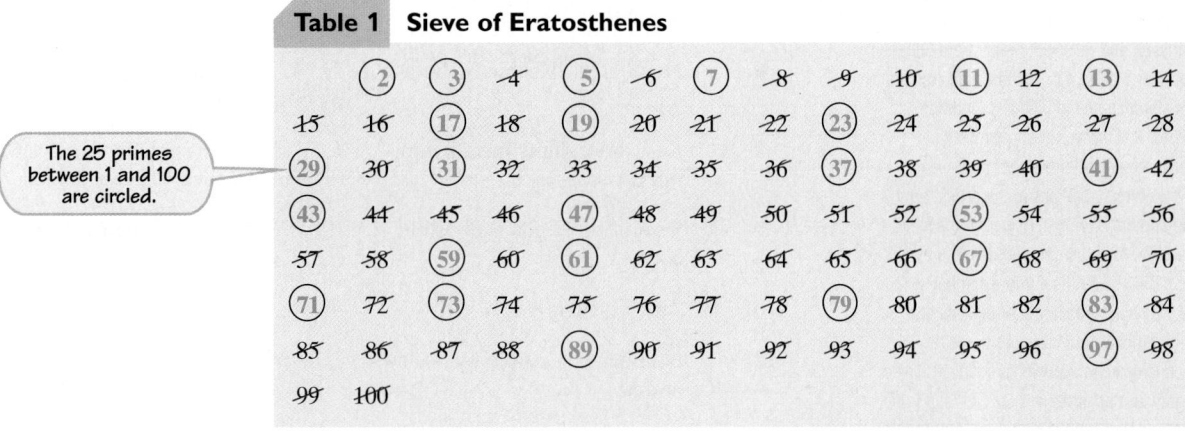

The 25 primes between 1 and 100 are circled.

▮▮ **EXAMPLE 3** Identifying Prime and Composite Numbers

Decide whether each number is prime or composite.

(a) 97   **(b)** 59,872   **(c)** 697

SOLUTION

(a) Because 97 is circled in **Table 1**, it is prime. If 97 had a smaller prime factor, 97 would have been crossed out as a multiple of that factor.

(b) The number 59,872 is even, so it is divisible by 2. It is composite.

There is only one even prime, the number 2 itself.

(c) For 697 to be composite, there must be a number other than 697 and 1 that divides into it with remainder 0. Start by trying 2, and then 3. Neither works. There is no need to try 4. (If 4 divides with remainder 0 into a number, then 2 will also.) Try 5. There is no need to try 6 or any succeeding even number. (Why?) Try 7. Try 11. (Why not try 9?) Try 13. Keep trying numbers until one works, or until a number is tried whose square exceeds the given number, 697. Try 17.

$$697 \div 17 = 41$$

The number 697 is composite, since

$$697 = 17 \cdot 41.$$ ▮▮▮

An aid in determining whether a natural number is divisible by another natural number is called a **divisibility test**. **Table 2** shows tests for divisibility by the natural numbers 2 through 12 (except for 7 and 11, which are covered in the exercises).

In the October 1, 1994 issue of *Science News*, Ivars Peterson gave a fascinating account of the discovery of a 75-year-old **factoring machine** ("Cranking Out Primes: Tracking Down a Long-lost Factoring Machine"). In 1989, Jeffrey Shallit of the University of Waterloo in Ontario came across an article in an obscure 1920 French journal, in which the author, Eugene Olivier Carissan, reported his invention of the factoring apparatus. Shallit and two colleagues embarked on a search for the machine. They contacted all telephone subscribers in France named Carissan and received a reply from Eugene Carissan's daughter. The machine was still in existence and in working condition, stored in a drawer at an astronomical observatory in Floirac, near Bordeaux.

Peterson explains in the article how the apparatus works. Using the machine, Carissan took just ten minutes to prove that 708,158,977 is a prime number, and he was able to factor a 13-digit number. While this cannot compare to what technology can accomplish today, it was a significant achievement for Carissan's day.

Table 2 **Divisibility Tests for Natural Numbers**

Divisible By	Test	Example
2	Number ends in 0, 2, 4, 6, or 8. (The last digit is even.)	9,489,994 ends in 4; it is divisible by 2.
3	Sum of the digits is divisible by 3.	897,432 is divisible by 3, since $8 + 9 + 7 + 4 + 3 + 2 = 33$ is divisible by 3.
4	Last two digits form a number divisible by 4.	7,693,432 is divisible by 4, since 32 is divisible by 4.
5	Number ends in 0 or 5.	890 and 7635 are divisible by 5.
6	Number is divisible by both 2 and 3.	27,342 is divisible by 6 since it is divisible by both 2 and 3.
8	Last three digits form a number divisible by 8.	1,437,816 is divisible by 8, since 816 is divisible by 8.
9	Sum of the digits is divisible by 9.	428,376,105 is divisible by 9 since sum of the digits is 36, which is divisible by 9.
10	The last digit is 0.	897,463,940 is divisible by 10.
12	Number is divisible by both 4 and 3.	376,984,032 is divisible by 12.

▌▌ **EXAMPLE 4** Applying Divisibility Tests

In each case, decide whether the first number is divisible by the second.

(a) 2,984,094; 4   **(b)** 4,119,806,514; 9

SOLUTION

(a) The last two digits form the number 94. Since 94 is not divisible by 4, the given number is not divisible by 4.

(b) The sum of the digits is

$$4 + 1 + 1 + 9 + 8 + 0 + 6 + 5 + 1 + 4 = 39,$$

which is not divisible by 9. The given number is, therefore, not divisible by 9. ▮▮▮

The Fundamental Theorem of Arithmetic

A *composite* number can be thought of as "composed" of smaller factors. For example, 42 is composite since $42 = 6 \cdot 7$. If the smaller factors are all primes, then we have a *prime factorization*. For example, $42 = 2 \cdot 3 \cdot 7$.

> **The Fundamental Theorem of Arithmetic**
>
> Every natural number can be expressed in one and only one way as a product of primes (if the order of the factors is disregarded). This unique product of primes is called the **prime factorization** of the natural number.

Because a prime natural number is not composed of smaller factors, its prime factorization is simply itself. For example, $17 = 17$.

▌▌ **EXAMPLE 5** Finding the Unique Prime Factorization of a Composite Number

Find the prime factorization of the number 1320.

SOLUTION

We use a "factor tree." The factor tree can start with $1320 = 2 \cdot 660$, as shown below on the left. Then $660 = 2 \cdot 330$, and so on, until every branch of the tree ends with a prime. All the resulting prime factors are shown circled in the diagram.

Alternatively, the same factorization is obtained by repeated division by primes, as shown on the right. (In general, you would divide by the primes 2, 3, 5, 7, 11, and so on, each as many times as possible, until the answer is no longer composite.)

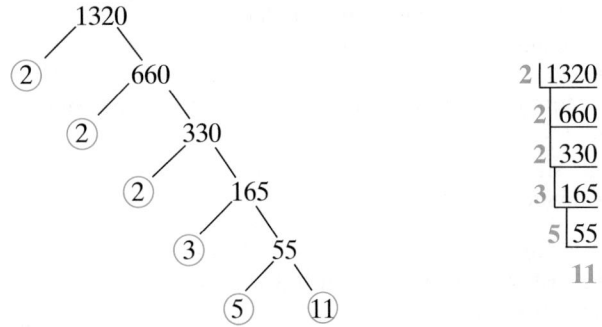

By either method, the prime factorization, in exponential form, is

$$1320 = 2^3 \cdot 3 \cdot 5 \cdot 11. \quad {\scriptstyle 2 \cdot 2 \cdot 2 \,=\, 2^3}$$

▮▮▮

The following program, written by Charles W. Gantner and provided courtesy of Texas Instruments, can be used on the TI-83/84 Plus calculator to list all primes less than or equal to a given natural number *N*.

```
PROGRAM: PRIMES
: Disp "INPUT N ≥ 2"
: Disp "TO GET"
: Disp "PRIMES ≤ N"
: Input N
: 2 → T
: Disp T
: 1 → A
: Lbl 1
: A + 2 → A
: 3 → B
: If A > N
: Stop
: Lbl 2
: If B ≤ √(A)
: Goto 3
: Disp A
: Pause
: Goto 1
: Lbl 3
: If A/B ≤ int (A/B)
: Goto 1
: B + 2 → B
: Goto 2
```

```
prgmPRIMES

INPUT N≥2
TO GET
PRIMES ≤ N
?6
```

```
TO GET
PRIMES ≤ N
?6
                  2
                  3
                  5
               Done
```

The display indicates that the primes less than or equal to 6 are 2, 3, and 5.

5.1 EXERCISES

Decide whether each statement is true *or* false.

1. Every natural number is divisible by 1.

2. There are no even prime numbers.

3. If *n* is a natural number and $9|n$, then $3|n$.

4. If *n* is a natural number and $5|n$, then $10|n$.

5. 1 is the least prime number.

6. Every natural number is both a factor and a multiple of itself.

7. If 16 divides a natural number, then 2, 4, and 8 must also divide that natural number.

8. The prime number 53 has exactly two natural number factors.

Find all natural number factors of each number.

9. 12

10. 20

11. 28

12. 172

Use divisibility tests to decide whether the given number is divisible by each number.

(a) 2   (b) 3   (c) 4   (d) 5   (e) 6   (f) 8
(g) 9   (h) 10   (i) 12

13. 321

14. 540

15. 36,360

16. 123,456,789

17. (a) In constructing the Sieve of Eratosthenes for 2 through 100, we said that any composite in that range had to be a multiple of some prime less than or equal to 7 (since the next prime, 11, is greater than the square root of 100). Explain.

   (b) To extend the Sieve of Eratosthenes to 200, what is the largest prime whose multiples would have to be considered?

   (c) Complete this statement: In seeking prime factors of a given number, we need only consider all primes up to and including the _____ _____ of that number, since a prime factor greater than the _____ _____ can only occur if there is at least one other prime factor less than the _____ _____.

   (d) Complete this statement: If no prime less than or equal to $\sqrt{n}$ divides *n*, then *n* is a _____ number.

18. (a) Continue the Sieve of Eratosthenes in **Table 1** from 101 to 200 and list the primes between 100 and 200. How many are there?

   (b) From your list in part (a), verify that the numbers 197 and 199 are both prime.

19. List two primes that are consecutive natural numbers. Can there be any others?

20. Can there be three primes that are consecutive natural numbers? Explain.

21. For a natural number to be divisible by both 2 and 5, what must be true about its last digit?

22. Consider the divisibility tests for 2, 4, and 8 (all powers of 2). Use inductive reasoning to predict the divisibility test for 16. Then, use the test to show that 456,882,320 is divisible by 16.

23. Redraw the factor tree of **Example 5,** assuming that you first observe that $1320 = 12 \cdot 110$, then that $12 = 3 \cdot 4$ and $110 = 10 \cdot 11$. Complete the process and give the resulting prime factorization.

24. Explain how your result in **Exercise 23** illustrates the fundamental theorem of arithmetic.

Find the prime factorization of each composite number.

25. 168

26. 300

27. 468

28. 931

Here is a divisibility test for 7.

(a) *Double the last digit of the given number, and subtract this value from the given number with the last digit omitted.*

(b) *Repeat the process of part (a) as many times as necessary until it is clear whether the number obtained is divisible by 7.*

(c) *If the final number obtained is divisible by 7, then the given number also is divisible by 7. If the final number is not divisible by 7, then neither is the given number.*

Use this divisibility test to determine whether each number is divisible by 7.

29. 214,256

30. 549,311

31. 584,854

32. 325,951

Here is a divisibility test for 11.

(a) *Starting at the left of the given number, add together every other digit.*

(b) *Add together the remaining digits.*

(c) *Subtract the smaller of the two sums from the larger. (If they are the same, the difference is 0.)*

(d) *If the final number obtained is divisible by 11, then the given number also is divisible by 11. If the final number is not divisible by 11, then neither is the given number.*

Use this divisibility test to determine whether each number is divisible by 11.

33. 6,524,846

34. 108,410,313

35. 470,933,815

36. 819,224,306

37. Consider the divisibility test for the composite number 6, and make a conjecture for the divisibility test for the composite number 15.

38. Give two factorizations of the number 75 that are not prime factorizations.

Determine all possible digit replacements for x so that the first number is divisible by the second. For example, 37, 58x is divisible by 2 if

$$x = 0, 2, 4, 6, \text{ or } 8.$$

39. 398,87x; 2

40. 2,45x,765; 3

41. 64,537,84x; 4

42. 2,143,89x; 5

43. 985,23x; 6

44. 23, x54,470; 10

There is a method to determine the **number of divisors** *of a composite number. To do this, write the composite number in its prime factored form, using exponents. Add 1 to each exponent and multiply these numbers. Their product gives the number of divisors of the composite number. For example,*

$$24 = 2^3 \cdot 3 = 2^3 \cdot 3^1.$$

Now add 1 to each exponent:

$$3 + 1 = 4, \ 1 + 1 = 2.$$

Multiply $4 \cdot 2$ *to get 8. There are 8 divisors of 24. (Because 24 is rather small, this can be verified easily. The divisors are 1, 2, 3, 4, 6, 8, 12, and 24, a total of eight as predicted.)*

Find the number of divisors of each composite number.

45. 42

46. 308

47. $5^8 \cdot 29^2$

48. $2^4 \cdot 7^2 \cdot 13^3$

Leap years occur when the year number is divisible by 4. An exception to this occurs when the year number is divisible by 100 (that is, it ends in two zeros). In such a case, the number must be divisible by 400 in order for the year to be a leap year. Determine which years are leap years.

49. 1776

50. 1894

51. 2200

52. 2400

53. Why is the following *not* a valid divisibility test for 8? "A number is divisible by 8 if it is divisible by both 4 and 2." Support your answer with an example.

54. Choose any three consecutive natural numbers, multiply them together, and divide the product by 6. Repeat this several times, using different choices of three consecutive numbers. Make a conjecture concerning the result.

55. Explain why the product of three consecutive natural numbers must be divisible by 6.

56. Choose any 6-digit number consisting of three digits followed by the same three digits in the same order (for example, 467,467). Divide by 13. Divide by 11. Divide by 7. What do you notice? Why do you think this happens?

5.2   LARGE PRIME NUMBERS

The Infinitude of Primes • The Search for Large Primes

The Infinitude of Primes

One important basic result about prime numbers was proved by Euclid around 300 B.C., namely that there are infinitely many primes. This means that no matter how large a prime we identify, there are always others even larger. Euclid's proof remains today as one of the most elegant proofs in all of mathematics. (An *elegant* mathematical proof is one that demonstrates the desired result in a most direct, concise manner. Mathematicians strive for elegance in their proofs.) It is called a **proof by contradiction.**

A statement can be proved by contradiction as follows: Assume that the negation of the statement is true and use that assumption to produce some sort of contradiction, or absurdity. Logically, the fact that the negation of the original statement leads to a contradiction means that the original statement must be true.

To understand better a particular part of the proof that there are infinitely many primes, first examine the following argument.

Suppose that $M = 2 \cdot 3 \cdot 5 \cdot 7 + 1 = 211$. Now M is the product of the first four prime numbers, plus 1. If we divide 211 by each of the primes 2, 3, 5, and 7, the remainder is always 1.

$$
\begin{array}{cccc}
105 & 70 & 42 & 30 \\
2\overline{)211} & 3\overline{)211} & 5\overline{)211} & 7\overline{)211} \\
\underline{210} & \underline{210} & \underline{210} & \underline{210} \\
1 & 1 & 1 & 1
\end{array}
$$

All remainders are 1.

So 211 is not divisible by any of the primes 2, 3, 5, and 7.

Now we can present Euclid's proof that there are infinitely many primes. If *there is no largest prime number*, then there must be infinitely many primes.

▌▌ **EXAMPLE 1** Proving the Infinitude of Primes

Prove by contradiction that there are infinitely many primes.

SOLUTION

Suppose there is a largest prime number, called P. Form the number M such that

$$M = p_1 \cdot p_2 \cdot p_3 \cdots \cdot P + 1,$$

where $p_1, p_2, p_3, \ldots, P$ represent all the primes less than or equal to P. Now the number M must be either prime or composite.

1. Suppose that M is prime.
    M is obviously larger than P, so if M is prime, it is larger than the assumed largest prime P. We have reached a *contradiction*.

2. Suppose that M is composite.
    If M is composite, it must have a prime factor. But none of $p_1, p_2, p_3, \ldots, P$ are factors of M, because division by each will leave a remainder of 1. (Recall the above argument.) So if M has a prime factor, it must be greater than P. But this is a *contradiction*, because P is the assumed largest prime.

In either case 1 or 2, we reach a contradiction. The whole argument was based upon the assumption that a largest prime exists, but as this leads to contradictions, there must be no largest prime, or equivalently, ***there are infinitely many primes.*** ▌▌▌

We could never investigate all infinitely many primes directly. So, historically, people have observed properties of the smaller, familiar, ones and then tried to either "disprove" the property (usually by finding counterexamples) or prove it (usually by some deductive argument).

Here is one way to **partition** the natural numbers (divide them into subsets).

Set A: all natural numbers of the form $4k$

Set B: all natural numbers of the form $4k + 1$

Set C: all natural numbers of the form $4k + 2$

Set D: all natural numbers of the form $4k + 3$

In each case, k is some whole number, except that for set A, k cannot be 0. All natural numbers are now accounted for. Any number of the form $4k + 4$ would be in subset A, because

$$4k + 4 = 4(k + 1).$$

Any number of the form $4k + 5$ would be in subset B, because

$$4k + 5 = 4(k + 1) + 1,$$

and so on. The subset A consists of all the multiples of 4. Each of these is divisible by 4, hence, each is not a prime. Now consider C. Because

$$4k + 2 = 2(2k + 1),$$

each member is divisible by 2, hence, each is not a prime (except for 2 itself).

Under this partitioning, all primes must be in either B or D.

Marin Mersenne (1588–1648), in his *Cogitata Physico-Mathematica* (1644), claimed that M_n was prime for n = 2, 3, 5, 7, 13, 17, 19, 31, 67, 127, and 257, and composite for all other prime numbers n less than 257. Other mathematicians at the time knew that Mersenne could not have actually tested all these values, but no one else could prove or disprove them either. It was more then 300 years later before all primes up to 257 were legitimately checked out, and Mersenne was finally revealed to have made five errors:

M_{61} is prime.

M_{67} is composite.

M_{89} is prime.

M_{107} is prime.

M_{257} is composite.

▮▮ **EXAMPLE 2** Partitioning the Natural Numbers

List the first eight members of each of the infinite sets A, B, C, and D.

SOLUTION

$A = \{4, 8, 12, 16, 20, 24, 28, 32, \dots\}$
$B = \{1, 5, 9, 13, 17, 21, 25, 29, \dots\}$
$C = \{2, 6, 10, 14, 18, 22, 26, 30, \dots\}$
$D = \{3, 7, 11, 15, 19, 23, 27, 31, \dots\}$ ▮▮▮

As mentioned earlier, sets A and C contain no primes. All primes must lie in sets B and D. (In fact, there are infinitely many primes in each.)

▮▮ **EXAMPLE 3** Identifying Primes of the Forms $4k + 1$ and $4k + 3$

Identify all primes *specifically listed* in the following infinite sets of **Example 2.**

(a) set B **(b)** set D

SOLUTION

(a) 5, 13, 17, 29   **(b)** 3, 7, 11, 19, 23, 31 ▮▮▮

Pierre de Fermat (profiled on **page 200**) proved that every prime number of the form $4k + 1$ can be expressed as the sum of two squares.

▮▮ **EXAMPLE 4** Expressing Primes as Sums of Squares

Express each prime in the solution of **Example 3(a)** as a sum of two squares.

SOLUTION

$5 = 1^2 + 2^2;$ $13 = 2^2 + 3^2;$ $17 = 1^2 + 4^2;$ $29 = 2^2 + 5^2$ ▮▮▮

The Search for Large Primes

Identifying larger and larger prime numbers and factoring large composite numbers into their prime components is of great practical importance today, because it is the basis of modern **cryptography systems,** or secret codes. Various codes have been used for centuries in military applications. Today the security of vast amounts of industrial, business, and personal data also depends upon the theory of prime numbers. See the **Extension** following **Section 5.4.**

No reasonable formula has ever been found that will consistently generate prime numbers, much less "generate all primes." The most useful attempt, named to honor the French monk Marin Mersenne (1588–1648), is given below.

At one time, $2^{11,213} - 1$ was the largest known **Mersenne prime.** To honor its discovery, the Urbana, Illinois, post office used the cancellation picture above.

Mersenne Numbers and Mersenne Primes

For $n = 1, 2, 3, \dots$, the **Mersenne numbers** are those generated by the formula

$$M_n = 2^n - 1.$$

(1) If n is composite, then M_n is also composite.

(2) If n is prime, then M_n may be either prime or composite.

The prime values of M_n are called the **Mersenne primes.** Large primes being verified currently are commonly Mersenne primes.

Long before Mersenne's time, there was general agreement on statement (1) in the box. (**Exercises 23–25** show how to find a factor of $2^n - 1$ whenever n is composite.) However, some early writers did not agree with statement (2), believing instead (incorrectly) that a prime n would always produce a prime M_n.

▮▮ **EXAMPLE 5** Finding Mersenne Numbers
_____

Find each Mersenne number M_n for $n = 2, 3$, and 5.

SOLUTION

$$M_2 = 2^2 - 1 = 3 \qquad 2^2 = 2 \cdot 2 = 4$$
$$M_3 = 2^3 - 1 = 7 \qquad 2^3 = 2 \cdot 2 \cdot 2 = 8$$
$$M_5 = 2^5 - 1 = 31 \qquad 2^5 = 2 \cdot 2 \cdot 2 \cdot 2 \cdot 2 = 32$$

Note that all three values, 3, 7, and 31, are indeed primes. ▮▮▮

It turns out that $M_7 = 2^7 - 1 = 127$ is also a prime (see **Exercise 18(a)** of **Section 5.1**), but it was discovered in 1536 that

$$M_{11} = 2^{11} - 1 = 2047 \quad \text{is not prime (since it is } 23 \cdot 89 \text{).}$$

So prime values of n do not always produce prime M_n. Which prime values of n *do* produce prime Mersenne numbers (the so-called **Mersenne primes**)? No way was ever found to identify, in general, which prime values of n result in Mersenne primes. It is a matter of checking out each prime n value individually—not an easy task given that the Mersenne numbers rapidly become very large.

The Mersenne prime search yielded results slowly. By about 1600, M_n had been verified as prime for all prime n up to 19 (except for 11, as mentioned above). The next one was M_{31}, verified by Euler sometime between 1752 and 1772.

In 1876, French mathematician Edouard Lucas used a clever test he had developed to show that M_{127} (a 39-digit number) is prime. In the 1930s Lucas's method was further simplified by D. H. Lehmer, and the testing of Mersenne numbers for primality has been done ever since with the Lucas-Lehmer test. In 1952 an early computer verified that M_{521}, M_{607}, M_{1279}, M_{2203}, and M_{2281} are primes.

Over the last half century, most new record-breaking primes have been identified by computer algorithms devised and implemented by mathematicians and programmers. In 1996, the **Great Internet Mersenne Prime Search (GIMPS)** was launched and now involves about 50,000 personal computers worldwide. Of the 47 Mersenne primes presently known, the GIMPS program has discovered the thirteen largest ones. The latest one found (as of summer 2010),

$$M_{42,643,801} = 2^{42,643,801} - 1,$$

has 12,837,064 digits. Read the margin note **Prime Does Pay** to learn of a larger one, discovered earlier.

During the same general period that Mersenne was thinking about prime numbers, Pierre de Fermat (about 1601–1665) conjectured that the formula

$$2^{2^n} + 1$$

would always produce a prime, for any whole number value of n. **Table 3** on the next page shows how this formula generates the first four **Fermat numbers,** which are all primes. The fifth Fermat number (from $n = 4$) is likewise prime. Fermat had verified these first five by around 1630. But the sixth Fermat number (from $n = 5$) turns out to be 4,294,967,297, which is *not* prime. (See **Exercises 15 and 16.**) As of summer 2010, no more primes have been found among the Fermat numbers, and only F_0 to F_{11} have been completely factored.

Prime Does Pay On April 12, 2009, the 47th known Mersenne prime was identified by Odd Magnar Strindmo, from Melhus, Norway. The number,

$$2^{42,643,801} - 1, \quad \text{has} \quad 12,837,064 \text{ digits.}$$

Exceeding ten million digits, it would have qualified for a $100,000 award from The Electronic Frontier Foundation—except that it wasn't the first with that many digits. That award went to Edson Smith of the UCLA Department of Mathematics, who discovered the 45th known Mersenne prime on August 23, 2008. His number,

$$2^{43,112,609} - 1, \quad \text{has} \quad 12,978,189 \text{ digits}$$

and is still (as of summer 2010) the largest Mersenne prime known.

The Foundation now offers $150,000 to the first person or group to discover a 100-million-digit prime. But at present GIMPS participation rates, that discovery could take ten years or more.

If you would like to join the **Great Internet Mersenne Prime Search** (or just learn more about it), check out www.mersenne.org.

Distributed Computing is a way of achieving great computer power by having lots of individual machines do separate parts of the computation. One example is the **Great Internet Mersenne Prime Search (GIMPS),** described in this section. Another example is **SETI@home (Search for Extraterrestrial Intelligence),** which assigns the analysis of signal data from small patches of the "sky" to participants. (The movie *Contact* was fiction, but still the search goes on.)

A third example, **Folding@home,** based at Stanford University, investigates the folding of proteins in living organisms into complex shapes and how they interact with other biological molecules.

Table 3   The Generation of Fermat Numbers

n	2^n	2^{2^n}	$2^{2^n} + 1$
0	1	2	3
1	2	4	5
2	4	16	17
3	8	256	257

Of historical note are a couple of polynomial formulas that produce primes. (A *polynomial* in a given variable involves adding or subtracting integer multiples of whole number powers of the variable. Discussed in **Section 7.6,** polynomials are among the most basic mathematical functions.) In 1732, Leonhard Euler offered the formula

$$n^2 - n + 41, \quad \text{Euler's formula}$$

which generates primes for n up to 40 and fails at $n = 41$. In 1879, E. B. Escott produced more primes with the formula

$$n^2 - 79n + 1601, \quad \text{Escott's formula}$$

which first fails at $n = 80$.

▐▐   **EXAMPLE 7**   Finding Numbers Using Euler's and Escott's Formulas

Find the first five numbers produced by each of the polynomial formulas of Euler and Escott.

SOLUTION
Table 4 shows the required numbers.

Table 4   A Few Polynomial-Generated Prime Numbers

n	Euler formula $n^2 - n + 41$	Escott formula $n^2 - 79n + 1601$
1	41	1523
2	43	1447
3	47	1373
4	53	1301
5	61	1231

All values found here are primes. (Use **Table 1** to verify the Euler values.)   ▐▐▐

Actually, it is not hard to prove that there can be no polynomial that will consistently generate primes. More complicated mathematical formulas exist for generating primes, but none produced so far can be practically applied in a reasonable amount of time, even using the fastest computers.

5.2 EXERCISES

Decide whether each statement is true *or* false.

1. Euclid's proof of the infinitude of primes is a proof by contradiction.

2. In the ancient times of Euclid, mathematicians had not achieved elegance in their proofs.

3. Every natural number of the form $4k + 1$ is prime.

4. Every natural number of the form $4k + 3$ is prime.

5. The number $2^{11} - 1$ is an example of a Mersenne prime.

6. As of early 2010, only five Fermat primes had ever been found.

7. Find the next two primes, of the form $4k + 1$, *not* listed specifically in **Example 3(a),** and express them as sums of squares.

8. Recall the first few perfect squares: 1, 4, 9, 16, 25. Try writing the numbers of the form $4k + 3$ listed in **Example 3(b)** as sums of two squares. Then complete this statement: The primes tested, of the form $4k + 3$, _____ be expressed as the sum of two squares. (Fermat claimed, but did not prove, that *no* prime of the form $4k + 3$ was the sum of two squares. Euler proved it 100 years later.)

9. Explain what is meant by a "proof by contradiction."

10. Does **Example 4** prove that every prime of the form $4k + 1$ can be expressed as a sum of two squares? Explain why or why not.

11. Verify that Euler's polynomial prime-generating formula $n^2 - n + 41$ fails to produce a prime for $n = 41$.

12. Evaluate Euler's polynomial formula for **(a)** $n = 42$, and **(b)** $n = 43$.

13. Choose the correct completion: For $n > 41$, Euler's formula produces a prime
    A. never.   **B.** sometimes.   **C.** always.
    (*Hint:* If no prime less than or equal to $\sqrt{n}$ divides n, then n is prime.)

14. Recall that Escott's formula, $n^2 - 79n + 1601$, fails to produce a prime for $n = 80$. Evaluate this formula for $n = 81$ and $n = 82$. Then complete the following statement: For $n > 80$, Escott's formula produces a prime
    A. never.   **B.** sometimes.   **C.** always.

15. **(a)** Evaluate the Fermat number F_4: $2^{2^n} + 1$ for $n = 4$.

    (b) In seeking possible prime factors of the Fermat number of part (a), what is the largest potential prime factor that one would have to try? (As stated in the text, this "fifth" Fermat number is in fact prime.)

16. **(a)** Verify the value given in the text for the "sixth" Fermat number (i.e., $2^{2^5} + 1$).

    (b) Divide this Fermat number by 641. (Euler discovered this factorization in 1732, proving that the sixth Fermat number is not prime.)

17. Write a short report on the Great Internet Mersenne Prime Search (GIMPS).

18. Write a short report identifying the 44th and 46th known Mersenne primes and how, when, and by whom they were found.

19. The Mersenne margin note on **page 187** cites a 1644 claim that was not totally resolved for some 300 years. Find out when, and by whom, Mersenne's five errors were demonstrated. (*Hint:* One was mentioned in the margin note on **page 181**.)

20. In Euclid's proof that there is no largest prime, we formed a number M by taking the product of primes and adding 1. Observe the pattern below.

$M = 2 + 1 = 3$	(3 is prime)
$M = 2 \cdot 3 + 1 = 7$	(7 is prime)
$M = 2 \cdot 3 \cdot 5 + 1 = 31$	(31 is prime)
$M = 2 \cdot 3 \cdot 5 \cdot 7 + 1 = 211$	(211 is prime)
$M = 2 \cdot 3 \cdot 5 \cdot 7 \cdot 11 + 1 = 2311$	(2311 is prime)

    It seems as though this pattern will always yield a prime number. Now evaluate
    $$M = 2 \cdot 3 \cdot 5 \cdot 7 \cdot 11 \cdot 13 + 1.$$

21. Is the final value of M computed in **Exercise 20** prime or composite? If it is composite, give its prime factorization.

22. Explain in your own words the proof by Euclid that there is no largest prime.

The text stated that the Mersenne number M_n is composite whenever n is composite. Exercises 23–26 develop one way you can always find a factor of such a Mersenne number.

23. For the composite number $n = 6$, find
    $$M_n = 2^n - 1.$$

24. Notice that $p = 3$ is a prime factor of $n = 6$. Find $2^p - 1$ for $p = 3$. Is $2^p - 1$ a factor of $2^n - 1$?

25. Complete this statement: If p is a prime factor of n, then _____ is a factor of the Mersenne number $2^n - 1$.

26. Find $M_n = 2^n - 1$ for $n = 10$.

27. Use the statement of **Exercise 25** to find two distinct factors of M_{10}.

28. Do you think this procedure will always produce *prime* factors of M_n for composite n? (*Hint:* Consider $n = 22$ and its prime factor $p = 11$, and recall the statement following **Example 5**.) Explain.

5.3 SELECTED TOPICS FROM NUMBER THEORY

Perfect Numbers • Deficient and Abundant Numbers • Amicable (Friendly) Numbers
• Goldbach's Conjecture • Twin Primes • Fermat's Last Theorem

Perfect Numbers

The mathematician **Albert Wilansky,** when phoning his brother-in-law, Mr. Smith, noticed an interesting property concerning Smith's phone number (493–7775). The number 4,937,775 is composite, and its prime factorization is

$$3 \cdot 5 \cdot 5 \cdot 65{,}837.$$

When the digits of the phone number are added, the result, 42, is equal to the sum of the digits in the prime factors: $3 + 5 + 5 + 6 + 5 + 8 + 3 + 7 = 42$. Wilansky termed such a number a **Smith number.** In 1985 it was proved that there are infinitely many Smith numbers, but there still are many unanswered questions about them.

In **Chapter 1,** we introduced figurate numbers, a topic investigated by the Pythagoreans, a group of Greek mathematicians and musicians who held their meetings in secret. In this section we examine some of the other special numbers that fascinated the Pythagoreans and are still studied by mathematicians today.

Divisors of a natural number were covered in **Section 5.1.** The **proper divisors** of a natural number include all divisors of the number except the number itself. For example, the proper divisors of 8 are 1, 2, and 4. (8 is *not* a proper divisor of 8.)

> **Perfect Numbers**
>
> A natural number is said to be **perfect** if it is equal to the sum of its proper divisors.

Is 8 perfect? No, because $1 + 2 + 4 = 7$, and $7 \neq 8$. The least perfect number is 6, because the proper divisors of 6 are 1, 2, and 3, and

$$1 + 2 + 3 = 6. \quad \text{6 is perfect.}$$

▌▌ **EXAMPLE 1** Verifying a Perfect Number

Show that 28 is a perfect number.

SOLUTION

The proper divisors of 28 are 1, 2, 4, 7, and 14. The sum of these is 28:

$$1 + 2 + 4 + 7 + 14 = 28.$$

By the definition, 28 is perfect. ▗▗▗

The numbers 6 and 28 are the two least perfect numbers. The next two are 496 and 8128. The pattern of these first four perfect numbers led early writers to conjecture that

1. The *n*th perfect number contains exactly *n* digits.
2. The even perfect numbers end in the digits 6 and 8, alternately.

⎫ Conjectures
⎬ NOT NECESSARILY
⎭ TRUE

(**Exercises 39–41** will help you evaluate these conjectures.)

There still are many unanswered questions about perfect numbers. Euclid showed that the following is true.

If $2^n - 1$ is prime, then $2^{n-1}(2^n - 1)$ is perfect, and conversely.

Because the prime values of $2^n - 1$ are the Mersenne primes (discussed in the previous section), this means that for every new Mersenne prime discovered, another perfect number is automatically revealed. (Hence, as of summer 2010, there were also 47 known perfect numbers.) It is also known that the following is true.

All even perfect numbers must take the form $2^{n-1}(2^n - 1)$.

It is strongly suspected that no odd perfect numbers exist. (Any odd one would have at least eight different prime factors and would have at least 300 decimal digits.) Therefore, Euclid and the early Greeks most likely identified the form of all perfect numbers.

Deficient and Abundant Numbers

Earlier we saw that 8 is not perfect because it is not equal to the sum of its proper divisors (8 ≠ 7). Next we define two alternative categories for natural numbers that are *not* perfect.

A number is said to be a **weird number** if it is abundant without being equal to the sum of any set of its own proper divisors. For example, 70 is weird because it is abundant (1 + 2 + 5 + 7 + 10 + 14 + 35 = 74 > 70), but the set of proper divisors

$$\{1, 2, 5, 7, 10, 14, 35\}$$

contains no subset whose elements add up to 70.

Deficient and Abundant Numbers

A natural number is **deficient** if it is greater than the sum of its proper divisors. It is **abundant** if it is less than the sum of its proper divisors.

Based on this definition, a *deficient number* is one with proper divisors that add up to less than the number itself, while an *abundant number* is one with proper divisors that add up to more than the number itself. For example, because the proper divisors of 8 (1, 2, and 4) add up to 7, which is less than 8, the number 8 is deficient.

EXAMPLE 2 Identifying Deficient and Abundant Numbers

Decide whether each number is deficient or abundant.

(a) 12   **(b)** 10

SOLUTION

(a) The proper divisors of 12 are 1, 2, 3, 4, and 6. The sum of these divisors is 16. Because 16 > 12, the number 12 is abundant.

(b) The proper divisors of 10 are 1, 2, and 5. Since 1 + 2 + 5 = 8, and 8 < 10, the number 10 is deficient.   ■■■

Amicable (Friendly) Numbers

Suppose that we add the proper divisors of 284.

$$1 + 2 + 4 + 71 + 142 = \mathbf{220}$$

Their sum is 220. Now, add the proper divisors of **220**.

$$1 + 2 + 4 + 5 + 10 + 11 + 20 + 22 + 44 + 55 + 110 = 284$$

The sum of the proper divisors of 220 is 284, while the sum of the proper divisors of 284 is 220. Number pairs with this property are said to be *amicable,* or *friendly*.

An extension of the idea of amicable numbers results in **sociable numbers.** In a chain of sociable numbers, the sum of the proper divisors of each number is the next number in the chain, and the sum of the proper divisors of the last number in the chain is the first number. Here is a 5-link chain of sociable numbers:

12,496

14,288

15,472

14,536

14,264.

The number 14,316 starts a 28-link chain of sociable numbers.

Amicable or Friendly Numbers

The natural numbers a and b are **amicable,** or **friendly,** if the sum of the proper divisors of a is b, and the sum of the proper divisors of b is a.

The smallest pair of amicable numbers, 220 and 284, was known to the Pythagoreans, but it was not until 1636 that Fermat found the next pair, 17,296 and 18,416. Many more pairs were found over the next few decades, but it took a 16-year-old Italian boy named Nicolo Paganini to discover in the year 1866 that the pair of amicable numbers 1184 and 1210 had been overlooked for centuries!

Today, powerful computers continually extend the lists of known amicable pairs. The last time we checked, nearly twelve million pairs were known. It still is unknown, however, if there are infinitely many such pairs. No one has found an amicable pair without prime factors in common, but the possibility of such a pair has not been eliminated.

A Dull Number? The Indian mathematician **Srinivasa Ramanujan** (1887–1920) developed many ideas in number theory. His friend and collaborator on occasion was G. H. Hardy, also a number theorist and professor at Cambridge University in England.

A story has been told about Ramanujan that illustrates his genius. Hardy once mentioned to Ramanujan that he had just taken a taxicab with a rather dull number: 1729. Ramanujan countered by saying that this number isn't dull at all; it is the smallest natural number that can be expressed as the sum of two cubes in two different ways:

$$1^3 + 12^3 = 1729$$
and $$9^3 + 10^3 = 1729.$$

Show that 85 can be written as the sum of two *squares* in two ways.

Goldbach's Conjecture

The mathematician Christian Goldbach (1690–1764) stated the following conjecture (guess), which is one of the most famous unsolved problems in mathematics.

> **Goldbach's Conjecture (Not Proved)**
>
> Every even number greater than 2 can be written as the sum of two prime numbers.
>
> *Examples:* $8 = 5 + 3$
> $10 = 5 + 5 \text{ (or } 10 = 7 + 3)$

Mathematicians have tried to prove the conjecture but have not succeeded. However, the conjecture has been verified (as of late 2010) for numbers up to 2×10^{18}.

▌▌ **EXAMPLE 3**   Expressing Numbers as Sums of Primes

Write each even number as the sum of two primes.

(a) 18   **(b)** 60

SOLUTION

(a) $18 = 5 + 13$. Another way of writing it is $7 + 11$. Notice that $1 + 17$ is *not* valid because by definition 1 is not a prime number.

(b) $60 = 7 + 53$. Can you find other ways? Why is $3 + 57$ not valid?   ▌▌▌

Twin Primes

Prime numbers that differ by 2 are called **twin primes.** Some twin prime pairs are 3 and 5, 5 and 7, 11 and 13, and so on. Like Goldbach's conjecture, the following conjecture about twin primes has never been proved.

> **Twin Prime Conjecture (Not Proved)**
>
> There are infinitely many pairs of twin primes.

Mathematics professor Gregory Larkin, played by Jeff Bridges, woos colleague Rose Morgan (Barbra Streisand) in the 1996 film *The Mirror Has Two Faces*. Larkin's research and book focus on the **twin prime conjecture,** which he correctly states in a dinner scene. He is amazed that his nonmathematician friend actually understands what he is talking about.

You may wish to verify that there are eight such pairs less than 100, using the Sieve of Eratosthenes in **Table 1.** As of summer 2010, the largest known twin primes were

$$65,516,468,355 \cdot 2^{333,333} \pm 1. \quad \text{Each contains 100,355 digits.}$$

Recall from **Section 5.2** that Euclid's proof of the infinitude of primes used numbers of the form

$$p_1 \cdot p_2 \cdot p_3 \cdots \cdot p_n + 1,$$

where all the ps are prime. It may seem that any such number must be prime, but that is not so. (See **Exercises 20 and 21** of **Section 5.2.**) However, this form often does produce primes (as does the same form with the plus replaced by a minus). When *all* the primes up to p_n are included, the resulting numbers, if prime, are called **primorial primes.** They are denoted

$$p\# \pm 1.$$

For example, $5\# + 1 = 2 \cdot 3 \cdot 5 + 1 = 31$ is a primorial prime. (In late 2010, the largest known primorial prime was $392,113\# + 1$, a number with 169,966 digits.) The primorial primes are a popular place to look for twin primes.

Sophie Germain (1776–1831) studied at the École Polytechnique in Paris in a day when female students were not admitted. A **Sophie Germain prime** is a prime p for which $2p + 1$ also is prime. Lately, large Sophie Germain primes have been discovered at the rate of one or more per year. As of late 2010, the largest one known was $183{,}027 \cdot 2^{265{,}440} - 1$, which has 79,911 digits.

Source: www.utm.edu

▌▌ **EXAMPLE 4** Verifying Twin Primes

Verify that the primorial formula $p\# \pm 1$ produces twin prime pairs for both **(a)** $p = 3$ and **(b)** $p = 5$.

SOLUTION

(a) $3\# \pm 1 = 2 \cdot 3 \pm 1 = 6 \pm 1 = 5$ and 7 Twin primes

> Multiply, then add and subtract.

(b) $5\# \pm 1 = 2 \cdot 3 \cdot 5 \pm 1 = 30 \pm 1 = 29$ and 31 Twin primes   ▪▪▪

Fermat's Last Theorem

In any right triangle with shorter sides (legs) a and b, and longest side (hypotenuse) c, the equation $a^2 + b^2 = c^2$ will hold true. This is the famous Pythagorean theorem. For example,

$$3^2 + 4^2 = 5^2 \qquad a = 3, b = 4, c = 5$$
$$9 + 16 = 25 \qquad \text{Apply the exponents.}$$
$$25 = 25. \qquad \text{True}$$

It is known that there are infinitely many such triples (a, b, c) that satisfy the equation $a^2 + b^2 = c^2$. Is something similar true of the equation

$$a^n + b^n = c^n$$

for natural numbers $n \geq 3$? Pierre de Fermat, who is profiled in a margin note on **page 200,** thought that not only were there not infinitely many such triples, but that there were, in fact, none. He made the following claim in the 1600s.

Fermat's Last Theorem (Proved in the 1990s)
For *any* natural number $n \geq 3$, there are *no* triples (a, b, c) that satisfy the equation $$a^n + b^n = c^n.$$

Fermat's assertion was the object of some 350 years of attempts by mathematicians to provide a suitable proof. While it was verified for many specific cases (Fermat himself proved it for $n = 3$), a proof of the general case could not be found until the Princeton mathematician Andrew Wiles announced a proof in the spring of 1993. Although some flaws were discovered in his argument, Wiles was able, by the fall of 1994, to repair and even improve the proof.

There were probably about 100 mathematicians around the world qualified to understand the Wiles proof. *Today Fermat's Last Theorem finally is regarded by the mathematics community as officially proved.*

The popular animated television series *The Simpsons* provides not only humor and social commentary but also lessons in mathematics. One episode depicted the equation

$$1782^{12} + 1841^{12} = 1922^{12},$$

which, according to **Fermat's Last Theorem**, cannot be true. Your calculator may indicate that the equation is true, but this is because it cannot accurately display powers of this size. Actually, 1782^{12} must be an *even* number because *an even number to any power is even.* Also, 1841^{12} must be *odd,* because *an odd number to any power is odd.* So the sum on the left must be *odd,* because

$$even + odd = odd.$$

Similarly, 1922^{12} must be *even.* So the equation states that an odd number equals an even number, which is impossible. (See www.simpsonsmath.com)

▌▌ **EXAMPLE 5** Applying a Theorem Proved by Fermat

One of the theorems legitimately proved by Fermat is as follows:

> *Every odd prime can be expressed as the difference of two squares in one and only one way.*

Express each odd prime as the difference of two squares.

(a) 3   **(b)** 7

SOLUTION

(a) $3 = 4 - 1 = 2^2 - 1^2$ **(b)** $7 = 16 - 9 = 4^2 - 3^2$ ▪▪▪

For Further Thought

Curious and Interesting

One of the most remarkable books on number theory is *The Penguin Dictionary of Curious and Interesting Numbers* (1986) by David Wells. This book contains fascinating numbers and their properties, including the following.

- There are only three sets of three digits that form prime numbers in all possible arrangements: {1, 1, 3}, {1, 9, 9}, {3, 3, 7}.

- Find the sum of the cubes of the digits of 136:

$$1^3 + 3^3 + 6^3 = 244.$$

  Repeat the process with the digits of 244:

$$2^3 + 4^3 + 4^3 = 136.$$

  We're back to where we started.

- 635,318,657 is the least number that can be expressed as the sum of two fourth powers in two ways:

$$635{,}318{,}657 = 59^4 + 158^4 = 133^4 + 134^4.$$

- The number 24,678,050 has an interesting property:

$$24{,}678{,}050 = 2^8 + 4^8 + 6^8 + 7^8 + 8^8 + 0^8$$
$$+ 5^8 + 0^8.$$

- The number 54,748 has a similar interesting property:

$$54{,}748 = 5^5 + 4^5 + 7^5 + 4^5 + 8^5.$$

- The number 3435 has this property:

$$3435 = 3^3 + 4^4 + 3^3 + 5^5.$$

For anyone whose curiosity is piqued by such facts, this book is for you!

For Group or Individual Investigation

Have each student in the class choose a three-digit number that is a multiple of 3. Add the cubes of the digits. Repeat the process until the same number is obtained over and over. Then, have the students compare their results. What is curious and interesting about this process?

5.3 EXERCISES

Decide whether each statement in Exercises 1–10 is true *or* false.

1. There are infinitely many prime numbers.

2. The prime numbers 2 and 3 are twin primes.

3. There is no perfect number between 496 and 8128.

4. $2^n - 1$ is prime if and only if $2^{n-1}(2^n - 1)$ is perfect.

5. Any prime number must be deficient.

6. The equation $17 + 51 = 68$ verifies Goldbach's conjecture for the number 68.

7. There are more Mersenne primes known than there are perfect numbers.

8. The number 31 cannot be represented as the difference of two squares.

9. The number $2^6(2^7 - 1)$ is perfect.

10. Any natural number greater than 1 is one and only one of the following: perfect, deficient, or abundant.

11. The proper divisors of 496 are 1, 2, 4, 8, 16, 31, 62, 124, and 248. Use this information to verify that 496 is perfect.

12. The proper divisors of 8128 are 1, 2, 4, 8, 16, 32, 64, 127, 254, 508, 1016, 2032, and 4064. Use this information to verify that 8128 is perfect.

13. As mentioned in the text, when $2^n - 1$ is prime,

$$2^{n-1}(2^n - 1)$$

    is perfect. By letting $n = 2, 3, 5$, and 7, we obtain the first four perfect numbers. Show that $2^n - 1$ is prime for $n = 13$, and then find the decimal digit representation for the fifth perfect number.

14. In the summer of 2010, the largest known prime number was $2^{43{,}112{,}609} - 1$. Use the formula in **Exercise 13** to write an expression for the perfect number generated by this prime number.

15. It has been proved that the reciprocals of *all* the positive divisors of a perfect number have a sum of 2. Verify this for the perfect number 6.

16. Consider the following equations.

$$6 = 1 + 2 + 3$$
$$28 = 1 + 2 + 3 + 4 + 5 + 6 + 7$$

    Show that a similar equation is valid for the third perfect number, 496.

Determine whether each number is abundant or deficient.

17. 45   **18.** 48

19. 88   **20.** 64

21. There are four abundant numbers between 1 and 25. Find them. (*Hint:* They are all even, and no prime number is abundant.)

22. Explain why a prime number must be deficient.

23. The first odd abundant number is 945. Its proper divisors are 1, 3, 5, 7, 9, 15, 21, 27, 35, 45, 63, 105, 135, 189, and 315. Use this information to verify that 945 is abundant.

24. Explain in your own words the terms *perfect number, abundant number,* and *deficient number.*

25. Nicolo Paganini's numbers 1184 and 1210 are amicable. The proper divisors of 1184 are 1, 2, 4, 8, 16, 32, 37, 74, 148, 296, and 592. The proper divisors of 1210 are 1, 2, 5, 10, 11, 22, 55, 110, 121, 242, and 605. Use the definition of amicable (friendly) numbers to show that they are indeed amicable.

26. An Arabian mathematician of the ninth century stated the following.

If the three numbers

$$x = 3 \cdot 2^{n-1} - 1,$$
$$y = 3 \cdot 2^n - 1,$$
and $$z = 9 \cdot 2^{2n-1} - 1$$

are all prime and $n \geq 2$, then $2^n xy$ and $2^n z$ are amicable numbers.

(a) Use $n = 2$, and show that the result is the least pair of amicable numbers, namely 220 and 284.

(b) Use $n = 4$ to obtain another pair of amicable numbers.

Write each even number as the sum of two primes. (There may be more than one way to do this.)

27. 16   **28.** 20

29. 30   **30.** 34

31. Joseph Louis Lagrange (1736–1813) conjectured that every odd natural number greater than 5 can be written as a sum $a + 2b$, where a and b are both primes.

(a) Verify this for the odd natural number 11.

(b) Verify that the odd natural number 17 can be written in this form in four different ways.

32. Another unproved conjecture in number theory states that every natural number multiple of 6 can be written as the difference of two primes. Verify this for 6, 12, and 18.

Find one pair of twin primes between the two numbers given.

33. 30, 50   **34.** 85, 105

While Pierre de Fermat probably is best known for his now famous "last theorem," he did provide proofs of many other theorems in number theory. Exercises 35–38 investigate some of these theorems.

35. If p is prime and the natural numbers a and p have no common factor except 1, then $a^{p-1} - 1$ is divisible by p.

(a) Verify this for $p = 5$ and $a = 3$.

(b) Verify this for $p = 7$ and $a = 2$.

36. Every odd prime can be expressed as the difference of two squares in one and only one way.

(a) Find this one way for the prime number 5.

(b) Find this one way for the prime number 11.

37. There is only one solution in natural numbers for $a^2 + 2 = b^3$, and it is $a = 5, b = 3$. Verify this solution.

38. There are only two solutions in integers for $a^2 + 4 = b^3$. One solution is $a = 2, b = 2$. Find the other solution.

The first four perfect numbers were identified in the text: 6, 28, 496, *and* 8128. *The next two are* 33,550,336 *and* 8,589,869,056. *Use this information about perfect numbers to work Exercises 39–41.*

39. Verify that each of these six perfect numbers ends in either 6 or 28. (In fact, this is true of all even perfect numbers.)

40. Is conjecture (1) in the text (that the nth perfect number contains exactly n digits) true or false? Explain.

41. Is conjecture (2) in the text (that the even perfect numbers end in the digits 6 and 8, alternately) true or false? Explain.

According to the Web site www.shyamsundergupta.com/amicable.htm, *a natural number is* **happy** *if the process of repeatedly summing the squares of its decimal digits finally ends in 1. For example, the least natural number (greater than 1) that is happy is 7, as shown here.*

$$7^2 = 49, \quad 4^2 + 9^2 = 97, \quad 9^2 + 7^2 = 130,$$
$$1^2 + 3^2 + 0^2 = 10, \quad 1^2 + 0^2 = 1.$$

An amicable pair is a **happy amicable pair** *if and only if both members of the pair are happy numbers. (The first 5000 amicable pairs include only 111 that are happy amicable pairs.) For each amicable pair, determine whether neither, one, or both of the members are happy, and whether the pair is a happy amicable pair.*

42. 220 and 284   **43.** 1184 and 1210

44. 10,572,550 and 10,854,650

45. 35,361,326 and 40,117,714

46. If the early Greeks knew the form of all even perfect numbers, namely $2^{n-1}(2^n - 1)$, then why did they not discover all the ones that are known today?

47. Explain why the primorial formula $p\# \pm 1$ does not result in a pair of twin primes for the prime value $p = 2$.

48. (a) What two numbers does the primorial formula produce for $p = 7$?

 (b) Which, if either, of these numbers is prime?

49. Choose the correct completion: The primorial formula produces twin primes

 A. never.   **B.** sometimes.   **C.** always.

*See the margin note (on **page 194**) defining a Sophie Germain prime, and complete this table.*

	p	$2p + 1$	Is p a Sophie Germain prime?
50.	2	____	____
51.	3	____	____
52.	5	____	____
53.	7	____	____
54.	11	____	____
55.	13	____	____

Factorial primes *are of the form* $n! \pm 1$ *for natural numbers n. (n! denotes "n factorial," the product of all natural numbers up to n, not just the primes as in the primorial primes. For example,* $4! = 1 \cdot 2 \cdot 3 \cdot 4 = 24$*.) As of late 2010, the largest verified factorial prime was* $34{,}790! - 1$*, which has 142,891 digits. Find the missing entries in this table.*

	n	$n!$	$n! - 1$	$n! + 1$	Is $n! - 1$ prime?	Is $n! + 1$ prime?
	2	2	1	3	no	yes
56.	3	____	____	____	____	____
57.	4	____	____	____	____	____
58.	5	____	____	____	____	____

59. Explain why the factorial prime formula does not give twin primes for $n = 2$.

Based on the preceding table, complete each statement with one of the following:

A. *never,*   **B.** *sometimes, or*   **C.** *always.*

When applied to particular values of n, the factorial prime formula $n! \pm 1$ produces

60. no primes ____   **61.** exactly one prime ____

62. twin primes ____

5.4 GREATEST COMMON FACTOR AND LEAST COMMON MULTIPLE

Greatest Common Factor • Least Common Multiple

Greatest Common Factor

The *greatest common factor* is defined as follows.

> **Greatest Common Factor**
>
> The **greatest common factor (GCF)** of a group of natural numbers is the largest natural number that is a factor of all the numbers in the group.
>
> *Examples:*   18 is the GCF of 36 and 54, because 18 is the largest natural number that divides both 36 and 54.
>
>   1 is the GCF of 7 and 16.

The greatest common factor is often called the *greatest common divisor*, and may be symbolized GCD or gcd.

Greatest common factors can be found by using prime factorizations. To determine the GCF of 36 and 54, first write the prime factorization of each number (perhaps by using factor trees or repeated division).

$$36 = 2^2 \cdot 3^2$$
$$54 = 2^1 \cdot 3^3$$

The GCF is the product of the primes common to the factorizations, with each prime raised to the power indicated by the *least* exponent that it has in any factorization. Here, the prime 2 has 1 as the least exponent (in $54 = 2^1 \cdot 3^3$), while the prime 3 has 2 as the least exponent (in $36 = 2^2 \cdot 3^2$).

$$GCF = 2^1 \cdot 3^2 = 2 \cdot 9 = 18,$$

We summarize as follows.

Finding the Greatest Common Factor (Prime Factors Method)

Step 1 Write the prime factorization of each number.

Step 2 Choose all primes common to *all* factorizations, with each prime raised to the *least* exponent that it has in any factorization.

Step 3 Form the product of all the numbers in Step 2. This product is the greatest common factor.

EXAMPLE 1 Finding the Greatest Common Factor by the Prime Factors Method

Find the greatest common factor of 360 and 2700.

SOLUTION
Write the prime factorization of each number.

$$360 = 2^3 \cdot 3^2 \cdot 5 \qquad 2700 = 2^2 \cdot 3^3 \cdot 5^2$$

Find the primes common to both factorizations, with each prime having as its exponent the *least* exponent from either product.

Use the least exponents.

$$GCF = 2^2 \cdot 3^2 \cdot 5 = 180$$

The greatest common factor of 360 and 2700 is 180. ■■■

gcd(360,2700)
180

The calculator shows that the greatest common divisor (factor) of 360 and 2700 is 180. Compare with **Example 1.**

EXAMPLE 2 Finding the Greatest Common Factor by the Prime Factors Method

Find the greatest common factor of 720, 1000, and 1800.

SOLUTION
Write the prime factorization for each number.

$$720 = 2^4 \cdot 3^2 \cdot 5$$
$$1000 = 2^3 \cdot 5^3$$
$$1800 = 2^3 \cdot 3^2 \cdot 5^2$$

Use the smallest exponent on each prime common to the factorizations.

$$GCF = 2^3 \cdot 5 = 40$$

(The prime 3 is not used in the greatest common factor because it does not appear in the prime factorization of 1000.) ■■■

▮▮ **EXAMPLE 3**   Finding the Greatest Common Factor by the Prime Factors Method

Find the greatest common factor of 80 and 63.

SOLUTION

$$80 = 2^4 \cdot 5$$
$$63 = 3^2 \cdot 7$$

There are no primes in common here, so the GCF is 1. The number 1 is the largest number that will divide into both 80 and 63. ▮▮▮

Two numbers, such as 80 and 63, with a greatest common factor of 1 are called **relatively prime numbers**—that is, they are prime *relative* to one another. (They have no common factors other than 1.)

Another method of finding the greatest common factor involves dividing the numbers by common prime factors.

Finding the Greatest Common Factor (Dividing by Prime Factors Method)

Step 1   Write the numbers in a row.

Step 2   Divide each of the numbers by a common prime factor. Try 2, then try 3, and so on.

Step 3   Divide the quotients by a common prime factor. Continue until no prime will divide into all the quotients.

Step 4   The product of the primes in Steps 2 and 3 is the greatest common factor.

▮▮ **EXAMPLE 4**   Finding the Greatest Common Factor by Dividing by Prime Factors

Find the greatest common factor of 12, 18, and 60.

SOLUTION

Write the numbers in a row and divide by 2.

$$\begin{array}{r|rrr} 2 & 12 & 18 & 60 \\ \hline & 6 & 9 & 30 \end{array}$$

The numbers 6, 9, and 30 are not all divisible by 2, but they are divisible by 3.

$$\begin{array}{r|rrr} 2 & 12 & 18 & 60 \\ \hline 3 & 6 & 9 & 30 \\ \hline & 2 & 3 & 10 \end{array}$$

No prime divides into 2, 3, and 10, so the greatest common factor of the numbers 12, 18, and 60 is given by the product of the primes on the left, 2 and 3.

$$\begin{array}{r|rrr} 2 & 12 & 18 & 60 \\ \hline 3 & 6 & 9 & 30 \\ \hline & 2 & 3 & 10 \end{array}$$
$$2 \cdot 3 = 6$$

The GCF of 12, 18, and 60 is 6. ▮▮▮

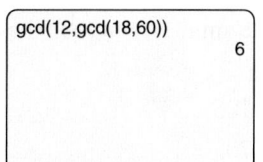

This screen uses the fact that $\gcd(a, b, c) = \gcd(a, \gcd(b, c))$. Compare with **Example 4**.

Another method of finding the greatest common factor of two numbers (but not more than two) is called the **Euclidean algorithm.***

▌▌ **EXAMPLE 5** Finding the Greatest Common Factor Using the Euclidean Algorithm

Use the Euclidean algorithm to find the greatest common factor of 90 and 168.

SOLUTION

Step 1 Begin by dividing the larger, 168, by the smaller, 90. Disregard the quotient, but note the remainder.

Step 2 Divide the smaller of the two numbers by the remainder obtained in Step 1. Once again, note the remainder.

Step 3 Continue dividing the successive remainders as many times as necessary to obtain a remainder of 0.

Step 4 The *last positive remainder* in this process is the greatest common factor of 90 and 168. It can be seen that their GCF is 6.

$$
\begin{array}{r} 1 \\ 90\overline{)168} \\ 90 \\ \hline 78 \end{array}
$$

$$
\begin{array}{r} 1 \\ 78\overline{)90} \\ 78 \\ \hline 12 \end{array}
$$

$$
\begin{array}{r} 6 \\ 12\overline{)78} \\ 72 \\ \hline 6 \end{array}
$$ Greatest common factor

$$
\begin{array}{r} 2 \\ 6\overline{)12} \\ 12 \\ \hline 0 \end{array}
$$

▌▌▌

The Euclidean algorithm is particularly useful if the two numbers are difficult to factor into primes. We summarize the algorithm here.

> **Finding the Greatest Common Factor (Euclidean Algorithm)**
>
> To find the greatest common factor of two unequal numbers, divide the larger by the smaller. Note the remainder, and divide the previous divisor by this remainder. Continue the process until a remainder of 0 is obtained. The greatest common factor is the last positive remainder obtained.

Pierre de Fermat (about 1601–1665), a government official who did not interest himself in mathematics until he was past 30, devoted leisure time to its study. He was a worthy scholar, best known for his work in number theory. His other major contributions involved certain applications in geometry and his original work in probability.

Much of Fermat's best work survived only on loose sheets or jotted, without proof, in the margins of works that he read.

Least Common Multiple

Closely related to the idea of the greatest common factor is the concept of the *least common multiple.*

> **Least Common Multiple**
>
> The **least common multiple (LCM)** of a group of natural numbers is the smallest natural number that is a multiple of all the numbers in the group.
>
> *Example:* 30 is the LCM of 15 and 10 because 30 is the smallest number that appears in both sets of multiples.
>
> Multiples of 15: $\{15, \mathbf{30}, 45, 60, 75, 90, 105, \ldots\}$
>
> Multiples of 10: $\{10, 20, \mathbf{30}, 40, 50, 60, 70, \ldots\}$

---

*For a proof that this process does indeed give the greatest common factor, see *Elementary Introduction to Number Theory, Second Edition,* by Calvin T. Long, pp. 34–35.

lcm(15,10)

30

The least common multiple of 15 and 10 is 30.

The set of natural numbers that are multiples of *both* 15 and 10 form the set of *common multiples*:

$$\{30, 60, 90, 120, \ldots\}.$$

While there are infinitely many common multiples, the *least* common multiple is observed to be 30.

A method similar to the first one given for the greatest common factor may be used to find the least common multiple of a group of numbers.

Finding the Least Common Multiple (Prime Factors Method)

Step 1 Write the prime factorization of each number.

Step 2 Choose all primes belonging to *any* factorization, with each prime raised to the power indicated by the *greatest* exponent that it has in any factorization.

Step 3 Form the product of all the numbers in Step 2. This product is the least common multiple.

▌▌ **EXAMPLE 6** Finding the Least Common Multiple by the Prime Factors Method

Find the least common multiple of 135, 280, and 300.

SOLUTION

Write the prime factorizations:

$$135 = 3^3 \cdot 5, \quad 280 = 2^3 \cdot 5 \cdot 7, \quad \text{and} \quad 300 = 2^2 \cdot 3 \cdot 5^2.$$

Form the product of all the primes that appear in *any* of the factorizations. Use the *greatest* exponent from any factorization.

Use the greatest exponents.

$$\text{LCM} = 2^3 \cdot 3^3 \cdot 5^2 \cdot 7 = 37{,}800$$

The least natural number divisible by 135, 280, and 300 is 37,800.   ▪▪▪

lcm(135,lcm(280,300))

37800

The least common multiple of 135, 280, and 300 is 37,800. Compare with **Example 6.**

The least common multiple of a group of numbers can also be found by dividing by prime factors. The process is slightly different than that for finding the GCF.

Finding the Least Common Multiple (Dividing by Prime Factors Method)

Step 1 Write the numbers in a row.

Step 2 Divide each of the numbers by a common prime factor. Try 2, then try 3, and so on.

Step 3 Divide the quotients by a common prime factor. When no prime will divide all quotients, but a prime will divide some of them, divide where possible and bring any nondivisible quotients down. Continue until no prime will divide any two quotients.

Step 4 The product of all prime divisors from Steps 2 and 3 as well as all remaining quotients is the least common multiple.

▮▮ EXAMPLE 7 | Finding the Least Common Multiple by Dividing by Prime Factors

Find the least common multiple of 12, 18, and 60.

SOLUTION

Proceed just as in **Example 4** to obtain the following.

$$
\begin{array}{r|rrr}
2 & 12 & 18 & 60 \\
3 & 6 & 9 & 30 \\
\hline
 & 2 & 3 & 10
\end{array}
$$

Now, even though no prime will divide 2, 3, and 10, the prime 2 will divide 2 and 10. Divide the 2 and the 10 and bring down the 3.

$$
\begin{array}{r|rrr}
2 & 12 & 18 & 60 \\
3 & 6 & 9 & 30 \\
2 & 2 & 3 & 10 \\
\hline
 & 1 & 3 & 5
\end{array}
\qquad 2 \cdot 3 \cdot 2 \cdot 1 \cdot 3 \cdot 5 = 180
$$

The LCM of 12, 18, and 60 is 180. ▮▮▮

It is shown in more advanced courses that the least common multiple of two numbers m and n can be obtained by dividing their product by their greatest common factor.

Finding the Least Common Multiple (Formula)

The least common multiple of m and n can be computed as follows.

$$
LCM = \frac{m \cdot n}{GCF \text{ of } m \text{ and } n}
$$

(This method works only for two numbers, not for more than two.)

▮▮ EXAMPLE 8 | Finding the Least Common Multiple by Formula

Use the formula to find the least common multiple of 90 and 168.

SOLUTION

In **Example 5** we used the Euclidean algorithm to find that the greatest common factor of 90 and 168 is 6. Therefore, the formula gives us

$$
\text{Least common multiple of 90 and 168} = \frac{90 \cdot 168}{6} = 2520.
$$
▮▮▮

```
(90*168)/gcd(90,168)
                 2520
```

This supports the result in **Example 8**.

PROBLEM-SOLVING HINT Problems that deal with questions such as "How many objects will there be in each group if each group contains the same number of objects?" and "When will two events occur at the same time?" can sometimes be solved using the ideas of greatest common factor and least common multiple.

▮▮ EXAMPLE 9 Finding Common Starting Times of Movie Cycles

The King Theatre and the Star Theatre run movies continuously, and each starts its first feature at 1:00 P.M. If the movie shown at the King lasts 80 minutes and the movie shown at the Star lasts 2 hours, when will the two movies start again at the same time?

SOLUTION

First, convert 2 hours to 120 minutes. The question can be restated as follows: "What is the smallest number of minutes it will take for the two movies to start at the same time again?" This is equivalent to asking, "What is the least common multiple of 80 and 120?"

Using any of the methods described in this section, we find that the least common multiple of 80 and 120 is 240. Therefore, it will take 240 minutes, or $\frac{240}{60} = 4$ hours for the movies to start again at the same time. By adding 4 hours to 1:00 P.M., we find that they will start together again at 5:00 P.M.   ▮▮▮

▮▮ EXAMPLE 10 Finding the Greatest Common Size of Stacks of Cards

Joshua Hornsby has 450 football cards and 840 baseball cards. He wants to place them in stacks on a table so that each stack has the same number of cards, and no stack has different types of cards within it. What is the greatest number of cards that he can have in each stack?

SOLUTION

Here, we are looking for the greatest number that will divide evenly into 450 and 840. This is, of course, the greatest common factor of 450 and 840. Using any of the methods described in this section, we find that

greatest common factor of 450 and 840 = 30.

Therefore, the greatest number of cards he can have in each stack is 30.   ▮▮▮

5.4 EXERCISES

Decide whether each statement is true *or* false.

1. Two even natural numbers cannot be relatively prime.

2. Two different prime numbers must be relatively prime.

3. If p is a prime number, then the greatest common factor of p and p^2 is p.

4. If p is a prime number, then the least common multiple of p and p^2 is p^3.

5. There is no prime number p such that the greatest common factor of p and 2 is 2.

6. The set of all common multiples of two given natural numbers is finite.

7. Two natural numbers must have at least one common factor.

8. The least common multiple of two different primes is their product.

9. Two composite numbers may be relatively prime.

10. The set of all common factors of two given natural numbers is finite.

Use the prime factors method to find the greatest common factor of each group of numbers.

11. 60 and 140

12. 400 and 110

13. 540 and 1200

14. 136 and 544

15. 52, 39, and 78

16. 138, 184, and 437

Use the method of dividing by prime factors to find the greatest common factor of each group of numbers.

17. 72 and 90

18. 166 and 415

19. 410 and 360

20. 384 and 222

21. 12, 18, and 36

22. 450, 1155, and 630

Use the Euclidean algorithm to find the greatest common factor of each group of numbers.

23. 32 and 56

24. 35 and 60

25. 24 and 108

26. 72 and 126

27. 480 and 400

28. 280 and 360

29. Explain in your own words how to find the greatest common factor of a group of numbers.

30. Explain in your own words how to find the least common multiple of a group of numbers.

Use the prime factors method to find the least common multiple of each group of numbers.

31. 54 and 30

32. 12 and 32

33. 90 and 50

34. 28 and 70

35. 30, 40, and 70

36. 24, 36, and 48

Use the method of dividing by prime factors to find the least common multiple of each group of numbers.

37. 24 and 32

38. 35 and 56

39. 45 and 75

40. 48, 54, and 60

41. 16, 120, and 216

42. 210, 385, and 2310

*Use the formula given in the text on **page 202** and the results of **Exercises 23–28** to find the least common multiple of each group of numbers.*

43. 32 and 56

44. 35 and 60

45. 24 and 108

46. 72 and 126

47. 480 and 400

48. 280 and 360

49. If p, q, and r are different primes, and a, b, and c are natural numbers such that $a > b > c$,

  (a) what is the greatest common factor of $p^a q^c r^b$ and $p^b q^a r^c$?

  (b) what is the least common multiple of $p^b q^a$, $q^b r^c$, and $p^a r^b$?

50. Find **(a)** the greatest common factor and **(b)** the least common multiple of $2^{31} \cdot 5^{17} \cdot 7^{21}$ and $2^{34} \cdot 5^{22} \cdot 7^{13}$. Leave your answers in prime factored form.

It is possible to extend the Euclidean algorithm in order to find the greatest common factor of more than two numbers. For example, if we wish to find the greatest common factor of 150, 210, and 240, we can first use the algorithm to find the greatest common factor of two of these (say, for example, 150 and 210). Then we find the greatest common factor of that result and the third number, 240. The final result is the greatest common factor of the original group of numbers.

Use the Euclidean algorithm as just described to find the greatest common factor of each group of numbers.

51. 150, 210, and 240

52. 12, 75, and 120

53. 90, 105, and 315

54. 48, 315, and 450

55. 144, 180, and 192

56. 180, 210, and 630

*If we allow repetitions of prime factors, we can use Venn diagrams (**Chapter 2**) to find the greatest common factor and the least common multiple of two numbers. For example, consider $36 = 2^2 \cdot 3^2$ and $45 = 3^2 \cdot 5$. Their greatest common factor is $3^2 = 9$, and their least common multiple is $2^2 \cdot 3^2 \cdot 5 = 180$.*

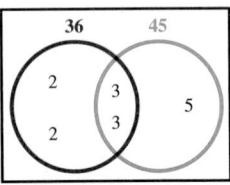

Intersection gives 3, 3.
Union gives 2, 2, 3, 3, 5.

*Use this method to find **(a)** the greatest common factor and **(b)** the least common multiple of the two numbers given.*

57. 12 and 18

58. 27 and 36

59. 54 and 72

60. Suppose that the least common multiple of p and q is q. What can we say about p and q?

61. Suppose that the least common multiple of p and q is pq. What can we say about p and q?

62. Suppose that the greatest common factor of p and q is p. What can we say about p and q?

63. Recall some of your early experiences in mathematics (for example, in the elementary grade classroom). What topic involving fractions required the use of the least common multiple? Give an example.

64. Recall some of your experiences in elementary algebra. What topics required the use of the greatest common factor? Give an example.

*Refer to **Examples 9 and 10** to solve each problem.*

65. *Inspecting Calculators* Karen Helfrich and Dorelle Less work on an assembly line, inspecting electronic calculators. Karen inspects the electronics of every sixteenth calculator, while Dorelle inspects the workmanship of every thirty-sixth calculator. If they both start working at the same time, which calculator will be the first that they both inspect?

66. *Night Off for Security Guards* Ross Craycraft and Jody Campbell work as security guards at a publishing company. Ross has every sixth night off, and Jody has every tenth night off. If both are off on July 1, what is the next night that they will both be off together?

67. *Stacking Coins* Lucy Bannister has 240 pennies and 288 nickels. She wants to place the pennies and nickels in stacks so that each stack has the same number of coins, and each stack contains only one denomination of coin. What is the largest number of coins that she can place in each stack?

68. *Bicycle Racing* Whitney Baer and Kim Davison are in a bicycle race, following a circular track. If they start at the same place and travel in the same direction, and Whitney completes a revolution every 40 seconds and Kim completes a revolution every 45 seconds, how long will it take them before they reach the starting point again simultaneously?

69. *Selling Books* Scott Day sold some books at $24 each, and used the money to buy some concert tickets at $50 each. He had no money left over after buying the tickets. What is the least amount of money he could have earned from selling the books? What is the least number of books he could have sold?

70. *Sawing Lumber* Terri Edwards has some pieces of two-by-four lumber. Some are 60 inches long, and some are 72 inches long. All of them must be sawn into shorter pieces. If all sawn pieces must be the same length, what is the longest such piece so that no lumber is left over?

EXTENSION Modern Cryptography

Basics of Cryptography • The Diffie-Hellman-Merkle Key Exchange Scheme
• RSA Public Key Cryptography

John Forbes Nash, Jr., profiled on **page 517**, was portrayed by Russell Crowe in the 2001 movie *A Beautiful Mind.* As a young American mathematician, Nash did brilliant work in several areas. One was real world code-breaking. An interactive session based on code-breaking, and more information on the movie, are available at www.abeautifulmind.com/main.html.

Basics of Cryptography **Cryptography** involves secret codes, ways of disguising information in order that a "sender" can transmit it to an intended "receiver" so that an "adversary" who somehow intercepts the transmission will be unable to discern its meaning. As is customary, we will refer to the sender and receiver (in either order) as Alice and Bob (*A* and *B*) and to the adversary as Eve (*E*). Converting a message to disguised form is called **encryption**, and converting it back to original form is called **decryption.**

Cryptography became more crucial as the extent of military, diplomatic, then industrial, and now even personal applications expanded. As the "code makers" became more adept at designing their systems, the "code breakers" became more adept at compromising those systems.

The basis of a cryptography system is normally some mathematical function, the "encryption algorithm," that encrypts (disguises) the message. (*Functions* are discussed in **Chapter 8.**) An example of a simple (and very insecure) encryption algorithm is the following:

> Replace every letter of the alphabet with the letter that *follows* it.
> (Replace z with a.)

Then the message "zebra" would be encrypted as "afcsb." Analyzing one or more intercepted messages encrypted using this function, and trying various possibilities, would enable an adversary to quickly determine the function, and its inverse, which would be the following:

> Replace every letter of the alphabet with the letter that *precedes* it.
> (Replace a with z.)

More advanced systems also use a **key,** which is some additional information needed to perform the algorithm correctly. By the middle of the twentieth century, state-of-the-art requirements for an effective cryptography system were as follows.

> **Basic Requirements of a Cryptography System**
>
> **1.** A *secret* algorithm (or function) for encrypting and decrypting data
>
> **2.** A *secret* key that provides additional information necessary for a receiver to carry out the decrypting process

The difficulty with requirement 1 was that all encryption functions at the time were two-way functions. Once an adversary obtained the encryption algorithm, the inverse (that is, the decryption algorithm) could be deduced mathematically.

The difficulty with requirement 2 was that the security of the key frequently dropped off after a period of use. This meant that Bob and Alice must exchange a new key fairly often so that their communications would continue to be safe. But this measure may be self-defeating, because every key exchange may be vulnerable to interception. This dilemma became known as the **key exchange problem** (or the **key distribution problem** in the case of multiple intended receivers).

In the 1970s, researchers discovered how to construct a *one-way* function that overcame both difficulties. It is an *exponential function* (**Section 8.6**), and is given by

$$C = M^k \ (\text{mod } n),$$

with the calculation carried out modulo n. The achievement of an essentially one-way, rather than two-way, function, is made possible by the theory of large prime numbers, the nature of modular arithmetic (introduced in the **Chapter 4 Extension**), and the present state of computer hardware and algorithms.

The Diffie-Hellman-Merkle Key Exchange Scheme

First the key exchange problem was solved by the **Diffie-Hellman-Merkle key exchange scheme** (announced in 1976 and named for the Stanford University team of Whitfield Diffie, Martin Hellman, and Ralph Merkle). Basically, it works as follows.

The Diffie-Hellman-Merkle Key Exchange Scheme

Alice and Bob can establish a key (a number) that they both will know, but that Eve cannot find out, even if she observes the communications between Bob and Alice as they set up their key. Alice and Bob can agree to use the function $C = M^k \ (\text{mod } n)$ with specific values for M and n. (They can agree to all this by mail, telephone, e-mail, or even casual conversation. It won't matter if Eve finds out.) Then they carry out the following sequence of individual steps.

Alice's Actions	*Bob's Actions*
Step 1 Choose a value of a. (Keep this value secret.)	**Step 1** Choose a value of b. (Keep this value secret.)
Step 2 Compute $\alpha = M^a \ (\text{mod } n)$.	**Step 2** Compute $\beta = M^b \ (\text{mod } n)$.
Step 3 Send the value of α to Bob.	**Step 3** Send the value of β to Alice.
Step 4 Receive the value of β from Bob.	**Step 4** Receive the value of α from Alice.
Step 5 Compute the key: $$K = \beta^a \ (\text{mod } n).$$	**Step 5** Compute the key: $$K = \alpha^b \ (\text{mod } n).$$

By this procedure, Alice and Bob will arrive at the same key value K because

$$\beta^a = (M^b)^a \qquad \beta = M^b$$
$$= M^{ba} \qquad \text{Rule of exponents: } (a^m)^n = a^{mn}$$
$$= M^{ab} \qquad \text{Commutative property: } ab = ba$$
$$= (M^a)^b \qquad \text{Rule of exponents: } (a^m)^n = a^{mn}$$
$$= \alpha^b. \qquad \alpha = M^a$$

We illustrate the basic procedures using much smaller numbers than would be used in practice so that our computations can be done on a handheld calculator.

```
16807/13
              1292.846154
Ans-1292
              .8461538462
Ans*13
                        11
```

The display shows that the residue of 16,807, modulo 13, is 11.

Modular arithmetic, as discussed in the **Chapter 4 Extension,** will be essential here. Given a modulus n, every natural number a is "equivalent" (actually congruent) to the remainder obtained when a is divided by n. This remainder is called the **residue** of a, modulo n. To find the residue can be thought of as to "mod." In **Example 1** to follow, for instance, one of the calculations will be to find the residue of 16,807, modulo 13. The calculator routine from the **Chapter 4 Extension (page 172)** applies as follows.

Step 1 Divide 16,807 by 13, obtaining 1292.846154.

Step 2 Subtract the integer part of the quotient, obtaining 0.846154. . . .

Step 3 Multiply by 13, obtaining 11. (Round if necessary.)

So, we see that $16{,}807 \equiv 11 \pmod{13}$. We have shown that $16{,}807 = 1292 \cdot 13 + 11$.

    (*Note:* In the work that follows, we carry out some lengthy sequences of modular arithmetic. We sometimes use the equals symbol, $=$, rather than the congruence symbol, $\equiv$, and when the modulus is understood, we sometimes omit the designation $(\bmod\ n)$.)

Calculator Routine for Finding the Residue of a, Modulo n

In a modular system, the residue modulo n for a number a can be found by completing these three steps, in turn.

Step 1 Divide a by the modulus n.

Step 2 Subtract the integer part of the quotient to obtain only the fractional part.

Step 3 Multiply the fractional part of the quotient by n.

The final result is the residue modulo n.

▮▮ **EXAMPLE 1** Using the Diffie-Hellman-Merkle Key Exchange Scheme

Establish a common key for Alice and Bob by using specific values for M, n, a, and b, and completing the steps outlined earlier for the Diffie-Hellman-Merkle key exchange scheme.

SOLUTION

Suppose Alice and Bob agree to use the values $M = 7$ and $n = 13$.

Alice's Actions	*Bob's Actions*
Step 1 Choose a value of a, say 5. (Alice keeps this value secret.)	***Step 1*** Choose a value of b, say 8. (Bob keeps this value secret.)
Step 2 $\alpha = M^a \pmod{n}$ $= 7^5 \pmod{13}$ $= 16{,}807 \pmod{13}$ $= 11$	***Step 2*** $\beta = M^b \pmod{n}$ $= 7^8 \pmod{13}$ $= 5{,}764{,}801 \pmod{13}$ $= 3$
Step 3 Send $\alpha = 11$ to Bob.	***Step 3*** Send $\beta = 3$ to Alice.
Step 4 Receive $\beta = 3$.	***Step 4*** Receive $\alpha = 11$.
Step 5 Compute the key: $K = \beta^a \pmod{n}$ $= 3^5 \pmod{13}$ $= 243 \pmod{13}$ $= 9$.	***Step 5*** Compute the key: $K = \alpha^b \pmod{n}$ $= 11^8 \pmod{13}$ $= 214{,}358{,}881 \pmod{13}$ $= 9$.

```
11^8
              214358881
Ans/13
             16489144.69
Ans-16489144
                  .692308
Ans*13
                 9.000004
```

The display shows the calculation of K in the right column. (Ignore the tiny roundoff error.)

Both Alice and Bob arrived at the same key value, $K = 9$, which they can use for encrypting future communications to one another. ▮▮▮

When the **RSA code** was first introduced in 1977, Martin Gardner's "Mathematical Games" column in *Scientific American* challenged researchers to decode a message using an *n* with 129 digits. With the aid of number theory, it took 600 mathematicians in 25 different countries only 17 years to factor *n* into 64- and 65-digit prime factors, as shown here.

114,381,625,757,888,867,669,235,779,976,
146,612,010,218,296,721,242,362,562,561,
842,935,706,935,245,733,897,830,597,123,
563,958,705,058,989,075,147,599,290,026,
879,543,541 = 3,490,529,510,847,650,949,
147,849,619,903,898,133,417,764,638,493,
387,843,990,820,577 × 32,769,132,993,
266,709,549,961,988,190,834,461,413,177,
642,967,992,942,539,798,288,533

The decoded message said, "The magic words are squeamish ossifrage."

Today, RSA users select much larger values of *p* and *q*, resulting in an *n* of well over 300 digits. It is thought that breaking such an encryption would take all the computers in the world, working together, more time than the age of the universe.

Suppose, at Step 3 in **Example 1,** Eve intercepts Bob's transmission of the value $\beta = 3$ to Alice. This will not help her, because she cannot deduce Bob's value of *b* that generated β. In fact it could have been any of the values

$$8, 20, 32, 44, 56, \ldots,$$

an infinite list of possibilities. (In practice, all the numbers in this list would be vastly greater.) Also, Eve does not know what exponent Alice will apply to 3 to obtain the key. The value

$$a = 5$$

is Alice's secret, never communicated to anyone else, not even Bob, so Eve cannot know what key Alice will obtain. The same argument applies if Eve intercepts Alice's transmission to Bob of the value

$$\alpha = 11.$$

(She is stymied even if she intercepts both transmissions.)

RSA Public Key Cryptography At practically the same time that Diffie, Hellman, and Merkle solved the key exchange problem, another team of researchers, Ron Rivest, Adi Shamir, and Leonard Adleman, at MIT, used the same type of mathematical function to eliminate the need for key exchange. Their scheme, known as RSA (from their surnames), is called **public key cryptography.** Anyone who wants the capability of receiving encrypted data simply makes known their public key, which anyone else can then use to encrypt messages to them. The beauty of the system is that the receiver possesses another private key, necessary for decrypting but never released to anyone else.

What makes RSA successful is that we have the mathematical understanding to identify very large prime numbers, and to multiply them to obtain a product. But if the prime factors are large enough, it is impossible, given the present state of knowledge, for anyone to determine the two original factors, even using very powerful computers.

Using RSA, Alice can receive encrypted messages from Bob in such a way that Eve cannot discern their meaning even if she intercepts them. We show here a complete outline of all the basic procedures, from setting up the scheme to encrypting and then decrypting a message.

RSA Basics: A Public Key Cryptography Scheme

Alice (the receiver) completes the following steps.

Step 1 Choose two prime numbers, *p* and *q*, which she keeps secret.

Step 2 Compute the *modulus n* (which is the product $p \cdot q$).

Step 3 Compute $\ell = (p - 1)(q - 1)$.

Step 4 Choose the *encryption exponent e*, which can be any integer between 1 and ℓ that is relatively prime to ℓ, that is, has no common factors with ℓ.

Step 5 Find her *decryption exponent d*, a number satisfying

$$e \cdot d = 1 \ (\mathrm{mod} \ \ell).$$

She keeps *d* secret.

Step 6 Provide Bob with her *public key*, which consists of the modulus *n* and the encryption exponent *e*.

(Bob's steps are on the next page.)

RSA Basics: A Public Key Cryptography Scheme (Cont.)

Now Bob (the sender) completes the following steps. (Recall that the purpose of all this is for Bob to be able to send Alice secure messages.)

Step 7 Convert the message to be sent to Alice into a number M (sometimes called the *plaintext*).

Step 8 Encrypt M, that is, use Alice's public key (n and e) to generate the encrypted message C (sometimes called the *ciphertext*) according to the formula

$$C = M^e \,(\text{mod } n).$$

Step 9 Transmit C to Alice.

When Alice receives C, she completes the final step:

Step 10 Decrypt C, that is, use her private key, consisting of n (also part of her public key) and d, to reproduce the original plaintext message M according to the formula

$$M = C^d \,(\text{mod } n).$$

EXAMPLE 2 Devising a Public Encryption Key

Use the values $p = 7$ and $q = 13$ (arbitrarily chosen primes) to devise Alice's public key by completing Steps 2–4 of the above outline of RSA basics.

A **brilliant number** (defined only in the last few years) is a product of two primes with equal numbers of digits. Is the product n in **Example 2** brilliant?

SOLUTION

Step 2 $n = p \cdot q = 7 \cdot 13 = 91$

Step 3 $\ell = (p - 1)(q - 1) = 6 \cdot 12 = 72$

Step 4 There are many choices here, but a prime less than 72 and relatively prime to 72 will meet the requirements. We arbitrarily choose $e = 11$.

Alice's public key is $n = 91$, $e = 11$. (Prime factors p and q must be kept secret.)

▮▮▮

EXAMPLE 3 Finding a Private Decryption Key

Complete Step 5 of the RSA basics outline to find Alice's private decryption key.

SOLUTION

Step 5 The decryption exponent d must satisfy

$$e \cdot d = 1 \,(\text{mod } \ell) \quad \text{or} \quad 11d = 1 \,(\text{mod } 72).$$

One way to satisfy this equation is to check the powers of 11 until we find one equal (actually congruent) to 1, modulo 72:

> Mod 72 congruences

$$11^1 = 11, \quad 11^2 = 121 = 49, \quad 11^3 = 1331 = 35,$$
$$11^4 = 14,641 = 25, \quad 11^5 = 161,051 = 59, \quad 11^6 = 1,771,561 = 1.$$

(The residues were found using the calculator routine given before **Example 1**.) Because we found that $11^6 = 1$, we take $d = 11^5 = 59$. This way,

$$e \cdot d = 11 \cdot 11^5 = 11^6 = 1, \quad \text{as required.}$$

Alice's private key is $n = 91$, $d = 59$.

▮▮▮

James Ellis, Clifford Cocks, and Malcolm Williamson all worked for Britain's Government Communications Headquarters in the 1970s. They actually discovered the mathematics of public key cryptography several years before the work at Stanford and MIT was announced (and subsequently patented). The British work was classified top secret and never came to light until some twenty years later, at approximately the same time that RSA Data Security, the company that had been built on U.S. RSA patents, was sold for $200 million.

EXAMPLE 4 Encrypting a Message for Transmission

Complete Steps 7 and 8 of the RSA basics outline to encrypt the message "HI" for Bob to send Alice. Use Alice's public key found in **Example 2:** $n = 91, e = 11$.

SOLUTION

Step 7 A simple way to convert "HI" to a number is to note that H and I are the 8th and 9th letters of the English alphabet. Simply let the plaintext message be $M = 89$.

Step 8 Now compute the ciphertext C: $C = M^e \pmod{n} = 89^{11} \pmod{91}$.

Here, 89^{11} is too large to be handled as we did the powers of 11 in **Example 3.** But we can use a trick here, expressing 11 as $1 + 2 + 8$. (1, 2, and 8 are the unique powers of 2 that sum to 11. So we are doing something like what we did when discussing the binary system in **Section 4.4.**) Now we can rewrite 89^{11} in terms of smaller powers and then make use of rules of exponents (**Section 7.5**).

$$89^{11} = 89^{1+2+8} \qquad 1 + 2 + 8 = 11$$
$$= 89^1 \cdot 89^2 \cdot 89^8 \quad \text{Rule of exponents: } a^{n+m} = a^n \cdot a^m$$

Now we "mod before we multiply," in other words, we compute the residue of individual factors first, then multiply those results. This keeps the numbers smaller.

$$89^1 = \mathbf{89} \qquad\qquad \text{Definition of first power}$$
$$89^2 = 7921 = \mathbf{4} \qquad \text{Mod}$$
$$89^8 = 3.936588806E15 \quad \text{Calculator result}$$

This last factor is too large to handle like the others. Due to the way we "split up" the exponent, subsequent powers of 89 can be written as powers of earlier ones.

$$89^8 = (89^2)^4 \quad \text{Rule of exponents: } a^{m \cdot n} = (a^m)^n$$
$$= 4^4 \qquad\quad 89^2 = 4 \text{ from above.}$$
$$= 256 \qquad\; \text{Evaluate } 4^4.$$
$$= \mathbf{74} \qquad\;\; \text{Mod}$$

Finally we obtain

$$89^{11} = \mathbf{89} \cdot \mathbf{4} \cdot \mathbf{74} \quad \text{Substitute.}$$
$$= 26{,}344 \qquad\;\; \text{Multiply.}$$
$$= 45. \qquad\qquad \text{Mod}$$

The plaintext $M = 89$ (for the message "HI") has been converted to the ciphertext $C = 45$. ■■■

Let's see if Alice can successfully decrypt the message 45 when she receives it.

EXAMPLE 5 Decrypting a Received Message

Complete Step 10 of the RSA basics outline to decrypt the message $C = 45$ from **Example 4.** Use Alice's private key, found in **Example 3:** $d = 59$ (also, $n = 91$).

SOLUTION

Step 10 The decryption formula gives

$$M = C^d \pmod{n}$$
$$= 45^{59} \pmod{91} \qquad\qquad\qquad\qquad \text{Substitute.}$$
$$= 45^{1+2+8+16+32} \pmod{91} \qquad\qquad \text{Use sum of powers of 2.}$$
$$= 45 \cdot 45^2 \cdot 45^8 \cdot 45^{16} \cdot 45^{32} \pmod{91}. \quad \text{Rule of exponents: } a^{m+n} = a^m \cdot a^n$$

Start with the smaller powers and "mod" each factor individually.

$$45^2 = 2025 = 23$$
$$45^8 = (45^2)^4 = 23^4 = 279{,}841 = 16$$
$$45^{16} = (45^8)^2 = 16^2 = 256 = 74$$
$$45^{32} = (45^{16})^2 = 74^2 = 5476 = 16$$

Inserting these values in the product for M, we get

$$M = 45 \cdot 23 \cdot 16 \cdot 74 \cdot 16$$
$$= 19{,}607{,}040$$
$$= 89.$$

We have correctly decrypted $C = 45$ to obtain

$$M = 89 = \text{HI}.$$

▮▮▮

EXTENSION EXERCISES

Find the residue in each case.

1. 45 (mod 6) **2.** 67 (mod 10)

3. 225 (mod 13) **4.** 418 (mod 15)

5. 5^9 (mod 12) **6.** 4^{11} (mod 9)

7. 8^7 (mod 11) **8.** 14^5 (mod 13)

9. 8^{27} (mod 17) **10.** 45^7 (mod 23)

11. 11^{14} (mod 18) **12.** 14^9 (mod 19)

Finding a Common Key *Find Alice and Bob's common key K by using the Diffie-Hellman-Merkle key exchange scheme with the given values of M, n, a, and b.*

	M	**n**	**a**	**b**
13.	5	13	7	6
14.	11	9	5	4
15.	5	11	6	7
16.	17	5	6	3

Apply the RSA scheme to find each missing value.

	p	**q**	**n**	**ℓ**
17.	5	11	___	___
18.	11	3	___	___
19.	5	13	___	___
20.	17	7	___	___

Encrypting Plaintext *Given the modulus n, the encryption exponent e, and the plaintext M, use RSA encryption to find the ciphertext C in each case.*

	n	**e**	**M**
21.	55	7	15
22.	33	7	8
23.	65	5	16
24.	119	11	12

Decrypting Ciphertext *Given the prime factors p and q, the encryption exponent e, and the ciphertext C, apply the RSA algorithm to find* **(a)** *the decryption exponent d and* **(b)** *the plaintext message M.*

	p	**q**	**e**	**C**
25.	5	11	3	30
26.	11	3	13	24
27.	5	13	35	17
28.	17	7	5	40

29. Describe the breakthrough represented by Diffie-Hellman-Merkle and RSA as opposed to all earlier forms of cryptography.

30. Explain why RSA would fail if mathematicians could (using computers) factor arbitrarily large numbers.

5.5 THE FIBONACCI SEQUENCE AND THE GOLDEN RATIO

The Fibonacci Sequence • The Golden Ratio

The Fibonacci Sequence

The solution of Fibonacci's rabbit problem is examined in **Chapter 1, pages 19–20.**

One of the most famous problems in elementary mathematics comes from the book *Liber Abaci*, written in 1202 by Leonardo of Pisa, a.k.a. Fibonacci. The problem is as follows:

> A man put a pair of rabbits in a cage. During the first month the rabbits produced no offspring, but each month thereafter produced one new pair of rabbits. If each new pair thus produced reproduces in the same manner, how many pairs of rabbits will there be at the end of one year?

The solution of this problem leads to a sequence of numbers known as the **Fibonacci sequence.** Here are the first fifteen terms of the Fibonacci sequence:

$$1, 1, 2, 3, 5, 8, 13, 21, 34, 55, 89, 144, 233, 377, 610.$$

After the first two terms (both 1) in the sequence, each term is obtained by adding the two previous terms. For example, the third term is obtained by adding $1 + 1$ to get 2, the fourth term is obtained by adding $1 + 2$ to get 3, and so on. This can be described by a mathematical formula known as a **recursion formula.**

If F_n represents the Fibonacci number in the nth position in the sequence, then

$$F_1 = 1$$
$$F_2 = 1$$
$$F_n = F_{n-2} + F_{n-1}, \quad \text{for } n \geq 3.$$

Using the recursion formula $F_n = F_{n-2} + F_{n-1}$, we obtain

$$F_3 = F_1 + F_2 = 1 + 1 = 2, \quad F_4 = F_2 + F_3 = 1 + 2 = 3, \quad \text{and so on.}$$

The Fibonacci sequence exhibits many interesting patterns, and by inductive reasoning we can make many conjectures about these patterns. However, simply observing a finite number of examples does not provide a proof of a statement. Proofs of the properties of the Fibonacci sequence often involve mathematical induction (covered in college algebra texts). Here we simply observe the patterns and do not attempt to provide proofs.

The **Fibonacci Association** is a research organization dedicated to investigation into the **Fibonacci sequence** and related topics. Check your library to see if it has the journal *Fibonacci Quarterly*. The first two journals of 1963 contain a basic introduction to the Fibonacci sequence.

▌▌ **EXAMPLE 1** Observing a Pattern of the Fibonacci Numbers

Find the sum of the squares of the first n Fibonacci numbers for $n = 1, 2, 3, 4, 5$, and examine the pattern. Generalize this relationship.

SOLUTION

$$1^2 = 1 = 1 \cdot 1 = F_1 \cdot F_2$$
$$1^2 + 1^2 = 2 = 1 \cdot 2 = F_2 \cdot F_3$$
$$1^2 + 1^2 + 2^2 = 6 = 2 \cdot 3 = F_3 \cdot F_4$$
$$1^2 + 1^2 + 2^2 + 3^2 = 15 = 3 \cdot 5 = F_4 \cdot F_5$$
$$1^2 + 1^2 + 2^2 + 3^2 + 5^2 = 40 = 5 \cdot 8 = F_5 \cdot F_6$$

The sum of the squares of the first n Fibonacci numbers seems to always be the product of F_n and F_{n+1}. This has been proved to be true, in general, using mathematical induction. ▌▌▌

The following program for the TI-83/84 Plus utilizes the *Binet form* of the *n*th Fibonacci number (see **Exercises 33–38**) to determine its value.

    PROGRAM: FIB
    : ClrHome
    : Disp "WHICH TERM"
    : Disp "OF THE"
    : Disp "SEQUENCE DO"
    : Disp "YOU WANT?"
    : Input N
    : (1 + √(5))/2 → A
    : (1 − √(5))/2 → B
    : (A^N − B^N)/√(5) → F
    : Disp F

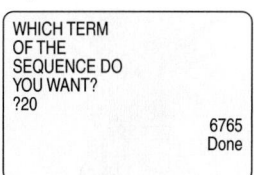

    WHICH TERM
    OF THE
    SEQUENCE DO
    YOU WANT?
    ?20
                            6765
                            Done

This screen indicates that the twentieth Fibonacci number is 6765.

Fibonacci Fun To observe one of the many interesting properties of the Fibonacci sequence, do the following.

1. Choose any term after the first and square it.
2. Multiply the terms before and after the term chosen in step 1.
3. Subtract the smaller value from the larger.
4. What is your result?

Try this procedure beginning with several different Fibonacci terms. **The result is always the same.**

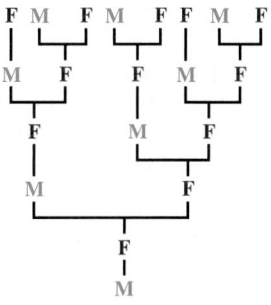

Figure 1

▌▌ **EXAMPLE 2** Observing the Fibonacci Sequence in a Long Division Problem

Observe the steps of the long division algorithm used to find the first few decimal places of the reciprocal of 89, the eleventh Fibonacci number. Locate occurrences of the terms of the Fibonacci sequence in the algorithm.

SOLUTION

$$
\begin{array}{r}
.011235\ldots \\
89\overline{)1.000000\ldots} \\
\underline{89} \\
110 \\
\underline{89} \\
210 \\
\underline{178} \\
320 \\
\underline{267} \\
530 \\
\underline{445} \\
850\ldots
\end{array}
$$

Notice that after the 0 in the tenths place, the next five digits are the first five terms of the Fibonacci sequence. In addition, as indicated in color in the process, the digits 1, 1, 2, 3, 5, 8 appear in the division steps. Now, look at the digits next to the ones in color, beginning with the second "1"; they, too, are 1, 1, 2, 3, 5, ...

If the division process is continued past the final step shown above, the pattern seems to stop, since to ten decimal places, $\frac{1}{89} \approx 0.0112359551$. (The decimal representation actually begins to repeat later in the process, since $\frac{1}{89}$ is a rational number.) However, the sum below indicates how the Fibonacci numbers are actually "hidden" in this decimal.

$$
\begin{array}{l}
0.01 \\
0.001 \\
0.0002 \\
0.00003 \\
0.000005 \\
0.0000008 \\
0.00000013 \\
0.000000021 \\
0.0000000034 \\
0.00000000055 \\
\underline{0.000000000089} \\
\end{array}
$$

$$\frac{1}{89} = 0.0112359550.\ldots$$

▌▌▌

Fibonacci patterns have been found in numerous places in nature. For example, male honeybees (drones) hatch from eggs that have not been fertilized, so a male bee has only one parent, a female. On the other hand, female honeybees hatch from fertilized eggs, so a female has two parents, one male and one female. **Figure 1** shows several generations of ancestors for a male honeybee.

Notice that in the first generation, starting at the bottom, there is 1 bee, in the second there is 1 bee, in the third there are 2 bees, and so on. These are the terms of the Fibonacci sequence. Furthermore, beginning with the second generation, the numbers of female bees form the sequence, and beginning with the third generation, the numbers of male bees also form the sequence.

A fraction such as

$$1 + \cfrac{1}{1 + \cfrac{1}{1 + \cfrac{1}{1 + \ddots}}}$$

is called a **continued fraction**. This continued fraction can be evaluated as follows.

Let $\quad x = 1 + \cfrac{1}{1 + \cfrac{1}{1 + \ddots}}$

Then $\qquad x = 1 + \dfrac{1}{x}$

$$x^2 = x + 1$$

$$x^2 - x - 1 = 0.$$

By the quadratic formula from algebra,

$$x = \frac{1 \pm \sqrt{1 - 4(1)(-1)}}{2(1)}$$

$$x = \frac{1 \pm \sqrt{5}}{2}.$$

Notice that the positive solution is the **golden ratio**.

Successive terms in the Fibonacci sequence also appear in some plants. For example, the photo (below on the left) shows the double spiraling of a daisy head, with 21 clockwise spirals and 34 counterclockwise spirals. These numbers are successive terms in the sequence.

Most pineapples (see the photo below on the right) exhibit the Fibonacci sequence in the following way: Count the spirals formed by the "scales" of the cone, first counting from lower left to upper right. Then count the spirals from lower right to upper left. You should find that in one direction you get 8 spirals, and in the other you get 13 spirals, once again successive terms of the Fibonacci sequence. Many pinecones exhibit 5 and 8 spirals, and the cone of the giant sequoia has 3 and 5 spirals.

The Golden Ratio

If we consider the quotients of successive Fibonacci numbers, a pattern emerges.

$$\frac{1}{1} = 1 \qquad \frac{5}{3} = 1.666\ldots \qquad \frac{21}{13} \approx 1.615384615 \qquad \frac{89}{55} = 1.618181818\ldots$$

$$\frac{2}{1} = 2 \qquad \frac{8}{5} = 1.6 \qquad \frac{34}{21} \approx 1.619047619$$

$$\frac{3}{2} = 1.5 \qquad \frac{13}{8} = 1.625 \qquad \frac{55}{34} \approx 1.617647059$$

These quotients seem to be approaching some "limiting value" close to 1.618. In fact, as we go farther into the sequence, these quotients approach the number

$$\frac{1 + \sqrt{5}}{2}, \quad \text{Golden ratio}$$

known as the **golden ratio,** and often symbolized by ϕ, the Greek letter phi.

The golden ratio appears over and over in art, architecture, music, and nature. Its origins go back to the days of the ancient Greeks, who thought that a golden rectangle exhibited the most aesthetically pleasing proportion.

A **golden rectangle** is one that can be divided into a square and another (smaller) rectangle the same shape as the original rectangle. (See **Figure 2**.) If we let the smaller rectangle have length L and width W, as shown in the figure, then we see that the original rectangle has length $L + W$ and width L. Both rectangles (being "golden") have their lengths and widths in the golden ratio, ϕ, so we have

$$\frac{L}{W} = \frac{L + W}{L}$$

$$\frac{L}{W} = \frac{L}{L} + \frac{W}{L} \quad \text{Write the right side as the sum of two fractions.}$$

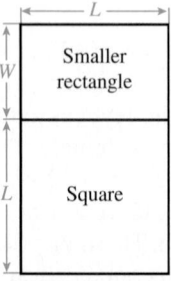

Figure 2

$$\phi = 1 + \frac{1}{\phi} \qquad \text{Substitute } \tfrac{L}{W} = \phi, \tfrac{L}{L} = 1, \text{ and } \tfrac{W}{L} = \tfrac{1}{\phi}.$$

$$\phi^2 = \phi + 1 \qquad \text{Multiply both sides by } \phi.$$

$$\phi^2 - \phi - 1 = 0. \qquad \text{Write in standard quadratic form.}$$

Using the quadratic formula from algebra, the positive solution of this equation is found to be $\frac{1 + \sqrt{5}}{2} \approx 1.618033989$, the golden ratio.

The Parthenon (see the photo), built on the Acropolis in ancient Athens during the fifth century B.C., is an example of architecture exhibiting many distinct golden rectangles.

To see an interesting connection between the terms of the Fibonacci sequence, the golden ratio, and a phenomenon of nature, we can start with a rectangle measuring 89 by 55 units. (See **Figure 3**.) This is a very close approximation to a golden rectangle. Within this rectangle a square is then constructed, 55 units on a side. The remaining rectangle is also approximately a golden rectangle, measuring 55 units by 34 units. Each time this process is repeated, a square and an approximate golden rectangle are formed.

As indicated in **Figure 3**, vertices of the square may be joined by a smooth curve known as a *spiral*. This spiral resembles the outline of a cross section of the shell of the chambered nautilus, as shown in the photo.

A Golden Rectangle in Art The rectangle outlining the figure in *St. Jerome* by Leonardo da Vinci is an example of a golden rectangle.

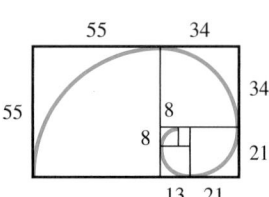

Figure 3

For Further Thought

Mathematical Animation

The 1959 animated film *Donald in Mathmagic Land* has endured for over 50 years as a classic. It provides a 25-minute trip with Donald Duck, led by the Spirit of Mathematics, through the world of mathematics. Several minutes of the film are devoted to the golden ratio (or, as it is termed there, the golden section).

Disney provides animation to explain the golden ratio in a way that the printed word simply cannot do. The golden ratio is seen in architecture, nature, and the human body.

For Group or Individual Investigation

1. Verify the following Fibonacci pattern in the conifer family. Obtain a pineapple, and count spirals formed by the "scales" of the cone, first counting from lower left to upper right. Then count the spirals from lower right to upper left. What do you find?

2. Two popular sizes of index cards are 3″ by 5″ and 5″ by 8″. Why do you think that these are industry-standard sizes?

3. Divide your height by the height to your navel. Find a class average. What value does this come close to?

5.5 EXERCISES

Answer each question concerning the Fibonacci sequence or the golden ratio.

1. The sixteenth Fibonacci number is 987 and the seventeenth Fibonacci number is 1597. What is the value of the eighteenth Fibonacci number?

2. Recall that F_n represents the Fibonacci number in the nth position in the sequence. What are the only two values of n such that $F_n = n$?

3. $F_{22} = 17{,}711$ and $F_{24} = 46{,}368$. What is the value of F_{23}?

4. If two successive terms of the Fibonacci sequence are both odd, is the next term even or odd?

5. What is the exact value of the golden ratio?

6. What is the approximate value of the golden ratio to the nearest thousandth?

In each of Exercises 7–14, a pattern is established involving terms of the Fibonacci sequence. Use inductive reasoning to make a conjecture concerning the next equation in the pattern, and verify it. You may wish to refer to the first few terms of the sequence given in the text.

7. $1 = 2 - 1$
   $1 + 1 = 3 - 1$
   $1 + 1 + 2 = 5 - 1$
   $1 + 1 + 2 + 3 = 8 - 1$
   $1 + 1 + 2 + 3 + 5 = 13 - 1$

8. $1 = 2 - 1$
   $1 + 3 = 5 - 1$
   $1 + 3 + 8 = 13 - 1$
   $1 + 3 + 8 + 21 = 34 - 1$
   $1 + 3 + 8 + 21 + 55 = 89 - 1$

9. $1 = 1$
   $1 + 2 = 3$
   $1 + 2 + 5 = 8$
   $1 + 2 + 5 + 13 = 21$
   $1 + 2 + 5 + 13 + 34 = 55$

10. $1^2 + 1^2 = 2$
    $1^2 + 2^2 = 5$
    $2^2 + 3^2 = 13$
    $3^2 + 5^2 = 34$
    $5^2 + 8^2 = 89$

11. $2^2 - 1^2 = 3$
    $3^2 - 1^2 = 8$
    $5^2 - 2^2 = 21$
    $8^2 - 3^2 = 55$

12. $2^3 + 1^3 - 1^3 = 8$
    $3^3 + 2^3 - 1^3 = 34$
    $5^3 + 3^3 - 2^3 = 144$
    $8^3 + 5^3 - 3^3 = 610$

13. $1 = 1^2$
    $1 - 2 = -1^2$
    $1 - 2 + 5 = 2^2$
    $1 - 2 + 5 - 13 = -3^2$
    $1 - 2 + 5 - 13 + 34 = 5^2$

14. $1 - 1 = -1 + 1$
    $1 - 1 + 2 = 1 + 1$
    $1 - 1 + 2 - 3 = -2 + 1$
    $1 - 1 + 2 - 3 + 5 = 3 + 1$
    $1 - 1 + 2 - 3 + 5 - 8 = -5 + 1$

15. Every natural number can be expressed as a sum of Fibonacci numbers, where no number is used more than once. For example, $25 = 21 + 3 + 1$. Express each of the following in this way.

    (a) 37   (b) 40   (c) 52

16. It has been shown that if m divides n, then F_m is a factor of F_n. Show that this is true for the following values of m and n.

    (a) $m = 2, n = 6$ (b) $m = 3, n = 9$
    (c) $m = 4, n = 8$

17. It has been shown that if the greatest common factor of m and n is r, then the greatest common factor of F_m and F_n is F_r. Show that this is true for the following values of m and n.

    (a) $m = 10, n = 4$ (b) $m = 12, n = 6$
    (c) $m = 14, n = 6$

18. For any prime number p except 2 or 5, either F_{p+1} or F_{p-1} is divisible by p. Show that this is true for the following values of p.

    (a) $p = 3$ (b) $p = 7$ (c) $p = 11$

19. Earlier we saw that if a term of the Fibonacci sequence is squared and then the product of the terms on each side of the term is found, there will always be a difference of 1. Follow the steps below, choosing the seventh Fibonacci number, 13.

    (a) Square 13. Multiply the terms of the sequence two positions away from 13 (i.e., 5 and 34). Subtract the smaller result from the larger, and record your answer.

    (b) Square 13. Multiply the terms of the sequence three positions away from 13. Once again, subtract the smaller result from the larger, and record your answer.

    (c) Repeat the process, moving four terms away from 13.

    (d) Make a conjecture about what will happen when you repeat the process, moving five terms away. Verify your answer.

20. *A Number Trick* Here is a number trick that you can perform. Ask someone to pick any two numbers at random and to write them down. Ask the person to determine a third number by adding the first and second, a fourth number by adding the second and third, and so on, until ten numbers are determined. Then ask the person to add these ten numbers. You will be able to give the sum before the person even completes the list, because the sum will always be 11 times the seventh number in the list. Verify that this is true, by using x and y as the first two numbers arbitrarily chosen. (*Hint:* Remember the distributive property from algebra.)

*Another Fibonacci-type sequence that has been studied by mathematicians is the **Lucas sequence,** named after a French mathematician of the nineteenth century. The first ten terms of the Lucas sequence are*

$$1, 3, 4, 7, 11, 18, 29, 47, 76, 123.$$

21. What is the eleventh term of the Lucas sequence?

22. Choose any term of the Lucas sequence and square it. Then multiply the terms on either side of the one you chose. Subtract the smaller result from the larger. Repeat this for a different term of the sequence. Do you get the same result? Make a conjecture about this pattern.

23. The first term of the Lucas sequence is 1. Add the first and third terms. Record your answer. Now add the first, third, and fifth terms and record your answer. Continue this pattern, each time adding another term that is in an *odd* position in the sequence. What do you notice about all of your sums?

24. The second term of the Lucas sequence is 3. Add the second and fourth terms. Record your answer. Now add the second, fourth, and sixth terms and record your answer. Continue this pattern, each time adding another term that is in an *even* position of the sequence. What do you notice about all of your sums?

25. Many interesting patterns exist among the terms of the Fibonacci sequence and the Lucas sequence. Make a conjecture about the next equation that would appear in each of the lists and then verify it.

(a) $1 \cdot 1 = 1$
$1 \cdot 3 = 3$
$2 \cdot 4 = 8$
$3 \cdot 7 = 21$
$5 \cdot 11 = 55$

(b) $1 + 2 = 3$
$1 + 3 = 4$
$2 + 5 = 7$
$3 + 8 = 11$
$5 + 13 = 18$

(c) $1 + 1 = 2 \cdot 1$
$1 + 3 = 2 \cdot 2$
$2 + 4 = 2 \cdot 3$
$3 + 7 = 2 \cdot 5$
$5 + 11 = 2 \cdot 8$

(d) $1 + 4 = 5 \cdot 1$
$3 + 7 = 5 \cdot 2$
$4 + 11 = 5 \cdot 3$
$7 + 18 = 5 \cdot 5$
$11 + 29 = 5 \cdot 8$

26. In the text we illustrate that the quotients of successive terms of the Fibonacci sequence approach the golden ratio. Make a similar observation for the terms of the Lucas sequence; that is, find the decimal approximations for the quotients

$$\frac{3}{1}, \frac{4}{3}, \frac{7}{4}, \frac{11}{7}, \frac{18}{11}, \frac{29}{18},$$

and so on, using a calculator. Then make a conjecture about what seems to be happening.

*Recall the **Pythagorean theorem** from geometry: If a right triangle has legs of lengths a and b and hypotenuse of length c, then*

$$a^2 + b^2 = c^2.$$

*Suppose that we choose any four successive terms of the Fibonacci sequence. Multiply the first and fourth. Double the product of the second and third. Add the squares of the second and third. The three results obtained form a **Pythagorean triple** (three numbers that satisfy the equation $a^2 + b^2 = c^2$). Find the Pythagorean triple obtained this way using the four given successive terms of the Fibonacci sequence.*

27. 1, 1, 2, 3   **28.** 1, 2, 3, 5   **29.** 2, 3, 5, 8

30. Look at the values of the hypotenuse (c) in the answers to **Exercises 27–29.** What do you notice about each of them?

31. The following array of numbers is called **Pascal's triangle.**

```
              1
            1   1
          1   2   1
        1   3   3   1
      1   4   6   4   1
    1   5  10  10   5   1
  1   6  15  20  15   6   1
```

This array is important in the study of counting techniques and probability (see later chapters) and appears in algebra in the binomial theorem. If the triangular array is written in a different form, as follows, and the sums along the diagonals as indicated by the dashed lines are found, there is an interesting occurrence. What do you find when the numbers are added?

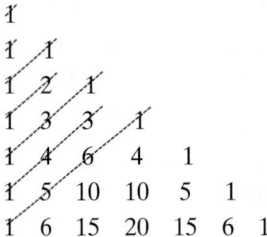

32. Write a paragraph explaining some of the occurrences of the Fibonacci sequence and the golden ratio in your everyday surroundings.

Exercises 33–38 require a scientific calculator.

33. The positive solution of the equation $x^2 - x - 1 = 0$ is $\frac{1 + \sqrt{5}}{2}$, as indicated in the text. The negative solution is $\frac{1 - \sqrt{5}}{2}$. Find the decimal approximations for both. What similarity do you notice between the two decimals?

34. In some cases, writers define the golden ratio to be the *reciprocal* of $\frac{1 + \sqrt{5}}{2}$. Find a decimal approximation for the reciprocal of $\frac{1 + \sqrt{5}}{2}$. What similarity do you notice between the decimals for $\frac{1 + \sqrt{5}}{2}$ and its reciprocal?

A remarkable relationship exists between the two solutions of $x^2 - x - 1 = 0$,

$$\phi = \frac{1 + \sqrt{5}}{2} \quad and \quad \overline{\phi} = \frac{1 - \sqrt{5}}{2},$$

and the Fibonacci numbers. To find the nth Fibonacci number without using the recursion formula, use a calculator to evaluate

$$\frac{\phi^n - \overline{\phi}^n}{\sqrt{5}}.$$

For example, to find the thirteenth Fibonacci number, evaluate

$$\frac{\left(\dfrac{1 + \sqrt{5}}{2}\right)^{13} - \left(\dfrac{1 - \sqrt{5}}{2}\right)^{13}}{\sqrt{5}}$$

*This form is known as the **Binet form** of the nth Fibonacci number. Use the Binet form and a calculator to find the nth Fibonacci number for each of the following values of n.*

35. $n = 14$ **36.** $n = 20$

37. $n = 22$ **38.** $n = 25$

COLLABORATIVE INVESTIGATION

Investigating an Interesting Property of Number Squares

In this group activity we will investigate a property of certain square arrangements of numbers. Begin by dividing up the class into groups of three or four students. Each student in the group should prepare a square of numbers like the one that follows:

1	2	3	4	5
6	7	8	9	10
11	12	13	14	15
16	17	18	19	20
21	22	23	24	25

Topics for Discussion

1. Each student should do the following individually:

> Choose any number in the first row. Circle it, and cross out all entries in the column below it. (For example, if you circle 4, cross out 9, 14, 19, and 24.) Now circle any remaining number in the second row, and cross out all entries in the column below it.
>
> Repeat this procedure for the third and fourth rows, and then circle the final remaining number in the fifth row.

Now each student in the group should add the circled numbers and compare his or her sum with all others in the group. What do you notice?

2. Verify that the sum in **Exercise 1** is equal to

$$\frac{1}{5}(1 + 2 + 3 + 4 + \cdots + 5^2).$$

3. Suppose **Exercise 1** was done as shown here:

1	②	3	4	5
6	⁊	⑧	9	10
11	⅟2	⅟3	14	⑮
⑯	⅟7	⅟8	19	2⁄0
2⁄1	2⁄2	2⁄3	㉔	2⁄5

Notice that summing the circled entries is just like summing

$$1 + 2 + 3 + 4 + 5,$$

except that

> 3 is replaced by 3 + 5,
> 5 is replaced by 5 + 10,
> 1 is replaced by 1 + 15,
> 4 is replaced by 4 + 20.

We can express this as

$$\begin{aligned} \text{sum} &= (1 + 2 + 3 + 4 + 5) \\ &\quad + (5 + 10 + 15 + 20) \\ &= 15 + 50, \quad \text{or} \quad 65. \end{aligned}$$

4. Explain why, whatever entries you choose to circle in the various rows, the sum is always the same.

5. Prepare a similar square of the natural numbers 1 through 36. Then repeat **Exercise 1.** Discuss your results. Verify that the sum is equal to

$$\frac{1}{6}(1 + 2 + 3 + 4 + \cdots + 6^2).$$

6. As a group, fill in the entries in this equation for the 6 by 6 square.

$$\begin{aligned} \text{sum} &= (\underline{\quad} + \underline{\quad} + \underline{\quad} + \underline{\quad} + \underline{\quad} + \underline{\quad}) \\ &\quad + (\underline{\quad} + \underline{\quad} + \underline{\quad} + \underline{\quad} + \underline{\quad}) \end{aligned}$$

7. As a group, predict the sum of the circled numbers in a 7 by 7 square by expressing it as follows. (Do not actually construct the square. Just generalize the pattern observed in the 5 by 5 and 6 by 6 cases.)

$$\begin{aligned} \text{sum} &= (\underline{\quad} + \underline{\quad} + \underline{\quad} + \underline{\quad} + \underline{\quad} + \\ &\quad \underline{\quad}) + (\underline{\quad} + \underline{\quad} + \underline{\quad} + \underline{\quad} + \\ &\quad \underline{\quad} + \underline{\quad}) \end{aligned}$$

Verify that the sum is equal to

$$\frac{1}{7}(1 + 2 + 3 + 4 + \cdots + 7^2).$$

8. Each individual should now prepare another 5 by 5 square and repeat **Exercise 1,** except this time start with a number in the first *column* and cross out remaining numbers in *rows*. In your group, discuss and explain what you observe. In particular, how do the individuals' answers compare, and how do they compare with the **Exercise 1** answers?

CHAPTER 5 TEST

In Exercises 1–6, decide whether each statement is true *or* false.

1. No two prime numbers differ by 1.

2. There are infinitely many prime numbers.

3. If a natural number is divisible by 9, then it must also be divisible by 3.

4. If p and q are different primes, 1 is their greatest common factor and pq is their least common multiple.

5. For all natural numbers n, 1 is a factor of n and n is a multiple of n.

6. If a natural number is not perfect, then it must be abundant.

7. Use divisibility tests to determine whether the number

$$656{,}723{,}600$$

is divisible by each of the following.

(a) 2 (b) 3 (c) 4
(d) 5 (e) 6 (f) 8
(g) 9 (h) 10 (i) 12

8. Decide whether each number is prime, composite, or neither.

(a) 87 (b) 97 (c) 1

9. Give the prime factorization of 2520.

10. In your own words state the Fundamental Theorem of Arithmetic.

11. Decide whether each number is perfect, deficient, or abundant.

(a) 36 (b) 8 (c) 28

12. Which of the following statements is false?

A. There are no known odd perfect numbers.

B. Every even perfect number must end in 6 or 28.

C. Goldbach's Conjecture for the number 8 is illustrated by the equation $8 = 7 + 1$.

13. Give a pair of twin primes between 50 and 70.

14. Find the greatest common factor of 135 and 216.

15. Find the least common multiple of 15, 45, and 50.

16. *Day Off for Fast-food Workers* Both Katherine Chong and Josh Dunlap work at a fast-food outlet. Katherine has every sixth day off and Josh has every fourth day off. If they are both off on Wednesday of this week, what will be the day of the week that they are next off together?

17. The twenty-third Fibonacci number is 28,657 and the twenty-fourth Fibonacci number is 46,368. What is the twenty-fifth Fibonacci number?

18. Make a conjecture about the next equation in the following list, and verify it.

$$\begin{aligned} 8 - (1 + 1 + 2 + 3) &= 1 \\ 13 - (1 + 2 + 3 + 5) &= 2 \\ 21 - (2 + 3 + 5 + 8) &= 3 \\ 34 - (3 + 5 + 8 + 13) &= 5 \\ 55 - (5 + 8 + 13 + 21) &= 8 \end{aligned}$$

19. Choose the correct completion of this statement: If p is a prime number, then $2^p - 1$ is prime

A. never   **B.** sometimes   **C.** always.

20. Give the first eight terms of a Fibonacci-type sequence with first term 1 and second term 5.

21. Choose any term after the first in the sequence of **Exercise 20.** Square it. Multiply the two terms on either side of it. Subtract the smaller result from the larger. Now repeat the process with a different term. Make a conjecture about what this process will yield for any term of the sequence.

22. Which one of the following is the *exact* value of the golden ratio?

A. $\dfrac{1 + \sqrt{5}}{2}$ **B.** $\dfrac{1 - \sqrt{5}}{2}$ **C.** 1.6   **D.** 1.618

23. Briefly state what Fermat's Last Theorem says, and describe the circumstances of its proof, including the approximate time interval involved.

24. Write a brief explanation of the acronym GIMPS. Include a definition and several examples of the term represented by the letters MP.

THE REAL NUMBERS AND THEIR REPRESENTATIONS

6

The 1997 film *Smilla's Sense of Snow* stars Julia Ormond as a brilliant young scientist who has a passion for snow and mathematics. In a conversation, she speaks of her love of numbers.

To me, the number system is like human life. First you have the natural numbers, the ones that are whole and positive, like the numbers of a small child. Consciousness expands and a child discovers longing. Do you know the mathematical expression for longing? Negative numbers, the formalization of the feeling that you're missing something. Then the child discovers the in-between spaces, between stones, between people, between numbers, and that produces fractions. But it's like a kind of madness, because it doesn't even stop there. It never stops. There are numbers that we can't even begin to comprehend. Mathematics is a vast, open landscape....

In this chapter we study the rational and the irrational numbers, which together form the real number system.

221

6.1 REAL NUMBERS, ORDER, AND ABSOLUTE VALUE

Sets of Real Numbers • Order in the Real Numbers • Additive Inverses and Absolute Value • Applications

The Origins of Zero The Mayan Indians of Mexico and Central America had one of the earliest numeration systems that included a symbol for zero. The very early Babylonians had a positional system, but they placed only a space between "digits" to indicate a missing power. When the Greeks absorbed Babylonian astronomy, they used the letter omicron, o, of their alphabet or ō to represent "no power," or "zero." The Greek numeration system was gradually replaced by the Roman numeration system.

The original Hindu word for zero was *sunya*, meaning "void." The Arabs adopted this word as *sifr*, or "vacant." The word *sifr* passed into Latin as *zephirum*, which over the years became *zevero*, *zepiro*, and finally, *zero*.

Sets of Real Numbers

The mathematician Leopold Kronecker (1823–1891) once made the statement, "God made the integers, all the rest is the work of man." The *natural numbers* are those numbers with which we count discrete objects. By including 0 in the set, we obtain the set of *whole numbers*.

Natural Numbers

$\{1, 2, 3, 4, \ldots\}$ is the set of **natural numbers.**

Whole Numbers

$\{0, 1, 2, 3, \ldots\}$ is the set of **whole numbers.**

These numbers, along with many others, can be represented on **number lines** like the one pictured in **Figure 1**. We draw a number line by locating any point on the line and calling it 0. Choose any point to the right of 0 and call it 1. The distance between 0 and 1 gives a unit of measure used to locate other points, as shown in **Figure 1**. The numbers labeled and those continuing in the same way to the right correspond to the set of whole numbers.

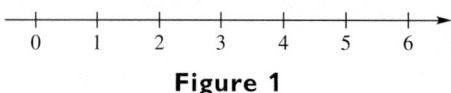

Figure 1

All the whole numbers starting with 1 are located to the right of 0 on the number line. But numbers may also be placed to the left of 0. These numbers, written $-1, -2, -3$, and so on, are shown in **Figure 2**. (The negative sign is used to show that the numbers are located to the *left* of 0.)

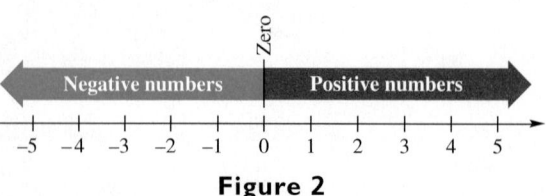

Figure 2

The numbers to the *left* of 0 are **negative numbers.** The numbers to the *right* of 0 are **positive numbers.** Positive numbers and negative numbers are called **signed numbers.** The number 0 itself is neither positive nor negative.

There are many practical applications of negative numbers. For example, temperatures sometimes fall below zero. The lowest temperature ever recorded in meteorological records was $-128.6°F$ at Vostok, Antarctica, on July 22, 1983. Altitudes below sea level can be represented by negative numbers. The shore surrounding the Dead Sea is 1312 feet below sea level. This can be represented as -1312 feet.

The history of the concept of zero is told in *Zero: The Biography of a Dangerous Idea,* by Charles Seife.

The whole numbers, their negatives, and zero make up the set of *integers*.

Integers

$\{\ldots, -3, -2, -1, 0, 1, 2, 3, \ldots\}$ is the set of **integers.**

Not all numbers are integers. For example, $\frac{1}{2}$ is a number *halfway* between the integers 0 and 1. Several numbers that are not integers are *graphed* in **Figure 3**. The **graph** of a number is a point on the number line representing that number. Think of the graph of a set of numbers as a "picture" of the set. All the numbers in **Figure 3** can be written as quotients of integers and are examples of *rational numbers*.

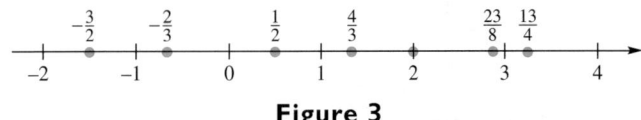

Figure 3

An integer, such as 2, is also a rational number. This is true because $2 = \frac{2}{1}$.

Rational Numbers

$\{x \mid x$ is a quotient of two integers, with denominator not equal to $0\}$ is the set of **rational numbers.**

(Read the part in the braces as "the set of all numbers x such that x is a quotient of two integers, with denominator not equal to 0.")

The set symbolism used in the definition of rational numbers,

$$\{x \mid x \text{ has a certain property}\},$$

is called **set-builder notation.** This notation is convenient to use when it is not possible, or practical, to list all the elements of the set.

There are other numbers on the number line that are not rational. For example, a square that measures one unit on a side has a diagonal whose length is the square root of 2, written $\sqrt{2}$. See **Figure 4**. It will be shown later that $\sqrt{2}$ cannot be written as a quotient of integers. Because of this, $\sqrt{2}$ is an *irrational number.*

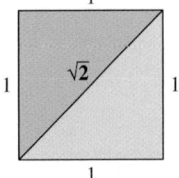

Figure 4

Irrational Numbers

$\{x \mid x$ is a number on the number line that is not rational$\}$ is the set of **irrational numbers.**

Irrational numbers include $\sqrt{3}$, $\sqrt{7}$, $-\sqrt{10}$, and π, which is the ratio of the distance around a circle (its *circumference*) to the distance across it (its *diameter*). All numbers that can be represented by points on the number line (the union of the sets of rational and irrational numbers) are called *real numbers*.

Real Numbers

$\{x \mid x$ is a number that can be represented by a point on the number line$\}$ is the set of **real numbers.**

Real numbers can be written as decimal numbers. Any rational number can be written as a decimal that will come to an end (terminate), or repeat in a fixed "block" of digits. For example, $\frac{2}{5} = 0.4$ and $\frac{27}{100} = 0.27$ are rational numbers with terminating decimals; $\frac{1}{3} = 0.3333\ldots$ and $\frac{3}{11} = 0.27272727\ldots$ are repeating decimals.

The decimal representation of an irrational number will neither terminate nor repeat. Decimal representations of rational and irrational numbers will be discussed further later in this chapter.

Figure 5 illustrates two ways to represent the relationships among the various sets of real numbers.

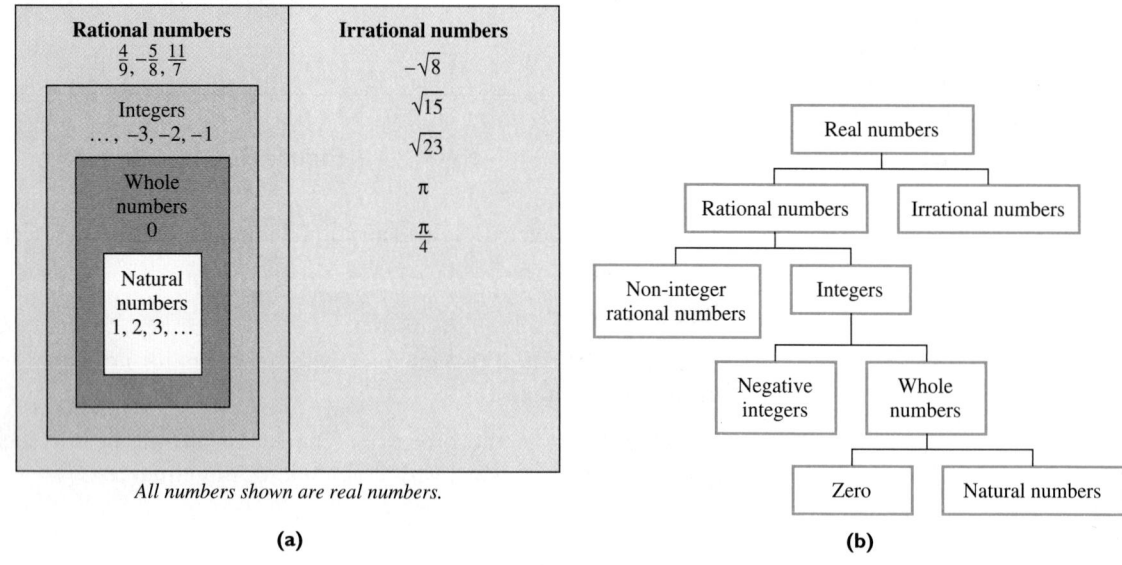

All numbers shown are real numbers.

(a)

(b)

Figure 5

▌▌ **EXAMPLE 1** Identifying Elements of a Set of Numbers

List the numbers in the set that belong to each set of numbers.

$$\left\{ -5, -\frac{2}{3}, 0, \sqrt{2}, \frac{13}{4}, 5, 5.8 \right\}$$

(a) natural numbers   **(b)** whole numbers   **(c)** integers

(d) rational numbers   **(e)** irrational numbers   **(f)** real numbers

SOLUTION

(a) The only natural number in the set is 5.

(b) The whole numbers consist of the natural numbers and 0. So, the elements of the set that are whole numbers are 0 and 5.

(c) The integers in the set are -5, 0, and 5.

(d) The rational numbers are $-5, -\frac{2}{3}, 0, \frac{13}{4}, 5$, and 5.8, because each of these numbers *can* be written as the quotient of two integers. For example, $5.8 = \frac{58}{10} = \frac{29}{5}$.

(e) The only irrational number in the set is $\sqrt{2}$.

(f) All the numbers in the set are real numbers. ▌▌▌

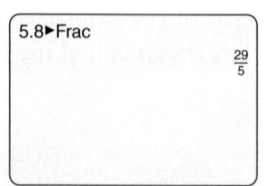

The TI-83/84 Plus calculator will convert a decimal to a fraction. See **Example 1(d).**

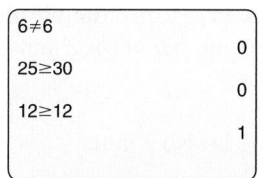

7 < 8
              1
8 > 2
              1
5 ≤ 9
              1

The calculator returns a 1 for each of these statements of inequality, signifying that each is true.

The symbol for equality, **=**, was first introduced by the Englishman Robert Recorde in his 1557 algebra text *The Whetstone of Witte.* He used two parallel line segments, because, he claimed, no two things can be more equal.

The symbols for order relationships, **<** and **>**, were first used by Thomas Harriot (1560–1621), another Englishman. These symbols were not immediately adopted by other mathematicians.

Order in the Real Numbers

Suppose that a and b represent two real numbers. If their graphs on the number line are the same point, they are **equal.** If the graph of a lies to the left of b, a **is less than** b, and if the graph of a lies to the right of b, a **is greater than** b. The **law of trichotomy** says that for two numbers a and b, one and only one of the following is true.

$$a = b, \quad a < b, \quad \text{or} \quad a > b$$

When read from left to right, the symbol $<$ means "is less than."

$$7 < 8 \quad \text{7 is less than 8.}$$

The symbol $>$ means "is greater than."

$$8 > 2 \quad \text{8 is greater than 2.}$$

Notice that the symbol always points to the lesser number.

Lesser number ⟶ $8 < 15$

The symbol $\leq$ means "is less than or equal to."

$$5 \leq 9 \quad \text{5 is less than or equal to 9.}$$

This statement is true, since $5 < 9$ is true. *If either the $<$ part or the $=$ part is true, then the inequality $\leq$ is true.* Also, $8 \leq 8$ is true since $8 = 8$ is true. But it is not true that $13 \leq 9$ because neither $13 < 9$ nor $13 = 9$ is true.

The symbol $\geq$ means "is greater than or equal to."

$$9 \geq 5 \quad \text{9 is greater than or equal to 5.}$$

This statement is true because $9 > 5$ is true.

■■ **EXAMPLE 2** Comparing Real Numbers

Determine whether each statement is *true* or *false.*

(a) $6 \neq 6$ **(b)** $5 < 19$ **(c)** $15 \leq 20$ **(d)** $25 \geq 30$ **(e)** $12 \geq 12$

6 ≠ 6
              0
25 ≥ 30
              0
12 ≥ 12
              1

The inequalities in **Example 2(a) and (d)** are false, as signified by the 0. The statement in **Example 2(e)** is true.

SOLUTION

(a) The statement $6 \neq 6$ is false, because 6 *is equal to* 6.

(b) Since 5 is indeed less than 19, this statement is true.

(c) The statement $15 \leq 20$ is true, since $15 < 20$.

(d) Both $25 > 30$ and $25 = 30$ are false, so $25 \geq 30$ is false.

(e) Since $12 = 12$, the statement $12 \geq 12$ is true.   ■ ■ ■

Additive Inverses and Absolute Value

For any nonzero real number x, there is exactly one number on the number line the same distance from 0 as x but on the opposite side of 0. In **Figure 6**, the numbers 3 and -3 are the same distance from 0 but are on opposite sides of 0. Thus, 3 and -3 are called **additive inverses, negatives,** or **opposites,** of each other.

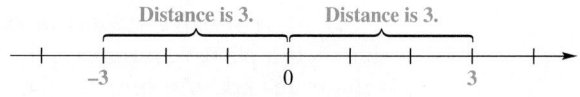

Figure 6

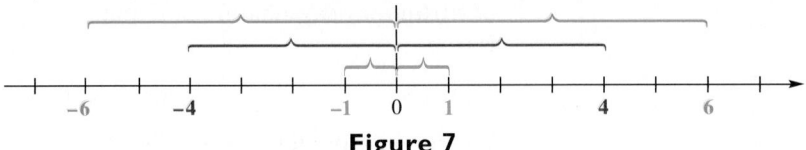

The TI-83/84 Plus distinguishes between the negative symbol (⁻) and the operation of subtraction.

The additive inverse of the number 0 is 0 itself. This makes 0 the only real number that is its own additive inverse. Other additive inverses occur in pairs. For example, 4 and −4, and 5 and −5, are additive inverses of each other. Several pairs of additive inverses are shown in **Figure 7**.

Figure 7

The additive inverse of a number can be indicated by writing the symbol − in front of the number. With this symbol, the additive inverse of 7 is written −7. The additive inverse of −4 is written −(−4) and can be read "the opposite of −4" or "the negative of −4." **Figure 7** suggests that 4 is an additive inverse of −4. Since a number can have only one additive inverse, the symbols 4 and −(−4) must represent the same number, which means that

$$-(-4) = 4.$$

Double Negative Rule

For any real number x, the following is true.

$$-(-x) = x$$

Table 1 shows several numbers and their additive inverses. An important property of additive inverses will be studied later in this chapter:

$$a + (-a) = (-a) + a = 0, \quad \text{for all real numbers } a.$$

As mentioned above, additive inverses are numbers that are the same distance from 0 (but in opposite directions) on the number line. See **Figure 7**. This idea can also be expressed by saying that a number and its additive inverse have the same absolute value. The **absolute value** of a real number can be defined as the distance between 0 and the number on the number line.

The symbol for the absolute value of the number x is $|x|$, read **"the absolute value of x."** For example, the distance between 2 and 0 on the number line is 2 units, so

$$|2| = 2.$$

Because the distance between −2 and 0 on the number line is also 2 units,

$$|-2| = 2.$$

Since distance is a physical measurement, which is never negative, ***the absolute value of a number is never negative.*** Since 0 is a distance of 0 units from 0, $|0| = 0.$

Table 1

Number	Additive Inverse
−4	−(−4) or 4
0	0
19	−19
$-\dfrac{2}{3}$	$\dfrac{2}{3}$

Formal Definition of Absolute Value

For any real number x, the absolute value of x is defined as follows.

$$|x| = \begin{cases} x & \text{if } x \geq 0 \\ -x & \text{if } x < 0 \end{cases}$$

If x is a positive number or 0, then its absolute value is x itself. For example, since 8 is a positive number, $|8| = 8$. ***If x is a negative number, then its absolute value is the additive inverse of x.*** For example, if $x = -9$, then $|-9| = -(-9) = 9$, since the additive inverse of −9 is 9.

The formal definition of absolute value can be confusing if it is not read carefully. The "$-x$" in the second part of the definition *does not* represent a negative number. Since x is negative in the second part, $-x$ represents the opposite of a negative number, that is, a positive number.

■■■ **EXAMPLE 3** Using Absolute Value

Simplify by finding the absolute value.

(a) $|5|$ **(b)** $|-5|$ **(c)** $-|5|$

(d) $-|-14|$ **(e)** $|8-2|$ **(f)** $-|8-2|$

SOLUTION

(a) $|5| = 5$ **(b)** $|-5| = -(-5) = 5$

(c) $-|5| = -(5) = -5$ **(d)** $-|-14| = -(14) = -14$

(e) $|8-2| = |6| = 6$ **(f)** $-|8-2| = -|6| = -6$ ■■■

Example 3(e) shows that absolute value bars also serve as grouping symbols. *Perform any operations that appear inside absolute value symbols before finding the absolute value.*

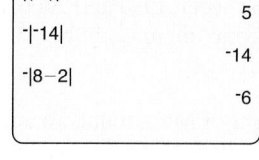

This screen supports the results of
Example 3(b), (d), and (f).

Applications

■■■ **EXAMPLE 4** Interpreting Change Using a Table

The projected annual rates of change in employment (in percent) in some of the fastest growing and in some of the most rapidly declining industries from 2002 through 2012 are shown in **Table 2**. What industry in the list is expected to see the greatest change? the least change?

Table 2	
Industry (2002–2012)	**Annual Rate of Change (in percent)**
Software publishers	5.3
Care services for the elderly	4.5
Child day-care services	3.6
Cut-and-sew apparel manufacturing	−12.2
Fabric mills	−5.9
Metal ore mining	−4.8

Source: U.S. Bureau of Labor Statistics.

SOLUTION

We want the greatest *change,* without regard to whether the change is an increase or a decrease. Look for the number in the list with the greatest absolute value. That number is found in cut-and-sew apparel manufacturing, since

$$|-12.2| = 12.2.$$

Similarly, the least change is in the child day-care services industry:

$$|3.6| = 3.6.$$ ■■■

6.1 EXERCISES

Give a number that satisfies the given condition.

1. An integer between 4.5 and 5.5

2. A rational number between 2.8 and 2.9

3. A whole number that is not positive and is less than 1

4. A whole number greater than 4.5

5. An irrational number that is between $\sqrt{13}$ and $\sqrt{15}$

6. A real number that is neither negative nor positive

Decide whether each statement is true *or* false.

7. Every natural number is positive.

8. Every whole number is positive.

9. Every integer is a rational number.

10. Every rational number is a real number.

List all numbers from each set that are **(a)** *natural numbers;* **(b)** *whole numbers;* **(c)** *integers;* **(d)** *rational numbers;* **(e)** *irrational numbers;* **(f)** *real numbers.*

11. $\left\{ -9, -\sqrt{7}, -1\frac{1}{4}, -\frac{3}{5}, 0, \sqrt{5}, 3, 5.9, 7 \right\}$

12. $\left\{ -5.3, -5, -\sqrt{3}, -1, -\frac{1}{9}, 0, 1.2, 1.8, 3, \sqrt{11} \right\}$

13. Explain the different sets of numbers introduced in this section, and give an example of each kind.

14. What two possible situations exist for the decimal representation of a rational number?

Use an integer to express each number in boldface print representing a change or measurement in the following applications.

15. **Height of the New York Times Tower** The New York Times Tower is **1046** feet high. (*Source:* Council on Tall Buildings and Urban Habitat.)

16. **Population of North Dakota** Between 1990 and 2000, the population of North Dakota increased by **3400**. (*Source:* U.S. Census Bureau.)

17. **Height of Mt. Arenal** The height of Mt. Arenal, an active volcano in Costa Rica, is **5436** feet above sea level. (*Source: The New York Times Almanac.*)

18. **Boiling Point of Chlorine** The boiling point of chlorine is approximately **30**° below 0° Fahrenheit.

19. **Melting Point of Fluorine** The melting point of fluorine gas is **220**° below 0° Celsius.

20. **Population of D.C.** Between 1990 and 2000, the population of the District of Columbia decreased by **31,841**. (*Source:* U.S. Census Bureau.)

21. **Windchill** When the wind speed is **30** miles per hour and the actual temperature is **15**° Fahrenheit, the windchill factor is **5**° below 0° Fahrenheit.

22. **Elevation of New Orleans** The city of New Orleans lies **8** feet below sea level. (*Source:* U.S. Geological Survey, *Elevations and Distances in the United States.*)

23. **Depths and Heights of Seas and Mountains** The chart gives selected depths and heights of bodies of water and mountains.

Bodies of Water	Average Depth in Feet (as a negative number)	Mountains	Altitude in Feet (as a positive number)
Pacific Ocean	−12,925	McKinley	20,320
South China Sea	−4802	Point Success	14,150
Gulf of California	−2375	Matlalcueyetl	14,636
Caribbean Sea	−8448	Ranier	14,410
Indian Ocean	−12,598	Steele	16,644

Source: The World Almanac and Book of Facts.

(a) List the bodies of water in order, starting with the deepest and ending with the shallowest.

(b) List the mountains in order, starting with the lowest and ending with the highest.

(c) *True or false:* The absolute value of the depth of the Pacific Ocean is greater than the absolute value of the depth of the Indian Ocean.

(d) *True or false:* The absolute value of the depth of the Gulf of California is greater than the absolute value of the depth of the Caribbean Sea.

24. *Percent Change* The graph shows the percent change in domestic car sales from January 2004 to January 2005 for various automakers.

(a) Which automaker had the greatest change in sales? What was that change?

(b) Which automaker had the least change in sales? What was the change?

(c) *True* or *false:* The absolute value of the percent change for Ford was greater than the absolute value of the percent change for General Motors.

(d) *True* or *false:* The percent change for Toyota was more than four times greater than the percent change for Mazda.

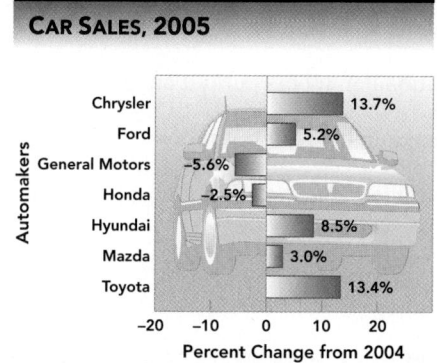

CAR SALES, 2005

Chrysler 13.7%
Ford 5.2%
General Motors −5.6%
Honda −2.5%
Hyundai 8.5%
Mazda 3.0%
Toyota 13.4%

Percent Change from 2004

Source: Chicago Tribune.

Graph each group of numbers on a number line.

25. −2, −6, −4, 3, 4

26. −5, −3, −2, 0, 4

27. $\frac{1}{4}, 2\frac{1}{2}, -3\frac{4}{5}, -4, -1\frac{5}{8}$

28. $5\frac{1}{4}, 4\frac{5}{9}, -2\frac{1}{3}, 0, -3\frac{2}{5}$

29. Match each expression in Column I with its value in Column II. Some choices in Column II may not be used.

I	II
(a) $\|-7\|$	**A.** 7
(b) $-(-7)$	**B.** −7
(c) $-\|-7\|$	**C.** neither A nor B
(d) $-\|-(-7)\|$	**D.** both A and B

30. Fill in the blanks with the correct values: The opposite of −2 is ____, while the absolute value of −2 is ____. The additive inverse of −2 is ____, while the additive inverse of the absolute value of −2 is ____.

Find **(a)** *the additive inverse (or opposite) of each number and* **(b)** *the absolute value of each number.*

31. −2   **32.** −8

33. 6   **34.** 11

35. 7 − 4   **36.** 8 − 3

37. 7 − 7   **38.** 3 − 3

39. Use the results of **Exercises 35 and 36** to complete the following: If $a - b > 0$, then the absolute value of $a - b$ in terms of a and b is ____.

40. Look at **Exercises 37 and 38** and use the results to complete the following: If $a - b = 0$, then the absolute value of $a - b$ is ____.

Select the lesser of the two given numbers.

41. −12, −4   **42.** −9, −14

43. −8, −1   **44.** −15, −16

45. 3, $\|-4\|$ **46.** 5, $\|-2\|$

47. $\|-3\|, \|-4\|$ **48.** $\|-8\|, \|-9\|$

49. $-\|-6\|, -\|-4\|$

50. $-\|-2\|, -\|-3\|$

51. $\|5 - 3\|, \|6 - 2\|$

52. $\|7 - 2\|, \|8 - 1\|$

Decide whether each statement is true *or* false.

53. $6 > -(-2)$ **54.** $-8 > -(-2)$

55. $-4 \leq -(-5)$ **56.** $-6 \leq -(-3)$

57. $\|-6\| < \|-9\|$ **58.** $\|-12\| < \|-20\|$

59. $-\|8\| > \|-9\|$ **60.** $-\|12\| > \|-15\|$

61. $\|-5\| \geq -\|-9\|$ **62.** $-\|-12\| \leq -\|-15\|$

63. $\|6 - 5\| \geq \|6 - 2\|$ **64.** $\|13 - 8\| \leq \|7 - 4\|$

65. *Population Change* The table shows the percent change in population from 2000 through 2006 for selected states.

(a) Which state had the greatest change in population? What was this change? Was it an increase or a decrease?

State	Percent Change
Alabama	3.4
Iowa	1.9
Louisiana	−4.1
Michigan	1.6
North Dakota	−1.0
West Virginia	0.6

Source: U.S. Census Bureau.

(b) Which state had the least change in population? What was this change? Was it an increase or a decrease?

66. *Balance of Trade* The table gives the net trade balance, in millions of dollars, for selected U.S. trade partners for January 2006.

Country	Trade Balance (in millions of dollars)
India	−1257
China	−17,911
Netherlands	756
France	−85
Turkey	−78

Source: U.S. Census Bureau.

A negative balance means that imports to the United States exceeded exports from the United States, while a positive balance means that exports exceeded imports.

(a) Which country had the greatest discrepancy between exports and imports? Explain.

(b) Which country had the least discrepancy between exports and imports? Explain.

67. *Comparing Employment Data* Refer to the table in Example 4. Of the fabric mills and software publishing industries, which annual employment rate shows the greater change (without regard to sign)?

68. Students often say "Absolute value is always positive." Is this true? If not, explain why.

Give three numbers between −6 and 6 that satisfy each given condition.

69. Positive real numbers but not integers

70. Real numbers but not positive numbers

71. Real numbers but not whole numbers

72. Rational numbers but not integers

73. Real numbers but not rational numbers

74. Rational numbers but not negative numbers

6.2 OPERATIONS, PROPERTIES, AND APPLICATIONS OF REAL NUMBERS

Operations • Order of Operations • Properties of Addition and Multiplication of Real Numbers • Applications of Real Numbers

Operations

The result of adding two numbers is called their **sum.** The numbers being added are called **addends** (or **terms**).

Adding Real Numbers

Like Signs Add two numbers with the *same* sign by adding their absolute values. The sign of the sum (either + or −) is the same as the sign of the two numbers.

Unlike Signs Add two numbers with *different* signs by subtracting the lesser absolute value from the greater to find the absolute value of the sum. The sum is positive if the positive number has the greater absolute value. The sum is negative if the negative number has the greater absolute value.

For example, to add −12 and −8, first find their absolute values.

$$|-12| = 12 \quad \text{and} \quad |-8| = 8$$

Since −12 and −8 have the *same* sign, add their absolute values: 12 + 8 = 20. Give the sum the sign of the two numbers. Since both numbers are negative, the sum is negative and

$$-12 + (-8) = -20.$$

Find $-17 + 11$ by subtracting the absolute values, because these numbers have different signs.

$$|-17| = 17 \quad \text{and} \quad |11| = 11$$
$$17 - 11 = 6$$

Give the result the sign of the number with the larger absolute value.

$$-17 + 11 = -6$$

Negative since $|-17| > |11|$

▮▮ EXAMPLE 1 Adding Signed Numbers

Find each sum.

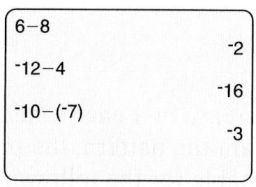

(a) $-6 + (-3)$ **(b)** $-12 + (-4)$ **(c)** $4 + (-1)$

(d) $-9 + 16$ **(e)** $-16 + 12$ **(f)** $-4 + 4$

SOLUTION

(a) $-6 + (-3) = -(6 + 3) = -9$ **(b)** $-12 + (-4) = -(12 + 4) = -16$

(c) $4 + (-1) = 3$ **(d)** $-9 + 16 = 7$

(e) $-16 + 12 = -4$ **(f)** $-4 + 4 = 0$ The sum of additive inverses is 0. ▮▮▮

The calculator supports the results of **Example 1(a), (c), and (e).**

The result of subtracting two numbers is called their **difference.** In $a - b$, a is called the **minuend,** and b is called the **subtrahend.** Compare the two statements below.

$$7 - 5 = 2 \quad \text{and} \quad 7 + (-5) = 2$$

In a similar way, $9 - 3 = 9 + (-3)$. That is, to subtract 3 from 9, add the additive inverse of 3 to 9. These examples suggest the following rule for subtraction.

> ### Definition of Subtraction
>
> For all real numbers a and b,
>
> $$a - b = a + (-b).$$
>
> (Change the sign of the subtrahend and add.)

▮▮ EXAMPLE 2 Subtracting Signed Numbers

Find each difference.

(a) $6 - 8$ **(b)** $-12 - 4$ **(c)** $-10 - (-7)$ **(d)** $15 - (-3)$

SOLUTION

Change to addition.

Change sign of the subtrahend and add.

(a) $6 - 8 = 6 + (-8) = -2$

Change to addition.

Sign is changed.

(b) $-12 - 4 = -12 + (-4) = -16$

The calculator supports the results of **Example 2(a), (b), and (c).**

(c) $-10 - (-7) = -10 + [-(-7)]$ This step can be omitted.

$$= -10 + 7$$
$$= -3$$

(d) $15 - (-3) = 15 + 3 = 18$ ▮▮▮

Practical Arithmetic From the time of Egyptian and Babylonian merchants, practical aspects of arithmetic complemented mystical (or "Pythagorean") tendencies. This was certainly true in the time of **Adam Riese** (1489–1559), a "reckon master" influential when commerce was growing in Northern Europe. He championed new methods of reckoning using Hindu-Arabic numerals and quill pens. (The Roman methods then in common use moved counters on a ruled board.) Riese thus fulfilled Fibonacci's efforts 300 years earlier to supplant Roman numerals and methods.

The result of multiplying two numbers is called their **product.** The two numbers being multiplied are called **factors.** Any rules for multiplication with negative real numbers should be consistent with the usual rules for multiplication of positive real numbers and zero. To inductively obtain a rule for multiplying a positive real number and a negative real number, observe the pattern of products below.

$$4 \cdot 5 = 20$$
$$4 \cdot 4 = 16$$
$$4 \cdot 3 = 12$$
$$4 \cdot 2 = 8$$
$$4 \cdot 1 = 4$$
$$4 \cdot 0 = 0$$
$$4 \cdot (-1) = ?$$

What number must be assigned as the product $4 \cdot (-1)$ so that the pattern is maintained? The numbers just to the left of the equality signs decrease by 1 each time, and the products to the right decrease by 4 each time. To maintain the pattern, the number to the right in the bottom equation must be 4 less than 0, which is -4, so

$$4 \cdot (-1) = -4.$$

The pattern continues with

$$4 \cdot (-2) = -8$$
$$4 \cdot (-3) = -12$$
$$4 \cdot (-4) = -16,$$

and so on. In the same way,

$$-4 \cdot 2 = -8$$
$$-4 \cdot 3 = -12$$
$$-4 \cdot 4 = -16,$$

and so on. A similar observation can be made about the product of two negative real numbers. Look at the pattern that follows.

$$-5 \cdot 4 = -20$$
$$-5 \cdot 3 = -15$$
$$-5 \cdot 2 = -10$$
$$-5 \cdot 1 = -5$$
$$-5 \cdot 0 = 0$$
$$-5 \cdot (-1) = ?$$

The numbers just to the left of the equality signs decrease by 1 each time. The products on the right increase by 5 each time. To maintain the pattern, the product $-5 \cdot (-1)$ must be 5 more than 0, so it seems reasonable for the following to be true.

$$-5 \cdot (-1) = 5$$

Continuing this pattern gives the following.

$$-5 \cdot (-2) = 10$$
$$-5 \cdot (-3) = 15$$
$$-5 \cdot (-4) = 20$$
$$\vdots$$

These observations lead to the following rules for multiplication.

$(+) \cdot (+) = +$
$(-) \cdot (-) = +$
$(+) \cdot (-) = -$
$(-) \cdot (+) = -$

Multiplying Real Numbers

Like Signs Multiply two numbers with the *same* sign by multiplying their absolute values to find the absolute value of the product. The product is positive.

Unlike Signs Multiply two numbers with *different* signs by multiplying their absolute values to find the absolute value of the product. The product is negative.

▮▮ **EXAMPLE 3** Multiplying Signed Numbers

Find each product.

(a) $-9 \cdot 7$ **(b)** $14 \cdot (-5)$ **(c)** $-8 \cdot (-4)$

SOLUTION

(a) $-9 \cdot 7 = -63$ **(b)** $14 \cdot (-5) = -70$ **(c)** $-8 \cdot (-4) = 32$ ▮▮▮

The symbol (∗) represents multiplication on this screen. The display supports the results of **Example 3**.

The result of dividing two numbers is called their **quotient.** In the quotient $a \div b$ (or $\frac{a}{b}$), where $b \neq 0$, a is called the **dividend** (or numerator), and b is called the **divisor** (or denominator). For real numbers a, b, and c,

$$\text{if} \quad \frac{a}{b} = c, \quad \text{then} \quad a = b \cdot c.$$

To illustrate this, consider the quotient $\frac{10}{-2}$. The value of this quotient is obtained by asking, "What number multiplied by -2 gives 10?" From our discussion of multiplication, the answer to this question must be "-5." Therefore,

$$\frac{10}{-2} = -5, \quad \text{because} \quad 10 = -2 \cdot (-5).$$

Similarly, $\qquad \frac{-10}{2} = -5 \quad \text{and} \quad \frac{-10}{-2} = 5.$

These facts, along with the fact that the quotient of two positive numbers is positive, lead to the following rules for division.

$(+)/(+) = +$
$(-)/(-) = +$
$(+)/(-) = -$
$(-)/(+) = -$

Dividing Real Numbers

Like Signs Divide two numbers with the *same* sign by dividing their absolute values to find the absolute value of the quotient. The quotient is positive.

Unlike Signs Divide two numbers with *different* signs by dividing their absolute values to find the absolute value of the quotient. The quotient is negative.

▌▌ **EXAMPLE 4** Dividing Signed Numbers

Find each quotient.

(a) $\dfrac{15}{-5}$ **(b)** $\dfrac{-100}{-25}$ **(c)** $\dfrac{-60}{3}$

SOLUTION

(a) $\dfrac{15}{-5} = -3$ This is true because $-5 \cdot (-3) = 15$.

(b) $\dfrac{-100}{-25} = 4$ **(c)** $\dfrac{-60}{3} = -20$ ▌▌▌

If 0 is divided by a nonzero number, the quotient is 0.

$$\frac{0}{a} = 0, \quad \text{for } a \neq 0$$

This is true because $a \cdot 0 = 0$. However, we cannot divide by 0. There is a good reason for this. Whenever a division is performed, we want to obtain one and only one quotient. Now consider this division problem.

$$\frac{7}{0}$$

We must ask ourselves "What number multiplied by 0 gives 7?" There is no such number, since the product of 0 and any number is zero. Now consider this quotient.

$$\frac{0}{0}$$

There are infinitely many answers to the question, "What number multiplied by 0 gives 0?" Since division by 0 does not yield a *unique* quotient, it is not permitted.

> **Division by Zero**
>
> *Division by 0 is undefined.*

Order of Operations

Given a problem such as $5 + 2 \cdot 3$, should 5 and 2 be added first or should 2 and 3 be multiplied first? When a problem involves more than one operation, we use the following rules for **order of operations.**

> **Order of Operations**
>
> *If parentheses or square brackets are present:*
>
> **Step 1** Work separately above and below any **fraction bar.**
>
> **Step 2** Use the rules below within each set of **parentheses or square brackets.** Start with the innermost set and work outward.
>
> *If no parentheses or brackets are present:*
>
> **Step 1** Apply any **exponents.**
>
> **Step 2** Do any **multiplications or divisions** in the order in which they occur, working from left to right.
>
> **Step 3** Do any **additions or subtractions** in the order in which they occur, working from left to right.

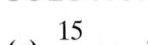

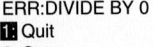

The division operation is represented by a slash (/). This screen supports the results of **Example 4.**

ERR:DIVIDE BY 0
1: Quit
2: Goto

Dividing by zero leads to this message on the TI-83/84 Plus.

5+2*3

What result does the calculator give? The order of operations determines the answer. (See **Example 5(a).**)

The sentence **"Please excuse my dear Aunt Sally"** is often used to help us remember the rule for order of operations. The letters **P, E, M, D, A, S** are the first letters of the words of the sentence, and they stand for *parentheses, exponents, multiply, divide, add, subtract.* (Remember also that M and D have equal priority, as do A and S. Operations with equal priority are performed in order from left to right.)

When evaluating an exponential expression that involves a negative sign, be aware that $(-a)^n$ and $-a^n$ do not necessarily represent the same quantity. For example, if $a = 2$ and $n = 6$,

$$(-2)^6 = (-2)(-2)(-2)(-2)(-2)(-2) = 64 \quad \text{The base is } -2.$$

while

$$-2^6 = -(2 \cdot 2 \cdot 2 \cdot 2 \cdot 2 \cdot 2) = -64. \quad \text{The base is 2.}$$

$(-2)^6$
-2^6
64
-64

Notice the difference in the two expressions. This supports $(-2)^6 \neq -2^6$.

▌▌ EXAMPLE 5 Using the Order of Operations

Use the order of operations to simplify each expression.

(a) $5 + 2 \cdot 3$

(b) $4 \cdot 3^2 + 7 - (2 + 8)$

(c) $\dfrac{2(8 - 12) - 11(4)}{5(-2) - 3}$

(d) -4^4

(e) $(-4)^4$

(f) $(-8)(-3) - [4 - (3 - 6)]$

SOLUTION

(a) $5 + 2 \cdot 3 = 5 + 6 \quad$ Multiply.

$= 11 \quad$ Add.

Be careful!
Multiply first.

(b) $4 \cdot 3^2 + 7 - (2 + 8) = 4 \cdot 3^2 + 7 - 10 \quad$ Work within parentheses first.

3^2 means $3 \cdot 3$, not $3 \cdot 2$.

$= 4 \cdot 9 + 7 - 10 \quad$ Apply the exponent.

$= 36 + 7 - 10 \quad$ Multiply.

$= 43 - 10 \quad$ Add.

$= 33 \quad$ Subtract.

(c) $\dfrac{2(8 - 12) - 11(4)}{5(-2) - 3} = \dfrac{2(-4) - 11(4)}{5(-2) - 3} \quad$ Work separately above and below fraction bar.

$= \dfrac{-8 - 44}{-10 - 3} \quad$ Multiply.

$= \dfrac{-52}{-13} \quad$ Subtract.

$= 4 \quad$ Divide.

(d) $-4^4 = -(4 \cdot 4 \cdot 4 \cdot 4) = -256$

The base is 4, not -4.

(e) $(-4)^4 = (-4)(-4)(-4)(-4) = 256$

The base is -4 here.

$5+2*3$
-4^4
$-8*3-(4-(3-6))$
11
-256
17

The calculator supports the results in
Example 5(a), (d), and (f).

(f) $-8(-3) - [4 - (3 - 6)] = -8(-3) - [4 - (-3)] \quad$ Work within parentheses.

Start here.

$= -8(-3) - [4 + 3] \quad$ Definition of subtraction

$= -8(-3) - 7 \quad$ Work within brackets.

$= 24 - 7 \quad$ Multiply.

$= 17 \quad$ Subtract. ■■■

Properties of Addition and Multiplication of Real Numbers

Properties of Addition and Multiplication

For real numbers a, b, and c, the following properties hold.

Closure Properties	$a + b$ **and** ab **are real numbers.**
Commutative Properties	$a + b = b + a$ $ab = ba$
Associative Properties	$(a + b) + c = a + (b + c)$
	$(ab)c = a(bc)$

Identity Properties

There is a real number 0 such that
$$a + 0 = a \quad \text{and} \quad 0 + a = a.$$

There is a real number 1 such that
$$a \cdot 1 = a \quad \text{and} \quad 1 \cdot a = a.$$

Inverse Properties

For each real number a, there is a single real number $-a$ such that
$$a + (-a) = 0 \quad \text{and} \quad (-a) + a = 0.$$

For each nonzero real number a, there is a single real number $\frac{1}{a}$ such that
$$a \cdot \frac{1}{a} = 1 \quad \text{and} \quad \frac{1}{a} \cdot a = 1.$$

Distributive Property of Multiplication with Respect to Addition

$$a(b + c) = ab + ac$$
$$(b + c)a = ba + ca$$

The set of real numbers is said to be closed with respect to the operations of addition and multiplication. This means that the sum of two real numbers and the product of two real numbers are themselves real numbers. The commutative properties state that two real numbers may be added or multiplied in either order without affecting the result. The associative properties allow us to group terms or factors in any manner we wish without affecting the result.

The number 0 is the **identity element for addition.** It may be added to any real number to obtain that real number. Similarly, 1 is the **identity element for multiplication.** Multiplying a real number by 1 will always yield that real number.

Each real number a has an **additive inverse,** $-a$, such that the sum of a and its additive inverse is the additive identity element 0. Each nonzero real number a has a **multiplicative inverse,** or **reciprocal,** $\frac{1}{a}$, such that the product of a and its multiplicative inverse is the multiplicative identity element 1.

The distributive property allows us to change certain products to sums and certain sums to products.

```
X+Y=Y+X
                     1
X+(Y+Z)=(X+Y)+Z
                     1
5(X+Y)=5X+5Y
                     1
```

No matter what values are stored in X, Y, and Z, the commutative, associative, and distributive properties assure us that these statements are true.

EXAMPLE 6   Identifying Properties of Addition and Multiplication

Identify the property of addition or multiplication illustrated in each statement.

(a) $5 + 7$ is a real number.

(b) $5 + (6 + 8) = (5 + 6) + 8$

(c) $8 + 0 = 8$

(d) $-4\left(-\dfrac{1}{4}\right) = 1$

(e) $4 + (3 + 9) = 4 + (9 + 3)$

(f) $5(x + y) = 5x + 5y$

SOLUTION

(a) The statement that the sum of two real numbers is also a real number is an example of the *closure property of addition*.

(b) Because the grouping of the terms is different on the two sides of the equation, this illustrates the *associative property of addition*.

(c) Adding 0 to a number yields the number itself. This is an example of the *identity property of addition*.

(d) Multiplying a number by its reciprocal yields 1, and this illustrates the *inverse property of multiplication*.

(e) The order of the addends (terms) 3 and 9 is different, so this is justified by the *commutative property of addition*.

(f) The factor 5 is distributed to the terms *x* and *y*. This is an example of the *distributive property of multiplication with respect to addition*.   ▮▮▮

Applications of Real Numbers

The usefulness of negative numbers can be seen by considering situations that arise in everyday life. For example, we need negative numbers to express the temperatures on January days in Anchorage, Alaska, where they often drop below zero. The phrases "in the red" and "in the black" mean losing money and making money, respectively. These descriptions go back to the days when bookkeepers used red ink to represent losses and black ink to represent gains.

PROBLEM-SOLVING HINT When problems deal with gains and losses, the gains may be interpreted as positive numbers and the losses as negative numbers. Temperatures below 0° are negative, and those above 0° are positive. Altitudes above sea level are considered positive, and those below sea level are considered negative.

▮▮ **EXAMPLE 7**   Analyzing Change in Annual Returns

Figure 8 shows annual returns in percent for Class A shares of the AIM Charter Fund.

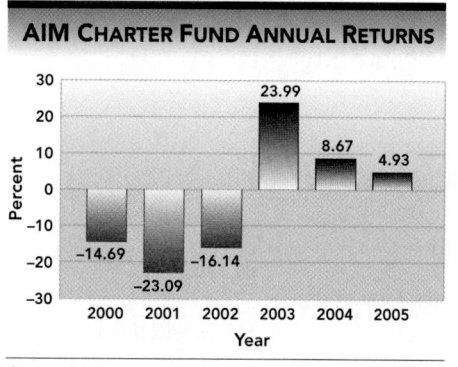

AIM CHARTER FUND ANNUAL RETURNS

Source: AIM.

Figure 8

Use a signed number to represent the change in the percent returns, shown in **Figure 8** on the preceding page, for the following years.

(a) 2002 to 2003   **(b)** 2003 to 2004

SOLUTION

(a) To find this change, we start with the percent from 2003 and subtract from it the percent from 2002.

$$23.99 \quad - \quad (-16.14) \quad = \quad \textbf{40.13}$$

The 2003 percent   The 2002 percent   A positive number indicates an increase.

(b) Use the same procedure as in part (a).

$$8.67 \quad - \quad 23.99 \quad = \quad \boldsymbol{-15.32}$$

The 2004 percent   The 2003 percent   A negative number indicates a decrease. ▮▮▮

▮▮ **EXAMPLE 8** Determining Difference of Temperatures
_____

The record high temperature in the United States was 134° Fahrenheit, recorded at Death Valley, California, in 1913. The record low was −80°F, at Prospect Creek, Alaska, in 1971. See **Figure 9**. How much greater was the highest temperature than the lowest temperature? (*Source: The World Almanac and Book of Facts.*)

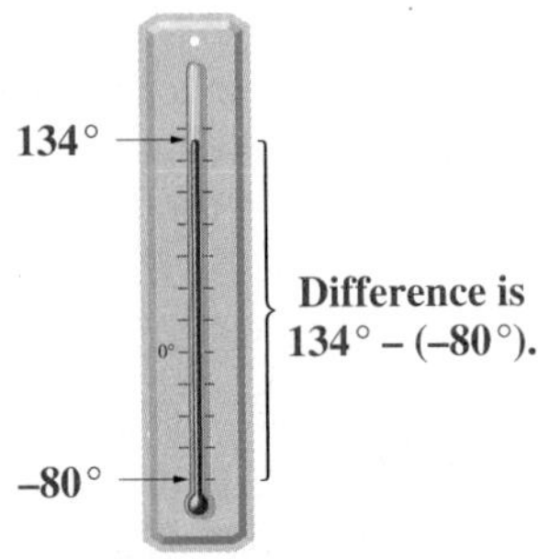

134° ——

Difference is 134° − (−80°).

0° —

−80° ——

Figure 9

SOLUTION

We must subtract the lower temperature from the higher temperature.

$$134 - (-80) = 134 + 80 \quad \text{Use the definition of subtraction.}$$
$$= 214 \quad \text{Add.}$$

The difference of the two temperatures is 214°F. ▮▮▮

6.2 EXERCISES

Fill in each blank with the correct response.

1. The sum of two negative numbers will always be a _____ number.
    (positive/negative)

2. The sum of a number and its opposite will always be ____.

3. To simplify the expression $8 + [-2 + (-3 + 5)]$, I should begin by adding _____ and _____, according to the rules for order of operations.

4. If I am adding a positive number and a negative number, and the negative number has the larger absolute value, the sum will be a_____ number.
    (positive/negative)

5. Explain in words how to add signed numbers. Consider the various cases and give examples.

6. Explain in words how to multiply signed numbers.

Perform the indicated operations, using the order of operations as necessary.

7. $-12 + (-8)$ **8.** $-5 + (-2)$

9. $12 + (-16)$ **10.** $-6 + 17$

11. $-12 - (-1)$ **12.** $-3 - (-8)$

13. $-5 + 11 + 3$ **14.** $-9 + 16 + 5$

15. $12 - (-3) - (-5)$ **16.** $15 - (-6) - (-8)$

17. $-9 - (-11) - (4 - 6)$

18. $-4 - (-13) + (-5 + 10)$

19. $(-12)(-2)$ **20.** $(-3)(-5)$

21. $9(-12)(-4)(-1)(3)$ **22.** $-5(-17)(2)(-2)(4)$

23. $\dfrac{-18}{-3}$ **24.** $\dfrac{-100}{-50}$ **25.** $\dfrac{36}{-6}$

26. $\dfrac{52}{-13}$ **27.** $\dfrac{0}{12}$ **28.** $\dfrac{0}{-7}$

29. $-6 + [5 - (3 + 2)]$ **30.** $-8[4 + (7 - 8)]$

31. $-4 - 3(-2) + 5^2$ **32.** $-6 - 5(-8) + 3^2$

33. $(-8 - 5)(-2 - 1)$ **34.** $\dfrac{(-10 + 4) \cdot (-3)}{-7 - 2}$

35. $-8(-2) - [(4^2) + (7 - 3)]$

36. $-7(-3) - [2^3 - (3 - 4)]$

37. $\dfrac{(-6 + 3) \cdot (-4)}{-5 - 1}$

38. $\dfrac{2(-5 + 3)}{-2^2} - \dfrac{(-3^2 + 2)(3)}{3 - (-4)}$

39. $\dfrac{2(-5) + (-3)(-2^2)}{-3^2 + 9}$ **40.** $\dfrac{3(-4) + (-5)(-2)}{2^3 - 2 + (-6)}$

41. $-\dfrac{1}{4}[3(-5) + 7(-5) + 1(-2)]$

42. $\dfrac{5 - 3\left(\dfrac{-5 - 9}{-7}\right) - 6}{-9 - 11 + 3 \cdot 7}$

43. Which of the following expressions are undefined?

  A. $\dfrac{8}{0}$ **B.** $\dfrac{9}{6 - 6}$ **C.** $\dfrac{4 - 4}{5 - 5}$ **D.** $\dfrac{0}{-1}$

44. If you have no money in your pocket and you divide it equally among your three siblings, how much does each get? Use this situation to explain division of zero by a positive integer.

Identify the property illustrated by each statement.

45. $6 + 9 = 9 + 6$ **46.** $8 \cdot 4 = 4 \cdot 8$

47. $9 + (-9) = 0$ **48.** $12 + 0 = 12$

49. $9 \cdot 1 = 9$ **50.** $\left(\dfrac{1}{-3}\right) \cdot (-3) = 1$

51. $7 + (2 + 5) = (7 + 2) + 5$

52. $(3 \cdot 5) \cdot 4 = 4 \cdot (3 \cdot 5)$

53. $0 + 283 = 283$

54. $6 \cdot (4 \cdot 2) = (6 \cdot 4) \cdot 2$

55. $2 \cdot (4 + 3) = 2 \cdot 4 + 2 \cdot 3$

56. $9 \cdot 6 + 9 \cdot 8 = 9 \cdot (6 + 8)$

57. $0 = -8 + 8$

58. $19 + 12$ is a real number.

59. $19 \cdot 12$ is a real number.

60. One of the authors received an email message from an old friend, Frank Capek. Frank said that his grandson had to evaluate $9 + 15 \div 3$. Frank and his wife, Barbara, said that the answer is 8, but the grandson said that the correct answer is 14. The grandson's reasoning is "There is a rule called the Order of Process so that you proceed from right to left rather than from left to right."

  (a) What is the correct answer?

  (b) Is the grandson's reasoning correct? Explain.

Exercises 61–68 are designed to explore the properties of real numbers in further detail.

61. **(a)** Evaluate $6 - 8$ and $8 - 6$.

  (b) By the results of part (a), we may conclude that subtraction is not a(n) _____ operation.

  (c) Are there *any* real numbers a and b for which $a - b = b - a$? If so, give an example.

62. **(a)** Evaluate $4 \div 8$ and $8 \div 4$.

  (b) By the results of part (a), we may conclude that division is not a(n) _____ operation.

  (c) Are there *any* real numbers a and b for which $a \div b = b \div a$? If so, give an example.

63. Many everyday occurrences can be thought of as operations that have opposites or inverses. For example, the inverse operation for "going to sleep" is "waking up." For each of the given activities, specify its inverse activity.

  (a) cleaning up your room

  (b) earning money

  (c) increasing the volume on your MP3 player

64. Many everyday activities are commutative; that is, the order in which they occur does not affect the outcome. For example, "putting on your shirt" and "putting on your pants" are commutative operations. Decide whether the given activities are commutative.

  (a) putting on your shoes; putting on your socks

  (b) getting dressed; taking a shower

  (c) combing your hair; brushing your teeth

65. The following conversation actually took place between one of the authors of this text and his son, Jack, when Jack was four years old.

DADDY: "Jack, what is $3 + 0$?"
JACK: "3"
DADDY: "Jack, what is $4 + 0$?"
JACK: "4 . . . and Daddy, *string* plus zero equals *string!*"
What property of addition of real numbers did Jack recognize?

66. The phrase *defective merchandise counter* is an example of a phrase that can have different meanings depending upon how the words are grouped (think of the associative properties). For example, (*defective merchandise*) *counter* is a location at which we would return an item that does not work, while *defective* (*merchandise counter*) is a broken place where items are bought and sold. For each of the following phrases, determine why the associative property does not hold.

(a) difficult test question

(b) woman fearing husband

(c) man biting dog

67. The distributive property holds for multiplication with respect to addition. Does the distributive property hold for addition with respect to multiplication? That is, is $a + (b \cdot c) = (a + b) \cdot (a + c)$ true for all values of a, b, and c? (*Hint:* Let $a = 2$, $b = 3$, and $c = 4$.)

68. Suppose that a student shows you the following work.
$$-3(4 - 6) = -3(4) - 3(6) = -12 - 18 = -30$$
The student has made a very common **error** in applying the distributive property. Explain the student's mistake, and work the problem correctly.

Each expression in Exercises 69–76 is equal to either 81 *or* −81. *Decide which of these is the correct value.*

69. -3^4 **70.** $-(3^4)$ **71.** $(-3)^4$

72. $-(-3^4)$ **73.** $-(-3)^4$ **74.** $[-(-3)]^4$

75. $-[-(-3)]^4$ **76.** $-[-(-3^4)]$

77. *Federal Budget Outlays* The bar graph shows federal budget outlays for the U.S. Treasury Department for the years 2006 through 2009. Use a signed number to represent the change in outlay for each time period.

(a) 2006 to 2007

(b) 2007 to 2008

(c) 2008 to 2009

(d) 2006 to 2009

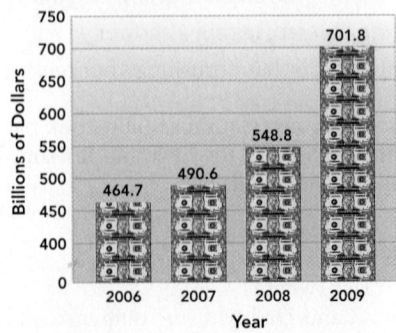

Source: U.S. Office of Management and Budget.

78. *Heights of Mountains and Depths of Trenches* The chart shows the heights in feet of some selected mountains and the depths in feet (as negative numbers) of some selected ocean trenches.

Mountain	Height	Trench	Depth
Foraker	17,400	Philippine	−32,995
Wilson	14,246	Cayman	−24,721
Pikes Peak	14,110	Java	−23,376

Source: The World Almanac and Book of Facts.

(a) How much higher is Mt. Foraker than the bottom of the Philippine Trench?

(b) What is the difference between the height of Pikes Peak and the depth of the Java Trench?

(c) How much deeper is the Cayman Trench than the Java Trench?

(d) How much deeper is the Philippine Trench than the Cayman Trench?

79. *Social Security Finances* The table shows Social Security tax revenue and cost of benefits (in billions of dollars).

Year	Tax Revenue	Cost of Benefits
2000	538	409
2010*	916	710
2020*	1479	1405
2030*	2041	2542

*Projected
Source: Social Security Board of Trustees.

(a) Find the difference between Social Security tax revenue and cost of benefits for each year shown in the table.

(b) Interpret your answer for 2030.

80. *House of Representatives* Based on census population projections for 2020, New York will lose 5 seats in the U.S. House of Representatives, Pennsylvania will lose 4 seats, and Ohio will lose 3. Write a signed number that represents the total projected change in the number of seats for these three states. (*Source:* Population Reference Bureau.)

81. *House of Representatives* Michigan is projected to lose 3 seats in the U.S. House of Representatives and Illinois 2 in 2020. The states projected to gain the most seats are California with 9, Texas with 5, Florida with 3, Georgia with 2, and Arizona with 2. Write a signed number that represents the algebraic sum of these changes. (*Source:* Population Reference Bureau.)

82. *Checking Account Balance* Christine MacKrell's checking account balance is $54.00. She then takes a gamble by writing a check for $89.00. What is her new balance? (Write the balance as a signed number.)

83. *Checking Account Balance* In August, Kimberly Manzi began with a checking account balance of $904.89. Her checks and deposits for August are given below:

Checks	Deposits
$35.84	$85.00
$26.14	$120.76
$3.12	

Assuming no other transactions, what was her account balance at the end of August?

84. *Checking Account Balance* In September, David Lopez began with a checking account balance of $904.89. His checks and deposits for September are given below:

Checks	Deposits
$41.29	$80.59
$13.66	$276.13
$84.40	

Assuming no other transactions, what was his account balance at the end of September?

85. *Difference in Elevations* The top of Mt. Whitney, visible from Death Valley, has an altitude of 14,494 feet above sea level. The bottom of Death Valley is 282 feet below sea level. Using 0 as sea level, find the difference of these two elevations. (*Source: World Almanac and Book of Facts.*)

86. *Altitude of Hikers* The surface, or rim, of a canyon is at altitude 0. On a hike down into the canyon, a party of hikers stops for a rest at 130 meters below the surface. They then descend another 54 meters. What is their new altitude? (Write the altitude as a signed number.)

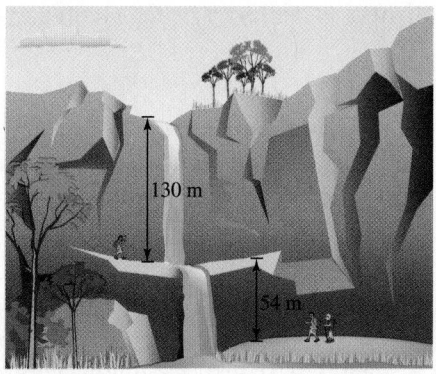

87. *Drastic Temperature Change* On January 23, 1943, the temperature rose 49°F in two minutes in Spearfish, South Dakota. If the starting temperature was −4°F, what was the temperature two minutes later? (*Source: Guinness World Records.*)

88. *Drastic Temperature Change* The greatest change in temperature ever recorded within a 24-hour period occurred in Browning, Montana, on January 23–24, 1916. The temperature fell 100°F from a starting temperature of 44°F. What was the low temperature during this period? (*Source: Guinness World Records.*)

89. *Extreme Temperatures in Alabama* The lowest temperature ever recorded in Alabama was −27°F. The highest temperature ever recorded there was 139°F more than the lowest. What was this highest temperature? (*Source: National Climatic Data Center.*)

90. *Extreme Temperatures in Iowa* The lowest temperature ever recorded in Iowa was −47°F. The highest temperature ever recorded there was 165°F more than the lowest temperature. What was this highest temperature? (*Source: National Climatic Data Center.*)

91. *Low Temperatures in Illinois and Minnesota* The lowest temperature recorded in Illinois was −36°F in 1999. The record low in Minnesota was set in 1996 and was 24°F lower than −36°F. What was the record low in Minnesota? (*Source: The World Almanac and Book of Facts.*)

92. *Low Temperatures in New Mexico and Utah* The lowest temperature ever recorded in New Mexico was −50°F in 1951. The lowest temperature ever recorded in Utah was in 1985 and was 19°F lower than New Mexico's record low. What is the record low temperature for Utah? (*Source: National Climatic Data Center.*)

93. *Breaching of Humpback Whales* Mark and Debbie noticed that one of their favorite whales, "Pineapple," breached 15 feet above the surface of the ocean while her mate cruised 12 feet below the surface. What is the difference between these two levels?

94. *Highest Point in Louisiana* The highest point in Louisiana is Driskill Mountain, at an altitude of 535 feet. The lowest point is at Spanish Fort, 8 feet below sea level. Using zero as sea level, find the difference between these two elevations. (*Source: The World Almanac and Book of Facts.*)

95. *Birth Date of a Greek Mathematician* A certain Greek mathematician was born in 428 B.C. Her father was born 41 years earlier. In what year was her father born?

96. *Birth Date of a Roman Philosopher* A certain Roman philosopher was born in 325 B.C. Her mother was born 35 years earlier. In what year was her mother born?

Home Prices *Median sales prices for existing single-family homes in the United States for the years 2003 through 2007 are shown in the table. Complete the table, determining the change from one year to the next by subtraction.*

	Year	Median Sales Price	Change from Previous Year
	2003	$180,200	
97.	2004	$195,200	
98.	2005	$219,000	
99.	2006	$221,900	
100.	2007	$217,900	

Source: National Association of Realtors.

6.3 RATIONAL NUMBERS AND DECIMAL REPRESENTATION

Definition and the Fundamental Property • Operations with Rational Numbers • Density and the Arithmetic Mean • Decimal Form of Rational Numbers

Definition and the Fundamental Property

The set of real numbers is composed of two important mutually exclusive subsets: the rational numbers and the irrational numbers. (Two sets are *mutually exclusive* if they contain no elements in common.)

Recall from **Section 6.1** that quotients of integers are called **rational numbers.** Think of the rational numbers as being made up of all the fractions (quotients of integers with denominator not equal to zero) and all the integers. Any integer can be written as the quotient of two integers. For example, the integer 9 can be written as the quotient $\frac{9}{1}$, or $\frac{18}{2}$, or $\frac{27}{3}$, and so on. Also, -5 can be expressed as a quotient of integers as $\frac{-5}{1}$ or $\frac{-10}{2}$, and so on. (How can the integer 0 be written as a quotient of integers?)

Benjamin Banneker (1731–1806) spent the first half of his life tending a farm in Maryland. He gained a reputation locally for his mechanical skills and abilities in mathematical problem solving. In 1772 he acquired astronomy books from a neighbor and devoted himself to learning astronomy, observing the skies, and making calculations. In 1789 Banneker joined the team that surveyed what is now the District of Columbia.

Banneker published almanacs yearly from 1792 to 1802. He sent a copy of his first almanac to Thomas Jefferson along with an impassioned letter against slavery. Jefferson subsequently championed the cause of this early African-American mathematician.

> **Rational Numbers**
>
> **Rational numbers** = $\{x \mid x \text{ is a quotient of two integers, with denominator not } 0\}$

A rational number is said to be in **lowest terms** if the greatest common factor of the numerator (top number) and the denominator (bottom number) is 1. Rational numbers are written in lowest terms by using the *fundamental property of rational numbers.*

> **Fundamental Property of Rational Numbers**
>
> If a, b, and k are integers with $b \neq 0$ and $k \neq 0$, then the following is true.
>
> $$\frac{a \cdot k}{b \cdot k} = \frac{a}{b}$$

▌▌ **EXAMPLE 1** Writing a Fraction in Lowest Terms

Write $\frac{36}{54}$ in lowest terms.

SOLUTION

The greatest common factor of 36 and 54 is 18.

$$\frac{36}{54} = \frac{2 \cdot \mathbf{18}}{3 \cdot \mathbf{18}} = \frac{2}{3}$$

> Use the fundamental property with $k = 18$.

▌▌▌

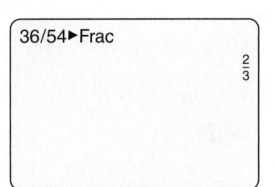

36/54▶Frac
$\frac{2}{3}$

The calculator gives 36/54 in lowest terms, as illustrated in **Example 1**.

In **Example 1**, we see that $\frac{36}{54} = \frac{2}{3}$. If we multiply the numerator of the fraction on the left by the denominator of the fraction on the right, we obtain $36 \cdot 3 = 108$. If we multiply the denominator of the fraction on the left by the numerator of the fraction on the right, we obtain $54 \cdot 2 = 108$. The result is the same in both cases.

One way of determining whether two fractions are equal is to perform this test. If the product of the **"extremes"** (36 and 3 in this case) equals the product of the **"means"** (54 and 2), the fractions are equal. This test for equality of rational numbers is called the **cross-product test.**

Cross-Product Test for Equality of Rational Numbers

For rational numbers $\frac{a}{b}$ and $\frac{c}{d}$, $b \neq 0$, $d \neq 0$, the following is true.

$$\frac{a}{b} = \frac{c}{d} \quad \text{if and only if} \quad a \cdot d = b \cdot c$$

Operations with Rational Numbers

The operation of addition of rational numbers can be illustrated by the sketches in **Figure 10**. The rectangle at the top left is divided into three equal portions, with one of the portions in color. The rectangle at the top right is divided into five equal parts, with two of them in color.

The total of the areas in color is represented by the sum

$$\frac{1}{3} + \frac{2}{5}.$$

To evaluate this sum, the areas in color must be redrawn in terms of a common unit. Since the least common multiple of 3 and 5 is 15, redraw both rectangles with 15 parts. See **Figure 11**. In the figure, 11 of the small rectangles are in color, so

$$\frac{1}{3} + \frac{2}{5} = \frac{5}{15} + \frac{6}{15} = \frac{11}{15}.$$

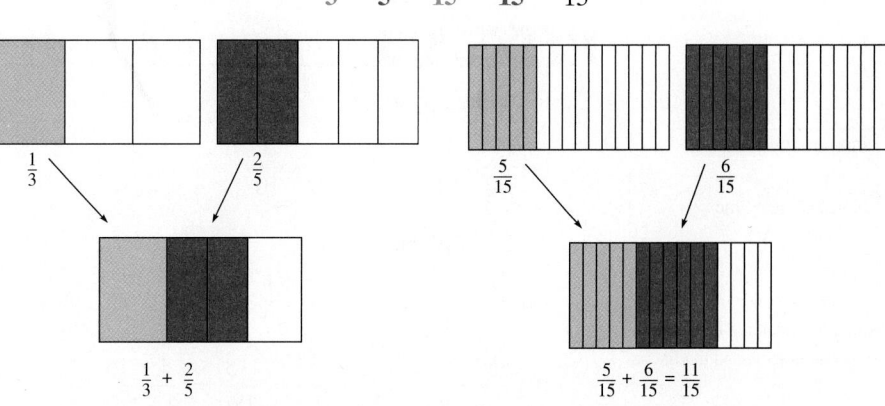

Figure 10　　　　　　　**Figure 11**

A similar example could be given for the difference of rational numbers.

Adding and Subtracting Rational Numbers

If $\frac{a}{b}$ and $\frac{c}{d}$ are rational numbers, then the following are true.

$$\frac{a}{b} + \frac{c}{d} = \frac{ad + bc}{bd} \quad \text{and} \quad \frac{a}{b} - \frac{c}{d} = \frac{ad - bc}{bd}$$

This formal definition is seldom used in practice. We usually first rewrite the fractions with the least common multiple of their denominators, called the **least common denominator (LCD).**

▮▮ **EXAMPLE 2**   Adding and Subtracting Rational Numbers

Perform each operation.

(a) $\dfrac{2}{15} + \dfrac{1}{10}$ **(b)** $\dfrac{173}{180} - \dfrac{69}{1200}$

SOLUTION

```
2/15+1/10▶Frac
                    7
                    ──
                    30
173/180−69/1200▶Frac
                    3253
                    ────
                    3600
```

The results of **Example 2** are illustrated in this screen.

(a) Since $30 \div 15 = 2,$

$$\frac{2}{15} = \frac{2 \cdot 2}{15 \cdot 2} = \frac{4}{30}$$

and since $30 \div 10 = 3,$

$$\frac{1}{10} = \frac{1 \cdot 3}{10 \cdot 3} = \frac{3}{30}.$$

The LCD is 30.

Thus,

$$\frac{2}{15} + \frac{1}{10} = \frac{4}{30} + \frac{3}{30} = \frac{7}{30}.$$

(b) The least common multiple of 180 and 1200 is 3600.

$$\frac{173}{180} - \frac{69}{1200} = \frac{3460}{3600} - \frac{207}{3600} = \frac{3460 - 207}{3600} = \frac{3253}{3600}$$

▮▮▮

Multiplying Rational Numbers

If $\frac{a}{b}$ and $\frac{c}{d}$ are rational numbers, then the following is true.

$$\frac{a}{b} \cdot \frac{c}{d} = \frac{ac}{bd}$$

▮▮ **EXAMPLE 3**   Multiplying Rational Numbers

Find each product.

(a) $\dfrac{3}{4} \cdot \dfrac{7}{10}$ **(b)** $\dfrac{5}{18} \cdot \dfrac{3}{10}$

```
(3/4)*(7/10)▶Frac
                    21
                    ──
                    40
(5/18)*(3/10)▶Frac
                    1
                    ──
                    12
```

To illustrate the results of **Example 3,** we use parentheses around the fraction factors.

SOLUTION

(a) $\dfrac{3}{4} \cdot \dfrac{7}{10} = \dfrac{3 \cdot 7}{4 \cdot 10} = \dfrac{21}{40}$

(b) $\dfrac{5}{18} \cdot \dfrac{3}{10} = \dfrac{5 \cdot 3}{18 \cdot 10} = \dfrac{15}{180} = \dfrac{1 \cdot 15}{12 \cdot 15} = \dfrac{1}{12}$

6.3   Rational Numbers and Decimal Representation   ▮▮▮ 245

In practice, a multiplication problem such as

$$\frac{5}{18} \cdot \frac{3}{10}$$

in part (b) is often solved by using slash marks to indicate that common factors have been divided out of the numerator and denominator.

$$\frac{\overset{1}{\cancel{5}}}{\underset{6}{\cancel{18}}} \cdot \frac{\overset{1}{\cancel{3}}}{\underset{2}{\cancel{10}}} = \frac{1}{6} \cdot \frac{1}{2} \quad\quad \text{3 is divided out of 3 and 18.}$$

$$\text{5 is divided out of 5 and 10.}$$

$$= \frac{1}{12}$$

▮▮▮

In a fraction, the fraction bar indicates the operation of division. The multiplicative inverse of the nonzero number b is $\frac{1}{b}$. We define division using multiplicative inverses.

Definition of Division

If a and b are real numbers, $b \neq 0$, then the following is true.

$$\frac{a}{b} = a \cdot \frac{1}{b}$$

You probably have heard the rule, "To divide fractions, invert the divisor and multiply." To illustrate this rule, suppose that you have $\frac{7}{8}$ of a gallon of milk and you wish to find how many quarts you have. Since a quart is $\frac{1}{4}$ of a gallon, you must ask yourself, "How many $\frac{1}{4}$s are there in $\frac{7}{8}$?" This would be interpreted as

$$\frac{7}{8} \div \frac{1}{4}, \quad \text{or} \quad \frac{\frac{7}{8}}{\frac{1}{4}}.$$

The fundamental property of rational numbers can be extended to rational number values of a, b, and k.

$$\frac{a}{b} = \frac{a \cdot k}{b \cdot k} = \frac{\frac{7}{8} \cdot 4}{\frac{1}{4} \cdot 4} = \frac{\frac{7}{8} \cdot 4}{1} = \frac{7}{8} \cdot \frac{4}{1} \quad \text{Let } a = \tfrac{7}{8}, b = \tfrac{1}{4}, \text{ and } k = 4 \left(\text{the reciprocal of } b = \tfrac{1}{4}\right).$$

We began with the division problem $\frac{7}{8} \div \frac{1}{4}$, which, through a series of equivalent expressions, led to the multiplication problem $\frac{7}{8} \cdot \frac{4}{1}$. So dividing by $\frac{1}{4}$ is equivalent to multiplying by its reciprocal, $\frac{4}{1}$.

$$\frac{7}{8} \cdot \frac{4}{1} = \frac{28}{8} = \frac{7}{2} \quad \text{Definition of multiplication of fractions}$$

Thus there are $\frac{7}{2}$, or $3\frac{1}{2}$, quarts in $\frac{7}{8}$ gallon.*

Early U.S. cents and **half cents** used fractions to denote their denominations. The half cent used $\frac{1}{200}$ and the cent used $\frac{1}{100}$. (See **Exercise 18** for a photo of an interesting error coin.)

The coins shown here were part of the collection of Louis E. Eliasberg, Sr. **Louis Eliasberg** was the only person ever to assemble a complete collection of United States coins. The Eliasberg gold coins were auctioned in 1982, while the copper, nickel, and silver coins were auctioned in two sales in 1996 and 1997. The half cent pictured sold for $506,000 and the cent sold for $27,500. The cent shown in **Exercise 18** went for a mere $2970.

---

*$3\frac{1}{2}$ is a **mixed number.** Mixed numbers are covered in the exercises for this section.

> **Dividing Rational Numbers**
>
> If $\frac{a}{b}$ and $\frac{c}{d}$ are rational numbers, where $\frac{c}{d} \neq 0$, then the following is true.
>
> $$\frac{a}{b} \div \frac{c}{d} = \frac{a}{b} \cdot \frac{d}{c} = \frac{ad}{bc}$$

▌▌ **EXAMPLE 4**   Dividing Rational Numbers

Find each quotient.

(a) $\dfrac{3}{5} \div \dfrac{7}{15}$ **(b)** $\dfrac{-4}{7} \div \dfrac{3}{14}$ **(c)** $\dfrac{2}{9} \div 4$ **(d)** $-9 \div \dfrac{3}{5}$

SOLUTION

(a) $\dfrac{3}{5} \div \dfrac{7}{15} = \dfrac{3}{5} \cdot \dfrac{15}{7} = \dfrac{45}{35} = \dfrac{9 \cdot 5}{7 \cdot 5} = \dfrac{9}{7}$

(b) $\dfrac{-4}{7} \div \dfrac{3}{14} = \dfrac{-4}{7} \cdot \dfrac{14}{3} = \dfrac{-56}{21} = \dfrac{-8 \cdot 7}{3 \cdot 7} = \dfrac{-8}{3} = -\dfrac{8}{3}$ ◁ $\dfrac{-a}{b}, \dfrac{a}{-b}$, and $-\dfrac{a}{b}$ are all equal.

(c) $\dfrac{2}{9} \div 4 = \dfrac{2}{9} \div \dfrac{4}{1} = \dfrac{2}{9} \cdot \dfrac{1}{4} = \dfrac{\overset{1}{2}}{9} \cdot \dfrac{1}{\underset{2}{4}} = \dfrac{1}{18}$

(d) $-9 \div \dfrac{3}{5} = \dfrac{\overset{-3}{-9}}{1} \cdot \dfrac{5}{\underset{1}{3}} = -15$ ▪▪▪

Calculator screen:
```
(-4/7)/(3/14)▶Frac
                -8/3
(2/9)/4▶Frac
                1/18
```
This screen supports the results in
Example 4(b) and (c).

Density and the Arithmetic Mean

There is no integer between two consecutive integers, such as 3 and 4. However, a rational number can always be found between any two distinct rational numbers. For this reason, the set of rational numbers is said to be *dense*.

> **Density Property of the Rational Numbers**
>
> If r and t are distinct rational numbers, with $r < t$, then there exists a rational number s such that
>
> $$r < s < t.$$

Repeated applications of the density property lead to the following conclusion.

> ***There are infinitely many rational numbers between two distinct rational numbers.***

One example of a rational number that is between two distinct rational numbers is the *arithmetic mean*. To find the **arithmetic mean,** or **average,** of n numbers, we add the numbers and then divide the sum by n. For two numbers, the number that lies halfway between them is their average.

▐▐ **EXAMPLE 5** Finding the Arithmetic Mean (Average)

Find the rational number halfway between $\frac{2}{3}$ and $\frac{5}{6}$ (that is, their arithmetic mean, or average).

SOLUTION

First, find their sum.

> Find a common denominator.

$$\frac{2}{3} + \frac{5}{6} = \frac{4}{6} + \frac{5}{6} = \frac{9}{6}, \text{ or } \frac{3}{2}$$

Now divide the sum, $\frac{3}{2}$, by 2.

$$\frac{3}{2} \div 2 = \frac{3}{2} \cdot \frac{1}{2} = \frac{3}{4} \quad \text{To divide, multiply by the reciprocal of the divisor.}$$

The number $\frac{3}{4}$ is halfway between $\frac{2}{3}$ and $\frac{5}{6}$. ▐▐▐

▐▐ **EXAMPLE 6** Finding the Arithmetic Mean (Average)

Table 3 shows the number of female civilian workers, in thousands, for some selected states. What is the average number, in thousands, for this group of states?

SOLUTION

To find this average, divide the sum by the number of states, 6.

$$\frac{2918 + 320 + 2016 + 869 + 571 + 1427}{6} = \frac{8121}{6} = 1353.5$$

The average number of female civilian workers for the group of states is about 1354 thousand (or 1,354,000). ▐▐▐

It is also true that between any two *real* numbers there is another *real* number. Thus, as in the case of the rational numbers, the set of real numbers is dense.

Decimal Form of Rational Numbers

Rational numbers can be expressed as decimals. Decimal numerals have place values that are powers of 10. The place values are as shown here.

Table 3

State	Number (in thousands)
Illinois	2918
Maine	320
North Carolina	2016
Oregon	869
Utah	571
Wisconsin	1427

Source: U.S. Bureau of Labor Statistics.

... | 4 | 8 | 3 | • | 0 | 3 | 9 | 4 | 7 | 5 | ...

(Hundreds, Tens, Ones, Decimal point, Tenths, Hundredths, Thousandths, Ten-Thousandths, Hundred-thousandths, Millionths)

The decimal numeral 483.039475 is read "four hundred eighty-three and thirty-nine thousand, four hundred seventy-five millionths."

A rational number in the form $\frac{a}{b}$ can be expressed as a decimal most easily by entering it into a calculator. For example, to write $\frac{3}{8}$ as a decimal, enter 3, then enter the operation of division, then enter 8. Press the equals key to find the following equivalence.

$$\frac{3}{8} = 0.375$$

This same result may be obtained by long division, as shown in the margin. By this result, the rational number $\frac{3}{8}$ is the same as the decimal 0.375. A decimal such as 0.375, which stops, is called a **terminating decimal.**

$$\frac{1}{4} = 0.25, \quad \frac{7}{10} = 0.7, \quad \text{and} \quad \frac{89}{1000} = 0.089 \quad \text{Examples of terminating decimals}$$

```
      0.375            0.3636...
  8) 3.000        11) 4.00000...
     24               33
     ──               ──
     60               70
     56               66
     ──               ──
     40               40
     40               33
     ──               ──
      0               70
                      66
                      ──
                      40
```

2/3
.6666666667

While 2/3 has a repeating decimal representation (2/3 = 0.6̄), the calculator rounds off in the final decimal place displayed.

Not all rational numbers can be represented by terminating decimals. For example, convert $\frac{4}{11}$ into a decimal by dividing 11 into 4 using a calculator. The display shows

$$0.3636363636, \quad \text{or perhaps} \quad 0.363636364.$$

However, we see that the long division process, shown in the margin on the previous page, indicates that we will actually get 0.3636 . . . , with the digits 36 repeating over and over indefinitely. To indicate this, we write a bar (called a *vinculum*) over the "block" of digits that repeats.

$$\frac{4}{11} = 0.\overline{36} \quad \text{0.}\overline{36}\text{ means 0.3636....}$$

A decimal such as 0.$\overline{36}$, which continues indefinitely, is called a **repeating decimal.**

$$\frac{5}{11} = 0.\overline{45}, \quad \frac{1}{3} = 0.\overline{3}, \quad \text{and} \quad \frac{5}{6} = 0.8\overline{3} \quad \text{Examples of repeating decimals}$$

Because of the limitations of the display of a calculator, and because some rational numbers have repeating decimals, it is important to be able to interpret calculator results accordingly when obtaining repeating decimals.

While we distinguish between *terminating* and *repeating* decimals in this book, some mathematicians prefer to consider all rational numbers as repeating decimals. This can be justified by thinking this way: if the division process leads to a remainder of 0, then zeros repeat without end in the decimal form. For example, we can consider the decimal form of $\frac{3}{4}$ as follows.

$$\frac{3}{4} = 0.75\overline{0}$$

5/11
.4545454545
1/3
.3333333333
5/6
.8333333333

Although only ten decimal digits are shown, all three fractions have decimals that repeat endlessly.

By considering the possible remainders that may be obtained when converting a quotient of integers to a decimal, we can draw an important conclusion about the decimal form of rational numbers. If the remainder is never zero, the division will produce a repeating decimal. This happens because each step of the division process must produce a remainder that is less than the divisor. Since the number of different possible remainders is less than the divisor, the remainders must eventually begin to repeat. This makes the digits of the quotient repeat, producing a repeating decimal.

Decimal Representation of Rational Numbers

Any rational number can be expressed as either a terminating decimal or a repeating decimal.

To determine whether the decimal form of a quotient of integers will terminate or repeat, we use the following rule.

Criteria for Terminating and Repeating Decimals

A rational number $\frac{a}{b}$ *in lowest terms* results in a **terminating decimal** if the only prime factor of the denominator is 2 or 5 (or both).

A rational number $\frac{a}{b}$ *in lowest terms* results in a **repeating decimal** if a prime other than 2 or 5 appears in the prime factorization of the denominator.

Simon Stevin (1548–1620) worked as a bookkeeper in Belgium and became an engineer in the Netherlands army. He is usually given credit for the development of **decimals.**

Justification of this rule is based on the fact that the prime factors of 10 are 2 and 5, and the decimal system uses ten as its base.

To find a baseball player's batting average, we divide the number of hits by the number of at-bats. A surprising paradox exists concerning averages. It is possible for Player *A* to have a higher batting average than Player *B* in each of two successive years, yet for the two-year period, Player *B* can have a higher total batting average. Look at the chart.

Year	Joe Shlabotnik	Scott Bailes
1998	$\frac{20}{40} = .500$	$\frac{90}{200} = .450$
1999	$\frac{60}{200} = .300$	$\frac{10}{40} = .250$
Two-year total	$\frac{80}{240} = .333$	$\frac{100}{240} = .417$

In both individual years, Shlabotnik had a higher average, but for the two-year period, Bailes had the higher average. This is an example of **Simpson's paradox** from statistics. (See also the **Chapter 12** opener, on **page 629.**)

▮▮ **EXAMPLE 7** Determining Whether a Decimal Terminates or Repeats

Determine whether the decimal form terminates or repeats.

(a) $\dfrac{7}{8}$ **(b)** $\dfrac{13}{150}$ **(c)** $\dfrac{6}{75}$

SOLUTION

(a) The rational number $\frac{7}{8}$ is in lowest terms. Its denominator is 8, and since 8 factors as 2^3, the decimal form will terminate. No primes other than 2 or 5 divide the denominator.

(b) The rational number $\frac{13}{150}$ is in lowest terms with denominator $150 = 2 \cdot 3 \cdot 5^2$. Since 3 appears as a prime factor of the denominator, the decimal form will repeat.

(c) First write the rational number $\frac{6}{75}$ in lowest terms.

$$\frac{6}{75} = \frac{2}{25} \quad \text{Denominator is 25.}$$

Since $25 = 5^2$, the decimal form will terminate.   ▮▮▮

We have seen that a rational number will be represented by either a terminating or a repeating decimal. Must a terminating decimal or a repeating decimal represent a rational number? The answer is *yes*. For example, the terminating decimal 0.6 represents a rational number.

$$0.6 = \frac{6}{10} = \frac{3}{5}$$

▮▮ **EXAMPLE 8** Writing Terminating Decimals as Quotients of Integers

Write each terminating decimal as a quotient of integers.

(a) 0.437   **(b)** 8.2

SOLUTION

(a) $0.437 = \dfrac{437}{1000}$ Read as "four hundred thirty-seven thousandths" and then write as a fraction.

(b) $8.2 = 8 + \dfrac{2}{10} = \dfrac{82}{10} = \dfrac{41}{5}$ Read as a decimal, write as a sum, and then add.   ▮▮▮

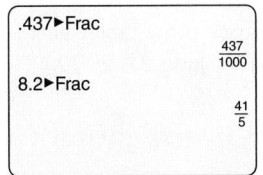

The results of **Example 8** are supported in this screen.

We now show how to convert a repeating decimal to a quotient of integers.

▮▮ **EXAMPLE 9** Writing a Repeating Decimal as a Quotient of Integers

Find a quotient of two integers equal to $0.\overline{85}$.

SOLUTION

Step 1 Let $x = 0.\overline{85}$, so $x = 0.858585\ldots$.

Step 2 Multiply both sides of the equation $x = 0.858585\ldots$ by 100. (Use 100 since there are **two** digits in the part that repeats, and $100 = 10^2$.)

$$x = 0.858585\ldots$$
$$100x = 100(0.858585\ldots)$$
$$100x = 85.858585\ldots$$

Step 3 Subtract the expressions in Step 1 from the final expressions in Step 2.

$$100x = 85.858585\ldots \qquad \text{(Recall that } x = 1x \text{ and } 100x - x = 99x.\text{)}$$
$$\underline{x = 0.858585\ldots}$$
$$99x = 85 \qquad \text{Subtract.}$$

Step 4 Solve the equation $99x = 85$ by dividing both sides by 99.

$$99x = 85$$
$$\frac{99x}{99} = \frac{85}{99} \qquad \text{Divide by 99.}$$
$$x = \frac{85}{99} \qquad \tfrac{99x}{99} = x$$
$$0.\overline{85} = \frac{85}{99} \qquad x = 0.\overline{85}$$

When checking with a calculator, remember that the calculator will only show a finite number of decimal places and may round off in the final decimal place shown.

▐▐▐

$1 = 0.99999^{9999999}$

Terminating or Repeating? One of the most baffling truths of elementary mathematics is the following:

$$1 = 0.9999\ldots.$$

Most people believe that $0.\overline{9}$ has to be less than 1, but this is not the case. The following argument shows why. Let $x = 0.9999\ldots$ Then

$$10x = 9.9999\ldots$$
$$\underline{x = 0.9999\ldots}$$
$$9x = 9 \qquad \text{Subtract.}$$
$$x = 1. \qquad \text{Divide.}$$

Therefore, $1 = 0.9999\ldots$ Similarly, it can be shown that any terminating decimal can be represented as a repeating decimal with an endless string of 9s. For example, $0.5 = 0.49999\ldots$ and $2.6 = 2.59999\ldots$ This is a way of justifying that any rational number may be represented as a repeating decimal.

For Further Thought

The Influence of Spanish Coinage on Stock Prices

Until August 28, 2000, when decimalization of the U.S. stock market began, market prices were reported with fractions having denominators with powers of 2, such as $17\frac{3}{4}$ and $112\frac{5}{8}$. Did you ever wonder why this was done?

During the early years of the United States, prior to the minting of its own coinage, the Spanish eight-reales coin, also known as the Spanish milled dollar, circulated freely in the states. Its fractional parts, the four reales, two reales, and one real, were known as **pieces of eight,** and were described as such in pirate and treasure lore. When the New York Stock Exchange was founded in 1792, it chose to use the Spanish milled dollar as its price basis, rather than the decimal base as proposed by Thomas Jefferson that same year.

In the September 1997 issue of *COINage*, Tom Delorey's article "The End of 'Pieces of Eight'" gives the following account:

As the Spanish dollar and its fractions continued to be legal tender in America alongside the decimal coins until 1857, there was no urgency to change the system—and by the time the Spanish-American money was withdrawn

in 1857, pricing stocks in eighths of a dollar—and no less—was a tradition carved in stone. Being somewhat a conservative organization, the NYSE saw no need to fix what was not broken.

All prices on the U.S. stock markets are now reported in decimals. (*Source:* "Stock price tables go to decimal listings," *The Times Picayune,* June 27, 2000.)

For Group or Individual Investigation

Consider this: Have you ever heard this old cheer? "Two bits, four bits, six bits, a dollar. All for the (home team), stand up and holler." The term **two bits** refers to 25 cents. Discuss how this cheer is based on the Spanish eight-reales coin.

6.3 EXERCISES

Choose the expression(s) that is (are) equivalent to the given rational number.

1. $\dfrac{4}{8}$

    A. $\dfrac{1}{2}$ **B.** $\dfrac{8}{4}$ **C.** 0.5   **D.** $0.5\overline{0}$ **E.** $0.\overline{55}$

2. $\dfrac{2}{3}$

    A. 0.67   **B.** $0.\overline{6}$ **C.** $\dfrac{20}{30}$ **D.** $0.666\ldots$ **E.** 0.6

3. $\dfrac{5}{9}$

    A. 0.56   **B.** 0.55   **C.** $0.\overline{5}$ **D.** $\dfrac{9}{5}$ **E.** $1\dfrac{4}{5}$

4. $\dfrac{1}{4}$

    A. 0.25   **B.** $0.24\overline{9}$ **C.** $\dfrac{25}{100}$ **D.** 4   **E.** $\dfrac{10}{400}$

Write each fraction in lowest terms.

5. $\dfrac{16}{48}$ **6.** $\dfrac{21}{28}$ **7.** $-\dfrac{15}{35}$ **8.** $-\dfrac{8}{48}$

Write each fraction in three other ways.

9. $\dfrac{3}{8}$ **10.** $\dfrac{9}{10}$

11. $-\dfrac{5}{7}$ **12.** $-\dfrac{7}{12}$

13. Write a fraction in lowest terms that represents the portion of each figure that is in color.

(a) 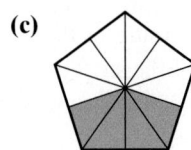   **(b)**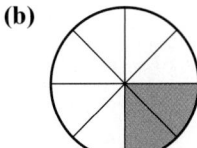

(c)   **(d)**

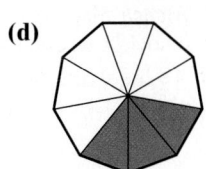

14. Write a fraction in lowest terms that represents the region described in parts (a)–(d).

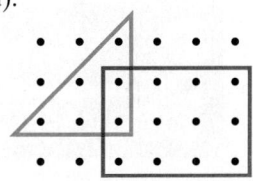

(a) the dots in the rectangle as a part of the dots in the entire figure

(b) the dots in the triangle as a part of the dots in the entire figure

(c) the dots in the rectangle as a part of the dots in the union of the triangle and the rectangle

(d) the dots in the intersection of the triangle and the rectangle as a part of the dots in the union of the triangle and the rectangle

15. Refer to the figure for **Exercise 14** and write a description of the region that is represented by the fraction $\dfrac{1}{12}$.

16. *Batting Averages* In a softball league, Paul Lewis got 8 hits in 20 at-bats, and Josh LaRoche got 12 hits in 30 at-bats. Which player (if either) had the higher batting average?

17. *Batting Averages* After ten games, the following statistics were obtained.

Player	At-bats	Hits	Home Runs
Anne Kelly	40	9	2
Christine O'Brien	36	12	3
Leah Goldberg	11	5	1
Otis Taylor	16	8	0
Carol Britz	20	10	2

Answer using estimation skills as necessary.

(a) Which player got a hit in exactly $\dfrac{1}{3}$ of his or her at-bats?

(b) Which player got a hit in just less than $\dfrac{1}{2}$ of his or her at-bats?

(c) Which player got a home run in just less than $\dfrac{1}{10}$ of his or her at-bats?

(d) Which player got a hit in just less than $\dfrac{1}{4}$ of his or her at-bats?

(e) Which two players got hits in exactly the same fractional parts of their at-bats? What was the fractional part, reduced to lowest terms?

18. Refer to the margin note discussing the use of common fractions on early U.S. copper coinage. The photo here shows an error near the bottom that occurred on an 1802 large cent. Discuss the error and how it represents a mathematical impossibility.

Perform the indicated operations and express answers in lowest terms. Use the order of operations as necessary.

19. $\dfrac{3}{8} + \dfrac{1}{8}$ **20.** $\dfrac{7}{9} + \dfrac{1}{9}$ **21.** $\dfrac{5}{16} + \dfrac{7}{12}$

22. $\dfrac{1}{15} + \dfrac{7}{18}$ **23.** $\dfrac{2}{3} - \dfrac{7}{8}$ **24.** $\dfrac{13}{20} - \dfrac{5}{12}$

25. $\dfrac{5}{8} - \dfrac{3}{14}$ **26.** $\dfrac{19}{15} - \dfrac{7}{12}$ **27.** $\dfrac{3}{4} \cdot \dfrac{9}{5}$

28. $\dfrac{3}{8} \cdot \dfrac{2}{7}$ **29.** $-\dfrac{2}{3} \cdot -\dfrac{5}{8}$ **30.** $-\dfrac{2}{4} \cdot \dfrac{3}{9}$

31. $\dfrac{5}{12} \div \dfrac{15}{4}$ **32.** $\dfrac{15}{16} \div \dfrac{30}{8}$

33. $-\dfrac{9}{16} \div -\dfrac{3}{8}$ **34.** $-\dfrac{3}{8} \div \dfrac{5}{4}$

35. $\left(\dfrac{1}{3} \div \dfrac{1}{2}\right) + \dfrac{5}{6}$ **36.** $\dfrac{2}{5} \div \left(-\dfrac{4}{5} \div \dfrac{3}{10}\right)$

37. *Recipe for Grits* The following chart appears on a package of Quaker® Quick Grits.

Microwave		Stove Top		
Servings	**1**	**1**	**4**	**6**
Water	$\dfrac{3}{4}$ cup	1 cup	3 cups	4 cups
Grits	3 Tbsp	3 Tbsp	$\dfrac{3}{4}$ cup	1 cup
Salt (optional)	dash	dash	$\dfrac{1}{4}$ tsp	$\dfrac{1}{2}$ tsp

(a) How many cups of water would be needed for 6 microwave servings?

(b) How many cups of grits would be needed for 5 stove-top servings? (*Hint:* 5 is halfway between 4 and 6.)

38. *U.S. Immigrants* Approximately 34 million people living in the United States in 2004 were born in other countries.

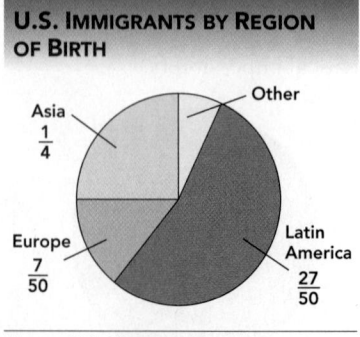

U.S. IMMIGRANTS BY REGION OF BIRTH

Asia $\dfrac{1}{4}$ Other

Europe $\dfrac{7}{50}$ Latin America $\dfrac{27}{50}$

Source: U.S. Census Bureau.

The circle graph in the previous column gives the fractional number from each region of birth for these immigrants.

(a) What fractional part of the immigrants were from other regions?

(b) What fractional part of the immigrants were from Latin America or Asia?

(c) How many (in millions) were from Europe?

*The **mixed number** $2\frac{5}{8}$ represents the sum $2 + \frac{5}{8}$. We can convert $2\frac{5}{8}$ to a fraction as follows:*

$$2\frac{5}{8} = 2 + \frac{5}{8} = \frac{2}{1} + \frac{5}{8} = \frac{16}{8} + \frac{5}{8} = \frac{21}{8}.$$

The fraction $\frac{21}{8}$ can be converted back to a mixed number by dividing 8 into 21. The quotient is 2, the remainder is 5, and the divisor is 8.

   Convert each mixed number to a fraction, and convert each fraction to a mixed number.

39. $4\dfrac{1}{3}$ **40.** $3\dfrac{7}{8}$ **41.** $2\dfrac{9}{10}$

42. $\dfrac{18}{5}$ **43.** $\dfrac{27}{4}$ **44.** $\dfrac{19}{3}$

It is possible to add mixed numbers by first converting them to fractions, adding, and then converting the sum back to a mixed number. For example,

$$2\frac{1}{3} + 3\frac{1}{2} = \frac{7}{3} + \frac{7}{2} = \frac{14}{6} + \frac{21}{6} = \frac{35}{6} = 5\frac{5}{6}.$$

The other operations with mixed numbers may be performed in a similar manner.

   Perform each operation and express your answer as a mixed number.

45. $3\dfrac{1}{4} + 2\dfrac{7}{8}$ **46.** $6\dfrac{1}{5} - 2\dfrac{7}{15}$

47. $-4\dfrac{7}{8} \cdot 3\dfrac{2}{3}$ **48.** $-4\dfrac{1}{6} \div 1\dfrac{2}{3}$

Solve each problem.

49. *Socket Wrench Measurements* A hardware store sells a 22-piece socket wrench set. The measure of the largest socket is $\frac{3}{4}$ in., while the measure of the smallest socket is $\frac{3}{16}$ in. What is the difference between these measures?

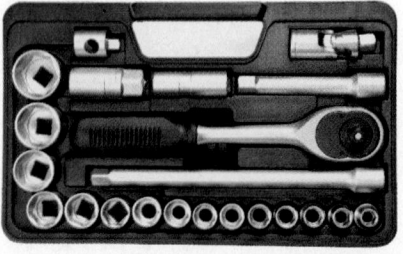

50. *Swiss Cheese Hole Sizes*   Under existing standards, most of the holes in Swiss cheese must have diameters between $\frac{11}{16}$ and $\frac{13}{16}$ in. To accommodate new high-speed slicing machines, the USDA wants to reduce the minimum size to $\frac{3}{8}$ in. How much smaller is $\frac{3}{8}$ in. than $\frac{11}{16}$ in.? (*Source:* U.S. Department of Agriculture.)

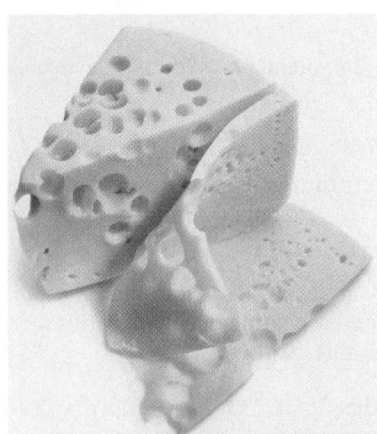

A quotient of quantities containing fractions (*with denominators not zero*) is called a **complex fraction.** *There are two methods that are used to simplify a complex fraction.*

Method 1   *Simplify the numerator and denominator separately. Then rewrite as a division problem, and proceed as you would when dividing fractions.*

Method 2   *Multiply both the numerator and denominator by the least common denominator of all the fractions found within the complex fraction. (This is, in effect, multiplying the fraction by 1, which does not change its value.) Apply the distributive property, if necessary, and simplify.*

Use one of the methods above to simplify each complex fraction.

51. $\dfrac{\frac{1}{2} + \frac{1}{4}}{\frac{1}{2} - \frac{1}{4}}$

52. $\dfrac{\frac{2}{3} + \frac{1}{6}}{\frac{2}{3} - \frac{1}{6}}$

53. $\dfrac{\frac{5}{8} - \frac{1}{4}}{\frac{1}{8} + \frac{3}{4}}$

54. $\dfrac{\frac{3}{16} - \frac{1}{2}}{\frac{5}{16} + \frac{1}{8}}$

55. $\dfrac{\frac{7}{11} + \frac{3}{10}}{\frac{1}{11} - \frac{9}{10}}$

56. $\dfrac{\frac{11}{15} + \frac{1}{9}}{\frac{13}{15} - \frac{2}{3}}$

The expressions in Exercises 57 and 58 are called ***continued fractions.*** *Write each in the form $\frac{p}{q}$ reduced to lowest terms.* (*Hint: Start at the bottom and work up.*)

57. $2 + \dfrac{1}{1 + \dfrac{1}{3 + \dfrac{1}{2}}}$

58. $4 + \dfrac{1}{2 + \dfrac{1}{1 + \dfrac{1}{3}}}$

Find the rational number halfway between the two given rational numbers.

59. $\dfrac{1}{2}, \dfrac{3}{4}$ **60.** $\dfrac{1}{3}, \dfrac{5}{12}$ **61.** $\dfrac{3}{5}, \dfrac{2}{3}$

62. $\dfrac{7}{12}, \dfrac{5}{8}$ **63.** $-\dfrac{2}{3}, -\dfrac{5}{6}$ **64.** $-3, -\dfrac{5}{2}$

Solve each problem.

65. *Average Annual Salary*   The table shows the average annual salary in the eight highest-paying metropolitan areas in the United States. Find the average of these amounts to the nearest dollar.

Metropolitan Area	Average Annual Salary
San Jose, CA	$63,056
New York, NY	$57,708
San Francisco, CA	$56,602
New Haven, CT, area	$51,170
Middlesex, NJ, area	$50,457
Jersey City, NJ	$49,562
Newark, NJ	$48,781
Washington, DC, area	$48,430

Source: Bureau of Labor Statistics.

66. *Tourism Earnings*   The top five countries for tourism earnings in 2007 are shown in the table. Find the average of these figures.

Country	Receipts (in billions of dollars)
U.S.	96.7
Spain	57.6
France	54.3
Italy	42.7
China	37.2

Source: World Tourism Organization.

In the March 1973 issue of The Mathematics Teacher *there appeared an article by Laurence Sherzer, an eighth-grade mathematics teacher, that immortalized one of his students, Robert McKay. To find a number (not necessarily their average) between two positive rational numbers $\frac{a}{b}$ and $\frac{c}{d}$, McKay claimed, simply add the numerators and add the denominators.*

For example, to find a rational number between $\frac{1}{3}$ and $\frac{1}{4}$, add $1 + 1 = 2$ to get the numerator and $3 + 4 = 7$ to get the denominator. Therefore, by ***McKay's theorem,*** $\frac{2}{7}$ *is between $\frac{1}{3}$ and $\frac{1}{4}$. Sherzer provided a proof of this method in the article. In Exercises 67–74 on the next page, use McKay's theorem to find a rational number between the two given rational numbers.*

67. $\dfrac{5}{6}$ and $\dfrac{9}{13}$

68. $\dfrac{10}{11}$ and $\dfrac{13}{19}$

69. $\dfrac{4}{13}$ and $\dfrac{9}{16}$

70. $\dfrac{6}{11}$ and $\dfrac{13}{14}$

71. $\dfrac{7}{6}$ and $\dfrac{9}{8}$

72. $\dfrac{11}{5}$ and $\dfrac{12}{11}$

73. 2 and 3

74. 3 and 4

75. Apply McKay's theorem to any pair of consecutive integers, and make a conjecture about what always happens in this case.

76. Explain in your own words how to find the rational number that is one-fourth of the way between two different rational numbers.

Convert each rational number into either a repeating or a terminating decimal. Use a calculator if your instructor so allows.

77. $\dfrac{3}{4}$

78. $\dfrac{7}{8}$

79. $\dfrac{3}{16}$

80. $\dfrac{9}{32}$

81. $\dfrac{3}{11}$

82. $\dfrac{9}{11}$

83. $\dfrac{2}{7}$

84. $\dfrac{11}{15}$

Convert each terminating decimal into a quotient of integers. Write each in lowest terms.

85. 0.4

86. 0.9

87. 0.85

88. 0.105

89. 0.934

90. 0.7984

*Use the method of **Example 7** to decide whether each rational number would yield a repeating or a terminating decimal. (Hint: Write in lowest terms before trying to decide.)*

91. $\dfrac{8}{15}$

92. $\dfrac{8}{35}$

93. $\dfrac{13}{125}$

94. $\dfrac{3}{24}$

95. $\dfrac{22}{55}$

96. $\dfrac{24}{75}$

97. Follow through on all parts of this exercise in order.
   (a) Find the decimal for $\frac{1}{3}$.
   (b) Find the decimal for $\frac{2}{3}$.
   (c) By adding the decimal expressions obtained in parts (a) and (b), obtain a decimal expression for
   $\frac{1}{3} + \frac{2}{3} = \frac{3}{3} = 1$.
   (d) State your result. Read the margin note on terminating and repeating decimals in this section, which refers to this idea.

98. It is a fact that $\frac{1}{3} = 0.333\ldots$. Multiply both sides of this equation by 3. Does your answer bother you? See the margin note on terminating and repeating decimals in this section.

*Use the method of **Example 9** to write each rational number as a quotient of integers in lowest terms.*

99. (a) 0.8 **(b)** $0.7\overline{9}$ **100. (a)** 0.75 **(b)** $0.74\overline{9}$

101. (a) 0.66 **(b)** $0.65\overline{9}$

102. Based on your results in **Exercises 99–101,** predict the lowest terms form of the rational number $0.4\overline{9}$.

6.4   IRRATIONAL NUMBERS AND DECIMAL REPRESENTATION

Definition and Basic Concepts • Irrationality of $\sqrt{2}$ and Proof by Contradiction • Operations with Square Roots • The Irrational Numbers $\pi, \phi,$ and e

Definition and Basic Concepts

Every rational number has a decimal form that terminates or repeats, and every repeating or terminating decimal represents a rational number. However,

$$0.102001000200001000002\ldots$$

does not terminate and does not repeat. (It is true that there is a pattern in this decimal, but no single block of digits repeats indefinitely.)*

The irrational number $\sqrt{2}$ was discovered by the Pythagoreans in about 500 B.C. This discovery was a great setback to their philosophy that everything is based upon the whole numbers. The Pythagoreans kept their findings secret, and legend has it that members of the group who divulged this discovery were sent out to sea, and, according to Proclus (410–485), "perished in a shipwreck, to a man."

*In this section, we will assume that the digits of a number such as this continue indefinitely in the pattern established. The next few digits would be 000000100000002, and so on.

Tsu Ch'ung-chih (about 500 A.D.), the Chinese mathematician honored on the above stamp, investigated the digits of π. **Aryabhata,** his Indian contemporary, gave 3.1416 as the value.

Irrational Numbers

Irrational numbers = $\{x \mid x$ is a number represented by a nonrepeating, nonterminating decimal$\}$

As the name implies, an irrational number cannot be represented as a quotient of integers.

The decimal number mentioned at the bottom of the previous page is an irrational number. Other irrational numbers include $\sqrt{2}$, $\dfrac{1 + \sqrt{5}}{2}$ (ϕ, from **Section 5.5**), π (the ratio of the circumference of a circle to its diameter), and e (a constant *approximately equal to* 2.71828). There are infinitely many irrational numbers.

Irrationality of $\sqrt{2}$ and Proof by Contradiction

Figure 12 illustrates how a point with coordinate $\sqrt{2}$ can be located on a number line.

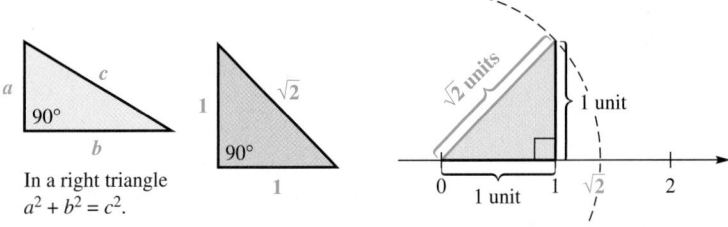

In a right triangle $a^2 + b^2 = c^2$.

Figure 12

The proof that $\sqrt{2}$ is irrational is a classic example of a **proof by contradiction.** We begin by assuming that $\sqrt{2}$ is rational, which leads to a contradiction, or absurdity. The method is also called **reductio ad absurdum** (Latin for "reduce to the absurd"). In order to understand the proof, we consider three preliminary facts:

1. When a rational number is written in lowest terms, the greatest common factor of the numerator and denominator is 1.
2. If an integer is even, then it has 2 as a factor and may be written in the form $2k$, where k is an integer.
3. If a perfect square is even, then its square root is even.

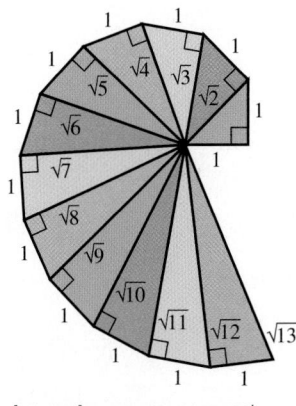

An interesting way to represent the lengths corresponding to $\sqrt{2}$, $\sqrt{3}$, $\sqrt{4}$, $\sqrt{5}$, and so on, is shown in the figure. Use the **Pythagorean theorem** to verify the lengths in the figure.

▐▐ **THEOREM**

Statement: $\sqrt{2}$ is an irrational number.
Proof: Assume that $\sqrt{2}$ is a rational number. Then by definition,

$$\sqrt{2} = \frac{p}{q}, \quad \text{for some integers } p \text{ and } q.$$

Furthermore, assume that $\frac{p}{q}$ is the form of $\sqrt{2}$ that is written in lowest terms, so the greatest common factor of p and q is 1.

$$2 = \frac{p^2}{q^2} \quad \text{Square both sides of the equation.}$$

$$2q^2 = p^2 \quad \text{Multiply by } q^2.$$

The last equation, $2q^2 = p^2$, indicates that 2 is a factor of p^2. So p^2 is even, and thus p is even. Since p is even, it may be written in the form $2k$, where k is an integer.

Now, substitute $2k$ for p in the last equation and simplify.

$$2q^2 = (2k)^2 \quad \text{Let } p = 2k.$$

$$2q^2 = 4k^2 \quad (2k)^2 = 2k \cdot 2k = 4k^2$$

$$q^2 = 2k^2 \quad \text{Divide by 2.}$$

Since q^2 has 2 as a factor, q^2 must be even, and thus q must be even. This leads to a contradiction: p and q cannot both be even because they would then have a common factor of 2. It was assumed that their greatest common factor is 1.

Therefore, since the original assumption that $\sqrt{2}$ is rational has led to a contradiction, it must follow that $\sqrt{2}$ is irrational. ▌▌▌

Operations with Square Roots

In everyday mathematical work, nearly all of our calculations deal with rational numbers, usually in decimal form. However, we must sometimes perform operations with irrational numbers.

$$\sqrt{2}, \quad \sqrt{3}, \quad \text{and} \quad \sqrt{13} \quad \text{Examples of square roots that are irrational}$$

$$\sqrt{4} = 2, \quad \sqrt{36} = 6, \quad \text{and} \quad \sqrt{100} = 10 \quad \text{Examples of square roots that are rational}$$

If n is a positive integer that is not the square of an integer, then $\sqrt{n}$ is an irrational number.

A calculator with a square root key can give approximations of square roots of numbers that are not perfect squares. To show that they are approximations, we use the $\approx$ symbol to indicate "is approximately equal to." Some such calculator approximations are as follows.

$$\sqrt{2} \approx 1.414213562, \quad \sqrt{6} \approx 2.449489743, \quad \text{and} \quad \sqrt{1949} \approx 44.14748011$$

Recall that $\sqrt{a}$, for $a \geq 0$, is the nonnegative number whose square is a. That is, $\left(\sqrt{a}\right)^2 = a$. We will now look at some simple operations with square roots.

Notice that

$$\sqrt{4} \cdot \sqrt{9} = 2 \cdot 3 = 6$$

and

$$\sqrt{4 \cdot 9} = \sqrt{36} = 6.$$

Thus, $\sqrt{4} \cdot \sqrt{9} = \sqrt{4 \cdot 9}$. This is a particular case of the following product rule.

Product Rule for Square Roots

For nonnegative real numbers a and b, the following is true.

$$\sqrt{a} \cdot \sqrt{b} = \sqrt{a \cdot b}$$

Just as every rational number $\frac{a}{b}$ can be written in *lowest terms* (by using the fundamental property of rational numbers), every square root radical has a *simplified form*.

Northern Exposure ran between 1990 and 1995 on the CBS network. In the episode "Nothing's Perfect" (10/12/92), the local disc jockey Chris Stevens (played by John Corbett) meets and develops a relationship with a mathematician (played by Wendel Meldrum) after accidentally running over her dog. Her area of research is **computation of the decimal digits of pi.** She mentions that a string of eight 8s appears in the decimal relatively early in the expansion. This string starts at position 46,663,520 counting from the first digit after the decimal point.

> **Conditions Necessary for the Simplified Form of a Square Root Radical**
>
> A square root radical is in **simplified form** if the following three conditions are met.
>
> **1.** The number under the radical **(radicand)** has no factor (except 1) that is a perfect square.
> **2.** The radicand has no fractions.
> **3.** No denominator contains a radical.

▮▮ **EXAMPLE 1** Simplifying a Square Root Radical (Product Rule)

Simplify $\sqrt{27}$.

SOLUTION

Since 9 is a factor of 27 and 9 is a perfect square, $\sqrt{27}$ is not in simplified form. The first condition of simplified form is not met. We simplify as follows.

$$\sqrt{27} = \sqrt{9 \cdot 3}$$

Simplified form → $= \sqrt{9} \cdot \sqrt{3}$ Use the product rule.

$$= 3\sqrt{3} \qquad \sqrt{9} = 3 \text{ since } 3^2 = 9. \qquad ▮▮▮$$

Expressions such as $\sqrt{27}$ and $3\sqrt{3}$ represent the *exact value* of the square root of 27. If we use the square root key of a calculator, we find

$$\sqrt{27} \approx 5.196152423.$$

If we find $\sqrt{3}$ and then multiply the result by 3, we get

$$3\sqrt{3} \approx 3(1.732050808) \approx 5.196152423.$$

Notice that these approximations are the same, as we would expect. The work in **Example 1** provides the mathematical justification that they are indeed equal.

> **Quotient Rule for Square Roots**
>
> For nonnegative real numbers a and positive real numbers b, the following is true.
>
> $$\frac{\sqrt{a}}{\sqrt{b}} = \sqrt{\frac{a}{b}}$$

▮▮ **EXAMPLE 2** Simplifying Square Root Radicals (Quotient Rule)

Simplify each radical.

(a) $\sqrt{\dfrac{25}{9}}$ **(b)** $\sqrt{\dfrac{3}{4}}$ **(c)** $\sqrt{\dfrac{1}{2}}$

SOLUTION

(a) Because the radicand contains a fraction, the radical expression is not simplified.

$$\sqrt{\frac{25}{9}} = \frac{\sqrt{25}}{\sqrt{9}} = \frac{5}{3} \qquad \text{Use the quotient rule.}$$

Near the end of the 2008 movie *Harold & Kumar Escape From Guantanamo Bay,* Kumar (Kal Penn), an excellent **mathematics student,** is involved in an incident at the wedding of his former girlfriend Vanessa (Danneel Harris), greatly embarrassing her. When she confronts him, he asks if he could do something to embarrass himself to make her feel better. She says that nothing could do so, but he goes on to recite a "nerdy" yet beautiful poem dealing with the square root of three, written by the late David Feinberg. The text of the poem can be found on the internet by searching "David Feinberg Square Root of 3." There are references to irrational numbers, integers, an approximation for the square root of 3, and the product rule for square root radicals.

In the second season of the original *Star Trek* series, the episode "Wolf in the Fold" told the story of an alien entity that had taken over the computer of the starship *Enterprise.* To drive the entity out of the computer, Captain Kirk suggested the following to Mr. Spock:

KIRK: Spock, don't you have a compulsory scan unit built into the computer banks?
SPOCK: Yes we do, Captain, but with the entity in control . . . .
KIRK: Well aren't there certain mathematical problems which simply cannot be solved?
SPOCK: Indeed. If we can focus the attention of the computer on one of them . . . .
KIRK: That ought to do it.

Later, they are able to do just that:

SPOCK: Ready?
KIRK: Implement.
SPOCK: Computer, this is a class "A" compulsory directive. Compute to the last digit the value of pi.
COMPUTER: No, no, no, no, no, ...
SPOCK (TO KIRK): As we know, the value of pi is a transcendental figure without resolution. The computer banks will work on this problem to the exclusion of all else until we order it to stop.
KIRK: Yes, that should keep that thing busy for a while.

The alien could not comply, because pi (π) is an irrational number, and its decimal representation has no last digit. As a result, ingenuity and mathematics saved the *Enterprise.*

(b) $\sqrt{\dfrac{3}{4}} = \dfrac{\sqrt{3}}{\sqrt{4}} = \dfrac{\sqrt{3}}{2}$ Use the quotient rule.

(c) $\sqrt{\dfrac{1}{2}} = \dfrac{\sqrt{1}}{\sqrt{2}} = \dfrac{1}{\sqrt{2}}$ $\boxed{\text{This is not yet simplified.}}$

This expression is not simplified, since condition 3 of simplified form is not met. To give an equivalent expression with no radical in the denominator, we use a procedure called **rationalizing the denominator.** Multiply $\dfrac{1}{\sqrt{2}}$ by $\dfrac{\sqrt{2}}{\sqrt{2}}$, which is a form of 1, the identity element for multiplication.

$$\frac{1}{\sqrt{2}} = \frac{1}{\sqrt{2}} \cdot \frac{\sqrt{2}}{\sqrt{2}} = \frac{\sqrt{2}}{2}$$ $\sqrt{2} \cdot \sqrt{2} = 2$

$\boxed{\text{This is the simplified form of } \sqrt{\tfrac{1}{2}}.}$ ■■■

Is $\sqrt{4} + \sqrt{9} = \sqrt{4 + 9}$ a true statement? The answer is *no*, since

$$\sqrt{4} + \sqrt{9} = 2 + 3 = 5, \quad \text{while} \quad \sqrt{4 + 9} = \sqrt{13}, \quad \text{and} \quad 5 \neq \sqrt{13}.$$

Square root radicals may be combined, however, if they have the same radicand. Such radicals are **like radicals.** We add (and subtract) like radicals using the distributive property.

■■ **EXAMPLE 3** Adding and Subtracting Square Root Radicals

Add or subtract as indicated.

(a) $3\sqrt{6} + 4\sqrt{6}$ **(b)** $\sqrt{18} - \sqrt{32}$

SOLUTION

(a) Since both terms contain $\sqrt{6}$, they are like radicals, and may be combined.

$$3\sqrt{6} + 4\sqrt{6} = (3 + 4)\sqrt{6}$$ Distributive property
$$= 7\sqrt{6}$$ Add.

(b) If we simplify $\sqrt{18}$ and $\sqrt{32}$, then this operation can be performed.

$$\sqrt{18} - \sqrt{32} = \sqrt{9 \cdot 2} - \sqrt{16 \cdot 2}$$ Factor so that perfect squares are in the radicands.
$$= \sqrt{9} \cdot \sqrt{2} - \sqrt{16} \cdot \sqrt{2}$$ Product rule
$$= 3\sqrt{2} - 4\sqrt{2}$$ Take square roots.
$$= (3 - 4)\sqrt{2}$$ Distributive property
$$= -1\sqrt{2}$$ Subtract.
$$= -\sqrt{2}$$ $-1 \cdot a = -a$ ■■■

From **Example 3,** we see that like radicals may be added or subtracted by adding or subtracting their coefficients (the numbers by which they are multiplied) and keeping the same radical. Observe these examples.

$$9\sqrt{7} + 8\sqrt{7} = 17\sqrt{7} \quad \text{(since } 9 + 8 = 17\text{)}$$

$$4\sqrt{3} - 12\sqrt{3} = -8\sqrt{3} \quad \text{(since } 4 - 12 = -8\text{)}$$

In the statements of the product and quotient rules for square roots, the radicands could not be negative. While $-\sqrt{2}$ is a real number, for example, $\sqrt{-2}$ is not. There is no real number whose square is -2. The same may be said for any negative radicand. In order to handle this situation, mathematicians have extended our number system to include *complex numbers,* discussed in the **Extension** at the end of this chapter.

The Irrational Numbers π, ϕ, and e

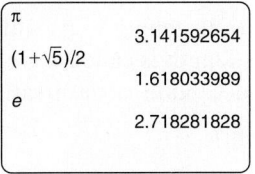

π	3.141592654
(1+√5)/2	
	1.618033989
e	
	2.718281828

Figure 13

Figure 13 shows approximations for three of the most interesting and important irrational numbers in mathematics. The first of these, π, represents the ratio of the circumference of a circle to its diameter. The second, ϕ, is the Golden Ratio, covered in detail in **Section 5.5.** Its exact value is $\dfrac{1+\sqrt{5}}{2}$. The third is e, a fundamental number in our universe. It is the base of the *natural exponential* and *natural logarithmic* functions, as seen in **Section 8.6.** The letter e was chosen to honor Leonhard Euler, who published extensive research on the number in 1746.

Pi (π)

$$\pi \approx 3.14159265358979323846264338327 9$$

The computation of the digits of π has fascinated mathematicians since ancient times. Archimedes was the first to explore it extensively, and as of October 20, 2005, its value had been computed to 1,241,100,000,000 decimal digits. Yasumasa Kanada of the University of Tokyo and the brothers Gregory and David Chudnovsky are among today's foremost pi researchers. The book *A History of π* by Petr Beckmann is a classic and now in its third edition. Numerous Web sites, including the following, are devoted to the history and methods of computation of pi.

> www.joyofpi.com/
>
> www.math.utah.edu/~alfeld/Archimedes/Archimedes.html
>
> www.super-computing.org/
>
> www.pbs.org/wgbh/nova/sciencenow/3210/04.html

One of the methods of computing pi involves the topic of *infinite series*.

This poem, dedicated to **Archimedes** ("the immortal Syracusan"), allows us to learn the first 31 digits of the decimal representation of π. By replacing each word with the number of letters it contains, with a decimal point following the initial 3, the decimal is found. The poem was written by A. C. Orr, and appeared in the *Literary Digest* in 1906.

> *Now I, even I, would celebrate*
> *In rhymes unapt, the great*
> *Immortal Syracusan, rivaled nevermore,*
> *Who in his wondrous lore*
> *Passed on before,*
> *Left men his guidance*
> *How to circles mensurate.*

▮▮ EXAMPLE 4 Computing the Digits of Pi Using an Infinite Series

It is shown in higher mathematics that the *infinite series*

$$1 - \frac{1}{3} + \frac{1}{5} - \frac{1}{7} + \frac{1}{9} + \dots \text{ "converges" to } \frac{\pi}{4}.$$

That is, as more and more terms are considered, its value becomes closer and closer to $\frac{\pi}{4}$. With a calculator, approximate the value of pi using twenty-one terms of this series.

SOLUTION

Figure 14 on the next page shows the necessary calculation on the TI-83/84 Plus calculator. The sum of the first twenty-one terms is multiplied by 4, to obtain the approximation 3.189184782. (This series converges slowly. While this is only correct to the first decimal place, better approximations are obtained using more terms of the series.)

In 1767 **J. H. Lambert** proved that π is irrational (and thus its decimal will never terminate and never repeat). Nevertheless, the 1897 Indiana state legislature considered a bill that would have *legislated* the value of π. In one part of the bill, the value was stated to be 4, and in another part, 3.2. Amazingly, the bill passed the House, but the Senate postponed action on the bill indefinitely.

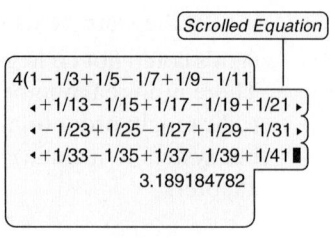

Scrolled Equation

$$4(1-1/3+1/5-1/7+1/9-1/11$$
$$\blacktriangleleft +1/13-1/15+1/17-1/19+1/21 \blacktriangleright$$
$$\blacktriangleleft -1/23+1/25-1/27+1/29-1/31 \blacktriangleright$$
$$\blacktriangleleft +1/33-1/35+1/37-1/39+1/41 \blacksquare$$
$$3.189184782$$

Figure 14   ■■■

A rectangle that satisfies the condition that the ratio of its length to its width is equal to the ratio of the sum of its length and width to its length is called a **Golden Rectangle.** This ratio is called the **Golden Ratio.** Its exact value is the irrational number $\dfrac{1 + \sqrt{5}}{2}$. It is represented by the Greek letter ϕ (phi).

Phi (ϕ)

$$\phi = \frac{1 + \sqrt{5}}{2} \approx 1.6180339887498948482045868343 65$$

Two readily accessible books on phi are *The Divine Proportion, A Study in Mathematical Beauty* by H. E. Huntley, and the more recent *The Golden Ratio* by Mario Livio. Some popular Web sites devoted to this irrational number are the following.

www.mcs.surrey.ac.uk/Personal/R.Knott/Fibonacci/

www.goldennumber.net/

www.mathforum.org/dr.math/faq/faq.golden.ratio.html

www.geom.uiuc.edu/~demo5337/s97b/art.htm

■┃ **EXAMPLE 5** Computing the Digits of Phi Using the Fibonacci Sequence

The first twelve terms of the Fibonacci sequence are

$$1, 1, 2, 3, 5, 8, 13, 21, 34, 55, 89, 144.$$

Each term after the first two terms is obtained by adding the two previous terms. Thus, the thirteenth term is $89 + 144 = 233$. As one goes farther and farther out in the sequence, the ratio of a term to its predecessor gets closer and closer to ϕ. How far out must one go in order to approximate ϕ so that the first five decimal places agree?

SOLUTION

After 144, the next three Fibonacci numbers are 233, 377, and 610. **Figure 15** shows that $\frac{610}{377} \approx 1.618037135$, which agrees with ϕ to the fifth decimal place. ■■■

The irrational number e is a fundamental constant in mathematics. In **Section 8.6,** e is the base of exponential and logarithmic functions.

233/144	
	1.618055556
377/233	
	1.618025751
610/377	
	1.618037135

Figure 15

---

e

$$e \approx 2.718281828459045235360287471353$$

The nature of *e* has made it less understood by the layman than π (or even ϕ, for that matter). The 1994 book *e: The Story of a Number* by Eli Maor has attempted to rectify this situation. The following Web sites also give information on *e*.

www.mathforum.org/dr.math/faq/faq.e.html

www-groups.dcs.st-and.ac.uk/~history/HistTopics/e.html

http://antwrp.gsfc.nasa.gov/htmltest/gifcity/e.1mil

www.math.toronto.edu/mathnet/answers/ereal.html

Example 6 illustrates another infinite series, this one converging to *e*.

▌▌ **EXAMPLE 6** Computing the Digits of *e* Using an Infinite Series

The infinite series

$$2 + \frac{1}{1 \cdot 2} + \frac{1}{1 \cdot 2 \cdot 3} + \frac{1}{1 \cdot 2 \cdot 3 \cdot 4} + \ldots \text{ converges to } e.$$

Use a calculator to approximate *e* using the first seven terms of this series.

SOLUTION

Figure 16 shows the sum of the first seven terms. (The denominators have all been multiplied out.) The sum is 2.718253968, which agrees with *e* to four decimal places. This series converges more rapidly than the one for π in **Example 4.** ▌▌▌

Scrolled Equation

2+1/2+1/6+1/24+1/120+1/720 ▸
◂ +1/5040
2.718253968

Figure 16

6.4 EXERCISES

Identify each number as rational *or* irrational.

1. $\dfrac{4}{9}$ 2. $\dfrac{7}{8}$ 3. $\sqrt{10}$

4. $\sqrt{14}$ 5. 1.618   6. 2.718

7. $0.\overline{41}$ 8. $0.\overline{32}$ 9. π

10. *e*   11. 3.14159   12. $\dfrac{22}{7}$

13. 0.878778777877778 …   14. $\dfrac{1 + \sqrt{5}}{2}$

15. (a) Find the sum.

$$\begin{array}{r} 0.272772777277772\ldots \\ +0.616116111611116\ldots \end{array}$$

(b) Based on the result of part (a), we can conclude that the sum of two _____ numbers may be a(n) _____ number.

16. (a) Find the sum.

$$\begin{array}{r} 0.010110111011110\ldots \\ +0.252552555255552\ldots \end{array}$$

(b) Based on the result of part (a), we can conclude that the sum of two _____ numbers may be a(n) _____ number.

Use a calculator to find a rational decimal approximation for each irrational number. Give as many places as your calculator shows.

17. $\sqrt{39}$ 18. $\sqrt{44}$ 19. $\sqrt{15.1}$ 20. $\sqrt{33.6}$

21. $\sqrt{884}$ 22. $\sqrt{643}$ 23. $\sqrt{\dfrac{9}{8}}$ 24. $\sqrt{\dfrac{6}{5}}$

*Use the methods of **Examples 1 and 2** to simplify each expression. Then, use a calculator to approximate both the given expression and the simplified expression. (Both should be the same.)*

25. $\sqrt{50}$ 26. $\sqrt{32}$

27. $\sqrt{75}$ 28. $\sqrt{150}$

29. $\sqrt{288}$ 30. $\sqrt{200}$

31. $\dfrac{5}{\sqrt{6}}$ 32. $\dfrac{3}{\sqrt{2}}$

33. $\sqrt{\dfrac{7}{4}}$ 34. $\sqrt{\dfrac{8}{9}}$

35. $\sqrt{\dfrac{7}{3}}$ 36. $\sqrt{\dfrac{14}{5}}$

*Use the method of **Example 3** to perform the indicated operations.*

37. $\sqrt{17} + 2\sqrt{17}$

38. $3\sqrt{19} + \sqrt{19}$

39. $5\sqrt{7} - \sqrt{7}$

40. $3\sqrt{27} - \sqrt{27}$

41. $3\sqrt{18} + \sqrt{2}$

42. $2\sqrt{48} - \sqrt{3}$

43. $-\sqrt{12} + \sqrt{75}$

44. $2\sqrt{27} - \sqrt{300}$

Exercises 45–58 deal with π, ϕ, or e. Use a calculator or computer as necessary.

45. Move one matchstick to make the equation approximately true. (*Source:* www.joyofpi.com)

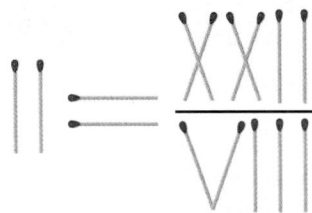

46. Find the square root of $\frac{2143}{22}$ using a calculator. Then find the square root of that result. Compare your result to the decimal given for π in the margin note. What do you notice?

47. Use a calculator to find the first eight digits in the decimal for $\frac{355}{113}$. Compare the result to the decimal for π given in the text. What do you notice?

48. You may have seen the statements "use $\frac{22}{7}$ for π" and "use 3.14 for π." Since $\frac{22}{7}$ is the quotient of two integers, and 3.14 is a terminating decimal, do these statements suggest that π is rational?

49. In the Bible (I Kings 7:23), a verse describes a circular pool at King Solomon's temple, about 1000 B.C. The pool is said to be ten cubits across, "and a line of 30 cubits did compass it round about." What value of π does this imply?

50. The ancient Egyptians used a method for finding the area of a circle that is equivalent to a value of 3.1605 for π. Write this decimal as a mixed number.

51. The computation of π has fascinated mathematicians and laymen for centuries. In the nineteenth century, the British mathematician William Shanks spent many years of his life calculating π to 707 decimal places. It turned out that only the first 527 were correct. Use an Internet search to find the 528th decimal digit of π (following the whole number part 3.).

52. One of the reasons for computing so many digits of π is to determine how often each digit appears and to identify any interesting patterns among the digits. Gregory and David Chudnovsky have spent a great deal of time looking for patterns in the digits. For example, six 9s in a row appear relatively early in the decimal, within the first 800 decimal places. Use an Internet search to find the positions of these six 9s in a row.

53. The expression $\frac{2 \cdot 2 \cdot 4 \cdot 4 \cdot 6 \cdot 6 \cdot 8 \cdots}{1 \cdot 3 \cdot 3 \cdot 5 \cdot 5 \cdot 7 \cdot 7 \cdots}$ converges to $\frac{\pi}{2}$. Use a calculator to evaluate only the digits of the expression as shown here, and then multiply by 2. What value for an approximation for π does this give (to one decimal place)?

54. A **mnemonic device** is a scheme whereby one is able to recall facts by memorizing something completely unrelated to the facts. One way of learning the first few digits of the decimal for π is to memorize a sentence (or several sentences) and count the letters in each word of the sentence. For example, "See, I know a digit," will give the first 5 digits of π: "See" has 3 letters, "I" has 1 letter, "know" has 4 letters, "a" has 1 letter, and "digit" has 5 letters. So the first five digits are 3.1415.

Verify that the following mnemonic devices work.

(a) "May I have a large container of coffee?"

(b) "See, I have a rhyme assisting my feeble brain, its tasks ofttimes resisting."

(c) "How I want a drink, alcoholic of course, after the heavy lectures involving quantum mechanics."

55. Use a calculator to find the decimal approximations for $\phi = \frac{1 + \sqrt{5}}{2}$ and its **conjugate**, $\frac{1 - \sqrt{5}}{2}$. Comment on the similarities and differences in the two decimals.

56. In some literature, the Golden Ratio is defined to be the reciprocal of $\frac{1 + \sqrt{5}}{2}$, which is $\frac{2}{1 + \sqrt{5}}$. Use a calculator to find a decimal approximation for $\frac{2}{1 + \sqrt{5}}$ and compare it to ϕ as defined in this text. What do you observe?

57. An approximation for e is 2.718281828. A student noticed that there seems to be a repetition of four digits in this number (1, 8, 2, 8) and concluded that e is rational, because repeating decimals represent rational numbers. Was the student correct? Why or why not?

58. Use a calculator with an exponential key to find values for the following: $(1.1)^{10}$, $(1.01)^{100}$, $(1.001)^{1000}$, $(1.0001)^{10,000}$, and $(1.00001)^{100,000}$. Compare your results to the approximation given for e in this section. What do you find?

Solve each problem. Use a calculator as necessary, and give approximations to the nearest tenth unless specified otherwise.

59. ***Period of a Pendulum*** The period of a pendulum in seconds depends on its length, L, in feet, and is given by the formula

$$P = 2\pi\sqrt{\frac{L}{32}}.$$

If a pendulum is 5.1 feet long, what is its period? Use 3.14 for π.

60. Radius of an Aluminum Can The radius of the circular top or bottom of an aluminum can with surface area S and height h is given by

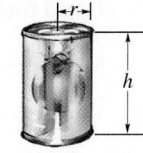

$$r = \frac{-h + \sqrt{h^2 + 0.64S}}{2}.$$

What radius should be used to make a can with height 12 inches and surface area 400 square inches?

61. Distance to the Horizon Jack Adrian, a friend of one of the authors of this text, has a beautiful 14th floor condo, with a stunning view, in downtown Chicago. The floor is 150 feet above the ground. Knowing that this author is a mathematics teacher, Jack emailed the author and told him that he recalled once having studied a formula for calculating the distance to the horizon, but could not remember it. He wanted to know how far he can see from his condo. The author responded:

> *To find the distance to the horizon in miles, take the square root of the height of your view and multiply that result by 1.224. That will give you the number of miles to the horizon.*

Assuming Jack's eyes are 6 feet above his floor, the total height from the ground is $150 + 6 = 156$ feet. To the nearest tenth of a mile, how far can he see to the horizon?

62. Electronics Formula The formula $I = \sqrt{\dfrac{2P}{L}}$ relates the coefficient of self-induction L (in henrys), the energy P stored in an electronic circuit (in joules), and the current I (in amps). Find the value of I if $P = 120$ joules and $L = 80$ henrys.

63. Area of the Bermuda Triangle **Heron's formula** gives a method of finding the area of a triangle if the lengths of its sides are known. Suppose that a, b, and c are the lengths of the sides. Let s denote one-half of the perimeter of the triangle (called the **semiperimeter**); that is,

$$s = \frac{1}{2}(a + b + c).$$

Then the area A of the triangle is given by

$$A = \sqrt{s(s - a)(s - b)(s - c)}.$$

Find the area of the Bermuda Triangle, if the "sides" of this triangle measure approximately 850 miles, 925 miles, and 1300 miles. Give your answer to the nearest thousand square miles.

64. Area Enclosed by the Vietnam Veterans' Memorial The Vietnam Veterans' Memorial in Washington, D.C., is in the shape of an unenclosed isosceles triangle with equal sides of length 246.75 feet. If the triangle were enclosed, the third side would have length 438.14 feet. Use Heron's formula from the previous exercise to find the area of this enclosure to the nearest hundred square feet. (*Source:* Information pamphlet obtained at the Vietnam Veterans' Memorial.)

65. Perfect Triangles A **perfect triangle** is a triangle whose sides have whole number lengths and whose area is numerically equal to its perimeter. Use Heron's formula to show that the triangle with sides of length 9, 10, and 17 is perfect.

66. Heron Triangles A **Heron triangle** is a triangle having integer sides and area. Use Heron's formula to show that each of the following is a Heron triangle.

(a) $a = 11, b = 13, c = 20$

(b) $a = 13, b = 14, c = 15$

(c) $a = 7, b = 15, c = 20$

67. Diagonal of a Box The length of the diagonal of a box is given by

$$D = \sqrt{L^2 + W^2 + H^2},$$

where L, W, and H are the length, the width, and the height of the box. Find the length of the diagonal, D, of a box that is 4 feet long, 3 feet wide, and 2 feet high.

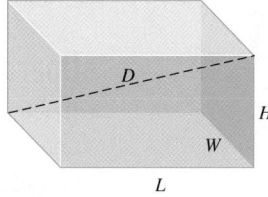

68. Rate of Return on an Investment If an investment of P dollars grows to A dollars in two years, the annual rate of return on the investment is given by

$$r = \frac{\sqrt{A} - \sqrt{P}}{\sqrt{P}}.$$

First rationalize the denominator and then find the annual rate of return (as a decimal) if \$50,000 increases to \$58,320.

69. Accident Reconstruction Police sometimes use the following procedure to estimate the speed at which a car was traveling at the time of an accident. A police officer drives the car involved in the accident under conditions similar to those during which the accident took place and then skids to a stop. If the car is driven at 30 miles per hour, then the speed at the time of the accident is given by

$$s = 30\sqrt{\frac{a}{p}}.$$

Here, a is the length of the skid marks left at the time of the accident and p is the length of the skid marks in the police test. Find s for the following values of a and p.

(a) $a = 862$ feet; $p = 156$ feet

(b) $a = 382$ feet; $p = 96$ feet

(c) $a = 84$ feet; $p = 26$ feet

70. Law of Tensions In the study of sound, one version of the law of tensions is

$$f_1 = f_2 \sqrt{\frac{F_1}{F_2}}.$$

Find f_1 to the nearest unit if $F_1 = 300$, $F_2 = 60$, and $f_2 = 260$.

The concept of square (second) root can be extended to **cube (third) root, fourth root,** *and so on. If $n \geq 2$ and a is a nonnegative number, $\sqrt[n]{a}$ represents the nonnegative number whose nth power is a. For example,*

$$\sqrt[3]{8} = 2 \quad because \quad 2^3 = 8,$$

$$\sqrt[3]{1000} = 10 \quad because \quad 10^3 = 1000,$$

$$\sqrt[4]{81} = 3 \quad because \quad 3^4 = 81, \quad and \ so \ on.$$

Find each root.

71. $\sqrt[3]{64}$

72. $\sqrt[3]{125}$

73. $\sqrt[3]{343}$

74. $\sqrt[3]{729}$

75. $\sqrt[3]{216}$

76. $\sqrt[3]{512}$

77. $\sqrt[4]{1}$

78. $\sqrt[4]{16}$

79. $\sqrt[4]{256}$

80. $\sqrt[4]{625}$

81. $\sqrt[4]{4096}$

82. $\sqrt[4]{2401}$

Use a calculator to approximate each root. Give as many places as your calculator shows. (Hint: To find the fourth root, find the square root of the square root.)

83. $\sqrt[3]{43}$

84. $\sqrt[3]{87}$

85. $\sqrt[3]{198}$

86. $\sqrt[4]{2107}$

87. $\sqrt[4]{10,265.2}$

88. $\sqrt[4]{863.5}$

89. $\sqrt[4]{968.1}$

90. $\sqrt[4]{12,966.4}$

6.5   APPLICATIONS OF DECIMALS AND PERCENTS

Operations with Decimals • Rounding Decimals • Percent • Applications

Operations with Decimals

Because calculators have, for the most part, replaced paper-and-pencil methods for operations with decimals and percent, we will only briefly mention these latter methods. *We strongly suggest that the work in this section be done with a calculator at hand.*

Addition and Subtraction of Decimals

To add or subtract decimal numbers, line up the decimal points in a column and perform the operation.

EXAMPLE 1   Adding and Subtracting Decimal Numbers

Find each of the following.

(a) $0.46 + 3.9 + 12.58$ **(b)** $12.1 - 8.723$

SOLUTION

(a)
$$\begin{array}{r} 0.46 \\ 3.90 \\ +12.58 \\ \hline 16.94 \end{array}$$
Line up decimal points.
Attach a zero as a placeholder.
← Sum

(b)
$$\begin{array}{r} 12.100 \\ -8.723 \\ \hline 3.377 \end{array}$$
Attach zeros.
← Difference

```
.46+3.9+12.58
                16.94
12.1-8.723
                3.377
```

This screen supports the results in **Example 1.**

■■■

Recall that when two numbers are multiplied, the numbers are called **factors** and the answer is called the **product.** When two numbers are divided, the number being divided is called the **dividend,** the number doing the dividing is called the **divisor,** and the answer is called the **quotient.**

Multiplication and Division of Decimals

Multiplication   To multiply decimals, multiply in the same manner as integers are multiplied. The number of decimal places to the right of the decimal point in the product is the *sum* of the numbers of places to the right of the decimal points in the factors.

Division   To divide decimals, move the decimal point to the right the same number of places in the divisor and the dividend so as to obtain a whole number in the divisor. Divide in the same manner as integers are divided. The number of decimal places to the right of the decimal point in the quotient is the same as the number of places to the right in the dividend.

▮▮ **EXAMPLE 2** Multiplying and Dividing Decimal Numbers

Find each of the following.

(a) 4.613×2.52 **(b)** $65.175 \div 8.25$

SOLUTION

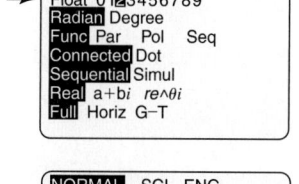

Here the TI-83/84 Plus is set to round the answer to two decimal places.

(a)
$$
\begin{array}{r}
4.613 \quad \leftarrow \text{3 decimal places} \\
\times \quad 2.52 \quad \leftarrow \text{2 decimal places} \\
\hline
9226 \\
23065 \\
9226 \\
\hline
11.62476 \quad \leftarrow \text{3 + 2 = 5 decimal places}
\end{array}
$$

(b)
$$
8.25 \overline{)65.175} \rightarrow 825 \overline{)6517.5}
$$
$$
\begin{array}{r}
7.9 \\
\hline
5775 \\
7425 \\
7425 \\
\hline
0
\end{array}
$$

Bring the decimal point straight up in the answer.

Rounding Decimals

▮▮ **EXAMPLE 3** Rounding a Decimal Number

Round 3.917 to the nearest hundredth.

SOLUTION

The hundredths place in 3.917 contains the digit 1.

3.917
↑ Hundredths place

To round this decimal, locate 3.91 and 3.92 on a number line as in **Figure 17**.

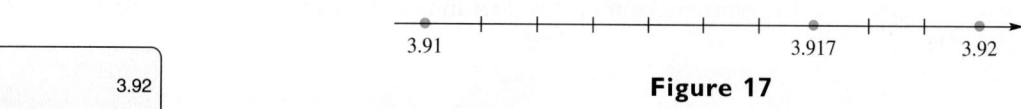

Figure 17

The calculator rounds 3.917 to the nearest hundredth.

The distance from 3.91 to 3.92 is divided into ten equal parts. The seventh of these ten parts locates the number 3.917. As the number line shows, 3.917 is closer to 3.92 than it is to 3.91, so 3.917 rounded to the nearest hundredth is 3.92.   ▮▮▮

The calculator rounds 3.915 *up* to 3.92.

If the number line method of **Example 3** were used to round 3.915 to the nearest hundredth, a problem would develop—the number 3.915 is exactly halfway between 3.91 and 3.92. An arbitrary decision is then made to round *up*: 3.915 rounded to the nearest hundredth is 3.92. (Some disciplines have guidelines so that in certain cases, a *downward* roundoff is made. We will not investigate these.)

Rules for Rounding Decimals
Step 1 Locate the **place** to which the number is being rounded.
Step 2 Look at the next **digit to the right** of the place to which the number is being rounded.
Step 3A If this digit is **less than 5,** drop all digits to the right of the place to which the number is being rounded. Do *not change* the digit in the place to which the number is being rounded.
Step 3B If this digit is **5 or greater,** drop all digits to the right of the place to which the number is being rounded. *Add one* to the digit in the place to which the number is being rounded.

▮▮ EXAMPLE 4 Rounding a Decimal Number

Round 14.39656 to the nearest thousandth.

SOLUTION

Step 1 Use an arrow to locate the place to which the number is being rounded.

$$14.39656$$

↑ Thousandths place

Step 2 Check to see if the first digit to the right of the arrow is 5 or greater.

14.396 ⑤ 6   Digit to the right of the arrow is 5.
↑

Step 3 Since the digit to the right of the arrow is 5 or greater, increase by 1 the digit to which the arrow is pointing. Drop all digits to the right of the arrow.

14.39656   Drop.
↑
14.397   Increase by 1.

With the calculator set to round to three decimal places, the result of **Example 4** is supported.

Finally, 14.39656 rounded to the nearest thousandth is 14.397.   ▮▮▮

Percent

One of the main applications of decimals comes from problems involving percents. The word **percent** means **"per hundred."** The symbol % represents "percent."

Percent
$$1\% = \frac{1}{100} = 0.01$$

In *The Producers,* Leo Bloom (Gene Wilder) and Max Bialystock (Zero Mostel) scheme to make a fortune by overfinancing what they think will be a Broadway flop. After enumerating the **percent** of profits all of Max's little old ladies have been offered in the production, reality sets in.

MAX: Leo, how much percentage of a play can there be altogether?

LEO: Max, you can only sell 100% of anything.

MAX: And how much for *Springtime for Hitler* have we sold?

LEO: 25,000%.

MAX (reaching for Leo's blue security blanket): 25,000% . . . . Give me that blue thing.

In *Willy Wonka and the Chocolate Factory,* upon preparing a mixture in his laboratory, Wilder delivers the following impossible **percent** analysis as he drinks his latest concoction.

WILLY WONKA: Invention, my dear friends, is 93% perspiration, 6% electricity, 4% evaporation, and 2% butterscotch ripple.

FEMALE VOICE: That's 105%.

MALE VOICE: Any good?

WILLY WONKA: Yes!

▌▌ EXAMPLE 5 Converting Percents to Decimals

Convert each percent to a decimal.

(a) 98%   **(b)** 3.4%   **(c)** 0.2%   **(d)** 150%

SOLUTION

(a) $98\% = 98(1\%) = 98(0.01) = 0.98$

(b) $3.4\% = 3.4(1\%) = 3.4(0.01) = 0.034$

(c) $0.2\% = 0.2(1\%) = 0.2(0.01) = 0.002$

(d) $150\% = 150(1\%) = 150(0.01) = 1.5$ ▮▮▮

▌▌ EXAMPLE 6 Converting Decimals to Percents

Convert each decimal to a percent.

(a) 0.13   **(b)** 0.532   **(c)** 2.3   **(d)** 0.07

SOLUTION

(a) $0.13 = 13(0.01) = 13(1\%) = 13\%$

(b) $0.532 = 53.2(0.01) = 53.2(1\%) = 53.2\%$

(c) $2.3 = 230(0.01) = 230(1\%) = 230\%$

(d) $0.07 = 7(0.01) = 7(1\%) = 7\%$ ▮▮▮

Converting between Decimals and Percents

To convert a percent to a decimal, drop the percent symbol (%) and move the decimal point two places to the left, inserting zeros as placeholders if necessary.

To convert a decimal to a percent, move the decimal point two places to the right, inserting zeros as placeholders if necessary, and attach the percent symbol (%).

▌▌ EXAMPLE 7 Converting Fractions to Percents

Convert each fraction to a percent.

(a) $\dfrac{3}{5}$ **(b)** $\dfrac{14}{25}$

SOLUTION

(a) First write $\frac{3}{5}$ as a decimal. Dividing 3 by 5 gives $\frac{3}{5} = 0.6 = 60\%$.

(b) $\dfrac{14}{25} = \dfrac{14 \cdot 4}{25 \cdot 4} = \dfrac{56}{100} = 0.56 = 56\%$ ▮▮▮

Converting a Fraction to a Percent

To convert a fraction to a percent, convert the fraction to a decimal, and then convert the decimal to a percent.

The percent symbol, %, probably evolved from a symbol introduced in an Italian manuscript of 1425. Instead of "per 100," "P 100," or "P cento," which were common at that time, the author used "Pͣ." By about 1650 the ͣ had become $\frac{0}{0}$, so "per $\frac{0}{0}$" was often used. Finally the "per" was dropped, leaving $\frac{0}{0}$ or %.

Source: Historical Topics for the Mathematics Classroom, the Thirty-first Yearbook of the National Council of Teachers of Mathematics, 1969.

In the following examples involving percents, three methods are shown. The second method in each case involves using cross-products. The third method involves the percent key of a basic calculator. (Keystrokes may vary among models.)

▌▌ **EXAMPLE 8** Finding a Percent of a Number

Find 18% of 250.

SOLUTION

Method 1 The key word "of" translates as "times."

$$(18\%)(250) = (0.18)(250) = 45$$

Method 2 Think "18 is to 100 as what (x) is to 250?" This translates as follows.

$$\frac{18}{100} = \frac{x}{250}$$

$$100x = 18 \cdot 250 \qquad \tfrac{a}{b} = \tfrac{c}{d} \text{ if and only if } ad = bc.$$

$$x = \frac{18 \cdot 250}{100} \qquad \text{Divide by 100.}$$

$$x = 45 \qquad \text{Simplify.}$$

Method 3 Use the percent key on a calculator with the following keystrokes.

With any of these methods, we find that 18% of 250 is 45.   ▌▌▌

▌▌ **EXAMPLE 9** Finding What Percent One Number Is of Another

What percent of 500 is 75?

SOLUTION

Method 1 Let the phrase "what percent" be represented by $x \cdot 1\%$ or $0.01x$. Again the word "of" translates as "times," while "is" translates as "equals."

$$0.01x \cdot 500 = 75$$

$$5x = 75 \qquad \text{Multiply on the left side.}$$

$$x = 15 \qquad \text{Divide by 5.}$$

Method 2 Think "What (x) is to 100 as 75 is to 500?"

$$\frac{x}{100} = \frac{75}{500}$$

$$500x = 7500 \qquad \text{Cross-products}$$

$$x = 15 \qquad \text{Divide by 500.}$$

Method 3 Use the following keystrokes on a calculator.

In each case, 15 is the percent, so we conclude that 75 is 15% of 500.   ▌▌▌

▐▐ **EXAMPLE 10** Finding a Number of Which a Given Number Is a Given Percent

38 is 5% of what number?

SOLUTION

Method 1

$$38 = 0.05x$$

$$x = \frac{38}{0.05} \quad \text{Divide by 0.05.}$$

$$x = 760 \quad \text{Simplify.}$$

Method 2   Think "38 is to what number (x) as 5 is to 100?"

$$\frac{38}{x} = \frac{5}{100}$$

$$5x = 3800 \quad \text{Cross-products}$$

$$x = 760 \quad \text{Divide by 5.}$$

Method 3   Use the following keystrokes on a calculator.

③ ⑧ ÷ ⑤ %   **760**   Final display

Each method shows us that 38 is 5% of 760.   ▮▮▮

There are various shortcuts that can be used to work with percents. Suppose that you need to compute 20% of 50. Here are two such shortcuts.

1. You think "20% means $\frac{1}{5}$, and to find $\frac{1}{5}$ of something I divide by 5, so 50 divided by 5 is 10. The answer is 10."

2. You think "20% is twice 10%, and to find 10% of something I move the decimal point one place to the left. So, 10% of 50 is 5, and 20% is twice 5, or 10. The answer is 10."

Applications

▐▐ **EXAMPLE 11** Interpreting Percents from a Graph

In 2007, Americans spent about $41.2 billion on their pets. Use the graph in **Figure 18** to determine how much of this amount was spent on pet food.

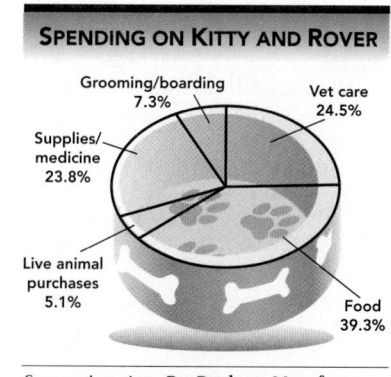

SPENDING ON KITTY AND ROVER

Grooming/boarding 7.3%
Vet care 24.5%
Supplies/medicine 23.8%
Live animal purchases 5.1%
Food 39.3%

Source: American Pet Products Manufacturers Association, Inc.

Figure 18

Dotty

SOLUTION

According to the graph on the preceding page, 39.3% was spent on food. Let x represent this amount in billions of dollars. We use Method 2 of **Example 8.**

$$\frac{x}{41.2} = 0.393 \qquad \text{39.3\% = 0.393}$$

$$x = 41.2(0.393) \qquad \text{Multiply by 41.2.}$$

$$x \approx 16.2 \qquad \text{Nearest tenth}$$

Therefore, about $16.2 billion was spent on pet food.   ▌▌▌

   In many applications we are asked to find the percent increase or percent decrease from one quantity to another. The following guidelines are helpful.

Finding Percent Increase or Decrease

1. To find the **percent increase from a to b,** where $b > a$, subtract a from b, and divide this result by a. Convert to a percent.

   Example: The percent increase from 4 to 7 is $\frac{7-4}{4} = \frac{3}{4} = 75\%$.

2. To find the **percent decrease from a to b,** where $b < a$, subtract b from a, and divide this result by a. Convert to a percent.

   Example: The percent decrease from 8 to 6 is $\frac{8-6}{8} = \frac{2}{8} = \frac{1}{4} = 25\%$.

▌▌ **EXAMPLE 12** Solving Problems about Percent Increase or Decrease

(a) An electronics store marked up a laptop computer from their cost of $1200 to a selling price of $1464. What was the percent markup?

(b) The enrollment in a community college declined from 12,750 during one school year to 11,350 the following year. Find the percent decrease to the nearest tenth.

SOLUTION

(a) "Markup" is a name for an increase. Let $x = $ the percent increase (as a decimal).

$$x = \frac{1464 - 1200}{1200} \qquad \text{Substitute the given values.}$$

Subtract to find the amount of increase.   *Use the original cost.*

$$x = \frac{264}{1200}$$

$$x = 0.22 \qquad \text{Use a calculator.}$$

The computer was marked up 22%.

(b) Let $x = $ the percent decrease (as a decimal).

$$\text{percent decrease} = \frac{\text{amount of decrease}}{\text{original amount}}$$

$$x = \frac{12{,}750 - 11{,}350}{12{,}750} \qquad \text{Substitute the given values.}$$

Subtract to find the amount of decrease.   *Use the original enrollment.*

$$x = \frac{1400}{12{,}750}$$

$$x \approx 0.11 \qquad \text{Use a calculator.}$$

The college enrollment decreased by about 11%.   ▌▌▌

When calculating a percent increase or a percent decrease, be sure to use the original number (before the increase or decrease) as the base. A common error is to use the final number (*after* the increase or decrease) in the denominator of the fraction.

For Further Thought

It's Time to End Decimal Point Abuse

Using a decimal point erroneously with a ¢ symbol is seen almost on a daily basis. Think about it . . . $.99 represents $\frac{99}{100}$ of a dollar, or 99 cents, while 99¢ also represents 99 cents (since ¢ is the symbol for *cent*). So what does .99¢ represent? That's right, $\frac{99}{100}$ of one cent!

Look at the photos provided by one of the authors. An order of spicy nuggets at Wendy's is advertised for .99¢. What do you think would happen if you gave the clerk a dime and asked for ten orders and change? You would most likely get a dumbfounded look. A similar response would probably be forthcoming if you asked for Sierra Mist, which costs even less: .79¢. To vacuum your car, it costs .50¢, a mere half cent. At The Floor Place, fabulous floors really do cost less . . . a lot less: less than half a cent per square foot for Berber flooring. Now here's a deal: a 2-liter bottle of Coca Cola for .09¢! (No doubt, the 1 preceding the decimal point fell off. Even then, one such bottle would cost only a tiny bit more than one penny.) At Winn Dixie, one pound of bananas costs .69¢.

For Group or Individual Investigation

Assume that the products shown in the photos are actually being sold for the indicated prices. Answer each of the following.

1. How many orders of spicy nuggets should you get for $1.00? How much change would Wendy's owe you?

2. How much does one ounce of Sierra Mist cost?

3. If you deposit two quarters to have your car vacuumed, how many times should you be able to vacuum?

4. You want to cover your room area with 400 square feet of Berber flooring. How much will this cost?

5. How many 2 liter bottles of Coca Cola would nine cents get you?

6. If 3 bananas weigh a total of 1 pound, how many can you get for a penny?

6.5 EXERCISES

Decide whether each statement is true *or* false.

1. 300% of 12 is 36.

2. 25% of a quantity is the same as $\frac{1}{4}$ of that quantity.

3. When 759.367 is rounded to the nearest hundredth, the result is 759.40.

4. When 759.367 is rounded to the nearest hundred, the result is 759.37.

5. To find 50% of a quantity, we may simply divide the quantity by 2.

6. A soccer team that has won 12 games and lost 8 games has a winning percentage of 60%.

7. If 70% is the lowest passing grade on a quiz that has 50 items of equal value, then answering at least 35 items correctly will assure you of a passing grade.

8. 30 is more than 40% of 120.

9. .99¢ = 99 cents

10. If an item usually costs $70.00 and it is discounted 10%, then the discount price is $7.00.

Calculate each of the following using either a calculator or paper-and-pencil methods, as directed by your instructor.

11. 8.53 + 2.785

12. 9.358 + 7.2137

13. 8.74 − 12.955

14. 2.41 − 3.997

15. 25.7 × 0.032

16. 45.1 × 8.344

17. 1019.825 ÷ 21.47

18. −262.563 ÷ 125.03

19. $\dfrac{118.5}{1.45 + 2.3}$

20. 2.45(1.2 + 3.4 − 5.6)

Government Spending   *For 2005, total U.S. government spending was about $2500 billion (or $2.5 trillion). The circle graph shows how the spending was divided.*

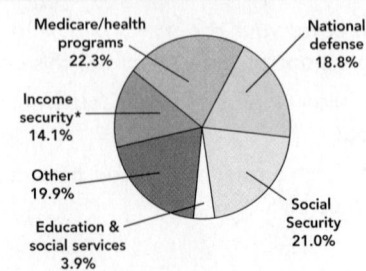

2005 U.S. GOVERNMENT SPENDING

Medicare/health programs 22.3%
National defense 18.8%
Income security* 14.1%
Other 19.9%
Education & social services 3.9%
Social Security 21.0%

*Includes pensions for government workers, unemployment compensation, food stamps, and other such programs.

Source: Office of Management and Budget.

21. About how much was spent on Social Security?

22. About how much did the U.S. government spend on education and social services in 2005?

Postage Stamp Pricing   *Refer to* **For Further Thought** *on decimal point abuse. At one time, the United States Postal Service sold rolls of 33-cent stamps that featured fruit berries. One such stamp is shown on the left. On the right is a photo of the pricing information found on the cellophane wrapper of such a roll.*

100 STAMPS PSA
.33¢ ea. TOTAL $33.00
FRUIT BERRIES
ITEM 7757
BCA

23. Look at the second line of the pricing information. According to the price listed *per stamp*, how many stamps should you be able to purchase for one cent?

24. The total price listed is the amount the Postal Service actually charges. If you were to multiply the listed price *per stamp* by the number of stamps, what should the total price be?

Pricing of Pie and Coffee   *The photos here were taken at a flea market near Natchez, MS. The handwritten signs indicate that a piece of pie costs .10¢ and a cup of coffee ("ffee") costs .5¢. Assuming these are the actual prices, answer the questions in Exercises 25–28.*

25. How much will 10 pieces of pie and 10 cups of coffee cost?

26. How much will 20 pieces of pie and 10 cups of coffee cost?

27. How many pieces of pie can you get for $1.00?

28. How many cups of coffee can you get for $1.00?

Exercises 29–32 are based on formulas found in Auto Math Handbook: Mathematical Calculations, Theory, and Formulas for Automotive Enthusiasts, *by John Lawlor (1991, HP Books).*

29. *Blood Alcohol Concentration* The Blood Alcohol Concentration (BAC) of a person who has been drinking is given by the formula

$$\text{BAC} = \frac{(\text{ounces} \times \text{percent alcohol} \times 0.075)}{\text{body weight in lb}}$$
$$- (\text{hours of drinking} \times 0.015).$$

Suppose a policeman stops a 190-pound man who, in two hours, has ingested four 12-ounce beers, each having a 3.2 percent alcohol content. The formula would then read

$$\text{BAC} = \frac{[(4 \times 12) \times 3.2 \times 0.075]}{190} - (2 \times 0.015).$$

(a) Find this BAC.

(b) Find the BAC for a 135-pound woman who, in three hours, has drunk three 12-ounce beers, each having a 4.0 percent alcohol content.

30. *Approximate Automobile Speed* The approximate speed of an automobile in miles per hour (MPH) can be found in terms of the engine's revolutions per minute (rpm), the tire diameter in inches, and the overall gear ratio by the formula

$$\text{MPH} = \frac{\text{rpm} \times \text{tire diameter}}{\text{gear ratio} \times 336}.$$

If a certain automobile has an rpm of 5600, a tire diameter of 26 inches, and a gear ratio of 3.12, what is its approximate speed (MPH)?

31. *Engine Horsepower* Horsepower can be found from indicated mean effective pressure (mep) in pounds per square inch, engine displacement in cubic inches, and revolutions per minute (rpm) using the formula

$$\text{Horsepower} = \frac{\text{mep} \times \text{displacement} \times \text{rpm}}{792{,}000}.$$

Suppose that an engine has displacement of 302 cubic inches and indicated mep of 195 pounds per square inch at 4000 rpm. What is its approximate horsepower?

32. *Torque Approximation* To determine the torque at a given value of rpm, the formula below applies:

$$\text{Torque} = \frac{5252 \times \text{horsepower}}{\text{rpm}}.$$

If the horsepower of a certain vehicle is 400 at 4500 rpm, what is the approximate torque?

Round each number to the nearest **(a)** *tenth;* **(b)** *hundredth. Always round from the original number.*

33. 78.414   **34.** 3689.537   **35.** 0.0837

36. 0.0658   **37.** 12.68925   **38.** 43.99613

Convert each decimal to a percent.

39. 0.42   **40.** 0.87   **41.** 0.365   **42.** 0.792

43. 0.008   **44.** 0.0093   **45.** 2.1   **46.** 8.9

Convert each fraction to a percent.

47. $\dfrac{1}{5}$ **48.** $\dfrac{2}{5}$ **49.** $\dfrac{1}{100}$ **50.** $\dfrac{1}{50}$

51. $\dfrac{3}{8}$ **52.** $\dfrac{5}{6}$ **53.** $\dfrac{3}{2}$ **54.** $\dfrac{7}{4}$

55. Explain the difference between $\frac{1}{2}$ of a quantity and $\frac{1}{2}\%$ of the quantity.

56. Group I shows some common percents, found in many everyday situations. In Group II are fractional equivalents of these percents. Match the fractions in Group II with their equivalent percents in Group I.

I		**II**	
(a) 25%	**(b)** 10%	**A.** $\dfrac{1}{3}$	**B.** $\dfrac{1}{50}$
(c) 2%	**(d)** 20%	**C.** $\dfrac{3}{4}$	**D.** $\dfrac{1}{10}$
(e) 75%	**(f)** $33\frac{1}{3}\%$	**E.** $\dfrac{1}{4}$	**F.** $\dfrac{1}{5}$

57. Fill in each blank with the correct numerical response.

(a) 5% means _____ in every 100.

(b) 25% means 6 in every _____.

(c) 200% means _____ for every 4.

(d) 0.5% means _____ in every 100.

(e) _____ % means 12 for every 2.

58. The Venn diagram shows the number of elements in the four regions formed.

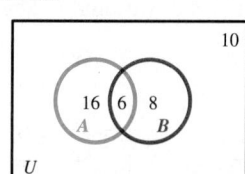

(a) What percent of the elements in the universe are in $A \cap B$?

(b) What percent of the elements in the universe are in A but not in B?

(c) What percent of the elements in $A \cup B$ are in $A \cap B$?

(d) What percent of the elements in the universe are in neither A nor B?

59. *Discount and Markup* Suppose that an item regularly costs $60.00 and it is discounted 20%. If it is then marked up 20%, is the resulting price $60.00? If not, what is it?

60. The figures in **Exercise 13** of **Section 6.3** are reproduced here. Express the fractional parts represented by the shaded areas as percents.

(a) 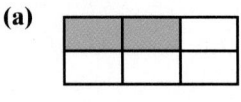 **(b)**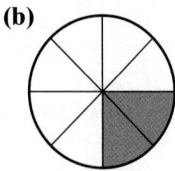

(c) 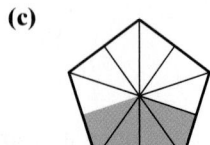 **(d)**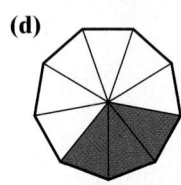

Win-Loss Record *Exercises 61 and 62 deal with winning percentage in the standings of sports teams.*

61. At the end of the regular 2009 Major League Baseball season, the standings of the East Division of the American League were as shown. Winning percentage is commonly expressed as a decimal rounded to the nearest thousandth. To find the winning percentage of a team, divide the number of wins (W) by the total number of games played (W + L). Find the winning percentage of each team.

Team	W	L	Pct.
New York Yankees	103	59	.636
Boston	95	67	
Tampa Bay	84	78	
Toronto	75	87	
Baltimore	64	98	

Source: World Almanac and Book of Facts.

(a) Boston   **(b)** Tampa Bay
(c) Toronto   **(d)** Baltimore

62. Repeat **Exercise 61** for the following standings for the East Division of the National League.

Team	W	L	Pct.
Philadelphia	93	69	
Florida	87	75	.537
Atlanta	86	76	
New York Mets	70	92	
Washington	59	103	

Source: World Almanac and Book of Facts.

(a) Philadelphia   **(b)** Atlanta
(c) New York Mets   **(d)** Washington

Work each problem involving percent.

63. What is 26% of 480?   **64.** Find 38% of 12.

65. Find 10.5% of 28.   **66.** What is 48.6% of 19?

67. What percent of 30 is 45?

68. What percent of 48 is 20?

69. 25% of what number is 150?

70. 12% of what number is 3600?

71. 0.392 is what percent of 28?

72. 78.84 is what percent of 292?

Solve each problem involving percent increase or decrease.

73. ***Percent Increase*** After 1 year on the job, Grady got a raise from $10.50 per hour to $11.34 per hour. What was the percent increase in his hourly wage?

74. ***Percent Discount*** Clayton bought a ticket to a rock concert at a discount. The regular price of the ticket was $70.00, but he paid only $59.50. What was the percent discount?

75. ***Percent Decrease*** Between July 1, 2000, and July 1, 2007, the estimated population of Pittsfield, Massachusetts declined from 134,953 to 129,798. What was the percent decrease to the nearest tenth? (*Source:* U.S. Census Bureau.)

76. ***Percent Increase*** Between July 1, 2000, and July 1, 2007, the estimated population of Anchorage, Alaska grew from 320,391 to 362,340. What was the percent increase to the nearest tenth? (*Source:* U.S. Census Bureau.)

77. ***Percent Discount*** In April 2008, the audio CD of the Original Broadway Cast Recording of the musical *Wicked* was available at www.amazon.com for $9.97. The list price (full price) of this CD was $18.98. To the nearest tenth, what was the percent discount? (*Source:* www.amazon.com)

78. ***Percent Discount*** In April 2008, the DVD of the movie *Alvin and the Chipmunks* was released. This DVD had a list price of $29.99 and was for sale at www.amazon.com at $15.99. To the nearest tenth, what was the percent discount? (*Source:* www.amazon.com)

Use mental techniques to answer the questions in Exercises 79–82. Try to avoid using paper and pencil or a calculator.

79. ***Allowance Increase*** Carly Murray's allowance was raised from $4.00 per week to $5.00 per week. What was the percent of the increase?
    A. 25%   **B.** 20%   **C.** 50%   **D.** 30%

80. ***Boat Purchase and Sale*** Susan Nassy bought a boat five years ago for $5000 and sold it this year for $2000. What percent of her original purchase did she lose on the sale?
    A. 40%   **B.** 50%   **C.** 20%   **D.** 60%

81. Population of Alabama The 2000 U.S. census showed that the population of Alabama was 4,447,000, with 26.0% represented by African Americans. What is the best estimate of the African American population in Alabama? (*Source:* U.S. Census Bureau.)

   A. 500,000   **B.** 1,500,000

   C. 1,100,000   **D.** 750,000

82. Population of Hawaii The 2000 U.S. census showed that the population of Hawaii was 1,212,000, with 21.4% of the population being of two or more races. What is the best estimate of this population of Hawaii? (*Source:* U.S. Census Bureau.)

   A. 240,000   **B.** 300,000

   C. 21,400   **D.** 24,000

Gasoline Prices *The line graph shows the average price, adjusted for inflation, that Americans have paid for a gallon of gasoline for selected years between 1958 and 2008. Use this information in Exercises 83 and 84.*

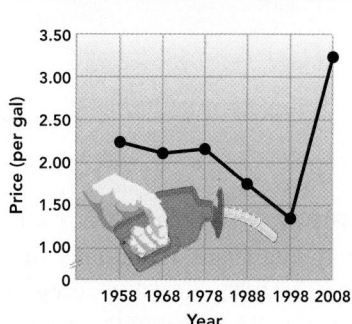

AVERAGE GASOLINE PRICES

Source: www.inflationdata.com

83. By what percent did prices increase from 1998 to 2008?

84. By what percent did prices decrease from 1978 to 1988?

Metabolic Units *One way to measure a person's cardio fitness is to calculate how many METs, or metabolic units, he or she can reach at peak exertion. One MET is the amount of energy used when sitting quietly. To calculate ideal METs, we can use one of the following expressions.*

$$14.7 - age \cdot 0.13$$

$$14.7 - age \cdot 0.11$$

(*Source: New England Journal of Medicine,* August, 2005.)

85. A 40-year-old woman wishes to calculate her ideal MET.

   (a) Write the expression using her age.

   (b) Calculate her ideal MET. (*Hint:* Use the order of operations.)

   (c) Researchers recommend that a person reach approximately 85% of their MET when exercising. Calculate 85% of the ideal MET from part (b). Then refer to the following table. What activity can the woman do that is approximately this value?

Activity	METs	Activity	METs
Golf (with cart)	2.5	Skiing (water or downhill)	6.8
Walking (3 mph)	3.3	Swimming	7.0
Mowing lawn (power mower)	4.5	Walking (5 mph)	8.0
Ballroom or square dancing	5.5	Jogging	10.2
Cycling	5.7	Rope skipping	12.0

Source: Harvard School of Public Health.

86. Repeat parts **(a)–(c)** of **Exercise 85** for a 55-year-old man.

87. Value of 1916-D Mercury Dime The 1916 Mercury dime minted in Denver is quite rare. In 1979 its value in Extremely Fine condition was $625. The 2010 value had increased to $6200. What was the percent increase in the value of this coin from 1979 to 2010? (*Sources: A Guide Book of United States Coins; Coin World Coin Values.*)

88. Value of 1903-O Morgan Dollar In 1963, the value of a 1903 Morgan dollar minted in New Orleans in typical Uncirculated condition was $1500. Due to a discovery of a large hoard of these dollars late that year, the value plummeted. Its value in 2010 was $550. What was the percent decrease in its value from 1963 to 2010? (*Sources: A Guide Book of United States Coins; Coin World Coin Values.*)

Tipping Procedure *It is customary in our society to "tip" waiters and waitresses when dining in restaurants. One common rate for tipping is 15%. A quick way of figuring a tip that will give a close approximation of 15% is as follows:*

Step 1 *Round off the bill to the nearest dollar.*

Step 2 *Find 10% of this amount by moving the decimal point one place to the left.*

Step 3 *Take half of the amount obtained in Step 2 and add it to the result of Step 2.*

This will give you approximately 15% of the bill. The amount obtained in Step 3 is 5%, and 10% + 5% = 15%. Use the method above to find an approximation of 15% for each restaurant bill.

89. $29.57   **90.** $38.32

91. $5.15   **92.** $7.89

Suppose that you get extremely good service and decide to tip 20%. You can use the first two steps listed, and then in Step 3, double the amount you obtained in Step 2. Use this method to find an approximation of 20% for each restaurant bill.

93. $59.96   **94.** $40.24

95. $180.43   **96.** $199.86

97. *Say Again?* A television reporter once asked a professional wrist-wrestler what percent of his sport was physical and what percent was mental. The athlete responded "I would say it's 50% physical and 90% mental." Comment on this response.

98. *Are You Sure?* According to *The Yogi Book*, consisting of quotations by baseball Hall-of-Famer Yogi Berra, he claims that "90% of the game is half mental." Comment on this statement.

EXTENSION Complex Numbers

Basic Concepts and the Imaginary Unit • Products and Quotients
• Complex Numbers and Powers of *i*

Basic Concepts and the Imaginary Unit Numbers such as $\sqrt{-5}$ and $\sqrt{-16}$ were called *imaginary* by early mathematicians. Eventually, their use made it necessary to expand the set of real numbers to form the set of **complex numbers.**

Consider the equation $z^2 + 1 = 0$. It has no real number solution, since any solution must be a number whose square is -1. In the set of real numbers all squares are nonnegative numbers, because the product of either two positive numbers or two negative numbers is positive and $0^2 = 0$. To provide a solution for the equation $z^2 + 1 = 0$, a new number i is defined so that the following is true.

$$i^2 = -1, \quad \text{which implies that} \quad i = \sqrt{-1}.$$

The number i is called the **imaginary unit.** This definition of i makes it possible to define the square root of any negative number as follows.

Gauss and the Complex Numbers In about 1831 **Carl Gauss** was able to show that numbers of the form $a + bi$ can be represented as points on the plane just as real numbers are. He shared this contribution with **Robert Argand**, a bookkeeper in Paris, who wrote an essay on the geometry of the complex numbers in 1806. This went unnoticed at the time.

$\sqrt{-b}$

For any positive real number b, $\sqrt{-b} = i\sqrt{b}$.

 EXAMPLE 1 Writing Square Roots Using *i*

Write each number as a product of a real number and *i*.

(a) $\sqrt{-100}$ **(b)** $\sqrt{-2}$

SOLUTION

(a) $\sqrt{-100} = i\sqrt{100} = 10i$ **(b)** $\sqrt{-2} = \sqrt{2}i = i\sqrt{2}$ ▌▌▌

An Imaginary Tale: The Story of √−1
by Paul J. Nahin provides a historical
account of the development of complex
numbers.

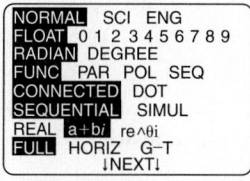

When the TI-83/84 Plus calculator is in
complex mode, denoted by $a + bi$, it will
perform complex number arithmetic.

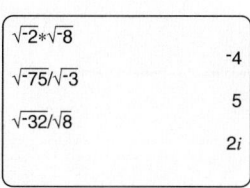

This screen supports the results of
Examples 2(b), 3(a), and 3(b).

In **Example 1(b),** it is easy to mistake $\sqrt{2}i$ for $\sqrt{2i}$, with the i under the radical. For this reason, it is common to write $\sqrt{2}\,i$ as $i\sqrt{2}$.

Products and Quotients When finding a product such as $\sqrt{-4} \cdot \sqrt{-9}$, the product rule for radicals cannot be used, since that rule applies only when both radicals represent real numbers. For this reason, always change $\sqrt{-b}$ (where $b > 0$) to the form $i\sqrt{b}$ before performing any multiplications or divisions.

$$\sqrt{-4} \cdot \sqrt{-9} = i\sqrt{4} \cdot i\sqrt{9} = i \cdot 2 \cdot i \cdot 3 = 6i^2$$

Since $i^2 = -1$,

$$6i^2 = 6(-1) = -6.$$

An *incorrect* use of the product rule for radicals would give a wrong answer.

$$\sqrt{-4} \cdot \sqrt{-9} = \sqrt{(-4)(-9)} = \sqrt{36} = 6 \quad \text{Incorrect}$$

This same reasoning holds for quotients as well.

▮▮ **EXAMPLE 2** Multiplying Expressions Involving i

Multiply.

(a) $\sqrt{-3} \cdot \sqrt{-7}$ **(b)** $\sqrt{-2} \cdot \sqrt{-8}$ **(c)** $\sqrt{-5} \cdot \sqrt{6}$

SOLUTION

(a) $\sqrt{-3} \cdot \sqrt{-7} = i\sqrt{3} \cdot i\sqrt{7} = i^2\sqrt{3 \cdot 7} = (-1)\sqrt{21} = -\sqrt{21}$

(b) $\sqrt{-2} \cdot \sqrt{-8} = i\sqrt{2} \cdot i\sqrt{8} = i^2\sqrt{2 \cdot 8} = (-1)\sqrt{16} = (-1)4 = -4$

(c) $\sqrt{-5} \cdot \sqrt{6} = i\sqrt{5} \cdot \sqrt{6} = i\sqrt{30}$ ▮▮▮

▮▮ **EXAMPLE 3** Dividing Expressions Involving i

Divide.

(a) $\dfrac{\sqrt{-75}}{\sqrt{-3}}$ **(b)** $\dfrac{\sqrt{-32}}{\sqrt{8}}$

SOLUTION

(a) $\dfrac{\sqrt{-75}}{\sqrt{-3}} = \dfrac{i\sqrt{75}}{i\sqrt{3}} = \sqrt{\dfrac{75}{3}} = \sqrt{25} = 5$

(b) $\dfrac{\sqrt{-32}}{\sqrt{8}} = \dfrac{i\sqrt{32}}{\sqrt{8}} = i\sqrt{\dfrac{32}{8}} = i\sqrt{4} = 2i$ ▮▮▮

Complex Numbers and Powers of i *Complex numbers* are defined as follows.

Complex Numbers

If a and b are real numbers, then any number of the form $a + bi$ is called a **complex number.**

---

real(3+7i)

      3

imag(3+7i)

      7

The TI-83/84 Plus calculator identifies the real and imaginary parts of $3 + 7i$.

In the complex number $a + bi$, the number a is called the **real part** and b is called the **imaginary part.*** When $b = 0$, $a + bi$ is a real number, so the real numbers are a subset of the complex numbers. Complex numbers of the form bi, where $b \neq 0$, are called **pure imaginary numbers.** In spite of their name, such numbers are very useful in applications, particularly in work with electricity.

An interesting pattern emerges when we consider various powers of i. By definition, $i^0 = 1$, and $i^1 = i$. We have seen that $i^2 = -1$, and greater powers of i can be found as shown in the following list.

$$i^3 = i \cdot i^2 = i(-1) = -i \qquad\qquad i^6 = i^2 \cdot i^4 = (-1) \cdot 1 = -1$$

$$i^4 = i^2 \cdot i^2 = (-1)(-1) = 1 \qquad i^7 = i^3 \cdot i^4 = (-i) \cdot 1 = -i$$

$$i^5 = i \cdot i^4 = i \cdot 1 = i \qquad\qquad i^8 = i^4 \cdot i^4 = 1 \cdot 1 = 1$$

A few powers of i are listed here.

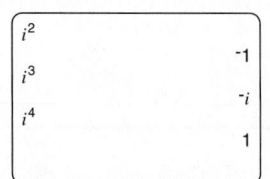

The calculator computes powers of i. Compare to the powers in the chart.

Powers of i			
$i^1 = i$	$i^5 = i$	$i^9 = i$	$i^{13} = i$
$i^2 = -1$	$i^6 = -1$	$i^{10} = -1$	$i^{14} = -1$
$i^3 = -i$	$i^7 = -i$	$i^{11} = -i$	$i^{15} = -i$
$i^4 = 1$	$i^8 = 1$	$i^{12} = 1$	$i^{16} = 1$

The powers of i rotate through the four numbers $i, -1, -i,$ and 1. Larger powers of i can be simplified by using the fact that $i^4 = 1$. For example, consider i^{75}.

$$i^{75} = (i^4)^{18} \cdot i^3 = 1^{18} \cdot i^3 = 1 \cdot i^3 = -i$$

Simplifying Large Powers of i

Step 1 Divide the exponent by 4.

Step 2 Observe the remainder obtained in Step 1. The large power of i is the same as i raised to the power determined by this remainder. Refer to the previous chart to complete the simplification. (If the remainder is 0, the power simplifies to $i^0 = 1$.)

∎∎ **EXAMPLE 4** Simplifying Powers of i

Simplify each power of i.

(a) i^{12} **(b)** i^{39}

SOLUTION

(a) $i^{12} = (i^4)^3 = 1^3 = 1$

(b) To find i^{39}, start by dividing 39 by 4 (Step 1), as shown in the margin. The remainder is 3. So $i^{39} = i^3 = -i$ (Step 2).

Another way to simplify i^{39} is as follows.

$$i^{39} = i^{36} \cdot i^3 = (i^4)^9 \cdot i^3 = 1^9 \cdot (-i) = -i$$ ∎∎∎

$$\begin{array}{r} 9 \\ 4\overline{)39} \\ \underline{36} \\ 3 \end{array} \longleftarrow \text{Remainder}$$

---

*In some texts, bi is called the imaginary part.

EXTENSION EXERCISES

*Use the method of **Examples 1–3** to write each expression as a real number or a product of a real number and i.*

1. $\sqrt{-144}$ **2.** $\sqrt{-196}$ **3.** $-\sqrt{-225}$

4. $-\sqrt{-400}$ **5.** $\sqrt{-3}$ **6.** $\sqrt{-19}$

7. $\sqrt{-75}$ **8.** $\sqrt{-125}$

9. $\sqrt{-5} \cdot \sqrt{-5}$ **10.** $\sqrt{-3} \cdot \sqrt{-3}$

11. $\sqrt{-9} \cdot \sqrt{-36}$ **12.** $\sqrt{-4} \cdot \sqrt{-81}$

13. $\sqrt{-16} \cdot \sqrt{-100}$ **14.** $\sqrt{-81} \cdot \sqrt{-121}$

15. $\dfrac{\sqrt{-200}}{\sqrt{-100}}$ **16.** $\dfrac{\sqrt{-50}}{\sqrt{-2}}$

17. $\dfrac{\sqrt{-54}}{\sqrt{6}}$ **18.** $\dfrac{\sqrt{-90}}{\sqrt{10}}$

19. $\dfrac{\sqrt{-288}}{\sqrt{-8}}$ **20.** $\dfrac{\sqrt{-48} \cdot \sqrt{-3}}{\sqrt{-2}}$

*Use the method of **Example 4** to simplify each power of i.*

21. i^8 **22.** i^{16} **23.** i^{42} **24.** i^{86}

25. i^{47} **26.** i^{63} **27.** i^{101} **28.** i^{141}

COLLABORATIVE INVESTIGATION

Budgeting to Buy a Car

You are shopping for a sports car and have put aside a certain amount of money each month for a car payment. Your instructor will assign this amount to you. After looking through a variety of resources, you have narrowed your choices to the cars listed in the table.

Year/Make/ Model	Retail Price	Fuel Tank Size (in gallons)	Miles per Gallon (city)	Miles per Gallon (highway)
2010 Ford Mustang	$31,395	16.0	16	24
2010 Ford Taurus SEL	$29,220	19.0	17	25
2010 Toyota Camry Hybrid	$26,150	17.2	33	34
2010 Mazda MX-5 Miata	$26,250	12.7	21	28
2010 Honda CR-V EX-L	$26,495	15.3	21	28
2010 Chevrolet Malibu Hybrid	$25,555	16.0	26	34

Source: www.edmunds.com

As a group, work through the following steps to determine which car you can afford to buy.

A. Decide which cars you think are within your budget.

B. Select one of the cars you identified in part A. Have each member of the group calculate the monthly payment for this car using a different financing option. Use the formula given below, where *P* is principal, *r* is interest rate, and *m* is the number of monthly payments, along with the financing options table.

Financing Options

Time (in years)	Interest Rate
4	2.0%
5	3.5%
6	5.0%

$$\text{Monthly Payment} = \frac{\dfrac{Pr}{12}}{1 - \left(\dfrac{12}{12 + r}\right)^m}$$

C. Have each group member determine the amount of money paid in interest over the duration of the loan for his or her financing option.

D. Consider fuel expenses.

   1. Assume you will travel an average of 75 miles in the city and 400 miles on the highway each week. How many gallons of gas will you need to buy each month?

   2. Using typical prices for gas in your area at this time, how much money will you need to have available for buying gas?

E. Repeat parts B–D as necessary until your group can reach a consensus on the car you will buy and the financing option you will use. Write a paragraph to explain your choices.

CHAPTER 6 TEST

1. Consider $\{-4, -\sqrt{5}, -\frac{3}{2}, -0.5, 0, \sqrt{3}, 4.1, 12\}$. List the elements of the set that belong to each of the following.
   (a) natural numbers
   (b) whole numbers
   (c) integers
   (d) rational numbers
   (e) irrational numbers
   (f) real numbers

2. Match each set in (a)–(d) with the correct set-builder notation description in A–D.
   (a) $\{\ldots, -4, -3, -2, -1\}$
   (b) $\{3, 4, 5, 6, \ldots\}$
   (c) $\{1, 2, 3, 4, \ldots\}$
   (d) $\{-12, \ldots, -2, -1, 0, 1, 2, \ldots, 12\}$

   A. $\{x | x$ is an integer with absolute value less than or equal to 12$\}$
   B. $\{x | x$ is an integer greater than 2.5$\}$
   C. $\{x | x$ is a negative integer$\}$
   D. $\{x | x$ is a positive integer$\}$

3. Decide whether each statement is *true* or *false*.
   (a) The absolute value of a number must be positive.
   (b) $|-7| = -(-7)$
   (c) $\frac{2}{5}$ is an example of a real number that is not an integer.
   (d) Every real number is either positive or negative.

Perform the indicated operations. Use the order of operations as necessary.

4. $6^2 - 4(9 - 1)$

5. $\dfrac{(-8 + 3) - (5 + 10)}{7 - 9}$

6. $(-3)(-2) - [5 + (8 - 10)]$

7. **Changes in Foreclosures** The graph shows the percent change in U.S. foreclosure filings from 2008 to 2009 for various states. Use this graph to answer parts (a)–(d) at the top of the next column. (Consider absolute value.)

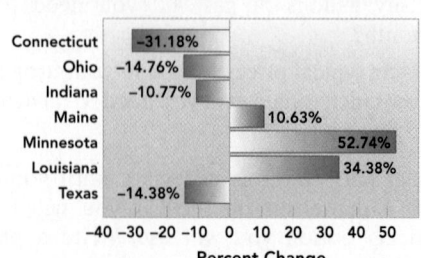

PERCENT CHANGE IN FORECLOSURES

Connecticut	−31.18%
Ohio	−14.76%
Indiana	−10.77%
Maine	10.63%
Minnesota	52.74%
Louisiana	34.38%
Texas	−14.38%

Percent Change

Source: Realty Trac, Inc.

(a) Which state had the greatest change in foreclosures? What was that change?
(b) Which state had the least change in foreclosures? What was that change?
(c) *True* or *false:* The absolute value of the percent change for Texas was greater than the absolute value of the percent change for Ohio.
(d) *True* or *false:* The percent change for Minnesota was more than four times greater than the percent change for Maine.

8. **Altitude of a Plane** The surface of the Dead Sea has altitude 1299 ft below sea level. Victoria LoCascio is flying 80 ft above that surface. How much altitude must she gain to clear a 3852 ft pass by 225 ft? (*Source: The World Almanac and Book of Facts.*)

9. **Median Home Prices** Median pricings for existing homes in the United States for the years 2004 through 2009 are shown in the table. Complete the table, determining the change from one year to the next by subtraction.

	Year	Median-Priced Existing Homes	Change from Previous Year
	2004	$195,200	
	2005	$219,000	$23,800
(a)	2006	$221,900	
(b)	2007	$217,900	
(c)	2008	$196,600	
(d)	2009	$177,500	

Source: National Association of Realtors.

10. Match each statement in (a)–(f) with the property that justifies it in A–F.
    (a) $7 \cdot (8 \cdot 5) = (7 \cdot 8) \cdot 5$
    (b) $3x + 3y = 3(x + y)$
    (c) $8 \cdot 1 = 1 \cdot 8 = 8$
    (d) $7 + (6 + 9) = (6 + 9) + 7$
    (e) $9 + (-9) = -9 + 9 = 0$
    (f) $5 \cdot 8$ is a real number.

    A. Distributive property
    B. Identity property
    C. Closure property
    D. Commutative property
    E. Associative property
    F. Inverse property

11. **Basketball Shot Statistics** Six players on the local high school basketball team had shooting statistics as shown in the table on the next page. Answer each question, using estimation skills as necessary.

Player	Field Goal Attempts	Field Goals Made
Ed Moura	40	13
Jack Pritchard	10	4
Chuck Miller	20	8
Ben Whitney	6	4
Charlie Dawkins	7	2
Jason McElwain ("J-Mac")	7	6

(a) Which players made more than half of their attempts?

(b) Which players made just less than $\frac{1}{3}$ of their attempts?

(c) Which player made exactly $\frac{2}{3}$ of his attempts?

(d) Which two players made the same fractional parts of their attempts? What was the fractional part, reduced to lowest terms?

(e) Which player made the greatest fractional part of his attempts?

Perform each operation. Write your answer in lowest terms.

12. $\frac{3}{16} + \frac{1}{2}$

13. $\frac{9}{20} - \frac{3}{32}$

14. $\frac{3}{8} \cdot \left(-\frac{16}{15}\right)$

15. $\frac{7}{9} \div \frac{14}{27}$

16. Convert each rational number into a repeating or terminating decimal. Use a calculator if your instructor so allows.

(a) $\frac{9}{20}$

(b) $\frac{5}{12}$

17. Convert each decimal into a quotient of integers, reduced to lowest terms.

(a) 0.72

(b) $0.\overline{58}$

18. Identify each number as rational or irrational.

(a) $\sqrt{10}$

(b) $\sqrt{16}$

(c) 0.01

(d) $0.\overline{01}$

(e) 0.0101101110...

(f) π

*For each of the following, **(a)** use a calculator to find a decimal approximation and **(b)** simplify the radical according to the guidelines in this chapter.*

19. $\sqrt{150}$

20. $\frac{13}{\sqrt{7}}$

21. $2\sqrt{32} - 5\sqrt{128}$

22. A student using her powerful new calculator states that the *exact* value of $\sqrt{65}$ is 8.062257748. Is she correct? If not, explain.

23. Work each of the following using either a calculator or paper-and-pencil methods, as directed by your instructor.

(a) 4.6 + 9.21

(b) 12 − 3.725 − 8.59

(c) 86(0.45)

(d) 236.439 ÷ (−9.73)

24. Round 9.0449 to the following place values:

(a) hundredths

(b) thousandths.

25. (a) Find 18.5% of 90.

(b) What number is 145% of 70?

26. Consider the figure.

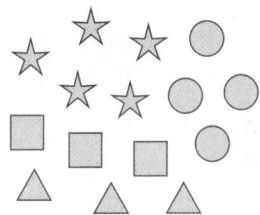

(a) What percent of the total number of shapes are circles?

(b) What percent of the total number of shapes are not stars?

27. *Sales of Books* Use estimation techniques to answer the following: In 2008, Carol Merrigan sold $300,000 worth of books. In 2009, she sold $900,000. Her 2009 sales were _____ of her 2008 sales.

A. 30%   **B.** $33\frac{1}{3}\%$ **C.** 200%   **D.** 300%

28. *Creature Comforts* From a list of "everyday items" often taken for granted, adults were recently surveyed as to those items they wouldn't want to live without. Complete the results shown in the table if 2400 adults were surveyed.

Item	Percent That Wouldn't Want to Live Without	Number That Wouldn't Want to Live Without
Toilet paper	69%	
Zipper	42%	
Frozen Food		384
Self-stick note pads		144

(Other items included tape, hairspray, pantyhose, paper clips, and Velcro.)

Source: Market Facts for Kleenex Cottonelle.

29. *Composition of U.S. Workforce*   The U.S. Bureau of Labor Statistics reported the composition of the U.S. workforce for the year 2006. The total number of people in the workforce for that year was 148,847,000. To the nearest thousand, how many of these were in the Hispanic category?

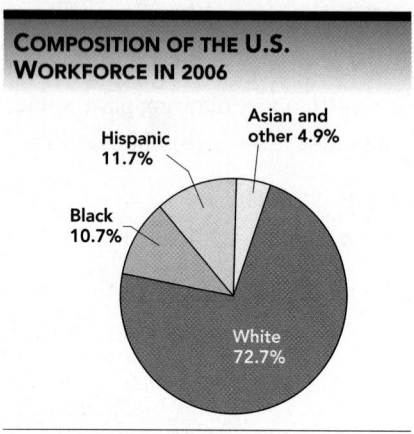

COMPOSITION OF THE U.S. WORKFORCE IN 2006

Hispanic 11.7%

Asian and other 4.9%

Black 10.7%

White 72.7%

Source: U.S. Bureau of Labor Statistics.

30. *Medicare Funding*   Projections have indicated that funding for Medicare will not cover its costs unless the program changes. The line graph shows projections for the years 2004 through 2013. What signed number represents how much the funding will have changed from 2004 to 2013?

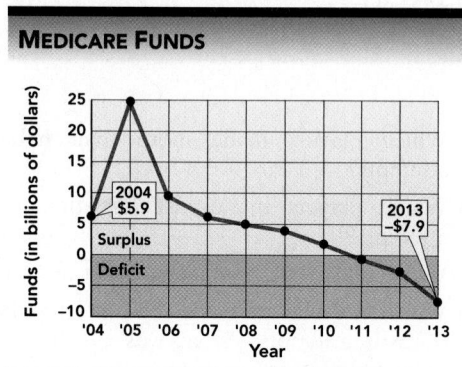

MEDICARE FUNDS

Funds (in billions of dollars)

2004 $5.9

Surplus

Deficit

2013 –$7.9

'04 '05 '06 '07 '08 '09 '10 '11 '12 '13
Year

Source: Centers for Medicare and Medicaid Services.

THE BASIC CONCEPTS OF ALGEBRA

The 2004 movie *Mean Girls* stars Lindsay Lohan as Cady Heron. A scene in the school cafeteria features Cady sitting with The Plastics (the "mean girls" of the title). Regina George, played by Rachel McAdams, is reading a candy bar wrapper.

REGINA: 120 calories and 48 calories from fat. What percent is that? I'm only eating food with less than 30% calories from fat.

CADY: It's 40%. (Responding to a quizzical look from Regina.) Well, 48 over 120 equals x over 100, and then you cross-multiply and get the value of x.

REGINA: Whatever. I'm getting cheese fries.

In her correct solution, Cady turns a percent problem into a proportion, which is an example of a linear equation. In this chapter, we learn how to solve linear equations and investigate other topics from elementary algebra.

7.1 LINEAR EQUATIONS

Solving Linear Equations • Special Kinds of Linear Equations • Literal Equations and Formulas • Models

al-jabr, algebrista, algebra The word **algebra** comes from the title of the work *Hisâb al-jabr w'al muquâbalah*, a ninth-century treatise by the Arab Mohammed ibn Mûsâ al-Khowârizmî. The title translates as "the science of reunion and reduction," or more generally, "the science of transposition and cancellation."

In the title of Khowârizmî's book, *jabr* ("restoration") refers to transposing negative quantities across the equals symbol in solving equations. From Latin versions of Khowârizmî's text, **"al-jabr"** became the broad term covering the art of equation solving. (The prefix *al* means "the.")

Solving Linear Equations

An **algebraic expression** involves only the basic operations of addition, subtraction, multiplication, division (except by 0), raising to powers, or taking roots on any collection of variables and numbers.

$$8x + 9, \quad \sqrt{y} + 4, \quad \text{and} \quad \frac{x^3 y^8}{z} \qquad \text{Examples of algebraic expressions}$$

An **equation** is a statement that two algebraic expressions are equal. A *linear equation in one variable* involves only real numbers and one variable.

$$x + 1 = -2, \quad x - 3 = 5, \quad \text{and} \quad 2x + 5 = 10 \qquad \text{Examples of linear equations}$$

Linear Equation in One Variable

An equation in the variable x is **linear** if it can be written in the form

$$Ax + B = C,$$

where A, B, and C are real numbers, with $A \neq 0$.

A linear equation in one variable is also called a **first-degree equation,** because the greatest power on the variable is one.

If the variable in an equation is replaced by a real number that makes the statement true, then that number is a **solution** of the equation. For example, 8 is a solution of the equation

$$x - 3 = 5,$$

because replacing x with 8 gives a true statement. An equation is **solved** by finding its **solution set,** the set of all solutions. The solution set of the equation $x - 3 = 5$ is $\{8\}$.

Equivalent equations are equations with the same solution set. Equations generally are solved by starting with a given equation and producing a series of simpler equivalent equations. For example,

$$8x + 1 = 17, \quad 8x = 16, \quad \text{and} \quad x = 2 \qquad \text{Equivalent equations}$$

are equivalent equations because each has the same solution set, $\{2\}$. We use the addition and multiplication properties of equality to produce equivalent equations.

Addition Property of Equality

For all real numbers A, B, and C, the equations

$$A = B \qquad \text{and} \qquad A + C = B + C$$

are equivalent. (The same number may be added to both sides of an equation without changing the solution set.)

algebrista, algebra In Spain under Moslem rule, the word **algebrista** referred to the person who restored (reset) broken bones. Signs outside barber shops read *Algebrista y Sangrador* (bonesetter and bloodletter). Such services were part of the barber's trade. The traditional red-and-white striped barber pole symbolizes blood and bandages.

> **Multiplication Property of Equality**
>
> For all real numbers A, B, and C, where $C \neq 0$, the equations
>
> $$A = B \quad \text{and} \quad AC = BC$$
>
> are equivalent. (Both sides of an equation may be multiplied by the same nonzero number without changing the solution set.)

▌▌ **EXAMPLE 1** Using the Addition and Multiplication Properties to Solve a Linear Equation

Solve $4x - 2x - 5 = 4 + 6x + 3$.

SOLUTION

The distributive property allows us to combine *like terms*, such as $4x$ and $2x$.

$$4x - 2x - 5 = 4 + 6x + 3 \qquad \text{Our goal is to isolate } x \text{ on one side.}$$

$$2x - 5 = 7 + 6x \qquad \begin{array}{l}\text{Combine like terms;}\\ 4x - 2x = (4-2)x = 2x\end{array}$$

$$2x - 5 + 5 = 7 + 6x + 5 \qquad \text{Add 5.}$$

$$2x = 12 + 6x \qquad \text{Combine like terms.}$$

$$2x - 6x = 12 + 6x - 6x \qquad \text{Subtract } 6x.$$

$$-4x = 12 \qquad \text{Combine like terms.}$$

$$\frac{-4x}{-4} = \frac{12}{-4} \qquad \text{Divide by } -4.$$

$$x = -3 \qquad \text{Simplify.}$$

Check that -3 is the solution by substituting it for x in the *original* equation.

Check:

$$4x - 2x - 5 = 4 + 6x + 3 \qquad \text{Original equation}$$

$$4(-3) - 2(-3) - 5 \overset{?}{=} 4 + 6(-3) + 3 \qquad \text{Let } x = -3.$$

$$-12 + 6 - 5 \overset{?}{=} 4 - 18 + 3 \qquad \text{Multiply.}$$

(This is **not** the solution.)——$-11 = -11$ ✓ True

The true statement indicates that $\{-3\}$ is the solution set. ▮▮▮

> **Solving a Linear Equation in One Variable**
>
> *Step 1* **Clear fractions.** Eliminate any fractions by multiplying both sides of the equation by a common denominator.
>
> *Step 2* **Simplify each side separately.** Use the distributive property to clear parentheses, and combine like terms as needed.
>
> *Step 3* **Isolate the variable terms on one side.** Use the addition property of equality to transform the equation so that all terms with variables are on one side and all numbers are on the other.
>
> *Step 4* **Transform so that the coefficient of the variable is 1.** Use the multiplication property of equality to obtain an equation with only the variable (with coefficient 1) on one side.
>
> *Step 5* **Check.** Substitute the solution into the original equation.

Notice in **Example 1** that because subtraction and division are defined in terms of addition and multiplication, respectively, we were able to subtract the same number from both sides of the equation, and divide both sides by the same nonzero number, without affecting the solution set.

▮▮ **EXAMPLE 2** Using the Distributive Property to Solve a Linear Equation

Solve $2(x - 5) + 3x = x + 6$.

The problem-solving strategy of guessing and checking, discussed in **Chapter 1**, was actually used by the early Egyptians in equation solving. This method, called the **Rule of False Position,** involved making an initial guess at the solution of an equation, and then following up with an adjustment in the likely event that the guess was incorrect. For example (using our modern notation), if the equation

$$6x + 2x = 32$$

was to be solved, an initial guess might have been $x = 3$. Substituting 3 for x gives

$$6(3) + 2(3) \stackrel{?}{=} 32$$
$$18 + 6 \stackrel{?}{=} 32$$
$$24 = 32. \quad \textbf{False}$$

The guess, 3, gives a value (24) which is smaller than the desired value (32). Since 24 is $\frac{3}{4}$ of 32, the guess, 3, is $\frac{3}{4}$ of the actual solution. The actual solution, therefore, must be 4, since 3 is $\frac{3}{4}$ of 4.

Use the methods explained in this section to verify this result.

SOLUTION

Step 1 Because there are no fractions in this equation, Step 1 does not apply.

Step 2 Use the distributive property to simplify and combine terms on the left side.

$$2(x - 5) + 3x = x + 6$$
$$2x - 10 + 3x = x + 6 \quad \text{Distributive property}$$
$$5x - 10 = x + 6 \quad \text{Combine like terms.}$$

Step 3 Next, use the addition property of equality.

$$5x - 10 + 10 = x + 6 + 10 \quad \text{Add 10.}$$
$$5x = x + 16 \quad \text{Combine like terms.}$$
$$5x - x = x + 16 - x \quad \text{Subtract } x.$$
$$4x = 16 \quad \text{Combine like terms.}$$

Step 4 Use the multiplication property of equality to isolate x on the left.

$$\frac{4x}{4} = \frac{16}{4} \quad \text{Divide by 4.}$$
$$x = 4 \quad \text{Simplify.}$$

Step 5 Check that the solution set is $\{4\}$ by substituting 4 for x in the original equation. ***You should always check your work.*** ▮▮▮

▮▮ **EXAMPLE 3** Solving a Linear Equation with Fractions

Solve $\dfrac{x + 7}{6} + \dfrac{2x - 8}{2} = -4$.

SOLUTION

Step 1 $\quad 6\left(\dfrac{x + 7}{6} + \dfrac{2x - 8}{2}\right) = 6(-4)$ — Multiply each side by the least common denominator (LCD), 6, to eliminate the fractions.

Step 2

Multiply each term by 6.

$$6\left(\frac{x + 7}{6}\right) + 6\left(\frac{2x - 8}{2}\right) = 6(-4) \quad \text{Distributive property}$$
$$x + 7 + 3(2x - 8) = -24 \quad \text{Multiply.}$$
$$x + 7 + 6x - 24 = -24 \quad \text{Distributive property}$$
$$7x - 17 = -24 \quad \text{Combine like terms.}$$

François Viète (1540–1603) was a lawyer at the court of Henry IV of France and studied equations. Viète simplified the notation of algebra and was among the first to use letters to represent numbers.

Step 3
$$7x - 17 + 17 = -24 + 17 \quad \text{Add 17.}$$
$$7x = -7 \quad \text{Combine like terms.}$$

Step 4
$$\frac{7x}{7} = \frac{-7}{7} \quad \text{Divide by 7.}$$
$$x = -1 \quad \text{Simplify.}$$

Step 5   *Check:*
$$\frac{x + 7}{6} + \frac{2x - 8}{2} = -4 \quad \text{Original equation}$$
$$\frac{-1 + 7}{6} + \frac{2(-1) - 8}{2} \overset{?}{=} -4 \quad \text{Let } x = -1.$$
$$\frac{6}{6} + \frac{-10}{2} \overset{?}{=} -4 \quad \text{Simplify each fraction.}$$
$$1 - 5 \overset{?}{=} -4$$
$$-4 = -4 \quad \checkmark \quad \text{True}$$

The solution -1 checks, so the solution set is $\{-1\}$.   ▋▋▋

▋▋ **EXAMPLE 4**   Solving a Linear Equation with Decimals

Solve $0.06x + 0.09(15 - x) = 0.07(15)$.

SOLUTION

Because each decimal number is in hundredths, multiply both sides of the equation by 100. This is done by moving the decimal points two places to the right. (To multiply the second term, $0.09(15 - x)$, by 100, multiply $100(0.09)$ first to get 9, so the product $100(0.09)(15 - x)$ becomes $9(15 - x)$.)

$$0.06x + 0.09(15 - x) = 0.07(15) \quad \text{Original equation}$$
$$0.06x + 0.09(15 - x) = 0.07(15) \quad \text{Multiply each term by 100.}$$
$$6x + 9(15 - x) = 7(15)$$
$$6x + 9(15) - 9x = 105 \quad \text{Distributive property; multiply.}$$
$$-3x + 135 = 105 \quad \text{Combine like terms; multiply.}$$
$$-3x + 135 - 135 = 105 - 135 \quad \text{Subtract 135.}$$
$$-3x = -30 \quad \text{Combine like terms.}$$
$$\frac{-3x}{-3} = \frac{-30}{-3} \quad \text{Divide by } -3.$$
$$x = 10 \quad \text{Simplify.}$$

Check to verify that the solution set is $\{10\}$.   ▋▋▋

Special Kinds of Linear Equations

The preceding equations had solution sets containing one element. For example,

$$2(x - 5) + 3x = x + 6 \quad \text{has solution set} \quad \{4\}.$$

Some equations that appear to be linear have no solutions, while others have an infinite number of solutions. **Table 1** on the next page gives the names of these types of equations.

Algebra dates back to the Babylonians of 2000 B.C. The Egyptians also worked problems in algebra, but the problems were not as complex as those of the Babylonians. In about the sixth century, the Hindus developed methods for solving problems involving interest, discounts, and partnerships.

Many Hindu and Greek works on mathematics were preserved only because Moslem scholars from about 750 to 1250 made translations of them. For example, Mohammed ibn Mûsâ al-Khowârizmî wrote books on algebra and on the Hindu numeration system (the one we use) that had tremendous influence in Western Europe. His name is remembered today in the word *algorithm*.

Sofia Kovalevskaya (1850–1891) was the most widely known Russian mathematician in the late nineteenth century. She did most of her work in the theory of **differential equations**— equations invaluable for expressing rates of change. For example, in biology, the rate of growth of a population, say of microbes, can be precisely stated by differential equations.

Kovalevskaya studied privately because public lectures were not open to women. She eventually received a degree (1874) from the University of Göttingen, Germany. In 1884 she became a lecturer at the University of Stockholm and later was appointed professor of higher mathematics.

Table 1   Types of Equations

Type of Equation	Number of Solutions	Indication When Solving
Conditional	One	Final line is $x = $ a number. (See **Example 5(a)**.)
Identity	Infinite; solution set {all real numbers}	Final line is true, such as $0 = 0$. (See **Example 5(b)**.)
Contradiction	None; solution set $\emptyset$	Final line is false, such as $0 = 1$. (See **Example 5(c)**.)

▋▋ **EXAMPLE 5**   Recognizing Conditional Equations, Identities, and Contradictions

Solve each equation. Decide whether it is a *conditional equation*, an *identity*, or a *contradiction*.

(a) $5x - 9 = 4(x - 3)$ **(b)** $5x - 15 = 5(x - 3)$ **(c)** $5x - 15 = 5(x - 4)$

SOLUTION

(a)
$$5x - 9 = 4(x - 3)$$
$$5x - 9 = 4x - 12 \qquad \text{Distributive property}$$
$$5x - 9 - 4x = 4x - 12 - 4x \qquad \text{Subtract } 4x.$$
$$x - 9 = -12 \qquad \text{Combine like terms.}$$
$$x - 9 + 9 = -12 + 9 \qquad \text{Add 9.}$$
$$x = -3 \qquad \text{Solution set } \{-3\}$$

The solution set has one element, so $5x - 9 = 4(x - 3)$ is a conditional equation.

(b) $5x - 15 = 5(x - 3)$
$$5x - 15 = 5x - 15 \qquad \text{Distributive property}$$
$$0 = 0 \qquad \text{Subtract } 5x \text{ and add 15.}$$

The final line, $0 = 0$, indicates that the solution set is {all real numbers}, and the equation $5x - 15 = 5(x - 3)$ is an identity. (*Note:* The first step yielded $5x - 15 = 5x - 15$, which is true for all values of x, implying an identity there.)

(c)
$$5x - 15 = 5(x - 4)$$
$$5x - 15 = 5x - 20 \qquad \text{Distributive property}$$
$$5x - 15 - 5x = 5x - 20 - 5x \qquad \text{Subtract } 5x.$$
$$-15 = -20 \qquad \text{False}$$

Because the result, $-15 = -20$, is *false*, the equation has no solution. The solution set is $\emptyset$, so the equation $5x - 15 = 5(x - 4)$ is a contradiction. ▋▋▋

Literal Equations and Formulas

An equation involving *variables* (or letters), such as $cx + d = e$, is called a **literal equation.** The most useful examples of literal equations are *formulas*. The solution of a problem in algebra often depends on the use of a mathematical statement or **formula** in which more than one letter is used to express a relationship.

$$d = rt, \quad I = prt, \quad \text{and} \quad P = 2L + 2W \qquad \text{Examples of formulas}$$

In some cases, a formula must be solved for one of its variables. This process is called **solving for a specified variable.** The steps used are similar to those used in solving linear equations.

When you are solving for a specified variable, the key is to treat that variable as if it were the only one. Treat all other variables like numbers (constants).

Solving for a Specified Variable

Step 1   Transform the equation so that all terms containing the specified variable are on one side of the equation and all terms without that variable are on the other side.

Step 2   If necessary, use the distributive property to combine the terms with the specified variable. The result should be the product of a sum or difference and the variable.

Step 3   Divide both sides by the factor that is multiplied by the specified variable.

▌▌ **EXAMPLE 6** Solving for a Specified Variable

Solve the formula $P = 2L + 2W$ for W.

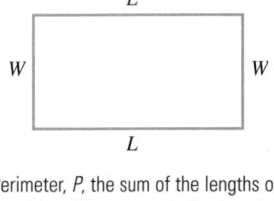

L

W   *W*

L

Perimeter, *P*, the sum of the lengths of the sides of the rectangle, is given by

$P = 2L + 2W.$

Figure 1

SOLUTION

Solve the formula for the perimeter (distance around) of a rectangle (**Figure 1**) for W by isolating W on one side of the equals symbol.

Step 1 $P = 2L + 2W$

$P - 2L = 2L + 2W - 2L$ Subtract 2L.

$P - 2L = 2W$

Step 2   Step 2 is not needed here.

Step 3 $\dfrac{P - 2L}{2} = \dfrac{2W}{2}$ Divide both sides by 2.

$\dfrac{P - 2L}{2} = W,$ or $W = \dfrac{P}{2} - L$ $\dfrac{a - b}{c} = \dfrac{a}{c} - \dfrac{b}{c}$ ▌▌▌

Models

A **mathematical model** is an equation (or inequality) that describes the relationship between two quantities. A *linear model* is a linear equation.

▌▌ **EXAMPLE 7** Modeling the Prevention of Indoor Pollutants

If a range hood removes contaminants at a flow rate of F liters of air per second, then the percent P of contaminants that are also removed from the surrounding air can be modeled by the linear equation

$$P = 1.06F + 7.18,$$

where $10 \leq F \leq 75$. What flow rate F must a range hood have to remove 50% of the contaminants from the air? (*Source:* Rezvan, R. L., "Effectiveness of Local Ventilation in Removing Simulated Pollutants from Point Sources," 65–75. In *Proceedings of the Third International Conference on Indoor Air Quality and Climate*, 1984.)

SOLUTION

$$P = 1.06F + 7.18$$

$$50 = 1.06F + 7.18 \quad \text{Let } P = 50.$$

$$5000 = 106F + 718 \quad \text{Multiply by 100.}$$

$$4282 = 106F \quad \text{Subtract 718.}$$

$$F \approx 40.40 \quad \text{Divide by 106.}$$

The flow rate must be approximately 40.40 L of air per second. ▮▮▮

For Further Thought

The Axioms of Equality

When we solve an equation, we must make sure that it remains "balanced"—that is, any operation that is performed on one side of an equation must also be performed on the other side in order to ensure that the set of solutions remains the same.

Underlying the rules for solving equations are four axioms of equality, listed below. For all real numbers a, b, and c,

1. **Reflexive axiom** $a = a$

2. **Symmetric axiom**   If $a = b$, then $b = a$.

3. **Transitive axiom**   If $a = b$ and $b = c$, then $a = c$.

4. **Substitution axiom**   If $a = b$, then a may replace b in any statement without affecting the truth or falsity of the statement.

A relation, such as equality, which satisfies the first three of these axioms (reflexive, symmetric, and transitive), is called an equivalence relation.

For Group or Individual Investigation

1. Give an example of an everyday relation that does not satisfy the symmetric axiom.

2. Does the transitive axiom hold in sports competition, with the relation "defeats"?

3. Give an example of a relation that does not satisfy the transitive axiom.

7.1 EXERCISES

1. Which equations are linear equations in x?
   - **A.** $2x + x - 1 = 0$ **B.** $8 = x^2$
   - **C.** $6x + 2 = 9$ **D.** $\frac{1}{2}x - \frac{1}{x} = 0$

2. Which of the equations in **Exercise 1** are not linear equations in x? Explain why.

3. Decide whether 12 is a solution of $3(x + 4) = 4x$ by substituting 12 for x. If it is not a solution, explain why.

4. Use substitution to decide whether -2 is a solution of $5(x + 4) - 3(x + 6) = 7(x + 1)$. If it is not a solution, explain why.

5. If two equations are equivalent, they have the same _____ _____ .

6. The equation $4[x + (2 - 3x)] = 2(4 - 4x)$ is an identity. Let x represent the number of letters in your last name. Is this number a solution of this equation? Check your answer.

7. Which expression is equivalent to $0.06(10 - x)(100)$?
   - **A.** $0.06 - 0.06x$ **B.** $60 - 6x$
   - **C.** $6 - 6x$ **D.** $6 - 0.06x$

8. Describe in your own words the steps used to solve a linear equation.

Solve each equation.

9. $7x + 8 = 1$ 10. $5x - 4 = 21$

11. $8 - 8x = -16$ 12. $9 - 2x = 15$

13. $7x - 5x + 15 = x + 8$

14. $2x + 4 - x = 4x - 5$

15. $12x + 15x - 9 + 5 = -3x + 5 - 9$

16. $-4x + 5x - 8 + 4 = 6x - 4$

17. $2(x + 3) = -4(x + 1)$

18. $4(x - 9) = 8(x + 3)$

19. $3(2x + 1) - 2(x - 2) = 5$

20. $4(x - 2) + 2(x + 3) = 6$

21. $2x + 3(x - 4) = 2(x - 3)$

22. $6x - 3(5x + 2) = 4(1 - x)$

23. $6x - 4(3 - 2x) = 5(x - 4) - 10$

24. $-2x - 3(4 - 2x) = 2(x - 3) + 2$

25. $-[2x - (5x + 2)] = 2 + (2x + 7)$

26. $-[6x - (4x + 8)] = 9 + (6x + 3)$

27. $-3x + 6 - 5(x - 1) = -(2x - 4) - 5x + 5$

28. $4(x + 2) - 8x - 5 = -3x + 9 - 2(x + 6)$

29. $-[3x - (2x + 5)] = -4 - [3(2x - 4) - 3x]$

30. $2[-(x - 1) + 4] = 5 + [-(6x - 7) + 9x]$

31. $-(9 - 3x) - (4 + 2x) - 4 = -(2 - 5x) - x$

32. $(2 - 4x) - (3 - 4x) + 4 = -(-3 + 6x) + x$

33. $(2x - 6) - (3x - 4) = -(-4 + x) - 4x + 6$

34. $(3x - 4) - (5x - 8) = -(x + 12) - 6x + 1$

35. To solve the linear equation

$$0.05x + 0.12(x + 5000) = 940,$$

we can multiply both sides by a power of 10 so that all coefficients are integers. What is the smallest power of 10 that will accomplish this goal?

36. Suppose that in solving the equation

$$\frac{1}{3}x + \frac{1}{2}x = \frac{1}{6}x,$$

you begin by multiplying both sides by 12, rather than the *least* common denominator, 6. Should you get the correct solution anyway? Explain.

Solve each equation.

37. $\dfrac{3x}{4} + \dfrac{5x}{2} = 13$

38. $\dfrac{8x}{3} - \dfrac{2x}{4} = -13$

39. $\dfrac{x - 8}{5} + \dfrac{8}{5} = -\dfrac{x}{3}$

40. $\dfrac{2x - 3}{7} + \dfrac{3}{7} = -\dfrac{x}{3}$

41. $\dfrac{4x + 1}{3} = \dfrac{x + 5}{6} + \dfrac{x - 3}{6}$

42. $\dfrac{2x + 5}{5} = \dfrac{3x + 1}{2} + \dfrac{-x + 7}{2}$

43. $0.05x + 0.12(x + 5000) = 940$

44. $0.09x + 0.13(x + 300) = 61$

45. $0.02(50) + 0.08x = 0.04(50 + x)$

46. $0.20(14{,}000) + 0.14x = 0.18(14{,}000 + x)$

47. $0.05x + 0.10(200 - x) = 0.45x$

48. $0.08x + 0.12(260 - x) = 0.48x$

49. The equation $x + 2 = x + 2$ is called a(n) _____, because its solution set is {all real numbers}. The equation $x + 1 = x + 2$ is called a(n) _____, because its solution set is ∅.

50. Which equation is a conditional equation?

    A. $2x + 1 = 3$ **B.** $x = 3x - 2x$

    C. $3x + 1 = 3x$ **D.** $\dfrac{1}{2}x = \dfrac{1}{2}x$

Decide whether each equation is conditional, an identity, or a contradiction. Give the solution set.

51. $-2x + 5x - 9 = 3(x - 4) - 5$

52. $-6x + 2x - 11 = -2(2x - 3) + 4$

53. $6x + 2(x - 2) = 9x + 4$

54. $-4(x + 2) = -3(x + 5) - x$

55. $-11x + 4(x - 3) + 6x = 4x - 12$

56. $3x - 5(x + 4) + 9 = -11 + 15x$

57. $7[2 - (3 + 4x)] - 2x = -9 + 2(1 - 15x)$

58. $4[6 - (1 + 2x)] + 10x = 2(10 - 3x) + 8x$

59. If we solve $\mathcal{A} = \frac{1}{2}bh$ for h, one possible correct answer is

$$h = \frac{2\mathcal{A}}{b}.$$

Which of the formulas is *not* equivalent to this?

    A. $h = 2\left(\dfrac{\mathcal{A}}{b}\right)$ **B.** $h = 2\mathcal{A}\left(\dfrac{1}{b}\right)$

    C. $h = \dfrac{\mathcal{A}}{\frac{1}{2}b}$ **D.** $h = \dfrac{\frac{1}{2}\mathcal{A}}{b}$

60. One source for geometric formulas gives the formula for the perimeter of a rectangle as

$$P = 2L + 2W,$$

while another gives it as

$$P = 2(L + W).$$

Are these equivalent? If so, what property justifies their equivalence?

Mathematical Formulas Solve each formula for the specified variable.

61. $d = rt$; for t (distance)

62. $I = prt$; for r (simple interest)

63. $\mathcal{A} = bh$; for b (area of a parallelogram)

64. $P = 2L + 2W$; for L (perimeter of a rectangle)

65. $P = a + b + c$; for a (perimeter of a triangle)

66. $V = LWH$; for W (volume of a rectangular solid)

67. $\mathcal{A} = \dfrac{1}{2}bh$; for b (area of a triangle)

68. $C = 2\pi r$; for r (circumference of a circle)

69. $S = 2\pi rh + 2\pi r^2$; for h (surface area of a right circular cylinder)

70. $\mathcal{A} = \dfrac{1}{2}h(B + b)$; for B (area of a trapezoid)

71. $C = \dfrac{5}{9}(F - 32)$; for F (Fahrenheit to Celsius)

72. $F = \dfrac{9}{5}C + 32$; for C (Celsius to Fahrenheit)

73. $V = \dfrac{1}{3}\pi r^2 h$; for h (volume of a cone)

74. $V = \dfrac{1}{3}Bh$; for h (volume of a right pyramid)

Work each problem involving a linear model.

75. *Tuition and Fees* The linear model

$$y = 226.9x - 449{,}700$$

describes the amount y in dollars for average tuition and fees at public colleges and universities during the years 1985 through 2008, where x is the year. (*Source:* The College Board.)

(a) Use the model to estimate tuition and fees in 2006.

(b) Use the model to determine the year in which tuition and fees reach $7150.

---

76. *Tuition and Fees* The linear model

$$y = 837.7x - 1{,}657{,}993$$

describes the amount y in dollars for average tuition and fees at private colleges and universities during the years 1985 through 2008, where x is the year. (*Source:* The College Board.)

(a) Use the model to estimate tuition and fees in 2005.

(b) Use the model to determine the year in which tuition and fees reach $27,000.

77. *Indoor Air Quality and Control* The excess lifetime cancer risk R is a measure of the likelihood that an individual will develop cancer from a particular pollutant. For example, if $R = 0.01$ then a person has a 1% increased chance of developing cancer during a lifetime. (This would translate into 1 case of cancer for every 100 people during an average lifetime.) The value of R for formaldehyde, a highly toxic indoor air pollutant, can be calculated using the linear model

$$R = kd,$$

where k is a constant, and d is the daily dose in parts per million. The constant k for formaldehyde can be calculated using the formula

$$k = \frac{0.132B}{W},$$

where B is the total number of cubic meters of air a person breathes in one day, and W is a person's weight in kilograms. (*Source:* Hines, A., T. Ghosh, S. Loyalka, and R. Warder, *Indoor Air: Quality & Control*, Prentice-Hall, 1993; Ritchie, I., and R. Lehnen, "An Analysis of Formaldehyde Concentration in Mobile and Conventional Homes," *J. Env. Health* 47: 300–305.)

(a) Find k for a person who breathes in 20 cubic meters of air per day and weighs 75 kilograms.

(b) Mobile homes in Minnesota were found to have a mean daily dose d of 0.42 part per million. Calculate R using the value of k found in part (a).

(c) For every 5000 people, how many cases of cancer could be expected each year from these levels of formaldehyde? Assume an average life expectancy of 72 years.

78. *Indoor Air Quality and Control* (See **Exercise 77.**) For nonsmokers exposed to environmental tobacco smoke (passive smokers), $R = 0.0015$.

(a) If the average life expectancy is 72 years, what is the excess lifetime cancer risk from secondhand tobacco smoke per year?

(b) Write a linear equation that will model the expected number of cancer cases C per year if there are x passive smokers.

(c) Estimate the number of cancer cases each year per 100,000 passive smokers.

7.2 APPLICATIONS OF LINEAR EQUATIONS

Translating Words into Symbols • Guidelines for Applications • Finding Unknown Quantities • Mixture and Interest Problems • Monetary Denomination Problems • Motion Problems

Translating Words into Symbols

PROBLEM-SOLVING HINT Usually there are key words and phrases in a verbal problem that translate into mathematical expressions involving addition, subtraction, multiplication, and division.

Translating from Words to Mathematical Expressions

Verbal Expression	Mathematical Expression (where x and y are numbers)
Addition	
The **sum** of a number and 7	$x + 7$
6 **more than** a number	$x + 6$
3 **plus** a number	$3 + x$
24 **added to** a number	$x + 24$
A number **increased by** 5	$x + 5$
The **sum** of two numbers	$x + y$
Subtraction	
2 **less than** a number	$x - 2$
12 **minus** a number	$12 - x$
A number **decreased by** 12	$x - 12$
The **difference between** two numbers	$x - y$
A number **subtracted from** 10	$10 - x$
Multiplication	
16 **times** a number	$16x$
A number **multiplied by** 6	$6x$
$\frac{2}{3}$ **of** a number (as applied to fractions and percent)	$\frac{2}{3}x$
Twice (2 times) a number	$2x$
The **product** of two numbers	xy
Division	
The **quotient** of 8 and a number	$\dfrac{8}{x}$ $(x \neq 0)$
A number **divided by** 13	$\dfrac{x}{13}$
The **ratio** of two numbers or the **quotient** of two numbers	$\dfrac{x}{y}$ $(y \neq 0)$

The symbol of equality, **=** , is often indicated by the word *is*. In fact, since equal mathematical expressions represent different names for the same number, words that indicate the idea of "sameness" translate as =. For example,

If the product of a number and 12 is decreased by 7, the result is 105

translates to the mathematical equation

$$12x - 7 = 105,$$

where *x* represents the unknown number. (Why would $7 - 12x = 105$ be incorrect?)

Guidelines for Applications

To solve applied problems, the following six steps are helpful.

George Polya's problem-solving **procedure** can be adapted to applications of algebra as seen in the steps in the box. Steps 1 and 2 make up the first stage of Polya's procedure (*Understand the Problem*), Step 3 forms the second stage (*Devise a Plan*), Step 4 comprises the third stage (*Carry Out the Plan*), and Steps 5 and 6 form the last stage (*Look Back*).

Solving an Applied Problem

Step 1 **Read** the problem carefully until you understand what is given and what is to be found.

Step 2 **Assign a variable** to represent the unknown value, using diagrams or tables as needed. Write down what the variable represents. If necessary, express any other unknown values in terms of the variable.

Step 3 **Write an equation** using the variable expression(s).

Step 4 **Solve** the equation.

Step 5 **State the answer.** Does it seem reasonable?

Step 6 **Check** the answer in the words of the *original* problem.

Finding Unknown Quantities

PROBLEM-SOLVING HINT A common type of problem involves finding two quantities when the sum of the quantities is known. Choose a variable to represent one of the unknowns and then represent the other quantity in terms of the same variable, using information from the problem. Then write an equation based on the words of the problem.

■■ **EXAMPLE 1** Finding Numbers of Strikeouts

Two outstanding major league pitchers in recent years are Randy Johnson and Johan Santana. In 2004, they combined for a total of 555 strikeouts. Johnson had 25 more strikeouts than Santana. How many strikeouts did each pitcher have? (*Source: World Almanac and Book of Facts.*)

SOLUTION

Step 1 **Read** the problem. We are asked to find the number of strikeouts each pitcher had.

Step 2 **Assign a variable** to represent the number of strikeouts for one of the men.

Let s = the number of strikeouts for Johan Santana.

We must also find the number of strikeouts for Randy Johnson. Because he had 25 more strikeouts than Santana,

$s + 25$ = the number of strikeouts for Johnson.

Johan Santana

Here is an application of linear equations, taken from the **Greek Anthology** (about 500 A.D.), a group of 46 number problems.

Demochares has lived a fourth of his life as a boy, a fifth as a youth, a third as a man, and has spent 13 years in his dotage. How old is he?

(Answer: 60 years old)

Step 3   **Write an equation.** The sum of the numbers of strikeouts is 555.

Santana's strikeouts	+	Johnson's strikeouts	=	Total
↓		↓		↓
s	$+$	$(s + 25)$	$=$	555

Step 4   **Solve** the equation.

$$s + (s + 25) = 555$$

$$2s + 25 = 555 \qquad \text{Combine like terms.}$$

$$2s + 25 - 25 = 555 - 25 \qquad \text{Subtract 25.}$$

$$2s = 530 \qquad \text{Combine like terms.}$$

$$\frac{2s}{2} = \frac{530}{2} \qquad \text{Divide by 2.}$$

Don't stop here.

$$s = 265$$

Step 5   **State the answer.** We let s represent the number of strikeouts for Santana, so Santana had 265. Then the number of strikeouts for Johnson is

$$s + 25 = 265 + 25 = 290. \quad \text{———} \quad \boxed{\textit{Be sure to find the second answer.}}$$

Step 6   **Check.** 290 is 25 more than 265, and the sum of 265 and 290 is 555.   ▮▮▮

▮▮ EXAMPLE 2   Finding Lengths of Pieces of Wood

A woodworking project calls for three pieces of wood. The longest piece must be twice the length of the middle-sized piece, and the shortest piece must be 10 inches shorter than the middle-sized piece. If the three pieces are to be cut from a board 70 inches long, how long can each piece be?

SOLUTION

Step 1   **Read** the problem. Three lengths must be found.

Step 2   **Assign a variable.** Because the middle-sized piece appears in both comparisons, let x represent the length, in inches, of the middle-sized piece.

$$x = \text{the length of the middle-sized piece,}$$
$$2x = \text{the length of the longest piece, and}$$
$$x - 10 = \text{the length of the shortest piece. See \textbf{Figure 2}.}$$

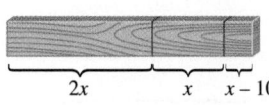

$$\underbrace{\quad}_{2x} \quad \underbrace{\quad}_{x} \quad \underbrace{\quad}_{x-10}$$

Figure 2

Step 3   **Write an equation.**

Longest	plus	middle-sized	plus	shortest	is	total length.
↓	↓	↓	↓	↓	↓	↓
$2x$	$+$	x	$+$	$(x - 10)$	$=$	70

Step 4   **Solve.**

$$4x - 10 = 70 \qquad \text{Combine like terms.}$$

$$4x - 10 + 10 = 70 + 10 \qquad \text{Add 10.}$$

$$4x = 80 \qquad \text{Combine like terms.}$$

$$\frac{4x}{4} = \frac{80}{4} \qquad \text{Divide by 4.}$$

$$x = 20$$

Problems involving age have been around since antiquity. The *Greek Anthology* gives the only information known about the life of the mathematician **Diophantus:**

Diophantus passed $\frac{1}{6}$ of his life in childhood, $\frac{1}{12}$ in youth, and $\frac{1}{7}$ more as a bachelor. Five years after his marriage was born a son who died 4 years before his father, at $\frac{1}{2}$ his father's final age.

Try to write an equation and solve it to show that Diophantus was 84 years old when he died.

Step 5   **State the answer.** The middle-sized piece is 20 inches long, the longest piece is $2(20) = 40$ inches long, and the shortest piece is $20 - 10 = 10$ inches long.

Step 6   **Check.** The sum of the lengths is 70 inches. All conditions of the problem are satisfied.   ▌▌▌

Mixture and Interest Problems

PROBLEM-SOLVING HINT Percents often are used in problems involving mixing different concentrations of a substance or different interest rates. In each case, to get the amount of pure substance or the interest, we multiply.

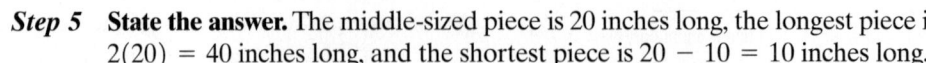

Mixture Problems	Interest Problems (annual)
base × rate (%) = percentage	principal × rate (%) = interest
$b \times r = p$	$P \times r = I$

In an equation, the percent should be written as a decimal.

▌▌ **EXAMPLE 3** Using Percents in Applications

(a) If a chemist has 40 liters of a 35% acid solution, how much pure acid is there?

(b) If $1300 is invested for one year at 2% simple interest, how much interest is earned in one year?

SOLUTION

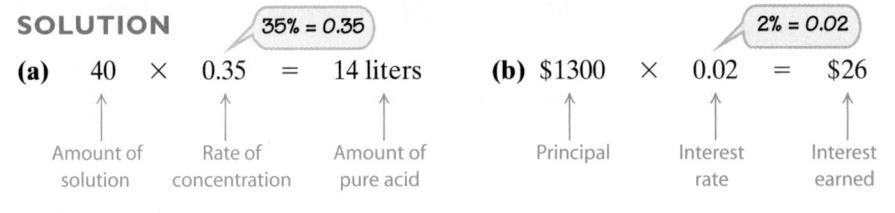

(a) $35\% = 0.35$

$$40 \times 0.35 = 14 \text{ liters}$$

Amount of solution — Rate of concentration — Amount of pure acid

(b) $2\% = 0.02$

$$\$1300 \times 0.02 = \$26$$

Principal — Interest rate — Interest earned   ▌▌▌

PROBLEM-SOLVING HINT A table enables us to set up more easily an equation for a problem, which is usually the most difficult step.

▌▌ **EXAMPLE 4** Solving a Mixture Problem

A chemist must mix 8 liters of a 40% acid solution with some 70% solution to obtain a 50% solution. How much of the 70% solution should be used?

SOLUTION

Step 1   **Read** the problem. We must find the amount of 70% solution to be used.

Step 2   **Assign a variable.** Let $x =$ the number of liters of 70% solution to be used. The information in the problem is illustrated in **Figure 3**.

In the 1941 movie *Buck Privates,* Slicker Smith (Bud Abbott) tells Herbie Brown (Lou Costello) that he is really dumb. To prove it, he challenges Herbie to answer this question:

Suppose you're 40 years old and you're in love with a little girl that's 10 years old. You're 4 times as old as that little girl. Now, you couldn't marry that little girl, could you? So you wait 5 years. Now you're 45 and she's 15. You're three times as old as the little girl. You still can't marry her, so you wait another 15 years. Now you're twice as old as that little girl. How long will you have to wait before she catches up to you?

Watch the movie to hear Herbie's clever answer.

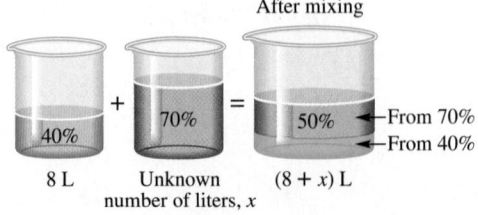

After mixing

40%   +   70%   =   50%   ←From 70%
                                      ←From 40%

8 L   Unknown $(8 + x)$ L
       number of liters, x

Figure 3

Use the given information to complete the table.

Percent (as a decimal)	Number of Liters	Liters of Pure Acid
40% = 0.40	8	0.40(8) = 3.2
70% = 0.70	x	0.70x
50% = 0.50	8 + x	0.50(8 + x)

Sum must equal

The numbers in the right column were found by multiplying the strengths and the numbers of liters. The number of liters of pure acid in the 40% solution plus the number of liters of pure acid in the 70% solution must equal the number of liters of pure acid in the 50% solution.

Step 3 **Write an equation.**

$$3.2 + 0.70x = 0.50(8 + x)$$

Step 4 **Solve.**

$$3.2 + 0.70x = 4 + 0.50x \quad \text{Distributive property}$$

$$0.20x = 0.8 \quad \text{Subtract 3.2 and 0.50}x.$$

$$x = 4 \quad \text{Divide by 0.20.}$$

Step 5 **State the answer.** The chemist should use 4 liters of the 70% solution.

Step 6 **Check.** 8 liters of 40% solution plus 4 liters of 70% solution is

$$8(0.40) + 4(0.70) = \text{6 liters}$$

of acid. Similarly, 8 + 4 or 12 liters of 50% solution has

$$12(0.50) = \text{6 liters}$$

of acid in the mixture. The total amount of pure acid is 6 liters both before and after mixing, so the answer checks. ▌▌▌

Example 5 uses the formula for simple interest, $I = Prt$. When $t = 1$, the formula becomes $I = Pr$, as shown in the Problem-Solving Hint on the previous page.

▌▌ **EXAMPLE 5** Solving an Investment Problem

After winning the state lottery, Theo Lieber has $40,000 to invest. He will put part of the money in an account paying 4% interest and the remainder into stocks paying 6% interest. His accountant tells him that the total annual income from these investments should be $2040. How much should he invest at each rate?

SOLUTION

Step 1 **Read** the problem again. We must find the two amounts.

Step 2 **Assign a variable.**

Let $\quad x =$ the amount to invest at 4%.

Then $\quad 40{,}000 - x =$ the amount to invest at 6%.

The formula for interest is $I = prt$. Here the time, t, is 1 year.

Rate (as a decimal)	Principal	Interest
4% = 0.04	x	0.04x
6% = 0.06	40,000 − x	0.06(40,000 − x)
	40,000	2040

← Totals

The 1995 action thriller *Die Hard: With a Vengeance* features John McClane (Bruce Willis) and Zeus Carver (Samuel L. Jackson) matching wits with villain Simon Gruber (Jeremy Irons) who is planting bombs around New York. To keep a bomb from detonating, McClane and Carver must dial a number that requires solving the following riddle.

As I was going to St. Ives,
I met a man with seven wives,
Every wife had seven sacks,
Every sack had seven cats,
Every cat had seven kits.
Kits, cats, sacks, and wives,
How many were going to
St. Ives?

The rhyme is a derivation of an old application found in the **Rhind papyrus,** an Egyptian manuscript that dates back to about 1650 B.C. **Leonardo of Pisa (Fibonacci)** also included a similar problem in *Liber Abaci* in 1202.

The answer to the question is 1. Only "I" was *going* to St. Ives.

Step 3 **Write an equation.** The last column of the table gives the equation.

Interest at 4%	plus	Interest at 6%	is	Total interest
↓	↓	↓	↓	↓
$0.04x$	$+$	$0.06(40{,}000 - x)$	$=$	2040

Step 4 **Solve** the equation. We do so without clearing decimals.

$$0.04x + 0.06(40{,}000) - 0.06x = 2040 \qquad \text{Distributive property}$$
$$0.04x + 2400 - 0.06x = 2040 \qquad \text{Multiply.}$$
$$-0.02x + 2400 = 2040 \qquad \text{Combine like terms.}$$
$$-0.02x = -360 \qquad \text{Subtract 2400.}$$
$$x = 18{,}000 \qquad \text{Divide by } -0.02.$$

Step 5 **State the answer.** Theo should invest \$18,000 at 4%. At 6%, he should invest \$40,000 − \$18,000 = \$22,000.

Step 6 **Check** by finding the annual interest at each rate.

$$0.04(\$18{,}000) = \$720 \quad \text{and} \quad 0.06(\$22{,}000) = \$1320$$
$$\$720 + \$1320 = \$2040, \quad \text{as required.} \qquad \blacksquare\blacksquare\blacksquare$$

Monetary Denomination Problems

PROBLEM-SOLVING HINT Problems that involve money are similar to mixture and investment problems.

Money Problems
Number × Value of one = Total value

For example, if a jar contains 37 quarters, the monetary value of the coins is

$$37 \quad \times \quad \$0.25 \quad = \quad \$9.25.$$

↑	↑	↑
Number of coins	Denomination	Monetary value

▮▮ **EXAMPLE 6** Solving a Monetary Denomination Problem

For a bill totaling \$5.65, a cashier received 25 coins consisting of nickels and quarters. How many of each denomination did the cashier receive?

SOLUTION

Step 1 **Read** the problem. We must find the number of each denomination.

Step 2 **Assign a variable.**

Let $x =$ the number of nickels.

Then $25 - x =$ the number of quarters.

Denomination	Number of Coins	Value	
\$0.05	x	$0.05x$	←
\$0.25	$25 - x$	$0.25(25 - x)$	← Sum must equal
	25	5.65	←

Step 3 **Write an equation.** The last column of the table gives the following.

$$0.05x + 0.25(25 - x) = 5.65$$

Step 4 **Solve.** $5x + 25(25 - x) = 565$ Multiply by 100.

$$5x + 625 - 25x = 565$$ Distributive property

$$-20x = -60$$ Subtract 625. Combine like terms.

$$x = 3$$ Divide by -20.

Step 5 **State the answer.** The cashier has 3 nickels and $25 - 3 = 22$ quarters.

Step 6 **Check.** The cashier has $3 + 22 = 25$ coins, and the value of the coins is

$$\$0.05(3) + \$0.25(22) = \$5.65, \quad \text{as required.} \quad ▮▮▮$$

Motion Problems

If an automobile travels at an average rate of 50 miles per hour for two hours, then it travels $50 \times 2 = 100$ miles. This is an example of the basic relationship

distance = rate × time.

This is given by the formula $d = rt$. By solving, in turn, for r and t, we obtain two other equivalent forms of the formula. The three forms are given below.

Distance, Rate, Time Relationship

$$d = rt \qquad r = \frac{d}{t} \qquad t = \frac{d}{r}$$

▮▮ **EXAMPLE 7** Using the Distance, Rate, Time Relationship

(a) The speed of sound is 1088 feet per second at sea level at 32°F. In 5 seconds under these conditions, how far does sound travel?

(b) The winner of the first Indianapolis 500 race (in 1911) was Ray Harroun, driving a Marmon Wasp at an average speed of 74.59 miles per hour. How long did it take for him to complete the 500-mile course? (*Source: The Universal Almanac 1997*, John W. Wright, General Editor.)

(c) At the 2008 Olympic Games in Beijing, China, Australian swimmer Leisel Jones set an Olympic record in the women's 100-m breast stroke, swimming the event in 65.17 seconds. What was her rate? (*Source: World Almanac and Book of Facts.*)

SOLUTION

(a)
$$1088 \quad \times \quad 5 \quad = \quad 5440 \text{ feet}$$
$$\text{Rate} \quad \times \quad \text{Time} \quad = \quad \text{Distance}$$

Leisel Jones

(b) To complete the 500 miles, it took Harroun

$$\text{Distance} \longrightarrow \frac{500}{74.59} = 6.70 \text{ hours} \quad (\text{rounded}). \longleftarrow \text{Time}$$
$$\text{Rate} \longrightarrow$$

Here, we found time given rate and distance, using $t = \frac{d}{r}$. To convert 0.70 hour to minutes, multiply by 60 to get $0.70(60) = 42$ minutes. The race took him 6 hours, 42 minutes to complete.

Can we average averages? A car travels from A to B at 40 miles per hour and returns at 60 miles per hour. What is its rate for the entire trip?

The correct answer is not 50 miles per hour, as you might expect. Remembering the distance, rate, time relationship and letting $x=$ the distance between A and B, we can simplify a complex fraction to find the correct answer.

$$\frac{\text{Average rate for}}{\text{entire trip}} = \frac{\text{Total distance}}{\text{Total time}}$$

$$= \frac{x + x}{\dfrac{x}{40} + \dfrac{x}{60}}$$

$$= \frac{2x}{\dfrac{3x}{120} + \dfrac{2x}{120}}$$

$$= \frac{2x}{\dfrac{5x}{120}}$$

$$= 2x \cdot \frac{120}{5x}$$

$$= 48$$

The average rate for the entire trip is 48 miles per hour.

(c) Her rate is found by dividing distance by time.

$$\text{Rate} = \frac{\text{Distance}}{\text{Time}} \longrightarrow \frac{100}{65.17} = 1.53 \text{ meters per second (rounded)} \quad \blacksquare\blacksquare\blacksquare$$

PROBLEM-SOLVING HINT Motion problems use the distance formula,

$$d = rt.$$

In this formula, *when rate (or speed) is given in miles per hour, time must be given in hours.* To solve such problems, *draw a sketch* to illustrate what is happening in the problem, and *make a table* to summarize the given information.

▌▌ **EXAMPLE 8** Solving a Motion Problem

Greg Sabo can bike from home to work in $\frac{3}{4}$ hour. By bus, the trip takes $\frac{1}{4}$ hour. If the bus travels 20 mph faster than Greg rides his bike, how far is it to his workplace?

SOLUTION

Step 1 **Read** the problem. We must find the distance between Greg's home and his workplace.

Step 2 **Assign a variable.** Although the problem asks for a distance, it is easier here to let x be his speed when he rides his bike to work. Then the speed of the bus is $x + 20$.

$$d = rt = x \cdot \frac{3}{4} = \frac{3}{4}x, \quad \text{Distance of trip by bike}$$

and

$$d = rt = (x + 20) \cdot \frac{1}{4} = \frac{1}{4}(x + 20) \quad \text{Distance of trip by bus}$$

We summarize this information in a table.

	Rate	**Time**	**Distance**	
Bike	x	$\dfrac{3}{4}$	$\dfrac{3}{4}x$	
Bus	$x + 20$	$\dfrac{1}{4}$	$\dfrac{1}{4}(x + 20)$	Same distance

Step 3 **Write an equation.** The key to setting up the correct equation is to recognize that the distance in each case is the *same*. See **Figure 4**.

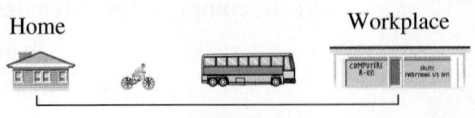

Home   Workplace

Figure 4

$$\frac{3}{4}x = \frac{1}{4}(x + 20) \quad \text{The distance is the same.}$$

Step 4   Solve. $4\left(\dfrac{3}{4}x\right) = 4\left(\dfrac{1}{4}\right)(x + 20)$ Multiply by 4.

$$3x = x + 20 \qquad \text{Multiply.}$$

$$2x = 20 \qquad \text{Subtract } x.$$

$$x = 10 \qquad \text{Divide by 2.}$$

Step 5   State the answer. The required distance is given by $d = rt$.

$$d = \frac{3}{4}x = \frac{3}{4}(10) = \frac{30}{4} = \textbf{7.5 miles} \quad \text{Distance by bike}$$

Step 6   Check by finding the distance by bus.

$$d = \frac{1}{4}(x + 20) = \frac{1}{4}(10 + 20) = \frac{30}{4} = \textbf{7.5 miles} \quad \text{Distance by bus}$$

This yields the same result. It is 7.5 miles to his workplace.   ▌▌▌

PROBLEM-SOLVING HINT In motion problems such as the one in **Example 8,** once you have filled in two pieces of information in each row of the table, you should automatically fill in the third piece of information, using the appropriate form of the formula relating distance, rate, and time.

7.2 EXERCISES

Decide whether each of the following translates into an expression or an equation.

1. the product of a number and 6

2. 39% of a number

3. $\frac{2}{3}$ of a number is 36.

4. 9 is 5 more than a number.

5. the ratio of a number and 24

6. 48 divided by a number is 12.

7. Rework **Example 6,** letting the variable represent the number of quarters. Is the answer to the problem the same?

8. Explain why $19 - x$ is *not* a correct translation of "19 less than a number."

Translate each verbal phrase into a mathematical expression. Use x to represent the unknown number.

9. a number decreased by 12

10. 7 more than a number

11. the product of 6 less than a number and 4 more than the number

12. the quotient of a number and 9

13. the ratio of 25 and a nonzero number

14. $\frac{6}{7}$ of a number

15. Write a few sentences describing the six steps for problem solving.

16. Which is *not* a valid translation of "30% of a number"?

  A. $0.30x$ **B.** $0.3x$ **C.** $\dfrac{3x}{10}$ **D.** 0.30

Unknown Numbers   *Let x represent the number, write an equation for the sentence, and then solve.*

17. If 2 is added to five times a number, the result is equal to 5 more than four times the number. Find the number.

18. If four times a number is added to 8, the result is three times the number added to 5. Find the number.

19. If 2 is subtracted from a number and this difference is tripled, the result is 6 more than the number. Find the number.

20. If 3 is added to a number and this sum is doubled, the result is 2 more than the number. Find the number.

21. The sum of three times a number and 7 more than the number is the same as the difference between -11 and twice the number. What is the number?

22. If 4 is added to twice a number and this sum is multiplied by 2, the result is the same as if the number is multiplied by 3 and 4 is added to the product. What is the number?

Use the methods of **Examples 1 and 2** *or your own method to solve each problem.*

23. *Concert Revenues* Bon Jovi and Bruce Springsteen had the two top-grossing North American concert tours for 2008, together generating $415.3 million in ticket sales. If Bruce Springsteen took in $6.1 million less than Bon Jovi, how much did each tour generate? (*Source:* www.billboard.com)

24. *Automobile Sales* The Toyota Camry was the top-selling passenger car in the United States in 2007, followed by the Honda Accord. Honda Accord sales were 81 thousand less than Toyota Camry sales, and 865 thousand of these two cars were sold. How many of each model of car were sold? (*Source: World Almanac and Book of Facts.*)

25. *NBA Record* In the 2008–2009 NBA regular season, the Boston Celtics won two more than three times as many games as they lost. The Celtics played 82 games. How many wins and losses did the team have? (*Source:* www.nba.com)

26. *MLB Record* In the 2008 Major League Baseball season, the Tampa Bay Rays won 33 fewer than twice as many games as they lost. They played 162 regular season games. How many wins and losses did the team have? (*Source:* www.mlb.com)

27. *U.S. Senate* During the 111th Congress (beginning in 2009), the U.S. Senate had a total of 98 Democrats and Republicans. There were 18 fewer Republicans than Democrats. How many Democrats and Republicans were there in the Senate? (*Source: World Almanac and Book of Facts.*)

28. *U.S. House of Representatives* The total number of Democrats and Republicans in the U.S. House of Representatives during the 111th Congress was 435. There were 31 more Democrats than Republicans. How many members of each party were there? (*Source: World Almanac and Book of Facts.*)

29. *Submarine Sandwich* Nagaraj Nanjappa has a party-length sandwich that is 59 inches long and is to be cut into three pieces. The middle piece will be 5 inches longer than the shortest piece, and the shortest piece will be 9 inches shorter than the longest piece. How long will the pieces be?

30. *Office Manager Duties* In one week, an office manager booked 55 tickets, divided among three airlines. He booked 7 more tickets on American Airlines than United Airlines. On Southwest Airlines, he booked 4 more than twice as many tickets as on United. How many tickets did he book on each airline?

31. *U.S. Olympic Medals* China earned a total of 100 medals at the 2008 Beijing Olympics. The number of gold medals was 23 more than the number of bronze medals. The number of bronze medals was 7 more than the number of silver medals. How many of each kind of medal did China earn? (*Source: World Almanac and Book of Facts.*)

32. *Textbook Editor Duties* Textbook editor Christine O'Brien spent $7\frac{1}{2}$ hours making telephone calls, writing e-mails, and attending meetings. She spent twice as much time attending meetings as making telephone calls, and $\frac{1}{2}$ hour longer writing e-mails than making telephone calls. How many hours did she spend on each task?

Use basic formulas, as in **Example 3,** *to solve each problem.*

33. Acid Mixture How much pure acid is in 500 milliliters of a 14% acid solution?

34. Alcohol Mixture How much pure alcohol is in 300 liters of a 30% alcohol solution?

35. Interest Earned If $10,000 is invested for one year at 2.5% simple interest, how much interest is earned?

36. Interest Earned If $50,000 is invested at 3% simple interest for 2 years, how much interest is earned?

37. Monetary Value of Coins What is the monetary amount of 497 nickels?

38. Monetary Value of Coins What is the monetary amount of 89 half-dollars?

Use the method of **Example 4** *or your own method to solve each problem.*

39. Alcohol Mixture In a chemistry class, 12 liters of a 12% alcohol solution must be mixed with a 20% solution to get a 14% solution. How many liters of the 20% solution are needed?

Strength	Liters of Solution	Liters of Alcohol
12%	12	
20%		
14%		

40. Alcohol Mixture How many liters of a 10% alcohol solution must be mixed with 40 liters of a 50% solution to get a 40% solution?

Strength	Liters of Solution	Liters of Alcohol
	x	
	40	
40%		

41. Antifreeze Mixture A car radiator needs a 40% antifreeze solution. The radiator now holds 20 liters of 20% solution. How many liters of this should be drained and replaced with 100% antifreeze to get the desired strength?

42. Chemical Mixture A tank holds 80 liters of a chemical solution. Currently, the solution has a strength of 30%. How much of this should be drained and replaced with a 70% solution to get a final strength of 40%?

43. Insecticide Mixture How much water must be added to 3 gallons of a 4% insecticide solution to reduce the concentration to 3%? (*Hint:* Water is 0% insecticide.)

44. Alcohol Mixture in First Aid Spray A medicated first aid spray on the market is 78% alcohol by volume. If the manufacturer has 50 liters of the spray containing 70% alcohol, how much pure alcohol should be added so that the final mixture is the required 78% alcohol? (*Hint:* Pure alcohol is 100% alcohol.)

Use the method of **Example 5** *or your own method to solve each problem. Assume all rates and amounts are annual.*

45. Investments at Different Rates John Allen earned $12,000 last year by giving tennis lessons. He invested part at 3% simple interest and the rest at 4%. He earned a total of $440 in interest. How much did he invest at each rate?

Rate (as a Decimal)	Principal	Interest in One Year
0.03		
0.04		
	12,000	440

46. Investments at Different Rates Kim Hobbs won $60,000 on a slot machine in Las Vegas. She invested part at 2% simple interest and the rest at 3%. She earned a total of $1600 in interest. How much was invested at each rate?

Rate (as a Decimal)	Principal	Interest in One Year
0.02	x	$0.02x$
	$60,000 - x$	
		1600

47. Investments at Different Rates Derrick Nantz invested some money at 4.5% simple interest and $1000 less than twice this amount at 3%. His total income from the interest was $1020. How much was invested at each rate?

48. Investments at Different Rates Dee Dee Myers invested some money at 3.5% simple interest, and $5000 more than 3 times this amount at 4%. She earned $1440 in interest. How much did she invest at each rate?

49. Investments at Different Rates Dave Morris has $29,000 invested in stocks paying 5%. How much additional money should he invest in certificates of deposit paying 2% so that the average return on the two investments is 3%?

50. Investments at Different Rates Terry McGinnis placed $15,000 in an account paying 6%. How much additional money should she deposit at 4% so that the average return on the two investments is 5.5%?

*Use the method of **Example 6** or your own method to solve each problem.*

51. Coin Mixture Mike Easley has a box of coins that he uses when playing poker with his friends. The box currently contains 44 coins, consisting of pennies, dimes, and quarters. The number of pennies is equal to the number of dimes, and the total value is $4.37. How many of each denomination of coin does he have in the box?

Denomination	Number of Coins	Value	
0.01	x	$0.01x$	
	x		
0.25			
	44	4.37	Totals

52. Coin Mixture Kathy Diamond found some coins while looking under her sofa pillows. There were equal numbers of nickels and quarters, and twice as many half-dollars as quarters. If she found $2.60 in all, how many of each denomination of coin did she find?

Denomination	Number of Coins	Value	
0.05	x	$0.05x$	
	x		
0.50	$2x$		
		2.60	Total

53. Attendance at a School Play For opening night of a school production of *The Mousetrap*, 410 tickets were sold. Students paid $3 each, while nonstudents paid $7 each. If a total of $1650 was collected, how many students and how many nonstudents attended?

54. Attendance at a Concert A total of 1100 people attended a James Taylor concert. Floor tickets cost $40 each, while balcony tickets cost $28 each. If a total of $41,600 was collected, how many of each type of ticket were sold?

55. Attendance at a Sporting Event At the local minor league hockey arena home games, Row 1 seats cost $35 each and Row 2 seats cost $30 each. The 105 seats in these rows were sold out for the season. The total receipts for them were $3420. How many of each type of seat were sold?

56. Coin Mixture In the nineteenth century, the United States minted two-cent and three-cent pieces. Frances Steib has three times as many three-cent pieces as two-cent pieces, and the face value of these coins is $1.76. How many of each denomination does she have?

57. Stamp Denominations In May 2009, U.S. first-class mail rates increased to 44 cents for the first ounce, plus 17 cents for each additional ounce. If Sabrina spent $17.45 for a total of 55 stamps of these two denominations, how many stamps of each denomination did she buy? (*Source:* U.S. Postal Service.)

58. Movie Ticket Prices A movie theater has two ticket prices: $9 for adults and $6 for children. If the box office took in $4716 from the sale of 600 tickets, how many tickets of each kind were sold?

Use the formula d = rt in Exercises 59–62.

59. Distance Between Cities A small plane traveled from Warsaw to Rome, averaging 164 miles per hour. The trip took two hours. What is the distance from Warsaw to Rome?

60. Distance Between Cities A driver averaged 53 miles per hour and took 10 hours to travel from Memphis to Chicago. What is the distance between Memphis and Chicago?

61. Suppose that an automobile averages 55 miles per hour, and travels for 30 minutes. Is the distance traveled $55 \cdot 30 = 1650$ miles? If not, give the correct distance.

62. Which of the following choices is the best *estimate* for the average speed of a trip of 350 miles that lasted 6.8 hours?

A. 50 miles per hour   **B.** 30 miles per hour

C. 60 miles per hour   **D.** 40 miles per hour

*Use the method of **Example 8** or your own method to solve each problem.*

63. Travel Times of Trains A train leaves Little Rock, Arkansas, and travels north at 85 kilometers per hour. Another train leaves at the same time and travels south at 95 kilometers per hour. How long will it take before they are 315 kilometers apart?

	Rate	Time	Distance
First train	85	t	
Second train			

64. Travel Times of Steamers Two steamers leave a port on a river at the same time, traveling in opposite directions. Each is traveling 22 miles per hour. How long will it take for them to be 110 miles apart?

	Rate	Time	Distance
First steamer		t	
Second steamer	22		

65. *Travel Times of Commuters* Nancy and Mark commute to work, traveling in opposite directions. Nancy leaves the house at 9:00 A.M. and averages 35 miles per hour. Mark leaves at 9:15 A.M. and averages 40 miles per hour. At what time will they be 140 miles apart?

66. *Travel Times of Bicyclers* Jeff leaves his house on his bicycle at 7:30 A.M. and averages 5 miles per hour. His wife, Joan, leaves at 8:00 A.M., following the same path and averaging 8 miles per hour. At what time will Joan catch up with Jeff?

67. *Time Traveled by a Pleasure Boat* A pleasure boat on the Mississippi River traveled from New Roads, LA, to New Orleans with a stop at White Castle. On the first part of the trip, the boat traveled at an average speed of 10 miles per hour. From White Castle to New Orleans the average speed was 15 miles per hour. The entire trip covered 100 miles. How long did the entire trip take if the two parts each took the same number of hours?

68. *Time Traveled on a Visit* Steve leaves Nashville to visit his cousin David in Napa, 80 miles away. He travels at an average speed of 50 miles per hour. One-half hour later David leaves to visit Steve, traveling at an average speed of 60 miles per hour. How long after David leaves will they meet?

69. *Distance Traveled to Work* When Glen Spencer drives his car to work, the trip takes 30 minutes. When he rides the bus, it takes 45 minutes. The average speed of the bus is 12 miles per hour less than his speed when driving. Find the distance he travels to work.

70. *Distance Traveled to School* Theresa Stevens can get to school in 15 minutes if she rides her bike. It takes her 45 minutes if she walks. Her speed when walking is 10 miles per hour slower than her speed when riding. How far does she travel to school?

Automobile Racing In Exercises 71–74, find the time. Use a calculator and round your answers to the nearest thousandth. (Source: The World Almanac and Book of Facts.)

	Event and Year	Participant	Distance	Rate
71.	Indianapolis 500, 2009	Helio Castroneves (Honda)	500 miles	150.318 mph
72.	Daytona 500, 2009	Matt Kenseth (Ford)	500 miles	132.816 mph
73.	Indianapolis 500, 1980	Johnny Rutherford (Hy-Gain McLaren/Goodyear)	255 miles*	148.725 mph
74.	Indianapolis 500, 1975	Bobby Unser (Jorgensen Eagle)	435 miles*	149.213 mph

*rain-shortened

Olympic Results In Exercises 75–78, find the rate. Use a calculator and round your answers to the nearest hundredth. All events were at the Beijing 2008 Olympics. (Source: World Almanac and Book of Facts.)

	Event	Participant	Distance	Time
75.	100-m hurdles, Women	Dawn Harper, USA	100 meters	12.54 seconds
76.	400-m hurdles, Women	Melanie Walker, Jamaica	400 meters	52.64 seconds
77.	400-m hurdles, Men	Angelo Taylor, USA	400 meters	47.25 seconds
78.	400-m run, Men	LaShawn Merritt, USA	400 meters	43.75 seconds

7.3 RATIO, PROPORTION, AND VARIATION

Writing Ratios • Unit Pricing • Solving Proportions • Direct Variation
• Inverse Variation • Joint and Combined Variation

Writing Ratios

One of the most frequently used mathematical concepts in everyday life is *ratio*. A baseball player's batting average is actually a ratio. The slope, or pitch, of a roof on a building may be expressed as a ratio. Ratios provide a way of comparing two numbers or quantities.

> **Ratio**
>
> A **ratio** is a quotient of two quantities. The ratio of the number a to the number b is written
>
> $$a \text{ to } b, \qquad \frac{a}{b}, \qquad \text{or} \qquad a\!:\!b.$$

When ratios are used in comparing units of measure, the units should be the same.

During the first season (1960) of **The Andy Griffith Show,** the episode "Opie's Charity" featured a conversation between Opie and Andy during which Andy explained to Opie that his donation of three cents to the underprivileged children's drive at school was "a piddlin' amount."

ANDY: I was reading here just the other day where there's somewhere like 400 needy boys in this county alone, or one and a half boys per square mile.
OPIE: There is?
ANDY: Sho' is.
OPIE: I've never seen one, Pa.
ANDY: Never seen one what?
OPIE: A half a boy.
ANDY: Well it's not really a half a boy. It's **a ratio.**
OPIE: Horatio who?
ANDY: Not *Horatio,* a ratio. It's mathematics. Arithmetic. Look now Opie, just forget that part of it. Forget the part about the half a boy.
OPIE: It's pretty hard to forget a thing like that, Pa.
ANDY: Well try.
OPIE: Poor Horatio.

EXAMPLE 1 Writing Ratios

Write a ratio for each word phrase.

(a) 5 hours to 3 hours   **(b)** 6 hours to 3 days

SOLUTION

(a) The ratio of 5 hr to 3 hr is

$$\frac{5 \text{ hr}}{3 \text{ hr}} = \frac{5}{3}. \quad \boxed{\text{The ratio is 5 to 3.}}$$

(b) To find the ratio of 6 hr to 3 days, first convert 3 days to hours.

$$3 \text{ days} = 3 \text{ days} \cdot \frac{24 \text{ hr}}{1 \text{ day}} = 72 \text{ hr}$$

The ratio of 6 hr to 3 days is found as follows.

$$\frac{6 \text{ hr}}{3 \text{ days}} = \frac{6 \text{ hr}}{72 \text{ hr}} = \frac{6}{72} = \frac{1}{12} \quad \text{The ratio is 1 to 12.}$$

Unit Pricing

Ratios can be applied in unit pricing, to see which size of an item offered in different sizes produces the best price per unit. To do this, set up the ratio of the price of the item to the number of units on the label. Then divide to obtain the price per unit.

▌▌ EXAMPLE 2 | Finding Price per Unit

A supermarket charges the following for a jar of extra crunchy peanut butter.

Peanut Butter

Size	Price
18-oz	$1.78
28-oz	$2.97
40-oz	$3.98

Which size is the best buy? That is, which size has the lowest unit price?

SOLUTION

Write ratios comparing the price for each size jar to the number of units (ounces) per jar. The results in **Table 2** are rounded to the nearest thousandth.

Table 2

Size	Unit Cost (dollars per ounce)	
18-oz	$\dfrac{\$1.78}{18} = \$0.099$	← The best buy
28-oz	$\dfrac{\$2.97}{28} = \$0.106$	
40-oz	$\dfrac{\$3.98}{40} = \$0.100$	

Because the 18-oz size produces the lowest unit cost, it is the best buy. Thus, buying the largest size does not always provide the best buy. ■■■

Solving Proportions

> **Proportion**
>
> A **proportion** is a statement that says that two ratios are equal.

For example, $\dfrac{3}{4} = \dfrac{15}{20}$ Proportion

is a proportion that says that the ratios $\frac{3}{4}$ and $\frac{15}{20}$ are equal. In the proportion

$$\frac{a}{b} = \frac{c}{d} \quad (b, d \neq 0),$$

a, b, c, and d are the **terms** of the proportion. The a and d terms are called the **extremes,** and the b and c terms are called the **means.** We read the proportion $\frac{a}{b} = \frac{c}{d}$ as "a is to b as c is to d." Multiply each side of this proportion by the common denominator, bd.

Vanishing
point

Image on film

Lens

Object

When you look a long way down a straight road or railroad track, it seems to narrow as it vanishes in the distance. The point where the sides seem to touch is called the **vanishing point.**

The same thing occurs in the lens of a camera, as shown in the figure. Suppose I represents the length of the image, O the length of the object, d the distance from the lens to the film, and D the distance from the lens to the object.

$$\frac{\text{Image length}}{\text{Object length}} = \frac{\text{Image distance}}{\text{Object distance}}$$

or

$$\frac{I}{O} = \frac{d}{D}$$

Given the length of the image on the film and its distance from the lens, the length of the object determines the distance the lens must be from the object.

In the 1994 movie *Little Big League*, young Billy Heywood (Luke Edwards) inherits the Minnesota Twins baseball team and becomes manager. Before the biggest game of the year, he can't keep his mind on his job, because a homework problem is giving him trouble.

If Joe can paint a house in 3 hours, and Sam can paint the same house in 5 hours, how long does it take for them to do it together?

One of his players provides a method to solve the problem, where *a* and *b* are the individual times. He claims that the expression $\frac{a \times b}{a + b}$ gives the correct answer. With $a = 5$ and $b = 3$, the answer he gives is

$$\frac{5 \times 3}{5 + 3} = \frac{15}{8} = 1\frac{7}{8} \text{ hours.}$$

The player's expression and answer are correct. Suppose *a* and *b* are the individual times. Then the hourly rates for the players are $\frac{1}{a}$ and $\frac{1}{b}$ job per hour. Multiplying rate by time worked gives the fractional part of the job performed by each player. Let *x* represent the time they must work together to complete one whole job.

$$\frac{1}{a}x + \frac{1}{b}x = 1$$
Linear equation

$$ab\left(\frac{1}{a}x + \frac{1}{b}x\right) = ab \cdot 1$$
Multiply by *ab*.

$$bx + ax = ab$$
Distributive property

$$x(a + b) = ab$$
Distributive property

$$x = \frac{ab}{a + b}$$
Divide by $a + b$.

$$bd \cdot \frac{a}{b} = bd \cdot \frac{c}{d} \qquad \text{Multiply each side by } bd.$$

$$\frac{b}{b}(d \cdot a) = \frac{d}{d}(b \cdot c) \qquad \text{Associative and commutative properties}$$

$$ad = bc \qquad \text{Commutative and identity properties}$$

We can also find the products *ad* and *bc* by multiplying diagonally.

$$\frac{a}{b} = \frac{c}{d}$$

For this reason, *ad* and *bc* are called **cross products.**

Cross Products

If $\dfrac{a}{b} = \dfrac{c}{d}$, then the cross products *ad* and *bc* are equal.

Also, if $ad = bc$, then $\dfrac{a}{b} = \dfrac{c}{d}$ (as long as $b \neq 0$, $d \neq 0$).

For a proportion to be true, the product of the extremes must equal the product of the means. If $\frac{a}{c} = \frac{b}{d}$, then $ad = cb$, or $ad = bc$. This means that these two corresponding proportions are equivalent:

The proportion $\dfrac{a}{b} = \dfrac{c}{d}$ *can also be written as* $\dfrac{a}{c} = \dfrac{b}{d}$ $(c \neq 0)$.

Sometimes one form is more convenient to work with than the other.

▮▮ **EXAMPLE 3** Solving Proportions

Solve the proportion $\dfrac{x}{63} = \dfrac{5}{9}$.

SOLUTION

$$\frac{x}{63} = \frac{5}{9}$$

$$9x = 63 \cdot 5 \qquad \text{Set the cross products equal.}$$

$$9x = 315 \qquad \text{Multiply.}$$

$$x = 35 \qquad \text{Divide by 9.}$$

The solution set is $\{35\}$. ▮▮▮

▮▮ **EXAMPLE 4** Solving an Equation Using Cross Products

Solve $\dfrac{x - 2}{5} = \dfrac{x + 1}{3}$.

SOLUTION

Find the cross products, and set them equal to each other.

$$3(x - 2) = 5(x + 1) \quad \text{Cross products}$$

Be sure to use parentheses.

$$3x - 6 = 5x + 5 \quad \text{Distributive property}$$

$$3x = 5x + 11 \quad \text{Add 6.}$$

$$-2x = 11 \quad \text{Subtract } 5x.$$

$$x = -\frac{11}{2} \quad \text{Divide by } -2.$$

The solution set is $\left\{-\frac{11}{2}\right\}$. ▮▮▮

▮▮ EXAMPLE 5 Using a Proportion to Predict Population

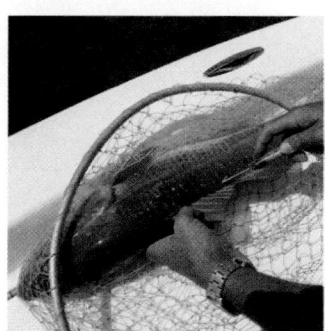

Biologists catch a sample of fish in a lake and mark each specimen with a harmless tag. Later, they catch a similar sample of fish from the same areas of the lake and determine the proportion of previously tagged fish in the new sample. The total fish population is estimated by assuming that the proportion of tagged fish in the new sample is the same as the proportion of tagged fish in the entire lake.

Suppose biologists tag 300 fish on May 1. When they return on June 1 and take a new sample of 400 fish, 5 of the 400 were previously tagged. Estimate the number of fish in the lake.

SOLUTION

Let x represent the number of fish in the lake. Set up and solve a proportion.

Tagged fish on May 1 ⟶ $\dfrac{300}{x} = \dfrac{5}{400}$ ⟵ Tagged fish in the June 1 sample

Total fish in the lake ⟶ ⟵ Total number in the June 1 sample

$$5x = 120{,}000 \quad \text{Cross products}$$

$$x = 24{,}000 \quad \text{Divide by 5.}$$

Based on this sampling procedure, there are about 24,000 fish in the lake. ▮▮▮

Direct Variation

Suppose that a carpet cleaning service charges $49.99 per room to shampoo a carpet. **Table 3** shows the relationship between the number of rooms cleaned and the cost of the total job for 1 through 5 rooms.

If we divide the cost of the job by the number of rooms, in each case we obtain the quotient, or ratio, 49.99 (dollars per room). Suppose that we let x represent the number of rooms and y represent the cost for cleaning that number of rooms. Then the relationship between x and y is given by the equation

$$\frac{y}{x} = 49.99, \quad \text{or} \quad y = 49.99x.$$

This relationship between x and y is an example of *direct variation*.

Table 3

Number of Rooms	Cost of the Job
1	$ 49.99
2	$ 99.98
3	$149.97
4	$199.96
5	$249.95

Direct Variation

y varies directly as x, or y is directly proportional to x, if there exists a nonzero constant k such that

$$y = kx, \quad \text{or, equivalently,} \quad \frac{y}{x} = k.$$

The constant k is a numerical value called the **constant of variation.**

EXAMPLE 6 Solving a Direct Variation Problem

Suppose y varies directly as x, and $y = 50$ when $x = 20$. Find y when $x = 14$.

SOLUTION

Since y varies directly as x, there exists a constant k such that $y = kx$. Find k by replacing y with 50 and x with 20.

$$y = kx \qquad \text{Variation equation}$$

$$50 = k \cdot 20 \qquad \text{Substitute the given values.}$$

$$\frac{5}{2} = k \qquad \text{Divide by 20. Express in lowest terms.}$$

Since $y = kx$ and $k = \frac{5}{2}$,

$$y = \frac{5}{2}x.$$

Now find y when $x = 14$.

$$y = \frac{5}{2} \cdot 14 = 35$$

The value of y is 35 when $x = 14$. ■■■

Another Way of Thinking

In **Example 6**, because the ratio of y to x is constant, you may want to simply write the equation as

$$\frac{50}{20} = \frac{y}{14}$$

and solve for y.

EXAMPLE 7 Solving a Direct Variation Problem

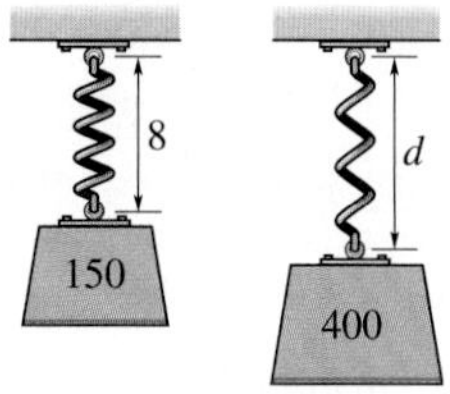

Hooke's law for an elastic spring states that the distance a spring stretches is directly proportional to the force applied. If a force of 150 pounds stretches a certain spring 8 centimeters, how much will a force of 400 pounds stretch the spring? See **Figure 5**.

SOLUTION

If d is the distance the spring stretches and f is the force applied, then $d = kf$ for some constant k.

$$d = kf \qquad \text{Variation equation}$$

$$8 = k \cdot 150 \qquad \text{Let } d = 8 \text{ and } f = 150.$$

$$k = \frac{8}{150} = \frac{4}{75} \qquad \text{Find } k.$$

Thus $d = \frac{4}{75} f$.

For a force of 400 pounds,

$$d = \frac{4}{75}(400) = \frac{64}{3}. \qquad \text{Let } f = 400.$$

The spring will stretch $\frac{64}{3}$ centimeters if a force of 400 pounds is applied. ■■■

Figure 5

Solving a Variation Problem

Step 1 Write the variation equation.

Step 2 Substitute the initial values and solve for k.

Step 3 Rewrite the variation equation with the value of k from Step 2.

Step 4 Substitute the remaining values, solve for the unknown, and find the required answer.

In some cases one quantity will vary directly as a *power* of another.

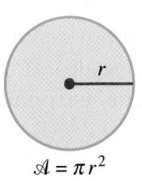

$$\mathcal{A} = \pi r^2$$

Figure 6

Direct Variation as a Power

y varies directly as the nth power of x if there exists a nonzero real number k such that

$$y = kx^n.$$

An example of direct variation as a power involves the area of a circle. See **Figure 6.** The formula for the area of a circle is $\mathcal{A} = \pi r^2$. Here, π is the constant of variation, and the area $\mathcal{A}$ varies directly as the square of the radius r.

▐▐ **EXAMPLE 8** Solving a Direct Variation Problem

The distance a body falls from rest varies directly as the square of the time it falls (here we disregard air resistance). If a skydiver falls 64 feet in 2 seconds, how far will she fall in 8 seconds?

SOLUTION

Step 1 If d represents the distance the skydiver falls and t the time it takes to fall, then d is a function of t, and, for some constant k, $d = kt^2$.

Step 2 To find the value of k, use the fact that the skydiver falls 64 feet in 2 seconds.

$$d = kt^2 \qquad \text{Formula}$$
$$64 = k(2)^2 \qquad \text{Let } d = 64 \text{ and } t = 2.$$
$$k = 16 \qquad \text{Evaluate } k.$$

Step 3 With this result, the variation equation becomes

$$d = 16t^2.$$

Step 4 Now let $t = 8$ to find the number of feet the skydiver will fall in 8 seconds.

$$d = 16t^2 = 16(8)^2 = 1024 \quad \text{Let } t = 8.$$

$8^2 = 8 \cdot 8 = 64$

The skydiver will fall 1024 feet in 8 seconds. ▐▐▐

Inverse Variation

In direct variation where $k > 0$, as x increases, y increases, and similarly as x decreases, y decreases. Another type of variation is *inverse variation*.

Inverse Variation

y varies inversely as x if there exists a nonzero real number k such that

$$y = \frac{k}{x}, \quad \text{or, equivalently,} \quad xy = k.$$

Also, **y varies inversely as the nth power of x** if there exists a nonzero real number k such that

$$y = \frac{k}{x^n}.$$

Johann Kepler (1571–1630) established the importance of the **ellipse** in 1609, when he discovered that the orbits of the planets around the sun were elliptical, not circular.

Halley's comet, which has been studied since 467 B.C., has an elliptical orbit which is long and narrow, with one axis much longer than the other. This comet was named for the British astronomer and mathematician **Edmund Halley** (1656–1742), who predicted its return after observing it in 1682. The comet appears regularly every 76 years.

▌▌ **EXAMPLE 9** Solving an Inverse Variation Problem

The weight of an object above Earth varies inversely as the square of its distance from the center of Earth. A space vehicle in an elliptical orbit has a maximum distance from the center of Earth (apogee) of 6700 miles. Its minimum distance from the center of Earth (perigee) is 4090 miles. See **Figure 7** (not to scale). If an astronaut in the vehicle weighs 57 pounds at its apogee, what does the astronaut weigh at the perigee?

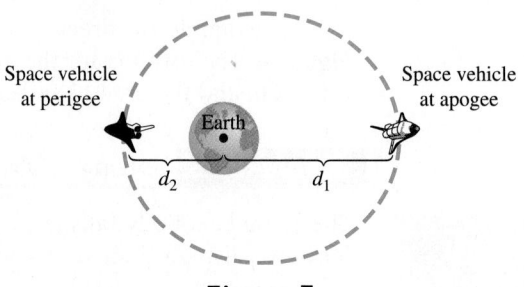

Figure 7

SOLUTION

If w is the weight and d is the distance from the center of Earth, then

$$w = \frac{k}{d^2}, \quad \text{for some constant } k.$$

At the apogee the astronaut weighs 57 pounds and the distance from the center of Earth is 6700 miles. Use these values to find k.

$$57 = \frac{k}{(6700)^2} \qquad \text{Let } w = 57 \text{ and } d = 6700.$$

$$k = 57(6700)^2 \qquad \text{Multiply by } (6700)^2. \text{Rewrite.}$$

Then the weight at the perigee with $d = 4090$ miles is

$$w = \frac{57(6700)^2}{(4090)^2} \approx 153 \text{ pounds.} \qquad \text{Use a calculator.} \qquad ▪▪▪$$

Joint and Combined Variation

If one variable varies as the product of several other variables (perhaps raised to powers), the first variable is said to **vary jointly** as the others.

▌▌ **EXAMPLE 10** Solving a Joint Variation Problem

The strength of a rectangular beam varies jointly as its width and the square of its depth. If the strength of a beam 2 inches wide by 10 inches deep is 1000 pounds per square inch, what is the strength of a beam 4 inches wide and 8 inches deep?

SOLUTION

If S represents the strength, w the width, and d the depth, then, for some constant k, $S = kwd^2$.

$$S = kwd^2 \qquad \boxed{10^2 = 10 \cdot 10 = 100}$$

$$1000 = k(2)(10)^2 \qquad \text{Let } S = 1000, w = 2, \text{ and } d = 10.$$

$$1000 = 200k \qquad \text{Apply the exponent. Multiply.}$$

$$k = 5 \qquad \text{Divide by 200. Rewrite.}$$

Thus, $S = 5wd^2$. Find S for $w = 4$ and $d = 8$ by substitution.

$$S = 5(4)(8)^2 = 1280 \quad \text{Let } w = 4 \text{ and } d = 8.$$

The strength of the beam is 1280 pounds per square inch.   ▮▮▮

Combined variation problems involve combinations of direct and inverse variation.

▮▮ **EXAMPLE 11** Solving a Combined Variation Problem

Grady Sizemore

Body mass index, or BMI, is used by physicians to assess a person's level of fatness. BMI varies directly as an individual's weight in pounds and inversely as the square of the individual's height in inches. A person who weighs 118 lb and is 64 in. tall has a BMI of 20.25. (The BMI is usually rounded to the nearest whole number.) Grady Sizemore of the Cleveland Indians weighs 200 pounds and is 6 feet, 2 inches tall. Find his BMI. (*Source: Washington Post;* www.mlb.com)

SOLUTION

Let B represent the BMI, w the weight, and h the height. Use the given information to determine k.

$$B = \frac{kw}{h^2} \quad \begin{array}{l} \longleftarrow \text{ BMI varies directly as the weight.} \\ \longleftarrow \text{ BMI varies inversely as the square of the height.} \end{array}$$

$$20.25 = \frac{k(118)}{64^2} \quad \text{Let } B = 20.25, w = 118, \text{ and } h = 64.$$

$$k = \frac{20.25(64^2)}{118} \quad \text{Multiply by } 64^2. \text{ Divide by } 118.$$

$$k \approx 703 \quad \text{Use a calculator.}$$

For Sizemore, use $k = 703$, $w = 200$, and $h = (6 \times 12) + 2 = 74$, to find B.

$$B = \frac{703(200)}{74^2} \approx 25.68 \approx 26 \quad \text{Nearest whole number}$$

Grady's BMI is 26.   ▮▮▮

7.3 EXERCISES

Determine the ratio and write it in lowest terms.

1. 50 feet to 80 feet

2. 12 miles to 36 miles

3. 17 dollars to 68 dollars

4. 600 people to 500 people

5. 288 inches to 12 feet

6. 60 inches to 2 yards

7. 5 days to 40 hours

8. 75 minutes to 4 hours

9. Which ratio is not the same as the ratio 2 to 5?
   A. 0.4   **B.** 4 to 10   **C.** 20 to 50   **D.** 5 to 2

10. Give three ratios that are equivalent to the ratio 4 to 3.

11. Explain the distinction between *ratio* and *proportion*. Give examples.

12. Suppose that someone told you to use cross products in order to multiply fractions. How would you explain to the person what is wrong with his or her thinking?

Decide whether each proportion is true *or* false.

13. $\dfrac{5}{35} = \dfrac{8}{56}$

14. $\dfrac{4}{12} = \dfrac{7}{21}$

15. $\dfrac{120}{82} = \dfrac{7}{10}$

16. $\dfrac{27}{160} = \dfrac{18}{110}$

17. $\dfrac{\frac{1}{2}}{5} = \dfrac{1}{10}$

18. $\dfrac{\frac{1}{3}}{6} = \dfrac{1}{18}$

Solve each equation.

19. $\dfrac{x}{4} = \dfrac{175}{20}$

20. $\dfrac{49}{56} = \dfrac{x}{8}$

21. $\dfrac{3x - 2}{5} = \dfrac{6x - 5}{11}$

22. $\dfrac{5 + x}{3} = \dfrac{x + 7}{5}$

23. $\dfrac{3x + 1}{7} = \dfrac{2x - 3}{6}$

24. $\dfrac{2x + 7}{3} = \dfrac{x - 1}{4}$

Solve each problem. In Exercises 25–31, assume all items are equally priced.

25. *Price of Candy Bars* If 16 candy bars cost $20.00, how much do 24 candy bars cost?

26. *Price of Ringtones* If 12 ringtones cost $30.00, how much do 8 ringtones cost?

27. *Price of Oil* Eight quarts of oil cost $14.00. How much do 5 quarts of oil cost?

28. *Price of Tires* Four tires cost $398.00. How much do 7 tires cost?

29. *Price of Jeans* If 9 pairs of jeans cost $121.50, find the cost of 5 pairs.

30. *Price of Shirts* If 7 shirts cost $87.50, find the cost of 11 shirts.

31. *Price of Gasoline* If 6 gallons of premium unleaded gasoline cost $17.82, how much would it cost to completely fill a 15-gallon tank?

32. *Sales Tax* If sales tax on a $16.00 DVD is $1.40, how much would the sales tax be on a $120.00 Blu-ray disc player?

33. *Distance Between Cities* The distance between Kansas City, Missouri, and Denver is 600 miles. On a certain wall map, this is represented by a length of 2.4 feet. On the map, how many feet would there be between Memphis and Philadelphia, two cities that are actually 1000 miles apart?

34. *Distance Between Cities* The distance between Singapore and Tokyo is 3300 miles. On a certain wall map, this distance is represented by 11 inches. The actual distance between Mexico City and Cairo is 7700 miles. How far apart are they on the same map?

35. *Distance Between Cities* A wall map of the United States has a distance of 8.5 inches between Memphis and Denver, two cities that are actually 1040 miles apart. The actual distance between St. Louis and Des Moines is 333 miles. How far apart are St. Louis and Des Moines on the map?

36. *Distance Between Cities* A wall map of the United States has a distance of 8.0 inches between New Orleans and Chicago, two cities that are actually 912 miles apart. The actual distance between the cities of Milwaukee and Seattle is 1940 miles. How far apart are Milwaukee and Seattle on the map?

37. *Distance Between Cities* On a world globe, the distance between Capetown and Bangkok, two cities that are actually 10,080 kilometers apart, is 12.4 inches. The actual distance between Moscow and Berlin is 1610 kilometers. How far apart are Moscow and Berlin on this globe?

38. *Distance Between Cities* On a world globe, the distance between Rio de Janeiro and Hong Kong, two cities that are actually 17,615 kilometers apart, is 21.5 inches. The actual distance between Paris and Stockholm is 1605 kilometers. How far apart are Paris and Stockholm on this globe?

39. *Cleaning Mixture* According to the directions on a bottle of Armstrong® Concentrated Floor Cleaner, for routine cleaning, $\frac{1}{4}$ cup of cleaner should be mixed with 1 gallon of warm water. How much cleaner should be mixed with $10\frac{1}{2}$ gallons of water?

40. *Cleaning Mixture* The directions on the bottle mentioned in **Exercise 39** also specify that for extra-strength cleaning, $\frac{1}{2}$ cup of cleaner should be used for each gallon of water. For extra-strength cleaning, how much cleaner should be mixed with $15\frac{1}{2}$ gallons of water?

41. *Exchange Rate (Dollars and Euros)* The euro is the common currency used by most European countries, including Italy. On August 15, 2009, the exchange rate between euros and U.S. dollars was 1 euro to $1.4294. Ashley went to Rome and exchanged her U.S. currency for euros, receiving 300 euros. How much in U.S. dollars did she exchange? (*Source:* www.xe.com/ucc)

42. *Exchange Rate (U.S. and Mexico)* If 8 U.S. dollars can be exchanged for 103.0 Mexican pesos, how many pesos, to the nearest hundredth, can be obtained for $65?

43. *Tagging Fish for a Population Estimate* Louisiana biologists tagged 250 fish in the oxbow lake False River on October 5. On a later date they found 7 tagged fish in a sample of 350. Estimate the total number of fish in False River to the nearest hundred.

44. *Tagging Fish for a Population Estimate* On May 13 researchers at Spirit Lake tagged 420 fish. When they returned a few weeks later, their sample of 500 fish contained 9 that were tagged. Give an approximation of the fish population in Spirit Lake to the nearest hundred.

Merchandise Pricing *A supermarket was surveyed to find the prices charged for items in various sizes. Find the best buy (based on price per unit) for each item.*

45. Granulated Sugar

Size	Price
4-lb	$1.79
10-lb	$4.29

46. Ground Coffee

Size	Price
15-oz	$3.43
34.5-oz	$6.98

47. Salad Dressing

Size	Price
16-oz	$2.44
32-oz	$2.98
48-oz	$4.95

48. Black Pepper

Size	Price
2-oz	$2.23
4-oz	$2.49
8-oz	$6.59

49. Vegetable Oil

Size	Price
16-oz	$1.66
32-oz	$2.59
64-oz	$4.29
128-oz	$6.49

50. Mouthwash

Size	Price
8.5-oz	$0.99
16.9-oz	$1.87
33.8-oz	$2.49
50.7-oz	$2.99

51. Tomato Ketchup

Size	Price
14-oz	$1.39
24-oz	$1.55
36-oz	$1.78
64-oz	$3.99

52. Grape Jelly

Size	Price
12-oz	$1.05
18-oz	$1.73
32-oz	$1.84
48-oz	$2.88

*Two triangles are **similar** if they have the same shape (but not necessarily the same size). Similar triangles have sides that are proportional. The figure shows two similar triangles.*

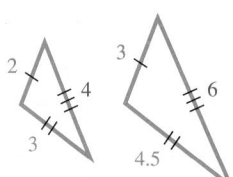

Notice that the ratios of the corresponding sides are all equal to $\frac{3}{2}$:

$$\frac{3}{2} = \frac{3}{2} \qquad \frac{4.5}{3} = \frac{3}{2} \qquad \frac{6}{4} = \frac{3}{2}.$$

If we know that two triangles are similar, we can set up a proportion to solve for the length of an unknown side. Use a proportion to find the lengths x and y given that the pair of triangles are similar.

53.

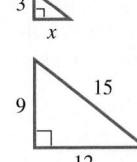

54.

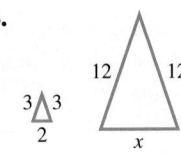

55.

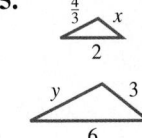

56.

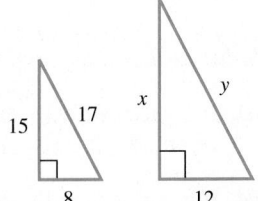

For the problems in Exercises 57 and 58, **(a)** *draw a sketch consisting of two right triangles, depicting the situation described, and* **(b)** *solve the problem. (Source: Guinness World Records.)*

57. George Washington's Chair An enlarged version of the chair used by George Washington at the Constitutional Convention casts a shadow 18 feet long at the same time a vertical pole 12 feet high casts a shadow 4 feet long. How tall is the chair?

58. Candle at an Exhibition One of the tallest candles ever constructed was exhibited at the 1897 Stockholm Exhibition. If it cast a shadow 5 feet long at the same time a vertical pole 32 feet high cast a shadow 2 feet long, how tall was the candle?

Consumer Price Index *The Consumer Price Index, issued by the U.S. Bureau of Labor Statistics, provides a means of determining the purchasing power of the U.S. dollar from one year to the next. Using the period from 1982 to 1984 as a measure of 100.0, the Consumer Price Index for selected years from 1995 to 2007 is shown here.*

Year	Consumer Price Index
1995	152.4
1997	160.5
1999	166.6
2001	177.1
2003	184.0
2005	195.3
2007	207.3

Source: Bureau of Labor Statistics.

To use the Consumer Price Index to predict a price in a particular year, we can set up a proportion and compare it with a known price in another year, as follows:

$$\frac{\text{Price in year } A}{\text{Index in year } A} = \frac{\text{Price in year } B}{\text{Index in year } B}.$$

Use the Consumer Price Index figures in the table to find the amount that would be charged for using the same amount of electricity that cost $225 in 1995. Give your answer to the nearest dollar.

59. in 1997   **60.** in 1999

61. in 2003   **62.** in 2007

Solve each problem involving variation.

63. If x varies directly as y, and $x = 27$ when $y = 6$, find x when $y = 2$.

64. If z varies directly as x, and $z = 30$ when $x = 8$, find z when $x = 4$.

65. If m varies directly as p^2, and $m = 20$ when $p = 2$, find m when $p = 5$.

66. If a varies directly as b^2, and $a = 48$ when $b = 4$, find a when $b = 7$.

67. If p varies inversely as q^2, and $p = 4$ when $q = \frac{1}{2}$, find p when $q = \frac{3}{2}$.

68. If z varies inversely as x^2, and $z = 9$ when $x = \frac{2}{3}$, find z when $x = \frac{5}{4}$.

69. Interest on an Investment The interest on an investment varies directly as the rate of interest. If the interest is $48 when the interest rate is 5%, find the interest when the rate is 4.2%.

70. Area of a Triangle For a constant base length, the area of a triangle varies directly as its height. Find the area of a triangle with a height of 6 inches, if the area is 10 square inches when the height is 4 inches.

71. Speed of a Car Over a specified distance, rate varies inversely with time. If a car goes a certain distance in one-half hour at 30 miles per hour, what rate is needed to go the same distance in three-fourths of an hour?

72. Length of a Rectangle For a constant area, the length of a rectangle varies inversely as the width. The length of a rectangle is 27 feet when the width is 10 feet. Find the length of a rectangle with the same area if the width is 18 feet.

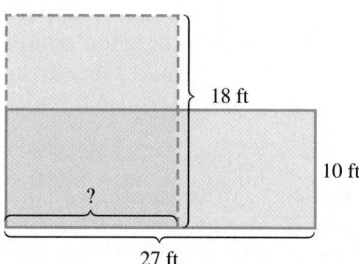

73. Weight of a Moose The weight of an object on the moon varies directly as the weight of the object on Earth. According to *Guinness World Records*, "Shad," a goat owned by a couple in California, weighs 352 pounds. Shad would weigh about 59 pounds on the moon. A bull moose weighing 1800 pounds was shot in Canada. How much would the moose have weighed on the moon?

74. Voyage in a Paddleboat According to *Guinness World Records*, the longest recorded voyage in a paddle boat is 2226 miles in 103 days by the foot power of two boaters down the Mississippi River. Assuming a constant rate, how far would they have gone if they had traveled 120 days? (Distance varies directly as time.)

75. *Pressure Exerted by a Liquid* The pressure exerted by a certain liquid at a given point varies directly as the depth of the point beneath the surface of the liquid. The pressure at a depth of 10 feet is 50 pounds per square inch. What is the pressure at a depth of 20 feet?

76. *Pressure of a Gas in a Container* If the volume is constant, the pressure of a gas in a container varies directly as the temperature. (Temperature must be measured in *Kelvin* (K), a unit of measurement used in physics.) If the pressure is 5 pounds per square inch at a temperature of 200 degrees K, what is the pressure at a temperature of 300 degrees K?

77. *Pressure of a Gas in a Container* If the temperature is constant, the pressure of a gas in a container varies inversely as the volume of the container. If the pressure is 10 pounds per square foot in a container with volume 3 cubic feet, what is the pressure in a container with volume 1.5 cubic feet?

78. *Force Required to Compress a Spring* The force required to compress a spring varies directly as the change in the length of the spring. If a force of 12 pounds is required to compress a certain spring 3 inches, how much force is required to compress the spring 5 inches?

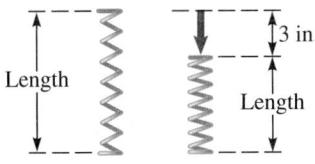

79. *Falling Body* For a body falling freely from rest (disregarding air resistance), the distance the body falls varies directly as the square of the time. If an object is dropped from the top of a tower 400 feet high and hits the ground in 5 seconds, how far did it fall in the first 3 seconds?

80. *Illumination from a Light Source* The illumination produced by a light source varies inversely as the square of the distance from the source. If the illumination produced 4 feet from a light source is 75 foot-candles, find the illumination produced 9 feet from the same source.

81. *Volume of Gas* Natural gas provides 35.8% of U.S. energy. (*Source*: U.S. Energy Department.) The volume of gas varies inversely as the pressure and directly as the temperature. If a certain gas occupies a volume of 1.3 liters at 300 K and a pressure of 18 newtons, find the volume at 340 K and a pressure of 24 newtons.

82. *Skidding Car* The force needed to keep a car from skidding on a curve varies inversely as the radius of the curve and jointly as the weight of the car and the square of the rate. If 242 pounds of force keep a 2000-pound car from skidding on a curve of radius 500 feet at 30 miles per hour, what force would keep the same car from skidding on a curve of radius 750 feet at 50 miles per hour?

83. *Load Supported by a Column* The maximum load that a cylindrical column with a circular cross section can hold varies directly as the fourth power of the diameter of the cross section and inversely as the square of the height. A 9-meter column 1 meter in diameter will support 8 metric tons. How many metric tons can be supported by a column 12 meters high and $\frac{2}{3}$ meter in diameter?

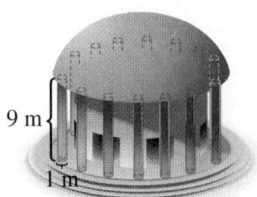

9 m

1 m

Load = 8 metric tons

Fish Weight-Estimation *Girth is the distance around the body of a fish.* (*Source:* Sacramento Bee, November 9, 2000.)

84. The weight of a bass varies jointly as its girth and the square of its length. A prize-winning bass weighed in at 22.7 pounds and measured 36 inches long with a 21-inch girth. How much would a bass 28 inches long with an 18-inch girth weigh?

85. The weight of a trout varies jointly as its length and the square of its girth. One angler caught a trout that weighed 10.5 pounds and measured 26 inches long with an 18-inch girth. Find the weight of a trout that is 22 inches long with a 15-inch girth.

86. Bill Veeck was the owner of several major league baseball teams in the 1950s and 1960s. He was known to often sit in the stands and enjoy games with his paying customers. Here is a quote attributed to him:

> *"I have discovered in 20 years of moving around a ballpark, that the knowledge of the game is usually in inverse proportion to the price of the seats."*

Explain in your own words the meaning of this statement. (To prove his point, Veeck once allowed the fans—as shown in the photo—to vote on managerial decisions.)

7.4 LINEAR INEQUALITIES

Number Lines and Interval Notation • Addition Property of Inequality • Multiplication Property of Inequality • Solving Linear Inequalities • Applications • Three-Part Inequalities

Archimedes, one of the greatest mathematicians of antiquity, was born in the Greek city of Syracuse about 287 B.C.

A colorful story about Archimedes relates his reaction to one of his discoveries. While taking a bath, he noticed that an immersed object, if heavier than a fluid, "will, if placed in it, descend to the bottom of the fluid, and the solid will, when weighed in the fluid, be lighter than its true weight by the weight of the fluid displaced." This discovery so excited him that he ran through the streets shouting "Eureka!" ("I have found it!") without bothering to clothe himself!

Archimedes met his death at age 75 during the pillage of Syracuse. He was using a sand tray to draw geometric figures when a Roman soldier came upon him. He ordered the soldier to move clear of his "circles," and the soldier obliged by killing him.

Number Lines and Interval Notation

Inequalities are algebraic expressions related by any of these symbols.

< "is less than"	≤ "is less than or equal to"
> "is greater than"	≥ "is greater than or equal to"

Unless otherwise specified, we solve an inequality by finding all real number solutions for it. For example, the solution set of $x \leq 2$ includes *all real numbers* that are less than or equal to 2, not just the *integers* less than or equal to 2.

We show the solution set of this inequality by graphing the real numbers satisfying $x \leq 2$. We do this by placing a square bracket at 2 on a number line and drawing an arrow from the bracket to the left (to show that all numbers less than 2 are also part of the graph).* See **Figure 8**.

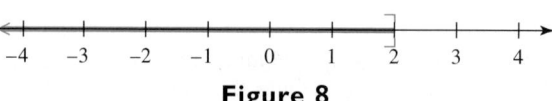

Figure 8

The set of numbers less than or equal to 2 is an example of an **interval** on the number line. To write intervals, we use **interval notation.** For example, using this notation, the interval of all numbers less than or equal to 2 is written as $(-\infty, 2]$. Interval notation often uses the **infinity symbol, ∞.** The **negative infinity symbol, $-\infty$,** does not indicate a number. It is used to show that the interval includes all real numbers less than 2. As on the number line, the square bracket indicates that 2 is part of the solution. *A parenthesis is always used next to the infinity symbol.*

The set of real numbers is written in interval notation as $(-\infty, \infty)$. Examples of other sets written in interval notation are shown in **Table 4** on the next page. In these intervals, assume that $a < b$.

---

*Some texts use solid circles rather than square brackets to indicate that the end point is included on a number line graph. [Open circles are also used to indicate noninclusion rather than parentheses, as described in **Example 1(a).**]

Table 4

Type of Interval	Set-Builder Notation	Interval Notation	Graph
Open interval	$\{x \mid a < x < b\}$	(a, b)	
Closed interval	$\{x \mid a \le x \le b\}$	$[a, b]$	
Half-open (or half-closed) interval	$\{x \mid a \le x < b\}$	$[a, b)$	
	$\{x \mid a < x \le b\}$	$(a, b]$	
Disjoint interval	$\{x \mid x < a \text{ or } x > b\}$	$(-\infty, a) \cup (b, \infty)$	
Infinite interval	$\{x \mid x > a\}$	(a, ∞)	
	$\{x \mid x \ge a\}$	$[a, \infty)$	
	$\{x \mid x < a\}$	$(-\infty, a)$	
	$\{x \mid x \le a\}$	$(-\infty, a]$	
	$\{x \mid x \text{ is a real number}\}$	$(-\infty, \infty)$	

EXAMPLE 1   Graphing Intervals Written in Interval Notation on a Number Line

Write each inequality in interval notation and graph the interval.

(a) $x > -5$ **(b)** $-1 \le x < 3$

SOLUTION

(a) The statement $x > -5$ says that x can be any number greater than -5 but cannot be -5. The interval is written $(-5, \infty)$. On a graph we place a parenthesis at -5 and draw an arrow to the right, as shown in **Figure 9**. The parenthesis at -5 indicates that -5 is not part of the graph.

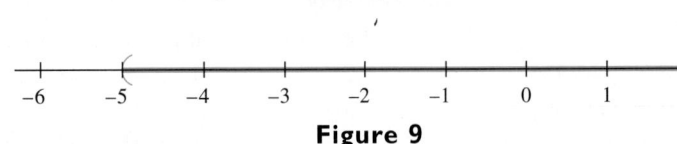

Figure 9

(b) The statement $-1 \le x < 3$ is read "-1 is less than or equal to x *and x is less than* 3." Thus, we want the set of numbers that are *between* -1 and 3, with -1 included and 3 excluded. In interval notation, we write $[-1, 3)$, using a square bracket at -1 because -1 is part of the graph, and a parenthesis at 3 because 3 is not part of the graph. The graph is shown in **Figure 10**.

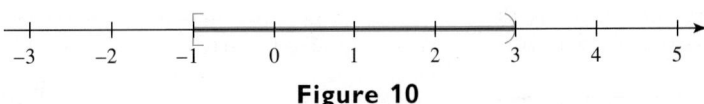

Figure 10

▌▌▌

Addition Property of Inequality

> **Linear Inequality in One Variable**
>
> A **linear inequality in one variable** can be written in the form
>
> $$Ax + B < C,$$
>
> where A, B, and C are real numbers, with $A \neq 0$. (The symbol $<$ may be replaced by $>$, $\leq$, or $\geq$.)

$$x + 5 < 2, \qquad x - 3 \geq 5, \qquad \text{and} \qquad 2x + 5 \leq 10 \qquad \text{\small Examples of linear inequalities}$$

Consider the true inequality $2 < 5$ and add 4 to each side

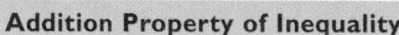

$$2 < 5 \qquad \text{\small True}$$
$$2 + 4 < 5 + 4 \qquad \text{\small Add 4 to each side.}$$
$$6 < 9 \qquad \text{\small True}$$

Start over and subtract 8 from each side.

$$2 - 8 < 5 - 8 \qquad \text{\small Subtract 8 from each side.}$$
$$-6 < -3 \qquad \text{\small True}$$

These examples suggest the **addition property of inequality.**

> **Addition Property of Inequality**
>
> For any real number expressions A, B, and C, the inequalities
>
> $$A < B \qquad \text{and} \qquad A + C < B + C$$
>
> have exactly the same solutions.
>   That is, the same number may be added to each side of an inequality without changing the solutions.

The same number may also be *subtracted* from each side of an inequality.

▌▌ **EXAMPLE 2** Using the Addition Property of Inequality

Solve $7 + 3x > 2x - 5$.

SOLUTION

Follow the same general procedure as in solving linear equations.

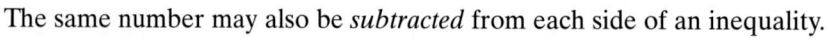

$$7 + 3x > 2x - 5$$
$$7 + 3x - 2x > 2x - 5 - 2x \qquad \text{\small Subtract 2x.}$$
$$7 + x > -5 \qquad \text{\small Combine like terms.}$$
$$7 + x - 7 > -5 - 7 \qquad \text{\small Subtract 7.}$$
$$x > -12 \qquad \text{\small Combine like terms.}$$

The solution set is $(-12, \infty)$. Its graph is shown in **Figure 11**.

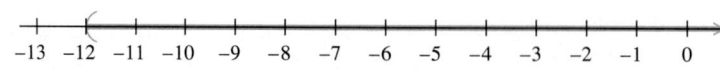

Figure 11

Amalie ("Emmy") Noether (1882–1935) was an outstanding mathematician in the field of **abstract algebra.** She studied and worked in Germany at a time when it was very difficult for a woman to do so. At the University of Erlangen in 1900, Noether was one of only two women. Although she could attend classes, professors could and did deny her the right to take the exams for their courses. Not until 1904 was Noether allowed to officially register. She completed her doctorate four years later.

    In 1916 Emmy Noether went to Göttingen to work with David Hilbert on the general theory of relativity. But even with Hilbert's backing and prestige, it was three years before the faculty voted to make Noether a *Privatdozent,* the lowest rank in the faculty. In 1922 Noether was made an unofficial professor (or assistant). She received no pay for this post, although she was given a small stipend to lecture in algebra.

▌▌▌

Multiplication Property of Inequality

The addition property of inequality cannot be used to solve inequalities such as

$$4x \geq 28.$$

These inequalities require the *multiplication property of inequality*. To see how this property works, we look at some examples.

Multiply each side of the true inequality $3 < 7$ by the positive number 2.

$3 < 7$	True
$2(3) < 2(7)$	Multiply each side by 2.
$6 < 14$	True

Now multiply each side of $3 < 7$ by the negative number -5.

$3 < 7$	True
$-5(3) < -5(7)$	Multiply each side by -5.
$-15 < -35$	False

To get a true statement when multiplying each side by -5, we must reverse the direction of the inequality symbol.

$3 < 7$	True
$-5(3) > -5(7)$	Multiply by -5. Reverse the inequality symbol.
$-15 > -35$	True

In summary, the **multiplication property of inequality** has two parts.

Multiplication Property of Inequality

Let A, B, and C be real number expressions, with $C \neq 0$.

1. If C is *positive*, then the inequalities

$$A < B \quad \text{and} \quad AC < BC$$

have the same solutions.

2. If C is *negative*, then the inequalities

$$A < B \quad \text{and} \quad AC > BC$$

have the same solutions.

That is, each side of an inequality may be multiplied by the same positive number without changing the solutions. *If the multiplier is negative, we must reverse the direction of the inequality symbol.*

The multiplication property of inequality also permits *division* of each side of an inequality by the same nonzero number.

Note the following differences for positive and negative numbers.

1. When each side of an inequality is multiplied or divided by a *positive number,* the direction of the inequality symbol *does not change.*

2. *Reverse the direction of the inequality symbol only when multiplying or dividing each side by a negative number.*

In **Example 3** that follows, notice how the inequality symbol is reversed *only* for part (b), where both sides of the inequality are divided by a negative number.

▮▮ **EXAMPLE 3** Using the Multiplication Property of Inequality

Solve each inequality and graph the solution set.

(a) $3x < -18$ **(b)** $-4x \geq 8$

SOLUTION

(a) $3x < -18$

> 3 is a positive number, so the inequality symbol does not change.

$$\frac{3x}{3} < \frac{-18}{3}$$ Divide by 3, a *positive* number.

$$x < -6$$

The solution set is $(-\infty, -6)$. The graph is shown in **Figure 12**.

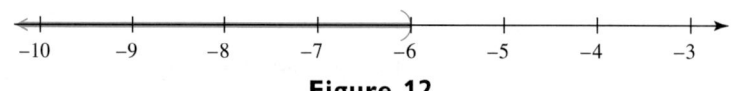

Figure 12

(b) $-4x \geq 8$

$$\frac{-4x}{-4} \leq \frac{8}{-4}$$ Divide by -4, a *negative* number. Reverse the inequality symbol.

> Reverse the inequality when multiplying or dividing by a negative number.

$$x \leq -2$$

The solution set $(-\infty, -2]$ is graphed in **Figure 13**.

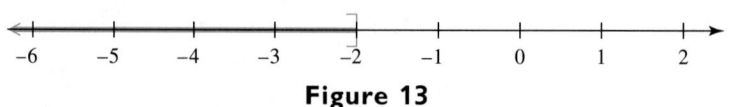

Figure 13   ▮▮▮

Solving Linear Inequalities

> **Solving a Linear Inequality in One Variable**
>
> ***Step 1*** **Simplify each side separately.** Use the distributive property to clear parentheses and combine like terms on each side as needed.
>
> ***Step 2*** **Isolate the variable terms on one side.** Use the addition property of inequality to get all terms with variables on one side of the inequality and all numbers on the other side.
>
> ***Step 3*** **Isolate the variable.** Use the multiplication property of inequality to change the inequality in the variable x to the form
>
> $$x < k, \quad x > k, \quad x \leq k, \quad \text{or} \quad x \geq k, \quad \text{where } k \text{ is a number.}$$
>
> *Remember: Reverse the direction of the inequality symbol only when multiplying or dividing each side of an inequality by a negative number.*

▌▌ **EXAMPLE 4** Solving a Linear Inequality

Solve $5(x - 3) - 7x \geq 4(x - 3) + 9$. Give the solution set in interval form, and then graph.

SOLUTION

Step 1

$$5(x - 3) - 7x \geq 4(x - 3) + 9$$

$$5x - 15 - 7x \geq 4x - 12 + 9 \qquad \text{Distributive property}$$

$$-2x - 15 \geq 4x - 3 \qquad \text{Combine like terms.}$$

Step 2

$$-2x - 15 - 4x \geq 4x - 3 - 4x \qquad \text{Use the addition property of inequality and subtract } 4x.$$

$$-6x - 15 \geq -3$$

$$-6x - 15 + 15 \geq -3 + 15 \qquad \text{Add 15.}$$

$$-6x \geq 12 \qquad \text{Combine like terms.}$$

Step 3

$$\frac{-6x}{-6} \leq \frac{12}{-6} \qquad \text{Use the multiplication property of inequality. Divide by } -6, \text{ a } \textit{negative} \text{ number. Reverse the symbol.}$$

Remember to reverse the inequality symbol.

$$x \leq -2$$

The solution set is $(-\infty, -2]$. Its graph is shown in **Figure 14**.

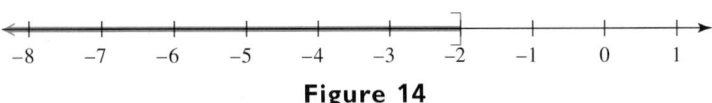

Figure 14 ▌▌▌

Applications

> **PROBLEM-SOLVING HINT** The table gives some of the more common phrases that suggest inequality along with examples and translations.
>
> | Phrase | Example | Inequality |
> |---|---|---|
> | Is greater than | A number *is greater than* 4. | $x > 4$ |
> | Is less than | A number *is less than* -12. | $x < -12$ |
> | Is at least | A number *is at least* 6. | $x \geq 6$ |
> | Is at most | A number *is at most* 8. | $x \leq 8$ |
>
> We use the same six problem-solving steps from **Section 7.2,** changing Step 3 to "Write an inequality" instead of "Write an equation."

The next example shows an application of algebra that is important to anyone who has ever asked,

"What score can I make on my next test and have a (particular grade) in this course?"

It uses the idea of finding the average of a number of grades. ***In general, to find the average of n numbers, add the numbers, and then divide by n.***

▌▌ **EXAMPLE 5** | Finding an Average Test Score

Josh has test grades of 86, 88, and 78 on his first three tests in calculus. If he wants an average of at least 80 after his fourth test, what are the possible scores he can make on his fourth test?

SOLUTION

Step 1 **Read** the problem again.

Step 2 **Assign a variable.** Let $x =$ Josh's score on his fourth test.

Step 3 **Write an inequality.** To find his average after 4 tests, add the test scores and divide by 4.

$$\underbrace{\frac{86 + 88 + 78 + x}{4}}_{\text{Average}} \underbrace{\geq 80}_{\substack{\text{is at} \\ \text{least 80.}}}$$

Step 4 **Solve.**

$$\frac{252 + x}{4} \geq 80 \qquad \text{Add the known scores.}$$

$$4\left(\frac{252 + x}{4}\right) \geq 4(80) \qquad \substack{\text{Multiply by 4 to clear} \\ \text{the fraction.}}$$

$$252 + x \geq 320$$

$$252 + x - 252 \geq 320 - 252 \qquad \text{Subtract 252.}$$

$$x \geq 68 \qquad \text{Combine like terms.}$$

Step 5 **State the answer.** He must score 68 or more on the fourth test to have an average of *at least* 80.

Step 6 **Check.** Determine whether this minimum score of 68 gives an average of 80.

$$\frac{86 + 88 + 78 + 68}{4} = \frac{320}{4} = 80 \checkmark$$

▌▌▌

▌▌ **EXAMPLE 6** | Using a Linear Inequality to Solve a Rental Problem

A rental company charges $15.00 to rent a chain saw, plus $2.00 per hour. Ken Pott can spend no more than $35.00 to clear some logs from his yard. For how long can he rent the saw to stay within budget?

SOLUTION

Let $h =$ the number of hours he can rent the saw. He must pay $15.00, plus 2.00h$, to rent the saw for h hours, and this amount must be *no more than* $35.00.

$$\underbrace{15 + 2h}_{\substack{\text{Cost of} \\ \text{renting}}} \underbrace{\leq}_{\substack{\text{is no} \\ \text{more than}}} \underbrace{35}_{\text{35 dollars.}}$$

$$15 + 2h - 15 \leq 35 - 15 \qquad \text{Subtract 15.}$$

$$2h \leq 20$$

$$h \leq 10 \qquad \text{Divide by 2.}$$

Ken can use the saw for a maximum of 10 hours. (Of course, he may use it for less time, as indicated by the inequality $h \leq 10$.) ▌▌▌

Three-Part Inequalities

Inequalities that say that one number is *between* two other numbers are **three-part inequalities.** For example,

$$-3 < 5 < 7 \quad \text{says that 5 is between } -3 \text{ and 7.}$$

For some applications, it is necessary to work with an inequality such as

$$3 < x + 2 < 8, \quad \text{where } x + 2 \text{ is between 3 and 8.}$$

To solve this inequality, we subtract 2 from each of the three parts.

$$3 - 2 < x + 2 - 2 < 8 - 2 \quad \text{Subtract 2 from each part.}$$

$$1 < x < 6$$

The idea is to use "is less than" to get the inequality in the form

> The symbols must point in the same direction and toward the lesser number.

a number $< x <$ **another number.**

▌▌ EXAMPLE 7 Solving Three-Part Inequalities

Solve $4 \leq 3x - 5 < 6$. Give the solution set in interval form, and then graph.

SOLUTION

$$4 \leq 3x - 5 < 6$$

$$4 + 5 \leq 3x - 5 + 5 < 6 + 5 \qquad \text{Add 5 to each part.}$$

$$9 \leq 3x < 11 \qquad \text{Simplify.}$$

> Remember to divide all three parts by 3.

$$\frac{9}{3} \leq \frac{3x}{3} < \frac{11}{3} \qquad \text{Divide each part by 3.}$$

$$3 \leq x < \frac{11}{3} \qquad \text{Simplify.}$$

The solution set is $\left[3, \frac{11}{3}\right)$. Its graph is shown in **Figure 15**.

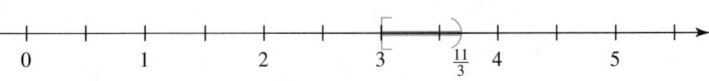

Figure 15   ▐▐▐

7.4 EXERCISES

In Exercises 1–6, match each set in Group I with the correct graph or interval notation in A–F in Group II.

I

1. $\{x \mid x \leq 3\}$

2. $\{x \mid x > 3\}$

3. $\{x \mid x < 3\}$

4. $\{x \mid x \geq 3\}$

5. $\{x \mid -3 \leq x \leq 3\}$

6. $\{x \mid -3 < x < 3\}$

II

A.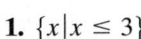

B.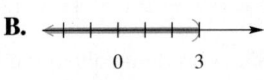

C. $(3, \infty)$

D. $(-\infty, 3]$

E. $(-3, 3)$

F. $[-3, 3]$

7. How does one determine whether to use parentheses or brackets when graphing the solution set of an inequality?

8. Describe the steps used to solve a linear inequality. Explain when it is necessary to reverse the inequality symbol.

Solve each inequality. Give the solution set in both interval and graph forms.

9. $4x + 1 \geq 21$

10. $5x + 2 \geq 52$

11. $\dfrac{3x - 1}{4} > 5$

12. $\dfrac{5x - 6}{8} < 8$

13. $-4x < 16$

14. $-2x > 10$

15. $-\dfrac{3}{4}x \geq 30$

16. $-1.5x \leq -\dfrac{9}{2}$

17. $-1.3x \geq -5.2$

18. $-2.5x \leq -1.25$

19. $\dfrac{2x - 5}{-4} > 5$

20. $\dfrac{3x - 2}{-5} < 6$

21. $x + 4(2x - 1) \geq x$

22. $x - 2(x - 4) \leq 3x$

23. $-(4 + x) + 2 - 3x < -14$

24. $-(9 + x) - 5 + 4x \geq 4$

25. $-3(x - 6) > 2x - 2$

26. $-2(x + 4) \leq 6x + 16$

27. $\dfrac{2}{3}(3x - 1) \geq \dfrac{3}{2}(2x - 3)$

28. $\dfrac{7}{5}(10x - 1) < \dfrac{2}{3}(6x + 5)$

29. $-\dfrac{1}{4}(x + 6) + \dfrac{3}{2}(2x - 5) < 10$

30. $\dfrac{3}{5}(x - 2) - \dfrac{1}{4}(2x - 7) \leq 3$

31. $3(2x - 4) - 4x < 2x + 3$

32. $7(4 - x) + 5x < 2(16 - x)$

33. $8\left(\dfrac{1}{2}x + 3\right) < 8\left(\dfrac{1}{2}x - 1\right)$

34. $10x + 2(x - 4) < 12x - 10$

35. A student solved the inequality

$$5x < -20$$

by dividing both sides by 5 and reversing the direction of the inequality symbol. His reasoning was that since −20 is a negative number, reversing the direction of the symbol was required. Is this correct? Explain why or why not.

36. Match each set given in interval notation with its description.

(a) $(0, \infty)$ **A.** positive real numbers

(b) $[0, \infty)$ **B.** negative real numbers

(c) $(-\infty, 0]$ **C.** nonpositive real numbers

(d) $(-\infty, 0)$ **D.** nonnegative real numbers

Solve each inequality. Give the solution set in both interval and graph forms.

37. $-4 < x - 5 < 6$

38. $-1 < x + 1 < 8$

39. $-9 \leq x + 5 \leq 15$

40. $-4 \leq x + 3 \leq 10$

41. $-6 \leq 2x + 4 \leq 16$

42. $-15 < 3x + 6 < -12$

43. $-19 \leq 3x - 5 \leq 1$

44. $-16 < 3x + 2 < -10$

45. $-1 \leq \dfrac{2x - 5}{6} \leq 5$

46. $-3 \leq \dfrac{3x + 1}{4} \leq 3$

47. $4 \leq 5 - 9x < 8$

48. $4 \leq 3 - 2x < 8$

Tornado Activity *In Exercises 49–52, answer the questions based on the graph.*

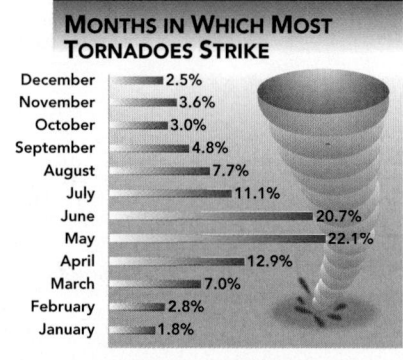

MONTHS IN WHICH MOST TORNADOES STRIKE

December	2.5%
November	3.6%
October	3.0%
September	4.8%
August	7.7%
July	11.1%
June	20.7%
May	22.1%
April	12.9%
March	7.0%
February	2.8%
January	1.8%

Source: The USA Today Weather Book.

49. In which months did the percent of tornadoes exceed 7.7%?

50. In which months was the percent of tornadoes at least 12.9%?

51. The data used to determine the graph were based on the number of tornadoes sighted in the United States during a twenty-year period. A total of 17,252 tornadoes were reported. In which months were fewer than 1500 reported?

52. How many more tornadoes occurred during March than October? (Use the total given in **Exercise 51.**)

Egg Production *In Exercises 53–56, answer the questions based on the graph.*

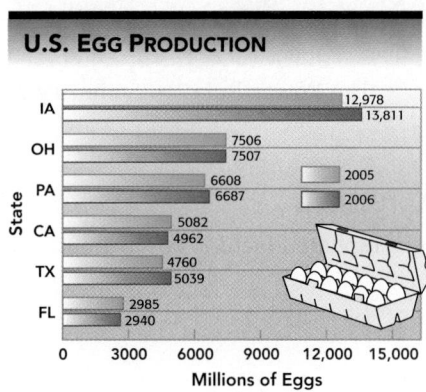

U.S. EGG PRODUCTION

State	2005	2006
IA	12,978	13,811
OH	7506	7507
PA	6608	6687
CA	5082	4962
TX	4760	5039
FL	2985	2940

Millions of Eggs

Source: U.S. Department of Agriculture.

53. In which states and in which years was production *at least* 6687 million?

54. In which states and in which years was production *at most* 4962 million?

55. If x represents 2006 egg production for Texas (TX) and y represents 2006 egg production for California (CA), which is true: $x < y$ or $x > y$?

56. If x represents 2005 egg production for Ohio (OH) and y represents 2006 egg production for OH, which is true: $x < y$ or $x > y$?

Solve each problem.

57. Taxicab Fare In a city, taxicabs charge $3.00 for the first $\frac{1}{5}$ mile and $0.50 for each additional $\frac{1}{5}$ mile. Frank Steed has only $7.50. What is the maximum distance he can travel (not including a tip for the cabbie)?

58. Taxicab Fare Fifteen years ago taxicab fares in the city in **Exercise 57** were $0.90 for the first $\frac{1}{7}$ mile and $0.10 for each additional $\frac{1}{7}$ mile. Based on the information given there and the answer you found, how much farther could Frank have traveled at that time?

59. Grade Average Hollis Sherman earned scores of 90 and 82 on his first two tests in English Literature. What score must he make on his third test to keep an average of 84 or greater?

60. Grade Average Beth Anderson scored 92 and 96 on her first two tests in Methods in Photography. What score must she make on her third test to keep an average of 90 or greater?

61. Car Rental A couple wishes to rent a car for one day. Agency A wants $29.95 per day and 28¢ per mile, while Agency B wants $34.95 per day and 25¢ per mile. For how many miles would the price to rent from Agency B exceed the price to rent from Agency A?

62. Car Rental John and Suzanne Gainey went to California for a week. They needed to rent a car, so they checked out two rental firms. Agency A wanted $28 per day, with no mileage fee. Agency B wanted $108 per week and 14¢ per mile. How many miles would they have to drive before the Agency A price is less than the Agency B price?

63. Body Mass Index A BMI (body mass index) between 19 and 25 is considered healthy. Use the formula

$$\text{BMI} = \frac{703 \times (\text{weight in pounds})}{(\text{height in inches})^2}$$

to find the weight range w, to the nearest pound, that gives a healthy BMI (body mass index) for each height. (*Source:* www.bmi-calculator.net)

(a) 72 inches   **(b)** Your height in inches

64. Target Heart Rate To achieve the maximum benefit from exercising, the heart rate in beats per minute should be in the target heart rate (THR) zone. For a person aged A, the formula is

$$0.7(220 - A) \leq \text{THR} \leq 0.85(220 - A).$$

Find the THR to the nearest whole number for each age. (*Source:* Hockey, Robert V., *Physical Fitness: The Pathway to Healthful Living*, Times Mirror/Mosby College Publishing.)

(a) 35   **(b)** Your age

Profit/Cost Analysis *A product will produce a profit only when the revenue R from selling the product exceeds the cost C of producing it (R and C in dollars). Find the least whole number of units x that must be sold for the business to show a profit for the item described.*

65. Peripheral Visions, Inc. finds that the cost to produce x studio quality DVDs is

$$C = 20x + 100,$$

while the revenue produced from them is $R = 24x$.

66. Speedy Delivery finds that the cost to make x customer deliveries is

$$C = 3x + 2300,$$

while the revenue produced from them is $R = 5.50x$.

7.5 PROPERTIES OF EXPONENTS AND SCIENTIFIC NOTATION

Exponents and Exponential Expressions • The Product Rule • Zero and Negative Exponents • The Quotient Rule • The Power Rules • Summary of Rules for Exponents • Scientific Notation

The term **googol,** meaning 10^{100}, was coined by Professor Edward Kasner of Columbia University. A googol is made up of a 1 with one hundred zeros following it. This number exceeds the estimated number of electrons in the universe, which is 10^{79}.

The Web search engine Google is named after a googol. Sergey Brin, president and cofounder of Google, Inc., was a mathematics major. He chose the name Google to describe the vast reach of this search engine. (*Source: The Gazette,* March 2, 2001.) The term "googling" is now part of the English language.

If a googol isn't big enough for you, try a **googolplex:**

$$googolplex = 10^{googol}.$$

Exponents and Exponential Expressions

Exponents are used to write products of repeated factors. For example, the product $3 \cdot 3 \cdot 3 \cdot 3$ is written

$$\underbrace{3 \cdot 3 \cdot 3 \cdot 3}_{4 \text{ factors of } 3} = 3^{\overset{\text{Exponent}}{4}}.$$
$$\underset{\text{Base}}{}$$

The number 4 shows that 3 appears as a factor four times. The number 4 is the **exponent** and 3 is the **base.** The quantity 3^4 is called an **exponential expression.** Read 3^4 as "3 to the fourth power," or "3 to the fourth." Multiplying out the four 3s gives 81.

$$3^4 = 3 \cdot 3 \cdot 3 \cdot 3 = 81$$

Exponential Expression

If a is a real number and n is a natural number, then the exponential expression a^n is defined as

$$a^n = \underbrace{a \cdot a \cdot a \cdot \ldots \cdot a.}_{n \text{ factors of } a}$$

The number a is the *base* and n is the *exponent.*

▌▌ **EXAMPLE 1** Evaluating Exponential Expressions

Evaluate each exponential expression.

(a) 7^2 **(b)** 5^3 **(c)** $(-2)^4$ **(d)** $(-2)^5$ **(e)** 5^1

SOLUTION $\quad\boxed{7^2 = 7 \cdot 7, \text{ not } 7 \cdot 2.}$

(a) $7^2 = 7 \cdot 7 = 49$ Read 7^2 as "7 squared."

(b) $5^3 = 5 \cdot 5 \cdot 5 = 125$ Read 5^3 as "5 cubed."

(c) $(-2)^4 = (-2)(-2)(-2)(-2) = 16$

(d) $(-2)^5 = (-2)(-2)(-2)(-2)(-2) = -32$

(e) $5^1 = 5$ ▌▌▌

In the exponential expression $3z^7$, the base of the exponent 7 is z, *not* $3z$.

$$3z^7 = 3 \cdot z \cdot z \cdot z \cdot z \cdot z \cdot z \cdot z \qquad \text{Base is } z.$$

$$(3z)^7 = (3z)(3z)(3z)(3z)(3z)(3z)(3z) \qquad \text{Base is } 3z.$$

For $(-2)^6$, the parentheses around -2 indicate that the base is -2.

$$(-2)^6 = (-2)(-2)(-2)(-2)(-2)(-2) = 64 \qquad \text{Base is } -2.$$

$(-2)^6$

64

-2^6

-64

This screen supports the discussion preceding **Example 2.**

In the expression -2^6, the base is 2, *not* -2. The $-$ sign tells us to find the negative, or additive inverse, of 2^6. It acts as a symbol for the factor -1.

$$-2^6 = -(2 \cdot 2 \cdot 2 \cdot 2 \cdot 2 \cdot 2) = -64 \quad \text{Base is 2.}$$

Therefore, since $64 \neq -64$, $(-2)^6 \neq -2^6$.

▮▮ **EXAMPLE 2** Evaluating Exponential Expressions

Evaluate each exponential expression.

(a) -4^2 **(b)** -8^4 **(c)** $(-8)^4$

SOLUTION

(a) $-4^2 = -(4 \cdot 4) = -16$

(b) $-8^4 = -(8 \cdot 8 \cdot 8 \cdot 8) = -4096$

(c) $(-8)^4 = (-8)(-8)(-8)(-8) = 4096$

Note how parts (b) and (c) differ.   ▮▮▮

The Product Rule

Consider the product $2^5 \cdot 2^3$, which can be simplified as follows.

$$\overbrace{2^5 \cdot 2^3 = (2 \cdot 2 \cdot 2 \cdot 2 \cdot 2)(2 \cdot 2 \cdot 2) = 2^8}^{5 + 3 = 8}$$

This result—products of exponential expressions with the same base are found by adding exponents—is generalized as the **product rule for exponents.**

Product Rule for Exponents

If m and n are natural numbers and a is any real number, then

$$a^m \cdot a^n = a^{m+n}.$$

▮▮ **EXAMPLE 3** Applying the Product Rule

Apply the product rule for exponents in each case.

(a) $3^4 \cdot 3^7$ **(b)** $5^3 \cdot 5$ **(c)** $y^3 \cdot y^8 \cdot y^2$

(d) $(5y^2)(-3y^4)$ **(e)** $(7p^3q)(2p^5q^2)$

SOLUTION

(a) $3^4 \cdot 3^7 = 3^{4+7} = 3^{11}$ **(b)** $5^3 \cdot 5 = 5^3 \cdot 5^1 = 5^{3+1} = 5^4$

> Do not make the error of writing $3 \cdot 3 = 9$ as the base.

(c) $y^3 \cdot y^8 \cdot y^2 = y^{3+8+2} = y^{13}$ Product rule extended to three powers

(d) $(5y^2)(-3y^4) = 5(-3)y^2y^4$ Associative and commutative properties

$\qquad\qquad\quad = -15y^{2+4}$ Multiply; product rule

$\qquad\qquad\quad = -15y^6$ Add.

(e) $(7p^3q)(2p^5q^2) = 7(2)p^3p^5qq^2$

$\qquad\qquad\qquad = 14p^8q^3$ ▮▮▮

Zero and Negative Exponents

We now consider 0 as an exponent. How can we define an expression such as 4^0 so that it is consistent with the product rule? By the product rule, we should have

$$4^2 \cdot 4^0 = 4^{2+0} = 4^2.$$

For the product rule to hold true, 4^0 must equal 1. This leads to the definition of a^0 for any nonzero real number a.

> **Zero Exponent**
>
> If a is any nonzero real number, then $a^0 = 1.$

The expression 0^0 **is undefined.***

▮▮ **EXAMPLE 4** Applying the Definition of Zero Exponent

Evaluate each expression.

(a) 12^0 **(b)** $(-6)^0$ **(c)** -6^0

(d) $5^0 + 12^0$ **(e)** $(8k)^0, \quad k \neq 0$

SOLUTION

(a) $12^0 = 1$ **(b)** $(-6)^0 = 1$ Base is -6.

(c) $-6^0 = -(6^0) = -1$ Base is 6.   **(d)** $5^0 + 12^0 = 1 + 1 = 2$

(e) $(8k)^0 = 1, \quad k \neq 0$ ▮▮▮

We now define a negative exponent. Using the product rule again,

$$8^2 \cdot 8^{-2} = 8^{2+(-2)} = 8^0 = 1.$$

This indicates that 8^{-2} is the reciprocal of 8^2. But $\frac{1}{8^2}$ is the reciprocal of 8^2, and a number can have only one reciprocal. Therefore, it is reasonable to conclude that $8^{-2} = \frac{1}{8^2}$. We can generalize and make the following definition.

> **Negative Exponent**
>
> For any natural number n and any nonzero real number a,
>
> $$a^{-n} = \frac{1}{a^n}.$$

With this definition, and the ones given earlier for positive and zero exponents, the expression a^n is meaningful for any integer exponent n and any nonzero real number a.

▮▮ **EXAMPLE 5** Applying the Definition of Negative Exponents

Write the following expressions with only positive exponents. Assume that all variables represent nonzero real numbers.

(a) 2^{-3} **(b)** 3^{-2} **(c)** 6^{-1} **(d)** $(5z)^{-3}$

(e) $5z^{-3}$ **(f)** $(5z^2)^{-3}$ **(g)** $-m^{-2}$ **(h)** $(-m)^{-4}$

---

*In advanced studies, 0^0 is called an *indeterminate form.*

(sidebar)

$(\text{-}6)^0$

$\text{-}6^0$ 1

$5^0 + 12^0$ -1

               2

This screen supports the results in parts (b), (c), and (d) of **Example 4.**

SOLUTION

(a) $2^{-3} = \dfrac{1}{2^3} = \dfrac{1}{8}$

(b) $3^{-2} = \dfrac{1}{3^2} = \dfrac{1}{9}$

(c) $6^{-1} = \dfrac{1}{6^1} = \dfrac{1}{6}$

(d) $(5z)^{-3} = \dfrac{1}{(5z)^3}$ Base is 5z.

(e) $5z^{-3} = 5\left(\dfrac{1}{z^3}\right) = \dfrac{5}{z^3}$ Base is z.

(f) $(5z^2)^{-3} = \dfrac{1}{(5z^2)^3}$

(g) $-m^{-2} = -\dfrac{1}{m^2}$

(h) $(-m)^{-4} = \dfrac{1}{(-m)^4}$ ▮▮▮

▮▮ **EXAMPLE 6** Evaluating Exponential Expressions

Evaluate each expression.

(a) $3^{-1} + 4^{-1}$ (b) $5^{-1} - 2^{-1}$ (c) $\dfrac{1}{2^{-3}}$ (d) $\dfrac{2^{-3}}{3^{-2}}$

SOLUTION

(a) $3^{-1} + 4^{-1} = \dfrac{1}{3} + \dfrac{1}{4} = \dfrac{4}{12} + \dfrac{3}{12} = \dfrac{7}{12}$ $3^{-1} = \frac{1}{3}, 4^{-1} = \frac{1}{4}$

(b) $5^{-1} - 2^{-1} = \dfrac{1}{5} - \dfrac{1}{2} = \dfrac{2}{10} - \dfrac{5}{10} = -\dfrac{3}{10}$

(c) $\dfrac{1}{2^{-3}} = \dfrac{1}{\dfrac{1}{2^3}} = 1 \div \dfrac{1}{2^3} = 1 \cdot \dfrac{2^3}{1} = 2^3 = 8$

> To divide, multiply by the reciprocal of the divisor.

(d) $\dfrac{2^{-3}}{3^{-2}} = \dfrac{\dfrac{1}{2^3}}{\dfrac{1}{3^2}} = \dfrac{1}{2^3} \div \dfrac{1}{3^2} = \dfrac{1}{2^3} \cdot \dfrac{3^2}{1} = \dfrac{3^2}{2^3} = \dfrac{9}{8}$ ▮▮▮

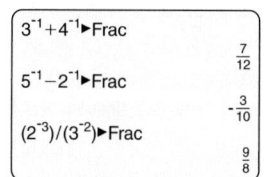

This screen supports the results in parts (a), (b), and (d) of **Example 6.**

Parts (c) and (d) of **Example 6** suggest the following generalizations.

Special Rules for Negative Exponents

If $a \neq 0$ and $b \neq 0$, then $\dfrac{1}{a^{-n}} = a^n$ and $\dfrac{a^{-n}}{b^{-m}} = \dfrac{b^m}{a^n}.$

The Quotient Rule

A quotient, such as $\dfrac{a^8}{a^3}$, can be simplified in much the same way as a product. (Assume that the denominator is not 0.) Using the definition of an exponent,

$$\dfrac{a^8}{a^3} = \dfrac{a \cdot a \cdot a \cdot a \cdot a \cdot a \cdot a \cdot a}{a \cdot a \cdot a} = a \cdot a \cdot a \cdot a \cdot a = a^5.$$

Notice that $8 - 3 = 5$. In the same way,

$$\dfrac{a^3}{a^8} = \dfrac{a \cdot a \cdot a}{a \cdot a \cdot a \cdot a \cdot a \cdot a \cdot a \cdot a} = \dfrac{1}{a^5} = a^{-5}.$$

Here, $3 - 8 = -5$. These examples suggest the **quotient rule for exponents.**

> **Quotient Rule for Exponents**
>
> If a is any nonzero real number and m and n are integers, then
>
> $$\frac{a^m}{a^n} = a^{m-n}.$$

▌▌ EXAMPLE 7 Applying the Quotient Rule

Apply the quotient rule for exponents in each case. Assume that all variables represent nonzero real numbers.

(a) $\dfrac{3^7}{3^2}$ **(b)** $\dfrac{p^6}{p^2}$ **(c)** $\dfrac{12^{10}}{12^9}$ **(d)** $\dfrac{7^4}{7^6}$ **(e)** $\dfrac{k^7}{k^{12}}$

SOLUTION

Numerator exponent

Denominator exponent

(a) $\dfrac{3^7}{3^2} = 3^{7-2} = 3^5$ **(b)** $\dfrac{p^6}{p^2} = p^{6-2} = p^4$

Subtract.

(c) $\dfrac{12^{10}}{12^9} = 12^{10-9} = 12^1 = 12$ **(d)** $\dfrac{7^4}{7^6} = 7^{4-6} = 7^{-2} = \dfrac{1}{7^2}$

> Use the definition of negative exponent.

(e) $\dfrac{k^7}{k^{12}} = k^{7-12} = k^{-5} = \dfrac{1}{k^5}$ ▐▐▐

▌▌ EXAMPLE 8 Applying the Quotient Rule

Write each quotient using only positive exponents. Assume that all variables represent nonzero real numbers.

(a) $\dfrac{2^7}{2^{-3}}$ **(b)** $\dfrac{8^{-2}}{8^5}$ **(c)** $\dfrac{6^{-5}}{6^{-2}}$ **(d)** $\dfrac{4}{4^{-1}}$ **(e)** $\dfrac{z^{-5}}{z^{-8}}$

SOLUTION

> Be careful when subtracting a negative number.

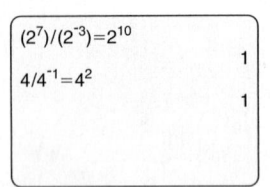

$(2^7)/(2^{-3})=2^{10}$

$4/4^{-1}=4^2$

This screen supports the results in parts (a) and (d) of **Example 8.**

(a) $\dfrac{2^7}{2^{-3}} = 2^{7-(-3)} = 2^{10}$ **(b)** $\dfrac{8^{-2}}{8^5} = 8^{-2-5} = 8^{-7} = \dfrac{1}{8^7}$

(c) $\dfrac{6^{-5}}{6^{-2}} = 6^{-5-(-2)} = 6^{-3} = \dfrac{1}{6^3}$ **(d)** $\dfrac{4}{4^{-1}} = \dfrac{4^1}{4^{-1}} = 4^{1-(-1)} = 4^2$

(e) $\dfrac{z^{-5}}{z^{-8}} = z^{-5-(-8)} = z^3$ ▐▐▐

The Power Rules

The expression $(3^4)^2$ can be simplified as

$$(3^4)^2 = 3^4 \cdot 3^4 = 3^{4+4} = 3^8, \quad \text{where } 4 \cdot 2 = 8.$$

This example suggests the first of the **power rules for exponents.** The other two parts can be demonstrated with similar examples.

> ### Power Rules for Exponents
>
> If a and b are real numbers, and m and n are integers, then
>
> $$(a^m)^n = a^{mn}, \quad (ab)^m = a^m b^m, \quad \text{and} \quad \left(\frac{a}{b}\right)^m = \frac{a^m}{b^m} \quad (b \neq 0).$$

In the statements of rules for exponents, we always assume that zero never appears to a negative power or to the power zero.

▌▌ **EXAMPLE 9** Applying the Power Rules

Use one or more power rules in each case. Assume that all variables represent nonzero real numbers.

(a) $(p^8)^3$ **(b)** $\left(\dfrac{2}{3}\right)^4$ **(c)** $(3y)^4$ **(d)** $(6p^7)^2$ **(e)** $\left(\dfrac{-2m^5}{z}\right)^3$

SOLUTION

(a) $(p^8)^3 = p^{8\cdot3} = p^{24}$ **(b)** $\left(\dfrac{2}{3}\right)^4 = \dfrac{2^4}{3^4} = \dfrac{16}{81}$

(c) $(3y)^4 = 3^4 y^4 = 81y^4$ **(d)** $(6p^7)^2 = 6^2 p^{7\cdot2} = 6^2 p^{14} = 36p^{14}$

(e) $\left(\dfrac{-2m^5}{z}\right)^3 = \dfrac{(-2)^3 m^{5\cdot3}}{z^3} = \dfrac{(-2)^3 m^{15}}{z^3} = \dfrac{-8m^{15}}{z^3}$ ▌▌▌

Notice that

$$6^{-3} = \left(\frac{1}{6}\right)^3 = \frac{1}{216} \quad \text{and} \quad \left(\frac{2}{3}\right)^{-2} = \left(\frac{3}{2}\right)^2 = \frac{9}{4}.$$

These are examples of two special rules for negative exponents.

> ### Special Rules for Negative Exponents
>
> If $a \neq 0$ and $b \neq 0$ and n is an integer, then
>
> $$a^{-n} = \left(\frac{1}{a}\right)^n \quad \text{and} \quad \left(\frac{a}{b}\right)^{-n} = \left(\frac{b}{a}\right)^n.$$

▌▌ **EXAMPLE 10** Applying Special Rules for Negative Exponents

Write each expression with only positive exponents, and then evaluate.

(a) $\left(\dfrac{3}{7}\right)^{-2}$ **(b)** $\left(\dfrac{4}{5}\right)^{-3}$

SOLUTION

(a) $\left(\dfrac{3}{7}\right)^{-2} = \left(\dfrac{7}{3}\right)^2 = \dfrac{49}{9}$ **(b)** $\left(\dfrac{4}{5}\right)^{-3} = \left(\dfrac{5}{4}\right)^3 = \dfrac{125}{64}$ ▌▌▌

$(3/7)^{-2}$▶Frac
  $\dfrac{49}{9}$
$(4/5)^{-3}$▶Frac
  $\dfrac{125}{64}$

This screen supports the results of **Example 10.**

Summary of Rules for Exponents

The definitions and rules of this section are summarized here.

Definitions and Rules for Exponents

For all integers m and n and all real numbers a and b,

Product Rule	$a^m \cdot a^n = a^{m+n}$
Quotient Rule	$\dfrac{a^m}{a^n} = a^{m-n} \quad (a \neq 0)$
Zero Exponent	$a^0 = 1 \quad (a \neq 0)$
Negative Exponent	$a^{-n} = \dfrac{1}{a^n} \quad (a \neq 0)$
Power Rules	$(a^m)^n = a^{mn} \qquad (ab)^m = a^m b^m$
	$\left(\dfrac{a}{b}\right)^m = \dfrac{a^m}{b^m} \quad (b \neq 0)$
Special Rules for Negative Exponents	$\dfrac{1}{a^{-n}} = a^n \; (a \neq 0) \quad \dfrac{a^{-n}}{b^{-m}} = \dfrac{b^m}{a^n} \quad (a, b \neq 0)$
	$a^{-n} = \left(\dfrac{1}{a}\right)^n \quad (a \neq 0)$
	$\left(\dfrac{a}{b}\right)^{-n} = \left(\dfrac{b}{a}\right)^n \quad (a, b \neq 0).$

▮▮ **EXAMPLE 11** Writing Expressions with No Negative Exponents

Simplify each expression so that no negative exponents appear in the final result. Assume that all variables represent nonzero real numbers.

(a) $3^2 \cdot 3^{-5}$ **(b)** $x^{-3} \cdot x^{-4} \cdot x^2$ **(c)** $(4^{-2})^{-5}$

(d) $(x^{-4})^6$ **(e)** $\dfrac{x^{-4} y^2}{x^2 y^{-5}}$ **(f)** $(2^3 x^{-2})^{-2}$

SOLUTION

(a) $3^2 \cdot 3^{-5} = 3^{2+(-5)} = 3^{-3} = \dfrac{1}{3^3}, \quad \text{or} \quad \dfrac{1}{27}$

(b) $x^{-3} \cdot x^{-4} \cdot x^2 = x^{-3+(-4)+2} = x^{-5} = \dfrac{1}{x^5}$

(c) $(4^{-2})^{-5} = 4^{-2(-5)} = 4^{10}$ **(d)** $(x^{-4})^6 = x^{(-4)6} = x^{-24} = \dfrac{1}{x^{24}}$

(e) $\dfrac{x^{-4} y^2}{x^2 y^{-5}} = \dfrac{x^{-4}}{x^2} \cdot \dfrac{y^2}{y^{-5}}$ **(f)** $(2^3 x^{-2})^{-2} = (2^3)^{-2} \cdot (x^{-2})^{-2}$

$\qquad\qquad = x^{-4-2} \cdot y^{2-(-5)}$ $\qquad\qquad\qquad = 2^{-6} x^4$

$\qquad\qquad = x^{-6} y^7$ $\qquad\qquad\qquad = \dfrac{x^4}{2^6}, \quad \text{or} \quad \dfrac{x^4}{64}$

$\qquad\qquad = \dfrac{y^7}{x^6}$

▮▮▮

Scientific Notation

Many of the numbers that occur in science are very large or very small. Writing these numbers is simplified by using *scientific notation*.

In the episode "Court-Martial" from the original *Star Trek* television series, Captain Kirk makes this statement during a scene on the bridge of the Enterprise:

Gentlemen, this computer has an auditory sensor. It can, in effect, hear sounds. By installing a booster we can increase that capability on an order of one to the fourth power. The computer should be able to bring us every sound occurring on the ship.

Can you identify the error in Kirk's statement? What do you think he might have really meant? (Think about scientific notation.)

Scientific Notation

A number is written in **scientific notation** when it is expressed in the form

$$a \times 10^n, \quad \text{where } 1 \le |a| < 10, \text{ and } n \text{ is an integer.}$$

Scientific notation requires that the number be written as a product of a number between 1 and 10 (or -1 and -10) and some integer power of 10. (1 and -1 are allowed as values of a, but 10 and -10 are not.) For example,

$$8000 = 8 \cdot 1000 = 8 \cdot 10^3, \quad \text{or} \quad 8 \times 10^3. \longleftarrow \text{ Scientific notation}$$

In scientific notation, it is customary to use $\times$ instead of a multiplication dot.

The steps involved in writing a number in scientific notation follow. (If the number is negative, ignore the negative sign, go through these steps, and then attach a negative sign to the result.)

Converting a Positive Number to Scientific Notation

Step 1 **Position the decimal point.** Place a caret, $\wedge$, to the right of the first nonzero digit, where the decimal point will be placed.

Step 2 **Determine the numeral for the exponent.** Count the number of digits from the decimal point to the caret. This number gives the absolute value of the exponent on 10.

Step 3 **Determine the sign for the exponent.** Decide whether multiplying by 10^n should make the result of Step 1 larger or smaller. The exponent should be positive to make the result larger. It should be negative to make the result smaller.

It is helpful to remember that for $n \ge 1$, $10^{-n} < 1$ and $10^n \ge 10$.

▌▌ **EXAMPLE 12** Converting to Scientific Notation

Convert each number from standard notation to scientific notation.

(a) 8,200,000   **(b)** 0.000072

SOLUTION

(a) Place a caret to the right of the 8 (the first nonzero digit) to mark the new location of the decimal point.

$$8_{\wedge}200{,}000$$

Count from the decimal point, which is understood to be after the last 0, to the caret.

$$8_{\wedge}200{,}000. \longleftarrow \text{ Decimal point}$$
$$\text{Count 6 places.}$$

Because the number 8.2 is to be made larger, the exponent on 10 is positive.

$$8{,}200{,}000 = 8.2 \times 10^6$$

```
8200000
             8.2E6
.000072
             7.2E⁻5
```

If a graphing calculator is set in scientific notation mode, it will give results as shown here. E6 means "times 10^6" and E-5 means "times 10^{-5}". Compare to the results of **Example 12.**

(b) $0.00007{,}2$ Count from left to right.

5 places

Since the number 7.2 is to be made smaller, the exponent on 10 is negative.

$$0.000072 = 7.2 \times 10^{-5}$$ ▊▊▊

Converting a Positive Number from Scientific Notation to Standard Notation

Multiplying a positive number by a positive power of 10 makes the number larger, so move the decimal point to the right if n is positive in 10^n.

Multiplying a positive number by a negative power of 10 makes the number smaller, so move the decimal point to the left if n is negative.

If n is zero, do not move the decimal point.

▊▊ **EXAMPLE 13** Converting from Scientific Notation

Convert each number from scientific notation to standard notation.

(a) 6.93×10^5 **(b)** 4.7×10^{-6} **(c)** -1.083×10^0

SOLUTION

(a) $6.93 \times 10^5 = 6.93000$ Attach 0s as necessary.

5 places

The decimal point was moved 5 places to the right.

$$6.93 \times 10^5 = 693{,}000$$

(b) $4.7 \times 10^{-6} = 000004.7$ Attach 0s as necessary.

6 places

The decimal point was moved 6 places to the left.

$$4.7 \times 10^{-6} = 0.0000047$$

(c) $-1.083 \times 10^0 = -1.083$ ▊▊▊

▊▊ **EXAMPLE 14** Using Scientific Notation in Computation

Evaluate $\dfrac{1{,}920{,}000 \times 0.0015}{0.000032 \times 45{,}000}$ by using scientific notation.

SOLUTION

$$\frac{1{,}920{,}000 \times 0.0015}{0.000032 \times 45{,}000} = \frac{1.92 \times 10^6 \times 1.5 \times 10^{-3}}{3.2 \times 10^{-5} \times 4.5 \times 10^4}$$ Express all numbers in scientific notation.

$$= \frac{1.92 \times 1.5 \times 10^6 \times 10^{-3}}{3.2 \times 4.5 \times 10^{-5} \times 10^4}$$ Commutative and associative properties

$$= \frac{1.92 \times 1.5}{3.2 \times 4.5} \times 10^4$$ Product and quotient rules

$\underbrace{\text{Don't stop here.}}$ $= 0.2 \times 10^4$ Simplify.

$$= (2 \times 10^{-1}) \times 10^4$$ Write 0.2 using scientific notation.

$$= 2 \times 10^3, \text{ or } 2000$$ Associative property; product rule; multiply.

▊▊▊

▮▮ **EXAMPLE 15** Using Scientific Notation in an Application

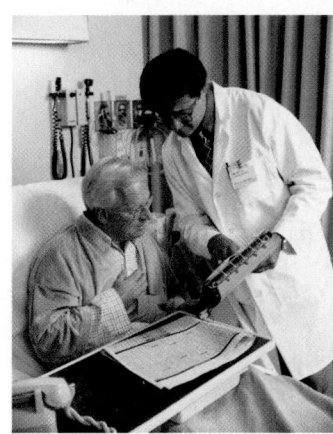

In 1990, the national health care expenditure in the United States was $714.0 billion. By 2005, this figure had risen by a factor of 2.8; that is, it almost tripled in 15 years. (*Source:* U.S. Centers for Medicare & Medicaid Services.)

(a) Write the 1990 health care expenditure using scientific notation.

(b) What was the expenditure in 2005?

SOLUTION

(a)   714.0 billion

$$= 714.0 \times 10^9 \qquad \text{1 billion} = 10^9$$

$$= (7.140 \times 10^2) \times 10^9 \quad \text{Write 714.0 in scientific notation.}$$

$$= 7.140 \times 10^{11} \qquad \text{Product rule}$$

In 1990, the expenditure was 7.140×10^{11}.

(b) Multiply the result in part (a) by 2.8.

$$(7.140 \times 10^{11}) \times 2.8$$

$$= (2.8 \times 7.140) \times 10^{11} \qquad \text{Commutative and associative properties}$$

$$= 19.992 \times 10^{11} \qquad \text{Round to three decimal places.}$$

$$= (1.9992 \times 10^1) \times 10^{11} \quad \text{Write 19.992 in scientific notation.}$$

$$= 1.9992 \times 10^{12} \qquad \text{Associative property; product rule; multiply.}$$

The 2005 expenditure was about $1,999,200,000,000 (almost $2 trillion). ▮▮▮

7.5 EXERCISES

Match the exponential expressions in Exercises 1–6 with their equivalent expressions in choices A–F below. Choices may be used once, more than once, or not at all.

1. $\left(\dfrac{5}{3}\right)^2$ **2.** $\left(\dfrac{3}{5}\right)^2$ **3.** $\left(-\dfrac{3}{5}\right)^{-2}$

4. $\left(-\dfrac{5}{3}\right)^{-2}$ **5.** $-\left(-\dfrac{3}{5}\right)^2$ **6.** $-\left(-\dfrac{5}{3}\right)^2$

A. $\dfrac{25}{9}$ **B.** $-\dfrac{25}{9}$ **C.** $\dfrac{9}{25}$

D. $-\dfrac{9}{25}$ **E.** none of these   **F.** all of these

Evaluate each exponential expression.

7. 5^4 **8.** 10^3

9. $(-2)^5$ **10.** $(-5)^4$

11. -2^3 **12.** -3^2

13. $-(-3)^4$ **14.** $-(-5)^2$

15. 7^{-2} **16.** 4^{-1}

17. -7^{-2} **18.** -4^{-1}

19. $\dfrac{2}{(-4)^{-3}}$ **20.** $\dfrac{2^{-3}}{3^{-2}}$

21. $\dfrac{5^{-1}}{4^{-2}}$ **22.** $\left(\dfrac{1}{2}\right)^{-3}$

23. $\left(\dfrac{1}{5}\right)^{-3}$ **24.** $\left(\dfrac{2}{3}\right)^{-2}$

25. $\left(\dfrac{4}{5}\right)^{-2}$ **26.** $3^{-1} + 2^{-1}$

27. $4^{-1} + 5^{-1}$ **28.** 8^0

29. 12^0 **30.** $(-23)^0$

31. $(-4)^0$ **32.** -2^0

33. $3^0 - 4^0$ **34.** $-8^0 - 7^0$

35. In order to raise a fraction to a negative power, we may change the fraction to its _____ and change the exponent to the ____ ____ of the original exponent.

36. Explain in your own words how to raise a power to a power.

37. Which one of the following is correct?

A. $-\dfrac{3}{4} = \left(\dfrac{3}{4}\right)^{-1}$ B. $\dfrac{3^{-1}}{4^{-1}} = \left(\dfrac{4}{3}\right)^{-1}$

C. $\dfrac{3^{-1}}{4} = \dfrac{3}{4^{-1}}$ D. $\dfrac{3^{-1}}{4^{-1}} = \left(\dfrac{3}{4}\right)^{-1}$

38. Which one of the following is incorrect?

A. $(3r)^{-2} = 3^{-2}r^{-2}$ B. $3r^{-2} = (3r)^{-2}$

C. $(3r)^{-2} = \dfrac{1}{(3r)^2}$ D. $(3r)^{-2} = \dfrac{r^{-2}}{9}$

Use the product, quotient, and power rules to simplify each expression. Write answers with only positive exponents. Assume that all variables represent nonzero real numbers.

39. $x^{12} \cdot x^4$

40. $\dfrac{x^{12}}{x^4}$

41. $\dfrac{5^{17}}{5^{16}}$

42. $\dfrac{3^{12}}{3^{13}}$

43. $\dfrac{3^{-5}}{3^{-2}}$

44. $\dfrac{2^{-4}}{2^{-3}}$

45. $\dfrac{9^{-1}}{9}$

46. $\dfrac{12}{12^{-1}}$

47. $t^5 t^{-12}$

48. $p^5 p^{-6}$

49. $(3x)^2$

50. $(-2x^{-2})^2$

51. $a^{-3}a^2a^{-4}$

52. $k^{-5}k^{-3}k^4$

53. $\dfrac{x^7}{x^{-4}}$

54. $\dfrac{p^{-3}}{p^5}$

55. $\dfrac{r^3 r^{-4}}{r^{-2} r^{-5}}$

56. $\dfrac{z^{-4} z^{-2}}{z^3 z^{-1}}$

57. $7k^2(-2k)(4k^{-5})$

58. $3a^2(-5a^{-6})(-2a)$

59. $(z^3)^{-2} z^2$

60. $(p^{-1})^3 p^{-4}$

61. $-3r^{-1}(r^{-3})^2$

62. $2(y^{-3})^4 (y^6)$

63. $(3a^{-2})^3 (a^3)^{-4}$

64. $(m^5)^{-2}(3m^{-2})^3$

65. $(x^{-5}y^2)^{-1}$

66. $(a^{-3}b^{-5})^2$

67. Which one of the following does *not* represent the reciprocal of x $(x \neq 0)$?

A. x^{-1} B. $\dfrac{1}{x}$ C. $\left(\dfrac{1}{x^{-1}}\right)^{-1}$ D. $-x$

68. Which one of the following is *not* in scientific notation?

A. 6.02×10^{23} B. 14×10^{-6}

C. 1.4×10^{-5} D. 3.8×10^3

Convert each number from standard notation to scientific notation.

69. 230

70. 46,500

71. 0.02

72. 0.0051

Convert each number from scientific notation to standard notation.

73. 6.5×10^3

74. 2.317×10^5

75. 1.52×10^{-2}

76. 1.63×10^{-4}

Use scientific notation to perform each of the following computations. Leave the answers in scientific notation.

77. $\dfrac{0.002 \times 3900}{0.000013}$

78. $\dfrac{0.009 \times 600}{0.02}$

79. $\dfrac{0.0004 \times 56,000}{0.000112}$

80. $\dfrac{0.018 \times 20,000}{300 \times 0.0004}$

81. $\dfrac{840,000 \times 0.03}{0.00021 \times 600}$

82. $\dfrac{28 \times 0.0045}{140 \times 1500}$

In Exercises 83–86, write the boldface numbers in scientific notation.

83. *U.S. Budget* The U.S. budget first passed **$1,000,000,000** in 1917. Seventy years later in 1987 it exceeded **$1,000,000,000,000** for the first time. President George W. Bush's budget request for fiscal 2009 was **$3,100,000,000,000.** If stacked in dollar bills, this amount would stretch **210,385** mi, almost 90% of the distance to the moon. (*Source: The New York Times.*)

84. *U.S. Area* By area, the largest of the fifty United States is Alaska, with land area of about **365,482,000** acres, while the smallest is Rhode Island, with land area of about **677,000** acres. The total land area of the United States is about **2,271,343,000** acres. (*Source: World Almanac and Book of Facts.*)

85. *NASA Budget* The budget for the Operating Plan in 2010 for the National Aeronautics and Space Administration was **$18.69 billion.** Write this amount in scientific notation. (*Source*: www.nasa.gov)

86. *Motor Vehicle Registrations* In 2007, there were about **247,264,600** motor vehicle registrations in the United States. Write this number in scientific notation. (*Source: U.S. Federal Highway Administration.*)

Astronomy Data *Each of the following statements (Exercises 87–90) comes from* Astronomy! A Brief Edition *by James B. Kaler (Addison-Wesley). If the number in the statement is in scientific notation, write it in standard notation without using exponents. If the number is in standard notation, write it in scientific notation.*

87. Multiplying this view over the whole sky yields a galaxy count of more than **10 billion.** (page 496)

88. The circumference of the solar orbit is . . . about **4.7 billion** km . . . . (in reference to the orbit of Jupiter, page 395)

89. The solar luminosity requires that **2×10^9** kg of mass be converted into energy every second. (page 327)

90. At maximum, a cosmic ray particle—a mere atomic nucleus of only **10^{-13}** cm across—can carry the energy of a professionally pitched baseball. (page 445)

Solve each problem.

91. *U.S. Population* In May 2008, the population of the United States was 304.1 million. (*Source: U.S. Census Bureau.*)

  (a) Write the May 2008 population using scientific notation.

  (b) Write $1 trillion, that is, $1,000,000,000,000, using scientific notation.

  (c) Using your answers from parts (a) and (b), calculate how much each person in the United States in the year 2008 would have had to contribute in order to make someone a trillionaire. Write this amount in standard notation to the nearest dollar.

92. *Powerball Lottery* In the early years of the Powerball Lottery, a player had to choose five numbers from 1 through 49 and one number from 1 through 42. It can be shown that there are about 8.009×10^7 different ways to do this. Suppose that a group of 2000 people decided to purchase tickets for all these numbers and each ticket cost $1.00. How much should each person have expected to pay? (*Source*: www.powerball.com)

93. *Distance of Uranus from the Sun* A parsec, a unit of length used in astronomy, is 1.9×10^{13} miles. The mean distance of Uranus from the sun is 1.8×10^7 miles. How many parsecs is Uranus from the sun?

94. *Number of Inches in a Mile* An inch is approximately 1.57828×10^{-5} mile. Find the reciprocal of this number to determine the number of inches in a mile.

95. *Speed of Light* The speed of light is approximately 3×10^{10} centimeters per second. How long will it take light to travel 9×10^{12} centimeters?

96. *Rocket from Earth to the Sun* The average distance from Earth to the sun is 9.3×10^7 miles. How long would it take a rocket, traveling at 2.9×10^3 miles per hour, to reach the sun?)

97. *Miles in a Light-Year* A *light-year* is the distance that light travels in one year. Find the number of miles in a light-year if light travels 1.86×10^5 miles per second.

98. *Time for Light to Travel* Use the information given in the previous two exercises to find the number of minutes necessary for light from the sun to reach Earth.

99. *Rocket from Venus to Mercury* The planet Mercury has an average distance from the sun of 3.6×10^7 miles, while the mean distance of Venus from the sun is 6.7×10^7 miles. How long would it take a spacecraft traveling at 1.55×10^3 miles per hour to travel from Venus to Mercury? Assume the trip could be timed so that its start and finish would occur when the respective planets are at their average distances from the sun and the same direction from the sun. (Give your answer in hours, without scientific notation.)

100. *Distance from an Object to the Moon* When the distance between the centers of the moon and Earth is 4.60×10^8 meters, an object on the line joining the centers of the moon and Earth exerts the same gravitational force on each when it is 4.14×10^8 meters from the center of Earth. How far is the object from the center of the moon at that point?

7.6 POLYNOMIALS AND FACTORING

Basic Terminology • Addition and Subtraction • Multiplication • Special Products • Factoring • Factoring Out the Greatest Common Factor • Factoring by Grouping • Factoring Trinomials • Factoring Special Binomials

Basic Terminology

A **term,** or **monomial,** is defined to be a number, a variable, or a product of numbers and variables. A **polynomial** is a term or a finite sum or difference of terms, with only nonnegative integer exponents permitted on the variables. If the terms of a polynomial contain only the variable x, then the polynomial is called a **polynomial in x.** (Polynomials in other variables are defined similarly.)

$$5x^3 - 8x^2 + 7x - 4, \quad 9p^5 - 3, \quad 8r^2, \quad \text{and} \quad 6 \qquad \text{Examples of polynomials}$$

The expression $9x^2 - 4x - \frac{6}{x}$ is not a polynomial because of the presence of $-\frac{6}{x}$. The terms of a polynomial cannot have variables in a denominator.

The greatest exponent in a polynomial in one variable is the **degree** of the polynomial. A nonzero constant has degree 0. (The polynomial 0 has no degree.) For example,

$$3x^6 - 5x^2 + 2x + 3 \quad \text{is a polynomial of degree 6.}$$

A polynomial can have more than one variable. A term containing more than one variable has degree equal to the sum of all the exponents appearing on the variables in the term. For example, $-3x^4y^3z^5$ is of degree $4 + 3 + 5 = 12$. The degree of a polynomial in more than one variable is equal to the greatest degree of any term appearing in the polynomial. By this definition, the polynomial

$$2x^4y^3 - 3x^5y + x^6y^2 \quad \text{is of degree 8}$$

because the x^6y^2 term has degree 8.

A polynomial containing exactly three terms is called a **trinomial** and one containing exactly two terms is a **binomial. Table 5** shows several polynomials and gives the degree and type of each.

Table 5

Polynomial	Degree	Type
$9p^7 - 4p^3 + 8p^2$	7	Trinomial
$29x^{11} + 8x^{15}$	15	Binomial
$-10r^6s^8$	14	Monomial
$5a^3b^7 - 3a^5b^5 + 4a^2b^9 - a^{10}$	11	None of these

Addition and Subtraction

Since the variables used in polynomials represent real numbers, a polynomial represents a real number. This means that all the properties of the real numbers hold for polynomials. Here is an application of the distributive property.

$$3m^5 - 7m^5 = (3 - 7)\, m^5 = -4m^5 \qquad \text{Combine like terms.}$$

Like terms are terms that have the exact same variable factors. Thus, polynomials are added by adding coefficients of like terms and are subtracted by subtracting coefficients of like terms.

▮▮ | **EXAMPLE 1** | Adding and Subtracting Polynomials

Add or subtract, as indicated.

(a) $(2y^4 - 3y^2 + y) + (4y^4 + 7y^2 + 6y)$

(b) $(-3m^3 - 8m^2 + 4) - (m^3 + 7m^2 - 3)$

(c) $(8m^4p^5 - 9m^3p^5) + (11m^4p^5 + 15m^3p^5)$

(d) $4(x^2 - 3x + 7) - 5(2x^2 - 8x - 4)$

SOLUTION

(a) $(2y^4 - 3y^2 + y) + (4y^4 + 7y^2 + 6y)$

$= (2 + 4)y^4 + (-3 + 7)y^2 + (1 + 6)y$ Combine like terms.

$= 6y^4 + 4y^2 + 7y$

(b) $(-3m^3 - 8m^2 + 4) - (m^3 + 7m^2 - 3)$

$= (-3 - 1)m^3 + (-8 - 7)m^2 + [4 - (-3)]$

$= -4m^3 - 15m^2 + 7$

(c) $(8m^4p^5 - 9m^3p^5) + (11m^4p^5 + 15m^3p^5)$

$= 19m^4p^5 + 6m^3p^5$

(d) $4(x^2 - 3x + 7) - 5(2x^2 - 8x - 4)$

$= 4x^2 - 4(3x) + 4(7) - 5(2x^2) - 5(-8x) - 5(-4)$ Distributive property

$= 4x^2 - 12x + 28 - 10x^2 + 40x + 20$ Associative property

$= -6x^2 + 28x + 48$ Combine like terms. ▮▮▮

As shown in **Examples 1(a), (b), and (d),** polynomials in one variable are often written with their terms in **descending powers.** The term of greatest degree is first, the one with the next greatest degree is second, and so on.

Multiplication

The associative and distributive properties, together with the properties of exponents, can also be used to find the product of two polynomials. For example,

$$(3x - 4)(2x^2 - 3x + 5)$$

$$= (3x - 4)(2x^2) - (3x - 4)(3x) + (3x - 4)(5)$$

$$= (3x)(2x^2) - 4(2x^2) - (3x)(3x) - (-4)(3x) + (3x)5 - 4(5)$$

$$= 6x^3 - 8x^2 - 9x^2 + 12x + 15x - 20$$

$$= 6x^3 - 17x^2 + 27x - 20.$$

It is sometimes more convenient to write such a product vertically, as follows.

$$2x^2 - 3x + 5$$

$$3x - 4$$

Be sure to place like terms in columns.

$$-8x^2 + 12x - 20 \longleftarrow -4(2x^2 - 3x + 5)$$

$$6x^3 - 9x^2 + 15x \longleftarrow 3x(2x^2 - 3x + 5)$$

$$6x^3 - 17x^2 + 27x - 20 \quad \text{Add in columns.}$$

▐▐ **EXAMPLE 2** Multiplying Polynomials Vertically

Multiply $(3p^2 - 4p + 1)(p^3 + 2p - 8)$.

SOLUTION

Multiply each term of the first polynomial by each term of the second and add.

$$
\begin{array}{r}
3p^2 - 4p + 1 \\
p^3 + 2p - 8 \\
\hline
-24p^2 + 32p - 8 \\
6p^3 - 8p^2 + 2p \\
3p^5 - 4p^4 + p^3 \\
\hline
3p^5 - 4p^4 + 7p^3 - 32p^2 + 34p - 8
\end{array}
$$

Multiply $3p^2 - 4p + 1$ by -8.

Multiply $3p^2 - 4p + 1$ by $2p$.

Multiply $3p^2 - 4p + 1$ by p^3.

Add in columns. ▐▐▐

The memory aid "FOIL" is a convenient way to find the product of two binomials. FOIL (for First, Outside, Inside, Last) gives the pairs of terms to be multiplied to get the product, as shown in the next examples.

▐▐ **EXAMPLE 3** Using the FOIL Method

Find each product.

(a) $(6m + 1)(4m - 3)$ **(b)** $(2x + 7)(2x - 7)$ **(c)** $(x^2 - 4)(x^2 + 4)$

SOLUTION

(a) $(6m + 1)(4m - 3)$

$$
\begin{array}{cccc}
 & \text{F} & \text{O} & \text{I} & \text{L}
\end{array}
$$

$= (6m)(4m) + (6m)(-3) + 1(4m) + 1(-3)$

$= 24m^2 - 18m + 4m - 3$

$= 24m^2 - 14m - 3$ Combine like terms.

(b) $(2x + 7)(2x - 7)$

$= 4x^2 - 14x + 14x - 49$ FOIL

$= 4x^2 - 49$ Combine like terms.

(c) $(x^2 - 4)(x^2 + 4) = x^4 + 4x^2 - 4x^2 - 16$

$= x^4 - 16$ ▐▐▐

The **special product**

$$(x + y)(x - y) = x^2 - y^2$$

can be used to solve some multiplication problems.

$$
\begin{aligned}
51 \times 49 &= (50 + 1)(50 - 1) \\
&= 50^2 - 1^2 \\
&= 2500 - 1 \\
&= 2499
\end{aligned}
$$

$$
\begin{aligned}
102 \times 98 &= (100 + 2)(100 - 2) \\
&= 100^2 - 2^2 \\
&= 10,000 - 4 \\
&= 9996
\end{aligned}
$$

Once these patterns are recognized, multiplications of this type can be done mentally.

Special Products

In **Example 3(a)**, the product of two binomials is a trinomial, while in **(b)** and **(c)** the product of two binomials is a binomial. *The product of two binomials of the forms $x + y$ and $x - y$ is always a binomial.* Check that the following is true.

> **Product of the Sum and Difference of Two Terms**
>
> $$(x + y)(x - y) = x^2 - y^2$$

The product $x^2 - y^2$ is called a **difference of two squares**.

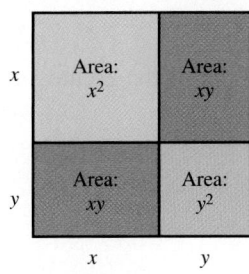

The **special product**

$$(x + y)^2 = x^2 + 2xy + y^2$$

can be illustrated geometrically using the diagram shown here. Each side of the large square has length $x + y$, so the area of the square is

$$(x + y)^2.$$

The large square is made up of two smaller squares and two congruent rectangles. The sum of the areas of these figures is

$$x^2 + 2xy + y^2.$$

Since these expressions represent the same quantity, they must be equal, thus giving us the pattern for squaring a binomial.

▮▮ **EXAMPLE 4** Finding Special Products

Find each product.

(a) $(3p + 11)(3p - 11)$ **(b)** $(5m^3 - 3)(5m^3 + 3)$

(c) $(9k - 11r^3)(9k + 11r^3)$

SOLUTION

(a) Using the pattern discussed earlier, replace x with $3p$ and y with 11.

$$(3p + 11)(3p - 11)$$
$$= (3p)^2 - 11^2$$
$$= 9p^2 - 121$$

(b) $(5m^3 - 3)(5m^3 + 3)$ **(c)** $(9k - 11r^3)(9k + 11r^3)$
$$= (5m^3)^2 - 3^2$$ $$= (9k)^2 - (11r^3)^2$$
$$= 25m^6 - 9$$ $$= 81k^2 - 121r^6$$ ▮▮▮

Squares of binomials are also special products.

Squares of Binomials

$$(x + y)^2 = x^2 + 2xy + y^2$$
$$(x - y)^2 = x^2 - 2xy + y^2$$

▮▮ **EXAMPLE 5** Finding Special Products

Find each product.

(a) $(2m + 5)^2$ **(b)** $(3x - 7y^4)^2$

SOLUTION

(a) $(2m + 5)^2 = (2m)^2 + 2(2m)(5) + (5)^2$
$$= 4m^2 + 20m + 25$$

> The square of a binomial has three terms. $(x + y)^2 \neq x^2 + y^2$

(b) $(3x - 7y^4)^2 = (3x)^2 - 2(3x)(7y^4) + (7y^4)^2$
$$= 9x^2 - 42xy^4 + 49y^8$$ ▮▮▮

Factoring

The process of finding polynomials whose product equals a given polynomial is called **factoring.** For example, since

$$4x + 12 = 4(x + 3),$$

both 4 and $x + 3$ are called **factors** of $4x + 12$. Also, $4(x + 3)$ is called a **factored form** of $4x + 12$. A polynomial that cannot be written as a product of two polynomials with integer coefficients is a **prime polynomial.** A polynomial is **factored completely** when it is written as a product of prime polynomials with integer coefficients.

Factoring is the inverse of multiplying, so a check requires that the product of the factored form yields the original polynomial.

Factoring Out the Greatest Common Factor

When factoring a polynomial, we first look for a monomial that is the greatest common factor (GCF) of all the terms of the polynomial.

$$6x^2y^3 + 9xy^4 + 18y^5$$

$$= (3y^3)(2x^2) + (3y^3)(3xy) + (3y^3)(6y^2) \quad \text{GCF} = 3y^3$$

$$= 3y^3(2x^2 + 3xy + 6y^2)$$

▌▌ EXAMPLE 6   Factoring Out the Greatest Common Factor

Factor out the greatest common factor from each polynomial.

(a) $9y^5 + y^2$ **(b)** $6x^2t + 8xt + 12t$

SOLUTION

(a) $9y^5 + y^2 = y^2 \cdot 9y^3 + y^2 \cdot 1$ The greatest common factor is y^2.

$$= y^2(9y^3 + 1)$$

(b) $6x^2t + 8xt + 12t$

$$= 2t(3x^2 + 4x + 6) \quad \text{GCF} = 2t$$ ▮▮▮

Factoring by Grouping

When a polynomial has more than three terms, it can sometimes be factored by a method called **factoring by grouping.**

$$ax + ay + 6x + 6y$$

$$= (ax + ay) + (6x + 6y) \quad \text{Group the terms.}$$

$$= a(x + y) + 6(x + y) \quad \text{Factor each group.}$$

$$= (x + y)(a + 6) \quad \text{Factor out } (x + y).$$

▌▌ EXAMPLE 7   Factoring by Grouping

Factor by grouping.

(a) $mp^2 + 7m + 3p^2 + 21$ **(b)** $2y^2 - 2z - ay^2 + az$

SOLUTION

(a) $mp^2 + 7m + 3p^2 + 21$

$$= (mp^2 + 7m) + (3p^2 + 21) \quad \text{Group the terms.}$$

$$= m(p^2 + 7) + 3(p^2 + 7) \quad \text{Factor each group.}$$

$$= (p^2 + 7)(m + 3) \quad p^2 + 7 \text{ is a common factor.}$$

(b) $2y^2 - 2z - ay^2 + az$

$$= (2y^2 - 2z) + (-ay^2 + az) \quad \text{Group the terms.}$$

$$= 2(y^2 - z) + a(-y^2 + z) \quad \text{Factor each group.}$$

The expression $-y^2 + z$ is the negative of $y^2 - z$, so factor out $-a$ instead of a.

$$= 2(y^2 - z) - a(y^2 - z) \quad \text{Factor out } -a.$$

$$= (y^2 - z)(2 - a) \quad \text{Factor out } y^2 - z.$$ ▮▮▮

Factoring Trinomials

Factoring trinomials requires using the FOIL method in an inverse manner.

▮▮ **EXAMPLE 8** Factoring Trinomials
_____

Factor each trinomial.

(a) $4y^2 - 11y + 6$ **(b)** $6p^2 - 7p - 5$

SOLUTION

(a) To factor this polynomial, we must find integers a, b, c, and d such that

$$4y^2 - 11y + 6 = (ay + b)(cy + d).$$

By using FOIL, we see that $ac = 4$ and $bd = 6$. The positive factors of 4 are 4 and 1 or 2 and 2. Since the middle term is negative, we consider only negative factors of 6. The possibilities are -2 and -3 or -1 and -6. Try various arrangements.

$$(2y - 1)(2y - 6) = 4y^2 - \mathbf{14y} + 6 \quad \text{Incorrect}$$
$$(2y - 2)(2y - 3) = 4y^2 - \mathbf{10y} + 6 \quad \text{Incorrect}$$
$$(y - 2)(4y - 3) = 4y^2 - \mathbf{11y} + 6 \quad \text{Correct}$$

The last trial gives the correct factorization.

(b) Again, we try various possibilities. The positive factors of 6 could be 2 and 3 or 1 and 6. As factors of -5 we have only -1 and 5 or -5 and 1.

$$(2p - 5)(3p + 1) = 6p^2 - \mathbf{13p} - 5 \quad \text{Incorrect}$$
$$(3p - 5)(2p + 1) = 6p^2 - \mathbf{7p} - 5 \quad \text{Correct}$$

Thus, $6p^2 - 7p - 5$ factors as $(3p - 5)(2p + 1)$.   ▮▮▮

Perfect square trinomials can be factored as follows.

Perfect Square Trinomials

$$x^2 + 2xy + y^2 = (x + y)^2$$
$$x^2 - 2xy + y^2 = (x - y)^2$$

▮▮ **EXAMPLE 9** Factoring Perfect Square Trinomials
_____

Factor each polynomial.

(a) $16p^2 - 40pq + 25q^2$ **(b)** $169x^2 + 104xy^2 + 16y^4$

SOLUTION

(a) Make sure that the middle term of the trinomial being factored, $-40pq$ here, is twice the product of the two terms in the binomial $4p - 5q$.

$$-40pq = 2(4p)(-5q)$$

Since $16p^2 = (4p)^2$ and $25q^2 = (5q)^2$, use the second pattern shown above.

$$16p^2 - 40pq + 25q^2 = (4p)^2 - 2(4p)(5q) + (5q)^2$$
$$= (4p - 5q)^2$$

(b) $169x^2 + 104xy^2 + 16y^4 = (13x + 4y^2)^2$, since $2(13x)(4y^2) = 104xy^2$.   ▮▮▮

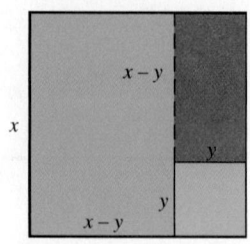

A **geometric proof** for the difference of squares property is shown above. (The proof is valid only for $x > y > 0$.)

$$x^2 - y^2 = x(x - y) + y(x - y)$$
$$= (x - y)(x + y)$$

Factor out $x - y$ in the second step.

Factoring Special Binomials

Difference of Squares

$$x^2 - y^2 = (x + y)(x - y)$$

▌▌ **EXAMPLE 10** Factoring Differences of Squares

Factor each polynomial.

(a) $4m^2 - 9$ **(b)** $256k^4 - 625m^4$ **(c)** $x^2 - 6x + 9 - y^4$

SOLUTION

(a) $4m^2 - 9$

$\quad = (2m)^2 - 3^2$ Difference of squares

$\quad = (2m + 3)(2m - 3)$

(b) $256k^4 - 625m^4$

$\quad = (16k^2)^2 - (25m^2)^2$ Difference of squares

$\quad = (16k^2 + 25m^2)(16k^2 - 25m^2)$

$\quad = (16k^2 + 25m^2)(4k + 5m)(4k - 5m)$

(c) $x^2 - 6x + 9 - y^4$

$\quad = (x^2 - 6x + 9) - y^4$ Group the first three terms.

$\quad = (x - 3)^2 - (y^2)^2$ Perfect square trinomial

$\quad = [(x - 3) + y^2][(x - 3) - y^2]$ Difference of squares

$\quad = (x - 3 + y^2)(x - 3 - y^2)$ ▌▌▌

Sum and Difference of Cubes

Sum of Cubes $x^3 + y^3 = (x + y)(x^2 - xy + y^2)$

Difference of Cubes $x^3 - y^3 = (x - y)(x^2 + xy + y^2)$

▌▌ **EXAMPLE 11** Factoring Sums and Differences of Cubes

Factor each polynomial.

(a) $x^3 + 27$ **(b)** $m^3 - 64n^3$ **(c)** $8q^6 + 125p^9$

SOLUTION

(a) $x^3 + 27$

$\quad = x^3 + 3^3$ Sum of cubes

$\quad = (x + 3)(x^2 - 3x + 9)$

(b) $m^3 - 64n^3$

$\quad = m^3 - (4n)^3$ Difference of cubes

$\quad = (m - 4n)[m^2 + m(4n) + (4n)^2]$

$\quad = (m - 4n)(m^2 + 4mn + 16n^2)$

(c) $8q^6 + 125p^9$

$\quad = (2q^2)^3 + (5p^3)^3$ Sum of cubes

$\quad = (2q^2 + 5p^3)[(2q^2)^2 - (2q^2)(5p^3) + (5p^3)^2]$

$\quad = (2q^2 + 5p^3)(4q^4 - 10q^2p^3 + 25p^6)$ ▌▌▌

7.6 EXERCISES

Find each sum or difference.

1. $(3x^2 - 4x + 5) + (-2x^2 + 3x - 2)$

2. $(4m^3 - 3m^2 + 5) + (-3m^3 - m^2 + 5)$

3. $(12y^2 - 8y + 6) - (3y^2 - 4y + 2)$

4. $(8p^2 - 5p) - (3p^2 - 2p + 4)$

5. $(6m^4 - 3m^2 + m) - (2m^3 + 5m^2 + 4m) + (m^2 - m)$

6. $-(8x^3 + x - 3) + (2x^3 + x^2) - (4x^2 + 3x - 1)$

7. $5(2x^2 - 3x + 7) - 2(6x^2 - x + 12)$

8. $8x^2y - 3xy^2 + 2x^2y - 9xy^2$

Find each product.

9. $(x + 3)(x - 8)$

10. $(y - 3)(y - 9)$

11. $(4r - 1)(7r + 2)$

12. $(5m - 6)(3m + 4)$

13. $4x^2(3x^3 + 2x^2 - 5x + 1)$

14. $2b^3(b^2 - 4b + 3)$

15. $(2m + 3)(2m - 3)$

16. $(8s - 3t)(8s + 3t)$

17. $(4m + 2n)^2$ **18.** $(a - 6b)^2$

19. $(5r + 3t^2)^2$ **20.** $(2z^4 - 3y)^2$

21. $(2z - 1)(-z^2 + 3z - 4)$

22. $(k + 2)(12k^3 - 3k^2 + k + 1)$

23. $(m - n + k)(m + 2n - 3k)$

24. $(r - 3s + t)(2r - s + t)$

25. $(a - b + 2c)^2$ **26.** $(k - y + 3m)^2$

27. Which one of the following is a trinomial in descending powers, having degree 6?
   A. $5x^6 - 4x^5 + 12$ **B.** $6x^5 - x^6 + 4$
   C. $2x + 4x^2 - x^6$ **D.** $4x^6 - 6x^4 + 9x + 1$

28. Give an example of a polynomial of four terms in the variable x, having degree 5, written in descending powers, lacking a fourth degree term.

29. The exponent in the expression 6^3 is 3. Explain why the degree of 6^3 is not 3. What is its degree?

30. Explain in your own words how to square a binomial.

Factor the greatest common factor from each polynomial.

31. $8m^4 + 6m^3 - 12m^2$

32. $2p^5 - 10p^4 + 16p^3$

33. $4k^2m^3 + 8k^4m^3 - 12k^2m^4$

34. $28r^4s^2 + 7r^3s - 35r^4s^3$

35. $2(a + b) + 4m(a + b)$

36. $4(y - 2)^2 + 3(y - 2)$

37. $2(m - 1) - 3(m - 1)^2 + 2(m - 1)^3$

38. $5(a + 3)^3 - 2(a + 3) + (a + 3)^2$

Factor each polynomial by grouping.

39. $6st + 9t - 10s - 15$

40. $10ab - 6b + 35a - 21$

41. $rt^3 + rs^2 - pt^3 - ps^2$

42. $2m^4 + 6 - am^4 - 3a$

43. $16a^2 + 10ab - 24ab - 15b^2$

44. $15 - 5m^2 - 3r^2 + m^2r^2$

45. $20z^2 - 8zx - 45zx + 18x^2$

46. $4 - 2y - 2x + xy$

47. $1 - a + ab - b$

48. Consider the polynomial $1 - a + ab - b$ from **Exercise 47.** The answer given in the answer section is $(1 - a)(1 - b)$. However, there are other acceptable factored forms. Which one of A–D is *not* a factored form of this polynomial?
   A. $(a - 1)(b - 1)$ **B.** $(-a + 1)(-b + 1)$
   C. $(-1 + a)(-1 + b)$ **D.** $(1 - a)(b + 1)$

Factor each trinomial.

49. $x^2 - 2x - 15$ **50.** $r^2 + 8r + 12$

51. $y^2 + 2y - 35$ **52.** $x^2 - 7x + 6$

53. $6a^2 - 48a - 120$ **54.** $8h^2 - 24h - 320$

55. $3m^3 + 12m^2 + 9m$

56. $9y^4 - 54y^3 + 45y^2$

57. $6k^2 + 5kp - 6p^2$

58. $14m^2 + 11mr - 15r^2$

59. $5a^2 - 7ab - 6b^2$

60. $12s^2 + 11st - 5t^2$

61. $21x^2 - xy - 2y^2$

62. $30a^2 + am - m^2$

63. $24a^4 + 10a^3b - 4a^2b^2$

64. $18x^5 + 15x^4z - 75x^3z^2$

65. $15x^2y^5 - 20x^3y^3 + 15xy^2$

66. $28m^4n^6 + 21m^6n^3 - 35m^3n^2$

Factor each perfect square trinomial. It may be necessary to factor out a common factor first.

67. $9m^2 - 12m + 4$

68. $16p^2 - 40p + 25$

69. $32a^2 - 48ab + 18b^2$

70. $20p^2 - 100pq + 125q^2$

71. $4x^2y^2 + 28xy + 49$

72. $9m^2n^2 - 12mn + 4$

Factor each difference of squares.

73. $x^2 - 36$

74. $t^2 - 64$

75. $y^2 - w^2$

76. $25 - w^2$

77. $9a^2 - 16$

78. $16q^2 - 25$

79. $25s^4 - 9t^2$

80. $36z^2 - 81y^4$

81. $p^4 - 625$

82. $m^4 - 81$

Factor each sum or difference of cubes.

83. $8 - a^3$

84. $r^3 + 27$

85. $125x^3 - 27$

86. $8m^3 - 27n^3$

87. $27y^9 + 125z^6$

88. $27z^3 + 729y^3$

Decide on a factoring method, and then factor the polynomial completely.

89. $x^2 + xy - 5x - 5y$

90. $8r^2 - 10rs - 3s^2$

91. $12m^2 + 16mn - 35n^2$

92. $36a^2 + 60a + 25$

93. $4z^2 + 28z + 49$

94. $6p^4 + 7p^2 - 3$

95. $1000x^3 + 343y^3$

96. $b^2 + 8b + 16 - a^2$

97. $125m^6 - 216$

98. $q^2 + 6q + 9 - p^2$

99. $p^4(m - 2n) + q(m - 2n)$

100. $216p^3 + 125q^3$

7.7 QUADRATIC EQUATIONS AND APPLICATIONS

Quadratic Equations • Zero-Factor Property • Square Root Property
• Quadratic Formula • Applications

Quadratic Equations

> **Quadratic Equation**
>
> An equation that can be written in the form
>
> $$ax^2 + bx + c = 0 \quad \text{Standard form}$$
>
> where a, b, and c are real numbers, with $a \neq 0$, is a **quadratic equation.** The form of the equation given above is called **standard form.**

Zero-Factor Property

The simplest method of solving a quadratic equation, but one that is not always easily applied, is by factoring. This method depends on the following property.

> **Zero-Factor Property**
>
> If $ab = 0$, then $a = 0$ or $b = 0$ or both.

When solving a quadratic equation by the zero-factor property, the equation must be in standard form before factoring.

▌▌ **EXAMPLE 1** Using the Zero-Factor Property

Solve $6x^2 + 7x = 3$.

SOLUTION

$$6x^2 + 7x = 3$$
$$6x^2 + 7x - 3 = 0 \qquad \text{Standard form}$$
$$(3x - 1)(2x + 3) = 0 \qquad \text{Factor.}$$
$$3x - 1 = 0 \quad \text{or} \quad 2x + 3 = 0 \qquad \text{Zero-factor property}$$
$$3x = 1 \quad \text{or} \quad 2x = -3 \qquad \text{Solve each equation.}$$
$$x = \frac{1}{3} \quad \text{or} \quad x = -\frac{3}{2} \qquad \text{Divide.}$$

Check by first substituting $\frac{1}{3}$ and then $-\frac{3}{2}$ in the original equation. The solution set is $\left\{\frac{1}{3}, -\frac{3}{2}\right\}$. ▮▮▮

Square Root Property

A quadratic equation of the form $x^2 = k$, $k \geq 0$, can be solved by factoring.

$$x^2 = k$$
$$x^2 - k = 0 \qquad \text{Subtract } k.$$
$$(x + \sqrt{k})(x - \sqrt{k}) = 0 \qquad \text{Factor, using radicals.}$$
$$x + \sqrt{k} = 0 \quad \text{or} \quad x - \sqrt{k} = 0 \qquad \text{Zero-factor property}$$
$$x = -\sqrt{k} \quad \text{or} \quad x = \sqrt{k} \qquad \text{Solve each equation.}$$

This leads to the square root property for solving equations.

Square Root Property

If $k \geq 0$, then the solutions of $x^2 = k$ are $x = \pm\sqrt{k}$.

If $k > 0$, the equation $x^2 = k$ has two real solutions. If $k = 0$, there is only one solution, 0. If $k < 0$, there are no real solutions. (However, in this case, there *are* imaginary solutions. Imaginary numbers are discussed briefly in the **Extensions** on complex numbers at the end of **Chapter 6** and this chapter.)

▌▌ **EXAMPLE 2** Using the Square Root Property

Use the square root property to solve each quadratic equation for real solutions.

(a) $x^2 = 25$ **(b)** $x^2 = 18$ **(c)** $x^2 = -3$ **(d)** $(x - 4)^2 = 12$

SOLUTION

(a) Since $\sqrt{25} = 5$, the solution set of the equation $x^2 = 25$ is $\{5, -5\}$, which may be abbreviated $\{\pm 5\}$.

Completing the square, used in deriving the quadratic formula, has important applications in algebra. To transform the expression $x^2 + kx$ into the square of a binomial, we add to it the square of half the coefficient of x, that is,

$$\left[\left(\tfrac{1}{2}\right)k\right]^2 = \frac{k^2}{4}.$$

We then get

$$x^2 + kx + \frac{k^2}{4} = \left(x + \frac{k}{2}\right)^2.$$

For example, to make $x^2 + 6x$ the square of a binomial, we add 9, since $9 = \left[\frac{1}{2}(6)\right]^2$. This results in the trinomial $x^2 + 6x + 9$, which is equal to $(x + 3)^2$.

The Greeks had a method of completing the square geometrically. For example, to complete the square for $x^2 + 6x$, begin with a square of side x. Add three rectangles of width 1 and length x to the right side and the bottom. Each rectangle has area $1x$ or x, so the total area of the figure is now $x^2 + 6x$. To fill in the corner (that is, "complete the square"), we add 9 1-by-1 squares as shown. The new completed square has sides of length $x + 3$ and area

$$(x + 3)^2 = x^2 + 6x + 9.$$

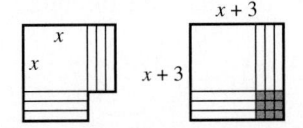

(b)
$$x^2 = 18$$
$$x = \pm\sqrt{18} \qquad \text{Square root property}$$
$$x = \pm\sqrt{9 \cdot 2} \qquad \text{Factor 18 as 9 · 2.}$$
$$x = \pm\sqrt{9} \cdot \sqrt{2} \qquad \text{Product rule for square roots}$$
$$x = \pm 3\sqrt{2} \qquad \sqrt{9} = 3$$

The solution set is $\{\pm 3\sqrt{2}\}$.

(c) Since $-3 < 0$, the equation $x^2 = -3$ has no real solutions. The solution set is $\emptyset$.

(d)
$$(x - 4)^2 = 12$$
$$x - 4 = \pm\sqrt{12} \qquad \text{Square root property}$$
$$x = 4 \pm \sqrt{12} \qquad \text{Add 4.}$$
$$x = 4 \pm \sqrt{4 \cdot 3} \qquad \text{Factor 12 as 4 · 3.}$$
$$x = 4 \pm 2\sqrt{3} \qquad \sqrt{4 \cdot 3} = 2\sqrt{3}$$

The solution set is $\{4 \pm 2\sqrt{3}\}$.   ▌▌▌

Quadratic Formula

By *completing the square* (see the margin note on **page 349**) we can derive one of the most important formulas in algebra, the *quadratic formula*.

$$ax^2 + bx + c = 0 \qquad \text{Standard quadratic equation } (a > 0)$$

$$x^2 + \frac{b}{a}x + \frac{c}{a} = 0 \qquad \text{Divide by } a.$$

$$x^2 + \frac{b}{a}x = -\frac{c}{a} \qquad \text{Add } -\frac{c}{a}.$$

$$x^2 + \frac{b}{a}x + \frac{b^2}{4a^2} = \frac{b^2}{4a^2} - \frac{c}{a} \qquad \text{Add } \frac{b^2}{4a^2}.$$

$$\left(x + \frac{b}{2a}\right)^2 = \frac{b^2 - 4ac}{4a^2} \qquad \text{Factor on the left. Combine terms on the right.}$$

$$x + \frac{b}{2a} = \pm\sqrt{\frac{b^2 - 4ac}{4a^2}} \qquad \text{Square root property}$$

$$x + \frac{b}{2a} = \pm\frac{\sqrt{b^2 - 4ac}}{\sqrt{4a^2}} \qquad \text{Quotient rule for square roots}$$

$$x = -\frac{b}{2a} \pm \frac{\sqrt{b^2 - 4ac}}{2a} \qquad \text{Subtract } \frac{b}{2a}.$$

> Be careful; $-b \pm \sqrt{b^2 - 4ac}$ is all written over 2a.

$$x = \frac{-b \pm \sqrt{b^2 - 4ac}}{2a} \qquad \text{Combine like terms. This is also valid for } a < 0.$$

A first-season episode of *Blue Collar TV* (2004) featured Bill Engvall paying a sarcastic tribute to an underappreciated figure in his life.

To my high school algebra teacher, for teaching me that x equals minus b plus or minus the square root of b squared minus 4ac all over 2a, because Lord knows I use that information EVERY DAY!

Bill's teacher evidently did a good job, because he used the word "all" before 2a. A common student error is to forget to write the $-b$ in the numerator with the radical expression in the **quadratic formula**. See **Exercise 42** in this section.

Quadratic Formula

The solutions of $ax^2 + bx + c = 0$, $a \neq 0$, are given by the **quadratic formula.**

$$x = \frac{-b \pm \sqrt{b^2 - 4ac}}{2a}$$

A Radical Departure from the Other Methods of Evaluating the Golden Ratio Recall from a previous chapter that the golden ratio is found in numerous places in mathematics, art, and nature. In a margin note there, we showed that *the "continued" fraction*

$$1 + \cfrac{1}{1 + \cfrac{1}{1 + \cfrac{1}{1 + \dots}}}$$

is equal to the golden ratio, $\frac{1 + \sqrt{5}}{2}$. Now consider this *"nested" radical:*

$$\sqrt{1 + \sqrt{1 + \sqrt{1 + \dots}}}$$

Let x represent this radical expression. Because it appears "within itself," we can write

$$x = \sqrt{1 + x}$$
$$x^2 = 1 + x$$
$$x^2 - x - 1 = 0.$$

Using the quadratic formula, with $a = 1$, $b = -1$, and $c = -1$, it can be shown that the positive solution of this equation, and thus the value of the nested radical is . . . (you guessed it!) the golden ratio.

▐▐ **EXAMPLE 3** Using the Quadratic Formula

Solve $x^2 - 4x + 2 = 0$.

SOLUTION

$$x = \frac{-b \pm \sqrt{b^2 - 4ac}}{2a} \qquad \text{Quadratic formula}$$

$$x = \frac{-(-4) \pm \sqrt{(-4)^2 - 4(1)(2)}}{2(1)} \qquad a = 1, b = -4, c = 2$$

$$x = \frac{4 \pm \sqrt{16 - 8}}{2} \qquad \text{Start to simplify.}$$

$$x = \frac{4 \pm 2\sqrt{2}}{2} \qquad \sqrt{16 - 8} = \sqrt{8} = 2\sqrt{2}$$

$$x = \frac{2(2 \pm \sqrt{2})}{2} \qquad \text{Factor out 2 in the numerator.}$$

> Factor, and then divide out the common factor.

$$x = 2 \pm \sqrt{2} \qquad \text{Divide out common factor.}$$

The solution set is $\{2 + \sqrt{2}, 2 - \sqrt{2}\}$, abbreviated $\{2 \pm \sqrt{2}\}$. ▐▐▐

▐▐ **EXAMPLE 4** Using the Quadratic Formula

Solve $2x^2 = x + 4$.

SOLUTION

First write the equation in standard form as $2x^2 - x - 4 = 0$.

$$x = \frac{-(-1) \pm \sqrt{(-1)^2 - 4(2)(-4)}}{2(2)} \qquad \text{Quadratic formula with } a = 2, b = -1, c = -4$$

$$x = \frac{1 \pm \sqrt{1 + 32}}{4} \qquad \text{Simplify the radicand.}$$

$$x = \frac{1 \pm \sqrt{33}}{4} \qquad \text{Add.}$$

The solution set is $\left\{\frac{1 \pm \sqrt{33}}{4}\right\}$. ▐▐▐

Applications

▐▐ **EXAMPLE 5** Applying a Quadratic Equation

Two cars left an intersection at the same time, one heading due north, and the other due west. Some time later, they were exactly 100 miles apart. The car headed north had gone 20 miles farther than the car headed west. How far had each car traveled?

SOLUTION

Step 1 **Read** the problem carefully.

Step 2 **Assign a variable.**

Let x = the distance traveled by the car headed west.

Then $(x + 20)$ = the distance traveled by the car headed north.

See **Figure 16**. The cars are 100 miles apart, so the hypotenuse of the right triangle equals 100.

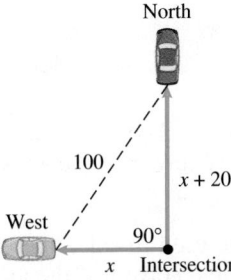

Figure 16

Évariste Galois (1811–1832), as a young Frenchman, agreed to fight a duel. He had been engaged for some time in mathematical research that centered on solving equations by using **group theory.** Now, anticipating the possibility of his death, he summarized the essentials of his discoveries in a letter to a friend. The next day Galois was killed. He was not yet 21 years old when he died.

Step 3 **Write an equation.**

$$c^2 = a^2 + b^2 \qquad \text{Pythagorean theorem}$$

$$100^2 = x^2 + (x + 20)^2 \qquad \text{Substitute.}$$

Step 4 **Solve.** $\qquad 10{,}000 = x^2 + x^2 + 40x + 400 \qquad \text{Square the binomial.}$

$$2x^2 + 40x - 9600 = 0 \qquad \text{Standard form}$$

$$x^2 + 20x - 4800 = 0 \qquad \text{Divide both sides by 2.}$$

Use the quadratic formula to find x.

$$x = \frac{-20 \pm \sqrt{20^2 - 4(1)(-4800)}}{2(1)} \qquad a = 1, b = 20, c = -4800$$

$$x = \frac{-20 \pm \sqrt{19{,}600}}{2} \qquad \text{Simplify under the radical.}$$

$$x = 60 \quad \text{or} \quad x = -80 \qquad \text{Use a calculator.}$$

Step 5 **State the answer.** Since distance cannot be negative, discard the negative solution. The required distances are 60 miles and $60 + 20 = 80$ miles.

Step 6 **Check.** Since $60^2 + 80^2 = 100^2$, the answer is correct. ▌▌▌

▌▌ **EXAMPLE 6** Applying a Quadratic Equation

If a rock on Earth is projected upward from the top of a 144-foot building with an initial velocity of 112 feet per second, its position (in feet above the ground) is given by $s = -16t^2 + 112t + 144$, where t is time in seconds after it was projected. How long does it take for the rock to hit the ground?

SOLUTION

When the rock hits the ground, its distance above the ground is 0. Find t when s is 0.

$$0 = -16t^2 + 112t + 144 \qquad \text{Let } s = 0.$$

$$0 = t^2 - 7t - 9 \qquad \text{Divide both sides by } -16.$$

$$t = \frac{7 \pm \sqrt{49 + 36}}{2} \qquad \text{Quadratic formula}$$

$$t = \frac{7 \pm \sqrt{85}}{2} \qquad \text{Add.} \quad \boxed{\text{This must be rejected.}}$$

$$t \approx 8.1 \quad \text{or} \quad t \approx -1.1 \qquad \text{Use a calculator.}$$

Since the rock cannot hit the ground before it is projected, discard the negative solution. The rock will hit the ground about 8.1 seconds after it is projected. ▌▌▌

Niels Henrik Abel (1802–1829) of Norway was identified in childhood as a mathematical genius but never received in his lifetime the professional recognition his work deserved. He proved that a general formula for solving **fifth-degree equations** does not exist. The quadratic formula (for equations of degree 2) is well known, and formulas do exist for solving third- and fourth-degree equations. Abel's accomplishment ended a search that had lasted for years.

7.7 EXERCISES

Fill in each blank with the correct response.

1. For the quadratic equation $5x^2 + 4x - 8 = 0$, the values of a, b, and c are, respectively, _____, _____, and _____.

2. To solve $3x^2 - 5x = -3$ by the quadratic formula, the first step is to add _____ to both sides of the equation.

3. Can the quadratic formula be used to solve the equation $2x^2 - 5 = 0$? Explain, and solve it if the answer is yes.

4. Can the quadratic formula be used to solve the equation $4x^2 + 3x = 0$? Explain, and solve it if the answer is yes.

Solve each equation by the zero-factor property.

5. $(x + 3)(x - 9) = 0$

6. $(x + 6)(x + 4) = 0$

7. $(2x - 7)(5x + 1) = 0$

8. $(7x - 3)(6x + 4) = 0$

9. $x^2 - x - 12 = 0$

10. $x^2 + 4x - 5 = 0$

11. $x^2 + 9x + 14 = 0$

12. $x^2 + 3x - 4 = 0$

13. $12x^2 + 4x = 1$

14. $15x^2 + 7x = 2$

15. $(x + 4)(x - 6) = -16$

16. $(x - 1)(3x + 2) = 4x$

Solve each equation by using the square root property. Give only real number solutions.

17. $x^2 = 64$

18. $x^2 = 16$

19. $x^2 = 24$

20. $x^2 = 48$

21. $x^2 = -5$

22. $x^2 = -10$

23. $(x - 4)^2 = 9$

24. $(x + 3)^2 = 25$

25. $(4 - x)^2 = 3$

26. $(3 + x)^2 = 11$

27. $(2x - 5)^2 = 13$

28. $(4x + 1)^2 = 19$

Solve each equation by the quadratic formula. Give only real number solutions.

29. $4x^2 - 8x + 1 = 0$

30. $x^2 + 2x - 5 = 0$

31. $2x^2 = 2x + 1$

32. $9x^2 + 6x = 1$

33. $x^2 - 1 = x$

34. $2x^2 - 4x = 5$

35. $4x(x + 1) = 1$

36. $4x(x - 1) = 19$

37. $(x + 2)(x - 3) = 1$

38. $(x - 5)(x + 2) = 6$

39. $x^2 - 6x = -14$

40. $x^2 = 2x - 2$

41. Why can't the quadratic formula be used to solve the equation $2x^3 + 3x - 4 = 0$?

42. A student gave the quadratic formula incorrectly as follows: $x = -b \pm \dfrac{\sqrt{b^2 - 4ac}}{2a}$. What is wrong with this?

*The expression $b^2 - 4ac$, the radicand in the quadratic formula, is called the **discriminant** of the quadratic equation*

$$ax^2 + bx + c = 0, \quad a \neq 0.$$

By evaluating it we can determine, without actually solving the equation, the number and nature of the solutions of the equation. Suppose that a, b, and c are integers. Then the chart below shows how the discriminant can be used to analyze the solutions.

Discriminant	Solutions
Positive, and the square of an integer	Two different rational solutions
Positive, but not the square of an integer	Two different irrational solutions
Zero	One rational solution (a double solution)
Negative	No real solutions

In Exercises 43–48, evaluate the discriminant, and then determine whether the equation has **(a)** *two different rational solutions,* **(b)** *two different irrational solutions,* **(c)** *one rational solution (a double solution), or* **(d)** *no real solutions.*

43. $x^2 + 6x + 9 = 0$

44. $4x^2 + 20x + 25 = 0$

45. $6x^2 + 7x - 3 = 0$

46. $2x^2 + x - 3 = 0$

47. $9x^2 - 30x + 15 = 0$

48. $2x^2 - x + 1 = 0$

49. When using the quadratic formula, if $b^2 - 4ac$ is positive, then the equation has _____ real solution(s). (how many?)

50. If a, b, and c are integers in $ax^2 + bx + c = 0$ and $b^2 - 4ac = 17$, then the equation has _____ irrational solution(s). (how many?)

Solve each problem. Use a calculator as necessary, and round the answer to the nearest tenth.

51. *Height of a Projectile* A building is 400 feet high. Suppose that a ball is projected upward from the top, and its position s in feet above the ground is given by the equation $s = -16t^2 + 45t + 400$, where t is the number of seconds elapsed. How long will it take for the ball to reach a height of 200 feet above the ground?

52. *Height of a Projectile* A high-rise condominium building is 407 feet high. Suppose that a ball is projected upward from the top and its position s in feet above the ground is given by the equation $s = -16t^2 + 75t + 407$, where t is the number of seconds elapsed. How long will it take for the ball to reach a height of 450 feet above the ground?

53. *Height of a Projectile* Refer to the equations in **Exercises 51 and 52.** Suppose that the first sentence in each problem did not give the height. How could you use the equation to determine the height?

54. *Position of a Flashlight Beam* A flashlight beam moves horizontally back and forth along a wall with the distance of the light on the wall from a starting point at t minutes given by $s = 100t^2 - 300t$. How long will it take before the light returns to the starting point?

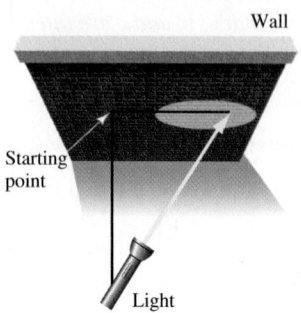

55. *Height of a Projectile* An object is projected directly upward from the ground. After t seconds its distance in feet above the ground is $s = 144t - 16t^2$.

(a) After how many seconds will the object be 128 feet above the ground? (*Hint*: Look for a common factor before solving the equation.)

(b) When does the object strike the ground?

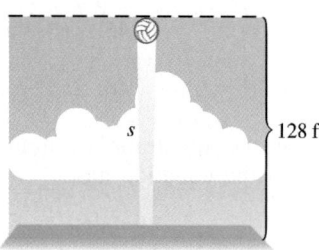

56. *Distance of a Skid* The formula $D = 100t - 13t^2$ gives the distance in feet a car going approximately 68 miles per hour will skid in t seconds. Find the time it would take for the car to skid 190 feet. (*Hint:* Your answer must be less than the time it takes the car to stop, which is 3.8 seconds.)

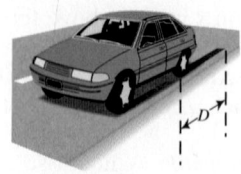

57. *Side Lengths of a Triangle* Find the lengths of the sides of the right triangle.

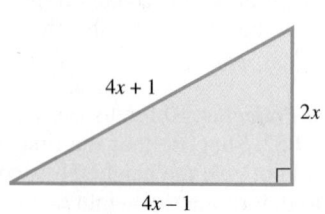

58. *Side Lengths of a Triangle* Find the lengths of the sides of the right triangle.

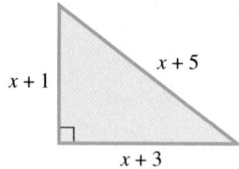

59. *Length of a Wire* Refer to **Exercise 51.** Suppose that a wire is attached to the top of the building and pulled tight. It is attached to the ground 100 feet from the base of the building, as shown in the figure. How long is the wire?

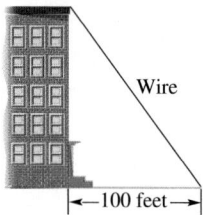

60. *Length of a Wire* Refer to **Exercise 52.** Suppose that a wire is attached to the top of the building and pulled tight. The length of the wire is twice the distance between the base of the building and the point on the ground where the wire is attached. How long is the wire?

61. *Distances Traveled by Ships* Two ships leave port at the same time, one heading due south and the other heading due east. Several hours later, they are 170 miles apart. If the ship traveling south travels 70 miles farther than the other, how many miles does each travel?

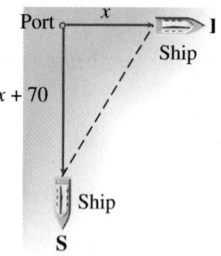

62. *Height of a Kite* Paulette Starney is flying a kite that is 30 feet farther above her hand than its horizontal distance from her. The string from her hand to the kite is 150 feet long. How far is the kite above her hand?

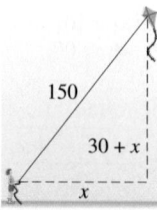

63. *Size of a Toy Piece* A toy manufacturer needs a piece of plastic in the shape of a right triangle with the longer leg 2 centimeters more than twice as long as the shorter leg, and the hypotenuse 1 centimeter more than the longer leg. How long should the three sides of the triangular piece be?

64. *Size of a Developer's Property* Hollis Sherman, a developer, owns a piece of land enclosed on three sides by streets, giving it the shape of a right triangle. The hypotenuse is 8 meters longer than the longer leg, and the shorter leg is 9 meters shorter than the hypotenuse. Find the lengths of the three sides of the property.

65. *Dimensions of Puzzle Pieces* Two pieces of a large wooden puzzle fit together to form a rectangle with a length 1 centimeter less than twice the width. The diagonal, where the two pieces meet, is 2.5 centimeters in length. Find the length and width of the rectangle.

66. *Leaning Ladder* A 13-foot ladder is leaning against a house. The distance from the bottom of the ladder to the house is 7 feet less than the distance from the top of the ladder to the ground. How far is the bottom of the ladder from the house?

67. *Dimensions of a Strip of Flooring Around a Rug* Kyle and Marin want to buy a rug for a room that is 15 feet by 20 feet. They want to leave an even strip of flooring uncovered around the edges of the room. How wide a strip will they have if they buy a rug with an area of 234 square feet?

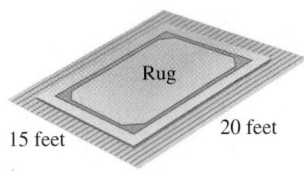

68. *Dimensions of a Border Around a Pool* A club swimming pool is 30 feet wide and 40 feet long. The club members want an exposed aggregate border in a strip of uniform width around the pool. They have enough material for 296 square feet. How wide can the strip be?

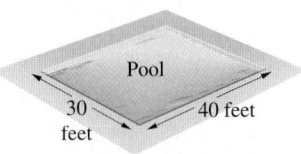

69. *Dimensions of a Garden* Arif's backyard is 20 meters by 30 meters. He wants to put a flower garden in the middle of the backyard, leaving a strip of grass of uniform width around the flower garden. Arif must have 184 square meters of grass. Under these conditions, what will the length and width of the garden be?

70. *Cardboard Box Dimensions* If a square piece of cardboard has 3-inch squares cut from its corners and then has the flaps folded up to form an open-top box, the volume of the box is given by the formula

$$V = 3(x - 6)^2,$$

where x is the length of each side of the original piece of cardboard in inches. What original length would yield a box with a volume of 432 cubic inches?

71. *Dimensions of a Piece of Sheet Metal* A rectangular piece of sheet metal has a length that is 4 inches less than twice the width. A square piece 2 inches on a side is cut from each corner. The sides are then turned up to form an uncovered box of volume 256 cubic inches. Find the length and width of the original piece of metal.

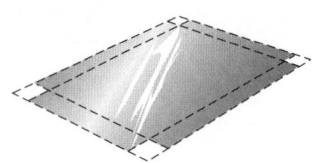

72. *Interest Rate* The formula

$$A = P(1 + r)^2$$

gives the amount A in dollars that P dollars will grow to in 2 years at interest rate r (where r is given as a decimal), using compound interest. What interest rate will cause $2000 to grow to $2142.25 in 2 years?

Recall that the corresponding sides of similar triangles are proportional. (Refer to Section 7.3 Exercises 53–56.) Use this fact to find the lengths of the indicated sides of each pair of similar triangles. Check all possible solutions in both triangles. Sides of a triangle cannot be negative.

73. Side AC

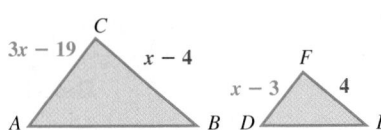

74. Side RQ

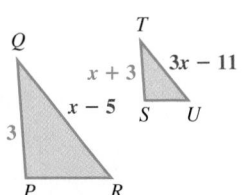

75. For centuries mathematicians wrestled with finding a formula that could solve cubic (third-degree) equations. In sixteenth-century Italy, Niccolo Tartaglia had developed a method of solving a cubic equation of the form

$$x^3 + mx = n.$$

Girolamo Cardano begged to know Tartaglia's method, and after he was told, he was sworn to secrecy. Nonetheless, Cardano published Tartaglia's method in his 1545 work *Ars Magna* (although he did give Tartaglia credit).

The formula for finding one real solution of the equation $x^3 + mx = n$ is

$$x = \sqrt[3]{\frac{n}{2} + \sqrt{\left(\frac{n}{2}\right)^2 + \left(\frac{m}{3}\right)^3}}$$
$$- \sqrt[3]{-\left(\frac{n}{2}\right) + \sqrt{\left(\frac{n}{2}\right)^2 + \left(\frac{m}{3}\right)^3}}.$$

Solve $x^3 + 9x = 26$ using this formula.

EXTENSION   Complex Solutions of Quadratic Equations

Review of i and $\sqrt{-b}$, where $b > 0$ • The Discriminant
• Solving a Quadratic Equation

Review of i and $\sqrt{-b}$, where $b > 0$ In the **Chapter 6 Extension,** we saw that the real number system is a subset of the complex number system. The imaginary unit i, where $i = \sqrt{-1}$, is defined so that $i^2 = -1$, and a number of the form $a + bi$, where a and b are real, is called a complex number.

A square root of a negative number can be written as the product of i and a real number. Here are some examples.

$$\sqrt{-4} = i \cdot \sqrt{4} = i \cdot 2 = 2i$$
$$\sqrt{-7} = i\sqrt{7}$$
$$\sqrt{-32} = i\sqrt{32} = i\sqrt{16 \cdot 2} = 4i\sqrt{2}$$

The Discriminant   In the quadratic formula

$$x = \frac{-b \pm \sqrt{b^2 - 4ac}}{2a},$$

the expression under the radical symbol, $b^2 - 4ac$, is called the **discriminant.** In **Section 7.7,** we focused on quadratic equations with discriminants that were positive or zero. If the discriminant is negative, then the equation has two nonreal solutions.

Discriminant

The discriminant of $ax^2 + bx + c = 0$ is $b^2 - 4ac$. If a, b, and c are integers, then the number and type of solutions are determined as follows.

Discriminant	Number and Type of Solutions
Positive, and the square of an integer	Two rational solutions
Positive, but not the square of an integer	Two irrational solutions
Zero	One rational solution
Negative	Two nonreal solutions

▌▌ **EXAMPLE 1** Using the Discriminant

Show that $x^2 + x + 4 = 0$ has two nonreal complex solutions.

SOLUTION

$$b^2 - 4ac = 1^2 - 4(1)(4) \quad \text{Here, } a = 1, b = 1, \text{ and } c = 4.$$

$$= -15 \quad \boxed{\text{Negative discriminant}}$$

Because $-15 < 0$, the equation has two nonreal solutions. ▌▌▌

Solving a Quadratic Equation

▌▌ **EXAMPLE 2** Solving a Quadratic Equation with Nonreal Solutions

Solve $(9x + 3)(x - 1) = -8$.

SOLUTION

$$(9x + 3)(x - 1) = -8$$

$$9x^2 - 6x - 3 = -8 \quad \text{Multiply.}$$

$$9x^2 - 6x + 5 = 0 \quad \text{Add 8.}$$

From the equation $9x^2 - 6x + 5 = 0$, we identify $a = 9$, $b = -6$, and $c = 5$.

$$x = \frac{-b \pm \sqrt{b^2 - 4ac}}{2a} \quad \text{Quadratic formula}$$

$$x = \frac{-(-6) \pm \sqrt{(-6)^2 - 4(9)(5)}}{2(9)} \quad \text{Substitute.}$$

$$x = \frac{6 \pm \sqrt{-144}}{18} \quad \boxed{\text{See the Chapter 6 Extension.}}$$

$$x = \frac{6 \pm 12i}{18} \quad \sqrt{-144} = 12i$$

$$x = \frac{6(1 \pm 2i)}{6(3)} \quad \text{Factor.}$$

$$x = \frac{1 \pm 2i}{3} \quad \text{Lowest terms}$$

$$x = \frac{1}{3} \pm \frac{2}{3}i \quad \text{Standard form } a + bi \text{ for a complex number}$$

The solution set is $\left\{\frac{1}{3} + \frac{2}{3}i, \frac{1}{3} - \frac{2}{3}i\right\}$. ▌▌▌

EXTENSION EXERCISES

*The following equations have nonreal solutions. Use the quadratic formula and the discussion of complex numbers in this **Extension** and the **Extension** in **Chapter 6** to solve them.*

1. $x^2 + 12 = 0$

2. $x^2 + 18 = 0$

3. $9x(x - 2) = -13$

4. $4x(x - 4) = -17$

5. $x^2 - 6x + 14 = 0$

6. $x^2 + 4x + 11 = 0$

7. $4x^2 - 4x = -7$

8. $9x^2 - 6x = -7$

9. $x(3x + 4) = -2$

10. $x(2x + 3) = -2$

COLLABORATIVE INVESTIGATION

How Does Your Walking Rate Compare to That of Olympic Race-Walkers?

Race-walking at speeds exceeding 8 miles per hour is a high-fitness, long-distance, competitive sport. The table below contains gold medal winners in the 2008 Olympic Games race-walking competition.

A. Complete the table by applying the proportion given below to find the race-walker's steps per minute. **Use 10 km ≈ 6.21 miles.** (Round all answers except those for steps per minute to the nearest thousandth. Round steps per minute to the nearest whole number.)

$$\frac{70 \text{ steps per minute}}{2 \text{ miles per hour}} = \frac{x \text{ steps per minute}}{y \text{ miles per hour}}$$

Event	Gold Medal Winner	Country	Time in Hours: Minutes: Seconds	Time in Minutes	Time in Hours	y Miles per Hour	x Steps per Minute
20-km Walk, Women	Olga Kaniskina	Russia	1:26:31				
20-km Walk, Men	Valeriy Borchin	Russia	1:19:01				
50-km Walk, Men	Alex Schwazer	Italy	3:37:09				

Source: The World Almanac and Book of Facts.

B. Using a stopwatch, take turns counting how many steps each member of the group takes in one minute while walking at a normal pace. Record the results in the table below. Then do it again at a fast pace. Record these results.

C. Use the proportion from part A to convert the numbers from part B to miles per hour and complete the chart.

1. Find the average speed for the group at a normal pace and at a fast pace.
2. What is the minimum number of steps per minute you would have to take to be a race-walker?
3. At a fast pace, did anyone in the group walk fast enough to be a race-walker? Explain how you decided.

	Normal Pace		Fast Pace	
Name	x Steps per Minute	y Miles per Hour	x Steps per Minute	y Miles per Hour

CHAPTER 7 TEST

Solve each equation.

1. $5x - 3 + 2x = 3(x - 2) + 11$

2. $\dfrac{2x - 1}{3} + \dfrac{x + 1}{4} = \dfrac{43}{12}$

3. Decide whether the equation

$$3x - (2 - x) + 4x = 7x - 2 - (-x)$$

is conditional, an identity, or a contradiction. Give its solution set.

4. Solve for v: $S = vt - 16t^2$.

Solve each application.

5. *Areas of Hawaiian Islands* Three islands in the Hawaiian island chain are Hawaii (the Big Island), Maui, and Kauai. Together, their areas total 5300 square miles. The island of Hawaii is 3293 square miles larger than the island of Maui, and Maui is 177 square miles larger than Kauai. What is the area of each island?

6. *Chemical Mixture* How many liters of a 20% solution of a chemical should Roxanne Roberts mix with 10 liters of a 50% solution to obtain a mixture that is 40% chemical?

7. *Speeds of Trains* A passenger train and a freight train leave a town at the same time and travel in opposite directions. Their speeds are 60 mph and 75 mph, respectively. How long will it take for them to be 297 miles apart?

8. *Merchandise Pricing* Which is the better buy for processed cheese slices: 16 slices for \$4.38 or 12 slices for \$3.30?

9. *Distance Between Cities* The distance between Boston and Milwaukee is 1050 miles. On a certain map this distance is represented by 21 inches. On the same map Seattle and Cincinnati are 46 inches apart. What is the actual distance between Seattle and Cincinnati?

10. *Current in a Circuit* The current in a simple electrical circuit is inversely proportional to the resistance. If the current is 80 amps when the resistance is 30 ohms, find the current when the resistance is 12 ohms.

Solve each inequality. Give the solution set in both interval and graph forms.

11. $-4x + 2(x - 3) \geq 4x - (3 + 5x) - 7$

12. $-10 < 3x - 4 \leq 14$

13. Which one of the following inequalities is equivalent to $x < -3$?

    A. $-3x < 9$ **B.** $-3x > -9$

    C. $-3x > 9$ **D.** $-3x < -9$

14. *Grade Average* Robert Murphy has scores of 83, 76, and 79 on his first three tests in Math 1031 (Survey of Mathematics). If he wants an average of at least 80 after his fourth test, what are the possible scores he can make on his fourth test?

Evaluate each exponential expression.

15. $\left(\dfrac{4}{3}\right)^2$ **16.** $-(-2)^6$

17. $\left(\dfrac{3}{4}\right)^{-3}$ **18.** $-5^0 + (-5)^0$

Use the properties of exponents to simplify each expression. Write answers with positive exponents only. Assume that all variables represent nonzero real numbers.

19. $9(4p^3)(6p^{-7})$ **20.** $\dfrac{m^{-2}(m^3)^{-3}}{m^{-4}m^7}$

21. Write each number in standard notation.

    (a) 6.93×10^8 **(b)** 1.25×10^{-7}

22. Use scientific notation to evaluate

$$\frac{(2,500,000)(0.00003)}{(0.05)(5,000,000)}.$$

Leave the answer in scientific notation.

23. *Time Traveled for a Radio Signal* The mean distance to Earth from Pluto is 4.58×10^9 kilometers. The first U.S. space probe to Pluto transmitted radio signals from Pluto to Earth at the speed of light, 3.00×10^5 kilometers per second. How long (in seconds) did it take for the signals to reach Earth?

Perform the indicated operations.

24. $(3k^3 - 5k^2 + 8k - 2) - (3k^3 - 9k^2 + 2k - 12)$

25. $(5x + 2)(3x - 4)$

26. $(4x^2 - 3)(4x^2 + 3)$

27. $(x + 4)(3x^2 + 8x - 9)$

28. Give an example of a polthat it is fifth degree, variable, with exactlycoefficient for its sec

Factor each polynomial completely.

29. $2p^2 - 5pq + 3q^2$

30. $100x^2 - 49y^2$

31. $27y^3 - 125x^3$

32. $4x + 4y - mx - my$

Solve each quadratic equation.

33. $6x^2 + 7x - 3 = 0$

34. $x^2 - 13 = 0$

35. $x^2 - x = 7$

36. *Time an Object Has Descended* The equation

$$s = 16t^2 + 15t$$

gives the distance s in feet an object dropped off a building has descended in t seconds. Find the time t when the object has descended 25 feet. Use a calculator and round the answer to the nearest hundredth.

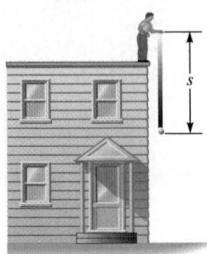

GRAPHS, FUNCTIONS, AND SYSTEMS OF EQUATIONS AND INEQUALITIES

8

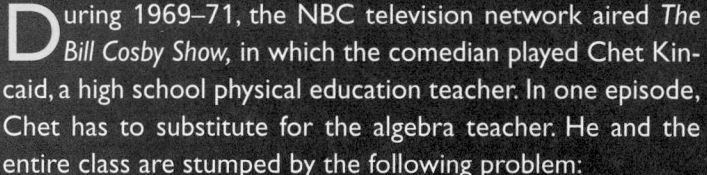

During 1969–71, the NBC television network aired *The Bill Cosby Show*, in which the comedian played Chet Kincaid, a high school physical education teacher. In one episode, Chet has to substitute for the algebra teacher. He and the entire class are stumped by the following problem:

How many pounds of candy that sells for $0.75 per pound must be mixed with candy that sells for $1.25 per pound to obtain 9 pounds of a mixture that should sell for $0.96 per pound?

Chet spends his weekend trying to solve this problem. (The title of the episode is "Let *x* Equal a Lousy Weekend.") He even visits the local candy store, where the owner says that in order to solve the problem, "you have to know algebra." The smartest student in the class, Eddie Tucker, is able to solve the problem correctly using a system of equations. See **page 429** for Eddie's answer.

361

8.1 THE RECTANGULAR COORDINATE SYSTEM AND CIRCLES

Rectangular Coordinates • Distance Formula • Midpoint Formula • Circles
• An Application

Double Descartes After the French postal service issued the above stamp in honor of **René Descartes,** sharp eyes noticed that the title of Descartes's most famous book was wrong. Thus a second stamp (see facing page) was issued with the correct title. The book in question, *Discourse on Method,* appeared in 1637. In it Descartes rejected traditional Aristotelian philosophy, outlining a universal system of knowledge that was to have the certainty of mathematics. For Descartes, method was *analysis,* going from self-evident truths step-by-step to more distant and more general truths. One of these truths is his famous statement, "I think, therefore I am." (Thomas Jefferson, also a rationalist, began the *Declaration* with the words, "We hold these truths to be self-evident.")

Rectangular Coordinates

Each pair of numbers (1, 2), (−1, 5), and (3, 7) is an example of an **ordered pair**—a pair of numbers written within parentheses in which the positions of the numbers are relevant. The two numbers are the **components** of the ordered pair.

An ordered pair is graphed using two number lines that intersect at right angles at the zero points, as shown in **Figure 1**. The common zero point is called the **origin.** The horizontal line, the **x-axis,** represents the first number in an ordered pair, and the vertical line, the **y-axis,** represents the second. The x-axis and the y-axis make up a **rectangular** (or **Cartesian**) **coordinate system.** The axes form four **quadrants,** numbered I, II, III, and IV as shown in **Figure 2**. (A point on an axis is not considered to be in any of the four quadrants.)

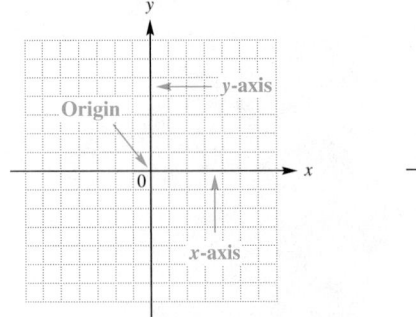

Figure 1

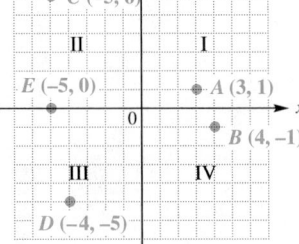

Figure 2

We locate, or plot, the point on the graph that corresponds to the ordered pair (3, 1) by moving three units from zero to the right along the x-axis, and then one unit up parallel to the y-axis, labeled *A* in **Figure 2**. The phrase "the point corresponding to the ordered pair (3, 1)" often is abbreviated "the point (3, 1)." The numbers in an ordered pair are called the **coordinates** of the corresponding point.

The parentheses used to represent an ordered pair also are used to represent an open interval (introduced in **Chapter 7**). The context of the discussion tells us whether we are discussing ordered pairs or open intervals.

Distance Formula

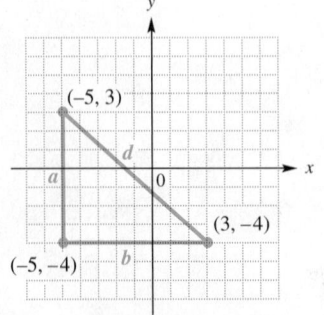

Figure 3

To find the distance between two points, say (3, −4) and (−5, 3), we use the Pythagorean theorem. In **Figure 3**, we see that the vertical line through (−5, 3) and the horizontal line through (3, −4) intersect at the point (−5, −4). Thus, the point (−5, −4) becomes the vertex of the right angle in a right triangle. By the Pythagorean theorem, the square of the length of the hypotenuse, *d*, in **Figure 3** is equal to the sum of the squares of the lengths of the two legs *a* and *b*.

$$d^2 = a^2 + b^2 \qquad \text{Equation of the Pythagorean theorem}$$

The length *a* is the distance between the endpoints of that leg. Since the x-coordinate of both points is −5, the side is vertical, and we can find *a* by finding the difference between the y-coordinates. Subtract −4 from 3 to get a positive value of *a*. Similarly, find *b* by subtracting −5 from 3.

$$a = 3 - (-4) = 7$$

> Use parentheses when subtracting a negative number.

$$b = 3 - (-5) = 8$$

Substitute these values into the equation.

$$d^2 = a^2 + b^2$$

$$d^2 = 7^2 + 8^2 \quad \text{Let } a = 7 \text{ and } b = 8.$$

$$d^2 = 49 + 64 \quad \text{Apply the exponents.}$$

$$d^2 = 113 \quad \text{Add.}$$

$$d = \sqrt{113} \quad \text{Square root property, } d > 0$$

Therefore, the distance between $(-5, 3)$ and $(3, -4)$ is $\sqrt{113}$.

This result can be generalized. **Figure 4** shows the two different points (x_1, y_1) and (x_2, y_2). To find a formula for the distance d between these two points, notice that the distance between (x_2, y_2) and (x_2, y_1) is given by $a = y_2 - y_1$, and the distance between (x_1, y_1) and (x_2, y_1) is given by $b = x_2 - x_1$. Thus,

$$d^2 = (x_2 - x_1)^2 + (y_2 - y_1)^2, \quad \text{Pythagorean theorem}$$

and by using the square root property, we obtain the distance formula.

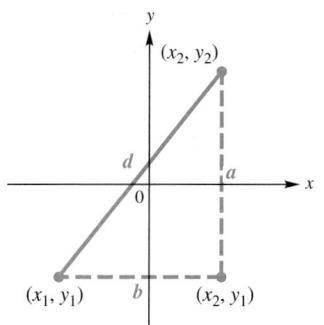

Figure 4

Distance Formula

The distance d between the points (x_1, y_1) and (x_2, y_2) is given by this formula.

$$d = \sqrt{(x_2 - x_1)^2 + (y_2 - y_1)^2}$$

This equation is the **distance formula.**

The small numbers 1 and 2 in the ordered pairs (x_1, y_1) and (x_2, y_2) are called **subscripts.** We read x_1 as "x sub 1." Subscripts are used to distinguish between different values of a variable that have a common property.

▌▌ **EXAMPLE 1** Finding the Distance between Two Points

Find the distance between the points $(-3, 5)$ and $(6, 4)$.

SOLUTION

Designating the points as (x_1, y_1) and (x_2, y_2) is arbitrary. Let us choose $(x_1, y_1) = (-3, 5)$ and $(x_2, y_2) = (6, 4)$.

$$d = \sqrt{(x_2 - x_1)^2 + (y_2 - y_1)^2} \quad \text{Distance formula}$$

> Begin with the x- and y-values of the same point.

$$= \sqrt{(6 - (-3))^2 + (4 - 5)^2} \quad x_2 = 6, y_2 = 4, x_1 = -3, y_1 = 5$$

$$= \sqrt{9^2 + (-1)^2} \quad \text{Simplify.}$$

$$= \sqrt{82}$$ ▌▌▌

Descartes wrote his *Geometry* as an application of his method. It was published as an appendix to the *Discourse*. His attempts to unify algebra and geometry influenced the creation of what became coordinate geometry and influenced the development of calculus by Newton and Leibniz in the next generation.

In 1649 Descartes went to Sweden to tutor Queen Christina. She preferred working in the unheated castle in the early morning. Descartes was used to staying in bed until noon. The rigors of the Swedish winter proved too much for him, and he died less than a year later.

Midpoint Formula

The **midpoint** of a line segment is the point on the segment that is equidistant from both endpoints. Given the coordinates of the two endpoints of a line segment, we can find the coordinates of the midpoint of the segment.

Midpoint Formula

The coordinates of the midpoint of the segment with endpoints (x_1, y_1) and (x_2, y_2) are as follows.

$$\left(\frac{x_1 + x_2}{2}, \frac{y_1 + y_2}{2}\right)$$

Thus, the coordinates of the midpoint of a line segment are found by calculating the averages of the x- and y-coordinates of the endpoints.

■■ **EXAMPLE 2** Finding the Midpoint of a Segment

Find the coordinates of the midpoint of the line segment with endpoints $(8, -4)$ and $(-9, 6)$.

SOLUTION

Using the midpoint formula, we find that the coordinates of the midpoint are

$$\left(\frac{8 + (-9)}{2}, \frac{-4 + 6}{2}\right) = \left(-\frac{1}{2}, 1\right). \qquad \begin{array}{l} x_1 = 8, x_2 = -9, \\ y_1 = -4, y_2 = 6 \end{array}$$

■■■

■■ **EXAMPLE 3** Applying the Midpoint Formula to Data

Figure 5 depicts how a graph might indicate the increase in the number of McDonald's restaurants worldwide from 20,000 in 1996 to 31,000 in 2006. Use the midpoint formula and the two given points to estimate the number of restaurants in 2001, and compare it to the actual (rounded) figure of 30,000.

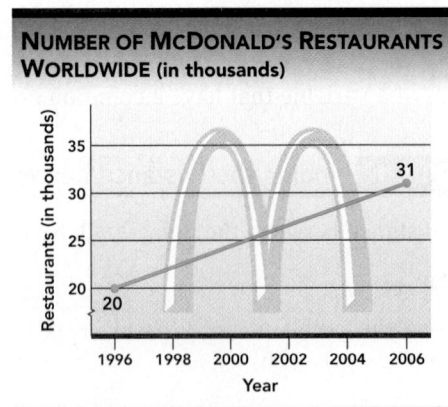

NUMBER OF McDONALD'S RESTAURANTS WORLDWIDE (in thousands)

Source: McDonald's Corp.; Hoovers.

Figure 5

SOLUTION

The year 2001 lies halfway between 1996 and 2006, so we must find the coordinates of the midpoint of the segment that has endpoints $(1996, 20)$ and $(2006, 31)$.

$$\left(\frac{\mathbf{1996} + \mathbf{2006}}{2}, \frac{\mathbf{20} + \mathbf{31}}{2}\right) = (2001, 25.5) \qquad \textit{y is in thousands.}$$

Thus, our estimate is 25,500, which is well below the actual figure of 30,000. (This discrepancy is due to McDonald's having an average increase of 2000 new stores per year between 1996 and 2001, and then an average increase of only 200 stores per year between 2001 and 2006. Graphs such as this can be misleading.) ■■■

Circles

An application of the distance formula leads to one of the most familiar shapes in geometry, the circle. A **circle** is the set of all points in a plane that lie a fixed distance from a fixed point. The fixed point is called the **center** and the fixed distance is called the **radius.**

▮▮ **EXAMPLE 4** Finding an Equation of a Circle

Find an equation of the circle with radius 3 and center at $(0, 0)$, and graph the circle.

SOLUTION

If the point (x, y) is on the circle, the distance from (x, y) to the center $(0, 0)$ is 3, as shown in **Figure 6**.

$$\sqrt{(x_2 - x_1)^2 + (y_2 - y_1)^2} = d \quad \text{Distance formula}$$

$$\sqrt{(x - 0)^2 + (y - 0)^2} = 3 \quad x_1 = 0, y_1 = 0, x_2 = x, y_2 = y, d = 3$$

$$x^2 + y^2 = 9 \quad \text{Square both sides.}$$

An equation of this circle is $x^2 + y^2 = 9$. It can be graphed by locating all points three units from the origin.   ▮▮▮

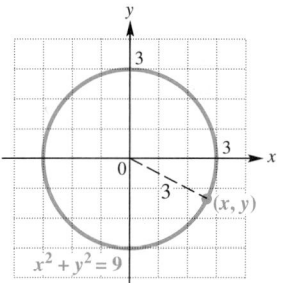

Figure 6

▮▮ **EXAMPLE 5** Finding an Equation of a Circle and Graphing

Find an equation for the circle that has its center at $(4, -3)$ and radius 5, and graph the circle.

SOLUTION

$$\sqrt{(x_2 - x_1)^2 + (y_2 - y_1)^2} = d \quad \text{Distance formula}$$

$$\sqrt{(x - 4)^2 + [y - (-3)]^2} = 5 \quad \text{Substitute in the distance formula.}$$

$$(x - 4)^2 + (y + 3)^2 = 25 \quad \text{Square both sides.}$$

The graph of this circle is shown in **Figure 7**.   ▮▮▮

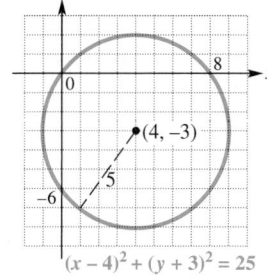

Figure 7

   Examples 4 and 5 can be generalized to get an equation of a circle with radius r and center at (h, k). If (x, y) is a point on the circle, the distance from the center (h, k) to the point (x, y) is r. Then by the distance formula,

$$\sqrt{(x - h)^2 + (y - k)^2} = r.$$

Squaring both sides gives the **center-radius form** of the equation of a circle.

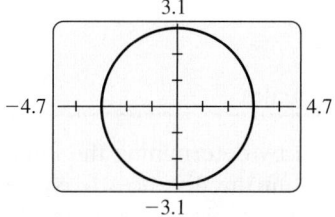

To graph $x^2 + y^2 = 9$, in **Example 4,** we solve for y to get

$$y_1 = \sqrt{9 - x^2} \text{ and } y_2 = -\sqrt{9 - x^2}.$$

Then we graph both in a square window.

Equation of a Circle

The equation of a circle of radius r with center at (h, k) is

$$(x - h)^2 + (y - k)^2 = r^2.$$

In particular, a circle of radius r with center at the origin has equation

$$x^2 + y^2 = r^2.$$

In these equations, r^2 will be greater than or equal to 0. If the constant on the right is 0, the graph is a single point. If it is negative, there is no graph.

▐▐ **EXAMPLE 6** Finding an Equation of a Circle

Find an equation of the circle with center at $(-1, 2)$ and radius 4.

SOLUTION

$$(x - h)^2 + (y - k)^2 = r^2 \quad \text{Equation of a circle}$$

$$[x - (-1)]^2 + (y - 2)^2 = 4^2 \quad \text{Let } h = -1, k = 2, \text{ and } r = 4.$$

Be careful with signs. $\quad (x + 1)^2 + (y - 2)^2 = 16$ ▐▐▐

In the equation found in **Example 5,** multiplying out $(x - 4)^2$ and $(y + 3)^2$ and then combining like terms gives the following.

$$(x - 4)^2 + (y + 3)^2 = 25$$

$$x^2 - 8x + 16 + y^2 + 6y + 9 = 25$$

$$x^2 + y^2 - 8x + 6y = 0$$

This result suggests that an equation that has both x^2- and y^2-terms with equal coefficients may represent a circle. The next example shows how to tell, using a method from algebra called **completing the square.**

▐▐ **EXAMPLE 7** Completing the Square and Graphing a Circle

Graph $x^2 + y^2 + 2x + 6y - 15 = 0$.

SOLUTION

Since the equation has x^2- and y^2-terms with equal coefficients, its graph might be that of a circle. To find the center and radius, complete the squares in x and y as follows. (See **page 350,** where completing the square is introduced.)

$$x^2 + y^2 + 2x + 6y = 15 \quad \text{Add 15 to both sides.}$$

$$(x^2 + 2x \quad) + (y^2 + 6y \quad) = 15 \quad \text{Rewrite in anticipation of completing the square.}$$

$$(x^2 + 2x + 1) + (y^2 + 6y + 9) = 15 + 1 + 9 \quad \text{Complete the squares in both } x \text{ and } y.$$

$$(x + 1)^2 + (y + 3)^2 = 25 \quad \text{Factor on the left and add on the right.}$$

The final equation shows that the graph is a circle with center at $(-1, -3)$ and radius 5. The graph is shown in **Figure 8**. ▐▐▐

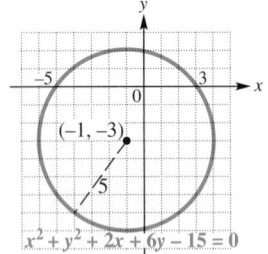

Figure 8

An Application

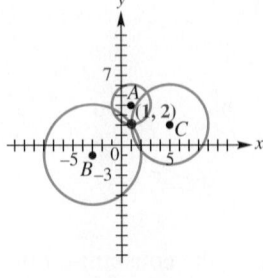

Figure 9

▐▐ **EXAMPLE 8** Locating the Epicenter of an Earthquake

Seismologists can locate the epicenter of an earthquake by determining the intersection of three circles. The radii of these circles represent the distances from the epicenter to each of three receiving stations. The centers of the circles represent the receiving stations.

Suppose receiving stations A, B, and C are located on a coordinate plane at the points $(1, 4)$, $(-3, -1)$, and $(5, 2)$. Let the distances from the earthquake epicenter to the stations be 2 units, 5 units, and 4 units, respectively. See **Figure 9**. Where on the coordinate plane is the epicenter located?

SOLUTION

Graph the three circles as shown in **Figure 9**. From the graph it appears that the epicenter is located at (1, 2). To check this algebraically, determine the equation for each circle and substitute $x = 1$ and $y = 2$.

Station *A*:	Station *B*:	Station *C*:
$(x - 1)^2 + (y - 4)^2 = 4$	$(x + 3)^2 + (y + 1)^2 = 25$	$(x - 5)^2 + (y - 2)^2 = 16$
$(1 - 1)^2 + (2 - 4)^2 = 4$	$(1 + 3)^2 + (2 + 1)^2 = 25$	$(1 - 5)^2 + (2 - 2)^2 = 16$
$0 + 4 = 4$	$16 + 9 = 25$	$16 + 0 = 16$
$4 = 4$	$25 = 25$	$16 = 16$

The point (1, 2) does lie on all three graphs. Thus, it must be the epicenter. ▮▮▮

For Further Thought

Phlash Phelps is the morning radio personality on Sirius XM Satellite Radio's *Sixties on Six* Decades channel. Phlash is an expert on U.S. geography and loves traveling around the country to strange, out-of-the-way locations. The photo shows Kurt Gilchrist and Phlash (seated) visiting a small Arizona settlement called *Nothing*. (Nothing is so small that it's not named on current maps.) The sign indicates that Nothing is 50 mi from Wickenburg, AZ, 75 mi from Kingman, AZ, 105 mi from Phoenix, AZ, and 180 mi from Las Vegas, NV.

For Group or Individual Investigation

Discuss how the concepts of **Example 8** can be used to locate Nothing, AZ, on a map of Arizona and southern Nevada.

8.1 EXERCISES

Fill in each blank with the correct response.

1. For any value of x, the point $(x, 0)$ lies on the _____-axis.

2. For any value of y, the point $(0, y)$ lies on the _____-axis.

3. The circle $x^2 + y^2 = 9$ has the point _____ as its center.

4. The point (___, 0) is the center of the circle

$$(x - 2)^2 + y^2 = 16.$$

Name the quadrant, if any, in which each point is located.

5. (a) $(1, 6)$

(b) $(-4, -2)$

(c) $(-3, 6)$

(d) $(7, -5)$

(e) $(-3, 0)$

6. (a) $(-2, -10)$

(b) $(4, 8)$

(c) $(-9, 12)$

(d) $(3, -9)$

(e) $(0, -8)$

7. Use the given information to determine the possible quadrants in which the point (x, y) must lie.

(a) $xy > 0$

(b) $xy < 0$

(c) $\dfrac{x}{y} < 0$

(d) $\dfrac{x}{y} > 0$

8. What must be true about one of the coordinates of any point that lies along an axis?

Locate the following points on the rectangular coordinate system, using a graph similar to **Figure 2**.

9. $(2, 3)$

10. $(-1, 2)$

11. $(-3, -2)$

12. $(1, -4)$

13. $(0, 5)$

14. $(-2, -4)$

15. $(-2, 4)$

16. $(3, 0)$

17. $(-2, 0)$

18. $(3, -3)$

19. *Tax Revenues* The graph indicates U.S. federal government tax revenues in billions of dollars.

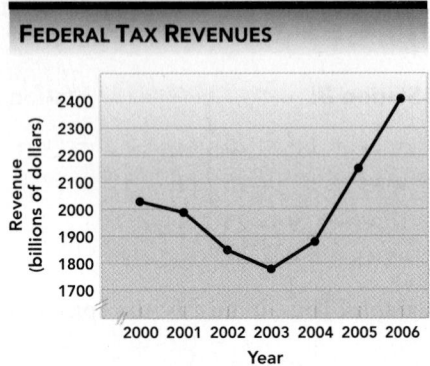

FEDERAL TAX REVENUES

Source: Office of Management and Budget.

(a) If (x, y) represents a point on the graph, what does x represent? What does y represent?

(b) Estimate revenue in 2006.

(c) Write an ordered pair (x, y) that gives approximate federal tax revenues in 2006.

20. *Medical Spending* The graph indicates spending in billions of dollars on medical care in the United States.

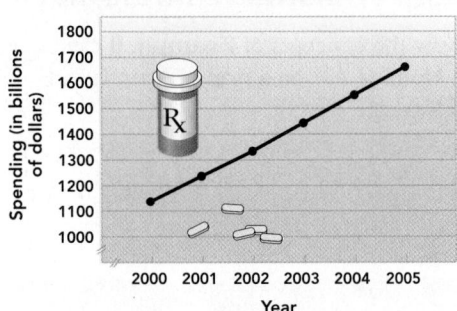

PERSONAL SPENDING ON MEDICAL CARE

Source: U.S. Centers for Medicare and Medicaid Services.

(a) If (x, y) represents a point on the graph, what does x represent? What does y represent?

(b) What was spending in 2003?

(c) In what year was spending about $1140 billion?

In Exercises 21–26, find
(a) *the distance between the pair of points, and*

(b) *the coordinates of the midpoint of the segment having the points as endpoints.*

21. $(3, 4)$ and $(-2, 1)$

22. $(-2, 1)$ and $(3, -2)$

23. $(-2, 4)$ and $(3, -2)$

24. $(1, -5)$ and $(6, 3)$

25. $(-3, 7)$ and $(2, -4)$

26. $(0, 5)$ and $(-3, 12)$

In Exercises 27–30, match each center-radius form of the equation of a circle with the correct graph from choices A–D.

27. $(x - 3)^2 + (y - 2)^2 = 25$

28. $(x - 3)^2 + (y + 2)^2 = 25$

29. $(x + 3)^2 + (y - 2)^2 = 25$

30. $(x + 3)^2 + (y + 2)^2 = 25$

A. 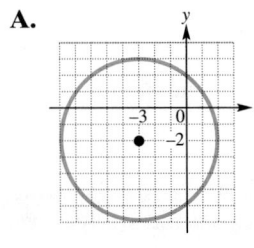 **B.**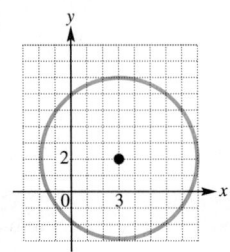

C. 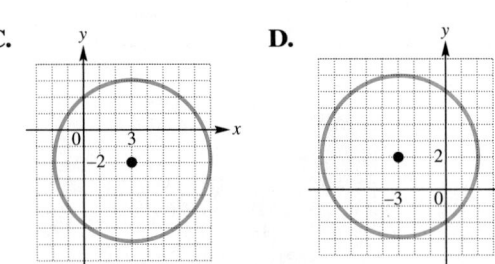 **D.**

Write an equation of the circle with the given center and radius.

31. $(0, 0); r = 6$ | **32.** $(0, 0); r = 5$

33. $(-1, 3); r = 4$ | **34.** $(2, -2); r = 3$

35. $(0, 4); r = \sqrt{3}$ | **36.** $(-2, 0); r = \sqrt{5}$

37. Suppose that a circle has an equation of the form $x^2 + y^2 = r^2$, $r > 0$. What is the center of the circle? What is the radius of the circle?

38. (a) How many points are there on the graph of $(x - 4)^2 + (y - 1)^2 = 0$? Explain your answer.

(b) How many points are there on the graph of $(x - 4)^2 + (y - 1)^2 = -1$? Explain your answer.

Find the center and the radius of each circle. (Hint: In Exercises 43 and 44 divide both sides by the greatest common factor.)

39. $x^2 + y^2 + 4x + 6y + 9 = 0$

40. $x^2 + y^2 - 8x - 12y + 3 = 0$

41. $x^2 + y^2 + 10x - 14y - 7 = 0$

42. $x^2 + y^2 - 2x + 4y - 4 = 0$

43. $3x^2 + 3y^2 - 12x - 24y + 12 = 0$

44. $2x^2 + 2y^2 + 20x + 16y + 10 = 0$

Graph each circle.

45. $x^2 + y^2 = 36$

46. $x^2 + y^2 = 81$

47. $(x - 2)^2 + y^2 = 36$

48. $x^2 + (y + 3)^2 = 49$

49. $(x + 2)^2 + (y - 5)^2 = 16$

50. $(x - 4)^2 + (y - 3)^2 = 25$

51. $(x + 3)^2 + (y + 2)^2 = 36$

52. $(x - 5)^2 + (y + 4)^2 = 49$

Find **(a)** *the distance between P and Q and* **(b)** *the coordinates of the midpoint of the segment joining P and Q.*

53.   **54.**

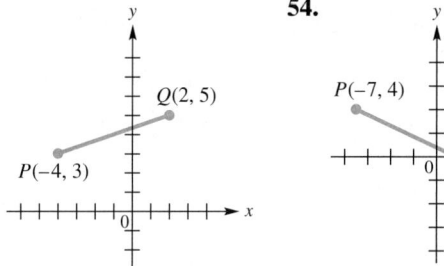

Solve each problem.

55. *Bachelor's Degree Attainment* The graph shows a straight line that approximates the percentage of Americans 25 years and older who earned bachelor's degrees or higher during the years 1990–2006. Use the midpoint formula and the two given points to estimate the percent in 1998. Compare your answer with the actual percent of 24.4.

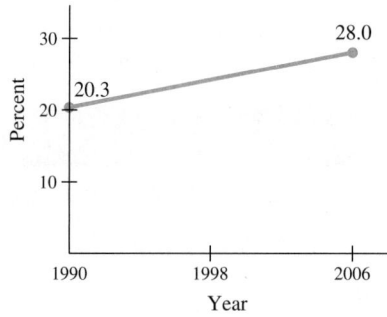

Percent of Bachelor's Degrees or Higher

Source: U.S. Census Bureau.

56. *Temporary Assistance for Needy Families (TANF)* The graph at the top of the next column shows an idealized linear relationship for the average monthly payment to needy families in the TANF program. Based on this information, what was the average payment to families in 2002, to the nearest dollar?

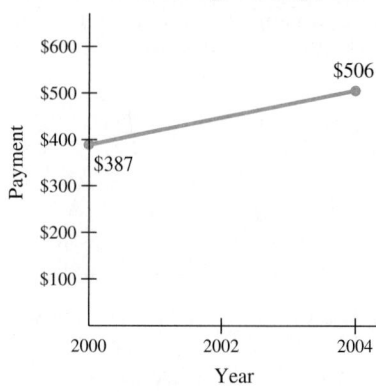

Average Monthly Payment to TANF Program Recipients

Source: Administration for Children and Families; U.S. Census Bureau.

57. *Poverty Level Income Cutoffs* The table lists how poverty level income cutoffs (in dollars) for a family of four have changed over time. Use the midpoint formula to approximate the poverty level cutoff in 1995.

Year	Income (in dollars)
1970	3968
1980	8414
1990	13,359
2000	17,603
2004	19,157

Source: U.S. Census Bureau.

58. *Public College Enrollment* Enrollments in public colleges for recent years are shown in the table. Use the midpoint formula to estimate the enrollments for **(a)** 1998 and **(b)** 2004.

Year	Enrollment (in thousands)
1995	11,092
2001	12,233
2007	13,555

Source: U.S. Census Bureau.

59. A student was asked to find the distance between the points $(5, 8)$ and $(2, 14)$, and wrote the following:

$$d = \sqrt{(5 - 8)^2 + (2 - 14)^2}.$$

Explain why this is incorrect.

60. An alternative form of the distance formula is

$$d = \sqrt{(x_1 - x_2)^2 + (y_1 - y_2)^2}.$$

Compare this to the form given in this section, and explain why the two forms are equivalent.

61. A circle can be drawn on a piece of posterboard by fastening one end of a string, pulling the string taut with a pencil, and tracing a curve as shown in the figure. Explain why this method works.

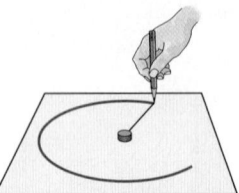

62. *Crawfish Racing* This figure shows how the crawfish race is held at the Crawfish Festival in Breaux Bridge, Louisiana. Explain why a circular "race-track" is appropriate for such a race.

63. *Epicenter of an Earthquake* Three receiving stations record the presence of an earthquake. The locations of the receiving stations and the distances to the epicenter are contained in the following three equations: $(x - 2)^2 + (y - 1)^2 = 25$, $(x + 2)^2 + (y - 2)^2 = 16$, and $(x - 1)^2 + (y + 2)^2 = 9$. Graph the circles and determine the location of the earthquake epicenter.

64. *Epicenter of an Earthquake* Show algebraically that if three receiving stations at $(1, 4)$, $(-6, 0)$, and $(5, -2)$ record distances to an earthquake epicenter of 4 units, 5 units, and 10 units, respectively, the epicenter would lie at $(-3, 4)$.

65. Can a circle have its center at $(2, 4)$ and be tangent to both axes? (*Tangent to* means touching at one point.) Explain.

66. Without actually graphing, state whether the graphs of $x^2 + y^2 = 4$ and $x^2 + y^2 = 25$ will intersect. Explain your answer.

67. If the coordinates of one endpoint of a line segment are $(3, -8)$ and the coordinates of the midpoint of the segment are $(6, 5)$, what are the coordinates of the other endpoint?

68. Suppose that the endpoints of a line segment have coordinates (x_1, y_1) and (x_2, y_2).

   (a) Show that the distance between (x_1, y_1) and $\left(\dfrac{x_1 + x_2}{2}, \dfrac{y_1 + y_2}{2}\right)$ is the same as the distance between (x_2, y_2) and $\left(\dfrac{x_1 + x_2}{2}, \dfrac{y_1 + y_2}{2}\right)$.

   (b) Show that the sum of the distances between (x_1, y_1) and $\left(\dfrac{x_1 + x_2}{2}, \dfrac{y_1 + y_2}{2}\right)$, and (x_2, y_2) and $\left(\dfrac{x_1 + x_2}{2}, \dfrac{y_1 + y_2}{2}\right)$ is equal to the distance between (x_1, y_1) and (x_2, y_2).

   (c) From the results of parts (a) and (b), what conclusion can be made?

69. Which one of the following has a circle as its graph?

   A. $x^2 - y^2 = 9$ **B.** $x^2 = 9 - y^2$

   C. $y^2 - x^2 = 9$ **D.** $-x^2 - y^2 = 9$

70. An **isosceles triangle** has at least two sides of equal length. Determine whether the triangle with vertices $(0, 0)$, $(3, 4)$, and $(7, 1)$ is isosceles.

▌ ▌ ▌ ▌ ▌ ▌ ▌ ▌ ▌ **8.2 LINES, SLOPE, AND AVERAGE RATE OF CHANGE**

Linear Equations in Two Variables • Intercepts • Slope • Parallel and Perpendicular Lines • Average Rate of Change

Linear Equations in Two Variables

Earlier we studied linear equations in a single variable. A solution of such an equation is a real number. A linear equation in *two* variables will have solutions written as ordered pairs. Equations with two variables will, in general, have an infinite number of solutions. To find ordered pairs that satisfy the equation, select any number for one of the variables, substitute it into the equation for that variable, and then solve for the other variable.

For example, suppose $x = 0$ in the equation $2x + 3y = 6$.

$$2x + 3y = 6 \quad \text{Given equation}$$
$$2(0) + 3y = 6 \quad \text{Let } x = 0.$$
$$0 + 3y = 6 \quad \text{Multiply.}$$
$$3y = 6 \quad \text{Add.}$$
$$y = 2 \quad \text{Divide by 3.}$$

This gives the ordered pair $(0, 2)$. Other ordered pairs satisfying $2x + 3y = 6$ include $(6, -2)$, $(3, 0)$, $(-3, 4)$, and $(9, -4)$.

The equation $2x + 3y = 6$ is graphed by plotting the ordered pairs mentioned above. These are shown in **Figure 10(a)**. The resulting points appear to lie on a straight line. If all the ordered pairs that satisfy the equation $2x + 3y = 6$ were graphed, they would form a straight line, as shown in **Figure 10(b)**. *The graph of any first-degree equation in two variables is a straight line.*

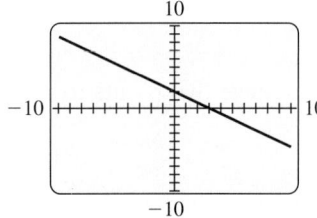

This is a calculator graph of the line shown in **Figure 10(b)**. We must first solve $2x + 3y = 6$ for y to input the equation.

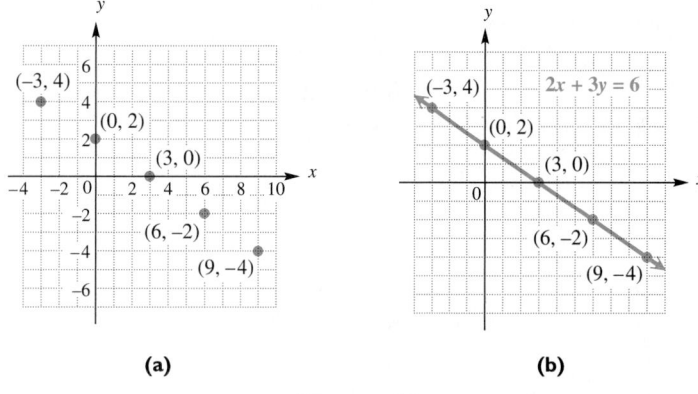

(a)   (b)

Figure 10

Linear Equation in Two Variables

An equation that can be written in the form

$$Ax + By = C \quad \text{(where } A \text{ and } B \text{ are not both 0)}$$

is a **linear equation in two variables.** This form is called **standard form.**

In this book, when we provide answers in standard form, we will do so with $A > 0$ (or if $A = 0$, then $B > 0$) and with A, B, and C having greatest common factor 1.

First-degree (linear) equations with one or two variables have straight-line graphs. Since a straight line is determined if any two different points on the line are known, finding two different points is sufficient to graph the line.

Intercepts

Two points that are useful for graphing lines are the x- and y-intercepts. The **x-intercept** is the point (if any) where the line crosses the x-axis, and the **y-intercept** is the point (if any) where the line crosses the y-axis. (*Note:* In many texts, the intercepts are defined as numbers and not as points. However, in this book we will refer to intercepts as points.) Intercepts can be found as follows.

Intercepts for Graphs of Linear Equations

To find the *x*-intercept, let $y = 0$ and solve for *x*.

To find the *y*-intercept, let $x = 0$ and solve for *y*.

▮▮ **EXAMPLE 1** Graphing an Equation Using Intercepts

Find the *x*- and *y*-intercepts of $4x - y = -3$, and graph the equation.

SOLUTION

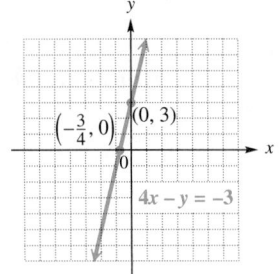

Figure 11

To find the *x*-intercept, let $y = 0$.

$$4x - 0 = -3 \quad \text{Let } y = 0.$$
$$4x = -3$$
$$x = -\frac{3}{4} \quad \text{x-intercept is } \left(-\frac{3}{4}, 0\right).$$

To find the *y*-intercept, let $x = 0$.

$$4(0) - y = -3 \quad \text{Let } x = 0.$$
$$-y = -3$$
$$y = 3 \quad \text{y-intercept is } (0, 3).$$

The intercepts are the two points $\left(-\frac{3}{4}, 0\right)$ and $(0, 3)$. Use these two points to draw the graph, as shown in **Figure 11**. ▮▮▮

A line may not have an *x*-intercept, or it may not have a *y*-intercept.

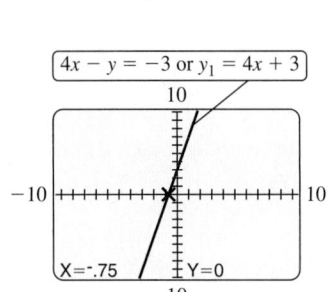

The display at the bottom of the screen supports the fact that $\left(-\frac{3}{4}, 0\right)$ is the *x*-intercept of the line in **Figure 11**. We could locate the *y*-intercept similarly.

▮▮ **EXAMPLE 2** Graphing Lines with a Single Intercept

Graph each line.

(a) $y = 2$ **(b)** $x = -1$

SOLUTION

(a) Writing the equation $y = 2$ as

$$0x + 1y = 2$$

shows that any value of *x*, including $x = 0$, gives $y = 2$, making the *y*-intercept $(0, 2)$. Since *y* is always 2, there is no value of *x* corresponding to $y = 0$, and so the graph has no *x*-intercept. The graph, shown in **Figure 12(a)**, is a horizontal line.

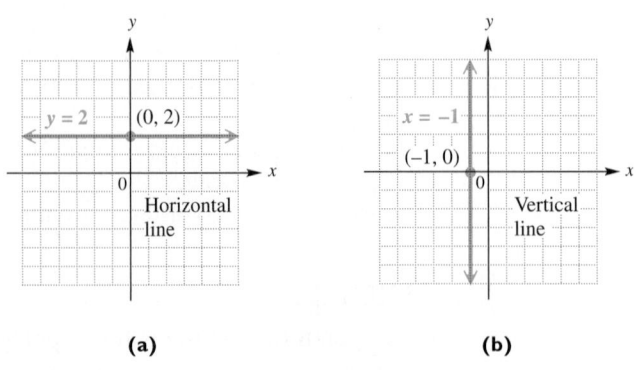

Figure 12

(b) In this equation, $x = -1$ for all *y*. No value of *y* makes $x = 0$. The graph has no *y*-intercept, and thus must be vertical, as shown in **Figure 12(b)**. ▮▮▮

Slope

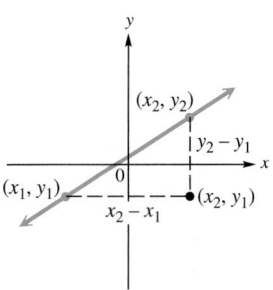

Figure 13

Two distinct points determine a unique line. A line also can be determined by a point on the line and some measure of the "steepness" of the line. The measure of the steepness of a line is called the *slope* of the line. One way to get a measure of the steepness of a line is to compare the vertical change in the line (the *rise*) to the horizontal change (the *run*) while moving along the line from one fixed point to another.

Suppose that (x_1, y_1) and (x_2, y_2) are two different points on a line. Then, moving along the line from (x_1, y_1) to (x_2, y_2), the y-value changes from y_1 to y_2, an amount equal to $y_2 - y_1$. As y changes from y_1 to y_2, the value of x changes from x_1 to x_2 by the amount $x_2 - x_1$. See **Figure 13**. The ratio of the change in y to the change in x is called the **slope** of the line. The letter m is used to denote the slope.

> **Slope Formula**
>
> If $x_1 \neq x_2$, the slope m of the line through the distinct points (x_1, y_1) and (x_2, y_2) is
>
> $$m = \frac{\text{rise}}{\text{run}} = \frac{\text{change in } y}{\text{change in } x} = \frac{y_2 - y_1}{x_2 - x_1}.$$

▮▮ EXAMPLE 3 Using the Slope Formula

Find the slope of the line that passes through the points $(2, -1)$ and $(-5, 3)$.

SOLUTION

Let $(2, -1) = (x_1, y_1)$ and $(-5, 3) = (x_2, y_2)$, and use the slope formula.

$$m = \frac{y_2 - y_1}{x_2 - x_1} = \frac{3 - (-1)}{-5 - 2} = \frac{4}{-7} = -\frac{4}{7}$$

> Start with the x- and y-values of the same point.

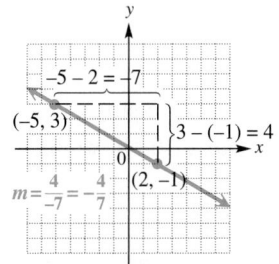

Figure 14

See **Figure 14**. Now let $(2, -1) = (x_2, y_2)$ and $(-5, 3) = (x_1, y_1)$.

$$m = \frac{-1 - 3}{2 - (-5)} = \frac{-4}{7} = -\frac{4}{7} \quad \text{The same answer}$$

This example suggests that the slope is the same no matter which point is considered first. Using similar triangles from geometry, we can show that the slope is the same for *any* two different points chosen on the line. ▮▮▮

▮▮ EXAMPLE 4 Finding Slopes of Vertical and Horizontal Lines

Find the slope, if possible, of each of the following lines.

(a) $x = -3$ **(b)** $y = 5$

SOLUTION

(a) By inspection, $(-3, 5)$ and $(-3, -4)$ are two points that satisfy the equation $x = -3$. Use these two points to find the slope.

$$m = \frac{-4 - 5}{-3 - (-3)} = \frac{-9}{0} \quad \text{Undefined slope}$$

Since division by zero is undefined, the slope is undefined. (This is why the definition of slope includes the restriction that $x_1 \neq x_2$.)

Visitors to Epcot Center at Walt Disney World in Florida love the ride **Test Track.** This sign at the beginning of the ride indicates an upward **slope** of about $\frac{1}{4}$.

(b) Find the slope by selecting two different points on the line, such as $(3, 5)$ and $(-1, 5)$, and by using the definition of slope.

$$m = \frac{5 - 5}{3 - (-1)} = \frac{0}{4} = 0 \quad \text{Zero slope} \qquad \blacksquare\blacksquare\blacksquare$$

In **Example 2,** $x = -1$ has a graph that is a vertical line, and $y = 2$ has a graph that is a horizontal line. Generalizing from those results and the results of **Example 4,** we can make the following statements about vertical and horizontal lines.

Vertical and Horizontal Lines

- A vertical line has an equation of the form $x = a$, where a is a real number, and its slope is undefined.
- A horizontal line has an equation of the form $y = b$, where b is a real number, and its slope is 0.

■■ **EXAMPLE 5** Graphing a Line Using Slope and a Point

Graph the line that has slope $\frac{2}{3}$ and passes through the point $(-1, 4)$.

SOLUTION

First locate the point $(-1, 4)$ on a graph as shown in **Figure 15.** Then,

$$m = \frac{\textbf{change in } y}{\textbf{change in } x} = \frac{2}{3}. \quad \text{Definition of slope}$$

Move *up* 2 units in the y-direction and then *right* 3 units in the x-direction to locate another point on the graph (labeled P). The line through $(-1, 4)$ and P is the required graph. ■■■

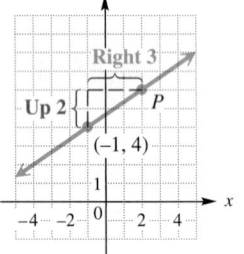

Figure 15

Figure 16

The line graphed in **Figure 14** has a negative slope, $-\frac{4}{7}$, and the line *falls* from left to right. In contrast, the line graphed in **Figure 15** has a positive slope, $\frac{2}{3}$, and it *rises* from left to right. These ideas can be generalized. (**Figure 16** shows lines of positive, zero, negative, and undefined slopes.)

Positive and Negative Slopes

- A line with a positive slope rises from left to right.
- A line with a negative slope falls from left to right.

Parallel and Perpendicular Lines

The slopes of a pair of parallel or perpendicular lines are related in a special way. The slope of a line measures the steepness of the line. Since parallel lines have equal steepness, their slopes also must be equal. Also, lines with the same slope are parallel.

Slopes of Parallel Lines

Two nonvertical lines with the same slope are parallel. Two nonvertical parallel lines have the same slope. Furthermore, any two vertical lines are parallel.

|| EXAMPLE 6 Determining Whether Two Lines Are Parallel

Determine whether the lines L_1, through $(-2, 1)$ and $(4, 5)$, and L_2, through $(3, 0)$ and $(0, -2)$, are parallel.

SOLUTION

The slope of L_1 is

$$m_1 = \frac{5 - 1}{4 - (-2)} = \frac{4}{6} = \frac{2}{3}.$$

The slope of L_2 is

$$m_2 = \frac{-2 - 0}{0 - 3} = \frac{-2}{-3} = \frac{2}{3}.$$

Because the slopes are equal, the lines are parallel.   ■■■

Perpendicular lines are lines that meet at right angles. It can be shown that the slopes of perpendicular lines have a product of -1, provided that neither line is vertical. For example, if the slope of a line is $\frac{3}{4}$, then any line perpendicular to it has slope $-\frac{4}{3}$, because $\left(\frac{3}{4}\right)\left(-\frac{4}{3}\right) = -1$.

> **Slopes of Perpendicular Lines**
>
> If neither is vertical, two perpendicular lines have slopes that are negative reciprocals—that is, their product is -1. Also, two lines with slopes that are negative reciprocals are perpendicular. Every vertical line is perpendicular to every horizontal line.

|| EXAMPLE 7 Determining Whether Two Lines Are Perpendicular

Determine whether the lines L_1, through $(0, -3)$ and $(2, 0)$, and L_2, through $(-3, 0)$ and $(0, -2)$, are perpendicular.

SOLUTION

The slope of L_1 is

$$m_1 = \frac{0 - (-3)}{2 - 0} = \frac{3}{2}.$$

The slope of L_2 is

$$m_2 = \frac{-2 - 0}{0 - (-3)} = -\frac{2}{3}.$$

Because the product of the slopes of the two lines is $\frac{3}{2}\left(-\frac{2}{3}\right) = -1$, the lines are perpendicular.   ■■■

Average Rate of Change

The slope formula applied to any two points on a line gives the **average rate of change** in y per unit change in x, where the value of y depends on the value of x.

For example, suppose the height of a boy increased from 60 to 68 inches between the ages of 12 and 16, as shown in **Figure 17**. We can find the boy's average growth rate (or average change in height) per year.

$$\begin{array}{c} \text{Change in height } y \longrightarrow \\ \text{Change in age } x \longrightarrow \end{array} \frac{68 - 60}{16 - 12} = \frac{8}{4} = 2 \text{ inches per year}$$

The boy may actually have grown more than 2 inches during some years and less than 2 inches during other years. If we plotted ordered pairs (age, height) for those years and drew a line connecting any two of those points, the average rate of change would likely be slightly different than that found above. However, using the data for ages 12 and 16, the boy's *average* change in height was 2 inches per year over these years.

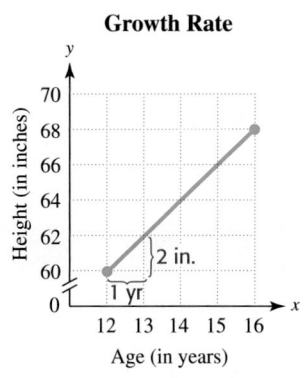

Figure 17

▌▌ **EXAMPLE 8** Interpreting Slope as Average Rate of Change

The graph in **Figure 18** approximates the average number of hours per year spent watching cable and satellite TV for each person in the United States during the years 2000 through 2005. Find the average rate of change in number of hours per year.

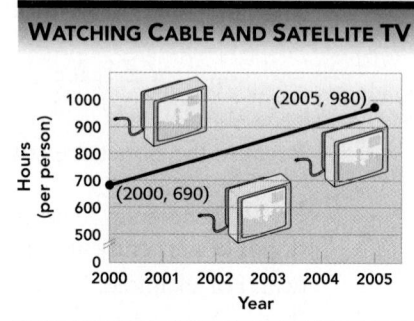

WATCHING CABLE AND SATELLITE TV

Source: Veronis Suhler Stevenson.

Figure 18

SOLUTION

To determine the average rate of change, we need two pairs of data. From the graph, if $x = 2000$, then $y = 690$ and if $x = 2005$, then $y = 980$. Thus, we have the ordered pairs (2000, 690) and (2005, 980). By the slope formula,

$$\text{average rate of change} = \frac{980 - 690}{2005 - 2000} = \frac{290}{5} = 58$$

> A positive slope indicates an increase.

This means that the average time per person spent watching cable and satellite TV *increased* by 58 hr per year from 2000 through 2005. ▌▌▌

▌▌ **EXAMPLE 9** Interpreting Slope as Average Rate of Change

During the year 2000, the average person in the United States spent 866 hr watching broadcast TV. In 2004, the average number of hours per person spent watching broadcast TV was 678. Find the average rate of change in number of hours per year. (*Source:* Veronis Suhler Stevenson.)

SOLUTION

To use the slope formula, we need two ordered pairs. Here, we let one ordered pair be (2000, 866) and the other be (2004, 678).

$$\text{average rate of change} = \frac{678 - 866}{2004 - 2000} = \frac{-188}{4} = -47$$

> A negative slope indicates a decrease.

The graph in **Figure 19** confirms that the line through the ordered pairs falls from left to right and, therefore, has negative slope. Thus, the average time per person spent watching broadcast TV *decreased* by 47 hr per year from 2000 through 2004. ▌▌▌

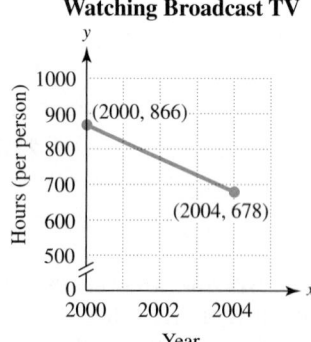

Watching Broadcast TV

Figure 19

8.2 EXERCISES

Complete the given ordered pairs for each equation. Then graph the equation.

1. $2x + y = 5$; (0,), (, 0), (1,), (, 1)

2. $3x - 4y = 24$; (0,), (, 0), (6,), (, −3)

3. $x - y = 4$; (0,), (, 0), (2,), (, −1)

4. $x + 3y = 12$; (0,), (, 0), (3,), (, 6)

5. $4x + 5y = 20$; (0,), (, 0), (3,), (, 2)

6. $2x - 5y = 12;\ (0,\ ),\ (\ ,0),\ (\ ,-2),\ (-2,\ )$

7. $3x + 2y = 8$

x	y
0	
	0
2	
	-2

8. $5x + y = 12$

x	y
0	
	0
	-3
2	

 9. Explain how to find the x-intercept of a linear equation in two variables.

 10. Explain how to find the y-intercept of a linear equation in two variables.

11. Which choice has a horizontal line as its graph?
  A. $2y = 6$ **B.** $2x = 6$
  C. $x - 4 = 0$ **D.** $x + y = 0$

12. What is the minimum number of points that must be determined in order to graph a linear equation in two variables?

For each equation, give the x-intercept and the y-intercept. Then graph the equation.

13. $3x + 2y = 12$

14. $2x + 5y = 10$

15. $5x + 6y = 10$

16. $3y + x = 6$

17. $2x - y = 5$

18. $3x - 2y = 4$

19. $x - 3y = 2$

20. $y - 4x = 3$

21. $y + x = 0$

22. $2x - y = 0$

23. $3x = y$

24. $x = -4y$

25. $x = 2$

26. $y = -3$

27. $y = 4$

28. $x = -2$

In Exercises 29–36 in the next column, match the equation with the figure in choices A–D below that most closely resembles its graph.

A. 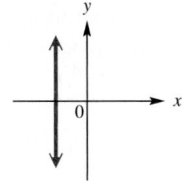   **B.**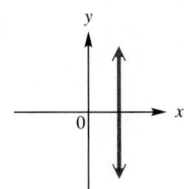

C. 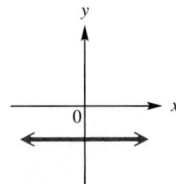   **D.**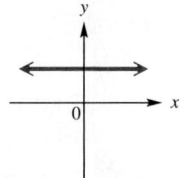

29. $y + 2 = 0$ **30.** $y + 4 = 0$

31. $x + 3 = 0$ **32.** $x + 7 = 0$

33. $y - 2 = 0$ **34.** $y - 4 = 0$

35. $x - 3 = 0$ **36.** $x - 7 = 0$

37. What is the slope (or pitch) of this roof?

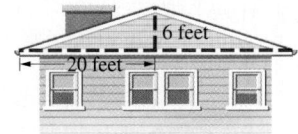

38. What is the slope (or grade) of this hill?

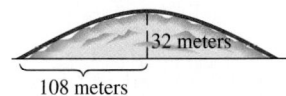

39. Use the coordinates of the indicated points to find the slope of each line.
  (a) 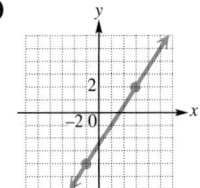   **(b)**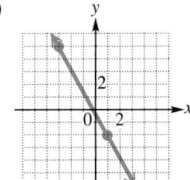

40. Tell whether the slope of the given line in (a) – (d) is positive, negative, zero, or undefined.
  (a) 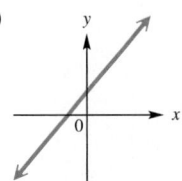   **(b)**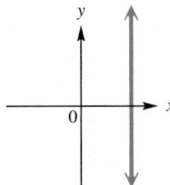

  (c) 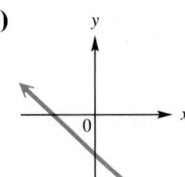   **(d)**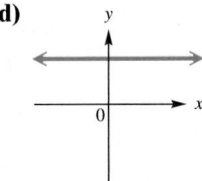

Find the slope of the line through each pair of points by using the slope formula.

41. $(-2, -3)$ and $(-1, 5)$ **42.** $(-4, 3)$ and $(-3, 4)$

43. $(8, 1)$ and $(2, 6)$ **44.** $(13, -3)$ and $(5, 6)$

45. $(2, 4)$ and $(-4, 4)$ **46.** $(-6, 3)$ and $(2, 3)$

47. Public School Data   Figure A depicts public school enrollment (in thousands) in grades 9–12 in the United States. **Figure B** below gives the (average) number of public school students per computer.

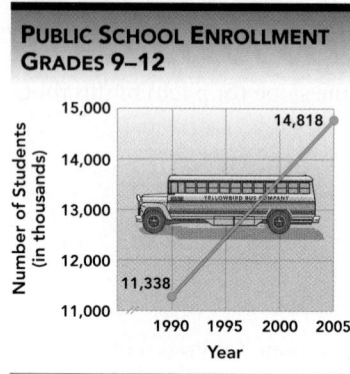

Source: U.S. Department of Education.

Figure A

(a) Use (1990, 11,338) and (2005, 14,818) to find the slope of the line in **Figure A**.

(b) The slope of the line in **Figure A** is _____.
(positive/negative)
This means that during the period represented, enrollment _____.
(increased/decreased)

(c) The slope of a line represents its *rate of change*. Based on **Figure A**, what was the increase in students *per year* during the period shown?

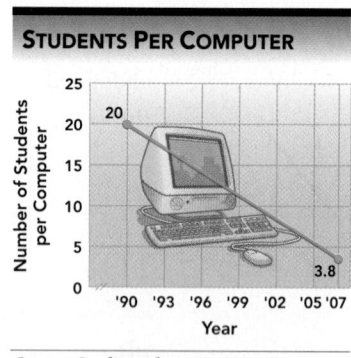

Source: Quality Education Data, Inc.

Figure B

(d) Use the two indicated points to find the slope of the line in **Figure B**.

(e) The slope of the line in **Figure B** is _____.
(positive/negative)
This means that during the period represented, the number of students per computer _____.
(increased/decreased)

(f) Based on **Figure B**, what was the decrease in students per computer *per year* during the period shown?

48. Use the results of **Exercise 47** to make a connection between the sign of the slope of a line and the increase or decrease in the quantity represented by y.

*Use the method of **Example 5** to graph each line.*

49. $m = \frac{1}{2}$,   through $(-3, 2)$

50. $m = \frac{2}{3}$,   through $(0, 1)$

51. $m = -\frac{5}{4}$,   through $(-2, -1)$

52. $m = -\frac{3}{2}$,   through $(-1, -2)$

53. $m = -2$,   through $(-1, -4)$

54. $m = 3$,   through $(1, 2)$

55. $m = 0$,   through $(2, -5)$

56. $m = 0$,   through $(2, 4)$

57. undefined slope,   through $(4, 2)$

58. undefined slope,   through $(-3, 1)$

Determine whether the lines described are parallel, perpendicular, *or* neither parallel nor perpendicular.

59. L_1 through $(4, 6)$ and $(-8, 7)$, and L_2 through $(7, 4)$ and $(-5, 5)$

60. L_1 through $(9, 15)$ and $(-7, 12)$, and L_2 through $(-4, 8)$ and $(-20, 5)$

61. L_1 through $(2, 0)$ and $(5, 4)$, and L_2 through $(6, 1)$ and $(2, 4)$

62. L_1 through $(0, -7)$ and $(2, 3)$, and L_2 through $(0, -3)$ and $(1, -2)$

63. L_1 through $(0, 1)$ and $(2, -3)$, and L_2 through $(10, 8)$ and $(5, 3)$

64. L_1 through $(1, 2)$ and $(-7, -2)$, and L_2 through $(1, -1)$ and $(5, -9)$

Use the concept of slope to solve each problem.

65. Steepness of an Upper Deck The upper deck at U.S. Cellular Field in Chicago has produced, among other complaints, displeasure with its steepness. It has been compared to a ski jump. It is 160 ft from home plate to the front of the upper deck and 250 ft from home plate to the back. The top of the upper deck is 63 ft above the bottom. What is its slope?

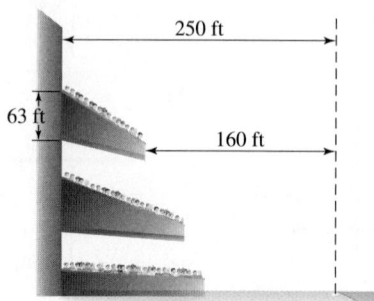

66. Grade (Slope) of a Ramp When designing the new TD Banknorth Garden arena in Boston to replace the old Boston Garden, architects were careful to design the ramps leading up to the entrances so that circus elephants would be able to walk up the ramps. The maximum grade (or slope) that an elephant will walk on is 13%. Suppose that such a ramp were constructed with a horizontal run of 150 ft. What would be the maximum vertical rise the architects could use?

Rate of Change *Find and interpret the average rate of change illustrated in each graph.*

67.

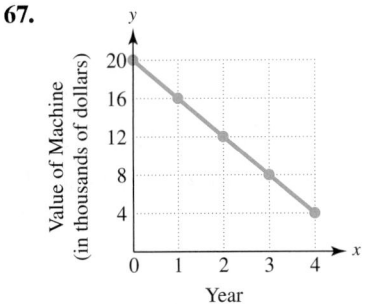

68.

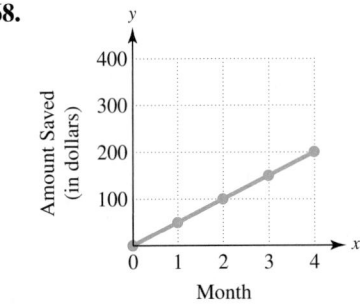

Use the idea of average rate of change to solve each problem. Round answers to the nearest thousandth.

69. Mobile Homes The graph at the top of the next column provides a good approximation of the number of mobile homes (in thousands) placed in use in the United States during 2000–2006.

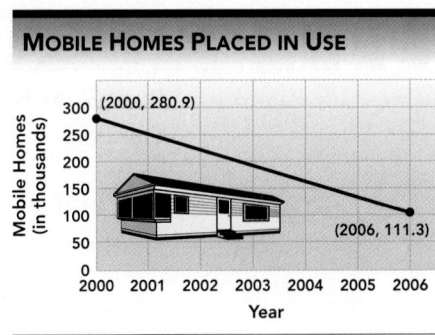

MOBILE HOMES PLACED IN USE

Source: U.S. Census Bureau.

(a) Use the given data to find the average rate of change per year during this period.

(b) How is a negative slope interpreted in this case?

70. Recreation Spending Personal spending on recreation in the United States (in billions of dollars) in recent years is closely approximated by the graph.

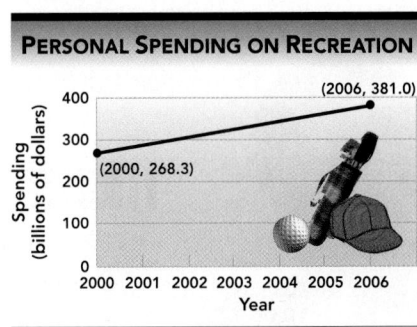

PERSONAL SPENDING ON RECREATION

Source: U.S. Department of Commerce.

(a) Use the given data to determine the average rate of change per year.

(b) How is a positive slope interpreted in this case?

71. The total amount spent on plasma TVs in the United States changed from $1590 million in 2003 to $5705 million in 2006. Find and interpret the average rate of change in sales, in millions of dollars per year. Round your answer to the nearest hundredth. (*Source:* Consumer Electronics Association.)

72. The total amount spent on analog TVs in the United States changed from $5836 million in 2003 to $1424 million in 2006. Find and interpret the average rate of change in sales, in millions of dollars per year. Round your answer to the nearest hundredth. (*Source:* Consumer Electronics Association.)

8.3 EQUATIONS OF LINES AND LINEAR MODELS

Point-Slope Form • Slope-Intercept Form • Summary of Forms of Linear
Equations • Linear Models

Point-Slope Form

If the slope of a line and a particular point on the line are known, it is possible to find an equation of the line. Suppose that the slope of a line is m and (x_1, y_1) is a particular point on the line. Let (x, y) be any other point on the line. Then, by the definition of slope,

$$m = \frac{y - y_1}{x - x_1}. \quad \text{Slope formula}$$

Multiplying both sides by $x - x_1$ gives the familiar *point-slope form* of the equation of the line.

Point-Slope Form

The equation of the line through (x_1, y_1) with slope m is written in **point-slope form** as follows.

$$y - y_1 = m(x - x_1)$$

▌▌ EXAMPLE 1 Finding an Equation Given the Slope and a Point

Find the standard form of an equation of the line with slope $\frac{1}{3}$, passing through the point $(-2, 5)$.

SOLUTION

$$y - y_1 = m(x - x_1) \quad \text{Point-slope form}$$

$$y - 5 = \frac{1}{3}[x - (-2)] \quad \text{Let } (x_1, y_1) = (-2, 5) \text{ and } m = \frac{1}{3}.$$

<u>Substitute carefully.</u>

$$y - 5 = \frac{1}{3}(x + 2)$$

$$3y - 15 = x + 2 \quad \text{Multiply by 3.}$$

$$x - 3y = -17 \quad \text{Standard form} \quad ▌▌▌$$

If two points on a line are known, it is possible to find an equation of the line. One method is to first find the slope using the slope formula, and then use the slope with one of the given points in the point-slope form.

▌▌ EXAMPLE 2 Finding an Equation Given Two Points

Find the standard form of an equation of the line passing through the points $(-4, 3)$ and $(5, -7)$.

SOLUTION

First find the slope, using the definition.

$$m = \frac{-7 - 3}{5 - (-4)} = -\frac{10}{9} \quad \begin{matrix} x_1 = -4, y_1 = 3, \\ x_2 = 5, y_2 = -7 \end{matrix}$$

Maria Gaetana Agnesi (1719–1799) did much of her mathematical work in coordinate geometry. She grew up in a scholarly atmosphere. Her father was a mathematician on the faculty at the University of Bologna. In a larger sense she was an heir to the long tradition of Italian mathematicians.

Maria was fluent in several languages by age 13, but she chose mathematics over literature. The curve shown below, called the **witch of Agnesi**, is studied in analytic geometry courses.

$$y = \frac{a^3}{x^2 + a^2}$$

Either $(-4, 3)$ or $(5, -7)$ may be used as (x_1, y_1) in the point-slope form of the equation of the line. If $(-4, 3)$ is used, then $-4 = x_1$ and $3 = y_1$.

$$y - y_1 = m(x - x_1) \qquad \text{Point-slope form}$$

$$y - 3 = -\frac{10}{9}[x - (-4)] \qquad (x_1, y_1) = (-4, 3) \text{ and } m = -\frac{10}{9}$$

$$y - 3 = -\frac{10}{9}(x + 4) \qquad \text{Definition of subtraction}$$

$$9(y - 3) = -10(x + 4) \qquad \text{Multiply by 9.}$$

$$9y - 27 = -10x - 40 \qquad \text{Distributive property}$$

$$10x + 9y = -13 \qquad \text{Standard form} \qquad\qquad ■■■$$

Slope-Intercept Form

Suppose that the slope m of a line is known, and the y-intercept of the line has coordinates $(0, b)$. Then we have the following.

$$y - y_1 = m(x - x_1) \qquad \text{Point-slope form}$$

$$y - b = m(x - 0) \qquad \text{Let } (x_1, y_1) = (0, b).$$

$$y - b = mx$$

$$y = mx + b \qquad \text{Add } b \text{ to both sides.}$$

This last result is known as the *slope-intercept form* of the equation of the line.

> **Slope-Intercept Form**
>
> The equation of a line with slope m and y-intercept $(0, b)$ is written in **slope-intercept form** as follows.
>
> $$y = mx + b$$
> $\qquad\quad\uparrow\qquad\uparrow$
> $\qquad$ Slope $\quad$ y-intercept is $(0, b)$.

Every linear equation (of a nonvertical line) has a *unique* (one and only one) slope-intercept form. In the next section, where we will study *linear functions,* the slope-intercept form will be necessary in specifying such functions.

EXAMPLE 3 Writing an Equation in Slope-Intercept Form

Write each of the following equations in slope-intercept form.

(a) the line $x - 3y = -17$ described in **Example 1**

(b) the line $10x + 9y = -13$ described in **Example 2**

SOLUTION

(a) Solve for y to obtain the slope-intercept form.

$$x - 3y = -17$$

$$-3y = -x - 17 \qquad \text{Subtract } x.$$

$$y = \frac{1}{3}x + \frac{17}{3} \qquad \text{Divide by } -3.$$

The slope is $\frac{1}{3}$ and the y-intercept is $\left(0, \frac{17}{3}\right)$.

(b)
$$10x + 9y = -13$$
$$9y = -10x - 13 \quad \text{Subtract } 10x.$$
$$y = -\frac{10}{9}x - \frac{13}{9} \quad \text{Divide by 9.}$$

The slope is $-\frac{10}{9}$ and the y-intercept is $\left(0, -\frac{13}{9}\right)$. ▮▮▮

If the slope-intercept form of the equation of a line is known, the method of graphing described in **Example 5** of **Section 8.2** can be used to graph the line.

▮▮ **EXAMPLE 4** Graphing a Line Using Slope and y-Intercept

Graph the line with the equation $y = -\frac{2}{3}x + 3$.

SOLUTION

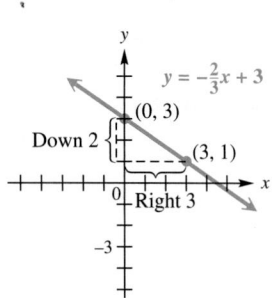

Figure 20

Because the equation is given in slope-intercept form, we can see that the slope is $-\frac{2}{3}$ and the y-intercept is $(0, 3)$. For now, interpret $-\frac{2}{3}$ as $\frac{-2}{3}$. Plot the point $(0, 3)$, and then, using the "rise over run" interpretation of slope, move *down* 2 units (because of the -2 in the numerator of the slope) and to the *right* 3 units (because of the 3 in the denominator). We arrive at the point $(3, 1)$.

Plot the point $(3, 1)$, and join the two points with a line, as shown in **Figure 20**. (We could also have interpreted $-\frac{2}{3}$ as $\frac{2}{-3}$ and obtained a different second point. However, the line would be the same.) ▮▮▮

▮▮ **EXAMPLE 5** Finding an Equation Using a Slope Relationship (Parallel Lines)

Find the slope-intercept form of the equation of the line parallel to the graph of $2x + 3y = 6$, passing through the point $(-4, 5)$. Graph both lines.

SOLUTION

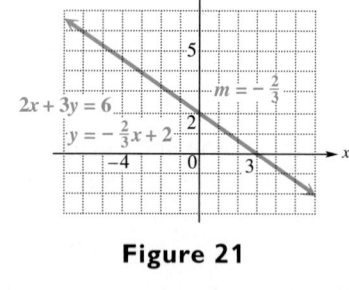

Figure 21

The slope of the line $2x + 3y = 6$, shown in **Figure 21**, can be found by solving for y.

$$2x + 3y = 6$$
$$3y = -2x + 6 \quad \text{Subtract } 2x.$$
$$y = -\frac{2}{3}x + 2 \quad \text{Divide by 3.}$$
$$\underset{\text{Slope}}{\uparrow}$$

The slope is given by the coefficient of x, so $m = -\frac{2}{3}$. The line through $(-4, 5)$ and parallel to $2x + 3y = 6$ must have the same slope. To find the required equation, use the point-slope form with $(x_1, y_1) = (-4, 5)$ and $m = -\frac{2}{3}$.

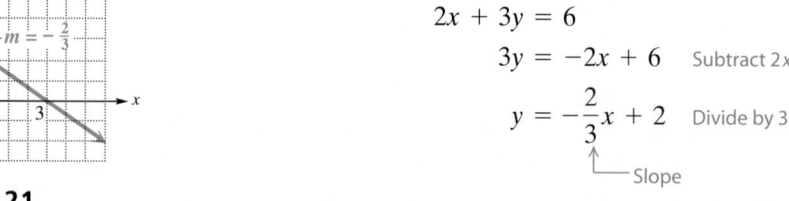

$$y - 5 = -\frac{2}{3}[x - (-4)] \quad y_1 = 5, m = -\frac{2}{3}, x_1 = -4$$
$$y - 5 = -\frac{2}{3}(x + 4) \quad \text{Definition of subtraction}$$
$$y - 5 = -\frac{2}{3}x - \frac{8}{3} \quad \text{Distributive property}$$
$$y = -\frac{2}{3}x - \frac{8}{3} + \frac{15}{3} \quad \text{Add } 5 = \frac{15}{3}.$$
$$y = -\frac{2}{3}x + \frac{7}{3} \quad \text{Combine like terms.}$$

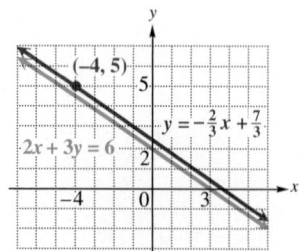

Figure 22

Both lines are shown in **Figure 22**. ▮▮▮

EXAMPLE 6 Finding an Equation Using a Slope Relationship (Perpendicular Lines)

Find the slope-intercept form of the equation of the line perpendicular to the graph of $2x + 3y = 6$, passing through the point $(-4, 5)$. Graph both lines.

SOLUTION

In **Example 5** we found that the slope of the line $2x + 3y = 6$ is $-\frac{2}{3}$. A line perpendicular to it must have a slope that is the negative reciprocal of $-\frac{2}{3}$, which is $\frac{3}{2}$. Use the point $(-4, 5)$ and slope $\frac{3}{2}$ in the point-slope form to obtain the equation of the perpendicular line shown in **Figure 23**.

$$y - 5 = \frac{3}{2}[x - (-4)] \quad \text{\scriptsize } y_1 = 5, m = \frac{3}{2}, x_1 = -4$$

$$y - 5 = \frac{3}{2}(x + 4) \qquad \text{Definition of subtraction}$$

$$y - 5 = \frac{3}{2}x + 6 \qquad \text{Distributive property}$$

$$y = \frac{3}{2}x + 11 \qquad \text{Add 5.} \qquad \blacksquare\blacksquare\blacksquare$$

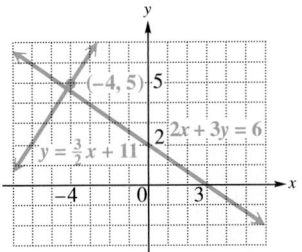

Figure 23

Summary of Forms of Linear Equations

A summary of the various forms of linear equations follows.

Summary of Forms of Linear Equations	
$Ax + By = C$	**Standard form** (A and B are not both 0.)
$x = a$	**Vertical line** Undefined slope and the x-intercept is $(a, 0)$.
$y = b$	**Horizontal line** Slope is 0 and the y-intercept is $(0, b)$.
$y = mx + b$	**Slope-intercept form** Slope is m and the y-intercept is $(0, b)$.
$y - y_1 = m(x - x_1)$	**Point-slope form** Slope is m and the line passes through (x_1, y_1).

Linear Models

Earlier examples and exercises gave equations that described real data. Now we show how such equations can be found. The process of writing an equation to fit a graph is called *curve-fitting*. The next example illustrates this concept for a straight line. The resulting equation is called a **linear model.**

EXAMPLE 7 Modeling Tuition Costs

Average annual tuition and fees for in-state students at public four-year colleges are shown in **Table 1**.

(a) Graph the data. Let $x = 0$ correspond to 1990, $x = 4$ correspond to 1994, and so on. What type of equation might model the data?

(b) Find an equation that models the data.

Table 1

Year	Cost (in dollars)
1990	2035
1994	2820
1996	3151
1998	3486
2000	3774
2002	4273
2004	4920

Source: U.S. National Center for Education Statistics.

(c) Use the equation from part (b) to approximate the cost of tuition and fees at public four-year colleges in 2006.

SOLUTION

(a) The points are plotted in **Figure 24**, where x corresponds to the year as described, and y represents the cost in dollars. It appears that a linear equation will model the data.

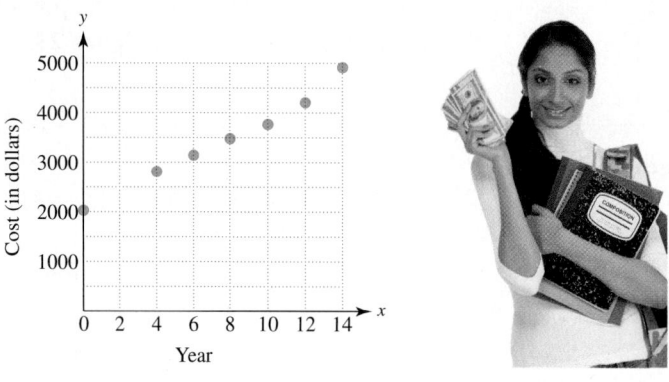

Figure 24

(b) Since the points in **Figure 24** lie approximately on a straight line, we can write a linear equation that models the relationship between year x and cost y. We choose two data points, $(0, 2035)$ and $(12, 4273)$, to find the slope of the line.

$$m = \frac{4273 - 2035}{12 - 0} = \frac{2238}{12} = 186.5$$

Start with the x- and y-values of the same point.

The slope 186.5 indicates that the cost of tuition and fees increased by about $186.50 per year from 1990 to 2002. We use this slope, the y-intercept $(0, \mathbf{2035})$, and the slope-intercept form to write an equation of the line. Thus,

$$y = \mathbf{186.5}x + \mathbf{2035}.$$

(c) The value $x = 16$ corresponds to the year 2006.

$$y = 186.5x + 2035 \qquad \text{Equation from part (b)}$$

$$y = 186.5(\mathbf{16}) + 2035 \qquad \text{Substitute 16 for } x.$$

$$y = 5019 \qquad \text{Multiply and then add.}$$

According to the model, average tuition and fees for in-state students at public four-year colleges in 2006 were about $5019. ■■■

In **Example 7,** if we had chosen different data points, we would have found a slightly different equation. However, all such equations should yield similar results, since the data points are approximately linear.

8.3 EXERCISES

Match each equation in Column I with the correct description given in Column II.

I

1. $y = 4x$

2. $y = \frac{1}{4}x$

3. $y = -2x + 1$

4. $y - 1 = -2(x - 4)$

II

A. slope $= -2$, through the point $(4, 1)$

B. slope $= -2$, y-intercept $(0, 1)$

C. passing through the points $(0, 0)$ and $(4, 1)$

D. passing through the points $(0, 0)$ and $(1, 4)$

In Exercises 5–12, match each equation with the graph that it most closely resembles in Choices A–H. (Hint: Determining the signs of m and b will help you make your decision.)

5. $y = 2x + 3$

6. $y = -2x + 3$

7. $y = -2x - 3$

8. $y = 2x - 3$

9. $y = 2x$

10. $y = -2x$

11. $y = 3$

12. $y = -3$

A.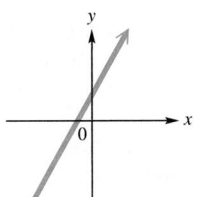

B.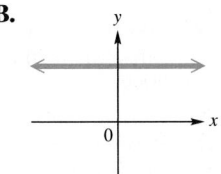

C.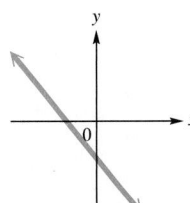

D.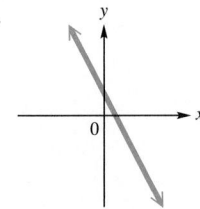

E.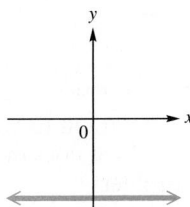

F.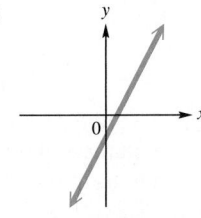

G.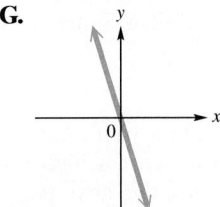

H.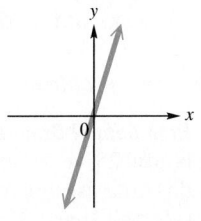

Use the geometric interpretation of slope (rise divided by run) to find the slope of each line. Then, by identifying the y-intercept from the graph, write the slope-intercept form of the equation of the line.

13.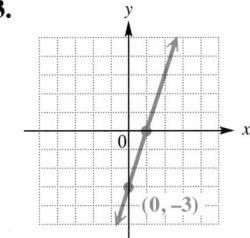

14.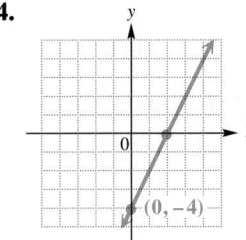

15.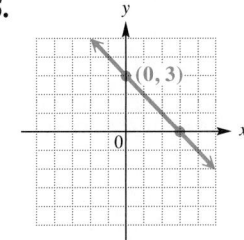

16.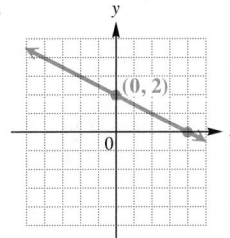

Write the slope-intercept form of the equation of the line satisfying the given conditions.

17. Through $(-2, 4)$;   slope $-\frac{3}{4}$

18. Through $(-1, 6)$;   slope $-\frac{5}{6}$

19. Through $(5, 8)$;   slope -2

20. Through $(12, 10)$;   slope 1

21. Through $(-5, 4)$;   slope $\frac{1}{2}$

22. Through $(7, -2)$;   slope $\frac{1}{4}$

23. x-intercept $(3, 0)$;   slope 4

24. x-intercept $(-2, 0)$;   slope -5

Write an equation for a line that satisfies the given conditions.

25. Through $(9, 5)$;   slope 0

26. Through $(-4, -2)$;   slope 0

27. Through $(9, 10)$;   undefined slope

28. Through $(-2, 8)$;   undefined slope

29. Through $(0.5, 0.2)$;   vertical

30. Through $\left(\frac{5}{8}, \frac{2}{9}\right)$;   vertical

31. Through $(-7, 8)$;   horizontal

32. Through $(2, 7)$;   horizontal

Write the equation, in slope-intercept form if possible, of the line passing through the two points.

33. $(3, 4)$ and $(5, 8)$

34. $(5, -2)$ and $(-3, 14)$

35. $(6, 1)$ and $(-2, 5)$

36. $(-2, 5)$ and $(-8, 1)$

37. $\left(-\frac{2}{5}, \frac{2}{5}\right)$ and $\left(\frac{4}{3}, \frac{2}{3}\right)$

38. $\left(\frac{3}{4}, \frac{8}{3}\right)$ and $\left(\frac{2}{5}, \frac{2}{3}\right)$

39. $(2, 5)$ and $(1, 5)$ **40.** $(-2, 2)$ and $(4, 2)$

41. $(7, 6)$ and $(7, -8)$ **42.** $(13, 5)$ and $(13, -1)$

43. $(1, -3)$ and $(-1, -3)$ **44.** $(-4, 6)$ and $(5, 6)$

Find the equation in slope-intercept form of the line satisfying the given conditions.

45. $m = 5$; $b = 15$

46. $m = -2$; $b = 12$

47. $m = -\frac{2}{3}$; $b = \frac{4}{5}$

48. $m = -\frac{5}{8}$; $b = -\frac{1}{3}$

49. Slope $\frac{2}{5}$; y-intercept $(0, 5)$

50. Slope $-\frac{3}{4}$; y-intercept $(0, 7)$

51. Explain why the point-slope form of an equation cannot be used to find the equation of a vertical line.

52. Which one of the following equations is in standard form, according to the definition of standard form given in this text?

    A. $3x + 2y - 6 = 0$ **B.** $y = 5x - 12$

    C. $2y = 3x + 4$ **D.** $6x - 5y = 12$

For each equation **(a)** *write in slope-intercept form,* **(b)** *give the slope of the line, and* **(c)** *give the y-intercept.*

53. $x + y = 12$ **54.** $x - y = 14$

55. $5x + 2y = 20$ **56.** $6x + 5y = 40$

57. $2x - 3y = 10$ **58.** $4x - 3y = 10$

Write the equation in slope-intercept form of the line satisfying the given conditions.

59. Through $(7, 2)$; parallel to $3x - y = 8$

60. Through $(4, 1)$; parallel to $2x + 5y = 10$

61. Through $(-2, -2)$; parallel to $-x + 2y = 10$

62. Through $(-1, 3)$; parallel to $-x + 3y = 12$

63. Through $(8, 5)$; perpendicular to $2x - y = 7$

64. Through $(2, -7)$; perpendicular to $5x + 2y = 18$

65. Through $(-2, 7)$; perpendicular to $x = 9$

66. Through $(8, 4)$; perpendicular to $x = -3$

Solve each problem. In part (a), give equations in slope-intercept form. (Round slope to the nearest tenth.)

67. *Digital Camera Sales* Total sales of digital cameras in the United States (in millions of dollars) are shown in the graph, where the year 2003 corresponds to $x = 0$.

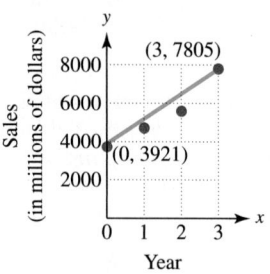

Source: Consumer Electronics Association.

    (a) Use the ordered pairs from the graph to write an equation that models the data. What does the slope tell us in the context of this problem?

    (b) Use the equation from part (a) to approximate the sales of digital cameras in the United States in 2007.

68. *Fax Machine Sales* Total sales of fax machines in the United States (in millions of dollars) are shown in the graph, where the year 2003 corresponds to $x = 0$.

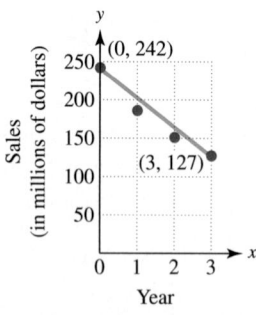

Source: Consumer Electronics Association.

    (a) Use the ordered pairs from the graph to write an equation that models the data. What does the slope tell us in the context of this problem?

    (b) Use the equation from part (a) to approximate the sales of fax machines in the United States in 2007.

Solve each problem.

69. *High School Graduates* The percentage of the U.S. population 25 years and older with at least a high school diploma is shown in the table on the next page for selected years.

High School Graduates

Year	Percent
1950	34.3
1960	41.1
1970	52.3
1980	66.5
1990	77.6
2000	84.1
2005	85.2

Source: U.S. Census Bureau.

(a) Let $x = 0$ represent 1950, $x = 10$ represent 1960, and so on. Use the data for 1950 and 2000 to find an equation that models the data.

(b) Use the equation from part (a) to approximate the percentage, to the nearest tenth, of the U.S. population 25 years and older who were at least high school graduates in 1995.

70. *Nuclear Waste* The table gives the heavy metal nuclear waste (in thousands of metric tons) from spent reactor fuel stored temporarily at reactor sites, awaiting permanent storage. (*Source*: "Burial of Radioactive Nuclear Waste under the Seabed," *Scientific American*, January 1998, p. 62.)

Heavy Metal Nuclear Waste

Year x	Waste y
1995	32
2000*	42
2010*	61
2020*	76

*Estimates by the U.S. Department of Energy.

Let $x = 0$ represent 1995, $x = 5$ represent 2000 (since $2000 - 1995 = 5$), and so on.

(a) Use $(0, 32)$ and $(25, 76)$ to find the equation of a line that approximates the other ordered pairs. Use the form $y = mx + b$.

(b) Use the equation from part (a) to estimate the amount of nuclear waste in 2008.

71. *Mail Delivery* The number of pieces of first class mail delivered in the United States is shown in the bar graph in the next column.

(a) Use the information given for the years 2003 and 2007, letting $x = 3$ represent 2003 and $x = 7$ represent 2007, and letting y represent the number of pieces of mail (in millions), to write an equation that models the data.

Source: U.S. Postal Service.

(b) Use the equation to approximate the number of pieces of first class mail delivered in 2005. How does this result compare to the actual value 98,071 million?

72. *Household Income* Median household income of all Americans is shown in the bar graph.

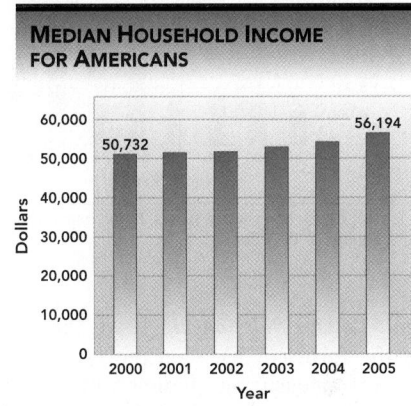

Source: U.S. Census Bureau.

(a) Use the years 2000 and 2005, letting $x = 0$ represent 2000, $x = 5$ represent 2005, and y represent the median income, to write an equation that models median household income.

(b) Use the equation to approximate the median income for 2003. How does your result compare to the actual value $52,680?

73. *Distant Galaxies* In the late 1920s, the famous observational astronomer Edwin P. Hubble (1889–1953) determined the distances to several galaxies and the velocities at which they were receding from Earth. Four galaxies with their distances in light-years and velocities in miles per second are listed in the table.

Galaxy	Distance	Velocity
Virgo	50	990
Ursa Minor	650	9300
Corona Borealis	950	15,000
Bootes	1700	25,000

Source: Sharov, A., and I. Novikov, *Edwin Hubble, the Discoverer of the Big Bang Universe*, Cambridge University Press, 1993.

(a) Let *x* represent distance and *y* represent velocity. Use the data for Virgo and Bootes to find an equation of a line that models the data.

(b) If the galaxy Hydra is receding at a speed of 37,000 miles per second, estimate its distance from Earth, using the equation from part (a).

74. *Air Conditioner Choices* The graph shows the recommended air conditioner size (in British thermal units) for selected room sizes in square feet. Use the information given for rooms of 150 square feet and 1400 square feet. Let *x* represent the number of square feet and *y* represent the corresponding Btu size air conditioner. Find a linear equation that models the data. Write it in slope-intercept form.

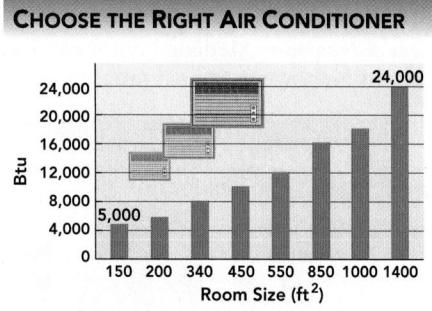

CHOOSE THE RIGHT AIR CONDITIONER

Source: Carey, Morris and James, Home Improvement for Dummies, IDG Books.

75. *Fahrenheit–Celsius Relationship* If we think of ordered pairs of the form (C, F), then the two most common methods of measuring temperature, Celsius and Fahrenheit, can be related as follows: When C = 0, F = 32, and when C = 100, F = 212. This exercise

explains how this information is used to find the formula that relates the two temperature scales.

(a) There is a linear relationship between Celsius and Fahrenheit temperatures. When C = 0°, F = _____, and when C = 100°, F = _____.

(b) Think of ordered pairs of temperatures (C, F), where C and F represent corresponding Celsius and Fahrenheit temperatures. The equation that relates the two scales has a straight-line graph that contains the two points determined in part (a). What are these two points?

(c) Find the slope of the line described in part (b).

(d) Think of the point-slope form of the equation in terms of C and F, where C replaces *x* and F replaces *y*. Use the slope from part (c) and one of the two points determined earlier to find the equation that gives F in terms of C.

(e) To obtain another form of the formula, use the equation you found in part (d) and solve for C in terms of F.

(f) The equation found in part (d) is graphed on the graphing calculator screen shown here. Observe the display at the bottom, and interpret it in the context of this exercise.

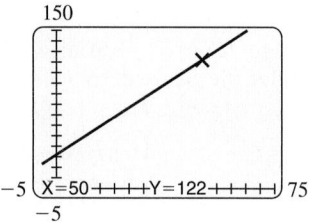

76. *Fahrenheit-Celsius Equality* For what temperature are the Fahrenheit and Celsius scales equal?

8.4 AN INTRODUCTION TO FUNCTIONS: LINEAR FUNCTIONS, APPLICATIONS, AND MODELS

Relations and Functions • Domain and Range • Graphs of Relations • Graphs of Functions • Function Notation • Linear Functions • Break-Even Analysis

Relations and Functions

We often describe one quantity in terms of another. To represent corresponding quantities, we can use ordered pairs.

For example, suppose that it is time to fill up your car's tank with gasoline. At your local station, 89-octane gas is selling for $3.10 per gallon. Experience has taught you that the final price you pay is determined by the number of gallons you buy multiplied by the price per gallon (in this case, $3.10). As you pump the gas, two sets of numbers spin by: the number of gallons pumped and the price for that number of gallons. **Table 2** on the next page uses ordered pairs to illustrate this situation.

Which grade of fuel was purchased? See **page 395** for the answer.

Table 2

Number of Gallons Pumped	Price for This Number of Gallons
0	$0.00 = 0 ($3.10)
1	$3.10 = 1 ($3.10)
2	$6.20 = 2 ($3.10)
3	$9.30 = 3 ($3.10)
4	$12.40 = 4 ($3.10)

If we let x denote the number of gallons pumped, then the price y in dollars can be found by the linear equation $y = 3.10x$. Theoretically, there are infinitely many ordered pairs (x, y) that satisfy this equation. In this application we are limited to nonnegative values for x, since we cannot have a negative number of gallons. There also is a practical maximum value for x in this situation, which varies from one car to another. What determines this maximum value?

In this example, the total price depends on the amount of gasoline pumped. For this reason, price is called the *dependent variable,* and the number of gallons is called the *independent variable.* Generalizing, if the value of the variable y depends on the value of the variable x, then y is the **dependent variable** and x the **independent variable.**

Independent variable ⎤   ⎡ Dependent variable
$$(x, y)$$

Because related quantities can be written using ordered pairs, the concept of *relation* can be defined as follows.

Relation

A **relation** is a set of ordered pairs.

For example, the sets

$$F = \{(1, 2), (-2, 5), (3, -1)\} \quad \text{and} \quad G = \{(-4, 1), (-2, 1), (-2, 0)\}$$

both are relations. A special kind of relation, called a *function,* is important in mathematics and its applications.

Function

A **function** is a relation in which for each value of the first component of the ordered pairs there is *exactly one value* of the second component.

Of the two examples of a relation just given, only set F is a function, because for each x-value, there is exactly one y-value. In set G, the last two ordered pairs have the same x-value paired with two different y-values, so G is a relation but not a function.

$$F = \{(1, 2), (-2, 5), (3, -1)\} \quad \text{Function}$$
Different x-values

$$G = \{(-4, 1), (-2, 1), (-2, 0)\} \quad \text{Not a function}$$
Same x-values

In a function, there is exactly one value of the dependent variable, the second component, for each value of the independent variable, the first component.

Another way to think of a function relationship is to think of the independent variable as an input and the dependent variable as an output. A calculator is an input-output machine, for example. To find 8^2, we must input 8, press the squaring key, and see that the output is 64. Inputs and outputs also can be determined from a graph or a table.

A third way to describe a function is to give a rule that tells how to determine the dependent variable for a specific value of the independent variable. Suppose the rule is given in words as "the dependent variable is twice the independent variable." As an equation, this can be written

$$y = 2x.$$

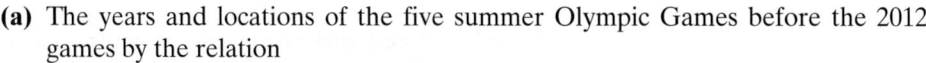

Dependent   Independent
variable   variable

▮▮ **EXAMPLE 1** Determining Independent and Dependent Variables

Determine the independent and dependent variables for each of the following functions. Give an example of an ordered pair belonging to the function.

(a) The years and locations of the five summer Olympic Games before the 2012 games by the relation

{(1992, Barcelona), (1996, Atlanta), (2000, Sydney), (2004, Athens), (2008, Beijing)}

(b) The procedure by which someone uses a calculator that finds square roots

(c) The graph in **Figure 25** that shows the relationship between the number of gallons of water in a small swimming pool and time in hours

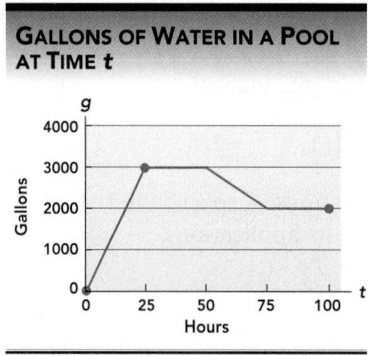

GALLONS OF WATER IN A POOL AT TIME t

Figure 25

Table 3	
Year	**Cell Phone Subscribers (in thousands)**
2002	140,766
2003	158,722
2004	182,140
2005	207,896
2006	233,041

Source: CTIA-The Wireless Association.

(d) The table of cell phone subscriptions shown in **Table 3**

(e) $y = 3x + 4$

SOLUTION

(a) The independent variable (the first component in each ordered pair) is the year. The dependent variable (the second component) is the city. For example, the ordered pair (2008, Beijing) belongs to this function.

(b) The independent variable (the input) is a nonnegative real number, because the square root of a negative number is not a real number. The dependent variable (the output) is the nonnegative square root. For example, (81, 9) belongs to this function. See **Figure 26**.

(c) The independent variable is time, in hours, and the dependent variable is the number of the gallons of water in the pool. One ordered pair is (25, 3000).

(d) The independent variable is the year and the dependent variable is the number of subscriptions. An example of an ordered pair is (2006, 233,041).

(e) The independent variable is x, and the dependent variable is y. When $x = 1$, $y = 3(1) + 4 = 7$, so one ordered pair is (1, 7). ▮▮▮

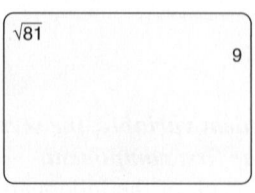

Figure 26

Domain and Range

> ### Domain and Range
>
> In a relation consisting of ordered pairs (x, y), the set of all values of the independent variable (x) is the **domain.** The set of all values of the dependent variable (y) is the **range.**

▮▮ **EXAMPLE 2** Determining Domain and Range

Give the domain and range of each function in **Example 1.**

SOLUTION

(a) The domain is the set of years,

$$\{1992, 1996, 2000, 2004, 2008\},$$

and the range is the set of cities,

$$\{\text{Barcelona, Atlanta, Sydney, Athens, Beijing}\}.$$

(b) Because we are taking square roots, the domain is restricted to *nonnegative* numbers: $[0, \infty)$. The range also is $[0, \infty)$.

(c) The domain is all possible values of t, the time in hours, which is the interval $[0, 100]$. The range is the number of gallons at time t, the interval $[0, 3000]$.

(d) The domain is the set of years,

$$\{2002, 2003, 2004, 2005, 2006\}.$$

The range is the set of subscriptions (in thousands),

$$\{140{,}766,\ 158{,}722,\ 182{,}140,\ 207{,}896,\ 233{,}041\}.$$

(e) In the defining equation (or rule), $y = 3x + 4$, x can be any real number, so the domain is $\{x \mid x$ is a real number$\}$, or $(-\infty, \infty)$. Because every real number y can be produced by some value of x, the range also is the set $\{y \mid y$ is a real number$\}$, or $(-\infty, \infty)$. ▮▮▮

Graphs of Relations

The **graph of a relation** is the graph of its ordered pairs. It gives a picture of the relation, which can be used to find its domain and range.

▮▮ **EXAMPLE 3** Determining Domain and Range

Give the domain and range of each relation.

(a) 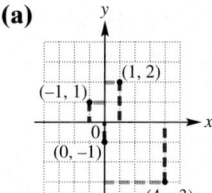 **(b)** 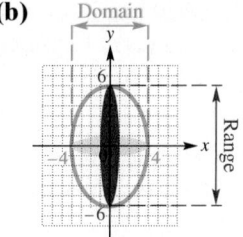 **(c)** 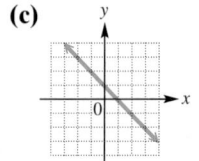 **(d)**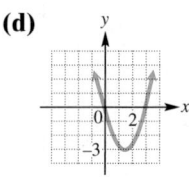

SOLUTION

(a) The domain is the set of x-values, $\{-1, 0, 1, 4\}$, and the range is the set of y-values, $\{-3, -1, 1, 2\}$.

(b) The *x*-values of the points on the graph include all numbers between −4 and 4, inclusive. The *y*-values include all numbers between −6 and 6, inclusive. Using interval notation, the domain is [−4, 4] and the range is [−6, 6].

(c) The arrowheads indicate that the line extends indefinitely left and right, as well as up and down. Therefore, both the domain and the range are the set of all real numbers, written (−∞, ∞).

(d) The arrowheads indicate that the graph extends indefinitely left and right, as well as upward. The domain is (−∞, ∞). Because there is a least *y*-value, −3, the range includes all real numbers greater than or equal to −3, written [−3, ∞).   ▮▮▮

We have seen that relations can be defined by equations, such as $y = 2x + 3$ and $y^2 = x$. It is sometimes necessary to determine the domain of a relation from its equation. In this book, the following agreement on the domain of a relation is assumed.

Agreement on Domain

The domain of a relation is assumed to be all real numbers that produce real numbers when substituted for the independent variable.

To illustrate this agreement, because any real number can be used as a replacement for *x* in $y = 2x + 3$, the domain of this function is the set of real numbers. The function defined by $y = \frac{1}{x}$ has all real numbers except 0 as domain, because *y* is undefined only if $x = 0$. And $g(x) = \sqrt{x}$ has a domain of all nonnegative numbers, since the square root of a negative number is not real.

In general, the domain of a function defined by an algebraic expression is all real numbers, except those numbers that lead to division by 0 or an even root of a negative number.

Graphs of Functions

Most of the relations we have seen in the examples are functions—that is, each *x*-value corresponds to exactly one *y*-value. Now we look at ways to determine whether a given relation, defined algebraically, is a function.

When *y* is a function of *x*, each value of *x* leads to only one value of *y*. Thus, any vertical line in the coordinate plane must intersect the graph in at most one point. This is the **vertical line test for a function.**

Vertical Line Test

If a vertical line intersects the graph of a relation in more than one point, then the relation is not a function.

For example, in the graph shown in **Figure 27(a)** *y* is not a function of *x*, since a vertical line can intersect the graph in more than one point. In **Figure 27(b)**, *y* is a function of *x*.

The vertical line test is a simple method for identifying a function defined by a graph. It is more difficult to decide whether a relation defined by an equation represents *y* as a function of *x*.

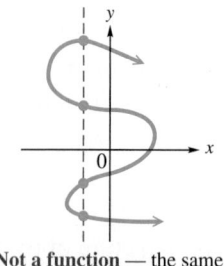

Not a function — the same
x-value corresponds to
four different *y*-values

(a)

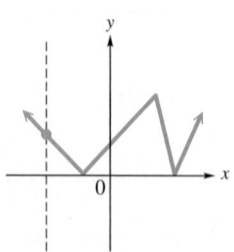

Function — each
x-value corresponds to
only one *y*-value

(b)

Figure 27

▐▐ **EXAMPLE 4** Determining Whether a Relation is a Function

Decide whether each equation defines a function, and give the domain.

(a) $y = x + 4$ **(b)** $y = \sqrt{2x - 1}$ **(c)** $y^2 = x$

(d) $y \leq x - 1$ **(e)** $y = \dfrac{5}{x - 1}$

SOLUTION

(a) In the defining equation, $y = x + 4$, y is always found by adding 4 to x. Thus, each value of x corresponds to just one value of y and the equation defines a function; x can be any real number, so the domain is $(-\infty, \infty)$.

(b) In the equation $y = \sqrt{2x-1}$, for any choice of x in the domain, there is exactly one corresponding value for y (the radical is a nonnegative number). Thus, this equation defines a function. Because the radicand cannot be negative, we must have $2x - 1 \geq 0$.

$$2x - 1 \geq 0$$
$$2x \geq 1 \quad \text{Add 1.}$$
$$x \geq \frac{1}{2} \quad \text{Divide by 2.}$$

The domain is $\left[\frac{1}{2}, \infty\right)$.

(c) The ordered pairs $(16, 4)$ and $(16, -4)$ both satisfy this equation. Since one value of x, 16, corresponds to two values of y, 4 and -4, this equation does not define a function. Because x is equal to the square of y, the values of x must always be nonnegative. The domain of the relation is $[0, \infty)$.

(d) By definition, y is a function of x if every value of x leads to exactly one value of y. In the inequality $y \leq x - 1$, a particular value of x, say 1, corresponds to many values of y. The ordered pairs $(1, 0)$, $(1, -1)$, $(1, -2)$, $(1, -3)$, and so on, all satisfy the inequality. For this reason, the inequality does not define a function. Any number can be used for x, so the domain is the set of real numbers $(-\infty, \infty)$.

(e) For the equation $y = \frac{5}{x - 1}$, given any value of x in the domain, we find y by subtracting 1, then dividing the result into 5. This process produces exactly one value of y for each value in the domain, so this equation defines a function.

The domain includes all real numbers except those that make the denominator 0. We find these numbers by setting the denominator equal to 0 and solving for x.

$$x - 1 = 0$$
$$x = 1 \quad \text{Add 1.}$$

Thus, the domain includes all real numbers *except* 1, written $(-\infty, 1) \cup (1, \infty)$. ▮▮▮

In summary, three variations of the definition of function are now given.

Variations of the Definition of Function

1. A **function** is a relation in which, for each value of the first component of the ordered pairs, there is exactly one value of the second component.

2. A **function** is a set of distinct ordered pairs in which no first component is repeated.

3. A **function** is a rule or correspondence that assigns exactly one range value to each distinct domain value.

Function Notation

When a function f is defined with a rule or an equation using x and y for the independent and dependent variables, we say "y is a function of x" to emphasize that y *depends on x.* For a function f, we use the notation

$$y = f(x),$$

called **function notation,** to express this and read $f(x)$ as "f of x." (In this notation the parentheses do not indicate multiplication.) For example, in function f, if $y = 2x - 7$, we write

> Do not read $f(x)$ as "f times x."

$f(x) = 2x - 7.$

Note that $f(x)$ is just another name for the dependent variable y. For example, if $y = f(x) = 9x - 5$, and $x = 2$, then we find y, or $f(2)$, by replacing x with 2.

$$y = f(2)$$
$$y = 9 \cdot 2 - 5$$
$$= 13$$

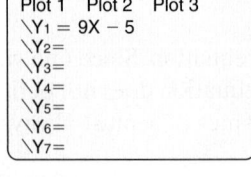

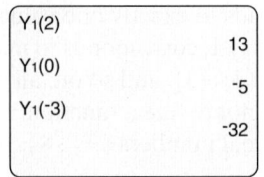

For $Y_1 = 9X - 5$, function notation capability of the TI-83/84 Plus supports the discussion here.

The statement "if $x = 2$, then $y = 13$" is written with function notation for f as

$$f(2) = 13.$$

Read $f(2)$ as "f of 2" or "f at 2." Also,

$$f(0) = 9 \cdot 0 - 5 = -5, \quad \text{and} \quad f(-3) = 9(-3) - 5 = -32.$$

These ideas and the symbols used to represent them can be explained as follows.

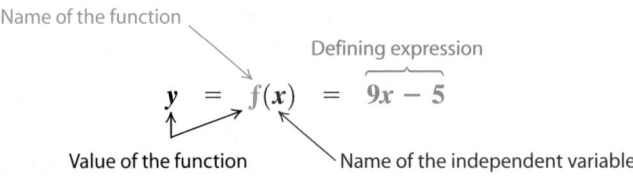

Name of the function

Defining expression

$$y \;=\; f(x) \;=\; 9x - 5$$

Value of the function

Name of the independent variable

▌▌ **EXAMPLE 5** Using Function Notation

Let $f(x) = -x^2 + 5x - 3$. Find the following.

(a) $f(2)$ **(b)** $f(-1)$ **(c)** $f(2x)$

SOLUTION

(a) $f(x) = -x^2 + 5x - 3$

$f(2) = -2^2 + 5 \cdot 2 - 3$ Replace x with 2.

> -2^2 means $-(2^2) = -4$.

$= -4 + 10 - 3$ Apply the exponent. Multiply.

$= 3$ Add and subtract.

(b) $f(-1) = -(-1)^2 + 5(-1) - 3$ Replace x with -1.

$= -1 - 5 - 3$ $-(-1)^2 = -(-1)(-1) = -1$

$= -9$ Subtract.

(c) $f(2x) = -(2x)^2 + 5(2x) - 3$ Replace x with $2x$.

$= -4x^2 + 10x - 3$ $-(2x)^2 = -2^2x^2 = -4x^2$

▌▌▌

Linear Functions

> **Linear Function**
>
> A function that can be written in the form
>
> $$f(x) = ax + b$$
>
> for real numbers a and b is a **linear function.**

Notice that the form $f(x) = ax + b$ defining a linear function is the same as that of the slope-intercept form of the equation of a line with a representing the slope. We know that the graph of $f(x) = ax + b$ will be a line with slope a and y-intercept $(0, b)$.

▮▮ **EXAMPLE 6** Graphing Linear Functions

Graph each linear function.

(a) $f(x) = -2x + 3$ **(b)** $f(x) = 3$

SOLUTION

(a) To graph the function, locate the y-intercept, $(0, 3)$. From this point, use the slope $-2 = \frac{-2}{1}$ to move down 2 and right 1. This second point is used to obtain the graph in **Figure 28**.

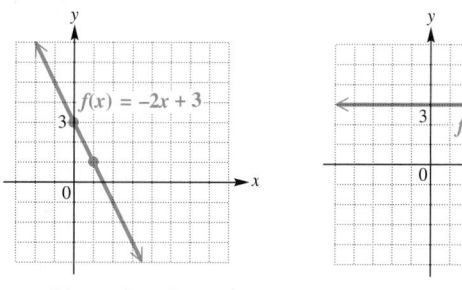

Linear function	Constant function
Figure 28	**Figure 29**

(b) From the previous section, we know that the graph of $y = 3$ is a horizontal line. Therefore, the graph of $f(x) = 3$ is a horizontal line with y-intercept $(0, 3)$ as shown in **Figure 29**. ▮▮▮

The function defined in **Example 6(b)** and graphed in **Figure 29** is an example of a constant function. A **constant function** is a linear function of the form

$$f(x) = b,$$

where b is a real number. The domain of any linear function is $(-\infty, \infty)$. The range of a nonconstant linear function (like in **Example 6(a)**) is also $(-\infty, \infty)$, while the range of the constant function $f(x) = b$ is $\{b\}$.

Break-Even Analysis

A company's cost of producing a product and the revenue from selling the product can be expressed as linear functions. The idea of **break-even analysis** then can be explained using the graphs of these functions.

1. When cost is greater than revenue earned, the company loses money.
2. When cost is less than revenue, the company makes money.
3. When cost equals revenue, the company breaks even.

Answer to the Gasoline Pumping question on page 388 Divide the sale amount by the number of gallons to find that the price per gallon is that of diesel fuel.

▮▮ **EXAMPLE 7** Analyzing Cost, Revenue, and Profit

Peripheral Visions, Inc., produces studio-quality DVDs of live concerts. The company places an ad in a trade newsletter. The cost of the ad is $100. Each DVD costs $20 to produce, and the company charges $24 per disk.

(a) Express the cost C as a function of x, the number of DVDs produced and sold.

(b) Express the revenue R as a function of x, the number of DVDs sold.

(c) When will the company break even? That is, for what value of x does revenue equal cost?

(d) Graph the cost and revenue functions on the same coordinate system, and interpret the graph.

SOLUTION

(a) The **fixed cost** is $100, and for each DVD produced, the **variable cost** is $20. Therefore, the cost C can be expressed as a function of x, the number of DVDs produced.

$$C(x) = 20x + 100 \quad (C \text{ in dollars})$$

(b) Each DVD sells for $24, so the revenue R is given by

$$R(x) = 24x \quad (R \text{ in dollars}).$$

(c) The company will just break even (no profit and no loss) if revenue just equals cost, or $R(x) = C(x)$. Solve this equation for x.

$$R(x) = C(x)$$
$$24x = 20x + 100 \quad \text{Substitute for } R(x) \text{ and } C(x).$$
$$4x = 100 \quad \text{Subtract 20x.}$$
$$x = 25 \quad \text{Divide by 4.}$$

If 25 DVDs are produced and sold, the company will break even.

(d) **Figure 30** shows the graphs of the two functions. At the break-even point, we see that when 25 DVDs are produced and sold, both the cost and the revenue are $600. If fewer than 25 DVDs are produced and sold (that is, when $x < 25$), the company loses money. When more than 25 DVDs are produced and sold (that is, when $x > 25$), there is a profit.

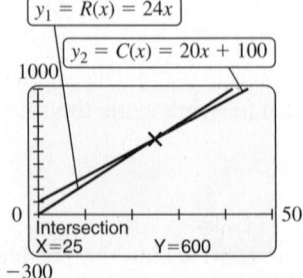

The break-even point is (25, 600), as indicated at the bottom of the screen. The calculator can find the point of intersection of the graphs. Compare with **Figure 30**.

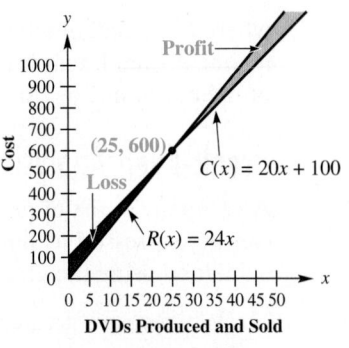

Figure 30

▮▮▮

8.4 EXERCISES

1. Define *function* and give an example.

2. Define *domain of a function* and give an example.

In Exercises 3–14, for each relation, decide whether it is a function, and give the domain and range.

3. $\{(0, 0), (1, 1), (2, 4), (4, 16)\}$

4. $\{(2, 5), (3, 7), (4, 9), (5, 11)\}$

5. $\{(1, 1), (1, -1), (2, 4), (2, -4), (3, 9), (3, -9)\}$

6. The set containing certain countries and their predicted life expectancy estimates for persons born in 2050 is $\{$(United States, 83.90), (Japan, 90.91), (Canada, 85.26), (Britain, 83.79), (France, 87.01), (Germany, 83.12), (Italy, 82.26)$\}$. (*Source*: Shripad Tuljapurkar, Mountain View Research, Los Altos, California.)

7. An input–output machine accepts positive real numbers as input, and outputs both their positive and negative square roots.

8.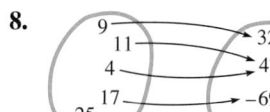

9. **U.S. Voting-Age Population (in millions)**

Hispanic	21.3
Native American	1.6
Asian American	8.2
African American	24.6
White	152.0

Source: U.S. Bureau of the Census.

10. $\{(x, y) \mid x = |y|\}$

11.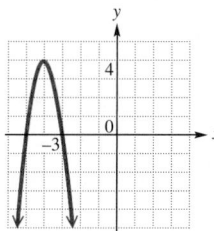

12.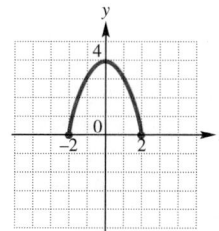

13.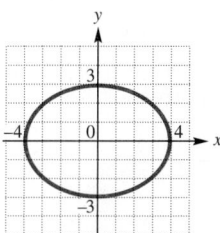

14.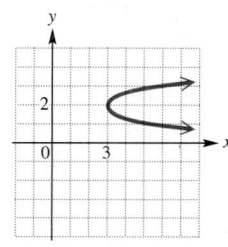

Decide whether the given relation defines y as a function of x. Give the domain.

15. $y = x^2$

16. $y = x^3$

17. $x = y^2$

18. $x = y^4$

19. $x + y < 4$

20. $x - y < 3$

21. $y = \sqrt{x}$

22. $y = -\sqrt{x}$

23. $y = \dfrac{1}{x}$

24. $y = \dfrac{-3}{x}$

25. $y = \sqrt{4x + 2}$

26. $y = \sqrt{9 - 2x}$

27. $y = \dfrac{2}{x - 2}$

28. $y = \dfrac{-7}{x - 7}$

29. **Pool Water Level** Refer to **Example 1, Figure 25**, to answer the questions.

   (a) What interval describes values of the dependent variable?

   (b) For how long is the water level increasing? Decreasing?

   (c) How many gallons are present after 90 hours?

   (d) Call this function g. What is $g(0)$? What does this mean in this example?

30. **Electricity Consumption** The graph shows the megawatts of electricity used on a record-breaking summer day in Sacramento, California.

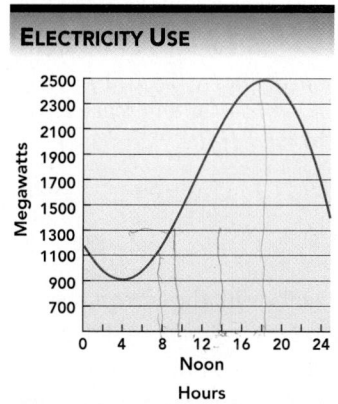

ELECTRICITY USE

Source: **Sacramento Municipal Utility District.**

   (a) Is this the graph of a function?

   (b) What is the domain?

   (c) Estimate the number of megawatts of electricity use at 8 A.M.

   (d) At what time was the most electricity used? The least electricity?

   (e) At about what time was electricity use 1300 megawatts?

31. Give an example of a function from everyday life. (*Hint:* Fill in the blanks: _____ depends on _____, so _____ is a function of _____.)

32. Choose the correct response: The notation $f(3)$ means
  A. the variable f times 3, or $3f$.
  B. the value of the dependent variable when the independent variable is 3.
  C. the value of the independent variable when the dependent variable is 3.
  D. f equals 3.

Let $f(x) = 3 + 2x$ and $g(x) = x^2 - 2$. Find each function value.

33. $f(1)$ **34.** $f(4)$ **35.** $g(2)$

36. $g(0)$ **37.** $g(-1)$ **38.** $g(-3)$

39. $f(-8)$ **40.** $f(-5)$ **41.** $f(0)$

42. $g(0)$ **43.** $f\left(-\dfrac{3}{2}\right)$ **44.** $g(\sqrt{2})$

Sketch the graph of each linear function. Give the domain and range.

45. $f(x) = -2x + 5$ **46.** $g(x) = 4x - 1$

47. $h(x) = \dfrac{1}{2}x + 2$ **48.** $F(x) = -\dfrac{1}{4}x + 1$

49. $G(x) = 2x$ **50.** $H(x) = -3x$

51. $f(x) = 5$ **52.** $g(x) = -4$

An equation that defines y as a function f of x is given.
(a) *Solve for y in terms of x, and replace y with the function notation f(x).* **(b)** *Find $f(3)$.*

53. $y + 2x^2 = 3$ **54.** $y - 3x^2 = 2$

55. $4x - 3y = 8$ **56.** $-2x + 5y = 9$

57. Fill in the blanks with the correct responses:
The equation $2x + y = 4$ has a straight _____ as its graph. One point that lies on the line is $(3, \underline{\quad})$. If we solve the equation for y and use function notation, we have a linear function $f(x) = \underline{\qquad}$. For this function, $f(3) = \underline{\quad}$, meaning that the point $(\underline{\quad}, \underline{\quad})$ lies on the graph of the function.

58. Which one of the following defines a linear function?

  A. $y = \dfrac{x - 5}{4}$ **B.** $y = \dfrac{1}{x}$

  C. $y = x^2$ **D.** $y = \sqrt{x}$

59. *Taxi Fares*
  (a) Suppose that a taxicab driver charges $2.50 per mile. Fill in the chart with the correct response for the price $f(x)$ she charges for a trip of x miles.

x	$f(x)$
0	
1	
2	
3	

  (b) The linear function that gives a rule for the amount charged is $f(x) =$ _____.
  (c) Graph this function for the domain $\{0, 1, 2, 3\}$.

60. *Cost to Mail a Package* A package weighing x pounds costs $f(x)$ dollars to mail to a given location, where
$$f(x) = 2.75x.$$

  (a) Evaluate $f(3)$.
  (b) Describe what 3 and the value $f(3)$ mean in part (a), using the terminology *independent variable* and *dependent variable*.
  (c) How much would it cost to mail a 5-lb package? Write the answer using function notation.

61. *Forensic Studies* Forensic scientists use the lengths of the tibia (t), the bone from the ankle to the knee, and the femur (r), the bone from the knee to the hip socket, to calculate the height of a person. A person's height (h) is determined from the lengths of these bones using functions defined by the following formulas. All measurements are in centimeters.

For men:	*For women:*
$h(r) = 69.09 + 2.24r$	$h(r) = 61.41 + 2.32r$
or $h(t) = 81.69 + 2.39t$	or $h(t) = 72.57 + 2.53t$

  (a) Find the height of a man with a femur measuring 56 centimeters.
  (b) Find the height of a man with a tibia measuring 40 centimeters.
  (c) Find the height of a woman with a femur measuring 50 centimeters.
  (d) Find the height of a woman with a tibia measuring 36 centimeters.

62. *Pool Size for Sea Otters* Federal regulations set standards for the size of the quarters of marine mammals. A pool to house sea otters must have a volume of "the square of the sea otter's average adult length (in meters) multiplied by 3.14 and by 0.91 meter." If x represents the sea otter's average adult length and $f(x)$ represents the volume of the corresponding pool size, this formula can be written as
$$f(x) = (0.91)(3.14)x^2.$$

Find the volume of the pool for each of the following adult lengths (in meters). Round answers to the nearest hundredth.

(a) 0.8   **(b)** 1.0

(c) 1.2   **(d)** 1.5

63. **Speeding Fines** Suppose that speeding fines are determined by the linear function

$$f(x) = 10(x - 65) + 50, \quad x > 65,$$

where $f(x)$ is the cost in dollars of the fine if a person is caught driving x miles per hour.

(a) Radar clocked a driver at 76 mph. How much was the fine?

(b) While balancing his checkbook, Johnny ran across a canceled check that his wife Gwen had written to the Department of Motor Vehicles for a speeding fine. The check was written for $100. How fast was Gwen driving?

(c) At what whole-number speed are tickets first given?

(d) For what speeds is the fine greater than $200?

64. **Expansion and Contraction of Gases** In 1787, Jacques Charles noticed that gases expand when heated and contract when cooled. Suppose that a particular gas follows the model

$$f(x) = \frac{5}{3}x + 455,$$

where x is the temperature in Celsius and $f(x)$ is the volume in cubic centimeters. (*Source*: Bushaw, D., et al., *A Sourcebook of Applications of School Mathematics*, MAA, 1980. Reprinted with permission.)

(a) Find the volume when the temperature is 27°C.

(b) What is the temperature when the volume is 605 cubic centimeters?

(c) Determine what temperature gives a volume of 0 cubic centimeters (that is, absolute zero, or the coldest possible temperature).

Cost and Revenue Models In Exercises 65–68, do the following.

(a) Express the cost C as a function of x, where x represents the quantity of items as given.

(b) Express the revenue R as a function of x.

(c) Determine the value of x for which revenue equals cost.

(d) Graph the equations

$$y = C(x) \quad and \quad y = R(x)$$

on the same axes, and interpret the graph.

65. Perian Herring stuffs envelopes for extra income during her spare time. Her initial cost to obtain the necessary information for the job was $200.00. Each envelope costs $0.02 and she gets paid $0.04 per envelope stuffed. Let x represent the number of envelopes stuffed.

66. Bart Stewart runs a copying service in his home. He paid $3500 for the copier and a lifetime service contract. Each sheet of paper he uses costs $0.01, and he gets paid $0.05 per copy he makes. Let x represent the number of copies he makes.

67. Frank Sesso operates a delivery service in a southern city. His start-up costs amounted to $2300. He estimates that it costs him (in terms of gasoline, wear and tear on his car, etc.) $3.00 per delivery. He charges $5.50 per delivery. Let x represent the number of deliveries he makes.

68. Jane Major bakes cakes and sells them at Louisiana parish fairs. Her initial cost for the Pointe Coupee Parish fair this year was $40.00. She figures that each cake costs $2.50 to make, and she charges $6.50 per cake. Let x represent the number of cakes sold. (Assume that there were no cakes left over.)

8.5 QUADRATIC FUNCTIONS, GRAPHS, AND MODELS

Quadratic Functions and Parabolas • Graphs of Quadratic Functions • Vertex of a Parabola • General Graphing Guidelines • A Model for Optimization

Quadratic Functions and Parabolas

We now look at *quadratic functions*, those defined by second-degree polynomials.

Quadratic Function

A function f is a **quadratic function** if

$$f(x) = ax^2 + bx + c,$$

where a, b, and c are real numbers, with $a \neq 0$.

The simplest quadratic function is defined by $f(x) = x^2$. Plotting the points in the table below and drawing a smooth curve through them gives the graph in **Figure 31**. This graph is called a **parabola.** Every quadratic function has a graph that is a parabola.

Parabolas are symmetric about a line (the y-axis in **Figure 31**). The line of symmetry for a parabola is called the **axis** of the parabola. The point where the axis intersects the parabola is the **vertex** of the parabola. The vertex is the lowest (or highest) point of a vertical parabola.

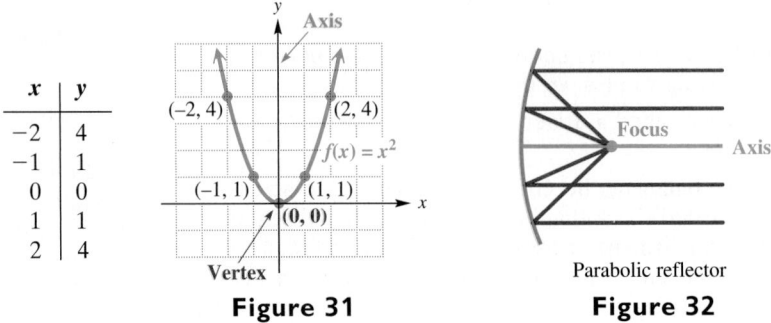

Figure 31	Figure 32

The **focus** of a parabola is a point on its axis that determines the curvature. See **Figure 32**. When the parabolic reflector of a solar oven is aimed at the sun, the light rays bounce off the reflector and collect at the focus, creating intense heat at that point.

Graphs of Quadratic Functions

The first example shows how the constant a affects the graph of a function of the form $g(x) = ax^2$.

▮▮ **EXAMPLE 1** Graphing Quadratic Functions $\left(g(x) = ax^2\right)$

Graph the functions defined as follows. Compare with the graph of $f(x) = x^2$.

(a) $g(x) = -x^2$　　**(b)** $g(x) = \dfrac{1}{2}x^2$

SOLUTION

(a) For a given value of x, the corresponding value of $g(x)$ will be the negative of what it was for $f(x) = x^2$. (See the table of values with **Figure 33**.) Because of this, the graph of $g(x) = -x^2$ is the same shape as that of $f(x) = x^2$, but opens downward, as in **Figure 33**. *In general, the graph of $f(x) = ax^2 + bx + c$ opens downward whenever $a < 0$.*

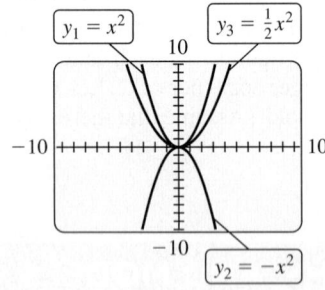

The screen illustrates the three graphs considered in **Example 1** and **Figures 33** and **34**.

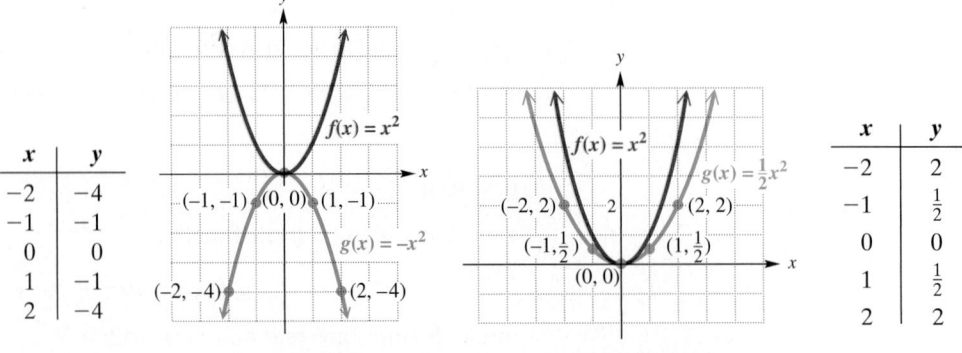

Figure 33	Figure 34

(b) Choose a value of x, and then find $g(x)$. The coefficient $\frac{1}{2}$ will cause the resulting value of $g(x)$ to be less than that of $f(x) = x^2$, making the parabola wider than the graph of $f(x) = x^2$. See **Figure 34**. In both parabolas of this example, the axis is the vertical line $x = 0$ and the vertex is the origin $(0, 0)$.   ▮▮▮

Vertical and horizontal shifts of the graph of $f(x) = x^2$ are called **translations.**

▮▮ **EXAMPLE 2** Graphing a Quadratic Function (Vertical Shift)

Graph $g(x) = x^2 - 4$. Compare with the graph of $f(x) = x^2$.

SOLUTION

By comparing the tables of values for $g(x) = x^2 - 4$ and $f(x) = x^2$ shown with **Figure 35**, we can see that for corresponding x-values, the y-values of g are each 4 less than those for f. This leads to a *vertical shift*. Thus, the graph of $g(x) = x^2 - 4$ is the same as that of $f(x) = x^2$, but translated 4 units down. See **Figure 35**. The vertex of this parabola (here the lowest point) is at $(0, -4)$. The axis of the parabola is the vertical line $x = 0$.

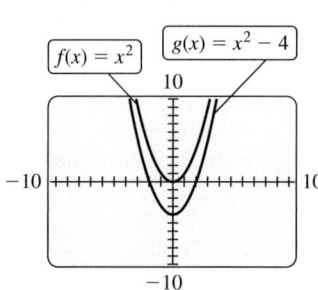

Compare with **Figure 35**.

$f(x) = x^2$

x	y
-2	4
-1	1
0	0
1	1
2	4

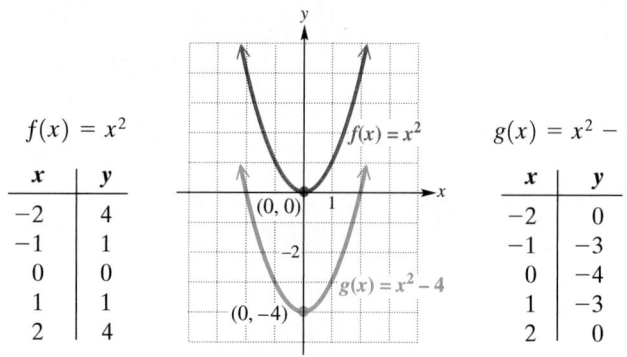

Figure 35   ▮▮▮

$g(x) = x^2 - 4$

x	y
-2	0
-1	-3
0	-4
1	-3
2	0

▮▮ **EXAMPLE 3** Graphing a Quadratic Function (Horizontal Shift)

Graph $g(x) = (x - 4)^2$. Compare with the graph of $f(x) = x^2$.

SOLUTION

Comparing the tables of values shown with **Figure 36** shows that the graph of $g(x) = (x - 4)^2$ is the same as that of $f(x) = x^2$, but translated 4 units to the right. This is a *horizontal shift*. The vertex is at $(4, 0)$. As shown in **Figure 36**, the axis of this parabola is the vertical line $x = 4$.

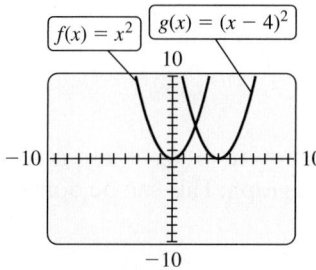

Compare with **Figure 36**.

$f(x) = x^2$

x	y
-2	4
-1	1
0	0
1	1
2	4

Figure 36   ▮▮▮

$g(x) = (x - 4)^2$

x	y
2	4
3	1
4	0
5	1
6	4

Errors frequently occur when horizontal shifts are involved. To determine the direction and magnitude of horizontal shifts, find the value of x that would cause the expression $x - h$ to equal 0. For example, the graph of

$$f(x) = (x - 5)^2 \quad \text{would be shifted 5 units to the } \textit{right,}$$

because $x = +5$ would cause $x - 5$ to equal 0. On the other hand, the graph of

$$f(x) = (x + 4)^2 \quad \text{would be shifted 4 units to the } \textit{left,}$$

because $x = -4$ would cause $x + 4$ to equal 0.

The following general principles apply for graphing functions of the form $f(x) = a(x - h)^2 + k$.

General Principles for Graphs of Quadratic Functions

1. The graph of the quadratic function defined by

$$f(x) = a(x - h)^2 + k, \quad a \neq 0,$$

is a parabola with vertex (h, k), and the vertical line $x = h$ as axis.

2. The graph opens upward if a is positive and downward if a is negative.

3. The graph is wider than that of $f(x) = x^2$ if $0 < |a| < 1$. The graph is narrower than that of $f(x) = x^2$ if $|a| > 1$.

▮▮ **EXAMPLE 4** Graphing a Quadratic Function Using General Principles

Graph $f(x) = -2(x + 3)^2 + 4$.

SOLUTION

The parabola opens downward (because $a < 0$), and is narrower than the graph of $f(x) = x^2$, since $a = -2$, and $|-2| > 1$. This parabola has vertex at $(-3, 4)$, as shown in **Figure 37**. To complete the graph, we plotted the additional ordered pairs $(-4, 2)$ and $(-2, 2)$.

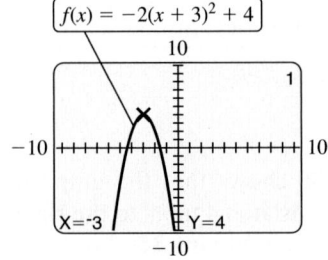

Compare with **Figure 37**. The vertex is $(-3, 4)$.

x	y
-4	2
-3	4
-2	2

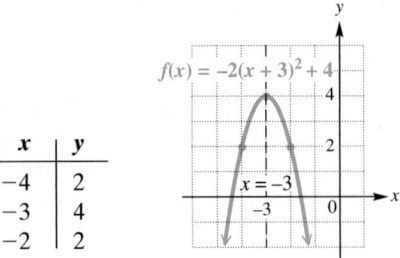

Figure 37   ▮▮▮

Vertex of a Parabola

When the equation of a parabola is given in the form $f(x) = ax^2 + bx + c$, it is necessary to locate the vertex in order to sketch an accurate graph. This can be done in two ways.

1. By completing the square (**Example 5**)

2. By using a formula which can be derived by completing the square (**Example 6**)

▌▌ **EXAMPLE 5** Finding the Vertex by Completing the Square

Find the vertex of the graph of $f(x) = x^2 - 4x + 5$.

SOLUTION

To find the vertex, we need to express $x^2 - 4x + 5$ in the form $(x - h)^2 + k$. This is done by completing the square. (See **pages 350 and 366.**) To simplify the notation, replace $f(x)$ with y.

$$y = x^2 - 4x + 5 \quad \text{Let } y = f(x).$$

$$y - 5 = x^2 - 4x \quad\quad\quad\quad \text{Transform so that the constant term is on the left.}$$

$$y - 5 + 4 = x^2 - 4x + 4 \quad \text{Half of } -4 \text{ is } -2; (-2)^2 = 4. \text{ Add 4 to both sides.}$$

$$y - 1 = (x - 2)^2 \quad\quad\quad \text{Combine terms on the left and factor on the right.}$$

$$y = (x - 2)^2 + 1 \quad \text{Add 1 to both sides.}$$

Now write the original equation as $f(x) = (x - 2)^2 + 1$. As shown earlier, the vertex of this parabola is $(2, 1)$. ▮▮▮

A formula for the vertex of the graph of the quadratic function $y = ax^2 + bx + c$ can be found by completing the square for the general form of the equation. In doing so, we begin by dividing by a, since the coefficient of x^2 must be 1.

$$y = ax^2 + bx + c \quad (a \neq 0)$$

$$\frac{y}{a} = x^2 + \frac{b}{a}x + \frac{c}{a} \quad\quad\quad\quad\quad \text{Divide by } a.$$

$$\frac{y}{a} - \frac{c}{a} = x^2 + \frac{b}{a}x \quad\quad\quad\quad\quad \text{Subtract } \frac{c}{a}.$$

$$\frac{y}{a} - \frac{c}{a} + \frac{b^2}{4a^2} = x^2 + \frac{b}{a}x + \frac{b^2}{4a^2} \quad \text{Add } \left(\frac{1}{2} \cdot \frac{b}{a}\right)^2 = \frac{b^2}{4a^2}.$$

$$\frac{y}{a} + \frac{b^2 - 4ac}{4a^2} = \left(x + \frac{b}{2a}\right)^2 \quad \begin{array}{l}\text{Combine terms on the left}\\\text{and factor on the right.}\end{array}$$

$$\frac{y}{a} = \left(x + \frac{b}{2a}\right)^2 - \frac{b^2 - 4ac}{4a^2} \quad \begin{array}{l}\text{Transform so that the}\\ y\text{-term is alone on the left.}\end{array}$$

$$y = a\left(x + \frac{b}{2a}\right)^2 + \frac{4ac - b^2}{4a} \quad \text{Multiply by } a.$$

$$y = a\underbrace{\left[x - \left(-\frac{b}{2a}\right)\right]}_{h}^2 + \underbrace{\frac{4ac - b^2}{4a}}_{k} \quad \begin{array}{l}\text{Write addition as subtraction}\\\text{of the opposite.}\end{array}$$

The final equation shows that the vertex (h, k) can be expressed in terms of a, b, and c. However, it is not necessary to memorize the expression for k, because it can be obtained by replacing x with $-\frac{b}{2a}$.

Vertex Formula

The vertex of the graph of $f(x) = ax^2 + bx + c \ (a \neq 0)$ has these coordinates.

$$\left(-\frac{b}{2a}, \ f\left(-\frac{b}{2a}\right)\right)$$

The trajectory of a shell fired from a cannon is a **parabola.** To reach the maximum range with a cannon, it is shown in calculus that the muzzle must be set at 45°. If the muzzle is elevated above 45°, the shell goes too high and falls too soon. If the muzzle is set below 45°, the shell is rapidly pulled to Earth by gravity.

Johann Kepler (1571–1630) established the importance of a curve called an **ellipse** in 1609, when he discovered that the orbits of the planets around the sun were elliptical, not circular. The orbit of Halley's comet, shown here, also is elliptical.

See **For Further Thought** at the end of this section for more on ellipses.

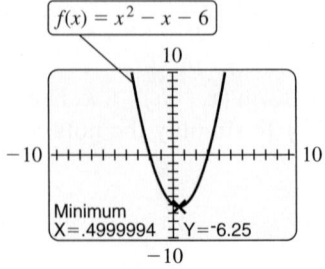

$f(x) = x^2 - x - 6$

Notice the slight discrepancy when we instruct the calculator to find the vertex (a *minimum* here). This reinforces the fact that **we must understand the concepts and not totally rely on technology!**

◼◼ **EXAMPLE 6** Finding the Vertex by Using the Formula

Use the vertex formula to find the vertex of the graph of the function

$$f(x) = x^2 - x - 6.$$

SOLUTION

For $f(x) = x^2 - x - 6$, or $1x^2 - 1x - 6$, the values are $a = 1$, $b = -1$, and $c = -6$. The x-coordinate of the vertex of the parabola is given by

$$-\frac{b}{2a} = -\frac{(-1)}{2(1)} = \frac{1}{2}.$$

The y-coordinate is $f\left(-\frac{b}{2a}\right) = f\left(\frac{1}{2}\right)$.

$$f\left(\frac{1}{2}\right) = \left(\frac{1}{2}\right)^2 - \frac{1}{2} - 6 = \frac{1}{4} - \frac{1}{2} - 6 = -\frac{25}{4}$$

Finally, the vertex is $\left(\frac{1}{2}, -\frac{25}{4}\right)$. ◼◼◼

General Graphing Guidelines

We now examine a general approach to graphing quadratic functions using intercepts and the vertex.

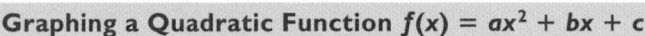

Graphing a Quadratic Function $f(x) = ax^2 + bx + c$

Step 1 **Decide whether the graph opens upward or downward.** Determine whether the graph opens upward (if $a > 0$) or opens downward (if $a < 0$) to aid in the graphing process.

Step 2 **Find the vertex.** Find the vertex either by using the formula or by completing the square.

Step 3 **Find the y-intercept.** Find the y-intercept by evaluating $f(0)$.

Step 4 **Find the x-intercepts.** Find the x-intercepts, if any, by solving $f(x) = 0$.

Step 5 **Complete the graph.** Find and plot additional points as needed, using the symmetry about the axis.

Galileo Galilei (1564–1642) died in the year Newton was born. His work was important in Newton's development of calculus. The idea of **function** is implicit in Galileo's analysis of the parabolic path of a projectile, where height and range are functions (in our terms) of the angle of elevation and the initial velocity.

According to legend, Galileo dropped objects of different weights from the tower of Pisa to disprove the Aristotelian view that heavier objects fall faster than lighter objects. He developed a formula for freely falling objects that is described by

$$d = 16t^2,$$

where d is the distance in feet that a given object falls (discounting air resistance) in a given time t, in seconds, regardless of weight.

◼◼ **EXAMPLE 7** Graphing a Quadratic Function Using General Guidelines

Graph the quadratic function $f(x) = x^2 - x - 6$.

SOLUTION

Step 1 From the equation, $a = 1 > 0$, so the graph of the function opens up.

Step 2 The vertex, $\left(\frac{1}{2}, -\frac{25}{4}\right)$, was found in **Example 6** using the vertex formula.

Step 3 To find the y-intercept, evaluate $f(0)$.

$$f(x) = x^2 - x - 6$$

$$f(0) = 0^2 - 0 - 6 \quad \text{Let } x = 0.$$

$$f(0) = -6 \quad \text{Simplify.}$$

The y-intercept is $(0, -6)$.

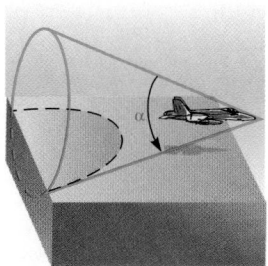

A sonic boom is a loud explosive sound caused by the shock wave that accompanies an aircraft traveling at supersonic speed. The sonic boom shock wave has the shape of a cone, and it intersects the ground in one branch of a curve known as a **hyperbola.** Everyone located along the hyperbolic curve on the ground hears the sound at the same time.

See **For Further Thought** on **page 406** for more on hyperbolas.

Step 4 Find any x-intercepts. Because the vertex $\left(\frac{1}{2}, -\frac{25}{4}\right)$ is in quadrant IV and the graph opens upward, there will be two x-intercepts. To find them, let $f(x) = 0$ and solve.

$$f(x) = x^2 - x - 6$$
$$0 = x^2 - x - 6 \qquad \text{Let } f(x) = 0.$$
$$0 = (x - 3)(x + 2) \qquad \text{Factor.}$$
$$x - 3 = 0 \quad \text{or} \quad x + 2 = 0 \qquad \text{Zero-factor property (Section 7.7)}$$
$$x = 3 \quad \text{or} \quad x = -2 \qquad \text{Solve for } x.$$

The x-intercepts are $(3, 0)$ and $(-2, 0)$.

Step 5 Plot the points found so far, and plot any additional points as needed. The symmetry of the graph is helpful here. The graph is shown in **Figure 38**.

x	y
-2	0
-1	-4
0	-6
$\frac{1}{2}$	$-\frac{25}{4}$
2	-4
3	0

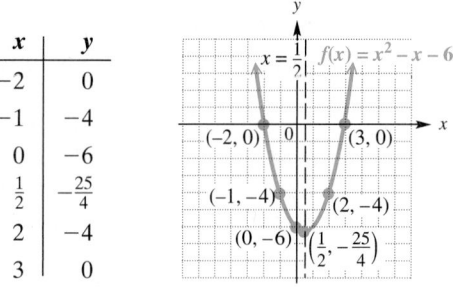

Figure 38 ▮▮▮

A Model for Optimization

As we have seen, the vertex of a vertical parabola is either the highest or the lowest point of the parabola. The y-value of the vertex gives the maximum or minimum value of y, while the x-value tells where that maximum or minimum occurs. Often a model can be constructed so that y can be *optimized*.

> **PROBLEM-SOLVING HINT** In some practical problems we want to know the least or greatest value of some quantity. When that quantity can be expressed using a quadratic function $f(x) = ax^2 + bx + c$, as in the next example, the vertex can be used to find the desired value.

▮▮ **EXAMPLE 8** Finding a Maximum Area

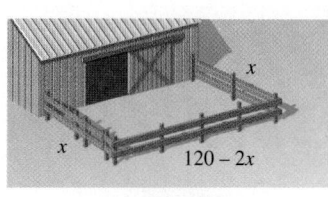

Figure 39

A farmer has 120 feet of fencing. He wants to put a fence around three sides of a rectangular plot of land, with the side of a barn forming the fourth side. Find the maximum area he can enclose. What dimensions give this area?

SOLUTION

Figure 39 shows the plot. Let x represent the width of the plot. Then, since there are 120 feet of fencing, we can represent the length in terms of x as follows.

$$x + x + \text{length} = 120 \qquad \text{Sum of the three fenced sides is 120 feet.}$$
$$2x + \text{length} = 120 \qquad \text{Combine terms.}$$
$$\text{length} = 120 - 2x \qquad \text{Subtract } 2x.$$

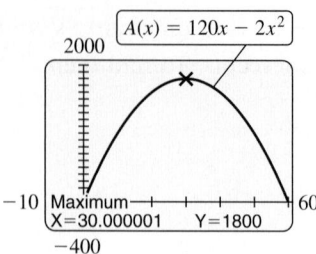

The vertex is (30, 1800), supporting the analytic result in **Example 8.**

The area $A(x)$ is modeled by the product of the length and width.

$$A(x) = (120 - 2x)x$$
$$= 120x - 2x^2$$

To make $120x - 2x^2$ (and thus the area) as large as possible, first find the vertex of the graph of the function $A(x) = 120x - 2x^2$.

$$A(x) = -2x^2 + 120x \quad \text{Standard form}$$

Here we have $a = -2$ and $b = 120$. The x-coordinate of the vertex is

$$-\frac{b}{2a} = -\frac{120}{2(-2)} = 30.$$

The vertex of the parabola is (**30**, **1800**). The vertex is a maximum point (since $a = -2 < 0$), so the maximum area that the farmer can enclose is

$$A(30) = -2(30)^2 + 120(30) = 1800 \quad \text{square feet.}$$

The farmer can enclose a maximum area of **1800** square feet, when the width of the plot is 30 feet and the length is $120 - 2(30) = 60$ feet. ■■■

Be careful when interpreting the meanings of the coordinates of the vertex in problems involving maximum or minimum values. The first coordinate, x, gives the value for which the *function value* is a maximum or a minimum. Read the problem carefully to determine whether you are asked to find the value of the independent variable, the dependent variable (that is, the function value), or both.

For Further Thought

The Conic Sections

The circle, introduced in the first section of this chapter, the parabola, the ellipse, and the hyperbola are known as **conic sections.** As seen in **Figure 40,** each of these geometric shapes can be obtained by intersecting a plane and an infinite cone (made up of two *nappes*).

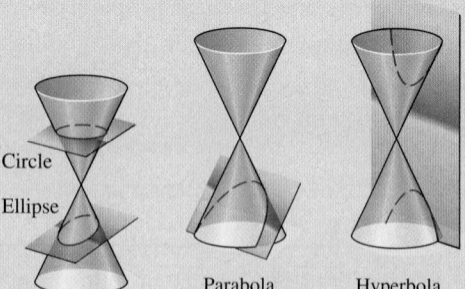

Figure 40

The Greek geometer Apollonius (c. 225 B.C.) was also an astronomer, and his classic work *Conic Sections* thoroughly investigated these figures. Apollonius is responsible for the names "ellipse," "parabola," and "hyperbola." The margin notes in this section show some ways that these figures appear in the world around us.

For Group or Individual Investigation

1. The terms *ellipse, parabola,* and *hyperbola* are similar to the terms *ellipsis, parable,* and *hyperbole.* What do these latter three terms mean? You might want to do some investigation as to the similarities between the mathematical terminology and these language-related terms.

2. Identify some places in the world around you where conic sections are encountered.

3. The accompanying photo shows how an ellipse can be drawn using tacks and string. Have a class member volunteer to go to the board and using string and chalk, modify the method to draw a circle. Then have two class members work together to draw an ellipse. (*Hint:* Press hard!)

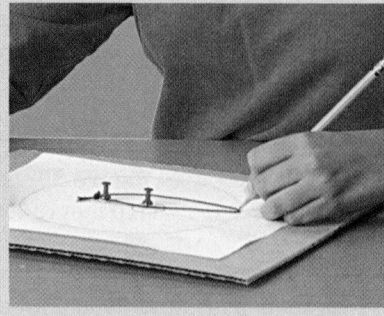

8.5 EXERCISES

In Exercises 1–6, match each equation with the figure in A–F that most closely resembles its graph.

A. 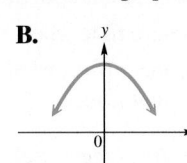   **B.** 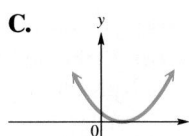   **C.**

D. 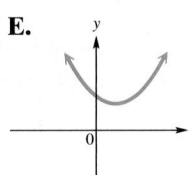   **E.** 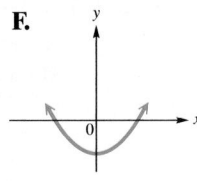   **F.**

1. $g(x) = x^2 - 5$

2. $h(x) = -x^2 + 4$

3. $F(x) = (x - 1)^2$

4. $G(x) = (x + 1)^2$

5. $H(x) = (x - 1)^2 + 1$

6. $K(x) = (x + 1)^2 + 1$

7. Explain in your own words the meaning of each term.
   (a) vertex of a parabola   **(b)** axis of a parabola.

8. Explain why the axis of the graph of a quadratic function cannot be a horizontal line.

Identify the vertex of the graph of each quadratic function.

9. $f(x) = -3x^2$

10. $f(x) = -0.5x^2$

11. $f(x) = x^2 + 4$

12. $f(x) = x^2 - 4$

13. $f(x) = (x - 1)^2$

14. $f(x) = (x + 3)^2$

15. $f(x) = (x + 3)^2 - 4$

16. $f(x) = (x - 5)^2 - 8$

17. Describe how the graph of each parabola in **Exercises 15 and 16** is shifted compared to the graph of $y = x^2$.

For each quadratic function, tell whether the graph opens upward or downward, and tell whether the graph is wider than, narrower than, or the same as the graph of $f(x) = x^2$.

18. $f(x) = -2x^2$

19. $f(x) = -3x^2 + 1$

20. $f(x) = 0.5x^2$

21. $f(x) = \frac{2}{3}x^2 - 4$

22. What does the value of a in $f(x) = a(x - h)^2 + k$ tell you about the graph of the function compared to the graph of $y = x^2$?

23. For $f(x) = a(x - h)^2 + k$, in what quadrant is the vertex if:
   (a) $h > 0, k > 0$;   **(b)** $h > 0, k < 0$;
   (c) $h < 0, k > 0$;   **(d)** $h < 0, k < 0$?

24. (a) What is the value of h if the graph of $f(x) = a(x - h)^2 + k$ has vertex on the y-axis?

   (b) What is the value of k if the graph of $f(x) = a(x - h)^2 + k$ has vertex on the x-axis?

Sketch the graph of each quadratic function using the methods described in this section. Indicate two points on each graph.

25. $f(x) = 3x^2$

26. $f(x) = -2x^2$

27. $f(x) = -\frac{1}{4}x^2$

28. $f(x) = \frac{1}{3}x^2$

29. $f(x) = x^2 - 1$

30. $f(x) = x^2 + 3$

31. $f(x) = -x^2 + 2$

32. $f(x) = -x^2 - 4$

33. $f(x) = 2x^2 - 2$

34. $f(x) = -3x^2 + 1$

35. $f(x) = (x - 4)^2$

36. $f(x) = (x - 3)^2$

37. $f(x) = 3(x + 1)^2$

38. $f(x) = -2(x + 1)^2$

39. $f(x) = (x + 1)^2 - 2$

40. $f(x) = (x - 2)^2 + 3$

Sketch the graph of each quadratic function. Indicate the coordinates of the vertex of the graph.

41. $f(x) = x^2 + 8x + 14$

42. $f(x) = x^2 + 10x + 23$

43. $f(x) = x^2 + 2x - 4$

44. $f(x) = 3x^2 - 9x + 8$

45. $f(x) = -2x^2 + 4x + 5$

46. $f(x) = -5x^2 - 10x + 2$

Solve each problem.

47. *Dimensions of an Exercise Run* Steve Stembridge has 100 meters of fencing material to enclose a rectangular exercise run for his dog. What width will give the enclosure the maximum area?

48. *Dimensions of a Parking Lot* Morgan's Department Store wants to construct a rectangular parking lot on land bordered on one side by a highway. It has 280 feet of fencing that is to be used to fence off the other three sides. What should be the dimensions of the lot if the enclosed area is to be a maximum? What is the maximum area?

49. *Height of a Projected Object* If an object on Earth is projected upward with an initial velocity of 32 feet per second, then its height after t seconds is given by

$$h(t) = -16t^2 + 32t.$$

Find the maximum height attained by the object and the number of seconds it takes to hit the ground.

50. *Height of a Projected Object* A projectile on Earth is fired straight upward so that its distance (in feet) above the ground *t* seconds after firing is given by

$$s(t) = -16t^2 + 400t.$$

Find the maximum height it reaches and the number of seconds it takes to reach that height.

51. *Height of a Projected Object* If air resistance is neglected, a projectile on Earth shot straight upward with an initial velocity of 40 meters per second will be at a height *s* in meters given by the function

$$s(t) = -4.9t^2 + 40t,$$

where *t* is the number of seconds elapsed after projection. After how many seconds will it reach its maximum height, and what is this maximum height? Round your answers to the nearest tenth.

52. *Height of a Projected Object* A space robot is projected from the moon with its height in feet given by

$$f(x) = -0.0013x^2 + 1.727x,$$

where *x* is time in seconds. Find the maximum height the robot can reach and the time it takes to get there. Round answers to the nearest tenth.

53. *Carbon Monoxide Exposure* Carbon monoxide (CO) combines with the hemoglobin of the blood to form carboxyhemoglobin (COHb), which reduces the transport of oxygen to tissues. Smokers routinely have a 4% to 6% COHb level in their blood, which can cause symptoms such as blood flow alterations, visual impairment, and poorer vigilance. The quadratic function defined by

$$T(x) = 0.00787x^2 - 1.528x + 75.89$$

approximates the exposure time in hours necessary to reach this 4% to 6% level, where $50 \le x \le 100$ is the amount of carbon monoxide present in the air in parts per million (ppm). (*Source: Indoor Air Quality Environmental Information Handbook: Combustion Sources,* U.S. Department of Energy.)

(a) A kerosene heater or a room full of smokers is capable of producing 50 ppm of carbon monoxide. How long would it take for a nonsmoking person to start feeling the symptoms mentioned?

(b) Find the carbon monoxide concentration necessary for a person to reach the 4% to 6% COHb level in 3 hours.

54. *Carbon Monoxide Exposure* Refer to **Exercise 53.** High concentrations of carbon monoxide (CO) can cause coma and death. The time required for a person to reach a COHb level capable of causing a coma can be approximated by

$$T(x) = 0.0002x^2 - 0.316x + 127.9.$$

T is the exposure time in hours necessary to reach that level and $500 \le x \le 800$ is the amount of carbon monoxide in parts per million (ppm). (*Source: Indoor Air Quality Environmental Information Handbook: Combustion Sources,* U.S. Department of Energy.)

(a) What is the exposure time when $x = 600$ ppm?

(b) Estimate the concentration of CO necessary to produce a coma in 4 hours.

55. *Automobile Stopping Distance* Selected values of the stopping distance *y* in feet of a car traveling *x* mph are given in the table.

Speed *x* (in mph)	Stopping Distance *y* (in feet)
20	46
30	87
40	140
50	240
60	282
70	371

Source: National Safety Institute Student Workbook.

The quadratic function defined by

$$f(x) = 0.056057x^2 + 1.06657x$$

is one model of the data. Find and interpret $f(45)$.

56. *Path of an Object on a Planet* When an object moves under the influence of constant force (without air resistance), its path is parabolic. This is the path of a ball thrown near the surface of a planet or other celestial object. Suppose two balls are simultaneously thrown upward at a 45° angle on two different planets. If their initial velocities are both 30 mph, then their *xy*-coordinates in feet can be expressed by the equation

$$y = x - \frac{g}{1922}x^2,$$

where *g* is the acceleration due to gravity. The value of *g* will vary with the mass and size of the planet. (*Source: Zeilik, M., S. Gregory, and E. Smith, Introductory Astronomy and Astrophysics,* Saunders College Publishers.)

On Earth, $g = 32.2$ and on Mars, $g = 12.6$. Find the two equations, and determine the difference in the horizontal distances traveled by the two balls.

8.6 EXPONENTIAL AND LOGARITHMIC FUNCTIONS, APPLICATIONS, AND MODELS

Exponential Functions and Applications • Logarithmic Functions and Applications • Exponential Models in Nature

Exponential Functions and Applications

In this section we introduce two new types of functions.

Exponential Function

An **exponential function** with base b, where $b > 0$ and $b \neq 1$, is a function f of the following form.

$$f(x) = b^x, \quad \text{where } x \text{ is any real number}$$

Notice that in the definition of exponential function, the base b is restricted to positive numbers, with $b \neq 1$.

Thus far, we have defined only integer exponents. In the definition of exponential function, we allow x to take on any real number value. By using methods not discussed in this book, expressions such as

$$2^{9/7}, \quad \left(\frac{1}{2}\right)^{1.5}, \quad \text{and} \quad 10^{\sqrt{3}}$$

can be approximated. A scientific or graphing calculator is capable of determining approximations for these numbers. See the screen in the margin.

The graphs of $f(x) = 2^x$, $g(x) = \left(\frac{1}{2}\right)^x$, and $h(x) = 10^x$ are shown in **Figure 41**. In each case, a table of selected points is given. The points are joined with a smooth curve. For each graph, the curve approaches but does not intersect the x-axis. For this reason, the x-axis is called the **horizontal asymptote** of the graph.

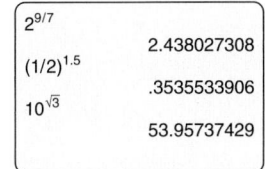

$2^{9/7}$	
$(1/2)^{1.5}$	2.438027308
$10^{\sqrt{3}}$	.3535533906
	53.95737429

Compare with the discussion in the text.

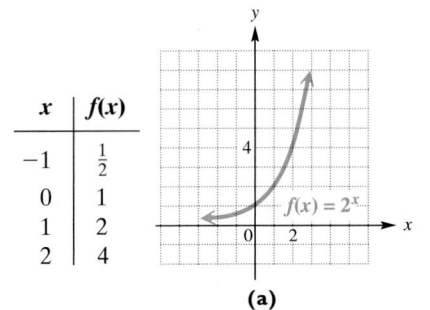

x	$f(x)$
-1	$\frac{1}{2}$
0	1
1	2
2	4

$f(x) = 2^x$

(a)

x	$g(x)$
-2	4
-1	2
0	1
1	$\frac{1}{2}$

$g(x) = \left(\frac{1}{2}\right)^x$

(b)

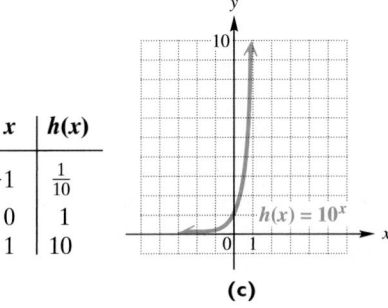

x	$h(x)$
-1	$\frac{1}{10}$
0	1
1	10

$h(x) = 10^x$

(c)

Figure 41

Characteristics of the Graph of $f(x) = b^x$

1. The graph always will contain the point $(0, 1)$, because $b^0 = 1$.

2. When $b > 1$, the graph will *rise* from left to right (as in **Figures 41(a) and (c)** above, with $b = 2$ and $b = 10$). When $0 < b < 1$, the graph will *fall* from left to right (as in **Figure 41(b)**, with $b = \frac{1}{2}$).

3. The x-axis is the horizontal asymptote.

4. The domain is $(-\infty, \infty)$ and the range is $(0, \infty)$.

Probably the most important exponential function has the base e. (See **Section 6.4.**) The number e is named after Leonhard Euler (1707–1783), and is approximately 2.718281828. It is an irrational number. As n gets larger without bound, the expression

$$\left(1 + \frac{1}{n}\right)^n \text{ approaches } e.$$

This is expressed as follows.

$$\text{As } n \to \infty, \quad \left(1 + \frac{1}{n}\right)^n \to e \approx 2.718281828.$$

See **Table 4**.

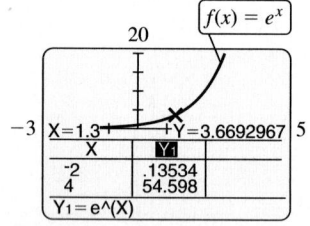

This table shows selected values for $Y_1 = \left(1 + \frac{1}{X}\right)^X$. Compare with **Table 4**.

Table 4

n	Approximate Value of $\left(1 + \dfrac{1}{n}\right)^n$
1	2
100	2.70481
1000	2.71692
10,000	2.71815
1,000,000	2.71828

Powers of e can be approximated on a scientific or graphing calculator. Some powers of e obtained on a calculator are

$$e^{-2} \approx 0.1353352832, \quad e^{1.3} \approx 3.669296668, \quad e^4 \approx 54.59815003.$$

The graph of the function $f(x) = e^x$ is shown in **Figure 42**.

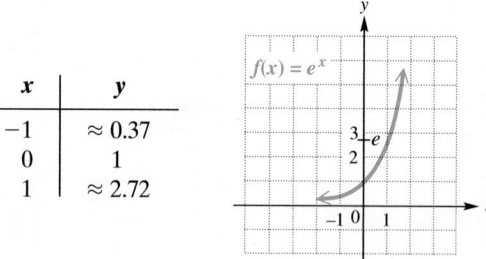

The values for e^{-2}, $e^{1.3}$, and e^4 are approximated in this split-screen graph of $f(x) = e^x$.

x	y
-1	≈ 0.37
0	1
1	≈ 2.72

Figure 42

A real-life application of exponential functions occurs in the computation of **compound interest.**

Compound Interest Formula

Suppose that a principal of P dollars is invested at an annual interest rate r (in percent, expressed as a decimal), compounded n times per year. Then the amount A accumulated after t years is given by the following formula.

$$A = P\left(1 + \frac{r}{n}\right)^{nt}$$

Following her success in *I Love Lucy*, **Lucille Ball** starred in *The Lucy Show*, which aired for six seasons on CBS in the 1960s. She worked for Mr. Mooney (Gale Gordon), who was very careful with his money.

In the September 26, 1966, show "Lucy, the Bean Queen," Lucy learned a lesson about **exponential growth.** Mr. Mooney had refused to lend her $1500 to buy furniture, because he claimed she did not know the value of money. He explained to her that if she were to save one penny on Day 1, two pennies on Day 2, four pennies on Day 3, and so on, she would have more than enough money to buy her furniture after only nineteen days. (You might want to verify this on your own.)

▐▐ **EXAMPLE 1** Applying the Compound Interest Formula

Suppose that $1000 is invested at an annual rate of 2%, compounded quarterly (four times per year). Find the total amount in the account after ten years if no withdrawals are made.

SOLUTION

$$A = P\left(1 + \frac{r}{n}\right)^{nt}$$ Compound interest formula

$$A = 1000\left(1 + \frac{0.02}{4}\right)^{4 \cdot 10}$$ $P = 1000, r = 0.02, n = 4, t = 10$

$$A = 1000(\mathbf{1.005})^{40}$$ Simplify.

$$A \approx 1000(\mathbf{1.22079})$$ Evaluate 1.005^{40} with a calculator.

$$A = 1220.79$$ To the nearest cent

$\approx$ means "is approximately equal to."

There would be $1220.79 in the account at the end of ten years.   ▐▐▐

The compounding formula given earlier applies if the financial institution compounds interest for a finite number of compounding periods annually. Theoretically, the number of compounding periods per year can get larger and larger (quarterly, monthly, daily, etc.), and if n is allowed to approach infinity, we say that interest is compounded *continuously.* The formula for **continuous compounding** involves the number e.

Continuous Compound Interest Formula

Suppose that a principal of P dollars is invested at an annual interest rate r (in percent, expressed as a decimal), compounded continuously. Then the amount A accumulated after t years is given by the following formula.

$$A = Pe^{rt}$$

▐▐ **EXAMPLE 2** Applying the Continuous Compound Interest Formula

Suppose that $5000 is invested at an annual rate of 2.5%, compounded continuously. Find the total amount in the account after four years if no withdrawals are made.

SOLUTION

$$A = Pe^{rt}$$ Continuous compound interest formula

$$A = 5000e^{0.025(4)}$$ $P = 5000, r = 0.025, t = 4$

$$A = 5000e^{0.1}$$ Simplify.

$$A \approx 5000(\mathbf{1.10517})$$ Use the e^x key on a calculator.

$$A = 5525.85$$ To the nearest cent

There will be $5525.85 in the account after four years.   ▐▐▐

The continuous compound interest formula is an example of an **exponential growth function**. In situations involving growth or decay of a quantity, the amount or number present at time t can often be approximated by a function of the form

$$A(t) = A_0 e^{kt},$$ If $k > 0$, there is exponential *growth*.
If $k < 0$, there is exponential *decay*.

where A_0 represents the amount or number present at time $t = 0$, and k is a constant.

A variation of **exponential growth** is found in the legend of a Persian king, who wanted to please his executive officer, the Grand Vizier, with a gift of his choice. The Grand Vizier explained that he would like to be able to use his chessboard to accumulate wheat. A single grain of wheat would be received for the first square on the board, two grains would be received for the second square, four grains for the third, and so on, doubling the number of grains for each of the 64 squares on the board. As unlikely as it may seem, the number of grains would total 18.5 quintillion!

Logarithmic Functions and Applications

Consider the statement

$$2^3 = 8.$$

Here 3 is the exponent (or power) to which the base 2 must be raised in order to obtain 8. The exponent 3 is called the *logarithm* with base 2 of 8, and this is written

$$3 = \log_2 8.$$

In general, we have the following relationship.

Definition of $\log_b x$

For $b > 0$, $b \neq 1$:

$$\text{If } b^y = x, \qquad \text{then} \qquad y = \log_b x.$$

Here $\log_b x$ is the exponent to which b must be raised in order to obtain x.

Table 5 illustrates the relationship between exponential equations and logarithmic equations.

Table 5

Exponential Equation	Logarithmic Equation
$3^4 = 81$	$4 = \log_3 81$
$10^5 = 100{,}000$	$5 = \log_{10} 100{,}000$
$\left(\frac{1}{2}\right)^{-4} = 16$	$-4 = \log_{1/2} 16$
$10^0 = 1$	$0 = \log_{10} 1$
$4^{-3} = \frac{1}{64}$	$-3 = \log_4 \frac{1}{64}$

A logarithm is an exponent.

The concept of inverse functions (studied in more advanced algebra courses) leads us to the definition of a second new function.

Logarithmic Function

A **logarithmic function with base b,** where $b > 0$ and $b \neq 1$, is a function g of the following form.

$$g(x) = \log_b x, \qquad \text{where } x > 0$$

The graph of the function $g(x) = \log_b x$ can be found by interchanging the roles of x and y in the function $f(x) = b^x$. Geometrically, this is accomplished by reflecting the graph of $f(x) = b^x$ about the line $y = x$.

The graphs of

$$F(x) = \log_2 x, \quad G(x) = \log_{1/2} x, \quad \text{and} \quad H(x) = \log_{10} x$$

are shown in **Figure 43** on the next page. The points in each table were obtained by interchanging the roles of x and y in the tables of points given in **Figure 41**.

$H(x) = \log_{10} x$

$F(x) = \log_2 x$

$G(x) = \log_{1/2} x$

Compare with **Figure 43** on the next page. Graphs of logarithmic functions with bases other than 10 and e are obtained with the use of the **change-of-base rule**:

$$\log_a x = \frac{\log x}{\log a} = \frac{\ln x}{\ln a}.$$

Alternatively, they can be drawn by using the capability that allows the user to obtain the graph of the inverse.

Note that $\log x$ denotes $\log_{10} x$ and $\ln x$ denotes $\log_e x$.

x	$F(x)$
$\frac{1}{2}$	-1
1	0
2	1
4	2

$F(x) = \log_2 x$

x	$G(x)$
4	-2
2	-1
1	0
$\frac{1}{2}$	1

$G(x) = \log_{1/2} x$

x	$H(x)$
$\frac{1}{10}$	-1
1	0
10	1

$H(x) = \log_{10} x$

(a) (b) (c)

Figure 43

The points are joined with a smooth curve, typical of the graphs of logarithmic functions. For each graph, the curve approaches but does not intersect the *y*-axis. Thus, the *y*-axis is called the **vertical asymptote** of the graph.

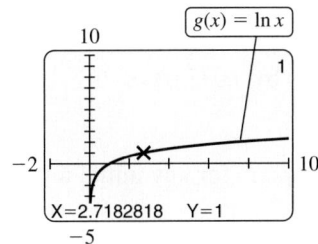

$g(x) = \ln x$

Notice that when

$$x = e \approx 2.7182818,$$
$$y = \ln e = 1.$$

Characteristics of the Graph of $g(x) = \log_b x$

1. The graph will always contain the point $(1, 0)$, because $\log_b 1 = 0$.

2. When $b > 1$, the graph will *rise* from left to right, from the fourth quadrant to the first (as in **Figure 43(a) and (c)**, with $b = 2$ and $b = 10$). When $0 < b < 1$, the graph will *fall* from left to right, from the first quadrant to the fourth (as in the illustration of **Figure 43(b)**, with $b = \frac{1}{2}$).

3. The *y*-axis is the vertical asymptote.

4. The domain is $(0, \infty)$ and the range is $(-\infty, \infty)$.

An important logarithmic function is the function with base *e*. If we interchange the roles of *x* and *y* in the graph of

$$f(x) = e^x \quad \textbf{(Figure 42)},$$

we obtain the graph of $g(x) = \log_e x$. The special symbol for the base *e* logarithm of *x* is *ln x*. That is,

$$\ln x = \log_e x.$$

Figure 44 shows the graph of $g(x) = \ln x$, which is called the **natural logarithmic function**.

The number *e* is named in honor of Leonhard Euler (1707–1783), the prolific Swiss mathematician. The value of *e* can be expressed as an **infinite series**.

$$e = 1 + \frac{1}{1} + \frac{1}{1 \cdot 2}$$
$$+ \frac{1}{1 \cdot 2 \cdot 3}$$
$$+ \frac{1}{1 \cdot 2 \cdot 3 \cdot 4} + \cdots$$

It can also be expressed using a **continued fraction.**

$$e = 2 + \cfrac{1}{1 + \cfrac{1}{2 + \cfrac{2}{3 + \cfrac{3}{4 + \cfrac{4}{\ddots}}}}}$$

x	y
≈ 0.37	-1
1	0
≈ 2.72	1

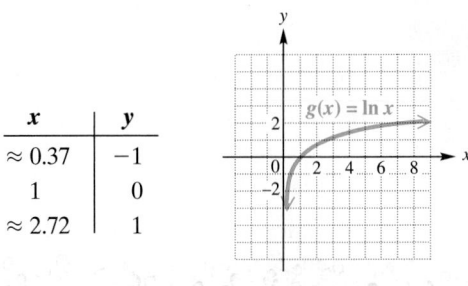

$g(x) = \ln x$

Figure 44

The expression $\ln e^k$ is the unique exponent to which the base *e* must be raised in order to obtain e^k. Thus, for all real numbers k,

$$\ln e^k = k.$$

This will be used in applications to follow.

▮▮ **EXAMPLE 3** Finding the Time for an Amount to Triple

Suppose that a certain amount P is invested at an annual rate of 3.5%, compounded continuously. How long will it take for the amount to triple?

SOLUTION

We wish to find the value of t in the continuous compound interest formula that will make the amount A equal to $3P$ (since we want the initial investment, P, to triple).

$$A = Pe^{rt} \qquad \text{Continuous compound interest formula}$$
$$3P = Pe^{0.035t} \qquad \text{Substitute } 3P \text{ for } A \text{ and } 0.035 \text{ for } r.$$
$$3 = e^{0.035t} \qquad \text{Divide both sides by } P.$$
$$\ln 3 = \ln e^{0.035t} \qquad \text{Take the natural logarithm of both sides.}$$
$$\ln 3 = 0.035t \qquad \text{Use the fact that } \ln e^k = k.$$
$$t = \frac{\ln 3}{0.035} \qquad \text{Divide both sides by } 0.035.$$

A calculator shows that $\ln 3 \approx 1.098612289$. Dividing this by 0.035 gives

$$t \approx 31.4$$

to the nearest tenth. Therefore, it would take about 31.4 years for any initial investment P to triple under the given conditions. ▮▮▮

The amount of time it would take for a given amount to double under given conditions is the **doubling time.** Verify that the doubling time for **Example 3** is $\frac{\ln 2}{0.035} \approx 19.8$ years.

Exponential Models in Nature

▮▮ **EXAMPLE 4** Modeling Population Growth

According to the U.S. Census Bureau, the world population reached 6 billion people on July 18, 1999, and was growing exponentially. By the end of 2000, the population had grown to 6.079 billion. The projected world population (in billions of people) x years after 2000, is given by the function defined by

$$f(x) = 6.079e^{0.0126x}.$$

(a) Based on this model, what was the world population in 2010?

(b) In what year did the world population reach 7 billion?

SOLUTION

(a) Since $x = 0$ represents the year 2000, in 2010 x would be $2010 - 2000 = 10$. We must find $f(x)$ when x is 10.

$$f(x) = 6.079e^{0.0126x} \qquad \text{Given function}$$
$$f(10) = 6.079e^{0.0126(10)} \qquad \text{Let } x = 10.$$
$$\approx 6.895 \qquad \text{Use a calculator.}$$

According to the model, the population was 6.895 billion at the end of 2010.

(b)

$$f(x) = 6.079e^{0.0126x} \quad \text{Given function}$$

$$7 = 6.079e^{0.0126x} \quad \text{Let } f(x) = 7.$$

$$\frac{7}{6.079} = e^{0.0126x} \quad \text{Divide by 6.079.}$$

$$\ln\left(\frac{7}{6.079}\right) = \ln e^{0.0126x} \quad \text{Take logarithms on both sides.}$$

$$\ln\left(\frac{7}{6.079}\right) = 0.0126x \quad \ln e^x = x$$

$$x = \frac{\ln\left(\frac{7}{6.079}\right)}{0.0126} \quad \text{Divide by 0.0126; rewrite.}$$

$$x \approx 11.2 \quad \text{Use a calculator.}$$

World population reached 7 billion 11.2 years after 2000, during the year 2011.

▊▊▊

Radioactive materials disintegrate according to exponential decay functions. The **half-life** of a substance that decays exponentially is the amount of time that it takes for the amount to decay to half its initial value.

▊▎ **EXAMPLE 5** Carbon 14 Dating

Carbon 14 is a radioactive form of carbon that is found in all living plants and animals. After a plant or animal dies, the radiocarbon disintegrates. Scientists determine the age of the remains by comparing the amount of carbon 14 present with the amount found in living plants and animals. The amount of carbon 14 present after x years is modeled by the exponential equation

$$y = y_0 e^{-0.0001216x},$$

where y_0 represents the initial amount.

(a) What is the half-life of carbon 14?

(b) If an initial sample contains 1 gram of carbon 14, how much will be left after 10,000 years?

SOLUTION

(a) To find the half-life, let $y = \frac{1}{2}y_0$ in the equation.

$$\frac{1}{2}y_0 = y_0 e^{-0.0001216x} \quad \text{Let } y = \frac{1}{2}y_0.$$

$$\frac{1}{2} = e^{-0.0001216x} \quad \text{Divide by } y_0.$$

$$\ln\left(\frac{1}{2}\right) = -0.0001216x \quad \text{Take the natural logarithm of both sides.}$$

$$x \approx 5700 \quad \text{Use a calculator.}$$

The half-life of carbon 14 is about 5700 years.

(b) Evaluate y for $x = 10,000$ and $y_0 = 1$.

$$y = 1e^{-0.0001216(10,000)} \approx 0.30 \quad \text{Use a calculator.}$$

There will be about 0.30 gram remaining.

▊▊▊

8.6 EXERCISES

Fill in each blank with the correct response.

1. For an exponential function $f(x) = a^x$, if $a > 1$, the graph _____ from left to right. If $0 < a < 1$, the
(rises/falls)
graph _____ from left to right.
(rises/falls)

2. The y-intercept of the graph of $y = a^x$ is _____.

3. The graph of the exponential function $f(x) = a^x$ _____ have an x-intercept.
(does/does not)

4. The point $(2, \underline{\quad})$ is on the graph of $f(x) = 3^{4x-3}$.

5. For a logarithmic function $g(x) = \log_a x$, if $a > 1$, the graph _____ from left to right. If $0 < a < 1$, the
(rises/falls)
graph _____ from left to right.
(rises/falls)

6. The x-intercept of the graph of $y = \log_a x$ is _____.

7. The graph of the logarithmic function $g(x) = \log_a x$ _____ have a y-intercept.
(does/does not)

8. The point $(98, \underline{\quad})$ lies on the graph of $g(x) = \log_{10}(x + 2)$.

Use a calculator to find an approximation for each number. Give as many digits as the calculator displays.

9. $9^{3/7}$

10. $14^{2/7}$

11. $(0.83)^{-1.2}$

12. $(0.97)^{3.4}$

13. $(\sqrt{6})^{\sqrt{5}}$

14. $(\sqrt{7})^{\sqrt{3}}$

15. $\left(\dfrac{1}{3}\right)^{9.8}$

16. $\left(\dfrac{2}{5}\right)^{8.1}$

Sketch the graph of each function.

17. $f(x) = 3^x$

18. $f(x) = 5^x$

19. $f(x) = \left(\dfrac{1}{4}\right)^x$

20. $f(x) = \left(\dfrac{1}{3}\right)^x$

Use a calculator to approximate each number. Give as many digits as the calculator displays.

21. e^3

22. e^4

23. e^{-4}

24. e^{-3}

In Exercises 25–28, rewrite the exponential equation as a logarithmic equation. In Exercises 29–32, rewrite the logarithmic equation as an exponential equation.

25. $4^2 = 16$

26. $5^3 = 125$

27. $\left(\dfrac{2}{3}\right)^{-3} = \dfrac{27}{8}$

28. $\left(\dfrac{1}{10}\right)^{-4} = 10,000$

29. $5 = \log_2 32$

30. $3 = \log_4 64$

31. $1 = \log_3 3$

32. $0 = \log_{12} 1$

Use a calculator to approximate each number. Give as many digits as the calculator displays.

33. $\ln 4$

34. $\ln 6$

35. $\ln 0.35$

36. $\ln 2.45$

Global Warming *This figure shows projected temperature increases using two graphs: one an exponential-type curve, and the other linear. From the figure, approximate the increase* **(a)** *for the exponential curve, and* **(b)** *for the linear graph for each of the years in Exercises 37–40.*

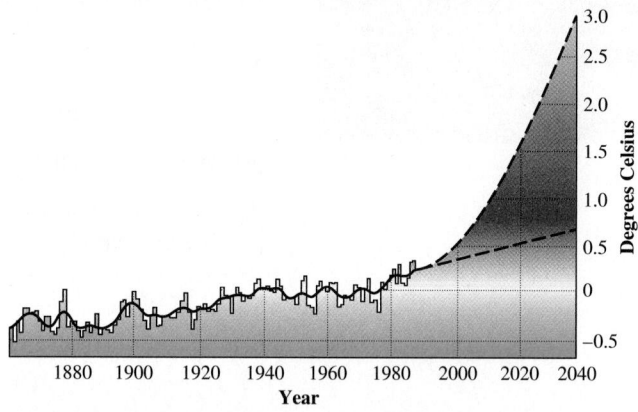

Source: "Zero Equals Average Global Temperature for the Period 1950–1979" by Dale D. Glasgow from National Geographic, October 1990. Reprinted by permission of the National Geographic Society.

37. 2000

38. 2010

39. 2020

40. 2040

Sketch the graph of each function. (Hint: Use the graphs of the exponential functions in Exercises 17–20 to help.)

41. $g(x) = \log_3 x$

42. $g(x) = \log_5 x$

43. $g(x) = \log_{1/4} x$

44. $g(x) = \log_{1/3} x$

Investment Determine the amount of money that will be accumulated in an account that pays compound interest, given the initial principal in each of the following.

45. $20,000 invested at 3% annual interest for 4 years compounded **(a)** annually; **(b)** semiannually.

46. $35,000 invested at 2.2% annual interest for 3 years compounded **(a)** annually; **(b)** quarterly.

47. $27,500 invested at 2.95% annual interest for 5 years compounded **(a)** daily ($n = 365$); **(b)** continuously.

48. $15,800 invested at 1.6% annual interest for 6.5 years compounded **(a)** quarterly; **(b)** continuously.

Comparing Investment Plans In Exercises 49 and 50, decide which of the two plans will provide a better yield. (Interest rates stated are annual rates.)

49. *Plan A:* $40,000 invested for 3 years at 1.5%, compounded quarterly

   Plan B: $40,000 invested for 3 years at 1.4%, compounded continuously

50. *Plan A:* $50,000 invested for 10 years at 1.75%, compounded daily ($n = 365$)

   Plan B: $50,000 invested for 10 years at 1.7%, compounded continuously

51. *Comparing Investments* Ronnie Virgets wants to invest $60,000 in a pension plan. One investment offers 7% compounded quarterly. Another offers 6.75% compounded continuously.

   (a) Which investment will earn more interest in 5 yr?

   (b) How much more will the better plan earn?

52. *Growth of an Account* If Ronnie (see **Exercise 51**) chooses the plan with continuous compounding, how long will it take for his $60,000 to grow to $80,000?

Solve each problem.

53. *Doubling Time* Find the doubling time of an investment earning 2.5% annual interest if interest is compounded continuously.

54. *Doubling Time* If interest is compounded continuously and the interest rate is tripled, what effect will this have on the time required for an investment to double?

55. *Growth of an Account* How long will it take an investment to triple, if interest is compounded continuously at 5% annually?

56. *Growth of an Account* What annual interest rate is required for an investment of $1000 to grow to $1200 in 4 years, if interest is compounded continuously?

57. *Atmospheric Pressure* The atmospheric pressure (in millibars) at a given altitude x (in meters) is approximated by the function

$$f(x) = 1013e^{-0.0001341x}.$$

(a) Predict the atmospheric pressure at 1500 meters.

(b) Predict the atmospheric pressure at 11,000 meters.

58. *World Population Growth* As seen in **Example 4,** the world population in billions closely fits the exponential function

$$f(x) = 6.079e^{0.0126x},$$

where x is the number of years since 2000.

(a) The world population was about 6.555 billion in 2006. How closely does the function approximate this value?

(b) Predict the population in 2015.

(c) Predict when the population will reach 8 billion.

59. *Population of Pakistan* The U.S. Census Bureau projects that the population of Pakistan, in thousands, will grow approximately according to the function

$$f(x) = 146{,}250(2)^{0.0176x},$$

where $x = 0$ represents the year 2000, $x = 25$ represents 2025, and $x = 50$ represents 2050.

(a) According to this model, what was the population of Pakistan in 2000?

(b) What will the population be in 2025?

(c) How will the population in 2025 compare to the population in 2000?

60. *Population of Brazil* The U.S. Census Bureau projects that the population of Brazil, in thousands, will grow approximately according to the function

$$f(x) = 176{,}000(2)^{0.008x},$$

where $x = 0$ represents the year 2000, $x = 25$ represents 2025, and $x = 50$ represents 2050.

(a) According to this model, what was the population of Brazil in 2000?

(b) What will the population be in 2025?

(c) How will the population in 2025 compare to the population in 2000?

61. *Decay of Lead* A sample of 500 grams of radioactive lead 210 decays to polonium 210 according to the function

$$A(t) = 500e^{-0.032t},$$

where t is time in years. Find the amount of the sample remaining after

(a) 4 years   **(b)** 8 years

(c) 20 years   **(d)** Find the half-life.

62. *Decay of Plutonium* Repeat **Exercise 61** for 500 grams of plutonium 241, which decays according to the function defined as follows, where t is time in years.

$$A(t) = A_0 e^{-0.053t}$$

63. *Decay of Radium* Find the half-life of radium 226, which decays according to the function defined as follows, where t is time in years.

$$A(t) = A_0 e^{-0.00043t}$$

64. *Decay of Iodine* How long will it take any quantity of iodine 131 to decay to 25% of its initial amount, knowing that it decays according to the function defined as follows, where t is time in days?

$$A(t) = A_0 e^{-0.087t}$$

65. *Carbon 14 Dating* Suppose an Egyptian mummy is discovered in which the amount of carbon 14 present is only about one-third the amount found in living human beings. About how long ago did the Egyptian die?

66. *Carbon 14 Dating* A sample from a refuse deposit near the Strait of Magellan had 60% of the carbon 14 of a contemporary living sample. How old was the sample?

67. *Carbon 14 Dating* Estimate the age of a specimen that contains 20% of the carbon 14 of a comparable living specimen.

68. *Value of a Copier* A small business estimates that the value $V(t)$ of a copier is decreasing according to the function defined by

$$V(t) = 5000(2)^{-0.15t},$$

where t is the number of years that have elapsed since the machine was purchased, and $V(t)$ is in dollars.

(a) What was the original value of the machine?

(b) What is the value of the machine 5 years after purchase? Give your answer to the nearest dollar.

(c) What is the value of the machine 10 years after purchase? Give your answer to the nearest dollar.

8.7 SYSTEMS OF EQUATIONS

Linear Systems in Two Variables • Elimination Method • Substitution Method
• Linear Systems in Three Variables

Linear Systems in Two Variables

During the first decade of the twenty-first century, the sale of digital cameras increased, while that of conventional cameras decreased. These trends can be seen in the graph in **Figure 45**. The two straight-line graphs intersect at the point in time when the two types of cameras had the *same* sales.

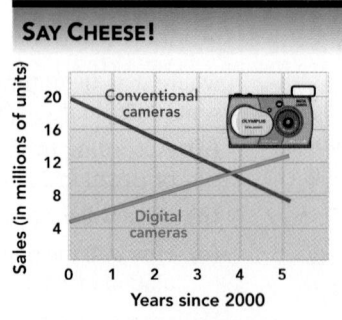

Source: Consumer Electronics Association.

Figure 45

$$2.5x + y = 19.4$$
$$-1.7x + y = 4.4$$

Linear system of equations

(Here, $x = 0$ represents 2000, $x = 1$ represents 2001, and so on. The variable y represents sales in millions of units.)

As shown beside **Figure 45**, we can use an equation to model the graph of digital camera sales (the blue equation) and another to model the graph of conventional camera sales (the red equation). Such a set of equations is called a **system of equations**. The point where the graphs in **Figure 45** intersect is a solution of each of the individual equations. It is also the solution of the linear system of equations.

The definition of a linear equation given earlier can be extended to more variables. Any equation of the form

$$a_1x_1 + a_2x_2 + \cdots + a_nx_n = b$$

for real numbers $a_1, a_2, \ldots, a_n$ (some of which may be 0), and b, is a **linear equation.** If all the equations in a system are linear, the system is a **linear system of equations,** or a **linear system.**

In **Figure 46**, the two linear equations $x + y = 5$ and $2x - y = 4$ are graphed in the same coordinate system. Notice that they intersect at the point $(3, 2)$. Because $(3, 2)$ is the only ordered pair that satisfies both equations at the same time, we say that $\{(3, 2)\}$ is the solution set of the system

$$x + y = 5$$
$$2x - y = 4.$$

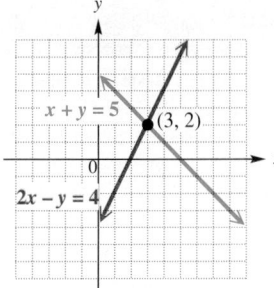

Figure 46

Because the graph of a linear equation in two variables is a line, there are three possibilities for the number of solutions in the solution set of a linear system.

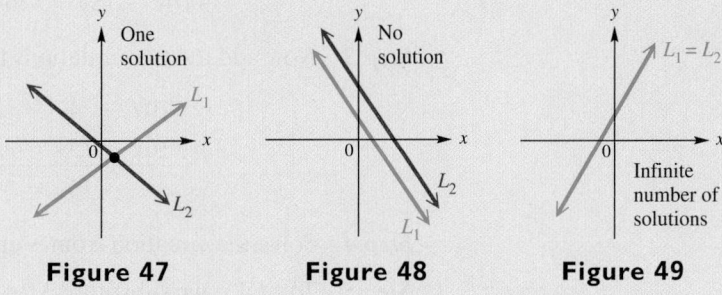

A graphing calculator supports our statement that (3, 2) is the solution of the system

$$x + y = 5$$
$$2x - y = 4.$$

Graphs of a Linear System in Two Variables (The Three Possibilities)

1. The two graphs intersect in a single point. The coordinates of this point give the only solution of the system. In this case, the system is **consistent** and the equations are **independent.** This is the most common case. See **Figure 47**.

2. The graphs are parallel lines. In this case, the system is **inconsistent** and the equations are **independent.** That is, there is no solution common to both equations of the system, and the solution set is $\emptyset$. See **Figure 48**.

3. The graphs are the same line. In this case, the system is **consistent** and the equations are **dependent,** because any solution of one equation of the system is also a solution of the other. The solution set is an infinite set of ordered pairs representing the points on the line. See **Figure 49**.

Figure 47 **Figure 48** **Figure 49**

Elimination Method

In most cases, we cannot rely on graphing to solve systems, so we use algebraic methods. The **elimination method** involves combining the two equations of the system so that one variable is eliminated. This is done using the following fact.

If $a = b$ and $c = d$, then $a + c = b + d$.

The solution of **systems of equations** of graphs more complicated than straight lines is the principle behind the **mattang**, a stick chart used by the people of the Marshall Islands in the Pacific. A mattang is made of roots tied together with coconut fibers, and it shows the wave patterns found when approaching an island.

Solving Linear Systems by Elimination

Step 1 **Write both equations in standard form** $Ax + By = C$.

Step 2 **Make the coefficients of one pair of variable terms opposites.** Multiply one or both equations by appropriate numbers so that the sum of the coefficients of either x or y is zero.

Step 3 **Add** the new equations to eliminate a variable. The sum should be an equation with just one variable.

Step 4 **Solve** the equation from Step 3.

Step 5 **Find the other value.** Substitute the result of Step 4 into either of the given equations and solve for the other variable.

Step 6 **Find the solution set.** Check the solution in both of the given equations. Then write the solution set.

▌▌ **EXAMPLE 1** Solving a System by Elimination (Two Variables)

Solve the system.

$$5x - 2y = 4 \quad \text{(1)}$$
$$2x + 3y = 13 \quad \text{(2)}$$

SOLUTION

Step 1 Both equations are already in standard form.

Step 2 Our goal is to add the two equations so that one of the variables is eliminated. To eliminate the variable x, we must first transform one or both equations so that the coefficients of x are opposites. Then, when we combine the equations, the term with x will have a coefficient of 0, and we will be able to solve for y. We begin by multiplying equation (1) by 2 and equation (2) by -5.

$$10x - 4y = 8 \quad \text{2 times each side of equation (1)}$$
$$-10x - 15y = -65 \quad \text{-5 times each side of equation (2)}$$

Step 3 Now add the two equations to eliminate x.

$$\begin{array}{r} 10x - 4y = 8 \\ \underline{-10x - 15y = -65} \\ -19y = -57 \quad \text{Add.} \end{array}$$

Step 4 Solve the equation from Step 3 to get $y = 3$. (Divide by -19.)

Step 5 To find x, we substitute 3 for y in either of the original equations.

$$2x + 3\mathbf{y} = 13 \quad \text{We use equation (2).}$$
$$2x + 3(\mathbf{3}) = 13 \quad \text{Let } y = 3.$$
$$2x + 9 = 13 \quad \text{Multiply.}$$
$$2x = 4 \quad \text{Subtract 9.}$$
$$x = 2 \quad \text{Divide by 2.}$$

Step 6 The solution appears to be $(2, 3)$. To check, substitute **2** for x and **3** for y in both of the original equations.

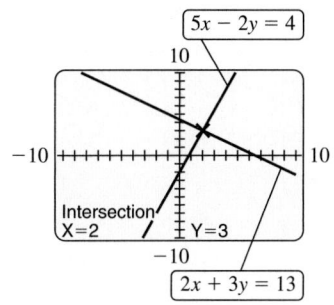

The solution in **Example 1** is supported by a graphing calculator. We solve each equation for y, graph them both, and find the point of intersection of the two lines: (2, 3).

Check:

$$5x - 2y = 4 \quad (1)$$
$$5(2) - 2(3) \stackrel{?}{=} 4$$
$$10 - 6 \stackrel{?}{=} 4$$
$$4 = 4 \checkmark \quad \text{True}$$

$$2x + 3y = 13 \quad (2)$$
$$2(2) + 3(3) \stackrel{?}{=} 13$$
$$4 + 9 \stackrel{?}{=} 13$$
$$13 = 13 \checkmark \quad \text{True}$$

The solution set is $\{(2, 3)\}$. ■■■

Substitution Method

Linear systems can also be solved by the **substitution method.** This method is most useful for solving linear systems in which one variable has coefficient 1 or -1.

Solving Linear Systems by Substitution

Step 1 **Solve for one variable in terms of the other.** Solve one of the equations for either variable. (If one of the variables has coefficient 1 or -1, choose it, since the substitution method is usually easier this way.)

Step 2 **Substitute** for that variable in the other equation. The result should be an equation with just one variable.

Step 3 **Solve** the equation from Step 2.

Step 4 **Find the other value.** Substitute the result from Step 3 into the equation from Step 1 to find the value of the other variable.

Step 5 **Find the solution set.** Check the solution in both of the given equations. Then write the solution set.

■■ **EXAMPLE 2** Solving a System by Substitution (Two Variables)

Solve the system.

$$3x + 2y = 13 \quad (1)$$
$$4x - y = -1 \quad (2)$$

SOLUTION

Step 1 First solve one of the equations for either x or y. Since the coefficient of y in equation (2) is -1, it is easiest to solve for y in equation (2).

$$-y = -1 - 4x \quad \text{Equation (2) rearranged}$$
$$y = 1 + 4x \quad \text{Multiply by } -1.$$

Step 2 Substitute $1 + 4x$ for y in equation (1) to obtain an equation in x.

$$3x + 2y = 13 \quad (1)$$
$$3x + 2(1 + 4x) = 13 \quad \text{Let } y = 1 + 4x.$$

Step 3 Solve for x in the equation just obtained.

$$3x + 2 + 8x = 13 \quad \text{Distributive property}$$
$$11x = 11 \quad \text{Combine terms; subtract 2.}$$
$$x = 1 \quad \text{Divide by 11.}$$

Step 4 Now solve for y. Because $y = 1 + 4x$, we find that $y = 1 + 4(1) = 5$.

Step 5 Check to see that the ordered pair $(1, 5)$ satisfies both of the original equations. The solution set is $\{(1, 5)\}$. ■■■

▐▐ EXAMPLE 3 Solving Systems of Special Cases

Solve each system.

(a) $3x - 2y = 4$ (1)

$-6x + 4y = 7$ (2)

(b) $-4x + y = 2$ (3)

$8x - 2y = -4$ (4)

SOLUTION

(a) Eliminate x by multiplying both sides of equation (1) by 2 and then adding.

$$6x - 4y = 8 \quad \text{2 times equation (1)}$$
$$\underline{-6x + 4y = 7} \quad \text{(2)}$$
$$0 = 15 \quad \text{False}$$

Both variables were eliminated here, leaving the false statement $0 = 15$, indicating that these two equations have no solutions in common. The system is inconsistent, with the empty set $\emptyset$ as the solution set.

(b) Eliminate x by multiplying both sides of equation (3) by 2 and then adding the result to equation (4).

$$-8x + 2y = 4 \quad \text{2 times equation (3)}$$
$$\underline{8x - 2y = -4} \quad \text{(4)}$$
$$0 = 0 \quad \text{True}$$

This true statement, $0 = 0$, indicates that a solution of one equation is also a solution of the other, so the solution set is an infinite set of ordered pairs. The two equations are dependent.

We write the solution set of a system of dependent equations as a set of ordered pairs by expressing x in terms of y as follows. Choose either equation and solve for x. We arbitrarily choose equation (3).

$$-4x + y = 2 \quad \text{(3)}$$
$$x = \frac{2 - y}{-4}$$
$$x = \frac{y - 2}{4} \quad \text{Multiply by } \tfrac{-1}{-1}.$$

The solution set can be written as

$$\left\{ \left(\frac{y - 2}{4}, y \right) \right\}.$$

By selecting values for y and calculating the corresponding values for x, individual ordered pairs of the solution set can be found. For example,

$$\text{if} \quad y = -2, \quad \text{then} \quad x = \frac{-2 - 2}{4} = -1$$

and the ordered pair $(-1, -2)$ is a solution. ▐▐▐

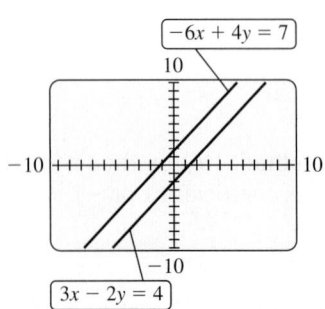

The graphs of the equations in **Example 3(a)** are parallel. There are no solutions.

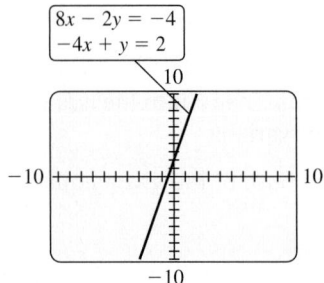

The graphs of the equations in **Example 3(b)** coincide. We see only one line. There are infinitely many solutions.

Linear Systems in Three Variables

A solution of an equation in three variables, such as

$$2x + 3y - z = 4,$$

is called an **ordered triple** and is written (x, y, z). For example, the ordered triples $(1, 1, 1)$ and $(10, -3, 7)$ are both solutions of the equation $2x + 3y - z = 4$, because the numbers in these ordered triples satisfy the equation when used as replacements for x, y, and z, respectively.

The methods of solving systems of two equations in two variables can be extended to solving systems of equations in three variables such as the following.

$$4x + 8y + z = 2$$
$$x + 7y - 3z = -14$$
$$2x - 3y + 2z = 3$$

System of three equations in three variables

(In some cases, one or more variables may be missing from one or more equations in a system. As examples, see **Exercises 47–52** on **page 426.**)

The graph of a linear equation with three variables is a *plane* and not a line. Because the graph of each equation of the system is a plane, whose graph is three-dimensional, graphing is not a practical method of solution. However, it does illustrate the number of solutions possible for such systems, as **Figure 50** shows.

Possibilities for Graphs of Linear Systems in Three Variables

1. The three planes may meet at a single, common point that forms the solution set of the system. See **Figure 50(a)**.

2. The three planes may have the points of a line in common so that the set of points along that line is the solution set of the system. See **Figure 50(b)**.

3. The three planes may coincide so that the solution set of the system is the set of all points on that plane. See **Figure 50(c)**.

4. The planes may have no points common to all three so that there is no solution for the system. See **Figure 50(d)–(g)**.

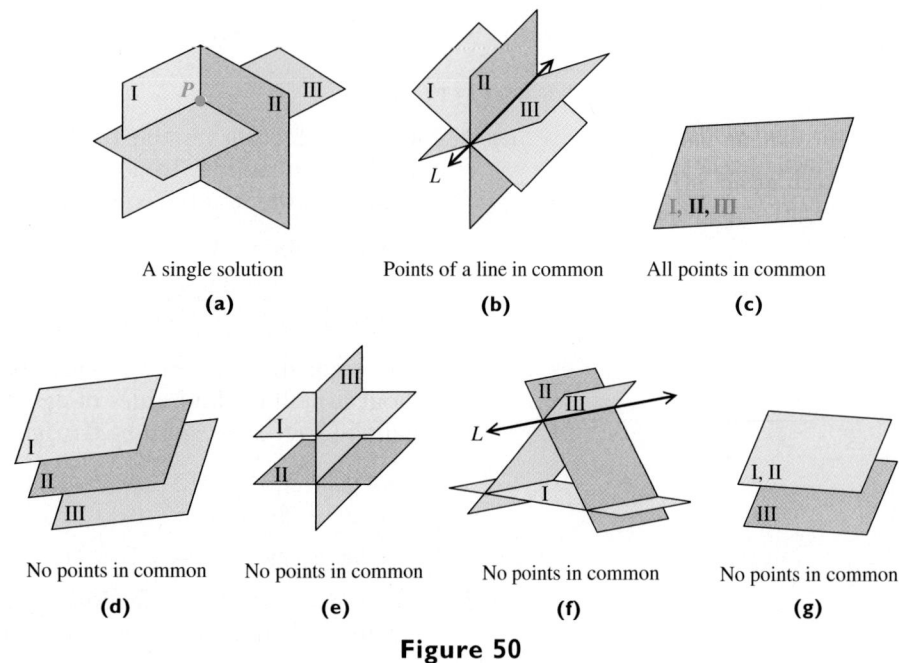

A single solution
(a)

Points of a line in common
(b)

All points in common
(c)

No points in common
(d)

No points in common
(e)

No points in common
(f)

No points in common
(g)

Figure 50

Systems in three variables are solved with an extension of the elimination method, summarized on the next page.

Solving Linear Systems in Three Variables by Elimination

Step 1 **Eliminate a variable.** Use the elimination method to eliminate any variable using any two of the given equations. The result is an equation in two variables.

Step 2 **Eliminate the same variable again.** Eliminate the *same* variable using any *other* two equations. The result is an equation in the same two variables as in Step 1.

Step 3 **Eliminate a different variable and solve.** Use the elimination method to eliminate a second variable using the two equations in two variables that result from Steps 1 and 2. The result is an equation in one variable that gives the value of that variable.

Step 4 **Find a second value.** Substitute the value of the variable found in Step 3 into either of the equations in two variables (found in Step 1 or Step 2) to find the value of a second variable.

Step 5 **Find a third value.** Use the values of the two variables from Steps 3 and 4 to find the value of the third variable by substituting into any of the original equations.

Step 6 **Find the solution set.** Check the solution in all of the original equations. Then write the solution set.

▮▮ **EXAMPLE 4** Solving a System (Three Variables)

Solve the system.

$$4x + 8y + z = 2 \qquad (1)$$
$$x + 7y - 3z = -14 \quad (2)$$
$$2x - 3y + 2z = 3 \qquad (3)$$

SOLUTION

Step 1 The choice of which variable to eliminate is arbitrary. Suppose we decide to begin by eliminating z. To do this, multiply both sides of equation (1) by 3 and then add the result to equation (2).

$$
\begin{array}{ll}
12x + 24y + 3z = 6 & \text{Multiply both sides of equation (1) by 3.}\\
\underline{x + 7y - 3z = -14} & (2)\\
13x + 31y = -8 & \text{Add.} \quad (4)
\end{array}
$$

Step 2 The new equation has only two variables, x and y. To get another equation without z, multiply both sides of equation (1) by -2 and add the result to equation (3). ***It is essential at this point to eliminate the same variable, z.***

$$
\begin{array}{ll}
-8x - 16y - 2z = -4 & \text{Multiply both sides of equation (1) by } -2.\\
\underline{2x - 3y + 2z = 3} & (3)\\
-6x - 19y = -1 & \text{Add.} \quad (5)
\end{array}
$$

Step 3 Now solve the system of equations from Steps 1 and 2 for x and y. (This step is possible only if the *same* variable is eliminated in the first two steps.)

$$
\begin{array}{ll}
78x + 186y = -48 & \text{Multiply both sides of (4) by 6.}\\
\underline{-78x - 247y = -13} & \text{Multiply both sides of (5) by 13.}\\
 -61y = -61 & \text{Add.}\\
 y = 1 & \text{Divide by } -61.
\end{array}
$$

Step 4 Substitute 1 for y in either equation from Steps 1 and 2.

$$-6x - 19y = -1 \quad \text{Using equation (5)}$$
$$-6x - 19(\mathbf{1}) = -1 \quad \text{Let } y = 1.$$
$$-6x - 19 = -1 \quad \text{Multiply.}$$
$$-6x = 18 \quad \text{Add 19.}$$
$$x = -3 \quad \text{Divide by } -6.$$

Step 5 Substitute -3 for x and 1 for y in one of the original equations to find z.

$$4x + 8y + z = 2 \quad \text{Using equation (1)}$$
$$4(\mathbf{-3}) + 8(\mathbf{1}) + z = 2 \quad \text{Let } x = -3 \text{ and } y = 1.$$
$$-4 + z = 2 \quad \text{Simplify.}$$
$$z = 6 \quad \text{Add 4.}$$

Step 6 It appears that the ordered triple $(-3, 1, 6)$ is the only solution of the system.

Check: $\quad 4x + 8y + z = 2 \quad$ (1)

$$4(-3) + 8(1) + 6 \stackrel{?}{=} 2$$

We show the check for equation (1). Check that the solution satisfies the other two equations.

$$-12 + 8 + 6 \stackrel{?}{=} 2$$
$$2 = 2 \quad \checkmark \text{ True}$$

The solution set is $\{(-3, 1, 6)\}$. ■■■

8.7 EXERCISES

Fill in the blanks with the correct responses.

1. If $(3, -6)$ is a solution of a linear system in two variables, then substituting _____ for x and _____ for y leads to true statements in *both* equations.

2. A solution of a system of independent linear equations in two variables is a(n) _____ _____ of numbers.

3. Which ordered pair could possibly be a solution of the graphed system of equations? Why?

A. $(3, 3)$
B. $(-3, 3)$
C. $(-3, -3)$
D. $(3, -3)$

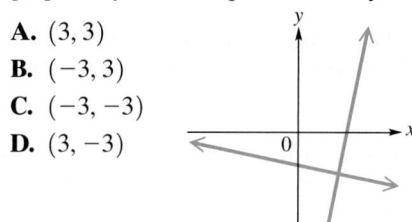

4. Which ordered pair could possibly be a solution of the graphed system of equations? Why?

A. $(3, 0)$
B. $(-3, 0)$
C. $(0, 3)$
D. $(0, -3)$

Decide whether the ordered pair is a solution of the given system.

5. $x + y - 6; \quad (5, 1)$
  $x - y = 4$

6. $x - y = 17; \quad (8, -9)$
  $x + y = -1$

7. $2x - y = 8; \quad (5, 2)$
  $3x + 2y = 20$

8. $3x - 5y = -12; \quad (-1, 2)$
  $x - y = 1$

Match each system in Exercises 9–12 with the correct graph in A–D below.

9. $x + y = 6$
  $x - y = 0$

10. $x + y = -6$
  $x - y = 0$

11. $x + y = 0$
  $x - y = -6$

12. $x + y = 0$
  $x - y = 6$

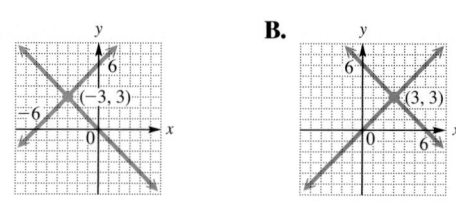

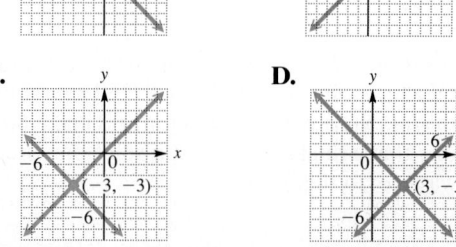

Solve each system by graphing.

13. $x + y = 4$
$2x - y = 2$

14. $x + y = -5$
$-2x + y = 1$

Solve each system by elimination.

15. $2x - 5y = 11$
$3x + y = 8$

16. $-2x + 3y = 1$
$-4x + y = -3$

17. $3x + 4y = -6$
$5x + 3y = 1$

18. $4x + 3y = 1$
$3x + 2y = 2$

19. $3x + 3y = 0$
$4x + 2y = 3$

20. $8x + 4y = 0$
$4x - 2y = 2$

21. $7x + 2y = 6$
$-14x - 4y = -12$

22. $x - 4y = 2$
$4x - 16y = 8$

23. $\dfrac{x}{2} + \dfrac{y}{3} = -\dfrac{1}{3}$
$\dfrac{x}{2} + 2y = -7$

24. $\dfrac{x}{5} + y = -\dfrac{12}{5}$
$\dfrac{x}{10} + \dfrac{y}{3} = -\dfrac{11}{30}$

25. $5x - 5y = 3$
$x - y = 12$

26. $2x - 3y = 7$
$-4x + 6y = 14$

Solve each system by substitution.

27. $4x + y = 6$
$y = 2x$

28. $2x - y = 6$
$y = 5x$

29. $3x - 4y = -22$
$-3x + y = 0$

30. $-3x + y = -5$
$x + 2y = 0$

31. $-x - 4y = -14$
$2x = y + 1$

32. $-3x - 5y = -17$
$4x = y - 8$

33. $5x - 4y = 9$
$3 - 2y = -x$

34. $6x - y = -9$
$4 + 7x = -y$

35. $x = 3y + 5$
$x = \dfrac{3}{2}y$

36. $x = 6y - 2$
$x = \dfrac{3}{4}y$

37. $\dfrac{1}{2}x + \dfrac{1}{3}y = 3$
$y = 3x$

38. $\dfrac{1}{4}x - \dfrac{1}{5}y = 9$
$y = 5x$

39. Explain what the following statement means: The solution set of the system

$$2x + y + z = 3$$
$$3x - y + z = -2 \quad \text{is } \{(-1, 2, 3)\}.$$
$$4x - y + 2z = 0$$

40. Write a system of three linear equations in three variables that has solution set $\{(3, 1, 2)\}$. Then solve the system. (*Hint:* Start with the solution and make up three equations that are satisfied by the solution. There are many ways to do this.)

Solve each system of equations in three variables.

41. $3x + 2y + z = 8$
$2x - 3y + 2z = -16$
$x + 4y - z = 20$

42. $-3x + y - z = -10$
$-4x + 2y + 3z = -1$
$2x + 3y - 2z = -5$

43. $2x + 5y + 2z = 0$
$4x - 7y - 3z = 1$
$3x - 8y - 2z = -6$

44. $5x - 2y + 3z = -9$
$4x + 3y + 5z = 4$
$2x + 4y - 2z = 14$

45. $x + y - z = -2$
$2x - y + z = -5$
$-x + 2y - 3z = -4$

46. $x + 2y + 3z = 1$
$-x - y + 3z = 2$
$-6x + y + z = -2$

47. $2x - 3y + 2z = -1$
$x + 2y + z = 17$
$2y - z = 7$

48. $2x - y + 3z = 6$
$x + 2y - z = 8$
$2y + z = 1$

49. $4x + 2y - 3z = 6$
$x - 4y + z = -4$
$-x + 2z = 2$

50. $2x + 3y - 4z = 4$
$x - 6y + z = -16$
$-x + 3z = 8$

51. $2x + y = 6$
$3y - 2z = -4$
$3x - 5z = -7$

52. $4x - 8y = -7$
$4y + z = 7$
$-8x + z = -4$

Camera Sales *Use the graph given in* **Figure 45** *at the beginning of this section (repeated here) to work Exercises 53–55.*

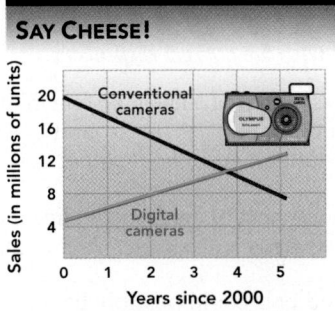

Source: Consumer Electronics Association.

53. For which years during the period 2000–2004 were sales of digital cameras less than sales of conventional cameras?

54. Estimate the year in which sales for the two types of cameras were the same. About what was this sales figure?

55. If $x = 0$ represents 2000 and $x = 4$ represents 2004, sales (y) in millions of units can be modeled by the linear equations in the following system.

$$2.5x + y = 19.4 \quad \text{Conventional cameras}$$

$$-1.7x + y = 4.4 \quad \text{Digital cameras}$$

Solve this system. Express values as decimals rounded to the nearest tenth. Write the solution as an ordered pair of the form (year, sales).

8.8 APPLICATIONS OF SYSTEMS

Introduction • Applications in Two Variables • An Application in Three Variables

Introduction

The chapter opener described a mixture problem posed in an episode of *The Bill Cosby Show*. Problems like this have been part of mathematics for thousands of years. Consider the one in the margin, which comes from a Hindu work that dates back to about A.D. 850. This problem can be solved by using a system of equations.

In this section we illustrate some strategies for solving applications using systems.

The mixed price of 9 citrons [a lemonlike fruit shown in the photo] and 7 fragrant wood apples is 107; again, the mixed price of 7 citrons and 9 fragrant wood apples is 101. O you arithmetician, tell me quickly the price of a citron and the price of a wood apple here, having distinctly separated those prices well.

The answer is on **page 432.**

> **PROBLEM-SOLVING HINT** Many problems involve more than one unknown quantity. Although some problems with two unknowns can be solved using just one variable, many times it is easier to use two variables. We write two equations that relate the unknown quantities. The system formed by the pair of equations can be solved using the methods of this section.

The following steps, based on the six-step problem-solving method first introduced in **Chapter 7,** give a strategy for solving problems using more than one variable.

> **Solving an Applied Problem by Writing a System of Equations**
>
> *Step 1* **Read** the problem carefully until you understand what is given and what is to be found.
>
> *Step 2* **Assign variables** to represent the unknown values, using diagrams or tables as needed. *Write down* what each variable represents.
>
> *Step 3* **Write a system of equations** that relates the unknowns.
>
> *Step 4* **Solve** the system of equations.
>
> *Step 5* **State the answer** to the problem. Does it seem reasonable?
>
> *Step 6* **Check** the answer in the words of the original problem.

Applications in Two Variables

▌▌ **EXAMPLE 1** Solving a Perimeter Problem

A rectangular soccer field may have a width between 50 and 100 yards and a length between 50 and 100 yards. Suppose that one particular field has a perimeter of 320 yards. Its length measures 40 yards more than its width. What are the dimensions of this field?

SOLUTION

Step 1 **Read** the problem again. We are asked to find the dimensions of the field.

Step 2 **Assign variables.** Let L = the length and W = the width.

Figure 51

Step 3 **Write a system of equations.** Because the perimeter is 320 yards, we find one equation by using the perimeter formula.

$$2L + 2W = 320$$

Because the length is 40 yards more than the width, we have

$$L = W + 40.$$

See **Figure 51**. We now have a system to solve.

$$2L + 2W = 320 \quad \text{(1)}$$
$$L = W + 40 \quad \text{(2)}$$

Step 4 **Solve** the system of equations. Since equation (2) is solved for L, we can substitute $W + 40$ for L in equation (1), and solve for W.

$$2L + 2W = 320 \quad \text{(1)}$$
$$2(W + 40) + 2W = 320 \quad L = W + 40$$
$$2W + 80 + 2W = 320 \quad \text{Distributive property}$$
$$4W + 80 = 320 \quad \text{Combine like terms.}$$
$$4W = 240 \quad \text{Subtract 80.}$$
$$W = 60 \quad \text{Divide by 4.}$$

Let $W = 60$ in the equation $L = W + 40$ to find L.

$$L = 60 + 40 = 100$$

Step 5 **State the answer.** The length is 100 yards, and the width is 60 yards. Both dimensions are within the ranges given in the problem.

Step 6 **Check.** The answer is correct, because the perimeter of this soccer field is

$$2(100) + 2(60) = 320 \text{ yards,}$$

and the length, 100 yards, is indeed 40 yards more than the width, because

$$100 - 40 = 60. \qquad \blacksquare\blacksquare\blacksquare$$

▌▌ **EXAMPLE 2** Solving a Problem about Ticket Prices

During recent National Hockey League and National Basketball Association seasons, two hockey tickets and one basketball ticket purchased at their average prices would have cost $148.79. One hockey ticket and two basketball tickets would have cost $148.60. What were the average ticket prices for the two sports? (*Source:* Team Marketing Report, Chicago.)

SOLUTION

Step 1 **Read** the problem again. There are two unknowns.

Step 2 **Assign variables.** Let h represent the average price for a hockey ticket and b represent the average price for a basketball ticket.

Step 3 **Write a system of equations.** Because two hockey tickets and one basketball ticket cost a total of $148.79, one equation for the system is

$$2h + b = 148.79.$$

By similar reasoning, the second equation is

$$h + 2b = 148.60.$$

Therefore, the system is as follows.

$$2h + b = 148.79 \quad \text{(1)}$$
$$h + 2b = 148.60 \quad \text{(2)}$$

Step 4 **Solve** the system of equations. We eliminate h.

$$\begin{aligned} 2h + b &= 148.79 \quad \text{(1)} \\ \underline{-2h - 4b} &= \underline{-297.20} \quad \text{Multiply each side of (2) by } -2. \\ -3b &= -148.41 \quad \text{Add.} \\ b &= 49.47 \quad \text{Divide by } -3. \end{aligned}$$

To find the value of h, let $b = 49.47$ in equation (2).

$$h + 2b = 148.60 \quad \text{(2)}$$
$$h + 2(49.47) = 148.60 \quad \text{Let } b = 49.47.$$
$$h + 98.94 = 148.60 \quad \text{Multiply.}$$
$$h = 49.66 \quad \text{Subtract 98.94.}$$

Step 5 **State the answer.** The average price for one basketball ticket was \$49.47. For one hockey ticket, the average price was \$49.66.

Step 6 **Check** that these values satisfy the conditions stated in the problem. ▮▮▮

We solved mixture problems earlier using one variable. Another approach is to use two variables and a system of equations.

▮▮ **EXAMPLE 3** Solving a Mixture Problem

How many ounces each of 5% hydrochloric acid and 20% hydrochloric acid must be combined to get 10 oz of solution that is 12.5% hydrochloric acid?

SOLUTION

Step 1 **Read** the problem. Two solutions of different strengths are being mixed together to get a specific amount of a solution with an "in-between" strength.

Step 2 **Assign variables.** Let x represent the number of ounces of 5% solution and y represent the number of ounces of 20% solution.

Solution to the Chapter Opener Problem Let x represent the number of pounds of \$0.75 candy, and let y represent the number of pounds of \$1.25 candy. The system to solve is

$$x + y = 9$$
$$0.75x + 1.25y = 0.96(9).$$

We find that there should be 5.22 pounds at \$0.75 per pound and 3.78 pounds at \$1.25 per pound.

Percent (as a decimal)	Ounces of Solution	Ounces of Pure Acid
5% = 0.05	x	$0.05x$
20% = 0.20	y	$0.20y$
12.5% = 0.125	10	$0.125(10)$

Summarize the information from the problem in a table.

Figure 52 also illustrates what is happening in the problem.

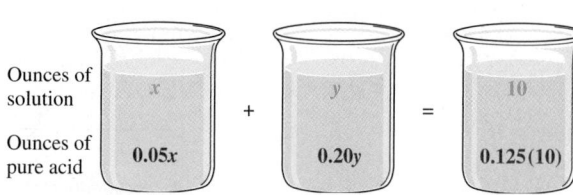

Ounces of solution

Ounces of pure acid

Figure 52

Step 3 **Write a system of equations.** When x ounces of 5% solution and y ounces of 20% solution are combined, the total number of ounces is 10.

$$x + y = 10 \quad \text{(1)}$$

The ounces of pure acid in the 5% solution ($0.05x$) plus the ounces of pure acid in the 20% solution ($0.20y$) should equal the total ounces of pure acid in the mixture, which is $0.125(10)$, or 1.25.

$$0.05x + 0.20y = 1.25 \quad \text{(2)}$$

Notice that these equations can be quickly determined by reading down in the table or using the labels in **Figure 52**.

Step 4 **Solve** the system of equations (1) and (2). We eliminate x.

$$
\begin{array}{rl}
5x + 20y = 125 & \text{Multiply each side of (2) by 100.} \\
\underline{-5x - 5y = -50} & \text{Multiply each side of (1) by } -5. \\
15y = 75 & \text{Add.} \\
y = 5 & \text{Divide by 15.}
\end{array}
$$

Because $y = 5$ and $x + y = 10$, x is also 5.

Step 5 **State the answer.** The desired mixture will require 5 ounces of the 5% solution and 5 ounces of the 20% solution.

Step 6 **Check** that these values satisfy both equations of the system. ■■■

Problems that use the distance formula $d = rt$ were introduced in **Chapter 7**. In many cases, these problems can be solved with systems of two linear equations.

■■ EXAMPLE 4 Solving a Motion Problem

Two executives in cities 400 miles apart leave at the same time to drive to a business meeting at a location on the line between their cities. They meet after 4 hours. Find the speed of each car if one car travels 20 miles per hour faster than the other.

SOLUTION

Step 1 **Read** the problem carefully.

Step 2 **Assign variables.**

Let x = the speed of the faster car,

and y = the speed of the slower car.

We use the formula $d = rt$. Each car travels for 4 hours, so the time, t, for each car is 4, as shown in the table.

	r	t	d
Faster car	x	4	$4x$	Find d from $d = rt$.
Slower car	y	4	$4y$	

Sketch what is happening in the problem. See **Figure 53**.

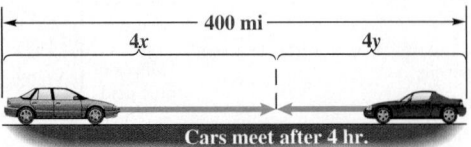

Figure 53

François Viète, a mathematician of sixteenth-century France, did much for the symbolism of mathematics. Before his time, different symbols were often used for different powers of a quantity. Viète used the same letter with a description of the power and the coefficient. According to Howard Eves in *An Introduction to the History of Mathematics*, Viète would have written

$$5BA^2 - 2CA + A^3 = D$$

as

*B*5 in *A* quad − *C* plano *2* in

A + *A* cub aequatur *D* solido.

Step 3 **Write two equations.** As shown in the figure, the total distance traveled by both cars is 400 miles.

$$4x + 4y = 400 \quad \text{(1)}$$

The faster car goes 20 miles per hour faster than the slower car.

$$x = 20 + y \quad \text{(2)}$$

Step 4 **Solve** this system of equations, by substitution.

$$4x + 4y = 400 \quad \text{(1)}$$
$$x = 20 + y \quad \text{(2)}$$

Replace *x* with 20 + *y* in equation (1) and solve for *y*.

$$4(20 + y) + 4y = 400 \quad \text{Let } x = 20 + y.$$
$$80 + 4y + 4y = 400 \quad \text{Distributive property}$$
$$80 + 8y = 400 \quad \text{Combine like terms.}$$
$$8y = 320 \quad \text{Subtract 80.}$$
$$y = 40 \quad \text{Divide by 8.}$$

Since *x* = 20 + *y*, and *y* = 40,

$$x = 20 + 40 = 60.$$

Step 5 **State the answer.** The speeds of the two cars are 40 miles per hour and 60 miles per hour.

Step 6 **Check** the answer. Because each car travels for 4 hours, the total distance traveled is

$$4(60) + 4(40) = 240 + 160 = 400 \text{ miles}, \quad \text{as required.} \qquad ▮▮▮$$

An Application in Three Variables

▮▮ **EXAMPLE 5** Solving a Problem Involving Prices

At Panera Bread, a loaf of honey wheat bread costs $2.95, a loaf of sunflower bread costs $2.99, and a loaf of French bread costs $5.79. On a recent day, three times as many loaves of honey wheat bread were sold as sunflower bread. The number of loaves of French bread sold was 5 less than the number of loaves of honey wheat bread sold. Total receipts for these breads were $87.89. How many loaves of each type of bread were sold? (*Source:* Panera Bread menu.)

Step 1 **Read** the problem again. There are three unknowns in this problem.

Step 2 **Assign variables** to represent the three unknowns.

Let *x* = the number of loaves of honey wheat bread,

y = the number of loaves of sunflower bread,

and *z* = the number of loaves of French bread.

Step 3 **Write a system of three equations.** Three times as many loaves of honey wheat bread were sold as sunflower bread, so

$$x = 3y, \quad \text{or} \quad x - 3y = 0. \quad \text{Subtract 3y.} \quad \text{(1)}$$

We need two more equations since there are three unknowns.

Number of loaves of French	equals	5 less than the number of loaves of honey wheat.
↓	↓	↓
z	$=$	$x - 5,$

$$-x + z = -5 \qquad \text{Subtract } x.$$
$$x - z = 5 \qquad \text{Multiply by } -1. \qquad (2)$$

Multiplying the cost of a loaf of each kind of bread by the total receipts.

$$2.95x + 2.99y + 5.79z = 87.89$$

Multiply each side of this equation by 100 to clear it of decimals.

$$295x + 299y + 579z = 8789 \quad (3)$$

Step 4 Solve the system of three equations,

$$x - 3y = 0 \qquad (1)$$
$$x - z = 5 \qquad (2)$$
$$295x + 299y + 579z = 8789. \qquad (3)$$

Use the method of **Section 8.7** to find that $x = 12, y = 4,$ and $z = 7.$

Solution to the Citron/Wood Apple Problem Let c represent the price of a single citron, and w represent the price of a wood apple. The system to solve is

$$9c + 7w = 107$$
$$7c + 9w = 101.$$

We find that the prices are 8 for a citron and 5 for a wood apple.

Step 5 State the answer. The solution set is $\{(12, 4, 7)\}$, so 12 loaves of honey wheat, 4 loaves of sunflower, and 7 loaves of French bread were sold.

Step 6 Check. Since $12 = 3 \cdot 4$, the number of loaves of honey wheat bread is three times the number of loaves of sunflower bread. Also, $12 - 7 = 5$, so the number of loaves of French bread is 5 less than the number of loaves of honey wheat bread. Multiply the appropriate cost per loaf by the number of loaves sold and add the results to check that total receipts were $87.89.

▐▐▐

8.8 EXERCISES

Solve each problem by using a system of equations.

1. Win-Loss Record During the 2009 Major League Baseball season, the Los Angeles Dodgers played 162 games. They won 28 more games than they lost. What was their win-loss record that year?

2009 MLB Final Standings National League West

Team	W	L
L.A. Dodgers	—	—
Colorado	92	70
San Francisco	88	74
San Diego	75	87
Arizona	—	—

Source: World Almanac and Book of Facts.

2. Win-Loss Record Refer to **Exercise 1.** During the same 162-game season, the Arizona Diamondbacks lost 22 more games than they won. What was the team's win-loss record?

3. Dimensions of a Basketball Court LeBron and Yao found that the width of their basketball court was 44 feet less than the length. If the perimeter was 288 feet, what were the length and the width of their court?

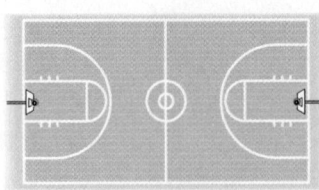

4. Dimensions of a Tennis Court Venus and Serena measured a tennis court and found that it was 42 feet longer than it was wide and had a perimeter of 228 feet. What were the length and the width of the tennis court?

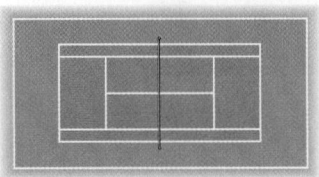

5. *Car Rental* On a 6-day trip, Michael Schmitz rented a car for $53 per day at weekday rates and $35 per day at weekend rates. If his total bill was $264, how many days did he rent at each rate? (*Source:* Enterprise.)

6. *Cost of Art Supplies* For an art project, Nicole McHam bought 8 sheets of colored paper and 3 marker pens for $6.50. She later needed 2 sheets of colored paper and 2 marker pens. These items cost $3.00. Find the cost of 1 marker pen and 1 sheet of colored paper.

7. *Dimensions of a Square and a Triangle* The side of a square is 4 centimeters longer than the side of an equilateral triangle. The perimeter of the square is 24 centimeters more than the perimeter of the triangle. Find the lengths of a side of the square and a side of the triangle.

8. *Dimensions of a Rectangle* The length of a rectangle is 7 feet more than the width. If the length were decreased by 3 feet and the width were increased by 2 feet, the perimeter would be 32 feet. Find the length and width of the original rectangle.

9. *Coffee Prices* At a business meeting at Panera Bread, the bill for two cappuccinos and three house lattes was $10.95. At another table, the bill for one cappuccino and two house lattes was $6.65. How much did each type of beverage cost? (*Source:* Panera Bread menu.)

10. *Top-Grossing Concerts* The top-grossing tour on the North American concert circuit for 2009 was U2, followed in second place by Bruce Springsteen and the E Street Band. Together, they took in $217.5 million from ticket sales. If Springsteen took in $28.5 million less than U2, how much did each band generate? (*Source:* Pollstar.)

11. *Travel Costs* New York City and Washington, D.C., were the two most expensive cities for business travel in 2009. On the basis of the average total costs per day for each city (which include a hotel room, car rental, and three meals), 2 days in New York and 3 days in Washington cost $2772, while 4 days in New York and 2 days in Washington cost $3488. What was the average cost per day in each city? (*Source:* Business Travel News.)

12. *Prices at Arby's* Andrew McGinnis works at Arby's. One day he sold 15 Junior Roast Beef sandwiches and 10 Big Montana sandwiches, totaling $75.25. Another day he sold 30 Junior Roast Beef sandwiches and 5 Big Montana sandwiches, totaling $84.65. How much did each type of sandwich cost? (*Source:* Arby's menu.)

13. *Ticket Prices* In 2009, the New York Yankees and the Boston Red Sox had the most expensive ticket prices in Major League Baseball. Two Yankees tickets and three Red Sox tickets purchased at their average prices cost $296.66, while three Yankees tickets and two Red Sox tickets cost $319.39. Find the average ticket price for a Yankees ticket and a Red Sox ticket. (*Source:* Team Marketing Report.)

14. *Cost of Clay* For his art class, Bryce bought 2 kilograms of dark clay and 3 kilograms of light clay, paying $22 for the clay. He later needed 1 kilogram of dark clay and 2 kilograms of light clay, costing $13 altogether. What was the cost per kilogram for each type of clay?

Fan Cost Index The Fan Cost Index (FCI) represents the cost of four average-price tickets, four small soft drinks, two small beers, four hot dogs, parking for one car, two game programs, and two souvenir caps to a sporting event. For example, in 2008, the FCI for Major League Baseball was $191.75. This was by far the least for the four major professional sports. (*Source:* www.teammarketing.com) Use the concept of FCI in Exercises 15 and 16.

15. For the 2008–2009 season, the FCI prices for the National Hockey League and the National Basketball Association totaled $580.16. The hockey FCI was $3.70 less than that of basketball. What were the FCIs for these sports?

16. In 2009, the FCI prices for Major League Baseball and the National Football League totaled $609.53. The football FCI was $215.75 more than that of baseball. What were the FCIs for these sports?

Formulas The formulas $p = br$ (percentage = base × rate) and $I = prt$ (simple interest = principal × rate × time) are used in the applications in Exercises 21–30. To prepare to use these formulas, work Exercises 17–20.

17. If a container of liquid contains 120 ounces of solution, what is the number of ounces of pure acid if the given solution contains the following acid concentrations?

  (a) 10%   **(b)** 25%

  (c) 40%   **(d)** 50%

18. If $50,000 is invested in an account paying simple annual interest, how much interest will be earned during the first year at the following rates?

  (a) 0.5%   **(b)** 1%

  (c) 1.25%   **(d)** 2.5%

19. If a pound of ham costs $2.29, give an expression for the cost of x pounds.

20. If a ticket to the movie *Avatar* costs $9 and y tickets are sold, give an expression for the amount collected.

21. *Acid Mixture* How many liters each of 15% acid and 33% acid should be mixed to obtain 40 liters of 21% acid?

Kind of Solution	Liters of Solution	Amount of Pure Acid
0.15	x	
0.33	y	
0.21	40	

22. Alcohol Mixture How many gallons each of 25% alcohol and 35% alcohol should be mixed to obtain 20 gallons of 32% alcohol?

Kind of Solution	Gallons of Solution	Amount of Pure Alcohol
0.25	x	$0.25x$
0.35	y	$0.35y$
0.32	20	$0.32(20)$

23. Antifreeze Mixture A truck radiator holds 18 liters of fluid. How much pure antifreeze must be added to a mixture that is 4% antifreeze in order to fill the radiator with a mixture that is 20% antifreeze?

24. Acid Mixture Pure acid is to be added to a 10% acid solution to obtain 27 liters of a 20% acid solution. What amounts of each should be used?

25. Fruit Drink Mixture A popular fruit drink is made by mixing fruit juices. Such a mixture with 50% juice is to be mixed with another mixture that is 30% juice to get 200 liters of a mixture that is 45% juice. How much of each should be used?

Kind of Juice	Number of Liters	Amount of Pure Juice
0.50	x	$0.50x$
0.30	y	
0.45		

26. Candy Mixture Erin Ryan plans to mix pecan clusters that sell for $3.60 per pound with chocolate truffles that sell for $7.20 per pound to get a mixture that she can sell in Valentine boxes for $4.95 per pound. How much of the $3.60 clusters and the $7.20 truffles should she use to create 80 pounds of the mix?

	Number of Pounds	Price per Pound	Value of Candy
Clusters	x	3.60	$3.60x$
Truffles	y	7.20	$7.20y$
Mixture	80	4.95	$4.95(80)$

27. Candy Mixture A grocer plans to mix candy that sells for $1.20 per pound with candy that sells for $2.40 per pound to get a mixture that he plans to sell for $1.65 per pound. How much of the $1.20 and $2.40 candy should he use if he wants 160 pounds of the mix?

28. Ticket Sales Tickets to a production of *West Side Story* at Northeastern State University cost $10.00 for general admission or $8.00 with student identification. If 184 people paid to see a performance and $1624 was collected, how many of each type of admission were sold?

29. Investment Mix An investor must invest a total of $15,000 in two accounts, one paying 4% simple annual interest, and the other 3%. If he wants to earn $550 annual interest, how much should he invest at each rate?

Principal	Rate	Interest
x	0.04	
y	0.03	
15,000		

30. Investment Mix A total of $3000 is invested, part at 2% simple interest and part at 4%. If the total annual return from the two investments is $100, how much is invested at each rate?

Principal	Rate	Interest
x	0.02	$0.02x$
y	0.04	$0.04y$
3000		100

Formulas *The formula* $d = rt$ *(distance = rate × time) is used in the applications in Exercises 33–36. To prepare to use this formula, work Exercises 31 and 32.*

31. If the speed of a boat in still water is 10 mph, and the speed of the current of a river is x mph, what is the speed of the boat

   (a) going upstream (that is, against the current, which slows the boat down);

   (b) going downstream (that is, with the current, which speeds the boat up)?

Downstream (with the current)

Upstream (against the current)

32. If the speed of a killer whale is 25 mph and the whale swims for y hours, give an expression for the number of miles the whale travels.

33. Speeds of Trains A train travels 150 miles in the same time that a plane covers 400 miles. If the speed of the plane is 20 miles per hour less than 3 times the speed of the train, find both speeds.

34. Speeds of Trains A freight train and an express train leave towns 390 miles apart at the same time, traveling toward one another. The freight train travels 30 mph slower than the express train. They pass one another 3 hours later. What are their speeds?

35. ***Speeds of Boat and Current*** In his motorboat, Tran travels upstream at top speed to his favorite fishing spot, a distance of 36 miles, in two hours. Returning, he finds that the trip downstream, still at top speed, takes only 1.5 hours. Find the speed of Tran's boat and the speed of the current.

36. ***Speeds of Snow Speeder and Wind*** Braving blizzard conditions on the planet Hoth, Luke Skywalker sets out at top speed in his snow speeder for a rebel base 3600 miles away. He travels into a steady headwind, and makes the trip in 2 hours. Returning, he finds that the trip back, still at top speed but now with a tailwind, takes only 1.5 hours. Find the top speed of Luke's snow speeder and the speed of the wind.

Solve each problem involving three unknowns.

37. ***Olympic Gold Medals*** In the 2008 Olympics in Beijing, Russia earned 5 fewer gold medals than bronze. The number of silver medals earned was 35 less than twice the number of bronze medals. Russia earned a total of 72 medals. How many of each kind of medal did Russia earn? (*Source: World Almanac and Book of Facts.*)

38. ***Voter Affiliations*** In a random sample of Americans of voting age conducted in 2010, 8% more people identified themselves as Independents than as Republicans, while 6% fewer identified themselves as Republicans than as Democrats. Of those sampled, 2% did not identify with any of the three categories. What percent of the people in the sample identified themselves with each of the three political affiliations? (*Source:* Gallup, Inc.)

39. ***Dimensions of a Triangle*** The perimeter of a triangle is 56 inches. The longest side measures 4 inches less than the sum of the other two sides. Three times the shortest side is 4 inches more than the longest side. Find the lengths of the three sides.

40. ***Dimensions of a Triangle*** The perimeter of a triangle is 70 centimeters. The longest side is 4 centimeters less than the sum of the other two sides. Twice the shortest side is 9 centimeters less than the longest side. Find the length of each side of the triangle.

41. ***Hardware Production*** A hardware supplier manufactures three kinds of clamps, types A, B, and C. Production restrictions require it to make 10 units more type C clamps than the total of the other types and twice as many type B clamps as type A. The shop must produce a total of 490 units of clamps per day. How many units of each type can be made per day?

42. ***Television Production*** A company produces three color television sets, models X, Y, and Z. Each model X set requires 2 hr of electronics work, 2 hr of assembly time, and 1 hr of finishing time. Each model Y requires 1, 3, and 1 hr of electronics, assembly, and finishing time, respectively. Each model Z requires 3, 2, and 2 hr of the same work, respectively. There are 100 hr available for electronics, 100 hr available for assembly, and 65 hr available for finishing per week. How many of each model should be produced each week if all available time must be used?

43. ***Harlem Globetrotter Ticket Prices*** Tickets for the Harlem Globetrotters show at Michigan State University in 2010 cost $16, $23, or, for VIP seats, $40. If nine times as many $16 tickets were sold as VIP tickets, and the number of $16 tickets sold was 55 more than the sum of the number of $23 tickets and VIP tickets, sales of all three kinds of tickets would total $46,575. How many of each kind of ticket would have been sold? (*Source:* Breslin Student Events Center.)

44. ***Concert Ticket Prices*** Three kinds of tickets are available for a Four Unplugged concert: "up close," "in the middle," and "far out." "Up close" tickets cost $10 more than "in the middle" tickets, while "in the middle" tickets cost $10 more than "far out" tickets. Twice the cost of an "up close" ticket is $20 more than 3 times the cost of a "far out" seat. Find the price of each kind of ticket.

NHL Point System *Starting with the 2005–2006 season, the National Hockey League adopted a new system for awarding points used to determine team standings. A team is awarded 2 points for a win (W), 0 points for a loss in regulation play (L), and 1 point for an overtime loss (OTL). Use this information in Exercises 45 and 46.*

45. During the 2008–2009 NHL regular season, the Boston Bruins played 82 games. Their wins and overtime losses resulted in a total of 116 points. They had 9 more losses in regulation play than overtime losses. How many wins, losses, and overtime losses did they have that year?

NHL Final Standings 2008–2009
Northeast Division, Eastern Conference

Team	GP	W	L	OTL	Points
Boston	82	—	—	—	116
Montreal	82	41	30	11	93
Buffalo	82	41	32	9	91
Ottawa	82	36	35	11	83
Toronto	82	34	35	13	81

Source: World Almanac and Book of Facts.

46. During the 2008–2009 NHL regular season, the Los Angeles Kings played 82 games. Their wins and overtime losses resulted in a total of 79 points. They had 14 more total losses (in regulation play and overtime) than wins. How many wins, losses, and overtime losses did they have that year?

NHL Final Standings 2008–2009
Pacific Division, Western Conference

Team	GP	W	L	OTL	Points
San Jose	82	53	18	11	117
Anaheim	82	42	33	7	91
Dallas	82	36	35	11	83
Phoenix	82	36	39	7	79
Los Angeles	82	—	—	—	79

Source: World Almanac and Book of Facts.

EXTENSION Using Matrix Row Operations to Solve Systems

Matrix Terminology • Matrix Row Operations • Gauss-Jordan Method

```
NAMES  MATH  EDIT
0↑cumSum(
A: ref(
B: rref(
C: rowSwap(
D: row+(
E: *row(
F: *row+(
```

Choices C, D, E, and F provide the user of the TI-83/84 Plus calculator a means of performing row operations on matrices.

Matrix Terminology The elimination method used to solve systems introduced in **Section 8.7** can be streamlined into a systematic method by using *matrices* (singular: *matrix*). Matrices can be used to solve linear systems, and matrix methods are particularly suitable for computer solutions of large systems of equations having many unknowns.

To begin, consider a system of three equations and three unknowns such as

$$a_1x + b_1y + c_1z = d_1$$
$$a_2x + b_2y + c_2z = d_2,$$
$$a_3x + b_3y + c_3z = d_3$$

written in an abbreviated form as
$$\begin{bmatrix} a_1 & b_1 & c_1 & d_1 \\ a_2 & b_2 & c_2 & d_2 \\ a_3 & b_3 & c_3 & d_3 \end{bmatrix}.$$

Such a rectangular array of numbers enclosed by brackets is called a **matrix.** Each number in the array is an **element** or **entry.** The matrix above has three **rows** (horizontal) and four **columns** (vertical) of entries, and is called a 3×4 (read "3 by 4") matrix. The constants in the last column of the matrix can be set apart from the coefficients of the variables by using a vertical line, as shown in the following **augmented matrix.**

$$\text{Rows} \begin{array}{l} \rightarrow \\ \rightarrow \\ \rightarrow \end{array} \begin{bmatrix} a_1 & b_1 & c_1 & d_1 \\ a_2 & b_2 & c_2 & d_2 \\ a_3 & b_3 & c_3 & d_3 \end{bmatrix} \text{Augmented matrix}$$

Columns

Matrix Row Operations The rows of this augmented matrix can be treated the same as the equations of a system of equations, since the augmented matrix is actually a short form of the system. Any transformation of the matrix that will result in an equivalent system is permitted. The following **matrix row operations** produce such transformations.

Matrix Row Operations

For any real number k and any augmented matrix of a system of linear equations, the following operations will produce the matrix of an *equivalent system*—that is, another system with the same solution set.

1. **Interchange any two rows of a matrix.**

2. **Multiply the elements of a row of a matrix by the same nonzero number k.**

3. **Add a common multiple of the elements of one row to the corresponding elements of another row.**

Gauss-Jordan Method

If the word "row" is replaced by "equation," it can be seen that the three row operations also apply to a system of equations, so that a system of equations can be solved by transforming its corresponding matrix into the matrix of an equivalent, simpler system. The goal is a matrix in the form

$$\begin{bmatrix} 1 & 0 & | & a \\ 0 & 1 & | & b \end{bmatrix} \quad \text{or} \quad \begin{bmatrix} 1 & 0 & 0 & | & a \\ 0 & 1 & 0 & | & b \\ 0 & 0 & 1 & | & c \end{bmatrix}$$

for systems with two or three equations respectively. On the left of the vertical bar there are ones down the diagonal from upper left to lower right and zeros elsewhere in the matrices. When these matrices are rewritten as systems of equations, the values of the variables are known. The **Gauss-Jordan method** is a systematic way of using the matrix row operations to change the augmented matrix of a system into the form that shows its solution.

EXAMPLE 1 Solving a Linear System Using Gauss-Jordan (Two Unknowns)

Solve the linear system.

$$3x - 4y = 1$$
$$5x + 2y = 19$$

SOLUTION

The equations should all be in the same form, with the variable terms in the same order on the left, and the constant term on the right. Begin by writing the augmented matrix.

$$\begin{bmatrix} 3 & -4 & | & 1 \\ 5 & 2 & | & 19 \end{bmatrix}$$

The goal is to transform this augmented matrix into one in which the values of the variables will be easy to see. That is, since each column in the matrix represents the coefficients of one variable, the augmented matrix should be transformed so that it is of the form

$$\begin{bmatrix} 1 & 0 & | & k \\ 0 & 1 & | & j \end{bmatrix}$$

for real numbers k and j. Once the augmented matrix is in this form, the matrix can be rewritten as a linear system to get

$$x = k$$
$$y = j.$$

The necessary transformations are performed as follows. It is best to work in columns beginning in each column with the element that is to become 1. In the augmented matrix,

$$\begin{bmatrix} 3 & -4 & | & 1 \\ 5 & 2 & | & 19 \end{bmatrix}$$

there is a 3 in the first row, first column position. Use row operation 2, multiplying each entry in the first row by $\frac{1}{3}$ to get a 1 in this position. (This step is abbreviated as $\frac{1}{3}$ R1.)

$$\begin{bmatrix} 1 & -\frac{4}{3} & | & \frac{1}{3} \\ 5 & 2 & | & 19 \end{bmatrix} \quad \frac{1}{3}\text{R1}$$

Introduce 0 in the second row, first column by multiplying each element of the first row by -5 and adding the result to the corresponding element in the second row, using row operation 3.

$$\begin{bmatrix} 1 & -\frac{4}{3} & | & \frac{1}{3} \\ 0 & \frac{26}{3} & | & \frac{52}{3} \end{bmatrix} \quad -5\text{R1} + \text{R2}$$

Obtain 1 in the second row, second column by multiplying each element of the second row by $\frac{3}{26}$, using row operation 2.

$$\begin{bmatrix} 1 & -\frac{4}{3} & | & \frac{1}{3} \\ 0 & 1 & | & 2 \end{bmatrix} \quad \frac{3}{26}\text{R2}$$

Finally, obtain 0 in the first row, second column by multiplying each element of the second row by $\frac{4}{3}$ and adding the result to the corresponding element in the first row.

$$\begin{bmatrix} 1 & 0 & | & 3 \\ 0 & 1 & | & 2 \end{bmatrix} \quad \frac{4}{3}\text{R2} + \text{R1}$$

This last matrix corresponds to the system

$$x = 3$$
$$y = 2,$$

that has the solution set $\{(3, 2)\}$. This solution could have been read directly from the third column of the final matrix. ■■■

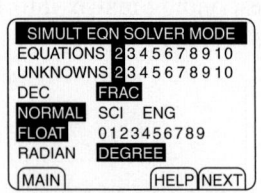

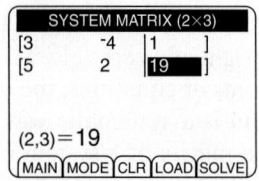

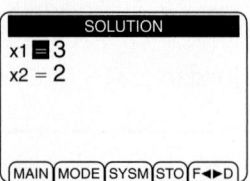

The TI-84 Plus has an application that solves simultaneous equations. Compare this to **Example 1.**

A linear system with three equations is solved in a similar way. Row operations are used to get 1s down the diagonal from left to right and 0s above and below each 1.

■■ **EXAMPLE 2** Solving a System Using Gauss-Jordan (Three Unknowns)

Use the Gauss-Jordan method to solve the system.

$$x - y + 5z = -6$$
$$3x + 3y - z = 10$$
$$x + 3y + 2z = 5$$

SOLUTION

Because the system is in proper form, begin by writing the augmented matrix of the linear system.

$$\begin{bmatrix} 1 & -1 & 5 & | & -6 \\ 3 & 3 & -1 & | & 10 \\ 1 & 3 & 2 & | & 5 \end{bmatrix}$$

The final matrix is to be of the form

$$\begin{bmatrix} 1 & 0 & 0 & | & m \\ 0 & 1 & 0 & | & n \\ 0 & 0 & 1 & | & p \end{bmatrix},$$

where m, n, and p are real numbers. This final form of the matrix gives the system $x = m$, $y = n$, and $z = p$, so the solution set is $\{(m, n, p)\}$.

There is already a 1 in the first row, first column. Introduce a 0 in the second row of the first column by multiplying each element in the first row by -3 and adding the result to the corresponding element in the second row, using row operation 3.

$$\begin{bmatrix} 1 & -1 & 5 & | & -6 \\ 0 & 6 & -16 & | & 28 \\ 1 & 3 & 2 & | & 5 \end{bmatrix} \quad -3R1 + R2$$

Now, to change the last element in the first column to 0, use row operation 3. Multiply each element of the first row by -1, then add the results to the corresponding elements of the third row.

$$\begin{bmatrix} 1 & -1 & 5 & | & -6 \\ 0 & 6 & -16 & | & 28 \\ 0 & 4 & -3 & | & 11 \end{bmatrix} \quad -1R1 + R3$$

The same procedure is used to transform the second and third columns. For both of these columns, first perform the step of getting 1 in the appropriate position of each column. Do this by multiplying the elements of the row by the reciprocal of the number in that position.

$$\begin{bmatrix} 1 & -1 & 5 & | & -6 \\ 0 & 1 & -\frac{8}{3} & | & \frac{14}{3} \\ 0 & 4 & -3 & | & 11 \end{bmatrix} \quad \frac{1}{6}R2$$

$$\begin{bmatrix} 1 & 0 & \frac{7}{3} & | & -\frac{4}{3} \\ 0 & 1 & -\frac{8}{3} & | & \frac{14}{3} \\ 0 & 4 & -3 & | & 11 \end{bmatrix} \quad R2 + R1$$

$$\begin{bmatrix} 1 & 0 & \frac{7}{3} & | & -\frac{4}{3} \\ 0 & 1 & -\frac{8}{3} & | & \frac{14}{3} \\ 0 & 0 & \frac{23}{3} & | & -\frac{23}{3} \end{bmatrix} \quad -4R2 + R3$$

$$\begin{bmatrix} 1 & 0 & \frac{7}{3} & | & -\frac{4}{3} \\ 0 & 1 & -\frac{8}{3} & | & -\frac{14}{3} \\ 0 & 0 & 1 & | & -1 \end{bmatrix} \quad \frac{3}{23}R3$$

$$\begin{bmatrix} 1 & 0 & 0 & | & 1 \\ 0 & 1 & -\frac{8}{3} & | & \frac{14}{3} \\ 0 & 0 & 1 & | & -1 \end{bmatrix} \quad -\frac{7}{3}R3 + R1$$

$$\begin{bmatrix} 1 & 0 & 0 & | & 1 \\ 0 & 1 & 0 & | & 2 \\ 0 & 0 & 1 & | & -1 \end{bmatrix} \quad \frac{8}{3}R3 + R2$$

The linear system associated with this final matrix is

$$x = 1$$
$$y = 2 \quad, \text{ and the solution set is } \quad \{(1, 2, -1)\}.$$
$$z = -1$$

■■■

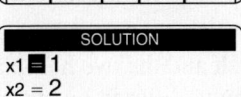

```
    SYSTEM MATRIX (3×4)
[1    -1    5    -6    ]
[3     3   -1    10    ]
[1     3    2    5     ]

(3,4)=5
 MAIN  MODE  CLR  LOAD  SOLVE


        SOLUTION
x1 ▆ 1
x2 = 2
x3 = -1


 MAIN  MODE  SYSM  STO  F◄►D
```

Compare to **Example 2.**

EXTENSION EXERCISES

Use the Gauss-Jordan method to solve each system of equations.

1. $x + y = 5$
$x - y = -1$

2. $x + 2y = 5$
$2x + y = -2$

3. $x + y = -3$
$2x - 5y = -6$

4. $3x - 2y = 4$
$3x + y = -2$

5. $2x - 3y = 10$
$2x + 2y = 5$

6. $4x + y = 5$
$2x + y = 3$

7. $3x - 7y = 31$
$2x - 4y = 18$

8. $5x - y = 14$
$x + 8y = 11$

9. $x + y - z = 6$
$2x - y + z = -9$
$x - 2y + 3z = 1$

10. $x + 3y - 6z = 7$
$2x - y + 2z = 0$
$x + y + 2z = -1$

11. $2x - y + 3z = 0$
$x + 2y - z = 5$
$2y + z = 1$

12. $4x + 2y - 3z = 6$
$x - 4y + z = -4$
$-x + 2z = 2$

13. $-x + y = -1$
$y - z = 6$
$x + z = -1$

14. $x + y = 1$
$2x - z = 0$
$y + 2z = -2$

15. $2x - y + 4z = -1$
$-3x + 5y - z = 5$
$2x + 3y + 2z = 3$

16. $5x - 3y + 2z = -5$
$2x + 2y - z = 4$
$4x - y + z = -1$

17. $x + y - 2z = 1$
$2x - y - 4z = -4$
$3x - 2y + z = -7$

18. $x + 3y - 6z = -26$
$3x + y - z = -10$
$2x - y - 3z = -16$

Solve each problem by writing a system and solving it by the Gauss-Jordan method.

19. *Company Revenue* In 2009, the two American telecommunication companies with the greatest revenues were AT&T and Verizon. The two companies had combined revenues of \$221.4 billion. AT&T's revenue was \$26.6 billion more than that of Verizon. What was the revenue for each company? (*Source: Fortune* magazine.)

20. *Perfume Supply* A department store display features three kinds of perfume: Felice, Vivid, and Joy. There are 10 more bottles of Felice than Vivid, and 3 fewer bottles of Joy than Vivid. Each bottle of Felice costs \$8, Vivid costs \$15, and Joy costs \$32. The total value of all the perfume is \$589. How many bottles of each are there?

8.9 LINEAR INEQUALITIES, SYSTEMS, AND LINEAR PROGRAMMING

Linear Inequalities in Two Variables • Systems of Inequalities • Linear Programming

Linear Inequalities in Two Variables

Linear inequalities with one variable were graphed on the number line in **Chapter 7.** Linear inequalities in two variables are graphed in a rectangular coordinate system.

> ### Linear Inequality in Two Variables
>
> An inequality that can be written as
>
> $$Ax + By < C \quad \text{or} \quad Ax + By > C,$$
>
> where A, B, and C are real numbers and A and B are not both 0, is a **linear inequality in two variables.** The symbols $\leq$ and $\geq$ may replace $<$ and $>$ in this definition.

A line divides the plane into three regions: the line itself and the two half-planes on either side of the line. Recall that the graphs of linear inequalities in one variable are *intervals* on the number line that may include an endpoint. The graphs of linear inequalities in two variables are *regions* in the real number plane and may include a *boundary line*. The **boundary line** for the inequality $Ax + By < C$ or $Ax + By > C$ is the graph of the *equation* $Ax + By = C$.

To graph a linear inequality, we follow these steps.

> **Graphing a Linear Inequality**
>
> *Step 1* **Draw the boundary.** Draw the graph of the straight line that is the boundary. Make the line solid if the inequality involves ≤ or ≥. Make the line dashed if the inequality involves < or >.
>
> *Step 2* **Choose a test point.** Choose any point not on the line as a test point.
>
> *Step 3* **Shade the appropriate region.** Shade the region that includes the test point if it satisfies the original inequality. Otherwise, shade the region on the other side of the boundary line.

▮▮ **EXAMPLE 1** Graphing a Linear Inequality

Graph $3x + 2y \geq 6$.

SOLUTION

First graph the straight line $3x + 2y = 6$. The graph of this line, the boundary of the graph of the inequality, is shown in **Figure 54**. The graph of the inequality $3x + 2y \geq 6$ includes the points of the line $3x + 2y = 6$, and either the points *above* the line $3x + 2y = 6$ or the points *below* that line. To decide which, select any point not on the line $3x + 2y = 6$ as a test point. The origin, $(0, 0)$, often is a good choice. Substitute the values from the test point $(0, 0)$ for x and y in the linear inequality $3x + 2y \geq 6$.

$$3(0) + 2(0) \overset{?}{\geq} 6$$
$$0 \geq 6 \quad \text{False}$$

Because the result is false, $(0, 0)$ does not satisfy the inequality, and so the solution set includes all points on the other side of the line. This region is shaded in **Figure 54**. ▮▮▮

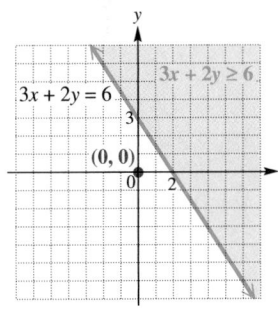

Figure 54

The TI-83/84 Plus allows us to shade the appropriate region for an inequality. Compare with **Figure 54**.

▮▮ **EXAMPLE 2** Graphing a Linear Inequality

Graph $x - 3y > 4$.

SOLUTION

First graph the boundary line, $x - 3y = 4$. The graph is shown in **Figure 55**. The points of the boundary line do not belong to the inequality $x - 3y > 4$ (since the inequality symbol is > and not ≥). For this reason, the line is dashed. To decide which side of the line is the graph of the solution set, choose any point that is not on the line, say $(1, 2)$. Substitute 1 for x and 2 for y in the original inequality.

$$1 - 3(2) \overset{?}{>} 4$$
$$-5 > 4 \quad \text{False}$$

Because of this false result, the solution set lies on the side of the boundary line that does *not* contain the test point $(1, 2)$. The solution set, graphed in **Figure 55**, includes only those points in the shaded region (not those on the line). ▮▮▮

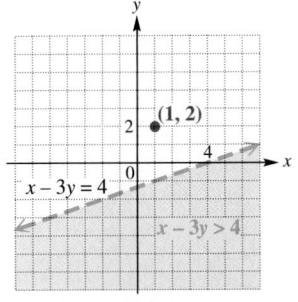

Figure 55

Systems of Inequalities

Systems of inequalities with two variables may be solved by graphing. A system of linear inequalities consists of two or more such inequalities, and the solution set of such a system consists of all points that make all the inequalities true at the same time.

> ### Graphing a System of Linear Inequalities
>
> **Step 1** **Graph each inequality in the same coordinate system.**   Graph each inequality in the system, using the method described in **Examples 1 and 2.**
>
> **Step 2** **Find the intersection of the regions of solutions.**   Indicate the intersection of the regions of solutions of the individual inequalities. This is the solution set of the system.

▮▮ **EXAMPLE 3** Graphing a System of Inequalities

Graph the solution set of the linear system.

$$3x + 2y \le 6$$
$$2x - 5y \ge 10$$

SOLUTION

Begin by graphing $3x + 2y \le 6$. To do this, graph $3x + 2y = 6$ as a solid line. Since $(0, 0)$ makes the inequality *true*, shade the region containing $(0, 0)$, as shown in **Figure 56**.

Now graph $2x - 5y \ge 10$. The solid line boundary is the graph of $2x - 5y = 10$. Since $(0, 0)$ makes the inequality *false*, shade the region that does not contain $(0, 0)$, as shown in **Figure 57**.

The solution set of the system is given by the intersection (overlap) of the regions of the graphs in **Figures 56 and 57**. The solution set is the shaded region in **Figure 58**, and includes portions of the two boundary lines.

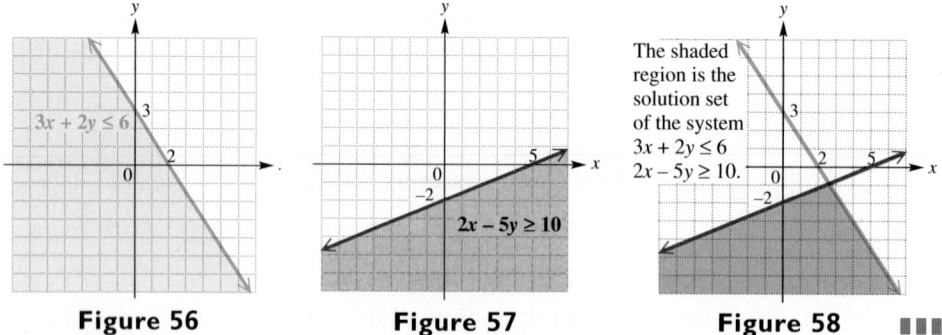

Figure 56   Figure 57   Figure 58   ▮▮▮

In practice, we usually do all the work in one coordinate system.

▮▮ **EXAMPLE 4** Graphing a System of Inequalities

Graph the solution set of the linear system.

$$2x + 3y \ge 12$$
$$7x + 4y \ge 28$$
$$y \le 6$$
$$x \le 5$$

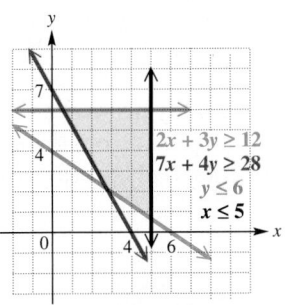

Figure 59

SOLUTION

Graph the four inequalities in one coordinate system and shade the region common to all four as shown in **Figure 59**. As shown, the boundary lines are all solid.   ▮▮▮

Linear Programming

One important application of mathematics to business and social science is **linear programming.** Linear programming is used to find an optimum value—for example, minimum cost or maximum profit. Procedures for solving linear programming problems were developed in 1947 by George Dantzig, while he was working on a problem of allocating supplies for the Air Force in a way that minimized total cost.

To solve a linear programming problem in general, use the following steps. (The terms *constraint, objective function, region of feasible solutions,* and *vertex* are defined in **Example 5**).

Solving a Linear Programming Problem

Step 1   Write all necessary constraints and the objective function.
Step 2   Graph the region of feasible solutions.
Step 3   Identify all vertices.
Step 4   Find the value of the objective function at each vertex.
Step 5   The solution is given by the vertex producing the optimum value of the objective function.

▌▌ **EXAMPLE 5** Maximizing Profit

The Smartski Company makes two products, DVD recorders and MP-3 players. Each DVD recorder gives a profit of $3, while each MP-3 player gives a profit of $7. The company must manufacture at least 1 DVD recorder per day to satisfy one of its customers, but no more than 5 because of production problems. Also, the number of MP-3 players produced cannot exceed 6 per day. As a further requirement, the number of DVD recorders cannot exceed the number of MP-3 players. How many of each should the company manufacture in order to obtain the maximum profit?

SOLUTION

Step 1 We translate the statements of the problem into symbols by letting

$$x = \text{number of DVD recorders to be produced daily}$$
$$y = \text{number of MP-3 players to be produced daily.}$$

According to the statement of the problem, the company must produce at least one DVD recorder (one or more), so

$$x \geq 1.$$

No more than 5 DVD recorders may be produced.

$$x \leq 5$$

No more than 6 MP-3 players may be made in one day.

$$y \leq 6$$

The number of DVD recorders may not exceed the number of MP-3 players.

$$x \leq y$$

The number of DVD recorders and of MP-3 players cannot be negative.

$$x \geq 0 \quad \text{and} \quad y \geq 0$$

George B. Dantzig (1914–2005) of Stanford University was one of the key people behind **operations research** (OR). As a management science, OR is not a single discipline. It draws from mathematics, probability theory, statistics, and economics. The name given to this "multiplex" shows its historical origins in World War II, when operations of a military nature called forth the efforts of many scientists to research their fields for applications to the war effort and to solve tactical problems.

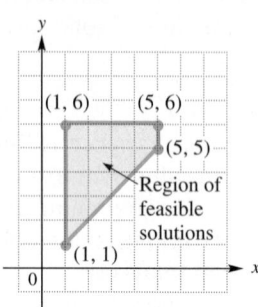

Figure 60

All restrictions, or **constraints,** placed on production can be summarized.

$$x \geq 1, \quad x \leq 5, \quad y \leq 6, \quad x \leq y, \quad x \geq 0, \quad y \geq 0$$

Because each DVD recorder gives a profit of $3, the daily profit from the production of x DVD recorders is $3x$ dollars. Also, the profit from the production of y MP-3 players is $7y$ dollars per day. The total daily profit is thus given by the following **objective function.**

$$\text{Profit} = 3x + 7y$$

Step 2 The maximum possible profit that the company can make, subject to these constraints, is found by sketching the graph of the solution set of the system. See **Figure 60**. The only feasible values of x and y are those that satisfy all constraints. These values correspond to points that lie on the boundary or in the shaded region, called the **region of feasible solutions.**

Step 3 The problem may now be stated as follows: find values of x and y in the region of feasible solutions as shown in **Figure 60** that will produce the maximum possible value of $3x + 7y$. It can be shown that any optimum value (maximum or minimum) will always occur at a **vertex** (or **corner point**) of the region of feasible solutions.

Step 4 Locate the point (x, y) that gives the maximum profit by checking the coordinates of the vertices, shown in **Figure 60** and in **Table 6**. Find the profit that corresponds to each coordinate pair.

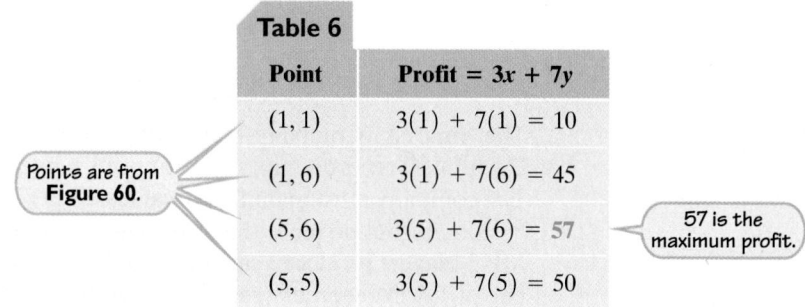

Table 6	
Point	**Profit $= 3x + 7y$**
$(1, 1)$	$3(1) + 7(1) = 10$
$(1, 6)$	$3(1) + 7(6) = 45$
$(5, 6)$	$3(5) + 7(6) = 57$
$(5, 5)$	$3(5) + 7(5) = 50$

Points are from **Figure 60**.

57 is the maximum profit.

Step 5 Choose the vertex that gives the maximum profit. The maximum profit of $57 is obtained when 5 DVD recorders and 6 MP-3 players are produced each day.   ▎▎▎

It Pays to Do Your Homework George Dantzig has told the story of how he obtained his degree without actually writing a thesis.

One day he arrived late to one of his classes and on the board were two problems. Assuming that they were homework problems, he worked on them and handed them in a few days later, apologizing to his professor for taking so long to do them.

Several weeks later he received an early morning visit from his professor. The problems had not been intended as homework problems; they were actually two famous *unsolved* problems in statistics! Later, when Dantzig began to think about a thesis topic, his professor told him that the two solutions would serve as his thesis.

8.9 EXERCISES

In Exercises 1–4, match each system of inequalities with the correct graph from choices A–D.

A. 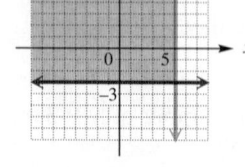   **B.** 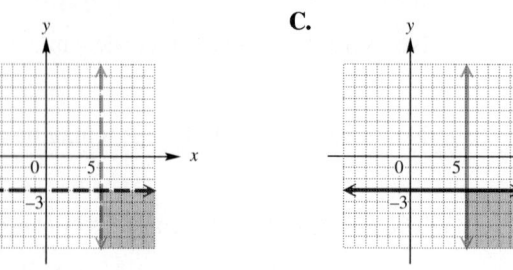   **C.** 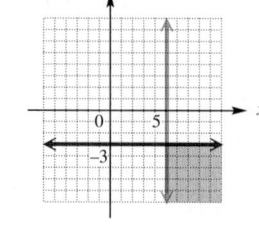   **D.**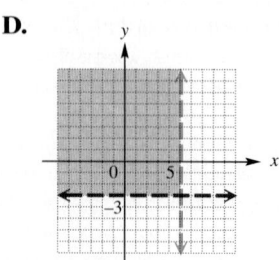

1. $x \geq 5$
  $y \leq -3$

2. $x \leq 5$
  $y \geq -3$

3. $x > 5$
  $y < -3$

4. $x < 5$
  $y > -3$

Graph each linear inequality.

5. $x + y \leq 2$

6. $x - y \geq -3$

7. $4x - y \leq 5$

8. $3x + y \geq 6$

9. $x + 3y \geq -2$

10. $4x + 6y \leq -3$

11. $x + 2y \leq -5$

12. $2x - 4y \leq 3$

13. $4x - 3y < 12$

14. $5x + 3y > 15$

15. $y > -x$

16. $y < x$

Graph each system of inequalities.

17. $x + y \leq 1$
    $x \geq 0$

18. $3x - 4y \leq 6$
    $y \geq 1$

19. $2x - y \geq 1$
    $3x + 2y \geq 6$

20. $x + 3y \geq 6$
    $3x - 4y \leq 12$

21. $-x - y < 5$
    $x - y \leq 3$

22. $6x - 4y < 8$
    $x + 2y \geq 4$

Exercises 23 and 24 show regions of feasible solutions. Find the maximum and minimum values of the given expressions.

23. $3x + 5y$

24. $40x + 75y$

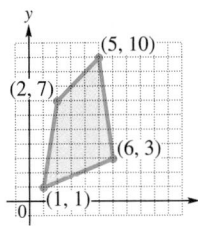

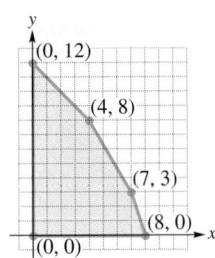

Use graphical methods to find values of x and y satisfying the given conditions. (It may be necessary to solve a system of equations in order to find vertices.) Find the value of the maximum or minimum as directed.

25. Find $x \geq 0$ and $y \geq 0$ such that

$$2x + 3y \leq 6$$
$$4x + y \leq 6$$

and $5x + 2y$ is maximized.

26. Find $x \geq 0$ and $y \geq 0$ such that

$$x + y \leq 10$$
$$5x + 2y \geq 20$$
$$2y \geq x$$

and $x + 3y$ is minimized.

27. Find $x \geq 2$ and $y \geq 5$ such that

$$3x - y \geq 12$$
$$x + y \leq 15$$

and $2x + y$ is minimized.

28. Find $x \geq 10$ and $y \geq 20$ such that

$$2x + 3y \leq 100$$
$$5x + 4y \leq 200$$

and $x + 3y$ is maximized.

Solve each linear programming problem.

29. *Refrigerator Shipping Costs* A manufacturer of refrigerators must ship at least 100 refrigerators to its two West coast warehouses. Each warehouse holds a maximum of 100 refrigerators. Warehouse A holds 25 refrigerators already, while warehouse B has 20 on hand. It costs $12 to ship a refrigerator to warehouse A and $10 to ship one to warehouse B. How many refrigerators should be shipped to each warehouse to minimize cost? What is the minimum cost?

30. *Food Supplement Costs* Renee McKim requires two food supplements, I and II. She can get these supplements from two different products, A and B. Product A provides 3 grams per serving of supplement I and 2 grams per serving of supplement II. Product B provides 2 grams per serving of supplement I and 4 grams per serving of supplement II. Her dietician, Dr. Dawson, has recommended that she include at least 15 grams of each supplement in her daily diet. If product A costs $0.25 per serving and product B costs $0.40 per serving, how can she satisfy her requirements most economically?

31. *Vitamin Pill Costs* Elizabeth Lamulle takes vitamin pills. Each day, she must have at least 16 units of Vitamin A, at least 5 units of Vitamin B_1, and at least 20 units of Vitamin C. She can choose between red pills costing 10¢ each that contain 8 units of A, 1 of B_1, and 2 of C; and blue pills that cost 20¢ each and contain 2 units of A, 1 of B_1, and 7 of C. How many of each pill should she take in order to minimize her cost and yet fulfill her daily requirements?

32. *Bolt Costs* A machine shop manufactures two types of bolts. Each can be made on any of three groups of machines, but the time required on each group differs, as shown in the table below.

		Machine Groups		
		I	**II**	**III**
Bolts	**Type A**	0.1 min	0.1 min	0.1 min
	Type B	0.1 min	0.4 min	0.5 min

Production schedules are made up one day at a time. In a day there are 240, 720, and 160 minutes available, respectively, on these machines. Type A bolts sell for $0.10 and type B bolts for $0.12. How many of each type of bolt should be manufactured per day to maximize revenue? What is the maximum revenue?

33. *Gasoline and Fuel Oil Costs* A manufacturing process requires that oil refineries manufacture at least 2 gallons of gasoline for each gallon of fuel oil. To meet the winter demand for fuel oil, at least 3 million gallons a day must be produced. The demand for gasoline is no more than 6.4 million gallons per day. If the price of gasoline is $2.90 per gallon and the price of fuel oil is $3.50 per gallon, how much of each should be produced to maximize revenue?

34. *Cake and Cookie Production* A bakery makes both cakes and cookies. Each batch of cakes requires two hours in the oven and three hours in the decorating room. Each batch of cookies needs one and a half hours in the oven

and two-thirds of an hour in the decorating room. The oven is available no more than 15 hours a day, while the decorating room can be used no more than 13 hours a day. How many batches of cakes and cookies should the bakery make in order to maximize profits if cookies produce a profit of $20 per batch and cakes produce a profit of $30 per batch?

35. *Aid to Earthquake Victims* Earthquake victims in China need medical supplies and bottled water. Each medical kit measures 1 cubic foot and weighs 10 pounds. Each container of water is also 1 cubic foot and weighs 20 pounds. The plane can only carry 80,000 pounds with a total volume of 6000 cubic feet. Each medical kit will aid 6 people, while each container of water will serve 10 people. How many of each should be sent in order to maximize the number of people aided?

36. *Aid to Earthquake Victims* If each medical kit could aid 4 people instead of 6, how would the results in **Exercise 35** change?

COLLABORATIVE INVESTIGATION

Tracking an Epidemic

The graph here shows a comparison of the number of African Americans and whites living with AIDS in the United States during 1993–2000. Form groups of 2–3 students each to work the following.

Topics for Discussion

1. The two lines were obtained by joining the data points that are of the form

   (year, number of people in thousands).

   Let $x = 0$ represent the year 1993, $x = 1$ represent 1994, and so on, and approximate the value of y for each year for African Americans. Estimate the missing values, and fill in the table. Remember that y is in thousands.

Year	Number of African Americans with AIDS (y, in thousands)
1993 ($x = 0$)	60
1994 ($x = 1$)	
1995 ($x = 2$)	
1996 ($x = 3$)	
1997 ($x = 4$)	
1998 ($x = 5$)	
1999 ($x = 6$)	
2000 ($x = 7$)	140

Now use any two data points to find an equation of the line describing these data.

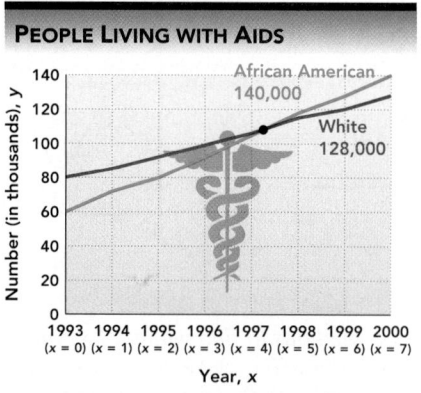

Source: U.S. Centers for Disease Control.

2. Repeat the procedure from part 1, applying the data from the line for whites living with AIDS.

Year	Number of Whites with AIDS (y, in thousands)
1993 ($x = 0$)	80
1994 ($x = 1$)	
1995 ($x = 2$)	
1996 ($x = 3$)	
1997 ($x = 4$)	
1998 ($x = 5$)	
1999 ($x = 6$)	
2000 ($x = 7$)	128

Now use any two data points to find an equation of the line describing these data.

3. The two equations from parts 1 and 2 form a system of two linear equations in two variables. Solve this system using any method you wish.

4. The x-coordinate of the solution of the system in part 3 should correspond to the year in which the two lines intersect. Look at the graph again. Does your x-value correspond the way it should?

5. Discuss why results of this activity might vary among groups performing it.

CHAPTER 8 TEST

1. Find the distance between the points $(-3, 5)$ and $(2, 1)$.

2. Find an equation of the circle whose center has coordinates $(-1, 2)$, with radius 3. Sketch its graph.

3. Find the x- and y-intercepts of the graph of $3x - 2y = 8$, and graph the equation.

4. Find the slope of the line passing through the points $(6, 4)$ and $(-1, 2)$.

5. Find the slope-intercept form of the equation of the line described.
   (a) passing through the point $(-1, 3)$, with slope $-\frac{2}{5}$
   (b) passing through $(-7, 2)$ and perpendicular to $y = 2x$
   (c) the line through $(-2, 3)$ and $(6, -1)$

6. Which one of the following has a positive slope and a negative y-coordinate for its y-intercept?

   A. 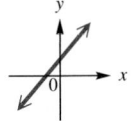   **B.**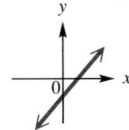

   C. 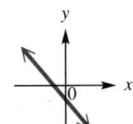   **D.**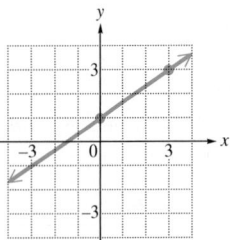

7. **Life Expectancy** The table shows life expectancy at birth, in years, for selected years from 1943 to 2003.

Year	Life Expectancy at Birth (in years)
1943	63.3
1953	68.8
1963	69.9
1973	71.4
1983	74.6
1993	75.5
2003	77.6

Source: Centers for Disease Control and Prevention.

(a) Use the information given for the years 1943 and 2003, letting $x = 0$ represent 1943 and $x = 60$ represent 2003. Let y represent life expectancy in years. Use these two years to write an equation that models life expectancy.

(b) Use the equation from part (a) to predict life expectancy in 2013.

(c) Use the midpoint formula to determine the life expectancy for the year halfway between 1973 and 1983.

8. **Compact Disc Sales** In 2000, 942.5 million compact discs (CDs) were sold in the United States. In 2006, 614.9 million CDs were sold. Find the average rate of change in CDs sold per year. (*Source:* Recording Industry Association of America.)

9. **Library Fines** It costs a borrower $0.05 per day for an overdue book, plus a flat $0.50 charge for all books borrowed. Let x represent the number of days the book is overdue, so y represents the total fine to the tardy user. Write an equation in the form $y = mx + b$ for this situation. Then give three ordered pairs with x-values of 1, 5, and 10 that satisfy the equation.

10. Write the slope-intercept form of the equation of the line shown.

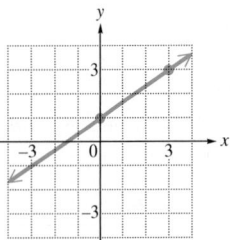

11. Consider the function $f(x) = x^2 - 3x + 12$.
    (a) Give its domain.
    (b) Find $f(-2)$.

12. Consider the function $f(x) = \dfrac{2}{x - 3}$.
    (a) Give its domain.
    (b) Find $f(3)$.

13. *Calculator Production* If the cost to produce x units of calculators is $C(x) = 50x + 5000$ dollars, while the revenue is $R(x) = 60x$ dollars, find the number of units of calculators that must be produced in order to break even. What is the revenue at the break-even point?

14. Graph the quadratic function

$$f(x) = -(x + 3)^2 + 4.$$

Give the axis, the vertex, the domain, and the range.

15. *Dimensions of a Parking Lot* Kirkwood Community College wants to construct a rectangular parking lot on land bordered on one side by a highway. It has 320 ft of fencing with which to fence off the other three sides. What should be the dimensions of the lot if the enclosed area is to be a maximum?

16. Use a scientific calculator to find an approximation of each of the following. Give as many digits as the calculator displays.

   (a) $5.1^{4.7}$ **(b)** $e^{-1.85}$

   (c) $\ln 23.56$

17. *Investment* Suppose that $12,000 is invested in an account that pays 2% annual interest, and is left untouched for 3 years. How much will be in the account if

   (a) interest is compounded quarterly (four times per year);

   (b) interest is compounded continuously?

18. *Decay of Plutonium-241* Suppose that the amount, in grams, of plutonium-241 present in a given sample is determined by the function

$$A(t) = 2.00e^{-0.053t},$$

where t is measured in years. Find the amount present in the sample after the given number of years.

   (a) 4   **(b)** 10   **(c)** 20

   (d) What was the initial amount present?

Solve each system by using elimination, substitution, or a combination of the two methods.

19. $2x + 3y = 2$
    $3x - 4y = 20$

20. $2x + y + z = 3$
     $x + 2y - z = 3$
    $3x - y + z = 5$

21. $2x + 3y - 6z = 11$
    $x - y + 2z = -2$
   $4x + y - 2z = 7$

Solve each problem by using a system of equations.

22. *Harrison Ford's Box Office Hits* Harrison Ford is one of Hollywood's biggest stars. As of January 2010, his two top-grossing films, *Star Wars Episode IV: A New Hope* and *Indiana Jones and the Kingdom of the Crystal Skull* earned $778 million together. If *Indiana Jones and the Kingdom of the Crystal Skull* grossed $144 million less than *Star Wars Episode IV: A New Hope,* how much did each film gross? (*Source:* www.the-numbers.com)

23. *Real Estate Commission* Doug Niles sells real estate. On three recent sales, he made 10% commission, 6% commission, and 5% commission. His total commissions on these sales were $17,000, and he sold property worth $280,000. If the 5% sale amounted to the sum of the other two, what were the three sales' prices?

24. Graph the solution set of the system of inequalities.

$$x + y \le 6$$
$$2x - y \ge 3$$

25. *Profit from Farm Animals* Callie Daniels raises only pigs and geese. She wants to raise no more than 16 animals, with no more than 12 geese. She spends $50 to raise a pig and $20 to raise a goose. She has $500 available for this purpose. Find the maximum profit she can make if she makes a profit of $80 per goose and $40 per pig. Indicate how many pigs and geese she should raise to achieve this maximum.

GEOMETRY

$r = 25$

r

$r = 30$

r

$r = 35$

r

MATT GROENING

On April 30, 2006, Episode 19 of the seventeenth season of the Fox television series *The Simpsons* dealt with the issue of gender, expectations, and curriculum in schools. In "Girls Just Want to Have Sums," Lisa Simpson's school is divided in two. She must attend the girls' school, where her mathematics class no longer poses a challenge. She disguises herself as a boy, infiltrates the boys' school, and proves that she can handle the more difficult classes offered there.

In one scene, the boys are asked by their teacher to determine the volume of a snowman. (See the figure above.) One boy responds to add the volumes of the spheres, because the radii are known. But Lisa corrects him, saying that he forgot the volume of the carrot nose: "one-third base times height" and gleefully follows with "Oh math, I have missed you!"

Formulas for perimeter, area, and volume are covered in this chapter, an introduction to geometry.

9.1 POINTS, LINES, PLANES, AND ANGLES

The Geometry of Euclid • Points, Lines, and Planes • Angles

Euclid's *Elements* as translated by Billingsley appeared in 1570 and was the first English language translation of the text—the most influential geometry text ever written.

Unfortunately, no copy of *Elements* exists that dates back to the time of Euclid (circa 300 B.C.), and most current translations are based upon a revision of the work prepared by Theon of Alexandria.

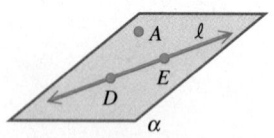

Figure 1

The Geometry of Euclid

Let no one unversed in geometry enter here.
—Motto over the door of Plato's Academy

To the ancient Greeks, mathematics meant geometry above all—a rigid kind of geometry from a modern-day point of view. The Greeks studied the properties of figures identical in shape and size (congruent figures) as well as figures identical in shape but not necessarily in size (similar figures). They absorbed ideas about area and volume from the Egyptians and Babylonians and established general formulas. The Greeks were the first to insist that statements in geometry be given rigorous proof.

The most basic ideas of geometry are **point, line,** and **plane.** In fact, it is not really possible to define them with other words. Euclid defined a point as "that which has no part," but this definition is vague. He defined a line as "that which has breadthless length." Again, this definition is vague. Based on our experience, however, we know what Euclid meant. The drawings that we use for points are dots. Lines have properties of no thickness and no width, and they extend indefinitely in two directions.

Euclid's definition of a plane, "a surface which lies evenly with the straight lines on itself," is represented by a flat surface, such as a tabletop or a page in a book.

Points, Lines, and Planes

There are certain universally accepted conventions and symbols used to represent points, lines, and planes. A capital letter usually represents a point. A line may be named by two capital letters representing points that lie on the line, or by a single (usually lowercase) letter, such as ℓ. Subscripts are sometimes used to distinguish one line from another when a lowercase letter is used. For example, ℓ_1 and ℓ_2 would represent two distinct lines. A plane may be named by three capital letters representing points that lie in the plane, or by a letter of the Greek alphabet, such as α (alpha), β (beta), or γ (gamma).

Figure 1 depicts a plane that may be represented either as α or as plane *ADE*. Contained in the plane is the line *DE* (or, equivalently, line *ED*), which is also labeled ℓ in the figure.

Selecting any point on a line divides the line into three parts: the point itself, and two **half-lines,** one on each side of the point. For example point *A* divides the line shown in **Figure 2** into three parts, *A* itself and two half-lines. Point *A* belongs to neither half-line. As the figure suggests, each half-line extends indefinitely in the direction opposite the other half-line.

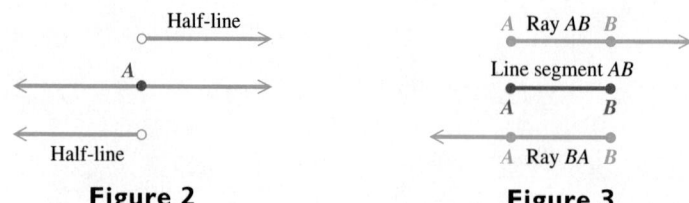

Figure 2   **Figure 3**

Including an initial point with a half-line gives a **ray.** A ray is named with two letters, one for the initial point of the ray, and one for another point contained in the half-line. In **Figure 3** ray *AB* has initial point *A* and extends in the direction of *B*. On the other hand, ray *BA* has *B* as its initial point and extends in the direction of *A*.

A **line segment** includes both endpoints and is named by its endpoints. **Figure 3** shows line segment AB, which may also be designated as line segment BA.

Table 1 shows these figures along with the symbols used to represent them.

Given any three points that are not in a straight line, a plane can be passed through the points. That is why **camera tripods** have three legs—no matter how irregular the surface, the tips of the three legs determine a plane. A camera support with four legs would wobble unless all four legs were carefully extended just the right amount.

Table 1

Name	Figure	Symbol
Line AB or line BA		$\overleftrightarrow{AB}$ or $\overleftrightarrow{BA}$
Half-line AB		$\overset{\circ}{\overrightarrow{AB}}$
Half-line BA		$\overset{\circ}{\overleftarrow{BA}}$
Ray AB		$\overrightarrow{AB}$
Ray BA		$\overleftarrow{BA}$
Segment AB or segment BA		$\overset{\cdot\cdot}{AB}$ or $\overset{\cdot\cdot}{BA}$

For a line, the symbol above the two letters shows two arrowheads, indicating that the line extends indefinitely in both directions. For half-lines and rays, only one arrowhead is used because these extend in only one direction. An open circle is used for a half-line to show that the endpoint is not included, while a solid circle is used for a ray to indicate the inclusion of the endpoint. Since a segment includes both endpoints and does not extend in either direction, solid circles are used to indicate endpoints of line segments.

The geometric definitions of "parallel" and "intersecting" apply to two or more lines or planes. (See **Figure 4**.) **Parallel lines** lie in the same plane and never meet, no matter how far they are extended. However, **intersecting lines** do meet.

If two distinct lines intersect, they intersect in one and only one point.

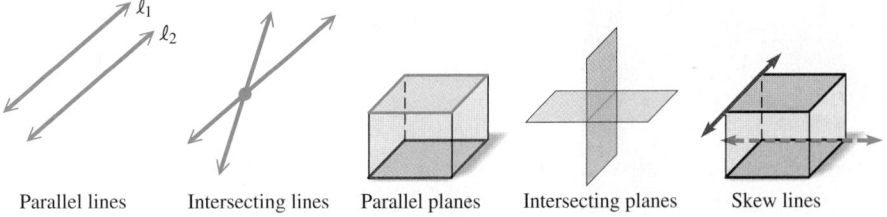

Parallel lines   Intersecting lines   Parallel planes   Intersecting planes   Skew lines

Figure 4

We use the symbol ∥ to denote parallelism. If ℓ_1 and ℓ_2 are parallel lines, as in **Figure 4**, then this may be indicated as

$$\ell_1 \| \ell_2.$$

Parallel planes also never meet, no matter how far they are extended. Two distinct **intersecting planes** form a straight line, the one and only line they have in common. **Skew lines** do not lie in the same plane, and they never meet, no matter how far they are extended.

Angles

An **angle** is the union of two rays that have a common endpoint. See **Figure 5**. The angle is formed by points on the rays themselves, and no other points. In **Figure 5**, point *X* is *not* a point on the angle. (It is said to be in the *interior* of the angle.)

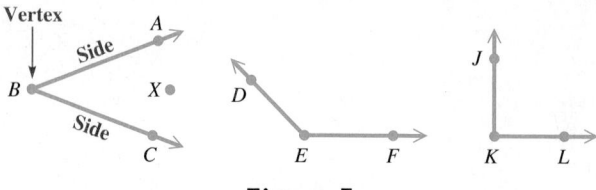

Figure 5

The rays forming an angle are called its **sides.** The common endpoint of the rays is the **vertex** of the angle. There are two standard ways of naming angles using letters. If no confusion will result, an angle can be named with the letter marking its vertex. Using this method, the angles in **Figure 5** can be named, respectively, angle *B*, angle *E*, and angle *K*.

Angles also can be named with three letters: the first letter names a point on one side of the angle; the middle letter names the vertex; the third names a point on the other side of the angle. In this system, the angles in the figure can be named angle *ABC,* angle *DEF,* and angle *JKL.* The symbol for representing an angle is ∡. Rather than writing "angle *ABC,*" we may write "∡*ABC.*"

An angle can be associated with an amount of rotation. For example, in **Figure 6(a)**, we let $\overrightarrow{BA}$ first coincide with $\overrightarrow{BC}$—as though they were the same ray. We then rotate $\overrightarrow{BA}$ (the endpoint remains fixed) in a counterclockwise direction to form ∡*ABC.*

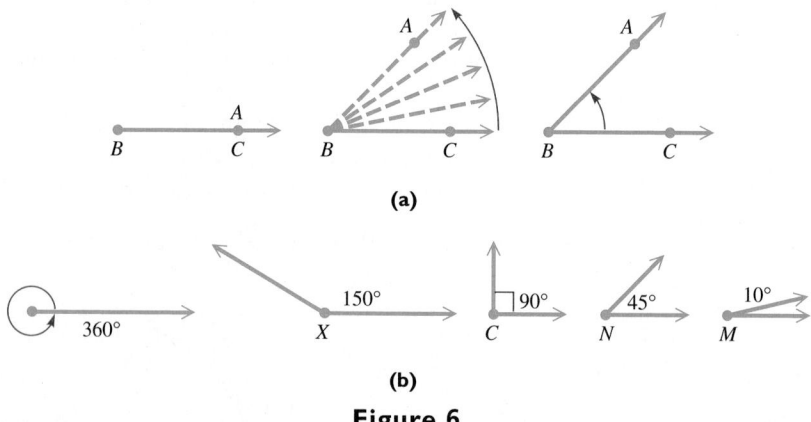

Figure 6

Angles are the key to the study of **geodesy,** the measurement of distances on the earth's surface.

Angles are measured by the amount of rotation, using a system that dates back to the Babylonians. Babylonian astronomers chose the number 360 to represent the amount of rotation of a ray back onto itself. Using 360 as the amount of rotation of a ray back onto itself, **one degree,** written 1°, is defined to be $\frac{1}{360}$ of a complete rotation. **Figure 6(b)** shows angles of various degree measures.

Angles are classified and named with reference to their degree measures. An angle whose measure is between 0° and 90° is called an **acute angle.** Angles *M* and *N* in **Figure 6(b)** are acute. An angle that measures 90° is called a **right angle.** Angle *C* in the figure is a right angle. The squared symbol ⌐ at the vertex denotes a right angle. Angles that measure more than 90° but less than 180° are said to be **obtuse angles** (angle *X*, for example). An angle that measures 180° is a **straight angle.** Its sides form a straight line.

A tool called a **protractor** can be used to measure angles. **Figure 7** shows a protractor measuring an angle whose measure is 135°.

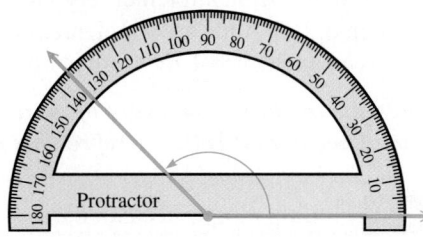

To use a protractor, position the hole (or dot) of the protractor on the vertex of the angle. With the 0-degree measure on the protractor placed on one side of the angle, the other side will show the degree measure of the angle.

Figure 7

When two lines intersect to form right angles they are called **perpendicular lines.** In **Figure 8**, the sides of ∡*NMP* have been extended to form another angle, ∡*RMQ*. The pair ∡*NMP* and ∡*RMQ* are called **vertical angles.** Another pair of vertical angles have been formed at the same time. They are ∡*NMQ* and ∡*PMR*.

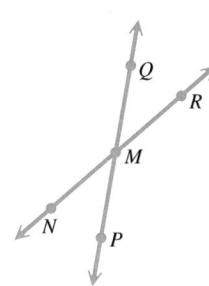

Figure 8

Property of Vertical Angles

Vertical angles have equal measures.

▌▌ EXAMPLE 1 Finding Angle Measures

Find the measure of each marked angle in the given figure.

(a) Figure 9   **(b) Figure 10**

SOLUTION

(a) Because the marked angles are vertical angles, they have the same measure.

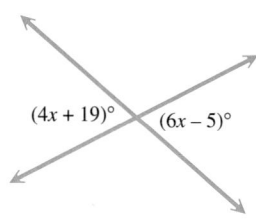

Figure 9

$$4x + 19 = 6x - 5 \qquad \text{Set measures equal.}$$
$$4x + 19 - 4x = 6x - 5 - 4x \quad \text{Subtract } 4x.$$
$$19 = 2x - 5 \qquad \text{Combine like terms.}$$
$$19 + 5 = 2x - 5 + 5 \qquad \text{Add 5.}$$
$$24 = 2x \qquad \text{Add.}$$

Don't stop here. $\qquad$ $\mathbf{12} = x$ $\qquad$ Divide by 2.

Since $x = 12$, one angle has measure $4(\mathbf{12}) + 19 = \mathbf{67}$ degrees. The other has the same measure, because $6(\mathbf{12}) - 5 = \mathbf{67}$ as well. Each angle measures 67°.

(b) The measures of the marked angles must add to 180°. They form a straight angle.

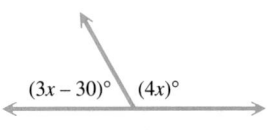

Figure 10

$$(3x - 30) + 4x = 180 \qquad \text{The angle sum is 180.}$$
$$7x - 30 = 180 \qquad \text{Combine like terms.}$$
$$7x - 30 + 30 = 180 + 30 \qquad \text{Add 30.}$$
$$7x = 210 \qquad \text{Add.}$$

Don't stop here. $\qquad$ $x = \mathbf{30}$ $\qquad$ Divide by 7.

To find the measures of the angles, replace x with 30 in the two expressions.

$$3x - 30 = 3(\mathbf{30}) - 30 = 90 - 30 = \mathbf{60}$$
$$4x = 4(\mathbf{30}) = \mathbf{120}$$

The two angle measures are 60° and 120°.   ▌▌▌

If the sum of the measures of two acute angles is 90°, the angles are said to be **complementary,** and each is called the *complement* of the other. For example, angles measuring 40° and 50° are complementary angles, because 40° + 50° = 90°. If two angles have a sum of 180°, they are **supplementary.** The *supplement* of an angle whose measure is 40° is an angle whose measure is 140°, because 40° + 140° = 180°.

If x represents the degree measure of an angle, 90 − x represents the measure of its complement, and 180 − x represents the measure of its supplement.

▮▮ **EXAMPLE 2** Finding Angle Measures

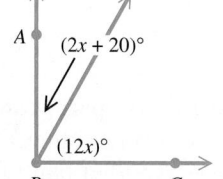

Figure 11

Find the measures of the angles in **Figure 11**, given that $\angle ABC$ is a right angle.

SOLUTION

The sum of the measures of the two acute angles is 90° (that is, they are complementary), because they form a right angle.

$$(2x + 20) + 12x = 90 \quad \text{The angle measures sum to 90°.}$$
$$14x + 20 = 90 \quad \text{Combine like terms.}$$
$$14x = 70 \quad \text{Subtract 20.}$$
$$x = 5 \quad \text{Divide by 14.}$$

The value of x is 5. Therefore, replace x with 5 in the two expressions.

$$2x + 20 = 2(5) + 20 = \mathbf{30}$$
$$12x = 12(5) = \mathbf{60}$$

The measures of the two angles are 30° and 60°. ▮▮▮

▮▮ **EXAMPLE 3** Using Complementary and Supplementary Angles

The supplement of an angle measures 10° more than three times its complement. Find the measure of the angle.

SOLUTION

Let x = the degree measure of the angle.

Then $180 - x$ = the degree measure of its supplement,

and $90 - x$ = the degree measure of its complement.

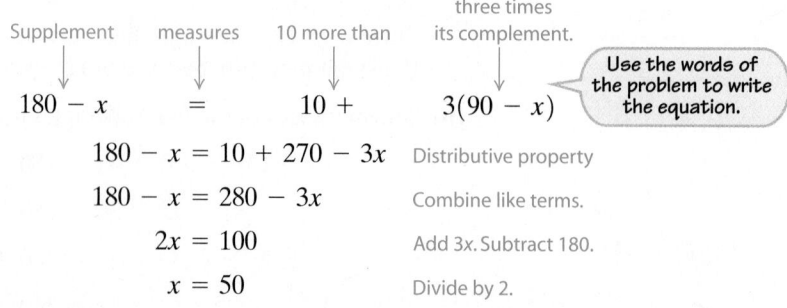

$$180 - x = 10 + 270 - 3x \quad \text{Distributive property}$$
$$180 - x = 280 - 3x \quad \text{Combine like terms.}$$
$$2x = 100 \quad \text{Add 3x. Subtract 180.}$$
$$x = 50 \quad \text{Divide by 2.}$$

The angle measures 50°. Because its supplement (130°) is 10° more than three times its complement (40°) (that is, 130 = 10 + 3(40) is true), the answer checks. ▮▮▮

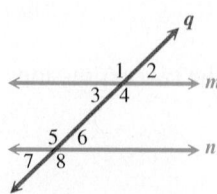

Figure 12

Parallel lines are lines that lie in the same plane and do not intersect. **Figure 12** shows parallel lines *m* and *n*. When a line *q* intersects two parallel lines, *q* is called a **transversal.** In **Figure 12**, the transversal intersecting the parallel lines forms eight angles, indicated by numbers. Angles 1 through 8 in the figure possess some special properties regarding their degree measures, as shown in **Table 2** on the next page.

Table 2

Name	Figure	Rule
Alternate interior angles	5 4 (also 3 and 6)	Angle measures are equal.
Alternate exterior angles	1 8 (also 2 and 7)	Angle measures are equal.
Interior angles on same side of transversal	4 6 (also 3 and 5)	Angle measures add to 180°.
Corresponding angles	2 6 (also 1 and 5, 3 and 7, 4 and 8)	Angle measures are equal.

A set of parallel lines with equidistant spacing intersects an identical set, but at a small angle. The result is a **moiré pattern,** named after the fabric *moiré* ("watered") *silk.* Moiré patterns are related to **periodic functions,** which describe regular recurring phenomena (wave patterns such as heartbeats or business cycles). Moirés thus apply to the study of electromagnetic, sound, and water waves, to crystal structure, and to other wave phenomena.

The converses of the above also are true. That is, if alternate interior angles are equal, then the lines are parallel. Similar results are valid for alternate exterior angles, interior angles on the same side of a transversal, and corresponding angles.

▍▍ **EXAMPLE 4** Finding Angle Measures

Find the measure of each marked angle in **Figure 13**, given that lines *m* and *n* are parallel.

SOLUTION

The marked angles are alternate exterior angles, which are equal.

$$3x + 2 = 5x - 40 \quad \text{Set angle measures equal.}$$
$$42 = 2x \qquad \text{Subtract . Add 40.}$$
$$21 = x \qquad \text{Divide by 2.}$$

Don't stop here.

Thus, $3x + 2 = 3 \cdot 21 + 2 = 65$ and $5x - 40 = 5 \cdot 21 - 40 = 65$.

So both angles measure 65°.

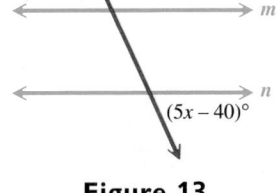

$(3x + 2)°$

m

n

$(5x - 40)°$

Figure 13

9.1 EXERCISES

Fill in each blank with the correct response.

1. The sum of the measures of two complementary angles is _____ degrees.

2. The sum of the measures of two supplementary angles is _____ degrees.

3. The measures of two vertical angles are _____.
(equal/not equal)

4. The measures of _____ right angles add up to the measure of a straight angle.

Decide whether each statement is true *or* false.

5. A line segment has two endpoints.

6. A ray has one endpoint.

7. If *A* and *B* are distinct points on a line, then ray *AB* and ray *BA* represent the same set of points.

8. If two lines intersect, they lie in the same plane.

9. If two lines are parallel, they lie in the same plane.

10. If two lines do not intersect, they must be parallel.

11. Segment *AB* and segment *BA* represent the same set of points.

12. There is no angle that is its own complement.

13. There is no angle that is its own supplement.

14. The origin of the use of the degree as a unit of measure of an angle goes back to the Egyptians.

Exercises 15–24 name portions of the line shown. For each exercise, **(a)** *give the symbol that represents the portion of the line named, and* **(b)** *draw a figure showing just the portion named, including all labeled points.*

15. line segment *AB*

16. ray *BC*

17. ray *CB*

18. line segment *AD*

19. half-line *BC*

20. half-line *AD*

21. ray *BA*

22. ray *DA*

23. line segment *CA*

24. line segment *DA*

Match the symbol in Group I with the symbol in Group II that names the same set of points, based on the figure.

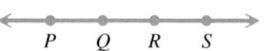

I		**II**	
25. $\overrightarrow{PQ}$	**26.** $\overset{\circ\!\!\!\!\!\frown}{QR}$	**A.** $\overset{\circ\!\!\!\!\!\frown}{QS}$	**B.** $\overrightarrow{RQ}$
27. $\overrightarrow{QR}$	**28.** $\overleftrightarrow{PQ}$	**C.** $\overleftrightarrow{SR}$	**D.** $\overrightarrow{QS}$
29. $\overrightarrow{RP}$	**30.** $\overset{\circ\!\!\!\!\!\frown}{SQ}$	**E.** $\overrightarrow{SP}$	**F.** $\overrightarrow{QP}$
31. $\overset{\bullet\!\!\!\!\frown\!\!\!\bullet}{PS}$	**32.** $\overset{\circ\!\!\!\!\!\frown}{PS}$	**G.** $\overleftrightarrow{RS}$	**H.** none of these

Lines, rays, half-lines, and segments may be considered sets of points. The **intersection** *(symbolized* ∩ *) of two sets is composed of all elements common to both sets, while the* **union** *(symbolized* ∪ *) of two sets is composed of all elements found in at least one of the two sets.*

Based on the figure below, specify each of the sets given in Exercises 33–40 in a simpler way.

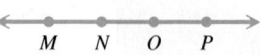

33. $\overrightarrow{MN} \cup \overrightarrow{NO}$

34. $\overrightarrow{MN} \cap \overrightarrow{NO}$

35. $\overrightarrow{MO} \cap \overrightarrow{OM}$

36. $\overrightarrow{MO} \cup \overrightarrow{OM}$

37. $\overrightarrow{OP} \cap O$

38. $\overrightarrow{OP} \cup O$

39. $\overrightarrow{NP} \cap \overrightarrow{OP}$

40. $\overrightarrow{NP} \cup \overrightarrow{OP}$

Give the measure of the complement of each angle.

41. 28°

42. 32°

43. 89°

44. 45°

45. *x*°

46. $(90 - x)°$

Give the measure of the supplement of each angle.

47. 132°

48. 105°

49. 26°

50. 90°

51. *y*°

52. $(180 - y)°$

Name all pairs of vertical angles in each figure.

53.

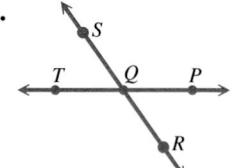

54.

55. In **Exercise 53**, if ∡*ABE* has a measure of 52°, find the measures of the angles.

(a) ∡*CBD*

(b) ∡*CBE*

56. In **Exercise 54**, if ∡*SQP* has a measure of 126°, find the measures of the angles.

(a) ∡*TQR*

(b) ∡*PQR*

Find the measure of each marked angle.

57.

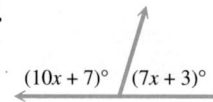

58.

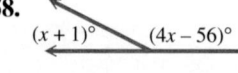

59.

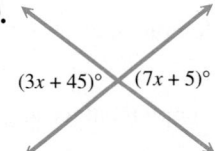

60.

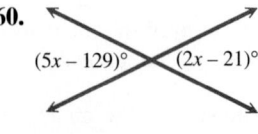

61.

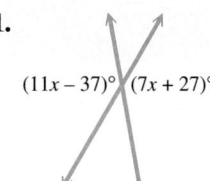

$(11x - 37)°$ $(7x + 27)°$

62.

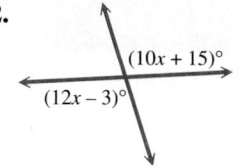

$(10x + 15)°$
$(12x - 3)°$

63.

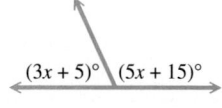

$(3x + 5)°$ $(5x + 15)°$

64.

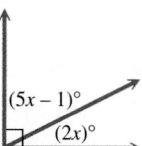

$(5x - 1)°$
$(2x)°$

65.

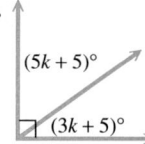

$(5k + 5)°$
$(3k + 5)°$

In Exercises 66–69, assume that lines m and n are parallel, and find the measure of each marked angle.

66.

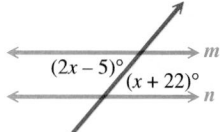

m
$(2x - 5)°$
$(x + 22)°$
n

67.

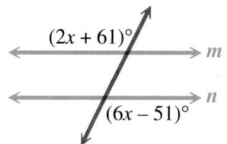

$(2x + 61)°$
m
n
$(6x - 51)°$

68.

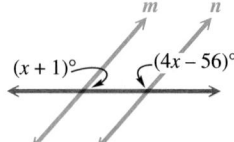

m n
$(x + 1)°$ $(4x - 56)°$

69.

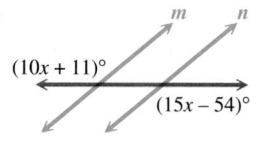

m n
$(10x + 11)°$
$(15x - 54)°$

Complementary and Supplementary Angles   *Solve each problem in Exercises 70–73.*

70. The supplement of an angle measures 25° more than twice its complement. Find the measure of the angle.

71. The complement of an angle measures 10° less than one-fifth of its supplement. Find the measure of the angle.

72. The supplement of an angle added to the complement of the angle gives 210°. What is the measure of the angle?

73. Half the supplement of an angle is 12° less than twice the complement of the angle. Find the measure of the angle.

74. The sketch shows parallel lines m and n cut by a transversal q. Complete the steps to prove that alternate exterior angles have the same measure.

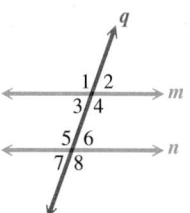

(a) Measure of ∡2 = measure of ∡ _____ , since they are vertical angles.

(b) Measure of ∡3 = measure of ∡ _____ , since they are alternate interior angles.

(c) Measure of ∡6 = measure of ∡ _____ , since they are vertical angles.

(d) By the results of parts (a), (b), and (c), the measure of ∡2 must equal the measure of ∡ _____ , showing that alternate _____ angles have equal measures.

75. Use the sketch to find the measure of each numbered angle. Assume that $m \| n$.

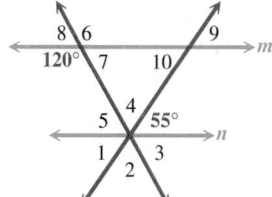

76. Complete these steps in the proof that vertical angles have equal measures. In this exercise, m (∡x) means "the measure of the angle x." Use the figure at the right.

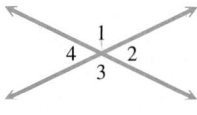

(a) m(∡1) + m(∡2) = _____ °

(b) m(∡2) + m(∡3) = _____ °

(c) Subtract the equation in part (b) from the equation in part (a) to get [m(∡1) + m(∡2)] − [m(∡2) + m(∡3)] = _____ ° − _____ °.

(d) m(∡1) + m(∡2) − m(∡2) − m(∡3) = _____ °

(e) m(∡1) − m(∡3) = _____ °

(f) m(∡1) = m(∡ _____)

9.2 CURVES, POLYGONS, AND CIRCLES

Curves • Triangles and Quadrilaterals • Circles

Curves

The term *curve* is used for describing figures in the plane. (See **Figure 14**.)

Simple; closed

Simple; not closed

Not simple; closed

Not simple; not closed

Figure 14

Simple Curve and Closed Curve

A **simple curve** can be drawn without lifting the pencil from the paper, and without passing through any point twice.

A **closed curve** has its starting and ending points the same and is drawn without lifting the pencil from the paper.

A simple closed figure is said to be **convex** if, for any two points A and B inside the figure, the line segment AB (that is, $\overrightarrow{AB}$) is always completely inside the figure. **Figure 15(a)** shows a convex figure and **(b)** shows one that is not convex.

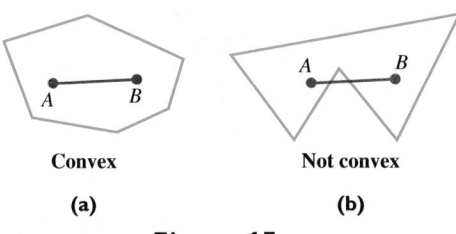

Convex   Not convex

(a)   (b)

Figure 15

Table 3	Classification of Polygons According to Number of Sides
Number of Sides	**Name**
3	triangle
4	quadrilateral
5	pentagon
6	hexagon
7	heptagon
8	octagon
9	nonagon
10	decagon

Among the most common types of curves in mathematics are those that are both simple and closed, and perhaps the most important of these are *polygons*. A **polygon** is a simple closed curve made up only of straight line segments. The line segments are called the *sides,* and the points at which the sides meet are called *vertices* (singular: *vertex*). Polygons are classified according to the number of line segments used as sides. **Table 3** gives the special names. ***In general, if a polygon has n sides, and no particular value of n is specified, it is called an n-gon.***

Some examples of polygons are shown in **Figure 16**. A polygon may or may not be convex. Polygons with all sides equal and all angles equal are **regular polygons.**

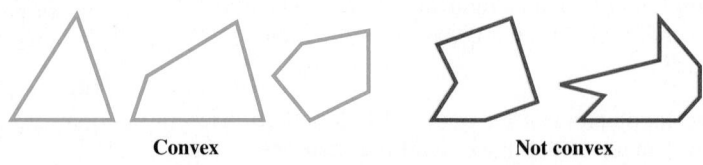

Convex   Not convex

Polygons are simple closed curves made up of straight line segments.

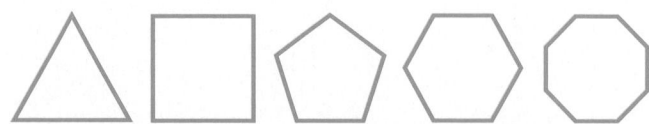

Regular polygons have equal sides and equal angles.

Figure 16

The puzzle-game above comes from China, where it has been a popular amusement for centuries. The figure on the left is a **tangram.** Any tangram is composed of the same set of seven tans (the pieces making up the square are shown on the right).

Mathematicians have described various properties of tangrams. While each tan is convex, only 13 convex tangrams are possible. All others, like the figure on the left, are not convex.

Triangles and Quadrilaterals

Triangles are classified by measures of angles as well as by number of equal sides, as shown in the following box. (Notice that tick marks are used in the bottom three figures to show how side lengths are related.)

Types of Triangles

	All Angles Acute	One Right Angle	One Obtuse Angle
Angles	Acute triangle	Right triangle	Obtuse triangle

	All Sides Equal	Two Sides Equal	No Sides Equal
Sides	Equilateral triangle	Isosceles triangle	Scalene triangle

Quadrilaterals are classified by sides and angles. An important distinction involving quadrilaterals is whether one or more pairs of sides are parallel.

Types of Quadrilaterals

Sample Figure	Definition
Trapezoid	A **trapezoid** is a quadrilateral with one pair of parallel sides.
Parallelogram	A **parallelogram** is a quadrilateral with two pairs of parallel sides.
Rectangle	A **rectangle** is a parallelogram with a right angle (and consequently, four right angles).
Square	A **square** is a rectangle with all sides having equal length.
Rhombus	A **rhombus** is a parallelogram with all sides having equal length.

An important property of triangles that was first proved by the Greek geometers deals with the sum of the measures of the angles of any triangle.

Angle Sum of a Triangle

The sum of the measures of the interior angles of any triangle is 180°.

While it is not an actual proof, a rather convincing argument for the truth of this statement can be given using any size triangle cut from a piece of paper. Tear each corner from the triangle, as suggested in **Figure 17(a)**. You should be able to rearrange the pieces so that the three angles form a straight angle, as shown in **Figure 17(b)**.

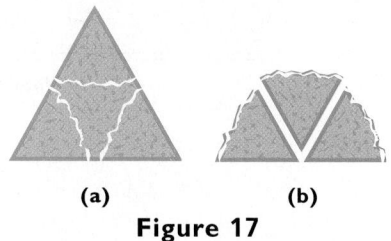

(a)   (b)

Figure 17

▮▮ **EXAMPLE 1** Finding Angle Measures in a Triangle

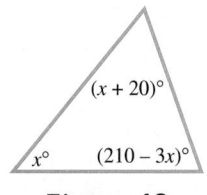

Figure 18

Find the measure of each angle in the triangle of **Figure 18**.

SOLUTION

By the angle sum relationship, the three angle measures must add up to 180°.

$$x + (x + 20) + (210 - 3x) = 180 \quad \text{Sum is 180.}$$
$$-x + 230 = 180 \quad \text{Combine like terms.}$$
$$-x = -50 \quad \text{Subtract 230.}$$
$$\boxed{\text{There are two more values to find.}} \rightarrow x = 50 \quad \text{Divide by } -1.$$

Because $x = 50$,

$$x + 20 = 50 + 20 = 70 \quad \text{and} \quad 210 - 3x = 210 - 3(50) = 60.$$

The three angles measure 50°, 70°, and 60°. Because $50° + 70° + 60° = 180°$, the answers satisfy the angle sum relationship. ▮▮▮

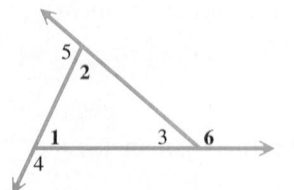

Figure 19

In the triangle shown in **Figure 19**, angles 1, 2, and 3 are called **interior angles,** while angles 4, 5, and 6 are called **exterior angles** of the triangle. Using the fact that the sum of the angle measures of any triangle is 180°, and a straight angle also measures 180°, the following property may be deduced.

Exterior Angle Measure

The measure of an exterior angle of a triangle is equal to the sum of the measures of the two opposite interior angles.

In **Figure 19**, the measure of angle 6 is equal to the sum of the measures of angles 1 and 2. Two other such statements can be made.

▍▍ EXAMPLE 2 Finding Interior and Exterior Angle Measures

Find the measures of interior angles A, B, and C of the triangle in **Figure 20**, and the measure of exterior angle BCD.

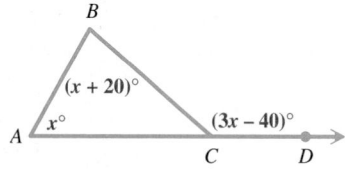

Figure 20

SOLUTION

By the property concerning exterior angles, the sum of the measures of interior angles A and B must equal the measure of angle BCD.

$$x + (x + 20) = 3x - 40$$

$$2x + 20 = 3x - 40 \quad \text{Combine like terms.}$$

$$-x = -60 \quad \text{Subtract } 3x. \text{ Subtract } 20.$$

$$x = 60 \quad \text{Divide by } -1.$$

Because the value of x is 60,

$$m(\text{Interior angle } A) = 60°$$

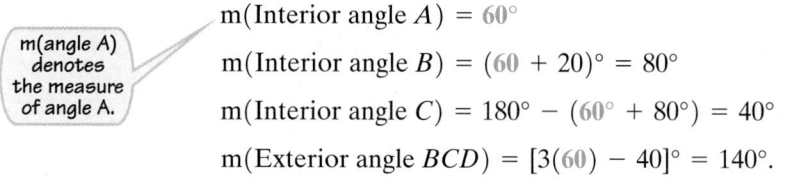

m(angle A) denotes the measure of angle A.

$$m(\text{Interior angle } B) = (60 + 20)° = 80°$$

$$m(\text{Interior angle } C) = 180° - (60° + 80°) = 40°$$

$$m(\text{Exterior angle } BCD) = [3(60) - 40]° = 140°. \qquad \blacksquare\blacksquare\blacksquare$$

Circles

A circle is a simple closed curve defined as follows.

Circle

A **circle** is a set of points in a plane, each of which is the same distance from a fixed point.

A circle may be physically constructed with compasses, where the spike leg remains fixed and the other leg swings around to construct the circle. A string may also be used to draw a circle. For example, loop a piece of chalk on one end of a piece of string. Hold the other end in a fixed position on a chalkboard, and pull the string taut. Then swing the chalk end around to draw a circle.

A circle, along with several lines and segments, is shown in **Figure 21**. The points P, Q, and R lie on the circle. Each lies the same distance from point O, which is called the **center** of the circle. (It is the "fixed point" referred to in the definition.) $\overrightarrow{OP}$, $\overrightarrow{OQ}$, and $\overrightarrow{OR}$ are segments whose endpoints are the center and a point on the circle. Each is called a **radius** of the circle (plural: **radii**). $\overrightarrow{PQ}$ is a segment whose endpoints both lie on the circle and is an example of a **chord.** The segment $\overleftrightarrow{PR}$ is a chord that passes through the center and is called a **diameter** of the circle. Notice that the measure of a diameter is twice that of a radius. A diameter such as $\overleftrightarrow{PR}$ in **Figure 21** divides a circle into two parts of equal size, each of which is called a **semicircle.**

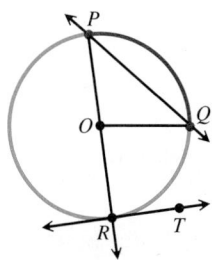

Figure 21

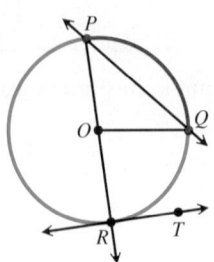

Figure 21 (repeated)

In **Figure 21,** $\overleftrightarrow{RT}$ is a line that touches (intersects) the circle in only one point, R, and is called a **tangent** to the circle. R is the point of tangency. $\overleftrightarrow{PQ}$, which intersects the circle in two points, is called a **secant** line. (What is the distinction between a chord and a secant?)

The portion of the circle shown in red in **Figure 21** is an **arc** of the circle. It consists of two endpoints (P and Q) and all points on the circle "between" these endpoints. The colored portion is called arc PQ (or QP), denoted in symbols as $\overarc{PQ}$ (or $\overarc{QP}$). An angle such as QPR, which has its vertex P on the circle and its sides $\overrightarrow{PQ}$ and $\overrightarrow{PR}$ is said to be **inscribed** in the circle, and it **intercepts** arc QR.

The Greeks were the first to insist that all propositions, or **theorems,** about geometry be given rigorous proofs before being accepted. One of the theorems receiving such a proof was this one.

> **Inscribed Angle**
>
> Any angle inscribed in a circle has degree measure half of that of its intercepted arc.

Figure 22(a) states this theorem symbolically. For example, if *arc PR* measures $80°$, then inscribed angle PQR measures $\left(\frac{80}{2}\right)° = 40°$. A special case of this theorem is indicated in **Figure 22(b)**. *Any angle inscribed in a semicircle is a right angle.*

Thales is credited with the first proof of the inscribed angle theorem. Legend records that he studied for a time in Egypt and then introduced geometry to Greece, where he attempted to apply the principles of Greek logic to his newly learned subject.

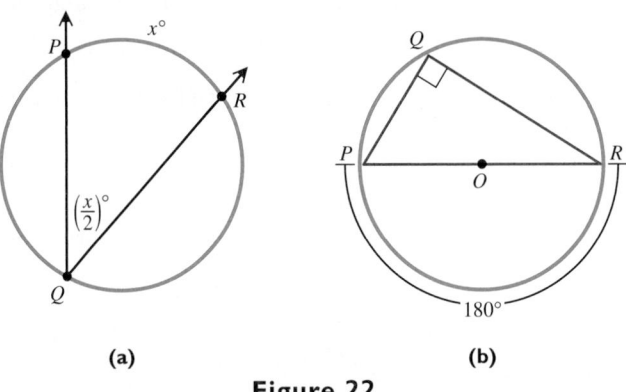

(a)   (b)

Figure 22

9.2 EXERCISES

Fill in each blank with the correct response.

1. A segment joining two points on a circle is called a(n) _____.

2. A segment joining the center of a circle and a point on the circle is called a(n) _____.

3. A regular triangle is called a(n) _____ triangle.

4. A chord that contains the center of a circle is called a(n) _____.

Decide whether each statement is true *or* false.

5. A rhombus is an example of a regular polygon.

6. If a triangle is isosceles, then it is not scalene.

7. A triangle can have more than one obtuse angle.

8. A square is both a rectangle and a parallelogram.

9. A square must be a rhombus.

10. A rhombus must be a square.

11. In your own words, explain the distinction between a square and a rhombus.

12. What common traffic sign in the United States is in the shape of an octagon?

Identify each curve as simple, closed, both, *or* neither.

13.

14.

15.

16.

17.

18.

19.

20.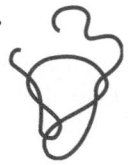

Decide whether each figure is convex *or* not convex.

21.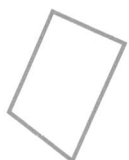

22.

23.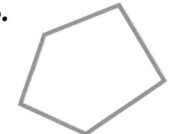

24.

25.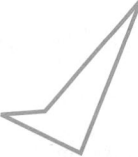

26.

Classify each triangle as acute, right, *or* obtuse. *Also classify each as* equilateral, isosceles, *or* scalene.

27.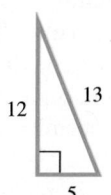

28.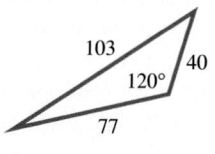

29.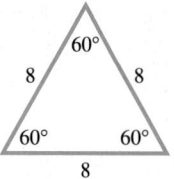

30.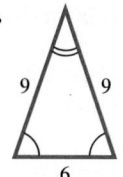

31.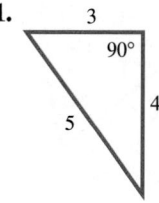

32.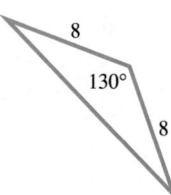

33.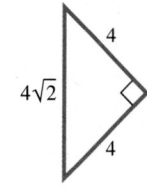

34.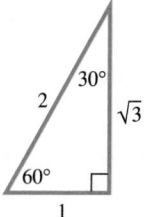

35.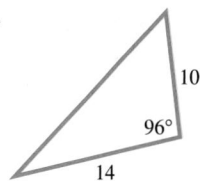

36.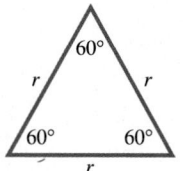

37.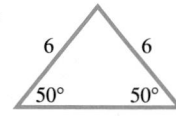

38.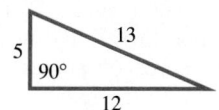

39. Give a definition of *isosceles right triangle.*

40. Can a triangle be both right and obtuse?

Find the measure of each angle in triangle ABC.

41.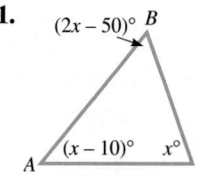

42.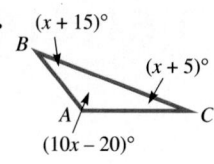

43.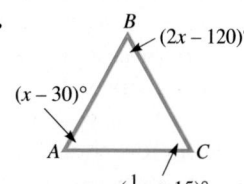

44.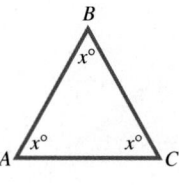

45. *Angle Measures* In triangle ABC, angles A and B have the same measure, while the measure of angle C is 24 degrees larger than the measure of each of A and B. What are the measures of the three angles?

46. *Angle Measures* In triangle *ABC*, the measure of angle *A* is 30 degrees more than the measure of angle *B*. The measure of angle *B* is the same as the measure of angle *C*. Find the measure of each angle.

In each triangle, find the measure of exterior angle BCD.

47.
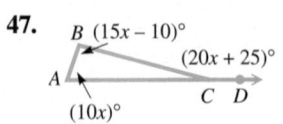

48.
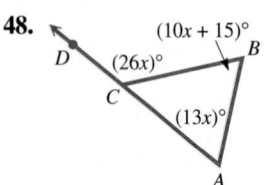

49.
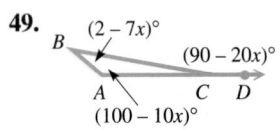

50.
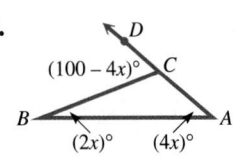

51. Using the points, segments, and lines in the figure, list all parts of the circle.

(a) center

(b) radii

(c) diameters

(d) chords

(e) secants

(f) tangents

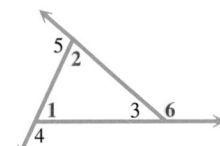

52. Refer to angles 1, 2, and 6 in the figure. Prove that the sum of the measures of angles 1 and 2 is equal to the measure of angle 6.

53. Go through the following argument provided by Richard Crouse in a letter to the editor of *Mathematics Teacher* in the February 1988 issue.

(a) Place the eraser end of a pencil on vertex *A* of the triangle and let the pencil coincide with side *AC* of the triangle.

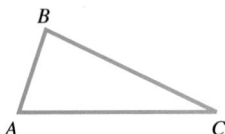

(b) With the eraser fixed at *A*, rotate the pencil counterclockwise until it coincides with side *AB*.

(c) With the pencil fixed at point *B*, rotate the eraser end counterclockwise until the pencil coincides with side *BC*.

(d) With the eraser fixed at point *C* (slide the pencil to this position), rotate the point end of the pencil counterclockwise until the pencil coincides with side *AC*.

(e) Notice that the pencil is now pointing in the opposite direction. What concept from this section does this exercise reinforce?

54. In the classic 1939 movie *The Wizard of Oz,* the Scarecrow, upon getting a brain, says the following: "The sum of the square roots of any two sides of an isosceles triangle is equal to the square root of the remaining side." Give an example to show that his statement is incorrect.

EXTENSION Geometric Constructions

Perpendicular Bisector • Perpendicular to a Line • Perpendicular Through a Line • Copied Angle

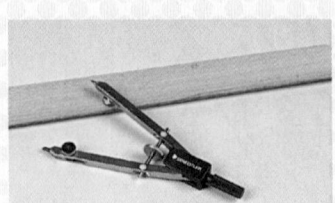

Compasses may be used to:

1. Swing a circular arc with given center and radius.

2. Reproduce a given length.

The Greeks did not study algebra as we do. To them geometry was the highest expression of mathematical science; their geometry was an abstract subject. Any practical application resulting from their work was nice but held no great importance.

To the Greeks, a geometrical construction also needed abstract beauty. A construction could not be polluted with such practical instruments as a ruler. The Greeks permitted only two tools in geometrical construction: compasses for drawing circles and arcs of circles, and a straightedge for drawing straight line segments. The straightedge, unlike a ruler, could have no marks on it. It was not permitted to line up points by eye.

Here are four basic constructions. Their justifications are based on the *congruence properties* of **Section 9.3.**

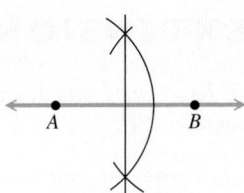

Perpendicular Bisector Construct the perpendicular bisector of a given line segment.

Let the segment have endpoints A and B. Adjust the compasses for any radius greater than half the length of AB. Place the point of the compasses at A and draw an arc, then draw another arc of the same size at B. The line drawn through the points of intersection of these two arcs is the desired perpendicular bisector. See **Figure 23**.

Figure 23

In his first effort as a director, Mel Gibson starred in the 1993 movie *The Man Without a Face*. As disfigured former teacher Justin McLeod, he tutors teenager Chuck Norstadt (portrayed by Nick Stahl). McLeod explains to Norstadt how to find the center of a circle using any three points on the circle as he sketches the diagram on a windowpane. His explanation is based on the fact that the **perpendicular bisector** of any chord of a circle passes through the center of the circle. See the figure.

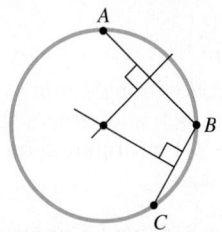

Perpendicular to a Line Construct a perpendicular from a point off a line to the line.

1. Let A be the point, r the line. Place the point of the compasses at A and draw an arc, cutting r in two points.

2. Swing arcs of equal radius from each of the two points on r which were constructed in (1). The line drawn through the intersection of the two arcs and point A is perpendicular to r. See **Figure 24**.

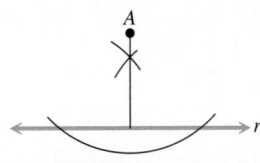

Figure 24

Perpendicular Through a Line Construct a perpendicular to a line at some given point on the line.

1. Let r be the line and A the point. Using any convenient radius on the compasses, place the point of the compasses at A and swing arcs that intersect r, as in **Figure 25**.

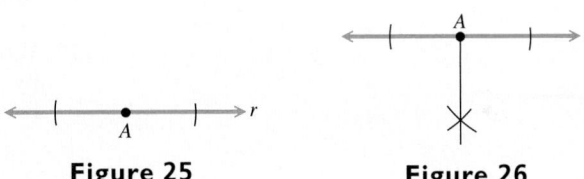

Figure 25   **Figure 26**

There were three constructions that the Greeks were not able to accomplish with **Euclidean tools,** specifically the compasses and unmarked straightedge. Now known as the **three famous problems of antiquity,** they are:
1. To trisect an arbitrary angle;
2. To construct the length of the edge of a cube having twice the volume of a given cube;
3. To construct a square having the same area as that of a given circle.

In the nineteenth century it was discovered that these constructions are, in fact, impossible to accomplish with Euclidean tools.

2. Increase the radius of the compasses, place the point of the compasses on the points obtained in (1) and draw arcs. A line through A and the intersection of the two arcs is perpendicular to r. See **Figure 26**.

Copied Angle Copy an angle.

1. In order to copy an angle ABC on line r, place the point of the compasses at B and draw an arc. Then place the point of the compasses on r' at some point P and draw the same arc, as in **Figure 27**.

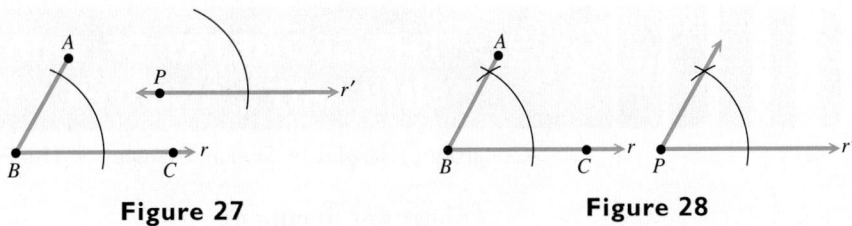

Figure 27   **Figure 28**

2. Measure, with your compasses, the distance between the points where the arc intersects the angle, and transfer this distance, as shown in **Figure 28**. Use a straightedge to join P to the point of intersection. The angle is now copied.

There are other basic constructions that can be found in books on plane geometry.

EXTENSION EXERCISES

In Exercises 1 and 2, construct the perpendicular bisector of segment PQ.

1.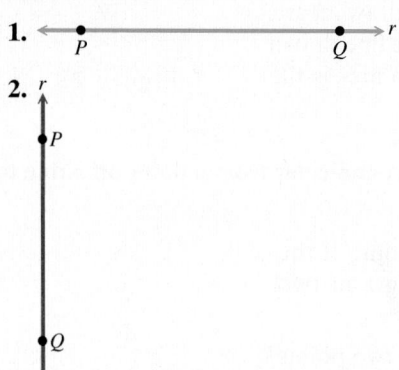

2.

3.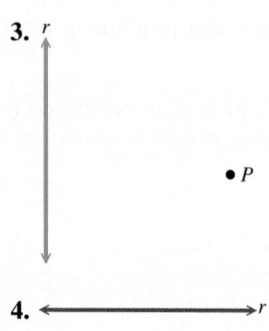

In Exercises 3 and 4, construct a perpendicular from P to the line r.

4.

5.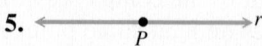

In Exercises 5 and 6, construct a perpendicular through the line r at P.

6.

In Exercises 7 and 8, copy the given angle.

7.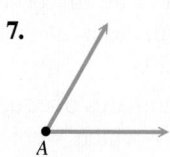

8.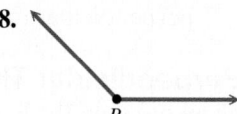

🖉 **9.** It is impossible to trisect the general angle using only Euclidean tools. Investigate this fact, and write a short report on it. Include in your report information on the construction tool called a *tomahawk.*

🖉 **10.** Write a report on this bronze relief titled **Geometria,** by Antonio de Pollaiolo, a Renaissance sculptor who lived in the fifteenth century.

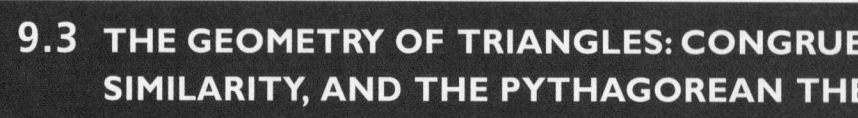

9.3 THE GEOMETRY OF TRIANGLES: CONGRUENCE, SIMILARITY, AND THE PYTHAGOREAN THEOREM

Congruent Triangles • Similar Triangles • The Pythagorean Theorem

Congruent Triangles

Triangles that are both the same size and the same shape are called **congruent triangles.** Informally speaking, if two triangles are congruent, then it is possible to pick up one of them and place it on top of the other so that they coincide exactly. An everyday example of congruent triangles would be the triangular supports for a child's swing set, machine-produced with exactly the same dimensions each time.

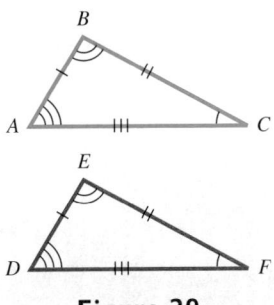

Figure 29

We use the "△" symbolism to designate triangles. **Figure 29** illustrates two congruent triangles, $\triangle ABC$ and $\triangle DEF$. The symbol $\cong$ denotes congruence, so

$$\triangle ABC \cong \triangle DEF.$$

Notice how the angles and sides are marked to indicate which angles are congruent and which sides are congruent. (Using precise terminology, we refer to angles or sides as being *congruent,* while the *measures* of congruent angles or congruent sides are *equal.* We will often use the terms "equal angles" or "equal sides" to describe angles of equal measure or sides of equal measure.)

In geometry the following properties are used to prove that two triangles are congruent.

Congruence Properties

Side-Angle-Side (SAS)   If two sides and the included angle of one triangle are equal, respectively, to two sides and the included angle of a second triangle, then the triangles are congruent.

Angle-Side-Angle (ASA)   If two angles and the included side of one triangle are equal, respectively, to two angles and the included side of a second triangle, then the triangles are congruent.

Side-Side-Side (SSS)   If three sides of one triangle are equal, respectively, to three sides of a second triangle, then the triangles are congruent.

Our knowledge of the mathematics of the Babylonians of Mesopotamia is based largely on archaeological discoveries of thousands of clay tablets. On the tablet labeled **Plimpton 322,** there are several columns of inscriptions that represent numbers. In one portion of the tablet (not shown here), the far right column is simply one that serves to number the lines, but two other columns represent values of hypotenuses and legs of right triangles with integer-valued sides.

Thus, it seems that while the famous theorem relating right-triangle side lengths is named for the Greek Pythagoras, the relationship was known more than 1000 years prior to the time of Pythagoras.

▮▮ **EXAMPLE 1** Proving Congruence

Refer to **Figure 30**.

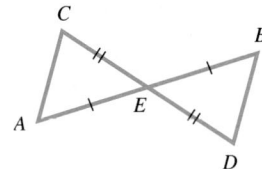

Figure 30

Given: $CE = ED$
        $AE = EB$

Prove: $\triangle ACE \cong \triangle BDE$

PROOF **STATEMENTS**	**REASONS**
1. $CE = ED$	1. Given
2. $AE = EB$	2. Given
3. $\angle CEA = \angle DEB$	3. Vertical angles are equal.
4. $\triangle ACE \cong \triangle BDE$	4. SAS congruence property

▮▮▮

▮▮ **EXAMPLE 2** Proving Congruence

Refer to **Figure 31**.

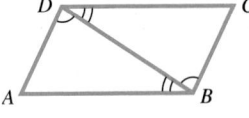

Figure 31

Given: $\angle ADB = \angle CBD$
        $\angle ABD = \angle CDB$

Prove: $\triangle ADB \cong \triangle CBD$

PROOF **STATEMENTS**	**REASONS**
1. $\angle ADB = \angle CBD$	1. Given
2. $\angle ABD = \angle CDB$	2. Given
3. $DB = DB$	3. Reflexive property (a quantity is equal to itself)
4. $\triangle ADB \cong \triangle CBD$	4. ASA congruence property

▮▮▮

▮▮ **EXAMPLE 3** Proving Congruence

Refer to **Figure 32**.

Given: $AD = CD$
$AB = CB$

Prove: $\triangle ABD \cong \triangle CBD$

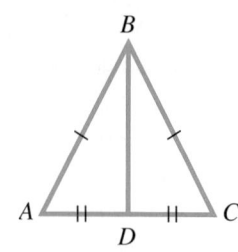

Figure 32

PROOF

STATEMENTS	REASONS
1. $AD = CD$	**1.** Given
2. $AB = CB$	**2.** Given
3. $BD = BD$	**3.** Reflexive property
4. $\triangle ABD \cong \triangle CBD$	**4.** SSS congruence property

▮▮▮

In **Example 3**, $\triangle ABC$ is an isosceles triangle. The results of that example allow us to make several important statements about an isosceles triangle. They are indicated symbolically in **Figure 33** and now stated.

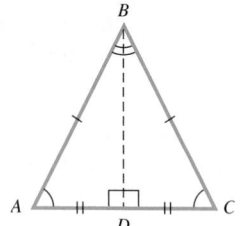

Figure 33

> **Important Statements about Isosceles Triangles**
>
> If $\triangle ABC$ is an isosceles triangle with $AB = CB$, and if D is the midpoint of the base AC, then the following properties hold.
>
> **1.** The base angles A and C are equal.
>
> **2.** Angles ABD and CBD are equal.
>
> **3.** Angles ADB and CDB are both right angles.

Similar Triangles

Many of the key ideas of geometry depend on **similar triangles,** pairs of triangles that are exactly the same shape but not necessarily the same size. **Figure 34** shows three pairs of similar triangles. (*Note:* The triangles do not need to be oriented in the same fashion in order to be similar.)

  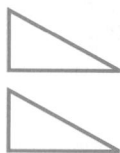

Figure 34

Suppose that a correspondence between two triangles ABC and DEF is set up as follows.

$\angle A$ corresponds to $\angle D$ side AB corresponds to side DE
$\angle B$ corresponds to $\angle E$ side BC corresponds to side EF
$\angle C$ corresponds to $\angle F$ side AC corresponds to side DF

For triangle ABC to be similar to triangle DEF, these conditions must hold.

1. Corresponding angles must have the same measure.

2. The ratios of the corresponding sides must be constant. That is, the corresponding sides are proportional.

By showing that either of these conditions holds in a pair of triangles, we may conclude that the triangles are similar.

▮▮ **EXAMPLE 4** Verifying Similarity

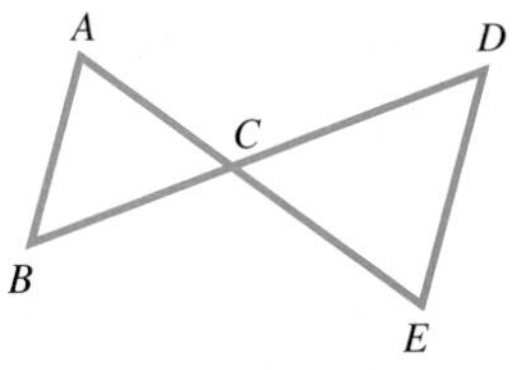

In **Figure 35**, $\overleftrightarrow{AB}$ is parallel to $\overleftrightarrow{ED}$. How can we verify that $\triangle ABC$ is similar to $\triangle EDC$?

SOLUTION

Because $\overleftrightarrow{AB}$ is parallel to $\overleftrightarrow{ED}$, the transversal $\overleftrightarrow{BD}$ forms equal alternate interior angles ABC and EDC. Also, transversal $\overleftrightarrow{AE}$ forms equal alternate interior angles BAC and DEC. We know that $\angle ACB = \angle ECD$, because they are vertical angles. Because the corresponding angles have the same measures in triangles ABC and EDC, the triangles are similar. ▮▮▮

Figure 35

Once we have shown that two angles of one triangle are equal to the two corresponding angles of a second triangle, it is not necessary to show the same for the third angle. Because, in any triangle, the sum of the angles equals 180°, we may conclude that the measures of the remaining angles *must* be equal. This leads to the following Angle-Angle similarity property.

> **Angle-Angle (AA) Similarity Property**
>
> If the measures of two angles of one triangle are equal to those of two corresponding angles of a second triangle, then the two triangles are similar.

▮▮ **EXAMPLE 5** Finding Side Lengths in Similar Triangles

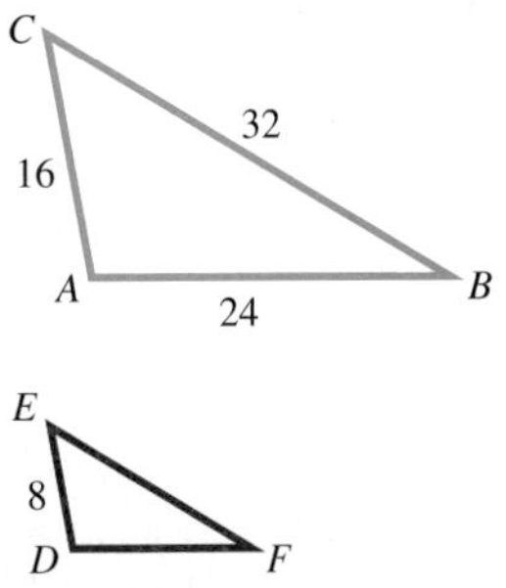

In **Figure 36**, $\triangle EDF$ is similar to $\triangle CAB$. Find the unknown side lengths in $\triangle EDF$.

SOLUTION

Side DF of the small triangle corresponds to side AB of the larger one, and sides DE and AC correspond. The fact that similar triangles have corresponding sides in proportion leads to the following equation.

Figure 36

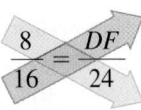

Using algebra, set the two cross-products equal. (As an alternative method of solution, multiply both sides by 48, the least common multiple of 16 and 24.)

$$8(24) = 16DF \qquad \text{Cross products are equal.}$$
$$192 = 16DF \qquad \text{Multiply.}$$
$$12 = DF \qquad \text{Divide by 16.}$$

Side DF has length 12.

Side EF corresponds to side CB. This leads to another proportion.

$$\frac{8}{16} = \frac{EF}{32}$$

$$\frac{1}{2} = \frac{EF}{32} \qquad \frac{8}{16} = \frac{1}{2}$$

$$2EF = 32 \qquad \text{Cross-products are equal.}$$

$$EF = 16 \qquad \text{Divide by 2.}$$

Side EF has length 16. ▮▮▮

EXAMPLE 6 Finding Side Lengths and Angle Measures in Similar Triangles

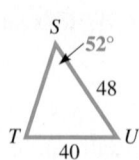

Find the measures of the unknown parts of the similar triangles STU and ZXY in **Figure 37**.

SOLUTION

Here angles X and T correspond, as do angles Y and U, and angles Z and S. Since angles Z and S correspond and since angle S is 52°, angle Z also must be 52°. The sum of the angles of any triangle is 180°. In the larger triangle, $X = 71°$ and $Z = 52°$.

$$X + Y + Z = 180 \quad \text{The angle sum is 180°.}$$
$$71 + Y + 52 = 180 \quad \text{Substitute, and solve for } y.$$
$$123 + Y = 180 \quad \text{Add.}$$
$$Y = 57 \quad \text{Subtract 123.}$$

Angle Y measures 57°. Because angles Y and U correspond, $U = 57°$ also.

Now find the unknown sides. Sides SU and ZY correspond, as do TS and XZ, and TU and XY, leading to the following proportions.

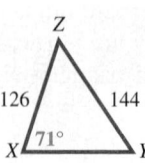

Figure 37

$\dfrac{SU}{ZY} = \dfrac{TS}{XZ}$	$\dfrac{XY}{TU} = \dfrac{ZY}{SU}$ Write the proportions.
$\dfrac{48}{144} = \dfrac{TS}{126}$	$\dfrac{XY}{40} = \dfrac{144}{48}$ Substitute.
$\dfrac{1}{3} = \dfrac{TS}{126}$	$\dfrac{XY}{40} = \dfrac{3}{1}$ Lowest terms
$3TS = 126$	$XY = 120$ Cross products are equal.
$TS = 42$	

Side TS has length 42, and side XY has length 120. ■■■

EXAMPLE 7 Finding the Height of a Flagpole

Lucie Wanersdorfer, the Lettsworth, LA postmaster, wants to measure the height of the office flagpole. She notices that at the instant when the shadow of the station is 18 feet long, the shadow of the flagpole is 99 feet long. The building is 10 feet high. What is the height of the flagpole?

SOLUTION

Figure 38 shows the information given in the problem. The two triangles shown there are similar, so corresponding sides are in proportion.

$$\frac{MN}{10} = \frac{99}{18} \quad \text{Write the proportion.}$$
$$\frac{MN}{10} = \frac{11}{2} \quad \text{Lowest terms}$$
$$2MN = 110 \quad \text{Cross products are equal.}$$
$$MN = 55 \quad \text{Divide by 2.}$$

The flagpole is 55 feet high. ■■■

Figure 38

The Pythagorean Theorem

In a right triangle, the side opposite the right angle (the longest side) is called the **hypotenuse.** The other two sides, which are perpendicular, are called the **legs.**

Pythagorean Theorem

If the two legs of a right triangle have lengths a and b, and the hypotenuse has length c, then

$$a^2 + b^2 = c^2.$$

That is, the sum of the squares of the lengths of the legs is equal to the square of the hypotenuse.

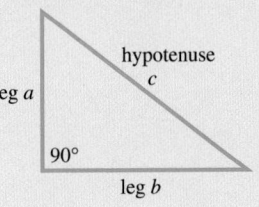

Pythagoras did not actually discover the theorem that was named after him. There is evidence that the Babylonians knew the concept quite well.

Figure 39 illustrates the theorem by using a tile pattern. The side of the square along the hypotenuse measures 5 units. Those along the legs measure 3 and 4 units. If $a = 3$, $b = 4$, and $c = 5$, the equation of the Pythagorean theorem is satisfied.

$$a^2 + b^2 = c^2 \qquad \text{Pythagorean theorem}$$
$$3^2 + 4^2 = 5^2 \qquad \text{Substitute.}$$
$$9 + 16 = 25 \qquad \text{Square.}$$
$$25 = 25 \quad \checkmark \quad \text{Add.}$$

Figure 39

The natural numbers 3, 4, and 5 form the **Pythagorean triple** $(3, 4, 5)$ because they satisfy the equation of the Pythagorean theorem. There are infinitely many such triples.

▮▮ **EXAMPLE 8** Using the Pythagorean Theorem

Find the length a in the right triangle shown in **Figure 40**.

SOLUTION

$$a^2 + b^2 = c^2 \qquad \text{Pythagorean theorem}$$
$$a^2 + 36^2 = 39^2 \qquad b = 36, c = 39$$
$$a^2 + 1296 = 1521 \qquad \text{Square.}$$
$$a^2 = 225 \qquad \text{Subtract 1296 from both sides.}$$
$$a = 15 \qquad \text{Choose the positive square root, because } a > 0.$$

Figure 40

Verify that $(15, 36, 39)$ is a Pythagorean triple as a check. ▮▮▮

The next example comes from the Cairo Mathematical Papyrus, an Egyptian document that dates back to about 300 B.C.

▮▮ **EXAMPLE 9** Finding a Ladder Height by Using the Pythagorean Theorem

A ladder of length 10 cubits has its foot 6 cubits from a wall. To what height does the ladder reach?

SOLUTION

As suggested by **Figure 41**, the ladder forms the hypotenuse of a right triangle, and the ground and wall form the legs. Let x represent the distance from the base of the wall to the top of the ladder.

$$x^2 + 6^2 = 10^2 \qquad \text{Be sure to substitute correctly.}$$
$$x^2 + 36 = 100 \qquad \text{Square.}$$
$$x^2 = 64 \qquad \text{Subtract 36.}$$
$$x = 8 \qquad \text{Choose the positive square root of 64, because } x \text{ represents a length.}$$

The ladder reaches a height of 8 cubits.

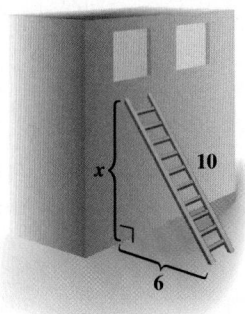

Figure 41 ▮▮▮

Probably the most famous mathematical statement in the history of motion pictures is heard in the 1939 classic *The Wizard of Oz.* Ray Bolger's character, the Scarecrow, wants a brain. When the Wizard grants him his "Th.D." (Doctor of Thinkology), the Scarecrow replies with a statement that has made mathematics teachers shudder for over 70 years. (See **Exercise 54** in **Section 9.2**.) His statement is quite impressive and sounds like the **Pythagorean theorem** but is totally incorrect. A triangle with sides of length 9, 9, and 4 provides a simple counterexample to his assertion.

The statement of the Pythagorean theorem is an *if. . . then* statement. If the antecedent (the statement following the word "if") and the consequent (the statement following the word "then") are interchanged, the new statement is called the *converse* of the original. Although the converse of a true statement may not be true, the *converse* of the Pythagorean theorem *is* also a true statement and can be used to determine if a triangle is a right triangle, given the lengths of the three sides.

> **Converse of the Pythagorean Theorem**
>
> If a triangle has sides of lengths a, b, and c, where c is the length of the longest side, and if $a^2 + b^2 = c^2$, then the triangle is a right triangle.

▮▮ **EXAMPLE 10** Applying the Converse of the Pythagorean Theorem

Following **Hurricane Katrina** in August 2005, the pine trees of southeastern Louisiana provided thousands of examples of **right triangles.** See the photo.

Suppose the vertical distance from the base of a broken tree to the point of the break is 55 inches. The length of the broken part is 144 inches. How far along the ground is it from the base of the tree to the point where the broken part touches the ground?

Jonathan Wooding has been contracted to complete an unfinished 8-foot-by-12-foot laundry room in an existing house. He finds that the previous contractor built the floor so that the length of its diagonal is 14 feet, 8 inches. Is the floor "squared off" properly?

SOLUTION

Because 14 feet, 8 inches $= 14\frac{2}{3}$ feet, he must check to see whether the following statement is true.

$$8^2 + 12^2 \stackrel{?}{=} \left(14\frac{2}{3}\right)^2 \qquad a^2 + b^2 = c^2$$

$$8^2 + 12^2 \stackrel{?}{=} \left(\frac{44}{3}\right)^2 \qquad 14\frac{2}{3} = \frac{44}{3}$$

$$208 \stackrel{?}{=} \frac{1936}{9} \qquad \text{Simplify.}$$

$$208 \neq 215\frac{1}{9} \qquad \text{The two values are not equal.}$$

He needs to fix the problem, since the diagonal, which measures 14 feet, 8 inches, should actually measure $\sqrt{208} \approx 14.4 \approx 14$ feet, 5 inches. ▮▮▮

For Further Thought

Proving the Pythagorean Theorem

The Pythagorean theorem has probably been proved in more different ways than any theorem in mathematics. A book titled *The Pythagorean Proposition*, by Elisha Scott Loomis, was first published in 1927. It contained more than 250 different proofs of the theorem.

One of the most popular proofs of the theorem follows. This proof requires two formulas for area.

The area $\mathcal{A}$ of a square is given by

$$\mathcal{A} = s^2,$$

where s is the length of a side of the square. The area $\mathcal{A}$ of a triangle is given by

$$\mathcal{A} = \frac{1}{2}bh,$$

where b is the base of the triangle and h is the height corresponding to that base. (In a right triangle, b and h are the legs.)

For Group or Individual Investigation

In the figure given on the next page, the area of the large square must always be the same, no matter how it is determined. It is made up of four right triangles and a smaller square.

(a) The length of a side of the large square is _____, so its area is (_____)² or _____.

(b) The area of the large square can also be found by obtaining the sum of the areas of the four right triangles and the smaller square. The area of each right triangle is _____, so the sum of the areas of the four right triangles is _____. The area of the smaller square is _____.

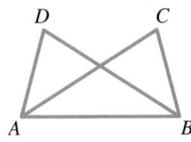

(c) The sum of the areas of the four right triangles and the smaller square is _____.

(d) Since the areas in (a) and (c) represent the area of the same figure, the expressions there must be equal. Setting them equal to each other we obtain

_____ = _____.

(e) Subtract $2ab$ from each side of the equation in (d) to obtain the desired result:

_____ = _____.

9.3 EXERCISES

*In Exercises 1–6, provide a STATEMENTS/REASONS proof similar to the ones in **Examples 1–3**.*

1. Given: $AC = BD$; $AD = BC$
   Prove: $\triangle ABD \cong \triangle BAC$

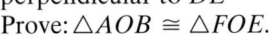

2. Given: $AC = BC$; $\angle ACD = \angle BCD$
   Prove: $\triangle ADC \cong \triangle BDC$

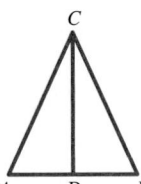

3. Given: $\overleftrightarrow{DB}$ is perpendicular to $\overleftrightarrow{AC}$; $AB = BC$
   Prove: $\triangle ABD \cong \triangle CBD$

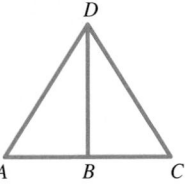

4. Given: $BC = BA$; $\angle 1 = \angle 2$
   Prove: $\triangle DBC \cong \triangle DBA$

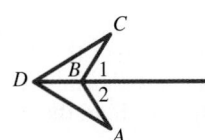

5. Given: $\angle BAC = \angle DAC$; $\angle BCA = \angle DCA$
   Prove: $\triangle ABC \cong \triangle ADC$.

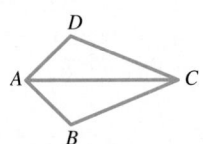

6. Given: $BO = OE$; $\overleftrightarrow{OB}$ is perpendicular to $\overleftrightarrow{AC}$; $\overleftrightarrow{OE}$ is perpendicular to $\overleftrightarrow{DE}$
   Prove: $\triangle AOB \cong \triangle FOE$.

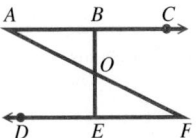

Exercises 7–10 refer to the given figure, which includes an isosceles triangle with $AB = BC$.

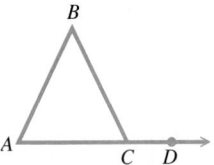

7. If $\angle B$ measures 46°, then $\angle A$ measures _____ and $\angle C$ measures _____.

8. If $\angle C$ measures 52°, what is the measure of $\angle B$?

9. What is the measure of $\angle BCD$ if $\angle B$ measures 40°?

10. What is the measure of $\angle B$ if $\angle BCD$ measures 100°?

11. Explain why all equilateral triangles must be similar.

12. Explain why two congruent triangles must be similar, but two similar triangles might not be congruent.

Name the corresponding angles and the corresponding sides for each of the following pairs of similar triangles.

13.

14.

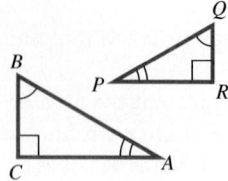

15.

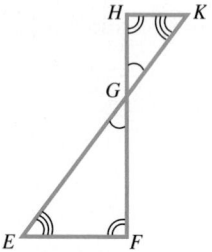

16.

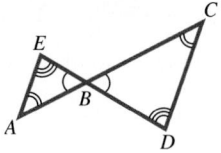

Find all unknown angle measures in each pair of similar triangles.

17.

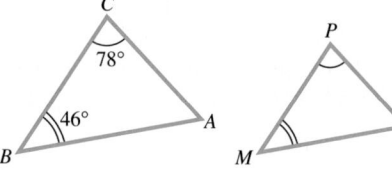

18.   **19.**

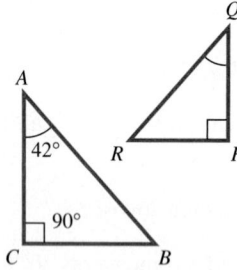 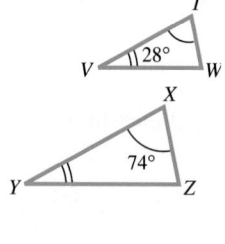

20.   **21.**

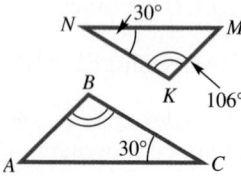 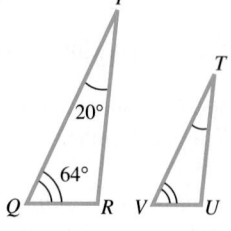

22.

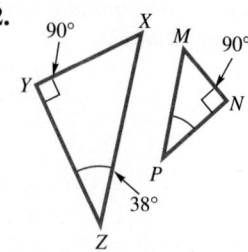

Find the unknown side lengths in each pair of similar triangles.

23.   **24.**

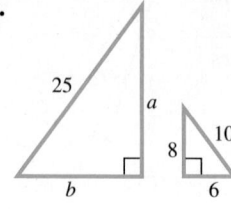 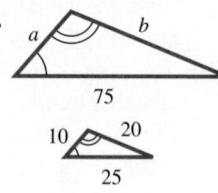

25.   **26.**

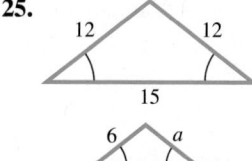 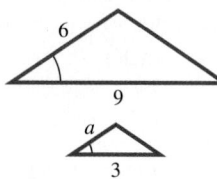

27.   **28.**

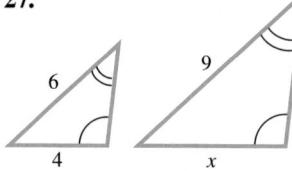 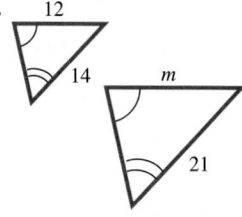

In each diagram, there are two similar triangles. Find the unknown measurement in each. (Hint: In the figure for Exercise 29, the side of length 100 in the smaller triangle corresponds to a side of length 100 + 120 = 220 in the larger triangle.)

29.   **30.**

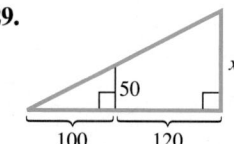 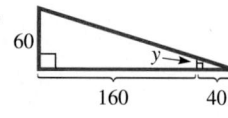

31.   **32.**

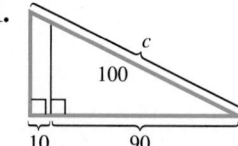 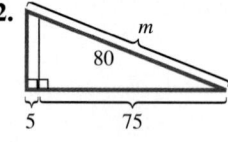

Solve each problem.

33. Height of a Tree A tree casts a shadow 45 m long. At the same time, the shadow cast by a vertical 2-m stick is 3 m long. Find the height of the tree.

34. Height of a Tower A forest fire lookout tower casts a shadow 180 ft long at the same time that the shadow of a 9-ft truck is 15 ft long. Find the height of the tower.

35. Lengths of Sides of a Photograph On a photograph of a triangular piece of land, the lengths of the three sides are 4 cm, 5 cm, and 7 cm, respectively. The shortest side of the actual piece of land is 400 m long. Find the lengths of the other two sides.

36. *Height of a Lighthouse Keeper* The Santa Cruz lighthouse is 14 m tall and casts a shadow 28 m long at 7 P.M. At the same time, the shadow of the lighthouse keeper is 3.5 m long. How tall is she?

37. *Height of a Building* A house is 15 ft tall. Its shadow is 40 ft long at the same time the shadow of a nearby building is 300 ft long. Find the height of the building.

38. *Height of the World's Tallest Human* Robert Wadlow was the tallest human being ever recorded. When a 6-ft stick cast a shadow 24 in., Robert would cast a shadow 35.7 in. How tall was he?

Find the unknown measurement. There are two similar triangles in each figure.

39.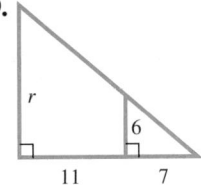

40.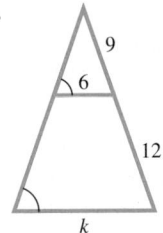

In Exercises 41–48, a and b represent the two legs of a right triangle, while c represents the hypotenuse. Find the lengths of the unknown sides.

41.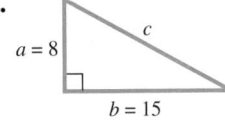

42.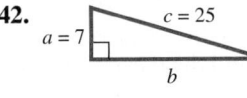

43.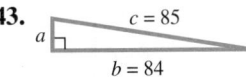

44.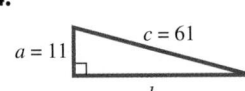

45. $a = 14$ m; $b = 48$ m

46. $a = 28$ km; $c = 100$ km

47. $b = 21$ in.; $c = 29$ in. **48.** $b = 120$ ft; $c = 169$ ft

49. Refer to **Exercise 54** in **Section 9.2**. Correct the Scarecrow's statement, using language similar to his.

50. Show that if $a^2 + b^2 = c^2$, then it is not necessarily true that $a + b = c$.

There are various formulas that will generate Pythagorean triples. For example, if we choose positive integers r and s, with r > s, then the set of equations

$$a = r^2 - s^2, \quad b = 2rs, \quad c = r^2 + s^2$$

generates a Pythagorean triple (a, b, c). Use the values of r and s given in each of Exercises 51–56 to generate a Pythagorean triple using this method.

51. $r = 2$, $s = 1$ **52.** $r = 3$, $s = 2$

53. $r = 4$, $s = 3$ **54.** $r = 3$, $s = 1$

55. $r = 4$, $s = 2$ **56.** $r = 4$, $s = 1$

57. Show that the formula given for **Exercises 51–56** actually satisfies $a^2 + b^2 = c^2$.

58. It can be shown that if $(x, x + 1, y)$ is a Pythagorean triple, then so is

$$(3x + 2y + 1, \quad 3x + 2y + 2, \quad 4x + 3y + 2).$$

Use this idea to find three more Pythagorean triples, starting with $(3, 4, 5)$. (*Hint:* Here, $x = 3$ and $y = 5$.)

If m is an odd positive integer greater than 1, then

$$\left(m, \frac{m^2 - 1}{2}, \frac{m^2 + 1}{2} \right)$$

is a Pythagorean triple. Use this to find the Pythagorean triple generated by each value of m in Exercises 59–62.

59. $m = 3$ **60.** $m = 5$

61. $m = 7$ **62.** $m = 9$

63. Show that the expressions in the directions for **Exercises 59–62** actually satisfy $a^2 + b^2 = c^2$.

64. Show why $(6, 8, 10)$ is the only Pythagorean triple consisting of consecutive even numbers.

For any integer n greater than 1,

$$(2n, n^2 - 1, n^2 + 1)$$

is a Pythagorean triple. Use this pattern to find the Pythagorean triple generated by each value of n in Exercises 65–68.

65. $n = 2$ **66.** $n = 3$

67. $n = 4$ **68.** $n = 5$

69. Show that the expressions in the directions for **Exercises 65–68** actually satisfy $a^2 + b^2 = c^2$.

70. Can an isosceles right triangle have sides with integer lengths? Why or why not?

Solve each problem. (You may wish to review quadratic equations from algebra.)

71. *Side Length of a Triangle* If the hypotenuse of a right triangle is 1 m more than the longer leg, and the shorter leg is 7 m, find the length of the longer leg.

72. *Side Lengths of a Triangle* The hypotenuse of a right triangle is 1 cm more than twice the shorter leg, and the longer leg is 9 cm less than three times the shorter leg. Find the lengths of the three sides of the triangle.

73. *Height of a Tree* At a point on the ground 30 ft from the base of a tree, the distance to the top of the tree is 2 ft more than twice the height of the tree. Find the height of the tree.

74. Dimensions of a Rectangle The length of a rectangle is 2 in. less than twice the width. The diagonal is 5 in. Find the length and width of the rectangle.

75. Height of a Break in Bamboo (Problem of the broken bamboo, from the Chinese work *Arithmetic in Nine Sections* (1261)) There is a bamboo 10 ft high, the upper end of which, being broken, reaches the ground 3 ft from the stem. Find the height of the break.

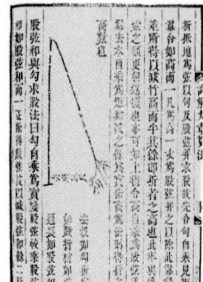

76. Depth of a Pond (Adapted from *Arithmetic in Nine Sections*) There grows in the middle of a circular pond 10 ft in diameter a reed which projects 1 ft out of the water. When it is drawn down it just reaches the edge of the pond. How deep is the water?

Squaring Off a Floor Under Construction *Imagine that you are a carpenter building the floor of a rectangular room. What must the diagonal of the room measure if your floor is to be squared off properly, given the dimensions in Exercises 77–80? Give your answer to the nearest inch.*

77. 12 ft by 15 ft   **78.** 14 ft by 20 ft

79. 16 ft by 24 ft   **80.** 20 ft by 32 ft

81. Proof of the Pythagorean Theorem by Similar Triangles In the figure, right triangles *ABC*, *CBD*, and *ACD* are similar. This may be used to prove the Pythagorean theorem. Fill in the blanks with the appropriate responses.

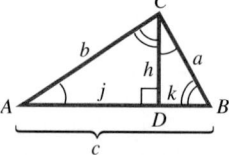

(a) By proportion, we have $\frac{c}{b} = $ ___ $/j$.

(b) By proportion, we also have $\frac{c}{a} = a/$ ___ .

(c) From part (a), $b^2 = $ ___ .

(d) From part (b), $a^2 = $ ___ .

(e) From the results of parts (c) and (d) and factoring, $a^2 + b^2 = c($ ___ $)$. Since ___ $= c$, it follows that _____ .

82. Animated Proof of the Pythagorean Theorem Go to

www.usna.edu/MathDept/mdm/pyth.html

to view an animation that provides a proof of the Pythagorean theorem.

These and other similar problems in this chapter have been adapted from Mathematics Teacher calendar problems.

*Exercises 83–90 require some ingenuity, but all can be solved using the concepts presented so far in this chapter.**

83. Value of a Measure in a Triangle In right triangle *ABC*, if *AD* = *DB* + 8, what is the value of *CD*?

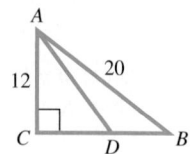

84. Angle Measure in a Triangle (A segment that *bisects* an angle divides the angle into two equal angles.) In the figure, angle *A* measures 50°. *OB* bisects angle *ABC*, and *OC* bisects angle *ACB*. What is the measure of angle *BOC*?

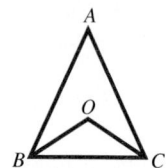

85. Unknown Length In triangle *VWZ*, *X* lies on $\overleftrightarrow{VZ}$ and *Y* lies on $\overleftrightarrow{WZ}$ with $\overleftrightarrow{XY}$ parallel to $\overleftrightarrow{VW}$ If *VZ* = 10, *XZ* = 8, and *WY* = 4, find the length *ZY*.

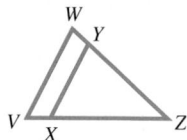

86. Unknown Length In right triangle *ABC* with right angle *C*, *BC* = 4 ft and *AC* = 3 ft. Point *R* is on $\overleftrightarrow{BC}$, equidistant from *A* and *B*. Find the length *CR*.

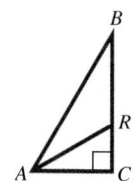

87. Unknown Angle Measure In the figure, *AD* = *AC* = *CB*. $\angle CAD$ is a right angle, and *C* lies on $\overleftrightarrow{BD}$ Find the measure of $\angle CAB$.

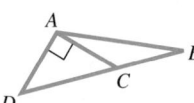

88. Unknown Length Triangle *CDE* is equilateral with *DE* = 60 units. *A* is the foot of the perpendicular from *D* to $\overleftrightarrow{CE}$, and *B* is the midpoint of $\overleftrightarrow{DA}$. Find the length *CB*.

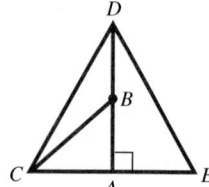

89. Unknown Angle Measure In the figure, *STRY* is a square and *TOR* is an equilateral triangle. Find the measure of $\angle TOS$ in degrees.

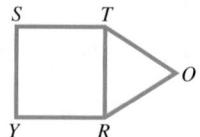

90. Unknown Length In the right triangle *ACD* with right angle *C*, *AB* + *AD* = *BC* + *DC*. If *BC* = 8 and *DC* = 10, find the length *AB*.

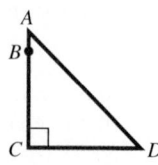

*Verify that the following constructions from the **Extension** following **Section 9.2** are valid. Use a STATEMENTS/ REASONS proof.*

91. Perpendicular Bisector   **92.** Perpendicular to a Line

93. Perpendicular through a Line   **94.** Copied Angle

9.4 PERIMETER, AREA, AND CIRCUMFERENCE

Perimeter of a Polygon • Area of a Polygon • Circumference of a Circle • Area of a Circle

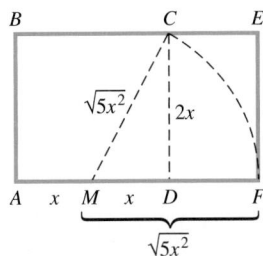

To construct a **golden rectangle,** one in which the ratio of the length to the width is equal to the ratio of the length plus the width to the length, begin with a square *ABCD.* With the point of the compasses at *M,* the midpoint of $\overrightarrow{AD}$, swing an arc of radius *MC* to intersect the extension of $\overrightarrow{AD}$ at *F.* Construct a perpendicular at *F,* and have it intersect the extension of $\overset{\leftrightarrow}{BC}$ at *E.* Then *ABEF* is a golden rectangle with ratio $(1 + \sqrt{5})/2$. (See **Section 5.5** for more on the golden ratio.)

To verify this construction, let *AM* = *x,* so that *AD* = *CD* = *2x.* Then, by the Pythagorean theorem,

$$MC = \sqrt{x^2 + (2x)^2}$$
$$= \sqrt{x^2 + 4x^2} = \sqrt{5x^2}.$$

Because *CF* is an arc of the circle with radius *MC,* *MF* = *MC* = $\sqrt{5x^2}$. Then the ratio of length *AF* to width *EF* is

$$\frac{AF}{EF} = \frac{x + \sqrt{5x^2}}{2x}$$
$$= \frac{x + x\sqrt{5}}{2x}$$
$$= \frac{x(1 + \sqrt{5})}{2x}$$
$$= \frac{1 + \sqrt{5}}{2}.$$

Similarly, it can be shown that
$$\frac{AF + EF}{AF} = \frac{1 + \sqrt{5}}{2}.$$

Perimeter of a Polygon

When working with a polygon, we are sometimes required to find the "distance around," or *perimeter,* of the polygon.

> ### Perimeter
>
> The **perimeter** of any polygon is the sum of the measures of the line segments that form its sides. Perimeter is measured in *linear units.*

The simplest polygon is a triangle. If a triangle has sides of lengths *a*, *b*, and *c*, then to find its perimeter we simply find the sum of *a*, *b*, and *c*, as shown below.

> ### Perimeter of a Triangle
>
> The perimeter *P* of a triangle with sides of lengths *a*, *b*, and *c* is given by the following formula.
>
> $$P = a + b + c$$
>
>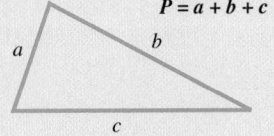

Because a rectangle is made up of two pairs of sides with the two sides in each pair equal in length, the formula for the perimeter of a rectangle may be stated as follows.

> ### Perimeter of a Rectangle
>
> The perimeter *P* of a rectangle with length ℓ and width *w* is given by the following formula.
>
> $$P = 2\ell + 2w, \quad \text{or equivalently,} \quad P = 2(\ell + w)$$
>
>

▎▎ **EXAMPLE 1** Using Perimeter to Determine Amount of Fencing Needed

A plot of land is in the shape of a rectangle. If it has length 50 feet and width 26 feet, how much fencing would be needed to completely enclose the plot?

SOLUTION

Since we must find the distance around the plot of land, the formula for the perimeter of a rectangle is needed.

$$P = 2\ell + 2w \qquad \text{Perimeter formula}$$
$$P = 2(\mathbf{50}) + 2(\mathbf{26}) \qquad \ell = 50, w = 26$$
$$P = 100 + 52 \qquad \text{Multiply.}$$
$$P = 152 \qquad \text{Add.}$$

The perimeter is 152 feet, so 152 feet of fencing is required.   ▮▮▮

A square is a rectangle with four sides of equal length. The formula for the perimeter of a square is a special case of the formula for the perimeter of a rectangle.

Perimeter of a Square

The perimeter P of a square with all sides of length s is given by the following formula.

$$P = 4s$$

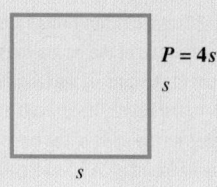

▮▮ **EXAMPLE 2** Using the Formula for Perimeter of a Square

A square has perimeter 54 inches. What is the length of each side?

SOLUTION

$$P = 4s \qquad \text{Perimeter formula}$$
$$\mathbf{54} = 4s \qquad P = 54$$
$$s = 13.5 \qquad \text{Divide by 4.}$$

Each side has a measure of 13.5 inches.   ▮▮▮

PROBLEM-SOLVING HINT The six-step method of solving an applied problem from **Section 7.2** can be used to solve problems involving geometric figures.

▮▮ **EXAMPLE 3** Finding Length and Width of a Rectangle

The length of a rectangular-shaped label is 1 centimeter more than twice the width. The perimeter is 110 centimeters. Find the length and the width.

SOLUTION

Step 1 **Read the problem.** We must find the length and the width.

Step 2 **Assign a variable.** Let w represent the width. Then $2w + 1$ can represent the length, because the length is 1 centimeter more than twice the width. **Figure 42** shows a diagram of the label.

Step 3 **Write an equation.** In the formula $P = 2\ell + 2w$, replace ℓ with $2w + 1$, and P with 110, because the perimeter is 110 centimeters.

$$110 = 2(2w + 1) + 2w$$

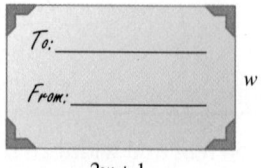

Figure 42

(not to scale)

Step 4 Solve the equation.

$$110 = 4w + 2 + 2w \qquad \text{Distributive property}$$
$$110 = 6w + 2 \qquad\qquad \text{Combine like terms.}$$
$$108 = 6w \qquad\qquad\quad \text{Subtract 2.}$$
$$18 = w \qquad\qquad\qquad \text{Divide by 6.}$$

Step 5 **State the answer.** Because $w = 18$, the width is 18 centimeters and the length is $2w + 1 = 2(18) + 1 = 37$ centimeters.

Step 6 **Check.** Because 37 is 1 more than twice 18, and because the perimeter is $2(37) + 2(18) = 110$, the answers are correct. ▮▮▮

Area of a Polygon

> ### Area
>
> The amount of plane surface covered by a polygon is called its **area.** Area is measured in *square units.*

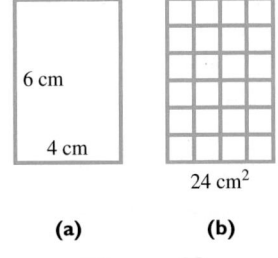

6 cm

4 cm

24 cm²

(a)   (b)

Figure 43

Defining the **area** of a figure requires a basic *unit of area.* One that is commonly used is the *square centimeter,* abbreviated cm^2. One square centimeter, or $1 \ cm^2$, is the area of a square one centimeter on a side. In place of $1 \ cm^2$, the basic unit of area could be $1 \ in.^2$, $1 \ ft^2$, $1 \ m^2$, or any appropriate unit.

As an example, we calculate the area of the rectangle shown in **Figure 43(a).** Using the basic $1 \ cm^2$ unit, **Figure 43(b)** shows that four squares, each 1 cm on a side, can be laid off horizontally while six such squares can be laid off vertically. A total of $4 \cdot 6 = 24$ of the small squares are needed to cover the large rectangle. Thus, the area of the large rectangle is $24 \ cm^2$.

We generalize to obtain a formula for the area of a rectangle. ($\mathscr{A}$ denotes area.)

> ### Area of a Rectangle
>
> The area $\mathscr{A}$ of a rectangle with length ℓ and width w is given by the following formula.
>
> $$\mathscr{A} = \ell w$$
>
>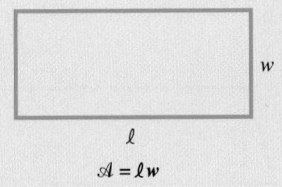

The formula for the area of a rectangle $\mathscr{A} = \ell w$ can be used to find formulas for the areas of other figures.

> ### Area of a Square
>
> The area $\mathscr{A}$ of a square with all sides of length s is given by the following formula.
>
> $$\mathscr{A} = s^2$$
>
>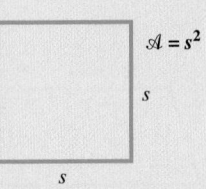

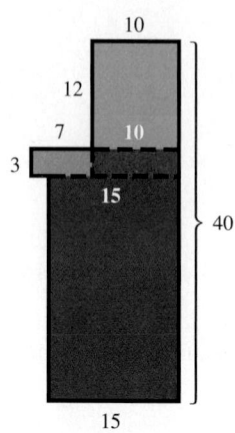

Figure 44

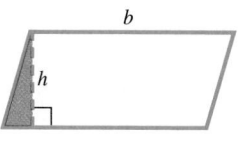

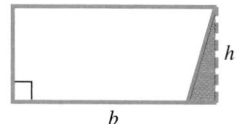

Figure 45

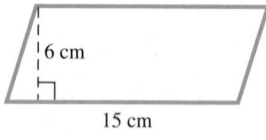

Figure 46

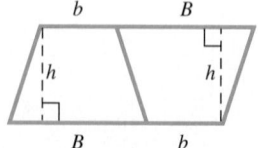

Figure 47

▮▮ **EXAMPLE 4** Using Area to Determine Amount of Carpet Needed

Figure 44 shows the floor plan of a building, made up of various rectangles. If each length given is in meters, how many square meters of carpet would be required to carpet the building?

SOLUTION

The dashed lines in the figure break up the floor area into rectangles. The areas of the various rectangles that result are as follows.

$$10 \text{ m} \cdot 12 \text{ m} = \textbf{120 m}^2, \qquad 3 \text{ m} \cdot 10 \text{ m} = \textbf{30 m}^2,$$
$$3 \text{ m} \cdot 7 \text{ m} = \textbf{21 m}^2, \qquad 15 \text{ m} \cdot 25 \text{ m} = \textbf{375 m}^2$$
$$(120 + 30 + 21 + 375) \text{ m}^2 = \textbf{546 m}^2,$$

$$\boxed{40 - 12 - 3 = 25}$$

The amount of carpet needed is 546 m². ▮▮▮

A **parallelogram** is a four-sided figure with both pairs of opposite sides parallel. Because a parallelogram need not be a rectangle, the formula for the area of a rectangle cannot be used directly for a parallelogram. However, this formula can be used indirectly, as shown in **Figure 45**. Cut off the triangle in color, and attach it at the right. The resulting figure is a rectangle with the same area as the original parallelogram.

The *height* of the parallelogram is the perpendicular distance between the top and bottom and is denoted by h in the figure. The width of the rectangle equals the height of the parallelogram, and the length of the rectangle is the base b of the parallelogram, so $\mathcal{A} = \text{length} \cdot \text{width}$ becomes $\mathcal{A} = \text{base} \cdot \text{height}$.

Area of a Parallelogram

The area $\mathcal{A}$ of a parallelogram with height h and base b is given by the following formula.

$$\mathcal{A} = bh$$

(*Note:* h represents the length of the perpendicular between the parallel sides and is not the length of a side.)

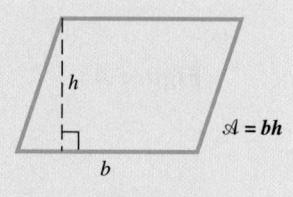

▮▮ **EXAMPLE 5** Using the Formula for Area of a Parallelogram

Find the area of the parallelogram in **Figure 46**.

SOLUTION

$$\begin{aligned}
\mathcal{A} &= bh && \text{Area formula} \\
&= 15 \text{ cm} \cdot 6 \text{ cm} && b = 15 \text{ cm}, h = 6 \text{ cm} \\
&= 90 \text{ cm}^2 && \text{Multiply.}
\end{aligned}$$

The area of the parallelogram is 90 cm². ▮▮▮

Figure 47 shows how we can find a formula for the area of a trapezoid. Notice that the figure as a whole is a parallelogram. It is made up of two trapezoids, each of which has height h, shorter base b, and longer base B. The area of the parallelogram is found by multiplying the height h by the base of the parallelogram, $b + B$—that is, $h(b + B)$. Because the area of the parallelogram is twice the area of each trapezoid, the area of each trapezoid is *half* the area of the parallelogram.

Area of a Trapezoid

The area $\mathcal{A}$ of a trapezoid with parallel bases b and B and height h is given by the following formula.

$$\mathcal{A} = \frac{1}{2}h(b + B)$$

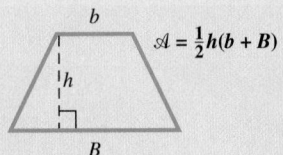

EXAMPLE 6 Using the Formula for Area of a Trapezoid

Find the area of the trapezoid in **Figure 48**.

SOLUTION

$$\mathcal{A} = \frac{1}{2}h(B + b) \qquad \text{Area formula}$$

$$= \frac{1}{2}(6 \text{ cm})(9 \text{ cm} + 3 \text{ cm}) \qquad h = 6 \text{ cm}, B = 9 \text{ cm}, b = 3 \text{ cm}$$

$$= \frac{1}{2}(6 \text{ cm})(12 \text{ cm}) \qquad \text{Add.}$$

$$= 36 \text{ cm}^2 \qquad \text{Multiply.}$$

The area of the trapezoid is 36 cm². ▮▮▮

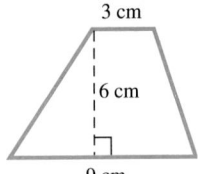

3 cm
6 cm
9 cm

Figure 48

The formula for the area of a triangle can be found from the formula for the area of a parallelogram. In **Figure 49** the triangle with vertices A, B, and C has been combined with another copy of itself, rotated 180° about the midpoint of $\overset{\leftrightarrow}{BC}$, to form a parallelogram. The area of this parallelogram is

$$\mathcal{A} = \text{base} \cdot \text{height, or } \mathcal{A} = bh.$$

However, the parallelogram has *twice* the area of the triangle, so the area of the triangle is *half* the area of the parallelogram.

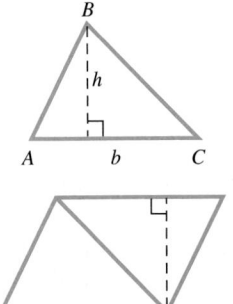

B
h
A   b   C

Figure 49

Area of a Triangle

The area $\mathcal{A}$ of a triangle with height h and base b is given by the following formula.

$$\mathcal{A} = \frac{1}{2}bh$$

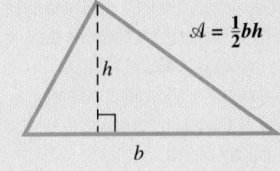

When applying the formula for the area of a triangle, remember that the height is the perpendicular distance between a vertex and the opposite side (or the extension of that side). See **Figure 50**.

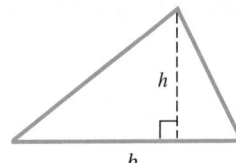
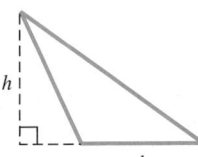

In each case, $\mathcal{A} = \frac{1}{2}bh$.

Figure 50

To use the formula for the area of a triangle, $A = \frac{1}{2}bh$, we must know the height from one of the sides of the triangle to the opposite vertex. Suppose that we know only the lengths of the three sides. Is there a way to determine the area from only this given information?

The answer is yes, and it leads us to the formula known as **Heron's formula.** Heron of Alexandria lived during the second half of the first century A.D., and although the formula is named after him, there is evidence that it was known to Archimedes several centuries earlier.

Let a, b, and c be lengths of the sides of any triangle. Let $s = \frac{1}{2}(a + b + c)$ represent the semiperimeter. Then the area A of the triangle is given by the formula

$$A = \sqrt{s(s - a)(s - b)(s - c)}.$$

The Vietnam Veterans' Memorial in Washington, D.C., is in the shape of an unenclosed isosceles triangle. The walls form a "V-shape," and each wall measures 246.75 feet. The distance between the ends of the walls is 438.14 feet. Use Heron's formula to show that the area enclosed by the triangular shape is approximately 24,900 ft².

▌▌ **EXAMPLE 7** Finding the Height of a Triangular Sail

The area of a triangular sail of a sailboat is 126 ft². The base of the sail is 12 ft. Find the height of the sail.

SOLUTION

Step 1 **Read.** We must find the height of the triangular sail.

Step 2 **Assign a variable.** Let h = the height of the sail in feet. See **Figure 51**.

Step 3 **Write an equation.** Using the information given in the problem, we substitute 126 ft² for A and 12 ft for b in the formula for the area of a triangle.

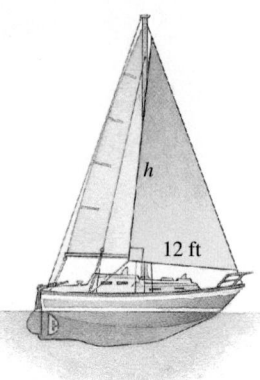

Figure 51

$$A = \frac{1}{2}bh \qquad \text{Area formula}$$

$$126 \text{ ft}^2 = \frac{1}{2}(\mathbf{12} \text{ ft})h \qquad A = 126 \text{ ft}^2, \ b = 12 \text{ ft}$$

Step 4 **Solve.**
$$126 \text{ ft}^2 = 6h \text{ ft} \qquad \text{Multiply.}$$
$$21 \text{ ft} = h \qquad \text{Divide by 6 ft.}$$

Step 5 **State the answer.** The height of the sail is 21 ft.

Step 6 **Check** to see that the values $A = 126$ ft², $b = 12$ ft, and $h = 21$ ft satisfy the formula for the area of a triangle. ▌▌▌

Circumference of a Circle

The distance around a circle is called its **circumference** (rather than "perimeter"). To understand the formula for the circumference of a circle, use a piece of string to measure the distance around a circle. Measure its diameter and then divide the circumference by the diameter. This quotient is the same, no matter what the size of the circle. The result of this measurement is an approximation for the number π.

$$\pi = \frac{\text{circumference}}{\text{diameter}} = \frac{C}{d}, \quad \text{or alternatively,} \quad C = \pi d$$

Circumference of a Circle

The circumference C of a circle of diameter d is given by the following formula.

$$C = \pi d$$

Also, since $d = 2r$, the circumference C of a circle of radius r is given by the following formula.

$$C = 2\pi r$$

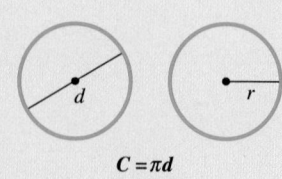

$C = \pi d$
$C = 2\pi r$

Recall that π is not a rational number. In this chapter we will use 3.14 as an approximation for π when one is required.

▮▮ **EXAMPLE 8** Finding the Circumference of a Circle

Find the circumference of each circle described. Use $\pi \approx 3.14$.

(a) A circle with diameter 12.6 centimeters

(b) A circle with radius 1.70 meters

SOLUTION

(a)
$$C = \pi d \qquad \text{Circumference formula}$$
$$\approx (3.14)(12.6 \text{ cm}) \qquad \pi \approx 3.14, \, d = 12.6 \text{ cm}$$
$$= 39.6 \text{ cm} \qquad \text{Multiply.}$$

The circumference is about 39.6 centimeters, rounded to the nearest tenth.

(b)
$$C = 2\pi r \qquad \text{Circumference formula}$$
$$\approx 2(3.14)(1.70 \text{ m}) \qquad \pi \approx 3.14, \, r = 1.70 \text{ m}$$
$$= 10.7 \text{ m} \qquad \text{Multiply.}$$

The circumference is approximately 10.7 meters. ▮▮▮

Area of a Circle

Start with a circle as shown in **Figure 52(a)**, divided into many equal pie-shaped pieces (**sectors**). Rearrange the pieces into an approximate rectangle as shown in **Figure 52(b)**. The circle has circumference $2\pi r$, so the "length" of the approximate rectangle is one-half of the circumference, or $\frac{1}{2}(2\pi r) = \pi r$, while its "width" is r. The area of the approximate rectangle is length times width, or $(\pi r)r = \pi r^2$. By choosing smaller and smaller sectors, the figure becomes closer and closer to a rectangle, so its area becomes closer and closer to πr^2.

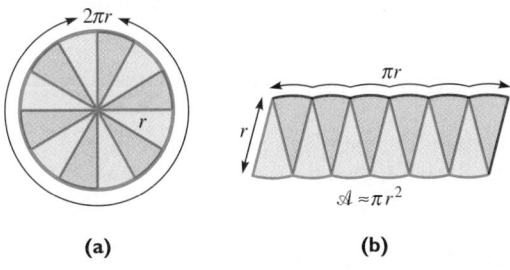

$2\pi r$

πr

r

r

$\mathcal{A} \approx \pi r^2$

(a) (b)

Figure 52

Area of a Circle

The area $\mathcal{A}$ of a circle with radius r is given by the following formula.

$$\mathcal{A} = \pi r^2$$

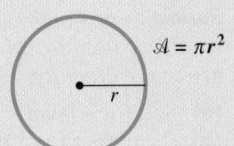

$\mathcal{A} = \pi r^2$

r

PROBLEM-SOLVING HINT The formula for the area of a circle can be used to determine the best value for the money the next time you purchase a pizza. The next example uses the idea of unit pricing.

Cast Away was one of the top films of 2000. It stars Tom Hanks as Chuck Noland, who, as the only survivor in a plane crash, is stranded for 4 years alone on a tropical island. Not long after the crash, speaking to his "friend" Wilson, a volleyball that had washed ashore, he used geometry to assess their chances of being found. Sketching a circle and performing an arithmetic calculation on the side of a rock, Chuck realizes their futility.

So, Wilson. We were en route from Memphis for eleven and a half hours at about 475 miles an hour. They think that we are right here. But we went out of radio contact and flew around that storm for about an hour. So that's a distance of what, 400 miles? Four hundred miles squared, that's 160,000, times pi, 3.14, ...

Chuck's calculation for the size of the search area is an application of the formula for the area of a circle, $\mathcal{A} = \pi r^2$. He looks to Wilson, and sighs,

. . . That's twice the size of Texas. They may never find us.

What was Chuck's answer? The land area of Texas is 261,797 square miles. Was he correct? The answer can be found on **page 484.**

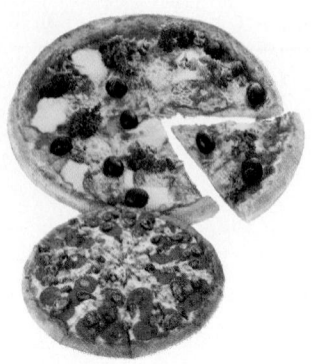

▮▮ **EXAMPLE 9** Using Area to Determine Better Value for Pizza

Paw-Paw Johnny's delivers pizza. The price of an 8-inch diameter pizza is $6.99, while the price of a 16-inch diameter pizza is $13.98. Which is the better buy?

SOLUTION

To determine which pizza is the better value for the money, we must first find the area of each, and divide the price by the area to determine the price per square inch.

8-inch diameter pizza area $= \pi(4 \text{ in.})^2 \approx 50.2 \text{ in.}^2$ ⠀ Radius is $(\frac{1}{2})(8 \text{ in.}) = 4$ in.

16-inch diameter pizza area $= \pi(8 \text{ in.})^2 \approx 201 \text{ in.}^2$ ⠀ Radius is $(\frac{1}{2})(16 \text{ in.}) = 8$ in.

The price per square inch for the 8-inch pizza is

$$\frac{\$6.99}{50.2} \approx 13.9\text{¢},$$

while the price per square inch for the 16-inch pizza is

$$\frac{\$13.98}{201} \approx 7.0\text{¢}.$$

Therefore, the 16-inch pizza is the better buy, since it costs approximately half as much per square inch. ▮▮▮

> 🎬 **Solution to Margin Note Problem** Chuck computes the approximate search area as 502,400 square miles. "Twice the size of Texas" is 2(261,797) = 523,594 square miles, so his analysis is correct.

9.4 EXERCISES

In Exercises 1–5, fill in each blank with the correct response.

1. The perimeter of an equilateral triangle with side length equal to _____ inches is the same as the perimeter of a rectangle with length 20 inches and width 16 inches.

2. A square with area 25 cm² has perimeter _____ cm.

3. If the area of a certain triangle is 48 square inches, and the base measures 8 inches, then the height must measure _____ inches.

4. If the radius of a circle is doubled, then its area is multiplied by a factor of _____.

5. Perimeter is to a polygon as _____ is to a circle.

6. *Perimeter or Area?* Decide whether perimeter or area would be used to solve a problem concerning the measure of the quantity.

   (a) Sod for a lawn
   (b) Carpeting for a bedroom
   (c) Baseboards for a living room
   (d) Fencing for a yard
   (e) Fertilizer for a garden
   (f) Tile for a bathroom
   (g) Determining the cost of planting rye grass in a lawn for the winter
   (h) Determining the cost of replacing a linoleum floor with a wood floor

Use the formulas of this section to find the area of each figure. In Exercises 19–22, use 3.14 as an approximation for π.

7.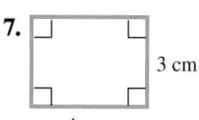
3 cm
4 cm

8.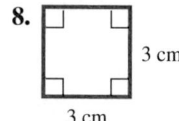
3 cm
3 cm

9.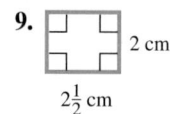
2 cm
$2\frac{1}{2}$ cm

10.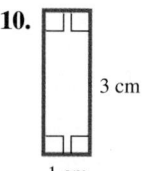
3 cm
1 cm

11.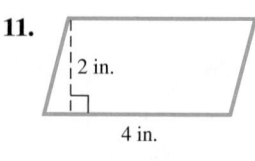
2 in.
4 in.
(a parallelogram)

12.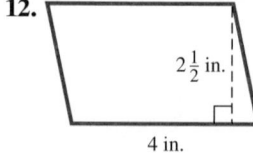
$2\frac{1}{2}$ in.
4 in.
(a parallelogram)

13.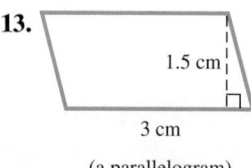
1.5 cm
3 cm
(a parallelogram)

14.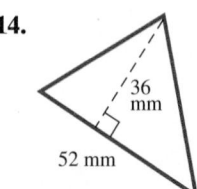
36 mm
52 mm

15.

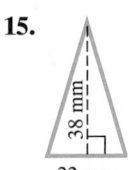

38 mm

22 mm

16.

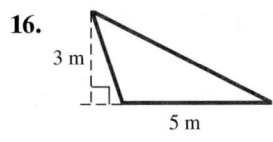

3 m

5 m

17.

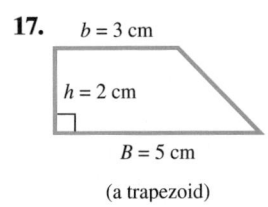

b = 3 cm

h = 2 cm

B = 5 cm

(a trapezoid)

18.

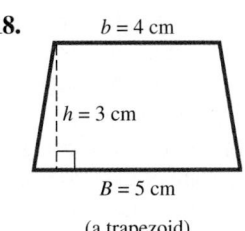

b = 4 cm

h = 3 cm

B = 5 cm

(a trapezoid)

19.

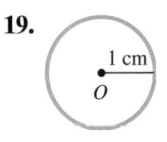

1 cm

O

20.

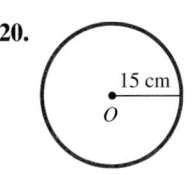

15 cm

O

21.

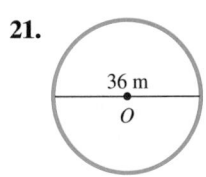

36 m

O

22.

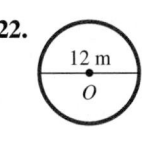

12 m

O

Solve each problem.

23. Window Side Length A stained-glass window in a church is in the shape of a square. The perimeter of the square is 7 times the length of a side in meters, decreased by 12. Find the length of a side of the window.

24. Dimensions of a Rectangle A video rental establishment displayed a rectangular cardboard stand-up advertisement for the movie *The Blind Side*. The length was 20 in. more than the width, and the perimeter was 176 in. What were the dimensions of the rectangle?

25. Dimensions of a Lot A lot is in the shape of a triangle. One side is 100 ft longer than the shortest side, while the third side is 200 ft longer than the shortest side. The perimeter of the lot is 1200 ft. Find the lengths of the sides of the lot.

26. Pennant Side Lengths A wall pennant is in the shape of an isosceles triangle. Each of the two equal sides measures 18 in. more than the third side, and the perimeter of the triangle is 54 in. What are the lengths of the sides of the pennant?

27. Radius of a Circular Foundation A hotel is in the shape of a cylinder, with a circular foundation. The circumference of the foundation is 6 times the radius, increased by 12.88 ft. Find the radius of the circular foundation. (Use 3.14 as an approximation for π.)

28. Radius of a Circle If the radius of a certain circle is tripled, with 8.2 cm then added, the result is the circumference of the circle. Find the radius of the circle. (Use 3.14 as an approximation for π.)

29. Area of Two Lots The survey plat in the figure below shows two lots that form a trapezoid. The measures of the parallel sides are 115.80 ft and 171.00 ft. The height of the trapezoid is 165.97 ft. Find the combined area of the two lots. Round your answer to the nearest hundredth of a square foot.

30. Area of a Lot Lot A in the figure is in the shape of a trapezoid. The parallel sides measure 26.84 ft and 82.05 ft. The height of the trapezoid is 165.97 ft. Find the area of Lot A. Round your answer to the nearest hundredth of a square foot.

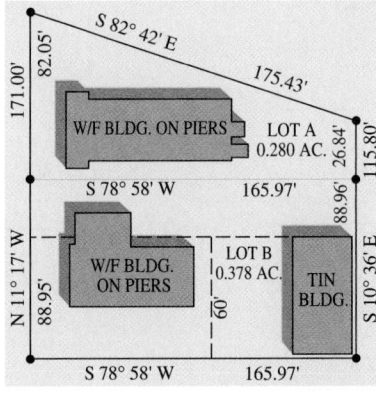

31. Perimeter or Area? In order to purchase fencing to go around a rectangular yard, would you need to use perimeter or area to decide how much to buy?

32. Perimeter or Area? In order to purchase fertilizer for the lawn of a yard, would you need to use perimeter or area to decide how much to buy?

In the chart below, one of the values r (radius), d (diameter), C (circumference), or $\mathcal{A}$ (area) is given for a particular circle. Find the remaining three values. Leave π in your answers.

	r	d	C	$\mathcal{A}$
33.	6 in.			
34.	9 in.			
35.		10 ft		
36.		40 ft		
37.			12π cm	
38.			18π cm	
39.				100π in.^{2}
40.				256π in.^{2}

Each figure has perimeter as indicated. (Figures are not necessarily to scale.) Find the value of x.

41. $P = 58$

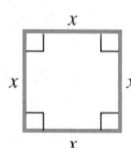

42. $P = 42$

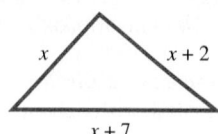

43. $P = 38$

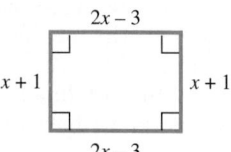

44. $P = 278$

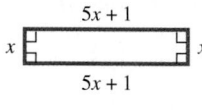

Each figure has area as indicated. Find the value of x.

45. $\mathscr{A} = 26.01$

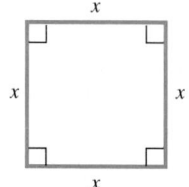

46. $\mathscr{A} = 28$

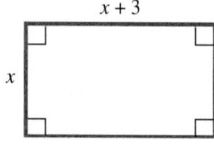

47. $\mathscr{A} = 15$

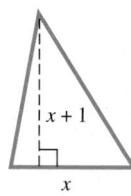

48. $\mathscr{A} = 30$

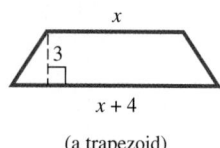

(a trapezoid)

Each circle has circumference or area as indicated. Find the value of x. Use 3.14 as an approximation for π.

49. $C = 37.68$

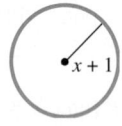

50. $C = 54.95$

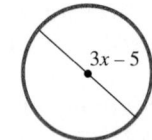

51. $\mathscr{A} = 28.26$

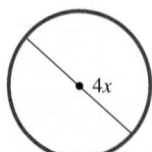

52. $\mathscr{A} = 18.0864$

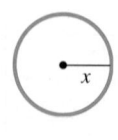

53. Work through the parts of this exercise in order, and use it to make a generalization concerning areas of rectangles.

   (a) Find the area of a rectangle 4 cm by 5 cm.

   (b) Find the area of a rectangle 8 cm by 10 cm.

(c) Find the area of a rectangle 12 cm by 15 cm.

(d) Find the area of a rectangle 16 cm by 20 cm.

(e) The rectangle in part (b) had sides twice as long as the sides of the rectangle in part (a). Divide the larger area by the smaller. By doubling the sides, the area increased _____ times.

(f) To get the rectangle in part (c), each side of the rectangle in part (a) was multiplied by _____. This made the larger area _____ times the size of the smaller area.

(g) To get the rectangle of part (d), each side of the rectangle of part (a) was multiplied by _____. This made the area increase to _____ times what it was originally.

(h) In general, if the length of each side of a rectangle is multiplied by n, the area is multiplied by _____.

*Job Cost Use the results of **Exercise 53** to solve each problem.*

54. A ceiling measuring 9 ft by 15 ft can be painted for $60. How much would it cost to paint a ceiling 18 ft by 30 ft?

55. Suppose carpet for a 10 ft by 12 ft room costs $200. Find the cost to carpet a room 20 ft by 24 ft.

56. A carpet cleaner charges $80 to shampoo an area 31 ft by 31 ft. What would be the charge for an area 93 ft by 93 ft?

57. Use the logic of **Exercise 53** to answer the following: If the radius of a circle is multiplied by n, then the area of the circle is multiplied by _____.

58. Use the logic of **Exercise 53** to answer the following: If the height of a triangle is multiplied by n and the base length remains the same, then the area of the triangle is multiplied by _____.

Total Area as the Sum of Areas By considering total area as the sum of the areas of all of its parts, the area of a figure such as those in Exercises 59–62 can be determined. Find the total area of each figure. Use 3.14 as an approximation for π in Exercises 61 and 62, and round to the nearest hundredth.

59.

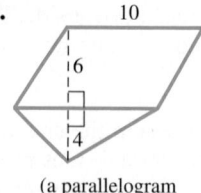

(a parallelogram and a triangle)

60.

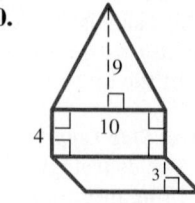

(a triangle, a rectangle, and a parallelogram)

61.

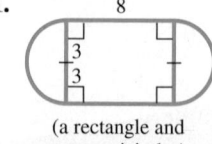

(a rectangle and two semicircles)

62.

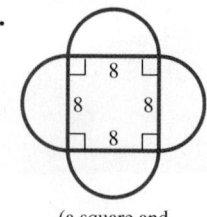

(a square and four semicircles)

Area of a Shaded Portion of a Plane Figure *The shaded areas of the figures in Exercises 63–68 may be found by subtracting the area of the unshaded portion from the total area of the figure. Use this approach to find the area of the shaded portion. Use 3.14 as an approximation for π in Exercises 66–68, and round to the nearest hundredth.*

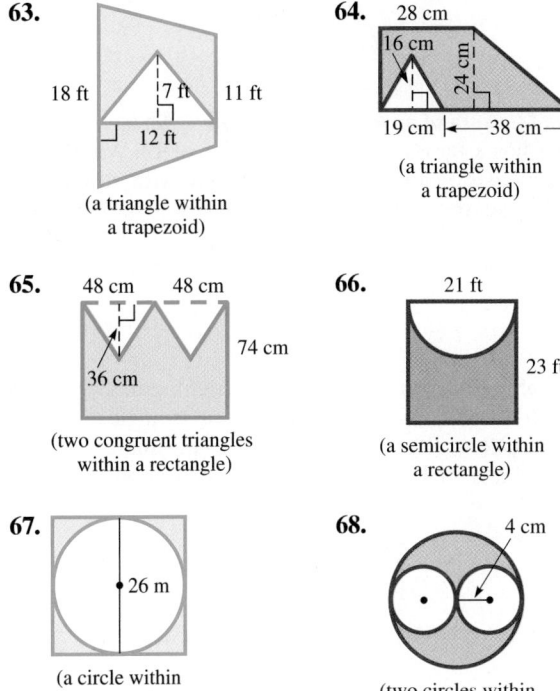

63.

18 ft   7 ft   11 ft
         12 ft

(a triangle within a trapezoid)

64. 28 cm

16 cm   24 cm

19 cm ⟵ 38 cm ⟶

(a triangle within a trapezoid)

65. 48 cm   48 cm

74 cm

36 cm

(two congruent triangles within a rectangle)

66. 21 ft

23 ft

(a semicircle within a rectangle)

67.

26 m

(a circle within a square)

68. 4 cm

(two circles within a circle)

Pizza Pricing *The following exercises show prices actually charged by Maw-Maw Gigi's, a local pizzeria. In each case, the dimension is the diameter of the pizza. Find the best buy.*

69. Cheese pizza: 10-in. pizza sells for $5.99, 12-in. pizza sells for $7.99, 14-in. pizza sells for $8.99.

70. Cheese pizza with two toppings: 10-in. pizza sells for $7.99, 12-in. pizza sells for $9.99, 14-in. pizza sells for $10.99.

71. All Feasts pizza: 10-in. pizza sells for $9.99, 12-in. pizza sells for $11.99, 14-in. pizza sells for $12.99.

72. Extravaganza pizza: 10-in. pizza sells for $11.99, 12-in. pizza sells for $13.99, 14-in. pizza sells for $14.99.

James Garfield's Proof of the Pythagorean Theorem *James A. Garfield, the twentieth president of the United States, provided a proof of the Pythagorean theorem using the figure at the top of the next column. Supply the required information in each of Exercises 73–76, in order, to follow his proof.*

73. Find the area of the trapezoid *WXYZ* using the formula for the area of a trapezoid.

74. Find the area of each of the right triangles *PWX*, *PZY*, and *PXY*.

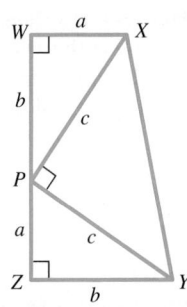

75. Since the sum of the areas of the three right triangles must equal the area of the trapezoid, set the expression from **Exercise 73** equal to the sum of the three expressions from **Exercise 74**.

76. Simplify the terms of the equation from **Exercise 75** as much as possible. What is the result?

A polygon can be inscribed within a circle or circumscribed about a circle. In the figure, triangle ABC is inscribed within the circle, while square WXYZ is circumscribed about it. These ideas will be used in some of the remaining exercises in this section and later in this chapter.

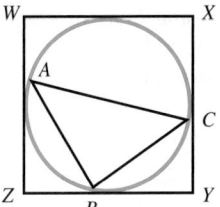

Exercises 77–90 require some ingenuity, but all may be solved using the concepts presented so far in this chapter.

77. *Diameter of a Circle* Given the circle with center *O* and rectangle *ABCO*, find the diameter of the circle.

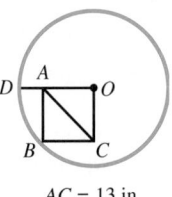

$AC = 13$ in.
$AD = 3$ in.

78. *Perimeter of a Triangle* What is the perimeter of $\triangle AEB$, if $AD = 20$ in., $DC = 30$ in., and $AC = 34$ in.?

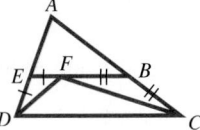

79. *Area of a Square* The area of square *PQRS* is 1250 square feet. *T*, *U*, *V*, and *W* are the midpoints of *PQ*, *QR*, *RS*, and *SP*, respectively. What is the area of square *TUVW*?

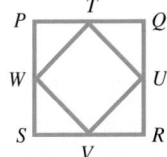

80. Area of a Quadrilateral The rectangle *ABCD* has length twice the width. If *P*, *Q*, *R*, and *S* are the midpoints of the sides, and the perimeter of *ABCD* is 96 in., what is the area of quadrilateral *PQRS*?

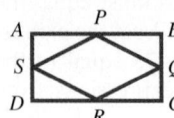

81. Area of a Shaded Region If *ABCD* is a square with each side measuring 36 in., what is the area of the shaded region?

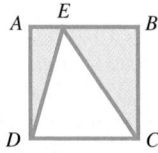

82. Perimeter of a Polygon Can the perimeter of the polygon shown be determined from the given information? If so, what is the perimeter?

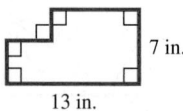

83. Area of a Shaded Region Express the area of the shaded region in terms of *r*, given that the circle is inscribed in the square.

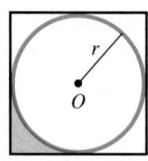

84. Area of a Trapezoid Find the area of trapezoid *ABCD*, given that the area of right triangle *ABE* is 30 in.².

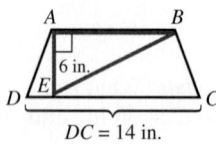

85. Area of a Quadrilateral Find the area of quadrilateral *ABCD*, if angles *A* and *C* are right angles.

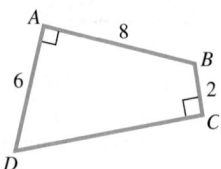

86. Area of a Triangle The perimeter of the isosceles triangle *ABC* (with *AB* = *BC*) is 128 in. The altitude *BD* is 48 in. What is the area of triangle *ABC*?

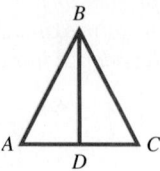

87. Base Measure of an Isosceles Triangle An isosceles triangle has a base of 24 and two sides of 13. What other base measure can an isosceles triangle with equal sides of 13 have and still have the same area as the given triangle?

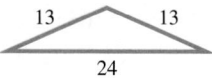

88. Area of a Pentagon In the figure, pentagon *PQRST* is formed by a square and an equilateral triangle such that *PQ* = *QR* = *RS* = *ST* = *PT*. The perimeter of the pentagon is 80. Find the area of the pentagon.

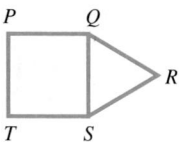

Exercises 89 and 90 refer to the given figure. The center of the circle is O.

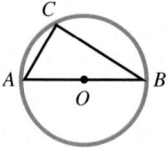

89. Radius of a Circle If $\overset{\frown}{AC}$ measures 6 in. and $\overset{\frown}{BC}$ measures 8 in., what is the radius of the circle?

90. Lengths of Chords of a Circle If $\overset{\frown}{AB}$ measures 13 cm, and the length of $\overset{\frown}{BC}$ is 7 cm more than the length of $\overset{\frown}{AC}$, what are the lengths of $\overset{\frown}{BC}$ and $\overset{\frown}{AC}$?

9.5 VOLUME AND SURFACE AREA

Space Figures • Volume and Surface Area of Space Figures

Space Figures

Polyhedral dice such as the ones shown here are often used in today's role-playing games.

The five regular polyhedra are also known as **Platonic solids,** named for the Greek philosopher Plato. He considered them as "building blocks" of nature and assigned fire to the tetrahedron, earth to the cube, air to the octahedron, and water to the icosahedron. Because the dodecahedron is different from the others due to its pentagonal faces, he assigned to it the cosmos (stars and planets). (*Source:* www.mathacademy.com) An animated view of the Platonic solids can be found at http://www.wikipedia.org/wiki/Platonic_solid

Thus far, this chapter has discussed only **plane figures**—figures that can be drawn completely in the plane of a sheet of paper. However, it takes the three dimensions of space to represent the solid world around us. For example, **Figure 53** shows a "box" (a **rectangular parallelepiped**). The *faces* of a box are rectangles. The faces meet at *edges;* the "corners" are called *vertices* (plural of vertex—the same word as for the "corner" of an angle).

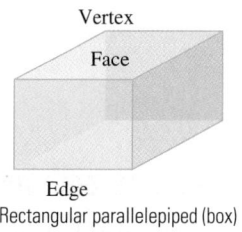

Rectangular parallelepiped (box)

Figure 53

Boxes are one kind of space figure belonging to an important group called **polyhedra,** the faces of which are made only of polygons. Perhaps the most interesting polyhedra are the *regular polyhedra.* Recall that a *regular polygon* is a polygon with all sides equal and all angles equal. A regular polyhedron is a space figure, the faces of which are only one kind of regular polygon. It turns out that there are only five different regular polyhedra. They are shown in **Figure 54.** A **tetrahedron** is composed of four equilateral triangles, each three of which meet in a point. Use the figure to verify that there are four faces, four vertices, and six edges.

Tetrahedron   Hexahedron (cube)   Octahedron   Dodecahedron   Icosahedron

Figure 54

The four remaining regular polyhedra are the **hexahedron,** the **octahedron,** the **dodecahedron,** and the **icosahedron.** The hexahedron, or cube, is composed of six squares, each three of which meet at a point. The octahedron is composed of groups of four regular triangles (i.e., equilateral) meeting at a point. The dodecahedron is formed by groups of three regular pentagons, while the icosahedron is made up of groups of five regular triangles.

Two other types of polyhedra are familiar space figures: pyramids and prisms. **Pyramids** are made of triangular sides and a polygonal base. **Prisms** have two faces in parallel planes; these faces are congruent polygons. The remaining faces of a prism are all parallelograms. (See **Figures 55(a)** and **(b)** on the next page.) By this definition, a box is also a prism.

Figure 55(c) shows space figures made up in part of circles, including *right circular cones* and *right circular cylinders.* It also shows how a circle can generate a *torus,* a doughnut-shaped solid that has interesting topological properties. See **Section 9.7.**

Tetrahedron

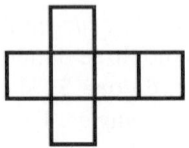

Hexahedron (cube)

Octahedron

Dodecahedron

Icosahedron

Patterns such as these may be used to construct three-dimensional models of the **regular polyhedra.** See

http://www.korthalsaltes.com

for some examples.

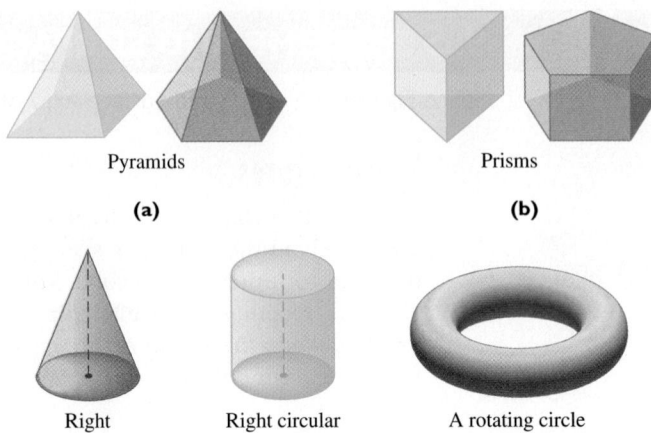

Pyramids
(a)

Prisms
(b)

Right
circular cone

Right circular
cylinder

A rotating circle
generates a torus.

(c)

Figure 55

Volume and Surface Area of Space Figures

While area is a measure of surface covered by a plane figure, **volume** is a measure of capacity of a space figure. Volume is measured in *cubic* units. For example, a cube with edge measuring 1 cm has volume 1 cubic cm, which is also written as 1 cm³, or 1 cc. The **surface area** is the total area that would be covered if the space figure were "peeled" and the peel laid flat. Surface area is measured in *square* units.

Volume and Surface Area of a Box

Suppose that a box has length ℓ, width w, and height h. Then the volume V and the surface area S are given by the following formulas.

$$V = \ell w h \quad \text{and} \quad S = 2\ell w + 2\ell h + 2hw$$

If the box is a cube with edge of length s, the formulas are as follows.

$$V = s^3 \quad \text{and} \quad S = 6s^2$$

$V = \ell wh$
$S = 2\ell w + 2\ell h + 2hw$

$V = s^3$
$S = 6s^2$

▌▌ **EXAMPLE 1** Using the Formulas for a Box

Find the volume V and the surface area S of the box shown in **Figure 56**.

SOLUTION

$$\begin{aligned} V &= \ell wh & \text{Volume formula} \\ &= 14 \cdot 7 \cdot 5 & \text{Substitute.} \\ &= 490 & \text{Multiply.} \end{aligned}$$

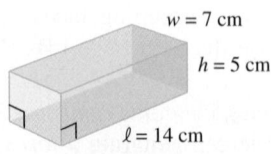

$w = 7$ cm
$h = 5$ cm
$\ell = 14$ cm
Figure 56

Volume is measured in cubic units, so the volume of the box is 490 cubic centimeters, or 490 cm³.

$$S = 2\ell w + 2\ell h + 2hw \qquad \text{Surface area formula}$$
$$= 2(14)(7) + 2(14)(5) + 2(5)(7) \quad \text{Substitute.}$$
$$= 196 + 140 + 70 \qquad \text{Multiply.}$$
$$= 406 \qquad \text{Add.}$$

Surface areas of space figures are measured in square units, so the surface area of the box is 406 square centimeters, or 406 cm². ▮▮▮

A typical tin can is an example of a **right circular cylinder.**

Volume and Surface Area of a Right Circular Cylinder

If a right circular cylinder has height h and radius of its base equal to r, then the volume V and the surface area S are given by the following formulas.

$$V = \pi r^2 h$$

and

$$S = 2\pi rh + 2\pi r^2$$

$$V = \pi r^2 h$$
$$S = 2\pi rh + 2\pi r^2$$

(In the formula for S, the areas of the top and bottom are included.)

▮▮ **EXAMPLE 2**   Using the Formulas for a Right Circular Cylinder

In **Figure 57**, the right circular cylinder has surface area 288π square inches, and the radius of its base is 6 inches. Find each measure.

(a) the height of the cylinder

(b) the volume of the cylinder

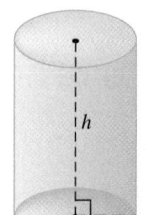

Right circular cylinder

Figure 57

SOLUTION

(a)
$$S = 2\pi rh + 2\pi r^2 \qquad \text{Surface area formula}$$
$$288\pi = 2\pi(6)h + 2\pi(6)^2 \quad S = 288\pi, \, r = 6$$
$$288\pi = 12\pi h + 72\pi \qquad \text{Multiply.}$$
$$216\pi = 12\pi h \qquad \text{Subtract } 72\pi.$$
$$h = 18 \qquad \text{Divide by } 12\pi.$$

The height is 18 inches.

(b)
$$V = \pi r^2 h \qquad \text{Volume formula}$$
$$= \pi(6)^2(18) \quad r = 6, \, h = 18$$
$$= 648\pi \qquad \text{Multiply.}$$

The exact volume is 648π in.³, or approximately 2030 in.³, using $\pi \approx 3.14$. ▮▮▮

The three-dimensional analogue of a circle is a **sphere.** It is defined by replacing the word "plane" with "space" in the definition of a circle (**Section 9.2**).

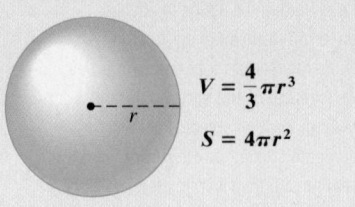

Volume and Surface Area of a Sphere

If a sphere has radius r, then the volume V and the surface area S are given by the following formulas.

$$V = \frac{4}{3}\pi r^3 \qquad \text{and} \qquad S = 4\pi r^2$$

$$V = \frac{4}{3}\pi r^3$$

$$S = 4\pi r^2$$

The **Moscow papyrus,** which dates back to about 1850 B.C., provides an example of inductive reasoning by the early Egyptian mathematicians. Problem 14 in the document reads:

You are given a truncated pyramid of 6 for the vertical height by 4 on the base by 2 on the top. You are to square this 4, result 16. You are to double 4, result 8. You are to square 2, result 4. You are to add the 16, the 8, and the 4, result 28. You are to take one-third of 6, result 2. You are to take 28 twice, result 56. See, it is 56. You will find it right.

What does all this mean? A *frustum* of a pyramid is that part of the pyramid remaining after its top has been cut off by a plane parallel to the base of the pyramid. The formula for finding the volume of the frustum of a pyramid with square bases is

$$V = \frac{1}{3}h(b^2 + bB + B^2),$$

where b is the length of the upper base, B is the length of the lower base, and h is the height (or altitude). The writer of the problem is giving a method of determining the volume of the frustum of a pyramid with square bases on the top and bottom, with bottom base side of length 4, top base side of length 2, and height equal to 6.

▮▮ EXAMPLE 3 Using the Volume Formula for a Sphere

Suppose that a spherical tank having radius 3 meters can be filled with liquid fuel for $200. How much will it cost to fill a spherical tank of radius 6 meters with the same fuel?

SOLUTION

Find the first volume, V_1.

$$\begin{aligned}
V_1 &= \frac{4}{3}\pi r^3 &&\text{Formula}\\
&= \frac{4}{3}\pi(3)^3 &&r = 3\\
&= \frac{4}{3}\pi(27) &&\text{Cube.}\\
&= 36\pi &&\text{Multiply.}
\end{aligned}$$

Find the second volume, V_2.

$$\begin{aligned}
V_2 &= \frac{4}{3}\pi r^3\\
&= \frac{4}{3}\pi(6)^3 &&r = 6\\
&= \frac{4}{3}\pi(216)\\
&= 288\pi
\end{aligned}$$

The volumes are 36π and 288π m³. Notice that by doubling the radius of the sphere from 3 meters to 6 meters, the volume has increased 8 times, because

$$V_2 = 288\pi = 8(36\pi) = 8V_1.$$

Therefore, the cost to fill the larger tank is eight times the cost to fill the smaller one: $8(\$200) = \$1600.$ ▮▮▮

The space figure shown in **Figure 58** is a **right circular cone.**

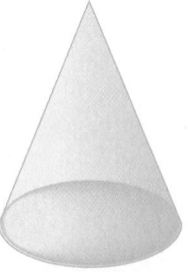

Right circular cone

Figure 58

Volume and Surface Area of a Right Circular Cone

If a right circular cone has height h and the radius of its circular base is r, then the volume V and the surface area S are given by the following formulas.

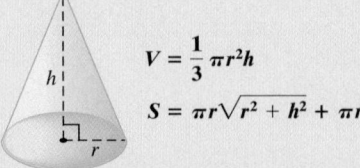

$$V = \frac{1}{3}\pi r^2 h$$

$$S = \pi r\sqrt{r^2 + h^2} + \pi r^2$$

$$V = \frac{1}{3}\pi r^2 h$$

and

$$S = \pi r\sqrt{r^2 + h^2} + \pi r^2$$

(In the formula for S, the area of the bottom is included.)

Pyramid

Figure 59

A **pyramid** is a space figure having a polygonal base and triangular sides. **Figure 59** shows a pyramid with a square base.

The **Transamerica Tower** in San Francisco is a pyramid with a square base. Each side of the base has a length of 52 meters, while the height of the building is 260 meters. The formula for the volume of a pyramid indicates that the volume of the building is about 234,000 cubic meters.

Volume of a Pyramid

If B represents the area of the base of a pyramid, and h represents the height (that is, the perpendicular distance from the top, or apex, to the base), then the volume V is given by the following formula.

$$V = \frac{1}{3}Bh$$

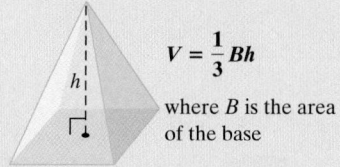

$V = \frac{1}{3}Bh$

where B is the area of the base

EXAMPLE 4 Comparing Volumes Using Ratios

What is the ratio of the volume of a right circular cone with radius of base r and height h to the volume of a pyramid having a square base, with each side of length r, and height h?

SOLUTION

First, use the formula for the volume of a cone.

$$V_1 = \text{Volume of the cone} = \frac{1}{3}\pi r^2 h$$

Because the pyramid has a square base, the area B of its base is r^2. Now use the formula for the volume of a pyramid.

$$V_2 = \text{Volume of the pyramid} = \frac{1}{3}Bh = \frac{1}{3}(r^2)h$$

Now find the ratio of the first volume to the second.

$$\frac{V_1}{V_2} = \frac{\frac{1}{3}\pi r^2 h}{\frac{1}{3}r^2 h} = \pi \quad \boxed{\text{The ratio is } \pi.}$$

▋▋▋

9.5 EXERCISES

Decide whether each statement is true *or* false.

1. A cube with volume 64 cubic inches has surface area 96 square inches.

2. A tetrahedron has the same number of faces as vertices.

3. A dodecahedron can be used as a model for a calendar for a given year, where each face of the dodecahedron contains a calendar for a single month, and there are no faces left over.

4. Each face of an octahedron is an octagon.

5. If you double the length of the edge of a cube, the new cube will have a volume that is twice the volume of the original cube.

6. The numerical value of the volume of a sphere is $\frac{r}{3}$ times the numerical value of its surface area, where r is the measure of the radius.

Find **(a)** *the volume and* **(b)** *the surface area of each space figure. When necessary, use* 3.14 *as an approximation for* π, *and round answers to the nearest hundredth.*

7.

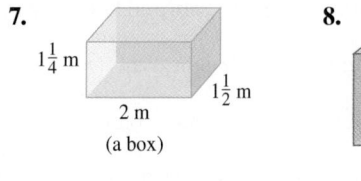

$1\frac{1}{4}$ m

2 m

$1\frac{1}{2}$ m

(a box)

8.

4 cm

6 cm

4 cm

(a box)

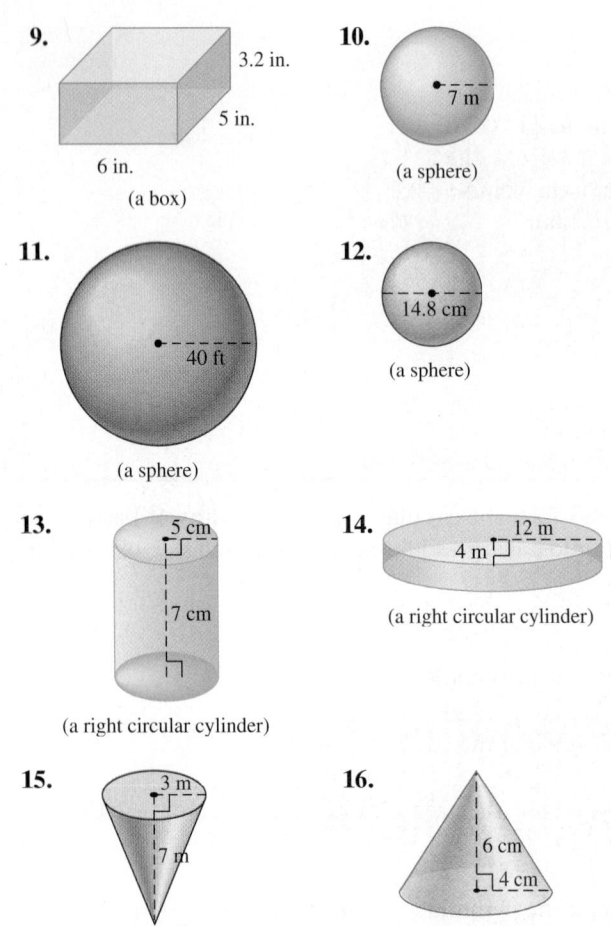

9.

3.2 in.
5 in.
6 in.
(a box)

10.

7 m
(a sphere)

11.

40 ft
(a sphere)

12.

14.8 cm
(a sphere)

13.

5 cm
7 cm
(a right circular cylinder)

14.

12 m
4 m
(a right circular cylinder)

15.

3 m
7 m
(a right circular cone)

16.

6 cm
4 cm
(a right circular cone)

Find the volume of each pyramid. In each case, the base is a rectangle.

17.

$h = 7$ in.
9 in.
8 in.

18.

$h = 10$ ft
4 ft
12 ft

Volumes of Common Objects   *Find each volume. Use 3.14 as an approximation for π when necessary.*

19. a coffee can, radius 6.3 cm and height 15.8 cm

20. a soup can, radius 3.2 cm and height 9.5 cm

21. a pork-and-beans can, diameter 7.2 cm and height 10.5 cm

22. a cardboard mailing tube, diameter 2 in. and height 40 in.

23. a coffee mug, diameter 9 cm and height 8 cm

24. a bottle of glue, diameter 3 cm and height 4.3 cm

25. the Great Pyramid of Cheops, near Cairo—its base is a square 230 m on a side, while the height is 137 m

26. a hotel in the shape of a cylinder with a base radius of 46 m and a height of 220 m

27. a road construction marker, a cone with height 2 m and base radius $\frac{1}{2}$ m

28. the conical portion of a witch's hat for a Halloween costume, with height 12 in. and base radius 4 in.

In the chart below, one of the values r (radius), d (diameter), V (volume), or S (surface area) is given for a particular sphere. Find the remaining three values. Leave π in your answers.

	r	*d*	*V*	*S*
29.	6 in.			
30.	9 in.			
31.		10 ft		
32.		40 ft		
33.			$\frac{32}{3}\pi$ cm^3	
34.			$\frac{256}{3}\pi$ cm^3	
35.				4π m^2
36.				144π m^2

Solve each problem.

37. Volume or Surface Area?   In order to determine the amount of liquid a spherical tank will hold, would you need to use volume or surface area?

38. Volume or Surface Area?   In order to determine the amount of leather it would take to manufacture a basketball, would you need to use volume or surface area?

39. Side Length of a Cube One of the three famous construction problems of Greek mathematics required the construction of an edge of a cube with twice the volume of a given cube. If the length of each side of the given cube is x, what would be the length of each side of a cube with twice the original volume?

40. Work through the parts of this exercise in order, and use them to make a generalization concerning volumes of spheres. Leave answers in terms of π.

   (a) Find the volume of a sphere having radius of 1 m.

   (b) Suppose the radius is doubled to 2 m. What is the volume?

   (c) When the radius was doubled, by how many times did the volume increase? (To find out, divide the answer for part (b) by the answer for part (a).)

   (d) Suppose the radius of the sphere from part (a) is tripled to 3 m. What is the volume?

(e) When the radius was tripled, by how many times did the volume increase?

(f) In general, if the radius of a sphere is multiplied by n, the volume is multiplied by _____.

Cost to Fill a Spherical Tank *If a spherical tank 2 m in diameter can be filled with a liquid for $300, find the cost to fill tanks of each diameter.*

41. 6 m   **42.** 8 m   **43.** 10 m

44. Use the logic of **Exercise 40** to answer the following: If the radius of a sphere is multiplied by n, then the surface area of the sphere is multiplied by _____.

Each of the following figures has volume as indicated. Find the value of x.

45. $V = 60$

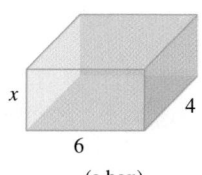

x
4
6
(a box)

46. $V = 450$

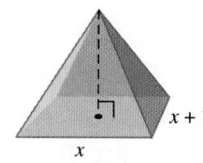

$x + 1$
x
$h = 15$
Base is a rectangle.
(a pyramid)

47. $V = 36\pi$

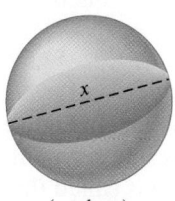

x
(a sphere)

48. $V = 245\pi$

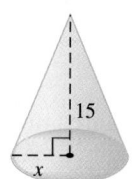

15
x
(a right circular cone)

Exercises 49–56 require some ingenuity, but all can be solved using the concepts presented so far in this chapter.

49. *Volume of a Box* The areas of the sides of a rectangular box are 30 in.², 35 in.², and 42 in.². What is the volume of the box?

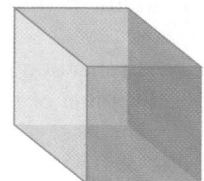

50. *Ratios of Volumes* In the figure, a right circular cone is inscribed in a hemisphere. What is the ratio of the volume of the cone to the volume of the hemisphere?

51. *Volume of a Sphere* A plane intersects a sphere to form a circle as shown in the figure. If the area of the circle formed by the intersection is 576π in.², what is the volume of the sphere?

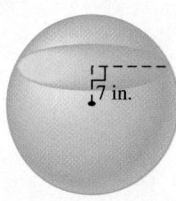

7 in.

52. *Change in Volume* If the height of a right circular cylinder is halved and the diameter is tripled, how is the volume changed?

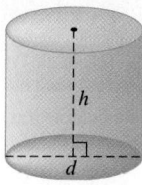

h
d

53. *Ratio of Area* What is the ratio of the area of the circumscribed square to the area of the inscribed square?

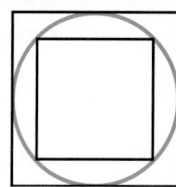

54. *Perimeter of a Square* Suppose the diameter of the circle shown is 8 in. What is the perimeter of the inscribed square $ABCD$?

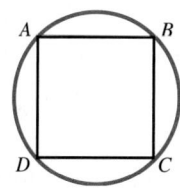

A B
D C

55. *Value of a Sum* In the circle shown with center O, the radius is 6. $QTSR$ is an inscribed square. Find the value of $PQ^2 + PT^2 + PR^2 + PS^2$.

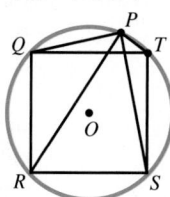

P
Q T
O
R S

56. *Ratio of Side Lengths* The square $JOSH$ is inscribed in a semicircle. What is the ratio of x to y?

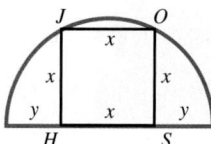

J O
x
x x
y x y
H S

Euler's Formula *Many crystals and some viruses are constructed in the shapes of regular polyhedra.*

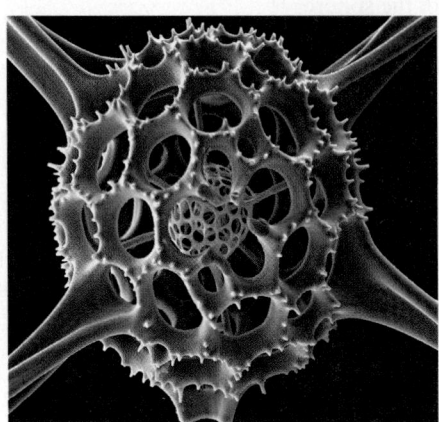

Radiolara virus

Leonhard Euler investigated a remarkable relationship among the numbers of faces (F), vertices (V) and edges (E) for the five regular polyhedra. Complete the chart in Exercises 57–61, and then draw a conclusion in Exercise 62.

	Polyhedron	Faces (F)	Vertices (V)	Edges (E)	Value of F + V − E
57.	Tetrahedron				
58.	Hexahedron (Cube)				
59.	Octahedron				
60.	Dodecahedron				
61.	Icosahedron				

62. Euler's formula is $F + V - E = $ _____ .

9.6 TRANSFORMATIONAL GEOMETRY

Reflections • Translations and Rotations • Size Transformations

In this chapter we have studied concepts of Euclidean geometry. Another branch of geometry, known as **transformational geometry,** investigates how one geometric figure can be transformed into another. In transformational geometry we are required to reflect, rotate, and change the size of figures using concepts that we now discuss.

Reflections

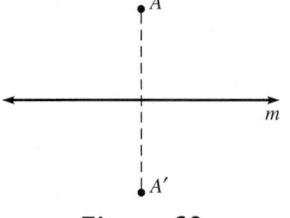

Figure 60

One way to transform one geometric figure into another is by reflection. In **Figure 60,** line m is perpendicular to the line segment AA' and bisects this line segment. We call point A' the **reflection image** of point A about line m. Line m is called the **line of reflection** for points A and A'. In the figure, we use a dashed line to connect points A and A' to show that these two points are images of each other under this transformation.

Point A' is the reflection image of point A only for line m. If a different line were used, A would have a different reflection image. Think of the reflection image of a point A about a line m as follows: Place a drop of ink at point A, and fold the paper along line m. The spot made by the ink on the other side of m is the reflection image of A. If A' is the image of A about line m, then A is the image of A' about the same line m.

To find the reflection image of a figure, find the reflection image of each point of the figure. The set of all reflection images of the points of the original figure is called the **reflection image** of the figure. **Figure 61** shows several figures (in black) and their reflection images (in color) about the lines shown.

An example of a **reflection.**

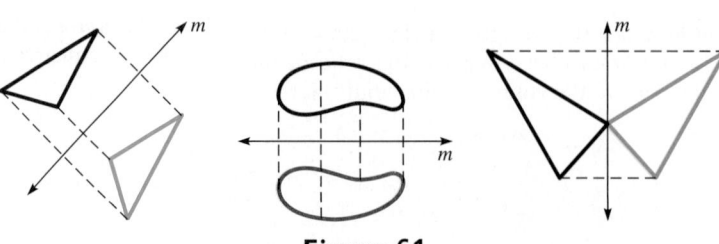

Figure 61

Each point in a plane has exactly one reflection image point with respect to a given line of reflection. Also, each reflection image point has exactly one original point. Thus, two distinct points cannot have the same reflection image. This means there is a *1-to-1 correspondence* between the set of points of the plane and the image points with respect to a given line of reflection. Any operation, such as reflection, in which there is a 1-to-1 correspondence between the points of the plane and their image points is called a **transformation.** We call reflection about a line the **reflection transformation.**

If a point A and its image, A', under a certain transformation are the same point, then point A is called an **invariant point** of the transformation. The only invariant points of the reflection transformation are the points of the line of reflection.

Three points that lie on the same straight line are called **collinear.** In **Figure 62**, points A, B, and C are collinear, and it can be shown that the reflection images A', B', and C', are also collinear. Thus, the reflection image of a line is also a line. We express this by saying that **reflection preserves collinearity.**

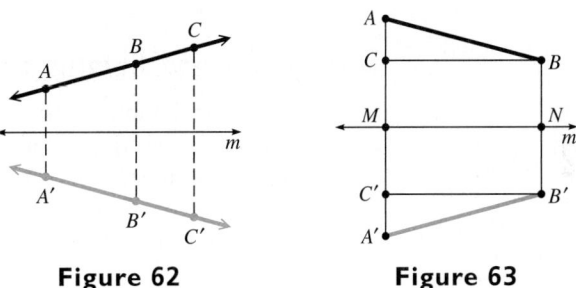

Figure 62   **Figure 63**

Distance is also preserved by the reflection transformation. Thus, in **Figure 63**, the distance between points A and B, written $|AB|$, is equal to the distance between the reflection images A' and B', or

$$|AB| = |A'B'|.$$

To prove this, we can use the definition of reflection image to verify that $|AM| = |MA'|$, and $|BN| = |NB'|$. Construct segments CB and $C'B'$, each perpendicular to BB'. Note that $CBB'C'$ is a rectangle. Because the opposite sides of a rectangle are equal and parallel, we have

$$|CB| = |C'B'|. \qquad \text{(Side)} \qquad \textbf{(1)}$$

Because $CBB'C'$ is a rectangle, we can also say

$$m \angle ACB = m \angle A'C'B' = 90° \qquad \text{(Angle)} \qquad \textbf{(2)}$$

where we use $m \angle ACB$ to represent the measure of angle ACB.

We know $|AM| = |MA'|$ and can show $|CM| = |MC'|$, so that

$$|AC| = |A'C'|. \qquad \text{(Side)} \qquad \textbf{(3)}$$

From statements (1), (2), and (3) above, we conclude that in triangles ABC and $A'B'C'$, two sides and the included angle of one are equal in measure to the corresponding two sides and angle of the other and, thus, are congruent by SAS (**Section 9.3**). Corresponding sides of congruent triangles are equal in length, so

$$|AB| = |A'B'|,$$

which is what we wanted to show. Hence, the distance between two points equals the distance between their reflection images, and, thus, reflection preserves distance. (The proof we have given is not really complete, because we have tacitly assumed that AB is not parallel to $A'B'$, and that A and B are on the same side of the line of reflection. Some modification would have to be made in the proof above to include these other cases.)

M.C. Escher (1898–1972) was a Dutch graphic artist, most recognized for spatial illusions, impossible buildings, repeating geometric patterns (tessellations), and his incredible techniques in woodcutting and lithography. He was a humble man who considered himself neither an artist nor a mathematician.

(*Sources:* M. C. Escher's Symmetry Drawing (Smaller and Smaller) and Waterfall © 2003 Cordon Art B.V., Baarn, Holland. All rights reserved; www.worldofescher.com.)

The figures shown in **Figure 64** are their own reflection images about the lines of reflection shown. In this case, the line of reflection is called a **line of symmetry** for the figure. **Figure 64(a)** has three lines of symmetry. A circle has every line through its center as a line of symmetry.

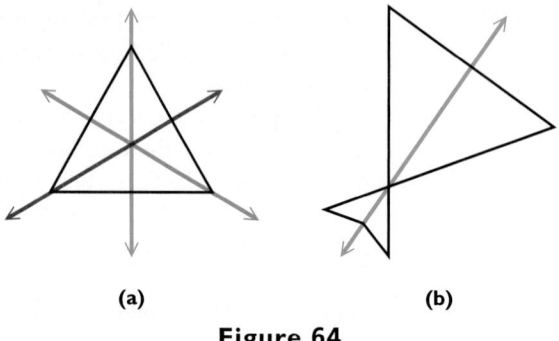

(a)   (b)

Figure 64

Translations and Rotations

We shall use the symbol r_m to represent a reflection about line m, and let us use $r_n \cdot r_m$ to represent a reflection about line m followed by a reflection about line n. We call $r_n \cdot r_m$ the **composition,** or **product,** of the two reflections r_n and r_m. **Figure 65** shows two examples of the composition of two reflections. In **Figure 65(a)**, lines m and n are parallel, while they intersect in **Figure 65(b)**.

How many kinds of **symmetry** do you see here?

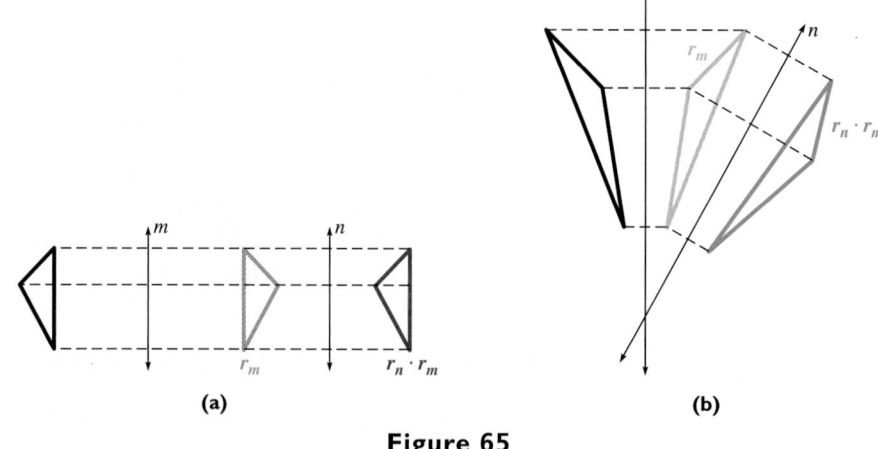

(a)   (b)

Figure 65

In **Figure 65(a)** both the original figure and its image under the composition of the two reflections appear to be oriented the same way and to have the same "tilt." In fact, it appears that the original figure could be slid along the dashed lines of **Figure 65(a)**, with no rotation, so as to cover the image. This composite transformation is called a **translation. Figure 66** shows a translation, and the image can be obtained as a composition of two reflections about parallel lines. Check that the distance between a point and its image under a translation is twice the distance between the two parallel lines. The distance between a point and its image under a translation is called the **magnitude** of the translation.

A translation of magnitude 0 leaves every point of the plane unchanged and, thus, is called the **identity translation.** A translation of magnitude k, followed by a similar translation of magnitude k but of opposite direction, returns a point to its original position, and, thus, these two translations are called **inverses** of each other. Check that there are no invariant points in a translation of magnitude $k > 0$.

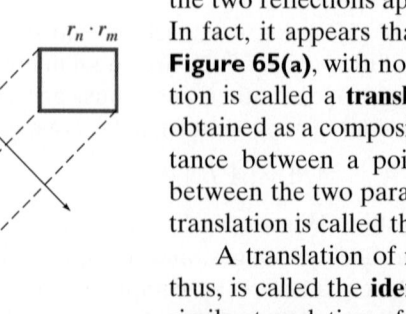

Figure 66

This **Escher pattern** fills the entire plane if we start with one fish and one ship and perform repeated translations in opposite directions.

A translation preserves collinearity (three points on the same line have image points that also lie on a line) and distance (the distance between two points is the same as the distance between the images of the points).

In **Figure 65(b)**, the original figure could be rotated so as to cover the image. Hence, we call the composition of two reflections about nonparallel lines a **rotation.** The point of intersection of these two nonparallel lines is called the **center of rotation.** The black triangle of **Figure 67** was reflected about line m and then reflected about line n, resulting in a rotation with center at B. The dashed lines in color represent the paths of the vertices of the triangle under the rotation. It can be shown that $m\measuredangle ABA'$ is twice as large as $m\measuredangle MBN$. The measure of angle ABA' is called the **magnitude** of the rotation.

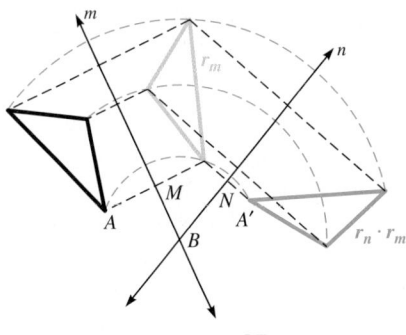

Figure 67

Rotations also preserve collinearity and distance. The identity transformation here is a rotation of $0°$ or $360°$, and rotations of, say, $240°$ and $120°$ (or in general, $x°$ and $360° - x°$, $0 \leq x \leq 360°$) are inverses of each other. The center of rotation is the only invariant point of any rotation except the identity rotation.

We have defined rotations as the composition of two reflections about nonparallel lines of reflection. We can also define a rotation by specifying its center, the angle of rotation, and a direction of rotation, as shown by the following example.

▮▮ **EXAMPLE 1** Finding an Image Under a Rotation

Find the image of a point P under a rotation transformation having center at a point Q and magnitude $135°$ clockwise.

SOLUTION

To find P', the image of P, first draw angle PQM having measure $135°$. Then draw an arc of a circle with center at Q and radius $|PQ|$. The point where this arc intersects side QM is P'. See **Figure 68**.

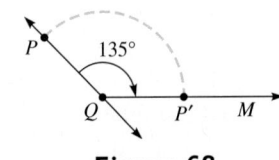

Figure 68   ▮▮▮

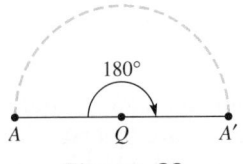

Figure 69

Figure 69 shows a rotation transformation having center Q and magnitude $180°$ clockwise. Point Q bisects the line segment from a point A to its image A', and for this reason this rotation is sometimes called a **point reflection.**

■■ **EXAMPLE 2** Finding Point Reflection Images

Find the point reflection images about point Q for each of the following figures.

SOLUTION

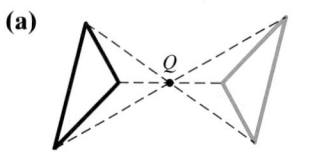

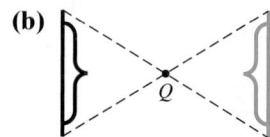

The point reflection images are shown in color. ■■■

Let r_m be a reflection about line m, and let T be a translation having nonzero magnitude and a direction parallel to m. Then the composition of T and r_m is called a **glide reflection,** as seen in **Figure 70**. Here a reflection followed by a translation is the same as a translation followed by a reflection, so that in this case

$$T \cdot r_m = r_m \cdot T.$$

Because a translation is the composition of *two* reflections, a glide reflection is the composition of *three* reflections. Because it is required that the translation have nonzero magnitude, there is no identity glide transformation.

All the transformations of this section discussed so far are **isometries,** or transformations in which the image of a figure has the same size and shape as the original figure. Any isometry is either a reflection or the composition of two or more reflections.

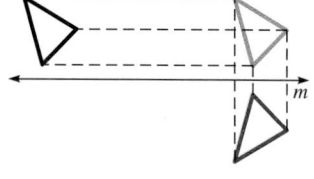

Figure 70

Size Transformations

Figure 71 shows a semicircle in black, a point M, and an image semicircle in color. Distance $A'M$ is twice the distance AM and distance $B'M$ is twice the distance BM. In fact, every point of the image semicircle, such as C', was obtained by drawing a line through M and C, and then locating C' such that $|MC'| = 2|MC|$.

Such a transformation is called a **size transformation** with center M and magnitude 2. We shall assume that a size transformation can have any positive real number k as magnitude. A size transformation having magnitude $k > 1$ is called a **dilation,** or **stretch.** A size transformation having magnitude $k < 1$ is called a **contraction,** or **shrink.**

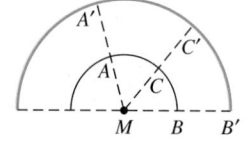

Figure 71

■■ **EXAMPLE 3** Applying Size Transformations

Apply a size transformation with center M and magnitude $\frac{1}{3}$ to the two triangles shown in black in **Figure 72**.

SOLUTION

To find the images of these triangles, we can find the image points of some sample points. For example, if we select point A on each of the original triangles, we can find the image points by drawing a line through A and M, and locating a point A' such that $|MA'| = \frac{1}{3}|MA|$. By doing this for all points of each of the black triangles, we get the images shown in color in **Figure 72**. ■■■

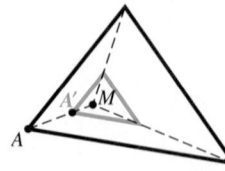

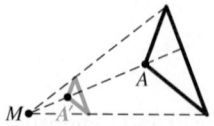

Figure 72

The identity transformation is a size transformation of magnitude 1, while size transformations of magnitude k and $\frac{1}{k}$, having the same center, are inverses of each other. The only invariant point of a size transformation of magnitude $k \neq 1$ is the center of the transformation.

▮▮ **EXAMPLE 4** Investigating Size Transformations

Does a size transformation **(a)** preserve collinearity? **(b)** preserve distance?

SOLUTION

(a) **Figure 73** shows three collinear points, A, B, and C, and their images under two different size transformations with center at M: one of magnitude 3 and one of magnitude $\frac{1}{3}$. In each case the image points appear to be collinear, and it can be proved that they are, using similar triangles. In fact, the image of a line not through the center of the transformation is a line parallel to the original line.

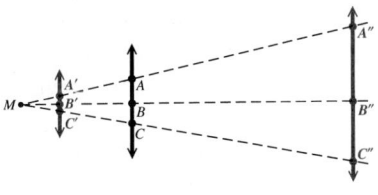

Figure 73

(b) As shown in **Figure 73**,

$$|AB| \neq |A'B'|.$$

Thus, a size transformation of magnitude $k \neq 1$ does not preserve distance and is not an isometry. ▮▮▮

Table 4 Summary of Transformations

	Reflection	Translation	Rotation	Glide Reflection	Size Transformation
Example					
Preserve collinearity?	Yes	Yes	Yes	Yes	Yes
Preserve distance?	Yes	Yes	Yes	Yes	No
Identity transformation?	None	Magnitude 0	Magnitude 360°	None	Magnitude 1
Inverse transformation?	None	Same magnitude; opposite direction	Same center; magnitude $360° - x°$	None	Same center; magnitude $\frac{1}{k}$
Composition of n reflections?	$n = 1$	$n = 2$, parallel	$n = 2$, nonparallel	$n = 3$	No
Isometry?	Yes	Yes	Yes	Yes	No
Invariant points?	Line of reflection	None	Center of rotation	None	Center of transformation

For Further Thought

Tessellations

The authors wish to thank Suzanne Alejandre for permission to reprint this article on tessellations, which first appeared at www.mathforum.org/sum95/suzanne/whattess.html.

tessellate (verb), **tessellation** (noun): from Latin *tessera* "a square tablet" or "a die used for gambling." Latin *tessera* may have been borrowed from Greek *tessares*, meaning "four," since a square tile has four sides. The diminutive of *tessera* was *tessella*, a small, square piece of stone or a cubical tile used in mosaics. Since a mosaic extends over a given area without leaving any region uncovered, the geometric meaning of the word "tessellate" is "to cover the plane with a pattern in such a way as to leave no region uncovered." By extension, space or hyperspace may also be tessellated.

Definition

A dictionary will tell you that the word "tessellate" means to form or arrange small squares in a checkered or mosaic pattern. The word "tessellate" is derived from the Ionic version of the Greek word "tesseres," which in English means "four." The first tilings were made from square tiles.

A regular polygon has 3 or 4 or 5 or more sides and angles, all equal. A **regular tessellation** means a tessellation made up of congruent regular polygons. [Remember: *Regular* means that the sides of the polygon are all the same length. *Congruent* means that the polygons that you put together are all the same size and shape.]

Only three regular polygons tessellate in the Euclidean plane: triangles, squares, or hexagons. We can't show the entire plane, but imagine that these are pieces taken from planes that have been tiled. Here are examples of

a tessellation of triangles

a tessellation of squares

a tessellation of hexagons

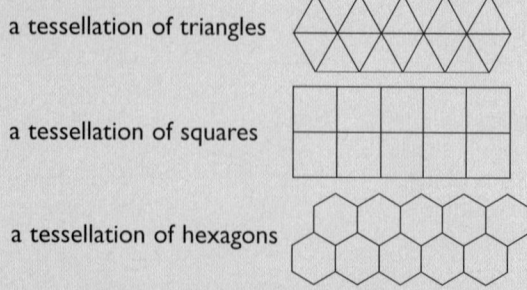

When you look at these three samples you can easily notice that the squares are lined up with each other while the triangles and hexagons are not. Also, if you look at six triangles at a time, they form a hexagon, so the tiling of triangles and the tiling of hexagons are

similar and they cannot be formed by directly lining shapes up under each other—a slide (or a glide!) is involved.

You can work out the interior measure of the angles for each of these polygons:

Shape	Angle Measure in Degrees
triangle	60
square	90
pentagon	108
hexagon	120
more than six sides	more than 120 degrees

Since the regular polygons in a tessellation must fill the plane at each vertex, the interior angle must be an exact divisor of 360 degrees. This works for the triangle, square, and hexagon, and you can show working tessellations for these figures. For all the others, the interior angles are not exact divisors of 360 degrees, and, therefore, those figures cannot tile the plane.

Naming Conventions

A tessellation of squares is named "4.4.4.4." Here's how: choose a vertex, and then look at one of the polygons that touches that vertex. How many sides does it have?

Since it's a square, it has four sides, and that's where the first "4" comes from. Now keep going around the vertex in either direction, finding the number of sides of the polygons until you get back to the polygon you started with. How many polygons did you count?

There are four polygons, and each has four sides.

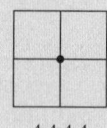

4.4.4.4

For a tessellation of regular congruent hexagons, if you choose a vertex and count the sides of the polygons that touch it, you'll see that there are three polygons and each has six sides, so this tessellation is called "6.6.6":

6.6.6

A tessellation of triangles has six polygons surrounding a vertex, and each of them has three sides: "3.3.3.3.3.3."

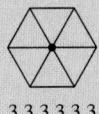

3.3.3.3.3.3

Semi-regular Tessellations

You can also use a variety of regular polygons to make **semi-regular tessellations.**

A semi-regular tessellation has two properties, which are:

1. It is formed by regular polygons.
2. The arrangement of polygons at every vertex point is identical.

Here are the **eight** semi-regular tessellations:

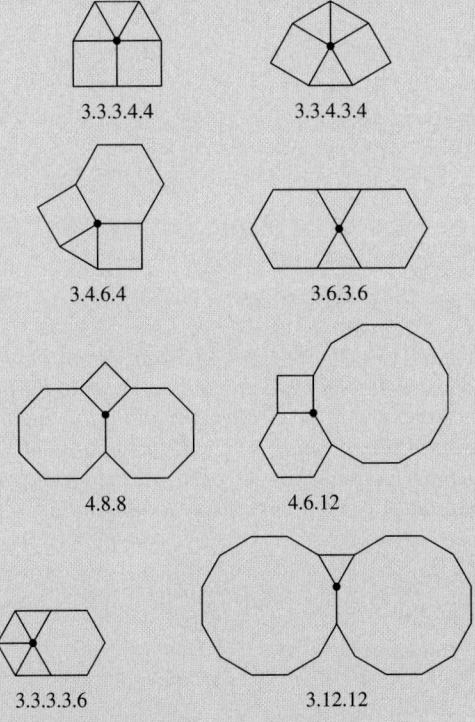

3.3.3.4.4   3.3.4.3.4

3.4.6.4   3.6.3.6

4.8.8   4.6.12

3.3.3.3.6   3.12.12

Interestingly, there are other combinations that seem like they should tile the plane because the arrangements of the regular polygons fill the space around a point. For example:

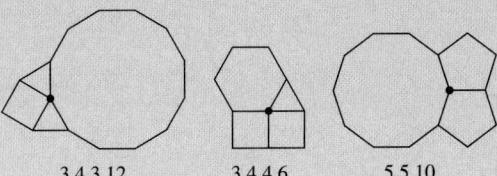

3.4.3.12   3.4.4.6   5.5.10

If you try tiling the plane with these units of tessellation you will find that they cannot be extended infinitely.

There is an infinite number of tessellations that can be made of patterns that do not have the same combination of angles at every vertex point. There are also tessellations made of polygons that do not share common edges and vertices.

For Group or Individual Investigation

1. Use the naming conventions to name each of these semi-regular tessellations.

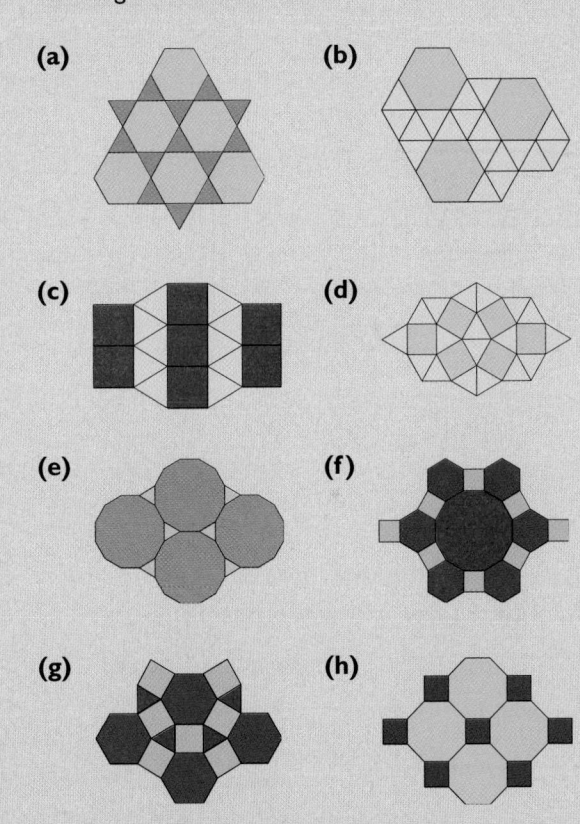

(a)   **(b)**

(c)   **(d)**

(e)   **(f)**

(g)   **(h)**

2. Why isn't this a semi-regular tessellation?

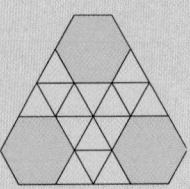

Tessellations (a) through (h) are courtesy of www.coolmath.com.

9.6 EXERCISES

Find the reflection images of the given figures about the given lines.

1.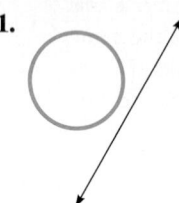

2.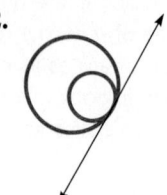

3.

4.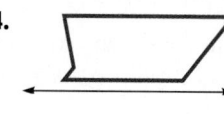

5.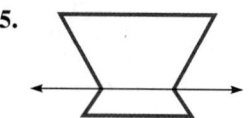

6.

7.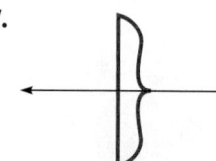

8.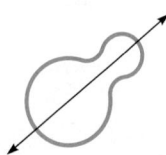

Find any lines of symmetry of the given figures.

9.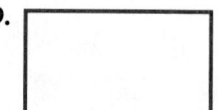

10.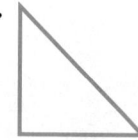

11.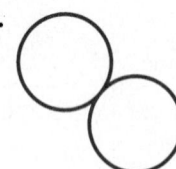

12.

First reflect the given figure about line m. Then reflect about line n.

13.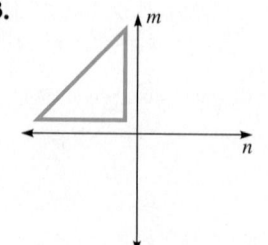

14.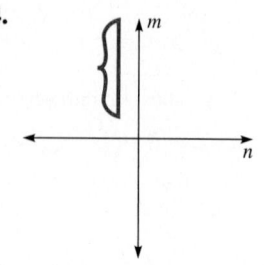

15.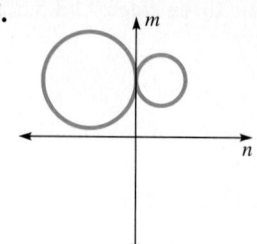

16.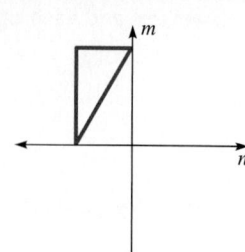

17.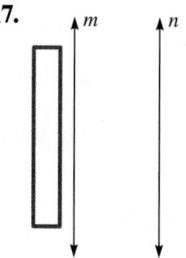

18.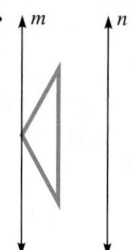

19.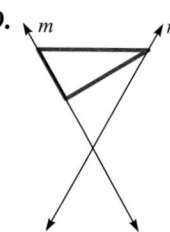

20.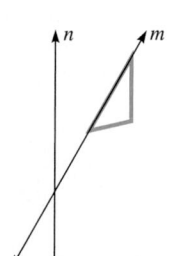

In Exercises 21–34, let T be a translation having magnitude 1.5 cm to the right in a direction parallel to the bottom edge of the page. Let r_m be a reflection about line m, and let R_P be a rotation about point P having magnitude 60° clockwise. In each of Exercises 21–32, perform the given transformations on point A of the figure below to obtain final image point A'.

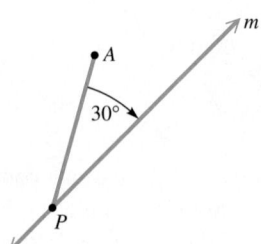

21. r_m

22. R_P

23. T

24. $r_m \cdot r_m$

25. $T \cdot T$

26. $R_P \cdot R_P$

27. $T \cdot R_P$

28. $T \cdot r_m$

29. $r_m \cdot T$

30. $R_P \cdot r_m$

31. $r_m \cdot R_P$

32. $R_P \cdot T$

33. Is $T \cdot r_m$ a glide reflection here?

34. Is $T \cdot r_m = r_m \cdot T$ true?

35. Suppose a rotation is given by $r_m \cdot r_n$, as shown in the figure below. Find the images of A, B, and C.

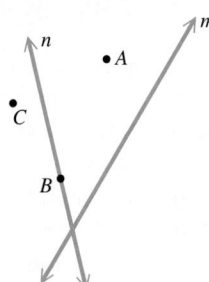

36. Does a glide reflection preserve
  (a) collinearity?   **(b)** distance?

Find the point reflection images of each of the following figures with the given points as center.

37.

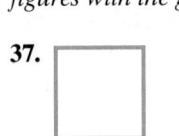

38.

39.

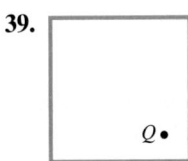

40.

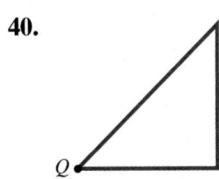

Perform the indicated size transformation.

41. magnitude 2; center M

42. magnitude $\frac{1}{2}$; center M

43. magnitude $\frac{1}{2}$; center M

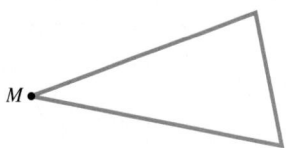

44. magnitude 2; center M

45. magnitude $\frac{1}{3}$; center M

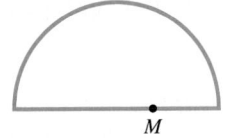

46. magnitude $\frac{1}{3}$; center M

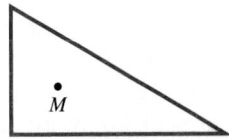

9.7   NON-EUCLIDEAN GEOMETRY, TOPOLOGY, AND NETWORKS

Euclid's Postulates and Axioms • The Parallel Postulate (Euclid's Fifth Postulate) • The Origins of Non-Euclidean Geometry • Topology • Networks

Euclid's Postulates and Axioms

The *Elements* of Euclid is quite possibly the most influential mathematics book ever written. (See the margin note on **page 450.**) It begins with definitions of basic ideas such as point, line, and plane. Euclid then gives five postulates providing the foundation of all that follows.

Next, Euclid lists five axioms that he views as general truths and not just facts about geometry. See **Table 5** on the next page. (To some of the Greek writers, postulates were truths about a particlar field, while axioms were general truths. Today, "axiom" is used in either case.) Using only these ten statements and the basic rules of logic, Euclid was able to prove a large number of "propositions" about geometric figures.

John Playfair (1748–1819) wrote his *Elements of Geometry* in 1795. Playfair's Axiom is: Given a line *k* and a point *P* not on the line, there exists one and only one line *m* through *P* that is parallel to *k*. This is equivalent to Euclid's Postulate 5.

Table 5

Euclid's Postulates	Euclid's Axioms
1. Two points determine one and only one straight line.	**6.** Things equal to the same thing are equal to each other.
2. A straight line extends indefinitely far in either direction.	**7.** If equals are added to equals, the sums are equal.
3. A circle may be drawn with any given center and any given radius.	**8.** If equals are subtracted from equals, the remainders are equal.
4. All right angles are equal.	**9.** Figures that can be made to coincide are equal.
5. Given a line *k* and a point *P* not on the line, there exists one and only one line *m* through *P* that is parallel to *k*.	**10.** The whole is greater than any of its parts.

The statement for Postulate 5 given above is actually known as Playfair's axiom on parallel lines, which is equivalent to Euclid's fifth postulate. To understand why this postulate caused trouble for so many mathematicians for so long, we must examine the original formulation.

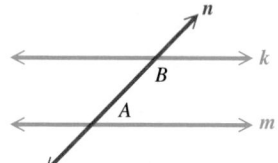

Figure 74

The Parallel Postulate (Euclid's Fifth Postulate)

In its original form, Euclid's fifth postulate states the following:

If two lines (k and m in **Figure 74***) are such that a third line, n, intersects them so that the sum of the two interior angles (A and B) on one side of line n is less than (the sum of) two right angles, then the two lines, if extended far enough, will meet on the same side of n that has the sum of the interior angles less than (the sum of) two right angles.*

Euclid's parallel postulate is quite different from the other nine postulates and axioms we listed. It is long and wordy, and difficult to understand without a sketch. It was commonly believed that this was not a postulate at all but a theorem to be proved. For more than 2000 years mathematicians tried repeatedly to prove it.

The most dedicated attempt came from an Italian Jesuit, Girolamo Saccheri (1667–1733). He attempted to prove the parallel postulate in an indirect way, by so-called "reduction to absurdity." He would assume the postulate to be false and then show that the assumption leads to a contradiction of something true (an absurdity). Such a contradiction would thus prove the statement true. Saccheri began with a quadrilateral, as in **Figure 75**. He assumed angles *A* and *B* to be right angles and sides *AD* and *BC* to be equal. His plan was as follows:

A Saccheri quadrilateral

Figure 75

1. To assume that angles *C* and *D* are obtuse angles, and to show that this leads to a contradiction.

2. To assume that angles *C* and *D* are acute angles, and to show that this also leads to a contradiction.

3. Then if *C* and *D* can be neither acute nor obtuse angles, they must be right angles.

4. If *C* and *D* are both right angles, then it can be proved that the fifth postulate is true. It thus is a theorem rather than a postulate.

Saccheri had no trouble with part 1. However, he did not actually reach a contradiction in the second part but produced some theorems so "repugnant" that he convinced himself he had vindicated Euclid. In fact, he published a book called in English *Euclid Freed of Every Flaw*. However, today we know that the fifth postulate is indeed an axiom and not a theorem. It is *consistent* with Euclid's other axioms.

The ten axioms of Euclid describe the world around us with remarkable accuracy. We now realize that the fifth postulate is necessary in Euclidean geometry to establish *flatness*. That is, the axioms of Euclid describe the geometry of *plane surfaces*. By changing the fifth postulate, we can describe the geometry of other surfaces. So, other geometric systems exist as much as Euclidean geometry exists, and they can even be demonstrated in our world. A system of geometry in which the fifth postulate is changed is called a **non-Euclidean geometry.**

The Origins of Non-Euclidean Geometry

One non-Euclidean system was developed by three people working separately at about the same time. Early in the nineteenth century Carl Friedrich Gauss worked out a consistent geometry replacing Euclid's fifth postulate. He never published his work, however, because he feared the ridicule of people who could not free themselves from habitual ways of thinking.

Nikolai Ivanovich Lobachevski (1793–1856) published a similar system in 1830 in the Russian language. At the same time, Janos Bolyai (1802–1860), a Hungarian army officer, worked out a similar system, which he published in 1832, not knowing about Lobachevski's work. Bolyai never recovered from the disappointment of not being the first and did no further work in mathematics.

Lobachevski replaced Euclid's fifth postulate with the following.

Angles C and D in the quadrilateral of Saccheri are acute angles. Lobachevski's replacement

This postulate of Lobachevski can be rephrased as follows.

*Through a point P off a line k (**Figure 76**), at least two different lines can be drawn parallel to k.*

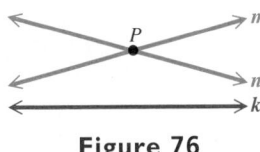

Figure 76

Compare this form of Lobachevski's postulate to the geometry of Euclid, where only one line can be drawn through *P* and parallel to *k*. At first glance, the postulate of Lobachevski does not agree with what we know about the world around us. But this is only because we think of our immediate surroundings as being flat.

Many of the theorems of Euclidean geometry are valid for the geometry of Lobachevski, but many are not. For example, in Euclidean geometry, the sum of the measures of the angles in any triangle is 180°. In Lobachevskian geometry, the sum of the measures of the angles in any triangle is *less* than 180°. Also, triangles of different sizes can never have equal angles, so similar triangles do not exist.

The geometry of Euclid can be represented on a plane. Since any portion of the earth that we are likely to see looks flat, Euclidean geometry is very useful for describing the everyday world around us. The non-Euclidean geometry of Lobachevski can be represented as a surface called a **pseudosphere.** This surface is formed by revolving a curve called a **tractrix** about the line *AB* in **Figure 77**.

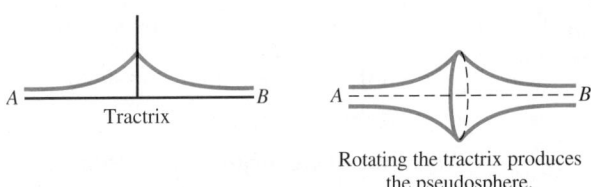

Rotating the tractrix produces
the pseudosphere.

Figure 77

Georg Friedrich Bernhard Riemann
(1826–1866) was a German mathematician. Though he lived a short time and published few papers, his work forms a basis for much modern mathematics. He made significant contributions to the theory of functions and the study of complex numbers as well as to geometry. Most calculus books today use the idea of a "Riemann sum" in defining the integral.

Riemann achieved a complete understanding of the non-Euclidean geometries of his day, expressing them on curved surfaces and showing how to extend them to higher dimensions.

A second non-Euclidean system was developed by Georg Riemann (1826–1866). He pointed out the difference between a line that continues indefinitely and a line having infinite length. For example, a circle on the surface of a sphere continues indefinitely but does not have infinite length. Riemann developed the idea of geometry on a sphere and replaced Euclid's fifth postulate with the following.

> *Angles C and D of the Saccheri quadrilateral are obtuse angles.*   Riemann's replacement

In terms of parallel lines, Riemann's postulate is stated this way.

> *Through a point P off a line k, no line can be drawn that is parallel to k.*

Riemannian geometry is important in navigation. "Lines" in this geometry are really *great circles,* or circles whose centers are at the center of the sphere. The shortest distance between two points on a sphere lies along an arc of a great circle. Great circle routes on a globe don't look at all like the shortest distance when the globe is flattened out to form a map, but this is part of the distortion that occurs when the earth is represented as a flat surface. See **Figure 78**. The sides of a triangle drawn on a sphere would be arcs of great circles. And, in Riemannian geometry, the sum of the measures of the angles in any triangle is *more* than 180°.

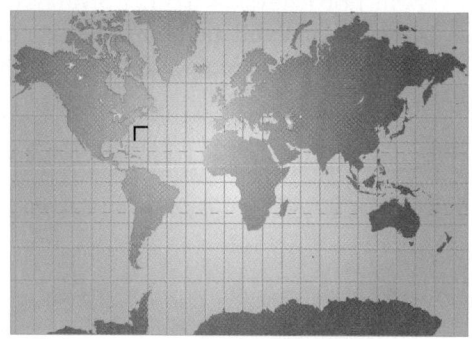

Figure 78

Topology

The plane and space figures studied in the Euclidean system are carefully distinguished by differences in size, shape, angularity, and so on. For a given figure such properties are permanent, and, thus, we can ask sensible questions about congruence and similarity. Suppose we studied "figures" made of rubber bands, as it were, "figures" that could be stretched, bent, or otherwise distorted without tearing or scattering. **Topology** does just that.

Topological questions concern the basic structure of objects rather than size or arrangement. For example, a typical topological question has to do with the number of holes in an object, a basic structural property that does not change during deformation. You cannot deform a rubber ball to get a rubber band without tearing it—making a hole in it. Thus the two objects are not topologically equivalent. On the other hand, a doughnut and a coffee cup are topologically equivalent, because one could be stretched to form the other without changing the basic structural property.

Topology and geometry software,
including games for users age 10 and up, can be found at www.geometrygames.org, a site developed by Jeff Weeks. Included are Torus Games, Kali, KaleidoTile, and investigations into Curved Spaces.

▌▌ **EXAMPLE 1** Determining Topological Equivalence

Decide if the figures in each pair are topologically equivalent.

(a) a football and a cereal box   **(b)** a doughnut and an unzipped coat

SOLUTION

(a) If we assume that a football is made of a perfectly elastic substance such as rubber or dough, it could be twisted or kneaded into the same shape as a cereal box. Thus, the two figures are topologically equivalent.

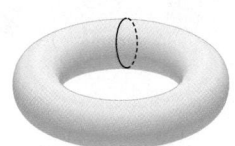

Torus One of the most useful figures in topology is the torus, a doughnut-like surface. Its properties are different from those of a sphere, for example. Imagine a sphere covered with hair. You cannot comb the hairs in a completely smooth way. One fixed point remains, as you can find on your own head. In the same way, on the surface of Earth the winds are not a smooth system. There is a calm point somewhere. However, the hair on a torus could be combed smooth.

(b) A doughnut has one hole, while the coat has two (the sleeve openings). Thus, a doughnut could not be stretched and twisted into the shape of the coat without tearing another hole in it. Because of this, a doughnut and the coat are not topologically equivalent. ■■■

In topology, figures are classified according to their **genus**—that is, the number of cuts that can be made without cutting the figures into two pieces. The genus of an object is the number of holes in it. See **Figure 79**.

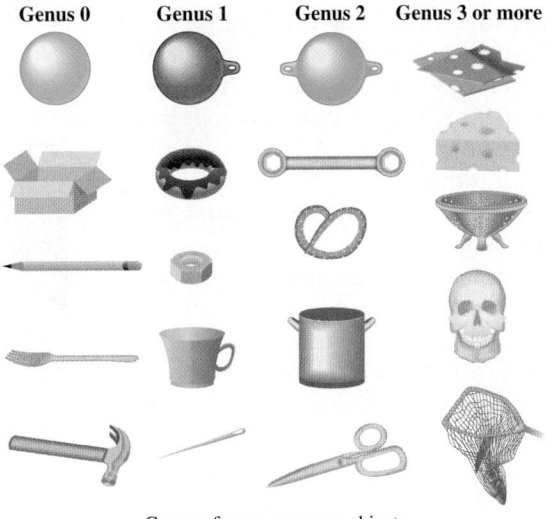

Genus of some common objects

Figure 79

Networks*

Another branch of modern geometry is *graph theory*. One topic of study in graph theory is *networks*. A **network** is a diagram showing the various paths (or **arcs**) between points (called **vertices,** or **nodes**). A network can be thought of as a set of arcs and vertices. **Figure 80** shows two examples of networks.

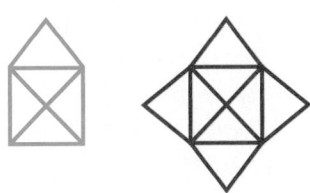

Figure 80

The study of networks began formally with the so-called Königsberg Bridge problem as solved by Leonhard Euler (1707–1783). In Königsberg, Germany, the River Pregel flowed through the middle of town. There were two islands in the river. During Euler's lifetime, there were seven bridges connecting the islands and the two banks of the river.

A competition developed to see if anyone could find a route that crossed each of the seven bridges exactly once. The problem concerns what topologists today call the *traversability* of a network. No one could find a solution.

---

*Chapter 15 is an entire chapter on Graph Theory, of which networks is one topic.

For Further Thought

Two Interesting Topological Surfaces

Two examples of topological surfaces are the **Möbius strip** and the **Klein bottle.** The Möbius strip is a single-sided surface named after August Ferdinand Möbius (1790–1868), a pupil of Gauss.

To construct a Möbius strip, cut out a rectangular strip of paper, perhaps 3 cm by 25 cm. Paste together the two 3-cm ends after giving the paper a half-twist. To see how the strip now has only one side, mark an x on the strip and then mark another x on what appears to be the other "side." Begin at one of the x's you have drawn, and trace a path along the strip. You will eventually come to the other x without crossing the edge of the strip.

A branch of chemistry called chemical topology studies the structures of chemical configurations. A recent advance in this area was the synthesis of the first molecular Möbius strip, which was formed by joining the ends of a double-stranded strip of carbon and oxygen atoms.

A mathematician confided
That a Möbius strip is one-sided.
And you'll get quite a laugh
If you cut one in half,
For it stays in one piece when divided.

Möbius strip

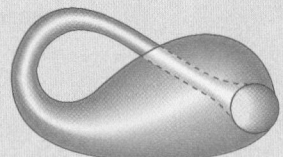
Klein bottle

Whereas a Möbius strip results from giving a paper *strip* a half-twist and then connecting it to itself, if we could do the same thing with a paper *tube* we would obtain a Klein bottle, named after Felix Klein (1849–1925). Klein produced important results in several areas, including non-Euclidean geometry and the early beginnings of group theory.

From www.kleinbottle.com

A mathematician named Klein
Thought the Möbius strip was divine.
Said he, "If you glue
The edges of two
You'll get a weird bottle like mine."

For Group or Individual Investigation

1. The Möbius strip has other interesting properties. With a pair of scissors, cut the strip lengthwise. Do you get two strips? Repeat the process with what you have obtained from the first cut. What happens?

2. Now construct another Möbius strip, and start cutting lengthwise about $\frac{1}{3}$ of the way from one edge. What happens?

3. What would be the advantage of a conveyor belt with the configuration of a Möbius strip?

The Königsberg Bridge problem became so famous that in 1735 it reached Euler, who was then at the court of the Russian empress Catherine the Great. In trying to solve the problem, Euler began by drawing a network representing the system of bridges, as in **Figure 81** on the next page.

Euler noticed that three routes meet at vertex A. Because 3 is an odd number, he called A an **odd vertex.** As three routes meet at A, it must be a starting or an ending point for any traverse of the network. Otherwise, when you got to A on your second trip there would be no way to get out. An **even vertex,** one where an even number of routes meet, need not be a starting or an ending point. (Why is this?)

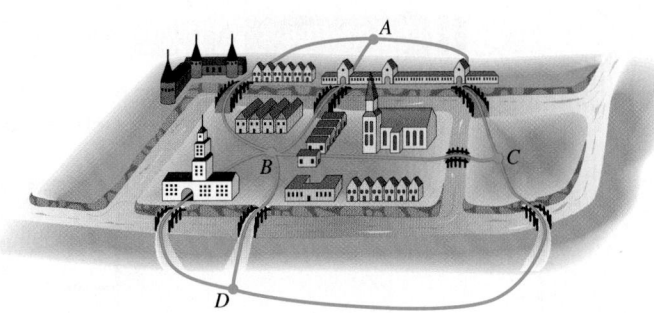

Figure 81

In **Figure 81**, three paths also meet at *C* and *D*, with five paths meeting at *B*. Thus, *B, C,* and *D* are also odd vertices. An odd vertex must be a starting or an ending point of a traverse. Thus, all four vertices *A, B, C,* and *D* must be starting or ending points. Because a network can have only two starting or ending points (one of each), this network cannot be traversed. The residents of Königsberg were trying to do the impossible.

Euler's result can be summarized as follows.

How should an artist paint a realistic view of railroad tracks going off to the horizon? In reality, the tracks are always at a constant distance apart, but they cannot be drawn that way except from overhead. The artist must make the tracks converge at a point. Only in this way will the scene look "real."

Beginning in the fifteenth century, artists led by Leone Battista Alberti, Leonardo da Vinci, and Albrecht Dürer began to study the problems of representing three dimensions in two. What artists initiated, mathematicians developed into a geometry different from that of Euclid—**projective geometry.**

Gerard Desargues (1591–1661), a French architect and engineer, published in 1636 and 1639 a treatise and proposals about perspective and had, thus, invented projective geometry. However, his geometric innovations were hidden for nearly 200 years. A manuscript by Desargues turned up in 1845, about 30 years after Jean-Victor Poncelet had rediscovered projective geometry.

Results on Vertices and Traversability

1. The number of odd vertices of any network is *even.* (That is, a network must have 2*n* odd vertices, where *n* = 0, 1, 2, 3, …)

2. A network with no odd vertices or exactly two odd vertices can be traversed. In the case of exactly two, start at one odd vertex and end at the other.

3. A network with more than two odd vertices cannot be traversed.

▌▌ **EXAMPLE 2** Deciding Whether Networks Are Traversable

Decide whether the networks in **Figures 82** and **83** are traversable.

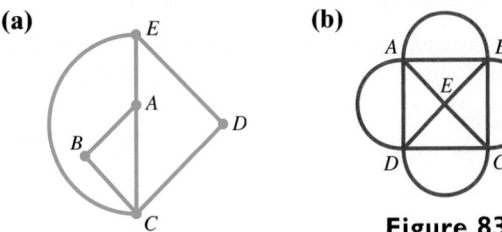

(a)   **(b)**

Figure 82   **Figure 83**

SOLUTION

(a) Because there are exactly two odd vertices (*A* and *E*) in **Figure 82**, this network can be traversed. One way to traverse the network is to start at *A*, go through *B* to *C*, then back to *A*. (It is acceptable to go through a vertex as many times as needed.) Then go to *E*, to *D*, to *C*, and finally go back to *E*. It is traversable.

(b) In **Figure 83**, vertices *A, B, C,* and *D* are all odd because five routes meet at each of them. This network is not traversable.

▌▌▌

▮▮ **EXAMPLE 3** Applying Traversability Concepts to a Floor Plan

Figure 84 shows the floor plan of a house. Is it possible to travel through this house, going through each door exactly once?

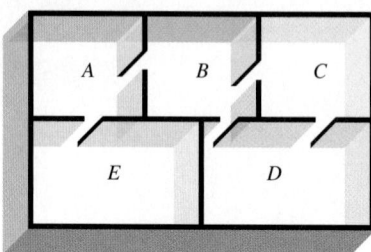

Figure 84

SOLUTION

Rooms *A*, *C*, and *D* have even numbers of doors, while rooms *B* and *E* have odd numbers of doors. If we think of the rooms as the vertices of a graph, then the fact that we have exactly two odd vertices means that it is possible to travel through each door of the house exactly once. One can start in either room *B* or room *E*. **Figure 85** shows how this can be done starting in room *E*.

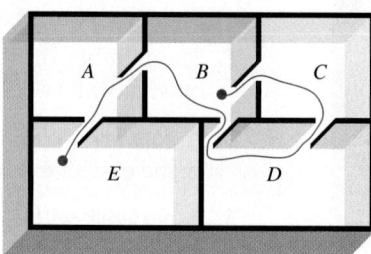

Figure 85   ▮▮▮

9.7 EXERCISES

The chart on the next page characterizes certain properties of Euclidean and non-Euclidean geometries. Study it, and use it to respond to Exercises 1–10.

1. In which geometry is the sum of the measures of the angles of a triangle equal to 180°?

2. In which geometry is the sum of the measures of the angles of a triangle greater than 180°?

3. In which geometry is the sum of the measures of the angles of a triangle less than 180°?

4. In a quadrilateral *ABCD* in Lobachevskian geometry, the sum of the measures of the angles must be _____ 360°.
(less than/greater than)

5. In a quadrilateral *ABCD* in Riemannian geometry, the sum of the measures of the angles must be _____ 360°.
(less than/greater than)

6. Suppose that *m* and *n* represent lines through *P* that are both parallel to *k*. In which geometry is this possible?

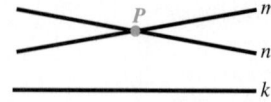

7. Suppose that *m* and *n* below *must* meet at a point. In which geometry is this possible?

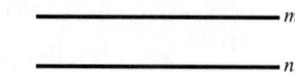

8. A globe representing the earth is a model for a surface in which geometry?

9. In which geometry is this statement possible? "Triangle *ABC* and triangle *DEF* are such that $\angle A = \angle D$, $\angle B = \angle E$, and $\angle C = \angle F$, and they have different areas."

EUCLIDEAN	NON-EUCLIDEAN	
Dates back to about 300 B.C.	Lobachevskian (about 1830)	Riemannian (about 1850)
	Lines have *infinite* length.	Lines have *finite* length.
Geometry on a plane	Geometry on a surface like a pseudosphere	Geometry on a sphere
Angles *C* and *D* of a Saccheri quadrilateral are *right* angles.	Angles *C* and *D* are *acute* angles.	Angles *C* and *D* are *obtuse* angles.
Given point *P* off line *k*, exactly *one* line can be drawn through *P* and parallel to *k*.	*More than one* line can be drawn through *P* and parallel to *k*.	*No* line can be drawn through *P* and parallel to *k*.
Typical triangle *ABC*	Typical triangle *ABC*	Typical triangle *ABC*
Two triangles can have the same size angles but different size sides (similarity as well as congruence).	Two triangles with the same size angles must have the same size sides (congruence only).	

10. Draw a figure (on a sheet of paper) as best you can showing the shape formed by the north pole *N* and two points *A* and *B* lying at the equator of a model of the earth.

Topological Equivalence *Someone once described a topologist as "a mathematician who doesn't know the difference between a doughnut and a coffee cup." This is due to the fact that both are of genus 1—they are topologically equivalent.*

Based on this interpretation, would a topologist know the difference between each pair of objects?

11. a spoon and a fork

12. a mixing bowl and a colander

13. a slice of American cheese and a slice of Swiss cheese

14. a compact disc and a phonograph record

In Exercises 15–22 each figure may be topologically equivalent to none or some of the objects labeled A–E. List all topological equivalences (by letter) for each figure.

A.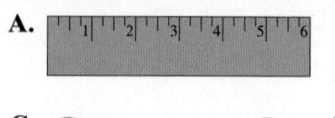

B.

C.

D.

E.

15.

(a pair of scissors)

16.

(a carrot)

17.

(a calculator)

18.

(a nut)

19.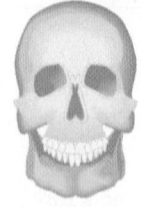

(a pyramid)

20.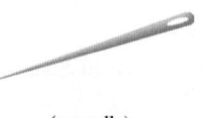

(a coin)

21.

(a skull)

22.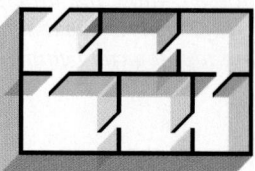

(a needle)

Give the genus of each object.

23. a compact disc

24. a phonograph record

25. a sheet of loose-leaf paper made for a three-ring binder

26. a sheet of loose-leaf paper made for a two-ring binder

27. a wedding band

28. a postage stamp

For each network, decide whether each lettered vertex is even *or* odd.

29.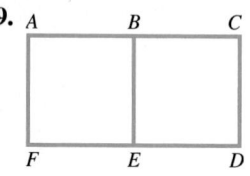

30.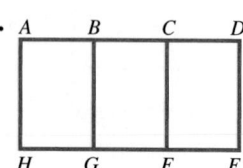

31.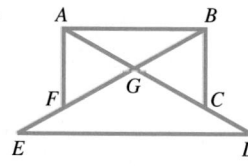

32.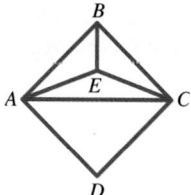

33.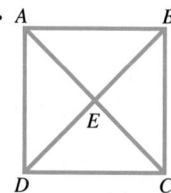

34.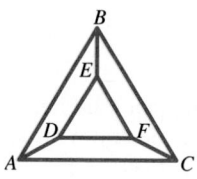

Decide whether each network is traversable. If a network is traversable, show how it can be traversed.

35.

36.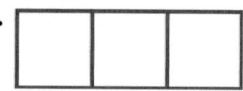

37.

38.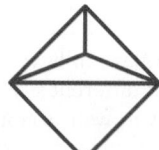

39.

40.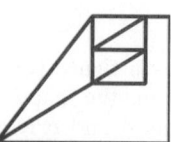

Is it possible to walk through each door of the following houses exactly once? If the answer is "yes," show how it can be done.

41.

42.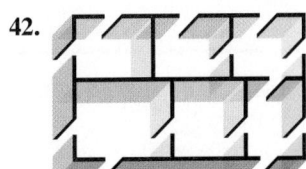

43.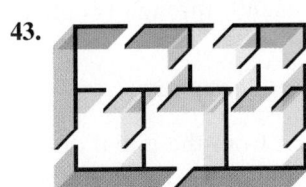

44.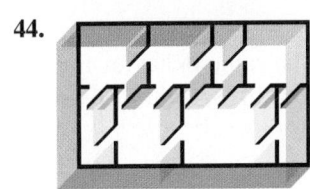

45. Pappus, a Greek mathematician in Alexandria about A.D. 320, wrote a commentary on the geometry of the times. We will work out a theorem of his about a hexagon inscribed in two intersecting lines. First we need to define an old word in a new way: a **hexagon** consists of any six lines in a plane, no three of which meet in the same point. In the figure in the next column, the vertices of several hexagons are labeled with numbers. Thus 1–2 represents a line segment joining vertices 1 and 2. Segments 1–2 and 4–5 are opposite sides of a hexagon, as are 2–3 and 5–6, and 3–4 and 6–1.

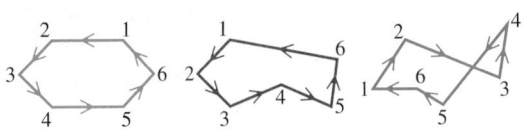

(a) Draw an angle less than 180°.

(b) Choose three points on one side of the angle. Label them 1, 5, 3 in that order, beginning with the point nearest the vertex.

(c) Choose three points on the other side of the angle. Label them 6, 2, 4 in that order, beginning with the point nearest the vertex.

(d) Draw line segments 1–6 and 3–4. Draw lines through the segments so they extend to meet in a point. Call it *N*.

(e) Let lines through 1–2 and 4–5 meet in point *M*.

(f) Let lines through 2–3 and 5–6 meet in *P*.

(g) Draw a straight line through points *M*, *N*, and *P*.

(h) Write in your own words a theorem generalizing your result.

46. The following theorem comes from projective geometry:

Theorem of Desargues in a Plane In a plane, if two triangles are placed so that lines joining corresponding vertices meet in a point, then corresponding sides, when extended, will meet in three collinear points. (*Collinear* points are points lying on the same line.)

Draw a figure that illustrates Desargues' theorem.

9.8 CHAOS AND FRACTAL GEOMETRY

Chaos • Fractals

Chaos

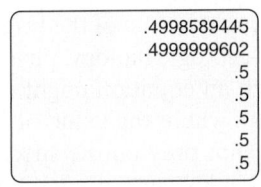

These two screens show how the TI-83 calculator can produce the sequence described. (The TI-84 plus produces a slightly different display, with the same results.)

Does Chaos Rule the Cosmos?
—One of the ten great unanswered questions of science, as found in the November 1992 issue of *Discover*

Consider the equation $y = kx(1 - x)$. Choosing $k = 2$ gives the equation $y = 2x(1 - x)$, which can be "iterated" by starting with an arbitrary x-value between 0 and 1, calculating the resulting y-value, substituting that y-value back in as x, calculating the resulting y-value, substituting that y-value back in as x, calculating another y-value, and so on. For example, a starting value of $x = 0.8$ produces the following sequence (which you can verify with a calculator):

$$0.8, 0.32, 0.435, 0.492, 0.500, 0.500, 0.500, \quad \text{and so on.}$$

The sequence seems to begin randomly but quickly stabilizes at the value 0.500. A different initial x-value would produce another sequence that would also "converge" to 0.500. The value 0.500 can be called an *attractor* for the sequence generated by the equation $y = 2x(1 - x)$. The values of the sequence are "attracted" toward 0.500.

▮▮ EXAMPLE 1 Finding Attractors

For the equation $y = kx(1 - x)$ with $k = 3$, begin with $x = 0.7$ and iterate with a calculator. What pattern emerges? How many attractors are there?

SOLUTION

Using a TI-83/84 Plus calculator, we find that the seventeenth through twentieth iterations give this sequence of terms.

$$0.6354387337, \quad 0.6949690482, \quad 0.6359612107, \quad 0.6945436475$$

The sequence apparently converges in a manner different from the initial discussion, alternating between values near 0.636 and 0.695. Therefore, for $k = 3$, the sequence tends alternately toward *two* distinct attractors. ▮▮▮

It happens that the equation in **Example 1** exhibits the same behavior for any initial value of x between 0 and 1. You are asked to show this for several cases in the exercises.

▮▮ EXAMPLE 2 Finding Attractors

In the equation of **Example 1,** change the multiplier k to 3.5, and find the forty-fourth through fifty-first terms. What pattern emerges? How many attractors are there?

SOLUTION

Again, using a TI-83/84 Plus calculator, and rounding to three decimal places, we get

$$0.383, 0.827, 0.501, 0.875, 0.383, 0.827, 0.501, 0.875.$$

This sequence seems to stabilize around *four* alternating attractors, approximately 0.383, 0.827, 0.501, and 0.875. ▮▮▮

Notice that in our initial discussion, for $k = 2$, the sequence converged to *one* attractor. In **Example 1,** for $k = 3$, it converged to *two* attractors, and in **Example 2,** for $k = 3.5$, it converged to *four* attractors.

If k is increased further, it turns out that the number of attractors doubles over and over again, more and more often. In fact, this doubling has occurred infinitely many times before k even gets as large as 4. When we look closely at groups of these doublings we find that they are always similar to earlier groups but on a smaller scale. This is called *self-similarity,* or *scaling,* an idea that is not new but has taken on new significance in recent years. Somewhere before k reaches 4, the resulting sequence becomes apparently totally random, with no attractors and no stability. This type of condition is one instance of what has come to be known in the scientific community as **chaos.** This name came from an early paper by the mathematician James A. Yorke, of the University of Maryland at College Park.

The equation $y = kx(1 - x)$ does not look all that complicated, but the intricate behavior exhibited by it and similar equations has occupied some of the brightest minds (not to mention computers) in various fields—ecology, biology, physics, genetics, economics, mathematics—since about 1960. Such an equation might represent, for example, the population of some animal species where the value of k is determined by factors (such as food supply or predators that prey on the species) that affect the increase or decrease of the population. Under certain conditions there is a long-run steady-state population (a single attractor). Under other conditions the population will eventually fluctuate between two alternating levels (two attractors), or four, or eight, and so on. But after a certain value of k, the long-term population becomes totally chaotic and unpredictable.

n	$u(n)$	
0	.7	
1	.63	
2	.6993	
3	.63084	
4	.69864	

$u(n) = 3u(n-1)(1-\ldots$

n	$u(n)$	
14	.69588	
15	.63489	
16	.69542	
17	.63544	
18	.69497	
19	.63596	
20	.69454	

$u(n) = .6945436475$

n	$u(n)$	
0	.7	
1	.735	
2	.68171	
3	.75943	
4	.63943	

$u(n) = 3.5u(n-1)(\ldots$

n	$u(n)$	
45	.82694	
46	.50088	
47	.875	
48	.38282	
49	.82694	
50	.50088	
51	.875	

$u(n) = .8749972636$

These screens support the discussion in **Examples 1 and 2.**

John Nash, a notable modern American mathematician (born in 1928), first came to the attention of the general public through his biography *A Beautiful Mind* (and the movie of the same name). In 1958 Nash narrowly lost out to René Thom (pictured below), topologist and inventor of catastrophe theory, for the Fields Medal. This is the mathematical equivalent of the Nobel prize.

Although his brilliant career was sadly interrupted by mental illness for a period of about thirty years, in 1994 Nash was awarded "the Central Bank of Sweden Prize in Economic Science in Memory of Alfred Nobel," generally regarded as equivalent to the Nobel prize. This award was for Nash's equilibrium theorem, published in his doctoral thesis in 1950. It turned out that Nash's work established a significant new way of analyzing rational conflict and cooperation in economics and other social sciences.

As long as k is small enough, there will be some number of attractors and the long-term behavior of the sequence (or population) is the same regardless of the initial x-value. But once k is large enough to cause chaos, the long-term behavior of the system will change drastically when the initial x-value is changed only slightly. For example, consider the following two sequences, both generated from $y = 4x(1 - x)$.

$$0.600, 0.960, 0.154, 0.520, 0.998, 0.006, 0.025, \ldots \quad \text{Starting with } x = 0.600$$
$$0.610, 0.952, 0.184, 0.601, 0.959, 0.157, 0.529, \ldots \quad \text{Starting with } x = 0.610$$

The fact that the two sequences wander apart from one another is partly due to roundoff errors along the way. But Yorke and others have shown that even "exact" calculations of the iterates would quickly produce divergent sequences just because of the slightly different initial values. This type of "sensitive dependence on initial conditions" was discovered (accidentally) back in the 1960s by Edward Lorenz when he was looking for an effective computerized model of weather patterns. He discerned the implication that any long-range weather predicting schemes might well be hopeless.

Patterns like those in the sequences above are more than just numerical oddities. Similar patterns apply to a great many phenomena in the physical, biological, and social sciences, many of them seemingly common natural systems that have been studied for hundreds of years. The measurement of a coastline, the description of the patterns in a branching tree, or a mountain range, or a cloud formation, or intergalactic cosmic dust, the prediction of weather patterns, the turbulent behavior of fluids of all kinds, the circulatory and neurological systems of the human body, fluctuations in populations and economic systems—these and many other phenomena remain mysteries, concealing their true nature somewhere beyond the reach of even our brightest minds and our biggest and fastest computers.

Continuous phenomena are easily dealt with. A change in one quantity produces a predictable change in another. (For example, a little more pressure on the gas pedal produces a little more speed.) Mathematical functions that represent continuous events can be graphed by unbroken lines or curves, or perhaps smooth, gradually changing surfaces. The governing equations for such phenomena are "linear," and extensive mathematical methods of solving them have been developed. On the other hand, erratic events associated with certain other equations are harder to describe or predict. The science of chaos, made possible by modern computers, continues to open up new ways to deal with such events.

One early attempt to deal with discontinuous processes in a new way, generally acknowledged as a forerunner of chaos theory, was that of the French mathematician René Thom, who, in the 1960s, applied the methods of topology. To emphasize the feature of sudden change, Thom referred to events such as a heartbeat, a buckling beam, a stock market crash, a riot, or a tornado, as *catastrophes*. He proved that all catastrophic events (in our four-dimensional space-time) are combinations of seven elementary catastrophes. (In higher dimensions the number quickly approaches infinity.)

Each of the seven elementary catastrophes has a characteristic topological shape. Two examples are shown in **Figure 86**. The figure on the left is called a *cusp*. The figure on the right is an *elliptic umbilicus* (a belly button with an oval cross-section). Thom's work became known as **catastrophe theory.**

Computer graphics have been indispensable in the study of chaotic processes. The plotting of large numbers of points has revealed patterns that would otherwise

René Thom

Figure 86

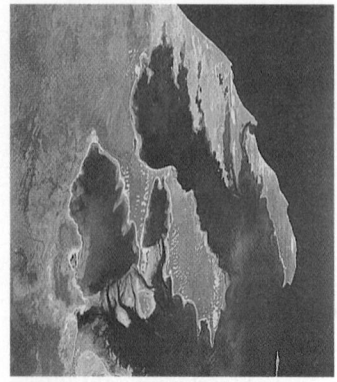

The surface of the earth, consisting of continents, mountains, oceans, valleys, and so on, has **fractal dimension** 2.2.

Aside from providing a geometric structure for chaotic processes in nature, fractal geometry is viewed by many as a significant art form. (To appreciate why, see the 1986 publication *The Beauty of Fractals*, by H. O. Peitgen and P. H. Richter, which contains 184 figures, many in color.) Peitgen and others have also published *Fractals for the Classroom: Strategic Activities Volume One* (Springer-Verlag, 1991).

have not been observed. (The underlying reasons for many of these patterns, however, have still not been explained.) The images shown in **Figure 87** are created using chaotic processes.

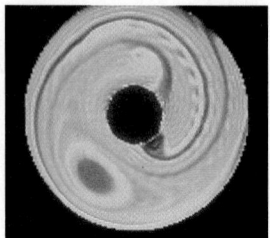 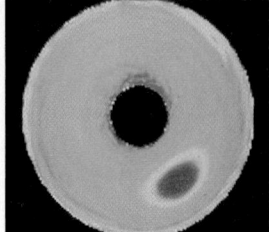

Figure 87

Fractals

If there is one structure that has provided a key for the new study of nonlinear processes, it is **fractal geometry,** developed over a period of years mainly by the IBM mathematician Benoit Mandelbrot (1924–2010). For his work in this field, and at the recommendation of the National Science Foundation, Columbia University awarded him the 1985 Bernard Medal for Meritorious Service to Science.

Lines have a single dimension. Plane figures have two dimensions, and we live in a three-dimensional spatial world. In a paper published in 1967, Mandelbrot investigated the idea of measuring the length of a coastline. He concluded that such a shape defies conventional Euclidean geometry and that rather than having a natural number dimension, it has a "fractional dimension." A coastline is an example of a *self-similar shape*—a shape that repeats itself over and over on different scales. From a distance, the bays and inlets cannot be individually observed, but as one moves closer they become more apparent. The branching of a tree, from twig to limb to trunk, also exhibits a shape that repeats itself.

In the early twentieth century, the German mathematician H. von Koch investigated the so-called Koch snowflake. It is shown in **Figure 88**. Starting with an equilateral triangle, each side then gives rise to another equilateral triangle. The process continues over and over, indefinitely, and a curve of infinite length is produced. The mathematics of Koch's era was not advanced enough to deal with such figures. However, using Mandelbrot's theory, it is shown that the Koch snowflake has dimension of about 1.26. This figure is obtained using a formula that involves logarithms. (Logarithms were introduced briefly in **Chapter 8.**)

Figure 88

The theory of fractals is today being applied to many areas of science and technology. It has been used to analyze the symmetry of living forms, the turbulence of liquids, the branching of rivers, and price variation in economics. Hollywood has used fractals in the special effects found in some blockbuster movies. **Figure 89** shows an example of a computer-generated fractal design.

An interesting account of the science of chaos is found in the popular 1987 book *Chaos*, by James Gleick. Mandelbrot has published two books on fractals. They are *Fractals: Form, Chance, and Dimension* (1975), and *The Fractal Geometry of Nature* (1982).

Figure 89

9.8 EXERCISES

Exercises 1–25 are taken from an issue of Student Math Notes, *published by the National Council of Teachers of Mathematics. They were written by Dr. Tami S. Martin, Mathematics Department, Illinois State University, and the authors wish to thank N.C.T.M. and Tami Martin for permission to reproduce this activity. Because the exercises should be done in numerical order, answers to all exercises (both even- and odd-numbered) appear in the answer section of the student edition of this book.*

Most of the mathematical objects you have studied have dimensions that are whole numbers. For example, such solids as cubes and icosahedrons have dimension three. Squares, triangles, and many other planar figures are two-dimensional. Lines are one-dimensional, and points have dimension zero. Consider a square with side of length one. Gather several of these squares by cutting out or using patterning blocks.

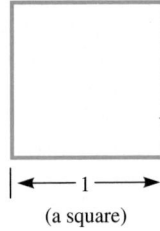

|←——— 1 ———→|

(a square)

The size of a figure is calculated by counting the number of replicas *(small pieces) that make it up. Here, a replica is the original square with edges of length one.*

1. What is the least number of these squares that can be put together edge to edge to form a larger square?

The original square is made up of one small square, so its size is one.

2. What is the size of the new square?

3. What is the length of each edge of the new square?

Similar figures have the same shape but are not necessarily the same size. The **scale factor** *between two similar figures can be found by calculating the ratio of corresponding edges:*

$$\frac{\text{new length}}{\text{old length}}.$$

4. What is the scale factor between the large square and the small square?

5. Find the ratio $\frac{\text{new size}}{\text{old size}}$ for the two squares.

6. Form an even larger square that is three units long on each edge. Compare this square to the small square.

What is the scale factor between the two squares? What is the ratio of the new size to the old size?

7. Form an even larger square that is four units long on each edge. Compare this square to the small square. What is the scale factor between the two squares? What is the ratio of the new size to the old size?

8. Complete the table for squares.

Scale Factor	2	3	4	5	6	10
Ratio of new size to old size						

9. How are the two rows in the table related?

Consider an equilateral triangle. The length of an edge of the triangle is one unit. The size of this triangle is one.

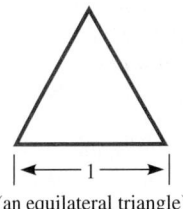

|←——— 1 ———→|

(an equilateral triangle)

10. What is the least number of equilateral triangles that can be put together edge to edge to form a similar larger triangle?

11. Complete the table for triangles.

Scale Factor	2	3	4	5	6	10
Ratio of new size to old size						

12. How does the relationship between the two rows in this table compare with the one you found in the table for squares?

One way to define the dimension, d, of a figure relates the scale factor, the new size, and the old size:

$$(\text{scale factor})^d = \frac{\text{new size}}{\text{old size}}.$$

Using a scale factor of two for squares or equilateral triangles, we can see that $2^d = \frac{4}{1}$; that is, $2^d = 4$. Because $2^2 = 4$, the dimension, d, must be two. This definition of dimension confirms what we already know—that squares and equilateral triangles are two-dimensional figures.

13. Use this definition and your completed tables to confirm that the square and the equilateral triangle are two-dimensional figures for scale factors other than two.

Consider a cube, with edges of length one. Let the size of the cube be one.

14. What is the least number of these cubes that can be put together face to face to form a larger cube?

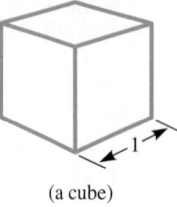

(a cube)

15. What is the scale factor between these two cubes? What is the ratio of the new size to the old size for the two cubes?

16. Complete the table for cubes.

Scale Factor	2	3	4	5	6	10
Ratio of new size to old size						

17. How are the two rows in the table related?

18. Use the definition of dimension and a scale factor of two to verify that a cube is a three-dimensional object.

We have explored scale factors and sizes associated with two- and three-dimensional figures. Is it possible for mathematical objects to have fractional dimensions? Consider each figure formed by replacing the middle third of a line segment of length one by one upside-down V, each of whose two sides are equal in length to the segment removed. The first four stages in the development of this figure are shown.

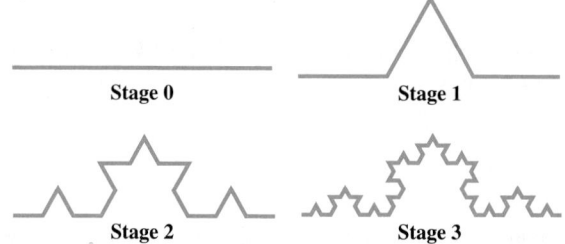

Finding the scale factor for this sequence of figures is difficult, because the overall length of a representative portion of the figure remains the same while the number of pieces increases. To simplify the procedure, follow these steps.

Step 1 *Start with any stage (e.g., Stage 1).*

Step 2 *Draw the next stage (e.g., Stage 2) of the sequence and "blow it up" so that it contains an exact copy of the preceding stage (in this example, Stage 1).*

Notice that Stage 2 contains four copies, or replicas, of Stage 1 and is three times as long as Stage 1.

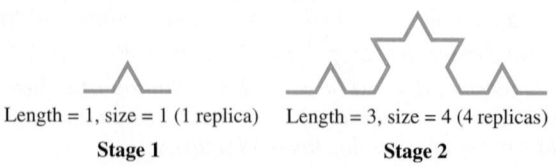

Length = 1, size = 1 (1 replica)   Length = 3, size = 4 (4 replicas)

Stage 1   **Stage 2**

19. The scale factor is equal to the ratio $\frac{\text{new length}}{\text{old length}}$ between any two consecutive stages. The scale factor between Stage 1 and Stage 2 is _____.

20. The size can be determined by counting the number of replicas of Stage 1 found in Stage 2. Old size = 1, new size = ____.

Use the definition of dimension to compute the dimension, d, of the figure formed by this process: $3^d = \frac{4}{1}$; that is, $3^d = 4$. Since $3^1 = 3$ and $3^2 = 9$, for $3^d = 4$ the dimension of the figure must be greater than one but less than two: $1 < d < 2$.

21. Use your calculator to estimate d. Remember that d is the exponent that makes 3^d equal 4. For example, because d must be between 1 and 2, try $d = 1.5$. But $3^{1.5} = 5.196\ldots$, which is greater than 4; thus, d must be smaller than 1.5. Continue until you approximate d to three decimal places. (Use logarithms for maximum accuracy.)

*The original figure was a one-dimensional line segment. By iteratively adding to the line segment, an object of dimension greater than one but less than two was generated. Objects with fractional dimension are known as **fractals**. Fractals are infinitely self-similar objects formed by repeated additions to, or removals from, a figure. The object attained at the limit of the repeated procedure is the fractal.*

   Next consider a two-dimensional object with sections removed iteratively. In each stage of the fractal's development, a triangle is removed from the center of each triangular region.

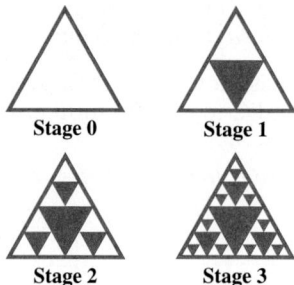

Stage 0   Stage 1

Stage 2   Stage 3

Use the process from the last example to help answer the following questions.

22. What is the scale factor of the fractal?

23. Old size = 1, new size = ____.

24. The dimension of the fractal is between what two whole number values?

25. Use the definition of dimension and your calculator to approximate the dimension of this fractal to three decimal places.

Use a calculator to determine the pattern of attractors for the equation $y = kx(1 - x)$ for the given value of k and the given initial value of x.

26. $k = 3.25$,
   $x = 0.7$

27. $k = 3.4$,
   $x = 0.8$

28. $k = 3.55$,
   $x = 0.7$

COLLABORATIVE INVESTIGATION

Generalizing the Angle Sum Concept

The sum of the measures of the angles of a triangle is 180°. This fact can be extended to determine a formula for the sum of the measures of the angles of any convex polygon. To begin this investigation, divide into groups of three or four students each. Prepare on a sheet of paper six figures as shown on the right.

Now we define a diagonal from vertex A to be a segment from A to a non-adjacent vertex. The triangle in Figure I has no diagonals, but the polygons in Figures II through VI do have them.

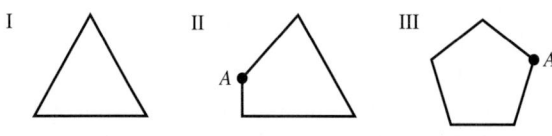

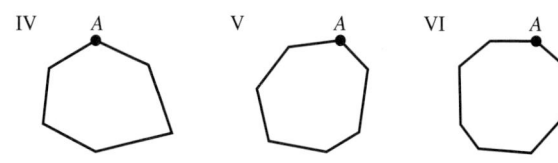

Topics for Discussion

1. Choose someone in the group to draw all possible diagonals from vertex A in each figure.

2. Now complete **Table 6** as a group.

Table 6

Polygon	Number of Sides	Number of Triangles, t	Number of Degrees in Each Triangle	Sum of the Measures of All Angles of the Polygon, $t \cdot 180°$
I				
II				
III				
IV				
V				
VI				

3. Based on the table you completed, answer the following in order.

   (a) As suggested by the table, the number of triangles that a convex polygon can be divided into is _____ less than the number of sides.

   (b) Thus, if a polygon has s sides, it can be divided into _____ triangles.

   (c) From the table we see that the sum of the measures of all the angles of a polygon can be found from the expression $t \cdot 180°$. Thus, if a polygon has s sides, the sum of the measures of all the angles of the polygon is given by the expression

   $$(\underline{\quad} - \underline{\quad}) \cdot \underline{\quad}°.$$

4. Use your discovery from **Exercise 3(c)** to find the sum of the measures of all the angles of

   (i) a nonagon (ii) a decagon (iii) a 12-sided polygon.

CHAPTER 9 TEST

1. Consider a 38° angle. Answer each of the following.

   (a) What is the measure of its complement?

   (b) What is the measure of its supplement?

   (c) Classify it as acute, obtuse, right, or straight.

Find the measure of each marked angle.

2.

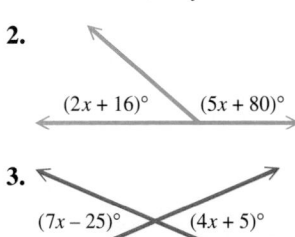

$(2x + 16)°$ $(5x + 80)°$

3.

$(7x - 25)°$ $(4x + 5)°$

4.

$(4x + 6)°$

$(10x)°$

In Exercises 5 and 6, assume that lines m and n are parallel, and find the measure of each marked angle.

5.

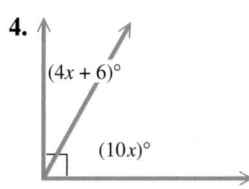

$(7x + 11)°$ n

$(3x - 1)°$ m

6.

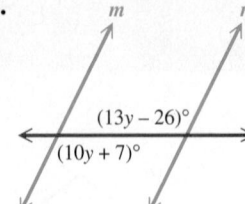

$(13y - 26)°$
$(10y + 7)°$

7. Explain why a rhombus must be a parallelogram, but a parallelogram might not be a rhombus.

8. Which one of the statements A–D is false?

   A. A square is a rhombus.

   B. The acute angles of a right triangle are complementary.

   C. A triangle may have both a right angle and an obtuse angle.

   D. A trapezoid may have nonparallel sides of the same length.

Identify each of the following curves as simple, closed, both, *or* neither.

9.

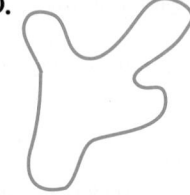

10.

11. Find the measure of each angle in the triangle.

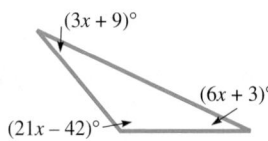

$(3x + 9)°$
$(6x + 3)°$
$(21x - 42)°$

Find the area of each of the following figures.

12.

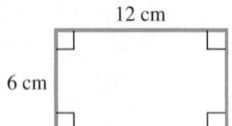

12 cm
6 cm

13.

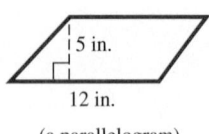

5 in.
12 in.
(a parallelogram)

14.

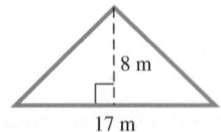

8 m
17 m

15.

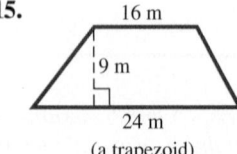

16 m
9 m
24 m
(a trapezoid)

16. If a circle has area 144π square inches, what is its circumference?

17. *Circumference of a Dome* The Rogers Centre in Toronto, Canada, is the first stadium with a hard-shell, retractable roof. The steel dome is 630 feet in diameter. To the nearest foot, what is the circumference of this dome?

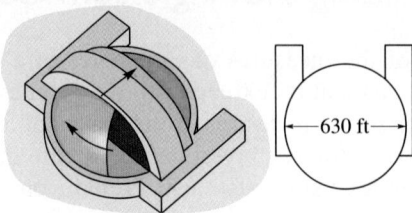

630 ft

18. *Area of a Shaded Figure* What is the area of the colored portion of the figure? Use 3.14 as an approximation for π.

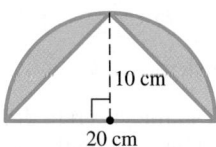

10 cm
20 cm
(a triangle within a semicircle)

19. Given: $\angle CAB = \angle DBA$; $DB = CA$
Prove: $\triangle ABD \cong \triangle BAC$

D C
A B

20. *Height of a Pole* If a 30-ft pole casts a shadow 45 ft long, how tall is a pole whose shadow is 30 ft long at the same time?

21. *Diagonal of a Rectangle* What is the measure of a diagonal of a rectangle that has width 20 m and length 21 m?

22. First reflect the given figure about line *n*, and then about line *m*.

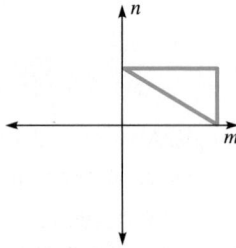

n
m

23. Find the point reflection image of the given figure with the given point as center.

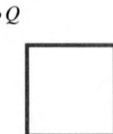

• Q

Find **(a)** *the volume and* **(b)** *the surface area of each of the following space figures. When necessary, use 3.14 as an approximation for* π.

24.

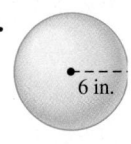

6 in.

(a sphere)

25.

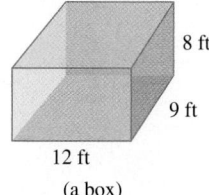

8 ft

9 ft

12 ft

(a box)

26.

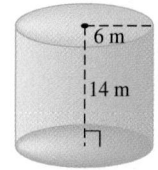

6 m

14 m

(a right circular cylinder)

27. List several main distinctions between Euclidean geometry and non-Euclidean geometry.

28. *Topological Equivalence* Are the following pairs of objects topologically equivalent?

  (a) a page of a book and the cover of the same book

  (b) a pair of glasses with the lenses removed, and the Mona Lisa

29. Decide whether it is possible to traverse the network shown. If it is possible, show how it can be done.

(a)

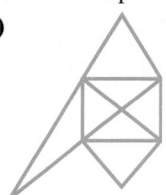

(b)

30. Use a calculator to determine the attractors for the sequence generated by the equation

$$y = 2.1x(1 - x),$$

with initial value of $x = 0.6$.

COUNTING METHODS

10

February 7, 2010, Miami, FL. Super Bowl XLIV pits the National Football Conference (NFC) New Orleans Saints against the American Football Conference (AFC) Indianapolis Colts. The Saints, led by quarterback Drew Brees (the game's MVP), eventually win an exciting game 31 to 17.

Before the game starts, the coin toss by Emmitt Smith, under the watchful eye of referee Scott Green, is called "heads" by the visiting Saints and comes up heads.

ANNOUNCER: "Can you believe this? (For) thirteen straight years the NFC has won the toss. The odds of any one side winning thirteen straight coin tosses is about 8100 to 1."

Was the announcer correct? The methods of this chapter enable us to count those odds exactly. The answer is on page 537.

10.1 COUNTING BY SYSTEMATIC LISTING

Counting • One-Part Tasks • Product Tables for Two-Part Tasks • Tree Diagrams for Multiple-Part Tasks • Other Systematic Listing Methods

Counting

In this chapter, "counting" means finding the number of objects, of some certain type, that exist. Among many possible reasons to ask and answer such a question, a major one is to be able to calculate the likelihood that some event may occur, that is the *probability* of the event. (Probability is the subject of **Chapter 11.**)

The methods of counting presented in this section involve listing the possible results for a given task. This approach is practical only for fairly short lists. When listing possible results, it is extremely important to use a *systematic* approach, so that no possibilities are missed.

One-Part Tasks

The results for simple, one-part tasks can often be listed easily. For the task of tossing a single fair coin, for example, the list is *heads, tails,* with two possible results. If the task is to roll a single fair die (a cube with faces numbered 1 through 6), the different results are 1, 2, 3, 4, 5, 6, a total of six possibilities.

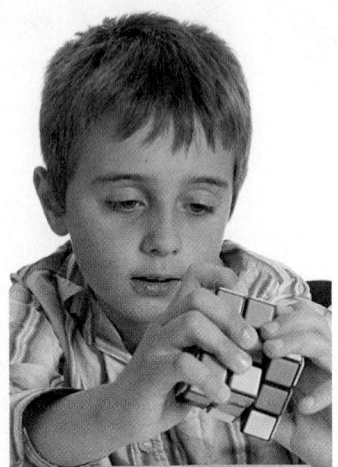

Counting methods can be used to find the number of moves required to solve a Rubik's Cube. The scrambled cube must be modified so that each face is a solid color. Rubik's royalties from sales of the cube in Western countries made him Hungary's richest man.

Although the craze over the cube of the early 1980s has waned, certain groups have remained intensely interested in not only solving the scrambled cube, but doing so as fast as possible. And the 30-year search for an exact number of moves (called face turns) that is guaranteed to suffice in all cases while no smaller number will suffice finally ended in July of 2010. That number is now known to be 20.

Even so, it is not yet known if an "efficient" algorithm exists for finding an actual solution in every case. So the cube still conceals mysteries for computer scientists to pursue.

Today, the cube's popularity is rivaled, among many people, by Sudoku puzzles.

▮▮ **EXAMPLE 1** Selecting a Club President

Consider a club N with five members:

$$N = \{\text{Alan, Bill, Cathy, David, Evelyn}\}, \quad \text{abbreviated as} \quad N = \{A, B, C, D, E\}.$$

In how many ways can this group select a president (assuming all members are eligible)?

SOLUTION

The task in this case is to select one of the five members as president. There are five possible results:

$$A, \ B, \ C, \ D, \text{ and } E.$$ ▮▮▮

Product Tables for Two-Part Tasks

▮▮ **EXAMPLE 2** Building Numbers from a Set of Digits

Determine the number of two-digit numbers that can be written using only the digits 1, 2, and 3.

SOLUTION

This task consists of two parts:

1. Choose a first digit.   **2.** Choose a second digit.

The results for a two-part task can be pictured in a **product table** such as **Table 1**. From the table we obtain our list of possible results:

$$11, \ 12, \ 13, \ 21, \ 22, \ 23, \ 31, \ 32, \ 33.$$

There are nine possibilities. ▮▮▮

Table 1

		Second Digit	
	1	**2**	**3**
First Digit **1**	11	12	13
2	21	22	23
3	31	32	33

▌▌ **EXAMPLE 3** Rolling a Pair of Dice

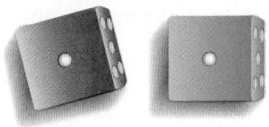

Determine the number of different possible results when two ordinary dice are rolled.

SOLUTION

Assume the dice are easily distinguishable. Perhaps one is red and the other green. Then the task consists of two parts:

1. Roll the red die.   **2.** Roll the green die.

The product table in **Table 2** shows that there are thirty-six possible results.

Table 2 Rolling Two Fair Dice						
	Green Die					
	1	**2**	**3**	**4**	**5**	**6**
1	(1, 1)	(1, 2)	(1, 3)	(1, 4)	(1, 5)	(1, 6)
2	(2, 1)	(2, 2)	(2, 3)	(2, 4)	(2, 5)	(2, 6)
3	(3, 1)	(3, 2)	(3, 3)	(3, 4)	(3, 5)	(3, 6)
4	(4, 1)	(4, 2)	(4, 3)	(4, 4)	(4, 5)	(4, 6)
5	(5, 1)	(5, 2)	(5, 3)	(5, 4)	(5, 5)	(5, 6)
6	(6, 1)	(6, 2)	(6, 3)	(6, 4)	(6, 5)	(6, 6)

(Red Die labels the rows at left.)

▌▌▌

You will want to refer to **Table 2** *when various dice-rolling problems occur in the remainder of this chapter and the next.*

▌▌ **EXAMPLE 4** Electing Two Club Officers

Find the number of ways that club N of **Example 1** can elect both a president and a secretary. Assume that all members are eligible, but that no one can hold both offices.

SOLUTION

Again, the required task has two parts:

1. Determine the president.   **2.** Determine the secretary.

Constructing **Table 3** gives us the possibilities (where, for example, AB denotes president A and secretary B, while BA denotes president B and secretary A).

Table 3 Electing Two Officers					
	Secretary				
	A	**B**	**C**	**D**	**E**
A		AB	AC	AD	AE
B	BA		BC	BD	BE
C	CA	CB		CD	CE
D	DA	DB	DC		DE
E	EA	EB	EC	ED	

(President labels the rows at left.)

Notice that certain entries (down the main diagonal, from upper left to lower right) are omitted from the table, since the cases AA, BB, and so on would imply one person holding both offices. Altogether, there are twenty possibilities.   ▌▌▌

▌▌ **EXAMPLE 5** Selecting Committees for a Club

Find the number of ways that club N can appoint a committee of two members to represent them at an association conference.

SOLUTION

The required task again has two parts. In fact, we can refer to **Table 3** again, but this time, the order of the two letters (people) in a given pair really makes no difference. For example, BD and DB are the same committee. (In **Example 4,** BD and DB were different results since the two people would be holding different offices.)

In the case of committees, we can eliminate not only the main diagonal entries but also all entries below the main diagonal. The resulting list contains ten possibilities:

$$AB, \quad AC, \quad AD, \quad AE, \quad BC, \quad BD, \quad BE, \quad CD, \quad CE, \quad DE.$$ ▌▌▌

Tree Diagrams for Multiple-Part Tasks

> **PROBLEM-SOLVING HINT** A task that has more than two parts is not easy to analyze with a product table. Another helpful device is the **tree diagram.**

▌▌ **EXAMPLE 6** Building Numbers from a Set of Digits

Find the number of three-digit numbers that can be written using only the digits 1, 2, and 3, assuming that **(a)** repeated digits are allowed and **(b)** repeated digits are not allowed.

SOLUTION

(a) The task of constructing such a number has three parts:

    1. Select the first digit.   **2.** Select the second digit.   **3.** Select the third digit.

As we move from left to right through the tree diagram in **Figure 1**, the tree branches at the first-stage to all possibilities for the first digit. Then each first-stage branch again branches, or splits, at the second stage, to all possibilities for the second digit. Finally, the third-stage branching shows the third-digit possibilities. The list of possible results (twenty-seven of them) is shown in **Figure 1**.

(b) For the case of nonrepeating digits, we could construct a whole new tree diagram, as in **Figure 2**, or we could simply go down the list of numbers from the first tree diagram and strike out any that contain repeated digits. In either case we obtain only six possibilities.

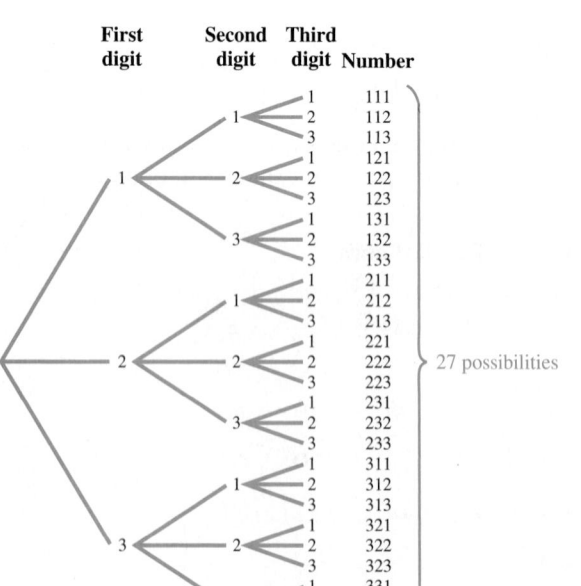

Tree diagram for three-digit numbers using digits 1, 2, and 3

Figure 1

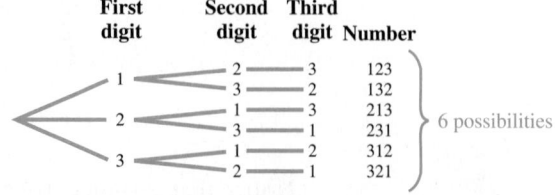

Tree diagram for nonrepeating three-digit numbers using digits 1, 2, and 3

Figure 2 ▌▌▌

Notice the distinction between parts (a) and (b) of **Example 6.** There are twenty-seven possibilities when "repetitions (of digits) are allowed," but only six possibilities when "repetitions are not allowed."

Here is another way to phrase the problem of **Example 6:**

> A three-digit number is to be determined by placing three slips of paper (marked 1, 2, and 3) into a hat and drawing out three slips in succession. Find the number of possible results if the drawing is done **(a)** *with replacement* and **(b)** *without replacement.*

Drawing "with replacement" means drawing a slip, recording its digit, and replacing the slip into the hat so that it is again available for subsequent draws.

> ***Drawing "with replacement" has the effect of "allowing repetitions," while drawing "without replacement" has the effect of "not allowing repetitions."***

The words "repetitions" and "replacement" are important in the statement of a problem. In **Example 2,** since no restrictions were stated, we assumed that *repetitions* (of digits) *were allowed,* or equivalently that digits were to be selected *with replacement.*

▋ ▋ EXAMPLE 7   Selecting Switch Settings on a Printer

Pamela DeMar's computer printer allows for optional settings with a panel of four on-off switches in a row. How many different settings can she select if no two adjacent switches can both be off?

SOLUTION

This situation is typical of user-selectable options on various devices, including computer equipment, garage door openers, and other appliances. In **Figure 3**, we denote "on" and "off" with 1 and 0, respectively. The number of possible settings is eight.

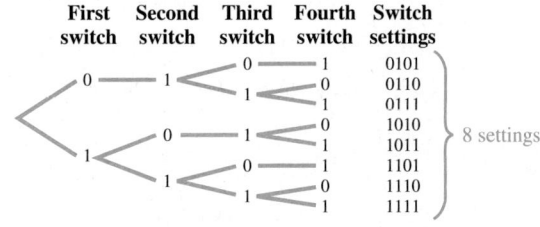

Tree diagram for printer settings
Figure 3

Notice that each time a switch is indicated as off (0), the next switch can only be on (1). This is to satisfy the restriction that no two adjacent switches can both be off.

▋▋▋

▋ ▋ EXAMPLE 8   Seating Attendees at a Concert

Arne, Bobbette, Chuck, and Deirdre have tickets for four reserved seats in a row at a concert. In how many different ways can they seat themselves so that Arne and Bobbette will sit next to each other?

SOLUTION

Here we have a four-part task:

> Assign people to the first, second, third, and fourth seats.

The tree diagram in **Figure 4** on the next page avoids repetitions, because no person can occupy more than one seat. Also, once *A* or *B* appears in the tree, the other one *must* occur at the next stage. (Why is this?) No splitting occurs from stage three to stage four because by that time there is only one person left unassigned. The right column in the figure shows the twelve possible seating arrangements.

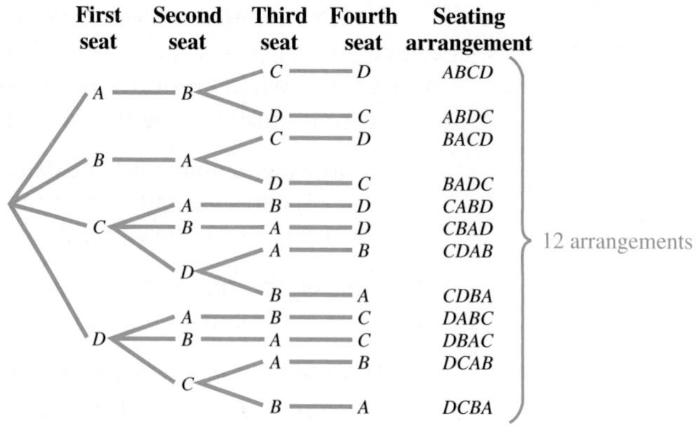

First seat	Second seat	Third seat	Fourth seat	Seating arrangement

Tree diagram for concert seating

Figure 4   ▌▌▌

Although we have applied tree diagrams only to tasks with three or more parts, they can also be used for two-part or even simple, one-part tasks. Product tables, on the other hand, are practical only for two-part tasks.

Other Systematic Listing Methods

There are additional systematic ways to produce complete listings of possible results besides product tables and tree diagrams.

In **Example 4,** where we used a product table (**Table 3**) to list all possible president-secretary pairs for the club $N = \{A, B, C, D, E\}$, we could have systematically constructed the same list using a sort of alphabetical or left-to-right approach.

First, consider the results where A is president. Any of the remaining members (B, C, D, or E) could then be secretary. That gives us the pairs AB, AC, AD, and AE. Next, assume B is president. The secretary could then be A, C, D, or E. We get the pairs BA, BC, BD, and BE. Continuing in order, we get the complete list just as in **Example 4:**

$$AB, \quad AC, \quad AD, \quad AE, \quad BA, \quad BC, \quad BD, \quad BE, \quad CA, \quad CB,$$
$$CD, \quad CE, \quad DA, \quad DB, \quad DC, \quad DE, \quad EA, \quad EB, \quad EC, \quad ED.$$

▌▌ **EXAMPLE 9**   Counting Triangles in a Figure

How many different triangles (of any size) can be traced in **Figure 5**?

SOLUTION

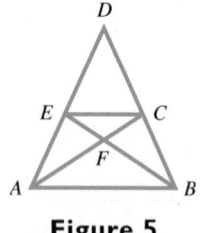

Figure 5

One systematic approach is to label points as shown, begin with A, and proceed in alphabetical order to write all three-letter combinations, then cross out the ones that are not triangles in the figure.

$$ABC, \quad ABD, \quad ABE, \quad ABF, \quad ACD, \quad ACE, \quad A\cancel{CF}, \quad A\cancel{DE}, \quad A\cancel{DF}, \quad AEF,$$
$$\cancel{BCD}, \quad BCE, \quad BCF, \quad BDE, \quad \cancel{BDF}, \quad \cancel{BEF}, \quad CDE, \quad \cancel{CDF}, \quad CEF, \quad \cancel{DEF}$$

Finally, there are twelve different triangles in the figure. Why are ACB and CBF (and many others) not included in the list?

Another method might be first to identify the triangles consisting of a single region each: DEC, ECF, AEF, BCF, ABF. Then list those consisting of two regions each: AEC, BEC, ABE, ABC; and those with three regions each: ACD, BED. There are no triangles with four regions, but there is one with five: ABD. The total is again twelve. Can you think of other systematic ways of getting the same list?   ▌▌▌

Notice that in the first method shown in **Example 9,** the labeled points were considered in alphabetical order. In the second method, the single-region triangles were listed by using a top-to-bottom and left-to-right order. Using a definite system helps to ensure that we get a complete list.

10.1 EXERCISES

Electing Officers of a Club *Refer to* **Examples 1 and 4,** *involving the club*

$$N = \{\text{Alan, Bill, Cathy, David, Evelyn}\}.$$

Assuming all members are eligible, but that no one can hold more than one office, list and count the different ways the club could elect each group of officers.

1. a president and a treasurer

2. a president and a treasurer if the president must be a female

3. a president and a treasurer if the two officers must be the same sex

4. a president, a secretary, and a treasurer, if the president and treasurer must be women

5. a president, a secretary, and a treasurer, if the president must be a man and the other two must be women

6. a president, a secretary, and a treasurer, if all three officers must be men

Appointing Committees *List and count the ways club N could appoint a committee of three members under each condition.*

7. There are no restrictions.

8. The committee must include more men than women.

Refer to **Table 2** *(the product table for rolling two dice). Of the 36 possibilities, determine the number for which the sum (for both dice) is the following.*

9. 2   10. 3   11. 4

12. 5   13. 6   14. 7

15. 8   16. 9   17. 10

18. 11   19. 12   20. odd

21. even

22. from 6 through 8 inclusive

23. between 6 and 10

24. less than 5

25. Construct a product table showing all possible two-digit numbers using digits from the set

$$\{2, 3, 5, 7\}.$$

Of the sixteen numbers in the product table for Exercise 25, list the ones that belong to each category.

26. even numbers

27. numbers with repeating digits

28. multiples of 3

29. prime numbers

30. Construct a tree diagram showing all possible results when three fair coins are tossed. Then list the ways of getting each result.
    (a) at least two heads
    (b) more than two heads
    (c) no more than two heads
    (d) fewer than two heads

31. Extend the tree diagram of **Exercise 30** for four fair coins. Then list the ways of getting each result.
    (a) more than three tails
    (b) fewer than three tails
    (c) at least three tails
    (d) no more than three tails

Determine the number of triangles (of any size) in each figure.

32.

33.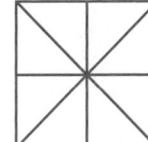

34.

35.

Determine the number of squares (of any size) in each figure.

36.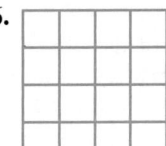

37.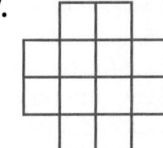

38.

39.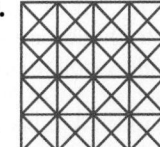

Consider only the smallest individual cubes and assume solid stacks (no gaps). Determine the number of cubes in each stack that are not visible from the perspective shown.

40. **41.**

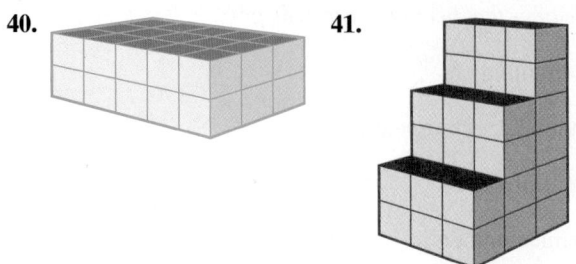

42. **43.**

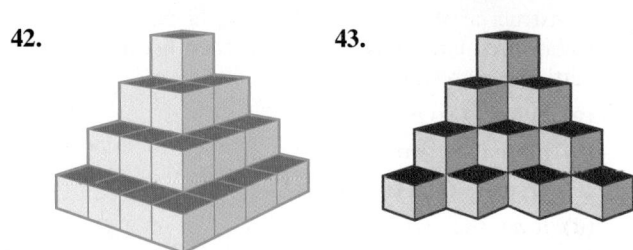

44. In the plane figure illustrated here, only movement that tends downward is allowed. Find the total number of paths from *A* to *B*.

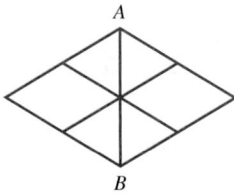

45. Find the number of paths from *A* to *B* in the figure illustrated here if the directions on various segments are restricted as shown.

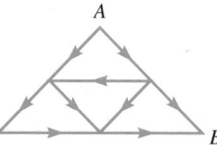

In each of Exercises 46–48, determine the number of different ways the given number can be written as the sum of two primes.

46. 30   **47.** 40   **48.** 95

49. Rolling Unusual Dice An unusual die has the numbers 2, 2, 3, 3, 5, and 8 on its six faces. Two of these dice are rolled, and the two numbers on the top faces are added. How many different sums are possible? (*Mathematics Teacher* calendar problem)

50. Shaking Hands in a Group A group of six strangers sat in a circle, and each one got acquainted only with the person to the left and the person to the right. Then all six people stood up and each one shook hands (once) with each of the others who was still a stranger. How many handshakes occurred?

51. Number of Games in a Chess Tournament Fifty people enter a single-elimination chess tournament. (If you lose one game, you're out.) Assuming no ties occur, what is the number of games required to determine the tournament champion?

52. Sums of Digits How many positive integers less than 100 have the sum of their digits equal to a perfect square?

53. Sums of Digits How many three-digit numbers have the sum of their digits equal to 22?

54. Integers Containing the Digit 2 How many integers between 100 and 400 contain the digit 2?

55. Filling an Order A customer ordered fifteen Zingers. Zingers are placed in packages of four, three, or one. In how many different ways can this order be filled? (*Mathematics Teacher* calendar problem)

56. Selecting Dinner Items Michael Bailey and friends are dining at the Clam Shell Restaurant this evening, where a complete dinner consists of three items:

(1) soup (clam chowder or minestrone) or salad (fresh spinach or shrimp),

(2) sourdough rolls or bran muffin, and

(3) entree (lasagna, lobster, or roast turkey).

Michael selects his meal subject to the following restrictions. He cannot stomach more than one kind of seafood at a sitting. Also, whenever he tastes minestrone, he cannot resist having lasagna as well. Use a tree diagram to determine the number of different choices Michael has.

Setting Options on a Computer Printer *For Exercises 57–59, refer to* **Example 7.** *How many different settings could Pamela choose in each case?*

57. No restrictions apply to adjacent switches.

58. No two adjacent switches can be off *and* no two adjacent switches can be on.

59. There are five switches rather than four, and no two adjacent switches can be on.

60. Building Numbers from Sets of Digits Determine the number of odd, nonrepeating three-digit numbers that can be written using only the digits 0, 1, 2, and 3.

61. Lattice Points on a Line Segment A line segment joins the points

$$(8, 12) \quad \text{and} \quad (53, 234)$$

in the Cartesian plane. Including its endpoints, how many lattice points does this line segment contain? (A *lattice point* is a point with integer coordinates.)

62. *Lengths of Segments Joining Lattice Points* In the pattern that follows, dots are one unit apart horizontally and vertically. If a segment can join any two dots, how many segments can be drawn with each length?

(a) 1   **(b)** 2   **(c)** 3   **(d)** 4   **(e)** 5

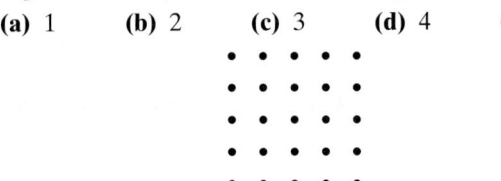

63. *Counting Matchsticks in a Grid* Uniform-length matchsticks are used to build a rectangular grid as shown here. If the grid is 12 matchsticks high and 25 matchsticks wide, how many matchsticks are used?

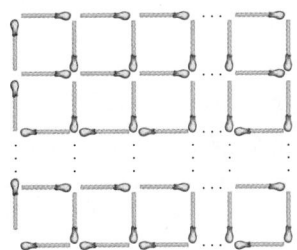

64. *Patterns in Floor Tiling* A square floor is to be tiled with square tiles as shown at the top of the next column, with blue tiles on the main diagonals and red tiles everywhere else. (In all cases, both blue and red tiles must be used and the two diagonals must have a common blue tile at the center of the floor.)

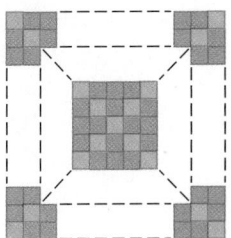

(a) If 81 blue tiles will be used, how many red tiles will be needed?

(b) For what numbers in place of 81 would this problem still be solvable?

(c) Find an expression in k giving the number of red tiles required in general.

65. *Shaking Hands in a Group* Chris Heister and his son were among four father-and-son pairs who gathered to trade baseball cards. As each person arrived, he shook hands with anyone he had not known previously. Each person ended up making a different number of new acquaintances (0–6), except Chris and his son, who each met the same number of people. How many hands did Chris shake?

*In Exercises 66 and 67, restate the given counting problem in two ways, first **(a)** using the word* repetition, *and then **(b)** using the word* replacement.

66. Example 2

67. Example 4

10.2 USING THE FUNDAMENTAL COUNTING PRINCIPLE

Uniformity and the Fundamental Counting Principle • Factorials
• Arrangements of Objects

Uniformity and the Fundamental Counting Principle

In **Section 10.1,** we obtained complete lists of all possible results for various tasks. However, if the total number of possibilities is all we need to know, then an actual listing usually is unnecessary and often is difficult or tedious to obtain, especially when the list is long.

Figure 6 repeats **Figure 2** of **Section 10.1** (for **Example 6(b)**), which shows all possible nonrepeating three-digit numbers using only the digits 1, 2, and 3.

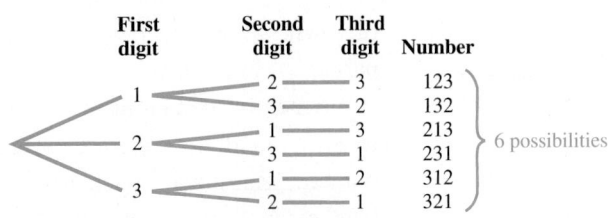

Figure 6

The tree diagram in **Figure 6** is "uniform" in the sense that a given part of the task can be done in the same number of ways no matter which choices were selected for previous parts. For example, there are always two choices for the second digit. (If the first digit is 1, the second can be 2 or 3. If the first is 2, the second can be 1 or 3. If the first is 3, the second can be 1 or 2.)

Example 6(a) of **Section 10.1** addressed the same basic situation:

> *Find the number of three-digit numbers that can be written using the digits 1, 2, and 3.*

In that case repetitions were allowed. With repetitions allowed, there were many more possibilities (27 rather than 6—see **Figure 1** of **Section 10.1**). But the uniformity criterion mentioned above still applied. No matter what the first digit is, there are three choices for the second (1, 2, 3). And no matter what the first and second digits are, there are three choices for the third. This uniformity criterion can be stated in general as follows.

Uniformity Criterion for Multiple-Part Tasks

A multiple-part task is said to satisfy the **uniformity criterion** if the number of choices for any particular part is the same *no matter which choices were selected for previous parts.*

The uniformity criterion is not always satisfied. Refer to **Example 7** (and **Figure 3**) of **Section 10.1**. After the first switch (two possibilities), other switches had either one or two possible settings depending on how previous switches were set. (This "nonuniformity" arose, in that case, from the requirement that no two adjacent switches could both be off.)

In the many cases where uniformity does hold, we can avoid having to construct a tree diagram by using the **fundamental counting principle,** stated as follows.

Fundamental Counting Principle

When a task consists of k separate parts and satisfies the uniformity criterion, if the first part can be done in n_1 ways, the second part can then be done in n_2 ways, and so on through the kth part, which can be done in n_k ways, then the total number of ways to complete the task is given by the product

$$n_1 \cdot n_2 \cdot n_3 \cdot \ldots \cdot n_k.$$

PROBLEM-SOLVING HINT A problem-solving strategy suggested in **Chapter 1** was: "*If a formula applies, use it.*" The fundamental counting principle provides a formula that applies to a variety of problems. The trick is to visualize the "task" at hand as being accomplished in a sequence of two or more separate parts.

A helpful technique when applying the fundamental counting principle is to write out all the separate parts of the task, with a blank for each one. Reason out how many ways each part can be done, and enter these numbers in the blanks. Finally, multiply these numbers together.

Richard Dedekind (1831–1916) studied at the University of Göttingen, where he was Gauss's last student. His work was not recognized during his lifetime, but his treatment of the infinite and of what constitutes a real number are influential even today.

While on vacation in Switzerland, Dedekind met Georg Cantor (profiled on **page 44**). Dedekind was interested in Cantor's work on infinite sets. Perhaps because both were working in new and unusual fields of mathematics, such as number theory, and because neither received the professional attention he deserved during his lifetime, the two struck up a lasting friendship.

▮▮ **EXAMPLE 1** Counting the Two-Digit Numbers

How many two-digit numbers are there in our (base-ten) system of counting numbers? (**While 40 is a two-digit number, 04 is not.**)

SOLUTION

Our "task" here is to select, or construct, a two-digit number. Set up the work as follows.

Part of task	Select first digit	Select second digit
Number of ways	_____	_____

There are nine choices for the first digit (1 through 9). Since there were no stated or implied restrictions, we assume that repetition of digits is allowed. Therefore, no matter which nonzero digit is used as the first digit, all nine choices are available for the second digit. Also, unlike the first digit, the second digit may be zero, so we have ten choices for the second digit. We can now fill in the blanks and multiply.

Part of task	Select first digit		Select second digit	
Number of ways	9	·	10	= 90

There are 90 two-digit numbers. (As a check, notice that they are the numbers from 10 through 99, a total of $99 - 10 + 1 = 90$.) ▮▮▮

▮▮ **EXAMPLE 2** Building Two-Digit Numbers with Restrictions

Find the number of two-digit numbers that do not contain repeated digits.

SOLUTION

The basic task is again to select a two-digit number, and there are two parts:

1. Select the first digit.   **2.** Select the second digit.

But a new restriction applies—no repetition of digits. There are nine choices for the first digit (1 through 9). Then nine choices remain for the second digit, since one nonzero digit has been used and cannot be repeated, but zero is now available. The total number is $9 \cdot 9 = 81$. ▮▮▮

▮▮ **EXAMPLE 3** Electing Club Officers with Restrictions

In how many ways can Club N of the previous section elect a president and a secretary if no one may hold more than one office and the secretary must be a man?

SOLUTION

Recall that $N = \{A, B, C, D, E\} = \{$Alan, Bill, Cathy, David, Evelyn$\}$. Considering president first, there are five choices (no restrictions). But now we have a problem with finding the number of choices for secretary. If a woman was selected president (C or E), there are three choices for secretary (A, B, and D). If a man was selected president, only two choices (the other two men) remain for secretary. ***In other words, the uniformity criterion is not met and our attempt to apply the fundamental counting principle has failed.***

All is not lost, however. To find the total number of ways, we can consider secretary first. There are three choices (A, B, and D). Now, no matter which man was chosen secretary, both of the other men, and both women, are available for president (four choices in every case). In this order, we satisfy the uniformity criterion and can use the fundamental counting principle. The total number of ways to elect a president and a secretary is $3 \cdot 4 = 12$. ▮▮▮

PROBLEM-SOLVING HINT **Example 3** suggests a useful problem-solving strategy: Whenever one or more parts of a task have special restrictions, try considering that part (or those parts) before other parts.

▮▮ **EXAMPLE 4** Counting Three-Digit Numbers with Restrictions

How many nonrepeating odd three-digit counting numbers are there?

SOLUTION

The most restricted digit is the third, since it must be odd. There are five choices (1, 3, 5, 7, and 9). Next, consider the first digit. It can be any nonzero digit except the one already chosen as the third digit. There are eight choices. Finally, the second digit can be any digit (including 0) except for the two (nonzero) digits already used. There are eight choices.

Part of task	Select third digit	Select first digit	Select second digit	
Number of ways	5 ·	8 ·	8	= 320

There are 320 nonrepeating odd three-digit counting numbers. ▮▮▮

▮▮ **EXAMPLE 5** Counting License Plates

In some states, auto license plates have contained three letters followed by three digits. How many such licenses are possible?

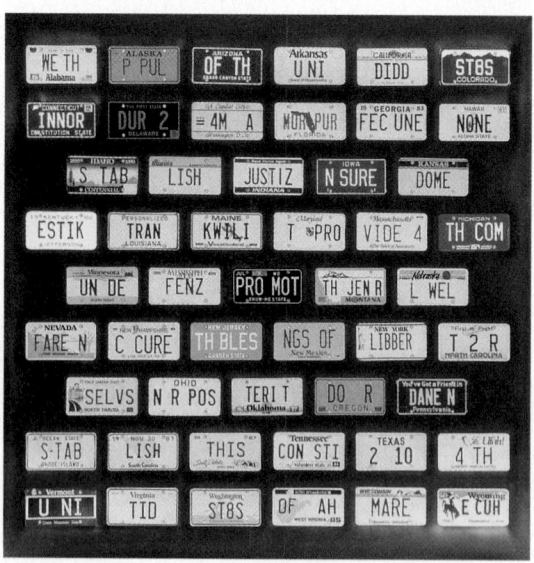

SOLUTION

The basic task is to design a license plate with three letters followed by three digits. There are six component parts to this task. Since there are no restrictions on letters or digits, the fundamental counting principle gives

$$26 \cdot 26 \cdot 26 \cdot 10 \cdot 10 \cdot 10 = 26^3 \cdot 10^3 = 17{,}576{,}000 \text{ possible licenses.}$$

(In practice, a few of the possible sequences of letters are considered undesirable and are not used.) ▮▮▮

▮▮ EXAMPLE 6 │ Building Numbers with Specified Digits

A four-digit number is to be constructed using only the digits 1, 2, and 3.

(a) How many such numbers are possible?

(b) How many of these numbers are odd and less than 2000?

SOLUTION

(a) To construct such a number, we must select four digits, in succession, from the given set of three digits, where the selection is done with replacement (since repetition of digits is apparently allowed). The number of possibilities is

$$3 \cdot 3 \cdot 3 \cdot 3 = 3^4 = 81 \quad \text{Fundamental counting principle}$$

(b) The number is less than 2000 only if the first digit is 1 (just one choice) and is odd only if the fourth digit is 1 or 3 (two choices). The second and third digits are unrestricted (three choices for each). The answer is

$$1 \cdot 3 \cdot 3 \cdot 2 = 18.$$

As a check, can you list the eighteen possibilities?   ▮▮▮

> **PROBLEM-SOLVING HINT** Two of the problem-solving strategies of **Chapter 1** were to "*First solve a similar simpler problem,*" and to "*Look for a pattern.*" In fact, a counting problem may sometimes prove to be essentially the same, or at least fit the same pattern, as another problem already solved.

▮▮ EXAMPLE 7 │ Distributing Golf Clubs

Vern has four antique wood head golf clubs that he wants to give to his three sons, Mark, Chris, and Scott.

(a) How many ways can the clubs be distributed?

(b) How many choices are there if the power driver must go to Mark and the number 3 wood must go to either Chris or Scott?

SOLUTION

(a) The task is to distribute four clubs among three sons. Consider the clubs in succession, and, for each one, ask how many sons could receive it. In effect, we must select four sons, in succession, from the list Mark, Chris, Scott, selecting with replacement. Compare this with **Example 6(a),** in which we selected four digits, in succession, from the digits 1, 2, and 3, selecting with replacement. In this case, we are selecting sons rather than digits, but the pattern is the same and the numbers are the same. Again our answer is

$$3^4 = 81.$$

(b) Just as in **Example 6(b),** one part of the task is now restricted to a single choice and another part is restricted to two choices. As in that example, the number of possibilities is

$$1 \cdot 3 \cdot 3 \cdot 2 = 18.$$ ▮▮▮

Answer to the Chapter Opener Question The Super Bowl announcer was pretty close. Since each coin must fall in one of two ways (heads or tails), the 13 consecutive NFC wins was just one of

$$2^{13} = 8192 \text{ possibilities.}$$

▮▮ **EXAMPLE 8** Seating Attendees at a Concert

Rework **Example 8** of **Section 10.1,** this time using the fundamental counting principle.

SOLUTION

Recall that Arne, Bobbette, Chuck, and Deirdre (A, B, C, and D) are to seat themselves in four adjacent seats (say 1, 2, 3, and 4) so that A and B are side-by-side. One approach to accomplish this task is to make three successive decisions as follows.

1. Which pair of seats should A and B occupy? There are *three* choices (1 and 2, 2 and 3, 3 and 4, as illustrated in the margin).
2. Which order should A and B take? There are *two* choices (A left of B, or B left of A).
3. Which order should C and D take? There are *two* choices (C left of D, or D left of C, not necessarily right next to each other).

1	2	3	4
X	X	_	_
_	X	X	_
_	_	X	X

Seats available to A and B

(Why did we not ask which two seats C and D should occupy?) The fundamental counting principle now gives the total number of choices:

$$3 \cdot 2 \cdot 2 = 12 \quad \text{Same result as in Section 10.1}$$

▮▮▮

Factorials

This section began with a discussion of nonrepeating three-digit numbers using digits 1, 2, and 3. The number of possibilities was

$$3 \cdot 2 \cdot 1 = 6. \quad \text{Fundamental counting principle}$$

That product can also be thought of as the total number of distinct *arrangements* of the three digits 1, 2, and 3.

Similarly, the number of distinct arrangements of four objects, say A, B, C, and D, is

$$4 \cdot 3 \cdot 2 \cdot 1 = 24. \quad \text{Fundamental counting principle}$$

Since this type of product occurs so commonly in applications, we give it a special name and symbol as follows. For any counting number n, the product of *all* counting numbers from n down through 1 is called **n factorial,** and is denoted **$n!$**.

Short Table of Factorials Factorial values increase rapidly. The value of 100! is a number with 158 digits.

$$0! = 1$$
$$1! = 1$$
$$2! = 2$$
$$3! = 6$$
$$4! = 24$$
$$5! = 120$$
$$6! = 720$$
$$7! = 5040$$
$$8! = 40,320$$
$$9! = 362,880$$
$$10! = 3,628,800$$

Factorial Formula

For any counting number n, the quantity **n factorial** is given as follows.

$$n! = n(n - 1)(n - 2)\ldots2 \cdot 1$$

The first few factorial values are easily found by simple multiplication, but they rapidly become very large. The use of a calculator is advised in most cases.

PROBLEM-SOLVING HINT Sometimes expressions involving factorials can be evaluated easily by observing that, in general, $n! = n(n - 1)!$, $n! = n(n - 1)(n - 2)!$, and so on. For example,

$$8! = 8 \cdot 7!, \quad 12! = 12 \cdot 11 \cdot 10 \cdot 9!, \quad \text{and so on.}$$

This pattern is especially helpful in evaluating quotients of factorials, such as

$$\frac{10!}{8!} = \frac{10 \cdot 9 \cdot 8!}{8!} = 10 \cdot 9 = 90.$$

■■ **EXAMPLE 9** Evaluating Expressions Containing Factorials

Evaluate each expression.

(a) $3!$ **(b)** $6!$ **(c)** $(6 - 3)!$ **(d)** $6! - 3!$

(e) $\dfrac{6!}{3!}$ **(f)** $\left(\dfrac{6}{3}\right)!$ **(g)** $15!$ **(h)** $100!$

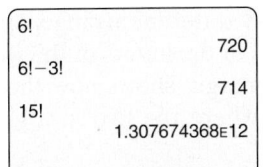

The results of **Example 9(b), (d), and (g)** are illustrated in this calculator screen.

SOLUTION

(a) $3! = 3 \cdot 2 \cdot 1 = 6$

(b) $6! = 6 \cdot 5 \cdot 4 \cdot 3 \cdot 2 \cdot 1 = 720$

(c) $(6 - 3)! = 3! = 6$

(d) $6! - 3! = 720 - 6 = 714$

(e) $\dfrac{6!}{3!} = \dfrac{6 \cdot 5 \cdot 4 \cdot 3!}{3!} = 6 \cdot 5 \cdot 4 = 120$ Note application of the Problem-Solving Hint.

(f) $\left(\dfrac{6}{3}\right)! = 2! = 2 \cdot 1 = 2$

(g) $15! = 1.307674368000 \times 10^{12}$ ← Done on a calculator

(h) $100! = 9.332621544 \times 10^{157}$ ← Too large for most calculators

Notice the distinction between parts (c) and (d) and between parts (e) and (f).   ■■■

So that factorials will be defined for all whole numbers, including zero, we define $0!$ as follows.

The definition $0! = 1$ is illustrated here.

> **Definition of Zero Factorial**
>
> $$0! = 1$$

(We will see later that this special definition makes other results easier to state.)

Arrangements of Objects

When finding the total number of ways to *arrange* a given number of distinct objects, we can use a factorial. The fundamental counting principle would do, but factorials provide a shortcut.

> **Arrangements of *n* Distinct Objects**
>
> The total number of different ways to arrange *n* distinct objects is *n!*.

■■ **EXAMPLE 10** Arranging Essays

Michelle Cook has seven essays to include in her English 1A folder. In how many different orders can she arrange them?

SOLUTION

The number of ways to arrange seven distinct objects is $7! = 5040$.   ■■■

▮▮ **EXAMPLE 11** Arranging Preschoolers

Tricia Caruso is taking thirteen preschoolers to the park. How many ways can the children line up, in single file, to board the van?

SOLUTION

Thirteen children can be arranged in $13! = 6{,}227{,}020{,}800$ different ways. ▮▮▮

D_1AD_2
D_2AD_1

D_1D_2A
D_2D_1A

AD_1D_2
AD_2D_1

In counting arrangements of objects that contain look-alikes, the normal factorial formula must be modified to find the number of truly different arrangements. For example, the number of distinguishable arrangements of the letters of the word DAD is not $3! = 6$ but rather $\frac{3!}{2!} = 3$. The listing in the margin shows how the six total arrangements consist of just three groups of two, where the two in a given group look alike.

Arrangements of n Objects Containing Look-Alikes

The number of **distinguishable arrangements** of n objects, where one or more subsets consist of look-alikes (say n_1 are of one kind, n_2 are of another kind, ..., and n_k are of yet another kind), is given by

$$\frac{n!}{n_1!\,n_2!\,\ldots\,n_k!}.$$

▮▮ **EXAMPLE 12** Counting Distinguishable Arrangements

Determine the number of distinguishable arrangements of the letters in each word.

(a) ATTRACT   **(b)** NIGGLING

SOLUTION

(a) For the letters of ATTRACT, the number of distinguishable arrangements is

$$7 \text{ letters total} \longrightarrow \frac{7!}{3!\,2!} = 420.$$
$$3 \text{ T's, 2 A's} \longrightarrow$$

(b) For the letters of NIGGLING, the number of distinguishable arrangements is

$$8 \text{ letters total} \longrightarrow \frac{8!}{2!\,2!\,3!} = 1680.$$
$$2 \text{ N's, 2 I's, 3 G's} \longrightarrow$$
▮▮▮

For Further Thought

Stirling's Approximation for *n*!

Although all factorial values are counting numbers, they can be approximated using **Stirling's formula,**

$$n! \approx \sqrt{2\pi n} \cdot n^n \cdot e^{-n},$$

which involves two famous irrational numbers, π and e. For example, while the exact value of $5!$ is $5 \cdot 4 \cdot 3 \cdot 2 \cdot 1 = 120$, the corresponding approximation is

$$5! \approx \sqrt{2\pi \cdot 5} \cdot 5^5 \cdot e^{-5} \approx 118.019168,$$

which is off by less than 2, an error of only 1.65%.

For Group or Individual Investigation

Use a calculator to fill in all values in the table on the next page. The column values are defined as follows.

$C = n!$ (exact value, by calculator)
$S \approx n!$ (Stirling's approximation, by calculator)
$D = $ Difference $(C - S)$
$P = $ Percentage difference $\left(\dfrac{D}{C} \cdot 100\%\right)$

n	C	S	D	P
1				
2				
3				
4				
5				
6				
7				
8				
9				
10				

Try to obtain percentage differences accurate to two decimal places.

Based on your calculations, answer each question.

1. In general, is Stirling's approximation too low or too high?

2. Observe the values in the table as *n* grows larger.

(a) Do the differences (*D*) get larger or smaller?

(b) Do the percentage differences (*P*) get larger or smaller?

(c) Does Stirling's formula become more accurate or less accurate?

10.2 EXERCISES

1. Explain the fundamental counting principle in your own words.

2. Describe how factorials can be used in counting problems.

For Exercises 3–6, n and m are counting numbers. Do the following: **(a)** *Tell whether the given statement is true in general, and* **(b)** *explain your answer, using specific examples.*

3. $(n + m)! = n! + m!$

4. $(n \cdot m)! = n! \cdot m!$

5. $(n - m)! = n! - m!$

6. $n! = n(n - 1)!$

Evaluate each expression without using a calculator.

7. $4!$

8. $6!$

9. $\dfrac{9!}{7!}$

10. $\dfrac{16!}{14!}$

11. $\dfrac{5!}{(5 - 2)!}$

12. $\dfrac{6!}{(6 - 3)!}$

13. $\dfrac{8!}{6!(8 - 6)!}$

14. $\dfrac{10!}{4!(10 - 4)!}$

15. $\dfrac{n!}{(n - r)!}$, where $n = 7$ and $r = 4$

16. $\dfrac{n!}{r!(n - r)!}$, where $n = 12$ and $r = 4$

Evaluate each expression using a calculator.

17. $10!$

18. $14!$

19. $\dfrac{12!}{5!}$

20. $\dfrac{13!}{(13 - 6)!}$

21. $\dfrac{20!}{10! \cdot 10!}$

22. $\dfrac{19!}{9! \cdot 10!}$

23. $\dfrac{n!}{(n - r)!}$, where $n = 17$ and $r = 8$

24. $\dfrac{n!}{r!(n - r)!}$, where $n = 24$ and $r = 18$

Arranging Letters   Find the number of distinguishable arrangements of the letters of each word.

25. GOOGOL

26. HEEBIE-JEEBIES

Settings on a Switch Panel   A panel containing three on–off switches in a row is to be set.

27. Assuming no restrictions on individual switches, use the fundamental counting principle to find the total number of possible panel settings.

28. Assuming no restrictions, construct a tree diagram to list all the possible panel settings of **Exercise 27.**

29. Now assume that no two adjacent switches can both be off. Explain why the fundamental counting principle does not apply.

30. Construct a tree diagram to list all possible panel settings under the restriction of **Exercise 29.**

31. *Rolling Dice* **Table 2** in the previous section shows that there are 36 possible outcomes when two fair dice are rolled. How many would there be if three fair dice were rolled?

32. *Counting Five-Digit Numbers* How many five-digit numbers are there in our system of counting numbers?

33. *Bowling* After rolling the first ball of a frame in a game of 10-pin bowling, how many different pin configurations can remain (assuming all configurations are physically possible)? (*Mathematics Teacher* calendar problem)

34. *Bowling* Answer the question of **Exercise 33** assuming that pins 1, 2, and 3 were knocked down on the first roll.

Matching Club Members with Tasks *Recall the club*

$$N = \{\text{Alan, Bill, Cathy, David, Evelyn}\}.$$

In how many ways could they do each of the following?

35. line up all five members for a photograph

36. schedule one member to work in the office on each of five different days, assuming members may work more than one day

37. select a male and a female to decorate for a party

38. select two members, one to open their next meeting and another to close it, given that Bill will not be present

Building Numbers with Specified Digits *In Exercises 39–42, counting numbers are to be formed using only the digits 3, 4, and 5. Determine the number of different possibilities for each type of number described.*

39. two-digit numbers

40. odd three-digit numbers

41. four-digit numbers with one pair of adjacent 4s and no other repeated digits (*Hint:* You may want to split the task of designing such a number into three parts, such as *(1)* position the pair of 4s, *(2)* position the 3, and *(3)* position the 5.)

42. five-digit numbers beginning and ending with 3 and with unlimited repetitions allowed

Selecting Dinner Items *The Gourmet de Coeur Restaurant offers five choices in the soup and salad category (two soups and three salads), two choices in the bread category, and four choices in the entree category. Find the number of dinners available in each case.*

43. One item is to be included from each of the three categories.

44. Only salad and entree are to be included.

Selecting Answers on a Test *Determine the number of possible ways to mark your answer sheet (with an answer for each question) for each test.*

45. a six-question true-or-false test

46. a ten-question multiple-choice test with five answer choices for each question

Selecting a College Class Schedule *Jessica Elbern's class schedule for next semester must consist of exactly one class from each of the four categories shown in the table at the top of the next column.*

For each situation in Exercises 47–52, use the table to determine the number of different sets of classes Jessica can take.

Category	Choices	Number of Choices
Economics	Free Markets Controlled Markets	2
Mathematics	History of Mathematics College Algebra Finite Mathematics	3
Education	Classroom Technology Group Dynamics Language Supervision Parent/Teacher Relations	4
Sociology	Social Problems Sociology of the Middle East Aging in America Minorities in America Women in American Culture	5

47. All classes shown are available.

48. She is not eligible for Free Markets or for Group Dynamics.

49. All sections of Minorities in America and Women in American Culture already are filled.

50. She does not have the prerequisites for Controlled Markets, College Algebra, or Language Supervision.

51. Funding has been withdrawn for three of the Education courses and for two of the Sociology courses.

52. She must complete Finite Mathematics and Social Problems next semester to fulfill her degree requirements.

53. *Selecting Clothing* Don Beville took two pairs of shoes, four pairs of pants, and six shirts on a trip. If all items are compatible, how many different outfits can he wear?

54. *Selecting Music Equipment* A music equipment outlet stocks ten different guitars, three guitar cases, six amplifiers, and five effects processors, with all items mutually compatible and all suitable for beginners. How many different complete setups could Lionel choose to start his musical career?

55. *Counting ZIP Codes* Tonya's ZIP code is 85726. How many ZIP codes altogether could be formed, each one using those same five digits?

56. *Listing Phone Numbers* John Cross keeps the phone numbers for his seven closest friends (three men and four women) in his digital phone memory. (Refer to **Example 8.**) How many ways can he list them if

(a) men are listed before women?

(b) men are all listed together?

(c) no two men are listed next to each other?

57. **Counting Telephone Area Codes** Until 1995, the rules for three-digit area codes in the United States were as follows:

- The first digit could not be 0 or 1.
- The second digit had to be 0 or 1.
- The third digit had no such restrictions.

In 1995, the restriction on the second digit of area codes was removed. How many area codes are currently possible? (*Mathematics Teacher* calendar problem)

Seating Arrangements at a Theater *In Exercises 58–61, Arne, Bobbette, Chuck, Deirdre, Ed, and Fran have reserved six seats in a row at the theater, starting at an aisle seat. (Refer to Example 8.)*

58. In how many ways can they arrange themselves? (*Hint:* Divide the task into the series of six parts shown below, performed in order.)

(a) If *A* is seated first, how many seats are available for him?

(b) Now, how many are available for *B*?

(c) Now, how many for *C*?

(d) Now, how many for *D*?

(e) Now, how many for *E*?

(f) Now, how many for *F*?

Now multiply together your six answers above.

59. In how many ways can they arrange themselves so that Arne and Bobbette will be next to each other?

Seats available to *A* and *B*

(*Hint:* Answer these questions, in order.)

(a) How many pairs of adjacent seats can *A* and *B* occupy?

(b) Now, given the two seats for *A* and *B*, in how many orders can they be seated?

(c) Now, how many seats are available for *C*?

(d) Now, how many for *D*?

(e) Now, how many for *E*?

(f) Now, how many for *F*?

Now multiply your six answers above.

60. In how many ways can they arrange themselves if the men and women are to alternate seats and a man must sit on the aisle? (*Hint:* Answer the questions at the top of the next column, in order.)

(a) How many choices are there for the person to occupy the first seat, next to the aisle? (It must be a man.)

(b) Now, how many choices of people may occupy the second seat from the aisle? (It must be a woman.)

(c) Now, how many for the third seat? (one of the remaining men)

(d) Now, how many for the fourth seat? (a woman)

(e) Now, how many for the fifth seat? (a man)

(f) Now, how many for the sixth seat? (a woman)

Now multiply your six answers above.

61. In how many ways can they arrange themselves if the men and women are to alternate with either a man or a woman on the aisle? (*Hint:* Answer these questions.)

(a) How many choices of people are there for the aisle seat?

(b) Now, how many are there for the second seat? (This person may not be of the same sex as the person on the aisle.)

(c) Now, how many choices are there for the third seat?

(d) Now, how many for the fourth seat?

(e) Now, how many for the fifth seat?

(f) Now, how many for the sixth seat?

Now multiply your six answers above.

62. Try working **Example 4** by considering digits in the order first, then second, then third. Explain what goes wrong.

63. Try working **Example 4** by considering digits in the order third, then second, then first. Explain what goes wrong.

64. Repeat **Example 4** but this time allow repeated digits. Does the order in which digits are considered matter in this case?

65. If all the six-digit numbers formed by using the digits 1, 2, 3, 4, 5, and 6, without repetition, are listed from least to greatest, which number will be 500th in the list? (*Mathematics Teacher* calendar problem)

66. The number $2^7 \cdot 3^4 \cdot 5 \cdot 7^2 \cdot 11^3$ is divisible by many perfect squares. How many? (*Mathematics Teacher* calendar problem)

67. How many of the anagrams [arrangements of the letters] of INDIANA are palindromes, that is arrangements that read the same forward and backward? *Hint:* One such palindrome is INADANI. (*Mathematics Teacher* calendar problem)

68. How many distinguishable rearrangements of the letters in the word CONTEST start with the two vowels? (*Mathematics Teacher* calendar problem)

▌ ▌ ▌ ▌ ▌ ▌▌ ▌▌ ▌▌▌

10.3 USING PERMUTATIONS AND COMBINATIONS

Permutations • Combinations • Guidelines on Which Method to Use

Permutations

Again recall the club

$$N = \{\text{Alan, Bill, Cathy, David, Evelyn}\} = \{A, B, C, D, E\},$$

and consider two questions:

1. How many ways can all the club members arrange themselves in a row for a photograph?
2. How many ways can the club elect a president, a secretary, and a treasurer if no one can hold more than one office?

From **Section 10.2,** the answer to the first question above is

$$5! = 5 \cdot 4 \cdot 3 \cdot 2 \cdot 1 = 120,$$

the number of possible arrangements of 5 distinct objects. We previously answered questions like the second one by using a tree diagram, or the fundamental counting principle. The answer is

$$5 \cdot 4 \cdot 3 = 60.$$

A good way to think of this second question is:

How many arrangements are there of five things taken three at a time?

The factors begin with 5 and proceed downward, just as in a factorial product, but do not go all the way to 1. (In this example the product stops when there are three factors.)

In the context of counting problems, arrangements are called **permutations.** The number of permutations of n distinct things taken r at a time is denoted $_nP_r$.* Since the number of objects being arranged cannot exceed the total number available, we assume that $r \leq n$. Applying the fundamental counting principle gives

$$_nP_r = n(n-1)(n-2)\ldots[n-(r-1)].$$

The first factor is $n - 0$, the second is $n - 1$, the third is $n - 2$, and so on. The rth factor, the last one in the product, will be the one with $r - 1$ subtracted from n, as shown above. We can express permutations, in general, in terms of factorials, to obtain a formula as follows.

$$
\begin{aligned}
_nP_r &= n(n-1)(n-2)\ldots[n-(r-1)] \\
&= n(n-1)(n-2)\ldots(n-r+1) && \text{Simplify the last factor.} \\
&= \frac{n(n-1)(n-2)\ldots(n-r+1)(n-r)(n-r-1)\ldots2\cdot1}{(n-r)(n-r-1)\ldots2\cdot1} && \begin{array}{l}\text{Multiply and divide by} \\ (n-r)(n-r-1)\ldots2\cdot1.\end{array} \\
&= \frac{n!}{(n-r)!} && \text{Definition of factorial}
\end{aligned}
$$

---

*Alternative notations are $P(n, r)$ and P_r^n.

Factorial Formula for Permutations

The number of **permutations,** or *arrangements,* of n distinct things taken r at a time, where $r \leq n$, can be calculated as follows.

$$_nP_r = \frac{n!}{(n-r)!}$$

Although we sometimes refer to a symbol such as $_4P_2$ as "a permutation"(see **Examples 1 and 2**), the symbol actually represents "the number of permutations of 4 distinct things taken 2 at a time" (or "the number of size-2 arrangements that can be selected from 4 distinct things").

▮▮ **EXAMPLE 1** Using the Factorial Formula for Permutations

Evaluate each permutation.

(a) $_4P_2$ **(b)** $_8P_5$ **(c)** $_5P_5$

SOLUTION

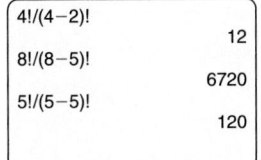

4!/(4−2)!
                        12
8!/(8−5)!
                      6720
5!/(5−5)!
                       120

This screen uses factorials to support the results of **Example 1**.

(a) $_4P_2 = \dfrac{4!}{(4-2)!} = \dfrac{4!}{2!} = \dfrac{24}{2} = 12$

(b) $_8P_5 = \dfrac{8!}{(8-5)!} = \dfrac{8!}{3!} = \dfrac{40{,}320}{6} = 6720$ $\dfrac{1 \cdot 2 \cdot 3 \cdot 4 \cdot 5 \cdot 6 \cdot 7 \cdot 8}{1 \cdot 2 \cdot 3} = 6720$

(c) $_5P_5 = \dfrac{5!}{(5-5)!} = \dfrac{5!}{0!} = \dfrac{120}{1} = 120$ ▮▮▮

Notice that $_5P_5$ is equal to $5!$. The following is true for all whole numbers n.

$$_nP_n = n!$$

(This is the number of arrangements of n distinct objects taken all n at a time.)

Most graphing and scientific calculators allow direct calculation of permutations, in which case the factorial formula is not needed.

▮▮ **EXAMPLE 2** Calculating Permutations Directly

Evaluate each permutation.

10 nPr 6
                    151200
20 nPr 0
                          1
18 nPr 12
              8.892185702E12

This screen uses the permutations feature to support the results of **Example 2**.

(a) $_{10}P_6$ **(b)** $_{28}P_0$ **(c)** $_{18}P_{12}$

SOLUTION

(a) $_{10}P_6 = 151{,}200$ **(b)** $_{28}P_0 = 1$ **(c)** $_{18}P_{12} = 8{,}892{,}185{,}702{,}400$

Concerning part (c), many calculators will not display this many digits, so you may obtain an answer such as 8.8921857×10^{12}.   ▮▮▮

PROBLEM-SOLVING HINT Permutations can be used any time we need to know the number of arrangements of r objects that can be selected from a collection of n objects. The word *arrangement* implies an ordering, so we use permutations only in cases when

1. repetitions are not allowed,   and   **2. order is important.**

Change ringing, the English way of ringing church bells, combines mathematics and music. Bells are rung first in sequence, 1, 2, 3, ... Then the sequence is permuted ("changed"). On six bells, 720 different "changes" (different permutations of tone) can be rung:
$$_6P_6 = 6!.$$
The church bells are swung by means of ropes attached to the wheels beside them. One ringer swings each bell, listening intently and watching the other ringers closely. If one ringer gets lost and stays lost, the rhythm of the ringing cannot be maintained; all the ringers have to stop.

A ringer can spend weeks just learning to keep a bell going and months learning to make the bell ring in exactly the right place. Errors of $\frac{1}{4}$ second mean that two bells are ringing at the same time. Even errors of $\frac{1}{10}$ second can be heard.

■ **EXAMPLE 3**   Building Numbers from a Set of Digits

How many nonrepeating three-digit numbers can be written using only the digits 3, 4, 5, 6, 7, and 8?

SOLUTION

Repetitions are not allowed since the numbers are to be "nonrepeating." (For example, 448 is not acceptable.) Also, order is important. (For example, 476 and 746 are *distinct* cases.) So we use permutations.

$$_6P_3 = 6 \cdot 5 \cdot 4 = 120$$

■■■

■ **EXAMPLE 4**   Designing Account Numbers

Suppose certain account numbers are to consist of two letters followed by four digits and then three more letters, where repetitions of letters or digits are not allowed *within* any of the three groups, but the last group of letters may contain one or both of those used in the first group. How many such accounts are possible?

SOLUTION

The task of designing such a number consists of three parts:

1. Determine the first set of two letters.
2. Determine the set of four digits.
3. Determine the final set of three letters.

Each part requires an arrangement without repetitions, which is a permutation. Multiply together the results of the three parts.

$$_{26}P_2 \cdot {}_{10}P_4 \cdot {}_{26}P_3 = \underbrace{650}_{\text{Part 1}} \cdot \underbrace{5040}_{\text{Part 2}} \cdot \underbrace{15{,}600}_{\text{Part 3}}$$

$$= 51{,}105{,}600{,}000$$

■■■

Combinations

We introduced permutations to evaluate the number of arrangements of n things taken r at a time, where repetitions are not allowed. The order of the items was important. Recall that club

$$N = \{\text{Alan, Bill, Cathy, David, Evelyn}\}$$

could elect three officers in $_5P_3 = 60$ different ways. With three-member committees, on the other hand, order is not important. The committees B, D, E and E, B, D are not different. The possible number of committees is not the number of arrangements of size 3. Rather, it is the number of *subsets* of size 3.

Recall that in the study of sets (**Chapter 2**), a **set** is a collection or group of things, commonly designated using a list within braces, as we have been designating the club

$$N = \{A, B, C, D, E\}.$$

The order of listing of the members (of any set) is unimportant. For example, $\{D, B, A, E, C\}$ is the same club. A **subset** of a set is a collection of some of the members. It may be all members of the original set, or even none of them, or anywhere in between. Again, the order of listing of the members is unimportant.

In the study of counting methods, subsets are called **combinations.** The number of combinations of n things taken r at a time (that is, the number of size r subsets, given a set of size n) is written $_nC_r$.*

> *Since there are n things available and we are choosing r of them, we can read $_nC_r$ as "n choose r."*

The size-3 committees (subsets) of the club (set) $N = \{A, B, C, D, E\}$ are:

$$\{A, B, C\}, \quad \{A, B, D\}, \quad \{A, B, E\}, \quad \{A, C, D\}, \quad \{A, C, E\},$$
$$\{A, D, E\}, \quad \{B, C, D\}, \quad \{B, C, E\}, \quad \{B, D, E\}, \quad \{C, D, E\}.$$

There are ten subsets of size 3, so ten is the number of three-member committees possible. Just as with permutations, repetitions are not allowed. For example, $\{E, E, B\}$ is not a valid three-member subset, just as EEB is not a valid three-member arrangement.

To see how to find the number of such subsets without listing them all, notice that each size-3 subset (combination) gives rise to six size-3 arrangements (permutations). For example, the single combination ADE yields these six permutations:

$$A, D, E \quad A, E, D \quad D, A, E \quad D, E, A \quad E, A, D \quad E, D, A.$$

There must be six times as many size-3 permutations as there are size-3 combinations, or, in other words, one-sixth as many combinations as permutations.

$$_5C_3 = \frac{_5P_3}{6} = \frac{60}{6} = 10$$

Again, the 6 appears in the denominator because there are six different ways to arrange a set of three things (since $3! = 3 \cdot 2 \cdot 1 = 6$). Generalizing from this example, we obtain a formula for evaluating numbers of combinations.

$$_nC_r = \frac{_nP_r}{r!} \qquad \text{\small r things can be arranged in $r!$ ways.}$$

$$= \frac{\dfrac{n!}{(n-r)!}}{r!} \qquad \text{\small Substitute the factorial formula for $_nP_r$.}$$

$$= \frac{n!}{r!(n-r)!} \qquad \text{\small Simplify algebraically.}$$

Factorial Formula for Combinations

The number of **combinations,** or *subsets,* of n distinct things taken r at a time, where $r \leq n$, can be calculated as follows.

$$_nC_r = \frac{_nP_r}{r!} = \frac{n!}{r!(n-r)!}$$

In **Examples 5 and 6,** we refer to $_nC_r$ as "a combination" even though it actually represents "the number of combinations of n distinct things taken r at a time" (or "the number of size-r subsets that can be selected from a set of n things").

---

*Alternative notations are $C(n, r)$, C_r^n, and $\binom{n}{r}$.

$$\begin{array}{cccccc} \mathcal{A} & \mathcal{B} & \mathcal{C} & \mathcal{D} & \mathcal{E} & \mathcal{F} \\ \text{\small Aaaaa} & \text{\small aaaab} & \text{\small aaaba.} & \text{\small aaabb.} & \text{\small aabaa.} & \text{\small aabab.} \\ \mathcal{G} & \mathcal{H} & \mathcal{I} & \mathcal{K} & \mathcal{L} & \mathcal{M} \\ \text{\small aabba} & \text{\small aabbb} & \text{\small abaaa.} & \text{\small abaab.} & \text{\small ababa.} & \text{\small ababb.} \\ \mathcal{N} & \mathcal{O} & \mathcal{P} & \mathcal{Q} & \mathcal{R} & \mathcal{S} \\ \text{\small abbaa.} & \text{\small abbab.} & \text{\small abbba.} & \text{\small abbbb.} & \text{\small baaaa.} & \text{\small baaab.} \\ \mathcal{T} & \mathcal{V} & \mathcal{W} & \mathcal{X} & \mathcal{Y} & \mathcal{Z} \\ \text{\small baaba.} & \text{\small baabb.} & \text{\small babaa.} & \text{\small babab.} & \text{\small babba.} & \text{\small babbb.} \end{array}$$

$\{\dot{A}Aaa\ BBbb\ CCcc\ DDdd\ EEee\ FFff$

$\{GGgg\ HHhh\ JIii\ KKkk\ LLll\ MMmm$

$\{NNnn\ OOoo\ PPpp\ QQqq\ RRrr\ SSss$

$\{TTtt\ VVvvuu\ WWww\ XXxx\ YYyy\ ZZzz$

"Bilateral cipher" (above) was invented by **Francis Bacon** early in the seventeenth century to code political secrets. This binary code, *a* and *b* in combinations of five, has 32 permutations. Bacon's "biformed alphabet" (bottom four rows) uses two type fonts to conceal a message in some straight text. The decoder deciphers a string of *as* and *bs*, groups them by fives, then deciphers letters and words. This code was applied to Shakespeare's plays in efforts to prove Bacon the rightful author.

EXAMPLE 5 Using the Factorial Formula for Combinations

Evaluate each combination.

(a) $_9C_7$ **(b)** $_{24}C_{18}$

SOLUTION

(a) $_9C_7 = \dfrac{9!}{7!(9-7)!} = \dfrac{9!}{7!\,2!} = \dfrac{362{,}880}{5040 \cdot 2} = 36$

(b) $_{24}C_{18} = \dfrac{24!}{18!(24-18)!} = \dfrac{24!}{18!\,6!} = 134{,}596$ ▮▮▮

```
9!/(7!*2!)
                        36
24!/(18!*6!)
                    134596
```
This screen uses factorials to support the results of **Example 5.**

EXAMPLE 6 Calculating Combinations Directly

Evaluate each combination.

(a) $_{14}C_6$ **(b)** $_{21}C_{15}$

SOLUTION

(a) $_{14}C_6 = 3003$ **(b)** $_{21}C_{15} = 54{,}264$ Use a calculator in each case. ▮▮▮

```
14 nCr 6
                      3003
21 nCr 15
                     54264
```
This screen uses the combinations feature to support the results of **Example 6.**

PROBLEM-SOLVING HINT Combinations have an important common property with permutations (repetitions are not allowed) and have an important distinction (order is *not* important with combinations). Combinations are applied only when

1. repetitions are not allowed, and **2. order is *not* important.**

EXAMPLE 7 Finding the Number of Subsets

Find the number of different subsets of size 2 in the set $\{a, b, c, d\}$. List them to check the answer.

SOLUTION

A subset of size 2 must have two distinct elements, so repetitions are not allowed. And since the order in which the elements of a set are listed makes no difference, order is not important. Use the combinations formula with $n = 4$ and $r = 2$.

$$_4C_2 = \dfrac{4!}{2!(4-2)!} = \dfrac{4!}{2!\,2!} = 6$$

The six subsets of size 2 are $\{a, b\}, \{a, c\}, \{a, d\}, \{b, c\}, \{b, d\}, \{c, d\}$. ▮▮▮

EXAMPLE 8 Finding the Number of Possible Poker Hands

A common form of poker involves "hands" (sets) of five cards each, dealt from a standard deck consisting of 52 different cards. How many different 5-card hands are possible?

SOLUTION

A 5-card hand must contain five distinct cards, so repetitions are not allowed. Also, the order is not important since a given hand depends only on the cards it contains, and not on the order in which they were dealt or the order in which they are displayed or played.

The set of 52 playing cards in the standard deck has four suits.

  ♠ spades   ♦ diamonds
  ♥ hearts   ♣ clubs

Ace is the unit card. Jacks, queens, and kings are "face cards." Each suit contains thirteen denominations: ace, 2, 3, . . . , 10, jack, queen, king. (In some games, ace rates above king, instead of counting as 1.)

Since order does not matter, use combinations (and a calculator).

$$_{52}C_5 = \frac{52!}{5!(52-5)!} = \frac{52!}{5!\,47!} = 2{,}598{,}960$$ ▮▮▮

▮▮ **EXAMPLE 9** Finding the Number of Subsets of Paintings

Keri Beers would like to buy ten different paintings but can afford only four of them. In how many ways can she make her selections?

SOLUTION

The four paintings selected must be distinct (repetitions are not allowed), and the order of the four chosen has no bearing in this case, so we use combinations.

$$_{10}C_4 = \frac{10!}{4!(10-4)!} = \frac{10!}{4!\,6!} = 210 \text{ ways}$$ ▮▮▮

Notice that, according to our formula for combinations,

$$_{10}C_6 = \frac{10!}{6!(10-6)!} = \frac{10!}{6!\,4!} = 210,$$

which is the same as $_{10}C_4$. In fact, **Exercise 62** asks you to prove the following fact, in general, for all whole numbers n and r, with $r \le n$.

$$_nC_r = {_nC_{n-r}}$$

Guidelines on Which Method to Use

The following table summarizes the similarities and differences between permutations and combinations, as well as the appropriate formulas for calculating their values.

Permutations	Combinations
Number of ways of selecting *r* items out of *n* items	
Repetitions are not allowed.	
Order is important.	Order is not important.
Arrangements of *n* items taken *r* at a time	Subsets of *n* items taken *r* at a time
$_nP_r = \dfrac{n!}{(n-r)!}$	$_nC_r = \dfrac{n!}{r!(n-r)!}$
Clue words: arrangement, schedule, order	Clue words: set, group, sample, selection

In cases where r items are to be selected from n items and repetitions are allowed, it is usually best to make direct use of the fundamental counting principle.

Most, if not all, of the exercises in this section will call for permutations and/or combinations. And in the case of multiple-part tasks, the fundamental counting principle may also be required. *In all cases, decide carefully whether order is important, since that determines whether to use permutations or combinations.*

PROBLEM-SOLVING HINT Many counting problems involve selecting some of the items from a given set of items. The particular conditions of the problem will determine which specific technique to use.

1. **If selected items can be repeated, use the fundamental counting principle.**
   Example: How many four-digit numbers are there?

   $$9 \cdot 10^3 = 9000$$

2. **If selected items cannot be repeated, and order is important, use permutations.**
   Example: How many ways can three of eight people line up at a ticket counter?

   $$_8P_3 = \frac{8!}{(8-3)!} = 336$$

3. **If selected items cannot be repeated, and order is *not* important, use combinations.**
   Example: How many ways can a committee of three be selected from a group of twelve people?

   $$_{12}C_3 = \frac{12!}{3!(12-3)!} = 220$$

▐▐ **EXAMPLE 10** Distributing Toys to Children

In how many ways can a mother distribute three different toys among her seven children if a child may receive anywhere from none to all three toys?

SOLUTION

Because a given child can be a repeat recipient, repetitions are allowed here, so we use the fundamental counting principle. Each of the three toys can go to any of the seven children. The number of possible distributions is $7 \cdot 7 \cdot 7 = 343$. ▐▐▐

▐▐ **EXAMPLE 11** Selecting Committees

How many different three-member committees could club N appoint so that exactly one woman is on the committee?

SOLUTION

Recall that $N = \{$Alan, Bill, Cathy, David, Evelyn$\}$. Two members are women; three are men. Although the question mentioned only that the committee must include exactly one woman, to complete the committee two men must be selected as well. The task of selecting the committee members consists of two parts:

1. Choose one woman.   2. Choose two men.

Because order is not important for committees, use combinations for the two parts. One woman can be chosen in $_2C_1 = \frac{2!}{1!1!} = 2$ ways, and two men can be chosen in $_3C_2 = \frac{3!}{2!1!} = 3$ ways. Finally, use the fundamental counting principle to obtain $2 \cdot 3 = 6$ different committees. This small number can be checked by listing.

$$\{C, A, B\}, \quad \{C, A, D\}, \quad \{C, B, D\}, \quad \{E, A, B\}, \quad \{E, A, D\}, \quad \{E, B, D\} \quad ▐▐▐$$

The illustration above is from the 1560s text **Logistica,** by the mathematician J. Buteo. Among other topics, the book discusses the number of possible throws of four dice and the number of arrangements of the cylinders of a combination lock. Note that "combination" is a misleading name for these locks since repetitions are allowed, and, also, order makes a difference.

███ **EXAMPLE 12** Selecting Attendees for an Event

Every member of the Alpha Beta Gamma fraternity would like to attend a special event this weekend, but only ten members will be allowed to attend. How many ways could the lucky ten be selected if there are a total of forty-eight members?

SOLUTION

In this case, ten distinct men are required (repetitions are not allowed), and the order of selection makes no difference, so we use combinations.

$$_{48}C_{10} = \frac{48!}{10! \, 38!} = 6,540,715,896 \quad \text{Use a calculator.} \quad ███$$

███ **EXAMPLE 13** Selecting Escorts

When the ten fraternity men of **Example 12** arrive at the event, four of them are selected to escort the four homecoming queen candidates. In how many ways can this selection be made?

SOLUTION

Of the ten, four distinct men are required, and order is important here because different orders will pair the men with different women. Use permutations.

$$_{10}P_4 = \frac{10!}{6!} = 5040 \text{ possible selections} \quad ███$$

███ **EXAMPLE 14** Dividing into Groups

In how many ways can the 9 members of a baseball lineup divide into groups of 4, 3, and 2 players?

SOLUTION

Order is not important within the groups. The players within a group are interchangeable in their order of listing. Use combinations.

First, 4 can be chosen from 9 in $_9C_4 = 126$ ways.

Then, 3 can be chosen from the remaining 5 in $_5C_3 = 10$ ways.

Then, 2 can be chosen from the remaining 2 in $_2C_2 = 1$ way.

The three groups also are not interchangeable. They all have different sizes. Apply the fundamental counting principle.

$$_9C_4 \cdot {_5C_3} \cdot {_2C_2} = 126 \cdot 10 \cdot 1 = 1260 \quad ███$$

███ **EXAMPLE 15** Dividing into Groups

In how many ways can the 9 players of **Example 14** divide into three groups of 3?

SOLUTION

After the pattern of **Example 14,** the answer may *seem* to be

$$_9C_3 \cdot {_6C_3} \cdot {_3C_3} = 84 \cdot 20 \cdot 1 = 1680.$$

However, this would impose an *unwanted order,* not within the groups, but *among* the groups. Ordering the three group selections was appropriate in **Example 14,** because those three groups were distinguishable. They were all different sizes. But here, all groups are size-3.

If the players are denoted $A, B, C, D, E, F, G, H,$ and I, then the list

(1) BIG, HEF, CAD **(2)** BIG, CAD, HEF **(3)** HEF, BIG, CAD
(4) HEF, CAD, BIG **(5)** CAD, BIG, HEF **(6)** CAD, HEF, BIG

contains six orderings of the same three groups. Since the product calculated above, from the fundamental counting principle, duplicates every set of three groups in this way, we must adjust that value by dividing by $3! = 6$ to obtain the true number of *unordered* sets of three groups. The idea is the same as when we adjust the number of arrangements—orderings—of n things taken r at a time to obtain the number of unordered sets of n things taken r at a time according to the formula

$$_nC_r = \frac{_nP_r}{r!}.$$

The number of ways 9 players can divide into three groups of 3 is

$$\frac{_9C_3 \cdot {}_6C_3 \cdot {}_3C_3}{3!} = \frac{1680}{6} = 280.$$ ▮▮▮

For Further Thought

Poker Hands

In 5-card poker, played with a standard 52-card deck, 2,598,960 different hands are possible. (See **Example 8.**) The desirability of the various hands depends upon their relative chance of occurrence, which, in turn, depends on the number of different ways they can occur, as shown in **Table 4.** Note that an ace can generally be positioned either below 2 (as a 1) or above king (as a 14). This is important in counting straight flush hands and straight hands.

Table 4   Categories of Hands in 5-Card Poker

Event E	Description of Event E	Number of Outcomes Favorable to E
Royal flush	Ace, king, queen, jack, and 10, all of the same suit	4
Straight flush	5 cards of consecutive denominations, all in the same suit (excluding royal flush)	36
Four of a kind	4 cards of the same denomination, plus 1 additional card	_____
Full house	3 cards of one denomination, plus 2 cards of a second denomination	3744
Flush	Any 5 cards all of the same suit (excluding royal flush and straight flush)	_____
Straight	5 cards of consecutive denominations (not all the same suit)	10,200
Three of a kind	3 cards of one denomination, plus 2 cards of two additional denominations	54,912
Two pairs	2 cards of one denomination, plus 2 cards of a second denomination, plus 1 card of a third denomination	_____
One pair	2 cards of one denomination, plus 3 additional cards of three different denominations	1,098,240
No pair	No two cards of the same denomination (and excluding any sort of flush or straight)	1,302,540
Total		**2,598,960**

For Group or Individual Investigation

As the table shows, a full house is a relatively rare occurrence. (Only four of a kind, straight flush, and royal flush are less likely.) To verify that there are 3744 different full house hands possible, carry out the following steps.

1. Explain why there are $_4C_3$ different ways to select three aces from the deck.

2. Explain why there are $_4C_2$ different ways to select two 8s from the deck.

3. If "aces and 8s" (three aces and two 8s) is one kind of full house, show that there are $_{13}P_2$ different kinds of full house altogether.

4. Multiply the expressions from Steps 1, 2, and 3 together. Explain why this product should give the total number of full house hands possible.

5. Find the three missing values in the right column of **Table 4**. (Answers are on **page 581**.)

6. Verify the right column total shown in **Table 4**.

10.3 EXERCISES

Evaluate each expression.

1. $_9P_3$

2. $_{12}P_5$

3. $_{11}C_7$

4. $_{14}C_6$

Determine the number of permutations (arrangements) of each of the following.

5. 20 things taken 4 at a time

6. 15 things taken 5 at a time

Determine the number of combinations (subsets) of each of the following.

7. 9 things taken 4 at a time

8. 13 things taken 6 at a time

Use a calculator to evaluate each expression.

9. $_{22}P_9$

10. $_{32}C_{12}$

11. Is it possible to evaluate $_8P_{10}$? Explain.

12. Is it possible to evaluate $_9C_{14}$? Explain.

13. Explain how permutations and combinations differ.

14. Explain how factorials are related to permutations.

15. *Permutations or Combinations?* Decide whether each object is a permutation or a combination.

(a) a telephone number

(b) a Social Security number

(c) a hand of cards in poker

(d) a committee of politicians

(e) the "combination" on a student gym locker combination lock

(f) a lottery choice of six numbers where the order does not matter

(g) an automobile license plate number

(h) an internet password

Exercises 16–23 can be solved with permutations even though the problem statements will not always include a form of the word "permutation," or "arrangement," or "ordering."

16. *Placing in a Race* How many different ways could first-, second-, and third-place finishers occur in a race with six runners competing?

17. *Arranging New Home Models* Tyler Aunan, a contractor, builds homes of eight different models and presently has five lots to build on. In how many different ways can he arrange homes on these lots? Assume five different models will be built.

18. *ATM PIN Numbers* An automated teller machine (ATM) requires a four-digit personal identification number (PIN), using the digits 0–9. (The first digit may be 0.) How many such PINs have no repeated digits?

19. *Electing Officers of a Club* How many ways can president and vice president be determined in a club with twelve members?

20. *Counting Prize Winners* First, second, and third prizes are to be awarded to three different people. If there are ten eligible candidates, how many outcomes are possible?

21. Counting Prize Winners How many ways can a teacher give five different prizes to five of her 25 students?

22. Scheduling Security Team Visits A security team visits 12 offices each night. How many different ways can the team order its visits?

23. Sums of Digits How many counting numbers have four distinct nonzero digits such that the sum of the four digits is

(a) 10?   **(b)** 11?

Exercises 24–31 can be solved with combinations even though the problem statements will not always include the word "combination" or "subset."

24. Sampling Cell Phones How many ways can a sample of five cell phones be selected from a shipment of twenty-four cell phones?

25. Detecting Defective Cell Phones If the shipment of **Exercise 24** contains six defective phones, how many of the size-five samples would not include any of the defective ones?

26. Committees of U.S. Senators How many different five-member committees could be formed from the 100 U.S. senators?

27. Selecting Hands of Cards Refer to the standard 52-card deck pictured on **page 549** and notice that the deck contains four aces, twelve face cards, thirteen hearts (all red), thirteen diamonds (all red), thirteen spades (all black), and thirteen clubs (all black). Of the 2,598,960 different five-card hands possible, decide how many would consist of the following cards.

(a) all diamonds   **(b)** all black cards

(c) all aces

28. Selecting Lottery Entries In a $\frac{7}{39}$ lottery, you select seven distinct numbers from the set 1 through 39, where order makes no difference. How many different ways can you make your selection?

29. Arranging New Home Models Tyler Aunan (the contractor) is to build six homes on a block in a new subdivision, using two different models, standard and deluxe. (All standard model homes are the same and all deluxe model homes are the same.)

(a) How many different choices does Tyler have in positioning the six houses if he decides to build three standard and three deluxe models?

(b) If Tyler builds two deluxes and four standards, how many different positionings can he use?

30. Choosing a Monogram Sheryl Jett wants to name her new baby so that his monogram (first, middle, and last initials) will be distinct letters in alphabetical order and he will share her last name. How many different monograms could she select?

31. Number of Paths from Point to Point In a certain city, there are seven streets going north–south and four streets going east–west. How many street paths start at the southwest corner of the city, end at the northeast corner of the city, and have the shortest possible length? (*Mathematics Teacher* calendar problem)

For Exercises 32–60, you may use permutations, combinations, the fundamental counting principle, or other counting methods as appropriate.

32. Selecting Lottery Entries In SuperLotto Plus, a California state lottery game, you select five distinct numbers from 1 to 47, and one MEGA number from 1 to 27, hoping that your selection will match a random list selected by lottery officials.

(a) How many different sets of six numbers can you select?

(b) Paul Burke always includes his age and his wife's age as two of the first five numbers in his Super-Lotto Plus selections. How many ways can he complete his list of six numbers?

33. Drawing Cards How many cards must be drawn (without replacement) from a standard deck of 52 to guarantee the following?

(a) Two of the cards will be of the same suit.

(b) Three of the cards will be of the same suit.

34. Flush Hands in Poker How many different 5-card poker hands would contain only cards of a single suit?

35. Identification Numbers in Research Subject identification numbers in a certain scientific research project consist of three letters followed by three digits and then three more letters. Assume repetitions are not allowed within any of the three groups, but letters in the first group of three may occur also in the last group of three. How many distinct identification numbers are possible?

36. Radio Station Call Letters Radio stations in the United States have call letters that begin with K or W (for west or east of the Mississippi River, respectively). Some have three call letters, such as WBZ in Boston, WLS in Chicago, and KGO in San Francisco. Assuming no repetition of letters, how many three-letter sets of call letters are possible? (Count all possibilities even though, practically, some may be inappropriate.)

37. Radio Station Call Letters Most stations that were licensed after 1927 have four call letters starting with K or W, such as WXYZ in Detroit or KRLD in Dallas. Assuming no repetitions, how many four-letter sets are possible? (Count all possibilities even though, practically, some may be inappropriate.)

38. Scheduling Games in a Basketball League Each team in an eight-team basketball league is scheduled to play each other team three times. How many games will be played altogether?

39. Scheduling Batting Orders in Baseball The Coyotes, a youth league baseball team, have seven pitchers, who only pitch, and twelve other players, all of whom can play any position other than pitcher. For Saturday's game, the coach has not yet determined which nine players to use nor what the batting order will be, except that the pitcher will bat last. How many different batting orders may occur?

40. Ordering Performers in a Music Recital A music class of five girls and four boys is having a recital. If each member is to perform once, how many ways can the program be arranged in each of the following cases?

(a) All girls must perform first.
(b) A girl must perform first and a boy must perform last.
(c) Elisa and Doug will perform first and last, respectively.
(d) The entire program will alternate between girls and boys.
(e) The first, fifth, and ninth performers must be girls.

41. Scheduling Daily Reading Carole begins each day by reading from one of seven inspirational books. How many ways can she arrange her reading for one week if the selection is done
(a) with replacement?   **(b)** without replacement?

42. Counting Card Hands How many of the possible 5-card hands from a standard 52-card deck would consist of the following cards?
(a) four clubs and one non-club
(b) two face cards and three non-face cards
(c) two red cards, two clubs, and a spade

43. Dividing People into Groups In how many ways could fifteen people be divided into five groups containing, respectively, one, two, three, four, and five people?

44. Dividing People into Groups In how many ways could fifteen people be divided into five groups of three people?

45. Dividing People into Groups In how many ways could eight people be divided into two groups of three people and a group of two people?

46. Points and Lines in a Plane If any two points determine a line, how many lines are determined by seven points in a plane, no three of which are collinear?

47. Points and Triangles in a Plane How many triangles are determined by twenty points in a plane, no three of which are collinear?

48. Counting Possibilities on a Combination Lock How many different three-number "combinations" are possible on a combination lock having 40 numbers on its dial? (*Hint:* "Combination" is a misleading name for these locks since repetitions are allowed and order makes a difference.)

49. Selecting Drivers and Passengers for a Trip Natalie Graham, her husband and son, and four additional friends are driving, in two vehicles, to the seashore.
(a) If all seven people can drive, how many ways can the two drivers be selected? (Everyone wants to drive the sports car, so it is important which driver gets which car.)
(b) If the sports car must be driven by Natalie, her husband, or their son, how many ways can the drivers now be determined?
(c) If the sports car will accommodate only two people, and there are no other restrictions, how many ways can both drivers and passengers be assigned to both cars?

50. *Winning the Daily Double in Horse Racing* You win the "daily double" by purchasing a ticket and selecting the winners of two specific races. If there are six and eight horses running in those races, respectively, how many tickets must you buy to guarantee a win?

51. *Winning the Trifecta in Horse Racing* Many race tracks offer a "trifecta" race. You win by selecting the correct first-, second-, and third-place finishers. If eight horses are entered, how many tickets must you purchase to guarantee that one of them will be a trifecta winner?

52. *Selecting Committees* Nine people are to be distributed among three committees of two, three, and four members, and a chairperson is to be selected for each committee. How many ways can this be done? (*Hint:* Break the task into the following sequence of parts.)

(a) Select the members of the two-person committee.

(b) Select the members of the three-person committee.

(c) Select the chair of the two-person committee.

(d) Select the chair of the three-person committee.

(e) Select the chair of the four-person committee.

53. *Selecting Committee Members* Repeat **Exercise 52** in case the three committees are to have three members each. (*Hint:* Use the same general sequence of task parts, but remember to adjust for *unwanted ordering* of the three committees.)

54. *Arranging New Home Models* (See **Exercise 29.**) Because of his good work, Tyler Aunan gets a contract to build homes on three additional blocks in the subdivision, with six homes on each block. He decides to build nine deluxe homes on these three blocks: two on the first block, three on the second, and four on the third. The remaining nine homes will be standard.

(a) Altogether on the three-block stretch, how many different choices does Tyler have for positioning the eighteen homes? (*Hint:* Consider the three blocks separately and use the fundamental counting principle.)

(b) How many choices would he have if he built 2, 3, and 4 deluxe models on the three different blocks as before, but not necessarily on the first, second, and third blocks in that order?

55. *Building Numbers from Sets of Digits*

(a) How many six-digit counting numbers use all six digits 4, 5, 6, 7, 8, and 9?

(b) Suppose all these numbers were arranged in increasing order: 456,789; 456,798; and so on. Which number would be 364th in the list?

56. *Arranging Five-letter Words* The 120 permutations of AHSME are arranged in dictionary order, as if each were an ordinary five-letter word. Find the last letter of the 86th word in the list. (*Mathematics Teacher* calendar problem)

57. *Arranging a Wedding Reception Line* At a wedding reception, the bride and groom, and four attendants will form a reception line. How many ways can they be arranged in each of the following cases?

(a) Any order will do.

(b) The bride and groom must be the last two in line.

(c) The groom must be last in line with the bride next to him.

58. *Assigning Student Grades* A professor teaches a class of 60 students and another class of 40 students. Five percent of the students in each class are to receive a grade of A. How many different ways can the A grades be distributed?

59. *Sums of Digits* How many counting numbers consist of four distinct nonzero digits such that the sum of the four digits is

(a) 12?   (b) 13?

60. *Screening Computer Processors* A computer company will screen a shipment of 30 processors by testing a random sample of five of them. How many different samples are possible?

61. Verify that $_{12}C_9 = {}_{12}C_3$.

62. Use the factorial formula for combinations to prove that in general,

$$_nC_r = {}_nC_{n-r}.$$

10.4 USING PASCAL'S TRIANGLE

Pascal's Triangle • Applications

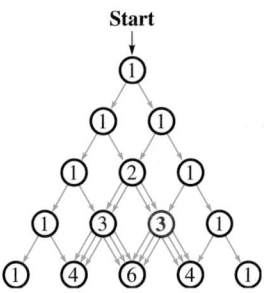

Start

Figure 7

Pascal's Triangle

The triangular array in **Figure 7** represents what we can call "random walks" that begin at START and proceed downward according to the following rule:

> At each circle (branch point), a coin is tossed. If it lands heads, we go downward to the left. If it lands tails, we go downward to the right. At each point, left and right are equally likely.

In each circle we have recorded the number of different routes that could bring us to that point. For example, the colored 3 can be reached as the result of three different coin-tossing sequences:

$$htt, \quad tht, \quad and \quad tth.$$

Another way to generate the same pattern of numbers is to begin with 1s down both diagonals and then fill in the interior entries by adding the two numbers just above a given position (to the left and right). For example, the colored 28 in **Table 5** is the result of adding 7 and 21 in the row above it.

Table 5	Pascal's Triangle											Row Sum
Row Number												
0						1						1
1					1		1					2
2				1		2		1				4
3			1		3		3		1			8
4		1		4		6		4		1		16
5	1		5		10		10		5		1	32
6		1	6	15		20		15	6	1		64
7	1	7	21		35		35		21	7	1	128
8	1	8	28	56		70		56	28	8	1	256
9	1	9	36	84	126		126	84	36	9	1	512
10	1	10	45	120	210	252	210	120	45	10	1	1024

By continuing to add pairs of numbers, we extend the array indefinitely downward, always beginning and ending each row with 1s. (The table shows just rows 0 through 10.) This unending "triangular" array of numbers is called **Pascal's triangle,** since Blaise Pascal wrote a treatise about it in 1653. There is evidence, though, that it was known as early as around 1100 and may have been studied in China or India still earlier.

At any rate, the "triangle" possesses many interesting properties. In counting applications, the most useful property is that, in general, entry number r in row number n is equal to $_nC_r$—the number of *combinations* of n things taken r at a time. This correspondence is shown (through row 7) in **Table 6** on the next page.

"Pascal's" triangle shown in the 1303 text
Szu-yuen Yu-chien (*The Precious Mirror of the Four Elements*) by the Chinese mathematician Chu Shih-chieh.

Table 6 Combination Values in Pascal's Triangle

Row Number

0	$_0C_0$
1	$_1C_0$ $_1C_1$
2	$_2C_0$ $_2C_1$ $_2C_2$
3	$_3C_0$ $_3C_1$ $_3C_2$ $_3C_3$
4	$_4C_0$ $_4C_1$ $_4C_2$ $_4C_3$ $_4C_4$
5	$_5C_0$ $_5C_1$ $_5C_2$ $_5C_3$ $_5C_4$ $_5C_5$
6	$_6C_0$ $_6C_1$ $_6C_2$ $_6C_3$ $_6C_4$ $_6C_5$ $_6C_6$
7	$_7C_0$ $_7C_1$ $_7C_2$ $_7C_3$ $_7C_4$ $_7C_5$ $_7C_6$ $_7C_7$

and so on

Having a copy of Pascal's triangle handy gives us another option for evaluating combinations. Any time we need to know the number of combinations of n things taken r at a time (that is, the number of subsets of size r in a set of size n), we can simply read entry number r of row number n. ***Keep in mind that the first row shown is row number 0.*** Also, the first entry of each row can be called entry number 0. This entry gives the number of subsets of size 0 (which is always 1 since there is only one empty set).

Applications

▌▌ **EXAMPLE 1** Applying Pascal's Triangle to Counting People

A group of ten people includes six women and four men. If five of these people are randomly selected to fill out a questionnaire, how many different samples of five people are possible?

SOLUTION

This is simply a matter of selecting a subset of five from a set of ten (or combinations of ten things taken five at a time).

$$_{10}C_5 = 252 \quad \text{See row 10 of Pascal's triangle in \textbf{Table 5.}}$$ ▌▌▌

▌▌ **EXAMPLE 2** Applying Pascal's Triangle to Counting People

Among the 252 possible samples of five people in **Example 1,** how many of them would consist of exactly two women and three men?

SOLUTION

Two women can be selected from six women in $_6C_2$ different ways, and three men can be selected from four men in $_4C_3$ different ways. These combination values can be read from Pascal's triangle. Then, since the task of obtaining two women and three men requires both individual parts, the fundamental counting principle tells us to multiply the two values.

$$_6C_2 \cdot {}_4C_3 = 15 \cdot 4 = 60 \quad \text{Rows 6 and 4 of Pascal's triangle}$$ ▌▌▌

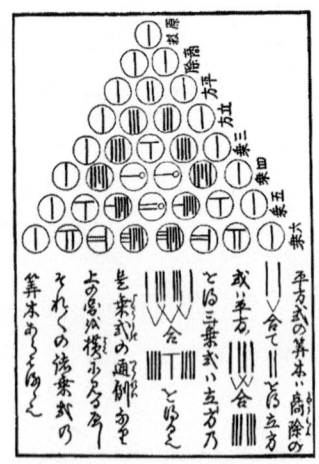

This **Japanese version** of the triangle dates from the eighteenth century. The "stick numerals" evolved from bamboo counting pieces used on a ruled board. Possibly Omar Khayyam, twelfth-century Persian mathematician and poet, may also have divined its patterns in pursuit of algebraic solutions. (The triangle lists the coefficients of the binomial expansion, explained in **For Further Thought** on **pages 559 and 560.**)

▮▮ **EXAMPLE 3** Applying Pascal's Triangle to Coin Tossing

If five fair coins are tossed, in how many different ways could exactly three heads be obtained?

SOLUTION

There are various "ways" of obtaining exactly three heads because the three heads can occur on different subsets of the coins. For example, hhtht and thhth are just two of many possibilities. When such a possibility is written down, exactly three positions are occupied by an h, the other two by a t. Each distinct way of choosing three positions from a set of five positions gives a different possibility. (Once the three positions for h are determined, each of the other two positions automatically receives a t.)

So our answer is just the number of size-three subsets of a size-five set, that is, the number of combinations of five things taken three at a time.

$$_5C_3 = 10 \quad \text{Row 5 of Pascal's triangle} \qquad \blacksquare\blacksquare\blacksquare$$

Notice that row 5 of Pascal's triangle also provides answers to several other questions about tossing five fair coins. They are summarized in **Table 7**.

Table 7 Tossing Five Fair Coins

Number of Heads n	Ways of Obtaining Exactly n Heads	Listing
0	$_5C_0 = 1$	ttttt
1	$_5C_1 = 5$	htttt, thttt, tthtt, tttht, tttth
2	$_5C_2 = 10$	hhttt, hthtt, htthh, htttt, thhtt, ththt, thtth, tthht, tthth, ttthh
3	$_5C_3 = 10$	hhhtt, hhtht, hhtth, hthht, hthth, htthh, thhht, thhth, ththh, tthhh
4	$_5C_4 = 5$	hhhht, hhhth, hhthh, hthhh, thhhh
5	$_5C_5 = 1$	hhhhh

To analyze the tossing of a different number of fair coins, we can simply take the pertinent numbers from a different row of Pascal's triangle. Repeated coin tossing is an example of a "binomial" experiment (because each toss has *two* possible outcomes, heads and tails).

For Further Thought

The Binomial Theorem

The combination values that comprise Pascal's triangle also arise in a totally different mathematical context. In algebra, "binomial" refers to a two-term expression such as

$$x + y, \quad \text{or} \quad a + 2b, \quad \text{or} \quad w^3 - 4.$$

The first few powers of the binomial $x + y$ are shown here.

$$(x + y)^0 = 1$$
$$(x + y)^1 = x + y$$
$$(x + y)^2 = x^2 + 2xy + y^2$$
$$(x + y)^3 = x^3 + 3x^2y + 3xy^2 + y^3$$
$$(x + y)^4 = x^4 + 4x^3y + 6x^2y^2 + 4xy^3 + y^4$$
$$(x + y)^5 = x^5 + 5x^4y + 10x^3y^2 + 10x^2y^3 + 5xy^4 + y^5$$

(continued)

For Further Thought (cont.)

The numerical coefficients of these expansions form the first six rows of Pascal's triangle. In our study of counting, we have called these numbers combinations, but in the study of algebra, they are called **binomial coefficients** and are usually denoted

$$\binom{n}{r} \quad \text{rather than} \quad {}_nC_r.$$

Generalizing the pattern of the powers shown on the preceding page yields the important result known as the **binomial theorem**.

Binomial Theorem

For any whole number n,

$$(x + y)^n = \binom{n}{0} \cdot x^n + \binom{n}{1} \cdot x^{n-1}y$$

$$+ \binom{n}{2} \cdot x^{n-2}y^2 + \binom{n}{3} \cdot x^{n-3}y^3 +$$

$$\cdots + \binom{n}{n-1} \cdot xy^{n-1} + \binom{n}{n} \cdot y^n,$$

where each binomial coefficient can be calculated by the formula

$$\binom{n}{r} = \frac{n!}{r!(n-r)!}.$$

Notice that, if $n = 0$, then the first term shown in the expansion is, at the same time, the last term, for

$$\binom{n}{0} \cdot x^n = \binom{0}{0} \cdot x^0 = \frac{0!}{0!0!} \cdot 1 = 1,$$

and $\binom{n}{n} \cdot y^n = \binom{0}{0} \cdot y^0 = \frac{0!}{0!0!} \cdot 1 = 1.$

EXAMPLE Applying the Binomial Theorem

Write out the binomial expansion for $(2a + 5)^4$.

SOLUTION

We take the initial coefficients from row 4 of Pascal's triangle and then simplify algebraically.

$(2a + 5)^4$ | Recall that $(xy)^n = x^n \cdot y^n$.

$$= \binom{4}{0} \cdot (2a)^4 + \binom{4}{1} \cdot (2a)^3 \cdot 5$$

$$+ \binom{4}{2} \cdot (2a)^2 \cdot 5^2 + \binom{4}{3} \cdot (2a) \cdot 5^3$$

$$+ \binom{4}{4} \cdot 5^4$$

$$= 1 \cdot 2^4 \cdot a^4 + 4 \cdot 2^3 \cdot a^3 \cdot 5 + 6 \cdot 2^2 \cdot a^2 \cdot 5^2$$

$$+ 4 \cdot 2 \cdot a \cdot 5^3 + 1 \cdot 5^4$$

$$= 16a^4 + 160a^3 + 600a^2 + 1000a + 625 \quad ▊▊▊$$

For Group or Individual Investigation

Write out the binomial expansion for each of the following powers.

1. $(x + y)^6$ 2. $(x + y)^7$
3. $(w + 4)^5$ 4. $(4x + 2y)^4$
5. $(u - v)^6$ (*Hint:* First change $u - v$ to $u + (-v)$.)
6. $(5m - 2n)^3$
7. How many terms are in the binomial expansion for $(x + y)^n$?
8. Identify the 15th term only of the expansion for $(a + b)^{18}$.

10.4 EXERCISES

Read each combination value directly from Pascal's triangle.

1. ${}_4C_2$ **2.** ${}_5C_3$ **3.** ${}_6C_3$ **4.** ${}_7C_5$

5. ${}_8C_5$ **6.** ${}_9C_6$ **7.** ${}_9C_2$ **8.** ${}_{10}C_7$

Selecting Committees of Congressmen *A committee of four Congressmen will be selected from a group of seven Democrats and three Republicans. Find the number of ways of obtaining each result.*

9. exactly one Democrat

10. exactly two Democrats

11. exactly three Democrats

12. exactly four Democrats

Tossing Coins *Suppose eight fair coins are tossed. Find the number of ways of obtaining each result.*

13. exactly three heads

14. exactly four heads

15. exactly five heads

16. exactly six heads

Selecting Classrooms Diana Baniak, searching for an Ecology class, knows that it must be in one of nine classrooms. Since the professor does not allow people to enter after the class has begun, and there is very little time left, she decides to try just four of the rooms at random.

17. How many different selections of four rooms are possible?

18. How many of the selections of **Exercise 17** will fail to locate the class?

19. How many of the selections of **Exercise 17** will succeed in locating the class?

20. What fraction of the possible selections will lead to "success"? (Give three decimal places.)

For a set of five objects, find the number of different subsets of each size. (Use row 5 of Pascal's triangle to find the answers.)

21. 0   **22.** 1

23. 2   **24.** 3

25. 4   **26.** 5

27. How many subsets (of any size) are there for a set of five elements?

28. For a given row in Pascal's triangle, let n be the row number and let s be the row sum.

   (a) Write an equation relating s and n.

   (b) Explain the relationship in part (a).

29. Which rows of Pascal's triangle have a single greatest entry?

30. What is the least four-digit number in Pascal's triangle? (*Mathematics Teacher* calendar problem)

Over the years, many interesting patterns have been discovered in Pascal's triangle.* We explore a few of them in Exercises 31–37.

31. Refer to **Table 5**.

   (a) Choose a row whose row number is prime. Except for the 1s in this row, what is true of all the other entries?

   (b) Choose a second prime row number and see if the same pattern holds.

   (c) Use the usual method to construct row 11 in **Table 5**, and verify that the same pattern holds in that row.

32. Name the next five numbers of the diagonal sequence in the figure. What are these numbers called? (See **Section 1.2**.)

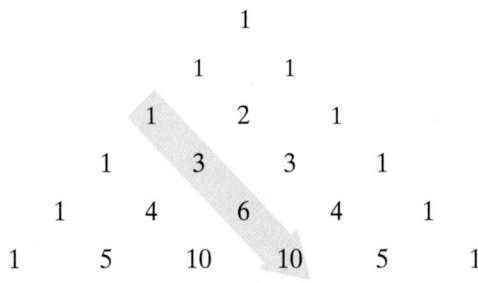

33. Complete the sequence of sums on the diagonals shown in the figure. What pattern do these sums make? What is the name of this important sequence of numbers? The presence of this sequence in the triangle apparently was not recognized by Pascal.

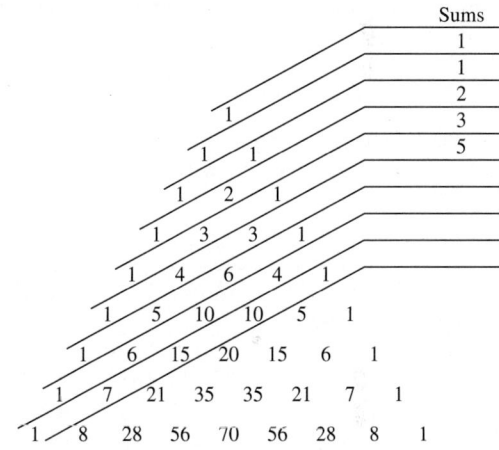

34. Construct another "triangle" by replacing every number in Pascal's triangle (rows **0** through **5**) by its remainder when divided by 2. What special property is shared by rows **2** and **4** of this new triangle?

35. What is the next row that would have the same property as rows **2** and **4** in **Exercise 34**?

36. How many even numbers are there in row **256** of Pascal's triangle? (Work **Exercises 34 and 35** first.)

37. The figure shows a portion of Pascal's triangle with several inverted triangular regions outlined. For any one of these regions, what can be said of the sum of the squares of the entries across its top row?

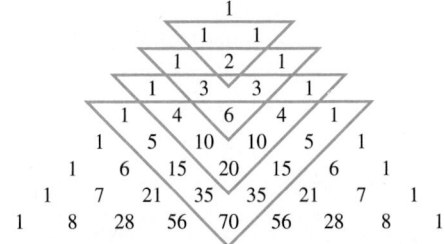

---

*For example, see the article "Serendipitous Discovery of Pascal's Triangle" by Francis W. Stanley in *The Mathematics Teacher*, February 1975.

38. More than a century before Pascal's treatise on the "triangle" appeared, another work by the Italian mathematician Niccolo Tartaglia (1506–1559) came out and included the table of numbers shown here.

1	1	1	1	1	1
1	2	3	4	5	6
1	3	6	10	15	21
1	4	10	20	35	56
1	5	15	35	70	126
1	6	21	56	126	252
1	7	28	84	210	462
1	8	36	120	330	792

Explain the connection between Pascal's triangle and Tartaglia's "rectangle."

39. It was stated in the text that each interior entry in Pascal's triangle can be obtained by adding the two numbers just above it (to the left and right). This fact, known as the "Pascal identity," can be written as

$$_nC_r = {_{n-1}C_{r-1}} + {_{n-1}C_r}.$$

Use the factorial formula for combinations (along with some algebra) to prove the Pascal identity.

The "triangle" that Pascal studied and published in his treatise was actually more like a truncated corner of Tartaglia's rectangle, as shown here.

1	1	1	1	1	1	1	1	1	1
1	2	3	4	5	6	7	8	9	
1	3	6	10	15	21	28	36		
1	4	10	20	35	56	84			
1	5	15	35	70	126				
1	6	21	56	126					
1	7	28	84						
1	8	36							
1	9								
1									

Each number in the truncated corner of Tartaglia's rectangle can be calculated in various ways. In each of Exercises 40–43, consider the number N to be located anywhere in the array. By checking several locations in the given array, determine how N is related to the sum of all entries in the shaded cells. Describe the relationship in words.

40.
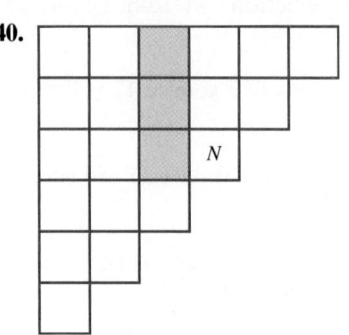

41.
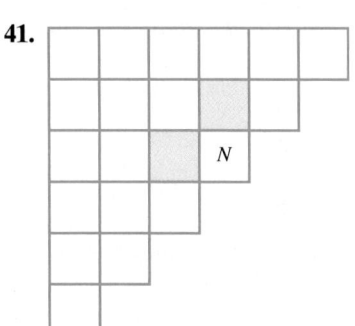

42.
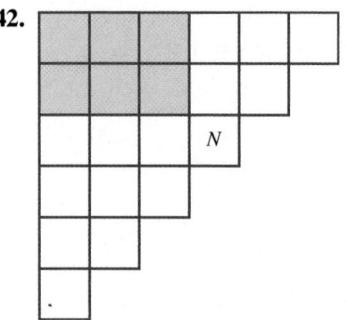

43.
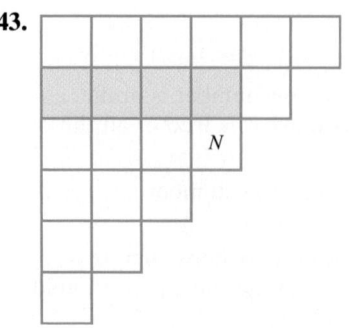

EXTENSION Magic Squares

Magic Square • Magic Sum Formula

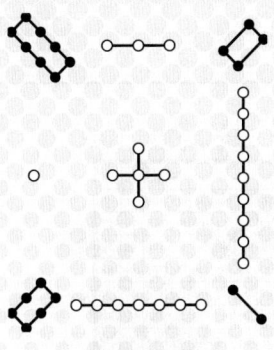

Figure 8

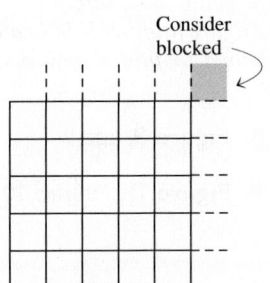

8	3	4
1	5	9
6	7	2

Figure 9

Magic Square The array of numbers known as Pascal's triangle has so many interesting patterns that we could almost think of it as a "magic" triangle. This **Extension** concerns another class of number arrays known as *magic squares*.

Legend has it that in about 2200 B.C. the Chinese Emperor Yu discovered on the bank of the Yellow River a tortoise whose shell bore the diagram in **Figure 8**. This so-called *lo-shu* is an early example of a **magic square.** If the numbers of dots are counted and arranged in a square fashion, the array in **Figure 9** is obtained. A magic square is a square array of numbers with the property that the sum along each row, column, and diagonal is the same. This common value is called the "magic sum." The **order** of a magic square is simply the number of rows (and columns) in the square. The magic square of **Figure 9** is an order 3 magic square.

Magic Sum Formula By using the formula for the sum of the first n terms of an arithmetic sequence, it can be shown that if a magic square of order n has entries $1, 2, 3, \ldots, n^2$, then the sum of *all entries* in the square is

$$\frac{n^2(n^2 + 1)}{2}.$$

Because there are n rows (and columns), the magic sum of the square may be found by dividing the above expression by n. This results in the following formula.

Magic Sum Formula

If a magic square of order n has entries $1, 2, 3, \ldots, n^2$, then the magic sum MS is given by the following formula.

$$\mathbf{MS} = \frac{n(n^2 + 1)}{2}$$

The magic sum of the square in **Figure 9** is

$$\mathrm{MS} = \frac{3(3^2 + 1)}{2} = 15. \quad \text{Let } n = 3 \text{ in the formula.}$$

We can construct an odd-order magic square using the "staircase method," attributed to an early French envoy, *de la Loubere*. The method is described below for an order 5 square, with entries $1, 2, 3, \ldots, 25$.

Begin by sketching a square divided into 25 cells into which the numbers 1–25 are to be entered. Proceed as described below, referring to **Figures 10 and 11**.

Step 1 Write 1 in the middle cell of the top row.

Step 2 Always try to enter numbers in sequence in the cells by moving diagonally from lower left to upper right. There are two exceptions to this:

   (a) If you go outside of the magic square, move all the way across the row or down the column to enter the number. Then proceed to move diagonally.

   (b) If you run into a cell that is already occupied (that is, you are "blocked"), drop down one cell from the last entry written and enter the next number there. Then proceed to move diagonally.

Step 3 Your last entry, 25, will be in the middle cell of the bottom row.

Figure 11 shows the completed magic square. Its magic sum is 65.

Consider
blocked

Figure 10

18	25	2	9	16
17	24	1	8	15	17
23	5	7	14	16	23
4	6	13	20	22	4
10	12	19	21	3	10
11	18	25	2	9

Figure 11

If magic squares catch your interest, a good source for further exploration is the website

http://mathforum.org/alejandre/magic.square.html.

Benjamin Franklin admitted that he would amuse himself while in the Pennysylvania Assembly with magic squares or circles "or any thing to avoid Weariness." He wrote about the usefulness of mathematics in the *Gazette* in 1735, saying that no employment can be managed without arithmetic, no mechanical invention without geometry. He also thought that mathematical demonstrations are better than academic logic for training the mind to reason with exactness and distinguish truth from falsity even outside of mathematics.

The square shown here is one developed by Franklin. It has a sum of 2056 in each row and diagonal, and, in Franklin's words, has the additional property "that a four-square hole being cut in a piece of paper of such size as to take in and show through it just 16 of the little squares, when laid on the greater square, the sum of the 16 numbers so appearing through the hole, wherever it was placed on the greater square should likewise make 2056." He claimed that it was "the most magically magic square ever made by any magician."

You might wish to verify the following property of this magic square: The sum of any four numbers that are opposite each other and at equal distances from the center is 514 (which is one-fourth of the magic sum).

EXTENSION EXERCISES

*Given a magic square, other magic squares may be obtained by rotating the given one. For example, starting with the magic square in **Figure 9**, a 90° rotation in a clockwise direction gives the magic square shown here.*

6	1	8
7	5	3
2	9	4

*Start with **Figure 9** and give the magic square obtained by each rotation described.*

1. 180° in a clockwise direction

2. 90° in a counterclockwise direction

*Start with **Figure 11** and give the magic square obtained by each rotation described.*

3. 90° in a clockwise direction

4. 180° in a clockwise direction

5. 90° in a counterclockwise direction

6. Try to construct an order-2 magic square containing the entries 1, 2, 3, 4. What happens?

Given a magic square, other magic squares may be obtained by adding or subtracting a constant value to or from each entry, multiplying each entry by a constant value, or dividing each entry by a nonzero constant value. In Exercises 7–10, start with the magic square whose figure number is indicated, and perform the operation described to find a new magic square. Give the new magic sum.

7. Figure 9, multiply by 3   **8. Figure 9**, add 7

9. Figure 11, divide by 2   **10. Figure 11**, subtract 10

According to a fanciful story by Charles Trigg in Mathematics Magazine *(September 1976, page 212), the Emperor Charlemagne (742–814) ordered a five-sided fort to be built at an important point in his kingdom. As good-luck charms, he had magic squares placed on all five sides of the fort. He had one restriction for these magic squares: all the numbers in them must be prime.*

Charlemagne's magic squares are given in Exercises 11–15, with one missing entry. Find the missing entry in each square.

11.

	71	257
47	269	491
281	467	59

12.

389		227
107	269	431
311	347	149

13.

389	227	191
71	269	
347	311	149

14.

401	227	179
47	269	491
359		137

15.

401	257	149
17		521
389	281	137

16. Compare the magic sums in **Exercises 11–15.** Charlemagne had stipulated that each magic sum should be the year in which the fort was built. What was that year?

Find the missing entries in each magic square.

17.

75	68	(a)
(b)	72	(c)
71	76	(d)

18.

1	8	13	(a)
(b)	14	7	2
16	9	4	(c)
(d)	(e)	(f)	15

19.

3	20	(a)	24	11
(b)	14	1	18	10
9	21	13	(c)	17
16	8	25	12	(d)
(e)	2	(f)	(g)	(h)

20.

3	36	2	35	31	4
10	12	(a)	26	7	27
21	13	17	14	(b)	22
16	(c)	23	(d)	18	15
28	30	8	(e)	25	9
(f)	1	32	5	6	34

21. Use the "staircase method" to construct a magic square of order 7, containing the entries 1, 2, 3, . . . , 49.

The magic square shown in the photograph is from a woodcut by Albrecht Dürer entitled Melancholia.

The two bottom center numbers give 1514, *the date of the woodcut. Refer to this magic square for Exercises 22–30.*

16	3	2	13
5	10	11	8
9	6	7	12
4	15	14	1

Dürer's Magic Square

22. What is the magic sum?

23. Verify: The sum of the entries in the four corners is equal to the magic sum.

24. Verify: The sum of the entries in any 2 by 2 square at a corner of the given magic square is equal to the magic sum.

25. Verify: The sum of the entries in the diagonals is equal to the sum of the entries not in the diagonals.

26. Verify: The sum of the squares of the entries in the diagonals is equal to the sum of the squares of the entries not in the diagonals.

27. Verify: The sum of the cubes of the entries in the diagonals is equal to the sum of the cubes of the entries not in the diagonals.

28. Verify: The sum of the squares of the entries in the top two rows is equal to the sum of the squares of the entries in the bottom two rows.

29. Verify: The sum of the squares of the entries in the first and third rows is equal to the sum of the squares of the entries in the second and fourth rows.

30. Find another interesting property of Dürer's magic square and state it.

31. A magic square of order 4 may be constructed as follows.

   (1) Lightly sketch in the diagonals of the blank magic square.

(2) Beginning at the upper left, move across each row from left to right, counting the cells as you go along. If the cell is on a diagonal, count it but do not enter its number. If it is not on a diagonal, enter its number.

(3) When this is completed, reverse the procedure, beginning at the bottom right and moving across from right to left. As you count the cells, enter the number if the cell is not occupied. If it is already occupied, count it but do not enter its number.

You should obtain a magic square similar to the one given for **Exercises 22–30.** How do they differ?

With chosen values for a, b, and c, an order-3 magic square can be constructed by substituting these values in the generalized form shown here.

$a+b$	$a-b-c$	$a+c$
$a-b+c$	a	$a+b-c$
$a-c$	$a+b+c$	$a-b$

Use the given values of a, b, and c to construct an order-3 magic square, using this generalized form.

32. $a = 5$, $b = 1$, $c = -3$

33. $a = 16$, $b = 2$, $c = -6$

34. $a = 5$, $b = 4$, $c = -8$

35. It can be shown that if an order-n magic square has least entry k, and its entries are consecutive counting numbers, then its magic sum is given by the formula

$$MS = \frac{n(2k + n^2 - 1)}{2}.$$

Construct an order-7 magic square with least entry 10 using the staircase method. Find its magic sum.

36. Use the formula of **Exercise 35** to find the missing entries in the following order-4 magic square whose least entry is 24.

(a)	38	37	27
35	**(b)**	30	32
31	33	**(c)**	28
(d)	26	25	**(e)**

In a 1769 letter from Benjamin Franklin to a Mr. Peter Collinson, Franklin exhibited the following semimagic square of order 8. (Note: A square is semimagic if it is magic except that one or both diagonals fail to give the magic sum.)

52	61	4	13	20	29	36	45
14	3	62	51	46	35	30	19
53	60	5	12	21	28	37	44
11	6	59	54	43	38	27	22
55	58	7	10	23	26	39	42
9	8	57	56	41	40	25	24
50	63	2	15	18	31	34	47
16	1	64	49	48	33	32	17

37. What is the magic sum?

Verify the following properties of this semimagic square.

38. The sums in the first half of each row and the second half of each row are both equal to half the magic sum.

39. The four corner entries added to the four center entries is equal to the magic sum.

40. The "bent diagonals" consisting of eight entries, going up four entries from left to right and down four entries from left to right, give the magic sum. (For example, starting with 16, one bent diagonal sum is $16 + 63 + 57 + 10 + 23 + 40 + 34 + 17$.)

If we use a "knight's move" (up two, right one) from chess, a variation of the staircase method gives the magic square shown here. (When blocked, we move to the cell just below the previous entry.)

10	18	1	14	22
11	24	7	20	3
17	5	13	21	9
23	6	19	2	15
4	12	25	8	16

Use a similar process to construct an order-5 magic square, starting with 1 in the cell described.

41. fourth row, second column (up two, right one; when blocked, move to the cell just below the previous entry)

42. third row, third column (up one, right two; when blocked, move to the cell just to the left of the previous entry)

43. The integers from 1 through 27 are placed in the cells of a 3 × 3 cube so that the sum in all nine rows and in all nine columns is the same. Finish the solution. (*Mathematics Teacher* calendar problem)

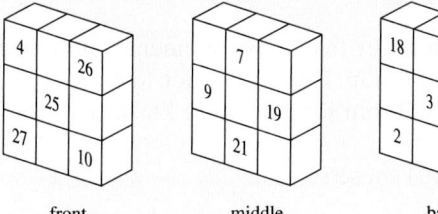

front   middle   back

44. Consider the "magic cube" of **Exercise 43.**
   (a) What is the magic sum?
   (b) How many three-cell "diagonals" does the cube contain?
   (c) Do the entries in all the diagonals also add to the magic sum?
   (d) How many rows does the cube *really* have?
   (e) Do all the additional rows also have the magic sum?

10.5   COUNTING PROBLEMS INVOLVING "NOT" AND "OR"

Problems Involving "Not"   •   Problems Involving "Or"

The counting techniques in this section, which can be thought of as *indirect techniques*, are based on some useful correspondences (from **Chapters 2 and 3**) between set theory, logic, and arithmetic, as shown in **Table 8**.

Table 8   Set Theory/Logic/Arithmetic Correspondences

	Set Theory	Logic	Arithmetic
Operation or NOT Connective (Symbol)	Complement (')	Not (~)	Subtraction (−)
Operation or Connective (Symbol)	Union (∪)	Or (∨)	Addition (+)

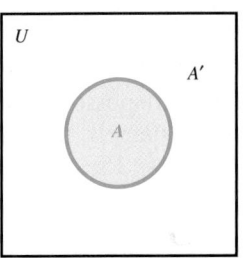

The complement of a set

Figure 12

Problems Involving "Not"

Suppose U is the set of all possible results of some type. (The "universal set U," comprises all possibilities as discussed in **Chapter 2**.) Let A be the set of all those results that satisfy a given condition. For any set S, its cardinal number is written $n(S)$, and its complement is written S'. **Figure 12** suggests that

$$n(A) + n(A') = n(U).$$

Also, $n(A) = n(U) - n(A')$ and $n(A') = n(U) - n(A).$

We focus here on the form that expresses the following indirect counting principle (based on the complement/not/subtraction correspondence from **Table 8**).

> **Complements Principle of Counting**
>
> The number of ways a certain condition can be satisfied is the total number of possible results minus the number of ways the condition would **not** be satisfied. Symbolically, if A is any set within the universal set U, then
>
> $$n(A) = n(U) - n(A').$$

▮▮ **EXAMPLE 1** Counting the Proper Subsets of a Set

For the set $S = \{a, b, c, d, e, f\}$, find the number of proper subsets.

SOLUTION

A proper subset of S is any subset with fewer than all six elements. Subsets of several different sizes would satisfy this condition. But, it is easier to consider the one subset that is not proper, namely S itself. From set theory, we know that set S has a total of

$$2^6 = 64 \text{ subsets.}$$

Thus, from the complements principle, the number of proper subsets is

$$64 - 1 = 63.$$

In words, the number of subsets that *are* proper is the total number of subsets minus the number of subsets that are *not* proper. ▮▮▮

Consider the tossing of three fair coins. Since each coin will land either heads (h) or tails (t), the possible results can be listed as follows.

hhh, hht, hth, thh, htt, tht, tth, ttt   Results of tossing three fair coins

(Even without the listing, we could have concluded that there would be eight possibilities. There are two possible outcomes for each coin, so the fundamental counting principle gives $2 \cdot 2 \cdot 2 = 2^3 = 8$.)

Suppose we wanted the number of ways of obtaining *at least* one head. In this case, "at least one" means one or two or three. Rather than dealing with all three cases, we can note that "at least one" is the opposite (or complement) of "fewer than one" (which is zero). Because there is only one way to get zero heads (ttt), and there are a total of eight possibilities, the complements principle gives the number of ways of getting at least one head:

$$8 - 1 = 7.$$

Indirect counting methods can often be applied to problems involving "at least," or "at most," or "less than," or "more than."

▮▮ **EXAMPLE 2** Counting Coin-Tossing Results

If four fair coins are tossed, in how many ways can at least one tail be obtained?

SOLUTION

By the fundamental counting principle, $2^4 = 16$ different results are possible. Exactly one of these fails to satisfy the condition of "at least one tail" (namely, no tails, or hhhh). So the answer (from the complements principle) is $16 - 1 = 15$. ▮▮▮

▮▮ **EXAMPLE 3** Counting Selections of Airliner Seats

Carol Britz and three friends are boarding an airliner just before departure time. There are only ten seats left, three of which are aisle seats. How many ways can the four people arrange themselves in available seats so that at least one of them sits on the aisle?

SOLUTION

The word "arrange" implies that order is important, so we shall use permutations. "At least one aisle seat" is the opposite (complement) of "no aisle seats." The total number of ways to arrange four people among ten seats is

$$_{10}P_4 = 5040.$$

The number of ways to arrange four people among seven (non-aisle) seats is

$$_7P_4 = 840.$$

Therefore, by the complements principle, the number of arrangements with at least one aisle seat is

$$\underset{\underset{5040}{\downarrow}}{_{10}P_4} - \underset{\underset{840}{\downarrow}}{_7P_4} = 4200. \qquad ■■■$$

Problems Involving "Or"

The complements principle is one way of counting indirectly. Another technique is to count the elements of a set by breaking that set into simpler component parts. If

$$S = A \cup B,$$

the cardinal number formula (from **Section 2.4**) says to find the number of elements in S by adding the number in A to the number in B. We must then subtract the number in the intersection $A \cap B$ if A and B are not disjoint, as in **Figure 13**. But if A and B are disjoint, as in **Figure 14**, the subtraction is not necessary.

The following principle reflects the union/or/addition correspondence from **Table 8**.

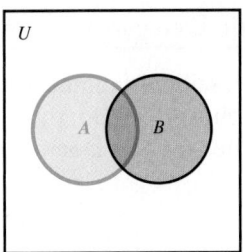

Nondisjoint sets

Figure 13

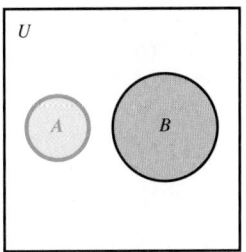

Disjoint sets

Figure 14

Additive Principle of Counting

The number of ways that one **or** the other of two conditions could be satisfied is the number of ways one of them could be satisfied plus the number of ways the other could be satisfied minus the number of ways they could both be satisfied together.

If A and B are any two sets, then

$$n(A \cup B) = n(A) + n(B) - n(A \cap B).$$

If sets A and B are disjoint, then

$$n(A \cup B) = n(A) + n(B).$$

■■ | **EXAMPLE 4**   Counting Card Hands

How many five-card poker hands consist of either <u>all clubs</u> or <u>all red cards</u>?

SOLUTION

No hand that satisfies one of these conditions could also satisfy the other, so the two sets of possibilities (all clubs, all red cards) are disjoint. Therefore the second formula of the additive principle applies.

$n(\text{all clubs or all red cards}) = n(\text{all clubs}) + n(\text{all red cards})$ Additive counting principle

$$= {}_{13}C_5 + {}_{26}C_5$$ 13 clubs, 26 red cards

$$= 1287 + 65{,}780$$ Substitute values.

$$= 67{,}067$$ Add.   ■■■

```
(10 nPr 4)−(7 nPr 4)
                 4200
(13 nCr 5)+(26 nCr 5)
                67067
```

Results in **Examples 3 and 4** are supported in this screen.

▮▮ EXAMPLE 5 Counting Selections from a Diplomatic Delegation

Table 9 categorizes a diplomatic delegation of 18 congressional members as to political party and gender. If one of the members is chosen randomly to be spokesperson for the group, in how many ways could that person be a Democrat or a woman?

Table 9	Men (*M*)	Women (*W*)	Totals
Republican (*R*)	5	3	8
Democrat (*D*)	4	6	10
Totals	9	9	18

SOLUTION

Since *D* and *W* are not disjoint (6 delegates are both Democrats and women), the first formula of the additive principle is required.

$$n(D \text{ or } W) = n(D \cup W) \qquad \text{Union/or correspondence}$$

$$= n(D) + n(W) - n(D \cap W) \qquad \text{Additive principle}$$

$$= 10 + 9 - 6 \qquad \text{Substitute values.}$$

$$= 13 \qquad \text{Add and subtract.}$$ ▮▮▮

(handwritten: subtract because counted both time; 6 is common between both)

▮▮ EXAMPLE 6 Counting Course Selections for a Degree Program

Chrissy Jenkins needs to take twelve more specific courses for a bachelors degree, including four in math, three in physics, three in computer science, and two in business. If five courses are randomly chosen from these twelve for next semester's program, how many of the possible selections would include at least two math courses?

SOLUTION

Of all the information given here, what is important is that there are four math courses and eight other courses to choose from, and that five of them are being selected for next semester. If *T* denotes the set of selections that include at least two math courses, then we can write

$$T = A \cup B \cup C$$

where   *A* = the set of selections with exactly two math courses,

    B = the set of selections with exactly three math courses,

and   *C* = the set of selections with exactly four math courses.

(In this case, *at least two* means exactly two **or** exactly three **or** exactly four.) The situation is illustrated in **Figure 15**. By previous methods, we know that

$$n(A) = {}_4C_2 \cdot {}_8C_3 = 6 \cdot 56 = 336,$$

$$n(B) = {}_4C_3 \cdot {}_8C_2 = 4 \cdot 28 = 112,$$

and $$n(C) = {}_4C_4 \cdot {}_8C_1 = 1 \cdot 8 = 8,$$

so that, by the additive principle,

$$n(T) = 336 + 112 + 8 = 456.$$ ▮▮▮

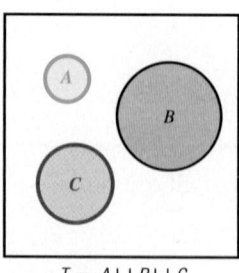

$T = A \cup B \cup C$

Figure 15

▌▌ **EXAMPLE 7** Counting Three-Digit Numbers with Conditions

How many three-digit counting numbers are multiples of 2 or multiples of 5?

SOLUTION

A multiple of 2 must end in an even digit (0, 2, 4, 6, or 8), so there are $9 \cdot 10 \cdot 5 = 450$ three-digit multiples of 2. A multiple of 5 must end in either 0 or 5, so there are $9 \cdot 10 \cdot 2 = 180$ of those. A multiple of both 2 and 5 is a multiple of 10 and must end in 0. There are $9 \cdot 10 \cdot 1 = 90$ of those. By the additive principle there are

$$450 + 180 - 90 = 540$$

possible three-digit numbers that are multiples of 2 or multiples of 5.   ▮▮▮

▌▌ **EXAMPLE 8** Counting Card-Drawing Results

A single card is drawn from a standard 52-card deck.

(a) In how many ways could it be a heart or a king?

(b) In how many ways could it be a club or a face card?

SOLUTION

(a) A single card can be both a heart and a king (the king of hearts), so use the first additive formula. There are thirteen hearts, four kings, and one card that is both a heart and a king.

$$13 + 4 - 1 = 16$$

(b) There are 13 clubs, 12 face cards, and 3 cards that are both clubs and face cards.

$$13 + 12 - 3 = 22$$ ▮▮▮

▌▌ **EXAMPLE 9** Counting Subsets of a Set with Conditions

How many subsets of a 25-element set have more than three elements?

SOLUTION

It would be a real job to count directly all subsets of size $4, 5, 6, \ldots, 25$. It is much easier to count those with three or fewer elements and apply the complements principle.

There is	$_{25}C_0 = 1$	size-0 subset.
There are	$_{25}C_1 = 25$	size-1 subsets.
There are	$_{25}C_2 = 300$	size-2 subsets.
There are	$_{25}C_3 = 2300$	size-3 subsets.

The total number of subsets (of all sizes, 0 through 25) is $2^{25} = 33{,}554{,}432$ (use a calculator). So the number with more than three elements must be

$$33{,}554{,}432 - (1 + 25 + 300 + 2300) = 33{,}554{,}432 - 2626$$

$$= 33{,}551{,}806.$$ ▮▮▮

In **Example 9,** we used both the additive principle (to get the number of subsets with no more than three elements) and the complements principle.

10.5 EXERCISES

How many proper subsets are there of each set?

1. {A, B, C, D}

2. {u, v, w, x, y, z}

Tossing Coins *If you toss seven fair coins, in how many ways can you obtain each result?*

3. at least one head ("At least one" is the complement of "none.")

4. at least two heads ("At least two" is the complement of "zero or one.")

5. at least two tails

6. at least one of each (a head and a tail)

Rolling Dice *If you roll two fair dice (say red and green), in how many ways can you obtain each result? (Refer to* **Table 2** *in* **Section 10.1.***)*

7. at least 2 on the green die

8. a sum of at least 3

9. a 4 on at least one of the dice

10. a different number on each die

Drawing Cards *If you draw a single card from a standard 52-card deck, in how many ways can you obtain each result?*

11. a card other than the ace of spades

12. a nonface card

Identifying Properties of Counting Numbers *How many two-digit counting numbers meet each requirement?*

13. not a multiple of 10

14. greater than 70 or a multiple of 10

15. Choosing Country Music Albums Jeanne Bronson's collection of ten country music albums includes *Southern Voice* by Tim McGraw. Jeanne will choose three of her albums to play on a drive to Nashville. (Assume order is not important.)

  (a) How many different sets of three albums could she choose?

  (b) How many of these sets would not include *Southern Voice*?

  (c) How many of them would include *Southern Voice*?

16. Choosing Broadway Hits The ten longest Broadway runs include *The Phantom of the Opera* and *Les Misérables.* Four of the ten are chosen randomly. (Assume order is not important.)

  (a) How many ways can the four be chosen?

  (b) How many of those groups of four would include neither of the two productions mentioned?

  (c) How many of them would include at least one of the two productions mentioned?

17. Choosing Days of the Week How many different ways could three distinct days of the week be chosen so that at least one of them begins with the letter S? (Assume order of selection is not important.)

18. Choosing School Assignments for Completion Diona Brown has nine major assignments to complete for school this week. Two of them involve writing essays. Diona decides to work on two of the nine assignments tonight. How many different choices of two would include at least one essay assignment? (Assume order is not important.)

Selecting Restaurants *Jason Ignacio wants to dine at four different restaurants during a summer getaway. If three of eight available restaurants serve seafood, find the number of ways that at least one of the selected restaurants will serve seafood given the following conditions.*

19. The order of selection is important.

20. The order of selection is not important.

21. Seating Arrangements on an Airliner Refer to **Example 3.** If one of the group decided at the last minute not to fly, then how many ways could the remaining three arrange themselves among the ten available seats so that at least one of them will sit on the aisle?

22. Identifying Properties of Counting Numbers Find the number of four-digit counting numbers containing at least one zero, under each of the following conditions.

  (a) Repeated digits are allowed.

  (b) Repeated digits are not allowed.

23. Counting Radio Call Letters Radio stations in the United States have call letters that begin with either K or W. Some have a total of three letters, and others have four letters. How many different call letter combinations are possible? Count all possibilities even though, practically, some may be inappropriate. (*Mathematics Teacher* calendar problem) (*Hint:* Do *not* apply combinations.)

24. Selecting Faculty Committees A committee of four faculty members will be selected from a department of twenty-five which includes professors Fontana and Spradley. In how many ways could the committee include at least one of these two professors?

25. Selecting Search and Rescue Teams A Civil Air Patrol unit of twelve members includes four officers. In how many ways can four members be selected for a search and rescue mission such that at least one officer is included?

26. Choosing Team Members Three students from a class of 12 will form a math contest team that must include at least 1 boy and at least 1 girl. If 160 different teams can be formed from the 12 students, which of the following can be the difference between the number of boys and the number of girls in the class?

A. 0 **B.** 2 **C.** 4 **D.** 6 **E.** 8

(*Mathematics Teacher* calendar problem)

Drawing Cards *If a single card is drawn from a standard 52-card deck, in how many ways could it be the following? (Use the additive principle.)*

27. a club or a jack

28. a face card or a black card

Counting Students Who Enjoy Music and Cinema *Of a group of 30 students, 25 enjoy music, 22 enjoy cinema, and 18 enjoy both music and cinema. How many of them enjoy the following?*

29. at least one of the two (Use the additive principle.)

30. neither of the two (complement of "at least one")

Counting Card Hands *Among the 2,598,960 possible 5-card poker hands from a standard 52-card deck, how many contain the following cards?*

31. at least one card that is not a heart (complement of "all hearts")

32. cards of more than one suit (complement of "all the same suit")

33. at least one face card (complement of "no face cards")

34. at least one club, but not all clubs (complement of "no clubs or all clubs")

35. Selecting Doughnuts A doughnut shop has a special on its Mix-n-Match selection, which allows customers to select three doughnuts from among the following varieties: plain, maple, frosted, chocolate, glazed, and jelly. How many different Mix-n-Match selections are possible? (*Mathematics Teacher* calendar problem)

36. Rolling Three Dice Three fair, standard six-faced dice of different colors are rolled. In how many ways can the dice be rolled such that the sum of the numbers rolled is 10? (*Mathematics Teacher* calendar problem)

The Size of Subsets of a Set *If a given set has ten elements, how many of its subsets have the given numbers of elements?*

37. at most two elements   **38.** at least eight elements

39. more than two elements

40. from three through seven elements

41. Counting License Numbers If license numbers consist of two letters followed by three digits, how many different licenses could be created having at least one letter or digit repeated? (*Hint:* Use the complements principle of counting.)

42. Drawing Cards If two cards are drawn from a 52-card deck without replacement (that is, the first card is not replaced in the deck before the second card is drawn), in how many different ways is it possible to obtain a king on the first draw and a heart on the second? (*Hint:* Split this event into the two disjoint components "king of hearts and then another heart" and "non-heart king and then heart." Use the fundamental counting principle on each component, then apply the additive principle.)

43. Extend the additive counting principle to three overlapping sets (as in the figure) to show that

$$n(A \cup B \cup C) = n(A) + n(B) + n(C)$$
$$- n(A \cap B) - n(A \cap C)$$
$$- n(B \cap C) + n(A \cap B \cap C).$$

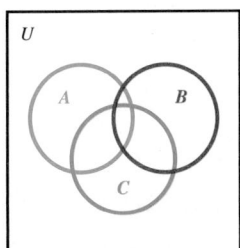

44. How many of the counting numbers 1 through 300 are *not* divisible by 2, 3, or 5? (*Hint:* Use the complements principle and the result of **Exercise 43.**)

Selecting National Monuments to Visit *Megan Lozano is planning a driving tour. While she is interested in seeing the twelve national monuments listed here, she will have to settle for seeing just three of them.*

New Mexico	Arizona	California
Gila Cliff Dwellings	Canyon de Chelly	Devils Postpile
Petroglyph	Organ Pipe Cactus	Joshua Tree
White Sands	Saguaro	Lava Beds
Aztec Ruins		Muir Woods
		Pinnacles

In how many ways could the three monuments chosen include the following? (Assume that order of selection is not important.)

45. sites in only one state

46. at least one site not in California

47. sites in fewer than all three states

48. sites in exactly two of the three states

Counting Categories of Poker Hands **Table 4** *in this chapter (**For Further Thought** in **Section 10.3**) described the various kinds of hands in 5-card poker. Verify each statement in Exercises 49–52. (Explain all steps of your argument.)*

49. There are four ways to get a royal flush.

50. There are 36 ways to get a straight flush.

51. There are 10,200 ways to get a straight.

52. There are 54,912 ways to get three of a kind.

53. Explain why the complements principle of counting is called an "indirect" method.

54. Explain the difference between the two formulas of the additive principle of counting.

COLLABORATIVE INVESTIGATION

Solving a Traveling Salesman Problem

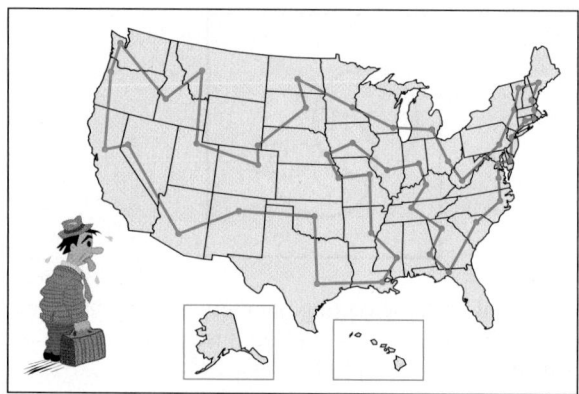

In 1985, Shen Lin came up with the route shown above for a salesman wanting to visit all capital cities in the forty-eight contiguous states, starting and ending at the same capital and traveling the shortest possible total distance. He could not prove that his 10,628-mile route was the shortest possible, but he offered $100 to anyone who could find a shorter one.

This is an example of a classic problem, the so-called **traveling salesman problem** (or **TSP**), which has many practical applications in business and industry but has baffled mathematicians for years. In the case above, there are 47! possible routes, although many of them can be quickly eliminated, leaving $\frac{24!}{3}$ possibilities to consider. This is still a 24-digit number, far too large for even state-of-the-art computers to analyze directly.

Although computer scientists have so far failed to find an "efficient algorithm" to solve the general traveling salesman problem, successes are periodically achieved for particular cases. In 2005, an optimal route was computed for a 33,810-city instance, which arose from a microchip layout problem.

A much smaller set (of seven cities, A through G), which can be completely analyzed using a calculator, is shown here.

Notice that certain routes clearly are *not* the shortest. For example, it is apparent that the route ACEDFGBA involves too much jumping back and forth across the diagram to result in the least possible total distance. (In fact, the total distance for this route is 360 miles, considerably more than necessary.) The fifteen distances given here (in miles) between pairs of cities should be sufficient data for computing the shortest possible route.

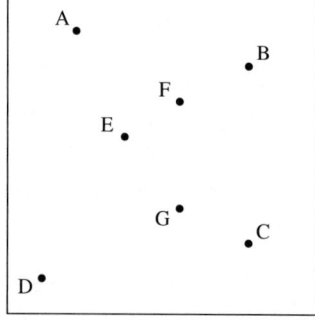

AB = 51	AF = 36	BF = 22	CG = 22	EF = 22
AD = 71	BC = 50	BG = 45	DE = 45	EG = 28
AE = 32	BE = 45	CD = 61	DG = 45	FG = 30

Topics for Discussion

Divide the class into groups of 3 or 4 students each. Each group is to do the following.

1. Study the drawing, and make a list of all routes that you think may be the shortest.

2. For each candidate route, add the appropriate seven terms to get a total distance.

3. Arrive at a group consensus as to which route is shortest.

Now bring the whole class back together, and do the following.

1. Make a list of routes, with total distances, that the various groups thought were shortest.

2. Observe whether the different groups all agreed on which route was shortest.

3. As a class, try to achieve a consensus on the shortest route. Do you think that someone else may be able to find a shorter one?

Optimal routes joining points, computed by traveling salesman theories (see the **Collaborative Investigation**), have been used to produce a variety of art. For example, the likeness shown at the right, based on the work of Andy Warhol, consists of a route that, if printed on $8\frac{1}{2}$-by-11-inch paper, would be 45.5 feet long.

Reproduced with permission from Robert Bosch.

CHAPTER 10 TEST

Counting Three-digit Numbers *If only digits* 0, 1, 2, 3, 4, 5, *and* 6 *may be used, find the number of possibilities in each category.*

1. three-digit numbers

2. odd three-digit numbers

3. three-digit numbers without repeated digits

4. three-digit multiples of five without repeated digits

5. ***Counting Triangles in a Figure*** Determine the number of triangles (of any size) in the figure shown here.

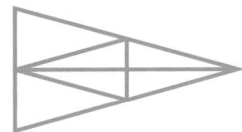

6. ***Tossing Coins*** Construct a tree diagram showing all possible results when a fair coin is tossed four times, if no two consecutive tosses can both be heads.

7. ***Sums of Digits*** How many nonrepeating four-digit numbers have the sum of their digits equal to 30?

8. ***Arranging People*** Tia, Jo, and four friends sit at a round table. How many ways can they be arranged if Tia and Jo refuse to sit next to each other? Assume that any rotation of a given arrangement, that is, when everyone moves the same number of seats in either clockwise or counterclockwise direction, is the same as the original arrangement. (*Mathematics Teacher* calendar problem)

Evaluate each expression.

9. 6!

10. $\dfrac{8!}{6!}$

11. $_{12}P_3$

12. $_8C_5$

13. ***Building Words from Sets of Letters*** How many five-letter "words" without repeated letters are possible using the English alphabet? (Assume that any five letters make a "word.")

14. ***Building Words from Sets of Letters*** Using the Russian alphabet (which has 32 letters), and allowing repeated letters, how many five-letter "words" are possible?

Scheduling Assignments *Eileen Burke has seven homework assignments to complete. She wants to do two of them on Thursday and the other five on Saturday.*

15. In how many ways can she order Thursday's work?

16. Assuming she finishes Thursday's work successfully, in how many ways can she order Saturday's work?

17. ***Arranging Letters*** Find the number of distinguishable arrangements of the letters of the word GOOGOL.

Selecting Groups of Basketball Players *If there are ten players on a basketball team, find the number of choices the coach has in selecting each of the following.*

18. four players to carry the team equipment

19. two players for guard positions and two for forward positions

20. five starters and five subs

21. two groups of four

22. a group of three or more of the players

Choosing Switch Settings Determine the number of possible settings for a row of five on–off switches under each condition.

23. There are no restrictions.

24. The first and fifth switches must be on.

25. The first and fifth switches must be set the same.

26. No two adjacent switches can both be off.

27. No two adjacent switches can be set the same.

28. At least two switches must be on.

Choosing Subsets of Letters Three distinct letters are to be chosen from the set

$$\{A, B, C, D, E, F, G\}.$$

Determine the number of ways to obtain a subset that includes each of the following.

29. the letter B

30. both A and E

31. either A or E, but not both

32. letters to spell the word AD

33. more consonants than vowels

34. **Number of Paths from Point to Point** A transit bus can travel in only two directions, north and east. From its starting point on the map shown, determine how many paths exist to reach the garage. (*Mathematics Teacher* calendar problem)

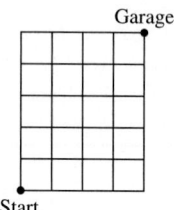

35. State the fundamental counting principle in your own words.

36. If $_nC_r = 495$ and $_nC_{r+1} = 220$, find the value of $_{n+1}C_{r+1}$.

37. If you write down the second entry of each row of Pascal's triangle (starting with row 1), what sequence of numbers do you obtain?

38. Explain why there are $r!$ permutations of n things taken r at a time corresponding to each combination of n things taken r at a time.

PROBABILITY

*S*uppose you're on a game show, and you're given the choice of three doors: Behind one of the doors is a car, and behind the other doors, goats. Of course, you want to win the car. You pick one of the doors, say Door 1, and the host, who knows what's behind the other doors, opens another door, say Door 3, to reveal a goat. He then says to you, "Do you want to change your choice?" Is it to your advantage to switch to Door 2?

This question appeared in *Parade* magazine in a column written by Marilyn vos Savant in the early 1990s. This probability problem, known as the Monty Hall Problem, was named after the host of the popular game show *Let's Make a Deal*. Marilyn's answer caused an incredible amount of discussion and argument among the general public at that time.

The answer and its justification can also be found at the interactive Web site www.math.ucsd.edu/~crypto/Monty/monty .html. *Would YOU switch doors?* (See page 613 for the answer.)

11.1 BASIC CONCEPTS

Historical Background • Probability • The Law of Large Numbers
• Probability in Genetics • Odds

If the **Pascal–Fermat correspondence** of 1654 marks the birth of probability theory, it wasn't an easy birth. In his 2010 book, *The Unfinished Game: Pascal, Fermat, and the Seventeenth-Century Letter that Made the World Modern* (see the photo above), Keith Devlin describes how the two "struggled for several weeks" to solve the unfinished game problem. In fact, this is no exception, but rather the rule, even for the greatest mathematicians. The reams of scratch work behind the elegant results are seldom seen and rarely published.

Historical Background

The modern mathematical theory of probability came mainly from the Russian scholars P. L. Chebyshev (1821–1922), A. A. Markov (1856–1922), and Andrei Nikolaevich Kolmogorov (1903–1987). But the basic ideas arose much earlier, mostly in questions of games and gambling. In 1654, two French mathematicians, Pierre de Fermat (about 1601–1665) and Blaise Pascal (1623–1662), corresponded with each other regarding a problem posed by the Chevalier de Méré, a gambler and member of the aristocracy.

> *If the two players of a game are forced to quit before the game is finished, how should the pot be divided?*

Pascal and Fermat solved the problem by developing basic methods of determining each player's chance, or probability, of winning.

The Dutch mathematician and scientist Christiaan Huygens (1629–1695) wrote a formal treatise on probability. It appeared in 1657 and was based on the Pascal–Fermat correspondence.

One of the first to apply probability to matters other than gambling was the French mathematician Pierre Simon de Laplace (1749–1827), who is usually credited with being the "father" of probability theory.

Probability

If you go to a supermarket and select five pounds of peaches at 89¢ per pound, you can easily predict the amount you will be charged at the checkout counter.

$$5 \cdot \$0.89 = \$4.45.$$

This is an example of a **deterministic phenomenon.** It can be predicted exactly on the basis of obtainable information, namely, in this case, number of pounds and cost per pound.

On the other hand, consider the problem faced by the produce manager of the market, who must order peaches to have on hand each day without knowing exactly how many pounds customers will buy during the day. Customer demand is an example of a **random phenomenon.** It fluctuates in such a way that its value (on a given day) cannot be predicted exactly with obtainable information.

The study of probability is concerned with such random phenomena. Even though we cannot be certain whether a given result will occur, we often can obtain a good measure of its *likelihood,* or **probability.** This chapter discusses various ways of finding and using probabilities.

Any observation, or measurement, of a random phenomenon is an **experiment.** The possible results of the experiment are **outcomes,** and the set of all possible outcomes is the **sample space.**

Usually we are interested in some particular collection of the possible outcomes. Any such subset of the sample space is an **event.** Outcomes that belong to the event are "favorable outcomes," or "successes." Any time a success is observed, we say that the event has "occurred." The probability of an event, being a numerical measure of the event's likelihood, is determined in one of two ways, either *theoretically* (mathematically) or *empirically* (experimentally).

Every event is a subset of the sample space.

"But is it probable," asked Pascal, "that probability gives assurance? Nothing gives certainty but truth; nothing gives rest but the sincere search for truth." When Pascal wrote that, he had gone to live at the Jansenist convent of Port-Royal after a carriage accident in 1654.

Pascal's notes on Christianity were collected after his death in the *Pensées* (thoughts). The above quotation is included. Another develops Pascal's "rule of the wager": If you bet God exists and live accordingly, you will have gained much even if God does not exist; if you bet the opposite and God does exist, you will have lost the reason for living right—hence everything.

▮▮ EXAMPLE 1 Finding Probability When Tossing a Coin

If a single coin is tossed, find the probability that it will land heads up.

SOLUTION

There is no apparent reason for one side of a coin to land up any more often than the other (in the long run), so we assume that heads and tails are equally likely.

The experiment here is the tossing of a single fair coin, the sample space is $S = \{h, t\}$, and the event whose probability we seek is $E = \{h\}$. Since one of the two equally likely outcomes is a head, the probability of heads is the quotient of 1 and 2.

$$\text{Probability (heads)} = \frac{1}{2}, \quad \text{written} \quad P(h) = \frac{1}{2} \quad \text{or} \quad P(E) = \frac{1}{2}. \quad \blacksquare\blacksquare\blacksquare$$

▮▮ EXAMPLE 2 Finding Probability When Tossing a Cup

If a Styrofoam cup is tossed, find the probability that it will land on its top.

SOLUTION

Intuitively, it seems that such a cup will land on its side much more often than on its top or its bottom. But just how much more often is not clear. To get an idea, we performed the experiment of tossing such a cup 50 times. It landed on its side 44 times, on its top 5 times, and on its bottom just 1 time. By the frequency of "success" in this experiment, we concluded for the cup we used that

$$P(\text{top}) \approx \frac{5}{50} = \frac{1}{10}. \quad \text{— (Write in lowest terms.)} \quad \blacksquare\blacksquare\blacksquare$$

In **Example 1** involving the tossing of a fair coin, the number of possible outcomes was obviously two, both were equally likely, and one of the outcomes was a head. No actual experiment was required. The desired probability was obtained *theoretically*. Theoretical probabilities apply to dice rolling, card games, roulette, lotteries, and so on, and apparently to many phenomena in nature.

Laplace, in his famous *Analytic Theory of Probability*, published in 1812, gave a formula that applies to any such theoretical probability, as long as the sample space S is finite and all outcomes are equally likely. (It is sometimes referred to as the *classical definition of probability*.)

Theoretical Probability Formula

If all outcomes in a sample space S are equally likely, and E is an event within that sample space, then the **theoretical probability** of event E is given by the following formula.

$$P(E) = \frac{\textbf{number of favorable outcomes}}{\textbf{total number of outcomes}} = \frac{n(E)}{n(S)}$$

On the other hand, **Example 2** involved the tossing of a cup, where the likelihoods of the various outcomes were not intuitively clear. It took an actual experiment to arrive at a probability value of $\frac{1}{10}$, and that value, based on a portion of all possible tosses of the cup, should be regarded as an approximation of the true theoretical probability. The value was found according to the *experimental*, or *empirical*, probability formula.

In 1827, **Robert Brown** (1773–1858), a Scottish physician and botanist, described the irregular motion of microscopic pollen grains suspended in water. Such "Brownian motion," as it came to be called, was not understood until 1905 when Albert Einstein explained it by treating molecular motion as a random phenomenon.

Empirical Probability Formula

If E is an event that may happen when an experiment is performed, then an **empirical probability** of event E is given by the following formula.

$$P(E) = \frac{\text{number of times event } E \text{ occurred}}{\text{number of times the experiment was performed}}$$

Usually it is clear in applications which probability formula should be used.

▋▋ **EXAMPLE 3** Finding the Probability of Having Daughters

Kathy Campbell wants to have exactly two daughters. Assuming that boy and girl babies are equally likely, find her probability of success if

(a) she has a total of two children. **(b)** she has a total of three children.

SOLUTION

(a) The equal likelihood assumption allows the use of theoretical probability. But how can we determine the number of favorable outcomes and the total number of possible outcomes?

One way is to use a tree diagram (see **Section 10.1**) to enumerate the possibilities, as shown in **Figure 1**. From the outcome column we obtain the sample space $S = \{gg, gb, bg, bb\}$. Only one outcome, marked with an arrow, is favorable to the event of exactly two daughters: $E = \{gg\}$.

$$P(E) = \frac{n(E)}{n(S)} = \frac{1}{4} \quad \text{Theoretical probability formula}$$

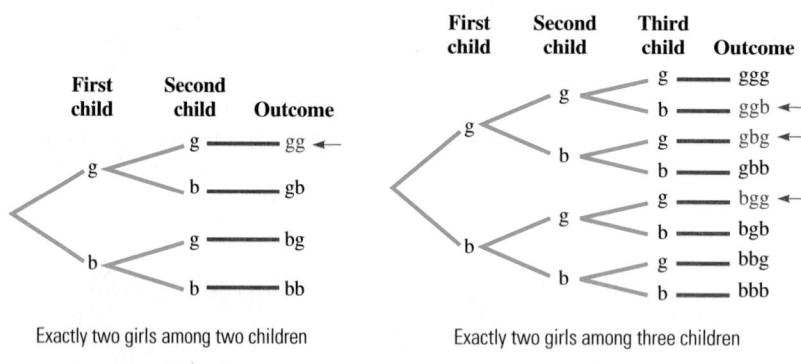

Exactly two girls among two children

Figure 1

Exactly two girls among three children

Figure 2

(b) For three children altogether, we construct another tree diagram, as shown in **Figure 2**. In this case, we see that

$$S = \{ggg, ggb, gbg, gbb, bgg, bgb, bbg, bbb\} \quad \text{and} \quad E = \{ggb, gbg, bgg\},$$

so $P(E) = \frac{3}{8}$. ▋▋▋

When dealing (or drawing) cards, as in the next example, the dealing is generally done "without replacement." Once dealt, a card is *not* replaced in the deck. So all cards in a hand are distinct. (Repetitions are *not* allowed.) In many cases, such as building three-digit numbers, repetition of digits *is* allowed. For example, 255 is a legitimate three-digit number. So digit selection is done "with replacement."

▌▌ **EXAMPLE 4** Finding Probability When Dealing Cards

Find the probability of being dealt each of the following hands in five-card poker. Use a calculator to obtain answers to eight decimal places.

(a) a full house (three of one denomination and two of another)

(b) a royal flush (the five highest cards—ace, king, queen, jack, ten—of a single suit)

SOLUTION

(a) **Table 1** summarizes the various possible kinds of five-card hands. (For more on card hands, see **Section 10.3.**) Since the 2,598,960 possible individual hands all are equally likely, we can enter the appropriate numbers from the table into the theoretical probability formula.

$$P(\text{full house}) - \frac{3744}{2{,}598{,}960} = \frac{6}{4165} \approx 0.00144058$$

(b) The table shows that there are four royal flushes, one for each suit.

$$P(\text{royal flush}) = \frac{4}{2{,}598{,}960} = \frac{1}{649{,}740} \approx 0.00000154 \qquad ▌▌▌$$

Examples 3 and 4 both utilized the theoretical probability formula because we were able to enumerate all possible outcomes and all were equally likely. In **Example 3,** however, the equal likelihood of girl and boy babies was *assumed*. In fact, male births typically occur a little more frequently. (At the same time, there usually are more females living at any given time, due to higher infant mortality rates among males and longer female life expectancy in general.) **Example 5** shows a way of incorporating such empirical information.

Table 1	Number of Poker Hands in 5-Card Poker; Nothing Wild
Event E	**Number of Outcomes Favorable to E**
Royal flush	4
Straight flush	36
Four of a kind	624
Full house	3744
Flush	5108
Straight	10,200
Three of a kind	54,912
Two pairs	123,552
One pair	1,098,240
No pair	1,302,540
Total	**2,598,960**

▌▌ **EXAMPLE 5** Finding the Probability of the Gender of a Resident

According to *Pocket World in Figures,* 2009 edition, published by *The Economist,* the U.S. population at the end of 2006 included 148.2 million males and 152.8 million females. If a person were selected randomly from the population in that year, what is the probability that the person would be a male?

SOLUTION

In this case, we calculate the empirical probability from the given experimental data.

$$P(\text{male}) = \frac{\text{number of males}}{\text{total number of persons}}$$

$$= \frac{148.2 \text{ million}}{148.2 \text{ million} + 152.8 \text{ million}}$$

$$\approx 0.492 \qquad ▌▌▌$$

The Law of Large Numbers

Recall the cup of **Example 2.** If we tossed it 50 more times, we would have 100 total tosses upon which to base an empirical probability of the cup landing on its top. The new value would likely be (at least slightly) different from what we obtained before. It would still be an empirical probability, but it would be "better" in the sense that it is based upon a larger set of outcomes.

The **law of large numbers** also can be stated as follows.

A theoretical probability really says nothing about one, or even a few, repetitions of an experiment, but only about the proportion of successes we would expect over the long run.

If, as we increase the number of tosses, the resulting empirical probability values approach some particular number, that number can be defined as the theoretical probability of that particular cup landing on its top. We could determine this "limiting" value only as the actual number of observed tosses approaches the total number of possible tosses of the cup. Since there are potentially an infinite number of possible tosses, we could never actually find the theoretical probability. But we can still assume such a number exists. And as the number of actual observed tosses increases, the resulting empirical probabilities should tend ever closer to the theoretical value.

This very important principle is known as the **law of large numbers** (or sometimes as the "law of averages").

Law of Large Numbers

As an experiment is repeated more and more times, the proportion of outcomes favorable to any particular event will tend to come closer and closer to the theoretical probability of that event.

▌▌ **EXAMPLE 6** Graphing a Sequence of Proportions

A fair coin was tossed 35 times, producing the following sequence of outcomes.

   tthhh, ttthh, hthtt, hhthh, ttthh, thttt, hhthh

Calculate the ratio of heads to total tosses after the first toss, the second toss, and so on through all 35 tosses, and plot these ratios on a graph.

SOLUTION

After the first toss, we have 0 heads out of 1 toss, for a ratio of $\frac{0}{1} = 0.00$. After two tosses, we have $\frac{0}{2} = 0.00$. After three tosses, we have $\frac{1}{3} \approx 0.33$. Verify that the first six ratios are

   0.00, 0.00, 0.33, 0.50, 0.60, 0.50.

The thirty-five ratios are plotted as points in **Figure 3**. The fluctuations away from 0.50 become smaller as the number of tosses increases, and the ratios appear to approach 0.50 toward the right side of the graph, in keeping with the law of large numbers.

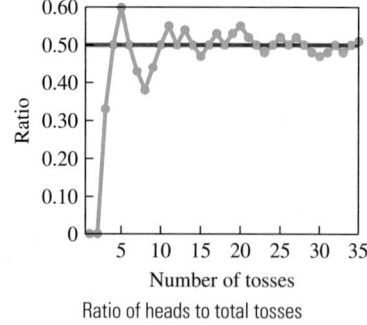

Number of tosses

Ratio of heads to total tosses

Figure 3

▌▌▌

Comparing Empirical and Theoretical Probabilities

A series of repeated experiments provides an *empirical probability* for an event, which, by *inductive reasoning*, is an *estimate* of the event's *theoretical probability*. (Increasing the number of repetitions increases the reliability of the estimate.)

Likewise, an established *theoretical probability* for an event enables us, by *deductive reasoning*, to *predict* the proportion of times the event will occur in a series of repeated experiments. (The prediction should be more accurate for larger numbers of repetitions.)

Probability in Genetics

Probabilities, both empirical and theoretical, have been valuable tools in many areas of science. An important early example was the work of the Austrian monk Gregor Mendel, who used the idea of randomness to help establish the study of genetics.

In an effort to understand the mechanism of character transmittal from one generation to the next in plants, Mendel counted the number of occurrences of various characteristics. He found that the flower color in certain pea plants obeyed this scheme:

Pure red crossed with pure white produces red.

Mendel theorized that red is "dominant" (symbolized with the capital letter R), while white is "recessive" (symbolized with the lowercase letter r). The pure red parent carried only genes for red (R), and the pure white parent carried only genes for white (r). The offspring would receive one gene from each parent, hence one of the four combinations shown in the body of **Table 2**. Because every offspring receives one gene for red, that characteristic dominates and the offspring exhibits the color red.

Gregor Johann Mendel (1822–1884) came from a peasant family who managed to send him to school. By 1847 he had been ordained and was teaching at the Abbey of St. Thomas. He finished his education at the University of Vienna and returned to the abbey to teach mathematics and natural science.

Mendel began to carry out experiments on plants in the abbey garden, notably pea plants, whose distinct traits (unit characters) he had puzzled over. In 1865 he published his results. His work was not appreciated at the time even though he had laid the foundation of **classical genetics.**

Table 2 First to Second Generation

		Second Parent	
		r	r
First Parent	R	Rr	Rr
	R	Rr	Rr

Table 3 Second to Third Generation

		Second Parent	
		R	r
First Parent	R	RR	Rr
	r	rR	rr

Now each of these second-generation offspring, though exhibiting the color red, still carries one of each gene. So when two of them are crossed, each third-generation offspring will receive one of the gene combinations shown in **Table 3**. Mendel theorized that each of these four possibilities would be equally likely and produced experimental counts that were close enough to support this hypothesis.

▮▮ **EXAMPLE 7** Finding Probabilities of Flower Colors

Referring to **Table 3**, determine the probability that a third-generation offspring will exhibit each flower color. Base the probabilities on the sample space of equally likely outcomes: $S = \{RR, Rr, rR, rr\}$.

(a) red **(b)** white

SOLUTION

(a) Since red dominates white, any combination with at least one gene for red (R) will result in red flowers. Since three of the four possibilities meet this criterion, $P(\text{red}) = \frac{3}{4}$.

(b) Only the combination rr has no gene for red, so $P(\text{white}) = \frac{1}{4}$. ▮▮▮

Odds

Whereas probability compares the number of favorable outcomes to the total number of outcomes, **odds** compare the number of favorable outcomes to the number of unfavorable outcomes. Odds are commonly quoted, rather than probabilities, in horse racing, lotteries, and most other gambling situations. And the odds quoted normally are odds "against" rather than odds "in favor."

Smoking 1.4 cigarettes
Spending 1 hour in a coal mine
Living 2 days in New York or Boston
Eating 40 teaspoons of peanut butter
Living 2 months with a cigarette smoker
Flying 1000 miles in a jet
Traveling 300 miles in a car
Riding 10 miles on a bicycle

Risk is the probability that a harmful event will occur. Almost every action or substance exposes a person to some risk, and the assessment and reduction of risk accounts for a great deal of study and effort in our world. The list above, from *Calculated Risk*, by J. Rodricks, contains activities that carry an annual increased risk of death by one chance in a million.

Odds

If all outcomes in a sample space are equally likely, a of them are favorable to the event E, and the remaining b outcomes are unfavorable to E, then the **odds in favor** of E are a to b, and the **odds against** E are b to a.

▮▮ **EXAMPLE 8** Finding the Odds of Getting an Intern Position

Theresa Cortesini has been promised one of six jobs, three of which would be intern positions at the state capitol. If she has equal chances for all six jobs, find the odds that she will get one of the intern positions.

SOLUTION

Since three possibilities are favorable and three are not, the odds of becoming an intern at the capitol are 3 to 3 (or 1 to 1 in reduced terms). Odds of 1 to 1 are often termed "even odds," or a "50–50 chance." ▮▮▮

▮▮ **EXAMPLE 9** Finding the Odds of Winning a Raffle

Bob Barickman has purchased 12 tickets for an office raffle in which the winner will receive an iPad. If 104 tickets were sold altogether and each has an equal chance of winning, what are the odds against Bob's winning the iPad?

SOLUTION

Bob has 12 chances to win and $104 - 12 = 92$ chances to lose, so the odds against winning are 92 to 12, or 23 to 3. (Divide both 92 and 12 by 4.) ▮▮▮

Converting between Probability and Odds

Let E be an event.

1. If $P(E) = \frac{a}{b}$, then the odds in favor of E are a to $(b - a)$.

2. If the odds in favor of E are a to b, then $P(E) = \frac{a}{a + b}$.

▮▮ **EXAMPLE 10** Converting from Probability to Odds

There is a 30% chance of rain tomorrow. Give this information in terms of odds.

SOLUTION

$$P(\text{rain}) = 0.30 = \frac{30}{100} = \frac{3}{10}$$

Convert the decimal fraction to a quotient of integers and reduce.

By conversion formula 1 above, the odds in favor of rain are 3 to $10 - 3$, or 3 to 7. Or, we can say the odds are 7 to 3 against rain tomorrow. ▮▮▮

▮▮ **EXAMPLE 11** Converting from Odds to Probability

In a certain sweepstakes, your odds of winning are 1 to 99,999. What is the probability that you will win?

SOLUTION

$$P(\text{win}) = \frac{1}{1 + 99,999} = \frac{1}{100,000} = 0.00001 \quad \text{Conversion formula 2}$$ ▮▮▮

11.1 EXERCISES

In Exercises 1–4, give the probability that the spinner shown would land on **(a)** *red,* **(b)** *yellow,* **(c)** *blue.*

1.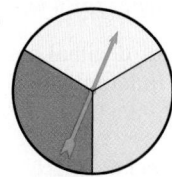

2.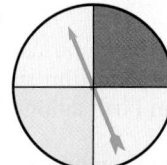

3.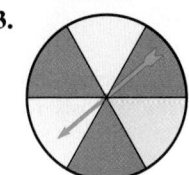

4.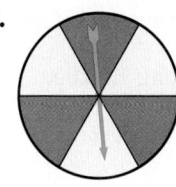

Solve each probability problem.

5. **Using Spinners to Generate Numbers** Suppose the spinner shown here is spun once, to determine a single-digit number, and we are interested in the event E that the resulting number is odd. Give each of the following.
   (a) the sample space
   (b) the number of favorable outcomes
   (c) the number of unfavorable outcomes
   (d) the total number of possible outcomes
   (e) the probability of an odd number
   (f) the odds in favor of an odd number

6. **Lining Up Preschool Children** Kim Lenaghan's group of preschool children includes nine girls and seven boys. If Kim randomly selects one child to be first in line, with E being the event that the one selected is a girl, give each of the following.
   (a) the total number of possible outcomes
   (b) the number of favorable outcomes
   (c) the number of unfavorable outcomes
   (d) the probability of event E
   (e) the odds in favor of event E

7. **Using Spinners to Generate Numbers** The spinner of **Exercise 5** is spun twice in succession to determine a two-digit number. Give each of the following.
   (a) the sample space
   (b) the probability of an odd number
   (c) the probability of a number with repeated digits
   (d) the probability of a number greater than 30
   (e) the probability of a prime number

8. **Probabilities in Coin Tossing** Two fair coins are tossed (say a dime and a quarter). Give each of the following.

(a) the sample space
(b) the probability of heads on the dime
(c) the probability of heads on the quarter
(d) the probability of getting both heads
(e) the probability of getting the same outcome on both coins

9. **Drawing Balls from an Urn** Anne Kelly randomly chooses a single ball from the urn shown here. Find the odds against each event.
   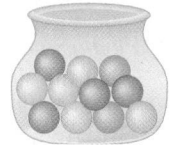
   (a) red   **(b)** yellow   **(c)** blue

10. **Random Selection of Club Officers** Five people (Alan, Bill, Cathy, David, and Evelyn) form a club $N = \{A, B, C, D, E\}$. If they choose a president randomly, find the odds against each result.
    (a) Cathy   **(b)** a woman
    (c) a person whose name begins with a consonant

11. **Random Selection of Fifties Music** Butch LeBeau has fifty hit singles from the fifties, including exactly one by Smiley Lewis, two by The Drifters, three by Bobby Darin, four by The Coasters, and five by Fats Domino. If Butch randomly selects one hit from his collection of fifty, find the probability it will be by each of the following.
    (a) Smiley Lewis   **(b)** The Drifters
    (c) Bobby Darin   **(d)** The Coasters
    (e) Fats Domino

12. **Probabilities in Coin Tossing** Three fair coins are tossed.
    (a) Write out the sample space.
    Determine the probability of each event.
    (b) no heads   **(c)** exactly one head
    (d) exactly two heads   **(e)** three heads

13. **Number Sums for Rolling Two Dice** The sample space for the rolling of two fair dice appeared in **Table 2** of **Section 10.1**. Reproduce that table, but replace each of the 36 equally likely ordered pairs with its corresponding sum (for the two dice). Then find the probability of rolling each sum.
    (a) 2   **(b)** 3   **(c)** 4
    (d) 5   **(e)** 6   **(f)** 7
    (g) 8   **(h)** 9   **(i)** 10
    (j) 11   **(k)** 12

In Exercises 14 and 15, give answers to three decimal places.

14. **Probability of Seed Germination** In a hybrid corn research project, 200 seeds were planted, and 175 of them germinated. Find the empirical probability that any particular seed of this type will germinate.

15. *Probability of Forest Land in California* According to *The World Almanac and Book of Facts 2010*, California has 155,959 square miles of land area, 51,250 square miles of which are forested. Find the probability that a randomly selected location in California will be forested.

16. *Probabilities of Two Daughters Among Four Children* In **Example 3,** what would be Kathy's probability of having exactly two daughters if she were to have four children altogether? (You may want to use a tree diagram to construct the sample space.)

17. *Rolling Altered Dice* A six-sided die has been altered so that the side that had been a single dot is now a blank face. Another die has a blank face instead of the face with four dots. What is the probability that a sum of 7 is rolled when the two dice are thrown? (*Mathematics Teacher* calendar problem)

18. *Probability of Location in a Tunnel* Mr. Davis is driving through a tunnel that is eight miles long. At this instant, what is the probability that he is at least six miles from one end of the tunnel? (*Mathematics Teacher* calendar problem)

Genetics in Snapdragons Mendel found no dominance in snapdragons (in contrast to peas) with respect to red and white flower color. When pure red and pure white parents are crossed (see **Table 2**), the resulting Rr combination (one of each gene) produces second-generation offspring with pink flowers. These second-generation pinks, however, still carry one red and one white gene, so when they are crossed the third generation is still governed by **Table 3**.

Find each probability for third-generation snapdragons.

19. *P*(red) 20. *P*(pink) 21. *P*(white)

Genetics in Pea Plants Mendel also investigated various characteristics besides flower color. For example, round peas are dominant over recessive wrinkled peas. First, second, and third generations can again be analyzed using **Tables 2 and 3**, where R represents round and r represents wrinkled.

22. Explain why crossing pure round and pure wrinkled first-generation parents will always produce round peas in the second-generation offspring.

23. When second-generation round pea plants (each of which carries both R and r genes) are crossed, find the probability that a third-generation offspring will have

   (a) round peas, (b) wrinkled peas.

Genetics of Cystic Fibrosis Cystic fibrosis *is one of the most common inherited diseases in North America (including the United States), occurring in about* 1 *of every* 2000 *Caucasian births and about* 1 *of every* 250,000 *non-Caucasian births. Even with modern treatment, victims usually die from lung damage by their early twenties.*

If we denote a cystic fibrosis gene with a C *and a disease-free gene with a* C *(since the disease is recessive), then only a*

cc *person will actually have the disease. Such persons would ordinarily die before parenting children, but a child can also inherit the disease from two* Cc *parents (who themselves are healthy, that is, have no symptoms but are "carriers" of the disease). This is like a pea plant inheriting white flowers from two red-flowered parents that both carry genes for white.*

24. Find the empirical probability (to four decimal places) that cystic fibrosis will occur in a randomly selected infant birth among U.S. Caucasians.

25. Find the empirical probability (to six decimal places) that cystic fibrosis will occur in a randomly selected infant birth among U.S. non-Caucasians.

26. Among 150,000 North American Caucasian births, about how many occurrences of cystic fibrosis would you expect?

Suppose that both partners in a marriage are cystic fibrosis carriers (a rare occurrence). Construct a chart similar to **Table 3** *and determine the probability of each of the following events.*

27. Their first child will have the disease.

28. Their first child will be a carrier.

29. Their first child will neither have nor carry the disease.

Suppose a child is born to one cystic fibrosis carrier parent and one non-carrier parent. Find the probability of each of the following events.

30. The child will have cystic fibrosis.

31. The child will be a healthy cystic fibrosis carrier.

32. The child will neither have nor carry the disease.

Genetics of Sickle-Cell Anemia Sickle-cell anemia *occurs in about* 1 *of every* 500 *black baby births and about* 1 *of every* 160,000 *non-black baby births. It is ordinarily fatal in early childhood. There is a test to identify carriers. Unlike cystic fibrosis, which is recessive, sickle-cell anemia is* **codominant.** *This means that inheriting two sickle-cell genes causes the disease, while inheriting just one sickle-cell gene causes a mild (non-fatal) version (which is called* **sickle-cell trait**). *This is similar to a snapdragon plant manifesting pink flowers by inheriting one red gene and one white gene.*

In Exercises 33 and 34, find the empirical probabilities of the given events.

33. A randomly selected black baby will have sickle-cell anemia. (Give your answer to three decimal places.)

34. A randomly selected non-black baby will have sickle-cell anemia. (Give your answer to six decimal places.)

35. Among 80,000 births of black babies, about how many occurrences of sickle-cell anemia would you expect?

Find the theoretical probability of each condition in a child both of whose parents have sickle-cell trait.

36. The child will have sickle-cell anemia.

37. The child will have sickle-cell trait.

38. The child will be healthy.

39. *Women's 100-Meter Run* In the history of track and field, no woman has broken the 10-second barrier in the 100-meter run.

   (a) From the statement above, find the empirical probability that a woman runner will break the 10-second barrier next year.

   (b) Can you find the theoretical probability for the event of part (a)?

   (c) Is it possible that the event of part (a) will occur?

40. Is there any way a coin could fail to be "fair"? Explain.

41. On page 27 of their book *Descartes' Dream*, Philip Davis and Reuben Hersh ask the question, "Is probability real or is it just a cover-up for ignorance?" What do you think? Are some things truly random, or is everything potentially deterministic?

42. If $P(E) = 0.37$, find

   (a) the odds in favor of E,   **(b)** the odds against E.

43. If the odds in favor of event E are 12 to 19, find $P(E)$.

44. If the odds against event E are 10 to 3, find $P(E)$.

Probabilities of Poker Hands *In 5-card poker, find the probability of being dealt each of the following. Give each answer to eight decimal places. (Refer to* **Table 1**.)

45. a straight flush   **46.** two pairs

47. four of a kind   **48.** four queens

49. a hearts flush (*not* a royal flush or a straight flush)

50. *Probabilities in Dart Throwing* If a dart hits the square target shown here at random, what is the probability that it will hit in a colored region? (*Hint:* Compare the area of the colored regions to the total area of the target.)

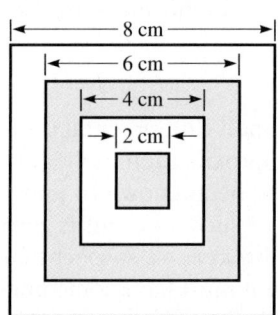

51. *Probabilities in Olympic Curling* In the Olympic event of curling, the scoring area (shown here) consists of four concentric circles on the ice with radii of 6 inches, 2 feet, 4 feet, and 6 feet.

If a team member lands a (43-pound) stone *randomly* within the scoring area, find the probability that it ends up centered on

   (a) red,   **(b)** white,   **(c)** blue.

52. *Drawing Cards* When drawing cards without replacement from a standard 52-card deck, find the maximum number of cards you could possibly draw and still get

   (a) fewer than three black cards,

   (b) fewer than six spades,

   (c) fewer than four face cards,

   (d) fewer than two kings.

The remaining exercises require careful thought to determine n(E) and n(S). (In some cases, you may want to employ counting methods from Chapter 10, such as the fundamental counting principle, permutations, or combinations.)

Probabilities of Seating Arrangements *Six people (three married couples) arrange themselves randomly in six consecutive seats in a row. Find the probability of each event in Exercises 53–56. (Hint: In each case the denominator of the probability fraction will be 6! = 720, the total number of ways to arrange six items.)*

53. Each man will sit immediately to the left of his wife.

54. Each man will sit immediately to the left of a woman.

55. The women will be in three adjacent seats.

56. The women will be in three adjacent seats, as will the men.

57. *Selecting Slopes* If two distinct numbers are chosen randomly from the set $\{-2, -\frac{4}{3}, -\frac{1}{2}, 0, \frac{1}{2}, \frac{3}{4}, 3\}$, find the probability that they will be the slopes of two perpendicular lines. (See **Section 8.2**.)

58. *Racing Bets* At most horse-racing tracks, the "trifecta" is a particular race in which you win if you correctly pick the "win," "place," and "show" horses (the first-, second-, and third-place winners), in their proper order. If five horses of equal ability are entered in today's trifecta race, and Tracy Light selects an entry, what is the probability that she will be a winner?

59. *Probabilities of Student Course Schedules* Suppose you plan to take three courses next term. If you select them randomly from a listing of twelve courses, five of which are science courses, what is the probability that all three courses you select will be science courses?

60. *Selecting Symphony Performances* Rhonda Goedeker randomly selects three symphony performances to attend this season, choosing from a schedule of ten performances, three of which will feature works by Beethoven. Find the probability that Rhonda will select all of the Beethoven programs.

Selecting Class Reports *Assuming that Ben, Jill, and Pam are three of the 26 members of the class, and that three of the class members will be chosen randomly to deliver their reports during the next class meeting, find the probability (to six decimal places) of each event.*

61. Ben, Jill, and Pam are selected, in that order.

62. Ben, Jill, and Pam are selected, in any order.

63. *Random Selection of Prime Numbers* If two distinct prime numbers are randomly selected from among the first eight prime numbers, what is the probability that their sum will be 24?

64. *Building Numbers from Sets of Digits* The digits 1, 2, 3, 4, and 5 are randomly arranged to form a five-digit number. Find the probability of each event.
(a) The number is even.
(b) The first and last digits of the number both are even.

65. *Random Sums* Two integers are randomly selected from the set $\{1, 2, 3, 4, 5, 6, 7, 8, 9\}$ and are added together. Find the probability that their sum is 11 if they are selected
(a) with replacement,   **(b)** without replacement.

66. *Random Sums and Products* Tamika selects two different numbers at random from the set $\{8, 9, 10\}$ and adds them. Carlos takes two different numbers at random from the set $\{3, 5, 6\}$ and multiplies them. What is the probability that Tamika's result is greater than Carlos's result? (*Mathematics Teacher* calendar problem)

67. *Divisibility of Random Products* When a fair six-sided die is tossed on a tabletop, the bottom face cannot be seen. What is the probability that the product of the numbers on the five faces that can be seen is divisible by 6? (*Mathematics Teacher* calendar problem)

68. *Building Fractions with Dice* Lisa has one red die and one green die, which she rolls to make up fractions. The green die is the numerator, and the red die is the denominator. Some of the fractions have terminating decimal representations. How many different terminating decimal results can these two dice represent? What is the probability of rolling a fraction with a terminating decimal representation? (*Mathematics Teacher* calendar problem)

Finding Palindromic Numbers *Numbers that are* **palindromes** *read the same forward and backward. For example, 30203 is a five-digit palindrome. If a single number is chosen randomly from each of the following sets, find the probability that it will be palindromic.*

69. the set of all two-digit numbers

70. the set of all three-digit numbers

Six people, call them A, B, C, D, E, and F, are randomly divided into three groups of two. Find the probability of each event. (Do not impose unwanted ordering among groups.)

71. *A* and *B* are in the same group, as are *C* and *D*.

72. *E* and *F* are in the same group.

11.2 EVENTS INVOLVING "NOT" AND "OR"

Properties of Probability • Events Involving "Not" • Events Involving "Or"

Properties of Probability

Recall that an empirical probability, based upon experimental observation, may be the best value available but still is only an approximation to the ("true") theoretical probability. For example, no human has ever been known to jump higher than 8.5 feet vertically, so the empirical probability of such an event is zero. Observing the rate at which high jump records have been broken, we suspect that the event is, in fact, possible and may one day occur. Hence it must have some nonzero theoretical probability, even though we have no way of assessing its exact value.

Recall also that the theoretical probability formula,

$$P(E) = \frac{n(E)}{n(S)},$$

is valid only when all outcomes in the sample space S are equally likely. For the experiment of tossing two fair coins, we can write $S = \{hh, ht, th, tt\}$ and compute

$$P(\text{both heads}) = \frac{1}{4}, \quad \text{which is } correct,$$

whereas if we define the sample space with non-equally likely outcomes as $S = \{\text{both heads, both tails, one of each}\}$, we are led to

$$P(\text{both heads}) = \frac{1}{3}, \quad \text{which is } incorrect.$$

(To convince yourself that $\frac{1}{4}$ is a better value than $\frac{1}{3}$, toss two fair coins 100 times or so to see what the empirical fraction seems to approach.)

For any event E within a sample space S, we know that $0 \leq n(E) \leq n(S)$. Dividing all members of this inequality by $n(S)$ gives

$$\frac{0}{n(S)} \leq \frac{n(E)}{n(S)} \leq \frac{n(S)}{n(S)}, \quad \text{or} \quad 0 \leq P(E) \leq 1.$$

In words, the probability of any event is a number from 0 through 1, inclusive.

If event E is *impossible* (cannot happen), then $n(E)$ must be 0 (E is the empty set), so $P(E) = 0$. If event E is *certain* (cannot help but happen), then $n(E) = n(S)$, so

$$P(E) = \frac{n(E)}{n(S)} = \frac{n(S)}{n(S)} = 1.$$

Pierre Simon de Laplace (1749–1827) began in 1773 to solve the problem of why Jupiter's orbit seems to shrink and Saturn's orbit seems to expand. Eventually Laplace worked out a complete theory of the solar system. *Celestial Mechanics* resulted from almost a lifetime of work. In five volumes, it was published between 1799 and 1825 and gained for Laplace the reputation "Newton of France."

Laplace's work on probability was actually an adjunct to his celestial mechanics. He needed to demonstrate that probability is useful in interpreting scientific data.

Properties of Probability

Let E be an event within the sample space S. That is, E is a subset of S. Then the following properties hold.

1. $0 \leq P(E) \leq 1$ (The probability of an event is a number from 0 through 1, inclusive.)

2. $P(\emptyset) = 0$ (The probability of an impossible event is 0.)

3. $P(S) = 1$ (The probability of a certain event is 1.)

▌▌ EXAMPLE 1 Finding Probability When Rolling a Die

When a single fair die is rolled, find the probability of each event.

(a) the number 2 is rolled   **(b)** a number other than 2 is rolled

(c) the number 7 is rolled   **(d)** a number less than 7 is rolled

SOLUTION

(a) Since one of the six possibilities is a 2, $P(2) = \frac{1}{6}$.

(b) There are five such numbers, 1, 3, 4, 5, and 6, so $P(\text{a number other than 2}) = \frac{5}{6}$.

(c) None of the possible outcomes is 7. Thus, $P(7) = \frac{0}{6} = 0$.

(d) Since all six of the possible outcomes are less than 7,

$$P(\text{a number less than 7}) = \frac{6}{6} = 1.$$

■ ■ ■

No probability in **Example 1** was less than 0 or greater than 1, which illustrates probability property 1. The "impossible" event of part (c) had probability 0, illustrating property 2. The "certain" event of part (d) had probability 1, illustrating property 3.

Events Involving "Not"

Table 4 repeats the information of **Table 8** of **Section 10.5,** with a third correspondence added in row 3. These correspondences are the basis for the probability rules. For example, the probability of an event *not* happening involves the *complement* and *subtraction,* according to row 1 of the table.

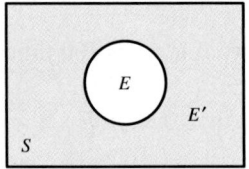

The logical connective "not" corresponds to "complement" in set theory.

$$P(not\ E) = P(S) - P(E)$$
$$= 1 - P(E)$$

Figure 4

Table 4   Set Theory/Logic/Arithmetic Correspondences

	Set Theory	**Logic**	**Arithmetic**
1. Operation or Connective (Symbol)	Complement (')	Not (~)	Subtraction (−)
2. Operation or Connective (Symbol)	Union (∪)	Or (∨)	Addition (+)
3. Operation or Connective (Symbol)	Intersection (∩)	And (∧)	Multiplication (·)

The rule for the probability of a complement follows and is illustrated in **Figure 4**.

> **Probability of a Complement (for Not E)**
>
> The probability that an event E will *not* occur is equal to one minus the probability that it *will* occur.
>
> $$P(\text{not } E) = 1 - P(E)$$

Notice that the events of **Examples 1(a) and (b),** namely "2" and "not 2," are complements of one another, and that their probabilities add up to 1. This illustrates the above probability rule. The equation

$$P(E) + P(E') = 1$$

is a rearrangement of the formula for the probability of a complement. Another form of the equation that is also useful at times follows.

$$P(E) = 1 - P(E')$$

▌▌ **EXAMPLE 2**   Finding the Probability of a Complement

When a single card is drawn from a standard 52-card deck, what is the probability that it will not be a king?

SOLUTION

$$P(\text{not a king}) = 1 - P(\text{king}) = 1 - \frac{4}{52} = \frac{48}{52} = \frac{12}{13}$$ ⟵ Remember to write in lowest terms. ▌▌▌

EXAMPLE 3 Finding the Probability of a Complement

If five fair coins are tossed, find the probability of obtaining at least two heads.

SOLUTION

There are $2^5 = 32$ possible outcomes for the experiment of tossing five fair coins. Most include at least two heads. In fact, only the outcomes

$$ttttt, \quad htttt, \quad thttt, \quad tthtt, \quad tttht, \quad \text{and} \quad tttth$$

do *not* include at least two heads. If E denotes the event "at least two heads," then E' is the event "not at least two heads,"

$$P(E) = 1 - P(E') = 1 - \frac{6}{32} = \frac{26}{32} = \frac{13}{16}$$ ▮▮▮

Mary Somerville (1780–1872) is associated with Laplace because of her brilliant exposition of his *Celestial Mechanics.*

Somerville studied Euclid thoroughly and perfected her Latin so she could read Newton's *Principia.* In about 1816 she went to London and soon became part of its literary and scientific circles.

Somerville's book on Laplace's theories came out in 1831 with great acclaim. Then followed a panoramic book, *Connection of the Physical Sciences* (1834). A statement in one of its editions suggested that irregularities in the orbit of Uranus might indicate that a more remote planet, not yet seen, existed. This caught the eye of the scientists who worked out the calculations for Neptune's orbit.

Events Involving "Or"

Examples 2 and 3 showed how the probability of an event can be approached *indirectly,* by first considering the complement of the event. Another indirect approach is to break the event into simpler component events. Row 2 of **Table 4** indicates that the probability of one event *or* another should involve the *union* and *addition.*

EXAMPLE 4 Selecting From a Set of Numbers

If one number is selected randomly from the set $\{1, 2, 3, 4, 5, 6, 7, 8, 9, 10\}$, find the probability that it will be

(a) odd or a multiple of 4   **(b)** odd or a multiple of 3.

SOLUTION

Define the following events:

$$\begin{aligned} S &= \{1, 2, 3, 4, 5, 6, 7, 8, 9, 10\} &&\text{Sample space} \\ A &= \{1, 3, 5, 7, 9\} &&\text{Odd outcomes} \\ B &= \{4, 8\} &&\text{Multiples of 4} \\ C &= \{3, 6, 9\} &&\text{Multiples of 3} \end{aligned}$$

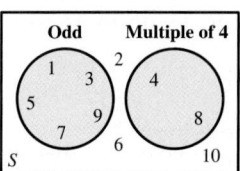

Figure 5

(a) **Figure 5** shows the positioning of the 10 integers within the sample space and within the pertinent sets A and B. The composite event "A or B" corresponds to the set $A \cup B = \{1, 3, 4, 5, 7, 8, 9\}$. By the theoretical probability formula,

$$P(A \text{ or } B) = \frac{7}{10}.$$ 〔Of 10 total outcomes, 7 are favorable.〕

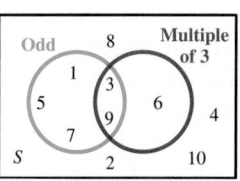

Figure 6

(b) **Figure 6** shows the situation.

〔Of 10 total outcomes, 6 are favorable.〕

$$P(A \text{ or } C) = \frac{6}{10} = \frac{3}{5}$$ ▮▮▮

Would an addition formula have worked in **Example 4**? Let's check.

Part (a): $P(A \text{ or } B) = P(A) + P(B) = \dfrac{5}{10} + \dfrac{2}{10} = \dfrac{7}{10}$ Correct

Part (b): $P(A \text{ or } C) = P(A) + P(C) = \dfrac{5}{10} + \dfrac{3}{10} = \dfrac{8}{10} = \dfrac{4}{5}$ Incorrect

The trouble in part (b) is that A and C are not disjoint sets. They have outcomes in common. Just as with the additive counting principle in **Chapter 10,** an adjustment must be made here to compensate for counting the common outcomes twice.

$$P(A \text{ or } C) = P(A) + P(C) - P(A \text{ and } C)$$

$$= \frac{5}{10} + \frac{3}{10} - \frac{2}{10} = \frac{6}{10} = \frac{3}{5} \qquad \text{Correct}$$

In probability theory, events that are disjoint sets are called *mutually exclusive events.*

Mutually Exclusive Events

Two events A and B are **mutually exclusive events** if they have no outcomes in common. (Mutually exclusive events cannot occur simultaneously.)

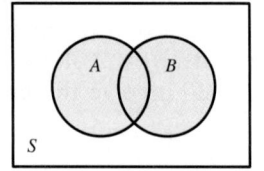

The logical connective "or" corresponds to "union" in set theory.

$P(A \text{ or } B)$
    $= P(A) + P(B) - P(A \text{ and } B)$

Figure 7

The results observed in **Example 4** are generalized as follows. The two possibilities are illustrated in **Figures 7 and 8**.

Addition Rule of Probability (for A or B)

If A and B are any two events, then

$$\mathbf{P(A \text{ or } B) = P(A) + P(B) - P(A \text{ and } B).}$$

If A and B are mutually exclusive, then

$$\mathbf{P(A \text{ or } B) = P(A) + P(B).}$$

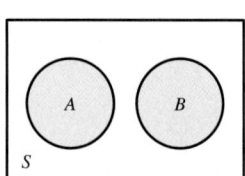

When A and B are mutually exclusive,

$P(A \text{ or } B) = P(A) + P(B).$

Figure 8

Actually, the first formula in the addition rule applies in all cases. (The third term on the right drops out when A and B are mutually exclusive, because $P(A \text{ and } B) = 0$.) Still it is good to remember the second formula in the preceding box for the many cases where the component events are mutually exclusive. In this section, we consider only cases where the event "A and B" is simple. We deal with more involved composites involving "and" in the next section.

▌▌ **EXAMPLE 5** Finding the Probability of an Event Involving "Or"

If a single card is drawn from a standard 52-card deck, what is the probability that it will be a spade or a red card?

SOLUTION

First note that "spade" and "red" cannot both occur, because there are no red spades. (All spades are black.) Therefore, we can use the formula for mutually exclusive events. There are 13 spades and 26 red cards in the deck.

$$P(\text{spade or red}) = P(\text{spade}) + P(\text{red}) = \frac{13}{52} + \frac{26}{52} = \frac{39}{52} = \frac{3}{4} \qquad ▉▉▉$$

We often need to consider composites of more than two events. When each event involved is mutually exclusive of all the others, we extend the addition rule to the appropriate number of components.

EXAMPLE 6 Treating Unions of Several Components

Amy Hogan plans to spend from 1 to 6 hours on her homework. If x represents the number of hours to be spent, then the probabilities of the various values of x, rounded to the nearest hour, are shown in **Table 5**. Find the probabilities that Amy will spend

(a) fewer than 3 hours **(b)** more than 2 hours

(c) more than 1 but no more than 5 hours **(d)** fewer than 5 hours.

Table 5

x	$P(x)$
1	0.05
2	0.10
3	0.20
4	0.40
5	0.10
6	0.15

SOLUTION

Because the time periods in **Table 5** are mutually exclusive of one another, we can simply add the appropriate component probabilities.

(a) $P(\text{fewer than 3}) = P(1 \text{ or } 2)$ Fewer than 3 means 1 or 2.

$= P(1) + P(2)$ Addition rule

$= 0.05 + 0.10$ Substitute values from **Table 5.**

$= 0.15$

(b) $P(\text{more than 2}) = P(3 \text{ or } 4 \text{ or } 5 \text{ or } 6)$ More than 2 means 3, 4, 5, or 6.

$= P(3) + P(4) + P(5) + P(6)$ Addition rule

$= 0.20 + 0.40 + 0.10 + 0.15$ Substitute values from **Table 5.**

$= 0.85$

(c) $P(\text{more than 1 but no more than 5})$

$= P(2 \text{ or } 3 \text{ or } 4 \text{ or } 5)$ 2, 3, 4, and 5 are more than 1 and no more than 5.

$= P(2) + P(3) + P(4) + P(5)$ Addition rule

$= 0.10 + 0.20 + 0.40 + 0.10$ Substitute values from **Table 5.**

$= 0.80$

(d) Although we could take a direct approach here, as in parts (a), (b), and (c), we will combine the complement rule with the addition rule.

$P(\text{fewer than 5}) = 1 - P(\text{not fewer than 5})$ Complement rule

$= 1 - P(5 \text{ or more})$ 5 or more is equivalent to not fewer than 5.

$= 1 - P(5 \text{ or } 6)$ 5 or more means 5 or 6.

$= 1 - [P(5) + P(6)]$ Addition rule

$= 1 - (0.10 + 0.15)$ Substitute values from **Table 5.**

$= 1 - 0.25$ Add inside the parentheses first.

$= 0.75$ ■■■

Table 5 in **Example 6** lists all possible time intervals so the corresponding probabilities add up to 1, a necessary condition for the way part (d) was done. The time spent on homework here is an example of a **random variable.** (It is "random" since we cannot predict which of its possible values will occur.)

A listing like **Table 5**, which shows all possible values of a random variable, along with the probabilities that those values will occur, is called a **probability distribution** for that random variable. Since *all* possible values are listed, they make up the entire sample space, and so the listed probabilities must add up to 1 (by probability property 3). Probability distributions will occur in **Exercises 32 and 33** of this section and will be discussed further in later sections.

██ EXAMPLE 7 Finding the Probability of an Event Involving "Or"

Find the probability that a single card drawn from a standard 52-card deck will be a diamond or a face card.

SOLUTION

The component events "diamond" and "face card" can occur simultaneously. (The jack, queen, and king of diamonds belong to both events.) So, we must use the first formula of the addition rule. We let D denote "diamond" and F denote "face card."

$$P(D \text{ or } F) = P(D) + P(F) - P(D \text{ and } F) \quad \text{Addition rule}$$

$$= \frac{13}{52} + \frac{12}{52} - \frac{3}{52} \quad \text{There are 13 diamonds, 12 face cards, and 3 that are both.}$$

$$= \frac{22}{52} \quad \text{Add and subtract.}$$

$$= \frac{11}{26} \quad \text{Write in lowest terms.} \quad ███$$

██ EXAMPLE 8 Finding the Probability of an Event Involving "Or"

Of 20 elective courses, Emily Horowitz plans to enroll in one, which she will choose by throwing a dart at the schedule of courses. If 8 of the courses are recreational, 9 are interesting, and 3 are both recreational and interesting, find the probability that the course Emily chooses will have at least one of these two attributes.

SOLUTION

If R denotes "recreational" and I denotes "interesting," then $P(R) = \frac{8}{20}$, $P(I) = \frac{9}{20}$, and $P(R \text{ and } I) = \frac{3}{20}$. R and I are not mutually exclusive.

$$P(R \text{ or } I) = \frac{8}{20} + \frac{9}{20} - \frac{3}{20} = \frac{14}{20} = \frac{7}{10} \quad \text{Addition rule; lowest terms} \quad ███$$

11.2 EXERCISES

1. **Determining Whether Events Are Mutually Exclusive** Amanda Crotts has three office assistants. If A is the event that at least two of them are men and B is the event that at least two of them are women, are A and B mutually exclusive?

2. **Determining Whether Events Are Mutually Exclusive** Jeanne Jalufka earned her college degree several years ago. Consider the following four events.

   Her alma mater is in the East.

   Her alma mater is a private college.

   Her alma mater is in the Northwest.

   Her alma mater is in the South.

   Are these events all mutually exclusive of one another?

3. Explain the difference between the two formulas in the addition rule of probability on **page 592,** illustrating each one with an appropriate example.

Probabilities for Rolling a Die For the experiment of rolling a single fair die, find the probability of each event.

4. not less than 2

5. not prime

6. odd or less than 5

7. even or prime

8. odd or even

9. less than 3 or greater than 4

Probability and Odds for Drawing a Card For the experiment of drawing a single card from a standard 52-card deck, find **(a)** *the probability, and* **(b)** *the odds in favor, of each event.*

10. not an ace

11. king or queen

12. club or heart

13. spade or face card

14. not a heart, or a 7

15. neither a heart nor a 7

Number Sums for Rolling a Pair of Dice *For the experiment of rolling an ordinary pair of dice, find the probability that the sum will be each of the following. (You may want to use a table showing the sum for each of the 36 equally likely outcomes.)*

16. 11 or 12

17. even or a multiple of 3

18. odd or greater than 9

19. less than 3 or greater than 9

20. Find the probability of getting a prime number in each case.

(a) A number is chosen randomly from the set $\{1, 2, 3, 4, \ldots, 12\}$.

(b) Two dice are rolled and the sum is observed.

21. Suppose, for a given experiment, A, B, C, and D are events, all mutually exclusive of one another, such that $A \cup B \cup C \cup D = S$ (the sample space). By extending the addition rule of probability on **page 592** to this case, and utilizing probability property 3, what statement can you make?

Probabilities of Poker Hands *If you are dealt a 5-card hand (this implies without replacement) from a standard 52-card deck, find the probability of getting each of the following. Refer to **Table 1** of **Section 11.1**, and give answers to six decimal places.*

22. a flush or three of a kind

23. a full house or a straight

24. a black flush or two pairs

25. nothing any better than two pairs

Probabilities in Golf Scoring   *The table gives golfer Brian Donahue's probabilities of scoring in various ranges on a par-70 course. In a given round, find the probability of each event in Exercises 26–30.*

26. 95 or higher

27. par or above

28. in the 80s

29. less than 90

30. not in the 70s, 80s, or 90s

31. What are the odds of Brian's scoring below par?

x	$P(x)$
Below 60	0.04
60–64	0.06
65–69	0.14
70–74	0.30
75–79	0.23
80–84	0.09
85–89	0.06
90–94	0.04
95–99	0.03
100 or above	0.01

32. **Drawing Balls from an Urn** Anne Kelly randomly chooses a single ball from the urn shown here, and x represents the color of the ball chosen. Construct a complete probability distribution for the random variable x.

33. Let x denote the sum of two distinct numbers selected randomly from the set $\{1, 2, 3, 4, 5\}$. Construct the probability distribution for the random variable x.

34. **Comparing Empirical and Theoretical Probabilities for Rolling Dice** Roll a pair of dice 50 times, keeping track of the number of times the sum is "less than 3 or greater than 9" (that is 2, 10, 11, or 12).

(a) From your results, calculate an empirical probability for the event "less than 3 or greater than 9."

(b) By how much does your answer differ from the *theoretical* probability of **Exercise 19?**

For Exercises 35–38, let A be an event within the sample space S, and let $n(A) = a$ and $n(S) = s$.

35. Use the complements principle of counting to find an expression for $n(A')$.

36. Use the theoretical probability formula to express $P(A)$ and $P(A')$.

37. Evaluate, and simplify, $P(A) + P(A')$.

38. What rule have you proved?

The remaining exercises require careful thought for the determination of $n(E)$ and $n(S)$. (In some cases, you may want to employ counting methods from Chapter 10, such as the fundamental counting principle, permutations, or combinations.)

Building Numbers from Sets of Digits   *Suppose we want to form three-digit numbers using the set of digits*

$$\{0, 1, 2, 3, 4, 5\}.$$

For example, 501 *and* 224 *are such numbers but* 035 *is not.*

39. How many such numbers are possible?

40. How many of these numbers are multiples of 5?

41. If one three-digit number is chosen at random from all those that can be made from the above set of digits, find the probability that the one chosen is not a multiple of 5.

42. *Multiplying Numbers Generated by Spinners* An experiment consists of spinning both spinners shown here and multiplying the resulting numbers together. Find the probability that the resulting product will be even.

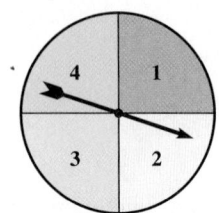
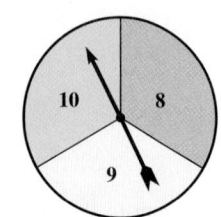

43. *Drawing Colored Marbles from Boxes* A bag contains fifty blue and fifty green marbles. Two marbles at a time are randomly selected. If both are green, they are placed in box A; if both are blue, in box B; if one is green and the other is blue, in box C. After all marbles are drawn, what is the probability that the numbers of marbles in box A and box B are the same? (*Mathematics Teacher* calendar problem)

44. *Random Births on the Same Day of the Week* What is the probability that, of three people selected at random, at least two were born on the same day of the week? (*Mathematics Teacher* calendar problem)

11.3 CONDITIONAL PROBABILITY; EVENTS INVOLVING "AND"

Conditional Probability • Events Involving "And"

Conditional Probability

Sometimes the probability of an event must be computed using the knowledge that some other event has happened (or is happening, or will happen—the timing is not important). This type of probability is called *conditional probability*.

Even **a rare occurrence** can sometimes cause widespread controversy. When Mattel Toys marketed a new talking Barbie doll a few years ago, some of the Barbies were programmed to say "Math class is tough." The National Council of Teachers of Mathematics (NCTM), the American Association of University Women (AAUW), and numerous consumers voiced complaints about the damage such a message could do to the self-confidence of children and to their attitudes toward school and mathematics. Mattel subsequently agreed to erase the phrase from the microchip to be used in future doll production.

Each Barbie was programmed to say four different statements, randomly selected from a pool of 270 prerecorded statements. Therefore, the probability of getting one that said "Math class is tough" was only

$$\frac{1 \cdot \,_{269}C_3}{\,_{270}C_4} \approx 0.015.$$

Other messages included in the pool were "I love school, don't you?," "I'm studying to be a doctor," and "Let's study for the quiz."

> ### Conditional Probability
>
> The probability of event B, computed on the assumption that event A has happened, is called the **conditional probability of B given A**, and is denoted
>
> $$P(B|A).$$

||| EXAMPLE 1   Selecting from a Set of Numbers

From the sample space $S = \{1, 2, 3, 4, 5, 6, 7, 8, 9, 10\}$, a single number is to be selected randomly. Find each probability given the events

  A: The selected number is odd,   and B: The selected number is a multiple of 3.

(a) $P(B)$ **(b)** $P(A \text{ and } B)$ **(c)** $P(B|A)$

SOLUTION

(a) $B = \{3, 6, 9\}$, so $P(B) = \frac{n(B)}{n(S)} = \frac{3}{10}$.

(b) A and B is the set $A \cap B = \{1, 3, 5, 7, 9\} \cap \{3, 6, 9\} = \{3, 9\}$.

$$P(A \text{ and } B) = \frac{n(A \cap B)}{n(S)} = \frac{2}{10} = \frac{1}{5}$$

(c) The given condition, that A occurs, effectively reduces the sample space from S to A, and the elements of the new sample space A that are also in B are the elements of $A \cap B$.

$$P(B|A) = \frac{n(A \cap B)}{n(A)} = \frac{2}{5}$$

|||

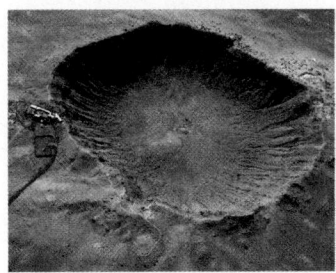

A **cosmic impact,** the collision of a meteor, comet, or asteroid with Earth, could be as catastrophic as full-scale nuclear war, killing a billion or more people. The Web site www.impact.arc .nasa.gov reports that a large enough object (1 kilometer or more in diameter) could even put the human species at risk of annihilation by causing drastic climate changes and destroying food crops.

The Spaceguard Survey has discovered more than half of the estimated number of near-Earth asteroids (NEAs) in this size range and hopes to locate 90% of them in the next decade. Although the risk of finding one on a collision course with the Earth is slight, it is anticipated that, if we did, we would be able to deflect it before impact.

The photo above shows a crater in Arizona, 4000 feet in diameter and 570 feet deep, thought to have been formed 20,000 to 50,000 years ago by a meteorite about 50 meters across, hitting the ground at several kilometers per second. (See http://en.wikipedia.org/wiki/Meteor_Crater.)

Example 1 illustrates some important points. First, because

$$\frac{n(A \cap B)}{n(A)} = \frac{\frac{n(A \cap B)}{n(S)}}{\frac{n(A)}{n(S)}} \qquad \text{Multiply numerator and denominator by } \frac{1}{n(S)}.$$

$$= \frac{P(A \cap B)}{P(A)}, \qquad \text{Theoretical probability formula}$$

the final line of the example gives the following convenient formula.

Conditional Probability Formula

The **conditional probability of B given A** is calculated as follows.

$$P(B|A) = \frac{P(A \cap B)}{P(A)} = \frac{P(A \text{ and } B)}{P(A)}$$

A second observation from **Example 1** is that the conditional probability of B, given A, was $\frac{2}{5}$, whereas the "unconditional" probability of B (with no condition given) was $\frac{3}{10}$, so the condition did make a difference.

▮▮ **EXAMPLE 2** Finding Probabilities of Boys and Girls in a Family

Given a family with two children, find the probabilities that

(a) both are girls, given that at least one is a girl, and

(b) both are girls, given that the older child is a girl.

(Assume boys and girls are equally likely.)

SOLUTION

We define the following events.

$$
\begin{aligned}
S &= \{gg, gb, bg, bb\} &&\text{Sample space} \\
A &= \{gg\} &&\text{Both are girls.} \\
B &= \{gg, gb, bg\} &&\text{At least one is a girl.} \\
C &= \{gg, gb\} &&\text{The older one is a girl.}
\end{aligned}
$$

Note that $A \cap B = \{gg\}$.

(a) $P(A|B) = \dfrac{P(A \text{ and } B)}{P(B)} = \dfrac{\frac{1}{4}}{\frac{3}{4}} = \dfrac{1}{4} \div \dfrac{3}{4} = \dfrac{1}{4} \cdot \dfrac{4}{3} = \dfrac{1}{3}$

(b) $P(A|C) = \dfrac{P(A \text{ and } C)}{P(C)} = \dfrac{\frac{1}{4}}{\frac{2}{4}} = \dfrac{1}{4} \div \dfrac{2}{4} = \dfrac{1}{4} \cdot \dfrac{4}{2} = \dfrac{1}{2}$ ▮▮▮

Sometimes a conditional probability is no different than the corresponding unconditional probability, in which case we call the two events *independent*.

Independent Events

Two events A and B are called **independent events** if knowledge about the occurrence of one of them has no effect on the probability of the other one, that is, if

$$P(B|A) = P(B), \quad \text{or, equivalently,} \quad P(A|B) = P(A).$$

▐▐ **EXAMPLE 3** Checking Events for Independence

A single card is to be drawn from a standard 52-card deck. (The sample space S has 52 elements.) Given the events

  A: The selected card is a face card,   and B: The selected card is black,

(a) Find $P(B)$.

(b) Find $P(B|A)$.

(c) Determine whether events A and B are independent.

SOLUTION

(a) There are 26 black cards in the 52-card deck.

$$P(B) = \frac{26}{52} = \frac{1}{2} \quad \text{Theoretical probability formula}$$

(b) $P(B|A) = \dfrac{P(B \text{ and } A)}{P(A)}$ Conditional probability formula

$\qquad = \dfrac{\frac{6}{52}}{\frac{12}{52}}$ Of 52 cards, 12 are face cards and 6 are black face cards.

$\qquad = \dfrac{6}{52} \cdot \dfrac{52}{12}$ To divide, multiply by the reciprocal.

$\qquad = \dfrac{1}{2}$ Calculate and write in lowest terms.

(c) Because $P(B|A) = P(B)$, events A and B are independent.   ▐▐▐

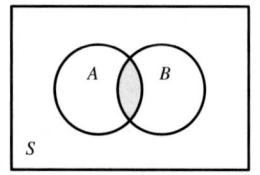

The logical connective "and" corresponds to "intersection" in set theory.

$$P(A \text{ and } B) = P(A) \cdot P(B|A)$$

Figure 9

Events Involving "And"

If we multiply both sides of the conditional probability formula by $P(A)$, we obtain an expression for $P(A \cap B)$, which applies to events of the form "A and B." The resulting formula is related to the fundamental counting principle of **Chapter 10**. It is illustrated in **Figure 9**.

Just as the calculation of $P(A \text{ or } B)$ is simpler when A and B are mutually exclusive, the calculation of $P(A \text{ and } B)$ is simpler when A and B are independent.

Multiplication Rule of Probability (for A and B)

If A and B are any two events, then

$$P(A \text{ and } B) = P(A) \cdot P(B|A).$$

If A and B are independent, then

$$P(A \text{ and } B) = P(A) \cdot P(B).$$

The first formula in the multiplication rule actually applies in all cases. ($P(B|A) = P(B)$ when A and B are independent.) Still, the independence of the component events is clear in many cases, so it is good to remember the second formula as well.

▌▌ **EXAMPLE 4** Selecting from a Set of Books

Each year, Jacqui Carper adds to her book collection a number of new publications that she believes will be of lasting value and interest. She has categorized each of her twenty acquisitions for 2011 as hardcover or paperback and as fiction or nonfiction. The numbers of books in the various categories are shown in **Table 6**.

Table 6   Year 2011 Books

	Fiction (F)	Nonfiction (N)	Totals
Hardcover (H)	3	5	8
Paperback (P)	8	4	12
Totals	11	9	20

If Jacqui randomly chooses one of these 20 books, find the probability it will be

(a) hardcover,   **(b)** fiction, given it is hardcover,   **(c)** hardcover and fiction.

SOLUTION

(a) Eight of the 20 books are hardcover, so $P(H) = \frac{8}{20} = \frac{2}{5}$.

(b) The given condition that the book is hardcover reduces the sample space to eight books. Of those eight, just three are fiction, so $P(F\,|\,H) = \frac{3}{8}$.

(c) $P(H \text{ and } F) = P(H) \cdot P(F\,|\,H) = \frac{2}{5} \cdot \frac{3}{8} = \frac{3}{20}$ Multiplication rule

It is easier here if we simply notice, directly from **Table 6**, that 3 of the 20 books are "hardcover and fiction." This verifies that the general multiplication rule of probability did give us the correct answer.   ▌▌▌

▌▌ **EXAMPLE 5** Selecting from a Set of Planets

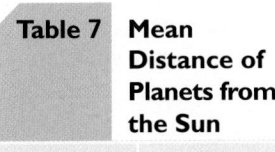

Table 7   Mean Distance of Planets from the Sun

Mercury	58
Venus	108
Earth	150
Mars	228
Jupiter	778
Saturn	1430
Uranus	2870
Neptune	4500

Table 7 lists the eight planets of our solar system together with their mean distances from the sun, in millions of kilometers. (Data is from *The World Almanac and Book of Facts 2010*.) Carrie Ayers must choose two distinct planets to cover in her astronomy report. If she selects randomly, find the probability that the first one selected is closer to the sun than Mars and the second is closer than Saturn.

SOLUTION

We define the events

   A: The first is closer than Mars,   and B: The second is closer than Saturn.

Then $P(A) = \frac{3}{8}$. (Three of the original eight choices are favorable.) If the planet selected first is closer than Mars, it is also closer than Saturn, and since that planet is no longer available, $P(B\,|\,A) = \frac{4}{7}$. (Four of the remaining seven are favorable.)

$$P(A \text{ and } B) = P(A) \cdot P(B\,|\,A) = \frac{3}{8} \cdot \frac{4}{7} = \frac{3}{14} \approx 0.214 \quad \text{Multiplication rule}$$ ▌▌▌

In **Example 5,** the condition that A had occurred changed the probability of B, since the selection was done, in effect, without replacement. (Repetitions were not allowed.) Events A and B were not independent. On the other hand, in the next example, the same events, A and B, will be independent.

▊▊ **EXAMPLE 6** Selecting from a Set of Planets

Carrie must again select two planets, but this time one is for an oral report, the other is for a written report, and they need not be distinct. (The same planet may be selected for both reports.) Again find the probability that, if she selects randomly, the first is closer than Mars and the second is closer than Saturn.

SOLUTION

Defining events A and B as in **Example 5,** we have $P(A) = \frac{3}{8}$, just as before. But the selection is now done *with* replacement. (Repetitions *are* allowed.) Event B is independent of event A, so we can use the second form of the multiplication rule.

$$P(A \text{ and } B) = P(A) \cdot P(B) = \frac{3}{8} \cdot \frac{5}{8} = \frac{15}{64} \approx 0.234 \quad \text{\small Answer is different than in \textbf{Example 5.}}$$ ▊▊▊

▊▊ **EXAMPLE 7** Selecting from a Deck of Cards

A single card is drawn from a standard 52-card deck. Let B denote the event that the card is black, and let D denote the event that it is a diamond. Are events B and D

(a) independent?   **(b)** mutually exclusive?

SOLUTION

(a) For the unconditional probability of D, we get $P(D) = \frac{13}{52} = \frac{1}{4}$. (Thirteen of the 52 cards are diamonds.) But for the conditional probability of D, given B, we have $P(D|B) = \frac{0}{26} = 0$. (None of the 26 black cards are diamonds.) Since the conditional probability $P(D|B)$ is different than the unconditional probability $P(D)$, B and D are not independent.

(b) Mutually exclusive events are events that cannot both occur for a given performance of an experiment. Since no card in the deck is both black and a diamond, B and D are mutually exclusive. ▊▊▊

▊▊ **EXAMPLE 8** Selecting from an Urn of Balls

Anne is still drawing balls from the same urn (shown at the side). This time she draws three balls, without replacement. Find the probability that she gets red, yellow, and blue balls, in that order.

SOLUTION

Using appropriate letters to denote the colors, and subscripts to indicate first, second, and third draws, the event can be symbolized R_1 and Y_2 and B_3.

$$P(R_1 \text{ and } Y_2 \text{ and } B_3) = P(R_1) \cdot P(Y_2|R_1) \cdot P(B_3|R_1 \text{ and } Y_2)$$
$$= \frac{4}{11} \cdot \frac{5}{10} \cdot \frac{2}{9} = \frac{4}{99} \approx 0.0404$$ ▊▊▊

▊▊ **EXAMPLE 9** Selecting from a Deck of Cards

If five cards are drawn without replacement from a standard 52-card deck, find the probability that they all are hearts.

SOLUTION

Each time a heart is drawn, the number of available cards decreases by one and the number of hearts decreases by one.

$$P(\text{all hearts}) = \frac{13}{52} \cdot \frac{12}{51} \cdot \frac{11}{50} \cdot \frac{10}{49} \cdot \frac{9}{48} = \frac{33}{66,640} \approx 0.000495$$ ▊▊▊

The search for extraterrestrial intelligence (SETI) may have begun in earnest as early as 1961 when Dr. Frank Drake presented an equation for estimating the number of possible civilizations in the Milky Way galaxy whose communications we might detect. Over the years, the effort has been advanced by many scientists, including the late astronomer and exobiologist Carl Sagan, who popularized the issue in TV appearances and in his book *The Cosmic Connection: An Extraterrestrial Perspective* (Dell Paperback). "There must be other starfolk," said Sagan. In fact, some astronomers have estimated the odds against life on Earth being the only life in the universe at one hundred billion billion to one.

Other experts disagree. Freeman Dyson, a noted mathematical physicist and astronomer, says in his book *Disturbing the Universe* that after considering the same evidence and arguments, he believes it is just as likely as not (even odds) that there never was any other intelligent life out there.

If you studied counting methods (**Chapter 10**), you may prefer to solve the problem of **Example 9** by using the theoretical probability formula and combinations. The total possible number of 5-card hands, drawn without replacement, is $_{52}C_5$, and the number of those containing only hearts is $_{13}C_5$.

$$P(\text{all hearts}) = \frac{_{13}C_5}{_{52}C_5} = \frac{\dfrac{13!}{5!8!}}{\dfrac{52!}{5!47!}} \approx 0.000495 \quad \text{Use a calculator.}$$

▌▌ EXAMPLE 10   Using Both Addition and Multiplication Rules

The local garage employs two mechanics, Arnie and Burt. Your consumer club has found that Arnie does twice as many jobs as Burt, Arnie does a good job three out of four times, and Burt does a good job only two out of five times. If you plan to take your car in for repairs, find the probability that a good job will be done.

SOLUTION

We define the events

A: work done by Arnie; B: work done by Burt; G: good job done.

Since Arnie does twice as many jobs as Burt, the (unconditional) probabilities of events A and B are, respectively, $\frac{2}{3}$ and $\frac{1}{3}$. Since Arnie does a good job three out of four times, the probability of a good job, given that Arnie did the work, is $\frac{3}{4}$. And since Burt does well two out of five times, the probability of a good job, given that Burt did the work, is $\frac{2}{5}$. (These last two probabilities are conditional.) These four values can be summarized.

$$P(A) = \frac{2}{3}, \quad P(B) = \frac{1}{3}, \quad P(G|A) = \frac{3}{4}, \quad \text{and} \quad P(G|B) = \frac{2}{5}.$$

Event G can occur in two mutually exclusive ways: Arnie could do the work and do a good job $(A \cap G)$, or Burt could do the work and do a good job $(B \cap G)$.

$$
\begin{aligned}
P(G) &= P(A \cap G) + P(B \cap G) & \text{Addition rule} \\
&= P(A) \cdot P(G|A) + P(B) \cdot P(G|B) & \text{Multiplication rule} \\
&= \frac{2}{3} \cdot \frac{3}{4} + \frac{1}{3} \cdot \frac{2}{5} & \text{Substitute the values.} \\
&= \frac{1}{2} + \frac{2}{15} = \frac{19}{30} \approx 0.633 & \blacksquare\blacksquare\blacksquare
\end{aligned}
$$

Multiply first, then add.

The tree diagram in **Figure 10** shows a graphical way to organize the work of **Example 10.** Use the given information to draw the tree diagram, then find the probability of a good job by adding the probabilities from the indicated branches of the tree.

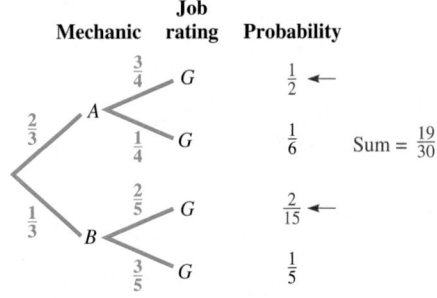

Garage mechanics experiment

Figure 10

▌▌ **EXAMPLE 11** Selecting Door Prizes

Rob Brown is among five door prize winners at a Christmas party. The five winners are asked to choose, without looking, from a bag which, they are told, contains five tokens, four of them redeemable for candy canes and one specific token redeemable for a $100 gift certificate. Can Rob improve his chance of getting the gift certificate by drawing first among the five people?

SOLUTION

We denote candy cane by C, gift certificate by G, and first draw, second draw, and so on by subscripts $1, 2, \ldots$. Then if Rob draws first, his probability of getting the gift certificate is

$$P(G_1) = \frac{1}{5}.$$

If he draws second, his probability of getting the gift certificate is

$$\begin{aligned} P(G_2) &= P(C_1 \text{ and } G_2) \\ &= P(C_1) \cdot P(G_2|C_1) \\ &= \frac{4}{5} \cdot \frac{1}{4} = \frac{1}{5}. \quad \text{Same result as above} \end{aligned}$$

For the third draw,

$$\begin{aligned} P(G_3) &= P(C_1 \text{ and } C_2 \text{ and } G_3) \\ &= P(C_1) \cdot P(C_2|C_1) \cdot P(G_3|C_1 \text{ and } C_2) \\ &= \frac{4}{5} \cdot \frac{3}{4} \cdot \frac{1}{3} = \frac{1}{5}. \quad \text{Same result as above} \end{aligned}$$

The probability of getting the gift certificate is $\frac{1}{5}$ when drawing fourth or fifth. The order in which the five winners draw does not affect Rob's chances. ▌▌▌

The **search for extraterrestrial intelligence (SETI)** has been mainly accomplished over the last decade through **SETI@HOME,** the largest distributed computing program on Earth. Most of the data are collected by the world's largest radio telescope, built into a 20-acre natural bowl in Aricebo, Puerto Rico (pictured above), and processed by millions of personal computers around the world.

To learn more, or for a chance to be the first to "contact" an extraterrestrial civilization, check out www.setiathome.ssl.berkeley.edu.

For Further Thought

The Birthday Problem

A classic problem (with a surprising result) involves the probability that a given group of people will include at least one pair of people with the same birthday (the same day of the year, not necessarily the same year). This problem can be analyzed using the probability of a complement formula (**Section 11.2**) and the multiplication rule of probability from this section. Suppose there are three people in the group.

P(at least one duplication of birthdays)

$= 1 - P$(no duplications) Complement formula

$= 1 - P$(2nd is different than 1st and 3rd is different than 1st and 2nd)

$= 1 - \dfrac{364}{365} \cdot \dfrac{363}{365}$ Multiplication rule

$\approx 1 - 0.992$

$= 0.008$

(To simplify the calculations, we have assumed 365 possible birth dates, ignoring February 29.)

By doing more calculations like the one above, we find that the smaller the group, the smaller the probability of a duplication. The larger the group, the larger the probability of a duplication. The table on the next page shows the probability of at least one duplication for numbers of people from 2 through 52.

For Group or Individual Investigation

1. Based on the data shown in the table, what are the odds in favor of a duplication in a group of 30 people?

2. Estimate from the table the least number of people for which the probability of duplication is at least $\frac{1}{2}$.

3. How small a group is required for the probability of a duplication to be *exactly* 0?

4. How large a group is required for the probability of a duplication to be *exactly* 1?

Number of People	Probability of at Least One Duplication	Number of People	Probability of at Least One Duplication	Number of People	Probability of at Least One Duplication
2	0.003	19	0.379	36	0.832
3	0.008	20	0.411	37	0.849
4	0.016	21	0.444	38	0.864
5	0.027	22	0.476	39	0.878
6	0.040	23	0.507	40	0.891
7	0.056	24	0.538	41	0.903
8	0.074	25	0.569	42	0.914
9	0.095	26	0.598	43	0.924
10	0.117	27	0.627	44	0.933
11	0.141	28	0.654	45	0.941
12	0.167	29	0.681	46	0.948
13	0.194	30	0.706	47	0.955
14	0.223	31	0.730	48	0.961
15	0.253	32	0.753	49	0.966
16	0.284	33	0.775	50	0.970
17	0.315	34	0.795	51	0.974
18	0.347	35	0.814	52	0.978

11.3 EXERCISES

For each experiment, determine whether the two given events are independent.

1. **Tossing Coins** A fair coin is tossed twice. The events are "head on the first" and "head on the second."

2. **Rolling Dice** A pair of dice are rolled. The events are "even on the first" and "odd on the second."

3. **Comparing Planets' Mean Distances from the Sun** Two planets are selected, without replacement, from the list in **Table 7**. The events are "the first selected planet is closer than Jupiter" and "the second selected planet is farther than Mars."

4. **Comparing Mean Distances from the Sun** Two celestial bodies are selected, with replacement, from the list in **Table 7**. The events are "the first selected body is closer than Earth" and "the second selected body is farther than Uranus."

5. **Guessing Answers on a Multiple-choice Test** The answers are all guessed on a twenty-question multiple-choice test. The events are "the first answer is correct" and "the last answer is correct."

6. **Selecting Committees of U.S. Senators** A committee of five is randomly selected from the 100 U.S. Senators. The events are "the first member selected is a Republican" and "the second member selected is a Republican." (Assume that there are both Republicans and non-Republicans in the Senate.)

Comparing Gender and Career Motivation of College Students *One hundred college seniors attending a career fair at a university were categorized according to gender and according to primary career motivation, as summarized here.*

	Primary Career Motivation			
	Money	Allowed to be Creative	Sense of Giving to Society	Total
Male	19	15	14	48
Female	12	23	17	52
Total	31	38	31	100

If one of these students is to be selected at random, find the probability that the student selected will satisfy each condition in Exercises 7–12.

7. female $\frac{52}{100}$

8. motivated primarily by creativity

9. not motivated primarily by money $\frac{19}{100}$

10. male and motivated primarily by money $\frac{19}{100}$

11. male, given that primary motivation is a sense of giving to society

12. motivated primarily by money or creativity, given that the student is female $\frac{12+23}{52} = \frac{35}{52}$ — condition

Selecting Pets *A pet store has seven puppies, including four poodles, two terriers, and one retriever. If Rebecka and Aaron, in that order, each select one puppy at random, with replacement (they may both select the same one), find the probability of each event in Exercises 13–16.*

13. both select a poodle

14. Rebecka selects a retriever, Aaron selects a terrier

15. Rebecka selects a terrier, Aaron selects a retriever

16. both select a retriever

Selecting Pets *Suppose two puppies are selected as earlier, but this time without replacement (Rebecka and Aaron cannot both select the same puppy). Find the probability of each event in Exercises 17–22.*

17. both select a poodle

18. Aaron selects a terrier, given Rebecka selects a poodle

— so one dog gone ← so ²⁄₆ dogs left

19. Aaron selects a retriever, given Rebecka selects a poodle

20. Rebecka selects a retriever

21. Aaron selects a retriever, given Rebecka selects a retriever *¹⁄₇ · ⁰⁄₆ =*

22. both select a retriever

Dealing Cards *Let two cards be dealt successively, without replacement, from a standard 52-card deck. Find the probability of each event in Exercises 23–27.*

23. spade second, given spade first

24. club second, given diamond first *¹³⁄₅₁ → 1 diamond already gone*

25. two face cards

26. no face cards *52 − 12 = 40*   *⁴⁰⁄₅₂ · ³⁹⁄₅₁ = one face card gone = 1 card is gone*

27. The first card is a jack and the second is a face card.

28. Given events A and B within the sample space S, the following sequence of steps establishes formulas that can be used to compute conditional probabilities. Justify each statement.

   (a) $P(A \text{ and } B) = P(A) \cdot P(B \mid A)$

   (b) Therefore, $P(B \mid A) = \dfrac{P(A \text{ and } B)}{P(A)}$.

   (c) Therefore, $P(B \mid A) = \dfrac{n(A \text{ and } B)/n(S)}{n(A)/n(S)}$.

   (d) Therefore, $P(B \mid A) = \dfrac{n(A \text{ and } B)}{n(A)}$.

Considering Conditions in Card Drawing *Use the results of Exercise 28 to find each probability when a single card is drawn from a standard 52-card deck.*

29. $P(\text{queen} \mid \text{face card})$

30. $P(\text{face card} \mid \text{queen})$

31. $P(\text{red} \mid \text{diamond})$

32. $P(\text{diamond} \mid \text{red})$

Investigating P(A and B) *Complete Exercises 33 and 34 to discover a general property of the probability of an event of the form A and B.*

33. If one number is chosen randomly from the integers 1 through 10, the probability of getting a number that is *odd and prime,* by the multiplication rule, is

$$P(\text{odd}) \cdot P(\text{prime} \mid \text{odd}) = \frac{5}{10} \cdot \frac{3}{5} = \frac{3}{10}.$$

   Compute the product $P(\text{prime}) \cdot P(\text{odd} \mid \text{prime})$, and compare to the product above.

34. What does **Exercise 33** imply, in general, about the probability of an event of the form A and B?

35. ***Gender in Sequences of Babies*** Two authors of this book each have three sons and no daughters. Assuming boy and girl babies are equally likely, what is the probability of this event?

36. ***Rolling Dice*** Three dice are tossed. What is the probability that the numbers shown will all be different? (*Mathematics Teacher* calendar problem)

The remaining exercises, and groups of exercises, may require concepts from earlier sections, such as the complements principle of counting and addition rules, as well as the multiplication rule of this section.

Probabilities in Warehouse Grocery Shopping *Therese Felser manages a grocery warehouse which encourages volume shopping on the part of its customers. Therese has discovered that, on any given weekday, 70 percent of the customer sales amount to more than $100. That is, any given sale on such a day has a probability of 0.70 of being for more than $100. (Actually, the conditional probabilities throughout the day would change slightly, depending on earlier sales, but this effect would be negligible for the first several sales of the day, so we can treat them as independent.)*
   Find the probability of each event in Exercises 37–40. (Give answers to three decimal places.)

37. The first two sales on Wednesday are both for more than $100.

38. The first three sales on Wednesday are all for more than $100.

39. None of the first three sales on Wednesday is for more than $100.

40. Exactly one of the first three sales on Wednesday is for more than $100.

Pollution from the Space Shuttle Launch Site *One problem encountered by developers of the space shuttle program is air pollution in the area surrounding the launch site. A certain direction from the launch site is considered critical in terms of hydrogen chloride pollution from the exhaust cloud. It has been determined that weather conditions would cause emission cloud movement in the critical direction only 5% of the time.*

In Exercises 41–44, find the probability for each event. Assume that probabilities for a particular launch in no way depend on the probabilities for other launches. (Give answers to two decimal places.)

41. A given launch will not result in cloud movement in the critical direction.

42. No cloud movement in the critical direction will occur during any of 5 launches.

43. Any 5 launches will result in at least one cloud movement in the critical direction.

44. Any 10 launches will result in at least one cloud movement in the critical direction.

Ordering Job Interviews *Three men and three women are waiting to be interviewed for jobs. If they are all selected in random order, find the probability of each event in Exercises 45–47.*

45. All the women will be interviewed first.

46. The first three interviewees will all be the same sex.

$\frac{6}{6} \cdot \frac{2}{5} \cdot \frac{1}{4} = $ *see note book* —

47. No man will be interviewed until at least two women have been interviewed.

48. **Cutting Up a Cube** A 4″ × 4″ × 4″ cube is painted and then cut into sixty-four 1″ × 1″ × 1″ cubes. A unit cube is then randomly selected and rolled. What is the probability that the top face of the rolled cube is painted? Express your answer as a common fraction. (*Mathematics Teacher* calendar problem)

49. **Tossing a Two-Headed Coin?** A gambler has two coins in his pocket—one fair coin and one two-headed coin. He selects a coin at random and flips it twice. If he gets two heads, what is the probability that he selected the fair coin? (*Mathematics Teacher* calendar problem)

50. In **Example 8,** where Anne draws three balls without replacement, what would be her probability of getting one of each color, where the order does not matter?

51. **Gender in Sequences of Babies** Assuming boy and girl babies are equally likely, find the probability that it would take

(a) at least three births to obtain two girls,

(b) at least four births to obtain two girls,

(c) at least five births to obtain two girls.

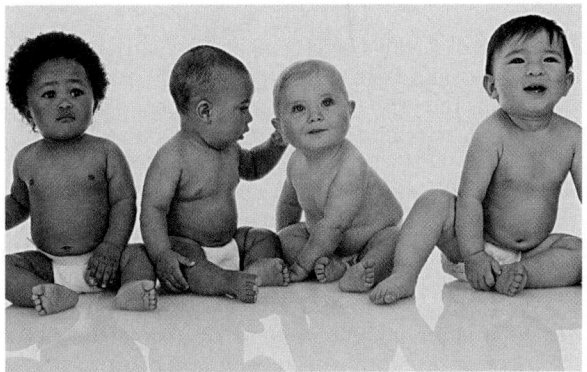

52. **Drawing Cards** Cards are drawn, without replacement, from an ordinary 52-card deck.

(a) How many must be drawn before the probability of obtaining at least one face card is greater than $\frac{1}{2}$?

(b) How many must be drawn before the probability of obtaining at least one king is greater than $\frac{1}{2}$?

Fair Decisions from Biased Coins *Many everyday decisions, like who will drive to lunch, or who will pay for the coffee, are made by the toss of a (presumably fair) coin and using the criterion "heads, you will; tails, I will." This criterion is not quite fair, however, if the coin is biased (perhaps due to slightly irregular construction or wear). John von Neumann suggested a way to make perfectly fair decisions even with a possibly biased coin. If a coin, biased so that*

$$P(h) = 0.5200 \quad \text{and} \quad P(t) = 0.4800,$$

is tossed twice, find each probability. (Give answers to four decimal places.)

53. $P(hh)$ **54.** $P(ht)$

55. $P(th)$ **56.** $P(tt)$

57. Having completed **Exercises 53–56,** can you suggest what von Neumann's scheme may have been?

Programming a Garage Door Opener *Kevin Frye installed a certain brand of automatic garage door opener that utilizes a transmitter control with six independent switches, each one set on or off. The receiver (wired to the door) must be set with the same pattern as the transmitter. (Exercises 58–61 are based on ideas similar to those of the "birthday problem" in the* **For Further Thought** *feature in this section.)*

58. How many different ways can Kevin set the switches?

59. If one of Kevin's neighbors also has this same brand of opener, and both of them set the switches randomly, what is the probability, to four decimal places, that they are able to open each other's garage doors?

60. If five neighbors with the same type of opener set their switches independently, what is the probability of at least one pair of neighbors using the same settings? (Give your answer to four decimal places.)

61. What is the minimum number of neighbors who must use this brand of opener before the probability of at least one duplication of settings is greater than $\frac{1}{2}$?

62. *Choosing Cards* There are three cards, one that is green on both sides, one that is red on both sides, and one that is green on one side and red on the other. One of the three cards is selected randomly and laid on the table. If it happens that the card on the table has a red side up, what is the probability that it is also red on the other side?

Weather Conditions on Successive Days *In November, the rain in a certain valley tends to fall in storms of several days' duration. The unconditional probability of rain on any given day of the month is 0.500. But the probability of rain on a day that follows a rainy day is 0.800, and the probability of rain on a day following a nonrainy day is 0.300. Find the probability of each event in Exercises 63–66. Give answers to three decimal places.*

63. rain on two randomly selected consecutive days in November

64. rain on three randomly selected consecutive days in November

65. rain on November 1 and 2, but not on November 3

66. rain on the first four days of November, given that October 31 was clear all day

Engine Failures in a Vintage Aircraft *In a certain four-engine vintage aircraft, now quite unreliable, each engine has a 10% chance of failure on any flight, as long as it is carrying its one-fourth share of the load. But if one engine fails, then the chance of failure increases to 20% for each of the other three engines. And if a second engine fails, each of the remaining two has a 30% chance of failure.*

Assuming that no two engines ever fail simultaneously, and that the aircraft can continue flying with as few as two operating engines, find each probability for a given flight of this aircraft. (Give answers to four decimal places.)

67. no engine failures

68. exactly one engine failure (any one of four engines)

69. exactly two engine failures (any two of four engines)

70. a failed flight

One-and-one Free Throw Shooting in Basketball *In basketball, "one-and-one" free throw shooting (commonly called foul shooting) is done as follows: if the player makes the first shot (1 point), he is given a second shot. If he misses the first shot, he is not given a second shot (see the tree diagram).*

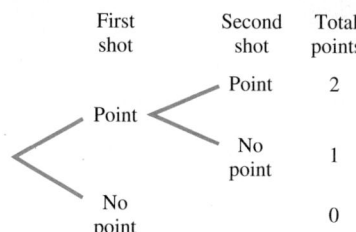

Christine Ellington, a basketball player, has a 70% foul shot record. (She makes 70% of her foul shots.) Find the probability that, on a given one-and-one foul shooting opportunity, Christine will score each number of points.

71. no points   **72.** one point

73. two points

74. *Comparing Empirical and Theoretical Probabilities in Dice Rolling* Roll a pair of dice until a sum of seven appears, keeping track of how many rolls it took. Repeat the process a total of 50 times, each time recording the number of rolls it took to get a sum of seven.

(a) Use your experimental data to compute an empirical probability (to two decimal places) that it would take at least three rolls to get a sum of seven.

(b) Find the theoretical probability (to two decimal places) that it would take at least three rolls to obtain a sum of seven.

75. Go to the Web site mentioned in the *cosmic impact* margin note in this section and write a report on the threat to humanity of cosmic impacts. Include an explanation of the abbreviation *NEO*.

11.4 BINOMIAL PROBABILITY

Binomial Probability Distribution • Binomial Probability Formula

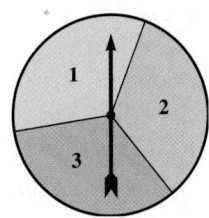

Binomial Probability Distribution

Suppose the spinner in the margin is spun twice. We are interested in the number of times a 2 is obtained. (Assume that 1, 2, and 3 all are equally likely on a given spin.) We can think of the outcome 2 as a "success," while a 1 or a 3 would be a "failure."

When the outcomes of an experiment are divided into just two categories, success and failure, the associated probabilities are called "binomial" (the prefix *bi* meaning *two*). Repeated performances of such an experiment, where the probability of success remains constant throughout all repetitions, are also known as repeated **Bernoulli trials** (after James Bernoulli). If we use an ordered pair to represent the result of each pair of spins, then the sample space for this experiment is

$$S = \{(1, 1), (1, 2), (1, 3), (2, 1), (2, 2), (2, 3), (3, 1), (3, 2), (3, 3)\}.$$

The nine outcomes in S are all equally likely. (This follows from the numbers 1, 2, and 3 being equally likely on a particular spin.)

If x denotes the number of 2s occurring on each pair of spins, then x is an example of a *random variable*. Although we cannot predict the result of any particular pair of spins, we can find the probabilities of various events from the sample space listing. In S, the number of 2s is 0 in four cases, 1 in four cases, and 2 in one case, as reflected in **Table 8**. Because the table includes all possible values of x, together with their probabilities, it is an example of a *probability distribution*. In this case, we have a **binomial probability distribution.** Notice that the probability column in **Table 8** has a sum of 1, in agreement with property 3 of probability (**Section 11.2**).

In order to develop a general formula for binomial probabilities, we can consider another way to obtain the probability values in **Table 8**. The various spins of the spinner are independent of one another, and on each spin the probability of success (S) is $\frac{1}{3}$ and the probability of failure (F) is $\frac{2}{3}$. We will denote success on the first spin by S_1, failure on the second by F_2, and so on.

Table 8	**Probability Distribution for the Number of 2s in Two Spins**
x	$P(x)$
0	$\frac{4}{9}$
1	$\frac{4}{9}$
2	$\frac{1}{9}$
	Sum $= \frac{9}{9} = 1$

$$
\begin{aligned}
P(x = 0) &= P(F_1 \text{ and } F_2) & \\
&= P(F_1) \cdot P(F_2) & \text{Multiplication rule} \\
&= \frac{2}{3} \cdot \frac{2}{3} & \text{Substitute values.} \\
&= \frac{4}{9} & \text{Multiply.}
\end{aligned}
$$

$$
\begin{aligned}
P(x = 1) &= P[(S_1 \text{ and } F_2) \text{ or } (F_1 \text{ and } S_2)] & \text{2 ways to get } x = 1 \\
&= P(S_1 \text{ and } F_2) + P(F_1 \text{ and } S_2) & \text{Addition rule} \\
&= P(S_1) \cdot P(F_2) + P(F_1) \cdot P(S_2) & \text{Multiplication rule} \\
&= \frac{1}{3} \cdot \frac{2}{3} + \frac{2}{3} \cdot \frac{1}{3} & \text{Substitute values.} \\
&= \frac{2}{9} + \frac{2}{9} & \text{Multiply.} \\
&= \frac{4}{9} & \text{Add.}
\end{aligned}
$$

James Bernoulli (1654–1705) is also known as Jacob or Jacques. He was charmed away from theology by the writings of Leibniz, became his pupil, and later headed the mathematics faculty at the University of Basel. His results in probability are contained in the *Art of Conjecture,* which was published in 1713, after his death, and which also included a reprint of the earlier Huygens paper. Bernoulli also made many contributions to calculus and analytic geometry.

$$P(x = 2) = P(S_1 \text{ and } S_2)$$

$$= P(S_1) \cdot P(S_2) \quad \text{Multiplication rule}$$

$$= \frac{1}{3} \cdot \frac{1}{3} \quad \text{Substitute values.}$$

$$= \frac{1}{9} \quad \text{Multiply.}$$

Notice the following pattern in the above calculations. There is only one way to get $x = 0$ (namely, F_1 and F_2). And there is only one way to get $x = 2$ (namely, S_1 and S_2). But there are two ways to get $x = 1$. One way is S_1 and F_2; the other is F_1 and S_2. There are two ways because the one success required can occur on the first spin or on the second spin. How many ways can exactly one success occur in two repeated trials? This question is equivalent to:

How many size-one subsets are there of the set of two trials?

The answer is $_2C_1 = 2$. (The expression $_2C_1$ denotes "combinations of 2 things taken 1 at a time." Combinations were discussed in **Section 10.3.**) Each of the two ways to get exactly one success has a probability equal to $\frac{1}{3} \cdot \frac{2}{3}$, the probability of success times the probability of failure.

If the same spinner is spun three times rather than two, then x, the number of successes (2s) could have values of 0, 1, 2, or 3. Then the number of ways to get exactly 1 success is $_3C_1 = 3$. They are: S_1 and F_2 and F_3, F_1 and S_2 and F_3, F_1 and F_2 and S_3. The probability of each of these three ways is $\frac{1}{3} \cdot \frac{2}{3} \cdot \frac{2}{3} = \frac{4}{27}$.

$$P(x = 1) = 3 \cdot \frac{4}{27} = \frac{12}{27} = \frac{4}{9}$$

Figure 11 shows all possibilities for three spins, and **Table 9** gives the associated probability distribution. In the tree diagram, the number of ways of getting two successes in three trials is 3, in agreement with the fact that $_3C_2 = 3$. Also the sum of the $P(x)$ column in **Table 9** is again 1.

Table 9	Probability Distribution for the Number of 2s in Three Spins	
x	$P(x)$	
0	$\frac{8}{27}$	
1	$\frac{12}{27}$	
2	$\frac{6}{27}$	
3	$\frac{1}{27}$	
	Sum $= \frac{27}{27} = 1$	

First spin	Second spin	Third spin	Number of successes	Probability
		S	3	$\frac{1}{3} \cdot \frac{1}{3} \cdot \frac{1}{3} = \frac{1}{27}$
	S	F	2	$\frac{1}{3} \cdot \frac{1}{3} \cdot \frac{2}{3} = \frac{2}{27}$
S		S	2	$\frac{1}{3} \cdot \frac{2}{3} \cdot \frac{1}{3} = \frac{2}{27}$
	F	F	1	$\frac{1}{3} \cdot \frac{2}{3} \cdot \frac{2}{3} = \frac{4}{27}$
	S	S	2	$\frac{2}{3} \cdot \frac{1}{3} \cdot \frac{1}{3} = \frac{2}{27}$
F		F	1	$\frac{2}{3} \cdot \frac{1}{3} \cdot \frac{2}{3} = \frac{4}{27}$
	F	S	1	$\frac{2}{3} \cdot \frac{2}{3} \cdot \frac{1}{3} = \frac{4}{27}$
		F	0	$\frac{2}{3} \cdot \frac{2}{3} \cdot \frac{2}{3} = \frac{8}{27}$

Tree diagram for three spins

Figure 11

PROBLEM-SOLVING HINT One of the problem-solving strategies from **Chapter 1** was "Look for a pattern." Having constructed complete probability distributions for binomial experiments with 2 and 3 repeated trials (and probability of success $\frac{1}{3}$), we can now generalize the observed pattern to any binomial experiment, as shown next.

Binomial Probability Formula

Define the following quantities.

$$n = \text{the number of repeated trials}$$
$$p = \text{the probability of success on any given trial}$$
$$q = 1 - p = \text{the probability of failure on any given trial}$$
$$x = \text{the number of successes that occur}$$

Note that p remains fixed throughout all n trials. This means that all trials are independent of one another. The random variable x (number of successes) can have any integer value from 0 through n. In general, x successes can be assigned among n repeated trials in ${}_nC_x$ different ways, since this is the number of different subsets of x positions among a set of n positions. Also, regardless of which x of the trials result in successes, there will always be x successes and $n - x$ failures, so we multiply x factors of p and $n - x$ factors of q together.

> **Binomial Probability Formula**
>
> When n independent repeated trials occur, where
>
> $$p = \text{probability of success} \quad \text{and} \quad q = \text{probability of failure}$$
>
> with p and q (where $q = 1 - p$) remaining constant throughout all n trials, the probability of exactly x successes is calculated as follows.
>
> $$P(x) = {}_nC_x\, p^x q^{n-x} = \frac{n!}{x!(n-x)!} p^x q^{n-x}$$

Binomial probabilities for particular values of n, p, and x can be found directly using tables, statistical software, and some handheld calculators. In the following examples, we use the formula derived above.

From the DISTR menu

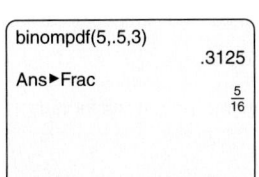

binompdf(5,.5,3)
                    .3125
Ans►Frac
                    $\frac{5}{16}$

The TI-83/84 Plus calculator will find the probability discussed in **Example 1**.

▐▌ **EXAMPLE 1** Finding Probability in Coin Tossing

Find the probability of obtaining exactly three heads in five tosses of a fair coin.

SOLUTION

Let heads be "success." Then this is a binomial experiment with $n = 5$, $p = \frac{1}{2}$, $q = \frac{1}{2}$, and $x = 3$.

$$P(3) = {}_5C_3\left(\frac{1}{2}\right)^3\left(\frac{1}{2}\right)^2 = 10 \cdot \frac{1}{8} \cdot \frac{1}{4} = \frac{5}{16} \quad \text{Binomial probability formula} \quad ▌▐▐$$

▐▌ **EXAMPLE 2** Finding Probability in Dice Rolling

Find the probability of obtaining exactly two 5s in six rolls of a fair die.

SOLUTION

Let 5 be "success." Then $n = 6$, $p = \frac{1}{6}$, $q = \frac{5}{6}$, and $x = 2$.

$$P(2) = {}_6C_2\left(\frac{1}{6}\right)^2\left(\frac{5}{6}\right)^4 = 15 \cdot \frac{1}{36} \cdot \frac{625}{1296} = \frac{3125}{15{,}552} \approx 0.201 \quad ▌▐▐$$

binompdf(6,1/6,2)
                    .200938786

This screen supports the answer in **Example 2.**

In the case of repeated independent trials, when an event involves more than one specific number of successes, we can employ the binomial probability formula along with the complement or addition rules.

▌▌ **EXAMPLE 3** Finding Probability of Female Children

A couple plans to have 5 children. Find the probability they will have more than 3 girls. (Assume girl and boy babies are equally likely.)

SOLUTION

Let a girl be "success." Then $n = 5, p = q = \frac{1}{2}$, and $x > 3$.

$$P(x > 3) = P(x = 4 \text{ or } 5) \qquad \text{More than 3 means 4 or 5.}$$
$$= P(4) + P(5) \qquad \text{Addition rule}$$
$$= {}_5C_4\left(\frac{1}{2}\right)^4\left(\frac{1}{2}\right)^1 + {}_5C_5\left(\frac{1}{2}\right)^5\left(\frac{1}{2}\right)^0 \qquad \text{Binomial probability formula}$$
$$= 5 \cdot \frac{1}{16} \cdot \frac{1}{2} + 1 \cdot \frac{1}{32} \cdot 1 \qquad \text{Simplify.}$$
$$= \frac{5}{32} + \frac{1}{32} = \frac{6}{32} = \frac{3}{16} = 0.1875$$

▌▌▌

binompdf(5,.5,4)+binompdf▸
◂(5,.5,5)
     .1875
Ans▶Frac
      $\frac{3}{16}$

This screen supports the answer in
Example 3.

▌▌ **EXAMPLE 4** Finding Probability of Hits in Baseball

Andrew Crowley, a baseball player, has a well-established career batting average of .300. In a brief series with a rival team, Andrew will bat 10 times. Find the probability that he will get more than two hits in the series.

SOLUTION

This "experiment" involves $n = 10$ repeated Bernoulli trials, with probability of success (a hit) given by $p = 0.3$ (which implies $q = 1 - 0.3 = 0.7$). Since, in this case, "more than 2" means

  "3 or 4 or 5 or 6 or 7 or 8 or 9 or 10" (eight different possibilities),

it will be less work to apply the complement rule.

$$P(x > 2) = 1 - P(x \le 2) \qquad \text{Complement rule}$$
$$= 1 - P(x = 0 \text{ or } 1 \text{ or } 2) \qquad \text{Only three different possibilities}$$
$$= 1 - [P(0) + P(1) + P(2)] \qquad \text{Addition rule}$$
$$= 1 - [{}_{10}C_0(0.3)^0(0.7)^{10} \qquad \text{Binomial probability formula}$$
$$+ {}_{10}C_1(0.3)^1(0.7)^9 + {}_{10}C_2(0.3)^2(0.7)^8]$$
$$\approx 1 - [0.0282 + 0.1211 + 0.2335] \qquad \text{Simplify.}$$
$$= 1 - 0.3828$$
$$= 0.6172$$

▌▌▌

[Scrolled Equation]

1−(binompdf(10,.3,0)+bin▸
◂ompdf(10,.3,1)+binompdf▸
◂(10,.3,2))
    .6172172136

This screen supports the answer in
Example 4.

11.4 EXERCISES

For Exercises 1–24, give all numerical answers as common fractions reduced to lowest terms. For Exercises 25–54, give all numerical answers to three decimal places.

Coin Tossing *If three fair coins are tossed, find the probability of each number of heads.*

1. 0   **2.** 1   **3.** 2

4. 3   **5.** 1 or 2   **6.** at least 1

7. no more than 1   **8.** fewer than 3

9. *Gender in Sequences of Babies* Assuming boy and girl babies are equally likely, find the probability that a family with three children will have exactly two boys.

10. *Relating Pascal's Triangle to Coin Tossing*   Pascal's triangle was shown in **Table 5** of **Section 10.4.** Explain how the probabilities in **Exercises 1–4** here relate to row 3 of the "triangle." (Recall that we referred to the top-most row of the triangle as "row number 0" and to the leftmost entry of each row as "entry number 0.")

11. Generalize the pattern in **Exercise 10** to complete the following statement. If *n* fair coins are tossed, the probability of exactly *x* heads is the fraction whose numerator is entry number _____ of row number _____ in Pascal's triangle, and whose denominator is the sum of the entries in row number _____.

Binomial Probability Applied to Tossing Coins Use the pattern noted in **Exercises 10 and 11** to find the probabilities of each number of heads when seven fair coins are tossed.

12. 0   13. 1   14. 2   15. 3

16. 4   17. 5   18. 6   19. 7

Binomial Probability Applied to Rolling Dice   A fair die is rolled three times. A 4 is considered "success," while all other outcomes are "failures." Find the probability of each number of successes.

20. 0   21. 1   22. 2   23. 3

24. **Exercises 10 and 11** established a way of using Pascal's triangle rather than the binomial probability formula to find probabilities of different numbers of successes in coin-tossing experiments. Explain why the same process would not work for **Exercises 20–23.**

For n repeated independent trials, with constant probability of success p for all trials, find the probability of exactly x successes in each of Exercises 25–28.

25. $n = 5$, $p = \frac{1}{3}$, $x = 4$

26. $n = 10$, $p = 0.7$, $x = 5$

27. $n = 20$, $p = \frac{1}{8}$, $x = 2$

28. $n = 30$, $p = 0.6$, $x = 22$

*For Exercises 29–31, refer to **Example 4.***

29. *Batting Averages in Baseball* Does Andrew's probability of a hit really remain constant at exactly 0.300 through all ten times at bat? Explain your reasoning.

30. *Batting Averages in Baseball* If Andrew's batting average is exactly .300 going into the series, and that value is based on exactly 1200 career hits out of 4000 previous times at bat, what is the greatest his average could possibly be (to three decimal places) when he goes up to bat the tenth time of the series? What is the least his average could possibly be when he goes up to bat the tenth time of the series?

31. Do you think the use of the binomial probability formula was justified in **Example 4,** even though *p* is not strictly constant? Explain your reasoning.

Random Selection of Answers on a Multiple-choice Test Beth Dahlke is taking a ten-question multiple-choice test for which each question has three answer choices, only one of which is correct. Beth decides on answers by rolling a fair die and marking the first answer choice if the die shows 1 or 2, the second if it shows 3 or 4, and the third if it shows 5 or 6. Find the probability of each event in Exercises 32–35.

32. exactly four correct answers

33. exactly seven correct answers

34. fewer than three correct answers

35. at least seven correct answers

Side Effects of Prescription Drugs   It is known that a certain prescription drug produces undesirable side effects in 35% of all patients who use it. Among a random sample of eight patients using the drug, find the probability of each event.

36. None have undesirable side effects.

37. Exactly one has undesirable side effects.

38. Exactly two have undesirable side effects.

39. More than two have undesirable side effects.

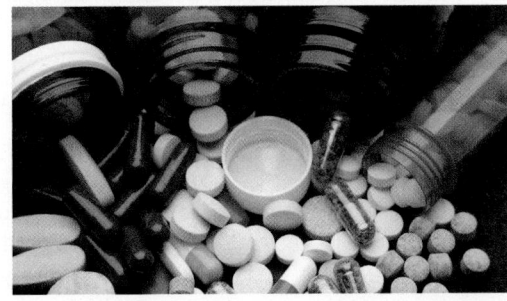

Likelihood of Capable Students Attending College In a certain state, it has been shown that only 60% of the high school graduates who are capable of college work actually enroll in colleges. Find the probability that, among nine capable high school graduates in this state, each number will enroll in college.

40. exactly 4   41. from 4 through 6

42. all 9   43. at least 3

44. *Student Ownership of Personal Computers*   At a large midwestern university, 90% of all students have their own personal computers. If five students at that university are selected at random, find the probability that exactly three of them have their own computers.

45. **Frost Survival Among Orange Trees** If it is known that 65% of all orange trees will survive a hard frost, then what is the probability that at least half of a group of six trees will survive such a frost?

46. **Rate of Favorable Media Coverage of an Incumbent President** During a presidential campaign, 64% of the political columns in a certain group of major newspapers were favorable to the incumbent president. If a sample of fifteen of these columns is selected at random, what is the probability that exactly ten of them will be favorable?

Selecting Balls From a Bag *A bag contains only white balls and black balls. Let p be the probability that a ball selected at random is black. Each time a ball is selected, it is placed back in the bag before the next ball is selected. Four balls are selected at random.*

47. What is the probability that two of the four balls are black and two are white? (*Mathematics Teacher* calendar problem) (*Hint:* Use the binomial probability formula to express the probability in terms of *p*.)

48. Evaluate the probability of **Exercise 47** in case the bag actually contains 15 black balls and 25 white balls. Give your answer to four decimal places.

Taking a Random Walk *Abby Gartland is parked at a mile marker on an east-west country road. She decides to toss a fair coin 10 times, each time driving 1 mile east if it lands heads up and 1 mile west if it lands tails up. The term "random walk" applies to this process, even though Abby drives rather than walks. It is a simplified model of Brownian motion, mentioned on* **page 580.** *(See also* **Exercises 9–12** *in the* **Extension** *at the end of this chapter.)*

In each of Exercises 49–56, find the probability that Abby's "walk" will end as described.

49. 10 miles east of the start

50. 6 miles east of the start

51. 6 miles west of the start

52. 5 miles west of the start

53. 2 miles east of the start

54. at least 2 miles east of the start

55. at least 2 miles from the start

56. exactly at the start

▌ ▌ ▌ ▌ ▌▌ **11.5 EXPECTED VALUE**

Expected Value • Games and Gambling • Investments • Business and Insurance

Expected Value

Table 10	
x	*P(x)*
1	0.05
2	0.10
3	0.20
4	0.40
5	0.10
6	0.15

The probability distribution in **Table 10**, from **Example 6** of **Section 11.2**, shows the probabilities assigned by Amy to the various lengths of time her homework may take on a given night. If Amy's friend Tara asks her how many hours her studies will take, what would be her best guess? Six different time values are possible, with some more likely than others. One thing Amy could do is calculate a "weighted average" by multiplying each possible time value by its probability and then adding the six products.

$$1(0.05) + 2(0.10) + 3(0.20) + 4(0.40) + 5(0.10) + 6(0.15)$$
$$= 0.05 + 0.20 + 0.60 + 1.60 + 0.50 + 0.90 = 3.85$$

Thus 3.85 hours is the **expected value** (or the **mathematical expectation**) of the quantity of time to be spent. Since the original time values in the table were rounded to the nearest hour, the expected value also should be rounded, to 4 hours.

> **Expected Value**
>
> If a random variable *x* can have any of the values $x_1, x_2, x_3, \ldots, x_n$, and the corresponding probabilities of these values occurring are $P(x_1), P(x_2), P(x_3), \ldots, P(x_n)$, then the **expected value of *x*** is calculated as follows.
>
> $$E(x) = x_1 \cdot P(x_1) + x_2 \cdot P(x_2) + x_3 \cdot P(x_3) + \cdots + x_n \cdot P(x_n)$$

EXAMPLE 1 Finding the Expected Number of Boys

Find the expected number of boys for a three-child family (that is, the expected value of the number of boys). Assume girls and boys are equally likely.

SOLUTION

The sample space for this experiment is

$$S = \{ \text{ggg, ggb, gbg, bgg, gbb, bgb, bbg, bbb} \}.$$

The probability distribution is shown in **Table 11**, along with the products and their sum, which gives the expected value.

Table 11

Number of Boys x	Probability $P(x)$	Product $x \cdot P(x)$
0	$\frac{1}{8}$	0
1	$\frac{3}{8}$	$\frac{3}{8}$
2	$\frac{3}{8}$	$\frac{6}{8}$
3	$\frac{1}{8}$	$\frac{3}{8}$

Expected value: $E(x) = \frac{12}{8} = \frac{3}{2}$

The expected number of boys is $\frac{3}{2}$, or 1.5. This result seems reasonable. Since boys and girls are equally likely, "half" the children are expected to be boys. ███

The expected value for the number of boys in the family could never actually occur. It is only a kind of long run average of the various values that *could* occur. (For more information on "averages," see **Section 12.2.**) If we record the number of boys in many different three-child families, then by the law of large numbers, as the number of observed families increases, the observed average number of boys should approach the expected value.

Games and Gambling

EXAMPLE 2 Finding Expected Winnings

A player pays $3 to play the following game: He tosses three fair coins and receives back "payoffs" of $1 if he tosses no heads, $2 for one head, $3 for two heads, and $4 for three heads. Find the player's expected net winnings for this game.

SOLUTION

Display the information as in **Table 12** on the next page. (Notice that, for each possible event, "net winnings" are "gross winnings" (payoff) minus cost to play.) Probabilities are derived from the sample space.

$$S = \{ \text{ttt, htt, tht, tth, hht, hth, thh, hhh} \}$$

The expected net loss of 50 cents is a long-run average only. On any particular play of this game, the player would lose $2 or lose $1 or break even or win $1. Over a long series of plays, say 100, there would be some wins and some losses, but the total net result would likely be around a $100 \cdot (\$0.50) = \$50$ *loss*.

Solution to the Chapter Opener Problem One way to look at the problem, given that the car is *not* behind Door 3, is that Doors 1 and 2 are now equally likely to contain the car. Thus, switching doors will neither help nor hurt your chances of winning the car.

However, there is another way to look at the problem. When you picked Door 1, the probability was $\frac{1}{3}$ that it contained the car. Being shown the goat behind Door 3 doesn't really give you any new information; after all, you knew that there was a goat behind at least one of the other doors. So seeing the goat behind Door 3 does nothing to change your assessment of the probability that Door 1 has the car. It remains $\frac{1}{3}$. But because Door 3 has been ruled out, the probability that Door 2 has the car is now $\frac{2}{3}$. Thus, you should switch.

Analysis of this problem depends on the psychology of the host. If we suppose that the host must *always* show you a losing door and then give you an option to switch, then you should switch. This was not specifically stated in the problem as posed above but was pointed out by many mathematicians who became involved in the discussion.

(The authors wish to thank David Berman of the University of New Orleans for his assistance with this explanation.)

For a convincing simulation of the Monty Hall problem, see http://www.grand-illusions.com/simulator/montysim.htm

Table 12

Number of Heads	Payoff	Net Winnings x	Probability $P(x)$	Product $x \cdot P(x)$
0	\$1	−\$2	$\frac{1}{8}$	−\$$\frac{2}{8}$
1	2	−1	$\frac{3}{8}$	−$\frac{3}{8}$
2	3	0	$\frac{3}{8}$	0
3	4	1	$\frac{1}{8}$	$\frac{1}{8}$

Expected value: $E(x) = -\$\frac{1}{2} = -\$0.50$

▮▮▮

A game in which the expected net winnings are zero is called a **fair game.** The game in **Example 2** has negative expected net winnings, so it is unfair against the player. A game with positive expected net winnings is unfair in favor of the player.

▮▮ **EXAMPLE 3** Finding the Fair Cost to Play a Game

The \$3 cost to play the game of **Example 2** makes the game unfair against the player (since the player's expected net winnings are negative). What cost would make this a fair game?

SOLUTION

We already computed, in **Example 2,** that the \$3 cost to play resulted in an expected net loss of \$0.50. Therefore we can conclude that the \$3 cost was 50 cents too high. A fair cost to play the game would then be \$3 − \$0.50 = \$2.50. ▮▮▮

The result in **Example 3** can be verified. Disregard the cost to play and find the expected *gross* winnings (by summing the products of payoff times probability).

$$E(\text{gross winnings}) = \$1 \cdot \frac{1}{8} + \$2 \cdot \frac{3}{8} + \$3 \cdot \frac{3}{8} + \$4 \cdot \frac{1}{8} = \frac{\$20}{8} = \$2.50$$

Expected gross winnings (payoff) are \$2.50, so this amount is a fair cost to play.

▮▮ **EXAMPLE 4** Finding the Fair Cost to Play a Game

In a certain state lottery, a player chooses three digits, in a specific order. (Leading digits may be 0, so numbers such as 028 and 003 are legitimate entries.) The lottery operators randomly select a three-digit sequence, and any player matching their selection receives a payoff of \$600. What is a fair cost to play this game?

SOLUTION

In this case, no cost has been proposed, so we have no choice but to compute expected *gross* winnings. The probability of selecting all three digits correctly is $\frac{1}{10} \cdot \frac{1}{10} \cdot \frac{1}{10} = \frac{1}{1000}$, and the probability of not selecting all three correctly is $1 - \frac{1}{1000} = \frac{999}{1000}$. The expected gross winnings are

$$E(\text{gross winnings}) = \$600 \cdot \frac{1}{1000} + \$0 \cdot \frac{999}{1000} = \$0.60.$$

Thus the fair cost to play this game is 60 cents. (In fact, the lottery charges \$1 to play, so players should expect to lose 40 cents per play *on the average.*) ▮▮▮

Roulette ("little wheel") was invented in France in the seventeenth or early eighteenth century. It has been a featured game of chance in the gambling casino of Monte Carlo.

The disk is divided into red and black alternating compartments, numbered 1 to 36 (but not in that order). There is a compartment also for 0 (and for 00 in the United States). In roulette, the wheel is set in motion, and an ivory ball is thrown into the bowl opposite to the direction of the wheel. When the wheel stops, the ball comes to rest in one of the compartments—the number and color determine who wins.

The players bet against the banker (person in charge of the pool of money) by placing money or equivalent chips in spaces on the roulette table corresponding to the wheel's colors or numbers. Bets can be made on one number or several, on odd or even, on red or black, or on combinations. The banker pays off according to the odds against the particular bet(s). For example, the classic payoff for a winning single number is $36 for each $1 bet.

State lotteries must be unfair against players because they are designed to help fund benefits (such as the state's school system) as well as to cover administrative costs and certain other expenses. Among people's reasons for playing may be a willingness to support such causes, but most people undoubtedly play for the chance to "beat the odds" and be one of the few net winners.

Gaming casinos are major business enterprises, by no means designed to break even; the games they offer are always unfair in favor of the house. The bias does not need to be great, however, since even relatively small average losses per player multiplied by large numbers of players can result in huge profits for the house.

▌ EXAMPLE 5 Finding Expected Winnings in Roulette

One simple type of *roulette* is played with an ivory ball and a wheel set in motion. The wheel contains thirty-eight compartments. Eighteen of the compartments are black, eighteen are red, one is labeled "zero," and one is labeled "double zero." (These last two are neither black nor red.) In this case, assume the player places $1 on either red or black. If the player picks the correct color of the compartment in which the ball finally lands, the payoff is $2; otherwise the payoff is zero. Find the expected net winnings.

SOLUTION

By the expected value formula, expected net winnings are

$$E(\text{net winnings}) = (\$1)\frac{18}{38} + (-\$1)\frac{20}{38} = -\$\frac{1}{19}.$$

The expected net *loss* here is $\$\frac{1}{19}$, or about 5.3¢, per play.   ▋▋▋

Investments

▌ EXAMPLE 6 Finding Expected Investment Profits

Nick Jovanovich has $5000 to invest and will commit the whole amount, for six months, to one of three technology stocks. A number of uncertainties could affect the prices of these stocks, but Nick is confident, based on his research, that one of only several possible profit scenarios will prove true of each one at the end of the six-month period. His complete analysis is shown in **Table 13**. (For example, stock *ABC* could lose $400, gain $800, or gain $1500.)

Table 13

Company *ABC*		Company *RST*		Company *XYZ*	
Profit or Loss x	Probability $P(x)$	Profit or Loss x	Probability $P(x)$	Profit or Loss x	Probability $P(x)$
−$400	0.2	$500	0.8	$0	0.4
800	0.5	1000	0.2	700	0.3
1500	0.3			1200	0.1
				2000	0.2

Find the expected profit (or loss) for each of the three stocks and select Nick's optimum choice based on these calculations. (The solution is on the next page.)

The first **Silver Dollar Slot Machine** was fashioned in 1929 by the Fey Manufacturing Company, San Francisco, inventors of the 3-reel, automatic payout machine (1895).

SOLUTION

Apply the expected value formula.

ABC: $-\$400 \cdot (0.2) + \$800 \cdot (0.5) + \$1500 \cdot (0.3) = \$770$

RST: $\$500 \cdot (0.8) + \$1000 \cdot (0.2) = \$600$

XYZ: $\$0 \cdot (0.4) + \$700 \cdot (0.3) + \$1200 \cdot (0.1) + \$2000 \cdot (0.2) = \$730$

The largest expected profit is $770. By this analysis, Nick should invest the money in stock ABC. ■■■

Of course, by investing in stock ABC, Nick may in fact *lose* $400 over the six months. The "expected" return of $770 is only a long-run average over many identical situations. Since this particular investment situation may never occur again, you may argue that using expected values is not the best approach for Nick to use.

An optimist would ignore most possibilities and focus on the *best* that each investment could do, while a pessimist would focus on the *worst* possibility for each investment.

■■ **EXAMPLE 7** Choosing Stock Investments

Decide which stock of **Example 6** Nick would pick in each case.

(a) He is an optimist.   **(b)** He is a pessimist.

SOLUTION

(a) Disregarding the probabilities, he would focus on the best case for each stock. Since ABC could return as much as $1500, RST as much as $1000, and XYZ as much as $2000, the optimum is $2000. He would buy stock XYZ (the best of the three *best* cases).

(b) In this situation, he would focus on the worst possible cases. Since ABC might return as little as $-$400$ (a $400 loss), RST as little as $500, and XYZ as little as $0, he would buy stock RST (the best of the three *worst* cases). ■■■

Business and Insurance

■■ **EXAMPLE 8** Finding Expected Lumber Revenue

Mike Crenshaw, a lumber wholesaler, is considering the purchase of a (railroad) carload of varied dimensional lumber. Mike calculates that the probabilities of reselling the load for $10,000, $9000, or $8000 are 0.22, 0.33, and 0.45, respectively. In order to ensure an *expected* profit of at least $3000, how much can Mike afford to pay for the load?

SOLUTION

The expected revenue (or income) from resales can be found in **Table 14**.

Table 14	Expected Lumber Revenue	
Income x	Probability $P(x)$	Product $x \cdot P(x)$
$10,000	0.22	$2200
9000	0.33	2970
8000	0.45	3600
	Expected revenue:	$8770

In general, we have the relationship

$$\text{profit} = \text{revenue} - \text{cost}.$$

Therefore, in terms of expectations,

$$\text{expected profit} = \text{expected revenue} - \text{cost}.$$

So $3000 = 8770 - \text{cost}$, or equivalently, $\text{cost} = 8770 - 3000 = 5770$. Mike can pay up to $5770 and still maintain an expected profit of at least $3000.   ▮▮▮

▮▮ **EXAMPLE 9** Analyzing an Insurance Decision

Jeff Marsalis, a farmer, will realize a profit of $150,000 on his wheat crop, unless there is rain before harvest, in which case he will realize only $40,000. The long-term weather forecast assigns rain a probability of 0.16. (The probability of no rain is $1 - 0.16 = 0.84$.) An insurance company offers crop insurance of $150,000 against rain for a premium of $20,000. Should Jeff buy the insurance?

SOLUTION

In order to make a wise decision, Jeff computes his expected profit under both options: to insure and not to insure. The complete calculations are summarized in the two "expectation" **Tables 15 and 16**.

For example, if insurance is purchased and it rains, Jeff's net profit is

$$\begin{bmatrix} \text{Insurance} \\ \text{proceeds} \end{bmatrix} + \begin{bmatrix} \text{Reduced} \\ \text{crop profit} \end{bmatrix} - \begin{bmatrix} \text{Insurance} \\ \text{premium} \end{bmatrix} \qquad \text{Net profit}$$

$$\$150,000 \quad + \quad \$40,000 \quad - \quad \$20,000 \quad = \quad \$170,000.$$

Table 15   Expectation when Insuring

	Net Profit x	Probability $P(x)$	Product $x \cdot P(x)$
Rain	$170,000	0.16	$27,200
No rain	130,000	0.84	109,200
			Expected profit: **$136,400**

Table 16   Expectation when Not Insuring

	Net Profit x	Probability $P(x)$	Product $x \cdot P(x)$
Rain	$40,000	0.16	$6400
No rain	150,000	0.84	126,000
			Expected profit: **$132,400**

By comparing expected profits ($136,400 > 132,400$), we conclude that Jeff is better off buying the insurance.   ▮▮▮

For Further Thought

Expected Value of Games of Chance

Slot machines are a popular game for those who want to lose their money with very little mental effort. We cannot calculate an expected value applicable to all slot machines since payoffs vary from machine to machine. But we can calculate the "typical expected value."

A player operates a slot machine by pulling a handle after inserting a coin or coins. Reels inside the machine then rotate, and come to rest in some random order. Assume that three reels show the pictures listed in **Table 17**. For example, of the 20 pictures on the first reel, 2 are cherries, 5 are oranges, 5 are plums, 2 are bells, 2 are melons, 3 are bars, and 1 is the number 7.

A picture of cherries on the first reel, but not on the second, leads to a payoff of 3 coins (*net* winnings: 2 coins); a picture of cherries on the first two reels, but not the third, leads to a payoff of 5 coins (*net* winnings: 4 coins). These and all other winning combinations are listed in **Table 18**.

Since, according to **Table 17**, there are 2 ways of getting cherries on the first reel, 15 ways of *not* getting cherries on the second reel, and 20 ways of getting anything on the third reel, we have a total of $2 \cdot 15 \cdot 20 = 600$ ways of getting a net payoff of 2. Since there are 20 pictures per reel, there are a total of $20 \cdot 20 \cdot 20 = 8000$ possible outcomes. Hence, the probability of receiving a net payoff of 2 coins is 600/8000.

This Cleveland Indians fan hit four 7s in a row on a progressive nickel slot machine at the Sands Casino in Las Vegas in 1988.

Table 17   Pictures on Reels

Pictures	Reels		
	1	2	3
Cherries	2	5	4
Oranges	5	4	5
Plums	5	3	3
Bells	2	4	4
Melons	2	1	2
Bars	3	2	1
7s	1	1	1
Totals	20	20	20

Table 18   Calculating Expected Loss on a Three-Reel Slot Machine

Winning Combinations	Number of Ways	Probability	Number of Coins Received	Net Winnings (in coins)	Probability Times Net Winnings
1 cherry (on first reel)	$2 \cdot 15 \cdot 20 = 600$	600/8000	3	2	1200/8000
2 cherries (on first two reels)	$2 \cdot 5 \cdot 16 = 160$	160/8000	5	4	640/8000
3 cherries	$2 \cdot 5 \cdot 4 = 40$	40/8000	10	9	360/8000
3 oranges	$5 \cdot 4 \cdot 5 = 100$	100/8000	10	9	900/8000
3 plums	$5 \cdot 3 \cdot 3 = 45$	45/8000	14	13	585/8000
3 bells	$\_ \cdot \_ \cdot \_ = \_\_$	___/8000	18	___	___/8000
3 melons (jackpot)	$\_ \cdot \_ \cdot \_ = \_\_$	___/8000	100	___	___/8000
3 bars (jackpot)	$\_ \cdot \_ \cdot \_ = \_\_$	___/8000	200	___	___/8000
3 7s (jackpot)	$\_ \cdot \_ \cdot \_ = \_\_$	___/8000	500	___	___/8000
Totals	___				6318/8000

Table 18 takes into account all *winning* outcomes, with the necessary products for finding expectation added in the last column. However, since a *nonwinning* outcome can occur in

8000 − 988 = 7012 ways (with winnings of −1 coin),

the product (−1) · 7012/8000 must also be included. Hence, the expected value of this particular slot machine is

$$\frac{6318}{8000} + (-1) \cdot \frac{7012}{8000} \approx -0.087 \text{ coin.}$$

On a machine costing one dollar per play, the expected *loss* (per play) is about

$$(0.087)(1 \text{ dollar}) = 8.7 \text{ cents.}$$

Actual slot machines vary in expected loss per dollar of play. But author Hornsby was able to beat a Las Vegas slot machine in 1988. (See the photo on **page 618**.)

Table 19 comes from an article by Andrew Sterrett in *The Mathematics Teacher* (March 1967), in which he discusses rules for various games of chance and calculates their expected values. He uses expected values to find expected times it would take to lose $1000 if you played continually at the rate of $1 per play and one play per minute.

For Group or Individual Investigation

1. Explain why the entries of the "Net Winnings" column of **Table 18** are all one fewer than the corresponding entries of the "Number of Coins Received" column.

2. Find the 29 missing values in **Table 18**. (Refer to **Table 17** for the values in the "Number of Ways" column.)

3. In order to make your money last as long as possible in a casino, which game should you play?

Table 19   Expected Time to Lose $1000

Game	Expected Value	Days	Hours	Minutes
Roulette (with one 0)	−$0.027	25	16	40
Roulette (with 0 and 00)	−$0.053	13	4	40
Chuck-a-luck	−$0.079	8	19	46
Keno (one number)	−$0.200	3	11	20
Numbers	−$0.300	2	7	33
Football pool (4 winners)	−$0.375	1	20	27
Football pool (10 winners)	−$0.658	1	1	19

11.5 EXERCISES

1. Explain in words what is meant by "expected value of a random variable."

2. Explain what a couple means by the statement, "We expect to have 1.5 sons."

3. *Tossing Coins*   Five fair coins are tossed. Find the expected number of heads.

4. *Drawing Cards*   Two cards are drawn, with replacement, from a standard 52-card deck. Find the expected number of diamonds.

Expected Winnings in a Die-rolling Game   For Exercises 5 and 6, a game consists of rolling a single fair die and pays off as follows: $3 for a 6, $2 for a 5, $1 for a 4, and no payoff otherwise.

5. Find the expected winnings for this game.

6. What is a fair price to pay to play this game?

Expected Winnings in a Die-rolling Game   For Exercises 7 and 8, consider a game consisting of rolling a single fair die, with payoffs as follows. If an even number of spots turns up, you receive as many dollars as there are spots up. But if an odd number of spots turns up, you must pay as many dollars as there are spots up.

7. Find the expected net winnings of this game.

8. Is this game fair, or unfair against the player, or unfair in favor of the player?

9. *Expected Winnings in a Coin-tossing Game*   A certain game involves tossing 3 fair coins, and it pays 10¢ for 3 heads, 5¢ for 2 heads, and 3¢ for 1 head. Is 5¢ a fair price to pay to play this game? (That is, does the 5¢ cost to play make the game fair?)

10. *Expected Winnings in Roulette* In a form of roulette slightly different from that in **Example 5,** a more generous management supplies a wheel having only thirty-seven compartments, with eighteen red, eighteen black, and one zero. Find the expected net winnings if you bet on red in this game.

11. *Expected Number of Absences in a Math Class* In a certain mathematics class, the probabilities have been empirically determined for various numbers of absentees on any given day. These values are shown in the table below. Find the expected number of absentees on a given day. (Give the answer to two decimal places.)

Number absent	0	1	2	3	4
Probability	0.18	0.26	0.29	0.23	0.04

12. *Expected Profit of an Insurance Company* An insurance company will insure a $200,000 home for its total value for an annual premium of $650. If the company spends $25 per year to service such a policy, the probability of total loss for such a home in a given year is 0.002, and you assume that either total loss or no loss will occur, what is the company's expected annual gain (or profit) on each such policy?

Profits from a College Foundation Raffle *A college foundation raises funds by selling raffle tickets for a new car worth* $36,000.

13. If 600 tickets are sold for $120 each, determine
   (a) the expected *net* winnings of a person buying one of the tickets,
   (b) the total profit for the foundation, assuming they had to purchase the car,
   (c) the total profit for the foundation, assuming the car was donated.

14. For the raffle described in **Exercise 13,** if 720 tickets are sold for $120 each, determine
   (a) the expected *net* winnings of a person buying one of the tickets,
   (b) the total profit for the foundation, assuming they had to purchase the car,
   (c) the total profit for the foundation, assuming the car was donated.

Winnings and Profits of a Raffle *Five thousand raffle tickets are sold. One first prize of* $1000, *two second prizes of* $500 *each, and three third prizes of* $100 *each will be awarded, with all winners selected randomly.*

15. If you purchased one ticket, what are your expected gross winnings?

16. If you purchased ten tickets, what are your expected gross winnings?

17. If the tickets were sold for $1 each, how much profit goes to the raffle sponsor?

18. *Expected Sales at a Theater Snack Bar* A children's theater found in a random survey that 58 customers bought one snack bar item, 49 bought two items, 31 bought three items, 4 bought four items, and 8 avoided the snack bar altogether. Use this information to find the expected number of snack bar items per customer. (Round your answer to the nearest tenth.)

19. *Expected Number of Children to Attend an Amusement Park* An amusement park, considering adding some new attractions, conducted a study over several typical days and found that, of 10,000 families entering the park, 1020 brought just one child (defined as younger than age twelve), 3370 brought two children, 3510 brought three children, 1340 brought four children, 510 brought five children, 80 brought six children, and 170 brought no children at all. Find the expected number of children per family attending this park. (Round your answer to the nearest tenth.)

20. *Expected Sums of Randomly Selected Numbers* Four cards are numbered 1 through 4. Two of these cards are chosen randomly (without replacement), and the numbers on them are added. Find the expected value of this sum.

21. *Prospects for Electronics Jobs in a City* In a certain California city, projections for the next year are that there is a 20% chance that electronics jobs will increase by 200, a 50% chance that they will increase by 300, and a 30% chance that they will decrease by 800. What is the expected change in the number of electronics jobs in that city in the next year?

22. *Expected Winnings in Keno* In one version of the game *keno,* the house has a pot containing 80 balls, numbered 1 through 80. A player buys a ticket for $1 and marks one number on it (from 1 to 80). The house then selects 20 of the 80 numbers at random. If the number selected by the player is among the 20 selected by the management, the player is paid $3.20. Find the expected net winnings for this game.

23. Refer to **Examples 6 and 7.** Considering the three different approaches (expected values, optimist, and pessimist), which one seems most reasonable to you, and why?

Contractor Decisions Based on Expected Profits *Lori Hales, a commercial building contractor, will commit her company to one of three projects depending on her analysis of potential profits or losses as shown here.*

Project A		Project B		Project C	
Profit or Loss x	**Probability** $P(x)$	**Profit or Loss** x	**Probability** $P(x)$	**Profit or Loss** x	**Probability** $P(x)$
$60,000	0.10	$0	0.20	$40,000	0.65
180,000	0.60	210,000	0.35	340,000	0.35
250,000	0.30	290,000	0.45		

Determine which project Lori should choose according to each approach.

24. expected values　　**25.** the optimist viewpoint

26. the pessimist viewpoint

Expected Winnings in a Game Show *A game show contestant is offered the option of receiving a computer system worth $2300 or accepting a chance to win either a luxury vacation worth $5000 or a boat worth $8000. If the second option is chosen the contestant's probabilities of winning the vacation or the boat are 0.20 and 0.15, respectively.*

27. If the contestant were to turn down the computer system and go for one of the other prizes, what would be the expected winnings?

28. Purely in terms of monetary value, what is the contestant's wiser choice?

Evaluating an Insurance Purchase *David Glenn, the promoter of an outdoor concert, expects a gate profit of $100,000, unless it rains, which would reduce the gate profit to $30,000. The probability of rain is 0.20. For a premium of $25,000 David can purchase insurance coverage that would pay him $100,000 in case of rain.*

Use this information for Exercises 29–32.

29. Find the expected net profit when the insurance is purchased.

30. Find the expected net profit when the insurance is not purchased.

31. Based on expected values, which is David's wiser choice in this situation?

32. If you were the promoter, would you base your decision on expected values? Explain your reasoning.

Expected Values in Book Sales *Jessica Lasda, an educational publisher representative, presently has five accounts, and her manager is considering assigning her three more accounts. The new accounts would bring potential volume to her business, and some of her present accounts have potential for growth as well. See the following table and continue on the next page.*

1	2	3	4	5	6
Account Number	**Existing Volume**	**Potential Additional Volume**	**Probability of Getting Additional Volume**	**Expected Value of Additional Volume**	**Existing Volume plus Expected Value of Additional Volume**
1	$10,000	$10,000	0.40	$4000	$14,000
2	30,000	0	—	—	30,000
3	25,000	15,000	0.20	3000	
4	35,000	0	—	—	
5	15,000	5,000	0.30		
6	0	30,000	0.10		
7	0	25,000	0.70		
8	0	45,000	0.60		

Use the previous table to work Exercises 33–37.

33. Compute the four missing expected values in column 5.

34. Compute the six missing amounts in column 6.

35. What is Jessica's total "expected" additional volume?

36. If Jessica achieved her expected additional volume in all accounts, what would be the total volume of all her accounts?

37. If Jessica achieved her expected additional volume in all accounts, by what percentage (to the nearest tenth of a percent) would she increase her total volume?

38. *Expected Winnings in Keno* Recall that in the game keno of **Exercise 22,** the house randomly selects 20 numbers from the counting numbers 1–80. In the variation called 6-spot keno, the player pays 60¢ for his ticket and marks 6 numbers of his choice. If the 20 numbers selected by the house contain at least 3 of those chosen by the player, he gets a payoff according to this scheme.

3 of the player's numbers among the 20	$0.35
4 of the player's numbers among the 20	2.00
5 of the player's numbers among the 20	60.00
6 of the player's numbers among the 20	1250.00

Find the player's expected net winnings in this game. [*Hint:* The four probabilities required here can be found using combinations (**Section 10.3**), the fundamental counting principle (**Section 10.2**), and the theoretical probability formula (**Section 11.1**).]

EXTENSION Estimating Probabilities by Simulation

Simulating Genetic Traits • Simulating Human Births

	Second Parent	
	R	**r**
First **R**	RR	Rr
Parent **r**	rR	rr

Simulation methods, also called **"Monte Carlo" methods,** require huge numbers of random digits, so computers are used to produce them. A computer, however, cannot toss coins. It must use an algorithmic process, programmed into the computer, which is called a **random number generator.** It is very difficult to avoid all nonrandom patterns in the results, so the digits produced are called "pseudorandom" numbers. They must pass a battery of tests of randomness before being "approved for use."

Computer scientists and physicists have been encountering unexpected difficulties with even the most sophisticated random number generators. Therefore, they must be carefully checked along with each new simulation application proposed.

Simulating Genetic Traits An important area within probability theory is the process called **simulation.** It is possible to study a complicated, or unclear, phenomenon by *simulating*, or imitating, it with a simpler phenomenon involving the same basic probabilities.

For example, recall from **Section 11.1** Mendel's discovery that when two Rr pea plants (red-flowered but carrying both red and white genes) are crossed, the offspring will have red flowers if an R gene is received from either parent or from both. This is because red is dominant and white is recessive. **Table 3**, reproduced here in the margin, shows that three of the four equally likely possibilities result in redflowered offspring.

Now suppose we want to estimate the probability that three offspring in a row will have red flowers. It is much easier (and quicker) to toss coins than to cross pea plants. And the equally likely outcomes, heads and tails, can be used to simulate the transfer of the equally likely genes, R and r. If we toss two coins, say a nickel and a penny, then we can interpret the results as follows.

hh ⇒ RR ⇒ red gene from first parent and red gene from second parent
    ⇒ red flowers

ht ⇒ Rr ⇒ red gene from first parent and white gene from second parent
    ⇒ red flowers

th ⇒ rR ⇒ white gene from first parent and red gene from second parent
    ⇒ red flowers

tt ⇒ rr ⇒ white gene from first parent and white gene from second parent
    ⇒ white flowers

Although nothing is certain for a few tosses, the law of large numbers indicates that larger and larger numbers of tosses should become better and better indicators of general trends in the genetic process.

▮▮ **EXAMPLE 1** Simulating Genetic Processes
_____

Toss two coins 50 times and use the results to approximate the probability that the crossing of Rr pea plants will produce three successive red-flowered offspring.

SOLUTION

We actually tossed two coins 50 times and got the following sequence.

> th, hh, th, tt, th, hh, ht, th, ht, th, hh, hh, tt, th, hh,
> ht, ht, ht, ht, th, hh, hh, hh, tt, ht, tt, hh, ht, ht, hh, tt,
> tt, tt, th, tt, tt, hh, ht, ht, ht, hh, tt, th, hh, tt, hh, ht,
> tt, tt, tt

By the color interpretation described on the previous page, this gives the following sequence of flower colors in the offspring.

> red–red–red–white–red–red–red–red–red–red–red–red–white–

Only "both tails" gives white. → red–red–red–red–red–red–red–red–red–red–white–red–white–

> red–red–red–red–white–white–white–red–white–white–red–red–

> red–red–red–white–red–red–white–red–red–white–white–white

We now have an experimental list of 48 sets of three successive plants, the 1st, 2nd, and 3rd entries, then the 2nd, 3rd, and 4th entries, and so on. Do you see why there are 48 in all?

Now we just count up the number of these sets of three that are "red-red-red." Since there are 20 of those, our empirical probability of three successive red offspring, obtained through simulation, is $\frac{20}{48} = \frac{5}{12}$, or about 0.417. By applying the multiplication rule of probability (with all outcomes independent of one another), we find that the theoretical value is $\left(\frac{3}{4}\right)^3 = \frac{27}{64}$, or about 0.422, so our approximation obtained by simulation is very close. ▮▮▮

Simulating Human Births
In human births boys and girls are (essentially) equally likely. Therefore, an individual birth can be simulated by tossing a fair coin, letting a head correspond to a girl and a tail to a boy.

▮▮ **EXAMPLE 2** Simulating Births with Coin Tossing
_____

A sequence of 40 actual coin tosses produced the results below.

> bbggb, gbbbg, gbgbb, bggbg, bbbbg, gbbgg, gbbgg, bgbbg

(For every head we have written g, for girl. For every tail, b, for boy.)

(a) How many pairs of two successive births are represented by the sequence?

(b) How many of those pairs consist of both boys?

(c) Find the empirical probability, based on this simulation, that two successive births both will be boys. Give your answer to three decimal places.

SOLUTION

(a) Beginning with the 1st–2nd pair and ending with the 39th–40th pair, there are 39 pairs.

(b) Observing the sequence of boys and girls, we count 11 pairs of two consecutive boys.

(c) Utilizing parts (a) and (b), we have $\frac{11}{39} \approx 0.282$. ▮▮▮

Pilots, astronauts, race car drivers, and others train in **simulators.** Some of these devices, which may be viewed as very technical, high-cost versions of video games, imitate conditions to be encountered later in the "real world." A simulator session allows estimation of the likelihood, or probability, of different responses that the learner would display under actual conditions. Repeated sessions help the learner to develop more successful responses before actual equipment and lives are put at risk.

Table 20
→51592
77876
36500
40571
04822
→53033
92080
01587
36006
63698
→17297
22841
→91979
96480
74949
76896
47588
45521
02472
55184
40177
84861
86937
20931
22454
→73219
→55707
48007
→65191
06772
94928
→15709
39922
96365
14655
65587
76905
12369
54219
89329
90060
06975
05050
69774
→78351
11464
84086
→51497
12307
68009

Another way to simulate births, and other phenomena, is with random numbers. The spinner in **Figure 12** can be used to obtain a table of random digits, like in **Table 20**. The 250 random digits generated have been grouped conveniently so that we can easily follow down a column or across a row to carry out a simulation.

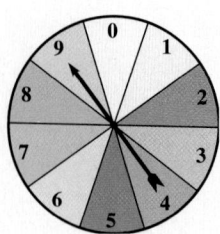

Figure 12

▮▮ **EXAMPLE 3** Simulating Births with Random Numbers

A couple plans to have five children. Use random number simulation to estimate the probability they will have more than three boys.

SOLUTION

Let each sequence of five digits, as they appear in **Table 20,** represent a family with five children, and (arbitrarily) associate odd digits with boys, even digits with girls. (Recall that 0 is even.) Verify that, of the fifty families simulated, only the ten marked with arrows have more than 3 boys (4 boys or 5 boys). Therefore, the estimated (empirical) probability is

$$P(\text{more than 3 boys}) = \frac{10}{50} = 0.20.$$ ▮▮▮

The theoretical value for the probability in **Example 3** above would be the same as that obtained in **Example 3** of **Section 11.4.** It was 0.1875. Our estimate above was fairly close. In light of the law of large numbers, a larger sampling of random digits (more than 50 simulated families) would likely yield a closer approximation.

▮▮ **EXAMPLE 4** Simulating Card Drawing with Random Numbers

Use random number simulation to estimate the probability that two cards drawn from a standard deck with replacement both will be of the same suit.

SOLUTION

Use this correspondence: 0 and 1 mean clubs, 2 and 3 mean diamonds, 4 and 5 mean hearts, 6 and 7 mean spades, 8 and 9 are disregarded. Now refer to **Table 20**. If we (arbitrarily) use the first digit of each five-digit group, omitting 8s and 9s, we obtain the sequence

5–7–3–4–0–5–0–3–6–1–2–7–7–4–4–0–5–4–2–2–

7–5–4–6–0–1–3–1–6–7–1–5–0–0–6–7–1–5–1–6.

First digits of all groups

This 40-digit sequence of digits yields the sequence of suits shown next.

5 gives hearts, 7 gives spades, 3 gives diamonds, and so on.

hearts–spades–diamonds–hearts–clubs–hearts–clubs–diamonds–spades–

clubs–diamonds–spades–spades–hearts–hearts–clubs–hearts–hearts–

diamonds–diamonds–spades–hearts–hearts–spades–clubs–clubs–

diamonds–clubs–spades–spades–clubs–hearts–clubs–clubs–spades–

spades–clubs–hearts–clubs–spades

Verify that, of the 39 successive pairs of suits (hearts–spades, spades–diamonds, diamonds–hearts, etc.), 9 of them are pairs of the same suit. This makes the estimated probability $\frac{9}{39} \approx 0.23$. (For comparison, the theoretical value is 0.25.) ▮▮▮

EXTENSION EXERCISES

1. **Simulating Pea Plant Reproduction with Coin Tossing** Explain why, in **Example 1,** fifty tosses of the coins produced only 48 sets of three successive offspring.

2. **Simulating Pea Plant Reproduction with Coin Tossing** Use the sequence of flower colors of **Example 1** to approximate the probability that *four* successive offspring all will have red flowers.

3. **Comparing the Likelihoods of Girl and Boy Births** Should the probability of two successive girl births be any different from that of two successive boy births?

4. **Finding Empirical Probability** Simulate 40 births by tossing coins yourself, and obtain an empirical probability for two successive girls.

5. **Simulating Boy and Girl Children with Random Numbers** Use **Table 20** to simulate fifty families with three children. Let 0–4 correspond to boys and 5–9 to girls, and use the middle three digits of the 5-digit groupings (159, 787, 650, and so on). Estimate the probability of exactly two boys in a family of three children. Compare with the theoretical probability, which is $\frac{3}{8} = 0.375$.

Simulating One-and-One Foul Shooting with Random Numbers
In Exercises 71–73 of Section 11.3, Christine, who had a 70% foul-shooting record, had probabilities of scoring 0, 1, or 2 points of 0.30, 0.21, and 0.49, respectively.

*Use **Table 20** (with digits 0–6 representing hit and 7–9 representing miss) to simulate 50 one-and-one shooting opportunities for Christine. Begin at the top left (5, 7, 3, etc., to the bottom), then move to the second column (1, 7, 6, etc.), going until 50 one-and-one opportunities are obtained. (Some "opportunities" involve one shot and one random digit, while others involve two shots and two random digits.) Keep a tally of the numbers of times 0, 1, and 2 points are scored.*

Number of Points	Tally
0	
1	
2	

From the tally, find the empirical probability (to two decimal places) of each event.

6. no points   7. 1 point   8. 2 points

Determining the Path of a Random Walk Using a Die and a Coin
Exercises 49–56 of Section 11.4 illustrated a simple version of the idea of a "random walk." Atomic particles released in nuclear fission also move in a random fashion. During World War II, John von Neumann and Stanislaw Ulam used simulation with random numbers to study particle motion in nuclear reactions. Von Neumann coined the name "Monte Carlo" for the methods used.

The figure suggests a model for random motion in two dimensions. Assume that a particle moves in a series of 1-unit "jumps," each one in a random direction, any one of 12 equally likely possibilities. One way to choose directions is to roll a fair die and toss a fair coin. The die determines one of the directions 1–6, coupled with heads on the coin. Tails on the coin reverses the direction of the die, so that the die coupled with tails gives directions 7–12. So 3h (meaning 3 with the die and heads with the coin) gives direction 3; 3t gives direction 9 (opposite to 3); and so on.

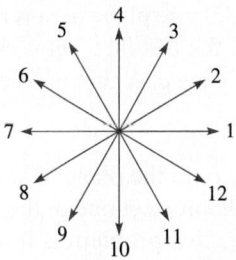

9. Simulate the motion described above with 10 rolls of a die (and tosses of a coin). Draw the 10-jump path you get. Make your drawing accurate enough so you can estimate (by measuring) how far from its starting point the particle ends up.

10. Repeat the experiment of **Exercise 9** four more times. Measure distance from start to finish for each of the 5 "random trips." Add these 5 distances and divide the sum by 5, to arrive at an "expected net distance" for such a trip.

For Exercises 11 and 12, consider another two-dimensional random walk governed by the following conditions.

- *Start out from a given street corner, and travel one block north. At each intersection:*
- *Turn left with probability $\frac{1}{6}$.*
- *Go straight with probability $\frac{2}{6}$ $(=\frac{1}{3})$.*
- *Turn right with probability $\frac{3}{6}$ $(=\frac{1}{2})$.*

   (Never turn around.)

11. **A Random Walk Using a Fair Die** Explain how a fair die could be used to simulate this random walk.

12. **A Random Walk Using a Random Number Table** Use **Table 20** to simulate this random walk. For every 1 encountered in the table, turn left and proceed for another block. For every 2 or 3, go straight and proceed for another block. For every 4, 5, or 6, turn right and proceed for another block. Disregard all other digits, that is, 0s, 7s, 8s, and 9s. (Do you see how this scheme satisfies the probabilities given before **Exercise 11**?) This time begin at the upper right corner of the table, running down the column 2, 6, 0, and so on, to the bottom. When this column of digits is used up, stop the "walk." Describe, in terms of distance and direction, where you have ended up relative to your starting point.

COLLABORATIVE INVESTIGATION

Finding Empirical Values of π

The information in this investigation was obtained from Burton's History of Mathematics: An Introduction, Third Edition, by David M. Burton, published by Wm. C. Brown, 1995, page 440.

The following problem was posed by Georges Louis Leclerc, Comte de Buffon (1707–1788) in his *Histoire Naturelle* in 1777. A large plane area is ruled with equidistant parallel lines, the distance between two consecutive lines of the series being *a*. A thin needle of length

$$\ell < a$$

is tossed randomly onto the plane. What is the probability that the needle will intersect one of these lines?

The answer to this problem is found using integral calculus, and the probability *p* is shown to be $p = \frac{2\ell}{\pi a}$. Solving for π gives us the formula

$$\pi = \frac{2\ell}{pa}, \qquad \textbf{(1)}$$

which can be used to approximate the value of π experimentally. This was first observed by Pierre Simon de Laplace, and such an experiment was carried out by Johann Wolf, a professor of astronomy at Bern, in about 1850. In this investigation, we will perform a similar experiment.

See http://webspace.ship.edu/deensley/mathdl/stats/Buffon.html for a dynamic illustration of this Buffon Needle Problem.

Topics for Discussion

Divide the class into groups of 3 or 4 students each. Each group will need the materials listed in the next column.

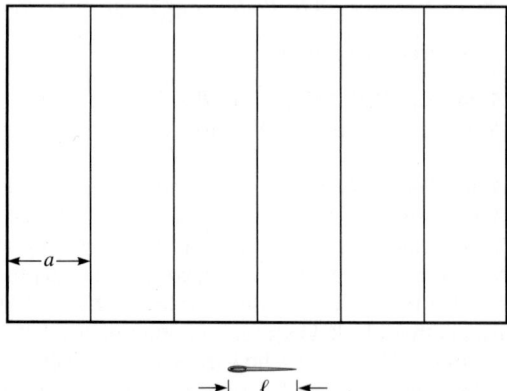

1. a sheet of paper with a series of parallel lines evenly spaced across it

2. a thin needle, or needlelike object, with a length less than the distance between adjacent parallel lines on the paper

Each group should carry out these steps:

1. Measure and record the distance between lines (*a*) and the length of the needle (ℓ), using the same units for both.

2. Assign one member to drop the needle onto the paper, another to determine whether the needle "hits" a line or not, and another to keep a tally of hits and misses.

3. Discuss ways to minimize bias so that the position and orientation of the dropped needle will be as random as possible.

4. Drop the needle 100 times, and record the number of hits.

5. Calculate the probability *p* = (number of hits)/100. Is this probability value theoretical or empirical?

6. Enter the calculated value of *p* and the measured values of *a* and ℓ into formula (1) to obtain a value of π. Round this value to four decimal places.

Now come back together as a class and record the various values obtained for π. Discuss the following questions.

1. The correct value of π, to four decimal places, is 3.1416. Which value of π, reported by the various groups, is most accurate? How far off is it?

2. Was it necessary to drop the needle 100 times, or could more or fewer tosses have been used?

3. Wolf tossed his needle 5000 times and it hit a line 2532 times, leading to an experimental value of π equal to 3.1596. How far off was Wolf's value?

4. How could the experiment be modified to produce "better" values for π?

5. Why could different groups use different ℓ to *a* ratios and still all obtain legitimate approximations for π?

6. Does the simulation method investigated here seem like a reasonable way to approximate π? Why, or why not?

CHAPTER 11 TEST

1. Explain the difference between *empirical* and *theoretical* probabilities.

2. State the *law of large numbers,* and use coin tossing to illustrate it.

Drawing Cards A single card is chosen at random from a standard 52-card deck. Find the odds against its being each of the following.

3. a heart

4. a red queen

5. a king or a black face card

Genetics of Cystic Fibrosis The chart represents genetic transmission of cystic fibrosis. C denotes a normal gene while c denotes a cystic fibrosis gene. (Normal is dominant.) Both parents in this case are Cc, which means that they inherited one of each gene, and are, therefore, carriers but do not have the disease.

		Second Parent	
		C	**c**
First Parent	**C**		Cc
	c		

6. Complete the chart, showing all four equally likely gene arrangements.

7. Find the probability that a child of these parents will also be a carrier without the disease.

8. What are the odds that a child of these parents actually will have cystic fibrosis?

Days Off for Pizza Parlor Workers The manager of a pizza parlor (which operates seven days a week) allows each of three employees to select one day off next week. Assuming the selection is done randomly and independently, find the probability of each event.

9. All three select different days.

10. All three select the same day, given that all three select a day beginning with the same letter.

11. Exactly two of them select the same day.

Building Numbers from Sets of Digits Two numbers are randomly selected without replacement from the set {1, 2, 3, 4, 5}. Find the probability of each event.

12. Both numbers are even.

13. Both numbers are prime.

14. The sum of the two numbers is odd.

15. The product of the two numbers is odd.

Selecting Committees A three-member committee is selected randomly from a group consisting of three men and two women.

16. Let *x* denote the number of men on the committee, and complete the probability distribution table.

x	*P(x)*
0	0
1	
2	
3	

17. Find the probability that the committee members are not all men.

18. Find the expected number of men on the committee.

Rolling Dice A pair of dice are rolled. Find the following.

19. the probability of "doubles" (the same number on both dice)

20. the odds in favor of a sum greater than 2

21. the odds against a sum of "7 or 11"

22. the probability of a sum that is even and less than 5

Making Par in Golf Ted Krischak has a 0.78 chance of making par on each hole of golf that he plays. Today he plans to play just three holes. Find the probability of each event. Round answers to three decimal places.

23. He makes par on all three holes.

24. He makes par on exactly two of the three holes.

25. He makes par on at least one of the three holes.

26. He makes par on the first and third holes but not on the second.

Drawing Cards Two cards are drawn, without replacement, from a standard 52-card deck. Find the probability of each event.

27. Both cards are red.

28. Both cards are the same color.

29. The second card is a queen, given that the first card is an ace

30. The first card is a face card and the second is black.

STATISTICS

The CBS television series, NUMB3RS, focused on how mathematics is used in solving crimes. In the December 5, 2008 episode Conspiracy Theory, agent Charlie Eppes wants to prove a point to one of his colleagues: "Go with what you know, not what you don't." He cites a case of Simpson's paradox, a puzzling statistical oddity.

In both these years, David Justice had a higher batting average than Derek Jeter. But if you factor in their uneven number of at-bats, Jeter beats him.

What we know is that for the two-year period, Jeter is the better hitter, despite the fact that for both individual years, Justice had higher averages. To verify the paradox for yourself, see For Further Thought on page 649.

12.1 VISUAL DISPLAYS OF DATA

Basic Concepts • Frequency Distributions • Grouped Frequency Distributions • Stem-and-Leaf Displays • Bar Graphs, Circle Graphs, and Line Graphs

Basic Concepts

Governments collect and analyze an amazing quantity of "statistics". The word itself comes from the Latin *statisticus,* meaning "of the state."

In statistical work, a **population** includes *all* items of interest, and a **sample** includes *some* (but ordinarily not all) of the items in the population. See the Venn diagram in the margin.

To predict the outcome of an approaching presidential election, we may be interested in a population of many millions of voter preferences (those of all potential voters in the country). As a practical matter, however, even national polling organizations with considerable resources will obtain only a relatively small sample, say 2000, of those preferences.

The study of statistics is divided into two main areas. **Descriptive statistics** has to do with collecting, organizing, summarizing, and presenting data (information). **Inferential statistics,** has to do with drawing inferences or conclusions (making conjectures) about populations based on information from samples.

The photos below show two random samples drawn from a large bowl of 10,000 colored beads. The 25-bead sample contains 9 green beads, from which we infer, by inductive reasoning, that the bowl (the population) must contain about $\frac{9}{25}$, or 36%, that is, about 3600 green beads.

A population of 10,000

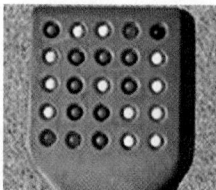
A random sample of 25

A random sample of 100

The 100-bead sample contains 28 green beads, leading to the inference that the population must contain about $\frac{28}{100}$, or 28%, that is, about 2800 green beads. This estimate, based on a larger sample, should be more accurate. In fact it is, since the bowl actually contains 30%, or 3000 green beads, and 2800 is closer to 3000 than 3600 is. (The "error" is one-third as much.)

Summarizing, if we know what a population is like, then probability theory enables us to predict what is likely to happen in a sample (deductive reasoning). If we know what a sample is like, then inferential statistics enables us to infer estimates about the population (inductive reasoning).

Information that has been collected but not yet organized or processed is called **raw data.** It is often **quantitative** (or **numerical**) but can also be **qualitative** (or **nonnumerical**), as illustrated in **Table 1**.

Population

Sample

EDIT CALC TESTS
1: 1-Var Stats
2: 2-Var Stats
3: Med-Med
4: LinReg(ax+b)
5: QuadReg
6: CubicReg
7: ↓QuartReg

EDIT CALC TESTS
7: ↑QuartReg
8: LinReg(a+bx)
9: LnReg
0: ExpReg
A: PwrReg
B: Logistic
C: SinReg

Various statistical options on the TI-83/84 Plus.

Table 1	Examples of Raw Data

Quantitative data: The number of siblings in ten different families: 3, 1, 2, 1, 5, 4, 3, 3, 8, 2

Qualitative data: The makes of six different automobiles: Toyota, Ford, Nissan, Toyota, Chevrolet, Honda

Quantitative data are generally more useful when they are **sorted,** or arranged in numerical order. In sorted form, the first list in **Table 1** appears as follows.

$$1, 1, 2, 2, 3, 3, 3, 4, 5, 8$$

Frequency Distributions

When a data set includes many repeated items, it can be organized into a **frequency distribution,** which lists the distinct data values (x) along with their frequencies (f). The frequency designates the number of times the corresponding item occurred in the data set.

It is also helpful to show the **relative frequency** of each distinct item. This is the fraction, or percentage, of the data set represented by the item. If n denotes the total number of items, and a given item, x, occurred f times, then the relative frequency of x is $\frac{f}{n}$. **Example 1** illustrates these ideas.

▌▌ **EXAMPLE 1** Constructing Frequency and Relative Frequency Distributions

The 25 members of a psychology class were polled as to the number of siblings in their individual families. Construct a frequency distribution and a relative frequency distribution for their responses, which are shown here.

$$2, 3, 1, 3, 3, 5, 2, 3, 3, 1, 1, 4, 2, 4, 2, 5, 4, 3, 6, 5, 1, 6, 2, 2, 2$$

SOLUTION

The data range from a low of 1 to a high of 6. The frequencies (obtained by inspection) and relative frequencies are shown in **Table 2**.

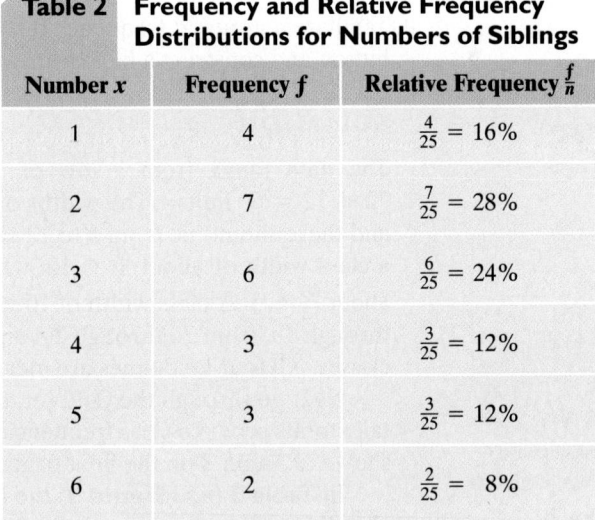

Table 2	Frequency and Relative Frequency Distributions for Numbers of Siblings	
Number x	**Frequency f**	**Relative Frequency $\frac{f}{n}$**
1	4	$\frac{4}{25} = 16\%$
2	7	$\frac{7}{25} = 28\%$
3	6	$\frac{6}{25} = 24\%$
4	3	$\frac{3}{25} = 12\%$
5	3	$\frac{3}{25} = 12\%$
6	2	$\frac{2}{25} = 8\%$

▌▌▌

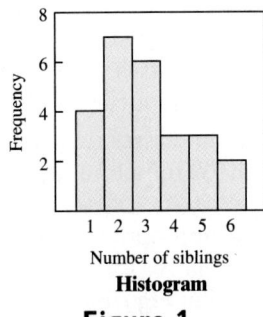

Number of siblings
Histogram
Figure 1

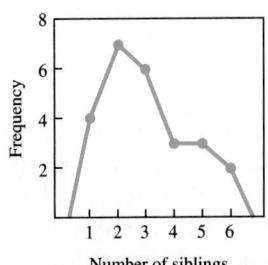

Number of siblings
Frequency polygon
Figure 2

The numerical data of **Table 2** can more easily be interpreted with the aid of a **histogram.** A series of rectangles, whose lengths represent the frequencies, are placed next to one another as shown in **Figure 1**. On each axis, horizontal and vertical, a label and the numerical scale should be shown.

The information shown in the histogram in **Figure 1** can also be conveyed by a **frequency polygon,** as in **Figure 2**. Simply plot a single point at the appropriate height for each frequency, connect the points with a series of connected line segments, and complete the polygon with segments that trail down to the axis beyond 1 and 6.

The frequency polygon is an instance of the more general *line graph,* used for many kinds of data, not just frequencies. Line graphs were first introduced in **Chapter 1.**

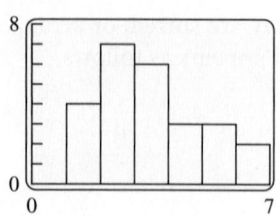

This histogram was generated with a graphing calculator using the data in **Table 2**. Compare with **Figure 1** on **page 631**.

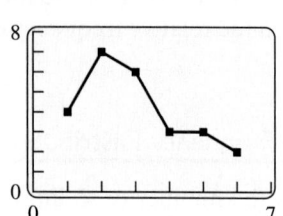

This line graph resembles the frequency polygon in **Figure 2** on **page 631**. It was generated with a graphing calculator using the data in **Table 2**.

Grouped Frequency Distributions

Data sets containing large numbers of items are often arranged into groups, or *classes*. All data items are assigned to their appropriate classes, and then a **grouped frequency distribution** can be set up and a graph displayed. Although there are no fixed rules for establishing the classes, most statisticians agree on a few general guidelines.

> ### Guidelines for the Classes of a Grouped Frequency Distribution
> 1. Make sure each data item will fit into one, and only one, class.
> 2. Try to make all classes the same width.
> 3. Make sure the classes do not overlap.
> 4. Use from 5 to 12 classes. (Too few or too many classes can obscure the tendencies in the data.)

▮▮ **EXAMPLE 2** Constructing a Histogram and a Frequency Polygon

Forty students, selected randomly in the school cafeteria one morning, were asked to estimate the number of hours they had spent studying in the past week (including both in-class and out-of-class time). Their responses are recorded here.

18	60	72	58	20	15	12	26	16	29
26	41	45	25	32	24	22	55	30	31
55	39	29	44	29	14	40	31	45	62
36	52	47	38	36	23	33	44	17	24

Tabulate a grouped frequency distribution and a grouped relative frequency distribution and construct a histogram and a frequency polygon for the given data.

SOLUTION

The data range from a low of 12 to a high of 72 (that is, over a range of $72 - 12 = 60$ units.). The widths of the classes should be uniform (by Guideline 2), and there should be from 5 to 12 classes (by Guideline 4). Five classes would imply a class width of about $\frac{60}{5} = 12$, while twelve classes would imply a class width of about $\frac{60}{12} = 5$. A class width of 10 will be convenient. We let our classes run from 10 through 19, from 20 through 29, and so on up to 70 through 79, for a total of seven classes. All four guidelines are met.

Next go through the data set, tallying each item into the appropriate class. The tally totals produce class frequencies, which in turn produce relative frequencies, as shown in **Table 3** on the next page. The histogram is displayed in **Figure 3**.

In **Table 3** (and **Figure 3**) the numbers 10, 20, 30, and so on are called the **lower class limits.** They are the smallest possible data values within the respective classes. The numbers 19, 29, 39, and so on are called the **upper class limits.** The common **class width** for the distribution is the difference of any two successive lower class limits (such as 30–20), or of any two successive upper class limits (such as 59–49). The class width for this distribution is 10, as noted earlier.

To construct a frequency polygon, notice that, in a *grouped* frequency distribution, the data items in a given class are generally not all the same. We can obtain the "middle" value, or **class mark,** by adding the lower and upper class limits and dividing this sum by 2. We locate all the class marks along the horizontal axis and plot points above the class marks. The heights of the plotted points represent the class frequencies. The resulting points are connected just as for an ordinary (nongrouped) frequency distribution. The result is shown in **Figure 4**.

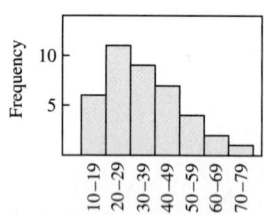

Weekly study times (in hours)
Grouped frequency histogram

Figure 3

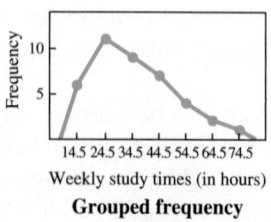

Weekly study times (in hours)
Grouped frequency polygon

Figure 4

Table 3	Grouped Frequency and Relative Frequency Distributions for Weekly Study Times		
Class Limits	Tally	Frequency f	Relative Frequency $\frac{f}{n}$
10–19	ⅢⅡ Ⅰ	6	$\frac{6}{40} = 15.0\%$
20–29	ⅢⅡ ⅢⅡ Ⅰ	11	$\frac{11}{40} = 27.5\%$
30–39	ⅢⅡ ⅢⅢ	9	$\frac{9}{40} = 22.5\%$
40–49	ⅢⅡ ⅡⅠ	7	$\frac{7}{40} = 17.5\%$
50–59	ⅢⅢ	4	$\frac{4}{40} = 10.0\%$
60–69	ⅡⅠ	2	$\frac{2}{40} = 5.0\%$
70–79	Ⅰ	1	$\frac{1}{40} = 2.5\%$
	Total: $n = 40$		

Stem-and-Leaf Displays

In **Table 3**, the tally marks give a good visual impression of how the data are distributed. In fact, the tally marks are almost like a histogram turned on its side. Nevertheless, once the tallying is done, the tally marks are usually dropped, and the grouped frequency distribution is presented as in **Table 4**.

The pictorial advantage of the tally marks is now lost. Furthermore, we cannot tell, from the grouped frequency distribution itself (or from the tally marks either, for that matter), what any of the original items were. We only know, for example, that there were seven items in the class 40–49. We do not know specifically what any of them were.

One way to avoid these shortcoming is to employ a tool of exploratory data analysis, the **stem-and-leaf display,** as shown in **Example 3**.

Table 4	Grouped Frequency Distribution for Weekly Study Times
Class Limits	Frequency
10–19	6
20–29	11
30–39	9
40–49	7
50–59	4
60–69	2
70–79	1

▋▋ **EXAMPLE 3** Constructing a Stem-and-Leaf Display

Present the study times data of **Example 2** in a stem-and-leaf display.

SOLUTION

See **Example 2** for the original raw data. We arrange the numbers in **Table 5**. The tens digits, to the left of the vertical line, are the "stems," while the corresponding ones digits are the "leaves." We have entered all items from the first row of the original data, from left to right, then the items from the second row through the fourth row.

Table 5	Stem-and-Leaf Display for Weekly Study Times									
1	8	5	2	6	4	7				
2	0	6	9	6	5	4	2	9	9	3	4
3	2	0	1	9	1	6	8	6	3		
4	1	5	4	0	5	7	4				
5	8	5	5	2							
6	0	2									
7	2										

Notice that the stem-and-leaf display of **Example 3** conveys at a glance the same pictorial impressions that a histogram would convey without the need for constructing the drawing. It also preserves the exact data values.

Bar Graphs, Circle Graphs, and Line Graphs

A frequency distribution of nonnumerical observations can be presented in the form of a **bar graph,** which is similar to a histogram except that the rectangles (bars) usually are not touching one another and sometimes are arranged horizontally rather than vertically. The bar graph of **Figure 5** shows the frequencies of occurrence of the vowels A, E, I, O, and U in this paragraph.

A graphical alternative to the bar graph is the **circle graph,** or **pie chart,** which uses a circle to represent the total of all the categories and divides the circle into sectors, or wedges (like pieces of pie), whose sizes show the relative magnitudes of the categories. The angle around the entire circle measures 360°. For example, a category representing 20% of the whole should correspond to a sector whose central angle is 20% of 360°, that is,

$$0.20(360°) = 72°.$$

A circle graph shows, at a glance, the relative magnitudes of various categories.

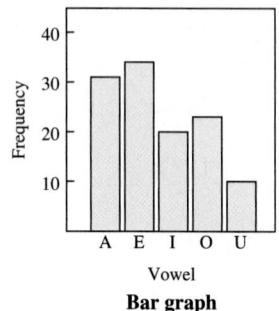

Bar graph

Figure 5

▮▮ **EXAMPLE 4** Constructing a Circle Graph

Cheri Goldberg found that, during her first semester of college, her expenses fell into categories as shown in **Table 6** below. Present this information in a circle graph.

SOLUTION

The central angle of the food sector is 0.30(360°) = 108°. Rent is 0.25(360°) = 90°. Calculate the other four angles similarly. Then draw a circle and mark off the angles with a protractor. The completed circle graph appears in **Figure 6**.

Table 6 Student Expenses	
Expense	**Percent of Total**
Food	30%
Rent	25%
Entertainment	15%
Clothing	10%
Books	10%
Other	10%

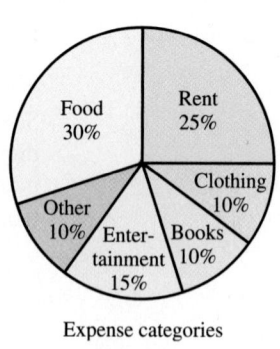

Expense categories

Figure 6 ▮▮▮

To demonstrate how a quantity *changes,* say with respect to time, use a **line graph.** Connect a series of line segments that rise and fall with time, according to the magnitude of the quantity being illustrated. To compare the patterns of change for two or more quantities, we can even plot multiple line graphs together in a "comparison line graph." (A line graph looks somewhat like a frequency polygon, but the quantities graphed are not necessarily frequencies.)

▌▌ **EXAMPLE 5** Constructing and Interpreting a Line Graph

Suppose Cheri, from **Example 4,** wanted to keep track of her major expenses, food and rent, over the course of four years of college (eight semesters), in order to see how each one's budget percentage changed with time and how the two compared. Use the data she collected (**Table 7**) to show this information in a line graph, and state any significant conclusions that are apparent from the graph.

Table 7	Food and Rent Expense Percentages	
Semester	**Food**	**Rent**
First	30%	25%
Second	31	26
Third	30	28
Fourth	29	29
Fifth	28	34
Sixth	31	34
Seventh	30	37
Eighth	29	38

SOLUTION

A comparison line graph for the given data (**Figure 7**) shows that the food percentage stayed fairly constant over the four years (at close to 30%), while the rent percentage, starting several points below food, rose steadily, surpassing food after the fourth semester and finishing significantly higher than food.

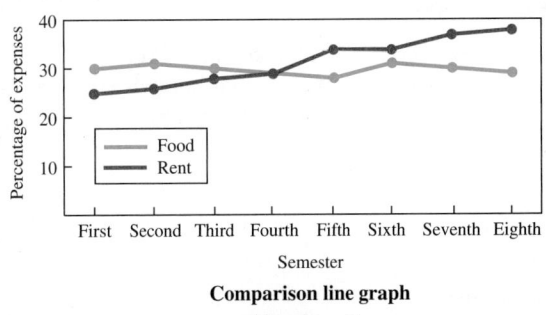

Comparison line graph

Figure 7   ▌▌▌

For Further Thought

Expected and Observed Frequencies

When fair coins are tossed, the results on particular tosses cannot be reliably predicted. As more and more coins are tossed, however, the proportions of heads and tails become more predictable. This is a consequence of the "law of large numbers."

    For example, if five coins are tossed, then the resulting number of heads, denoted *x*, is a "random

variable," whose possible values are

0, 1, 2, 3, 4, and 5.

If the five coins are tossed repeatedly, say 64 separate times, then the binomial probability formula can be used to get **expected frequencies** (or **theoretical frequencies**), as shown in the table on the next page. The first two columns of the table comprise the **expected frequency distribution** for 64 tosses of five fair coins.

(*continued*)

For Further Thought (cont.)

In an actual experiment, we could obtain **observed frequencies** (or **empirical frequencies**), which would most likely differ somewhat from the expected frequencies. But 64 repetitions of the experiment should be enough to provide fair consistency between expected and observed values.

For Group or Individual Investigation

Toss five coins a total of 64 times, keeping a record of the results.

1. Enter your experimental results in the third column of the table at the right, producing an **observed frequency distribution.**

2. Compare the second and third column entries.

3. Construct two histograms, one from the expected frequency distribution and one from your observed frequency distribution.

4. Compare the two histograms.

Number of Heads x	Expected Frequency e	Observed Frequency o
0	2	
1	10	
2	20	
3	20	
4	10	
5	2	

12.1 EXERCISES

In Exercises 1 and 2, use the given data to do the following:

(a) *Construct frequency and relative frequency distributions, in a table similar to* **Table 2**.

(b) *Construct a histogram.*

(c) *Construct a frequency polygon.*

1. **Preparation for Summer** According to *Newsmax* (May, 2010, page 76), the following are five popular "maintenance" activities performed as summer approaches.
   1. Prep the car for road trips.
   2. Clean up the house or apartment.
   3. Groom the garden.
   4. Exercise the body.
   5. Organize the wardrobe.

   The following data are the responses of 30 people who were asked, on June 1st, how many of the five they had accomplished.

   ```
   1  1  3  1  0  3  0  0  2  1
   2  2  0  0  5  3  4  0  1  0
   4  2  0  2  0  1  0  1  2  3
   ```

2. **Responses to "Pick a Number"** The following data are the responses of 28 people asked to "pick a number from 1 to 10."

   ```
   4   7  2  7  6  3   1
   7   4  9  8  5  6  10
   4  10  8  9  5  4   5
   9   2  6  6  6  8   7
   ```

In Exercises 3–6, use the given data to do the following:

(a) *Construct grouped frequency and relative frequency distributions, in a table similar to* **Table 3**. *(Follow the suggested guidelines for class limits and class width.)*

(b) *Construct a histogram.*

(c) *Construct a frequency polygon.*

3. **Exam Scores** The scores of the 54 members of a sociology lecture class on a 70-point exam were as follows.

   ```
   60  63  64  52  60  58  63  53  56
   64  48  54  64  57  51  67  60  49
   59  54  49  52  53  60  58  60  64
   52  56  56  58  66  59  62  50  58
   53  51  65  62  61  55  59  52  62
   58  61  65  56  55  50  61  55  54
   ```

   Use five classes with a uniform class width of 5 points, and use a lower limit of 45 points for the first class.

4. **Charge Card Account Balances** The following raw data represent the monthly account balances (to the nearest dollar) for a sample of 50 brand-new charge card users.

   ```
    78  175   46  138   79  118  90  163   88  107
   126  154   85   60   42   54  62  128  114   73
    67  119  116  145  129  130  81  105   96   71
   100  145  117   60  125  130  94   88  136  112
    85  165  118   84   74   62  81  110  108   71
   ```

   Use seven classes with a uniform width of 20 dollars, where the lower limit of the first class is 40 dollars.

5. Daily High Temperatures   The following data represent the daily high temperatures (in degrees Fahrenheit) for the month of June in a southwestern U.S. city.

79	84	88	96	102	104	99	97	92	94
85	92	100	99	101	104	110	108	106	106
90	82	74	72	83	107	111	102	97	94

Use nine classes with a uniform width of 5 degrees, where the lower limit of the first class is 70 degrees.

6. IQ Scores of College Freshmen   The following data represent IQ scores of a group of 50 college freshmen.

113	109	118	92	130	112	114	117	122	115
127	107	108	113	124	112	111	106	116	118
121	107	118	118	110	124	115	103	100	114
104	124	116	123	104	135	121	126	116	111
96	134	98	129	102	103	107	113	117	112

Use nine classes with a uniform width of 5, where the lower limit of the first class is 91.

In each of Exercises 7–10, construct a stem-and-leaf display for the given data. In each case, treat the ones digits as the leaves. For any single-digit data, use a stem of 0.

7. Games Won in the National Basketball Association   Approaching midseason, the teams in the National Basketball Association had won the following numbers of games.

27	20	29	11	26	11	12	7	26	18
22	19	14	13	22	9	25	11	10	15
38	10	22	23	31	8	24	15	24	15

8. Accumulated College Units   The students in a biology class were asked how many college units they had accumulated to date. Their responses are shown below.

12	4	13	12	21	22	15	17	33	24
32	42	26	11	53	62	42	25	13	8
54	18	21	14	19	17	38	17	20	10

9. Distances to School   The following data are the daily round-trip distances to school (in miles) for 30 randomly chosen students attending a community college in California.

16	30	10	11	18	26	34	18	8	12
21	14	5	22	4	25	9	10	6	21
12	18	9	16	44	23	4	13	36	8

10. Yards Gained in the National Football League   The following data represent net yards gained per game by National Football League running backs who played during a given week of the season.

25	19	36	73	37	88	67	33	54	123	79
19	39	45	22	58	7	73	30	43	24	36
65	43	33	55	40	29	112	60	94	86	62
52	29	18	25	41	3	49	102	16	32	46

Federal Government Receipts *The graph shows U.S. government receipts and outlays (both on-budget and off-budget) for 2001–2011. Refer to the graph for Exercises 11–15.*

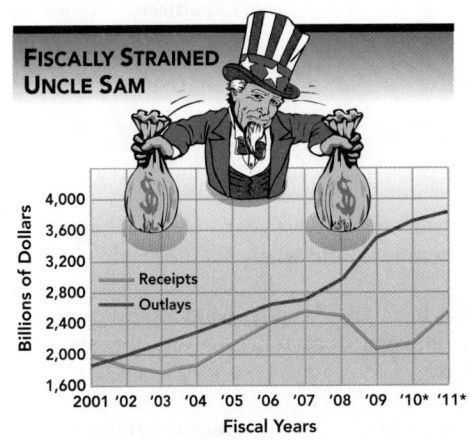

Source: Department of the Treasury, Office of Management and Budget.
*Data are estimates.

11. Of the period 2001–2011, list all years when receipts exceeded outlays.

12. Identify each of the following amounts and when it occurred.

   (a) the greatest one-year drop in receipts

   (b) the greatest one-year rise in outlays

13. In what years did receipts appear to climb faster than outlays?

14. About what was the greatest federal deficit, and in what year did it occur?

15. Plot a point for each year and draw a line graph showing the federal surplus (+) or deficit (−) over the years 2001–2011.

Reading Bar Graphs of Economic Indicators *The bar graphs here show trends in several economic indicators over the period 2004–2009. Refer to these graphs for Exercises 16–20.*

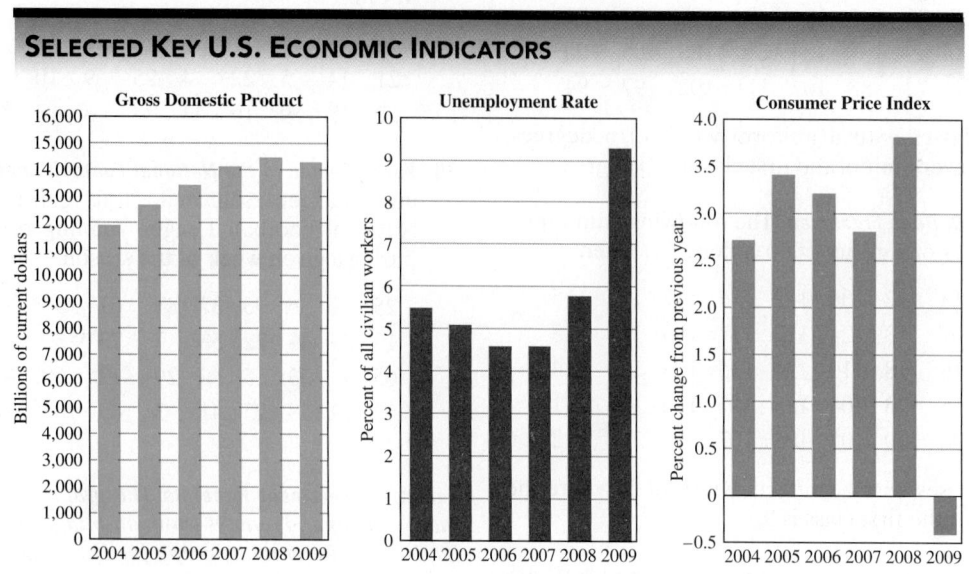

Sources: U.S. Department of Commerce, Bureau of Economic Analysis.
U.S. Department of Labor, Bureau of Labor Statistics.

16. About what was the gross domestic product in 2008?

17. Over the six-year period, about what was the highest consumer price index, and when did it occur?

18. What was the greatest year-to-year change in the unemployment rate, and when did it occur?

19. Observing these graphs, what would you say was the most unusual occurrence during the six years represented?

20. Explain why the gross domestic product would generally increase when the unemployment rate decreases.

Reading a Circle Graph of Government Spending *The circle graph below shows categories of planned federal spending from 2011 to 2020. Use the graph for Exercises 21 and 22.*

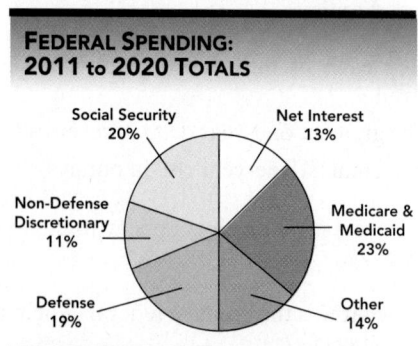

Source: Office of Management and Budget,
January 2010.

21. What is the greatest single expense category? To the nearest degree, what is the central angle of that category's sector?

22. If federal spending over the decade leading up to 2020 increased by about 7.5% per year (as it did over the preceding decade), total spending for the decade would be about $54,200 billion. Of that total, what amount would go to Social Security, Medicare, and Medicaid benefits (combined)?

23. *Sources of Job Training* A survey asked American workers how they were trained for their jobs. The percentages who responded in various categories are shown in the table below. Use the information in the table to draw a circle graph.

Principal Source of Training	Approximate Percentage of Workers
Trained in school	33%
Informal on-the-job training	25
Formal training from employers	12
Trained in military, or correspondence or other courses	10
No particular training, or could not identify any	20

Source: Bureau of Labor Statistics.

24. **Correspondence Between Education and Earnings** Data for 2008 showed that the average annual earnings of American workers corresponded to educational level as shown in the table below. Draw a bar graph that shows this information.

Educational Level	Median Weekly Earnings
Less than a high school diploma	$453
High school graduate	618
Some college, no degree	699
Associate degree	757
Bachelor's degree	1012
Master's degree	1233
Professional degree	1531
Doctoral degree	1561

Source: Bureau of Labor Statistics.

Net Worth of Retirement Savings *Claire Kozar, wishing to retire at age 60, is studying the comparison line graph here, which shows (under certain assumptions) how the net worth of her retirement savings (initially $400,000 at age 60) will change as she gets older and as she withdraws living expenses from savings. Refer to the graph for Exercises 25–28.*

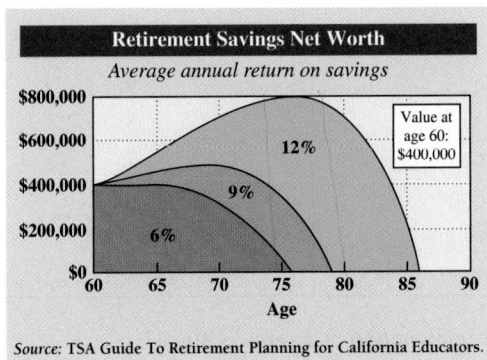

Retirement Savings Net Worth
Average annual return on savings
Source: TSA Guide To Retirement Planning for California Educators.

25. Assuming Claire can maintain an average annual return of 9%, how old will she be when her money runs out?

26. If she could earn an average of 12% annually, what maximum net worth would Claire achieve? At about what age would the maximum occur?

27. Suppose Claire reaches age 70, in good health, and the average annual return has proved to be 6%.

  (a) About how much longer can she expect her money to last?

  (b) What options might she consider in order to extend that time?

28. At age 77, about how many times more will Claire's net worth be if she averages a 12% return than if she averages a 9% return?

Sample Masses in a Geology Laboratory *Stem-and-leaf displays can be modified in various ways in order to obtain a reasonable number of stems. The following data, representing the measured masses (in grams) of thirty mineral samples in a geology lab, are shown in a **double-stem** display in **Table 8**.*

60.7	41.4	50.6	39.5	46.4
58.1	49.7	38.8	61.6	55.2
47.3	52.7	62.4	59.0	44.9
35.6	36.2	40.6	56.9	42.6
34.7	48.3	55.8	54.2	33.8
51.3	50.1	57.0	42.8	43.7

Table 8   Stem-and-Leaf Display for Mineral Sample Masses

(30–34)	3	4.7	3.8			
(35–39)	3	9.5	8.8	5.6	6.2	
(40–44)	4	1.4	4.9	0.6	2.6	2.8	3.7
(45–49)	4	6.4	9.7	7.3	8.3	
(50–54)	5	0.6	2.7	4.2	1.3	0.1
(55–59)	5	8.1	5.2	9.0	6.9	5.8	7.0
(60–64)	6	0.7	1.6	2.4		

29. Describe how the stem-and-leaf display of **Table 8** was constructed.

30. Explain why **Table 8** is called a "double-stem" display.

31. In general, how many stems (total) are appropriate for a stem-and-leaf display? Explain your reasoning.

32. **Record Temperatures** According to the National Climatic Data Center, the highest temperatures (in degrees Fahrenheit) ever recorded in the 50 states (as of August, 2006) were as follows.

112	100	128	120	134	118	106	110	109	112
100	118	117	116	118	121	114	114	105	109
107	112	114	115	118	117	118	125	106	110
122	108	110	121	113	120	119	111	104	111
120	113	120	117	105	110	118	112	114	115

Present these data in a double-stem display.

33. *Letter Occurrence Frequencies in the English Language*
The table below shows commonly accepted percentages of occurrence for the various letters in English language usage. (Code breakers have carefully analyzed these percentages as an aid in deciphering secret codes.)

For example, notice that E is the most commonly occurring letter, followed by T, A, O, N, and so on. The letters Q and Z occur least often. Referring to **Figure 5** in the text, would you say that the relative frequencies of occurrence of the vowels in the associated paragraph were typical or unusual? Explain your reasoning.

Letter	Percent	Letter	Percent
E	13	L	$3\frac{1}{2}$
T	9	C, M, U	3
A, O	8	F, P, Y	2
N	7	W, G, B	$1\frac{1}{2}$
I, R	$6\frac{1}{2}$	V	1
S, H	6	K, X, J	$\frac{1}{2}$
D	4	Q, Z	$\frac{1}{5}$

Frequencies and Probabilities of Letter Occurrence The percentages shown in *Exercise 33* are based on a very large sampling of English language text. Since they are based upon experiment, they are "empirical" rather than "theoretical." By converting each percent in that table to a decimal fraction, you can produce an **empirical probability distribution.**

For example, if a single letter is randomly selected from a randomly selected passage of text, the probability that it will be an E is 0.13. The probability that a randomly selected letter would be a vowel (A, E, I, O, or U) is

$$(0.08 + 0.13 + 0.065 + 0.08 + 0.03) = 0.385.$$

34. Rewrite the distribution shown in **Exercise 33** as an empirical probability distribution. Give values to three decimal places. Note that the 26 probabilities in this distribution—one for each letter of the alphabet—should add up to 1 (except for, perhaps, a slight round-off error).

35. **(a)** From your distribution of **Exercise 34,** construct an empirical probability distribution just for the vowels A, E, I, O, and U. (*Hint:* Divide each vowel's probability, from **Exercise 34,** by 0.385 to obtain a distribution whose five values add up to 1.) Give values to three decimal places.

   (b) Construct an appropriately labeled bar chart from your distribution of part (a).

36. Based on the occurrences of vowels in the paragraph represented by **Figure 5**, construct a probability distribution for the vowels. Give probabilities to three decimal places. The frequencies are:

   A–31,   E–34,   I–20,   O–23,   U–10.

37. Is the probability distribution of **Exercise 36** theoretical or empirical? Is it different from the distribution of **Exercise 35**? Which one is more accurate? Explain your reasoning.

38. *Frequencies and Probabilities of Study Times* Convert the grouped frequency distribution of **Table 3** to an empirical probability distribution, using the same classes and giving probability values to three decimal places.

39. *Probabilities of Study Times* Recall that the distribution of **Exercise 38** was based on weekly study times for a sample of 40 students. Suppose one of those students was chosen randomly. Using your distribution, find the probability that the study time in the past week for the student selected would have been in each of the following ranges.

   (a) 30–39 hours   **(b)** 40–59 hours

   (c) fewer than 30 hours   **(d)** at least 50 hours

Favorite Sports Among Recreation Students The 40 members of a recreation class were asked to name their favorite sports. The table shows the numbers who responded in various ways.

Sport	Number of Class Members
Sailing	9
Hang gliding	5
Snowboarding	7
Bicycling	3
Canoeing	12
Rafting	4

Use this information in Exercises 40– 42.

40. If a member of this class is selected at random, what is the probability that the favorite sport of the person selected is snowboarding?

41. **(a)** Based on the data in the table, construct a probability distribution, giving probabilities to three decimal places.

   (b) Is the distribution of part (a) theoretical or is it empirical?

   (c) Explain your answer to part (b).

42. Explain why a frequency polygon trails down to the axis at both ends while a line graph ordinarily does not.

12.2 MEASURES OF CENTRAL TENDENCY

Mean • Median • Mode • Central Tendency from Stem-and-Leaf Displays • Symmetry in Data Sets • Summary

A small video recycling business had the following daily sales over a six-day period.

$305, $285, $240, $376, $198, $264

A single number that is, in some sense representative of this whole set of numbers, a kind of "middle" value, would be a **measure of central tendency.**

Mean

Many calculators find the **mean** (as well as other statistical measures) automatically when a set of data items are entered. To recognize these calculators, look for a key marked $\boxed{\bar{x}}$, or perhaps $\boxed{\mu}$, or look in a menu such as "LIST" for a listing of mathematical measures.

The most common measure of central tendency is the **mean** (or **arithmetic mean**). The mean of a sample is denoted $\bar{x}$ (read "x bar"), while the mean of a complete population is denoted μ (the lower case Greek letter *mu*). For our purposes here, data sets are considered to be samples, so we use $\bar{x}$.

The mean of a set of data items is found by adding up all the items and then dividing the sum by the number of items. (The mean is what most people associate with the word "average.") Since adding up, or summing, a list of items is a common procedure in statistics, we use the symbol for "summation," Σ (the capital Greek letter *sigma*). Therefore, the sum of n items, say $x_1, x_2, \ldots, x_n$, can be denoted

$$\Sigma x = x_1 + x_2 + \cdots + x_n.$$

> **Mean**
>
> The **mean** of n data items $x_1, x_2, \ldots, x_n$, is calculated as follows.
>
> $$\bar{x} = \frac{\Sigma x}{n}$$

mean({305,285,240,376,198, ◂264})

                              278

A calculator can find the mean of items in a list. This screen supports the text discussion of daily sales figures.

We use this formula to find the central tendency of the daily sales figures above.

$$\text{Mean} = \bar{x} = \frac{\Sigma x}{n}$$

$$= \frac{305 + 285 + 240 + 376 + 198 + 264}{6} \quad \text{Add the daily sales.}$$
$$\qquad\qquad\qquad\qquad\qquad\qquad \text{Divide by the number of days.}$$

$$= \frac{1668}{6}, \quad \text{or} \quad 278$$

The mean value (the "average daily sales") for the week is $278.

▌▌ EXAMPLE 1 Finding the Mean of a List of Sales Figures

Last year's annual sales for eight different flower shops were as follows.

$374,910 $321,872 $242,943 $351,147
$382,740 $412,111 $334,089 $262,900

Find the mean annual sales for the eight shops.

SOLUTION

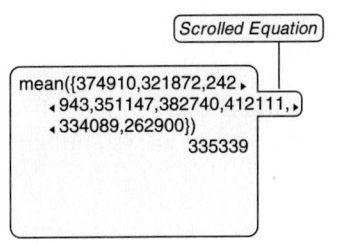

Scrolled Equation

mean({374910,321872,242◂ ◂943,351147,382740,412111,▸ ◂334089,262900})
                              335339

This screen supports the result in **Example 1.**

$$\bar{x} = \frac{\Sigma x}{n} = \frac{2{,}682{,}712}{8} = 335{,}339 \qquad \text{Add the sales.}$$
$$\qquad\qquad\qquad\qquad\qquad\qquad \text{Divide by the number of shops.}$$

The mean annual sales amount is $335,339. ▌▌▌

The following table shows the units and grades earned by one student last term.

Course	Grade	Units
Mathematics	A	3
History	C	3
Chemistry	B	5
Art	B	2
PE	A	1

In one common method of defining **grade-point average,** an A grade is assigned 4 points, with 3 points for B, 2 for C, and 1 for D. Compute grade-point average as follows.

Step 1 Multiply the number of units for a course and the number assigned to each grade.

Step 2 Add these products.

Step 3 Divide by the total number of units.

Course	Grade	Grade Points	Units	(Grade Points) · (Units)
Mathematics	A	4	3	12
History	C	2	3	6
Chemistry	B	3	5	15
Art	B	3	2	6
PE	A	4	1	4
			Totals: 14	43

$$\text{Grade-point average} = \frac{43}{14} = 3.07 \text{ (rounded)}$$

The calculation of a grade-point average is an example of a **weighted mean,** because the grade points for each course grade must be weighted according to the number of units of the course. (For example, five units of A is better than two units of A.) The number of units is called the **weighting factor.**

Weighted Mean

The **weighted mean** of n numbers, $x_1, x_2, \ldots, x_n$, that are weighted by the respective factors $f_1, f_2, \ldots, f_n$ is calculated as follows.

$$\overline{w} = \frac{\Sigma(x \cdot f)}{\Sigma f}$$

In words, the weighted mean of a group of (weighted) items is the sum of all products of items times weighting factors, divided by the sum of all weighting factors.

The weighted mean formula is commonly used to find the mean for a frequency distribution. In this case, the weighting factors are the frequencies.

Salary x	Number of Employees f
$12,000	8
$16,000	11
$18,500	14
$21,000	9
$34,000	2
$50,000	1

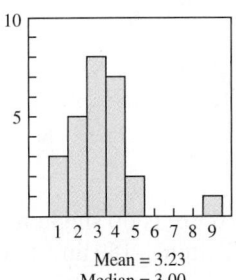

Scrolled Equation

mean({12000,16000,18500,▸
◂21000,34000,50000},{8,11,▸
◂14,9,2,1})
                18622.22222

In this screen supporting **Example 2**, the first list contains the salaries and the second list contains their frequencies.

▮▮ **EXAMPLE 2** Finding the Mean of a Frequency Distribution of Salaries

Find the mean salary for a small company that pays annual salaries to its employees as shown in the frequency distribution in the margin.

SOLUTION

According to the weighted mean formula, we can set up the work as follows.

Salary x	Number of Employees f	Salary · Number $x \cdot f$
$12,000	8	$ 96,000
$16,000	11	$176,000
$18,500	14	$259,000
$21,000	9	$189,000
$34,000	2	$ 68,000
$50,000	1	$ 50,000
Totals:	45	$838,000

$$\text{Mean salary} = \frac{\$838,000}{45} = \$18,622 \quad \text{(rounded)}$$ ▮▮▮

For some data sets the mean can be a misleading indicator of average. Consider Barry Matlock who runs a small business that employs five workers at the following annual salaries.

$$\$16,500, \quad \$16,950, \quad \$17,800, \quad \$19,750, \quad \$20,000$$

The employees, knowing that Barry accrues vast profits to himself, decide to go on strike and demand a raise. To get public support, they go on television and tell about their miserable salaries, pointing out the mean salary in the company.

$$\bar{x} = \frac{\$16,500 + \$16,950 + \$17,800 + \$19,750 + \$20,000}{5}$$

$$= \frac{\$91,000}{5}, \quad \text{or} \quad \$18,200 \quad \text{Mean salary (employees)}$$

The local television station schedules an interview with Barry to investigate. In preparation, Barry calculates the mean salary of *all* workers (including his own salary of $188,000).

$$\bar{x} = \frac{\$16,500 + \$16,950 + \$17,800 + \$19,750 + \$20,000 + \$188,000}{6}$$

$$= \frac{\$279,000}{6}, \quad \text{or} \quad \$46,500 \quad \text{Mean salary (including Barry's)}$$

When the TV crew arrives, Barry calmly assures them that there is no reason for his employees to complain since the company pays a generous mean salary of $46,500.

The employees, of course, would argue that when Barry included his own salary in the calculation, it caused the mean to be a misleading indicator of average. This was so because Barry's salary is not typical. It lies a good distance away from the general grouping of the items (salaries). An extreme value like this is referred to as an **outlier.** Since a single outlier can have a significant effect on the value of the mean, we say that the mean is "highly sensitive to extreme values."

Mean = 3.00
Median = 3.00

Mean = 3.23
Median = 3.00

The introduction of a single "outlier" above increased the mean by 8 percent but left the median unaffected.

Outliers should usually be considered as *possible* errors in the data.

Median

Another measure of central tendency, which is not so sensitive to extreme values, is the **median.** This measure divides a group of numbers into two parts, with half the numbers below the median and half above it.

Median

Find the **median** of a group of items as follows.

Step 1 Rank the items (that is, arrange them in numerical order from least to greatest).

Step 2 If the number of items is *odd,* the median is the middle item in the list.

Step 3 If the number of items is *even,* the median is the mean of the two middle items.

For Barry Matlock's business, all salaries (including Barry's), arranged in numerical order, are shown here.

$$\$16{,}500, \quad \$16{,}950, \quad \$17{,}800, \quad \$19{,}750, \quad \$20{,}000, \quad \$188{,}000$$

Thus, $\text{median} = \dfrac{\$17{,}800 + \$19{,}750}{2} = \dfrac{\$37{,}550}{2} = \$18{,}775.$

This figure is a representative average, based on all six salaries, that the employees would probably agree is reasonable.

▮▮ **EXAMPLE 3** Finding Medians of Lists of Numbers

Find the median of each list of numbers.

(a) 6, 7, 12, 13, 18, 23, 24   **(b)** 17, 15, 9, 13, 21, 32, 41, 7, 12

(c) 147, 159, 132, 181, 174, 253

SOLUTION

(a) This list is already in numerical order. The number of values in the list, 7, is odd, so the median is the middle value, or 13.

(b) First, place the numbers in numerical order from least to greatest.

$$7, 9, 12, 13, \underset{\underset{\text{Median}}{\uparrow}}{15}, 17, 21, 32, 41$$

The middle number can now be picked out. The median is 15.

(c) First write the numbers in numerical order.

$$132, 147, \mathbf{159}, \mathbf{174}, 181, 253$$

Since the list contains an even number of items, namely 6, there is no single middle item. Find the median by taking the mean of the two middle items, 159 and 174.

$$\frac{159 + 174}{2} = \frac{333}{2} = 166.5 \leftarrow \text{Median} \qquad ▮▮▮$$

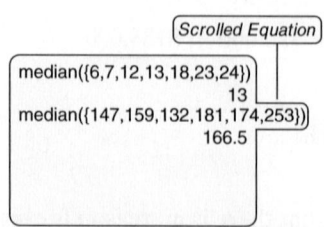

Scrolled Equation

median({6,7,12,13,18,23,24})
                            13
median({147,159,132,181,174,253})
                          166.5

The calculator can find the median of the entries in a list. This screen supports the results in **Examples 3(a) and (c).**

Locating the middle item (the median) of a frequency distribution, is a bit different. First find the total number of items in the set by adding the frequencies ($n = \Sigma f$). Then the median is the item whose *position* is given by the following formula.

Position of the Median in a Frequency Distribution

$$\text{Position of median} = \frac{n+1}{2} = \frac{\Sigma f + 1}{2}$$

This formula gives only the position, and not the actual value, of the median.

▌▌ **EXAMPLE 4**   Finding Medians for Frequency Distributions

Find the medians for the following distributions.

(a)
Value	1	2	3	4	5	6
Frequency	1	3	2	4	8	2

(b)
Value	2	4	6	8	10
Frequency	5	8	10	6	6

SOLUTION

(a) Arrange the work as follows. Tabulate the values and frequencies, and the **cumulative frequencies,** which tell, for each different value, how many items have that value or a lesser value.

Value	Frequency	Cumulative Frequency	
1	1	1	1 item 1 or less
2	3	4	1 + 3 = 4 items 2 or less
3	2	6	4 + 2 = 6 items 3 or less
4	4	10	6 + 4 = 10 items 4 or less
5	8	18	10 + 8 = 18 items 5 or less
6	2	20	18 + 2 = 20 items 6 or less

Total: 20

Adding the frequencies shows that there are 20 items total.

$$\text{position of median} = \frac{20+1}{2} = \frac{21}{2} = 10.5$$

The median, then, is the average of the tenth and eleventh items. To find these items, make use of the cumulative frequencies. Since the value 4 has a cumulative frequency of 10, the tenth item is 4 and the eleventh item is 5, making the median

$$\frac{4+5}{2} = \frac{9}{2} = 4.5.$$

median({1,2,3,4,5,6},{1,3,2, ▸
◂4,8,2})
4.5

(b)
Value	Frequency	Cumulative Frequency
2	5	5
4	8	13
6	10	23
8	6	29
10	6	35

Total: 35

There are 35 items total.

median({2,4,6,8,10},{5,8,10, ▸
◂6,6})
6

$$\text{position of median} = \frac{35+1}{2} = \frac{36}{2} = 18$$

These two screens support the results in
Example 4.

From the cumulative frequency column, the fourteenth through the twenty-third items are all 6s. This means the eighteenth item is a 6, so the median is 6.   ▮▮▮

Mode

The third important measure of central tendency is the **mode.** Suppose ten students earned the following scores on a business law examination.

$$74, 81, 39, 74, 82, 80, 100, 92, 74, 85$$

Notice that more students earned the score 74 than any other score.

> **Mode**
>
> The **mode** of a data set is the value that occurs most often.

▋▋ EXAMPLE 5 | Finding Modes for Sets of Data

Find the mode for each set of data.

(a) 51, 32, 49, 49, 74, 81, 92   **(b)** 482, 485, 483, 485, 487, 487, 489

(c) 10,708, 11,519, 10,972, 17,546, 13,905, 12,182

(d)

Value	19	20	22	25	26	28
Frequency	1	3	8	7	4	2

SOLUTION

(a) 51, 32, 49, 49, 74, 81, 92

The number 49 occurs more often than any other. Therefore, 49 is the mode. ***The numbers do not need to be in numerical order when looking for the mode.***

(b) 482, 485, 483, 485, 487, 487, 489

Both 485 and 487 occur twice. This list is said to have *two* modes, or to be **bimodal.**

(c) No number here occurs more than once. This list has no mode.

(d)

Value	Frequency
19	1
20	3
22	8 ← Greatest frequency
25	7
26	4
28	2

The frequency distribution shows that the most frequently occurring value (and, thus, the mode) is 22.

▋▋▋

It is traditional to include the mode as a measure of *central tendency*, because many important kinds of data sets do have their most frequently occurring values "centrally" located. However, there is no reason the mode cannot be one of the least values in the set or one of the greatest. In such a case, the mode really is not a good measure of "central tendency."

When the data items being studied are nonnumeric, the mode may be the only usable measure of central tendency. For example, the bar graph of **Figure 5** in **Section 12.1** showed frequencies of occurrence of vowels in a sample paragraph. Since A, E, I, O, and U are not numbers, they cannot be added, nor can they be numerically ordered. Thus, neither their mean nor their median exists. The mode, however, does exist. As the bar graph shows, the mode is the letter E.

Sometimes, a distribution is **bimodal** (literally, "two modes"), as in **Example 5(b).** In a large distribution, this term is commonly applied even when the two modes do not have exactly the same frequency. Three or more different items sharing the highest frequency of occurrence is not often useful information. We say that such a distribution has *no* mode.

Central Tendency from Stem-and-Leaf Displays

As shown in **Section 12.1,** data are sometimes presented in a stem-and-leaf display in order to give a graphical impression of their distribution. We can also calculate measures of central tendency from a stem-and-leaf display. The median and mode are more easily identified when the "leaves" are **ranked** (arranged in numerical order) on their "stems."

In **Table 9**, we have rearranged the leaves of **Table 5** in **Section 12.1** (which showed the weekly study times from **Example 2** of that section).

Table 9	Stem-and-Leaf Display for Weekly Study Times, with Leaves Ranked										
1	2	4	5	6	7	8					
2	0	2	3	4	4	5	6	6	9	9	9
3	0	1	1	2	3	6	6	8	9		
4	0	1	4	4	5	5	7				
5	2	5	5	8							
6	0	2									
7	2										

EXAMPLE 6	Finding the Mean, Median, and Mode from a Stem-and-Leaf Display

For the data in **Table 9**, find the following.

(a) the mean

(b) the median

(c) the mode

SOLUTION

(a) A calculator with statistical capabilities will automatically compute the mean. Otherwise, add all items (reading from the stem-and-leaf display) and divide by $n = 40$.

$$\text{mean} = \frac{12 + 14 + 15 + \cdots + 60 + 62 + 72}{40} = \frac{1395}{40} = 34.875$$

(b) In this case, $n = 40$ (an even number), so the median is the average of the twentieth and twenty-first items, in order. Counting leaves, we see that these will be the third and fourth items on the stem 3.

$$\text{median} = \frac{31 + 32}{2} = 31.5$$

(c) By inspection, we see that 29 occurred three times and no other value occurred that often.

$$\text{mode} = 29$$

▌▌▌

Symmetry in Data Sets

The most useful way to analyze a data set often depends on whether the distribution is **symmetric** or **nonsymmetric.** In a "symmetric" distribution, as we move out from the central point, the pattern of frequencies is the same (or nearly so) to the left and to the right. In a "nonsymmetric" distribution, the patterns to the left and right are different.

   Figure 8 shows several types of symmetric distributions, while **Figure 9** shows some nonsymmetric distributions. A nonsymmetric distribution with a tail extending out to the left, shaped like a J, is called **skewed to the left.** If the tail extends out to the right, the distribution is **skewed to the right.** Notice that a bimodal distribution may be either symmetric or nonsymmetric.

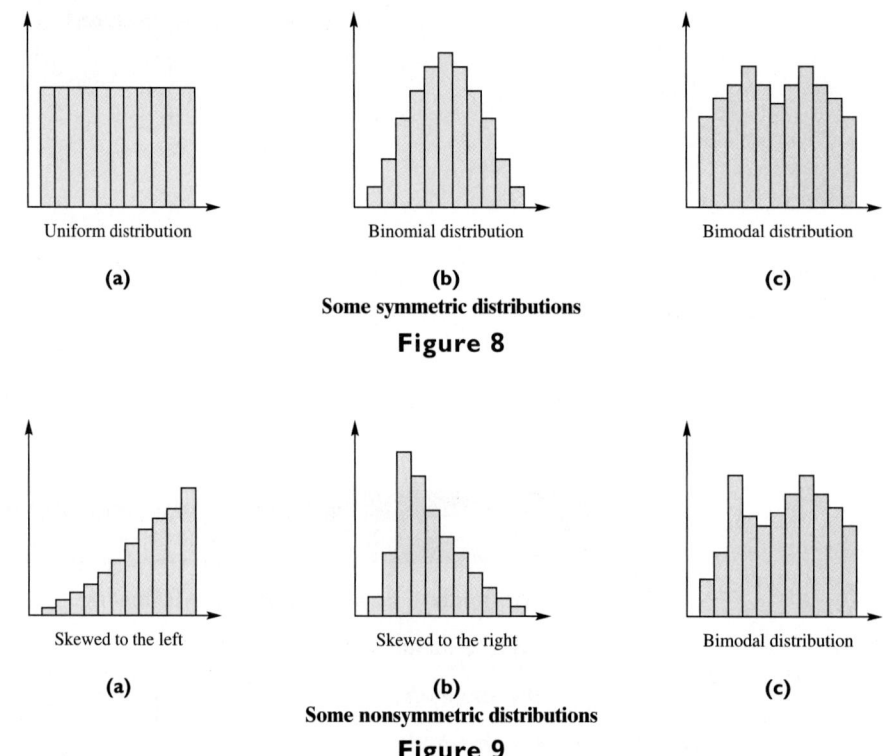

Uniform distribution	Binomial distribution	Bimodal distribution
(a)	**(b)**	**(c)**

Some symmetric distributions

Figure 8

Skewed to the left	Skewed to the right	Bimodal distribution
(a)	**(b)**	**(c)**

Some nonsymmetric distributions

Figure 9

Summary

We conclude this section with a summary of the measures presented and a brief discussion of their relative advantages and disadvantages.

Summary of the Common Measures of Central Tendency

The **mean** of a set of numbers is found by adding all the values in the set and dividing by the number of values.

The **median** is a kind of "middle" number. To find the median, first arrange the values in numerical order. For an *odd* number of values, the median is the middle value in the list. For an *even* number of values, the median is the mean of the two middle values.

The **mode** is the value that occurs most often. Some sets of numbers have two most frequently occurring values and are **bimodal**. Other sets have no mode at all (if no value occurs more often than the others or if more than two values occur most often).

Some helpful points of comparison follow.

1. For distributions of numeric data, the mean and median will always exist, while the mode may not exist. On the other hand, for nonnumeric data, it may be that none of the three measures exists, or that only the mode exists.

2. Because even a single change in the data may cause the mean to change, while the median and mode may not be affected at all, ***the mean is the most "sensitive" measure.***

3. In a symmetric distribution, the mean, median, and mode (if a single mode exists) will all be equal. In a nonsymmetric distribution, the mean is often unduly affected by relatively few extreme values and, therefore, may not be a good representative measure of central tendency. For example, distributions of salaries, family incomes, or home prices often include a few values that are much higher than the bulk of the items. In such cases, the median is a more useful measure.

4. ***The mode is the only measure covered here that must always be equal to one of the data items of the distribution.*** In fact, more of the data items are equal to the mode than to any other number. A fashion shop planning to stock only one hat size for next season would want to know the mode (the most common) of all hat sizes among their potential customers. Likewise, a designer of family automobiles would be interested in the most common family size. In examples like these, designing for the mean or the median might not be right for anyone.

For Further Thought

Simpson's Paradox

In baseball statistics, a player's "batting average" gives the average number of hits per time at bat. For example, a player who has gotten 84 hits in 250 times at bat has a batting average of $\frac{84}{250} = .336$. This "average" can be interpreted as the empirical probability of that player's getting a hit the next time at bat.

The following are actual comparisons of hits and at-bats for two major league players in the 1995, 1996, and 1997 seasons. The numbers illustrate a puzzling statistical occurrence known as **Simpson's paradox.** The example below, involving Dave Justice and Derek Jeter, was referred to in the "Conspiracy Theory" episode of the television series NUMB3RS. (*Source:* www.wikipedia.org)

For Group or Individual Investigation

1. Fill in the twelve blanks in the table, giving batting averages to three decimal places.

2. Which player had a better average in 1995?

3. Which player had a better average in 1996?

4. Which player had a better average in 1997?

5. Which player had a better average in 1995, 1996, and 1997 combined?

6. Did the results above surprise you? How can it be that one player's batting average leads another's for each of three years, and yet trails the other's for the combined years?

	Dave Justice			Derek Jeter		
	Hits	**At-bats**	**Batting Average**	**Hits**	**At-bats**	**Batting Average**
1995	104	411	_____	12	48	_____
1996	45	140	_____	183	582	_____
1997	163	495	_____	190	654	_____
Combined (1995–1997)	_____	_____	_____	_____	_____	_____

12.2 EXERCISES

For each list of data, calculate **(a)** *the mean,* **(b)** *the median,* *and* **(c)** *the mode or modes (if any). Round mean values to the nearest tenth.*

1. 7, 9, 12, 14, 34

2. 20, 27, 42, 45, 53, 62, 62, 64

3. 218, 230, 196, 224, 196, 233

4. 26, 31, 46, 31, 26, 29, 31

5. 3.1, 4.5, 6.2, 7.1, 4.5, 3.8, 6.2, 6.3

6. 14,320, 16,950, 17,330, 15,470

7. 0.78, 0.93, 0.66, 0.94, 0.87, 0.62, 0.74, 0.81

8. 0.53, 0.03, 0.28, 0.18, 0.39, 0.28, 0.14, 0.22, 0.04

9. 128, 131, 136, 125, 132, 128, 125, 127

10. 8.97, 5.64, 2.31, 1.02, 4.35, 7.68

Airline Fatalities in the United States *The table pertains to scheduled commercial carriers. Fatalities data include those on the ground except for the September 11, 2001, terrorist attacks. Use this information for Exercises 11–16.*

U.S. Airline Safety, 1999–2008

Year	Departures (millions)	Fatal Accidents	Fatalities
1999	10.9	2	12
2000	11.1	2	89
2001	10.6	6	531
2002	10.3	0	0
2003	10.2	2	22
2004	10.8	1	13
2005	10.9	3	22
2006	10.6	2	50
2007	10.7	0	0
2008	10.6	0	0

Source: The World Almanac and Book of Facts 2010.

For each category in Exercises 11–16, find **(a)** *the mean,* **(b)** *the median, and* **(c)** *the mode (if any).*

11. departures

12. fatal accidents

13. fatalities

The year 2001 was clearly an anomaly. If the data for that year are reduced by 4 fatal accidents and 265 fatalities, which of the three measures change and what are their new values for each of the following?

14. Exercise 12

15. Exercise 13

16. Following 2001, in what year did airline departures start to increase again?

Spending by U.S. Travelers *The table shows the top five U.S. states for domestic traveler spending in 2007.*

State	Spending (billions of dollars)
California	$96.2
Florida	68.9
New York	51.3
Texas	47.4
Nevada	34.5

Source: The World Almanac and Book of Facts 2010.

Find each of the following quantities for these five states.

17. the mean spending

18. the median spending

Measuring Elapsed Times *While doing an experiment, a physics student recorded the following sequence of elapsed times (in seconds) in a lab notebook.*

$$2.16, \ 22.2, \ 2.96, \ 2.20, \ 2.73, \ 2.28, \ 2.39$$

19. Find the mean.

20. Find the median.

The student from **Exercises 19 and 20,** *when reviewing the calculations later, decided that the entry 22.2 should have been recorded as 2.22, and made that change in the listing.*

21. Find the mean for the new list.

22. Find the median for the new list.

23. Which measure, the mean or the median, was affected more by correcting the error?

24. In general, which measure, mean or median, is affected less by the presence of an extreme value in the data?

Scores on Management Examinations *Rob Bates earned the following scores on his six management exams last semester.*

$$79, \ 81, \ 44, \ 89, \ 79, \ 90$$

25. Find the mean, the median, and the mode for Rob's scores.

26. Which of the three averages probably is the best indicator of Rob's ability?

27. If Rob's instructor gives him a chance to replace his score of 44 by taking a "make-up" exam, what must he score on the make-up to get an overall average (mean) of 85?

Exercises 28 and 29 give frequency distributions for sets of data values. For each set find the **(a)** *mean (to the nearest tenth),* **(b)** *median, and* **(c)** *mode or modes (if any).*

28.

Value	Frequency
12	3
14	1
16	8
18	4

29.

Value	Frequency
615	17
590	7
605	9
579	14
586	6
600	5

30. Average Employee Salaries A company has

5 employees with a salary of $19,500,

11 employees with a salary of $23,000,

7 employees with a salary of $28,300,

2 employees with a salary of $31,500,

4 employees with a salary of $38,900,

1 employee with a salary of $147,500.

Find the mean salary for the employees (to the nearest hundred dollars).

Grade-point Averages *Find the grade-point average for each of the following students. Assume* A = 4, B = 3, C = 2, D = 1, *and* F = 0. *Round to the nearest hundredth.*

31.

Units	Grade
4	C
7	B
3	A
3	F

32.

Units	Grade
2	A
6	B
5	C

Most Populous Countries *The table gives population (2009) and land area for the world's five most populous countries.*

Country	Population (millions)	Area (Thousands of square miles)
China	1339	3601
India	1157	1148
United States	307	3537
Indonesia	240	741
Brazil	199	3265

Source: World Almanac and Book of Facts 2010.

Use this information for Exercises 33–36.

33. Find the mean population (to the nearest million) for these 5 countries.

34. Find the mean area (to the nearest thousand square miles) for these 5 countries.

35. For each country, find the population density (to the nearest whole number of persons per square mile).

36. For the 5 countries combined, find the mean population density.

Personal Computer Use *Just six countries account for over half of all personal computers in use worldwide. The table shows figures for 2008. Use this information for Exercises 37 and 38.*

Country	PCs in use (millions)	Population (millions)
U.S.	303.8	264.10
China	1330.0	98.67
Japan	127.3	86.22
Germany	82.4	61.96
UK	60.9	47.04
France	64.7	43.11

Source: The World Almanac and Book of Facts 2010.

37. Estimate the mean number of PCs in use in 2008 for these six countries.

38. U.S. use was 22.19% of the worldwide total. How many PCs were in use in the world in 2008?

Crew, Passengers, and Hijackers on 9/11 Airliners *The table shows, for each hijacked flight on September 11, 2001, the numbers of crew members, passengers, and hijackers (not included as passengers). For each quantity in Exercises 39–41, find*

(a) *the mean,   and*   **(b)** *the median.*

Flight	Crew	Passengers	Hijackers
American #11	11	76	5
United #175	9	51	5
American #77	6	53	5
United #93	7	33	4

Source: www.911research.wtc7.net

39. number of crew members per plane

40. number of passengers per plane

41. total number of persons per plane

Olympic Medal Standings *The top ten medal-winning nations in the 2010 Winter Olympics at Vancouver, Canada, are shown in the table. Use the given information for Exercises 42–45.*

Medal Standings for the 2010 Winter Olympics

Nation	Gold	Silver	Bronze	Total
United States	9	15	13	37
Germany	10	13	7	30
Canada	14	7	5	26
Norway	9	8	6	23
Austria	4	6	6	16
Russia	3	5	7	15
South Korea	6	6	2	14
Sweden	5	2	4	11
China	5	2	4	11
France	2	3	6	11

Source: www.nbcolympics.com

Calculate the following for all nations shown.

42. the mean number of gold medals

43. the median number of silver medals

44. the mode, or modes, for the number of bronze medals

45. each of the following for the total number of medals
   (a) mean
   (b) median
   (c) mode or modes

In Exercises 46 and 47, use the given stem-and-leaf display to identify

(a) *the mean,*   **(b)** *the median,*   and   **(c)** *the mode (if any)* *for the data represented.*

46. Auto Repair Charges The display here represents prices (to the nearest dollar) charged by 23 different auto repair shops for a new alternator (installed). Give answers to the nearest cent.

```
 9 | 7
10 | 2  4
10 | 5  7  9
11 | 1  3  4  4
11 | 5  5  8  8  9
12 | 0  4  4
12 | 5  7  7  9
13 | 8
```

47. Scores on a Biology Exam The display here represents scores achieved on a 100-point biology exam by the 34 members of the class.

```
4 | 7
5 | 1  3  6
6 | 2  5  5  6  7  8  8
7 | 0  4  5  6  7  7  8  8  8  8  9
8 | 0  1  1  3  4  5  5
9 | 0  0  0  1  6
```

48. Calculating a Missing Test Score Katie Campbell's Business professor lost his grade book, which contained Katie's five test scores for the course. A summary of the scores (each of which was an integer from 0 to 100) indicates the following:

   The mean was 88.

   The median was 87.

   The mode was 92.

(The data set was not bimodal.) What is the least possible number among the missing scores?

49. Explain what an "outlier" is and how it affects measures of central tendency.

50. Consumer Preferences in Food Packaging A food processing company that packages individual cups of instant soup wishes to find out the best number of cups to include in a package. In a survey of 22 consumers, they found that five prefer a package of 1, five prefer a package of 2, three prefer a package of 3, six prefer a package of 4, and three prefer a package of 6.

   (a) Calculate the mean, median, and mode values for preferred package size.

   (b) Which measure in part (a) should the food processing company use?

   (c) Explain your answer to part (b).

51. *Scores on a Math Quiz* The following are scores earned by 15 college students on a 20-point math quiz.

0, 1, 3, 14, 14, 15, 16, 16, 17, 17, 18, 18, 18, 19, 20

(a) Calculate the mean, median, and mode values.

(b) Which measure in part (a) is most representative of the data?

In Exercises 52–55, begin a list of the given numbers, in order, starting with the least one. Continue the list only until the median of the listed numbers is a multiple of 4. Stop at that point and find **(a)** *the number of numbers listed, and* **(b)** *the mean of the listed numbers (to two decimal places).*

52. counting numbers   **53.** prime numbers

54. Fibonacci numbers (see **page 212**)   **55.** triangular numbers (see **pages 13–14**)

56. Seven consecutive whole numbers add up to 147. What is the result when their mean is subtracted from their median?

57. If the mean, median, and mode are all equal for the set {70, 110, 80, 60, x}, find the value of x.

58. Mike Coons wants to include a fifth counting number, n, along with the numbers 2, 5, 8, and 9 so that the mean and median of the five numbers will be equal. How many choices does Mike have for the number n, and what are those choices?

For Exercises 59–61, refer to the grouped frequency distribution shown here.

Class Limits	Frequency f
21–25	5
26–30	3
31–35	8
36–40	12
41–45	21
46–50	38
51–55	35
56–60	20

59. Is it possible to identify, based on the data shown in the table, any specific data items that occurred in this sample?

60. Is it possible to compute the actual mean for this sample?

61. Describe how you might approximate the mean for this sample. Justify your procedure.

62. *Average Employee Salaries* Refer to the salary data of **Example 2,** specifically the dollar amounts given in the salary column of the table. Explain what is wrong with simply calculating the mean salary by adding those six numbers and dividing the result by 6.

12.3 MEASURES OF DISPERSION

Range • Standard Deviation • Interpreting Measures of Dispersion • Coefficient of Variation

Table 10

	A	B
	5	1
	6	2
	7	7
	8	12
	9	13
Mean	7	7
Median	7	7

The mean is a good indicator of the central tendency of a set of data values, but it does not completely describe the data. Compare distribution A with distribution B in **Table 10**.

Both distributions have the same mean and the same median, but they are quite different. In the first, 7 is a fairly typical value, but in the second, most of the values differ considerably from 7. What is needed here is some measure of the **dispersion,** or *spread,* of the data. Two of the most common measures of dispersion, the *range* and the *standard deviation,* are discussed in this section.

Range

The **range** of a data set is a straightforward measure of dispersion.

Range

For any set of data, the **range** of the set is defined as follows.

Range = (greatest value in the set) − (least value in the set)

For a short list of data, calculation of the range is simple. For a more extensive list, it is more difficult to be sure you have accurately identified the greatest and least values.

Once the data are entered, a calculator with statistical functions may actually show the range (among other things), or at least sort the data and identify the minimum and maximum items. (The associated symbols may be something like ⎡MIN Σ⎤ and ⎡MAX Σ⎤, or min*X* and max*X*.) Given these two values, a simple subtraction produces the range.

▌▌ **EXAMPLE 1** Finding and Comparing Range Values

Find the ranges for distributions A and B in **Table 10**, and describe what they imply.

SOLUTION

In distribution A, the greatest value is 9 and the least is 5.

$$\text{Range} = \text{greatest} - \text{least} = 9 - 5 = 4$$

Distribution B is handled similarly.

$$\text{Range} = 13 - 1 = 12$$

We can say that even though the two distributions have identical averages, distribution B exhibits three times more dispersion, or *spread*, than distribution A. ▌▌▌

The range can be misleading if it is interpreted unwisely. For example, look at the points scored by Max and Molly on five different quizzes, as shown in **Table 11**. The ranges for the two students make it tempting to conclude that Max is more consistent than Molly. However, Molly is actually more consistent, with the exception of one very poor score. That score, 6, is an outlier which, if not actually recorded in error, must surely be due to some special circumstance. (Notice that the outlier does not seriously affect Molly's median score, which is more typical of her overall performance than is her mean score.)

Table 11

Quiz	Max	Molly
1	28	27
2	22	27
3	21	28
4	26	6
5	18	27
Mean	23	23
Median	22	27
Range	10	22

Standard Deviation

One of the most useful measures of dispersion, the *standard deviation*, is based on *deviations from the mean* of the data values.

▌▌ **EXAMPLE 2** Finding Deviations from the Mean

Find the deviations from the mean for all data values in the following sample.

$$32, 41, 47, 53, 57$$

SOLUTION

Add these values and divide by the total number of values, 5. The mean is 46. To find the deviations from the mean, subtract 46 from each data value.

Data value	32	41	47	53	57
Deviation	−14	−5	1	7	11

$$32 - 46 = -14 \qquad\qquad 57 - 46 = 11$$

To check your work, add the deviations. ***The sum of the deviations for a set of data is always 0.*** ▌▌▌

We cannot obtain a measure of dispersion by finding the mean of the deviations, because this number is always 0, since the positive deviations just cancel out the negative ones. To avoid this problem of positive and negative numbers canceling each other, we *square* each deviation.

The following chart shows the squares of the deviations for the data in **Example 2.**

Data value	32	41	47	53	57
Deviation	-14	-5	1	7	11
Square of deviation	196	25	1	49	121

$(-14) \cdot (-14) = 196 \qquad\qquad 11 \cdot 11 = 121$

An average of the squared deviations could now be found by dividing their sum by the number of data values n (5 in this case), which we would do if our data values composed a population. However, since we are considering the data to be a sample, we divide by $n - 1$ instead.*

The average that results is itself a measure of dispersion, called the **variance,** but a more common measure is obtained by taking the square root of the variance. This makes up, in a way, for squaring the deviations earlier, and gives a kind of average of the deviations from the mean, which is called the sample **standard deviation.** It is denoted by the letter s. (The standard deviation of a population is denoted σ, the lowercase Greek letter *sigma*.)

Continuing our calculations from the chart above, we obtain

$$s = \sqrt{\frac{196 + 25 + 1 + 49 + 121}{4}} = \sqrt{\frac{392}{4}} = \sqrt{98} \approx 9.90.$$

The algorithm (process) described above for finding the sample standard deviation can be summarized as follows.

Most calculators find square roots, such as $\sqrt{98}$, to as many digits as you need using a key like $\boxed{\sqrt{x}}$. In this book, we normally give from two to four significant figures for such calculations.

```
stdDev({32,41,47,53,57})
                9.899494937
√98
                9.899494937
```

This screen supports the text discussion. Note that the standard deviation reported agrees with the approximation for $\sqrt{98}$.

Calculation of Standard Deviation

Let a sample of n numbers $x_1, x_2, \ldots, x_n$ have mean $\bar{x}$. Then the **sample standard deviation, s,** of the numbers is calculated as follows.

$$s = \sqrt{\frac{\Sigma(x - \bar{x})^2}{n - 1}}$$

The individual steps involved in this calculation are as follows.

Step 1 Calculate $\bar{x}$, the mean of the numbers.

Step 2 Find the deviations from the mean.

Step 3 Square each deviation.

Step 4 Sum the squared deviations.

Step 5 Divide the sum in Step 4 by $n - 1$.

Step 6 Take the square root of the quotient in Step 5.

The preceding description helps show why standard deviation measures the amount of spread in a data set. For actual calculation purposes, we recommend the use of a scientific calculator, or a statistical calculator, that does all the detailed steps automatically. We illustrate both methods in **Example 3** on the next page.

---

*Although the reasons cannot be explained at this level, dividing by $n - 1$ rather than n produces a sample measure that is more accurate for purposes of inference. In most cases, the results using the two divisors are only slightly different.

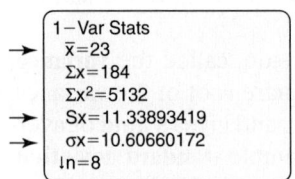

The sample in **Example 3** is stored in a list. (The last entry, 40, is not shown here.)

1–Var Stats
→ x̄=23
Σx=184
Σx²=5132
→ Sx=11.33893419
→ σx=10.60660172
↓n=8

The arrows point to the mean and the sample and population standard deviations. See **Example 3**.

∎∎ **EXAMPLE 3** Finding a Sample Standard Deviation

Find the standard deviation of the following sample by using **(a)** the step-by-step process, and **(b)** the statistical functions of a calculator.

$$7, 9, 18, 22, 27, 29, 32, 40$$

SOLUTION

(a) Carry out the six steps summarized above.

Step 1 Find the mean of the values.

$$\frac{7 + 9 + 18 + 22 + 27 + 29 + 32 + 40}{8} = 23$$

Step 2 Find the deviations from the mean.

Data value	7	9	18	22	27	29	32	40
Deviation	-16	-14	-5	-1	4	6	9	17

Step 3 Square each deviation.

Squares of deviations: 256   196   25   1   16   36   81   289

Step 4 Sum the squared deviations.

$$256 + 196 + 25 + 1 + 16 + 36 + 81 + 289 = 900$$

Step 5 Divide by $n - 1 = 8 - 1 = 7$: $\frac{900}{7} \approx 128.57$.

Step 6 Take the square root: $\sqrt{128.57} \approx 11.3$.

(b) Enter the eight data values. (The key for entering data may look something like $\boxed{\Sigma+}$. Find out which key it is on your calculator.) Then press the key for standard deviation. It may look like one of these.

$$\boxed{\text{STDEV}} \quad \text{or} \quad \boxed{\text{SD}} \quad \text{or} \quad \boxed{S_{n-1}} \quad \text{or} \quad \boxed{\sigma_{n-1}}$$

If your calculator also has a key that looks like σ_n, it is probably for *population* standard deviation, which involves dividing by n rather than by $n - 1$, as mentioned earlier.

The result should again be 11.3.

> If you mistakenly used the population standard deviation key, the result would be 10.6.

∎∎∎

For data given in the form of a frequency distribution, some calculators allow entry of both values and frequencies, or each value can be entered separately the number of times indicated by its frequency. Then press the standard deviation key.

The following example is included only to strengthen your understanding of frequency distributions and standard deviation, not as a practical algorithm for calculating.

Table 12

Value	Frequency
2	5
3	8
4	10
5	2

∎∎ **EXAMPLE 4** Finding the Standard Deviation of a Frequency Distribution

Find the sample standard deviation for the frequency distribution shown in **Table 12**.

SOLUTION

Complete the calculations as shown in **Table 13** on next page. To find the numbers in the "Deviation" column, first find the mean, and then subtract the mean from the numbers in the "Value" column.

stdDev({2,3,4,5},{5,8,10,2})
.9073771726
√19.76/24
.9073771726

The screen supports the result in **Example 4**.

Table 13

Value	Frequency	Value Times Frequency	Deviation	Squared Deviation	Squared Deviation Times Frequency
2	5	10	−1.36	1.8496	9.2480
3	8	24	−0.36	0.1296	1.0368
4	10	40	0.64	0.4096	4.0960
5	2	10	1.64	2.6896	5.3792
Sums	**25**	**84**			**19.76**

$$\bar{x} = \frac{84}{25} = 3.36 \qquad s = \sqrt{\frac{19.76}{24}} \approx \sqrt{0.8233} \approx 0.91 \qquad ▐▐▐$$

Central tendency and dispersion (or "spread tendency") are different and independent aspects of a set of data. Which one is more critical can depend on the specific situation.

For example, suppose tomatoes sell by the basket. Each basket costs the same, and each contains one dozen tomatoes. If you want the most fruit possible per dollar spent, you would look for the basket with the highest average weight per tomato (regardless of the dispersion of the weights). On the other hand, if the tomatoes are to be served on an hors d' oeuvre tray where "presentation" is important, you would look for a basket with uniform-sized tomatoes, that is a basket with the lowest weight dispersion (regardless of the average of the weights). See the illustration at the side.

Another situation involves target shooting (also illustrated at the side). The five hits on the top target are, *on average,* very close to the bulls eye, but the large dispersion (spread) implies that improvement will require much effort. On the other hand, the bottom target exhibits a poorer average, but the smaller dispersion means that improvement will require only a minor adjustment of the gun sights. (In general, consistent errors can be corrected more easily than more dispersed errors.)

Interpreting Measures of Dispersion

A main use of dispersion measures is to compare the amounts of spread in two (or more) data sets as we did with distributions A and B at the beginning of this section. A common technique in inferential statistics is to draw comparisons between populations by analyzing samples that come from those populations.

▐▐▐ **EXAMPLE 5** Comparing Populations Based on Samples

Two companies, *A* and *B*, sell 12-ounce jars of instant coffee. Five jars of each were randomly selected from markets, and the contents were carefully weighed, with the following results.

$$A: \quad 12.02, \quad 12.08, \quad 11.99, \quad 11.96, \quad 11.99$$
$$B: \quad 12.40, \quad 12.21, \quad 12.36, \quad 12.22, \quad 12.27$$

Find **(a)** which company provides more coffee in their jars, and **(b)** which company fills its jars more consistently.

SOLUTION

The mean and standard deviation values for both samples are shown in **Table 14**.

(a) Since $\bar{x}_B$ is greater than $\bar{x}_A$, we *infer* that Company B most likely provides more coffee (greater mean) per jar.

(b) Since s_A is less than s_B, we *infer* that Company A seems more consistent (smaller standard deviation).   ▐▐▐

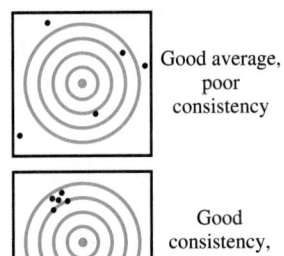

Higher average

Lower dispersion

The more desirable basket depends on your objective.

Good average, poor consistency

Good consistency, poor average

In this case, good consistency (lesser dispersion) is more desirable than a good average (central tendency).

Table 14

Sample A	Sample B
$\bar{x}_A = 12.008$	$\bar{x}_B = 12.292$
$s_A = 0.0455$	$s_B = 0.0847$

Pafnuty Lvovich Chebyshev (1821–1894) was a Russian mathematician known mainly for his work on the theory of prime numbers. Chebyshev and French mathematician and statistician **Jules Bienaymé** (1796–1878) independently developed an important inequality of probability now known as the Bienaymé–Chebyshev inequality.

The conclusions drawn in **Example 5** are tentative, because the samples were small. We could place more confidence in our inferences if we used larger samples, for then it would be more likely that the samples were accurate representations of their respective populations.

It is clear that a larger dispersion value means more "spread" than a smaller one. But it is difficult to say exactly what a single dispersion value says about a data set. *It is impossible* (though it would be nice) to make a general statement like: "Exactly half of the items of any distribution lie within one standard deviation of the mean of the distribution." Such a statement can be made only of specialized kinds of distributions. (See, for example, **Section 12.5** on the normal distribution.) There is, however, one useful result that does apply to all data sets, no matter what their distributions are like. This result is named for the Russian mathematician Pafnuty Lvovich Chebyshev.

Chebyshev's Theorem

For any set of numbers, regardless of how they are distributed, the fraction of them that lie within k standard deviations of their mean (where $k > 1$) is *at least*

$$1 - \frac{1}{k^2}.$$

Be sure to notice the words *at least* in the theorem. In certain distributions the fraction of items within k standard deviations of the mean may be more than $1 - \frac{1}{k^2}$, but in no case will it ever be less. The theorem is meaningful for any value of k greater than 1 (integer or noninteger).

▮▮ **EXAMPLE 6** Applying Chebyshev's Theorem

What is the minimum percentage of the items in a data set that lie within 3 standard deviations of the mean?

SOLUTION

With $k = 3$, we calculate as follows.

$\boxed{3^2 = 3 \cdot 3, \text{not } 3 \cdot 2}$ $1 - \frac{1}{3^2} = 1 - \frac{1}{9} = \frac{8}{9} \approx 0.889 = 88.9\%$ ← Minimum percentage   ▮▮▮

Coefficient of Variation

Look again at the top target pictured on **page 657.** The dispersion, or spread, among the five bullet holes may not be especially impressive if the shots were fired from 100 yards, but would be much more so at, say, 300 yards. There is another measure, the *coefficient of variation*, which takes this distinction into account. It is not strictly a measure of dispersion, as it combines central tendency and dispersion. It expresses the standard deviation as a percentage of the mean. ***Often this is a more meaningful measure than a straight measure of dispersion, especially when comparing distributions whose means are appreciably different.***

Coefficient of Variation

For any set of data, the **coefficient of variation** is calculated as follows.

$$V = \frac{s}{\bar{x}} \cdot 100 \quad \text{for a sample} \qquad \text{or} \qquad V = \frac{\sigma}{\mu} \cdot 100 \quad \text{for a population}$$

▌▌ EXAMPLE 7 Comparing Samples

Compare the dispersions in the two samples A and B.

$$A: 12, 13, 16, 18, 18, 20 \qquad B: 125, 131, 144, 158, 168, 193$$

Table 15

Sample A	Sample B
$\bar{x}_A = 16.167$	$\bar{x}_B = 153.167$
$s_A = 3.125$	$s_B = 25.294$
$V_A = 19.3$	$V_B = 16.5$

SOLUTION

Using a calculator, we obtain the values shown in **Table 15**. The values of V_A and V_B were found using the formula on the previous page. From the calculated values, we see that sample B has a much larger dispersion (standard deviation) than sample A. But sample A actually has the larger *relative* dispersion (coefficient of variation). The dispersion within sample A is larger as a percentage of the sample mean. ▌▌▌

For Further Thought

Measuring Skewness in a Distribution

Section 12.2 included a discussion of "symmetry in data sets." Here we present a common method of measuring the amount of "skewness," or nonsymmetry, inherent in a distribution.

In a skewed distribution, the mean will be farther out toward the tail than the median, as shown in the sketch.

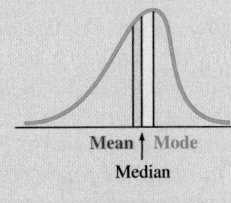

Mean ↑ Mode
Median

Skewed to the left

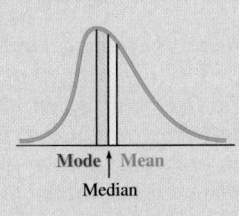

Mode ↑ Mean
Median

Skewed to the right

The degree of skewness can be measured by the **skewness coefficient**, which involves both central tendency and dispersion, and is calculated as follows.

$$SK = \frac{3 \cdot (\text{mean} - \text{median})}{\text{standard deviation}}$$

For Group or Individual Investigation

1. Under what conditions would the skewness coefficient be each of the following?

   (a) positive   **(b)** negative

2. Explain why the mean of a skewed distribution is always farther out toward the tail than the median.

3. In a skewed distribution, how many standard deviations apart are the mean and median in each case?

   (a) $SK = \frac{1}{2}$ **(b)** $SK = 1$ **(c)** $SK = 3$

12.3 EXERCISES

1. If your calculator finds both kinds of standard deviation, the sample standard deviation and the population standard deviation, which of the two will be a larger number for a given set of data? (*Hint:* Recall the difference between how the two standard deviations are calculated.)

2. If your calculator finds only one kind of standard deviation, explain how you would determine whether it is sample or population standard deviation (assuming your calculator manual is not available).

Find **(a)** *the range, and* **(b)** *the standard deviation for each sample in Exercises 3–12. Round answers to the nearest hundredth.*

3. 2, 5, 6, 8, 9, 11, 15

4. 6, 5, 10, 8, 9, 15, 22, 16, 5

5. 27, 34, 22, 41, 30, 25, 31

6. 57, 81, 55, 63, 77, 61, 84, 72, 65

7. 348, 326, 330, 308, 316, 322, 310, 319, 324, 330

8. 4.7, 5.3, 9.4, 6.6, 7.4, 6.2, 7.1, 8.0, 8.8, 7.9, 7.1, 7.4, 7.9, 8.1

9. 84.96, 84.60, 84.58, 84.48, 84.72, 85.62, 85.03, 85.10, 84.53

10. 312.3, 310.4, 309.3, 311.1, 310.8, 313.5, 312.6, 310.5, 311.0, 314.2

11.

Value	Frequency
13	3
10	4
7	7
4	5
1	2

12.

Value	Frequency
14	6
16	12
18	14
20	15
22	10
24	4
26	3

Use Chebyshev's theorem for Exercises 13–28.

Find the least possible fraction of the numbers in a data set lying within the given number of standard deviations of the mean. Give answers as standard fractions reduced to lowest terms.

13. 2   **14.** 4   **15.** $\dfrac{5}{2}$ **16.** $\dfrac{7}{4}$

Find the least possible percentage (to the nearest tenth of a percent) of the items in a distribution lying within the given number of standard deviations of the mean.

17. 3   **18.** 6   **19.** $\dfrac{5}{3}$ **20.** $\dfrac{9}{2}$

In a certain distribution of numbers, the mean is 80 and the standard deviation is 8. At least what fraction of the numbers are between the following pairs of numbers? Give answers as common fractions reduced to lowest terms.

21. 64 and 96   **22.** 56 and 104

23. 48 and 112   **24.** 40 and 120

In the same distribution (mean 80 and standard deviation 8), find the largest fraction of the numbers that could meet the following requirements. Give answers as common fractions reduced to lowest terms.

25. less than 64 or more than 96

26. less than 60 or more than 100

27. less than 52 or more than 108

28. less than 62 or more than 98

Bonus Pay for a Baseball Team *Mairead Jacoby owns a minor league baseball team. Each time the team wins a game, Mairead pays the nine starting players, the manager, and two coaches bonuses, which are certain percentages of their regular salaries. The amounts paid are listed here.*

$80,	$105,	$120,	$175,	$185,	$190,
$205,	$210,	$215,	$300,	$320,	$325

Use this distribution of bonuses for Exercises 29–34.

29. Find the mean of the distribution.

30. Find the standard deviation of the distribution.

31. How many of the bonus amounts are within one standard deviation of the mean?

32. How many of the bonus amounts are within two standard deviations of the mean?

33. What does Chebyshev's theorem say about the number of the amounts that are within two standard deviations of the mean?

34. Explain any discrepancy between your answers for **Exercises 32 and 33.**

In Exercises 35 and 36, two samples are given. In each case, **(a)** *find both sample standard deviations,* **(b)** *find both sample coefficients of variation,* **(c)** *decide which sample has the higher dispersion, and* **(d)** *decide which sample has the higher relative dispersion.*

35. *A:* 3, 7, 4, 3, 8   *B:* 10, 8, 10, 6, 7, 3, 5

36. *A:* 68, 72, 69, 65, 71, 72, 68, 71, 67, 67
     B: 26, 35, 30, 28, 31, 36, 38, 29, 34, 33

37. **Comparing Battery Lifetimes** Two brands of car batteries, both carrying 6-year warranties, were sampled and tested under controlled conditions. Five of each brand failed after the numbers of months shown here.

> Brand A: 74, 65, 70, 64, 71
> Brand B: 69, 70, 62, 72, 60

(a) Calculate both sample means.

(b) Calculate both sample standard deviations.

(c) Which brand apparently lasts longer?

(d) Which brand has the more consistent lifetime?

Lifetimes of Engine Control Modules *Chris Englert manages the service department of a trucking company. Each truck in the fleet utilizes an electronic engine control module. Long-lasting modules are desirable. A preventive replacement program also avoids costly breakdowns. For this purpose it is desirable that the modules be fairly consistent in their lifetimes, so that preventive replacements can be timed efficiently.*

Chris tested a sample of 20 Brand A modules, and they lasted 48,560 highway miles on the average (mean), with a standard deviation of 2116 miles. The listing below shows how long each of another sample of 20 Brand B modules lasted. Use these data for Exercises 38–40.

44,660,	51,300,	45,680,	48,840,	47,510,
61,220,	49,100,	48,660,	47,790,	47,210,
48,050,	49,920,	47,420,	45,880,	50,110,
52,910,	47,930,	45,800,	46,690,	49,240

38. According to the sampling, which brand of module has the longer average life (in highway miles)?

39. Which brand of module apparently has a more consistent (or uniform) length of life (in highway miles)?

40. If Brands A and B are the only modules available, which one should Chris purchase for the maintenance program? Explain your reasoning.

Utilize the following sample for Exercises 41–46.

> 13, 14, 17, 19, 21, 22, 25

41. Compute the mean and standard deviation for the sample (each to the nearest hundredth).

42. Now add 5 to each item of the given sample and compute the mean and standard deviation for the new sample.

43. Go back to the original sample. This time subtract 10 from each item, and compute the mean and standard deviation of the new sample.

44. Based on your answers for **Exercises 41–43,** make conjectures about what happens to the mean and standard deviation when all items of the sample have the same constant k added or subtracted.

45. Go back to the original sample again. This time multiply each item by 3, and compute the mean and standard deviation of the new sample.

46. Based on your answers for **Exercises 41 and 45,** make conjectures about what happens to the mean and standard deviation when all items of the sample are multiplied by the same constant k.

47. In **Section 12.2** we showed that the mean, as a measure of central tendency, is highly sensitive to extreme values. Which measure of dispersion, covered in this section, would be more sensitive to extreme values? Illustrate your answer with one or more examples.

A Cereal Marketing Survey A food distribution company conducted a survey to determine whether a proposed premium to be included in boxes of their cereal was appealing enough to generate new sales. Four cities were used as test markets, where the cereal was distributed with the premium, and four cities as control markets, where the cereal was distributed without the premium. The eight cities were chosen on the basis of their similarity in terms of population, per capita income, and total cereal purchase volume. The results follow.

		Percent Change in Average Market Share per Month
Test cities	1	+18
	2	+15
	3	+7
	4	+10
Control cities	1	+1
	2	−8
	3	−5
	4	0

48. Find the mean of the percent change in market share for the four test cities.

49. Find the mean of the percent change in market share for the four control cities.

50. Find the standard deviation of the percent change in market share for the test cities.

51. Find the standard deviation of the percent change in market share for the control cities.

52. Find the difference between the means of the test cities and the control cities. This difference represents the estimate of the percent change in sales due to the premium.

53. The two standard deviations from the test cities and the control cities were used to calculate an "error" of ± 7.95 for the estimate in **Exercise 52.** With this amount of error, what are the least and greatest estimates of the increase in sales?

(On the basis of the interval estimate of **Exercise 53** the company decided to mass produce the premium and distribute it nationally.)

For Exercises 54–56, refer to the grouped frequency distribution shown below. (Also refer to Exercises 59–61 in Section 12.2.)

Class Limits	Frequency f
21–25	5
26–30	3
31–35	8
36–40	12
41–45	21
46–50	38
51–55	35
56–60	20

54. Is it possible to identify any specific data items that occurred in this sample?

55. Is it possible to compute the actual standard deviation for this sample?

56. Describe how you might approximate the standard deviation for this sample. Justify your procedure.

57. Suppose the frequency distribution of **Example 4** involved 50 or 100 (or even more) distinct data values, rather than just four. Explain why the procedure of that example would then be very inefficient.

58. A "J-shaped" distribution can be skewed either to the right or to the left. (When skewed right, it is sometimes called a "reverse J" distribution.)

  (a) In a J-shaped distribution skewed to the right, which data item would be the mode, the greatest or the least item?

  (b) In a J-shaped distribution skewed to the left, which data item would be the mode, the greatest or the least item?

  (c) Explain why the mode is a weak measure of central tendency for a J-shaped distribution.

12.4 MEASURES OF POSITION

The z-Score • Percentiles • Deciles and Quartiles • The Box Plot

The **top ten jobs of 2010** did not vary much from recent earlier rankings despite the treacherous economy of 2008–2010. All ten require considerable education and/or training, and most require a good deal of mathematical ability. The rankings are based on the following five criteria.

(a) stress level
(b) working environment
(c) physical demands
(d) income
(e) hiring outlook

The rankings:

1. Actuary
2. Software Engineer
3. Computer Systems Analyst
4. Biologist
5. Historian
6. Mathematician
7. Paralegal Assistant
8. Statistician
9. Accountant
10. Dental Hygienist

To learn more, go to www.careercast.com

Measures of central tendency and measures of dispersion give us an effective way of characterizing an overall set of data. Central tendency indicates where, along a number scale, the overall data set is centered. Dispersion indicates how much the data set is spread out from the center point. And Chebyshev's theorem, stated in the previous section, tells us in a general sense what portions of the data set may be dispersed different amounts from the center point.

In some cases, we are interested in certain individual items within a data set, rather than in that set as a whole. So we would like to measure how an item fits into the collection, how it compares to other items in the collection, or even how it compares to another item in another collection. There are several common ways of creating such measures. Since they measure an item's position within the data set, they usually are called **measures of position.**

The z-Score

Each individual item in a sample can be assigned a **z-score,** which is defined as follows.

> **The z-score**
>
> If x is a data item in a sample with mean $\bar{x}$ and standard deviation s, then the **z-score** of x is calculated as follows.
>
> $$z = \frac{x - \bar{x}}{s}$$

Because $x - \bar{x}$ gives the amount by which x differs (or deviates) from the mean $\bar{x}$, $\frac{x - \bar{x}}{s}$ gives the number of standard deviations by which x differs from $\bar{x}$. Notice that z will be positive if x is greater than $\bar{x}$ but negative if x is less than $\bar{x}$. Chebyshev's theorem assures us that, in any distribution whatsoever, at least 89% (roughly) of the items will lie within three standard deviations of the mean. That is, at least 89% of the items will have z-scores between -3 and 3. In fact, many common distributions, especially symmetric ones, have considerably more than 89% of their items within three standard deviations of the mean (as we will see in the next section). Hence, a z-score greater than 3 or less than -3 is a rare occurrence.

▐▌ **EXAMPLE 1** Comparing Positions Using z-Scores

Two friends, Ann Kuick and Kay Allen, who take different history classes, had midterm exams on the same day. Ann's score was 86 while Kay's was only 78. Which student did relatively better, given the class data shown here?

	Ann	Kay
Class mean	73	69
Class standard deviation	8	5

SOLUTION

Calculate as follows.

Ann: $z = \dfrac{86 - 73}{8} = 1.625$ Kay: $z = \dfrac{78 - 69}{5} = 1.8$

Since Kay's z-score is higher, she was positioned relatively higher within her class than Ann was within her class. ▐▐▐

Percentiles

When you take the Scholastic Aptitude Test (SAT), or any other standardized test taken by large numbers of students, your raw score usually is converted to a **percentile** score, which is defined as follows.

Percentile

If approximately n percent of the items in a distribution are less than the number x, then x is the **nth percentile** of the distribution, denoted P_n.

For example, if you scored at the eighty-third percentile on the SAT, it means that you outscored approximately 83% of all those who took the test. (It does *not* mean that you got 83% of the answers correct.) Since the percentile score gives the position of an item within the data set, it is another "measure of position." The following example approximates percentiles for a fairly small collection of data.

▌▌ **EXAMPLE 2** Finding Percentiles
_____

The following are the numbers of dinner customers served by a restaurant on 40 consecutive days. (The numbers have been ranked least to greatest.)

46	51	52	55	56	56	58	59	59	59
61	61	62	62	63	63	64	64	64	65
66	66	66	67	67	67	68	68	69	69
70	70	71	71	72	75	79	79	83	88

For this data set, find **(a)** the thirty-fifth percentile, and **(b)** the eighty-sixth percentile.

SOLUTION

(a) The thirty-fifth percentile can be taken as the item below which 35 percent of the items are ranked. Since 35 percent of 40 is $0.35(40) = 14$, we take the fifteenth item, or 63, as the thirty-fifth percentile.

(b) Since 86 percent of 40 is $0.86(40) = 34.4$, we round *up* and take the eighty-sixth percentile to be the thirty-fifth item, or 72. ▌▌▌

Technically, percentiles originally were conceived as a set of 99 values $P_1, P_2, P_3, \ldots, P_{99}$ (not necessarily data items) along the scale that would divide the data set into 100 equal-sized parts. They were computed only for very large data sets. With smaller data sets, as in **Example 2,** dividing the data into 100 parts would necessarily leave many of those parts empty. However, the modern techniques of exploratory data analysis seek to apply the percentile concept to even small data sets. Thus, we use approximation techniques as in **Example 2.** Another option is to divide the data into a lesser number of equal-sized (or nearly equal-sized) parts.

Deciles and Quartiles

Deciles are the nine values (denoted $D_1, D_2, \ldots, D_9$) along the scale that divide a data set into ten (approximately) equal-sized parts, and **quartiles** are the three values (Q_1, Q_2, and Q_3) that divide a data set into four (approximately) equal-sized parts. Since deciles and quartiles serve to position particular items within portions of a distribution, they also are "measures of position." We can evaluate deciles by finding their equivalent percentiles.

$$D_1 = P_{10}, \quad D_2 = P_{20}, \quad D_3 = P_{30}, \quad \ldots, \quad D_9 = P_{90}$$

▌▌ **EXAMPLE 3** Finding Deciles

Find the fourth decile for the dinner customer data of **Example 2.**

SOLUTION

Refer to the ranked data table. The fourth decile is the fortieth percentile, and 40% of 40 is $0.40(40) = 16$. We take the fourth decile to be the seventeenth item, or 64. ▌▌▌

Although the three quartiles also can be related to corresponding percentiles, notice that the second quartile, Q_2, also is equivalent to the median, a measure of central tendency introduced in **Section 12.2.** A common convention for computing quartiles goes back to the way we computed the median.

Finding Quartiles

For any set of data (ranked in order from least to greatest):

The **second quartile, Q_2,** is just the median, the middle item when the number of items is odd, or the mean of the two middle items when the number of items is even.

The **first quartile, Q_1,** is the median of all items below Q_2.

The **third quartile, Q_3,** is the median of all items above Q_2.

▌▌ **EXAMPLE 4** Finding Quartiles

Find the three quartiles for the data of **Example 2.**

SOLUTION

Refer to the ranked data. The two middle data items are 65 and 66.

$$Q_2 = \frac{65 + 66}{2} = 65.5$$

The least 20 items (an even number) are all below Q_2, and the two middle items in that set are 59 and 61.

$$Q_1 = \frac{59 + 61}{2} = 60$$

The greatest 20 items are above Q_2.

$$Q_3 = \frac{69 + 70}{2} = 69.5$$ ▌▌▌

The Box Plot

A **box plot,** or **box-and-whisker plot,** involves the median (a measure of central tendency), the range (a measure of dispersion), and the first and third quartiles (measures of position), all incorporated into a simple visual display.

Box Plot

For a given set of data, a **box plot** (or **box-and-whisker plot**) consists of a rectangular box positioned above a numerical scale, extending from Q_1 to Q_3, with the value of Q_2 (the median) indicated within the box, and with "whiskers" (line segments) extending to the left and right from the box out to the minimum and maximum data items.

▌▌ EXAMPLE 5 Constructing a Box Plot

Construct a box plot for the weekly study times data of **Example 2** in **Section 12.1.**

SOLUTION

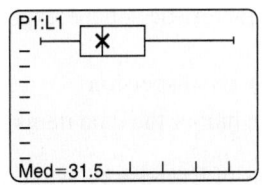

1 – Var Stats
↑n=40
minX=12
Q₁=24
Med=31.5
Q₃=44.5
maxX=72

This screen supports the results of
Example 5.

To determine the quartiles and the minimum and maximum values more easily, we use the stem-and-leaf display (with leaves ranked), given in **Table 9** of **Section 12.2.**

1	2 4 5 6 7 8
2	0 2 3 4 4 5 6 6 9 9 9
3	0 1 1 2 3 6 6 8 9
4	0 1 4 4 5 5 7
5	2 5 5 8
6	0 2
7	2

The median (determined earlier in **Example 6** of **Section 12.2**) is

$$\frac{31 + 32}{2} = 31.5.$$

From the stem-and-leaf display,

$$Q_1 = \frac{24 + 24}{2} = 24 \quad \text{and} \quad Q_3 = \frac{44 + 45}{2} = 44.5.$$

The minimum and maximum items are evident from the stem-and-leaf display. They are 12 and 72. The box plot is shown in **Figure 10.**

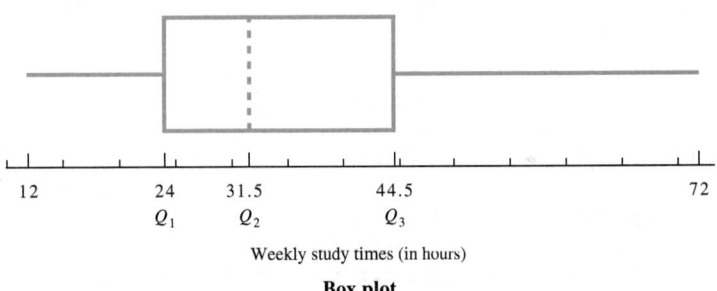

Weekly study times (in hours)

Box plot

Figure 10

▮▮▮

P1:L1

Med=31.5

This box plot corresponds to the results of **Example 5.** It indicates the median in the display at the bottom. The TRACE function of the TI-83/84 Plus will locate the minimum, maximum, and quartile values as well.

The box plot in **Figure 10** conveys the following important information:

1. central tendency (the location of the median);
2. the location of the middle half of the data (the extent of the box);
3. dispersion (the range is the extent of the whiskers); and
4. skewness (the nonsymmetry of both the box and the whiskers).

12.4 EXERCISES

Numbers of Restaurant Customers *Refer to the dinner customers data of* **Example 2.** *Approximate each of the following. (Use the methods illustrated in this section.)*

1. the fifteenth percentile

2. the seventy-fifth percentile

3. the third decile   4. the eighth decile

In Exercises 5–8, make use of z-scores.

5. ***Relative Positions on Geometry Quizzes*** In a geometry class, Neil Hunnewell scored 5 on a quiz for which the class mean and standard deviation were 4.6 and 2.1, respectively. Janet Hunnius scored 6 on another quiz for which the class mean and standard deviation were 4.9 and 2.3, respectively. Relatively speaking, which student did better?

6. *Relative Performances in Track Events* In Saturday's track meet, Edgar Espina, a high jumper, jumped 6 feet 3 inches. Conference high jump marks for the past season had a mean of 6 feet even and a standard deviation of 3.5 inches. Kurt Massey, Edgar's teammate, achieved 18 feet 4 inches in the long jump. In that event the conference season average (mean) and standard deviation were 16 feet 6 inches and 1 foot 10 inches, respectively. Relative to this past season in this conference, which athlete had a better performance on Saturday?

7. *Relative Lifetimes of Tires* The lifetimes of Brand A tires are distributed with mean 45,000 miles and standard deviation 4500 miles, while Brand B tires last for only 38,000 miles on the average (mean) with standard deviation 2080 miles. Nicole Britt's Brand A tires lasted 37,000 miles and Yvette Angel's Brand B tires lasted 35,000 miles. Relatively speaking, within their own brands, which driver got the better wear?

8. *Relative Ratings of Fish Caught* In a certain lake, the trout average 12 inches in length with a standard deviation of 2.75 inches. The bass average 4 pounds in weight with a standard deviation of 0.8 pound. If Tobi Casper caught an 18-inch trout and Katrina Bass caught a 6-pound bass, then relatively speaking, which catch was the better trophy?

Leading U.S. Trade Partners *Countries in the table are ranked by value of 2008 imports to the United States from the countries. Exports are from the United States to the countries. Use this information for Exercises 9–20.*

Country	Population (millions)	Trade Volume (billion U.S. $)	
		Imports	Exports
Canada	33	339	261
China	1339	338	70
Mexico	110	216	151
Japan	127	139	65
Germany	82	97	55
United Kingdom	61	59	54
Saudi Arabia	28	55	12
Venezuela	26	51	13
South Korea	48	48	35
France	64	44	29

Sources: The World Almanac and Book of Facts 2010, www.google.com

Compute z-scores (accurate to one decimal place) for Exercises 9–12.

9. Japan's population   **10.** imports from China

11. exports to Mexico

12. imports from Venezuela

In each of Exercises 13–16, determine which country occupied the given position.

13. the fifteenth percentile in population

14. the third quartile in exports

15. the fourth decile in imports

16. the first quartile in exports

17. Determine who was relatively higher: China in imports or Canada in exports.

18. Construct box plots for both exports and imports, one above the other in the same drawing.

19. What does your box plot of **Exercise 18** *for exports* indicate about the following characteristics of the exports data?
   (a) the central tendency   **(b)** the dispersion
   (c) the location of the middle half of the data items

20. Comparing your two box plots of **Exercise 18,** what can you say about the 2008 trade balance with this group of countries?

21. The text stated that, for *any* distribution of data, at least 89% of the items will be within three standard deviations of the mean. Why couldn't we just move some items farther out from the mean to obtain a new distribution that would violate this condition?

22. Describe the basic difference between a measure of central tendency and a measure of position.

This chapter has introduced three major characteristics, central tendency, dispersion, and position, and has developed various ways of measuring them in numerical data. In each of Exercises 23–26, a new measure is described. Explain in each case which of the three characteristics you think it would measure and why.

23. Midrange $= \dfrac{\text{minimum item} + \text{maximum item}}{2}$

24. Midquartile $= \dfrac{Q_1 + Q_3}{2}$

25. Interquartile range $= Q_3 - Q_1$

26. Semi-interquartile range $= \dfrac{Q_3 - Q_1}{2}$

27. The "skewness coefficient" was defined in **For Further Thought** in the previous section, and it is calculated as follows.

$$SK = \frac{3 \cdot (\bar{x} - Q_2)}{s}$$

Is this a measure of individual data items or of the overall distribution?

28. For the U.S. trade partners data preceding **Exercise 9,** calculate the skewness coefficient for **(a)** exports, and **(b)** imports.

29. From **Exercise 28,** how would you compare the skewness of exports versus imports?

30. In a national standardized test, Kimberly Austin scored at the ninety-second percentile. If 67,500 individuals took the test, about how many scored higher than Kimberly did?

31. Let the three quartiles (from least to greatest) for a large population of scores be denoted $Q_1, Q_2,$ and Q_3.

   (a) Is it necessarily true that

$$Q_2 - Q_1 = Q_3 - Q_2?$$

   (b) Explain your answer to part (a).

In Exercises 32–35, answer yes *or* no *and explain your answer. (Consult* **Exercises 23–26** *for definitions.)*

32. Is the midquartile necessarily the same as the median?

33. Is the midquartile necessarily the same as the midrange?

34. Is the interquartile range necessarily half the range?

35. Is the semi-interquartile range necessarily half the interquartile range?

	Raw Score	z-score
Omer	60	0.69
Alessandro	72	1.67

36. *Relative Positions on a Standardized Chemistry Test* Omer and Alessandro participated in the standardization process for a new statewide chemistry test. Within the large group participating, their raw scores and corresponding *z*-scores were as shown here.

Find the overall mean and standard deviation of the distribution of scores. (Give answers to two decimal places.)

Rating Passers in the National Football League Since the National Football League began keeping official statistics in 1932, the passing effectiveness of quarterbacks has been rated by several different methods. The current system, adopted in 1973, is based on four performance components: completions, touchdowns, yards gained, and interceptions, as percentages of the number of passes attempted. The computation can be accomplished using the following formula.

$$\text{Rating} = \frac{\left(250 \cdot \frac{C}{A}\right) + \left(1000 \cdot \frac{T}{A}\right) + \left(12.5 \cdot \frac{Y}{A}\right) + 6.25 - \left(1250 \cdot \frac{I}{A}\right)}{3},$$

where A = attempted passes,
        C = completed passes,
        T = touchdown passes,
        Y = yards gained passing,
and I = interceptions.

In addition to the weighting factors (coefficients) appearing in the formula, the four category ratios are limited to non-negative values with the following maximums.

$$0.775 \text{ for } \frac{C}{A}, \quad 0.11875 \text{ for } \frac{T}{A}, \quad 12.5 \text{ for } \frac{Y}{A}, \quad 0.095 \text{ for } \frac{I}{A}$$

These limitations are intended to prevent any one component of performance from having an undue effect on the overall rating. They are not often invoked but in special cases can have a significant effect.

   The preceding formula rates all passers against the same performance standard and is applied, for example, after a single game, an entire season, or a career. The ratings for the ten leading passers in the league for 2009 regular season play are ranked in the following table.

Rank	NFL Passer	Rating Points
1	Drew Brees, New Orleans	109.6
2	Brett Favre, Minnesota	107.2
3	Philip Rivers, San Diego	104.4
4	Aaron Rodgers, Green Bay	103.2
5	Ben Roethlisberger, Pittsburgh	100.5
6	Peyton Manning, Indianapolis	99.9
7	Matt Schaub, Houston	98.6
8	Tony Romo, Dallas	97.6
9	Tom Brady, New England	96.2
10	Kurt Warner, Arizona	93.2

Source: www.espn.go.com

Find the measures (to one decimal place) in Exercises 37–42.

37. the three quartiles

38. the third decile

39. the sixty-fifth percentile

40. the midrange (See **Exercise 23.**)

41. the midquartile (see **Exercise 24.**)

42. the interquartile range (See **Exercise 25.**)

43. Construct a box plot for the rating points data.

44. The eleventh-ranked passer in the 2009 regular season was Eli Manning of the New York Giants. Eli attempted 509 passes, completed 317, passed for 27 touchdowns, gained 4021 yards passing, and was intercepted 14 times. Compute his rating.

45. If Eli Manning had completed one more pass in 2009, what would his rating have been?

46. In the case of **Exercise 45,** how would Eli Manning have ranked for 2009?

47. Steve Young, of the San Francisco 49ers, set a full season rating record of 112.8 in 1994 and held that record until Peyton Manning achieved a rating of 121.1 in 2004. (As of 2010, Manning's all-time record holds.) If, in 2004, Manning had 336 completions, 49 touchdowns, and 4557 yards, for 497 attempts, how many times was he intercepted that year?

48. Refer to the passer rating formula and determine the highest rating possible (considered a "perfect" passer rating).

Archie Manning, father of NFL quarterbacks Peyton and Eli, signed this photo for author Hornsby's son, Jack.

12.5 THE NORMAL DISTRIBUTION

Discrete and Continuous Random Variables • Definition and Properties of a Normal Curve • A Table of Standard Normal Curve Areas • Interpreting Normal Curve Areas

Discrete and Continuous Random Variables

A random variable that can take on only certain fixed values is called a **discrete random variable.** For example, the number of heads in 5 tosses of a coin is discrete since its only possible values are 0, 1, 2, 3, 4, and 5. A variable whose values are not restricted in this way is a **continuous random variable.** For example, the diameter of camellia blossoms would be a continuous variable, spread over a scale perhaps from 5 to 25 centimeters. The values would not be restricted to whole numbers, or even to tenths, or hundredths, etc. A discrete random variable takes on only a countable number of values, whereas a continuous random variable takes on an uncountable number of values.

Most distributions discussed earlier in this chapter were *empirical* (based on observation). The distributions covered in this section are *theoretical* (based on theoretical probabilities). A knowledge of theoretical distributions enables us to identify when actual observations are inconsistent with stated assumptions, which is the key to inferential statistics.

The theoretical probability distribution for the discrete random variable "number of heads" when 5 fair coins are tossed is shown in **Table 16. Figure 11** shows the corresponding histogram. The probability values can be found using the binomial probability formula (**Section 11.4**) or using Pascal's triangle (**Section 10.4**).

The normal curve was first developed by **Abraham De Moivre** (1667–1754), but his work went unnoticed for many years. It was independently redeveloped by Pierre de Laplace (1749–1827) and Carl Friedrich Gauss (1777–1855). Gauss found so many uses for this curve that it is sometimes called the *Gaussian curve.*

Table 16 Probability Distribution

x	$P(x)$
0	0.03125
1	0.15625
2	0.31250
3	0.31250
4	0.15625
5	0.03125
Sum:	1.00000

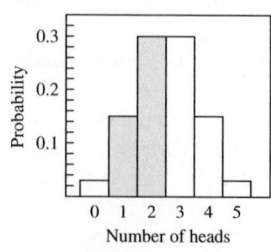

Figure 11

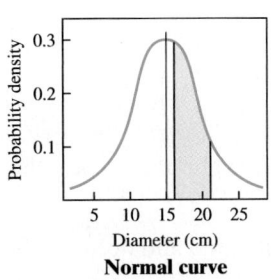

Normal curve

Figure 12

Since each rectangle in **Figure 11** is 1 unit wide, the *area* of the rectangle is also equal to the probability of the corresponding number of heads. The area, and thus the probability, for the event "1 head or 2 heads" is shaded in the figure. The graph consists of 6 distinct rectangles since "number of heads" is a *discrete* variable with 6 possible values. The sum of the 6 rectangular areas is exactly 1 square unit.

In contrast to the discrete "number of heads" distribution in **Table 16**, a probability distribution for camellia blossom diameters cannot be tabulated or graphed in quite the same way, since this variable is *continuous*. The graph would be smeared out into a "continuous" bell-shaped curve (rather than a set of rectangles) as shown in **Figure 12**. The vertical scale on the graph in this case shows what we call "probability density," the probability per unit along the horizontal axis.

Definition and Properties of a Normal Curve

The camellia blossom curve is highest at a diameter value of 15 cm, its center point, and drops off rapidly and equally toward a zero level in both directions. Such a symmetric, bell-shaped curve is called a **normal curve.** Any random variable whose graph has this characteristic shape is said to have a **normal distribution.**

The area under the curve along a certain interval is numerically equal to the probability that the random variable will have a value in the corresponding interval. The area of the shaded region in **Figure 12** is equal to the probability of a randomly chosen blossom having a diameter in the interval from the left extreme, say 16.4, to the right extreme, say 21.2. Normal curves are very important in the study of statistics because *a great many continuous random variables have normal distributions, and many discrete variables are distributed approximately normally.*

Each point on the horizontal scale of a normal curve lies some number of standard deviations from the mean (positive to the right, negative to the left). This number is the "standard score" for that point. It is the same as the z-score defined in **Section 12.4.** By relabeling the horizontal axis, as in **Figure 13**, we obtain the **standard normal curve**, which we can use to analyze *any* normal (or approximately normal) distribution. We relate the random variable value, x, to its z-score by

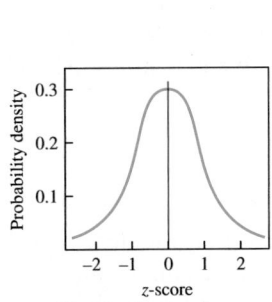

Standard normal curve

Figure 13

$$z = \frac{x - \overline{x}}{s}.$$

Figure 14 shows several of infinitely many possible normal curves. Each is completely characterized by its mean and standard deviation. Only one of these, the one marked S, is the *standard* normal curve. That one has mean 0 and standard deviation 1.

Close but Never Touching When a curve approaches closer and closer to a line, without ever actually meeting it (as a normal curve approaches the horizontal axis), the line is called an **asymptote**, and the curve approaches the line **asymptotically**.

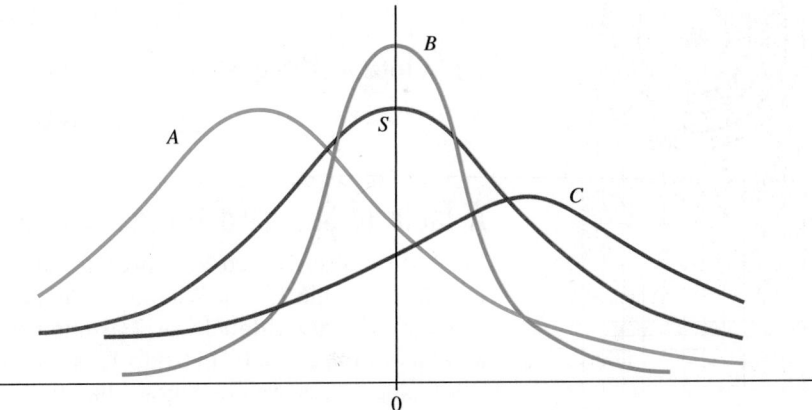

Normal curve S is standard, with mean = 0 and standard deviation = 1.
Normal curve A has mean < 0 and standard deviation = 1.
Normal curve B has mean = 0 and standard deviation < 1.
Normal curve C has mean > 0 and standard deviation > 1.

Figure 14

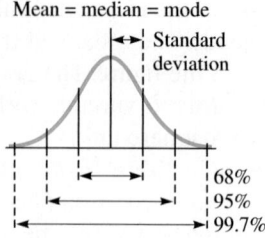

Figure 15

Several properties of normal curves are summarized below and are illustrated in **Figure 15**.

> **Properties of Normal Curves**
>
> The graph of a normal curve is bell-shaped and symmetric about a vertical line through its center.
>
> The mean, median, and mode of a normal curve are all equal and occur at the center of the distribution.
>
> *Empirical Rule* About 68% of all data values of a normal curve lie within 1 standard deviation of the mean (in both directions), about 95% within 2 standard deviations, and about 99.7% within 3 standard deviations.

The empirical rule indicates that a very small percentage of the items in a normal distribution will lie more than 3 standard deviations from the mean (approximately 0.3%, divided equally between the upper and lower tails of the distribution). As we move away from the center, the curve *never* actually touches the horizontal axis. No matter how far out we go, there is always a chance of an item occurring even farther out. Theoretically then, the range of a true normal distribution is infinite.

■■ **EXAMPLE 1** Applying the Empirical Rule

Suppose 300 chemistry students take a midterm exam and that the distribution of their scores can be treated as normal. Find the number of scores falling into each of the following intervals.

(a) Within 1 standard deviation of the mean

(b) Within 2 standard deviations of the mean

SOLUTION

(a) By the empirical rule, 68% of all scores lie within 1 standard deviation of the mean. Since there is a total of 300 scores, the number of scores within 1 standard deviation is as follows.

$$0.68(300) = 204 \quad \text{68\% = 0.68}$$

(b) A total of 95% of all scores lie within 2 standard deviations of the mean.

$$0.95(300) = 285 \quad \text{95\% = 0.95}$$

■■■

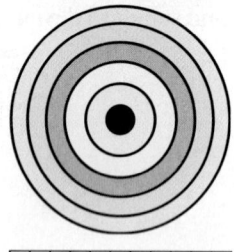

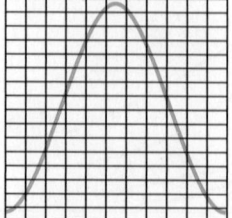

A normal distribution occurs in darts if the player, always aiming at the bull's-eye, tosses a fairly large number of times, and the aim on each toss is affected by independent random errors.

A Table of Standard Normal Curve Areas

Most questions we need to answer about normal distributions involve regions other than those within 1, 2, or 3 standard deviations of the mean. We might need the percentage of items within $1\frac{1}{2}$ or $2\frac{1}{5}$ standard deviations of the mean, or perhaps the area under the curve from 0.8 to 1.3 standard deviations above the mean.

In such cases, we need more than the empirical rule. The traditional approach is to refer to a table of area values, such as **Table 17**, which appears on **page 671.** Computer software packages designed for statistical uses usually will produce the required values on command and some advanced calculators also have this capability. Those tools are recommended. As an optional approach, we illustrate the use of **Table 17** here.

The column under *A* gives the proportion of the area under the entire curve that is between $z = 0$ and a positive value of z.

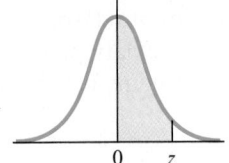

Because the curve is symmetric about the 0-value, the area between $z = 0$ and a *negative* value of z can be found by using the corresponding positive value of z.

Table 17 Areas Under the Standard Normal Curve

z	A	z	A	z	A	z	A	z	A	z	A
.00	.000	.56	.212	1.12	.369	1.68	.454	2.24	.487	2.80	.497
.01	.004	.57	.216	1.13	.371	1.69	.454	2.25	.488	2.81	.498
.02	.008	.58	.219	1.14	.373	1.70	.455	2.26	.488	2.82	.498
.03	.012	.59	.222	1.15	.375	1.71	.456	2.27	.488	2.83	.498
.04	.016	.60	.226	1.16	.377	1.72	.457	2.28	.489	2.84	.498
.05	.020	.61	.229	1.17	.379	1.73	.458	2.29	.489	2.85	.498
.06	.024	.62	.232	1.18	.381	1.74	.459	2.30	.489	2.86	.498
.07	.028	.63	.236	1.19	.383	1.75	.460	2.31	.490	2.87	.498
.08	.032	.64	.239	1.20	.385	1.76	.461	2.32	.490	2.88	.498
.09	.036	.65	.242	1.21	.387	1.77	.462	2.33	.490	2.89	.498
.10	.040	.66	.245	1.22	.389	1.78	.462	2.34	.490	2.90	.498
.11	.044	.67	.249	1.23	.391	1.79	.463	2.35	.491	2.91	.498
.12	.048	.68	.252	1.24	.393	1.80	.464	2.36	.491	2.92	.498
.13	.052	.69	.255	1.25	.394	1.81	.465	2.37	.491	2.93	.498
.14	.056	.70	.258	1.26	.396	1.82	.466	2.38	.491	2.94	.498
.15	.060	.71	.261	1.27	.398	1.83	.466	2.39	.492	2.95	.498
.16	.064	.72	.264	1.28	.400	1.84	.467	2.40	.492	2.96	.498
.17	.067	.73	.267	1.29	.401	1.85	.468	2.41	.492	2.97	.499
.18	.071	.74	.270	1.30	.403	1.86	.469	2.42	.492	2.98	.499
.19	.075	.75	.273	1.31	.405	1.87	.469	2.43	.492	2.99	.499
.20	.079	.76	.276	1.32	.407	1.88	.470	2.44	.493	3.00	.499
.21	.083	.77	.279	1.33	.408	1.89	.471	2.45	.493	3.01	.499
.22	.087	.78	.282	1.34	.410	1.90	.471	2.46	.493	3.02	.499
.23	.091	.79	.285	1.35	.411	1.91	.472	2.47	.493	3.03	.499
.24	.095	.80	.288	1.36	.413	1.92	.473	2.48	.493	3.04	.499
.25	.099	.81	.291	1.37	.415	1.93	.473	2.49	.494	3.05	.499
.26	.103	.82	.294	1.38	.416	1.94	.474	2.50	.494	3.06	.499
.27	.106	.83	.297	1.39	.418	1.95	.474	2.51	.494	3.07	.499
.28	.110	.84	.300	1.40	.419	1.96	.475	2.52	.494	3.08	.499
.29	.114	.85	.302	1.41	.421	1.97	.476	2.53	.494	3.09	.499
.30	.118	.86	.305	1.42	.422	1.98	.476	2.54	.494	3.10	.499
.31	.122	.87	.308	1.43	.424	1.99	.477	2.55	.495	3.11	.499
.32	.126	.88	.311	1.44	.425	2.00	.477	2.56	.495	3.12	.499
.33	.129	.89	.313	1.45	.426	2.01	.478	2.57	.495	3.13	.499
.34	.133	.90	.316	1.46	.428	2.02	.478	2.58	.495	3.14	.499
.35	.137	.91	.319	1.47	.429	2.03	.479	2.59	.495	3.15	.499
.36	.141	.92	.321	1.48	.431	2.04	.479	2.60	.495	3.16	.499
.37	.144	.93	.324	1.49	.432	2.05	.480	2.61	.495	3.17	.499
.38	.148	.94	.326	1.50	.433	2.06	.480	2.62	.496	3.18	.499
.39	.152	.95	.329	1.51	.434	2.07	.481	2.63	.496	3.19	.499
.40	.155	.96	.331	1.52	.436	2.08	.481	2.64	.496	3.20	.499
.41	.159	.97	.334	1.53	.437	2.09	.482	2.65	.496	3.21	.499
.42	.163	.98	.336	1.54	.438	2.10	.482	2.66	.496	3.22	.499
.43	.166	.99	.339	1.55	.439	2.11	.483	2.67	.496	3.23	.499
.44	.170	1.00	.341	1.56	.441	2.12	.483	2.68	.496	3.24	.499
.45	.174	1.01	.344	1.57	.442	2.13	.483	2.69	.496	3.25	.499
.46	.177	1.02	.346	1.58	.443	2.14	.484	2.70	.497	3.26	.499
.47	.181	1.03	.348	1.59	.444	2.15	.484	2.71	.497	3.27	.499
.48	.184	1.04	.351	1.60	.445	2.16	.485	2.72	.497	3.28	.499
.49	.188	1.05	.353	1.61	.446	2.17	.485	2.73	.497	3.29	.499
.50	.191	1.06	.355	1.62	.447	2.18	.485	2.74	.497	3.30	.500
.51	.195	1.07	.358	1.63	.448	2.19	.486	2.75	.497	3.31	.500
.52	.198	1.08	.360	1.64	.449	2.20	.486	2.76	.497	3.32	.500
.53	.202	1.09	.362	1.65	.451	2.21	.486	2.77	.497	3.33	.500
.54	.205	1.10	.364	1.66	.452	2.22	.487	2.78	.497	3.34	.500
.55	.209	1.11	.367	1.67	.453	2.23	.487	2.79	.497	3.35	.500

The table gives the fraction of all scores in a normal distribution that lie between the mean and z standard deviations from the mean. ***Because of the symmetry of the normal curve, the table can be used for values above the mean or below the mean.*** All of the items in the table can be thought of as corresponding to the area under the curve. The total area is arranged to be 1.000 square unit, with 0.500 square unit on each side of the mean. The table shows that at 3.30 standard deviations from the mean, essentially all of the area is accounted for. Whatever remains beyond is so small that it does not appear in the first three decimal places.

▋▋ **EXAMPLE 2** Applying the Normal Curve Table

Use **Table 17** to find the percent of all scores that lie between the mean and the following values.

(a) One standard deviation above the mean

(b) 2.45 standard deviations below the mean

SOLUTION

(a) Here $z = 1.00$ (the number of standard deviations, written as a decimal to the nearest hundredth). Refer to **Table 17**. Find 1.00 in the z column. The table entry is 0.341, so 34.1% of all values lie between the mean and one standard deviation above the mean.

   Another way of looking at this is to say that the area in color in **Figure 16** represents 34.1% of the total area under the normal curve.

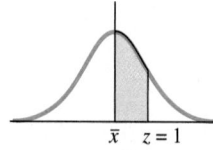

Figure 16

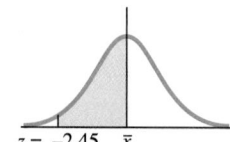

Figure 17

(b) Even though we go *below* the mean here (to the left), **Table 17** still works since the normal curve is symmetrical about its mean. Find 2.45 in the z column. A total of 0.493, or 49.3%, of all values lie between the mean and 2.45 standard deviations below the mean. This region is colored in **Figure 17**.   ▋▋▋

▋▋ **EXAMPLE 3** Finding Probabilities of Phone Call Durations

The time lengths of phone calls placed through a certain company are distributed normally with mean 6 minutes and standard deviation 2 minutes. If 1 call is randomly selected from phone company records, what is the probability that it will have lasted more than 10 minutes?

SOLUTION

Here 10 minutes is two standard deviations above the mean. The probability of such a call is equal to the area of the colored region in **Figure 18**.

   From **Table 17**, the area between the mean and two standard deviations above is 0.477 ($z = 2.00$). The total area to the right of the mean is 0.500. Find the area from $z = 2.00$ to the right by subtracting.

$$0.500 - 0.477 = 0.023$$

The probability of a call exceeding 10 minutes is 0.023, or 2.3%.   ▋▋▋

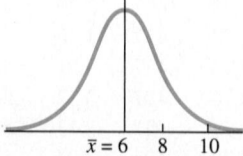

Figure 18

▮▮ **EXAMPLE 4** Finding Areas Under the Normal Curve

Find the total areas indicated in the regions in color in each of **Figures 19** and **20**.

SOLUTION

For **Figure 19**, find the area from 1.45 standard deviations below the mean to 2.71 standard deviations above the mean. From **Table 17**, $z = 1.45$ leads to an area of 0.426, while $z = 2.71$ leads to 0.497. The total area is the sum of these, or $0.426 + 0.497 = 0.923$.

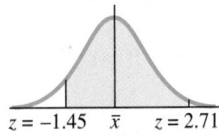

$z = -1.45 \quad \bar{x} \quad z = 2.71$

Figure 19

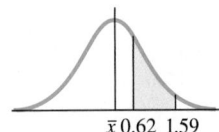

$\bar{x}\ 0.62\ 1.59$

Figure 20

To find the indicated area in **Figure 20**, refer again to **Table 17**. From the table, $z = 0.62$ leads to an area of 0.232, while $z = 1.59$ gives 0.444. To get the area between these two values of z, subtract the areas.

$$0.444 - 0.232 = 0.212$$

▮▮▮

Interpreting Normal Curve Areas

Examples 2–4 emphasize the *equivalence* of three quantities, as follows.

> **Meaning of Normal Curve Areas**
>
> In the standard normal curve, the following three quantities are equivalent.
>
> 1. **Percentage** (of total items that lie in an interval)
> 2. **Probability** (of a randomly chosen item lying in an interval)
> 3. **Area** (under the normal curve along an interval)

Which quantity we think of depends upon how a particular question is formulated. They are all evaluated by using *A*-values from **Table 17**.

In general, when we use **Table 17**, z is the z-score of a particular data item x. When one of these values is known and the other is required, as in **Examples 5 and 6**, we use the formula

$$z = \frac{x - \bar{x}}{s}.$$

▮▮ **EXAMPLE 5** Applying the Normal Curve to Driving Distances

In one area, the distribution of monthly miles driven by motorists has mean 1200 miles and standard deviation 150 miles. Assume that the number of miles is closely approximated by a normal curve, and find the percent of all motorists driving the following distances.

(a) Between 1200 and 1600 miles per month

(b) Between 1000 and 1500 miles per month

A Basic Consumer (T)issue It all started when a reporter on consumer issues for a Midwest TV station received a complaint that rolls of Brand X toilet paper manufactured by Company Y did not have the number of sheets claimed on the wrapper. Brand X is supposed to have 375 sheets, but three rolls of it were found by reporters to have 360, 361, and 363.

Shocked Company Y executives said that the **odds against** six rolls having fewer than 375 sheets each are 1 billion to 1. They counted sheets and found that several rolls of Brand X actually had 380 sheets each (machines count the sheets only in 10s). TV reporters made an independent count, and their results agreed with Company Y.

What happened the first time? Well, the reporters hadn't actually counted sheets, but had measured rolls and divided the length of a roll by the length of one sheet. Small variations in length can be expected, which add up over a roll, giving false results.

This true story perhaps points up the distinction in probability and statistics between **discrete values** and **continuous values**.

SOLUTION

(a) Start by finding how many standard deviations 1600 miles is above the mean. Use the formula for z.

$$z = \frac{1600 - 1200}{150} = \frac{400}{150} \approx 2.67$$

From **Table 17**, 0.496, or 49.6%, of all motorists drive between 1200 and 1600 miles per month.

(b) As shown in **Figure 21**, values of z must be found for both 1000 and 1500.

$$\text{For 1000:} \quad z = \frac{1000 - 1200}{150} = \frac{-200}{150} \approx -1.33$$

$$\text{For 1500:} \quad z = \frac{1500 - 1200}{150} = \frac{300}{150} = 2.00$$

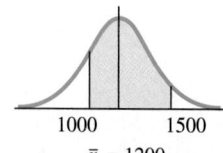

$\bar{x} = 1200$

Figure 21

From **Table 17**, $z = -1.33$ leads to an area of 0.408, while $z = 2.00$ gives 0.477. This means a total of

$$0.408 + 0.477 = 0.885, \quad \text{or} \quad 88.5\%,$$

of all motorists drive between 1000 and 1500 miles per month. ▌▌▌

▌▌ **EXAMPLE 6** Identifying a Data Value Within a Normal Distribution

A particular normal distribution has mean $\bar{x} = 81.7$ and standard deviation $s = 5.21$. What data value from the distribution would correspond to $z = -1.35$?

SOLUTION

Solve for x. $\qquad z = \dfrac{x - \bar{x}}{s}$ $\qquad$ *z*-score formula

$$-1.35 = \frac{x - 81.7}{5.21} \qquad \text{Substitute the given values for } z, \bar{x}, \text{ and } s.$$

$$-1.35(5.21) = \frac{x - 81.7}{5.21}(5.21) \qquad \text{Multiply each side by 5.21 to clear the fraction.}$$

$$-7.0335 = x - 81.7 \qquad \text{Simplify.}$$

$$74.6665 = x \qquad \text{Add 81.7.}$$

Rounding to the nearest tenth, the required data value is 74.7. ▌▌▌

▌▌ **EXAMPLE 7** Finding z-Values for Given Areas Under the Normal Curve

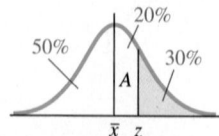

Figure 22

Assuming a normal distribution, find the z-value meeting each condition.

(a) 30% of the total area is to the right of z.

(b) 80% of the total area is to the left of z.

SOLUTION

(a) Because 50% of the area lies to the right of the mean, there must be 20% between the mean and z. (See **Figure 22**.) In **Table 17**, $A = 0.200$ corresponds to $z = 0.52$ or 0.53, or we could average the two: $z = 0.525$.

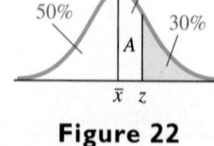

Figure 23

(b) This situation is shown in **Figure 23**. The 50% to the left of the mean plus 30% additional makes up the 80%. From **Table 17**, $A = 0.300$ implies $z = 0.84$. ▌▌▌

12.5 EXERCISES

Note: For problems requiring the calculation of z-scores or A-values, our answers are based on **Table 17**. *By using a calculator or computer package, you will sometimes obtain a slightly more accurate answer.*

Identify each variable quantity as discrete *or* continuous.

1. the number of heads in 50 tossed coins

2. the number of babies born in one day at a certain hospital

3. the average weight of babies born in a week

4. the heights of seedling pine trees at six months of age

5. the time as shown on a digital watch

6. the time as shown on a watch with a sweep hand

Measuring the Mass of Ore Samples *Suppose 100 geology students measure the mass of an ore sample. Due to human error and limitations in the reliability of the balance, not all the readings are equal. The results are found to closely approximate a normal curve, with mean 86 g and standard deviation 1 g.*

Use the symmetry of the normal curve and the empirical rule to estimate the number of students reporting readings in the following ranges.

7. more than 86 g

8. more than 85 g

9. between 85 and 87 g

10. between 84 and 87 g

Distribution of IQ Scores *On standard IQ tests, the mean is 100, with a standard deviation of 15. The results come very close to fitting a normal curve. Suppose an IQ test is given to a very large group of people. Find the percent of people whose IQ scores fall into each category.*

11. less than 100

12. greater than 115

13. between 70 and 130

14. more than 145

Find the percent of area under a normal curve between the mean and the given number of standard deviations from the mean. (Note that positive indicates above the mean, while negative indicates below the mean.)

15. 1.50

16. 0.92

17. −1.08

18. −2.25

Find the percent of the total area under a normal curve between the given values of z.

19. $z = 1.41$ and $z = 1.83$

20. $z = -1.74$ and $z = -1.14$

21. $z = -3.11$ and $z = 2.06$

22. $z = -1.98$ and $z = 1.02$

Find a value of z such that each condition is met.

23. 10% of the total area is to the right of z.

24. 4% of the total area is to the left of z.

25. 9% of the total area is to the left of z.

26. 23% of the total area is to the right of z.

Lifetimes of Lightbulbs *The Better lightbulb has an average life of 600 hr, with a standard deviation of 50 hr. The length of life of the bulb can be closely approximated by a normal curve. A warehouse manager buys and installs 10,000 such bulbs. Find the total number that can be expected to last each amount of time.*

27. at least 600 hr

28. between 600 and 675 hr

29. between 675 and 740 hr

30. between 490 and 720 hr

31. less than 740 hr

32. less than 510 hr

Weights of Chickens *The chickens at Benny and Ann Rice's farm have a mean weight of 1850 g with a standard deviation of 150 g. The weights of the chickens are closely approximated by a normal curve. Find the percent of all chickens having each weight.*

33. more than 1700 g

34. less than 1800 g

35. between 1750 and 1900 g

36. between 1600 and 2000 g

Filling Cereal Boxes *A certain dry cereal is packaged in 24-oz boxes. The machine that fills the boxes is set so that, on the average, a box contains 24.5 oz. The machine-filled boxes have contents weights that can be closely approximated by a normal curve. What percentage of the boxes will be underweight if the standard deviation is as follows?*

37. 0.5 oz

38. 0.4 oz

39. 0.3 oz

40. 0.2 oz

41. *Recommended Daily Vitamin Allowances* In nutrition, the recommended daily allowance of vitamins is a number set by the government to guide an individual's daily vitamin intake. Actually, vitamin needs vary drastically from person to person, but the needs are closely approximated by a normal curve. To calculate the recommended daily allowance, the government first finds the average need for vitamins among people in the population and the standard deviation. The **recommended daily allowance** is then defined as the mean plus 2.5 times the standard deviation. What fraction of the population will receive adequate amounts of vitamins under this plan?

Recommended Daily Vitamin Allowances *Find the recommended daily allowance for each vitamin if the mean need and standard deviation are as follows. (See **Exercise 41**.)*

42. mean need = 1800 units;
standard deviation = 140 units

43. mean need = 159 units;
standard deviation = 12 units

*Assume the following distributions are all normal, and use the areas under the normal curve given in **Table 17** to find the appropriate areas.*

44. *Filling Cartons with Milk* A machine that fills quart milk cartons is set up to average 32.2 oz per carton, with a standard deviation of 1.2 oz. What is the probability that a filled carton will contain less than 32 oz of milk?

45. *Finding Blood Clotting Times* The mean clotting time of blood is 7.47 sec, with a standard deviation of 3.6 sec. What is the probability that an individual's blood-clotting time will be less than 7 sec or greater than 8 sec?

46. *Sizes of Fish* The average length of the fish caught in Lake Amotan is 12.3 in., with a standard deviation of 4.1 in. Find the probability that a fish caught there will be longer than 18 in.

47. *Size Grading of Eggs* To be graded extra large, an egg must weigh at least 2.2 oz. If the average weight for an egg is 1.5 oz, with a standard deviation of 0.4 oz, how many of five dozen randomly chosen eggs would you expect to be extra large?

Distribution of Student Grades *Peter Davis teaches a course in marketing. He uses the following system for assigning grades to his students.*

Grade	Score in Class
A	Greater than $\bar{x} + 1.5s$
B	$\bar{x} + 0.5s$ to $\bar{x} + 1.5s$
C	$\bar{x} - 0.5s$ to $\bar{x} + 0.5s$
D	$\bar{x} - 1.5s$ to $\bar{x} - 0.5s$
F	Below $\bar{x} - 1.5s$

From the information in the table, what percent of the students receive the following grades?

48. A   **49.** B   **50.** C

51. Do you think this system would be more likely to be fair in a large freshman class in psychology or in a graduate seminar of five students? Why?

Normal Distribution of Student Grades *A teacher gives a test to a large group of students. The results are closely approximated by a normal curve. The mean is 75 with a standard deviation of 5. The teacher wishes to give As to the top 8% of the students and Fs to the bottom 8%. A grade of B is given to the next 15%, with Ds given similarly. All other students get Cs. Find the bottom cutoff (rounded to the nearest whole number) for the following grades. (Hint: Use **Table 17** to find z-scores from known A-values.)*

52. A   **53.** B   **54.** C   **55.** D

*A normal distribution has mean 76.8 and standard deviation 9.42. Follow the method of **Example 6** and find data values corresponding to the following values of z. Round to the nearest tenth.*

56. $z = 0.72$ **57.** $z = 1.44$

58. $z = -2.39$ **59.** $z = -3.87$

60. What percentage of the items lie within 1.25 standard deviations of the mean
   (a) in any distribution (using the results of Chebyshev's theorem)?
   (b) in a normal distribution (by **Table 17**)?

61. Explain the difference between the answers to parts (a) and (b) in **Exercise 60**.

EXTENSION Regression and Correlation

Linear Regression • Correlation

Table 18	Age vs. Income	
Resident	Age	Annual Income
A	19	2150
B	23	2550
C	27	3250
D	31	3150
E	36	4250
F	40	4200
G	44	4350
H	49	5000
I	52	4950
J	54	5650

Linear Regression One very important branch of inferential statistics, called **regression analysis,** is used to compare quantities or variables, to discover relationships that exist between them, and to formulate those relationships in useful ways.

Suppose a sociologist gathers data on a few (say ten) of the residents of a small village in a remote region in order to get an idea of how annual income (in dollars) relates to age in that village. The data are shown in **Table 18.**

The first step in analyzing these data is to graph the results, as shown in the **scatter diagram** of **Figure 24.** (Graphing calculators will plot scatter diagrams.)

Once a scatter diagram has been produced, we can draw a curve that best fits the pattern exhibited by the sample data points. This curve can have any one of many characteristic shapes, depending on how the quantities involved are related. The best-fitting curve for the sample points is called an **estimated regression curve.** If, as in the present discussion, the points in the scatter diagram seem to lie approximately along a straight line, the relation is assumed to be linear, and the line that best fits the data points is called the **estimated regression line.**

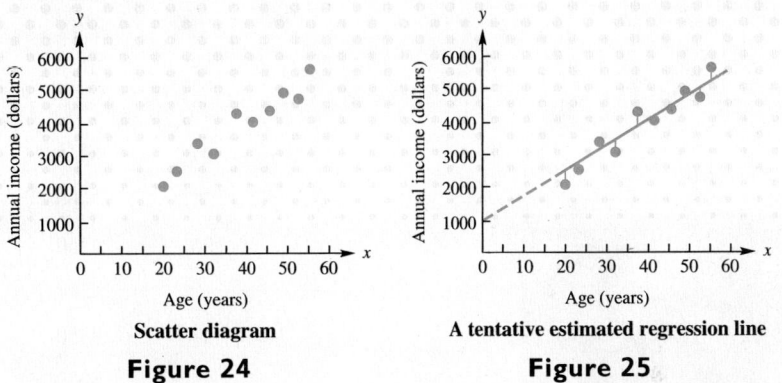

Scatter diagram

Figure 24

A tentative estimated regression line

Figure 25

If we let x denote age and y denote income in the data of **Table 18** and assume that the best-fitting curve is a line, then the equation of that line will take the form

$$y = ax + b,$$

where a is the slope of the line and b is the y-coordinate of the y-intercept (the y-value at which the line, if extended, would intersect the y-axis).

To completely identify the estimated regression line, we must find the values of the **regression coefficients** a and b, which requires some calculation. In **Figure 25**, a *tentative* line has been drawn through the scatter diagram.

For each x-value in the data set, the corresponding y-value usually differs from the value it would have if the data point were exactly on the line. These differences are shown in the figure by vertical segments. Choosing another line would make some of these differences greater and some lesser. The most common procedure is to choose the line where the sum of the squares of all these differences is minimized. This is called the **method of least squares,** and the resulting line is called the **least squares line.**

In the equation of the least squares line, the variable y' can be used to distinguish the *predicted* values (which would give points on the least squares line) from the *observed* values y (those occurring in the data set).

The least squares criterion mentioned above leads to specific values of a and b. We shall not give the details, which involve differential calculus, but the results are given here. (Σ—the Greek letter *sigma*—represents summation just as in earlier sections.)

Regression Coefficient Formulas

The **least squares line** $y' = ax + b$ that provides the best fit to the data points $(x_1, y_1), (x_2, y_2), \ldots, (x_n, y_n)$ has coefficient values as follows.

$$a = \frac{n(\Sigma xy) - (\Sigma x)(\Sigma y)}{n(\Sigma x^2) - (\Sigma x)^2} \qquad b = \frac{\Sigma y - a(\Sigma x)}{n}$$

▌▌ **EXAMPLE 1** Computing and Graphing a Least Squares Line

Find the equation of the least squares line for the age and income data given in **Table 18**. Graph the line.

SOLUTION

Start with the two columns on the left in **Table 19** (which just repeat the original data). Then find the products $x \cdot y$, and the squares x^2.

Table 19   Age and Income Calculations

x	y	$x \cdot y$	x^2
19	2150	40,850	361
23	2550	58,650	529
27	3250	87,750	729
31	3150	97,650	961
36	4250	153,000	1296
40	4200	168,000	1600
44	4350	191,400	1936
49	5000	245,000	2401
52	4950	257,400	2704
54	5650	305,100	2916
Sums: 375	39,500	1,604,800	15,433

From the table, $\Sigma x = 375$, $\Sigma y = 39,500$, $\Sigma xy = 1,604,800$, and $\Sigma x^2 = 15,433$. There are 10 pairs of values, so $n = 10$. Now find a with the formula given above.

$$a = \frac{10(1,604,800) - 375(39,500)}{10(15,433) - (375)^2} = \frac{1,235,500}{13,705} \approx 90.15$$

Finally, use this value of a to find b.

$$b = \frac{39,500 - 90.15(375)}{10} \approx 569.4$$

The equation of the least squares line can now be written.

$$y' = 90x + 569 \qquad \text{Coefficients are rounded.}$$

Letting $x = 20$ in this equation gives $y' = 2369$, and $x = 50$ implies $y' = 5069$. The two points $(20, 2369)$ and $(50, 5069)$ are used to graph the regression line in **Figure 26** on the next page. Notice that the intercept coordinates $(0, 569)$ also fit the extended line.

Francis Galton (1822–1911) learned to read at age three, was interested in mathematics and machines, but was an indifferent mathematics student at Trinity College, Cambridge. He became interested in researching methods of predicting weather. It was during this research that Galton developed early intuitive notions of **correlation** and **regression** and posed the problem of multiple regression.

Galton's key statistical work is *Natural Inheritance*. In it, he set forth his ideas on regression and correlation. He discovered the correlation coefficient while pondering Alphonse Bertillon's scheme for classifying criminals by physical characteristics. It was a major contribution to statistical method.

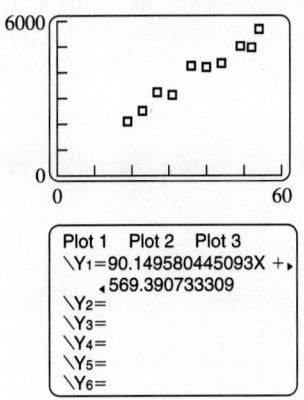

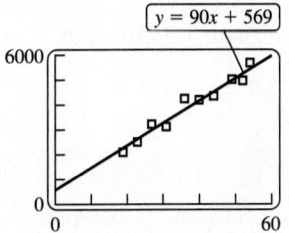

$y = 90x + 569$

The information in **Figure 26** and the accompanying discussion is supported in these screens.

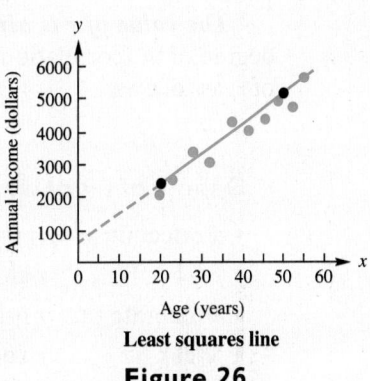

Least squares line

Figure 26   ■■■

A computer or a scientific, statistical, or graphing calculator is recommended for finding regression coefficients. (See the margin notes and the statistical options on **pages 630 and 631.**) Tedious calculations, such as in **Example 1,** can be avoided and the regression line produced automatically.

EXAMPLE 2   Predicting from a Least Squares Line

Use the result of **Example 1** to predict the income of a village resident who is 35 years old.

SOLUTION

$$y' = 90x + 569 \qquad \text{Equation from \textbf{Example 1}}$$
$$y' = 90(35) + 569 \qquad \text{Let } x = 35.$$
$$y' = 3719$$

Based on the given data, a 35-year-old will make about $3719 per year.   ■■■

Correlation Once an equation for the line of best fit (the least squares line) has been found, it is reasonable to ask, "Just how good is this line for predictive purposes?" If the points already observed fit the line quite closely, then future pairs of scores can be expected to do so. If the points are widely scattered about even the "best-fitting" line, then predictions are not likely to be accurate.

In general, the closer the *sample* data points lie to the least squares line, the more likely it is that the entire *population* of (x, y) points really do form a line, that is, that x and y really are related linearly. Also, the better the fit, the more confidence we can have that our least squares line (based on the sample) is a good estimator of the true population line.

One common measure of the strength of the linear relationship in the sample is called the **sample correlation coefficient,** denoted r. It is calculated from the sample data according to the following formula.

Sample Correlation Coefficient Formula

In linear regression, the strength of the linear relationship is measured by the correlation coefficient r, calculated as follows.

$$r = \frac{n(\Sigma xy) - (\Sigma x)(\Sigma y)}{\sqrt{n(\Sigma x^2) - (\Sigma x)^2} \cdot \sqrt{n(\Sigma y^2) - (\Sigma y)^2}}$$

The value of r is always between −1 and 1, or perhaps equal to −1 or 1. The degree of fit (correlation) can be described in general terms, according to the value of r, as follows.

Degree of Fit of an Estimated Regression Line to Sample Data Points

- Perfect fit: $r = 1$ or $r = -1$
- Strong fit: r close (but not equal) to 1 or −1
- Moderate fit: r not close to 0, and not close to 1 or −1
- Weak fit: r equal, or nearly equal, to 0

The sign (plus or minus) of r determines the type of linear relationship, if any, between the variables x and y.

Direct and Inverse Linear Relationships

- If $r > 0$, the regression line has positive slope. The relationship between x and y is ***direct***—as x increases, y also increases.
- If $r < 0$, the regression line has negative slope. The relationship between x and y is ***inverse***—as x increases, y decreases.
- If $r = 0$, no linear relationship between x and y is indicated.

▌▌ EXAMPLE 3 Finding a Correlation Coefficient

Find r for the age and income data of **Table 19** on **page 678.**

SOLUTION

Almost all values needed to find r were computed in **Example 1.**

$$n = 10 \quad \Sigma x = 375 \quad \Sigma y = 39{,}500 \quad \Sigma xy = 1{,}604{,}800 \quad \Sigma x^2 = 15{,}433$$

The only missing value is Σy^2. Squaring each y in the original data and adding the squares gives

$$\Sigma y^2 = 167{,}660{,}000.$$

Now use the formula to find that $r = 0.98$ (to two decimal places). This value of r, very close to 1, shows that age and income in this village are highly correlated. (The fit of the estimated regression line is strong.) The fact that r is positive indicates that the linear relationship is direct; as age increases, income also increases. ▌▌▌

> LinReg
> y=ax+b
> a=90.14958045
> b=569.3907333
> r²=.9572823948
> r=.9784080922

The slope a and y-intercept b of the regression equation, along with r^2 and r, are given. Compare with **Examples 1 and 3.**

▌▌ EXAMPLE 4 Analyzing the Aging Trend in the U.S. Population

The World Almanac and Book of Facts 2010 (page 622) reported the following U.S. Census Bureau data concerning the aging U.S. population over the last century.

Year	1910	1920	1930	1940	1950	1960	1970	1980	1990	2000	2010
Percent 65 and over	4.3	4.7	5.4	6.8	8.1	9.2	9.8	11.3	12.5	12.4	13.0

Let x represent time, in decades, from 1910, so $x = 0$ in 1910, $x = 1$ in 1920, $x = 2$ in 1930, and so on. Let y represent percent 65 and over in the population. Based on the data table, carry out the following.

(a) Plot a scatter diagram.

(b) Compute and graph the least squares regression line.

(c) Compute the correlation coefficient.

(d) Use the regression line to predict the percent 65 and over in 2050, and discuss the validity of the prediction.

SOLUTION

(a) The data points are plotted in **Figure 27**.

(b) We entered the x- and y-values into lists L1 and L2, respectively, in a calculator to obtain the equation of the least squares regression line.

$$y' = 0.97x + 4.03 \qquad \text{Coefficients are rounded.}$$

This line is shown in **Figure 27** as a dashed line.

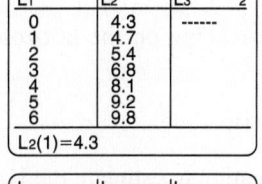

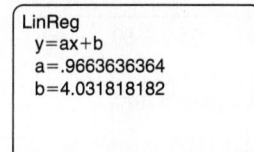

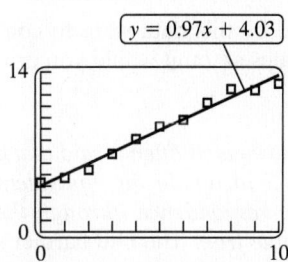

These screens support **Example 4(b)**.

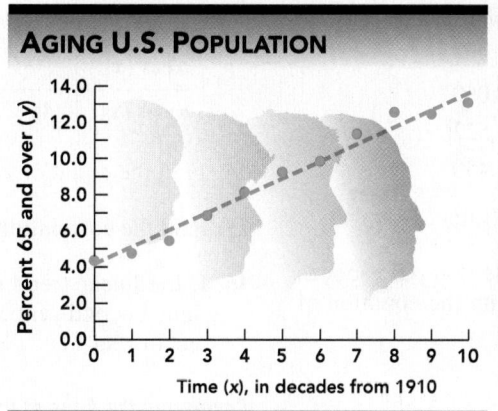

Figure 27

(c) $\Sigma x = 55$, $\Sigma x^2 = 385$, $n = 11$, $\Sigma y = 97.5$,
$\Sigma y^2 = 968.97$, $\Sigma(xy) = 593.8$

All values are from the calculator, using two-variable statistics.

$$r = \frac{n(\Sigma xy) - (\Sigma x)(\Sigma y)}{\sqrt{n(\Sigma x^2) - (\Sigma x)^2} \cdot \sqrt{n(\Sigma y^2) - (\Sigma y)^2}} \qquad \text{Correlation coefficient formula}$$

$$= \frac{11 \cdot 593.8 - 55 \cdot 97.5}{\sqrt{11 \cdot 385 - 55^2} \cdot \sqrt{11 \cdot 968.97 - 97.5^2}}$$

$$= 0.990211\ldots$$

$$r \approx 0.99$$

(d) $y' = 0.97x + 4.03 \qquad$ Estimated regression line

$\quad = 0.97 \cdot 14 + 4.03 \qquad$ The year 2050 corresponds to $x = 14$.

$y \approx 17.6 \qquad$ 17.61 has been rounded here.

Although the correlation was strong ($r \approx 0.99$) for the data points we had, it is risky to extrapolate a regression line too far out. There may be factors (such as declining numbers of baby boomers in the population) that may slow the aging phenomenon. (Incidentally, the Census Bureau projects 20.2% in 2050.) ▪▪▪

EXTENSION EXERCISES

Correlating Fertilizer and Corn Ear Size *In a study to determine the linear relationship between the length (in decimeters) of an ear of corn (y) and the amount (in tons per acre) of fertilizer used (x), the following values were determined.*

$$n = 10 \qquad \Sigma xy = 75$$
$$\Sigma x = 30 \qquad \Sigma x^2 = 100$$
$$\Sigma y = 24 \qquad \Sigma y^2 = 80$$

1. Find an equation for the least squares line.

2. Find the correlation coefficient.

3. If 3 tons per acre of fertilizer are used, what length (in decimeters) would the regression equation predict for an ear of corn?

Correlating Celsius and Fahrenheit Temperatures *In an experiment to determine the linear relationship between temperatures on the Celsius scale (y) and on the Fahrenheit scale (x), a student got the following results.*

$$n = 5 \qquad \Sigma xy = 28{,}050$$
$$\Sigma x = 376 \qquad \Sigma x^2 = 62{,}522$$
$$\Sigma y = 120 \qquad \Sigma y^2 = 13{,}450$$

4. Find an equation for the least squares line.

5. Find the reading on the Celsius scale that corresponds to a reading of 120° Fahrenheit, using the equation of **Exercise 4.**

6. Find the correlation coefficient.

Correlating Heights and Weights of Adult Men *A sample of 10 adult men gave the following data on their heights and weights.*

Height (inches) (x)	62	62	63	65	66
Weight (pounds) (y)	120	140	130	150	142

Height (inches) (x)	67	68	68	70	72
Weight (pounds) (y)	130	135	175	149	168

7. Find the equation of the least squares line.

8. Using the results of **Exercise 7,** predict the weight of a man whose height is 60 inches.

9. What would be the predicted weight of a man whose height is 70 inches?

10. Compute the correlation coefficient.

Correlating Reading Ability and IQs *The table below gives reading ability scores and IQs for a group of 10 individuals.*

Reading (x)	83	76	75	85	74
IQ (y)	120	104	98	115	87

Reading (x)	90	75	78	95	80
IQ (y)	127	90	110	134	119

11. Plot a scatter diagram with reading on the horizontal axis.

12. Find the equation of a regression line.

13. Use your regression line equation to estimate the IQ of a person with a reading score of 65.

Correlating Yearly Sales of a Company *Sales, in thousands of dollars, of a certain company are shown here.*

Year (x)	0	1	2	3	4	5
Sales (y)	48	59	66	75	80	90

14. Find the equation of the least squares line.

15. Find the correlation coefficient.

16. If the linear trend displayed by this data were to continue beyond year 5, what sales amount would you predict in year 7?

Comparing the Ages of Dogs and Humans *It often is said that a dog's age can be multiplied by 7 to obtain the equivalent human age. A more accurate correspondence (through the first 14 years) is shown in this table from* The Old Farmer's Almanac, *2000 edition, page 180.*

Dog age (x)	$\frac{1}{2}$	1	2	3	4	5	6	7
Equivalent human age (y)	10	15	24	28	32	36	40	44

Dog age (x)	8	9	10	11	12	13	14
Equivalent human age (y)	48	52	56	60	64	68	70.5

17. Plot a scatter diagram for the given data.

18. Find the equation of the regression line, and graph the line on the scatter diagram of **Exercise 17.**

19. Describe where the data points show the most pronounced departure from the regression line, and explain why this might be so.

20. Compute the correlation coefficient.

Statistics on the Westward Population Movement *The data show the increase in the percentage of U.S. population in the West since about the time of the California Gold Rush.*

Census Year	Time, in Decades from 1850 (x)	Percentage in West (y)
1850	0	0.8%
1870	2	2.6
1890	4	5.0
1910	6	7.7
1930	8	10.0
1950	10	13.3
1970	12	17.1
1990	14	21.2

Source: The World Almanac and Book of Facts 2000.

21. Taking x and y as indicated in the table, find the equation of the regression line.

22. Compute the correlation coefficient.

23. Describe the degree of correlation (for example, as strong, moderate, or weak).

24. Would you expect the linear trend apparent in the table to persist into the mid 21st century? Why or why not?

Comparing State Populations with Governors' Salaries *The table shows the ten most populous states (as of 2008) and the salaries of their governors (as of September 2009).*

Rank	State	Population, in Millions (x)	Governor's Salary, in Thousands of Dollars (y)
1	California	37	174
2	Texas	24	150
3	New York	19	179
4	Florida	18	130
5	Illinois	13	177
6	Pennsylvania	12	175
7	Ohio	11	142
8	Michigan	10	177
9	Georgia	10	139
10	North Carolina	9	140

Source: The World Almanac and Book of Facts 2010.

25. Find the equation of the estimated regression line.

26. Compute the correlation coefficient.

27. Describe the degree of correlation (for example, as strong, moderate, or weak).

28. What governor's salary would this linear model predict for a state with a population of 15 million citizens?

COLLABORATIVE INVESTIGATION

Combining Sets of Data

Divide your class into two separate groups, one consisting of the women and the other consisting of the men. Each group is to select a recorder to write the group's results. As a group, carry out the following tasks. (You may want to devise a way to allow the members of the groups to provide personal data anonymously.)

1. Record the number of members (n) in your group.

2. Collect shoe sizes (x) and heights in inches (y) for all members of the group.

3. Compute the mean, median, and mode(s), if any, for each of the two sets of data.

4. Compute the standard deviation of each of the two sets of data.

5. Construct a box plot for each of the two sets of data.

6. Plot a scatter diagram for the x-y data collected.

7. Find the equation of the least squares regression line

$$y' = ax + b.$$

8. Evaluate the correlation coefficient (*r*).

9. Evaluate the strength of the linear relationship between shoe size and height for your group.

Now re-combine your two groups into one. Discuss and carry out the following tasks.

1. If possible, compute the mean of the heights for the combined group, using only the means for the two individual groups and the number of members in each of the two groups. If this is not possible, explain why and describe how you *could* find the combined mean. Obtain the combined mean.

2. Do the same as in item 1 above for the median of the heights for the combined group.

3. Do the same for the mode of the heights for the combined group.

4. Fill in the table below, pertaining to heights, and discuss any apparent relationships among the computed statistics.

	Number of Members	Mean	Median	Mode
Women				
Men				
Combined				

CHAPTER 12 TEST

Cheaters Never Learn *The table here shows the results of an educational study of university physics students, comparing exam scores with students' rates of copying others' homework. The numbers in the table approximate letter grades on a 4-point scale (4.0 is an A, 3.0 is a B, and so on). Answer the questions in Exercises 1–4 in terms of copy rate.*

Copy Rate	Pretest	Exam 1	Exam 2	Exam 3	Final exam
<10%	2.70	2.75	2.90	2.80	2.95
10% to 30%	2.50	2.45	2.35	2.40	2.30
30% to 50%	2.45	2.43	2.30	2.10	2.00
>50%	2.40	2.05	1.70	1.80	1.60

Source: Table created using data from research reported in Physics Review-Special Topics-Physics Education *by David J. Palazzo, Young-Jin Lee, Rasil Warnakulasooriya, and David E. Pritchard of the Massachusetts Institute of Technology (MIT) physics faculty.*

1. Which students generally improved their exam performance over the course of the semester?

2. Which students did better on exam 3 than or exam 2?

3. Which students had lower scores consistently from one exam to the next throughout the semester?

4. Do you think that copying homework is generally a *cause* of lower exam scores? Explain.

5. *Crude Oil Production* The table in the right column above shows total 2008 production of crude oil (in millions of barrels) by the five top-producing states.

State	Total
Texas	398
Alaska	250
California	215
Louisiana	73
Oklahoma	64

Source: Energy Information Administration.

Use this information to determine each of the following.

(a) the mean production per state

(b) the range

(c) the standard deviation

(d) the coefficient of variation

(e) If 26 additional lesser producing states averaged (mean) 14 million barrels in 2008, what was the mean production for all 31 states?

Champion Trees *The table on the next page lists the 9 largest national champion trees, based on the formula*

$$T = G + H + 0.25C,$$

where $T = total points,$

  $G = girth$ (*circumference of trunk 4.5 feet above the ground*),

  $H = height,$

and $C = average \ crown \ spread.$

Tree Type	G (in.)	H (ft)	C (ft)	T	Location
Giant sequoia	1020	274	107	1321	Sequoia National Park, CA
Coast redwood	950	321	75	1290	Jedediah Smith Redwoods State Park, CA
Coast redwood	895	307	83	1223	Jedediah Smith Redwoods State Park, CA
Coast redwood	867	311	101	1203	Prairie Creek Redwoods State Park, CA
Western red cedar	761	159	45	931	Olympic National Park, WA
Sitka spruce	668	191	96	883	Olympic National Park, WA
Douglas-fir	512	301	65	829	Jedediah Smith Redwoods State Park, CA
Douglas-fir	505	281	71	804	Olympia National Forest, WA
Port-Orford cedar	522	242	35	773	Siskiyou National Forest, OR

Source: The World Almanac and Book of Facts 2010.

Use this information for Exercises 6 and 7.

6. For the nine trees listed, find the following.
   (a) the median height
   (b) the first quartile in girth
   (c) the eighth decile in total points

7. The tenth ranking tree in the country is a Common Bald Cypress on Cat Island, LA, with $G = 647$ inches, $H = 96$ feet, and $C = 74$ feet. For this tree, answer the following questions.
   (a) Find its total points.
   (b) Where would it have ranked based on girth alone?
   (c) How much taller would it have needed to be to displace the ninth ranked tree?
   (d) Assuming roughly a circular cross-section at 4.5 feet above the ground, approximate the diameter of the trunk (to the nearest foot) at that height.

Stimulus Bill The table shows seven major categories (in alphabetical order) of the 2009 congressional stimulus bill (total $787 billion).

Expenditure Category	Budgeted Amount ($ billions)
1. Education and Job Training	128.2
2. Energy	70.3
3. Environment	15.6
4. Health	152.0
5. Housing	20.5
6. Infrastructure	32.1
7. Transportation	48.2

Source: Congressional Budget Office.

8. Construct a bar graph for these data.

9. What percentage was assigned to health?

10. If $20 billion was allocated to health care–related information technology, what percentage of the total package went to *other* health categories?

11. What percentage was allocated to the three greatest categories combined?

Client Contacts of a Publisher's Representative Tami Dreyfus, a publishing company representative, recorded the following numbers of client contacts for twenty-two days in March. Use the given data for Exercises 12–14.

12	8	15	11	20	18	14	22	13	26	17
19	16	25	19	10	7	18	24	15	30	24

12. Construct grouped frequency and relative frequency distributions. Use five uniform classes of width 5 where the first class has a lower limit of 6. (Round relative frequencies to two decimal places.)

13. From your frequency distribution of **Exercise 12,** construct (a) a histogram and (b) a frequency polygon. Use appropriate scales and labels.

14. For the data above, how many uniform classes would be required if the first class had limits 7–9?

In Exercises 15–18, find the indicated measures for the following frequency distribution.

Value	8	10	12	14	16	18
Frequency	3	8	10	8	5	1

15. the mean

16. the median

17. the mode

18. the range

19. *Exam Scores in a Physics Class* The following data are exam scores achieved by the students in a physics class. Arrange the data into a stem-and-leaf display with leaves ranked.

79	43	65	84	77	70	52	61	80	66
68	48	55	78	71	38	45	64	67	73
77	50	67	91	84	33	49	61	79	72

Use the stem-and-leaf display shown here for Exercises 20–25.

2	3 3 4
2	6 7 8 9 9
3	0 1 1 2 3 3 3 4
3	5 6 7 8 8 9
4	1 2 2 4
4	5 7 9
5	2 4
5	8
6	0

Compute the measures required in Exercises 20–24.

20. the median

21. the mode(s), if any

22. the range

23. the third decile

24. the eighty-fifth percentile

25. Construct a box plot for the given data, showing values for the five important quantities on the numerical scale.

26. *Test Scores in a Training Institute* A certain training institute gives a standardized test to large numbers of applicants nationwide. The resulting scores form a normal distribution with mean 80 and standard deviation 5. Find the percent of all applicants with scores as follows. (Use the empirical rule.)

(a) between 70 and 90

(b) greater than 95 or less than 65

(c) less than 75

(d) between 85 and 90

Heights of Spruce Trees *In a certain young forest, the heights of the spruce trees are normally distributed with mean 5.5 meters and standard deviation 2.1 meters. If a single tree is selected randomly, find the probability (to the nearest thousandth) that its height will fall in each of the following intervals.*

27. less than 6.5 meters

28. between 6.2 and 9.4 meters

Season Statistics in Major League Baseball *The tables below show the 2009 statistics on games won for all three divisions of both major baseball leagues. In each case,*

$$n = \text{number of teams in the division,}$$
$$\bar{x} = \text{average (mean) number of games won,}$$
and $\quad s = \text{standard deviation of number of games won.}$

American League

East Division	Central Division	West Division
$n = 5$	$n = 5$	$n = 4$
$\bar{x} = 84.2$	$\bar{x} = 76.4$	$\bar{x} = 86.0$
$s = 15.5$	$s = 10.9$	$s = 9.0$

National League

East Division	Central Division	West Division
$n = 5$	$n = 6$	$n = 5$
$\bar{x} = 79.0$	$\bar{x} = 78.0$	$\bar{x} = 84.0$
$s = 14.1$	$s = 9.7$	$s = 10.9$

Refer to the preceding tables for Exercises 29–31.

29. Overall, who had the greatest winning average, the East teams, the Central teams, or the West teams?

30. Overall, where were the teams the least "consistent" in number of games won, East, Central, or West?

31. Find (to the nearest tenth) the average number of games won for all West Division teams.

32. The Boston Red Sox, in the East Division of the American League, and the Los Angeles Dodgers, in the West Division of the National League, each won 95 games. Use z-scores to determine which of these two teams did relatively better within its own division of 5 teams.

PERSONAL FINANCIAL MANAGEMENT

13

The second season of *The Andy Griffith Show* provided an episode that beautifully illustrated an application of the mathematics of finance. In "Mayberry Goes Bankrupt," Sheriff Taylor was reluctantly forced to evict kindly old gentleman Frank Myers from his home due to nonpayment of taxes. But Frank then produced a bond purchased for $100 in 1861 and paying 8.5% interest compounded annually. It had been stored away for 100 years. When the town banker told the Mayor he could not pay Frank, Andy explained why this was so.

> *Well, Mayor ... according to the computation machines down at the bank ... and they're good machines ... we ... owe Frank Myers $349,119.27. (To which Frank responds: I'll take it in cash.)*

By applying the formula for *compound interest* found in **Section 13.1,** you will find that the figure quoted is correct to the penny.

13.1 THE TIME VALUE OF MONEY

Interest • Simple Interest • Future Value and Present Value • Compound Interest
• Effective Annual Yield • Inflation

Interest

To determine the value of money, we consider not only the amount (number of dollars) but also the particular point in time that the value is to be determined. If we borrow an amount of money today, we will repay a larger amount later. This increase in value is known as **interest.** The money *gains value over time.*

The amount of a loan or a deposit is called the **principal.** The interest is usually computed as a percent of the principal. This percent is called the **rate of interest** (or the **interest rate,** or simply the **rate**). The rate of interest is always assumed to be an annual rate unless otherwise stated.

Interest calculated only on principal is called **simple interest.** Interest calculated on principal plus any previously earned interest is called **compound interest.**

Simple Interest

Simple interest is calculated according to the following formula.

> **Simple Interest**
>
> If P = principal, r = annual interest rate, and t = time (in years), then the **simple interest** I is calculated as follows.
>
> $$I = Prt$$

▌▌ **EXAMPLE 1** Finding Simple Interest

Find the simple interest paid to borrow $5350 for 5 months at 6%.

SOLUTION

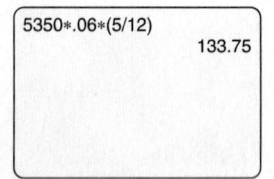

This is the computation required to solve
Example 1.

$$I = Prt \qquad \text{Simple interest formula}$$

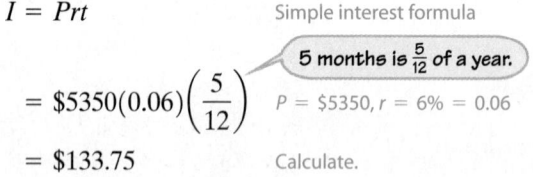

$$= \$5350(0.06)\left(\frac{5}{12}\right) \qquad P = \$5350, r = 6\% = 0.06$$

$$= \$133.75 \qquad \text{Calculate.}$$ ▌▌▌

Future Value and Present Value

In **Example 1,** at the end of 5 months the borrower would have to repay.

Principal   Interest
↓   ↓
$5350   + $133.75 = $5483.75.

The total amount repaid is sometimes called the **maturity value** (or simply the **value**) of the loan. We will generally refer to it as the **future value,** or **future amount,** since when a loan is being set up, repayment will be occurring in the future. We use A to denote future amount (or value). The original principal, denoted P, can also be thought of as **present value.**

Future value depends on principal (present value) and interest as follows.

$$A = P + I = P + Prt = P(1 + rt)$$

> ### Future Value for Simple Interest
>
> If a principal P is borrowed at simple interest for t years at an annual interest rate of r, then the **future value** of the loan, denoted A, is calculated as follows.
>
> $$A = P(1 + rt)$$

▌▌ **EXAMPLE 2** Finding Future Value for Simple Interest

James Albertone took out a simple interest loan for $210 to purchase textbooks and school supplies. If the annual interest rate is 6% and he must repay the loan after 8 months, find the future value (the maturity value) of the loan.

SOLUTION

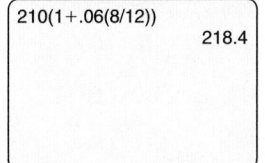

210(1+.06(8/12))

                    218.4

This is the computation required to solve **Example 2.**

$$A = P(1 + rt) \qquad \text{Future value formula}$$

$$= \$210\left[1 + 0.06\left(\frac{8}{12}\right)\right] \qquad P = \$210, r = 6\% = 0.06, t = \frac{8}{12}$$

$$= \$218.40 \qquad \text{Calculate.}$$

At the end of 8 months, James will need to repay $218.40.   ▌▌▌

Sometimes the future value is known, and we need to compute the present value. For this purpose, we solve the future value formula for P.

$$A = P(1 + rt) \qquad \text{Future value formula for simple interest}$$

$$P = \frac{A}{1 + rt} \qquad \text{Solve the formula for } P.$$

▌▌ **EXAMPLE 3** Finding Present Value for Simple Interest

Suppose that James (**Example 2**) is granted an 8-month *deferral* of the $210 payment rather than a loan. That is, instead of incurring interest for 8 months, he will have to pay just the $210 at the end of that period. If he has extra money right now, and if he can earn 2% simple interest on savings, what lump sum must he deposit now so that its value will be $210 after 8 months?

SOLUTION

210/(1+.02(8/12))

                    207.24

This is the computation required to solve **Example 3.**

$$P = \frac{A}{1 + rt} \qquad \text{Future value formula solved for } P$$

$$P = \frac{\$210}{1 + (0.02)\left(\frac{8}{12}\right)} = \$207.24 \qquad \text{Substitute known values and simplify.}$$

A deposit of $207.24 now, growing at 2% simple interest, will grow to $210 over an 8-month period.   ▌▌▌

Compound Interest

Interest paid on principal plus interest is called *compound interest*. After a certain period, the interest earned so far is *credited* (added) to the account, and the sum (principal plus interest) then earns interest during the next period.

███ **EXAMPLE 4** Comparing Simple and Compound Interest

Compare simple and compound interest for a $1000 deposit at 4% interest for 5 years.

SOLUTION

$$A = P(1 + rt) \qquad \text{Future value formula}$$

$$= \$1000(1 + 0.04 \cdot 5) \quad \text{\scriptsize P = \$1000, r = 4\% = 0.04, t = 5}$$

$$= \$1200 \qquad\qquad \text{Calculate.}$$

After 5 years, $1000 grows to $1200 subject to 4% simple interest.

The result of compounding (annually) for 5 years is shown in **Table 1**.

Table 1	A $1000 Deposit at 4% Interest Compounded Annually		
Year	Beginning Balance	Interest Earned $I = Prt$	Ending Balance
1	$1000.00	$1000.00(0.04)(1) = $40.00	$1040.00
2	$1040.00	$1040.00(0.04)(1) = $41.60	$1081.60
3	$1081.60	$1081.60(0.04)(1) = $43.26	$1124.86
4	$1124.86	$1124.86(0.04)(1) = $44.99	$1169.85
5	$1169.85	$1169.85(0.04)(1) = $46.79	$1216.64

Under annual compounding for 5 years, $1000 grows to $1216.64, which is $16.64 more than under simple interest. ███

Based on the compounding pattern of **Example 4,** we now develop a future value formula for compound interest. In practice, earned interest can be credited to an account at time intervals other than 1 year (usually more often). For example, it can be done semiannually, quarterly, monthly, or daily. This time interval is called the **compounding period** (or simply the **period**). Start with the following definitions:

P = original principal deposited, r = annual interest rate,

m = number of periods per year, n = total number of periods.

During each individual compounding period, interest is earned according to the simple interest formula, and as interest is added, the beginning principal increases from one period to the next. During the first period, the interest earned is given by

$$\text{Interest} = P(r)\left(\frac{1}{m}\right) \qquad \text{\scriptsize Interest = (Principal)(rate)(time), one period = \frac{1}{m} year}$$

$$= P\left(\frac{r}{m}\right). \qquad \text{\scriptsize Rewrite $(r)(\frac{1}{m})$ as $(\frac{r}{m})$.}$$

At the end of the first period, the account then contains

$$\text{\scriptsize Beginning amount \quad Interest}$$
$$\downarrow \qquad \downarrow$$
$$\text{Ending amount} = P + P\left(\frac{r}{m}\right)$$

$$= P\left(1 + \frac{r}{m}\right). \quad \text{\scriptsize Factor P from both terms.}$$

To borrow from the title of the Clint Eastwood classic *The Good, the Bad, and the Ugly*, the 1994 movie *Blank Check* includes a scene that qualifies as **ugly mathematics.** Twelve-year-old Preston Waters receives a check for $11.00 and uses his computer to determine how long it will take for this amount to grow to $1,000,000 at 3.45% annual interest.

While there is no information on the number of compounding periods, the answer given in the movie is incorrect for any number. The computer determines that it would take 342,506 years. Even with interest compounded just once a year, the time would "only" be 337 years.

King Hammurabi tried to hold interest rates at 20 percent for both silver and gold, but moneylenders ignored his decrees.

Now during the second period, the interest earned is given by

$$\text{Interest} = \left[P\left(1 + \frac{r}{m}\right)\right](r)\left(\frac{1}{m}\right) \quad \text{Interest = [Principal] (rate) (time)}$$

$$= P\left(1 + \frac{r}{m}\right)\left(\frac{r}{m}\right),$$

so that the account ends the second period containing

$$\text{Ending amount} = \overset{\text{Beginning amount}}{P\left(1 + \frac{r}{m}\right)} + \overset{\text{Interest}}{P\left(1 + \frac{r}{m}\right)\left(\frac{r}{m}\right)}$$

$$= P\left(1 + \frac{r}{m}\right)\left[1 + \frac{r}{m}\right] \quad \text{Factor } P(1 + \tfrac{r}{m}) \text{ from both terms.}$$

$$= P\left(1 + \frac{r}{m}\right)^2. \quad a \cdot a = a^2$$

Consider one more period, namely, the third. The interest earned is

$$\text{Interest} = \left[P\left(1 + \frac{r}{m}\right)^2\right](r)\left(\frac{1}{m}\right) \quad \text{Interest = [Principal](rate) (time)}$$

$$= P\left(1 + \frac{r}{m}\right)^2\left(\frac{r}{m}\right),$$

so the account ends the third period containing

$$\text{Ending amount} = \overset{\text{Beginning amount}}{P\left(1 + \frac{r}{m}\right)^2} + \overset{\text{Interest}}{P\left(1 + \frac{r}{m}\right)^2\left(\frac{r}{m}\right)}$$

$$= P\left(1 + \frac{r}{m}\right)^2\left[1 + \frac{r}{m}\right] \quad \text{Factor } P(1 + \tfrac{r}{m})^2 \text{ from both terms.}$$

$$= P\left(1 + \frac{r}{m}\right)^3. \quad a^2 \cdot a = a^3$$

Table 2 summarizes the preceding results.

	Table 2	**Compound Amount**	
Period Number	**Beginning Amount**	**Interest Earned During Period**	**Ending Amount**
1	P	$P\left(\frac{r}{m}\right)$	$P\left(1 + \frac{r}{m}\right)$
2	$P\left(1 + \frac{r}{m}\right)$	$P\left(1 + \frac{r}{m}\right)\left(\frac{r}{m}\right)$	$P\left(1 + \frac{r}{m}\right)^2$
3	$P\left(1 + \frac{r}{m}\right)^2$	$P\left(1 + \frac{r}{m}\right)^2\left(\frac{r}{m}\right)$	$P\left(1 + \frac{r}{m}\right)^3$
⋮	⋮	⋮	⋮
n	$P\left(1 + \frac{r}{m}\right)^{n-1}$	$P\left(1 + \frac{r}{m}\right)^{n-1}\left(\frac{r}{m}\right)$	$\mathbf{P\left(1 + \frac{r}{m}\right)^n}$

The lower right entry of **Table 2** provides the following formula.

The quantity

$$\left(1 + \frac{r}{m}\right)^n$$

can be evaluated using a key such as y^x on a scientific calculator or $\wedge$ on a graphing calculator.

Future Value for Compound Interest

If P dollars are deposited at an annual interest rate of r, compounded m times per year, and the money is left on deposit for a total of n periods, then the **future value, A** (the final amount on deposit), is calculated as follows.

$$A = P\left(1 + \frac{r}{m}\right)^n$$

▌▌ **EXAMPLE 5** Finding Future Value for Compound Interest

Find the future value (final amount on deposit) and the amount of interest earned for the following deposits.

(a) $12,450 at 3% compounded quarterly for 5 years

(b) $3419 at 4.1% compounded monthly for 30 months

SOLUTION

(a) Here $P = \$12{,}450$, $r = 3\% = 0.03$, and $m = 4$. Over 5 years,

$$n = 5m = (5)(4) = 20.$$

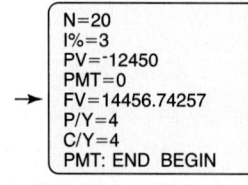

```
N=20
I%=3
PV=-12450
PMT=0
FV=14456.74257
P/Y=4
C/Y=4
PMT: END  BEGIN
```

The financial functions of the TI-83/84 Plus calculator allow the user to solve for a missing quantity regarding the time value of money. The arrow indicates the display that supports the future value answer in **Example 5(a).**

We use the future value formula and a calculator.

$$A = \$12{,}450\left(1 + \frac{0.03}{4}\right)^{20} = \$14{,}456.74$$

Now we subtract to find the interest earned.

$$\overset{\text{Future value}}{\downarrow} \quad \overset{\text{Present value}}{\downarrow}$$
$$\text{Interest earned} = \$14{,}456.74 - \$12{,}450$$
$$= \$2006.74$$

(b) Here $P = \$3419$, $r = 4.1\% = 0.041$, $m = 12$, and $n = 30$.

$$A = \$3419\left(1 + \frac{0.041}{12}\right)^{30} = \$3787.38$$

$$\overset{\text{Future value}}{\downarrow} \quad \overset{\text{Present value}}{\downarrow}$$
$$\text{Interest earned} = \$3787.38 - \$3419$$
$$= \$368.38 \qquad\qquad ▋▋▋$$

Compound interest problems sometimes require that we solve the formula for P to compute the present value when the future value is known.

$$A = P\left(1 + \frac{r}{m}\right)^n \qquad \text{Future value for compound interest}$$

$$P = \frac{A}{\left(1 + \frac{r}{m}\right)^n} \qquad \text{Solve the formula for } P.$$

The 1957 movie *The Pajama Game* was inspired by the Broadway musical of the same name. It was recently revived on Broadway and starred Harry Connick, Jr. The female lead in the movie, "Babe" Williams, was played by Doris Day. She and her coworkers at the Sleeptite Pajama Factory were attempting to get a $7\frac{1}{2}$ cent per hour raise.

The musical number **"Seven and a Half Cents"** features three computations, determining how much this seemingly small raise will earn in three time periods. Based on pencil and paper calculations, the lyrics state that in 5 years, the raise will amount to $852.74, in 10 years $1705.48, and in 20 years $3411.96. Assuming that the figure for 5 years is correct, is the one for 10 years also correct? Now, how about the one for 20 years? Oops!

▮▮ **EXAMPLE 6**   Finding Present Value for Compound Interest

Lisa Ashley will need $27,000 in 5 years to help pay for her college education. What lump sum, deposited today at 4% compounded quarterly, will produce the necessary amount?

SOLUTION

This question requires that we find the present value P based on the following.

Future value:	$A = \$27{,}000$
Annual rate:	$r = 4\% = 0.04$
Periods per year:	$m = 4$
Total number of periods:	$n = (5)(4) = 20$

$$P = \frac{A}{\left(1 + \frac{r}{m}\right)^n} \qquad \text{Future value formula solved for } P$$

$$P = \frac{\$27{,}000}{\left(1 + \frac{0.04}{4}\right)^{20}} \qquad \text{Substitute known values.}$$

$$P = \$22{,}127.70 \qquad \text{Calculate.}$$

Assuming interest of 4% compounded quarterly can be maintained, $27,000 can be attained 5 years in the future by depositing $22,127.70 today.   ▮▮▮

The next example uses logarithms. See the discussion of logarithms in **Section 8.6** (or your calculator manual).

▮▮ **EXAMPLE 7**   Finding the Time Required to Double a Principal Deposit

In a savings account paying 3% interest, compounded daily, when will the amount in the account be twice the original principal?

SOLUTION

The future value must equal two times the present value.

$$2P = P\left(1 + \frac{r}{m}\right)^n \qquad \text{Substitute } 2P \text{ for } A \text{ in the future value formula.}$$

$$2 = \left(1 + \frac{r}{m}\right)^n \qquad \text{Divide both sides by } P.$$

$$2 = \left(1 + \frac{0.03}{365}\right)^n \qquad \text{Substitute values of } r \text{ and } m.$$

$$\log 2 = \log\left(1 + \frac{0.03}{365}\right)^n \qquad \text{Take the logarithm of both sides.}$$

$$\log 2 = n \log\left(1 + \frac{0.03}{365}\right) \qquad \text{Use the power property of logarithms.}$$

$$n = \frac{\log 2}{\log\left(1 + \frac{0.03}{365}\right)} \qquad \text{Solve for } n.$$

$$n = 8434 \qquad \text{Round to the nearest whole number.}$$

Because n denotes the number of periods, which is days in this case, the required amount of time is 8434 days, or 23 years, 39 days (ignoring leap years).   ▮▮▮

Example 8 shows the importance of starting early to maximize the long-term advantage of compounding.

The power of compound interest is being put to use in the town of Union City, Michigan. Eli Hooker, chairman of the local Bicentennial Committee in 1976, saw that there was not enough money to put on a proper celebration that year. So, in order to help his town prepare for the tricentennial, in 2076, he collected twenty-five dollars apiece from 42 patriotic residents and deposited the money in a local bank. Compounded at seven percent, that money would grow to a million dollars by 2076.

Unfortunately, the million dollars won't be worth as much then as we might think. If the community decides to hire people to parade around in historical costumes, it might have paid them $4 per hour in 1976. The going wage in 2076, assuming 7% annual inflation for a hundred years, would be well over $3000 per hour.

▌▌ EXAMPLE 8 Comparing Retirement Plans

Compare the results at age 65 for the following two retirement plans. Both plans earn 8% annual interest throughout the account building period.

Plan A: Gina Fox begins saving at age 20, deposits $2000 on every birthday from age 21 to age 30 (10 deposits, or $20,000 total), and thereafter makes no additional contributions.

Plan B: Peter Harris waits until age 30 to start saving, makes deposits of $2000 on every birthday from age 31 to age 65 (35 deposits, or $70,000 total).

SOLUTION

Table 3 shows how both accounts build over the years. $20,000, deposited earlier, produces $83,744 more than $70,000, deposited later.

Table 3		
Age	**Plan A**	**Plan B**
20	0	0
25	11,733	0
30	28,973	0
35	42,571	11,733
40	62,551	28,973
45	91,908	54,304
50	135,042	91,524
55	198,422	146,212
60	291,547	226,566
65	428,378	344,634

In **Example 8,** the *early* deposits of Plan A outperformed the *greater number* of deposits of Plan B because the interest rate was high enough to result in a Plan A balance at age 30 that Plan B could never overtake, despite additional Plan B deposits from then on. If the interest rate had been 6% rather than 8%, Plan B would have overtaken Plan A (at age 57) and at age 65 would have come out ahead by $20,253 (to the nearest dollar).

Effective Annual Yield

Banks, credit unions, and others often advertise two rates: first, the actual annualized interest rate, or **nominal rate** (the "named" or "stated" rate), and second, the equivalent rate that would produce the same final amount, or future value, at the end of 1 year if the interest being paid were simple rather than compound. This is called the "effective rate," or more commonly the **effective annual yield.** (It may be denoted **APY** for **"annual percentage yield."**) Because the interest is normally compounded multiple times per year, the yield will usually be somewhat higher than the nominal rate.

▐▐ **EXAMPLE 9** Finding Effective Annual Yield

What is the effective annual yield of an account paying a nominal rate of 2.50%, compounded quarterly?

SOLUTION

From the given data, $r = 0.025$ and $m = 4$. Suppose we deposited $P = \$1$ and left it for 1 year ($n = 4$). Then the compound future value formula gives

$$A = 1 \cdot \left(1 + \frac{0.025}{4}\right)^4 \approx 1.0252.$$

The initial deposit of $1, after 1 year, has grown to $1.0252.

$$\text{Interest earned} = 1.0252 - 1 \qquad \text{Interest = future value − present value}$$

$$= 0.0252, \quad \text{or} \quad 2.52\%$$

A nominal rate of 2.50% results in an effective annual yield of 2.52%. ▐▐▐

Generalizing the procedure of **Example 9** gives the following formula.

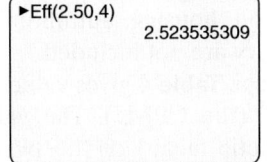

►Eff(2.50,4)
2.523535309

Financial calculators are programmed to compute effective interest rate. Compare to the result in **Example 9.**

Effective Annual Yield

A nominal interest rate of r, compounded m times per year, is equivalent to the following **effective annual yield.**

$$Y = \left(1 + \frac{r}{m}\right)^m - 1$$

When shopping for loans or savings opportunities, a borrower should seek the least yield available, while a depositor should look for the greatest.

▐▐ **EXAMPLE 10** Comparing Savings Rates

Christine Ellington wants to deposit $2800 into a savings account and has narrowed her choices to the three institutions represented here. Which is the best choice?

Institution	Rate on Deposits of $1000 to $5000
Friendly Credit Union	2.08% annual rate, compounded monthly
Premier Savings	2.09% annual yield
Neighborhood Bank	2.05% compounded daily

SOLUTION

Compare the effective annual yields for the three institutions.

Friendly: $\qquad Y = \left(1 + \dfrac{0.0208}{12}\right)^{12} - 1 = 0.0210 = 2.10\%$

Premier: $\qquad Y = 2.09\%$

Neighborhood: $\qquad Y = \left(1 + \dfrac{0.0205}{365}\right)^{365} - 1 = 0.0207 = 2.07\%$

The best of the three yields, 2.10%, is offered by Friendly Credit Union. ▐▐▐

Table 4	Consumer Price Index (CPI-U)*	
Year	Average CPI-U	Percent Change in CPI-U
1979	72.6	11.3
1980	82.4	13.5
1981	90.9	10.3
1982	96.5	6.2
1983	99.6	3.2
1984	103.9	4.3
1985	107.6	3.6
1986	109.6	1.9
1987	113.6	3.6
1988	118.3	4.1
1989	124.0	4.8
1990	130.7	5.4
1991	136.2	4.2
1992	140.3	3.0
1993	144.5	3.0
1994	148.2	2.6
1995	152.4	2.8
1996	156.9	3.0
1997	160.5	2.3
1998	163.0	1.6
1999	166.6	2.2
2000	172.2	3.4
2001	177.1	2.8
2002	179.9	1.6
2003	184.0	2.3
2004	188.9	2.7
2005	195.3	3.4
2006	201.6	3.2
2007	207.3	2.8
2008	215.3	3.8
2009	214.5	−0.4

Source: Bureau of Labor Statistics.

*The period 1982 to 1984: 100

Inflation

Interest reflects how money *gains value over time* when it is borrowed or lent. On the other hand, in terms of the equivalent number of goods or services that a given amount of money will buy, money normally *loses value over time.* This results in a periodic increase in the cost of living, which is called **price inflation.**

In the United States, the Bureau of Labor Statistics publishes **consumer price index (CPI)** figures, which reflect the prices of certain items purchased by large numbers of people. The items include such things as food, housing, automobiles, fuel, and clothing. Items such as yachts or expensive jewelry are not included.

Current data are published regularly at www.bls.gov/cpi. **Table 4** gives values of the primary index representing "all urban consumers" (the CPI-U). The value shown for a given year is actually the average (arithmetic mean) of the twelve monthly figures for that year. The table shows, for example, that the average CPI-U for 2007 (207.3) was 2.8% greater than the average value for 2006 (201.6).

Deflation is a *decrease* in price levels from one year to the next. A brief period of minor deflation, along with a general economic slowdown, usually is called a **recession.** (For example, in **Table 4**, note the 2009 rate of −0.4.)

Unlike account values under interest compounding, which make sudden jumps at just certain points in time (such as quarterly, monthly, or daily), price levels tend to fluctuate gradually over time. Thus, it is appropriate, for inflationary estimates, to use the formula for continuous compounding (introduced in **Section 8.6.**)

Future Value for Continuous Compounding

If an initial deposit of P dollars earns continuously compounded interest at an annual rate r for a period of t years, then the **future value, A,** is calculated as follows.

$$A = Pe^{rt}$$

▮▮ **EXAMPLE 11** Predicting Inflated Salary Levels

Suppose you earn a salary of $34,000 per year. About what salary would you need 20 years from now to maintain your purchasing power in case the inflation rate were to persist at each of the following levels?

(a) 2% (approximately the 1999 level)

(b) 13% (approximately the 1980 level)

SOLUTION

(a) In this case we can use the continuous compounding future value formula with $P = \$34{,}000$, $r = 0.02$, and $t = 20$, and the $\boxed{e^x}$ key on a calculator.

$$A = Pe^{rt} = (\$34{,}000)e^{(0.02)(20)} = \$50{,}722.04$$

The required salary 20 years from now would be about $51,000.

(b) For this level of inflation, we would have the following.

$$A = Pe^{rt} = (\$34{,}000)e^{(0.13)(20)} = \$457{,}767.09$$

The required salary 20 years from now would be about $458,000. ▮▮▮

To compare equivalent general price levels in any 2 years, we can use the proportion at the top of the next page. (A proportion is a statement that says that two ratios are equal. See **Section 7.3.**)

$34000e^{(.02*20)}$
                    50722.04
$34000e^{(.13*20)}$
                    457767.09

These are the computations required to solve the two parts of **Example 11.**

Inflation Proportion

For a given consumer product or service subject to average inflation, prices in two different years are related as follows.

$$\frac{\text{Price in year A}}{\text{Price in year B}} = \frac{\text{CPI in year A}}{\text{CPI in year B}}$$

■ EXAMPLE 12 Comparing a Tuition Increase to Average Inflation

Michael Dew's college tuition in 2009 was $9910. His uncle attended the same school in 1990 and paid $4990 in tuition. Compare the school's tuition increase to average inflation over the same period.

SOLUTION

Let x represent what we would expect the tuition to be in 2009 if it had increased at the average rate since 1990.

$$\frac{\text{Price in 2009}}{\text{Price in 1990}} = \frac{\text{CPI in 2009}}{\text{CPI in 1990}} \qquad \text{Inflation proportion}$$

$$\frac{x}{\$4990} = \frac{214.5}{130.7} \qquad \text{Substitute. CPI values are from \textbf{Table 4.}}$$

$$x = \frac{214.5}{130.7} \cdot \$4990 \qquad \text{Solve for } x.$$

$$x \approx \$8189$$

Now compare the actual 2009 tuition, $9910, with the expected figure, $8189.

$$\frac{\$9910}{\$8189} = 1.21 \qquad 1.21 = 100\% + 21\%$$

Over the period from 1990 to 2009, tuition at Michael's college increased approximately 21% more than the average CPI-U rate. ■■■

When working with quantities, such as inflation, where continual fluctuations and inexactness prevail, we often develop rough "rules of thumb" for obtaining quick estimates. One example is the estimation of the **years to double,** which is the number of years it takes for the general level of prices to double for a given annual rate of inflation. We can derive an estimation rule as follows.

$$A = Pe^{rt} \qquad \text{Future value formula}$$

$$2P = Pe^{rt} \qquad \text{Prices are to double.}$$

$$2 = e^{rt} \qquad \text{Divide both sides by } P.$$

$$\ln 2 = rt \qquad \text{Take the natural logarithm of both sides.}$$

$$t = \frac{\ln 2}{r} \qquad \text{Solve for } t.$$

$$t = \frac{100 \ln 2}{100r} \qquad \text{Multiply numerator and denominator by 100.}$$

$$\textbf{years to double} \approx \frac{\textbf{70}}{\textbf{annual inflation rate}} \qquad 100 \ln 2 \approx 70$$

(Because r is the inflation rate as a *decimal*, $100r$ is the inflation rate as a *percent.*)

The result above usually is called the **rule of 70.** The value it produces, if not a whole number, should be rounded *up* to the next whole number of years.

Monetary inflation devalues the currency just as **price inflation** does, but it does so through a direct increase in the money supply within the economy. An example in the United States was the issuance in 2009 and 2010 of massive government debt and massive government spending on "stimulus" programs. Debate persisted among economists as to whether actions of the government and central bank would accomplish their goals. Would economic recovery continue, or would major deflation occur? Most everyone agreed that the long-term result of monetary inflation would be more and more price inflation. Some deny that any real distinction exists, that due to complex interrelated economic forces, monetary and price inflation are essentially the same thing.

```
(100*ln(2))/2.3
              30.13683394
70/2.3
              30.43478261
```

Because 100 ln 2 ≈ 70, the two results shown here are approximately equal. See **Example 13** and the preceding discussion.

▍▍ **EXAMPLE 13** Estimating Years to Double by the Rule of 70

Estimate the years to double for an annual inflation rate of 2.3%.

SOLUTION

$$\text{Years to double} \approx \frac{70}{2.3} \approx 30.43 \quad \text{Rule of 70}$$

With a sustained inflation rate of 2.3%, prices would double in about 31 years. ▍▍▍

13.1 EXERCISES

In the following exercises, assume whenever appropriate that, unless otherwise known, there are 12 months per year, 30 days per month, and 365 days per year.

Find the simple interest owed for each loan.

1. $800 at 6% for 1 year

2. $3000 at 5% for 1 year

3. $920 at 7% for 9 months

4. $5400 at 7% for 4 months

5. $2675 at 7.3% for $2\frac{1}{2}$ years

6. $2620 at 4.82% for 22 months

Find the future value of each deposit if the account pays **(a)** *simple interest, and* **(b)** *interest compounded annually.*

7. $700 at 3% for 6 years

8. $2000 at 4% for 5 years

9. $2500 at 2% for 3 years

10. $3000 at 5% for 4 years

Solve each interest-related problem.

11. **Simple Interest on a Late Property Tax Payment** Andrew Draa was late on his property tax payment to the county. He owed $7500 and paid the tax 4 months late. The county charges a penalty of 5% simple interest. Find the amount of the penalty.

12. **Simple Interest on a Loan for Work Uniforms** Austin Caperton bought a new supply of delivery uniforms. He paid $922 for the uniforms and agreed to pay for them in 5 months at 6% simple interest. Find the amount of interest that he will owe.

13. **Simple Interest on a Small Business Loan** Kelly Kunert opened a security service on March 1. To pay for office furniture and guard dogs, Kelly borrowed $12,800 at the bank and agreed to pay the loan back in 10 months at 7% simple interest. Find the *total amount* required to repay the loan.

14. **Simple Interest on a Tax Overpayment** Paul Lewis is owed $530 by the Internal Revenue Service for overpayment of last year's taxes. The IRS will repay the amount at 4% simple interest. Find the *total amount* Paul will receive if the interest is paid for 8 months.

Find the missing final amount (future value) and/or interest earned.

	Principal	Rate	Compounded	Time	Final Amount	Compound Interest
15.	$ 975	4%	quarterly	4 years	$1143.26	_____
16.	$1150	7%	semiannually	6 years	$1737.73	_____
17.	$ 480	6%	semiannually	9 years	_____	$337.17
18.	$2370	5%	quarterly	5 years	_____	_____
19.	$7500	$3\frac{1}{2}$ %	annually	25 years	_____	_____
20.	$3450	2.4%	semiannually	10 years	_____	_____

For each deposit, find the future value (that is, the final amount on deposit) when compounding occurs (a) *annually,* (b) *semiannually, and* (c) *quarterly.*

	Principal	Rate	Time
21.	$2000	4%	3 years
22.	$5000	2%	7 years
23.	$18,000	1%	5 years
24.	$10,000	3%	9 years

Occasionally a savings account may actually pay interest compounded continuously. For each deposit, find the interest earned if interest is compounded (a) *semiannually,* (b) *quarterly,* (c) *monthly,* (d) *daily, and* (e) *continuously.*

	Principal	Rate	Time
25.	$850	1.6%	4 years
26.	$1550	2.8%	33 months (Assume 1003 days in parts (d) and (e).)

27. Describe the effect of interest being compounded more and more often. In particular, how good is continuous compounding?

Solve each interest-related problem.

28. Finding the Amount Borrowed in a Simple Interest Loan Jay Jenkins takes out a 7% simple interest loan today that will be repaid 15 months from now with a payoff amount of $815.63. What amount is Jay borrowing?

29. Finding the Amount Borrowed in a Simple Interest Loan What is the maximum amount Ginger Logan can borrow today if it must be repaid in 4 months with simple interest at 8% and she knows that at that time she will be able to repay no more than $1500?

30. In the development of the future value formula for compound interest in the text, at least four specific problem-solving strategies were employed. Identify (name) as many of them as you can and describe their use in this case.

Find the present value for each future amount.

31. $1000 (6% compounded annually for 5 years)

32. $14,000 (4% compounded quarterly for 3 years)

33. $9860 (8% compounded semiannually for 10 years)

34. $15,080 (5% compounded monthly for 4 years)

Finding the Present Value of a Compound Interest Retirement Account *Robyn Martin wants to establish an account that will supplement her retirement income beginning 30 years from now. For each interest rate find the lump sum she must deposit today so that $500,000 will be available at time of retirement.*

35. 5% compounded quarterly

36. 6% compounded quarterly

37. 5% compounded daily

38. 6% compounded daily

Finding the Effective Annual Yield in a Savings Account *Suppose a savings and loan pays a nominal rate of 2% on savings deposits. Find the effective annual yield if interest is compounded as stated in Exercises 39–45. (Give answers to the nearest thousandth of a percent.)*

39. annually

40. semiannually

41. quarterly

42. monthly

43. daily

44. 1000 times per year

45. 10,000 times per year

46. Judging from **Exercises 39–45,** what do you suppose is the effective annual yield if a nominal rate of 2% is compounded continuously? Explain your reasoning.

Comparing Savings Rates and Yields *The table shows the two best savings rates available on a certain online listing on May 25, 2010. Use this information in Exercises 47 and 48.*

	Rate	Yield
Sallie Mae	1.390%	1.400%
Capital One Direct Banking	1.340%	1.349%

47. If you deposit $30,000 with Sallie Mae, how much would you have in 1 year?

48. How often does compounding occur in the Capital One account: daily, monthly, quarterly, or semiannually?

Solve each problem.

49. Finding Years to Double How long would it take to double your money in an account paying 4% compounded quarterly? (Answer in years plus days, ignoring leap years.)

50. Comparing Principal and Interest Amounts After what time period would the interest earned equal the original principal in an account paying 2% compounded daily? (Answer in years plus days, ignoring leap years.)

51. Solve the effective annual yield formula for *r* to obtain a general formula for nominal rate in terms of yield and the number of compounding periods per year.

52. *Finding the Nominal Rate of a Savings Account* Ridgeway Savings compounds interest monthly, and the effective annual yield is 1.95%. What is the nominal rate?

53. *Comparing Bank Savings Rates* Bank A pays a nominal rate of 3.800% compounded daily on deposits. Bank B produces the same annual yield as the first but compounds interest only quarterly and pays no interest on funds deposited for less than an entire quarter.

(a) What nominal rate does Bank B pay (to the nearest thousandth of a percent)?

(b) Which bank should Nancy Dennis choose if she has $2000 to deposit for 10 months? How much more interest will she earn than in the other bank?

(c) Which bank should Dara Lanier choose for a deposit of $6000 for one year? How much interest will be earned?

Estimating the Years to Double by the Rule of 70 Use the rule of 70 *to estimate the years to double for each annual inflation rate.*

54. 1%   **55.** 2%

56. 8%   **57.** 9%

Estimating the Inflation Rate by the Rule of 70 Use the rule of 70 *to estimate the annual inflation rate (to the nearest tenth of a percent) that would cause the general level of prices to double in each time period.*

58. 5 years   **59.** 7 years

60. 16 years   **61.** 22 years

62. Derive a rule for estimating the "years to triple," that is, the number of years it would take for the general levels of prices to triple for a given annual inflation rate.

Estimating Future Prices for Constant Annual Inflation The year 2010 prices of several items are given below. Find the estimated future prices required to fill the blanks in the chart. (Give a number of significant figures consistent with the 2010 price figures provided.)

Item	2010 Price	2015 Price 2% Inflation	2025 Price 2% Inflation	2015 Price 10% Inflation	2025 Price 10% Inflation
63. Fast food meal	$ 5.89	_____	_____	_____	_____
64. House	$265,000	_____	_____	_____	_____
65. Small car	$ 18,500	_____	_____	_____	_____
66. Gallon of gasoline	$ 2.65	_____	_____	_____	_____

Estimating Future Prices for Variable Annual Inflation As seen in **Table 4**, *inflation rates do not often stay constant over a period of years. Assume that prices for the items below increased at the average annual rates shown in* **Table 4**. *Use the inflation proportion to find the missing prices in the last column of the chart. Round to the nearest dollar.*

Item	Price	Year Purchased	Price in 2009
67. Evening dress	$ 175	2000	_____
68. Desk	$ 450	2002	_____
69. Lawn tractor	$1099	1996	_____
70. Designer puppy	$ 250	1998	_____

Solve each interest-related problem.

71. *Finding the Present Value of a Future Equipment Purchase* Human gene sequencing is a major research area of biotechnology. PE Biosystems leased 300 of its sequencing machines to a sibling company, Celera. If Celera was able to earn 7% compounded quarterly on invested money, what lump sum did they need to invest in order to purchase those machines 18 months later at a price of $300,000 each? (*Source: Forbes,* February 21, 2000, p. 102.)

72. *Finding the Present Value of a Future Real Estate Purchase* A California couple are selling their small dairy farm to a developer, but they wish to defer receipt of the money until 2 years from now, when they will be in a lower tax bracket. Find the lump sum that the developer can deposit today, at 5% compounded quarterly, so that enough will be available to pay the couple $1,450,000 in 2 years.

13.2 CONSUMER CREDIT

Types of Consumer Credit • Installment Loans • Revolving Loans

Types of Consumer Credit

Consumer credit refers to borrowing money to finance purchases of cars, furniture, appliances, jewelry, electronics, and many other things. Technically, **real estate mortgages,** loans to finance home purchases, are also consumer credit, but they usually involve much larger amounts and longer repayment periods.

In this section we discuss two common types of consumer credit. The first type, **installment loans,** or **closed-end** credit, involves borrowing a set amount up front and paying a series of equal installments (payments) until the loan is paid off. Furniture, appliances, and cars commonly are financed through closed-end credit.

With the second type of consumer credit, **revolving loans,** or **open-end** credit, there is no fixed number of installments—the consumer continues paying until no balance is owed. With revolving loans, additional credit often is extended before the initial amount is paid off. Examples of open-end credit include most department store charge accounts and bank charge cards such as MasterCard and VISA.

Installment Loans

Installment loans, set up under closed-end credit, often are based on **add-on interest.** This means that interest is calculated by the simple interest formula $I = Prt$, and we simply "add on" this amount of interest to the principal borrowed to arrive at the total debt (or amount to be repaid).

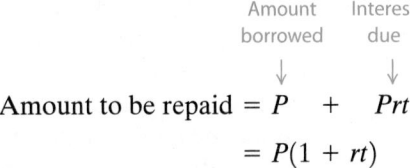

$$\text{Amount to be repaid} = P + Prt$$
$$= P(1 + rt)$$

The total debt is then equally divided among the payments (usually monthly) to be made over the t years.

Credit card debt among students has raised increasing concern in recent years among lawmakers, college officials, and consumer advocacy groups. As a result, hundreds of colleges have banned card marketers from campus, and new federal law brought significant new regulations effective in 2010.

A 2010 study by Sallie Mae (a college financing company) pegged average undergraduate credit card debt at $3,173. The National Center for Education Statistics reported that average total debt among graduating seniors (including credit cards and private and federal loans) was $27,803. (*Source:* www.thelantern.com, Ohio State University student newspaper)

▌▌ **EXAMPLE 1** Repaying an Add-On Loan

Mary Kaye Leonard buys $5400 worth of furniture and appliances for her first apartment. She pays $1100 down and agrees to pay the balance at a 7% add-on rate for 2 years. Find

(a) the total amount to be repaid,

(b) the monthly payment, and

(c) the total cost of the purchases, including finance charges.

SOLUTION

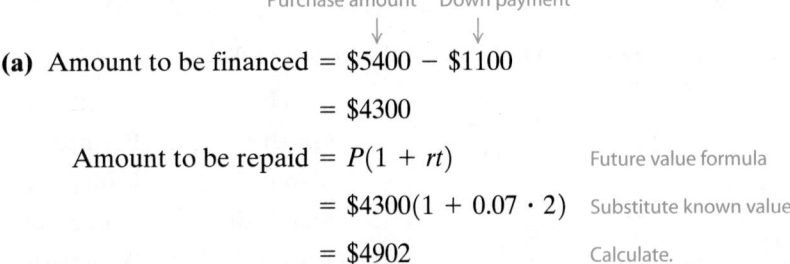

(a) Amount to be financed = $5400 − $1100

= $4300

Amount to be repaid = $P(1 + rt)$ Future value formula

= $4300(1 + 0.07 · 2)   Substitute known values.

= $4902   Calculate.

(b) Monthly payment $= \dfrac{\$4902}{24}$ ⟵ Amount to be repaid

⟵ Number of payments

$= \$204.25$

Down payment   Loan repayment

$\downarrow$ $\downarrow$

(c) Total cost of purchases $= \$1100 \;+\; \$4902$

$= \$6002$

Mary Kaye will end up paying $6002, which is 11.1% more than the price tag total. ▮▮▮

Notice that the repayment amount in **Example 1,** $P(1 + rt)$, was the same as the final amount A in a savings account paying a simple interest rate r for t years. (See **Section 13.1.**) But in the case of savings, the bank keeps all of your money for the entire time period. In **Example 1,** Mary Kaye did not keep the full principal amount for the full time period. She repaid it in 24 monthly installments. The 7% add-on rate turns out to be equivalent to a much higher "true annual interest" rate.

Revolving Loans

With a typical department store account, or bank card, a credit limit is established initially and the consumer can make many purchases during a month (up to the credit limit). The required monthly payment can vary from a set minimum (which may depend on the account balance) up to the full balance.

For purchases made in a store or other retail location, the customer may authorize adding the purchase price to his or her charge account by signing on a paper "charge slip," or perhaps on an electronic signature pad. Authorization also can be given by telephone or over the Internet for mail orders and other expenditures.

At the end of each billing period (normally once a month), the customer receives an **itemized billing,** a statement listing purchases and cash advances, the total balance owed, the minimum payment required, and perhaps other account information. Any charges beyond cash advanced and cash prices of items purchased are called **finance charges.** Finance charges may include interest, an annual fee, credit insurance coverage, a time payment differential, or carrying charges.

Most revolving credit plans calculate finance charges by the **average daily balance method.** The average daily balance is the *weighted mean* (see **Section 12.2**) of the various amounts of credit utilized for different parts of the billing period, with the weighting factors being the number of days that each credit amount applied.

▮▮ | **EXAMPLE 2** | Using the Average Daily Balance Method for Credit Card Charges

Learning the following rhyme will help you in problems like the one found in **Example 2.**

Thirty days hath September, April, June, and November. All the rest have thirty-one, Save February which has twenty-eight days clear, And twenty-nine in each leap year.

The activity in Jessica Lasda's MasterCard account for one billing period is shown below. If the previous balance (on March 3) was $209.46, and the bank charges 1.3% per month on the average daily balance, find

(a) the average daily balance for the next billing (April 3),

(b) the finance charge to appear on the April 3 billing, and

(c) the account balance on April 3.

March 3	Billing date	
March 12	Payment	$50.00
March 17	Clothes	$28.46
March 20	Mail order	$31.22
April 1	Auto parts	$59.10

SOLUTION

(a) First make a table that shows the beginning date of the billing period and the dates of all transactions in the billing period. Along with each of these, compute the running balance on that date.

Date	Running Balance
March 3	$209.46
March 12	$209.46 − $50 = $159.46
March 17	$159.46 + $28.46 = $187.92
March 20	$187.92 + $31.22 = $219.14
April 1	$219.14 + $59.10 = $278.24

Next, tabulate the running balance figures, along with the number of days until the balance changed. Multiply each balance amount by the number of days. The sum of these products gives the "sum of the daily balances."

Date	Running Balance	Number of Days Until Balance Changed	$\left(\begin{array}{c}\textbf{Running}\\\textbf{Balance}\end{array}\right) \cdot \left(\begin{array}{c}\textbf{Number}\\\textbf{of Days}\end{array}\right)$
March 3	$209.46	9	$1885.14
March 12	$159.46	5	$ 797.30
March 17	$187.92	3	$ 563.76
March 20	$219.14	12	$2629.68
April 1	$278.24	2	$ 556.48
		Totals: 31	$6432.36

$$\text{Average daily balance} = \frac{\text{Sum of daily balances}}{\text{Days in billing period}} = \frac{\$6432.36}{31} = \$207.50$$

Jessica will pay a finance charge based on the average daily balance of $207.50.

(b) The finance charge for the April 3 billing will be

$$1.3\% \text{ of } \$207.50 = 0.013 \cdot \$207.50 \qquad \text{\small 1.3\% = 1.3 × 0.01 = 0.013}$$

$$= \$2.70.$$

(c) The account balance on the April 3 billing will be the latest running balance plus the finance charge.

$$\$278.24 + \$2.70 = \$280.94 \qquad \blacksquare\blacksquare\blacksquare$$

Other features of revolving accounts can be at least as important as interest. For example:

1. Is an annual fee charged? If so, how much is it?

2. Is a special "introductory" rate offered? If so, how long will it last?

3. Are there other incentives, such as rebates, credits toward certain purchases, "free" airline miles, or return of interest charges for long-time use?

Credit cards and other revolving loans are relatively expensive credit. The monthly rate of 1.3% in **Example 2** is typical and is equivalent to an annual rate of 15.6%. A single card (like VISA or MasterCard), however, can be a great convenience, as most all merchants accept it and it eliminates the need to carry cash or write checks.

A wise practice, if at all possible, is *not* to carry a balance from month to month, but to pay the entire new balance by the due date each month. Since purchases made during the month are not billed until the next billing date, and the payment due date may be 20 days or more after the billing date, items can often be charged on a card without actually paying for them for nearly two months. To obtain this form of "free credit," resist the temptation to buy more than can be paid for by the next payment date.

13.2 EXERCISES

Round all monetary answers to the nearest cent unless directed otherwise. Assume that unless otherwise known, there are 12 months per year, 30 days per month, and 365 days per year

Financing an Appliance Purchase *Krishna Gil bought appliances costing $3450 at a store charging 8% add-on interest. She made a $500 down payment and agreed to monthly payments over two years.*

1. Find the total amount to be financed.

2. Find the total interest to be paid.

3. Find the total amount to be repaid.

4. Find the monthly payment.

5. Find the total cost, for appliances plus interest.

Financing a New Car Purchase *Suppose you want to buy a new car that costs $16,500. You have no cash—only your old car, which is worth $3000 as a trade-in.*

6. How much do you need to finance to buy the new car?

7. The dealer says the interest rate is 9% add-on for 3 years. Find the total interest.

8. Find the total amount to be repaid.

9. Find the monthly payment.

10. Find your total cost, for the new car plus interest.

In Exercises 11–16, use the add-on method of calculating interest to find the total interest and the monthly payment.

	Amount of Loan	Length of Loan	Interest Rate
11.	$4500	3 years	9%
12.	$2700	2 years	8%
13.	$ 750	18 months	7.4%
14.	$2450	30 months	9.2%
15.	$ 535	16 months	11.1%
16.	$ 798	29 months	10.3%

Work each problem.

17. **Finding the Monthly Payment for an Add-On Interest Furniture Loan** The Giordanos buy $8500 worth of furniture for their new home. They pay $3000 down. The store charges 10% add-on interest. The Giordanos will pay off the furniture in 30 monthly payments ($2\frac{1}{2}$ years). Find the monthly payment.

18. **Finding the Monthly Payment for an Add-On Interest Auto Loan** Find the monthly payment required to pay off an auto loan of $9780 over 3 years if the add-on interest rate is 9.3%.

19. **Finding the Monthly Payment for an Add-On Interest Home Electronics Loan** The total purchase price of a new home entertainment system is $14,240. If the down payment is $2900 and the balance is to be financed over 48 months at 10% add-on interest, what is the monthly payment?

20. **Finding the Monthly Payment for an Add-On Interest Loan** What are the monthly payments Donna De Simone pays on a loan of $1680 for a period of 10 months if 9% add-on interest is charged?

21. **Finding the Amount Borrowed in an Add-On Interest Car Loan** Joshua Eurich has misplaced the sales contract for his car and cannot remember the amount he originally financed. He does know that the add-on interest rate was 9.8% and the loan required a total of 48 monthly payments of $314.65 each. How much did Joshua borrow (to the nearest dollar)?

22. **Finding an Add-On Interest Rate** Susan Dratch is making monthly payments of $207.31 to pay off a $3\frac{1}{2}$ year loan for $6400. What is her add-on interest rate (to the nearest tenth of a percent)?

23. **Finding the Term of an Add-On Interest Loan** How long (in years) will it take Michael Garbin to pay off an $8000 loan with monthly payments of $172.44 if the add-on interest rate is 9.2%?

24. **Finding the Number of Payments of an Add-On Interest Loan** How many monthly payments must Jawann make on a $10,000 loan if he pays $417.92 a month and the add-on interest rate is 10.15%?

Finding Finance Charges *Find the finance charge for each charge account. Assume interest is calculated on the average daily balance of the account.*

	Average Daily Balance	Monthly Interest Rate
25.	$ 249.94	1.4%
26.	$ 350.75	1.5%
27.	$ 419.95	1.38%
28.	$ 450.21	1.26%
29.	$1073.40	1.425%
30.	$1320.42	1.375%

Finding Finance Charges and Account Balances Using the Average Daily Balance Method *For each credit card account, assume one month between billing dates (with the appropriate number of days) and interest of 1.3% per month on the average daily balance. Find* **(a)** *the average daily balance,* **(b)** *the monthly finance charge, and* **(c)** *the account balance for the next billing.*

31. Previous balance: $728.36

May 9	Billing date	
May 17	Payment	$200
May 30	Dinner	$ 46.11
June 3	Theater tickets	$ 64.50

32. Previous balance: $514.79

January 27	Billing date	
February 9	Candy	$11.08
February 13	Returns	$26.54
February 20	Payment	$59
February 25	Repairs	$71.19

33. Previous balance: $462.42

June 11	Billing date	
June 15	Returns	$106.45
June 20	Jewelry	$115.73
June 24	Car rental	$ 74.19
July 3	Payment	$115
July 6	Flowers	$ 68.49

34. Previous balance: $983.25

August 17	Billing date	
August 21	Mail order	$ 14.92
August 23	Returns	$ 25.41
August 27	Beverages	$ 31.82
August 31	Payment	$108
September 9	Returns	$ 71.14
September 11	Concert tickets	$110
September 14	Cash advance	$100

Finding Finance Charges *Assume no purchases or returns are made in Exercises 35 and 36.*

35. At the beginning of a 31-day billing period, Sandra Lazzaro has an unpaid balance of $720 on her credit card. Three days before the end of the billing period, she pays $600. Find her finance charge at 1.4% per month using the average daily balance method.

36. Anthony Marsella's VISA bill dated April 14 shows an unpaid balance of $1070. Five days before May 14, the end of the billing period, Anthony makes a payment of $900. Find his finance charge at 1.32% per month using the average daily balance method.

Analyzing a "90 Days Same as Cash" Offer *One version of the "90 Days Same as Cash" promotion was offered by a "major purchase card," which established an account charging 1.3167% interest per month on the account balance. Interest charges are added to the balance each month, becoming part of the balance on which interest is computed the next month.*

If you pay off the original purchase charge within 3 months, all interest charges are cancelled. Otherwise you are liable for all the interest. Suppose you purchase $2900 worth of carpeting under this plan.

37. Find the interest charge added to the account balance at the end of

(a) the first month,

(b) the second month,

(c) the third month.

38. Suppose you pay off the account 1 day late (3 months plus 1 day). What total interest amount must you pay? (Do not include interest for the one extra day.)

39. Treating the 3 months as $\frac{1}{4}$ year, find the equivalent simple interest rate for this purchase (to the nearest tenth of a percent).

Various Charges of a Bank Card Account *Beth Johnson's bank card account charges 1.1% per month on the average daily balance as well as the following special fees:*

Cash advance fee:	2% (*not less than $2 nor more than $10*)
Late payment fee:	$15
Over-the-credit-limit fee:	$5

In the month of June, Beth's average daily balance was $1846. She was on vacation during the month and did not get her account payment in on time, which resulted in a late payment and resulted in charges accumulating to a sum above her credit limit. She also used her card for six $100 cash advances while on vacation. Find the following based on account transactions in that month.

40. interest charges to the account

41. special fees charged to the account

Write out your response to each of the following.

42. Is it possible to use a bank credit card for your purchases without paying anything for credit? If so, explain how.

43. Obtain applications or descriptive brochures for several different bank card programs, compare their features (including those in fine print), and explain which deal would be best for you, and why.

44. Research and explain the difference, if any, between a "credit" card and a "debit" card.

45. Many charge card offers include the option of purchasing credit insurance coverage, which would make your monthly payments if you became disabled and could not work and/or would pay off the account balance if you died. Find out the details on at least one such offer, and discuss why you would or would not accept it.

46. Make a list of "special incentives" offered by bank cards you are familiar with, and briefly describe the pros and cons of each one.

47. One bank offered a card with a "low introductory rate" of 5.9%, good through the end of the year. And furthermore, you could receive back a percentage (up to 100%!) of all interest you pay, as shown in the table.

Use your card for:	2 years	5 years	10 years	15 years	20 years
Get back:	10%	25%	50%	75%	100%

(As soon as you take a refund, the time clock starts over.) Because you can eventually claim all your interest payments back, is this card a good deal? Explain.

48. Recall a car-buying experience you have had, or visit a new-car dealer and interview a salesperson. Describe the procedure involved in purchasing a car on credit.

Comparing Bank Card Accounts *Dorothy Laymon is considering two bank card offers that are the same in all respects except for the following:*

> *Bank A charges no annual fee and charges monthly interest of 1.18% on the unpaid balance.*

> *Bank B charges a $30 annual fee and monthly interest of 1.01% on the unpaid balance.*

From her records, Dorothy has found that the unpaid balance she tends to carry from month to month is quite consistent and averages $900.

49. Estimate her total yearly cost to use the card if she chooses the card from

  (a) Bank A

  (b) Bank B.

50. Which card is her better choice?

13.3 TRUTH IN LENDING

Annual Percentage Rate (APR) • Unearned Interest

Annual Percentage Rate (APR)

The Consumer Credit Protection Act, which was passed in 1968, has commonly been known as the **Truth in Lending Act.** In this section we discuss two major issues addressed in the law:

1. How can we tell the true annual interest rate a lender is charging?

2. How much of the finance charge are we entitled to save if we decide to pay off a loan sooner than originally scheduled?

Question 1 above arose because lenders were computing and describing the interest they charged in several different ways. For example, how does 1.5% per month at Sears compare to 9% per year add-on interest at a furniture store? Truth in Lending standardized the so-called true annual interest rate, or **annual percentage rate,** commonly denoted **APR.** All sellers (car dealers, stores, banks, insurance agents, credit card companies, and the like) must disclose the APR when asked, and the written contract must state the APR in all cases. This enables a borrower to more easily compare the true costs of different loans.

Theoretically, a borrower should not need to calculate APR, but it is possible to verify the value stated by the lender. Since the formulas for finding APR are quite involved, it is easiest to use a table provided by the Federal Reserve Bank. We show an abbreviated version in **Table 5** on the next page. It identifies APR values to the nearest half percent from 8.0% to 14.0%, for loans requiring *monthly* payments and extending over the most common lengths for consumer loans from 6 to 60 months.

Table 5 relates the following three quantities.

APR = true annual interest rate (shown across the top)

    n = total number of scheduled monthly payments (shown down the left side)

    h = finance charge per $100 of amount financed (shown in the body of the table)

Table 5 **Annual Percentage Rate (APR) for Monthly Payment Loans**

Number of Monthly Payments (*n*)	Annual Percentage Rate (APR)												
	8.0%	8.5%	9.0%	9.5%	10.0%	10.5%	11.0%	11.5%	12.0%	12.5%	13.0%	13.5%	14.0%
	(Finance charge per $100 of amount financed) (*h*)												
6	$2.35	$2.49	$2.64	$2.79	$2.94	$3.08	$3.23	$3.38	$3.53	$3.68	$3.83	$3.97	$4.12
12	4.39	4.66	4.94	5.22	5.50	5.78	6.06	6.34	6.62	6.90	7.18	7.46	7.74
18	6.45	6.86	7.28	7.69	8.10	8.52	8.93	9.35	9.77	10.19	10.61	11.03	11.45
24	8.55	9.09	9.64	10.19	10.75	11.30	11.86	12.42	12.98	13.54	14.10	14.66	15.23
30	10.66	11.35	12.04	12.74	13.43	14.13	14.83	15.54	16.24	16.95	17.66	18.38	19.10
36	12.81	13.64	14.48	15.32	16.16	17.01	17.86	18.71	19.57	20.43	21.30	22.17	23.04
48	17.18	18.31	19.45	20.59	21.74	22.90	24.06	25.23	26.40	27.58	28.77	29.97	31.17
60	21.66	23.10	24.55	26.01	27.48	28.96	30.45	31.96	33.47	34.99	36.52	38.06	39.61

▌▌ **EXAMPLE 1** Finding the APR for an Add-On Loan

Recall that Mary Kaye (in **Example 1** of **Section 13.2**) paid $1100 down on a $5400 purchase and agreed to pay the balance at a 7% add-on rate for 2 years. Find the APR for her loan.

SOLUTION

As shown previously, the total amount financed was

$$\underset{\downarrow}{\text{Purchase price}} \quad \underset{\downarrow}{\text{Down payment}}$$

$$\$5400 - \$1100 = \$4300.$$

The finance charge (interest) was

$$I = Prt = \$4300 \cdot 0.07 \cdot 2 = \$602.$$

Next find the finance charge per $100 of the amount financed. To do this, divide the finance charge by the amount financed, then multiply by $100.

$$\left(\begin{array}{c}\text{Finance charge per}\\ \$100 \text{ financed}\end{array}\right) = \frac{\text{Finance charge}}{\text{Amount financed}} \cdot \$100$$

$$= \frac{\$602}{\$4300} \cdot \$100, \quad \text{or} \quad \$14$$

This amount, $14, represents *h*, the finance charge per $100 of the amount financed. Because the loan was to be paid over 24 months, look down to the "24 monthly payments" row of **Table 5** (*n* = 24). Then look across the table for the *h*-value closest to $14.00, which is $14.10. From that point, read up the column to find the APR, 13.0% (to the nearest half percent). In this case, a 7% add-on rate is equivalent to an APR of 13.0%. ▌▌▌

```
5400−1100
                  4300
4300*.07*2
                  602
(602/4300)*100
                  14
```

These are the computations required in the solution of **Example 1.**

▌▌ EXAMPLE 2 Finding the APR for a Car Loan

After a down payment on her new car, Yvette Freeman still owed $7454. She agreed to repay the balance in 48 monthly payments of $185 each. What is the APR on her loan?

SOLUTION

First find the finance charge.

$$\underset{\substack{\uparrow \\ \text{Total} \\ \text{payments}}}{} \qquad \underset{\substack{\uparrow \\ \text{Amount} \\ \text{financed}}}{}$$

$$\text{Finance charge} = 48 \cdot \$185 - \$7454$$

$$= \$1426 \quad \boxed{\text{Multiply first. Then subtract.}}$$

Now find the finance charge per $100 financed as in **Example 1.**

$$\begin{pmatrix} \text{Finance charge per} \\ \$100 \text{ financed} \end{pmatrix} = \frac{\text{Finance charge}}{\text{Amount financed}} \cdot \$100$$

$$= \frac{\$1426}{\$7454} \cdot \$100, \quad \text{or} \quad \$19.13$$

Find the "48 payments" row of **Table 5,** read across to find the number closest to 19.13, which is 19.45. From there read up to find the APR, which is 9.0%. ▌▌▌

```
48*185−7454
                1426.00
(1426/7454)*100
                  19.13
```

These are the computations required in the solution of **Example 2.**

Unearned Interest

Question 2 at the beginning of the section arises when a borrower decides to pay off an installment loan earlier than originally scheduled. In such a case, it turns out that the lender has not loaned as much money for as long as planned and so he has not really "earned" the full finance charge originally disclosed.

If a loan is paid off early, the amount by which the original finance charge is reduced is called the **unearned interest.** We will discuss two common methods of calculating unearned interest, the **actuarial method** and the **rule of 78.** The Truth in Lending Act requires that the method for calculating this refund (or reduction) of finance charge be disclosed at the time the loan is initiated. Whichever method is used, the borrower may not, in fact, save all the unearned interest, since the lender is entitled to impose an **early payment penalty** to recover certain costs. A lender's intention to impose such a penalty in case of early payment also must be disclosed at initiation of the loan.

Rights and responsibilities apply to all credit accounts, and the consumer should read all disclosures provided by the lender. *The Fair Credit Billing Act* and *The Fair Credit Reporting Act* regulate, among other things, procedures for billing and for disputing bills, and for providing and disputing personal information on consumers.

If you have ever applied for a charge account, a personal loan, insurance, or a job, then information about where you work and live, how you pay your bills, and whether you've been sued, arrested, or have filed for bankruptcy appears in the files of Consumer Reporting Agencies (CRAs), which sell that information to creditors, employers, insurers, and other businesses.

For more detailed information on these and many other consumer issues, you may want to consult the Web site www.consumeraction.gov.

Unearned Interest—Actuarial Method

For an installment loan requiring *monthly* payments, which is paid off earlier than originally scheduled, let

R = regular monthly payment,

k = remaining number of scheduled payments (*after* current payment), and

h = finance charge per $100, corresponding to a loan with the same APR and k monthly payments.

Then the **unearned interest, u,** is calculated as follows.

$$u = kR\left(\frac{h}{\$100 + h}\right)$$

Once the unearned interest u is calculated (by any method), the amount required to pay off the loan early is easily found. It consists of the present regular payment due, plus k additional future payments, minus the unearned interest.

Payoff Amount

An installment loan requiring regular monthly payments R can be paid off early, along with the current payment. If the original loan had k additional payments scheduled (after the current payment), and the unearned interest is u, then, disregarding any possible prepayment penalty, the **payoff amount** is calculated as follows.

$$\text{Payoff amount} = (k + 1)R - u$$

▮▮ **EXAMPLE 3** Finding the Early Payoff Amount by the Actuarial Method

Yvette Freeman got an unexpected pay raise and wanted to pay off her car loan of **Example 2** at the end of 3 years rather than paying for 4 years as originally agreed.

(a) Find the unearned interest (the amount she will save by retiring the loan early).

(b) Find the "payoff amount" (the amount required to pay off the loan at the end of 3 years).

SOLUTION

(a) From **Example 2,** recall that $R = \$185$ and APR $= 9.0\%$. The current payment is payment number 36, so $k = 48 - 36 = 12$. Use **Table 5**, with 12 payments and APR 9.0%, to obtain $h = \$4.94$. Then use the actuarial method formula.

$$u = 12 \cdot \$185\left(\frac{\$4.94}{\$100 + \$4.94}\right) = \$104.51$$

By this method, Yvette will save $104.51 in interest by retiring the loan early.

(b) The payoff amount is found by using the appropriate formula.

$$\text{Payoff amount} = (12 + 1)\$185 - \$104.51 = \$2300.49$$

The required payoff amount at the end of 3 years is $2300.49. ▮▮▮

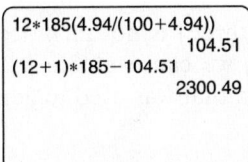

12*185(4.94/(100+4.94))
                  104.51
(12+1)*185−104.51
                  2300.49

These are the computations required in the solution of **Example 3.**

The actuarial method, because it is based on the APR value, probably is the better method. However, some lenders still use the second method, the **rule of 78.**

Unearned Interest—Rule of 78

For a closed-end loan requiring *monthly* payments, which is paid off earlier than originally scheduled, let

    F = original finance charge,

    n = number of payments originally scheduled, and

    k = remaining number of scheduled payments (*after* current payment).

Then the **unearned interest, u,** is calculated as follows.

$$u = \frac{k(k + 1)}{n(n + 1)} \cdot F$$

▮▮ **EXAMPLE 4** Finding the Early Payoff Amount by the Rule of 78

Again assume that the loan in **Example 2** is paid off at the time of the thirty-sixth monthly payment. This time however, instead of the actuarial method, use the rule of 78 to find

(a) the unearned interest, and   **(b)** the payoff amount.

SOLUTION

(a) From **Example 2,** the original finance charge is $F = \$1426$. Also, $n = 48$ and $k = 12$.

$$u = \frac{12(12 + 1)}{48(48 + 1)} \cdot \$1426 = \$94.58 \quad \text{Rule of 78}$$

By the rule of 78, Yvette will save $94.58 in interest, which is $9.93 *less* than her savings by the actuarial method.

(b)   Payoff amount $= (12 + 1)\$185 - \$94.58 = \$2310.42$

The payoff amount is $2310.42, which is $9.93 *more* than the payoff amount calculated by the actuarial method in **Example 3.**   ▮▮▮

(12*(12+1))/(48(48+1))*1426
                    94.58
(12+1)*185−94.58
                  2310.42

These are the computations required in the solution of **Example 4.**

When the rule of 78 was first introduced into financial law (by the Indiana legislature in 1935), loans were ordinarily written for 1 year or less, interest rates were relatively low, and loan amounts were less than they tend to be today. For these reasons the rule of 78 was acceptably accurate then. Today, however, with very accurate tables and/or calculators readily available, the rule of 78 is used much less often than previously.

Suppose we want to compute unearned interest accurately (so we don't trust the rule of 78), but the APR value, or the number of scheduled payments, or the number of remaining payments (or at least one of the three) is not included in **Table 5**. Then what? Actually, in the actuarial method, we can evaluate h (the finance charge per $100 financed) using the same formula that was used to generate **Table 5**.

Finance Charge per $100 Financed

If an installment loan requires n equal monthly payments and APR denotes the true annual interest rate for the loan (as a decimal), then h, the **finance charge per $100 financed**, is calculated as follows.

$$h = \frac{n \cdot \frac{\text{APR}}{12} \cdot \$100}{1 - \left(1 + \frac{\text{APR}}{12}\right)^{-n}} - \$100$$

▮▮ **EXAMPLE 5** Finding Unearned Interest and Early Payoff Amount

Mark Foss borrowed $4000 to pay for music equipment for his band. His loan contract states an APR of 9.8% and stipulates 28 monthly payments of $160.39 each. Mark decides to pay the loan in full at the time of his nineteenth scheduled payment. Find

(a) the unearned interest, and   **(b)** the payoff amount.

SOLUTION

(a) First find h from the finance charge formula just given.

> Remember to use the remaining number of payments, $28 - 19 = 9$, as the value of n.

$$h = \frac{9\left(\frac{0.098}{12}\right)(\$100)}{1 - \left(1 + \frac{0.098}{12}\right)^{-9}} - \$100 = \$4.13$$

Next use the actuarial formula for unearned interest.

Regular monthly payment:	$R = \$160.39$
Remaining number of payments:	$k = 28 - 19 = 9$
Finance charge per \$100:	$h = \$4.13$

$$u = 9 \cdot \$160.39 \cdot \frac{\$4.13}{\$100 + \$4.13} = \$57.25$$

The amount of interest Mark will save is \$57.25.

(b)   Payoff amount $= (9 + 1)(\$160.39) - \$57.25 = \$1546.65.$

To pay off the loan at the time of his nineteenth scheduled payment, Mark must pay \$1546.65.   ███

Side note:

```
(9*(.098/12)*100)/(1-(1+
  .098/12)^-9)-100
                    4.13
9*160.39*4.13/(100+4.13)
                   57.25
```

These are the computations required in the solution of **Example 5(a)**.

13.3 EXERCISES

Round all monetary answers to the nearest cent unless otherwise directed.

Finding True Annual Interest Rate *Find the APR (true annual interest rate), to the nearest half percent, for each loan.*

	Amount Financed	Finance Charge	Number of Monthly Payments
1.	\$1000	\$75	12
2.	\$1700	\$202	24
3.	\$6600	\$750	30
4.	\$5900	\$1150	48

Finding the Monthly Payment *Find the monthly payment for each loan.*

	Purchase Price	Down Payment	Finance Charge	Number of Monthly Payments
5.	\$3000	\$500	\$250	24
6.	\$4280	\$450	\$700	36
7.	\$3950	\$300	\$800	48
8.	\$8400	\$2500	\$1300	60

Finding True Annual Interest Rate *Find the APR (true annual interest rate), to the nearest half percent, for each loan.*

	Purchase Price	Down Payment	Add-on Interest Rate	Number of Payments
9.	\$4190	\$390	6%	12
10.	\$3250	\$750	7%	36
11.	\$7480	\$2200	5%	18
12.	\$12,800	\$4500	6%	48

Unearned Interest by the Actuarial Method *Each loan was paid in full before its due date.* **(a)** *Obtain the value of h from* **Table 5.** *Then* **(b)** *use the actuarial method to find the amount of unearned interest, and* **(c)** *find the payoff amount.*

	Regular Monthly Payment	APR	Remaining Number of Scheduled Payments After Payoff
13.	\$346.70	11.0%	18
14.	\$783.50	8.5%	12
15.	\$595.80	9.5%	6
16.	\$314.50	10.0%	24

Finding Finance Charge and True Annual Interest Rate *For each loan, find* **(a)** *the finance charge, and* **(b)** *the APR.*

17. John Lanza financed a $1990 computer with 24 monthly payments of $91.50 each.

18. Jessica Luther bought a horse trailer for $5090. She paid $1240 down and paid the remainder at $152.70 per month for $2\frac{1}{2}$ years.

19. Brandon Hight still owed $2000 on his new garden tractor after the down payment. He agreed to pay monthly payments for 18 months at 6% add-on interest.

20. Alfred Juarez paid off a $15,000 car loan over 3 years with monthly payments of $487.54 each.

Comparing the Actuarial Method and the Rule of 78 for Unearned Interest *Each loan was paid off early. Find the unearned interest by* **(a)** *the actuarial method, and* **(b)** *the rule of 78.*

	Amount Financed	Regular Monthly Payments	Total Number of Payments Scheduled	Remaining Number of Scheduled Payments After Payoff
21.	$3310	$201.85	18	6
22.	$10,230	$277.00	48	12
23.	$29,850	$641.58	60	12
24.	$16,730	$539.82	36	18

Unearned Interest by the Actuarial Method *Each loan was paid in full before its due date.* **(a)** *Obtain the value of h from the appropriate formula. Then* **(b)** *use the actuarial method to find the amount of unearned interest, and* **(c)** *find the payoff amount.*

	Regular Monthly Payment	APR	Remaining Number of Scheduled Payments After Payoff
25.	$212	8.6%	4
26.	$575	9.33%	8

Comparing Loan Choices *Laura Kennedy needs to borrow $5000 to pay for NBA season tickets for her family. She can borrow the amount from a finance company (at 6.5% add-on interest for 3 years) or from the credit union (36 monthly payments of $164.50 each). Use this information for Exercises 27–30.*

27. Find the APR (to the nearest half percent) for each loan and decide which one is Laura's better choice.

28. Laura takes the credit union loan. At the time of her thirtieth payment she pays it off. If the credit union uses the rule of 78 for computing unearned interest, how much will she save by paying in full now?

29. What would Laura save in interest if she paid in full at the time of the thirtieth payment and the credit union used the actuarial method for computing unearned interest?

30. Under the conditions of **Exercise 29**, what amount must Laura come up with to pay off her loan?

31. Describe why, in **Example 1**, the APR and the add-on rate differ. Which one is more legitimate? Why?

Approximating the APR of an Add-On Rate *To convert an add-on interest rate to its corresponding APR, some people recommend using the formula*

$$APR = \frac{2n}{n+1} \cdot r,$$

where r is add-on rate and n is total number of payments.

32. Apply the given formula to calculate the APR (to the nearest half percent) for the loan of **Example 1** ($r = 0.07, n = 24$).

33. Compare your APR value in **Exercise 32** to the value in **Example 1.** What do you conclude?

The Rule of 78 with Prepayment Penalty *A certain retailer's credit contract designates the rule of 78 for computing unearned interest and imposes a "prepayment penalty." In case of any payoff earlier than the due date, they will charge an additional 10% of the original finance charge. Find the least value of k (remaining payments after payoff) that would result in any net savings in each case.*

34. 24 payments originally scheduled

35. 36 payments originally scheduled

36. 48 payments originally scheduled

The actuarial method of computing unearned interest assumes that, throughout the life of the loan, the borrower is paying interest at the rate given by APR for money actually being used by the borrower. When contemplating complete payoff along with the current payment, think of k future payments as applying to a separate loan with the same APR and h being the finance charge per $100 of that loan. Refer to the following formula.

$$u = kR\left(\frac{h}{\$100 + h}\right)$$

37. Describe in words the quantity represented by

$$\frac{h}{\$100 + h}.$$

38. Describe in words the quantity represented by kR.

39. Explain why the product of the two quantities above represents unearned interest.

Write out your response to each exercise.

40. Why might a lender be justified in imposing a prepayment penalty?

41. Discuss reasons that a borrower may want to pay off a loan early.

42. Find out what federal agency you can contact if you have questions about compliance with the Truth in Lending Act. (Any bank, or retailer's credit department, should be able to help you with this, or you could try a Web search.)

43. Study the table at the right, which pertains to a 12-month loan. The column-3 entries are designed so that they are in the same ratios as the column-2 entries but will add up to 1 because their denominators are all equal to

$$1 + 2 + 3 + 4 + 5 + \ldots + 12 = \frac{12 \cdot 13}{2} = 78.$$

(This is the origin of the term "rule of 78.")

Month	Fraction of Loan Principal Used by Borrower	Fraction of Finance Charge Owed
1	12/12	12/78
2	11/12	11/78
3	10/12	10/78
4	9/12	9/78
5	8/12	8/78
6	7/12	7/78
7	6/12	6/78
8	5/12	5/78
9	4/12	4/78
10	3/12	3/78
11	2/12	2/78
12	1/12	1/78
		78/78 = 1

Suppose the loan is paid in full after eight months. Use the table to determine the unearned fraction of the total finance charge.

44. Find the fraction of unearned interest of **Exercise 43** by using the rule of 78 formula.

13.4 THE COSTS AND ADVANTAGES OF HOME OWNERSHIP

Fixed-Rate Mortgages • Adjustable-Rate Mortgages • Closing Costs • Taxes, Insurance, and Maintenance

Fixed-Rate Mortgages

Heating a house is another cost that may get you involved with banks and interest rates after you finally get a roof over your head. The roof you see above does more than keep off the rain. It holds solar panels, part of the solar heating system in the building.

For many decades, home ownership has been considered a centerpiece of the "American dream." For most people, a home represents the largest purchase of their lifetime, and it is certainly worth careful consideration.

A loan for a substantial amount, extending over a lengthy time interval (typically up to 30 years), for the purpose of buying a home or other property or real estate, and for which the property is pledged as security for the loan, is called a **mortgage.** (In some areas, a mortgage may also be called a **deed of trust** or a **security deed.**) The time until final payoff is called the **term** of the mortgage. The portion of the purchase price of the home that the buyer pays initially is called the **down payment.** The **principal amount of the mortgage** (the amount borrowed) is found by subtracting the down payment from the purchase price.

With a **fixed-rate mortgage,** the interest rate will remain constant throughout the term, and the initial principal balance, together with interest due on the loan, is repaid to the lender through regular (constant) periodic (we assume monthly) payments. This is called **amortizing** the loan. The regular monthly payment needed to amortize a loan depends on the amount financed, the term of the loan, and the interest rate, according to the formula on the next page.

Regular Monthly Payment

The **regular monthly payment** required to repay a loan of P dollars, together with interest at an annual rate r, over a term of t years, is calculated as follows.

$$R = \frac{P\left(\frac{r}{12}\right)}{1 - \left(\frac{12}{12 + r}\right)^{12t}}$$

EXAMPLE 1 Using a Formula to Find a Monthly Mortgage Payment

Find the monthly payment necessary to amortize a $75,000 mortgage at 5.5% annual interest for 15 years.

SOLUTION

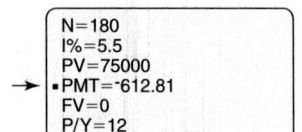

N=180
I%=5.5
PV=75000
→ ■PMT=⁻612.81
FV=0
P/Y=12
C/Y=12
PMT: END BEGIN

The arrow indicates a payment of $612.81, supporting the result of **Example 1.**

$$R = \frac{\$75,000\left(\frac{0.055}{12}\right)}{1 - \left(\frac{12}{12 + 0.055}\right)^{(12)(15)}} = \$612.81$$

■■■

With a programmable or financial calculator, you can store the formula above and minimize the work. Another option is to use a tool such as **Table 6**, which gives payment values (per $1000 principal) for typical ranges of mortgage terms and interest rates. The entries in the table are given to five decimal places so that accuracy to the nearest cent can be obtained for most normal mortgage amounts.

Table 6	Monthly Payments to Repay Principal and Interest on a $1000 Mortgage					
Annual rate **(r)**	**Term of Mortgage (Years)** **(t)**					
	5	**10**	**15**	**20**	**25**	**30**
4.0%	$18.41652	$10.12451	$7.39688	$6.05980	$5.27837	$4.77415
4.5%	18.64302	10.36384	7.64993	6.32649	5.55832	5.06685
5.0%	18.87123	10.60655	7.90794	6.59956	5.84590	5.36822
5.5%	19.10116	10.85263	8.17083	6.87887	6.14087	5.67789
6.0%	19.33280	11.10205	8.43857	7.16431	6.44301	5.99551
6.5%	19.56615	11.35480	8.71107	7.45573	6.75207	6.32068
7.0%	19.80120	11.61085	8.98828	7.75299	7.06779	6.65302
7.5%	20.03795	11.87018	9.27012	8.05593	7.38991	6.99215
8.0%	20.27639	12.13276	9.55652	8.36440	7.71816	7.33765
8.5%	20.51653	12.39857	9.84740	8.67823	8.05227	7.68913
9.0%	20.75836	12.66758	10.14267	8.99726	8.39196	8.04623
9.5%	21.00186	12.93976	10.44225	9.32131	8.73697	8.40854
10.0%	21.24704	13.21507	10.74605	9.65022	9.08701	8.77572
10.5%	21.49390	13.49350	11.05399	9.98380	9.44182	9.14739
11.0%	21.74242	13.77500	11.36597	10.32188	9.80113	9.52323
11.5%	21.99261	14.05954	11.68190	10.66430	10.16469	9.90291
12.0%	22.24445	14.34709	12.00168	11.01086	10.53224	10.28613

▌▌▐ EXAMPLE 2 Using a Table to Find a Monthly Mortgage Payment

Find the monthly payment necessary to amortize a $98,000 at 6.5% for 25 years.

SOLUTION

In **Table 6**, read down to the 6.5% row and across to the column for 25 years, to find the entry 6.75207. As this is the monthly payment amount needed to amortize a loan of $1000, and our loan is for $98,000, our required monthly payment is

$$98 \cdot \$6.75207 = \$661.70. \qquad \blacksquare\blacksquare\blacksquare$$

So that the borrower pays interest only on the money actually owed in a month, interest on real-estate loans is computed on the decreasing balance of the loan. Each equal monthly payment is first applied toward interest for the previous month. The remainder of the payment is then applied toward reduction of the principal amount owed.

Payments in the early years of a real-estate loan are mostly interest (typically 80% or more); only a small amount goes toward reducing the principal. The amount of interest decreases each month, so that larger and larger amounts of the payment will apply to the principal. During the last years of the loan, most of the monthly payment is applied toward the principal. (See **Table 8** on **page 716.**)

Once the regular monthly payment has been determined, as in **Examples 1 and 2,** an **amortization schedule** (or **repayment schedule**) can be generated. It will show the allotment of payments for interest and principal, and the principal balance, for one or more months during the life of the loan. Tables showing these breakdowns are available from lenders or can be produced on a computer spreadsheet. The following steps demonstrate how the computations work.

Step 1 Interest for the month $= \left(\dfrac{\text{Old balance}}{\text{of principal}}\right)\left(\dfrac{\text{Annual}}{\text{interest rate}}\right)\left(\dfrac{1}{12}\text{ year}\right)$

Step 2 Payment on principal $= \left(\dfrac{\text{Monthly}}{\text{payment}}\right) - \left(\dfrac{\text{Interest for}}{\text{the month}}\right)$

Step 3 New balance of principal $= \left(\dfrac{\text{Old balance}}{\text{of principal}}\right) - \left(\dfrac{\text{Payment on}}{\text{principal}}\right)$

This sequence of steps is done for the end of each month. The new balance obtained in Step 3 becomes the Step 1 old balance for the next month.

▌▌▐ EXAMPLE 3 Preparing an Amortization Schedule

The Petersons have a $60,000 mortgage with a term of 30 years and a 4.5% interest rate. Prepare an amortization schedule for the first 2 months of their mortgage.

SOLUTION

First get the monthly payment. We use **Table 6**. (You could also use the formula.)

Mortgage amount in $1000s ↓   Intersection of 4.5% row with 30-year column in **Table 6** ↓

$R = 60 \quad \cdot \quad \$5.06685 = \$304.01$

Now apply Steps 1–3.

Step 1 Interest for the month $= \$60{,}000(0.045)\left(\frac{1}{12}\right) = \$225$

Step 2 Payment on principal $= \$304.01 - \$225 = \$79.01$

Step 3 New balance of principal $= \$60{,}000 - \$79.01 = \$59{,}920.99$

Sidebar (left margin):

```
 N=300.00
 I%=6.50
 PV=98000.00
→ •PMT=⁻661.70
 FV=0.00
 P/Y=12.00
 C/Y=12.00
 PMT: END  BEGIN
```

Under the conditions of **Example 2,** the monthly payment is $661.70. Compare with the table method.

The book, *You Can Do the Math,* by Ron Lipsman of the University of Maryland, is a practical resource for most aspects of **personal financial management.** The associated Web site, www.math.umd.edu/~rll/cgi-bin/finance.html, provides "calculators," with which you can easily input your own values to get the results of many different financial computations.

Starting with an old balance of $59,920.99, repeat the steps for the second month.

Step 1 Interest for the month = $59,920.99$(0.045)\left(\frac{1}{12}\right)$ = $224.70

Step 2 Payment on principal = $304.01 − $224.70 = $79.31

Step 3 New balance of principal = $59,920.99 − $79.31 = **$59,841.68**

These calculations are summarized in **Table 7**.

Table 7	Amortization Schedule		
Payment Number	Interest Payment	Principal Payment	Balance of Principal
			$60,000.00
1	$225.00	$79.01	$59,920.99
2	$224.70	$79.31	**$59,841.68**

▪▪▪

Prevailing mortgage interest rates have varied considerably over the years. **Table 8** shows portions of the amortization schedule for the Petersons' loan of **Example 3** and shows what the corresponding values would have been had their interest rate been 14.5%. (Rates that high have not been seen for many years.) Notice how much interest is involved in this home mortgage. At the (low) 4.5% rate, $49,444.03 in interest was paid along with the $60,000 principal. At a rate of 14.5%, the interest alone would total the huge sum of $204,504.88, which is about 3.4 times greater than the mortgage principal.

Table 8	Amortization Schedules for a $60,000, 30-Year Mortgage						
4.5% Interest Monthly Payment: $304.01				14.5% Interest Monthly Payment: $734.73			
Payment Number	Interest Payment	Principal Payment	Balance of Principal	Payment Number	Interest Payment	Principal Payment	Balance of Principal
Initially →			60,000.00	Initially →			60,000.00
1	225.00	79.01	59,920.99	1	725.00	9.73	59,990.27
2	224.70	79.31	59,841.68	2	724.88	9.85	59,980.42
3	224.41	79.60	59,762.08	3	724.76	9.97	59,970.45
12	221.68	82.33	59,032.06	12	723.63	11.11	59,875.11
60	205.47	98.54	54,694.75	60	714.96	19.77	59,149.53
175	152.47	151.54	40,506.65	175	656.05	78.69	54,214.82
176	151.90	152.11	40,354.54	176	655.10	79.64	54,135.18
236	113.60	190.41	30,102.65	236	571.02	163.72	47,092.76
237	112.88	191.13	29,911.52	237	569.04	165.70	46,927.07
240	110.73	193.28	29,333.83	240	562.96	171.78	46,417.87
303	59.33	244.68	15,575.66	303	368.65	366.09	30,142.47
304	58.41	245.60	15,330.05	304	364.22	370.51	29,771.96
359	2.27	301.74	302.88	359	17.44	717.29	725.96
360	1.14	302.88	0.00	360	8.77	725.96	0.00
Totals:	49,444.03	60,000.00		**Totals:**	204,504.88	60,000.00	

Adjustable-Rate Mortgages

The lending industry uses many variations on the basic fixed-rate mortgage. An **adjustable-rate mortgage (ARM),** also known as a **variable-rate mortgage (VRM),** generally starts out with a lower rate than similar fixed-rate loans, but the rate changes periodically, reflecting changes in prevailing rates.

Quantities Governing Adjustable-rate Mortgages (ARMS)

- **Adjustment period**—Time interval between rate adjustments (typically 1, 3, or 5 years)
- **Index**—Standard fluctuating average that is the basis for the new, adjusted rate (typically the 1-, 3-, or 5-year U.S. Treasury security rate, or a national or regional "cost of funds" index)
- **Margin**—Additional amount added to the index by the lender (typically a few percentage points)
- **Discount**—Amount by which the *initial* rate may be less than the sum of the index and the margin (typically arranged between the seller and the lender)
- **Interest rate cap**—Limits on (interest) rate increases
- **Periodic cap**—Limit on rate increase per adjustment period (typically about 1% per 6 months or 2% per year)
- **Overall cap**—Limit on rate increases over the life of the loan (typically about 5% total)
- **Payment cap**—Limit on how much the payment can increase at each adjustment
- **Negative amortization**—An increasing loan principal (perhaps caused by a payment cap preventing the payment from covering a higher interest rate)
- **Convertibility feature**—A contractual ability to convert to a fixed-rate mortgage (usually at certain designated points in time)
- **Prepayment penalty**—Charges imposed by the lender if payments are made early

---

EXAMPLE 4   Comparing ARM Payments Before and After a Rate Adjustment

We pay $20,000 down on a $180,000 house and take out a 1-year ARM for a 30-year term. The lender uses the 1-year Treasury index (at 4%) and a 2% margin.

(a) Find the monthly payment for the first year.

(b) Suppose that after a year the 1-year Treasury index has increased to 5.1%. Find the monthly payment for the second year.

SOLUTION

$$\text{Cost of house} \qquad \text{Down payment}$$
$$\downarrow \qquad\qquad \downarrow$$

(a)   Mortgage amount $= \$180{,}000 - \$20{,}000 = \$160{,}000$

The first-year interest rate will be

ARM interest rate $=$ Index rate $+$ Margin $= 4\% + 2\% = 6\%.$

Now from **Table 6** (using 6% over 30 years) we obtain 5.99551.

First-year monthly payment $= 160 \cdot \$5.99551 = \$959.28$

(b) During the first year, a small amount of the mortgage principal has been paid, so in effect we will now have a new "mortgage amount." (Also, the term will now be 1 year less than the original term.) The amortization schedule for the first year (not shown here) yields a loan balance, after the twelfth monthly payment, of $158,035.19.

For the second year,

$$\text{ARM interest rate} = \text{Index rate} + \text{Margin} = 5.1\% + 2\% = 7.1\%.$$

Because 7.1% is not included in **Table 6**, we use the regular monthly payment formula with the new mortgage balance and 29 years for the remaining term.

$$\text{Second-year monthly payment} = \frac{P\left(\frac{r}{12}\right)}{1 - \left(\frac{12}{12 + r}\right)^{12t}} \qquad \text{Regular payment formula}$$

$$= \frac{\$158,035.19\left(\frac{0.071}{12}\right)}{1 - \left(\frac{12}{12 + 0.071}\right)^{(12)(29)}} \qquad \text{Substitute known values.}$$

$$= \$1072.74$$

The first ARM interest rate adjustment has caused the second-year monthly payment to rise to $1072.74, which is an increase of $113.46 over the initial monthly payment. ▮▮▮

A "seller buydown" occurs when the seller (a new-home builder, for example) pays the lender an amount in order to discount the buyer's loan. This reduces the initial rate and monthly payments, but it may be combined with higher initial fees or even an increase in the price of the house.

▮▮ **EXAMPLE 5** Discounting a Mortgage Rate

In **Example 4,** suppose that a seller buydown discounts our initial (first-year) rate by 1.5%. Find the first-year and second-year monthly payments.

SOLUTION

The 4% index rate is discounted to 2.5%. Adding the 2% margin yields a net first-year rate of 4.5% (rather than the 6% of **Example 4**), so the **Table 6** entry is 5.06685.

$$\text{First-year monthly payment} = 160(\$5.06685) = \$810.70$$

The amortization schedule shows a balance at the end of the first year of $157,418.79. The discount now expires, and the index has increased to 5.1%, so for the second year,

$$\text{ARM interest rate} = \text{Index rate} + \text{Margin} = 5.1\% + 2\% = 7.1\%.$$

(This is just as in **Example 4.**) Using the monthly payment formula, with $r = 7.1\%$ and $t = 29$,

$$\text{Second-year monthly payment} = \frac{\$157,418.79\left(\frac{0.071}{12}\right)}{1 - \left(\frac{12}{12 + 0.071}\right)^{(12)(29)}} \qquad \text{Substitute values in the monthly payment formula.}$$

$$= \$1068.55.$$

The initial monthly payment of $810.70 looks considerably better than the $959.28 of **Example 4,** but at the start of year two, monthly payments jump by $257.85. ▮▮▮

Making sure an ARM has adequate rate and payment caps will help avoid "payment shock." It is also wise to have convertibility and no prepayment penalty.

Refinancing means initiating a new home mortgage and paying off the old one. In times of relatively low rates, lenders often encourage homeowners to refinance. Because setting up a new loan will involve costs, make sure you have a good reason before refinancing. Some possible reasons:

1. The new loan may be comparable to the current loan with a rate low enough to recoup the costs in a few years.
2. You may want to pay down your balance faster by switching to a shorter-term loan.
3. You may want to borrow out equity to cover other major expenses, such as education for your children.
4. Your present loan may have a large balloon feature that necessitates refinancing.
5. You may be uncomfortable with your variable (hence uncertain) ARM and want to convert to a fixed-rate loan.

Closing Costs

Apart from principal and interest payments, buying a home involves a variety of one-time expenses called **closing costs,** or **settlement charges,** which are imposed when the loan is finalized (at "closing"). A buyer is entitled to a "good faith estimate" of these costs from the lender and, if desired, may shop for alternative providers of settlement services. Typical closing costs are illustrated in the following example.

▮▮ **EXAMPLE 6** Computing Total Closing Costs

For a $58,000 mortgage, the borrower was charged the following closing costs.

Loan origination fee (1% of mortgage amount)	$____
Broker loan fee	1455
Lender document and underwriting fees	375
Lender tax and wire fees	205
Fee to title company	200
Title insurance fee	302
Title reconveyance fee	65
Document recording fees	35

Compute the total closing costs for this mortgage.

SOLUTION

"Loan origination fees" are commonly referred to as **points**. Each "point" amounts to 1% of the mortgage amount. By imposing points, the lender can effectively raise the interest rate without raising monthly payments (because points are normally paid at closing rather than over the life of the loan). In this case, "one point" translates to $580. Adding this to the other amounts listed gives total closing costs of $3217.   ▮▮▮

As there is considerable potential for abuse in the area of closing costs, Truth in Lending regulations require the lender to provide clarifying information, including the APR for the loan. The APR, the cost of the loan as a yearly rate, will probably be higher than the stated interest rate since it must reflect all points and other fees paid directly for credit as well as the actual interest.

Taxes, Insurance, and Maintenance

The primary financial considerations for most new homeowners are the following.

1. Accumulating the down payment
2. Having sufficient cash and income to qualify for the loan
3. Making the mortgage payments

Three additional ongoing expenses are

taxes, insurance, and maintenance,

all of which should be anticipated realistically. They can be significant.

  Property taxes are collected by a county or other local government. Depending on location and the home value, they can range up to several thousand dollars annually. An advantage is that property taxes and mortgage interest are income tax deductible. Therefore, money expended for those items will decrease income taxes. This is one way that the government, through the tax code, encourages home ownership.

▌▌ **EXAMPLE 7** Taking Taxes into Account in Home Ownership

Darryl Graves is in a 30% combined state and federal income tax bracket. He has calculated that he can afford a net average monthly expenditure of $1400 for a home. Can he afford the home of his dreams, which would require a 20-year, $205,000 fixed-rate mortgage at 6% plus $1920 in annual property taxes?

SOLUTION

Let's "do the math."

Regular monthly mortgage payment = 205 · $7.16431

$\qquad\qquad\qquad\qquad\qquad\qquad\quad$ ≈ $1469

Monthly property taxes = $\dfrac{\$1920}{12}$ ← Annual taxes ← Months per year

$\qquad\qquad\qquad\qquad\quad$ = $160

Total monthly expense = $1469 + $160

$\qquad\qquad\qquad\qquad\quad$ = $1629

Because $1629 > $1400, it seems that Darryl cannot afford this home. But wait—remember that mortgage interest and property taxes are both income tax deductible. Let's consider further.

$$\text{Monthly interest} = \$205{,}000\,(0.06)\left(\frac{1}{12}\right) \qquad \text{Interest} = Prt$$

$$= \$1025$$

Of the $1469 mortgage payment, $1025 would be interest (initially).

Monthly deductible expenses = $1025 + $160

$\qquad\qquad\qquad\qquad\qquad\quad$ = $1185

Monthly income tax savings = $1185 · 30%

$\qquad\qquad\qquad\qquad\qquad\qquad$ ≈ $356

Net monthly cost of home = $1629 − $356

$\qquad\qquad\qquad\qquad\qquad\quad$ = $1273

By considering the effect of taxes, we see that the net monthly cost, $1273, is indeed within Darryl's $1400 affordability limit. ▌▌▌

Homeowner's insurance usually covers losses due to fire, storm damage, and other casualties. Some types, such as earthquake or hurricane coverage, could be unavailable or very expensive, depending on location. Also, all homes require **maintenance,** but these costs can vary greatly, depending mainly on the size, construction type, age, and condition of the home. These expenses are necessary in order to protect the home investment. They are not generally tax deductible.

Government-backed mortgages, including FHA (Federal Housing Administration) and VA (Veterans Administration) loans, carry a government guarantee to protect the lender in case the borrower fails to repay the loan. Those who do not qualify for these loans, and obtain a conventional loan instead, usually are required to buy private mortgage insurance (PMI) as part of the loan package.

This feature can be a surprise to first-time home purchasers. It was introduced to protect lenders but indirectly protects the buyers, who may lose a bundle if some catastrophe makes it impossible to make the payments.

Over the second half of the twentieth century the amount of credit life insurance in force (for the purpose of covering consumer debt) increased by over 500 times, while group life insurance increased by only about 200 times, ordinary life insurance increased by about 60 times, and industrial life insurance actually decreased. (*Source:* American Council of Life Insurance.)

▌▌ **EXAMPLE 8** | Including Insurance and Maintenance in Home Costs

In moving ahead with his home purchase, Darryl (**Example 7**) estimates that homeowner's insurance will be about $550 per year, and that maintenance will be about $650 per year. Will these additional expenses mean that he cannot afford the home?

SOLUTION

These items carry no tax advantage (they are not deductible), so the added monthly expense is simply

$$\text{Monthly insurance and maintenance expense} = \frac{\$550 + \$650}{12} = \$100.$$

With insurance and maintenance included, we obtain

$$\text{Adjusted monthly expense} = \$1273 + \$100 = \$1373,$$

which is still less than $1400. Darryl can still afford the purchase.   ▌▌▌

Payments for property taxes and homeowner's insurance are commonly made from a **reserve account** (also called an **escrow,** or **impound, account**) maintained by the mortgage lender. The borrower must pay enough each month, along with amortization costs, so that the reserve account will be sufficient to make the payments when they come due. (In some cases, the homeowner pays taxes directly to the taxing authority and insurance premiums directly to an insurance company, totally separate from mortgage payments to the lender.)

Examples 7 and 8 raise some reasonable questions.

1. Is it wise to buy a house close to your spending limit, in light of future uncertainties?

2. What about the fact that the interest portion of mortgage payments, and therefore the tax savings, will decrease over time?

3. Won't taxes, insurance, and maintenance costs likely increase over time, making it more difficult to keep up the payments?

Some possible responses follow.

1. Darryl may have built in sufficient leeway when he decided on his $1400 per month allowance.

2. **(a)** Look again at **Table 8** to see how slowly the interest portion drops.

   (b) Most people find that their income over time increases faster than expenses for a home that carries a fixed-rate mortgage. (A variable-rate mortgage is more risky and should have its initial rate locked in for as long as possible.)

   (c) Prevailing interest rates rise and fall over time. While rising rates will not affect a fixed-rate mortgage, falling rates may offer the opportunity to reduce mortgage expenses by refinancing. (See the margin note on refinancing for guidelines.)

3. Here again, increases in income will probably keep pace. While most things, including personal income, tend to follow inflation, the fixed-rate mortgage insures that mortgage amortization, a major item, will stay constant.

13.4 EXERCISES

Round all monetary answers to the nearest cent unless directed otherwise.

Monthly Payment on a Fixed-Rate Mortgage *Find the monthly payment needed to amortize principal and interest for each fixed-rate mortgage. You can use either the regular monthly payment formula or* **Table 6**, *as appropriate.*

	Loan Amount	Interest Rate	Term			Loan Amount	Interest Rate	Term
1.	$70,000	10.0%	20 years	**5.**		$227,750	12.5%	25 years
2.	$50,000	11.0%	15 years	**6.**		$95,450	15.5%	5 years
3.	$57,300	8.7%	25 years	**7.**		$132,500	7.6%	22 years
4.	$85,000	7.9%	30 years	**8.**		$205,000	5.5%	10 years

Amortization of a Fixed-Rate Mortgage *Complete the first one or two months (as required) of each amortization schedule for a fixed-rate mortgage.*

9. Mortgage: $58,500

Interest rate: 10.0%

Term of loan: 30 years

Amortization Schedule

Payment Number	Total Payment	Interest Payment	Principal Payment	Balance of Principal
1	(a) _____	(b) _____	(c) _____	(d) _____

10. Mortgage: $87,000

Interest rate: 8.5%

Term of loan: 20 years

Amortization Schedule

Payment Number	Total Payment	Interest Payment	Principal Payment	Balance of Principal
1	(a) _____	(b) _____	(c) _____	(d) _____

11. Mortgage: $143,200

Interest rate: 6.5%

Term of loan: 15 years

Amortization Schedule

Payment Number	Total Payment	Interest Payment	Principal Payment	Balance of Principal
1	(a) _____	(b) _____	(c) _____	(d) _____
2	(e) _____	(f) _____	(g) _____	(h) _____

12. Mortgage: $124,750

Interest rate: 9%

Term of loan: 25 years

Amortization Schedule

Payment Number	Total Payment	Interest Payment	Principal Payment	Balance of Principal
1	(a) _____	(b) _____	(c) _____	(d) _____
2	(e) _____	(f) _____	(g) _____	(h) _____

13. Mortgage: $113,650

Interest rate: 8.2%

Term of loan: 10 years

Amortization Schedule

Payment Number	Total Payment	Interest Payment	Principal Payment	Balance of Principal
1	(a) _____	(b) _____	(c) _____	(d) _____
2	(e) _____	(f) _____	(g) _____	(h) _____

14. Mortgage: $150,000
Interest rate: 6.25%
Term of loan: 16 years

Amortization Schedule

Payment Number	Total Payment	Interest Payment	Principal Payment	Balance of Principal
1	(a) _____	(b) _____	(c) _____	(d) _____
2	(e) _____	(f) _____	(g) _____	(h) _____

Finding Monthly Mortgage Payments *Find the total monthly payment, including taxes and insurance.*

	Mortgage	Interest Rate	Term of Loan	Annual Taxes	Annual Insurance
15.	$ 62,300	7%	20 years	$610	$220
16.	$ 51,800	10%	25 years	$570	$145
17.	$ 89,560	6.5%	10 years	$915	$409
18.	$ 72,890	5.5%	15 years	$1850	$545
19.	$115,400	8.8%	20 years	$1295.16	$444.22
20.	$128,100	11.3%	30 years	$1476.53	$565.77

Comparing Total Principal and Interest on a Mortgage *Suppose $140,000 is owed on a house. The monthly payment for principal and interest at 8.5% for 30 years is 140 · $7.68913 = $1076.48.*

21. How many monthly payments will be made over the 30-year period?

22. What is the total amount that will be paid for principal and interest?

23. The total interest charged is the total amount paid minus the amount financed. What is the total interest?

24. Which is more—the amount financed or the total interest paid? By how much?

Long-Term Effect of Interest Rates *You may remember seeing home mortgage interest rates fluctuate widely in a period of not too many years. The following exercises show the effect of changing rates. Refer to* **Table 8**, *which compared the amortization of a $60,000, 30-year mortgage for rates of 4.5% and 14.5%. Give values of each of the following for* **(a)** *a 4.5% rate, and* **(b)** *a 14.5% rate.*

25. monthly payments

26. percentage of first monthly payment that is principal

27. balance of principal after 1 year

28. balance of principal after 20 years

29. the first monthly payment that includes more toward principal than toward interest

30. amount of interest included in final monthly payment of mortgage

The Effect of the Term on Total Amount Paid *Suppose a $60,000 mortgage is to be amortized at 7.5% interest. Find the total amount of interest that would be paid for each term.*

31. 10 years   **32.** 20 years   **33.** 30 years   **34.** 40 years

The Effect of Adjustable Rates on the Monthly Payment *For each adjustable-rate mortgage, find* **(a)** *the initial monthly payment,* **(b)** *the monthly payment for the second adjustment period, and* **(c)** *the change in monthly payment at the first adjustment.*

	Beginning Balance	Term	Initial Index Rate	Margin	Adjustment Period	Adjusted Index Rate	Adjusted Balance	
35.	$75,000	20 years	6.5%	2.5%	1 year	8.0%	$73,595.52	*(The "adjusted balance" is the principal balance at the time of the first rate adjustment. Assume no caps apply.)*
36.	$44,500	30 years	7.2%	2.75%	3 years	6.6%	$43,669.14	

The Effect of Rate Caps on Adjustable-Rate Mortgages James Kinchen has a 1-year ARM for $50,000 over a 20-year term. The margin is 2% and the index rate starts out at 7.5% and increases to 10.0% at the first adjustment. The balance of principal at the end of the first year is $49,119.48. The ARM includes a periodic rate cap of 2% per adjustment period. (Use this information for Exercises 37–40.)

37. Find **(a)** the interest owed and **(b)** the monthly payment due for the first month of the first year.

38. Find **(a)** the interest owed and **(b)** the monthly payment due for the first month of the second year.

39. What is the monthly payment adjustment at the end of the first year?

40. If the index rate has dropped slightly at the end of the second year, will the third-year monthly payments necessarily drop? Why or why not?

Closing Costs of a Mortgage For Exercises 41–44, refer to the following list of closing costs for the purchase of a $175,000 house requiring a 20% down payment, and find each requested amount.

Title insurance premium	$240
Document recording fee	30
Loan fee (two points)	___
Appraisal fee	225
Prorated property taxes	685
Prorated fire insurance premium	295

41. the mortgage amount

42. the loan fee

43. the total closing costs

44. the total amount of cash required of the buyer at closing (including down payment)

Consider the scenario of **Example 7.** *Recalling that mortgage interest is income tax deductible, find (to the nearest dollar) the additional initial net monthly savings resulting from each strategy. (In each case, only the designated item changes. All other features remain the same.)*

45. Change the mortgage term from 20 years to 30 years.

46. Change the mortgage from fixed at 6% to an ARM with an initial rate of 5%.

For each of Exercises 47–50, find all of the following quantities for a $200,000 fixed-rate mortgage. (Give answers to the nearest dollar.)

(a) *Monthly mortgage payment (principal and interest)*

(b) *Monthly house payment (including property taxes and insurance)*

(c) *Initial monthly interest*

(d) *Income tax deductible portion of initial house payment*

(e) *Net initial monthly cost for the home (considering tax savings)*

Term of Mortgage	Interest Rate	Annual Property Tax	Annual Insurance	Owner's Income Tax Bracket
47. 15 years	5.5%	$960	$480	20%
48. 20 years	6.0%	$840	$420	25%
49. 10 years	6.5%	$1092	$540	30%
50. 30 years	7.5%	$1260	$600	40%

On the basis of material in this section, or your own research, give brief written responses to each problem.

51. Give other ways Darryl (**Examples 7 and 8**) could possibly decrease the initial net monthly payments for his home.

52. Suppose your ARM allows conversion to a fixed-rate loan at each of the first five adjustment dates. Describe circumstances under which you would want to convert.

53. Describe each type of mortgage.

   Graduated payment

   Balloon payment

   Interest-only

   Option ARM ("neg-am")

54. Should a home buyer always pay the smallest down payment that will be accepted? Explain.

55. Should a borrower always choose the shortest term available in order to minimize the total interest expense? Explain.

56. Under what conditions would an ARM probably be a better choice than a fixed-rate mortgage?

57. Why are second-year monthly payments (slightly) less in **Example 5** than in **Example 4** even though the term, 29 years, and the interest rate, 7.1%, are the same in both cases?

58. Do you think that the discount in **Example 5** actually makes the overall cost of the mortgage less? Explain.

59. Discuss the term "payment shock" mentioned at the end of **Example 5.**

60. Find out what is meant by each term and describe some of the features of each.

   FHA-backed mortgage

   VA-backed mortgage

   Conventional mortgage

13.5 FINANCIAL INVESTMENTS

Stocks • Bonds • Mutual Funds • Evaluating Investment Returns
• Building a Nest Egg

Stocks

In a general sense, an *investment* is a way of putting resources to work so that (hopefully) they will grow. Our main emphasis here will be on the basic mathematical aspects of a restricted class of financial investments, namely, *stocks, bonds,* and *mutual funds.*

Buying stock in a corporation makes you a part owner of the corporation. You then share in any profits the company makes, and your share of profits is called a **dividend.** If the company prospers (or if increasing numbers of investors believe it will prosper in the future), your stock will be attractive to others, so that you may, if you wish, sell your shares at a profit. The profit you make by selling for more than you paid is called a **capital gain.** A negative gain, or **capital loss,** results if you sell for less than you paid. By **return on investment,** we mean the net difference between what you receive (including your sale price and any dividends received) and what you paid (your purchase price plus any other expenses of buying and selling the stock).

|| EXAMPLE 1 Finding the Return on a Stock Ownership

Lauren Hileman bought 100 shares of stock in Company A on January 15, 2010, paying $30 per share. On January 15, 2011, she received a dividend of $0.50 per share, and the stock price had risen to $30.85 per share. (Ignore any costs other than the purchase price.) Find the following.

(a) Lauren's total cost for the stock

(b) The total dividend amount

(c) Lauren's capital gain if she sold the stock on January 15, 2011

(d) Lauren's total return on her one year of ownership of this stock

(e) The percentage return

SOLUTION

(a) Cost = ($30 per share) · (100 shares) = $3000

She paid $3000 total.

(b) Dividend = ($0.50 per share) · (100 shares) = $50

The dividend amount was $50.

Change in price per share   Number of shares

(c) Capital gain = ($30.85 − $30.00) · 100 = $0.85 · 100 = $85

The capital gain was $85.

Dividend   Capital gain

(d) Total return = $50 + $85 = $135

Total return on the investment was $135.

(e) Percentage return = $\dfrac{\text{Total return}}{\text{Total cost}} \cdot 100\% = \dfrac{\$135}{\$3000} \cdot 100\% = 4.5\%$

The percentage return on the investment was 4.5%.   ■■■

The **NASDAQ (National Association of Securities Dealers Advanced Quotations),** unlike the NYSE and other exchanges that actually carry out trading at specific locations, is an electronic network of brokerages established in 1971 to facilitate the trading of over-the-counter (unlisted) stocks. Most of the high-tech company stocks, which grew very rapidly as a group in the 1980s and especially the 1990s (and many of which declined as rapidly in 2000–2002), are (or were) listed on the Nasdaq market.

The price of a share of stock is determined by the law of supply and demand at institutions called **stock exchanges.** In the United States, the oldest and largest exchange is the New York Stock Exchange (NYSE), established in 1792 and located on Wall Street in New York City. Members of the public buy their stock through stockbrokers, people who have access to the exchange. Stockbrokers do business in offices throughout the country. They charge a fee for buying or selling stock.

Current prices and other information about particular stocks are published daily in many newspapers and on various Web sites, where information may be updated every few minutes. **Table 9** below shows examples of trading on the NYSE, on June 4, 2010. The exchange opens at 9:30 A.M. and closes at 4:00 P.M., Eastern time.

Observe the column headings and the numbers for the first company listed, Allstate, with market symbol ALL. The first four numbers show that the first sale of Allstate shares after 9:30 A.M. was for $29.62 per share, the highest sale during the trading day was for $29.77, the lowest was for $28.86, and the last sale before 4:00 P.M. was for $28.94 per share.

Moving across to the right, the next two numbers show that the closing price for the day was $1.23 lower than that of the previous day, that is 4.08% lower. The volume number indicates that 5,383,700 shares (to the nearest 100 shares) of Allstate stock were sold that day.

The next two numbers show that, over the last year, the greatest and least prices paid for ALL were $35.51 and $22.82, respectively. The following two numbers show that Allstate's current dividend is 80 cents per share and that represents a current yield of 2.76% (of the current stock closing price for the day).

PE is the **price-to-earnings ratio,** the current price per share divided by the earnings per share over the past 12 months. For ALL, this ratio was 12.58. Finally, the year-to-date percent change means that Allstate's price per share is now $3.66 less than it was at the start of this calendar year.

Table 9   Selected Stock Quotes (June 4, 2010)

Company	Symbol	Open	Daily Hi	Daily Lo	Close	Net Change	% Change	Volume (100s)	52-wk HI	52-wk LO	Div	% Yield	PE	YTD % Change
Allstate	ALL	29.62	29.77	28.86	28.94	−1.23	−4.08	53837	35.51	22.82	0.80	2.76	12.58	−3.66
Bank of America	BAC	15.50	15.73	15.25	15.35	−0.46	−2.91	1479077	19.86	11.20	0.04	0.26	...	1.93
CarMax	KMX	21.72	21.87	20.75	20.93	−1.46	−6.52	25150	26.50	21.10	...	...	16.74	−13.69
Caterpillar, Inc.	CAT	59.49	60.20	57.36	57.76	−3.35	−5.48	102585	72.83	30.01	1.68	2.91	29.62	1.35
Chevron	CVX	72.15	72.71	70.80	71.28	−2.63	−3.56	180765	83.41	60.88	2.88	4.04	10.82	−7.42
Deere	DE	58.37	59.33	56.50	56.88	−2.79	−4.68	51837	63.68	34.90	1.20	2.11	24.73	5.16
Duke Energy	DUK	15.87	15.88	15.58	15.61	−0.44	−2.74	99430	17.94	13.91	0.96	6.15	17.54	−9.30
FedEx	FDX	82.21	82.62	78.84	79.37	−4.61	−5.49	38621	97.75	49.76	0.44	0.55	...	−4.89
General Mills	GIS	74.28	74.28	73.04	73.30	−1.44	−1.93	33270	75.14	51.37	1.96	2.67	14.84	3.52
Harley-Davidson	HOG	28.33	28.35	27.16	27.35	−1.88	−6.43	58195	36.13	14.99	0.40	1.46	...	8.53
Kimberly-Clark	KMB	60.73	60.83	59.98	60.18	−1.10	−1.80	62518	67.03	50.42	2.64	4.39	13.52	−5.54
Pearson ADS	PSO	13.80	13.83	13.52	13.57	−0.52	−3.69	990	16.37	9.29	0.56	4.13	15.96	−5.50
Sara Lee	SLE	14.42	14.50	14.20	14.24	−0.38	−2.60	152351	15.06	8.72	0.44	3.09	20.06	16.91
Walt Disney	DIS	34.06	34.35	33.44	33.69	−1.02	−2.94	217056	37.98	22.05	0.35	1.04	17.64	4.47
Yum!Brands	YUM	41.36	41.60	40.70	40.86	−1.06	−2.53	47957	44.00	32.24	0.84	2.06	18.08	16.84

▌▌ EXAMPLE 2   Reading the Stock Table

Use the stock table (**Table 9**) to find the required amounts below.

(a) The highest price for the last 52 weeks for FedEx (FDX)

(b) The dividend for Kimberly-Clark (KMB)

SOLUTION

(a) Find the correct line from the stock table for FedEx.

The highest price for FedEx for the last 52 weeks was $97.75.

(b) The div value of 2.64 means that KMB paid a dividend of $2.64 per share.   ▌▌▌

▌▌ EXAMPLE 3   Finding the Cost of a Stock Purchase

Find the cost for 100 shares of Deere (DE) stock, purchased at the closing price for the day.

SOLUTION

From **Table 9**, the closing price for the day for Deere was $56.88 per share.

$$\underset{\substack{\text{Price per} \\ \text{share} \\ \downarrow}}{} \qquad \underset{\substack{\text{Number of} \\ \text{shares} \\ \downarrow}}{}$$

$$\text{Total cost} = \$56.88 \quad \cdot \quad 100 = \$5688.00$$

One hundred shares of this stock would cost $5688.00, plus any broker's fees.   ▌▌▌

Most stock purchases and sales are done through a broker, who has representatives at the exchange to execute a buy or sell order. The broker will charge a **commission** (the broker's fee) for executing an order. Before 1974, commission rates were set by stock exchange rules and were uniform from broker to broker. Since then, however, rates are competitive and vary considerably among brokers.

Full-service brokers, who offer research, professional opinions on buying and selling individual issues, and various other services, tend to charge the highest commissions on transactions they execute. Many **discount brokers,** on the other hand, merely buy and sell stock for their clients, offering little in the way of additional services.

During the 1990s, when it often seemed that almost any reasonable choice of stock would pay off for almost any investor, a number of online companies appeared, offering much cheaper transactions than were available through conventional brokers. Subsequently, most conventional brokerage firms, as well as the major discount brokerages, introduced their own automated (online) services. Investors today should compare a number of options before deciding which brokerage can best provide the stock investment services they need.

Commissions normally are a percentage of the value of a purchase or sale (called the **principal**). Some firms charge additional amounts in certain cases. For example, rates may depend on whether the order is for a **round lot** of shares (a multiple of 100) or an **odd lot** (any portions of an order for fewer than 100 shares). On the odd-lot portion, you may be charged an **odd-lot differential** (say, 10¢ per share). Also, it is possible to place a **limit order,** where the broker is instructed to execute a buy or sell if and when a stock reaches a predesignated price. An extra fee may be added to the commision on a limit order. One prominent discount brokerage does not charge these special fees but uses a tiered commission structure depending on the principal amount of the purchase or sale and distinguishes between **broker-assisted** and **automated** trades, as shown on the next page.

Typical Discount Commission Structure

Broker-Assisted Trade

Principal Amount	Commission
Up to $2499.99	$35 + 1.7% of principal
$2500.00–$6249.99	$65 + 0.66% of principal
$6250.00–$19,999.99	$76 + 0.34% of principal
$20,000.00–$49,999.99	$100 + 0.22% of principal
$50,000.00–$499,999.99	$155 + 0.11% of principal
$500,000.00 or more	$255 + 0.09% of principal

Automated Trade

Number of Shares	Commission
Up to 1000	$29.95
More than 1000	$0.03 per share

Also, the Securities and Exchange Commission (SEC), a federal agency that regulates stock markets, supports its own activities by charging the exchanges, based on volume of transactions. Typically this charge is passed on to investors, through brokers, in the form of an **SEC fee,** assessed on stock sales only (not purchases). As of June 2010, this fee was 1.69¢ per $1000 of principal (rounded *up* to the next cent). For example, to find the fee for a sale of $1600, first divide $1600 by $1000, then multiply by 1.69¢.

$$\text{SEC fee} = \frac{\$1600}{\$1000} \cdot \$0.0169 = \$0.02704, \quad \text{which is rounded up to \$0.03.}$$

1.69¢ = $0.0169

▮▮ **EXAMPLE 4** Finding Total Cost for a Broker-Assisted Stock Purchase

Find the total cost (including expenses) to Merideth Kolaski, who executes a broker-assisted purchase of 325 shares of Duke Energy stock at the average price of the day on June 4, 2010. Use the typical discount commission structure outlined above.

SOLUTION

Daily high Daily low

$$\text{Average price} = \frac{\$15.88 + \$15.58}{2} \quad \text{arithmetic mean}$$

$$= \$15.73$$

Price per share Number of shares

$$\text{Basic cost} = \$15.73 \quad \cdot \quad 325$$

$$= \$5112.25$$

Because this principal amount falls in the second tier of the commission structure, the broker's commission is $65 plus 0.66% of this amount.

$$\text{Broker's commission} = \$65 + 0.0066 \cdot \$5112.25 \quad \text{Multiply first, then add.}$$

$$= \$65 + \$33.74$$

$$= \$98.74$$

Basic cost Commission

$$\text{Total cost} = \$5112.25 + 98.74$$

$$= \$5210.99$$

The total cost to Merideth for this purchase is $5210.99. ▮▮▮

∎∎ EXAMPLE 5 Finding Proceeds for an Automated Stock Sale

Find the amount received by David Hertzenberg, when executing an automated sale of 500 shares of General Mills stock at the high price of the day on June 4, 2010.

SOLUTION

From **Table 9**, the basic price of the stock sold is

$$(\$74.28 \text{ per share}) \cdot (500 \text{ shares}) = \$37{,}140.00.$$

Because fewer than 1000 shares are sold, the commission is \$29.95. Find the SEC fee as described before **Example 4.**

$$\frac{\$37{,}140.00}{\$1000} \cdot \$0.0169 = \$0.627666$$

Round up to obtain an SEC fee of \$0.63. Then

$$
\underset{\text{Basic price}}{\downarrow} \quad \underset{\text{Commission}}{\downarrow} \quad \underset{\text{SEC fee}}{\downarrow}
$$

$$\text{Amount received} = \$37{,}140.00 - \$29.95 - \$0.63$$
$$= \$37{,}109.42.$$

David received \$37,109.42. ∎∎∎

Bonds

Rather than contributing your capital (money) to a company, you may prefer merely to *lend* money to the company, receiving an agreed-upon rate of interest for the use of your money. In this case you would buy a bond from the company rather than purchase stock. The bond (loan) is issued with a stated term (life span), after which the bond "matures" and the principal (or **face value**) is paid back to you. Over the term, the company pays you a fixed rate of interest, which depends upon prevailing interest rates at the time of issue (and to some extent on the company's credit rating), rather than on the underlying value of the company.

A corporate bondholder has no stake in company profits but is (quite) certain to receive timely interest payments. If a company is unable to pay both bond interest and stock dividends, the bondholders must be paid first.

∎∎ EXAMPLE 6 Finding the Return on a Bond Investment

Jerry Higgins invests \$10,000 in a 5-year corporate bond paying 6% annual interest, paid semiannually. Find the total return on this investment, assuming Jerry holds the bond to maturity (for the entire 5 years). Ignore any broker's fees.

SOLUTION

By the simple interest formula (see **Section 13.1**),

$$I = Prt = \$10{,}000(0.06)(5) = \$3000.$$

Notice that this amount, \$3000, is the *total* return, over the 5-year period, not the annual return. Also, the fact that interest is paid twice per year (3% of the face value each time) has no bearing here since compounding does not occur. ∎∎∎

Historically the overall rate of return over most time periods has been greater for stocks than for bonds. This fact (along with the general appeal of ownership) has led some investors to avoid bonds altogether. On the other hand, there are fewer uncertainties involved with bonds, and a bond investor's capital is subject to less risk. These facts can make bonds more attractive than stocks, especially for retired investors who depend on a steady stream of income from their investments. Many investors, however, seek to build a balanced portfolio that includes both stocks and bonds.

The **Wall Street reform bill of 2010** put forth "the most sweeping set of changes to the financial regulatory system since the 1930s." Prompted by the failure of a number of large financial and other companies and a steep international recession beginning in 2007, the bill created a new Consumer Financial Protection Bureau within the Federal Reserve, headed by a presidentially-appointed "independent" regulator, and with authority to write new rules to (theoretically) protect consumers from unfair or abusive practices in mortgages and credit cards. In fact, the bill creates vast bureaucratic control over virtually all financial areas discussed in this chapter.

Decade earlier, in 1999, Congressional repeal of many earlier legal and regulatory barriers had allowed large financial conglomerates to offer one-stop shopping for services in the areas of insurance, banking, and investments.

It took over a year for the Democrat-controlled Congress to bring the 2010 bill to a vote. According to the watchdog group Public Citizen, over that period the financial industry spent nearly $600 million to hire some 1,000 lobbyists to promote their interests.

Debate raged about whether the bill was really to help consumers or to control business (or perhaps a combination of the two). It was predicted that it would take about a year for the rules to be established and the impact to be felt.

(*Source: www.CNNMoney.com*)

Mutual Funds

A **mutual fund** is a pool of money collected by an investment company from many individuals and/or institutions and invested in many stocks, bonds, or money market instruments. By the late 1990s approximately $5 trillion was invested in more than 7000 separate mutual funds. By 2000 over 50 million U.S. households held mutual funds, and the largest category of these holdings was within retirement accounts.

Mutual Funds Versus Individual Stocks and Bonds

Advantages of Mutual Funds

1. *Simplicity*
   Let someone else do the work.

2. *Diversification*
   Being part of a large pool makes it easier to own interests in many different stocks, which decreases vulnerability to large losses in one particular stock or one particular sector of the economy.

3. *Access to New Issues*
   Initial public offerings (IPOs) can sometimes be very profitable. Whereas individual investors find it difficult to get in on these, the large overall assets of a mutual fund give its managers much more access.

4. *Economies of Scale*
   Large stock purchases usually incur smaller expenses per dollar invested.

5. *Professional Management*
   Professional managers may have the expertise to pick stocks and time purchases to achieve better the stated objectives of the fund.

6. *Indexing*
   With minimal management, an index fund can maintain a portfolio that mimics a popular index (such as the S&P 500). This makes it easy for individual fund investors to achieve returns at least close to those of the index.

Disadvantages of Mutual Funds

1. *Impact of One-Time Charges and Recurring Fees*
   Sales charges, management fees, "12b-1" fees (used to pay sales representatives), and fund expenses can mount and can be difficult to identify. And paying management fees does not guarantee getting *quality* management.

2. *Hidden Cost of Brokerage*
   Recurring fees and expenses are added to give the *expense ratio* of a fund. But commissions paid by the fund for stock purchases and sales are in addition to the expense ratio. (Since 1995, funds have been required to disclose their average commission costs in their annual reports.)

3. *Some Hidden Risks of Fund Ownership*
   (a) In the event of a market crash, getting out of the fund may mean accepting securities rather than cash, and these may be difficult to redeem for a fair price.
   (b) Managers may stray from the stated strategies of the fund.
   (c) Since tax liability is passed on to fund investors and depends on purchases and sales made by fund managers, investors may be unable to avoid inheriting unwanted tax basis.

Source: Forbes Guide to the Markets, John Wiley & Sons, Inc.

An abundance of information about **mutual funds** is available on the Internet. For example, the Investment Company Institute (ICI), the national association of the American investment company industry, provides material at the site www.ici.org/.

Because a mutual fund owns many different stocks, each share of the fund owns a fractional interest in each of those companies. In an "open-end" fund (by far the most common type), new shares are created and issued to buyers while the fund company absorbs the shares of sellers. Each day, the value of a share in the fund (called the ***net asset value,*** or ***NAV***) is determined as follows.

Net Asset Value of a Mutual Fund

If A = Total fund assets, L = Total fund liabilities, and N = Number of shares outstanding, then the **net asset value** is calculated as follows.

$$NAV = \frac{A - L}{N}$$

▋▋ **EXAMPLE 7** Finding the Number of Shares in a Mutual Fund Purchase

Suppose, on a given day, a mutual fund has $500 million worth of stock, $500,000 in cash (not invested), and $300,000 in other assets. Total liabilities amount to $4 million, and there are 25 million shares outstanding. If Elaine Jefferson invests $50,000 in this fund, how many shares will she obtain?

SOLUTION

$$A = \$500{,}000{,}000 + \$500{,}000 + \$300{,}000$$

$$= \$500{,}800{,}000$$

$$L = \$4{,}000{,}000$$

$$N = 25{,}000{,}000$$

$$NAV = \frac{A - L}{N} \qquad \text{Formula}$$

$$= \frac{\$500{,}800{,}000 - \$4{,}000{,}000}{25{,}000{,}000} \qquad \text{Substitute values of } A, L, \text{ and } N.$$

$$= \$19.872 \qquad \text{Calculate.}$$

Because $\frac{\$50{,}000}{\$19.872} \approx 2516$, Elaine's $50,000 investment will purchase (to the nearest whole number) 2516 shares. ▋▋▋

Evaluating Investment Returns

Regardless of the type of investment you have or are considering (stocks, bonds, mutual funds, or others), it is important to be able to accurately evaluate and compare returns (profits or losses). Even though past performance is never a guarantee of future returns, it is crucial information. A wealth of information on stock and bond markets and mutual funds is available in many publications (for example, the *Wall Street Journal, Investor's Business Daily,* and *Barron's Weekly*) and on numerous Internet sources (for example, www.nasdaq.com).

The most important measure of performance of an investment is the **annual rate of return.** This is not *necessarily* the same as percentage return, as calculated in **Example 1,** because annual rate of return depends on the time period involved. Some commonly reported periods are daily, seven-day, monthly, month-to-date, quarterly, quarter-to-date, annual, year-to-date, 2-year, 3-year, 5-year, 10-year, 20-year, and "since inception" (since the fund or other investment vehicle was begun).

Examples 8 and 9 illustrate some of the many complications that arise when one tries to evaluate and compare different investments.

▐▐ **EXAMPLE 8** Analyzing a Stock's Annual Rate of Return

Theo Lieber owns 50 shares of stock. His brokerage statement for the end of August showed that the stock closed that month at a price of $40 (per share) and the statement for the end of September showed a closing price of $40.12. For purposes of illustration, disregard any possible dividends, and assume that the money gained in a given month has no opportunity to earn additional returns. (Those earnings cannot be "reinvested.") Find the following.

(a) The value of these shares at the end of August

(b) Theo's monthly return on this stock

(c) The monthly percentage return

(d) The annual rate of return

SOLUTION

(a)
$$\text{Value} = \underset{\text{Price per share}}{\$40} \cdot \underset{\text{Number of shares}}{50} = \$2000$$

(b)
$$\text{Return} = \underset{\text{Change in price per share}}{(\$40.12 - \$40)} \cdot \underset{\text{Number of shares}}{50}$$
$$= \$6$$

(c)
$$\text{Percentage return} = \frac{\text{Total return}}{\text{Total value}} \cdot 100\%$$
$$= \frac{\$6}{\$2000} \cdot 100\%$$
$$= 0.3\%$$

(d) Because monthly returns do not earn more returns, we use an "arithmetic" return here. Simply add 0.3% twelve times (or multiply 0.3% by 12), to obtain 3.6%. The annual rate of return is 3.6%. ▐▐▐

▐▐ **EXAMPLE 9** Analyzing a Mutual Fund's Annual Rate of Return

Kathryn Lutterschmidt owns 80 shares of a mutual fund with a net asset value of $10 on October 1. Assume that the only return that the fund earns is dividends of 0.4% per month, which are automatically reinvested. Find the following.

(a) The value of Kathryn's holdings in this fund on October 1

(b) The monthly return   **(c)** The annual rate of return

SOLUTION

(a) Value = NAV · number of shares = $10 · 80 = $800

(b) Monthly return = 0.4% of $800 = $3.20

(c) In this case, monthly returns get reinvested. Compounding occurs. Therefore, we use a "geometric" return rather than arithmetic. To make this calculation, first find the "return relative," which is 1 plus the monthly rate of return:

$$1 + 0.4\% = 1 + 0.004 = 1.004.$$

Then multiply this return relative 12 times (raise it to the 12th power) to get an annual return relative: $1.004^{12} \approx 1.049$. Finally, subtract 1 and multiply by 100 to convert back to a percentage rate. The annual rate of return is 4.9%. ▐▐▐

A geometric return such as the one just found in **Example 9** often is called the "effective annual yield." (Notice that an arithmetic return calculation would have ignored the reinvestment compounding and would have understated the effective annual rate of return by 0.1%, because 12(0.4%) = 4.8%.)

Building a Nest Egg

The most important function of investing, for most people, is to build an account for some future use, probably for retirement living. In **Example 8** of **Section 13.1,** we compared two retirement programs, Plan A and Plan B, to emphasize the importance of starting a retirement investment program early in life. The performance of investments over time is generally governed by formulas based on the summation of geometric sequences, which is discussed in the **Extension** on investment fraud following this section. The formulas given here will be used without showing their derivations.

There are two major barriers to building a retirement nest egg (or college tuition fund, or legacy to leave to heirs or to charity, or whatever the goal is for accumulating wealth). These barriers are *inflation* and *(income) taxes*.

Table 4 (page 696) shows the actual historical inflation rates over 30 years (1979–2009). This reflects an average of about 4.0% per year. If we had invested for retirement over that time span, the inflation proportion (see **page 697**) indicates that we would have ended up in 2009 paying about $\frac{214.5}{72.6} = 3.0$ times as much for goods and services as when we started, in 1979.

This inflationary effect, if unanticipated, could make a sizable dent in retirement living, but there is a fairly painless way to make provision for it. Recall that the CPI reflects the (usually) rising trend in pricing, and that salaries and wages more or less follow along. Periodically (maybe once a year), we can simply increase contributions by enough to keep pace with inflation.

The formula below allows us to compute the future values of an account where regular deposits are systematically adjusted for inflation. If the inflation rate is i, then the amount R is deposited at the end of year 1, $R(1 + i)$ is deposited at the end of year 2, and so on, with the deposit at the end of the year n, in general, being $R(1 + i)^{n-1}$.

Future Value of an Inflation-Adjusted Retirement Account

Assume annual deposits into a retirement account, adjusted for inflation. If

i = annual rate of inflation,

R = initial deposit (at the end of year 1),

r = annual rate of return on money in the account,

and n = number of years deposits are made,

then the value V of the account at the end of n years is calculated as follows.

$$V = R\left[\frac{(1 + r)^n - (1 + i)^n}{r - i}\right]$$

▌▌ EXAMPLE 10 Adjusting a Retirement Account for Inflation

In **Example 8** of **Section 13.1,** Gina executed Plan A, depositing $2000 on each birthday from age 21 to age 30, then stopped depositing, and at age 65 had $428,378. Peter, with Plan B, waited until age 31 to make the first $2000 deposit, then deposited $2000 every year to age 65 and came out with only $344,634.

Compute the final account value, at age 65, for Peter's Plan B, assuming that the 35 annual deposits had been adjusted for a 4% annual inflation rate.

SOLUTION

Use the "inflation-adjusted" formula given in the box with $R = \$2000$, $r = 0.08$, $i = 0.04$, and $n = 35$. The final account value is

$$V = \$2000\left[\frac{(1 + 0.08)^{35} - (1 + 0.04)^{35}}{0.08 - 0.04}\right] \approx \$541{,}963.$$

With inflation adjustment, Plan B, by age 65, accumulates the amount \$541,963. ▌▌▌

   The second barrier to building wealth—taxes—is not so easily dealt with. You will find that the more you invest and the more you earn, the higher the percentage that our progressive tax system will claim of your earnings. Probably your most effective tool in softening (though not overcoming) this effect is to take full advantage of tax-deferred accounts, such as a TSA (Tax-Sheltered Annuity, or 403(b) Plan); an IRA (Individual Retirement Account, or 401(k) plan), especially if your employer will contribute matching funds; or, if self-employed, a SEP (Simplified Employee Pension) or a Keogh plan.

   With most tax-deferred retirement accounts, the accumulated money is all taxed when it is withdrawn (presumably during retirement years). Therefore, it may seem that tax deferral is not an advantage but simply puts off when the tax is paid, assuming your tax rate remains the same. To demonstrate the decided advantage of deferral, we will compare the two situations using the following formulas. For a fair comparison, we look at both account values *after all taxes have been paid*.

Tax-Deferred Versus Taxable Retirement Accounts

In both cases,

   $R =$ amount withheld annually from current salary to build the retirement account,

   $n =$ number of years contributions are made,

   $r =$ annual rate of return on money in the account,

   $t =$ marginal tax rate of account holder,

   $V =$ final value of the account, **following all accumulations and payment of all taxes.**

Tax-Deferred Account

   The entire amount R is contributed each year, all contributions, plus earnings, earn a return over the n years, at which time tax is paid on all money in the account. The final account value is calculated as follows.

$$V = \frac{(1 - t)R[(1 + r)^n - 1]}{r}$$

Taxable Account

   Each amount R withheld from salary is taxed up front, decreasing the amount of the annual deposit to $(1 - t)R$. Furthermore, annual earnings are also taxed at the end of each year. But at the end of the accumulation period, no more tax will be due. The final account value is calculated as follows.

$$V = \frac{R[(1 + r(1 - t))^n - 1]}{r}$$

▮▮ **EXAMPLE 11** Comparing Tax-Deferred and Taxable Retirement Accounts

Tara Culliney and Steve Day, both in a 20% marginal tax bracket, will each contribute $2000 annually for 20 years to retirement accounts that return 5% annually. Tara chooses a tax-deferred account, while Steve chooses a taxable account. Compare their final account values at the end of the accumulation period, after payment of all taxes.

SOLUTION

We have $R = \$2000$, $n = 20$, $r = 0.05$, and $t = 0.20 = 0.2$.

Tara: $\quad V = \dfrac{(1 - 0.2)\$2000[(1 + 0.05)^{20} - 1]}{0.05}$ Substitute values in the "tax-deferred" formula.

$\quad\quad\quad \approx \$52{,}906.$

Steve: $\quad V = \dfrac{\$2000[(1 + 0.05(1 - 0.2))^{20} - 1]}{0.05}$ Substitute values in the "taxable" formula.

$\quad\quad\quad \approx \$47{,}645.$

By deferring taxes, Tara ends up with $5261, or about 11%, more. ▮▮▮

Greater contributions, a longer accumulation period, a higher rate of return, and a higher tax bracket all will accentuate the positive effect of tax deferral.

Tax-deferred is not the same as "tax-free," which makes the result of **Example 12** less impressive than it may seem. This type of retirement income is taxed at the time it is withdrawn. People who sell tax-deferred plans stress that you will probably be in a lower tax bracket after retirement because of reduced income. But many find this is not so, especially compared to early career income, and especially if your retirement account investments have done very well, which could make your required withdrawals quite large. Besides, who can tell what general tax rates will be 30 years from now?

▮▮ **EXAMPLE 12** Comparing Tax-Deferred and Taxable Retirement Accounts

Repeat **Example 11,** but this time let $R = \$5000$, $n = 40$, $r = 0.10$, and $t = 0.40 = 0.4$.

SOLUTION

Tara: $\quad V = \dfrac{(1 - 0.4)\,\$5000\,[(1 + 0.10)^{40} - 1]}{0.10}$ Substitute values in the "tax-deferred" formula.

$\quad\quad\quad \approx \$1{,}327{,}778.$

Steve: $\quad V = \dfrac{\$5000[(1 + 0.10\,(1 - 0.4))^{40} - 1]}{0.10}$ Substitute values in the "taxable" formula.

$\quad\quad\quad \approx \$464{,}286.$

With these higher parameters, Tara's advantage is dramatic: $863,492, or about 186%, more. ▮▮▮

For Further Thought

Summary of Investments

The summary of various types of investments in **Table 10,** on the next page, is based on average cases and is intended only as a general comparison of investment opportunities. There are numerous exceptions to the characteristics shown. For example, though the table shows no selling fees for mutual funds, this is really true only for the so-called no-load funds. The "loaded" funds do charge "early redemption fees" or other kinds of sales charges. That is not to say that a no-load fund is necessarily better. For example, the absence of sales fees may be offset by higher "management fees."

These various costs, as well as other important factors, will be clearly specified in a fund's prospectus and should be studied carefully before a purchase decision is made. Some expertise is not entirely

(continued)

For Further Thought (cont.)

unnecessary for mutual fund investing, just less so than with certain other options, like direct stock purchases, raw land, or collectibles.

To use the table, read across the columns to find the general characteristics of the investment. "Liquidity" refers to the ability to get cash from the investment quickly.

For Group or Individual Investigation

List (a) some investment types you would recommend considering and (b) some you would recommend avoiding for a friend whose main investment objective is as follows.

1. Avoid losing money.
2. Avoid losing purchasing power.
3. Avoid having to learn about investments.
4. Avoid having to work on investments.
5. Be sure to realize a gain.
6. Be able to "cash in" at any time.
7. Get as high a return as possible.
8. Be able to "cash in" without paying fees.
9. Realize quick profits.
10. Realize growth over the long term.

Table 10 Summary of Investments

Investment	Protection of Principal	Protection Against Inflation	Rate of Return (%)	Certainty of Return	Selling Fees	Liquidity	Long-Term Growth	Requires Work from Investor	Expert Knowledge Required
Cash	excellent	none	0			excellent	no	no	no
Ordinary life insurance	good	poor	2–4	excellent	high	excellent	no	no	no
Savings bonds	excellent	poor	3–5	excellent	none	excellent	no	no	no
Bank savings	excellent	poor	2–4	excellent	none	excellent	no	no	no
Credit union	excellent	poor	3–4	excellent	none	excellent	no	no	no
Corporation bonds	good	poor	5–7	excellent	low	good	no	some	some
Tax-free municipal bonds	excellent	poor	2–5	excellent	medium	good	no	no	some
Corporation stock	good	good	3–12	good	medium	good	yes	some	some
Preferred stock	good	poor	4–8	excellent	medium	good	no	some	some
Mutual funds	good	good	3–12	good	none	good	yes	no	no
Your own home	good	good	4–10	good	medium	poor	yes	yes	no
Mortgages on the homes of others	fair	poor	5–8	fair	high	poor	no	yes	some
Raw land	fair	good	?	fair	medium	poor	yes	no	yes
Rental properties	good	good	4–8	fair	medium	poor	yes	yes	some
Stamps, coins, antiques	fair	good	0–10	fair	high	poor	yes	yes	yes
Your own business	fair	good	0–20	poor	high	poor	yes	yes	yes

13.5 EXERCISES

Refer to the stock table (**Table 9** *on page 726) for Exercises 1–36.*

Reading Stock Charts *Find each of the following.*

1. closing price for CarMax (KMX)

2. sales for the day for FedEx (FDX)

3. change from the previous day for Harley-Davidson (HOG)

4. closing price for Sara Lee (SLE)

5. 52-week high for Pearson ADS (PSO)

6. 52-week low for Walt Disney (DIS)

7. dividend for Allstate (ALL)

8. opening price for Bank of America (BAC)

9. sales for the day for General Mills (GIS)

10. percent change from the previous day for Caterpillar Inc. (CAT)

11. year-to-date percentage change for CarMax (KMX)

12. year-to-date percentage change for Yum!Brands (YUM)

13. price-to-earnings ratio for Caterpillar Inc. (CAT)

14. percentage yield for Chevron (CVX)

Finding Stock Costs *Find the basic cost (ignoring any broker fees) for each stock purchase, at the day's closing price.*

15. 600 shares of Chevron (CVX)

16. 100 shares of Sara Lee (SLE)

17. 500 shares of FedEx (FDX)

18. 800 shares of Allstate (ALL)

Finding Stock Costs *Find the cost, at the day's closing price, for each stock purchase. Include typical discount broker commissions as described in the text.*

	Stock Symbol	Number of Shares	Transaction Type
19.	PSO	60	broker-assisted
20.	GIS	70	broker-assisted
21.	BAC	355	automated
22.	CAT	585	automated
23.	HOG	2500	broker-assisted

	Stock Symbol	Number of Shares	Transaction Type
24.	DUK	1500	automated
25.	YUM	2400	automated
26.	DIS	20,000	broker-assisted

Finding Receipts for Stock Sales *Find the amount received by the sellers of each stock (at the day's closing prices). Deduct sales expenses as described in the text.*

	Stock Symbol	Number of Shares	Transaction Type
27.	ALL	400	broker-assisted
28.	KMX	600	broker-assisted
29.	CVX	500	automated
30.	DE	700	automated
31.	FDX	1350	automated
32.	KMB	2740	automated
33.	SLE	1480	broker-assisted
34.	PSO	1270	broker-assisted

Finding Net Results of Combined Transactions *For each combined transaction (executed at the closing price of the day), find the net amount paid out or taken in. Assume typical expenses as outlined in the text.*

35. Paul Burke bought 100 shares of Walt Disney and sold 20 shares of General Mills, both broker-assisted trades.

36. Rebecca Leidy bought 800 shares of Bank of America and sold 300 shares of Chevron, both automated trades.

Costs and Returns of Stock Investments *For each of the following stock investments, find* **(a)** *the total purchase price,* **(b)** *the total dividend amount,* **(c)** *the capital gain or loss,* **(d)** *the total return, and* **(e)** *the percentage return.*

	Number of Shares	Purchase Price per Share	Dividend per Share	Sale Price per Share
37.	40	$20.00	$2.00	$44.00
38.	20	$25.00	$1.00	$22.00
39.	100	$12.50	$1.08	$10.15
40.	200	$ 8.80	$1.12	$11.30

Total Return on Bond Investments *Find the total return earned by each bond in Exercises 41–44.*

	Face Value	Annual Interest Rate	Term to Maturity
41.	$ 1000	5.5%	5 years
42.	$ 5000	6.4%	10 years
43.	$10,000	7.11%	3 months
44.	$50,000	4.88%	6 months

Net Asset Value of a Mutual Fund *For each investment, find* **(a)** *the net asset value, and* **(b)** *the number of shares purchased.*

	Amount Invested	Total Fund Assets	Total Fund Liabilities	Total Shares Outstanding
45.	$ 3500	$875 million	$ 36 million	80 million
46.	$ 1800	$643 million	$102 million	50 million
47.	$25,470	$2.31 billion	$135 million	263 million
48.	$83,250	$1.48 billion	$ 84 million	112 million

Finding Monthly and Annual Investment Returns *For each investment, assume that there is no opportunity for reinvestment of returns. In each case find* **(a)** *the monthly return,* **(b)** *the annual return, and* **(c)** *the annual percentage return.*

	Amount Invested	Monthly Percentage Return
49.	$ 645	1.3%
50.	$ 895	0.9%
51.	$2498	2.3%
52.	$4983	1.8%

Effective Annual Rate of Return of Mutual Fund Investments *Assume that each mutual fund investment earns monthly returns that are reinvested and subsequently earn at the same rate. In each case find* **(a)** *the beginning value of the investment,* **(b)** *the first monthly return, and* **(c)** *the effective annual yield.*

	Beginning NAV	Number of Shares Purchased	Monthly Percentage Return
53.	$ 9.63	125	1.5%
54.	$12.40	185	2.3%
55.	$11.94	350	1.83%
56.	$18.54	548	2.22%

Finding Commissions *For each of the following trades, determine the missing amounts in columns* **(a), (b),** *and* **(c).**

	Number of Shares	Price per Share	(a) Principal Amount	(b) Broker-assisted Commission	(c) Automated Commission
57.	10	$1.00	_____	_____	_____
58.	10	$100.00	_____	_____	_____
59.	400	$1.00	_____	_____	_____
60.	400	$100.00	_____	_____	_____
61.	4000	$1.00	_____	_____	_____
62.	4000	$100.00	_____	_____	_____

63. Referring to **Exercises 57–62,** fill in the blanks in the following statement.

A broker-assisted purchase is cheaper than an automated purchase only when a relatively _____ number of shares are purchased for a relatively _____ price per share.
(large/small)   (high/low)

Inflation-Adjusted Retirement Accounts *Find the future value (to the nearest dollar) of each inflation-adjusted retirement account. Deposits are made at the end of each year.*

	Annual Inflation Rate	Initial Deposit	Annual Rate of Return	Number of Years
64.	2%	$1000	6%	20
65.	3%	$2000	5%	25
66.	4%	$2500	7%	30
67.	1%	$5000	6.5%	40

The Effect of Tax Deferral on Retirement Accounts *Find the final value, after all taxes are paid, for each account if* **(a)** *taxes are deferred, or* **(b)** *taxes are not deferred. In both cases, deposits are made at the end of each year.*

	Marginal Tax Rate	Regular Deferred Contribution	Annual Rate of Return	Number of Years
68.	10%	$500	7%	15
69.	15%	$1000	5%	30
70.	28%	$3000	10%	25
71.	35%	$1500	6%	10

72. Monthly Deposits Adjusted for Inflation In an inflation-adjusted retirement account, let i denote annual inflation, let r denote annual return, and let n denote number of years, as in the text, but suppose deposits are made monthly rather than yearly with initial deposit R.

(a) What expression represents the amount that would be deposited at the end of the second month?

(b) Modify the future value formula for an inflation-adjusted account to accommodate the more frequent deposits.

(c) Find (to the nearest dollar) the future value for monthly deposits of $100 (initially) for 20 years if $i = 0.03$ and $r = 0.06$.

73. Finding an Unknown Rate Given the compound interest formula

$$A = P\left(1 + \frac{r}{m}\right)^n,$$

do the following.

(a) Solve the formula for r.

(b) Find the annual rate r if $50 grows to $85.49 in 10 years with interest compounded quarterly. Give r to the nearest tenth of a percent.

74. Comparing Continuous with Annual Compounding It was suggested in the text that inflation is more accurately reflected by the continuous compounding formula than by periodic compounding. Compute the ratio

$$\frac{Pe^{rt}}{P(1 + r)^n} = \frac{e^{rt}}{(1 + r)^n}$$

to find how much (to the nearest tenth of a percent) continuous compounding exceeds annual compounding. Use a rate of 3% over a period of 30 years.

Spreading Mutual Fund Investments Among Asset Classes *Mutual funds (as well as other kinds of investments) normally are categorized into one of several "asset classes," according to the kinds of stocks or other securities they hold. Small capitalization funds are most aggressive, while cash is most conservative.*

Asset Classes
a. Aggressive Growth (small cap)
b. Growth
c. Growth & Income
d. Income
e. Cash

Many investors, often with the help of an advisor, try to construct their portfolios in accordance with their stages of life. Basically, the idea is that a younger person can afford to be more aggressive (and assume more risk) while an older investor should be more conservative (assuming less risk). The investment diagrams here show typical percentage ranges that might be recommended by an investment advisor.

In Exercises 75–78, divide the given investor's money into the five categories so as to position them right at the middle of the recommended ranges.

75. Candace Cooney, in her early investing years, with $20,000 to invest

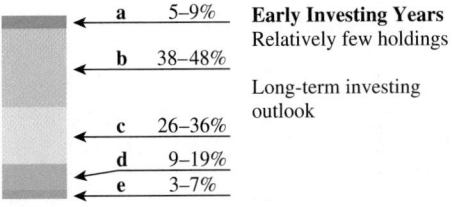

a 5–9%	**Early Investing Years** Relatively few holdings
b 38–48%	
	Long-term investing outlook
c 26–36%	
d 9–19%	
e 3–7%	

76. Stephen Jennings, in his good earning years, with $250,000 to invest

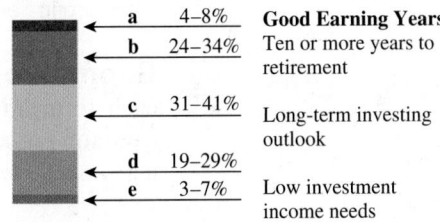

a 4–8%	**Good Earning Years** Ten or more years to retirement
b 24–34%	
c 31–41%	Long-term investing outlook
d 19–29%	
e 3–7%	Low investment income needs

77. Kevin Clarke, in his high income/saving years, with $400,000 to invest

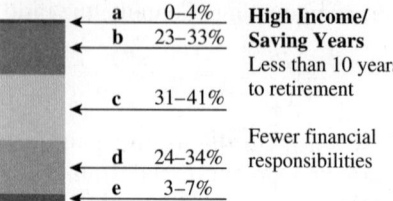

a 0–4%	**High Income/**
b 23–33%	**Saving Years**
	Less than 10 years
c 31–41%	to retirement
d 24–34%	Fewer financial responsibilities
e 3–7%	

78. Lauren Ellis, retired, with $845,000 to invest

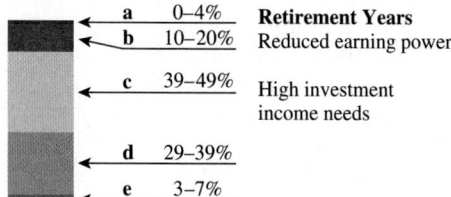

a 0–4%	**Retirement Years**
b 10–20%	Reduced earning power
c 39–49%	High investment income needs
d 29–39%	
e 3–7%	

The Effect of Taxes on Investment Returns *Income from municipal bonds generally is exempt from federal, and sometimes state, income tax. For an investor with a marginal combined state and federal tax rate of 35%, a taxable return of 6% would yield only 3.9% (65% of 6%). So at that tax rate, a tax-exempt return of 3.9% is equivalent to a taxable return of 6%. Find the tax-exempt rate of return that is equivalent to the given taxable rate of return for each investor.*

Investor	Marginal Combined Tax Rate	Taxable Rate of Return
79. Patrick Campbell	25%	5%
80. Jaclyn Autrey	30%	7%
81. Brandi Bankston	35%	8%
82. Chris Barker	40%	10%

Write responses to Exercises 83–90. Some research may be required.

83. Describe "dollar-cost averaging," and relate it to advantage number 1 of mutual funds as listed in the text.

84. From **Table 9** in the text, would you say that June 4, 2010, was a "good day" on Wall Street or a "bad day"?

85. Log onto www.napfa.org to research financial planners. Then report on what you would look for in a planner.

86. A great deal of research has been done in attempts to understand and predict trends in the stock market. Discuss the term *financial engineering*. Within this area of study, what is a *rocket scientist* (or *quant*)?

87. Regarding mutual funds, discuss the difference between a *front-end load* and a *contingent deferred sales charge*.

88. What is meant by *growth stock* and *income stock*?

89. With respect to investing in corporate America, describe the difference between being an owner and being a lender.

90. Comment on the graph shown here.

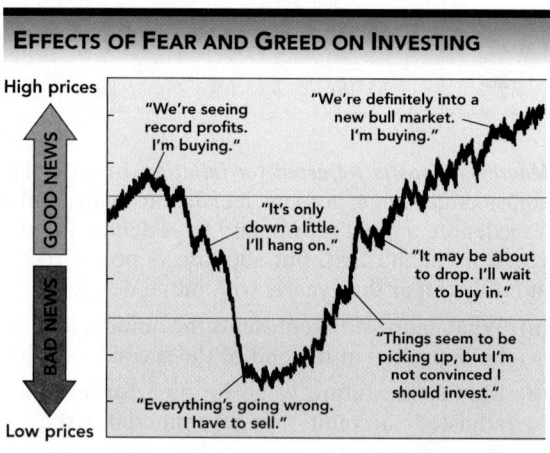

EXTENSION Ponzi Schemes and Other Investment Frauds*

Geometric Sequences • Pyramid Schemes • Ponzi Schemes

Geometric Sequences
In a **geometric sequence** (first seen in **Chapter 1**), each term after the first is generated by multiplying the previous term by the **common ratio,** a number remaining constant throughout the sequence. For example, a geometric sequence with first term 3 and common ratio 2 starts out as follows:

$$3, 6, 12, 24, 48, 96, \ldots.$$

*Sources: www.usatoday.com, www.moneymorning.com, www.nytimes.com, www.wikipedia.org

In general, if the first term is denoted a, the common ratio is denoted r, and there are n terms altogether, then the complete sequence is

$$a, ar, ar^2, ar^3, \ldots, ar^{n-1}.$$

(Verify by inductive reasoning that the nth term really is ar^{n-1}.)

The sum of all n terms of the geometric sequence above can be written

$$S = a + ar + ar^2 + \cdots + ar^{n-2} + ar^{n-1}.$$

Multiply both sides of this equation by r:

$$Sr = ar + ar^2 + ar^3 + \cdots + ar^{n-1} + ar^n.$$

Now position these two equations, one below the other, and subtract as follows.

$$
\begin{array}{llllll}
S = a & + ar & + ar^2 & + \cdots + ar^{n-2} & + ar^{n-1} \\
Sr = ar & + ar^2 & + ar^3 & + \cdots + ar^{n-1} & + ar^n \\
\hline
\end{array}
$$

$$S - Sr = (a - ar) + (ar - ar^2) + (ar^2 - ar^3) + \cdots + (ar^{n-2} - ar^{n-1}) + (ar^{n-1} - ar^n)$$

Now we can rearrange and regroup the terms on the right to obtain the following.

$$S - Sr = a + (ar - ar) + (ar^2 - ar^2) + \cdots + (ar^{n-1} - ar^{n-1}) - ar^n$$
$$= a + 0 + 0 + \cdots + 0 - ar^n$$

Notice that all terms on the right, except a and $-ar^n$, were arranged in pairs to cancel out. So we get the following.

$$S - Sr = a - ar^n$$
$$S(1 - r) = a(1 - r^n) \quad \text{Factor both sides.}$$
$$S = \frac{a(1 - r^n)}{1 - r} \quad \text{Solve for the sum } S.$$

The Sum of a Geometric Sequence

If a geometric sequence has first term a and common ratio r, and has n terms altogether, then the sum of all n terms is calculated as follows.

$$S = \frac{a(1 - r^n)}{1 - r}$$

The ability to recognize a geometric sequence and to sum its terms is very helpful in many applications, including detecting investment fraud.

Pyramid Schemes Most everyone has been invited, through email or otherwise, to pass on some message to two (or more) other people. Sometimes it is an innocent "chain letter." But if it involves sending money to someone, it is likely a **pyramid scheme.**

▮▮ **EXAMPLE 1** Analyzing Payoffs in a Pyramid Scheme

You receive a letter with a list of three names, along with the following instructions.

1. Send $1 to the top name on the list.

2. Remove that name and move the other two names up on the list.

3. Add your own name at the bottom of the list.

4. Send the same letter, with the new list, to two other people.

Suppose you decide to participate (become a member), both of your two recruits also participate, all of their four recruits participate, and all of their eight recruits participate. We call this the "each one recruits two" model. (It is also known, classically, as the 8-ball model.) You and the next three levels of participation are illustrated in **Figure 1**.

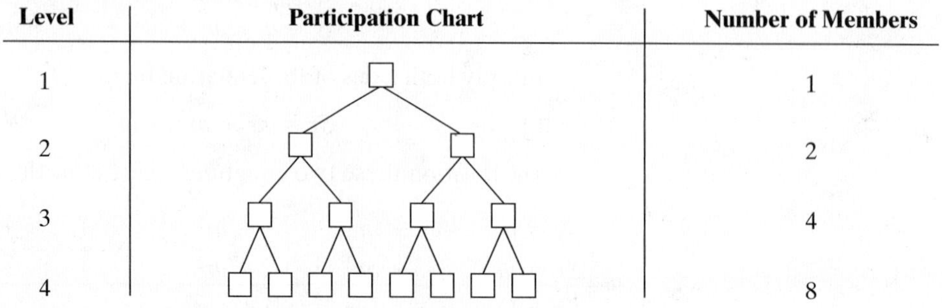

Level	Participation Chart	Number of Members
1		1
2		2
3		4
4		8

Participation chart for an 8-ball pyramid scheme

Figure 1

(a) With you and all your downstream recruits, how many members are there?

(b) How much money will you receive?

(c) What is your profit?

SOLUTION

(a) $1 + 2 + 4 + 8 = 15$

(b) You receive $1 from each level-4 member, for a total of $8.

Income Cost
↓   ↓

(c) Profit = $8 − $1 = $7 (minus two envelopes and two postage stamps)   ▐▐▐

Observe, from **Figure 1** of **Example 1,** that, beginning with one member at level 1, the number of members in a given level is double the number of members in the previous level.

▐▌ **EXAMPLE 2** Finding the Number of Members in a Pyramid Scheme

For each of the following numbers of levels, find the total number of members, from level 1 up to and including the given level. Use inductive reasoning in part (c).

(a) 4   **(b)** 7   **(c)** N

SOLUTION

(a) $1 + 2 + 4 + 8 = 15$ (or, $2^4 - 1$)

(b) $1 + 2 + 4 + 8 + 16 + 32 + 64 = 127$ (or, $2^7 - 1$)

(c) Assuming the pattern observed in parts (a) and (b) holds, the total number of members from level 1 through level N, inclusive, would be

$$2^N - 1.$$ ▐▐▐

The expression, $2^N - 1$, of **Example 2(c)** was derived inductively, but can also be deduced using the formula for the sum of a geometric sequence given earlier.

▐▌ **EXAMPLE 3** Deducing the Number of Members in a Pyramid Scheme

Use deductive reasoning to *prove* that $2^N - 1$ is the total number of members in an "each one recruits two" pyramid with N levels.

SOLUTION

The number of members in the N levels are $1, 2, 4, 8, \ldots,$ and 2^{N-1}. Their sum is the sum of a geometric sequence with

$$\text{first term } a = 1, \text{ common ratio } r = 2, \text{ number of terms } n = N.$$

So the sum is found as follows.

$$S = \frac{a(1 - r^n)}{1 - r} \qquad \text{Sum formula}$$

$$= \frac{1(1 - 2^N)}{1 - 2} \qquad \text{Substitute } a = 1, r = 2, n = N.$$

$$= \frac{2^N - 1}{2 - 1} \qquad \text{Multiply numerator and denominator by } -1.$$

$$= 2^N - 1 \qquad \text{Simplify.} \qquad\qquad ▮▮▮$$

Table 11 summarizes the various values involved as the pyramid builds downward.

Table 11	The Numbers in an "Each One Recruits Two" Pyramid Scheme	
Level Number n	**Number of Members in Level** n	**Total Number of Members in all Levels Up To and Including Level** n
1	$1 = 2^{1-1}$	$1 = 2^1 - 1$
2	$2 = 2^{2-1}$	$1 + 2 = 3 = 2^2 - 1$
3	$4 = 2^{3-1}$	$1 + 2 + 4 = 7 = 2^3 - 1$
4	$8 = 2^{4-1}$	$1 + 2 + 4 + 8 = 15 = 2^4 \quad 1$
5	$16 = 2^{5-1}$	$1 + 2 + 4 + 8 + 16 = 31 = 2^5 - 1$
.	.	.
.	.	.
.	.	.
N	2^{N-1}	$1 + 2 + 4 + 8 + 16 + \ldots + 2^{N-1} = 2^N - 1$

The pyramid must keep building downward indefinitely if all the members are to receive their profit. But a pyramid with, say, 20 levels requires

$$2^{20} - 1 = 1,048,575 \text{ members.}$$

And just 33 levels would involve

$$2^{33} - 1 = 8,589,934,591 \text{ members,}$$

which exceeds the population of the world. Therefore, every pyramid scheme must eventually fail, and most likely long before achieving 33 levels. And when it fails, the members in the last three levels will not get paid. This means that if failure occurs after N levels, then the number of members who lose their money is

$$2^{N-1} + 2^{N-2} + 2^{N-3}.$$

The fact that a **pyramid scheme** profits relatively few at the expense of many, most of whom don't really understand how it works, is part of why these schemes are illegal in the United States (and many other countries). If participants are provided goods or services comparable in value to their "entry fee," then the combination of promotion (recruiting) and selling (goods or services) can become (technically) a legal multi-level marketing (MLM) plan. But there is a fine line between legitimate business and fraud. The legal distinction rests on whether the recruitment exists to promote the product or the product exists to promote the recruitment.

We can now express the fraction of all participants who will lose money as follows.

$$\text{Fraction who lose} = \frac{2^{N-1} + 2^{N-2} + 2^{N-3}}{2^N - 1}$$

⟵ Number who lose
⟵ Number who participate

$$= \frac{2^{N-3}(2^2 + 2 + 1)}{2^N - 1}$$

Factor 2^{N-3} from numerator.

$$= \frac{2^{N-3}(7)}{2^N - 1}$$

Add.

Now deleting the −1 from the denominator makes the denominator (slightly) greater, hence the overall fraction lesser. So we can state the following.

$$\text{Fraction who lose} > \frac{2^{N-3}(7)}{2^N}$$

$$= \frac{7}{2^{N-(N-3)}}$$

Apply rule of exponents.

$$= \frac{7}{2^3}$$

Simplify exponent.

$$= \frac{7}{8}$$

Simplify.

No matter how many levels succeed, everyone in the last three levels loses, and these are more than $\frac{7}{8}$ of all participants.

Ponzi Schemes Pyramid schemes are relatively straightforward, though promoters tend to avoid the use of terms like "pyramid" and "scheme." **Ponzi schemes,** on the other hand, come in many varieties and usually involve financial instruments (like "derivatives") and terms (like "alternative asset classes") that can confuse even experienced investors. These scams always pretend to offer real investment returns of one kind or another, but in fact an investor's "returns" come only from his own money or from the deposits of later investors.

The name comes from the years following World War I, when an Italian immigrant, Charles Ponzi, realized that non-uniform international currency exchange rates and other factors made it possible, theoretically, to profit by buying postal reply coupons in Italy and exchanging them for U.S. stamps. There was a money-making potential in this, but over time, Ponzi solicited and received far more deposits ("investments") than could be placed in that market. His operation, mostly in the New England area, drew in more and more participants as he returned profits to early investors out of the deposits of later investors.

Charles Ponzi, like many other scheme operators who followed him, possessed personal attributes, including charm and salesmanship, that allowed him to accummulate much more than what was required just to pay out the profits demanded. As he seemed to be making good on his promises, most investors left both principal and profit to increase in the plan. On some days, he had thousands of zealous investors lined up to give him their money.

It is important, for the success of a Ponzi scheme, that the illusion of successful investment returns be maintained early on to build confidence and attract an ever-growing number of investors. And it helps if the true details of the operation are obscure and difficult or impossible to actually verify.

| EXAMPLE 4 | Finding the Minimum Number of Investors Needed to Support a Ponzi Scheme |

Ponzi promised investors a 50% profit within 45 days or a 100% profit within 90 days. Assuming that he started the year with one investor, who put in $1000, and that all investors always withdrew their 90-day profit and left their principal with Ponzi, how many investors would he need within a year?

SOLUTION

Consider the absolute minimum number of investors required at the end of each quarter (although this certainly was not Ponzi's objective).

- After one quarter (90 days) the single investor's $1000 could be paid back to him as his quarterly profit. So at that point no new investors are necessary.

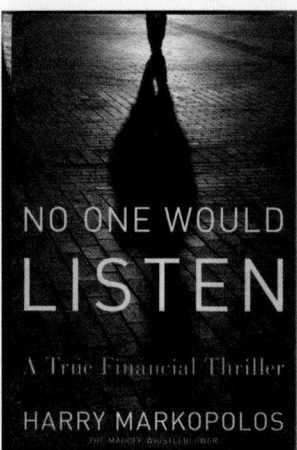

The 2010 book *No One Would Listen,* by Harry Markopolos, describes the longest running and largest Ponzi scheme ever revealed, as well as the futile efforts made by Markopolos, over a decade, to convince governmental regulators to take action against its operator, Bernard Madoff. (See **Exercises 23–25.**) Extensive resources, for the general reader and for classroom use, are available at www.noonewouldlisten.com.

- At the end of the second quarter, the investor wants another $1000 profit, and no money is available without an additional investor. So one investor must be added. His deposit can be used to pay the original investor.
- At the end of the third quarter, there are two investors, and no money. Two additional investors must be recruited to pay profits to the two previous investors.
- At the end of the fourth quarter (one year), four investors expect quarterly profit, so four new investors must be recruited.

Just to pay out profits, Ponzi would need to double his number of investors at the end of each quarter starting with the second. By the end of the year, 1 has doubled to 2, 2 to 4, and 4 to 8. He must end the year with 8 investors. Nothing is left for Ponzi. And if anyone wanted their principal back, he would be in trouble. ▋▋▋

▋▋ **EXAMPLE 5** Analyzing Cash Flow in a Ponzi Scheme

Suppose that investors are promised 100% profit per quarter. At the beginning of each quarter (90 days), 1000 investors contribute $1000 each, and all monies stay in until the end of the year. There are then four categories of investors.

1. those who have been in for 4 quarters

2. those who have been in for 3 quarters

3. those who have been in for 2 quarters

4. those who have been in for 1 quarter

At the end of the year, 10% of those in each category take out their profits, but leave their principal. What amount does that leave with the operator?

SOLUTION

The amount taken in during the year is $4000 \cdot \$1000 = \$4,000,000$. At the end of the year, the supposed profits would be: $4000 for each category 1 investor, $3000 for each category 2 investor, $2000 for each category 3 investor, and $1000 for each category 4 investor. Ten percent of each category take out their profits, and 10% of 1000 is 100, so the payout would then be

Category 1 Category 2 Category 3 Category 4
↓   ↓   ↓   ↓

$$100 \cdot \$4000 + 100 \cdot \$3000 + 100 \cdot \$2000 + 100 \cdot \$1000 = \$1,000,000.$$

The amount the operator retains is

$$\$4,000,000 - \$1,000,000 = \$3,000,000.$$ ▋▋▋

EXTENSION EXERCISES

Analyzing an "Each One Recruits Three" Pyramid Scheme For Exercises 1–11, consider a pyramid scheme just like in **Example 1,** *except that "each one recruits three," rather than two. (Work these all, in order.)*

1. Draw a chart like in **Example 1** showing the first four levels.

2. How many members are in each of the following levels?
   (a) 1   **(b)** 2   **(c)** 3   **(d)** 4

3. If the chart is extended, in general how many members are in level *N*?

4. If you are the top person in the chart, and each person's entry fee is $1, how much money will you receive?

5. What will your profit be?

6. What is the total number of members, from level 1 through each of the following levels, inclusive?
   (a) 1   **(b)** 2
   (c) 3   **(d)** 4
   (e) 5   **(f)** 6

7. Fill in the blanks in the following statements. The total number of members in levels 1 through N, inclusive, is $1 + 3 + 9 + \ldots + \underline{\hspace{1.5cm}}$. This is the sum of a \underline{\hspace{2.5cm}} sequence with $a = \underline{\hspace{0.5cm}}$, $r = \underline{\hspace{0.5cm}}$, and $n = \underline{\hspace{0.5cm}}$. So the total number of members is \underline{\hspace{1cm}}.

8. If the pyramid fails after level N, how many members will lose?

9. Suppose the scheme runs through level 6 and then fails. How many members lose?

10. Under the conditions of **Exercise 9**, what fraction of the members lose?

11. In an "each one recruits two" pyramid scheme, it was shown that more than $\frac{7}{8}$ of all members will lose. Use a similar analysis to characterize the fraction who will lose in an "each one recruits three" scheme.

12. Suppose you enter an "each one recruits two" pyramid scheme (at level 1), paying your $1 entry fee. If x denotes the number of level-4 recruits that eventually send you $1, then x is a random variable that can take on any of the values 0, 1, 2, 3, 4, 5, 6, 7, or 8. If the probability that any given person invited to join actually will join is $\frac{1}{2}$, then, using binomial probabilities gives the following probability distribution for x.

x	$P(x)$
0	0.34361
1	0.39270
2	0.19635
3	0.05610
4	0.01002
5	0.00114
6	0.00008
7	0.00000
8	0.00000

Find each of the following.

(a) the sum of these probability values

(b) your expected income

13. In **Exercise 12,** what is your expected profit?

14. If you were initiating a pyramid scheme, what would be the advantages and disadvantages of "each one recruits three" rather than two?

15. In a pyramid scheme, even if you and your three levels of recruits are embedded in a much larger chart, with multiple levels above you and many more below you, it is still only your four levels that affect your cost and income. Explain why this is so.

16. In an "each one recruits two" pyramid scheme, more than $\frac{7}{8}$ of all members will lose. What is the *greatest* fraction that could lose, and how could it happen?

17. Discuss places you have encountered "chain letters" or pyramid schemes with promises of money rewards for entering.

18. A number of other types of frauds have surfaced over the years. (Someone always has a new angle.) Research and write a report on "matrix schemes."

Finding the Required Number of Investors in a Ponzi Scheme Refer to **Example 4** for Exercises 19 and 20.

19. How many investors would be required by the end of two years with the same promised return of 100% per 90 days?

20. If the year began with 1000 investors, how many would be required at the end of each time period?

(a) one year   **(b)** two years   **(c)** three years

Exploring Cash Flow in a Ponzi Scheme Refer to **Example 5** for Exercises 21 and 22.

21. Suppose that at the end of the year, those 10% of investors actually invest another $1000 rather than taking out profit. Now what amount stays with the operator going into the second year?

22. Explain what factors may have convinced investors to put in more money and not take out profit.

Bernie Made Off with Billions. *As of mid 2010, the largest Ponzi scheme in history was operated by Bernard Madoff, a New York financier and former chairman of the NASDAQ Stock Market. When he was arrested in December of 2008, Mr. Madoff had swindled investors, including charities, foundations, large hedge funds, and funds of funds, as well as individuals, out of some $21 billion. He claimed to be trading in Standard & Poor's 500 Index options, but no one could tell what his fund actually held because he sold out of each option before reporting became mandatory.*

23. Assume that Charles Ponzi bilked his investors out of $4 million in 1920. If inflation averaged 3% from 1920 to 2008, compare the magnitudes of the Ponzi and Madoff scams in comparable dollars.

24. Speculate as to whether Bernard Madoff set out to swindle his investors in the beginning.

25. Considering the serious economic downturn in 2008, why do you think the Madoff scheme, and many others also, were discovered around the same time.

26. Research online or elsewhere to find out about other notable Ponzi schemes over the years. Can you identify any common traits among the operators?

COLLABORATIVE INVESTIGATION

To Buy or to Rent?

Divide your class into groups of at least four students each. Every group is to first read the following.

> Ian and Tami, a young couple with a child, live in a rented apartment. After taxes, Ian earns $38,180 per year and Tami's part-time job brings in $7000 per year. In the foreseeable future, their earnings probably will just keep pace with inflation. They are presently operating on the following monthly budget.

Rent	$1050
Food	600
Day care	525
Clothing	420
Utilities	120
Entertainment	300
Savings	450
Other	300

> They have accumulated $36,000 in savings.
>
> Having found a house they would like to buy, which is priced at $162,500, they have consulted several lenders and have discovered that, at best, purchasing the house would involve costs as shown here.

Down payment required (20%)	_____
Closing costs (required at closing):	
Loan fee (1 point)	_____
Appraisal fee	300
Title insurance premium	375
Document and recording fees	70
Prorated property taxes	650
Prorated fire insurance premium	270
Other	230

Total immediate costs: _____

Ongoing monthly ownership costs would be as follows.

Fixed-rate 30-year mortgage at 7.5%   _____

Taxes ($1350 annually)   _____

Fire insurance ($540 annually)   _____

> In order to own their own home, Ian and Tami are willing to cut their clothing and entertainment expenditures by 30% each and could decrease their savings allotments by 20%. (Some savings still will be necessary to provide for additional furnishings they would need and for expenses of an expanding family in the future.) They also figure that the new house and yard would require $130 monthly for maintenance and that utilities will be twice what they have been in the apartment. Other than that, their present budget allotments would remain the same.

Now divide your group into two "subgroups." The first subgroup is to answer these questions:

1. What amount would the home purchase cost Ian and Tami in immediate expenditures?

2. Do they have enough cash on hand?

The second subgroup is to answer these questions:

3. What amount would the house cost Ian and Tami on an ongoing monthly basis?

4. What amount will their monthly budget allow toward this cost?

5. Can they meet the monthly expenses of owning the house?

Within your group, decide whether Ian and Tami can afford to purchase the house. Select a representative to report your findings to the class.

Compare the evaluations of the various groups, and try to resolve any discrepancies.

CHAPTER 13 TEST

Find all monetary answers to the nearest cent. Use tables and formulas from the chapter as necessary.

Finding the Future Value of a Deposit *Find the future value of each deposit.*

1. $100 for 5 years at 6% simple interest

2. $50 for 2 years at 8% compounded quarterly

Solve each problem.

3. **Effective Annual Yield of an Account** Find the effective annual yield to the nearest hundredth of a percent for an account paying 3% compounded monthly.

4. **Years to Double by the Rule of 70** Use the rule of 70 to estimate the years to double at an inflation rate of 5%.

5. **Finding the Present Value of a Deposit** What amount deposited today in an account paying 4% compounded semiannually would grow to $100,000 in 10 years?

6. **Finding Bank Card Interest by the Average Daily Balance Method** Caroline DiJullio's MasterCard statement shows an average daily balance of $680. Find the interest due if the rate is 1.6% per month.

Analyzing a Consumer Loan *Jason Hoffa buys a turquoise necklace for his wife on their anniversary. He pays $4000 for the necklace with $1000 down. The dealer charges add-on interest of 7.5% per year. Jason agrees to make payments for 24 months. Use this information for Exercises 7–10.*

7. Find the total amount of interest he will pay.

8. Find the monthly payment.

9. Find the APR value (to the nearest half percent).

10. Find the unearned interest if he repays the loan in full with six payments remaining. Use the most accurate method available.

11. **True Annual Interest Rate in Consumer Financing** Newark Hardware wants to include financing terms in their advertising. If the price of a floor waxer is $150 and the finance charge with no down payment is $5 over a 6-month period (six equal monthly payments), find the true annual interest rate (APR).

12. Explain what a mutual fund is and discuss several of its advantages and disadvantages.

Finding the Monthly Payment on a Home Mortgage *Find the monthly payment required for each home loan.*

13. The mortgage is for $150,000 at a fixed rate of 7% for 20 years. Amortize principal and interest only, disregarding taxes, insurance, and other costs.

14. The purchase price of the home is $218,000. The down payment is 20%. Interest is at 8.5% fixed for a term of 30 years. Annual taxes are $1500 and annual insurance is $750.

Solve each problem.

15. **Cost of Points in a Home Loan** If the lender in **Exercise 14** charges two *points,* how much does that add to the cost of the loan?

16. Explain in general what *closing costs* are. Are they different from *settlement charges*?

17. **Adjusting the Rate in an Adjustable-Rate Mortgage** To buy your home you obtain a 1-year ARM with 2.25% margin and a 2% periodic rate cap. The index starts at 7.85% but has increased to 10.05% by the first adjustment date. What interest rate will you pay during the second year?

18. **Reading Stock Charts** According to the stock table (**Table 9** on **page 726**), how many shares of Sara Lee were traded on June 4, 2010?

Finding the Return on a Stock Investment *Laurie Campbell bought 1000 shares of stock at $12.75 per share. She received a dividend of $1.38 per share shortly after the purchase and another dividend of $1.02 per share one year later. Eighteen months after buying the stock she sold the 1000 shares for $10.36 per share.*

19. Find Laurie's total return on this stock.

20. Find her percentage return. Is this the *annual rate of return* on this stock transaction? Why or why not?

21. **The Final Value of a Retirement Account** $1800 is deposited at the end of each year in a tax-deferred retirement account. The account earns a 6% annual return, the account owner's marginal tax rate is 25%, and taxes are paid at the end of 30 years. Find the final value of the account.

22. What is meant by saying that a retirement account is "adjusted for inflation"?

Edward James Olmos as Jaime Escalante in Stand and Deliver   *What is his Bacon number? See* **page 802**.

The popular game *The Six Degrees of Kevin Bacon* was developed by three Albright College friends a number of years ago. The object of the game is to link actor Kevin Bacon to another actor or actress using movies, with six or fewer titles in the link. Thanks to the International Movie Data Base (www.imdb.com), this goal can be reached almost instantaneously. The minimum number of links necessary is called the *Bacon number* for the other performer. For example, Mae West has a Bacon number of three, as she can be linked to Kevin Bacon in three steps as follows:

- *Mae West was in Myra Breckinridge (1970) with Calvin Lockhart.*
- *Calvin Lockhart was in Wild at Heart (1990) with Sherilyn Fenn.*
- Sherilyn Fenn was in *Cavedweller (2004)* with Kevin Bacon.

The linking process used in *The Six Degrees of Kevin Bacon* can be applied to other situations (Web pages, for example) and can be modeled using concepts from *graph theory*.

Graph theory has many real-world applications, with particularly important ones related to the Internet and telecommunications. (*Sources:* www.imdb.com, www.oracleofbacon.org.)

15.1 BASIC CONCEPTS

Graphs • Walks, Paths, and Circuits • Complete Graphs and Subgraphs
• Graph Coloring

Graphs

Suppose a preschool teacher has ten children in her class: Andy, Claire, Dave, Erin, Glen, Katy, Joe, Mike, Sam, and Tim. The teacher wants to analyze the social interactions among these children. She observes with whom the children play during recess over a 2-week period and records her observations.

Child	Played with
Andy	no one
Claire	Dave, Erin, Glen, Katy, Sam
Dave	Claire, Erin, Glen, Katy
Erin	Claire, Dave, Katy
Glen	Claire, Dave, Sam
Katy	Claire, Dave, Erin
Joe	Mike, Tim
Mike	Joe
Sam	Claire, Glen
Tim	Joe

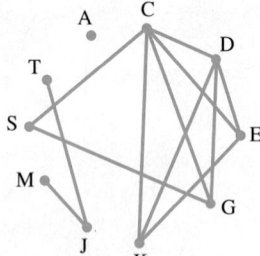

The **World Wide Web** is sometimes studied as a very large graph. The vertices are Web pages, with the edges links between pages. This graph is unimaginably large. It is very hard to even get a good estimate of how many vertices this graph has. In 2005 it was estimated that there were about 11.5 billion Web pages. By 2008 Google software engineers announced in a blog that they had found one trillion distinct URLs on the Web.

Despite these enormous numbers, because of the way the Web is connected, one can get from any randomly chosen Web page to any other using hyperlinks in an average of about 19 clicks. Even if the Web becomes 10 to 100 times larger, this would still be possible in only 20 or 21 clicks. Because of this, search engines such as Google can find keywords very quickly. (*Sources:* http://jmm.aaa.net.au/ articles/15080.htm; Antonio Gulli Universit di Pisa, Informatica; Alessio Signorini, University of Iowa, Computer Science; R. Albert, H. Jeong, and A.-L. Barabsi, *Nature* 401, 130–131, 1999.)

It is not easy to see patterns in the children's friend-ships from this list. Instead, the information may be shown in a diagram, as in **Figure 1**, where each letter is the first letter of a child's name. Such a diagram is called a *graph.** Each dot is called a **vertex** (plural **vertices**) of the graph. The lines between vertices are called **edges.**

In **Figure 1**, each vertex represents one of the pre-school children, and the edges show the relationship "play with each other." An edge must always begin and end at a vertex. We may have a vertex with no edges joined to it, such as A in **Figure 1**.

Figure 1

> **Graph**
>
> A **graph** is a collection of vertices (at least one) and edges. Each edge goes from a vertex to a vertex.

---

*Here *graph* will mean finite graph. A finite graph is a graph with finitely many edges and vertices.

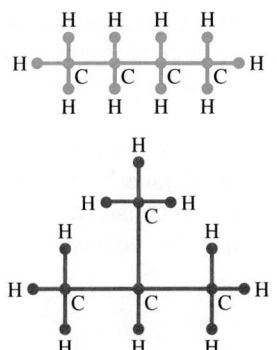

Why are they called graphs? The name was first used by chemist **A. Crum Brown.** He made a major breakthrough in chemistry in 1864 by inventing the now familiar diagrams to show different molecules with the same chemical composition. For example, both molecules illustrated above have chemical formula C_4H_{10}. Brown called his sketches **graphic formulae.** Mathematicians got involved in helping to classify all possible structures with a particular chemical composition and adopted the term "graph."

The graph in **Figure 1** has ten vertices and twelve edges. The only vertices of the graph are the dots. There is *no* vertex where edges TJ and SG intersect, since the intersection point does not represent one of the children. The positions of the vertices and the lengths of the edges have no significance. Also, the edges do not have to be drawn as straight lines. ***Only the relation between the vertices has significance, indicated by the presence or absence of an edge between them.***

Why not draw two edges for each friendship pair? For example, why not draw one edge showing that Tim plays with Joe and another edge showing that Joe plays with Tim? Since Tim and Joe play with each other, the extra edge would show no additional information. Graphs in which there is no more than one edge between any two vertices and in which no edge goes from a vertex to the same vertex are called **simple graphs.** See **Figure 2**.

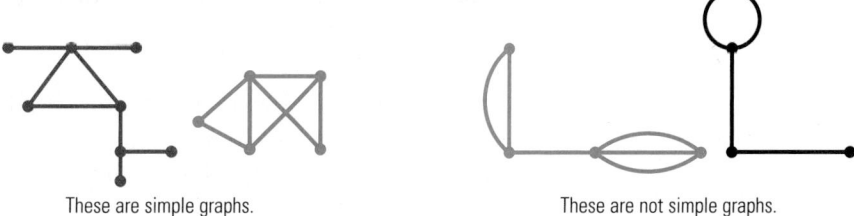

These are simple graphs.   These are not simple graphs.

Figure 2

In this chapter, the word **graph** *means simple graph, unless indicated otherwise.* (The meaning of "simple" here is different from its meaning in the phrase "simple curves" discussed with geometry in **Chapter 9.**)

From the graph in **Figure 1**, we can determine the size of a child's friendship circle by counting the number of edges coming from that child's vertex. There are five edges coming from the vertex labeled C, indicating that Claire plays with five different children. The number of edges joined to a vertex is called the **degree of the vertex.** In **Figure 1**, the degree of vertex C is 5, the degree of vertex M is 1, and the degree of vertex A is 0, as no edges are joined to A. (Here, the use of *degree* has nothing to do with its use in geometry in measuring the size of an angle.)

While **Figure 1** clarifies the friendship patterns of the preschoolers, the graph can be drawn in a different, more informative way as in **Figure 3**. The graph still has edges between the same pairs of vertices. We think of **Figure 3** as one graph, even though it has three pieces, since it represents a single situation. By drawing the graph in this way, we make the friendship patterns more apparent. Although the graph in **Figure 3** looks different from that in **Figure 1**, it shows the same relationships between the vertices. The two graphs are said to be *isomorphic*.

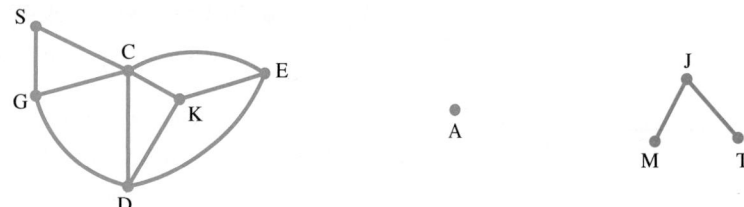

Figure 3

Isomorphic Graphs

Two graphs are **isomorphic** if there is a one-to-one matching between vertices of the two graphs with the property that whenever there is an edge between two vertices of either one of the graphs, there is an edge between the corresponding vertices of the other graph.

The word **isomorphism** comes from the Greek words *isos,* meaning "same," and *morphe,* meaning "form." Other words that come from the Greek root *isos* include

isobars: lines drawn on a map connecting places with the same barometric pressure;

isosceles: a triangle with two legs (*scelos*) of equal length; and

isomers: chemical compounds with the same chemical composition but different chemical structures.

A useful way to think about isomorphic graphs is to imagine a graph drawn with computer software that allows you to drag vertices without detaching any of the edges from their vertices. Any graph we can obtain by simply dragging vertices in this way will be isomorphic to the original graph.

Replacing a graph with an isomorphic graph sometimes can convey more about the relationships being examined. For example, it is clear from **Figure 3** on the previous page that there are no friendship links between the group consisting of Joe, Tim, and Mike, and the other children. We say that the graph is *disconnected.*

Connected and Disconnected Graphs

A graph is **connected** if we can move from each vertex of the graph to every other vertex of the graph *along edges of the graph.* If not, the graph is **disconnected.** The connected pieces of a graph are called the **components** of the graph.

Figure 3 shows clearly that the friendship relationships among the children in the preschool class have three components. Although the graph in **Figure 1** also is disconnected and includes three components, the way in which the graph is drawn does not make this as clear.

Using the graph in **Figure 3** to analyze the relationships in her class, the teacher might feel concerned that Tim, Mike, and Joe do not interact with the other children. Certainly she would feel concerned about Andy's isolation. She might observe that Claire seems to get along well with other children and encourage interaction between Claire and Tim, Mike, and Joe, and she might make a special attempt to encourage the children to include Andy in their games. Showing the friendship relationships as in **Figure 3** made it much easier to analyze them.

PROBLEM-SOLVING HINT Using different colors for different components can help determine how many components a graph has. We choose a color, begin at any vertex, and color all edges and vertices that we can get to from our starting vertex along edges of the graph. If the whole graph is not colored, we then choose a different color and an uncolored vertex, and repeat the process, continuing until the whole graph is colored.

▌▌ **EXAMPLE 1** Determining Number of Components

Is the graph in **Figure 4** connected or disconnected? How many components does the graph have?

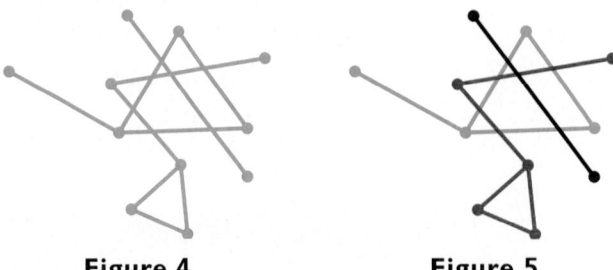

Figure 4   Figure 5

SOLUTION

Coloring the graph helps to solve the problem. The graph with color (**Figure 5**) shows three connected components. The original graph is disconnected. ▌▌▌

James Joseph Sylvester (1814–1897) was the first mathematician to use the word *graph* for these diagrams in the context of mathematics. Sylvester spent most of his life in Britain, but had an important influence on American mathematics from 1876 to 1884 as a professor at the newly founded Johns Hopkins University in Baltimore, Maryland. As a young man he worked as an actuary and lawyer in London, tutoring math on the side. One of his students was Florence Nightingale. His only published book, *The Laws of Verse*, was about poetry.

▌▌ EXAMPLE 2 Deciding Whether Graphs Are Isomorphic

Are the two graphs in **Figure 6** isomorphic? Justify your answer.

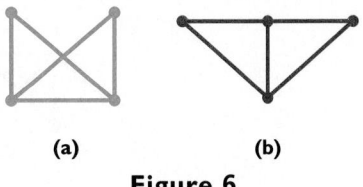

(a)   (b)

Figure 6

SOLUTION

These graphs are isomorphic. To show this, we label corresponding vertices with the same letters and color-code the matching edges in graphs (a) and (b) of **Figure 7**.

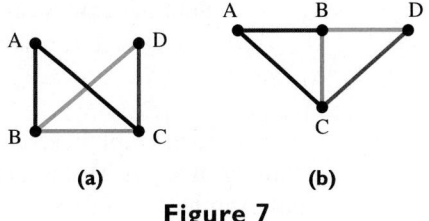

(a)   (b)

Figure 7   ▪▪▪

▌▌ EXAMPLE 3 Deciding Whether Graphs Are Isomorphic

Are the two graphs in **Figure 8** isomorphic?

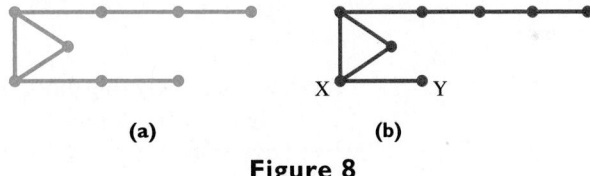

(a)   (b)

Figure 8

SOLUTION

These graphs are not isomorphic. If we imagine graph (a) drawn with our special computer software, we can see that no matter how we drag the vertices we can not get this graph to look exactly like graph (b). For example, graph (b) has vertex X of degree 3 joined to vertex Y of degree one. Neither of the vertices of degree 3 in graph (a) is joined to a vertex of degree one.   ▪▪▪

▌▌ EXAMPLE 4 Summing Degrees

For each graph in **Figure 9**, determine the number of edges and the sum of the degrees of the vertices. (Note that graph (b) is not a simple graph.)

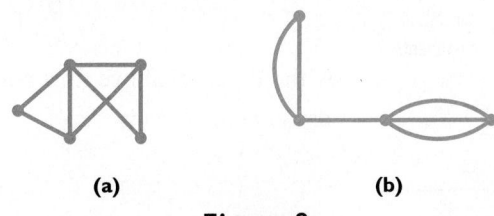

(a)   (b)

Figure 9

SOLUTION

Start by writing the degree of each vertex next to the vertex, as in **Figure 10**.

(a)   **(b)**

Figure 10

For graph (a): | For graph (b):
Number of edges = 7 | Number of edges = 6
Sum of degrees of vertices | Sum of degrees of vertices
= 2 + 3 + 2 + 3 + 4 = 14 | = 2 + 3 + 4 + 3 = 12   ▮▮▮

For each graph in **Example 4,** the sum of the degrees of the vertices is twice the number of edges. This is true for all graphs. Check that it is true for graphs in previous examples.

Sum of the Degrees Theorem

In any graph, the sum of the degrees of the vertices equals twice the number of edges.

To understand why this theorem is true, we think of any graph and imagine cutting each edge at its midpoint (without adding any vertices to the graph, however). Now we have precisely twice as many half edges as we had edges in our original graph. For each vertex, we count the number of half edges joined to the vertex. This is, of course, the degree of the vertex. We add these answers to determine the sum of the degrees of the vertices. We know that the number of half edges is twice the number of edges in our original graph. So, the sum of the degrees of the vertices in the graph is twice the number of edges in the graph.

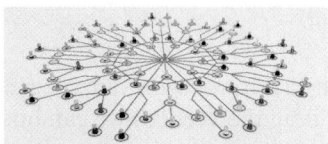

Networks are at the forefront of research in biology. Biologists have made enormous strides in understanding the structure of molecules in living organisms. It is now important to understand how these molecules interact with each other. This can be viewed as a network, or graph.

For example, current research aims to identify how proteins in cells interact with other proteins. Insights into such networks may help explain the growth of cancerous tumors. This may lead to better treatments for cancer. It was discovered that as graphs, these biological networks are surprisingly similar to the graphs representing the World Wide Web.

▮▮ **EXAMPLE 5** Using the Sum of the Degrees Theorem

A graph has precisely six vertices, each of degree 3. How many edges does this graph have?

SOLUTION

The sum of the degrees of the vertices of the graph is

$$3 + 3 + 3 + 3 + 3 + 3 = 18.$$

By the theorem above, this number is twice the number of edges, so the number of edges in the graph is

$$\frac{18}{2}, \quad \text{or} \quad 9. \qquad ▮▮▮$$

A **call graph** has telephone numbers as vertices, while edges represent a call placed from one number to another. A call graph for one company for just one day contained nearly 54 million vertices and 170 million edges. It had 3.7 million components. One of these was a giant component containing nearly 80% of the vertices.

▌▌ **EXAMPLE 6** Planning a Tour

Suppose we decide to explore the upper Midwest next summer. We plan to travel by Greyhound bus and would like to visit Grand Forks, Fargo, Bemidji, St. Cloud, Duluth, Minneapolis, Escanaba, and Green Bay. A check of the Greyhound website shows direct bus links between destinations as indicated.

City	Direct bus links with
Grand Forks	Bemidji, Fargo
Fargo	Grand Forks, St. Cloud, Minneapolis
Bemidji	Grand Forks, St. Cloud
St. Cloud	Bemidji, Fargo, Minneapolis
Duluth	Escanaba, Minneapolis
Minneapolis	Fargo, St. Cloud, Duluth, Green Bay
Escanaba	Duluth, Green Bay
Green Bay	Escanaba, Minneapolis

Draw a graph with vertices representing the destinations and edges representing the relation "there is a direct bus link." Is this a connected graph? Explain.

SOLUTION

Begin with eight vertices representing the eight destinations as in **Figure 11**. Use the bus link information to fill in the edges of the graph.

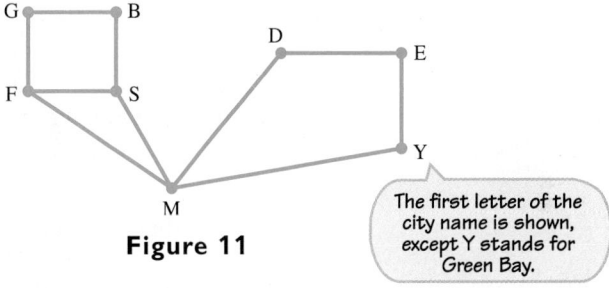

The first letter of the city name is shown, except Y stands for Green Bay.

Figure 11

Figure 11 is a connected graph. It shows that we can travel by bus from any of our chosen destinations to any other. ▌▌▌

Walks, Paths, and Circuits

Example 6 suggests several important ideas. For example, what trips could we take among the eight destinations, using only direct bus links? If we do not mind riding the same bus route more than once, we could take the following route.

$$M \rightarrow S \rightarrow F \rightarrow S \rightarrow B$$

Note that we used the St. Cloud to Fargo link twice. We could not take the $M \rightarrow D \rightarrow S$ route, however, since there is no direct bus link from Duluth to St. Cloud. Each possible route on the graph is called a *walk*.

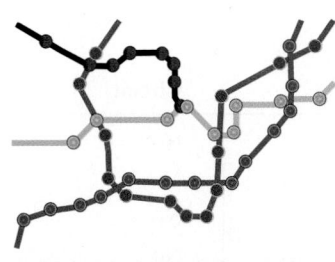

Maps of subway systems in large cities usually do not faithfully represent the positions of stations, nor the distances between them. They are essentially graphs with vertices representing stations and edges showing subway links.

Walk

A **walk** in a graph is a sequence of vertices, each linked to the next vertex by a specified edge of the graph.

This diagram shows a **Venn diagram** relationship among walks, paths, and circuits.

We can think of a walk as a route we can trace with a pencil without lifting the pencil from the graph.

$$M \rightarrow S \rightarrow F \rightarrow S \rightarrow B \quad \text{and} \quad F \rightarrow M \rightarrow D \rightarrow E \quad \text{Walks}$$

$$M \rightarrow D \rightarrow S \quad \text{Not a walk (There is no edge between D and S in \textbf{Figure 11}.)}$$

Suppose that the travel time for our trip is restricted, and we do not want to use any bus link more than once. A *path* is a special kind of walk.

Path
A **path** in a graph is a walk that uses no edge more than once.*

$$M \rightarrow S \rightarrow F \rightarrow M, \quad F \rightarrow M \rightarrow D \rightarrow E, \quad M \rightarrow S \rightarrow F \rightarrow M \rightarrow D \quad \text{Paths}$$

Trace these paths with a finger on the graph in **Figure 11**. Note that a path may use a *vertex* more than once.

$$B \rightarrow S \rightarrow F \rightarrow M \rightarrow S \rightarrow B \quad \text{Not a path (It uses edge BS more than once.)}$$

$$M \rightarrow D \rightarrow S \quad \text{Not a path (It is not even a walk.)}$$

Perhaps we want to begin and end our tour in the same city (and still not use any bus route more than once). A path such as this is known as a *circuit*. Two circuits we could take follow.

$$M \rightarrow S \rightarrow F \rightarrow M, \quad M \rightarrow S \rightarrow F \rightarrow M \rightarrow D \rightarrow E \rightarrow Y \rightarrow M \quad \text{Circuits}$$

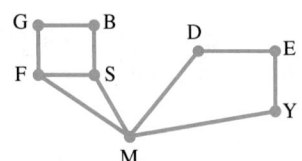

Figure 11 (repeated)

Circuit
A **circuit** in a graph is a path that begins and ends at the same vertex.

Notice that a circuit is a kind of path and, therefore, is also a kind of walk.

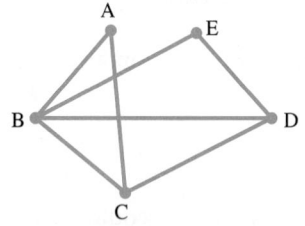

Figure 12

▮▮ **EXAMPLE 7** Classifying Walks

Using the graph in **Figure 12**, classify each sequence as a walk, a path, or a circuit.

(a) $E \rightarrow C \rightarrow D \rightarrow E$ **(b)** $A \rightarrow C \rightarrow D \rightarrow E \rightarrow B \rightarrow A$

(c) $B \rightarrow D \rightarrow E \rightarrow B \rightarrow C$ **(d)** $A \rightarrow B \rightarrow C \rightarrow D \rightarrow B \rightarrow A$

SOLUTION

	Walk	Path	Circuit
(a)	No (no edge E to C)	No[†]	No[†]
(b)	Yes	Yes	Yes
(c)	Yes	Yes	No
(d)	Yes	No (edge AB is used twice)	No[††]

[†] If a sequence of vertices is not a walk, it cannot possibly be either a path or a circuit.

[††] If a sequence of vertices is not a path, it cannot possibly be a circuit, since a circuit is defined as a special kind of path. ▮▮▮

*Some books call this a *trail* and use the term *path* for a walk that visits no vertex more than once.

When planning our trip, it would be useful to know the length of time the bus ride takes. We write the time for each bus ride on the graph, as shown in **Figure 13**.

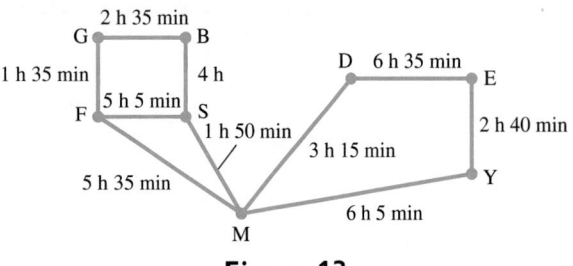

Figure 13

A graph with numbers on the edges as in **Figure 13** is known as a **weighted graph.** The numbers on the edges are called **weights.**

> **PROBLEM-SOLVING HINT** Drawing a sketch is a useful problem-solving strategy. **Example 8** illustrates how drawing a sketch can simplify a problem that at first seems complicated.

▌▌ **EXAMPLE 8**   Analyzing a Round-Robin Tournament

In a round-robin tournament, every contestant plays every other contestant. The winner is the contestant who wins the most games. Suppose six tennis players compete in a round-robin tournament. How many matches will be played?

SOLUTION

Draw a graph with six vertices to represent the six players. Then, as in **Figure 14**, draw an edge for each match between a pair of contestants. We can count the edges to find out how many matches must be played. Or, we can reason as follows: There are 6 vertices each of degree 5, so the sum of the degrees of the vertices in this graph is $6 \cdot 5$, or 30. We know that the sum of the degrees is twice the number of edges. Therefore, there are 15 edges in this graph and, thus, 15 matches in the tournament.   ▌▌▌

Complete Graphs and Subgraphs

The graph for **Example 8** in **Figure 14** is an example of a *complete graph*.

> **Complete Graph**
>
> A **complete graph** is a graph in which there is exactly one edge going from each vertex to each other vertex in the graph.

▌▌ **EXAMPLE 9**   Deciding Whether a Graph Is Complete

Decide whether each of the graphs in **Figure 15** is complete. If a graph is not complete, explain why it is not.

SOLUTION

Graph (a) is not complete. There is no edge from vertex A to vertex D. Graph (b) is complete. (Check that there is an edge from each of the ten vertices to each of the other nine vertices in the graph.)   ▌▌▌

Mazes have always fascinated people. Mazes are found on coins from ancient Knossos (Greece), in the sand drawings at Nazca in Peru, on Roman pavements, on the floors of renaissance cathedrals in Europe, and, of course, as hedge mazes in gardens. Graphs can be used to clarify the structure of mazes.

Figure 14

(a)

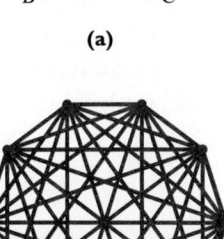

(b)
Figure 15

▌▌ **EXAMPLE 10** Finding a Complete Graph

Find a complete graph with four vertices in the preschoolers' friendship pattern depicted in **Figure 3**, repeated here.

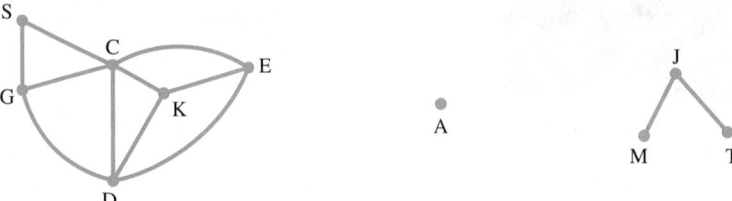

Figure 3 (repeated)

SOLUTION

Figure 16 shows a portion of the friendship graph from **Figure 3**. This is a complete graph with four vertices. ▌▌▌

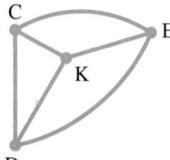

Figure 16

Figure 16 includes some complete graphs with three vertices. In general, a graph consisting of some of the vertices of the original graph and some of the original edges between those vertices is called a **subgraph.** Vertices or edges not included in the original graph cannot be in the subgraph. (Notice the similarity to the idea of subset, discussed earlier in the text.)

A subgraph may include anywhere from one to all the vertices of the original graph and anywhere from none to all the edges of the original graph. Notice that a subgraph is a graph, and recall that in a graph every edge goes from a vertex to a vertex. Therefore, no edge can be included in a subgraph without the vertices at both of its ends also being included.

- The subgraph shown in **Figure 16** is a complete graph, but a subgraph does not have to be complete. For example, the graphs in **Figures 17(a) and (b)** are both subgraphs of the graph in **Figure 3**.

- The graph in **Figure 17(b)** is a subgraph even though it has no edges. (However, we could not form a subgraph by taking edges without vertices. In a graph every edge goes from a vertex to a vertex.)

- The graph in **Figure 17(c)** is *not* a subgraph of the graph in **Figure 3**, since there was no edge between M and T in the original graph.

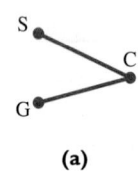

(a)

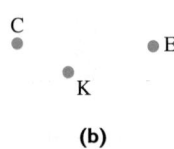

(b)

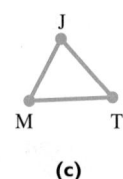

(c)

Figure 17

Graph Coloring

Tabatha works at the college learning center, and one of her tasks is to schedule study groups for the courses listed at the left below. Study groups for different courses must be scheduled at different times if there are students taking both courses. The column on the right shows, for each course, which of the other courses have students in common with it. For example, the first row shows that each of the courses statistics, chemistry, history, and physics has one or more students also taking algebra.

Course	Other courses taken by students in this course
Algebra	Statistics, Chemistry, History, Physics
History	Statistics, Chemistry, Biology, Algebra
Chemistry	Physics, Biology, Writing, Algebra, History
Biology	Physics, Statistics, Writing, History, Chemistry
Physics	Statistics, Algebra, Chemistry, Biology
Statistics	Writing, Algebra, History, Biology, Physics
Writing	Chemistry, Biology, Statistics

Stand and Deliver (1998) stars **James Edward Olmos** as Jaime Escalante, an inner-city high school mathematics teacher who inspires his students and defies all odds in successfully preparing them for the Advanced Placement calculus exam. Olmos is shown in the chapter opener photo.

The concept of Bacon number is described in the chapter opener. Olmos' Bacon number is two. Can you justify this result? (The answer is on **page 802**.)

Tabatha's task is to figure out the least number of time slots needed for the seven study groups and to decide which (if any) can be scheduled at the same time. We can draw a graph, with a vertex for each course and an edge between two vertices, *if there are students taking both courses*. See **Figure 18**.

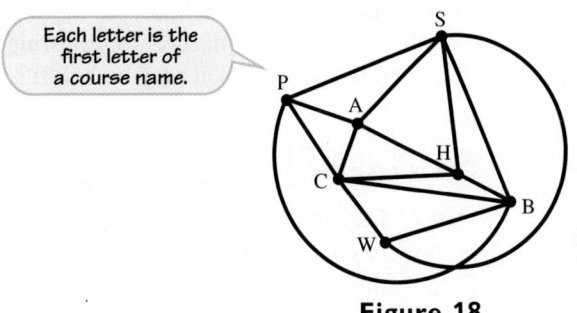

Figure 18

If there is an edge between two vertices, the corresponding courses have students in common, and the study groups must *not* meet at the same time. To show this we use a different color for each time slot for study groups. We will color the vertices with the different colors to show when the study groups could be scheduled.

To make sure that study groups are at different times if the courses have students in common, we must make sure that any two vertices joined by an edge have different colors. To ensure the least number of time slots, we use as few colors as possible. In **Figure 19**, we show one possible coloring of the vertices using three colors. We cannot color the graph as required with fewer than three colors.

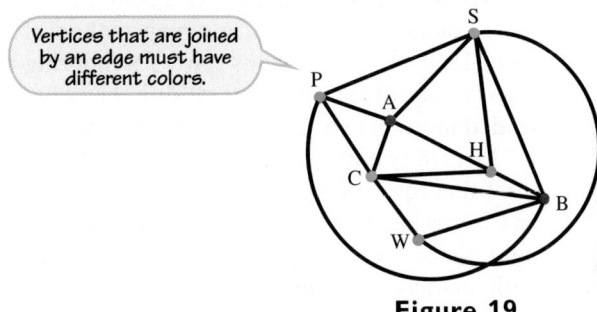

Figure 19

Tabatha can schedule the required study groups in no fewer than 3 time slots. She can schedule statistics and chemistry at one time, physics, history, and writing at a second time, and biology and algebra at a third time.

The method we used is called a *coloring** for the graph.

Coloring and Chromatic Number

A **coloring** for a graph is an assignment of a color to each vertex in such a way that vertices joined by an edge have different colors. The **chromatic number** of a graph is the least number of colors needed to make a coloring.

Using this terminology, Tabatha had to determine the chromatic number for the graph in **Figure 18**. The chromatic number was 3, which equaled the least number of time slots needed for the study groups.

———————————

*This is sometimes called a *vertex* coloring for the graph.

Have you ever had bad reception on your cell phone? This often occurs because signals are being sent at roughly the same frequency to too many cell phones located close together. Graph coloring can be used to help analyze this problem. However, with over 4 billion cell-phone subscribers in the world (United Nations International Telecommunications Union estimate in 2008) and a fairly narrow frequency range available for cell-phone transmission, many believe that governments should make more frequencies available for cell phone usage.

Answer to the Bacon Number Question

Olmos was not in a movie with Bacon, so Olmos' Bacon number must be greater than one.

• Edward James Olmos was in *My Family* (1995) with Bibi Besch.
• Bibi Besch was in *Tremors* (1990) with Kevin Bacon.

Thus, Olmos has a Bacon number of two.

The idea of using vertex coloring to solve problems like this is straightforward. Determining the chromatic number for a graph with many vertices or producing a coloring using the least possible number of colors can be difficult. No one has yet found an efficient method for finding the exact chromatic number for arbitrarily large graphs. (The term *efficient algorithm* has a specific, technical meaning for computer scientists. See **Section 15.3.**)

While the following method for coloring a graph may not give a coloring with the least number of colors, it may be helpful.

Coloring a Graph

Step 1 Choose a vertex with greatest degree, and color it. Use the same color to color as many vertices as you can without coloring two vertices the same color if they are joined by an edge.

Step 2 Choose a new color, and repeat what you did in Step 1 for vertices not already colored.

Step 3 Repeat Step 1 until all vertices are colored.

Graph coloring is used to solve many practical problems. It is useful in management science for solving scheduling problems, such as the study groups example above. Graph coloring is also related to allocating transmission frequencies to TV and radio stations and cell phone companies.

The coloring of graphs has an interesting history involving maps. Maps need to be colored so that territories with common boundaries have different colors. How many colors are needed? For map makers, four colors have always sufficed. In about 1850, mathematicians started pondering this. For over a hundred years, they were neither able to prove that four colors are always enough, nor find a map that needed more than four colors. This was called the **four-color problem.**

In 1976 two mathematicians, Kenneth Appel and Wolfgang Haken, provided a proof that four colors are always enough. This proof created a controversy in mathematics, as it relied on computer calculations so lengthy (fifty 24-hour days of computer time) that no person could check the entire proof. Because of this, some mathematicians still feel that the four-color theorem has not yet been proved, and many keep looking for a shorter proof.

The postmark shown above was used by the Urbana, IL, post office to commemorate the proof of the four-color theorem.

15.1 EXERCISES

For Exercises 1–6, determine how many vertices and how many edges each graph has.

1.

2.

3.

4.

5.

6.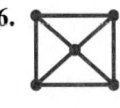

For each graph indicated, find the degree of each vertex in the graph. Then add the degrees to get the sum of the degrees of the vertices of the graph. What relationship do you notice between the sum of degrees and the number of edges?

7. Exercise 1   **8.** Exercise 2

9. Exercise 3   **10.** Exercise 4

*In Exercises 11–16, determine whether the two graphs are isomorphic. If so, label corresponding vertices of the two graphs with the same letters and color-code corresponding edges, as in **Example 2.** (Note that there is more than one correct answer for many of these exercises.)*

11.

    (a)   (b)

12.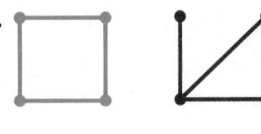

    (a)   (b)

13.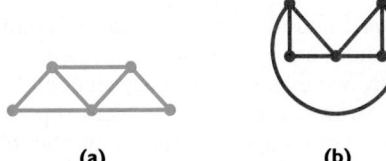

    (a)   (b)

14.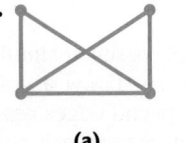

    (a)   (b)

15.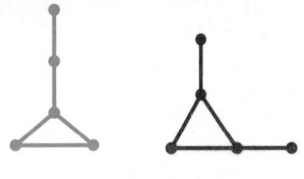

    (a)   (b)

16.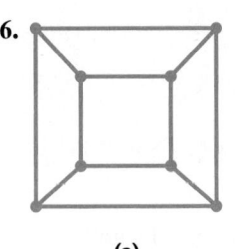

    (a)   (b)

In Exercises 17–22, determine whether the graph is connected or disconnected. Then determine how many components the graph has.

17.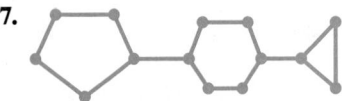

18.

19.

20.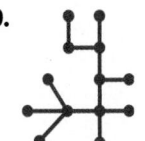

21.   **22.**

In Exercises 23–26, use the theorem that relates the sum of degrees to the number of edges to determine the number of edges in the graph (without drawing the graph).

23. A graph with 5 vertices, each of degree 4

24. A graph with 7 vertices, each of degree 4

25. A graph with 5 vertices, three of degree 1, one of degree 2, and one of degree 3

26. A graph with 8 vertices, two of degree 1, three of degree 2, one of degree 3, one of degree 5, and one of degree 6

In Exercises 27–29, refer to the following graph.

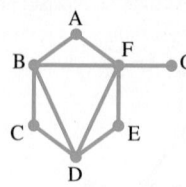

27. Which are walks in the graph? If not, why not?

(a) A → B → C

(b) B → A → D

(c) E → F → A → E

(d) B → D → F → B → D

(e) D → E

(f) C → B → C → B

28. Which are paths in the graph? If not, why not?

(a) B → D → E → F

(b) D → F → B → D

(c) B → D → F → B → D

(d) D → E → F → G → F → D

(e) B → C → D → B → A

(f) A → B → E → F → A

29. Which are circuits in the graph? If not, why not?

(a) A → B → C → D → E → F

(b) A → B → D → E → F → A

(c) C → F → E → D → C

(d) G → F → D → E → F

(e) F → D → F → E → D → F

In Exercises 30 and 31, refer to the following graph.

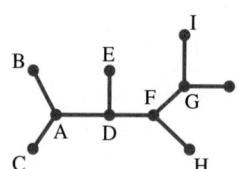

30. Which are walks in the graph? If not, why not?

(a) F → G → J → H → F

(b) D → F

(c) B → A → D → F → H

(d) B → A → D → E → D → F → H

(e) I → G → J

(f) I → G → J → I

31. Which are paths in the graph? If not, why not?

(a) A → B → C

(b) J → G → I → G → F

(c) D → E → I → G → F

(d) C → A

(e) C → A → D → E

(f) C → A → D → E → D → A → B

*In Exercises 32–37, refer to the following graph. In each case, determine whether the sequence of vertices is **(i)** a walk, **(ii)** a path, **(iii)** a circuit in the graph.*

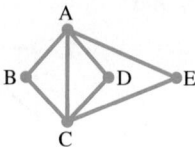

32. A → B → C → D → E

33. A → B → C

34. A → B → C → D → A

35. A → B → A → C → D → A

36. A → B → C → A → D → C → E → A

37. C → A → B → C → D → A → E

In Exercises 38–43, determine whether the graph is a complete graph. If not, explain why it is not complete.

38.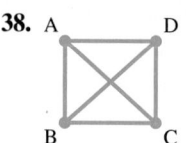

39.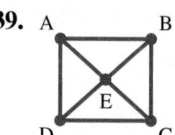

40.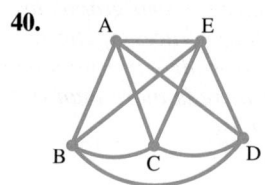

41.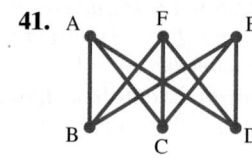

42.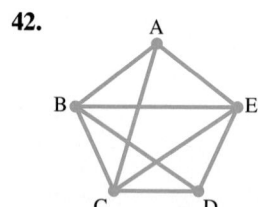

43.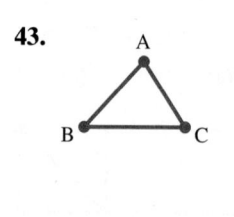

Solve each problem.

44. Chess Competition Students from two schools compete in chess. Each school has a team of four students. Each student must play one game against each student on the opposing team. Draw a graph with vertices representing the students, and edges representing the chess games. How many games must be played in the competition?

45. Chess Competition A chess master plays seven simultaneous games with seven other players. Draw a graph with vertices representing the players and edges representing the chess games. How many games are being played?

46. *Dancing Partners* At a party there were four males and five females. During the party each male danced with each female (and no female pair or male pair danced together). Draw a graph with vertices representing the people at the party and edges showing the relationship "danced with." How many edges are there in the graph?

47. *Number of Handshakes* There are six members on a hockey team (including the goalie). At the end of a hockey game, each member of the team shakes hands with each member of the opposing team. How many handshakes occur?

48. *Number of Handshakes* There are seven people at a business meeting. One of these shakes hands with four people, four shake hands with two people, and two shake hands with three people. How many handshakes occur? (*Hint:* Use the theorem that the sum of the degrees of the vertices in a graph is twice the number of edges.)

49. *Spread of a Rumor* A lawyer is preparing his argument in a libel case. He has evidence that a libelous rumor about his client was discussed in various telephone conversations among eight people. Two of the people involved had four telephone conversations in which the rumor was discussed, one person had three, four had two, and one had one such telephone conversation. How many telephone conversations were there in which the rumor was discussed among the eight people?

50. *Vertices and Edges of a Cube* Draw a graph with vertices representing the vertices (the corners) of a cube and edges representing the edges of the cube. In your graph, find a circuit that visits four different vertices. What figure does your circuit form on the actual cube?

51. *Vertices and Edges of a Tetrahedron* Draw a graph with vertices representing the vertices (or corners) of a tetrahedron and edges representing the edges of the tetrahedron. In the graph, identify a circuit that visits three different vertices. What figure does the circuit form on the actual tetrahedron?

52. *Students in the Same Class* Mary, Erin, Sue, Jane, Katy, and Brenda are friends at college. Mary, Erin, Sue, and Jane are in the same math class. Sue, Jane, and Katy take the same English composition class.

  (a) Draw a graph with vertices representing the six students and edges representing the relation "take a common class."

  (b) Is the graph connected or disconnected? How many components does the graph have?

  (c) In the graph, identify a subgraph that is a complete graph with four vertices.

  (d) In the graph, identify three different subgraphs that are complete graphs with three vertices. (There are several correct answers.)

53. Here is another theorem about graphs: *In any graph, the number of vertices with odd degree must be even.* Explain why this theorem is true. (*Hint:* Use the theorem about the relationship between the number of edges and the sum of degrees.)

54. Draw two nonisomorphic (simple) graphs with 6 vertices, with each vertex having degree 3.

55. Explain why the graphs in **Exercise 54** are not isomorphic.

56. *Analyzing a Cube with a Graph* Draw a graph whose vertices represent the *faces* of a cube and in which an edge between two vertices shows that the corresponding faces of the actual cube share a common boundary. What is the degree of each vertex in the graph? What does the degree of any vertex in the graph tell about the actual cube?

57. Graphs may be used to clarify the structure of mazes. Vertices represent entrances and points in the maze where there is a dead end or a choice of two or more edges by which to proceed. For example, the 1690 design for the hedge maze at Hampton Court in England and a corresponding graph are shown below.

    Write a paper on mazes. Use graphs to analyze the structures of the mazes. Perhaps focus on a particular kind of maze, such as mazes in gardens, mazes in art and architecture, or mazes in ancient cultures.

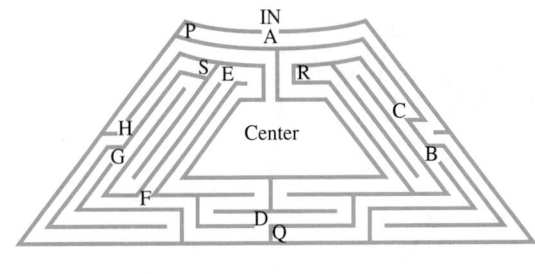

58. Graphs may be used to clarify the rhyme schemes in poetry. Vertices represent words at the end of a line, edges are drawn, and a path is used to indicate the rhyme scheme. For example, here is the first stanza of *Ode to Autumn* by John Keats, with the rhyme scheme analyzed using a graph:

Season of mists and mellow fruitfulness,	A
Close bosom-friend of the maturing sun;	B
Conspiring with him how to load and bless	A
With fruit the vines that round the thatch-eves run;	B
To bend with apples the moss'd cottage-trees	C
And fill all fruit with ripeness to the core;	D
To swell the gourd, and plump the hazel shells	E
With a sweet kernel; to set budding more,	D
And still more, later flowers for the bees,	C
Until they think that warm days will never cease,	C
For Summer has o'er brimm'd their clammy cells.	E

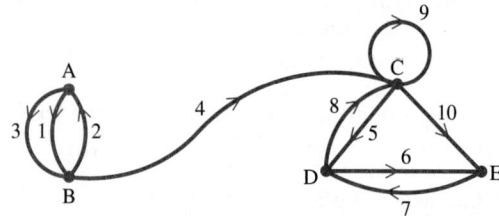

Write a paper on rhyme schemes in poetry, using graphs to illustrate. Focus either on a particular poet or on a particular type of poem.

In Exercises 59 through 64, color the graph using as few colors as possible. Determine the chromatic number of the graph. (Hint: The chromatic number is fixed, but there may be more than one correct coloring.)

59.
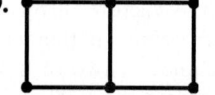

60.
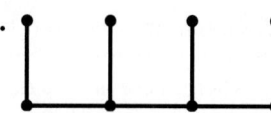

61.
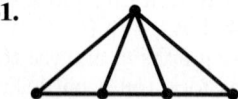

62.
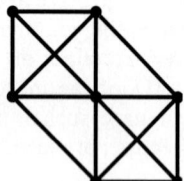

63.
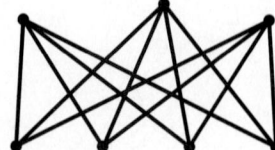

64.
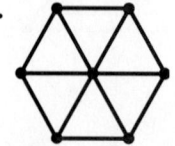

65. Color each graph using as few colors as possible. Use this to determine the chromatic number of the graph. (Graphs like these are called **cycles.**)

(a) 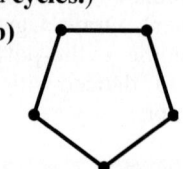   **(b)**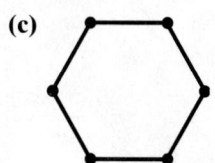

(c) 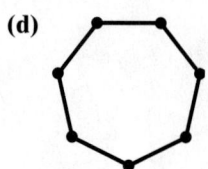   **(d)**

(e) Use the results from parts (a)–(d) to make a prediction about the chromatic number of a cycle. (*Hint:* Consider two cases.)

66. Sketch a complete graph with the specified number of vertices, color the graph with as few colors as possible, and use this to determine the chromatic number of the graph.

(a) 3 vertices

(b) 4 vertices

(c) 5 vertices

(d) Write a general principle by completing this statement: A complete graph with n vertices has chromatic number ____ .

(e) Why is the statement in part (d) true?

(f) Generalize further by completing this statement: If a graph has a *subgraph* that is a complete graph with n vertices, then the chromatic number of the graph must be at least ____ .

In Exercises 67–70, color the vertices using as few colors as possible. Then state the chromatic number of the graph. (Hint: It might help to first identify the largest subgraph that is a complete graph.)

67. 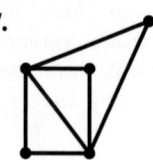   **68.**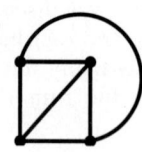

69. 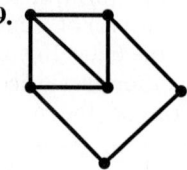   **70.**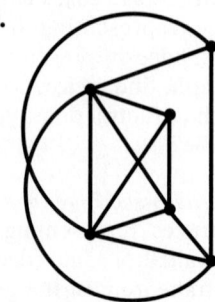

71. *Scheduling Meeting Times* Campus Life must schedule weekly meeting times for the six organizations listed below in such a way that organizations with members in common meet at different times. Use graph coloring to determine the least number of different meeting times and to decide which organizations should meet at the same time.

Organization	Members also belong to
Choir	Caribbean Club, Dance Club, Theater, Service Club
Caribbean Club	Dance Club, Service Club, Choir
Service Club	Forensics, Choir, Theater, Caribbean Club
Forensics	Dance Club, Service Club
Theater	Choir, Service Club
Dance Club	Choir, Caribbean Club, Forensics

72. *Assigning Frequencies to Transmitters* Interference can occur between radio stations. To avoid this, transmitters that are less than 60 miles apart must be assigned different broadcast frequencies. The transmitters for 7 radio stations are labeled A through G. The information below shows, for each transmitter, which of the others are within 60 miles. Use graph coloring to determine the least number of different broadcast frequencies that must be assigned to the 7 transmitters. Include a plan for which transmitters could broadcast on the same frequency to use this least number of frequencies.

Transmitter	Transmitters within 60 miles of this
A	B, E, F
B	A, C, E, F, G
C	B, D, G
D	C, F, G
E	A, B, F
F	A, B, D, E, G
G	B, C, D, F

73. *Inviting Colleagues to a Gathering* Tiffany wants to invite her work colleagues to her home. However, several of her colleagues do not get along with each other, as summarized in the list at the top of the next column. Tiffany plans to organize several gatherings, so that colleagues who do not get along are not there at the same time. Use graph coloring to determine the least number of gatherings needed to achieve this, and decide which colleagues should be invited each time.

- Joe does not get along with Brad and Phil.
- Caitlin does not get along with Lindsay and Brad.
- Lindsay does not get along with Phil.
- Mary does not get along with Lindsay.
- Eva gets along with everyone.

Graph Coloring In Exercises 74–76, the graph shows the vertices and edges of the figure specified. Color the vertices of each figure in such a way that vertices with an edge between them have different colors. Use graph coloring to find a way to do this, and specify the least number of colors needed.

74. Cube

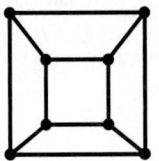

75. Octahedron

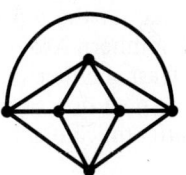

76. Dodecahedron

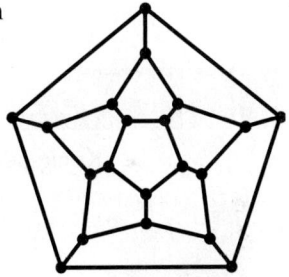

Graph Coloring In Exercises 77 and 78, draw a vertex for each region shown in the map. Draw an edge between two vertices if the two regions have a common boundary. (Do not draw an edge if the regions meet at just one point.) Then find a coloring for the graph, using as few colors as possible.

77.

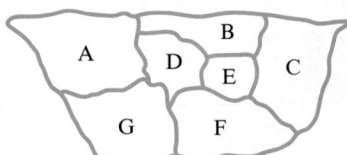

78.

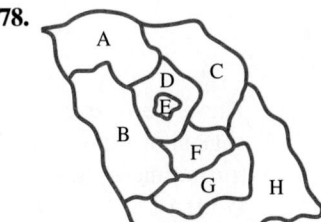

79. *Map Coloring* The map shows areas of upstate New York. Use graph coloring to determine the least number of colors that can be used to color the map so that areas with common boundaries have different colors.

80. *Map Coloring* The map at the top of the next column shows countries of Southern Africa. Use graph coloring to determine the least number of colors that can be used to color the map so that countries with common boundaries have different colors.

Map Drawing In Exercises 81–83, draw a map with the specified number of countries that can be colored using the stated number of colors, and no fewer. (Countries may not consist of disconnected pieces.) If it is not possible to draw such a map, say why not.

81. 6 countries, 3 colors   **82.** 6 countries, 4 colors

83. 6 countries, 5 colors

84. Write a short paper on the history of the four-color problem. Include discussion of the proof by Appel and Haken.

15.2 EULER CIRCUITS

Königsberg Bridge Problem • Fleury's Algorithm

Leonhard Euler (1707–1783) was a devoted father and grandfather. He had thirteen children and frequently worked on mathematics with children playing around him. He lost the sight in his right eye at age 31, a couple of years after writing the Königsberg bridge paper. He became completely blind at age 58, but produced more than half his mathematical work after that. Euler wrote nearly a thousand books and papers.

Königsberg Bridge Problem

In the early 1700s, the city of Königsberg was the capital of East Prussia. (Königsberg is now called Kaliningrad and is in Russia.) The river Pregel ran through the city in two branches with an island between the branches. **Figure 20** shows the city as it looked in the early 1700s.

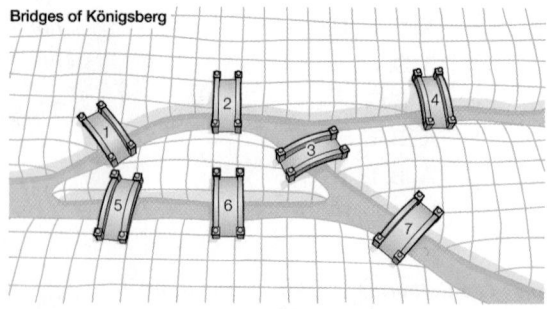

Figure 20

There were seven bridges joining various parts of the city. **Figure 21** on the next page shows a map of the river and bridges in the city. According to Leonhard Euler (pronounced "oiler"), the following problem was well known in his time (around 1730):

> Is it possible for a citizen of Königsberg to take a stroll through the city, crossing each bridge exactly once, and beginning and ending at the same place?

Try to find such a route on the map in **Figure 21**. (Do not cross the river anywhere except at the bridges shown on the map.)

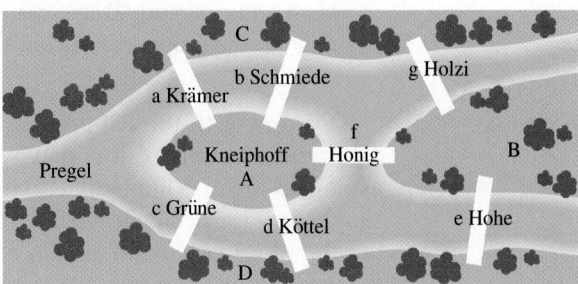

Figure 21

We can simplify the problem by drawing the map as a graph. See **Figure 22**. The graph focuses on the relations between the vertices. This is the relation "there is a bridge." In this graph we have *two* edges between vertices A and C and between vertices A and D. Thus, this graph is not a simple graph. We have labeled the edges with lowercase letters. Now try to find a route as required in the puzzle.

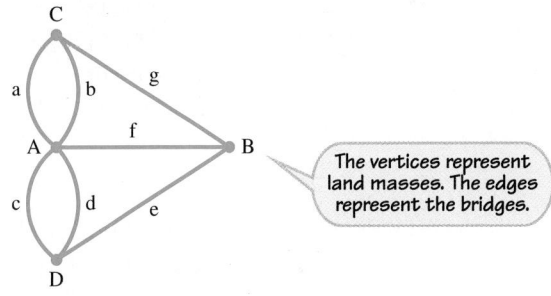

The vertices represent land masses. The edges represent the bridges.

Figure 22

The Königsberg bridge problem requires more than a path and more than a circuit. (Recall that a path is a walk that uses no edge more than once, and a circuit is a path that begins and ends at the same vertex.) The problem requires a circuit that uses *every* edge, *exactly* once. This is called an *Euler circuit.*

Euler Path and Euler Circuit

An **Euler path** in a graph is a path that uses every edge of the graph exactly once. An **Euler circuit** in a graph is a circuit that uses every edge of the graph exactly once.

▌▌ **EXAMPLE 1** Recognizing Euler Circuits

Consider the graph in **Figure 23**.

(a) Is $A \rightarrow B \rightarrow C \rightarrow D \rightarrow E \rightarrow F \rightarrow A$ an Euler circuit for this graph? Justify your answer.

(b) Does the graph have an Euler circuit?

SOLUTION

(a) $A \rightarrow B \rightarrow C \rightarrow D \rightarrow E \rightarrow F \rightarrow A$ is a circuit, but not an Euler circuit, since it does not use every edge of the graph. For example, the edge BD is not used in this circuit.

A university was founded in Königsberg in 1544. It was established as a Lutheran center of learning. Its most famous professor was the philosopher **Immanual Kant,** who was born in Königsberg in 1724. The university was completely destroyed during World War II.

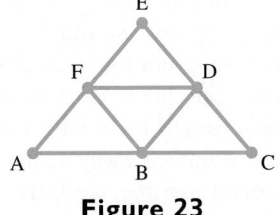

Figure 23

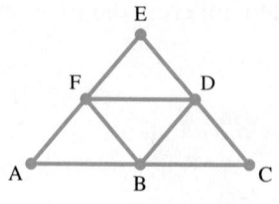

Figure 23 (repeated)

(b) In the graph in **Figure 23**, the circuit

$$A \rightarrow B \rightarrow C \rightarrow D \rightarrow E \rightarrow F \rightarrow D \rightarrow B \rightarrow F \rightarrow A$$

is an Euler circuit. Trace this path on the graph to check that it does use every edge of the graph exactly once.   ▌▌▌

Returning to the Königsberg bridge problem, it seemed that no route of the type required could be found. Why was this so? Euler published a paper in 1736 that explained why it is impossible to find a walk of the required kind, and he provided a simple way for deciding whether a given graph has an Euler circuit. Euler did not use the terms *graph* and *circuit*, but his paper was, in fact, the first paper on graph theory. In modern terms, Euler proved the first part of the theorem below. Part 2 was not proved until 1873.

> **Euler's Theorem**
>
> Suppose we have a connected graph.
>
> **1.** If the graph has an Euler circuit, then each vertex of the graph has even degree.
> **2.** If each vertex of the graph has even degree, then the graph has an Euler circuit.

What does Euler's theorem predict about the connected graph in **Figure 23**? The degrees of the vertices are as follows.

> A: 2   B: 4   C: 2   D: 4   E: 2   F: 4

Each vertex has even degree, so it follows from part 2 of the theorem that the graph has an Euler circuit. (We already knew this, since we found an Euler circuit for this graph in **Example 1**.)

What does Euler's theorem suggest about the Königsberg bridge problem? Note that the degree of vertex C in **Figure 22** is 3, which is an odd number, and the graph is connected. So, by part 1 of the theorem, the graph cannot have an Euler circuit. (In fact, the graph has many vertices with odd degree, but the presence of *any* vertex of odd degree indicates that the graph does not have an Euler circuit.)

Why is Euler's theorem true? Consider the first part of the theorem:

If a connected graph has an Euler circuit, then each vertex has even degree.

Suppose we have a connected graph with an Euler circuit in the graph. Suppose the circuit begins and ends at a vertex A. Imagine traveling along the Euler circuit, from A all the way back to A, putting an arrow on each edge in our direction of travel. (Of course, we travel along each edge exactly once.)

Now consider any vertex B in the graph. It has edges joined to it, each with an arrow. Some of the arrows point toward B, some point away from B. The number of arrows pointing toward B is the same as the number of arrows pointing away from B, for every time we visit B, we come in on one unused edge and leave via a different unused edge. In other words, we can pair off the edges joined to B, with each pair having one arrow pointing toward B and one arrow pointing away from B. Thus, the total number of edges joined to B must be an even number, and, therefore, the degree of B is even. A similar argument shows that our starting vertex, A, also has even degree.

The following is from Euler's paper on the **Königsberg bridge problem:** "I was told that while some denied the possibility of doing this and others were in doubt, no one maintained that it was actually possible. On the basis of the above, I formulated the following very general problem for myself: Given any configuration of the river and the branches into which it may divide, as well as any number of bridges, to determine whether or not it is possible to cross each bridge exactly once." (*Source:* Newman, James R. (ed.), "The Königsberg Bridges," *Scientific American*, July 1953, in *Readings from Scientific American: Mathematics in the Modern World*, 1968.)

By 1875 a new bridge had been built in Königsberg, joining the land areas we labeled C and D in **Figure 21**. It was now possible for a citizen of Königsberg to take a walk that used each bridge exactly once, provided he or she started at A and ended at B, or vice versa.

The second part of Euler's theorem states the following:

> *If each vertex of a connected graph has even degree,*
> *then the graph has an Euler circuit.*

To show that this is true, we will provide a recipe (Fleury's algorithm) for finding an Euler circuit in any such graph. First, however, we consider more examples of how Euler's theorem can be applied.

▮▮ **EXAMPLE 2** Using Euler's Theorem

Decide which of the graphs in **Figure 24** has an Euler circuit. Justify your answers.

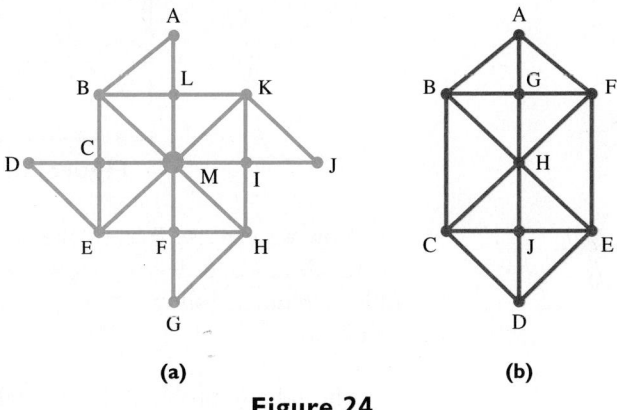

(a)   (b)

Figure 24

SOLUTION

(a) The graph in **Figure 24(a)** is connected. If we write the degree next to each vertex on the graph, as in **Figure 25**, we see that each vertex has even degree. Since the graph is connected, and each vertex has even degree, it follows from Euler's theorem that the graph has an Euler circuit.

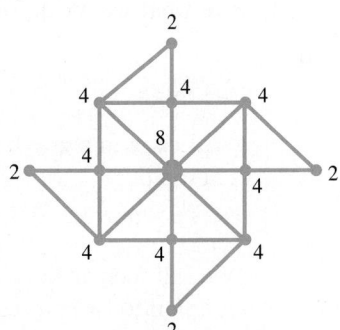

Figure 25

(b) In **Figure 24(b)**, check the degrees of the vertices. Note that vertex A has degree three, an odd degree. We need look no further. It follows from Euler's theorem that this connected graph does not have an Euler circuit. (All the other vertices in this graph except for D have even degree. However, if just one vertex has odd degree, then the graph does not have an Euler circuit.) ▮▮▮

PROBLEM-SOLVING HINT When solving a challenging problem, it is useful to ask whether the problem is related to another problem that you already know how to solve. **Example 3** on the next page illustrates this strategy.

▎▎ **EXAMPLE 3** Tracing Patterns

Beginning and ending at the same place, is it possible to trace the pattern shown in **Figure 26** below without lifting the pencil off the page and without tracing over any part of the pattern (except isolated points) more than once?

SOLUTION

The pattern in **Figure 26** is not a graph. (It has no vertices.) But what we are being asked to do is very much like being asked to find an Euler circuit. So we imagine that there are vertices at points where lines or curves of the pattern meet, obtaining the graph in **Figure 27**.

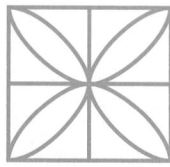
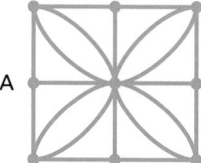

Figure 26   **Figure 27**

Now we can use Euler's theorem to decide whether we can trace the pattern. Vertex A has odd degree. Thus, by Euler's theorem, this graph does not have an Euler circuit. It follows that we cannot trace the original pattern in the manner required. ▎▎▎

The tracing problem in **Example 3** illustrates a practical problem that occurs when designing robotic arms to trace patterns. Automated machines that engrave identification tags for pets require such a mechanical arm.

Fleury's Algorithm

Fleury's algorithm can be used to find an Euler circuit in any connected graph in which each vertex has even degree. An algorithm is like a recipe—follow the steps and we achieve what we need. Before introducing Fleury's algorithm, we need a definition.

> **Cut Edge**
>
> A **cut edge** in a graph is an edge whose removal disconnects a component of the graph.

We call such an edge a cut edge, since removing the edge *cuts* a connected piece of a graph into two pieces.*

▎▎ **EXAMPLE 4** Identifying Cut Edges

Identify the cut edges in the graph in **Figure 28**.

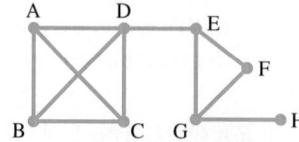

Figure 28

*Some mathematicians use "bridge" instead of "cut edge" to describe such an edge.

The word **algorithm** comes from the name of the Persian mathematician, **Abu Ja'far Muhammad ibn Musa Al-Khowârizmî,** who lived from about A.D. 780 to A.D. 850. One of the books he wrote was on the Hindu-Arabic system of numerals (the system we use today), and calculations using them. The Latin translation of this book was called *Algoritmi de numero Indorum,* meaning "Al-Khowârizmî on the Hindu Art of Reckoning."

SOLUTION

This graph has only one component, so we must look for edges whose removal would disconnect the graph.

DE is a cut edge. If we removed this edge, we would disconnect the graph into two components, obtaining the graph of **Figure 29(a)**. HG is also a cut edge. Its removal would disconnect the graph as shown in **Figure 29(b)**.

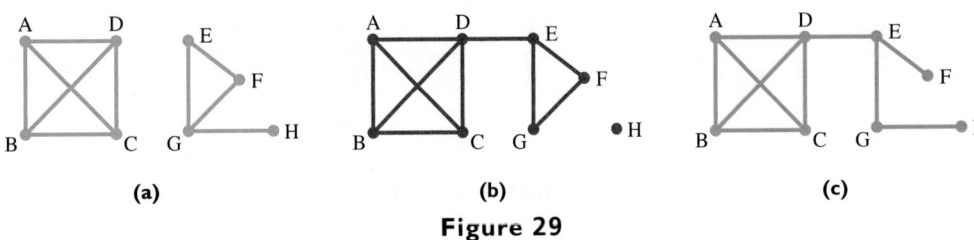

(a)　　　　　　　　　　**(b)**　　　　　　　　　　**(c)**

Figure 29

None of the other edges is a cut edge. We could remove any *one* of the other edges and still have a connected graph (that is, we would still have a path from each vertex of the graph to each other vertex). For example, if we remove edge GF, we end up with a graph that still is connected, as shown in **Figure 29(c)**. ■■■

Recall that Fleury's algorithm is for finding an Euler circuit in a connected graph in which each vertex has even degree.

> **Fleury's Algorithm**
>
> *Step 1* Start at any vertex. Go along any edge from this vertex to another vertex. *Remove this edge from the graph.*
>
> *Step 2* You are now on a vertex of the revised graph. Choose any edge from this vertex, subject to only one condition: do not use a cut edge (*of the revised graph*) unless you have no other option. Go along your chosen edge. *Remove this edge from the graph.*
>
> *Step 3* Repeat Step 2 until you have used all the edges and returned to the vertex at which you started.

EXAMPLE 5 Using Fleury's Algorithm

Find an Euler circuit for the graph in **Figure 30**.

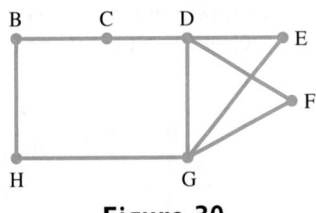

Figure 30

The **Tshokwe people of northeastern Angola** have a tradition involving continuous patterns in sand. The tracings are called *sona* and they have ritual significance. They are used as mnemonics for stories about the gods and ancestors. Elders trace the drawings while telling the stories. The sona shown here is called *skin of a leopard*. The men draw the grid of dots first, as an aid to recalling the sona. *Source:* Gerdes, Paul. *Geometry from Africa – Mathematical and Educational Explorations.* Mathematical Association of America, 1999, p. 171.

SOLUTION

First we must check that this graph does indeed have an Euler circuit. Check that the graph is connected and that each vertex has even degree.

We can start at any vertex. We choose C. We could go from C to B or from C to D. We go to D, removing the edge CD. (We show it scratched out, but we must think of this edge as gone.) Our path begins: C → D. The revised graph is shown in **Figure 31**.

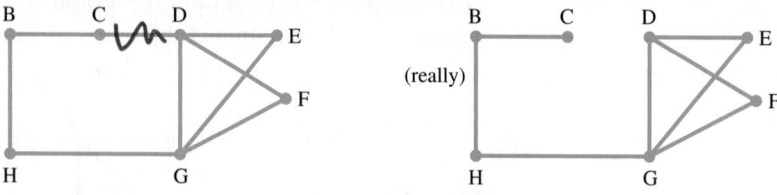

Figure 31

Note that none of the edges DE, DF, or DG is a cut edge for our current graph, so we can choose to go along any one of these. We go from D to G, removing edge DG. So far, our path is C → D → G. (Be sure to keep a record of this path.) **Figure 32** shows the revised graph.

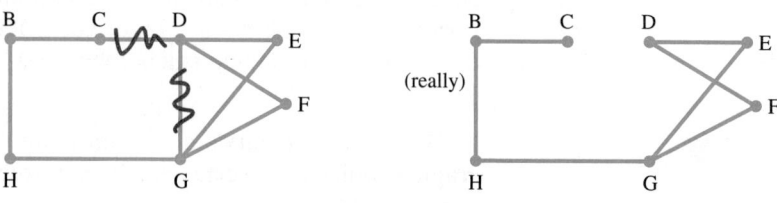

Figure 32

The remaining edges at G are GE, GF, and GH. Note, however, that GH is a cut edge for our revised graph, and we have other options. Thus, according to Fleury's algorithm, *we must not use GH at this stage*. (If we used GH now, we would never be able to get back to use the edges GF, GE, and so on.) We go from G to F. Our path is C → D → G → F, and we show our revised graph in **Figure 33**.

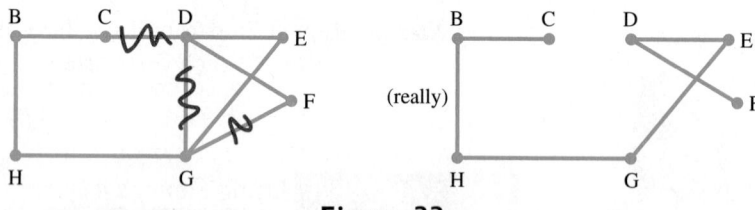

Figure 33

Now we have only one edge from F, namely, FD. This is a cut edge of the revised graph, but *since we have no other option* we may use this edge. Our path is C → D → G → F → D, and our revised graph is shown in **Figure 34**.

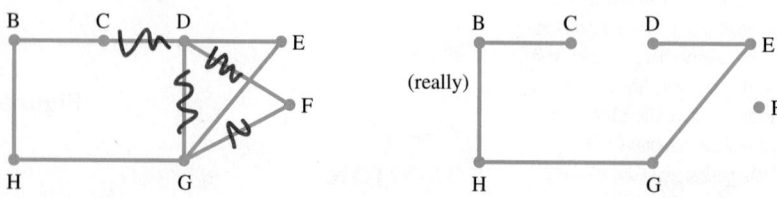

Figure 34

We have only one edge left at D, namely DE. It is a cut edge of the remaining graph, but since we have no other option, we may use it.

It is now clear how to complete the Euler circuit. (Be sure to return to the starting vertex.) The complete Euler circuit is:

$$C \rightarrow D \rightarrow G \rightarrow F \rightarrow D \rightarrow E \rightarrow G \rightarrow H \rightarrow B \rightarrow C.$$ ∎∎∎

If we start with a connected graph with all vertices having even degree, then Fleury's algorithm will always produce an Euler circuit for the graph. *Note that a graph that has an Euler circuit always has more than one Euler circuit.*

Even for a large graph, a computer can successfully apply Fleury's algorithm. This is not the case for all algorithms. (See **For Further Thought** on The Speed of Algorithms on **page 827**.)

Euler circuits have many practical applications. Consider planning a route for mail delivery. **Figure 35** shows a map of a rural district. In rural areas, mailboxes are placed along the same side of a road, so the mail delivery vehicle needs to travel along the road in one direction only. Suppose the roads off the main road in **Figure 35** show a mail delivery region.

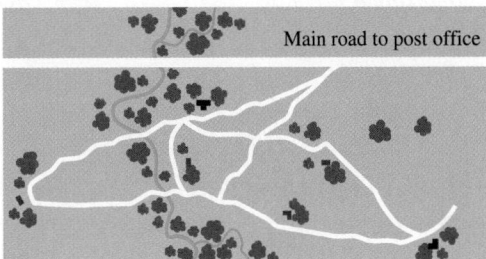

Figure 35

It would be ideal if the mail carrier could find an Euler circuit covering the delivery route. If such a circuit existed, it would minimize the distance traveled for the delivery. A glance at the map (thinking of road intersections as vertices) reveals that there is no Euler circuit for this route.

As the next best thing, the delivery vehicle should retrace its path as little as possible. For simplicity, we assume that the time to travel any of the stretches of road when not delivering mail is roughly the same. In **Figure 36**, we added dotted edges to indicate stretches of road to be covered twice. For this delivery route, it is easy to see that we effectively inserted as few edges as possible to obtain a graph that has an Euler circuit.

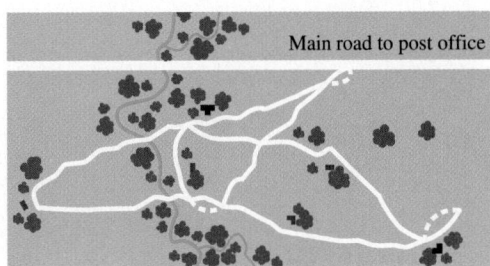

Figure 36

Now we can use Fleury's algorithm to find an Euler circuit on the graph in **Figure 36**, and this will give the most efficient route for mail delivery.

There are additional complications for mechanical brooms for **street sweeping.**

1. The mechanical brooms have to travel along each curb, in the direction of traffic flow (and some streets are one-way).

2. It takes time to switch the brooms from one side of the vehicle to the other.

3. Sweeping has to be coordinated with city parking so that there are no parked cars when sweeping is to be done.

For a simple delivery area such as this, it is not hard to choose an efficient route intuitively. For route planning in large cities, however, the techniques of this section offer significant savings on services such as mail delivery, mechanized street sweeping, snowplowing, and electric meter checking. In the 1980s a computerized system for planning street sweeping in Washington, D.C., resulted in a 20% savings. In large cities the street sweeping budget is tens of millions of dollars, so savings of 20% easily justify the initial cost of setting up a computerized system.

The study of Euler circuits began in the eighteenth century with a little mathematical puzzle, but the ideas developed provide efficient management techniques for our complex modern cities.

15.2 EXERCISES

In Exercises 1–3, a graph is shown and some sequences of vertices are specified. Determine which of these sequences show Euler circuits. If not, explain why not.

1.

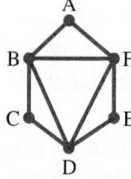

(a) A → B → C → D → A → B → C → D → A

(b) C → B → A → D → C

(c) A → C → D → B → A

(d) A → B → C → D

2.

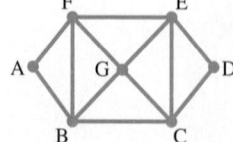

(a) A → B → C → D → E → F → A

(b) F → B → D → B

(c) A → B → C → D → E → F → B → D → F → A

(d) A → B → F → D → B → C → D → E → F → A

3.

(a) A → B → C → D → E → F → A

(b) A → B → C → D → E → G → C → E → F → G → B → F → A

(c) A → B → C → D → E → C → G → E → F → G → E → F → A

(d) A → B → G → E → D → C → G → F → B → C → E → F → A

In Exercises 4–8, use Euler's theorem to decide whether the graph has an Euler circuit. (Do not actually find an Euler circuit.) Justify each answer briefly.

4.

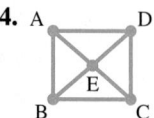

5.

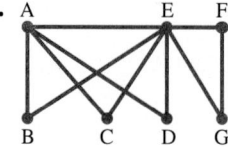

6.

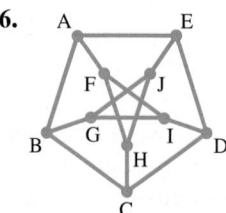

7.

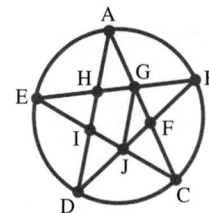

8.

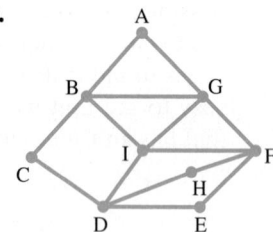

In Exercises 9 and 10, use Euler's theorem to determine whether it is possible to begin and end at the same place, trace the pattern without lifting your pencil, and trace over no line in the pattern more than once.

9.

10.

In Exercises 11–15, use Euler's theorem to determine whether the graph has an Euler circuit, justifying each answer. Then determine whether the graph has a circuit that visits each vertex exactly once, except that it returns to its starting vertex. If so, write down the circuit. (There may be more than one correct answer.)

11.
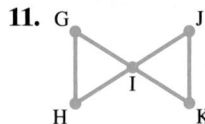

12.
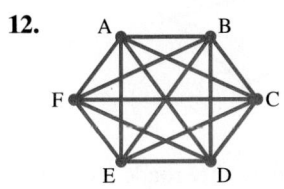

13.
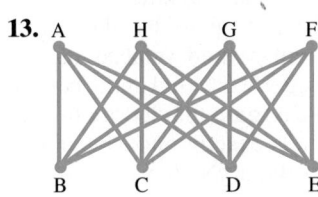

14.
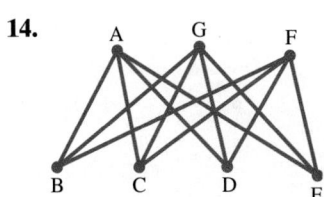

15.
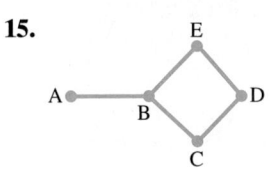

In Exercises 16–19, different floor tilings are shown. The material applied between tiles is called grout. For which of these floor tilings could the grout be applied beginning and ending at the same place, without going over any joint twice, and without lifting the tool? Justify each answer.

16.
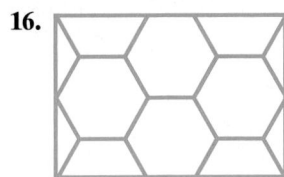

17.
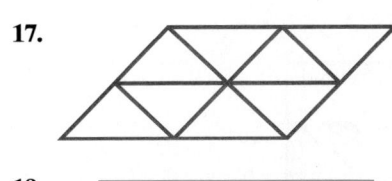

18.
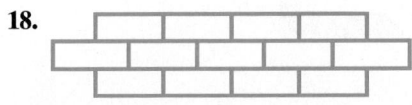

19.
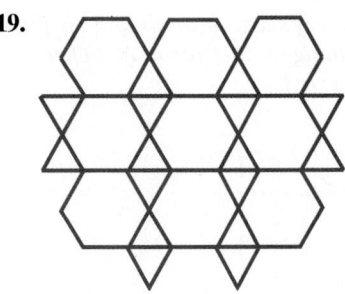

In Exercises 20–22, identify all cut edges in the graph. If there are none, say so.

20.
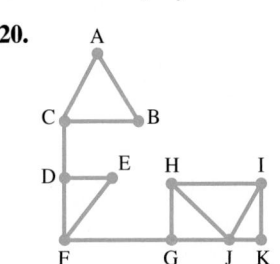

21.
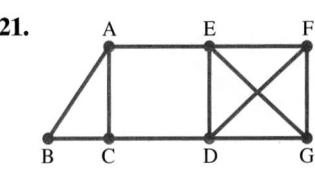

22.
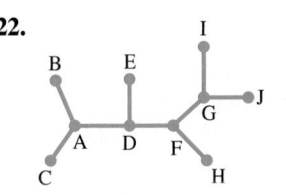

In Exercises 23–25, a graph is shown for which a student has been asked to find an Euler circuit starting at A. The student's revisions of the graph after the first few steps of Fleury's algorithm are shown, and in each case the student is now at B. For each graph, determine all edges that Fleury's algorithm permits the student to use for the next step.

23.
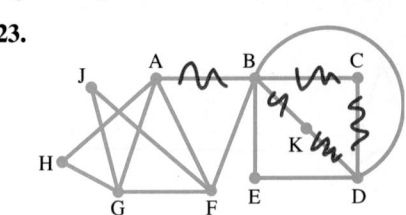

24. **25.**
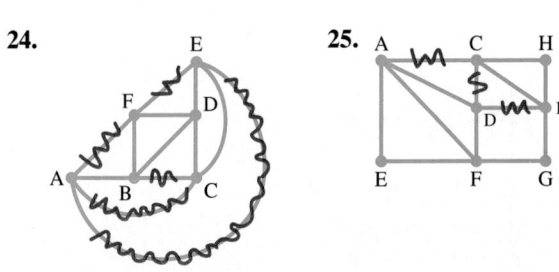

In Exercises 26–28, use Fleury's algorithm to find an Euler circuit for the graph, beginning and ending at A. (There are many different correct answers.)

26.

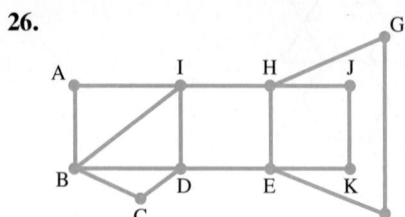

27.

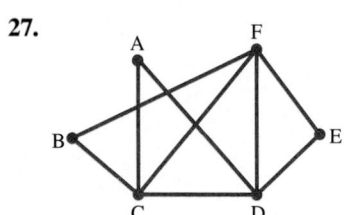

28.

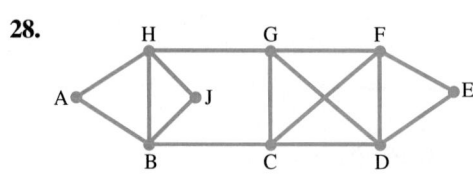

In Exercises 29–31, use Euler's theorem to determine whether the graph has an Euler circuit. If not, explain why not. If the graph does have an Euler circuit, use Fleury's algorithm to find an Euler circuit for the graph. (There are many different correct answers.)

29.

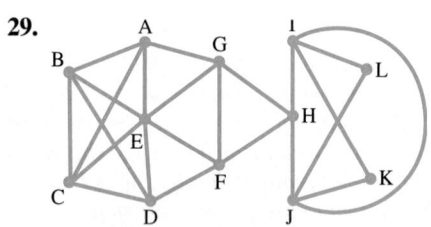

30.

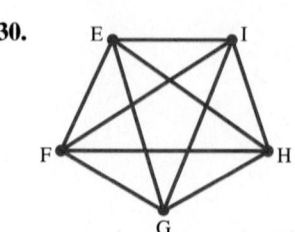

31.

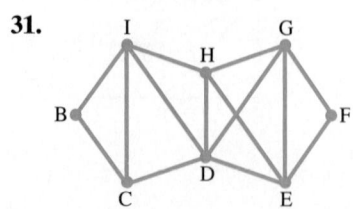

32. *Garden Design* The graph below shows the layout of the paths in a botanical garden. The edges represent the paths. Has the garden been designed in such a way that it is possible for a visitor to find a route that begins and ends at the entrance to the garden (represented by the vertex A) and that goes along each path exactly once? If so, use Fleury's algorithm to find such a route.

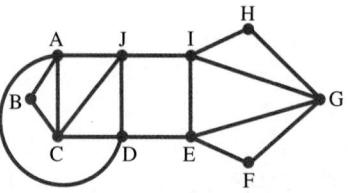

33. *Parking Pattern* The map shows the roads on which parking is permitted at a national monument. This is a pay and display facility. A security guard has the task of periodically checking that all parked vehicles have a valid parking ticket displayed. He is based at the central complex, labeled A. Is there a route that he can take to walk along each of the roads exactly once, beginning and ending at A? If so, use Fleury's algorithm to find such a route.

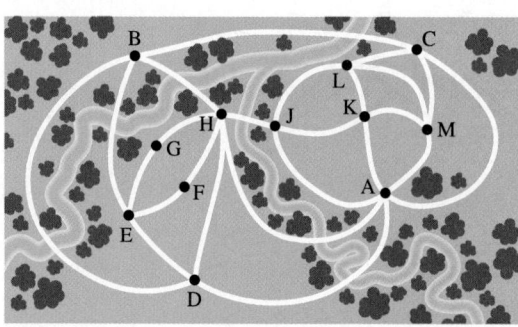

Building Floor Plans *In Exercises 34–36, the floor plan of a building is shown. For which of these is it possible to start outside, walk through each door exactly once, and end up back outside? Justify each answer. (Hint: Think of the rooms and "outside" as the vertices of a graph, and the doors as the edges of the graph.)*

34.

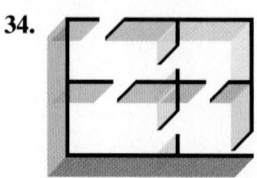

35.

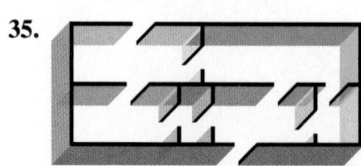

36.

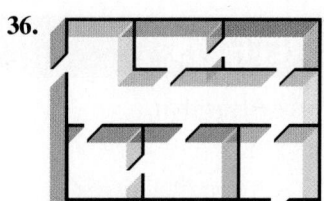

Exercises 37–44 are based on the following theorem:

1. *If a graph has an Euler path that begins and ends at different vertices, then these two vertices are the only vertices with odd degree. (All the rest have even degree.)*

2. *If exactly two vertices in a connected graph have odd degree, then the graph has an Euler path beginning at one of these vertices and ending at the other.*

In Exercises 37–40, determine whether the graph has an Euler path that begins and ends at different vertices. Justify your answer. If the graph has such a path, say at which vertices the path must begin and end.

37.

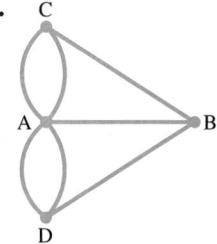

38.

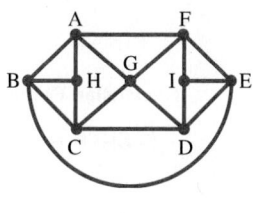

39.

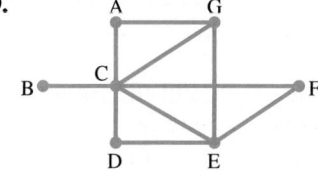

40.

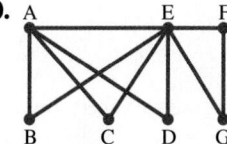

Building Floor Plans *In Exercises 41–43, refer to the floor plan indicated, and determine whether it is possible to start in one of the rooms of the building, walk through each door exactly once, and end up in a different room from the one you started in. Justify each answer.*

41. Refer to the floor plan shown in **Exercise 34.**

42. Refer to the floor plan shown in **Exercise 35.**

43. Refer to the floor plan shown in **Exercise 36.**

44. *New York City Bridges* The accompanying schematic map shows a portion of the New York City area, including tunnels and bridges.

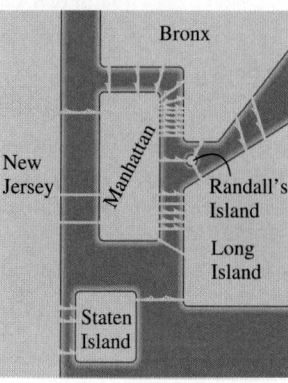

(a) Is it possible to take a drive around the New York City area using each tunnel and bridge exactly once, beginning and ending in the same place?

(b) Is it possible to take a drive around the New York City area using each tunnel and bridge exactly once, beginning and ending in different places? If so, where must the drive begin and end?

In Exercises 45–47, the graph does not have an Euler circuit. For each graph find a circuit that uses as many edges as possible. (There is more than one correct answer in each case.) How many edges did you use in the circuit?

45.

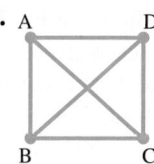

46.

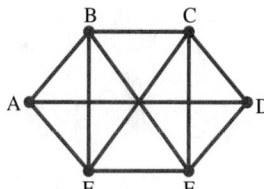

47.

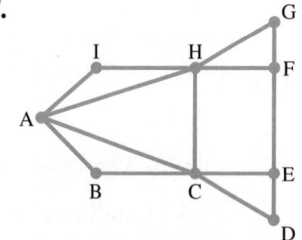

48. There are only five regular polyhedra: the cube, the tetrahedron, the octahedron, the dodecahedron, and the icosahedron. (See **Chapter 9.**) For which of these can you trace your finger along each edge exactly once, beginning and ending at the same vertex? Justify your answer using the ideas developed in this section.

49. Which *complete graphs* have Euler circuits? Justify your answer carefully.

50. Write a paper on the sand tracings of the Bushoong or Tshokwe people.

5.3 HAMILTON CIRCUITS AND ALGORITHMS

Hamilton Circuits • Minimum Hamilton Circuits • Brute Force Algorithm
• Nearest Neighbor Algorithm

Hamilton Circuits

In this section we examine *Hamilton circuits* in graphs. The story of Hamilton circuits is a story of very large numbers and of unsolved problems in both mathematics and computer science.

We start with a game, called the Icosian game, invented by Irish mathematician William Hamilton in the mid-nineteenth century. It uses a wooden board marked with the graph shown in **Figure 37**.

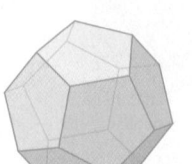

Dodecahedron

Hamilton sold the **Icosian game** idea to a games dealer for 25 British pounds. It went on the market in 1859, but it was not a huge success. A later version of the game, *A Voyage Around the World*, consisted of a regular dodecahedron with pegs at each of the 20 vertices. The vertices had names such as Brussels, Delhi, and Zanzibar. The aim was to travel to all vertices along the edges of the dodecahedron, visiting each vertex exactly once. We can show the vertices and edges of a dodecahedron precisely as in **Figure 37**.

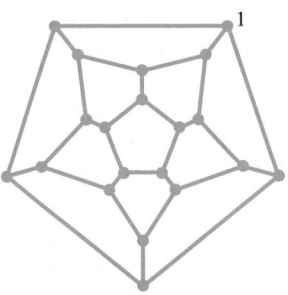

The Icosian Game

Figure 37

The game includes 20 pegs numbered 1 through 20. (The word *Icosian* comes from the Greek word for 20.) At each vertex of the graph there is a hole for a peg.

The simplest version of the game is as follows: Put the pegs into the holes in order, following along the edges of the graph, in such a way that peg 20 ends up in a hole that is joined by an edge to the hole of peg 1. Try this now, numbering the vertices in the graph in **Figure 37**, starting at vertex 1.

The Icosian game asks that we find a circuit in the graph, but the circuit need not be an Euler circuit. The circuit must visit each *vertex* exactly once, except for returning to the starting vertex to complete the circuit. (The circuit may or may not travel all edges of the graph.) Circuits such as this are called *Hamilton circuits*.

> **Hamilton Circuit**
>
> A **Hamilton circuit** in a graph is a circuit that visits each vertex exactly once (returning to the starting vertex to complete the circuit).

▐▐ **EXAMPLE 1** Identifying Hamilton Circuits

Which of the following are Hamilton circuits for the graph in **Figure 38**? Justify your answers briefly.

(a) A → B → E → D → C → F → A

(b) A → B → C → D → E → F → C →
E → B → F → A

(c) B → C → D → E → F → B

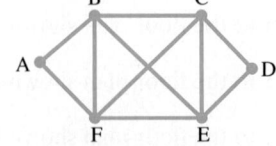

Figure 38

SOLUTION

(a) A → B → E → D → C → F → A is a Hamilton circuit for the graph. It visits each vertex of the graph exactly once, and then returns to the starting vertex. (Trace this circuit on the graph to check it.)

(b) A → B → C → D → E → F → C → E → B → F → A is not a Hamilton circuit, since it visits vertex B (and vertices C, E, and F) more than once. (This is, however, an Euler circuit for the graph.)

(c) B → C → D → E → F → B is not a Hamilton circuit since it does not visit all vertices in the graph. ▮▮▮

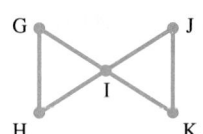

Figure 39

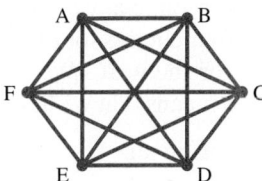

Figure 40

Some graphs, such as the graph in **Figure 39**, do not have a Hamilton circuit. There is no way to visit all the vertices and return to the starting vertex without visiting vertex I more times than allowed.

It can be difficult to determine whether a particular graph has a Hamilton circuit, since there is no theorem that gives necessary and sufficient conditions for a Hamilton circuit to exist. This remains an unsolved problem in Hamilton circuits. (Contrast the simple method provided by Euler's theorem for checking whether a graph has an Euler circuit.)

Fortunately, in many real-world applications of Hamilton circuits we are dealing with complete graphs, and any complete graph with three or more vertices does have a Hamilton circuit. (Recall our discussion of complete graphs in **Section 15.1**.) For example,

$$A \to B \to C \to D \to E \to F \to A$$

is a Hamilton circuit for the complete graph shown in **Figure 40**. We could form a Hamilton circuit for any complete graph with three or more vertices in a similar way.

Hamilton Circuits for Complete Graphs

Any complete graph with three or more vertices has a Hamilton circuit.

The graph in **Figure 40** has many Hamilton circuits. Try finding some that are different from the one given earlier.

How many Hamilton circuits does a complete graph have? Before we count, we need an agreement about when two sequences of vertices will be considered to be *different* Hamilton circuits. For example, the Hamilton circuits

$$B \to C \to D \to E \to F \to A \to B \quad \text{and} \quad A \to B \to C \to D \to E \to F \to A$$

visit the vertices in essentially the same order in the graph in **Figure 40**, although the sequences start with different vertices. If we mark the circuit on the graph, we can describe it starting at any vertex. For our purposes, it is convenient to consider the two sequences above as representing the same Hamilton circuit.

When Hamilton Circuits Are the Same

Hamilton circuits that differ *only* in their starting points will be considered to be the same circuit.

The Tutte graph, shown here, has no Hamilton circuit. This graph has a history connected to the four-color problem for map coloring (**Section 15.1**). In 1880 Peter Tate provided a "proof" for the four-color theorem. It was based on the assumption that every connected graph, with all vertices of degree three, and which can be drawn with edges crossing nowhere except at vertices, has a Hamilton circuit. But in 1946, Tutte produced the graph shown here, showing that Tate's basic assumption was wrong, and his proof was, therefore, invalid.

PROBLEM-SOLVING HINT Tree diagrams are often useful for counting.

Large Numbers 70! is the first factorial greater than 10^{100}. Most calculators will calculate numbers up to only about 10^{99}, so if you try calculating 70! you probably will get an error message. (Try it.) 10^{100} is called one googol, a name invented by a nine-year-old child when asked to name a very, very large number.

These numbers are unimaginably large. Consider:

$$25! \approx 2 \times 10^{25}$$
$$50! \approx 3 \times 10^{64}$$
$$100! \approx 9 \times 10^{157}$$

Comparison:

Approximate number of *meters* from Saturn to the sun: 10^{12}

Estimate of the number of *inches* to the farthest object in the universe: 10^{27}.

Approximate number of molecules we would have if we filled a sphere the size of the earth with water: 10^{49}.

The "clock" in the photo above indicates the U.S. population at a given time. Write the figure shown in scientific notation.

We begin by counting the number of Hamilton circuits in a complete graph with four vertices. (See **Figure 41**.) We can use the same starting point for all the circuits we count. We choose A as the starting point. From A we can go to any of the three remaining vertices (B, C, or D). No matter which vertex we choose, we then have two unvisited vertices for our next choice. Then there is only one way to complete the Hamilton circuit. We illustrate this counting procedure in **Figure 42**.

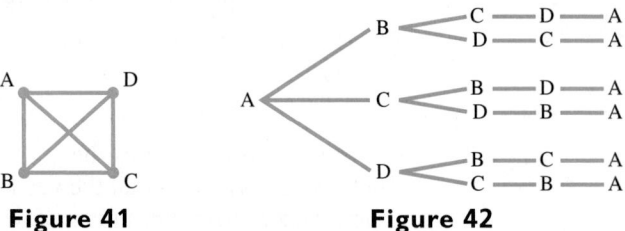

Figure 41   **Figure 42**

The tree diagram in **Figure 42** shows that we have $3 \cdot 2 \cdot 1$ Hamilton circuits in the graph. We write this as 3! (read "3 factorial"). See **Chapter 10**.

Returning to **Figure 40**, we can count the number of Hamilton circuits in the complete graph with 6 vertices. Start at vertex A. From A we can proceed to any of the five remaining vertices. No matter which we choose, we then have four choices for the next vertex along the circuit, three choices for the next, and two for the next. (We could draw a counting tree for this, but it would be rather large.) This means that we have

$$5 \cdot 4 \cdot 3 \cdot 2 \cdot 1 = 5! \quad \text{different Hamilton circuits in all.}$$

Likewise, we would find that a complete graph with 10 vertices has 9! Hamilton circuits. In general, for a complete graph the number of Hamilton circuits in the graph can be obtained by calculating the factorial of the number that is one less than the number of vertices.

Number of Hamilton Circuits in a Complete Graph

A complete graph with n vertices has $(n - 1)!$ Hamilton circuits.

As the number of vertices in a complete graph increases, the number of Hamilton circuits for that graph increases very quickly. Previously we considered how quickly exponential functions increase. Factorials increase quickly as well. For example,

$$25! = 15,511,210,043,330,985,984,000,000,$$

or approximately 1.6×10^{25}—more than a trillion trillion.

Minimum Hamilton Circuits

Consider that on a typical day, a UPS van might have to make deliveries to 100 different locations. For simplicity, assume that none are priority deliveries, so they can be made in any order. UPS wants to minimize the time to make these deliveries. Think of the 100 locations and the UPS distribution center as the vertices of a complete graph with 101 vertices.

In principle, the van can go from any of these locations directly to any other, shown by having an edge between each pair of vertices. Suppose we estimate the travel time between each pair of locations (of course, this would depend on distance and traffic conditions along the route). These estimates provide weights on the edges of the graph. The objective is to visit each location exactly once, to begin and end at the same place, and to take as little time as possible.

Traveling Salesman Problems and Archaeology Archaeologists often excavate sites in which there is no clear evidence to show which deposits were made earlier, and which later. Some archaeologists have used minimum Hamilton circuits to solve the problem. For example, if a site consists of a number of burials, they consider a complete graph with vertices representing the various burials, and weights on the edges corresponding roughly to how dissimilar the burials are. A minimum Hamilton circuit in this graph gives the best guess for the order in which the deposits were made.

In graph theory terms, we need a Hamilton circuit for the graph that has *least possible total weight*. The **total weight** of a circuit is the sum of the weights on the edges in the circuit. We call such a circuit a *minimum Hamilton circuit* for the graph.

> **Minimum Hamilton Circuit**
>
> In a weighted graph, a **minimum Hamilton circuit** is a Hamilton circuit with least possible total weight.

A problem whose solution requires us to find a minimum Hamilton circuit for a complete, weighted graph often is called a **traveling salesman problem** (or TSP). (See also the **Chapter 10 Collaborative Investigation.**) Think of the vertices of the complete graph as the cities that a salesperson must visit and the weights on the edges as the cost of traveling directly between the cities. To minimize costs, the salesperson needs a minimum Hamilton circuit for the graph.

Traveling salesman problems are relevant to efficient routing of telephone calls and Internet connections. As another example, to manufacture integrated circuit silicon chips, many lines have to be etched on a silicon wafer. Minimizing production time involves deciding the order in which to etch the lines, a traveling salesman problem. Likewise, to manufacture circuit boards for integrated circuits, laser-drilled holes must be made for connections. Again, the order for drilling the holes is a critical factor in production time.

Brute Force Algorithm

Suppose we are given a complete, weighted graph. How can we find a minimum Hamilton circuit for the graph? One way is to systematically list all the Hamilton circuits in the graph, find the total weight of each, and choose a circuit with least total weight. (In fact, it is sufficient to add up the weights on the edges for just half of the Hamilton circuits, since the total weight of a circuit is the same as the total weight of the circuit that uses the same edges in reverse order.)

The method just described is sometimes called the **brute force algorithm** since we find the solution by checking *all* the Hamilton circuits.

> **Brute Force Algorithm**
>
> *Step 1* Choose a starting point.
> *Step 2* List all the Hamilton circuits with that starting point.
> *Step 3* Find the total weight of each circuit.
> *Step 4* Choose a Hamilton circuit with least total weight.

▐▌ **EXAMPLE 2** Using the Brute Force Algorithm

Find a minimum Hamilton circuit for the complete, weighted graph shown in **Figure 43**.

SOLUTION

Choose a starting point, A. List all the Hamilton circuits starting at A. Since this is a complete graph with 4 vertices, there are

$$3! = 3 \cdot 2 \cdot 1 = 6 \text{ circuits.}$$

Thus, we must find 6 Hamilton circuits.

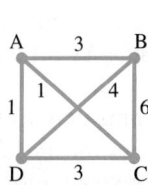

Figure 43

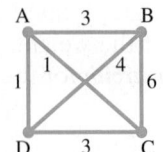

Figure 43 (repeated)

We need a systematic way of writing down all the Hamilton circuits. The counting tree of **Figure 43** provides a guide. We start by finding all the Hamilton circuits that begin A → B, then include those that begin A → C, and finally include those that begin A → D, as shown below. Once all the Hamilton circuits are listed, pair those that visit the vertices in precisely opposite orders. (Circuits in these pairs have the same total weight. This will save some adding.) Finally, determine the sum of the weights in each circuit.

Circuit	Total weight of the circuit
1. A → B → C → D → A	3 + 6 + 3 + 1 = 13
2. A → B → D → C → A	3 + 4 + 3 + 1 = **11** Minimum
3. A → C → B → D → A	1 + 6 + 4 + 1 = 12
4. A → C → D → B → A (opposite of 2)	11
5. A → D → B → C → A (opposite of 3)	12
6. A → D → C → B → A (opposite of 1)	13

We can now see that A → B → D → C → A is a minimum Hamilton circuit for the graph. The weight of this circuit is 11. ▮▮▮

In principle, the brute force algorithm provides a way to find a minimum Hamilton circuit in any complete, weighted graph. In practice, it takes far too long to obtain a complete, weighted graph with 7 vertices. There are 6!, or 720, Hamilton circuits in the graph, and we would have to calculate the total weight for half of these. That means we would have to do 360 separate calculations, in addition to listing the Hamilton circuits.

Most real-world problems involve a great deal more than 7 vertices. Manufacturing a large integrated circuit can involve a graph with almost one million vertices. Likewise, telecommunications companies routinely deal with graphs with millions of vertices. As the number of vertices in the graph increases, the task of finding a minimum Hamilton circuit using the brute force algorithm soon becomes too time-consuming for even our fastest computers. For example, if one of today's supercomputers had started using the brute force algorithm on a 100-vertex traveling salesman problem when the universe was created, it would still be far from done.

In contrast, Fleury's algorithm for finding an Euler circuit in a graph does not take too long for our computers, even for rather large graphs. Algorithms that do not take too much computer time are called **efficient algorithms.** Computer scientists have so far been unable to find an efficient algorithm for the traveling salesman problem, and they suspect that it is simply impossible to create such an algorithm.

The traveling salesman problem is just one of a collection of problems for which there is no known efficient algorithm. Many of these unsolved problems are related in such a way that an efficient algorithm for solving any one of them could be adapted to solve all of them. Probably the most important unsolved problem in computer science is either to find an efficient algorithm for the traveling salesman problem or to explain why no one could create such an algorithm. (We often refer to this as the P = NP problem.)

For the traveling salesman problem, there are some algorithms that do not take too much computer time and that give *reasonably good* solutions *most of the time.* Such algorithms are called **approximate algorithms,** since they give an approximate solution to the problem. We shall consider one such algorithm for the traveling salesman problem. The underlying idea is that from each vertex we proceed to a "nearest" available vertex.

William Rowan Hamilton (1805–1865) spent most of his life in Dublin, Ireland. He was good friends with the poet William Wordsworth, whom he met while touring England and Scotland. Hamilton tried writing poetry, but Wordsworth tactfully suggested that his talents were in mathematics rather than poetry. Catherine Disney was the first great love of his life, but under pressure from her parents, she married another man, much wealthier than Hamilton. Hamilton never seemed to quite get over this.

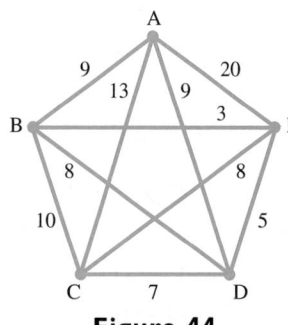

NP complete is a technical term in computer science describing problems for which all known algorithms take way too much time for large graphs for even the fastest imaginable computers. The traveling salesman problem and determining the chromatic number of a graph are NP complete. The popular puzzle SUDOKU also is in the class of NP complete problems.

Nearest Neighbor Algorithm

Nearest Neighbor Algorithm

Step 1   Choose a starting point for the circuit. Call this vertex A.

Step 2   Check all the edges joined to A, and choose one that has least weight. Proceed along this edge to the next vertex.

Step 3   At each vertex you reach, check the edges from there *to vertices not yet visited*. Choose one with least weight. Proceed along this edge to the next vertex.

Step 4   Repeat Step 3 until you have visited all the vertices.

Step 5   Return to the starting vertex.

EXAMPLE 3   Using the Nearest Neighbor Algorithm

A courier is based at the head office (A) and must deliver documents to four other offices (B, C, D, and E). The estimated time of travel (in minutes) between each of these offices is shown on the graph in **Figure 44**. The courier wants to visit the locations in an order that takes the least time. Use the nearest neighbor algorithm to find an approximate solution to this problem. Calculate the total time required to cover the chosen route.

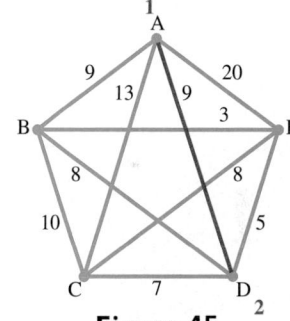

Figure 44   **Figure 45**

SOLUTION

Step 1   Choose a starting point. Let's start at A.

Step 2   Choose an edge with least weight joined to A. Both AB and AD have weight 9, which is less than the weights of the other two edges joined to A. We choose AD* and keep a record of the circuit as we form it.

$$A \xrightarrow{9} D$$

To help ensure that we do not visit a vertex twice, we number the vertices as we visit them and color the edges used, as in **Figure 45**.

Continue to number the vertices as we work through the rest of the solution.

Step 3   Now check edges joined to D, excluding DA (since we have already been to A). DC has weight 7, DB has weight 8, and DE has weight 5. DE has smallest weight, so proceed along DE to E. Our circuit begins this way.

$$A \xrightarrow{9} D \xrightarrow{5} E$$

---

*If using a computer to do this, we would instruct the computer to make a random choice between AB and AD.

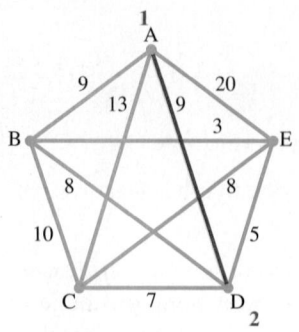

Figure 45 (repeated)

Step 4 Now repeat the process at E. Check all edges from E that go to a vertex not yet visited. EC has weight 8 and EB has weight 3. Proceed along EB to B. Our circuit so far is as follows.

$$A \xrightarrow{9} D \xrightarrow{5} E \xrightarrow{3} B$$

Step 5 We have one vertex not yet visited, C. We go next to C and now have visited all the vertices. We return to our starting point, A. Our Hamilton circuit is

$$A \xrightarrow{9} D \xrightarrow{5} E \xrightarrow{3} B \xrightarrow{10} C \xrightarrow{13} A.$$

Its total weight is $9 + 5 + 3 + 10 + 13 = 40$.

Our advice to the courier would thus be to visit the offices in the order shown in this circuit. This route will take about 40 minutes. ▉▉▉

We might think that we could get a quicker route for the courier just by looking at the graph, rather than following the rules of the algorithm. We would be right. The circuit we found in **Example 3** is not the minimum Hamilton circuit for the graph in **Figure 44**. (See below.) However, the point of an approximate algorithm is that a computer can implement it without taking too much time, and most of the time it will give a reasonably good solution to the problem.

If we had a computer performing the nearest neighbor algorithm for us, we could make a small adjustment that would give better results without taking too much longer. We could repeat the nearest neighbor algorithm for all possible starting points, and then choose from these the Hamilton circuit with least weight. If we do this for the example above, we obtain the results in **Table 1**.

Table 1

Starting Vertex	Circuit Using Nearest Neighbor	Total Weight
A	$A \to D \to E \to B \to C \to A$	$9 + 5 + 3 + 10 + 13 = 40$
B	$B \to E \to D \to C \to A \to B$	$3 + 5 + 7 + 13 + 9 = 37$
C	$C \to D \to E \to B \to A \to C$	$7 + 5 + 3 + 9 + 13 = 37$
D	$D \to E \to B \to A \to C \to D$	$5 + 3 + 9 + 13 + 7 = 37$
E	$E \to B \to D \to C \to A \to E$	$3 + 8 + 7 + 13 + 20 = 51$

With this information, we would recommend to the courier that he use a circuit with total weight 37, for example the circuit

$$D \to E \to B \to A \to C \to D.$$

This does not force him to start his journey at D. If he followed the route

$$A \to C \to D \to E \to B \to A,$$

he would be using the same edges as in $D \to E \to B \to A \to C \to D$, and his traveling time still would be 37 minutes.

Can we now be sure that we have found the minimum Hamilton circuit for the graph in **Figure 45**? No. This is still an *approximate* solution. If we check the total weights of all possible Hamilton circuits in the graph, we find the Hamilton circuit

$$A \xrightarrow{9} B \xrightarrow{3} E \xrightarrow{8} C \xrightarrow{7} D \xrightarrow{9} A$$

with total weight just 36 minutes. The nearest neighbor algorithm simply will not find this minimum Hamilton circuit for the graph. However, all we expect of an approximate algorithm is that it give a reasonably good solution for the problem in a reasonable amount of time.

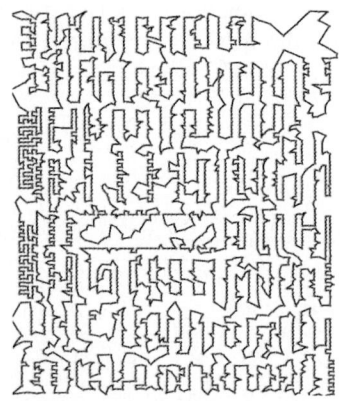

Records for Traveling Salesman Problems There is a race on to set records for exact solutions to traveling salesman problems. Computer scientists do this by using parallel processing and more sophisticated algorithms (all still exponential time algorithms—see **For Further Thought** on The Speed of Algorithms). The illustration shows the exact solution to a traveling salesman problem with 3038 vertices on a printed circuit board, obtained in 1993.

Here are some of the other records, showing the year each was set and the number of vertices in the graph.

1980: 318
1987: 666
1994: 7397
1998: 13,509
2001: 15,112
2004: 24,978
2006: 85,900

Source: www.tsp.gatech.edu/index.html

For Further Thought

The Speed of Algorithms

How do computer scientists classify the speed of algorithms? First, they write the number of steps a computer using the algorithm takes to solve a problem as a function of the "size" of the problem. We can think of the size of the problem as the number of vertices in the graph.

Let's suppose that our graph has n vertices. For some algorithms the number of steps is a **polynomial function of n,** for example $n^4 + 2n$. For other algorithms, the number of steps is an **exponential function of n,** for example 2^n. (See **Chapters 7 and 8** for more on polynomial and exponential functions.) As n increases, the number of steps increases much faster for exponential functions than for polynomial functions. Functions that involve factorials increase even faster.

In the table below we show approximate values for functions of the three types for different values of n. (We use scientific notation to make it easier to compare the sizes of the numbers.)

n	n^4	2^n	$n!$
5	6.3×10^2	3.2×10	1.2×10^2
10	1.0×10^4	1.0×10^3	3.6×10^6
15	5.1×10^4	3.3×10^4	1.3×10^{12}
20	1.6×10^5	1.0×10^6	2.4×10^{18}
25	3.9×10^5	3.4×10^7	1.6×10^{25}
30	8.1×10^5	1.1×10^9	2.7×10^{32}
40	2.6×10^6	1.1×10^{12}	8.2×10^{47}
50	6.3×10^6	1.1×10^{15}	3.0×10^{64}

In the first line of the table (where $n = 5$), n^4 gives the largest value. But as n gets larger, 2^n grows much faster than n^4, while $n!$ grows extremely fast. For example, if we double the size of n from 15 to 30, n^4 becomes a little more than 10 times as large, 2^n becomes about

3×10^4 or 30,000 times as large, while $n!$ becomes approximately 2×10^{20} times as large. 10^{20} is more than a billion billion.

Algorithms whose time functions grow no faster than a polynomial function are called **polynomial time algorithms.** These are *efficient* algorithms—they do not take too much computer time.

Algorithms whose time functions grow faster than any polynomial function are called **exponential time algorithms.** These are *not efficient* algorithms. They are by nature too time-consuming for our computers. Our silicon chip computers are getting faster each year, but even this increase in speed hardly puts a dent in the time required for a computer to implement an exponential time algorithm for a very large graph.

Because the brute force algorithm for the traveling salesman problem has a time function involving $n!$, which grows faster than an exponential function of n, this algorithm is an exponential time algorithm.

For Group or Individual Investigation

Use the table to help answer these questions:

1. By approximately what factor does n^4 grow if we double n from 10 to 20?

2. By approximately what factor does 2^n grow if we double n from 10 to 20?

3. By approximately what factor does $n!$ grow if we double n from 10 to 20?

4. Repeat Exercises 1–3 if we double n from 25 to 50.

5. Suppose it would take 2^{30} years using computers at their present speeds to solve a certain problem. (2^{30} is a little over one billion.) If we assume that computers double in speed each year, how long would we have to wait before we could solve the problem in 1 year?

15.3 EXERCISES

In Exercises 1 and 2, a graph is shown, and some paths in the graph are specified. Determine which paths are Hamilton circuits for the graph. If not, say why not.

1.

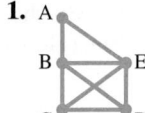

(a) $A \rightarrow E \rightarrow C \rightarrow D \rightarrow E \rightarrow B \rightarrow A$

(b) $A \rightarrow E \rightarrow C \rightarrow D \rightarrow B \rightarrow A$

(c) $D \rightarrow B \rightarrow E \rightarrow A \rightarrow B$

(d) $E \rightarrow D \rightarrow C \rightarrow B \rightarrow E$

2.

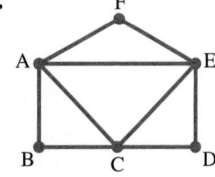

(a) $A \rightarrow B \rightarrow C \rightarrow D \rightarrow E \rightarrow C \rightarrow A \rightarrow E \rightarrow F \rightarrow A$

(b) $A \rightarrow C \rightarrow D \rightarrow E \rightarrow F \rightarrow A$

(c) $F \rightarrow A \rightarrow C \rightarrow E \rightarrow F$

(d) $C \rightarrow D \rightarrow E \rightarrow F \rightarrow A \rightarrow B$

In Exercises 3 and 4, determine whether each sequence of vertices is a circuit, whether it is an Euler circuit, and whether it is a Hamilton circuit. Justify your answers.

3.

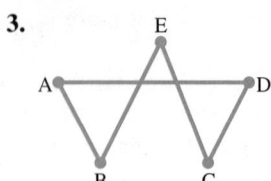

(a) A → B → C → D → E → A
(b) B → E → C → D → A → B
(c) E → B → A → D → A → D → C → E

4.

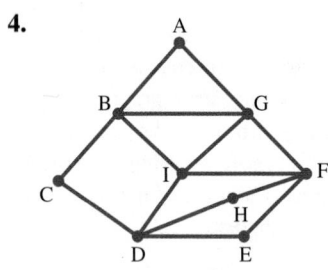

(a) A → B → C → D → E → F → G → A
(b) B → I → G → F → E → D → H → F → I → D → C → B → G → A → B
(c) A → B → C → D → E → F → G → H → I → A

In Exercises 5–10, determine whether the graph has a Hamilton circuit. If so, find one. (There are many different correct answers.)

5.

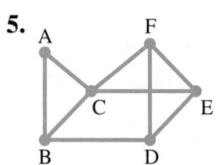

6.

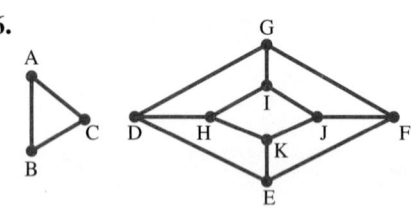

7.

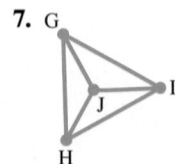

8.

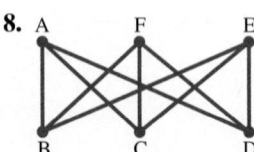

9.

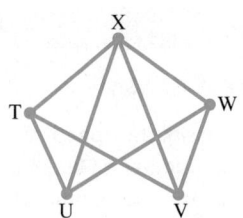

10.

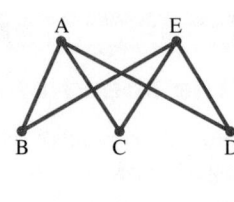

11. Draw a graph that has a Hamilton circuit but no Euler circuit. Specify the Hamilton circuit, and explain why the graph has no Euler circuit. (There are many different correct answers.)

12. Draw a graph that has an Euler circuit but no Hamilton circuit. Specify an Euler circuit in your graph. (There are many different correct answers.)

13. Draw a graph that has both an Euler circuit and a Hamilton circuit. Specify these circuits. (There are many different correct answers.)

14. Decide whether each statement is true or false. If the statement is false, give an example to show that it is false.

(a) A Hamilton circuit for a graph must visit each vertex in the graph.

(b) An Euler circuit for a graph must visit each vertex in the graph.

(c) A Hamilton circuit for a graph must use each edge in the graph.

(d) An Euler circuit for a graph must use each edge in the graph.

(e) A circuit cannot be both a Hamilton circuit and an Euler circuit.

(f) An Euler circuit must visit no vertex more than once, except the vertex where the circuit begins and ends.

In Exercises 15–20, determine whether an Euler circuit, a Hamilton circuit, or neither would solve the problem.

15. *Bandstands at a Festival* The vertices of a graph represent bandstands at a festival and the edges represent paths between the bandstands. A visitor wants to visit each bandstand exactly once, returning to her starting point when she is finished.

16. *Relay Team Running Order* The vertices of a complete graph represent the members of a five-person relay team. The team manager wants a circuit that will show the order in which the team members will run. (He will decide later who will start.)

17. *Paths in a Botanical Garden* The vertices of a graph represent places where paths in a botanical garden cross and the edges represent the paths. A visitor wants to walk along each path in the garden exactly once, returning to his starting point when finished.

18. *Traveling in Western Europe* The vertices of a graph represent the countries on the continent (Western Europe), with edges representing border crossings between the countries. A traveler wants to travel over each border crossing exactly once, returning to the first country visited for his flight home to the United States.

19. *Traveling in Africa* Vertices represent countries in sub-Saharan Africa, with an edge between two vertices if those countries have a common border. A traveler wants to visit each country exactly once, returning to the first country visited for her flight home to the United States.

20. *Reading X-Rays* In using X-rays to analyze the structure of crystals, an X-ray diffractometer measures the intensity of reflected radiation from the crystal in thousands of different positions. Consider the complete graph with vertices representing the positions where measurements must be taken. The researcher must decide the order in which to take these readings, with the diffractometer returning to its starting point when finished.

In Exercises 21–24, use a calculator, if necessary, to find the value.

21. 4!   **22.** 6!

23. 9!   **24.** 14!

In Exercises 25–28, determine how many Hamilton circuits there are in a complete graph with this number of vertices. (Leave answers in factorial notation.)

25. 10 vertices   **26.** 15 vertices

27. 18 vertices   **28.** 60 vertices

29. List all Hamilton circuits in the graph which start at P.

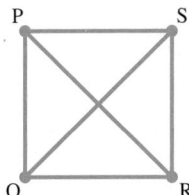

In Exercises 30–36, refer to the following graph. List all Hamilton circuits in the graph that start with the indicated vertices.

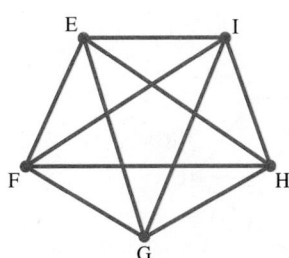

30. Starting E → F → G

31. Starting E → H → I

32. Starting E → I → H

33. Starting E → F

34. Starting E → I

35. Starting E → G

36. Starting at E

37. List all Hamilton circuits in the graph which start at A.

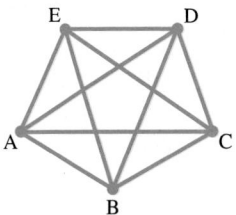

In Exercises 38–41, use the brute force algorithm to find a minimum Hamilton circuit for the graph. In each case determine the total weight of the minimum Hamilton circuit.

38.
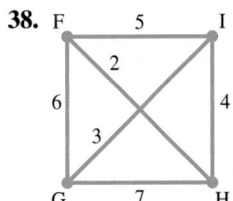

39.
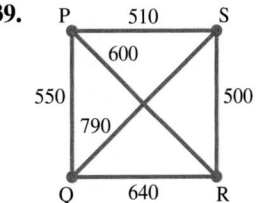

40.
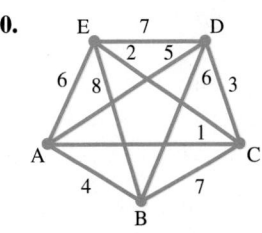

41.
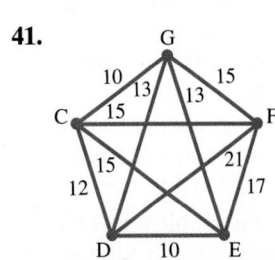

In Exercises 42–44, use the nearest neighbor algorithm starting at each of the indicated vertices to determine an approximate solution to the problem of finding a minimum Hamilton circuit for the graph. In each case, find the total weight of the circuit found.

42.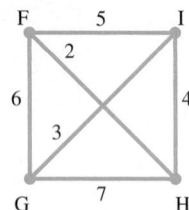
(a) Starting at F
(b) Starting at G
(c) Starting at H
(d) Starting at I

43.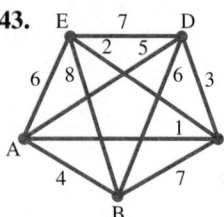
(a) Starting at A
(b) Starting at C
(c) Starting at D
(d) Starting at E

44.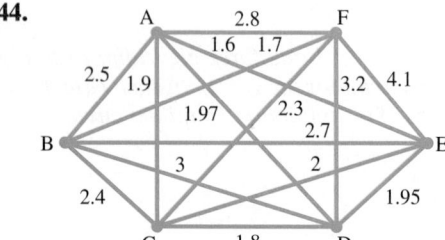

(a) Starting at A   (b) Starting at B
(c) Starting at C   (d) Starting at D
(e) Starting at E   (f) Starting at F

45. Refer to the accompanying graph. Complete parts (a)–(c) in order.

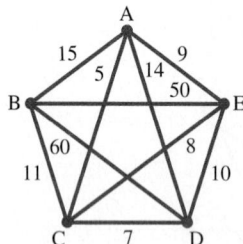

(a) Use the nearest neighbor algorithm starting at each of the vertices in turn to determine an approximate solution to the problem of finding a minimum Hamilton circuit for the graph. In each case, find the total weight of the circuit.

(b) Which of the circuits found in part (a) gives the best solution to the problem of finding a minimum Hamilton circuit for the graph?

(c) Just by looking carefully at the graph, find a Hamilton circuit in the graph that has lower total weight than any of the circuits found in part (a).

46. A graph is called a **complete bipartite graph** if the vertices can be separated into two groups in such a way that there are no edges between vertices in the same group, and there is an edge between each vertex in the first group and each vertex in the second group. An example is shown below.

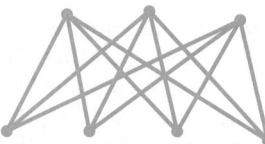

The notation we use for these graphs is $K_{m,n}$ where m and n are the numbers of vertices in the two groups. For example, the graph shown in this exercise is $K_{4,3}$ (or $K_{3,4}$). Answer the following in order:

(a) Draw $K_{2,2}$, $K_{2,3}$, $K_{2,4}$, $K_{3,3}$, and $K_{4,4}$.

(b) For each of the graphs you have drawn in part (a), find a Hamilton circuit or say that the graph has no Hamilton circuit.

(c) Make a conjecture: What must be true about m and n for $K_{m,n}$ to have a Hamilton circuit?

(d) What must be true about m and n for $K_{m,n}$ to have an Euler circuit? Justify your answer.

In Exercises 47–50, find all Hamilton circuits in the graph which start at A. (Hint: Use counting trees.)

47.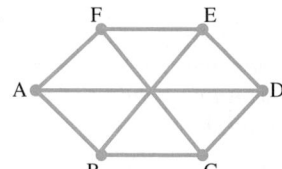

48.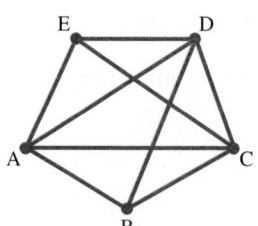

49.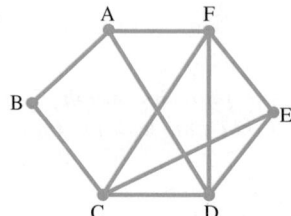

50.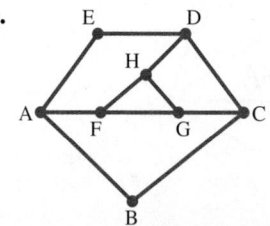

51. Paul A. M. Dirac proved the following theorem in 1952:

Suppose G is a (simple) graph with n vertices, n ≥ 3. If the degree of each vertex is greater than or equal to $\frac{n}{2}$, then the graph has a Hamilton circuit.

Refer to graphs (1)–(5) and answer parts (a)–(e) in order.

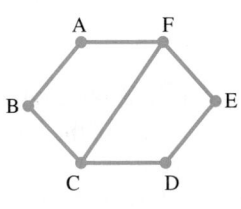

(1)

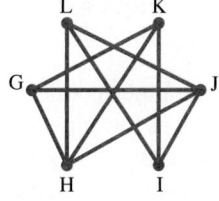

(2)

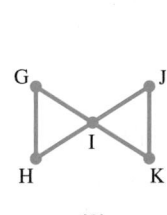

(3)

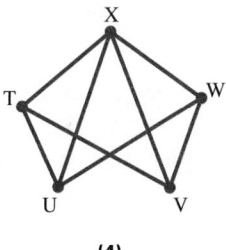

(4)

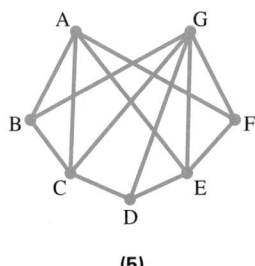

(5)

(a) Which of the graphs satisfy the condition that the degree of each vertex is greater than or equal to $\frac{n}{2}$?

(b) For which of the graphs can we conclude from **Dirac's theorem** that the graph has a Hamilton circuit?

(c) If a graph does *not* satisfy the condition that the degree of each vertex is greater than or equal to $\frac{n}{2}$, can we be sure that the graph does *not* have a Hamilton circuit? Justify your answer. (*Hint:* Study the accompanying graphs.)

(d) Is Dirac's theorem still true if $n < 3$? Justify your answer.

(e) Use Dirac's theorem to write a convincing argument that any complete graph with 3 or more vertices has a Hamilton circuit.

The graph below shows the Icosian game (described in the text) with the vertices labeled. In Exercises 52–54, find a Hamilton circuit for the graph in the specified version of the game. (We suggest you write numbers on the graph in the order in which you visit the vertices. There are different correct answers for these exercises.)

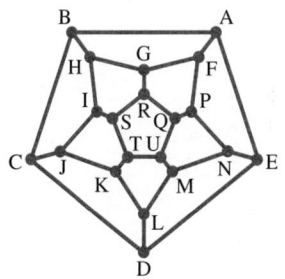

52. The circuit begins at A.

53. The circuit begins A → F.

54. The circuit begins A → B → H.

55. Refer to **Exercise 58** in **Section 15.1** for how one can analyze the rhyme scheme in poetry using graphs. Use this idea to write a paper on sestinas. Be sure to discuss what Hamilton circuits have to do with sestinas.

56. Find out what NP complete problems are, and write a paper on them. Include a careful description of at least one NP complete problem that is different from the traveling salesman problem.

15.4 TREES AND MINIMUM SPANNING TREES

Connected Graphs and Trees • Spanning Trees • Minimum Spanning Trees • Kruskal's Algorithm • Number of Vertices and Edges

Connected Graphs and Trees

Consider a problem that Peggy has in her garden. She wants to install an underground irrigation system. The system must connect the faucet (F) to outlets at various points in the garden, specifically the rose bed (R), perennial bed (P), daffodil bed (D), annuals bed (A), berry patch (B), vegetable patch (V), cut flower bed (C), and shade bed (S). These are shown as the vertices of the graph in **Figure 46** on the next page.

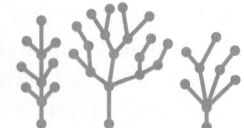

In graph theory, the botanical words go beyond trees. A **forest** is a graph with all components trees, as shown here. Later in this section you will find the words **root** and **leaf** applied to graphs. The terms **pruning** and **separating** arise in applications of trees to computer analysis of images.

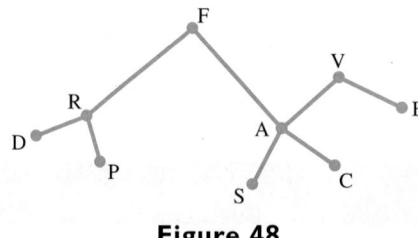

Figure 46

The irrigation system will have pipes connecting these points. For the irrigation system to work well, there should be as few pipes as possible connecting all the outlets.

Think about this problem in terms of a graph with edges representing pipes. Peggy wants water to flow from the faucet (F) to each of the outlets. This means that we need to create a *connected* graph that includes all the vertices in **Figure 46**. We discussed connected graphs in **Section 15.1.** Now that we are familiar with paths, we can give a definition more useful for our purposes here.

Connected Graph

A **connected graph** is one in which there is *at least one path* between each pair of vertices.

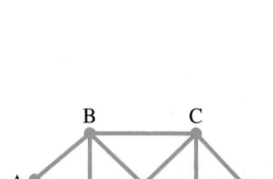

Figure 47

To see that this definition agrees with our earlier definition (on **page 794**), observe that if we select any pair of vertices in the connected graph in **Figure 47** (for example, A and C) then there is at least one path between them. (In fact, there are many paths between A and C.) Two examples are

$$A \rightarrow B \rightarrow E \rightarrow C$$

and
$$A \rightarrow F \rightarrow C.$$

Peggy needs a *connected* graph. Also she must use as few pipes as possible to connect all the outlets to the system. This means that the graph *must not contain any circuits*. If the graph had a circuit, we could remove one of the pipes in the circuit, and still have a connected system of pipes.

Figure 48 shows one possible solution to Peggy's problem.

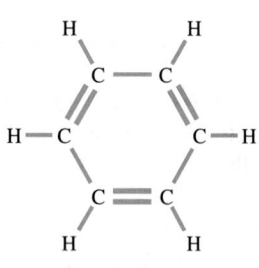

Benzene

It seems mathematician **Arthur Cayley** (see **page 835**) invented the term "tree" in graph theory in about 1857 in connection with problems related to counting all trees of certain types. Later he realized the relevancy of his work to nineteenth-century organic chemistry and in the 1870s published a note on this. Of course, not all molecules have treelike structures. Friedrich Kekulé's realization that the structure of benzene is *not* a tree is considered one of the most brilliant breakthroughs in organic chemistry.

Figure 48

There is a name for graphs that are connected and contain no circuits.

Tree

We call a graph a **tree** if the graph is *connected* and contains *no circuits.*

Just how fast are the fastest computers? Computer speeds are sometimes measured in **flops** (floating point operations per second). A speed of one gigaflop means that the computer can perform about one billion (10^9) calculations per second.

A modern desktop computer can perform at a few gigaflops. In 2009, the fastest computer was the Cray Jaguar, which could perform at almost 1800 teraflops. One teraflop is about one trillion (10^{12}) calculations per second. (*Source:* www.top500.org/lists.)

All five of the graphs shown in **Figure 49** are trees.

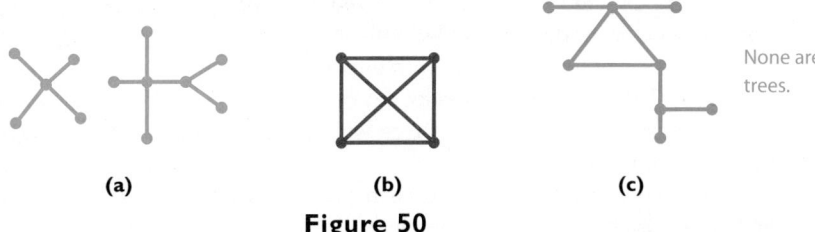

All are trees.

Figure 49

In contrast, none of the graphs shown in **Figure 50** is a tree. The graph in **Figure 50(a)** is not a tree, because it is not connected. Those in **Figures 50(b) and (c)** are not trees, because each contains at least one circuit.

(a)   (b)   (c)

None are trees.

Figure 50

Unique Path Property of Trees

In a tree there is always **exactly one path** from each vertex in the graph to any other vertex in the graph.

For example, starting with vertices S and B in the tree in **Figure 48**, there is exactly one path from vertex S to vertex B, namely, $S \rightarrow A \rightarrow V \rightarrow B$.

This property follows from the definition of a tree. For as a tree is connected, there is always at least one path between each pair of vertices. Also, if the graph is a tree, there cannot be two different paths between a pair of vertices. If there were, these together would contain a circuit.

It is the unique path property of trees that makes them so important in real-world applications. This also is the reason trees are not a very useful model for telephone networks. Each edge of a tree is a cut edge, so failure along one link would disrupt the service. Telephone companies rely on networks with many circuits to provide alternative routes for calls.

▌▌ **EXAMPLE 1** Renovating an Irrigation System

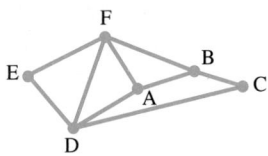

Figure 51

Joe has an old underground irrigation system in his garden, with connections at the faucet (F), outlets A through E in the garden, and existing underground pipes as shown in the graph in **Figure 51**. He wants to renovate this system, keeping only some of the pipes. Water must still be able to flow to each of the original outlets, and the graph of the irrigation system must be a tree. Design an irrigation system that meets Joe's objectives.

SOLUTION

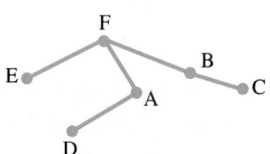

Figure 52

In graph theory terms, we need a *subgraph* of the graph in **Figure 51**. Since water still must be able to flow to each of the original outlets, we need a connected subgraph that *includes all the vertices of the original graph*. Finally, this subgraph must be a *tree*. Thus, we must remove edges (but no vertices) from the graph, without disconnecting the graph, to obtain a subgraph that is a tree. One way to achieve this is shown in **Figure 52**.   ▌▌▌

For Further Thought

Binary Coding

The unique path property of a tree can be used to make a code. We illustrate with a **binary code**, that is, one that uses 0s and 1s. (Recall from **Chapter 4** that when we represent numbers in binary form we use only the symbols 0 and 1.)

To set up the code we use a special kind of tree like that shown in the figure below. This tree is a **directed graph** (there are arrows on the edges). The vertex at the top (with no arrows pointing toward it) is called the **root** of the directed tree. The vertices with no arrows pointing away from them are called **leaves** of the directed tree. We label each leaf with a letter we want to encode. The diagram shown encodes only 8 letters, but we could easily draw a bigger tree with more leaves to represent more letters.

We now write a 0 on each branch that goes left and a 1 on each branch that goes right.

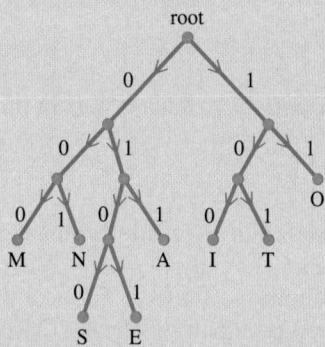

To show how the encoding works, we write the word MAT using the code. Follow the unique path from the root of the tree down to the appropriate leaf, noting in order the labels on the edges.

M is written 000.
A is written 011.
T is written 101.

So MAT is written 000011101.

We can easily translate this code using our tree. Let us see how we could decode 000011101. Referring to the tree, there is only one path from the root to a leaf that can give rise to those first three 0s, and that is the path leading to M. So we can begin to separate the code word into letters: 000–011101. Again following down from the root, the path 011 leads us unambiguously to A. So we have 000–011–101. The path 101 leads unambiguously to T.

The reason we can translate the string of 0s and 1s back to letters without ambiguity is that no letter has a code the same as the first part of the code for a different letter.

For Group Discussion

1. Use the binary encoding tree to write the binary code for each of the following words: ANT, SEAT

2. Use the encoding tree to find the word represented by each of the following codes: 0001111001 0100011101

3. Decode the following messages (commas are inserted to show separation of words).

   (a) 0110011010100, 100001, 1010101001101

   (b) 0101011101, 0001000011010100, 100001, 101100001

   (c) 011, 0000101011001, 1010101011000

   (d) 00001010101101, 0000101, 011101, 1010101011

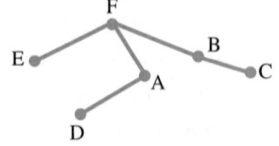

Figure 52 (repeated)

Spanning Trees

A subgraph of the type shown in **Figure 52** from **Example 1** is called a *spanning tree* for the graph. This kind of subgraph "spans" the graph in the sense that it connects all the vertices of the original graph into a subgraph.

> **Spanning Tree**
>
> A **spanning tree** for a graph is a subgraph that includes every vertex of the original graph, and is a tree.

We can find a spanning tree for any connected graph (think about that) and, if the original graph has at least one circuit, it will have several different spanning trees.

EXAMPLE 2 Finding Spanning Trees

Consider the graph shown in **Figure 53**. Find two different spanning trees for the graph.

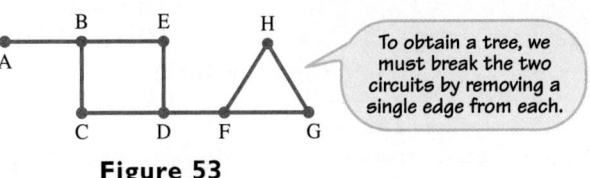

To obtain a tree, we must break the two circuits by removing a single edge from each.

Figure 53

Arthur Cayley (1821–1895) was a close friend of James Sylvester. (See **page 795**.) They worked together as lawyers at the courts of Lincolns Inn in London and discussed mathematics with each other during work hours. Cayley considered his work as a lawyer simply a way to support himself so that he could do mathematics. In the fourteen years he worked as a lawyer, he published 250 mathematical papers. At age 42, he took a huge paycut to become a mathematics professor at Cambridge University.

SOLUTION

There are several choices for which edges to remove. We could remove edges CD and FH, leaving the subgraph in **Figure 54(a)**. Alternatively, we could remove edges ED and FG, leaving the subgraph in **Figure 54(b)**. There are other correct solutions.

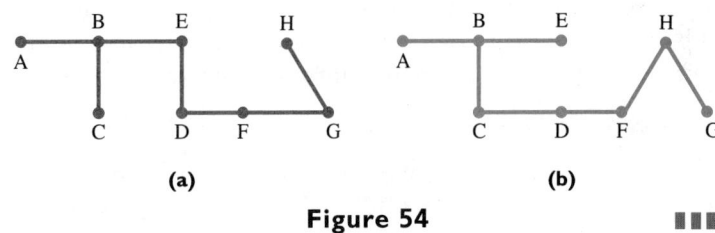

(a)   (b)

Figure 54   ▮▮▮

If two spanning trees use different edges from the original graph, we consider them to be different spanning trees even when they are isomorphic graphs. The subgraphs shown in **Figure 54** are *different* spanning trees, even though they happen to be isomorphic graphs. (Are they isomorphic? To decide, change the labels in graph (a) as follows: Interchange C and E, and interchange G and H. By dragging vertices without detaching edges, we can obtain graphs that look alike.)

Minimum Spanning Trees

Suppose there are six villages in a rural district. At present all the roads in the district are gravel roads. There is not enough funding to pave all the roads, but there is a pressing need to have good paved roads so that emergency vehicles can travel easily between the villages. The vertices in the graph in **Figure 55** represent the villages in the district, and the edges represent the existing gravel roads. Estimated costs for paving the different roads are shown, in millions of dollars. (These estimates take into account distances, as well as features of the terrain.)

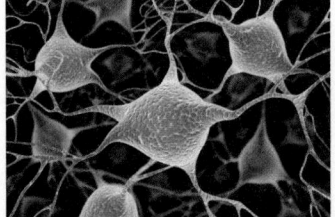

Computer analysis of images is a field of active research, particularly in medicine. (Computer analysis of images refers to having a computer detect relevant features of an image.) Some of this research uses minimum spanning trees. They have been used to identify protein fibers in photographs of cells. The computer detects some points lying on the fibers and then determines a minimum spanning tree to deduce the overall structure of the fiber. Some studies have used minimum spanning trees to analyze cancerous tissue.

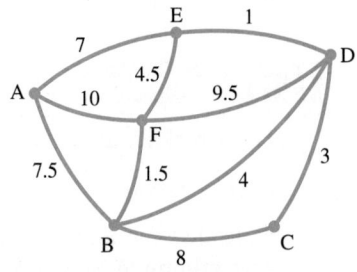

Figure 55

Minimum Spanning Trees in Astronomy
The structure of the universe may hold clues about the formation of the universe. The image shows the large-scale structure of the universe in a region comprising approximately 10% of the sky. It shows the distribution of about 2 million galaxies. Galaxies are not uniformly distributed throughout the universe. Instead they seem to be arranged in clusters, which are grouped together into superclusters, which themselves seem to be arranged in vast chains called filaments. As the image shows, there are voids between the filaments. Some astronomers are using spanning trees to help map the filamentary structure of the universe.

The district council wants to pave just enough roads so that emergency vehicles will be able to travel from any village to any other along paved roads, though possibly by a roundabout route. The council would like to achieve this at *lowest possible cost.*

The problem calls for exactly one path from each vertex in the graph to any other, so it requires a spanning tree. This spanning tree should have minimum total weight. (The total weight of a spanning tree is the sum of the weights of the edges in the tree.)

Minimum Spanning Tree

A spanning tree that has minimum total weight is called a **minimum spanning tree** for the graph.

Kruskal's Algorithm

Fortunately for the district planners, there is a good algorithm for finding a minimum spanning tree for any connected, weighted graph. It is called **Kruskal's algorithm.** (The algorithm is an efficient algorithm, since it does not take too much computer time for even very large graphs.)

Kruskal's Algorithm for Finding a Minimum Spanning Tree for Any Connected, Weighted Graph

Choose edges for the spanning tree as follows.

Step 1 First edge: Choose any edge with minimum weight.

Step 2 Next edge: Choose any edge with minimum weight from *those not yet selected.* (At this stage, the subgraph may look disconnected.)

Step 3 Continue to choose edges of minimum weight from those not yet selected, except *do not select any edge that creates a circuit* in the subgraph.

Step 4 Repeat Step 3 until the subgraph connects all vertices of the original graph.

Because Kruskal's algorithm gives a subgraph that is connected, includes all vertices of the original graph, and has no circuits, it certainly provides a spanning tree for the graph. Also, the algorithm always will give us a *minimum* spanning tree for the graph. The explanation for this fact is beyond the scope of this text.

Algorithms such as Kruskal's often are called *greedy* algorithms. Why might this be so?

▌▌ **EXAMPLE 3** Applying Kruskal's Algorithm

Use Kruskal's algorithm to find a minimum spanning tree for the graph in **Figure 55**.

SOLUTION

Note that the graph is connected, so Kruskal's algorithm applies. Choose an edge with minimum weight. ED has the least weight of all the edges, so it is selected first. We color the edge a different color to show that it has been selected. See **Figure 56** on the next page.

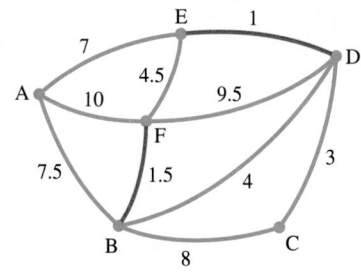

Figure 56   **Figure 57**

Of the remaining edges, BF has the least weight, so it is the second edge chosen, as shown in **Figure 57**. Note that it does not matter that at this stage the subgraph is not connected.

Continuing, we choose CD, then BD, as shown in **Figure 58**. Of the edges remaining, EF has the least weight. However, EF *would create a circuit* in the subgraph. So, ignore EF and note that, of the edges remaining, AE has the least weight. Thus, AE is included in the spanning tree, as shown in **Figure 59**.

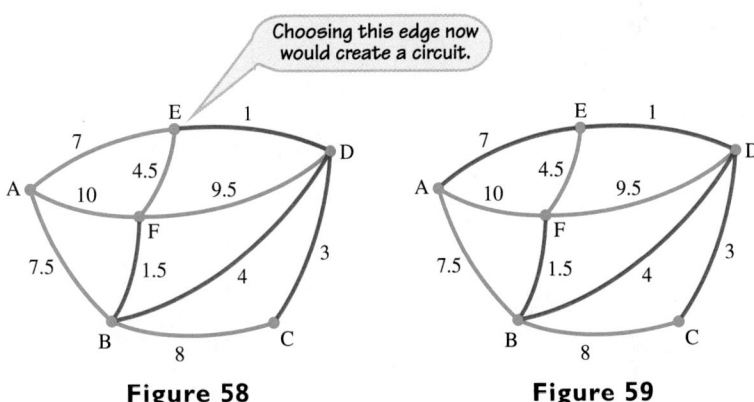

Figure 58   **Figure 59**

We now have a subgraph of the original that connects all vertices of the original graph into a tree. This subgraph is the required minimum spanning tree for the original graph. Its total weight is

$$1 + 1.5 + 3 + 4 + 7 = 16.5.$$

Thus, the district council can achieve its objective at a cost of 16.5 million dollars, by paving only the roads represented by edges in the minimum spanning tree.   ▌▌▌

Number of Vertices and Edges

There is an interesting relation between the number of vertices and the number of edges in a tree.

Weather data are complex, involving numerous readings of temperature, pressure, and wind velocity over huge areas, making accurate weather prediction difficult at best. Some current research uses minimum spanning trees to help computers interpret these data. For example, minimum spanning trees are used to identify developing cold fronts.

Number of Vertices and Edges in a Tree

If a graph is a tree, then the number of edges in the graph is one less than the number of vertices.

A tree with n vertices has $n - 1$ edges.

Consider the graphs shown in **Figure 60**. Information about these graphs is shown in **Table 2**. The first three graphs listed are not trees, and there is no uniform relation between the number of edges and the number of vertices for these graphs. In general, graphs may have more or fewer vertices than edges or an equal number of both. In contrast, the last three graphs listed are trees. The number of edges is indeed one less than the number of vertices for these trees.

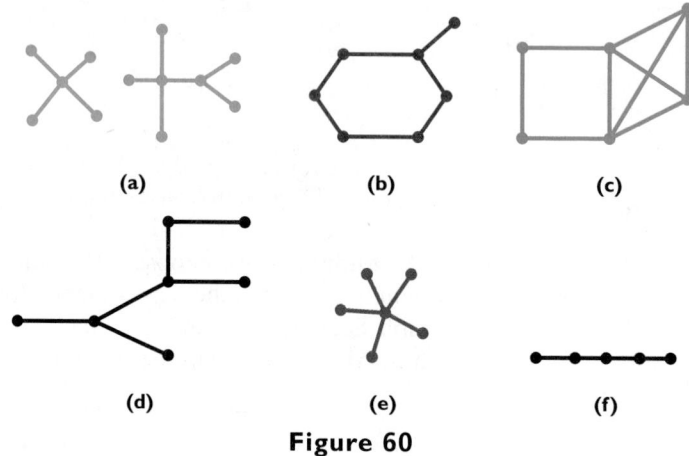

(a)   (b)   (c)

(d)   (e)   (f)

Figure 60

Table 2			
Graph	**Tree?**	**Number of Vertices**	**Number of Edges**
(a)	No	12	10
(b)	No	7	7
(c)	No	6	9
(d)	Yes	7	6	$6 = 7 - 1$
(e)	Yes	6	5	$5 = 6 - 1$
(f)	Yes	5	4	$4 = 5 - 1$

If we consider only connected graphs, there is a converse for the theorem on the previous page:

For a connected graph, if the number of edges is one less than the number of vertices, then the graph is a tree.

▍▍ **EXAMPLE 4**   Using the Vertex/Edge Relation

A chemist has synthesized a new chemical compound. She knows from her analyses that a molecule of the compound contains 54 atoms and that the molecule has a tree-like structure. How many chemical bonds are there in the molecule?

SOLUTION

Think of the atoms in the molecule as the vertices of a tree, and the bonds as edges of the tree. This tree has 54 vertices. Since the number of edges in a tree is one less than the number of vertices, the molecule must have 53 bonds. ▍▍▍

PROBLEM-SOLVING HINT Trial and error is a good problem-solving strategy. Choose an arbitrary proposed solution to the problem and check whether it works. If it does not work, we may gain insight into what to try next.

▮▮ **EXAMPLE 5** Finding a Graph with Specified Properties

Suppose a graph is a tree and has 15 vertices. What is the greatest number of vertices of degree 5 that this graph could have? Draw such a tree.

SOLUTION

Because the graph is a tree with 15 vertices, it must have 14 edges. Recall that the sum of the degrees of the vertices of a graph is twice the number of edges. Thus, the sum of the degrees of the vertices in the tree must be 2 · 14, which is 28.

Now we use trial and error. We want the greatest possible number of vertices with degree 5. Four vertices with degree 5 would contribute 20 to the total degree sum. This would leave 28 − 20 = 8 as the degree sum of the remaining 11 vertices, but this would mean that some of those vertices would have no edges joined to them. The graph would not be connected and would not be a tree.

If we try 3 vertices with degree 5, this would contribute 15 to the total degree sum. It would leave 28 − 15 = 13 as the degree sum for the remaining 12 vertices. We can draw a graph with these specifications, as in **Figure 61**. Thus, the greatest possible number of vertices of degree 5 in a tree with 15 vertices is 3.   ▮▮▮

Figure 61

15.4 EXERCISES

In Exercises 1–7, determine whether the graph is a tree. If not, explain why it is not.

1.

2.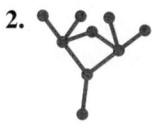

3.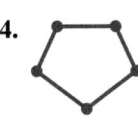

4.

5.

6. a complete graph with 6 vertices

7. a connected graph with all vertices having even degree

In Exercises 8–10, add edges (no vertices) to the graph to change the graph into a tree or explain why this is not possible. (Note: There may be more than one correct answer.)

8. A   B   C
       E   D
   G   H
       F
       I

9. J   K
        M
     L
       N   O   P

10. Q____R

S•   •T
      |
      •U

In Exercises 11–13, determine whether the graph described must be a tree.

11. Spread of a Rumor   A sociologist is investigating the spread of a rumor. He finds that 18 people know of the rumor. One of these people must have started the rumor, and each must have heard the rumor for the first time from one of the others. He draws a graph with vertices representing the 18 people and edges showing from whom each person first heard the rumor.

12. Internet Search Engine   You are using the Google search engine to search the Web for information on a topic for a paper. You start at the Google page and follow links you find, sometimes going back to a site you've already visited. To keep a record of the sites you visit, you show each site as a vertex of a graph. You draw an edge each time you connect for the *first* time to a *new* site.

13. Tracking Infectious Disease   A patient has a highly infectious disease. An employee of the Centers for Disease Control is trying to quarantine all people who have had contact over the past week with either the patient or with someone already included in the contact network. The employee draws a graph with vertices representing the patient and all people who have had contact as described. The edges of the graph represent the relation "the two people have had contact."

In Exercises 14–17, determine whether the statement is true *or* false. *If the statement is false, draw an example to show that it is false.*

14. Every graph with no circuits is a tree.

15. Every connected graph in which each edge is a cut edge is a tree.

16. Every graph in which there is a path between each pair of vertices is a tree.

17. Every graph in which each edge is a cut edge is a tree.

In Exercises 18–20, find three different spanning trees for each graph. (There are many different correct answers.)

18.
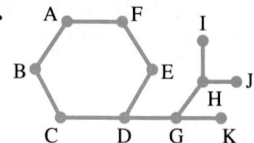

19.
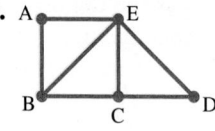

20.
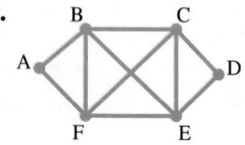

In Exercises 21–23, find all spanning trees for the graph.

21.
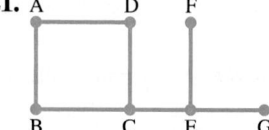

22.
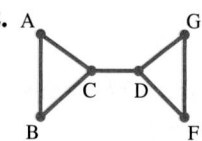

23.
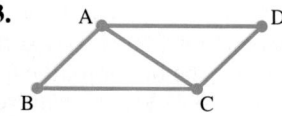

In Exercises 24–26, determine how many spanning trees the graph has.

24.

25.

26.
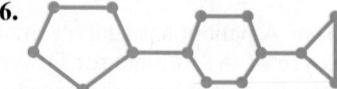

27. What is a general principle about the number of spanning trees in graphs such as those in **Exercises 24–26**?

28. Complete the parts of this exercise in order.

   (a) Find all the spanning trees of each of the following graphs.

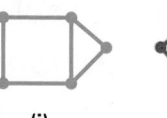 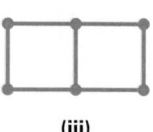

      (i)   **(ii)**   **(iii)**

   (b) For each of the following graphs, determine how many spanning trees the graph has.

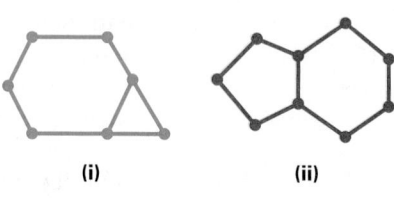

      (i)   **(ii)**

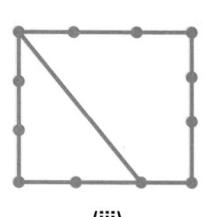

      (iii)

   (c) What is a general principle about the number of spanning trees in graphs of the kind shown in (a) and (b)?

In Exercises 29–32, use Kruskal's algorithm to find a minimum spanning tree for the graph. Find the total weight of this minimum spanning tree.

29.
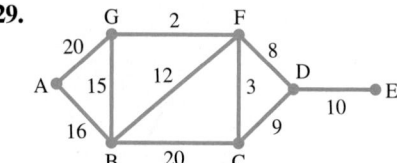

30.
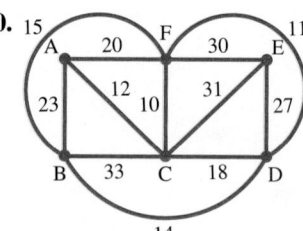

31.
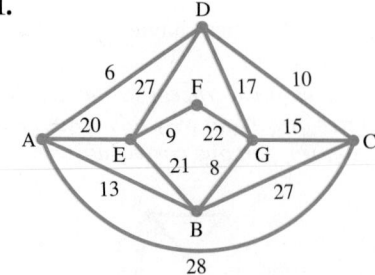

32.

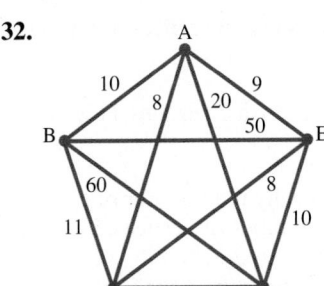

33. School Building Layout A school consists of 6 separate buildings, represented by the vertices in the graph.

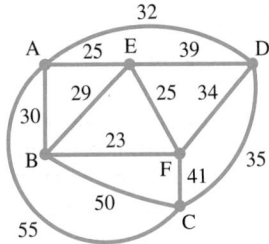

There are paths between some of the buildings as shown. The graph also shows the length in feet of each path. School administrators want to cover some of these paths with roofs so that students will be able to walk between buildings without getting wet when it rains. To minimize cost, they must select paths to be covered such that the total length to be covered is as small as possible. Use Kruskal's algorithm to determine which paths to cover. Also determine the total length of pathways to be covered.

34. Town Water Distribution A town council is planning to provide town water to an area that previously relied on private wells. Water will be fed into the area at the point represented by the vertex labeled A in the graph.

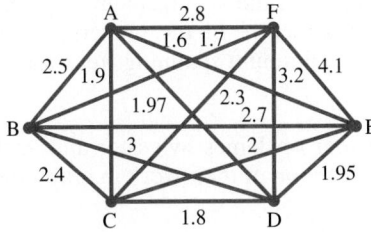

Water must be piped to each of five main distribution points, represented by the vertices labeled B through F in the accompanying graph. Town engineers have estimated the cost of laying the pipes to carry the water between each pair of points in millions of dollars, as indicated in the graph. They must now select which pipes should be laid, so that there is exactly one route for the water to be pumped from A to any one of the five distribution points (possibly via another distribution point), and they want to achieve this at minimum cost. Use Kruskal's algorithm to decide which pipes should be laid. Find the total cost of laying the pipes.

35. How many edges are there in a tree with 34 vertices?

36. How many vertices are there in a tree with 40 edges?

37. How many edges are there in a spanning tree for a complete graph with 63 vertices?

38. A connected graph has 27 vertices and 43 edges. How many edges must be removed to form a spanning tree for the graph?

39. We have said that we can always find at least one spanning tree for a connected graph and usually more than one. Could it happen that different spanning trees for the same graph have different numbers of edges? Justify your answer.

40. Suppose we have a tree with 9 vertices.
  (a) Determine the number of edges in the graph.
  (b) Determine the sum of the degrees of the vertices in the graph.
  (c) Determine the least possible number of vertices of degree 1 in this graph.
  (d) Determine the greatest possible number of vertices of degree 1 in this graph.
  (e) Answer parts (a) through (d) for a tree with n vertices.

41. Suppose we have a tree with 10 vertices.
  (a) Determine the number of edges in the graph.
  (b) Determine the sum of the degrees of the vertices in the graph.
  (c) Determine the least possible number of vertices of degree 4 in this graph.
  (d) Determine the greatest possible number of vertices of degree 4 in this graph.
  (e) Draw a graph to illustrate your answer in part (d).

42. Suppose we have a tree with 17 vertices.
  (a) Determine the number of edges in the graph.
  (b) Determine the sum of the degrees of the vertices in the graph.
  (c) Determine the greatest possible number of vertices of degree 5 in this graph.
  (d) Draw a graph to illustrate your answer in part (c).

43. Computer Network Layout A business has 23 employees, each with his or her own desk computer, all working in the same office. The managers want to network the computers. They need to install cables between individual computers so that every computer is linked into the network. Because of the way the office is laid out, it is not convenient to simply connect all the computers in one long line. Determine the least number of cables the managers need to install to achieve their objective.

44. ***Design of a Garden*** Maria Jimenez has 12 vegetable and flower beds in her garden and wants to build flagstone paths between the beds so that she can get from each bed along flagstone paths to every other bed. She also wants a path linking her front door to one of the beds. Determine the minimum number of flagstone paths she must build to achieve this.

Exercises 45–47 refer to the following situation: We start with a tree and then draw in extra edges and vertices. For each, say whether it is possible to draw in the number of edges and vertices specified to end up with a connected graph. If it is possible, determine whether the resulting graph must be a tree, may be a tree, or cannot possibly be a tree. Justify each answer briefly.

45. Draw in the same number of vertices as edges.

46. Draw in more vertices than edges.

47. Draw in more edges than vertices.

48. Starting with a tree, is it possible to draw in the same number of vertices as edges and end up with a disconnected graph? If so, give an example. If not, justify briefly.

Exercises 49–51 require the following theorem, proved by Cayley in 1889: **A complete graph with n vertices has n^{n-2} spanning trees.**

49. How many spanning trees are there for a complete graph with 3 vertices? Draw a complete graph with 3 vertices and find all the spanning trees.

50. How many spanning trees are there for a complete graph with 4 vertices? Draw a complete graph with 4 vertices and find all the spanning trees.

51. How many spanning trees are there for a complete graph with 5 vertices?

52. Find all nonisomorphic trees with 4 vertices. How many are there?

53. Find all nonisomorphic trees with 5 vertices. How many are there?

54. Find all nonisomorphic trees with 6 vertices. How many are there?

55. Find all nonisomorphic trees with 7 vertices. How many are there?

56. In this exercise, we explore why the number of edges in a tree is one less than the number of vertices. Since the statement is clearly true for a tree with only one vertex, we will consider a tree *with more than one vertex.*

Answer parts (a)–(h) in order.

(a) How many components does the tree have?

(b) Why must the tree have at least one edge?

(c) Remove one edge from the tree. How many components does the resulting graph have?

(d) You have not created any new circuits by removing the edge, so each of the components of the resulting graph is a tree. If the remaining graph still has edges, choose any edge and remove it. (You have now removed 2 edges from the original tree.) Altogether, how many components remain?

(e) Repeat the procedure described in (d). If you remove 3 edges from the original tree, how many components remain? If you remove 4 edges from your original tree, how many components remain?

(f) Repeat the procedure in (d) until you have removed all the edges from the tree. If you have to remove n edges to achieve this, determine an expression involving n for the number of components remaining.

(g) What *are* the components that remain when you have removed all the edges from the tree?

(h) What can you conclude about the number of vertices in a tree with n edges?

57. Write a paper on the arrangement of galaxies and the filamentary structure of the universe. Include discussion of how minimum spanning trees are used to analyze this.

58. Write a paper on James Sylvester and Arthur Cayley. Include discussion of their work in graph theory.

EXTENSION Route Planning

Introduction • Minimizing Deadheading

Introduction When planning routes for mail delivery, street sweeping, or snow-plowing, the roads in the region to be covered usually do not have an Euler circuit. Unavoidably, certain stretches of road must be traveled more than once. This is referred to as **deadheading.** Planners then try to find a route on which the driver will spend as little time as possible deadheading. We now explore how this can be done.

Minimizing Deadheading In **Example 1,** for simplicity we use street grids for which the distance from corner to corner in any direction is the same.

EXAMPLE 1 Finding an Euler Circuit on a Street Grid

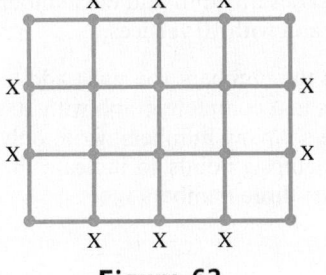

Figure 62

The street grid in **Figure 62** has every vertex of odd degree marked with an X. Insert edges coinciding with existing roads to change it to a graph with an Euler circuit.

SOLUTION

A certain amount of trial and error is needed to find the least number of edges that must be inserted to ensure that the street grid graph has an Euler circuit.

If we insert edges as shown in **Figure 63**, we obtain a graph that has an Euler circuit. (Check that all vertices now have even degree.) This solution introduces 11 edges, which turns out to be more deadheading than is necessary.

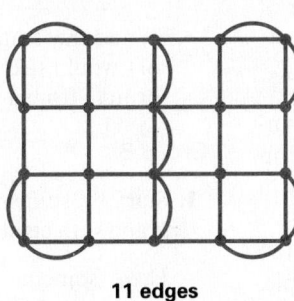

11 edges

Figure 63

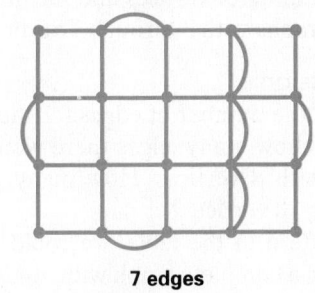

This represents the least amount of deadheading.

7 edges

Figure 64

If we insert edges as shown in **Figure 64**, with just 7 additional edges we obtain a graph with an Euler circuit. This is, in fact, the least number of edges that must be inserted (keeping to the street grid) to change the original street grid graph into a graph that has an Euler circuit. (There are different ways to insert the seven edges.)

▮▮▮

EXTENSION EXERCISES

1. In the graph shown here, we have inserted just six edges in the original street grid from **Example 1.** Why is this not a better solution than the one in **Figure 64**?

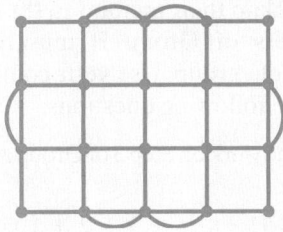

For each street grid in Exercises 2–4, insert edges to obtain a street grid that has an Euler circuit. Try to insert as few edges as possible.

2.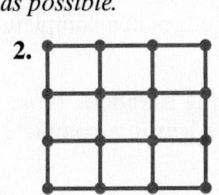

3.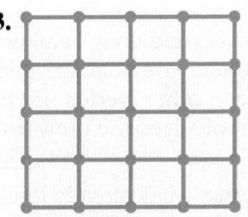

4.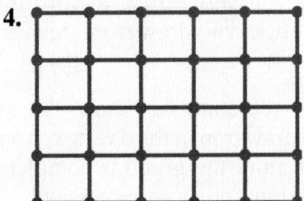

COLLABORATIVE INVESTIGATION

Finding the Number of Edges in a Complete Graph

In this investigation we explore two short methods for finding the number of edges in a complete graph with a specified number of vertices. By comparing the methods, we obtain a special sum formula that you encountered in **Chapter 1.**

Divide into groups of 4 or 5 students. Assign to each group member a different complete graph, with 4, 5, 6, or 7 vertices. Each member should sketch his or her complete graph and count the number of edges. Next, make a table showing the number of vertices and the number of edges in complete graphs with 3 through 7 vertices.

For Group Discussion
Is there a pattern in the number of edges for these complete graphs? Guess how many edges there would be in a complete graph with 8 vertices. How many are in a complete graph with 10 vertices?

If there is a pattern in the table, we could find the number of vertices in a complete graph with, for example, 100 vertices. Of course, completing the table all the way up to 100 would take a long time. A short way of determining the number of edges in a complete graph with any specified number of vertices can be used instead. Divide your group into two groups, A and B, and complete the following tasks.

Group A

1. Start by studying the number of edges in a complete graph with eight vertices. Proceed as follows.

   Have someone in the group draw the eight vertices (no edges yet).

   (a) Choose any one of the vertices and draw in all necessary edges *from this vertex*. (Remember, there must be an edge to every other vertex in the graph.) Record the number of edges you drew from this first vertex.   (a) ____

   (b) Now choose a different vertex—it is already joined to your first vertex by an edge. Draw in all necessary additional edges *from this vertex*. Record the number of *additional* edges you drew from this vertex.   (b) ____

   Continue this process, determining how many *addi-tional* edges you must draw from a third vertex, from a fourth vertex, and so on until the graph is complete. Record the number of additional edges in succession.

   (c) ____ (d) ____ (e) ____ (f) ____ (g) ____

   Now add your answers from (a) through (g) to find the total number of edges.

   Total number of edges = ____ + ____ + ____ + ____

   + ____ + ____ + ____ = ____

2. Repeat the procedure just described to find the number of edges in a complete graph with 10 vertices.

3. As in Step 1, write down the numbers you must add to find the number of edges in a complete graph with 100 vertices. (Since there are so many numbers, write only the first three numbers, ellipsis points to indicate the omission, and then the last three numbers.)

   Total number of edges = ____ + ____ + ____ + ...

   + ____ + ____ + ____

   To add these numbers by hand (or even with a calculator) would take a long time. Perhaps you remember a formula from a previous chapter?

Group B

1. Start by studying the number of edges in a complete graph with eight vertices. Proceed as follows.

   Have someone draw a graph with 8 vertices. Then answer the following.

   (a) Each vertex in your graph has the same degree. What is it?   (a) ____

   (b) Use your answer from (a) to find the sum of the degrees of the vertices in your graph.   (b) ____

   (c) Find the number of edges in the complete graph, by using the theorem from **Section 15.1** that relates the sum of degrees to the number of edges in the graph.   (c) ____

2. Repeat the procedure described above to find the number of edges in a complete graph with 10 vertices.

3. Repeat the procedure described above to find the number of edges in a complete graph with 100 vertices.

Group B should now rejoin Group A. The members of Group A must explain their method to the whole group. Then the members of Group B must explain their method to the whole group. Use your combined knowledge to answer the following questions.

1. By comparing the work on Step 3 of Group A and Group B, find the sum:

   $$99 + 98 + 97 + \ldots + 3 + 2 + 1 = \underline{\quad}$$

2. Determine the number of edges in a complete graph with 210 vertices.

3. Write a formula for the number of edges in a complete graph with *m* vertices.

4. Determine the sum of the following numbers. (*Hint:* Regard the sum as the number of edges in a complete graph.)

   $$155 + 154 + 153 + \ldots + 3 + 2 + 1 = \underline{\quad}$$

CHAPTER 15 TEST

In Exercises 1–4, refer to the following graph.

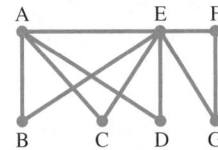

1. Determine how many vertices the graph has.

2. Determine the sum of the degrees of the vertices.

3. Determine how many edges the graph has.

4. Which of the following are paths in the graph? If not, why not?

   (a) B → A → C → E → B → A

   (b) A → B → E → A

   (c) A → C → D → E

5. Which of the following are circuits in the graph? If not, why not?

   (a) A → B → E → D → A

   (b) A → B → C → D → E → F → G → A

   (c) A → B → E → F → G → E → D → A → E → C → A

6. Draw a graph that has 2 components.

7. A graph has 10 vertices, 3 of degree 4, and the rest of degree 2. Use the theorem that relates the sum of degrees to the number of edges to determine the number of edges in the graph (without drawing the graph).

8. Determine whether graphs (a) and (b) are isomorphic. If they are, justify this by labeling corresponding vertices of the two graphs with the same letters and color-coding the corresponding edges.

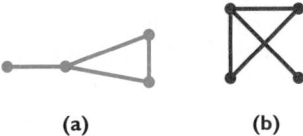

(a)   (b)

9. **Planning for Dinner** Julia is planning to invite some friends for dinner. She plans to invite John, Adam, Bill, Tina, Nicole, and Rita. John, Nicole, and Tina all know each other. Adam knows John and Tina. Bill also knows Tina, and he knows Rita. Draw a graph with vertices representing the six friends whom Julia plans to invite to dinner and edges representing the relationship "know each other." Is your graph connected or disconnected? Which of the guests knows the greatest number of other guests?

10. **Chess Competition** There are 8 contestants in a chess competition. Each contestant plays one chess game against every other contestant. The winner is the contestant who wins the most games. How many chess games will be played in the competition?

11. Is the accompanying graph a complete graph? Justify your answer.

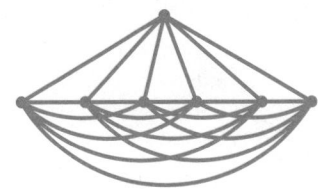

Color each graph using as few colors as possible. Use the result to determine the chromatic number of the graph.

12.   13.

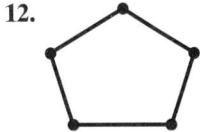   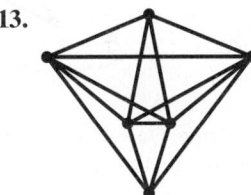

14. **Scheduling Exams** A teacher at a high school must schedule exams for the senior class. Subjects in which there are exams are listed on the left. Several students must take more than one of the exams, as shown on the right. Exams in subjects with students in common must not be scheduled at the same time. Use graph coloring to determine the least number of exam times needed, and to identify exams that can be given at the same times.

Exam	Students taking this must also take
History	English, Mathematics, Biology, Geography, Psychology
English	Mathematics, Psychology, History
Mathematics	Chemistry, Biology, History, English
Chemistry	Biology, Mathematics
Biology	Mathematics, Chemistry, History
Psychology	English, History, Geography
Geography	Psychology, History

15. Refer to the graph for **Exercises 1–4.** Which of the following are Euler circuits for the graph? If not, why not?

   (a) A → B → E → D → A

   (b) A → B → C → D → E → F → G → A

   (c) A → B → E → F → G → E → D → A → E → C → A

In Exercises 16 and 17, use Euler's theorem to decide whether the graph has an Euler circuit. (Do not actually find an Euler circuit.) Justify your answer briefly.

16.

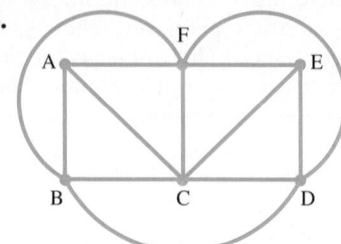

17.

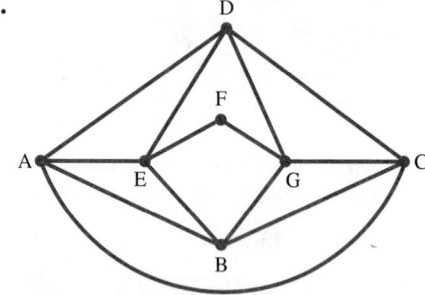

18. *Building Floor Plan*   The floor plan of a building is shown. Is it possible to start outside, walk through each door exactly once, and end up back outside? Justify your answer.

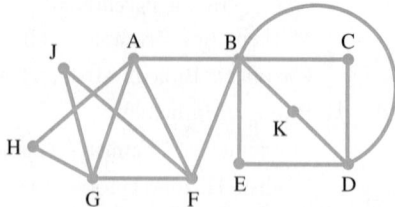

19. Use Fleury's algorithm to find an Euler circuit for the accompanying graph, beginning F → B.

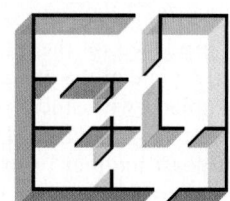

20. Refer to the graph for **Exercises 1–4.** Which of the following are Hamilton circuits for the graph? If not, why not?

(a) A → B → E → D → A

(b) A → B → C → D → E → F → G → A

(c) A → B → E → F → G → E → D → A → E → C → A

21. List all Hamilton circuits in the graph that start F → G. How many are there?

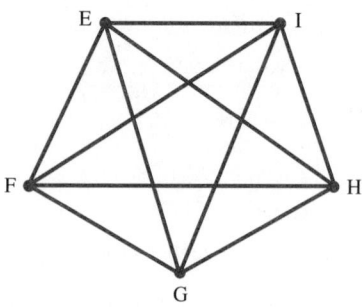

22. Use the brute force algorithm to find a minimum Hamilton circuit for the accompanying graph. Determine the total weight of the minimum Hamilton circuit.

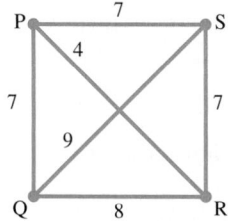

23. Use the nearest neighbor algorithm starting at A to find an approximate solution to the problem of finding a minimum Hamilton circuit for the graph below. Find the total weight of this circuit.

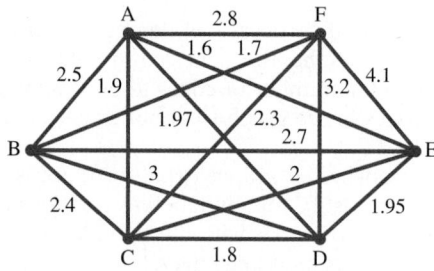

24. How many Hamilton circuits are there in a complete graph with 25 vertices? (Leave your answer as a factorial.)

25. *Rock Band Tour Plan*   The agent for a rock band based in Milwaukee is planning a tour for the band. He plans for the band to visit Minneapolis, Santa Barbara, Orlando, Phoenix, and St. Louis. Since the band members want to minimize the time they are away from home, they do not want to go to any of these cities more than once on the tour. Consider the complete graph with vertices representing the 6 cities mentioned. Does the problem of planning the tour require an Euler circuit, a Hamilton circuit, or neither for its solution?

26. Draw three nonisomorphic trees with 7 vertices.

In Exercises 27–29, decide whether the statement is true *or* false.

27. Every tree has a Hamilton circuit.

28. In a tree each edge is a cut edge.

29. Every tree is connected.

30. Find all the different spanning trees for the following graph.

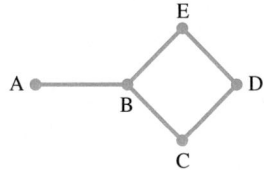

31. Use Kruskal's algorithm to find a minimum spanning tree for the following graph.

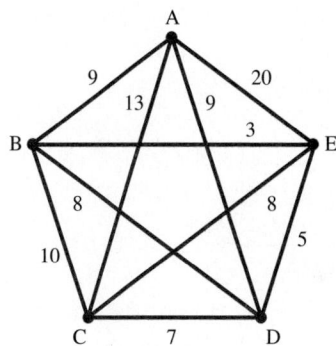

32. Determine the number of edges in a tree with 50 vertices.

APPENDIX: THE METRIC SYSTEM

The metric system was developed by a committee of the French Academy just after the French Revolution of 1789. The president of the committee was the mathematician Joseph Louis Lagrange. The advantages of the metric system can be seen when compared to our English system. In the English system, one inch is one-twelfth of a foot, while one foot is one-third of a yard. One mile is equivalent to 5280 feet, or 1760 yards. Obviously, there is no consistency in subdivisions.

In the metric system, prefixes are used to indicate multiplications or divisions by powers of ten. For example, the basic unit of length in the metric system is the *meter* (which is a little longer than one yard). To indicate one thousand meters, attach the prefix **"kilo-"** to get **kilo**meter. To indicate one one-hundredth of a meter, use the prefix **"centi-"** to obtain **centi**meter. A complete list of the prefixes of the metric system is shown in **Table 1**, with the most commonly used prefixes appearing in bold type.

Joseph Louis Lagrange (1736–1813) was born in Turin, Italy, and became a professor at age 19. In 1776 he came to Berlin at the request of Frederick the Great to take the position Euler left. A decade later Lagrange settled permanently in Paris. Napoleon was among many who admired and honored him.

Lagrange's greatest work was in the theory and application of **calculus.** He carried forward Euler's work of putting calculus on firm algebraic ground in his theory of functions. His *Analytic Mechanics* (1788) applied calculus to the motion of objects.

Lagrange's contributions to algebra had great influence on Galois and, hence, the theory of groups. He also wrote on number theory, proving that every integer is the sum of at most four squares.

Table 1	Metric Prefixes			
Prefix	**Multiple**		**Prefix**	**Multiple**
exa	1,000,000,000,000,000,000		deci	0.1
peta	1,000,000,000,000,000		**centi**	0.01
tera	1,000,000,000,000		**milli**	0.001
giga	1,000,000,000		micro	0.000001
mega	1,000,000		nano	0.000000001
kilo	1000		pico	0.000000000001
hecto	100		femto	0.000000000000001
deka	10		atto	0.000000000000000001

Length and Area

Lagrange urged the committee devising the metric system to find some natural measure for length from which weight and volume measures could be derived. It was decided that one **meter (m)** would be the basic unit of length, with a meter being defined as one ten-millionth of the distance from the equator to the North Pole.

To obtain measures longer than one meter, Greek prefixes were added. For measures smaller than a meter, Latin prefixes were used. A meter is a little longer than a yard (about 39.37 inches). A **centimeter (cm)** is one one-hundredth of a meter and is about $\frac{2}{5}$ of an inch. See **Figure 1**.

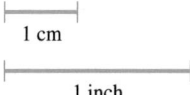

1 cm

1 inch

Figure 1

A Comparison of Distances

Length in Meters	Approximate Related Distances
10^{19}	Distance to the North Star
10^{12}	Distance of Saturn from the sun
10^{11}	Distance of Venus from the sun
10^{9}	Diameter of the sun
10^{8}	Diameter of Jupiter
10^{7}	Diameter of Earth; distance from Washington, D.C. to Tokyo
10^{6}	Distance from Chicago to Wichita, Kansas
10^{5}	Average distance across Lake Michigan
10^{4}	Average width of the Grand Canyon
10^{3}	Length of the Golden Gate Bridge
10^{2}	Length of a football field
10^{1}	Average height of a two-story house
10^{0}	Width of a door
10^{-1}	Width of your hand
10^{-2}	Diameter of a piece of chalk
10^{-3}	Thickness of a dime
10^{-4}	Thickness of a piece of paper
10^{-5}	Diameter of a red blood cell
10^{-7}	Thickness of a soap bubble
10^{-8}	Average distance between molecules of air in a room
10^{-9}	Diameter of a molecule of oil
10^{-14}	Diameter of an atomic nucleus
10^{-15}	Diameter of a proton

Because the metric system is based on decimals and powers of ten, conversions within the system involve multiplying and dividing by powers of ten. For example, to convert 2.5 m to centimeters, multiply 2.5 by 100 (since 100 cm = 1 m) to obtain 250 cm. On the other hand, to convert 18.6 cm to meters, divide by 100 to obtain 0.186 m. Other conversions are made in the same manner, using the meanings of the prefixes. Why is 42 m equal to 42,000 millimeters (mm)?

Long distances usually are measured in kilometers. A **kilometer (km)** is 1000 meters. (According to a popular dictionary, the word *kilometer* may be pronounced with the accent on either the first or the second syllable. Scientists usually stress the second syllable.) A kilometer is equal to about 0.6 mile. **Figure 2** shows the ratio of 1 kilometer to 1 mile.

Conversions from meters to kilometers, and vice versa, are made by multiplying or dividing by 1000 as necessary. For example, 37 kilometers equals 37,000 meters, while 583 meters equals 0.583 km.

The area of a figure can be measured in square metric units. **Figure 3** shows a square that is 1 cm on each side. Thus, it is a **square centimeter (cm²)**. One square meter (m²) is the area of a square with sides one meter long. How many cm² are in one m²?

According to Paul G. Hewitt, in *Conceptual Physics,* 7th edition (HarperCollins):

The distance from the equator to the North Pole was thought at the time to be close to 10,000 kilometers. One ten-millionth of this, the meter, was carefully determined and marked off by means of scratches on a bar of platinum-iridium alloy. This bar is kept at the International Bureau of Weights and Measures in France. The standard meter in France has since been calibrated in terms of the wavelength of light—it is 1,650,763.73 times the wavelength of orange light emitted by the atoms of the gas krypton-86. The meter is now defined as being the length of the path traveled by light in a vacuum during a time interval of 1/299,792,458 of a second.

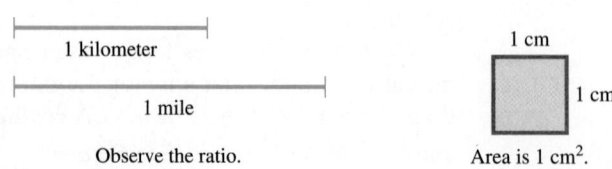

1 kilometer

1 mile

Observe the ratio.

Figure 2

1 cm

1 cm

Area is 1 cm².

Figure 3

In September 1999, the **Mars *Climate Orbiter*** was lost due to "a failure to use metric units in the coding of a ground software file. . . ." According to Edward Weiler, associate administrator for NASA's Office of Space Science, the metric conversion error that led to the loss "should have been caught five ways to Sunday," but it wasn't. (*Source*: "NASA's Mars Losses Spark Anger and Opportunity" by Leonard David, Washington Contributing Editor to www.space.com.)

Volume, Mass, and Weight

The volume of a three-dimensional figure is measured in cubic units. If, for example, the dimensions are given in centimeters, the volume may be determined by the appropriate formula from geometry, and it will be in **cubic centimeters (cm³).** See **Figure 4** for a sketch of a box whose volume is one cm³.

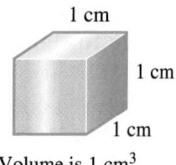

Volume is 1 cm³.

Figure 4

In the metric system, one **liter (L)** is the quantity assigned to the volume of a box that is 10 cm on a side. (See **Figure 5**.) A liter is a little more than a quart as seen in **Figure 6**. Notice the advantage of this definition over the equivalent one in the English system—using a ruler marked in centimeters, a volume of 1 liter (symbolized 1 L) can be constructed. On the other hand, given a ruler marked in inches, it would be difficult to construct a volume of 1 quart.

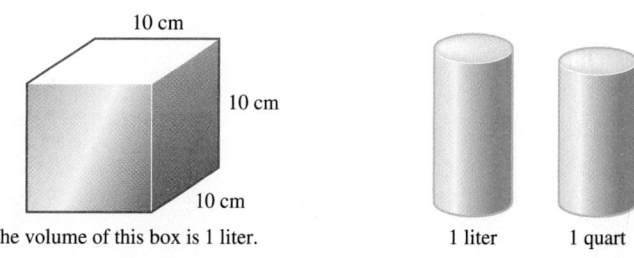

The volume of this box is 1 liter.   1 liter   1 quart

Figure 5   **Figure 6**

The prefixes mentioned earlier are used throughout the metric system, so one **milliliter (ml)** is one one-thousandth of a liter, one **centiliter (cl)** is one one-hundredth of a liter, one **kiloliter (kl)** is 1000 liters, and so on. Milliliters are used extensively in science and medicine. Many beverages now are sold by milliliters and by liters. For example, 750 ml is a common size for wine bottles, and many soft drinks now are sold in 1- and 2-liter bottles.

Because of the way a liter is defined as the volume of a box 10 cm on a side,

$$1\,L = 10\,cm \times 10\,cm \times 10\,cm = 1000\,cm^3 \quad or \quad \frac{1}{1000}\,L = 1\,cm^3.$$

Since $\frac{1}{1000}\,L = 1\,ml$, we have the following relationship.

$$1\,ml = 1\,cm^3$$

For example, the volume of a box which is 8 cm by 6 cm by 5 cm may be given as 240 cm³ or as 240 ml.

The box in **Figure 4** is 1 cm by 1 cm by 1 cm. The volume of this box is

$$1\,cm^3, \quad or \quad 1\,ml.$$

By definition, the mass of the water that fills such a box is **1 gram (g).** A nickel five-cent piece has a mass close to 5 grams, or 5 g. The volume of water used to define a gram is very small, so a gram is a very small mass. For everyday use, a **kilogram (kg),** or one thousand grams, is more practical. A kilogram weighs about 2.2 pounds. A common abbreviation for kilogram is the word **kilo.**

The original scale of **Anders Celsius** had the freezing point of water at 100° and the boiling point at 0°, but biologist Carl von Linne inverted the scale, giving us the familiar Celsius scale of today.

This photo shows that 13 feet, 6 inches is equal to 4.1 meters. Use this information and a proportion to show that one yard is equal to 0.91 meter.

Extremely small masses can be measured with **milligrams (mg)** and **centigrams (cg).** These measures are so small that they, like centiliters and milliliters, are used mainly in science and medicine.

Temperature

In the metric system temperature is measured in **degrees Celsius.** On the Celsius temperature scale, water freezes at 0° and boils at 100°. These two numbers are easier to remember than the corresponding numbers on the Fahrenheit scale, 32° and 212°. The thermometer in **Figure 7** shows some typical temperatures in both Fahrenheit and Celsius.

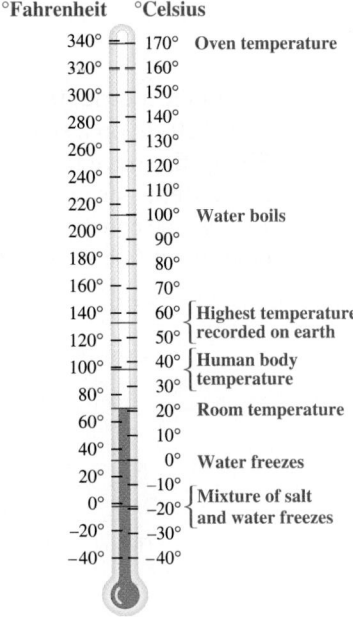

Figure 7

The formulas given below can be used to convert between Celsius and Fahrenheit temperatures.

Celsius-Fahrenheit Conversion Formulas

To convert a reading from Fahrenheit to Celsius, use $C = \frac{5}{9}(F - 32).$

To convert from Celsius to Fahrenheit, use $F = \frac{9}{5}C + 32.$

Metric Conversions

Due to legislation enacted by Congress, the metric system is used in the United States, and an ultimate goal is for the two systems to be in use, side-by-side, with public acceptance of both systems. Industries that export a great many goods are using the metric system, since this is compatible with most of the countries with which they trade.

Some scientific calculators are programmed to do conversions between the English and metric systems. Approximate conversions can be made with the aid of **Tables 2 and 3** on the next page.

Table 2 Metric to English		
To Convert from	**To**	**Multiply by**
meters	yards	1.0936
meters	feet	3.2808
meters	inches	39.37
kilometers	miles	0.6214
grams	pounds	0.0022
kilograms	pounds	2.20
liters	quarts	1.0567
liters	gallons	0.2642

Table 3 English to Metric		
To Convert from	**To**	**Multiply by**
yards	meters	0.9144
feet	meters	0.3048
inches	meters	0.0254
miles	kilometers	1.609
pounds	grams	454
pounds	kilograms	0.454
quarts	liters	0.9464
gallons	liters	3.785

APPENDIX EXERCISES

Perform each conversion by multiplying or dividing by the appropriate power of 10.

1. 8 m to millimeters

2. 14.76 m to centimeters

3. 8500 cm to meters

4. 250 mm to meters

5. 68.9 cm to millimeters

6. 3.25 cm to millimeters

7. 59.8 mm to centimeters

8. 3.542 mm to centimeters

9. 5.3 km to meters

10. 9.24 km to meters

11. 27,500 m to kilometers

12. 14,592 m to kilometers

Use a metric ruler to perform each measurement, first in centimeters, then in millimeters.

13. ├────────────────┤

14. ├──────────────────────┤

15. ├────────────────────────────┤

16. Based on your measurement of the line segment in **Exercise 13,** one inch is about how many centimeters? How many millimeters?

Perform each conversion by multiplying or dividing by the appropriate power of 10.

17. 6 L to centiliters

18. 4.1 L to milliliters

19. 8.7 L to milliliters

20. 12.5 L to centiliters

21. 925 cl to liters

22. 412 ml to liters

23. 8974 ml to liters

24. 5639 cl to liters

25. 8000 g to kilograms

26. 25,000 g to kilograms

27. 5.2 kg to grams

28. 12.42 kg to grams

29. 4.2 g to milligrams

30. 3.89 g to centigrams

31. 598 mg to grams

32. 7634 cg to grams

Use the formulas given in the text to perform each conversion. Round to the nearest degree.

33. 86°F to Celsius

34. 536°F to Celsius

35. −114°F to Celsius

36. −40°F to Celsius

37. 10°C to Fahrenheit

38. 25°C to Fahrenheit

39. −40°C to Fahrenheit

40. −15°C to Fahrenheit

Solve each problem. Refer to geometry formulas as necessary.

41. *Weight of Nickels* One nickel weighs 5 g. How many nickels are in 1 kg of nickels?

42. *Salt in Sea Water* Sea water contains about 3.5 g salt per 1000 ml of water. How many grams of salt would be in one liter of sea water?

43. *Weight of Helium* Helium weighs about 0.0002 g per milliliter. How much would one liter of helium weigh?

44. *Sugar Solution* About 1500 g sugar can be dissolved in a liter of warm water. How much sugar could be dissolved in one milliliter of warm water?

45. *Cost of Metal* Northside Foundry needed seven metal strips, each 67 cm long. Find the total cost of the strips, if they sell for $8.74 per meter.

46. *Cost of Lace* Uptown Dressmakers bought fifteen pieces of lace, each 384 mm long. The lace sold for $54.20 per meter. Find the cost of the fifteen pieces.

47. *Cost of Marble* Imported marble for desktops costs $174.20 per square meter. Find the cost of a piece of marble 128 cm by 174 cm.

48. *Cost of Paper* A special photographic paper sells for $63.79 per square meter. Find the cost to buy 80 pieces of the paper, each 9 cm by 14 cm.

49. *Volume of a Box* An importer received some special coffee beans in a box measuring 82 cm by 1.1 m by 1.2 m. Give the volume of the box, both in cubic centimeters and cubic meters.

50. *Volume of a Crate* A fabric center receives bolts of woolen cloth in crates measuring 1.5 m by 74 cm by 97 cm. Find the volume of a crate, both in cubic centimeters and cubic meters.

51. *Medicine Bottles* A medicine is sold in small bottles holding 800 ml each. How many of these bottles can be filled from a vat holding 160 L of the medicine?

52. *Bottles of Soda Pop* How many 2-liter bottles of soda pop would be needed for a wedding reception if 80 people are expected, and each drinks 400 ml of soda?

Perform each conversion. Use a calculator and/or the table in the text as necessary.

53. 982 yd to meters

54. 12.2 km to miles

55. 125 mi to kilometers

56. 1000 mi to kilometers

57. 1816 g to pounds

58. 1.42 lb to grams

59. 47.2 lb to grams

60. 7.68 kg to pounds

61. 28.6 L to quarts

62. 59.4 L to quarts

63. 28.2 gal to liters

64. 16 qt to liters

Metric measures are very common in medicine. Since we convert among metric measures by moving the decimal point, errors in locating the decimal point in medical doses are not unknown. Decide whether each dose of medicine seems reasonable *or* unreasonable.

65. Take 2 kg of aspirin three times a day.

66. Take 4 L of liquid Mylanta every evening just before bedtime.

67. Take 25 ml of cough syrup daily.

68. Soak your feet in 6 L of hot water.

69. Inject $\frac{1}{2}$ L of insulin every morning.

70. Apply 40 g of salve to a cut on your finger.

Select the most reasonable choice for each of the following.

71. length of an adult cow
   A. 1 m   **B.** 3 m   **C.** 5 m

72. length of a Lexus
   A. 1 m   **B.** 3 m   **C.** 5 m

73. distance from Seattle to Miami
   A. 500 km   **B.** 5000 km   **C.** 50,000 km

74. length across an average nose
 A. 3 cm   **B.** 30 cm   **C.** 300 cm

75. distance across a page of a book
 A. 1.93 mm   **B.** 19.3 mm   **C.** 193 mm

76. weight of a book
 A. 1 kg   **B.** 10 kg   **C.** 1000 kg

77. weight of a large automobile
 A. 1300 kg   **B.** 130 kg   **C.** 13 kg

78. volume of a 12-ounce bottle of beverage
 A. 35 ml   **B.** 355 ml   **C.** 3550 ml

79. height of a person
 A. 180 cm   **B.** 1800 cm   **C.** 18 cm

80. diameter of the earth
 A. 130 km   **B.** 1300 km   **C.** 13,000 km

81. length of a long freight train
 A. 8 m   **B.** 80 m   **C.** 800 m

82. volume of a grapefruit
 A. 1 L   **B.** 4 L   **C.** 8 L

83. the length of a pair of Levi jeans
 A. 70 cm   **B.** 700 cm   **C.** 7 cm

84. a person's weight
 A. 700 kg   **B.** 7 kg   **C.** 70 kg

85. diagonal measure of a small TV monitor
 A. 5 cm   **B.** 50 cm   **C.** 500 cm

86. width of a standard bedroom door
 A. 1 m   **B.** 3 m   **C.** 5 m

87. thickness of a marking pen
 A. 0.9 mm   **B.** 9 mm   **C.** 90 mm

88. length around the rim of a coffee mug
 A. 300 mm   **B.** 30 mm   **C.** 3000 mm

89. the temperature at the surface of a frozen lake
 A. 0°C   **B.** 10°C   **C.** 32°C

90. the temperature in the middle of Death Valley on a July afternoon
 A. 25°C   **B.** 40°C   **C.** 65°C

91. surface temperature of desert sand on a hot summer day
 A. 30°C   **B.** 60°C   **C.** 90°C

92. temperature of boiling water
 A. 100°C   **B.** 120°C   **C.** 150°C

93. air temperature on a day when you need a sweater
 A. 30°C   **B.** 20°C   **C.** 10°C

94. air temperature on a day when you go swimming
 A. 30°C   **B.** 15°C   **C.** 10°C

95. temperature when baking a cake
 A. 120°C   **B.** 170°C   **C.** 300°C

96. temperature of bath water
 A. 35°C   **B.** 50°C   **C.** 65°C

ANSWERS TO SELECTED EXERCISES

CHAPTER 1 THE ART OF PROBLEM SOLVING

1.1 Exercises *(pages 6–8)*

1. deductive **3.** inductive **5.** deductive **7.** deductive
9. inductive **11.** inductive **13.** Answers will vary.
15. 21 **17.** 3072 **19.** 63 **21.** $\frac{11}{12}$ **23.** 216 **25.** 52
27. 5 **29.** One such list is 10, 20, 30, 40, 50, ...
31. $(98{,}765 \times 9) + 3 = 888{,}888$
33. $3367 \times 15 = 50{,}505$
35. $33{,}334 \times 33{,}334 = 1{,}111{,}155{,}556$
37. $3 + 6 + 9 + 12 + 15 = \frac{15(6)}{2}$
39. $5(6) + 5(36) + 5(216) + 5(1296) + 5(7776) = 6(7776 - 1)$
41. $\frac{1}{2} + \frac{1}{4} + \frac{1}{8} + \frac{1}{16} + \frac{1}{32} = 1 - \frac{1}{32}$
43. 20,100 **45.** 320,400 **47.** 15,400 **49.** 2550
51. 1 (These are the numbers of chimes a clock rings, starting with 12 o'clock, if it rings the number of hours on the hour, and 1 chime on the half-hour.)
53. (a) The middle digit is always 9, and the sum of the first and third digits is always 9 (considering 0 as the first digit if the difference has only two digits). **(b)** Answers will vary. **55.** 142,857; 285,714; 428,571; 571,428; 714,285; 857,142. Each result consists of the same six digits, but in a different order. $142{,}857 \times 7 = 999{,}999$

1.2 Exercises *(pages 15–18)*

1. arithmetic; 56 **3.** geometric; 1215 **5.** neither
7. geometric; 8 **9.** neither **11.** arithmetic; 22
13. 79 **15.** 450 **17.** 4032 **19.** 32,758 **21.** 57; 99
23. $(4321 \times 9) - 1 = 38{,}888$
25. $999{,}999 \times 4 = 3{,}999{,}996$
27. $21^2 - 15^2 = 6^3$ **29.** $5^2 - 4^2 = 5 + 4$
31. $1 + 5 + 9 + 13 = 4 \times 7$ **33.** 45,150 **35.** 228,150
37. 2601 **39.** 250,000 **41.** $S = n(n + 1)$
43. Answers will vary. **45.** *row 1*: 28, 36; *row 2*: 36, 49, 64; *row 3*: 35, 51, 70, 92; *row 4*: 28, 45, 66, 91, 120; *row 5*: 18, 34, 55, 81, 112, 148; *row 6*: 8, 21, 40, 65, 96, 133, 176
47. $8(1) + 1 = 9 = 3^2$; $8(3) + 1 = 25 = 5^2$; $8(6) + 1 = 49 = 7^2$; $8(10) + 1 = 81 = 9^2$
49. The pattern is 1, 0, 1, 0, 1, 0, ...
51.

53. 256 **55.** 117 **57.** 235 **59.** $N_n = \dfrac{n(7n - 5)}{2}$
61. a square number **63.** a perfect cube **65.** 42
67. 419 **69.** $\frac{101}{2}$ **71.** 2048 **73.** $\frac{1}{2048}$ **75.** $\frac{5}{2048}$

1.3 Exercises *(pages 24–29)*

1. 32 **3.** 0 (The product of the first and last digits is the two-digit number between them.) **5.** 11 **7.** infinitely many (Any line through the center of the square will do this.) **9.** 48.5 in. **11.** 42 **13.** 6 **15.** If you multiply the two digits in the numbers in the first row, you will get the second row of numbers. The second row of numbers is a pattern of two numbers (8 and 24) repeating. **17.** I put the ring in the box and put my lock on the box. I send you the box. You put your lock on, as well, and send it back to me. I then remove my lock with my key and send the box (with your lock still on) back to you, so you can remove your lock with your key and get the ring. **19.** 59
21. You should choose a sock from the box labeled *red and green socks*. Because it is mislabeled, it contains only red socks or only green socks, determined by the sock you choose. If the sock is green, relabel this box *green socks*. Since the other two boxes were mislabeled, switch the remaining label to the other box and place the label that says *red and green socks* on the unlabeled box. No other choice guarantees a correct relabeling because you can remove only one sock.
23. D **25.** A
27. One example of a solution follows.

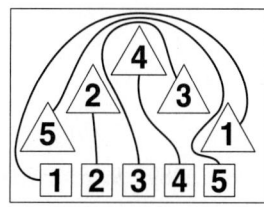

29.

9	7	2	14	11	5	4	12	13	3	6	10	15	1	8

(or the same arrangement reading right to left)
31. Here is one solution. **33.** D **35.** $\frac{1}{3}$

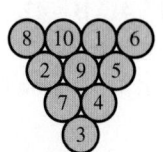

37. One possible sequence is shown here. The numbers represent the number of gallons in each bucket in each successive step.

Big	7	4	4	1	1	0	7	5	5
Small	0	3	0	3	0	1	1	3	0

39. 90 **41.** 55 mph **43.** 07 **45.** 437 **47.** 3
49. 21 stamps (5 five-cent stamps and 16 eight-cent stamps) **51.** 3 socks **53.** 35 **55.** 6
57. the nineteenth day **59.** 1967
61. Eve has $5, and Adam has $7.
63.

$$\begin{array}{r} 4\ 0\ 2 \\ \times \quad 3\ 9 \\ \hline 1\ 5,\ 6\ 7\ 8 \end{array}$$

65.

6	12	7	9
1	15	4	14
11	5	10	8
16	2	13	3

67. 25 pitches (The visiting team's pitcher retires 24 consecutive batters through the first eight innings, using only one pitch per batter. His team does not score either. Going into the bottom of the ninth tied 0–0, the first batter for the home team hits his first pitch for a home run. The pitcher threw 25 pitches and loses the game by a score of 1–0.) **69.** Q

71. Here is one solution.

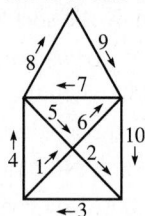

73. 6 ways **75.** 86 cm
77. Dan (36) is married to Jessica (29); James (30) is married to Cathy (31).
79. 12; All months have 28 days.
81. 3
85. The products always differ by 1.

83. 6

	X	X
X		X
X	X	

One of two possibilities

1.4 Exercises *(pages 33–36)*
1. 43.8 **3.** 2.3589 **5.** 7.48 **7.** 7.1289 **9.** 6340.338097
11. 1 **13.** 1.061858759 **15.** 2.221441469
17. 3.141592653 **19.** 0.7782717162 **21.** yes
23. positive **25.** 1 **27.** the same as **29.** 0
31. negative **33.** Answers will vary.
35. Answers will vary. **37.** 63 **39.** 14 **41.** B **43.** A
45. D **47.** 5% **49.** 260,000 **51.** 2005, 2006, 2007
53. 2001: about 165 billion lb; 2007: about 185 billion lb
55. from 2000 to 2005; about $0.85
57. The price of a gallon of gas was decreasing.

Chapter 1 Test *(pages 41–42)*
1. inductive **2.** deductive
3. The magic sum is 38.

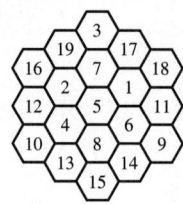

4. 65,359,477,124,183 × 68 = 4,444,444,444,444,444
5. 351 **6.** 31,375 **7.** 65; 65 = 1 + 7 + 13 + 19 + 25
8. 1, 8, 21, 40, 65, 96, 133, 176; The pattern is 1, 0, 1, 0, 1, 0, 1, 0, ...
9. The first two terms are both 1. Each term after the second is found by adding the two previous terms.
10. $\frac{1}{4}$ **11.** 9 **12.** 35
13. Answers will vary. One possible solution is
1 + 2 + 3 − 4 + 5 + 6 + 78 + 9 + 0 = 100.
14. 108 in., or 9 ft **15.** 3
16. The sum of the digits is always 9.
17. 9.907572861 (Answers may vary due to the model of calculator used.) **18.** 34.328125 **19.** B
20. (a) between 1998 and 1999, 1999 and 2000, and 2003 and 2004 **(b)** The unemployment rate was increasing.
(c) 2003: 6.0%; 2004: 5.5%; decline: 0.5%

CHAPTER 2 THE BASIC CONCEPTS OF SET THEORY

2.1 Exercises *(pages 47–49)*
1. F **3.** E **5.** B **7.** H **9.** {1, 2, 3, 4, 5, 6}
11. {0, 1, 2, 3, 4} **13.** {6, 7, 8, 9, 10, 11, 12, 13, 14}
15. {−15, −13, −11, −9, −7, −5, −3, −1}
17. {2, 4, 8, 16, 32, 64, 128, 256} **19.** {0, 2, 4, 6, 8, 10}
21. {21, 22, 23, . . . } **23.** {Lake Erie, Lake Huron, Lake Michigan, Lake Ontario, Lake Superior}
25. {5, 10, 15, 20, 25, . . . } **27.** $\left\{1, \frac{1}{2}, \frac{1}{3}, \frac{1}{4}, \frac{1}{5}, . . .\right\}$
In Exercises 29 and 31, there are other ways to describe the sets. 29. {$x \mid x$ is a rational number} **31.** {$x \mid x$ is an odd natural number less than 76} **33.** the set of single-digit integers **35.** the set of states of the United States
37. finite **39.** infinite **41.** infinite **43.** infinite
45. 8 **47.** 500 **49.** 26 **51.** 39 **53.** 28
55. Answers will vary. **57.** well defined
59. not well defined **61.** ∈ **63.** ∉ **65.** ∉ **67.** ∈
69. false **71.** true **73.** true **75.** true **77.** false
79. true **81.** true **83.** true **85.** false **87.** true
89. Answers will vary.

91. {2} and {3, 4} (Other examples are possible.)

93. {a, b} and {a, c} (Other examples are possible.)

95. (a) {Drew Barrymore, Leonardo DiCaprio, Samuel L. Jackson, Jim Carrey} **(b)** {Will Ferrell, Ewan McGregor}

2.2 Exercises *(pages 54–55)*

1. D **3.** B **5.** ⊄ **7.** ⊆ **9.** ⊆ **11.** ⊄ **13.** both

15. ⊆ **17.** both **19.** neither **21.** true **23.** false

25. true **27.** false **29.** true **31.** true **33.** false

35. true **37.** true **39.** false **41. (a)** 64 **(b)** 63

43. (a) 32 **(b)** 31 **45.** {5, 7, 9, 10} **47.** {2} **49.** ∅

51. {Higher cost, Lower cost, Educational, More time to see the sights in California, Less time to see the sights in California, Cannot visit relatives along the way, Can visit relatives along the way} **53.** {Higher cost, More time to see the sights in California, Cannot visit relatives along the way} **55.** ∅ **57.** {A, B, C, D, E} (All are present.)

59. {A, B, C}, {A, B, D}, {A, B, E}, {A, C, D}, {A, C, E}, {A, D, E}, {B, C, D}, {B, C, E}, {B, D, E}, {C, D, E}

61. {A}, {B}, {C}, {D}, {E} **63.** 32

65. $2^{25} - 1 = 33,554,431$ **67. (a)** 15 **(b)** 16; It is now possible to select *no* bills. **69. (a)** s **(b)** s **(c)** $2s$

(d) Adding one more element will always double the number of subsets, so the expression 2^n is true in general.

2.3 Exercises *(pages 65–68)*

1. B **3.** A **5.** E **7.** {a, c} **9.** {a, b, c, d, e, f}

11. {a, b, c, d, e, f, g} **13.** {b, d, f} **15.** {d, f}

17. {a, b, c, e, g} **19.** {a, c, e, g} **21.** {a} **23.** {e, g}

25. {e, g} **27.** {d, f} **29.** {e, b, g}

In Exercises 31–35, there may be other acceptable descriptions.

31. the set of all elements that either are in A, or are not in B and not in C **33.** the set of all elements that are in C but not in B, or are in A **35.** the set of all elements that are in A but not in C, or in B but not in C

37. {e, h, c, l, b} **39.** {l, b} **41.** {e, h, c, l, b} **43.** the set of all tax returns showing business income or filed in 2009

45. the set of all tax returns filed in 2009 without itemized deductions **47.** the set of all tax returns with itemized deductions or showing business income, but not selected for audit **49.** always true **51.** always true

53. not always true **55. (a)** {1, 3, 5, 2} **(b)** {1, 2, 3, 5}

(c) For any sets X and Y, $X \cup Y = Y \cup X$.

57. (a) {1, 3, 5, 2, 4} **(b)** {1, 3, 5, 2, 4} **(c)** For any sets X, Y, and Z, $X \cup (Y \cup Z) = (X \cup Y) \cup Z$.

59. (a) {4} **(b)** {4} **(c)** For any sets X and Y, $(X \cup Y)' = X' \cap Y'$. **61.** $X \cup \emptyset = X$; For any set X, $X \cup \emptyset = X$. **63.** true **65.** false **67.** true **69.** true

71. $A \times B = \{(2, 4), (2, 9), (8, 4), (8, 9), (12, 4), (12, 9)\}$; $B \times A = \{(4, 2), (4, 8), (4, 12), (9, 2), (9, 8), (9, 12)\}$

73. $A \times B = \{(d, p), (d, i), (d, g), (o, p), (o, i), (o, g), (g, p), (g, i), (g, g)\}$; $B \times A = \{(p, d), (p, o), (p, g), (i, d), (i, o), (i, g), (g, d), (g, o), (g, g)\}$

75. $n(A \times B) = 6$; $n(B \times A) = 6$

77. $n(A \times B) = 210$; $n(B \times A) = 210$ **79.** 6

81.
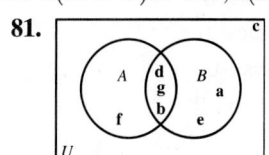

83.
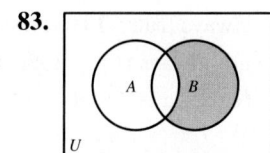

$B \cap A'$

85.
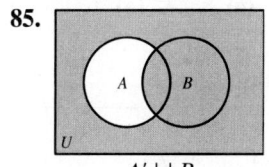

$A' \cup B$

87.
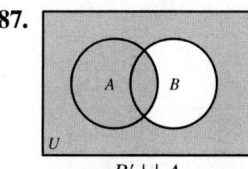

$B' \cup A$

89.
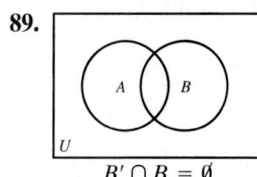

$B' \cap B = \emptyset$

91.
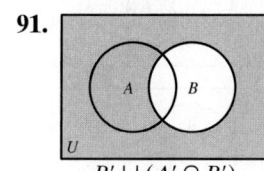

$B' \cup (A' \cap B')$

93.
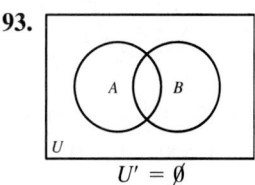

$U' = \emptyset$

95.
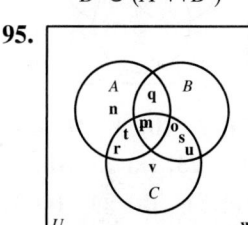

97.
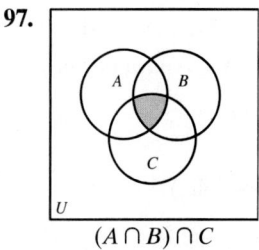

$(A \cap B) \cap C$

99.
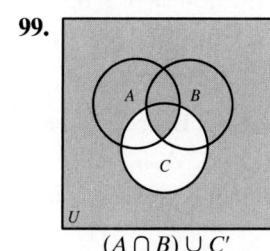

$(A \cap B) \cup C'$

101.
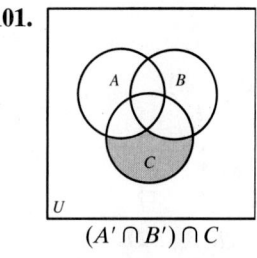

$(A' \cap B') \cap C$

103.
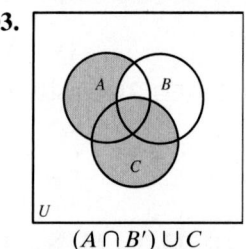

$(A \cap B') \cup C$

105.

$(A \cap B') \cap C'$

107.
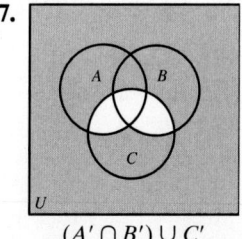

$(A' \cap B') \cup C'$

109. $A' \cap B'$, or $(A \cup B)'$
111. $(A \cup B) \cap (A \cap B)'$, or $(A \cup B) - (A \cap B)$,
or $(A - B) \cup (B - A)$
113. $(A \cap B) \cup (A \cap C)$, or $A \cap (B \cup C)$
115. $(A \cap B) \cap C'$, or $(A \cap B) - C$
117. $A \cap B = \emptyset$ **119.** This statement is true for any set A.
121. $A = \emptyset$ **123.** $A = \emptyset$ **125.** $A = \emptyset$ **127.** $B \subseteq A$
129. always true **131.** always true
133. not always true **135.** always true
137. (a) $\{x \mid x \text{ is a real number}\}$ **(b)** $\emptyset$

2.4 Exercises (pages 71–74)

1. (a) 5 **(b)** 7 **(c)** 0 **(d)** 2 **(e)** 8 **3. (a)** 1 **(b)** 3
(c) 4 **(d)** 0 **(e)** 2 **(f)** 8 **(g)** 2 **(h)** 6 **5.** 21
7. 7 **9.** 35

11.
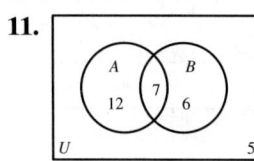

13.
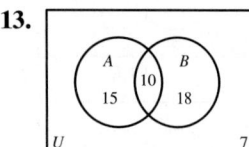

15.
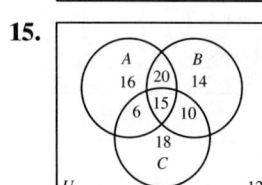

17.
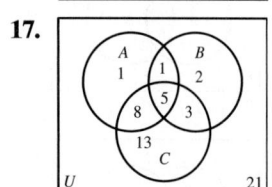

19. (a) 2 **(b)** 4 **21. (a)** 25 **(b)** 20 **(c)** 12 **(d)** 10
(e) 19 **23. (a)** 37 **(b)** 38 **25. (a)** 500 **(b)** 91
27. (a) 31 **(b)** 24 **(c)** 11 **(d)** 45 **29. (a)** 1
(b) 1, 2, 3, 4, 5, 6, 7, 8, 9, 10, 11, 12, 13, 14, 15
(c) 1, 2, 3, 4, 5, 9, 11 **(d)** 5, 8, 13 **31. (a)** 9 **(b)** 9
(c) 20 **(d)** 20 **(e)** 27 **(f)** 15 **33.** Answers will vary.

Extension Exercises (pages 79–80)

1. B; 1 **3.** A; $\aleph_0$ **5.** F; 0
7. (Other correspondences are possible.)

$$\{I, \quad II, \quad III\}$$
$$\updownarrow \quad \updownarrow \quad \updownarrow$$
$$\{x, \quad y, \quad z\}$$

9. (Other correspondences are possible.)

$$\{a, \quad d, \quad i, \quad t, \quad o, \quad n\}$$
$$\updownarrow \quad \updownarrow \quad \updownarrow \quad \updownarrow \quad \updownarrow \quad \updownarrow$$
$$\{a, \quad n, \quad s, \quad w, \quad e, \quad r\}$$

11. 11 **13.** 0 **15.** $\aleph_0$ **17.** $\aleph_0$ **19.** $\aleph_0$ **21.** 12
23. $\aleph_0$ **25.** both **27.** equivalent **29.** equivalent

31. $\{2, \quad 4, \quad 6, \quad 8, \quad \ldots, \quad 2n, \quad \ldots\}$
$\quad\;\;\, \updownarrow \quad \updownarrow \quad \updownarrow \quad \updownarrow \qquad\;\; \updownarrow$
$\quad\;\;\,\{1, \quad 2, \quad 3, \quad 4, \quad \ldots, \quad n, \quad \ldots\}$

33. $\{1{,}000{,}000, \quad 2{,}000{,}000, \quad 3{,}000{,}000, \quad \ldots, \quad 1{,}000{,}000n, \quad \ldots$
$\qquad\; \updownarrow \qquad\qquad \updownarrow \qquad\qquad \updownarrow \qquad\qquad\qquad\quad \updownarrow$
$\{ \quad 1, \qquad\qquad 2, \qquad\qquad 3, \qquad \ldots, \qquad\quad n, \qquad \ldots$

35. $\{2, \quad 4, \quad 8, \quad 16, \quad 32, \quad \ldots, \quad 2^n, \quad \ldots\}$
$\quad\;\;\, \updownarrow \quad \updownarrow \quad \updownarrow \quad \updownarrow \quad \updownarrow \qquad\quad \updownarrow$
$\quad\;\;\,\{1, \quad 2, \quad 3, \quad 4, \quad 5, \quad \ldots, \quad n, \quad \ldots\}$

37. This statement is not always true. For example, let
A = the set of counting numbers, B = the set of real
numbers.
39. This statement is not always true. For example, A
could be the set of all subsets of the set of reals. Then
$n(A)$ would be an infinite number *greater* than c.
41. (a) Rays emanating from point P will establish a
geometric pairing of the points on the semicircle with the
points on the line.

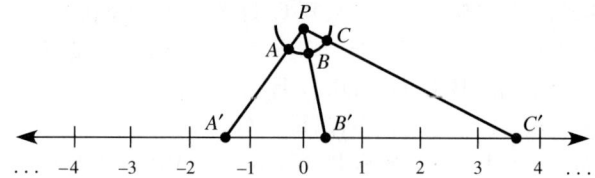

(b) The set of real numbers is infinite, having been
placed in a one-to-one correspondence with a proper
subset of itself.

43. $\{3, \quad 6, \quad 9, \quad 12, \quad \ldots, \quad 3n, \quad \ldots\}$
$\quad\;\;\, \updownarrow \quad \updownarrow \quad \updownarrow \quad \updownarrow \qquad\qquad \updownarrow$
$\quad\;\;\,\{6, \quad 9, \quad 12, \quad 15, \quad \ldots, \quad 3n + 3, \quad \ldots\}$

45. $\left\{\dfrac{3}{4}, \quad \dfrac{3}{8}, \quad \dfrac{3}{12}, \quad \dfrac{3}{16}, \quad \ldots, \quad \dfrac{3}{4n}, \quad \ldots\right\}$
$\quad\;\;\, \updownarrow \quad\; \updownarrow \quad\; \updownarrow \quad\; \updownarrow \qquad\qquad \updownarrow$
$\quad\;\;\,\left\{\dfrac{3}{8}, \quad \dfrac{3}{12}, \quad \dfrac{3}{16}, \quad \dfrac{3}{20}, \quad \ldots, \quad \dfrac{3}{4n + 4}, \quad \ldots\right\}$

47. $\left\{\dfrac{1}{9}, \quad \dfrac{1}{18}, \quad \dfrac{1}{27}, \quad \ldots, \quad \dfrac{1}{9n}, \quad \ldots\right\}$
$\quad\;\;\, \updownarrow \quad\; \updownarrow \quad\; \updownarrow \qquad\qquad \updownarrow$
$\quad\;\;\,\left\{\dfrac{1}{18}, \quad \dfrac{1}{27}, \quad \dfrac{1}{36}, \quad \ldots, \quad \dfrac{1}{9n + 9}, \quad \ldots\right\}$

49. Answers will vary. **51.** Answers will vary.

Chapter 2 Test (pages 81–82)

1. $\{a, b, c, d, e\}$ **2.** $\{a, b, d\}$ **3.** $\{c, f, g, h\}$ **4.** $\{a, c\}$
5. true **6.** false **7.** true **8.** true **9.** false **10.** true
11. true **12.** true **13.** 8 **14.** 15
Answers may vary in Exercises 15.–18. **15.** the set of
odd integers between -4 and 10 **16.** the set of months
of the year **17.** $\{x \mid x \text{ is a negative integer}\}$ **18.** $\{x \mid x$
is a multiple of 8 between 20 and 90$\}$ **19.** $\subseteq$ **20.** neither

21.
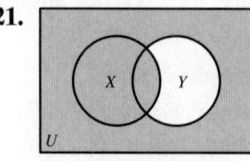
$X \cup Y'$

22.
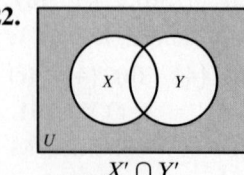
$X' \cap Y'$

23.
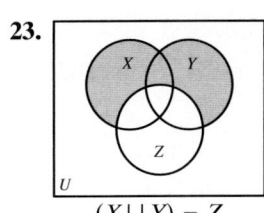
$(X \cup Y) - Z$

24.
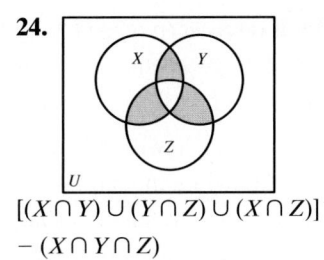
$[(X \cap Y) \cup (Y \cap Z) \cup (X \cap Z)]$
$- (X \cap Y \cap Z)$

25. {Electric razor}   **26.** {Adding machine, Barometer, Pendulum clock, Thermometer}   **27.** {Electric razor}
28. Answers will vary.   **29. (a)** 22   **(b)** 12   **(c)** 28
30. (a) 16   **(b)** 32   **(c)** 33   **(d)** 45   **(e)** 14   **(f)** 26

CHAPTER 3 INTRODUCTION TO LOGIC

3.1 Exercises *(pages 88–90)*

1. statement   **3.** not a statement   **5.** statement
7. statement   **9.** statement   **11.** not a statement
13. statement   **15.** compound   **17.** not compound
19. not compound   **21.** compound   **23.** Her aunt's name is not Hermione.   **25.** At least one dog does not have its day.   **27.** No book is longer than this book.
29. At least one computer repairman can play blackjack.
31. Someone does not love somebody sometime.
33. $x \leq 12$ **35.** $x < 5$ **37.** Answers will vary.
39. She does not have green eyes.   **41.** She has green eyes and he is 60 years old.   **43.** She does not have green eyes or he is 60 years old.   **45.** She does not have green eyes or he is not 60 years old.   **47.** It is not the case that she does not have green eyes and he is 60 years old.
49. $p \wedge \sim q$ **51.** $\sim p \vee q$ **53.** $\sim(p \vee q)$ or, equivalently, $\sim p \wedge \sim q$ **55.** Answers will vary.
57. C   **59.** A, B   **61.** A, C   **63.** B   **65.** true
67. true   **69.** true   **71.** true   **73.** false   **75.** Answers will vary.   **77.** Every person here has done that at one time or another.

3.2 Exercises *(pages 99–100)*

1. false   **3.** true   **5.** They must both be false.   **7.** T
9. T   **11.** F   **13.** T   **15.** T   **17.** T   **19.** It is a disjunction, because it means "$6 > 2$ or $6 = 2$."   **21.** T
23. F   **25.** T   **27.** T   **29.** F   **31.** F   **33.** T   **35.** T
37. T   **39.** 4   **41.** 16   **43.** 128   **45.** seven   **47.** FFTF
49. FTTT   **51.** TTTT   **53.** FFFT   **55.** TFFF
57. FFFFTFFF   **59.** FTFTTTTT
61. TTTTTTTTTTTTFTTT   **63.** You can't pay me now and you can't pay me later.   **65.** It is not summer or there is snow.   **67.** I did not say yes or she did not say no.   **69.** $6 - 1 \neq 5$ or $9 + 13 = 7$ **71.** Neither Prancer nor Vixen will lead Santa's reindeer sleigh next Christmas.

73. T   **75.** F   **77.**

p	q	$p \veebar q$
T	T	F
T	F	T
F	T	T
F	F	F

79. F   **81.** T   **83.** The lady is behind Door 2. *Reasoning:* Suppose that the sign on Door 1 is true. Then the sign on Door 2 would also be true, but this is impossible. So the sign on Door 2 must be true, and the sign on Door 1 must be false. Because the sign on Door 1 says the lady is in Room 1, and this is false, the lady must be behind Door 2.

3.3 Exercises *(pages 107–109)*

1. If you see it on the Internet, then you can believe it.
3. If an integer is divisible by 10, then it is divisible by 5.
5. If the soldier is a marine, then the soldier loves boot camp.   **7.** If it is a panda, then it does not live in Idaho.
9. If it is an opium-eater, then it has no self-command.
11. true   **13.** true   **15.** false   **17.** true   **19.** Answers will vary.   **21.** F   **23.** T   **25.** T   **27.** If they do not raise alpacas, then he trains dogs.   **29.** If she has a bird for a pet, then they raise alpacas and he trains dogs.   **31.** If he does not train dogs, then they do not raise alpacas or she has a bird for a pet.   **33.** $b \rightarrow p$ **35.** $p \rightarrow \sim s$
37. $p \wedge (s \rightarrow \sim b)$ **39.** $p \rightarrow s$ **41.** T   **43.** F
45. T   **47.** F   **49.** T   **51.** T   **53.** Answers will vary.
55. TTTF   **57.** TTFT   **59.** TTTT; tautology   **61.** TFTF
63. TTTTTTFT   **65.** TTTFTTTTTTTTTTTT
67. one   **69.** That is an authentic Rolex watch and I am not surprised.   **71.** The English measures are not converted to metric measures and the spacecraft does not crash on the surface of Saturn.   **73.** You want to be happy for the rest of your life and you make a pretty woman your wife.   **75.** You do not give your plants tender, loving care or they flourish.   **77.** She does or he will.   **79.** The person is not a resident of Pensacola or is a resident of Florida.   **81.** equivalent   **83.** equivalent
85. not equivalent   **87.** equivalent   **89.** equivalent
91. $(p \wedge q) \vee (p \wedge \sim q)$; The statement simplifies to p.
93. $p \vee (\sim q \wedge r)$ **95.** $\sim p \vee (p \vee q)$; The statement simplifies to T.
97. The statement simplifies to $p \wedge q$.

99. The statement simplifies to F.

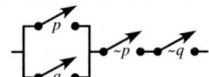

101. The statement simplifies to $(r \wedge \sim p) \wedge q$.

103. The statement simplifies to $p \vee q$.

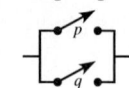

105. $525.60

3.4 Exercises *(pages 114–115)*

1. (a) If you were an hour, then beauty would be a minute.   **(b)** If beauty were not a minute, then you would not be an hour.   **(c)** If you were not an hour, then beauty would not be a minute.   **3. (a)** If you don't fix it, then it ain't broke.   **(b)** If it's broke, then fix it.
(c) If you fix it, then it's broke.   **5. (a)** If it is dangerous to your health, then you walk in front of a moving car.
(b) If you do not walk in front of a moving car, then it is not dangerous to your health.   **(c)** If it is not dangerous to your health, then you do not walk in front of a moving car.   **7. (a)** If they flock together, then they are birds of a feather.   **(b)** If they are not birds of a feather, then they do not flock together.   **(c)** If they do not flock together, then they are not birds of a feather.
9. (a) If he comes, then you built it.   **(b)** If you don't build it, then he won't come.   **(c)** If he doesn't come, then you didn't build it.   **11. (a)** $\sim q \rightarrow p$ **(b)** $\sim p \rightarrow q$
(c) $q \rightarrow \sim p$ **13. (a)** $\sim q \rightarrow \sim p$ **(b)** $p \rightarrow q$ **(c)** $q \rightarrow p$
15. (a) $(q \vee r) \rightarrow p$ **(b)** $\sim p \rightarrow (\sim q \wedge \sim r)$
(c) $(\sim q \wedge \sim r) \rightarrow \sim p$ **17.** Answers will vary.
19. If it is muddy, then I'll wear my galoshes.   **21.** If 19 is positive, then $19 + 1$ is positive.   **23.** If a number is an integer, then it is a rational number.   **25.** If I do logic puzzles, then I am driven crazy.   **27.** If Jeff Marsalis is to shave, then he must have a day's growth of beard.
29. If I go from Boardwalk to Baltic Avenue, then I pass GO.   **31.** If a number is a whole number, then it is an integer.   **33.** If their pitching improves, then the Nationals will win the pennant.   **35.** If the figure is a rectangle, then it is a parallelogram with a right angle.
37. If a triangle has two perpendicular sides, then it is a right triangle.   **39.** If a two-digit number whose units digit is 5 is squared, then the square will end in 25.
41. D   **43.** Answers will vary.   **45.** true   **47.** false
49. false   **51.** contrary   **53.** consistent   **55.** contrary
57. consistent   **59.** Answers will vary. One example is: That man is Otis Taylor. That man sells books.

3.5 Exercises *(pages 119–120)*

1. valid   **3.** invalid   **5.** valid   **7.** invalid   **9.** invalid
11. invalid   **13.** yes
15. All people with blue eyes have blond hair.
   Natalie Graham does not have blond hair.
   Natalie Graham does not have blue eyes.
17. invalid   **19.** valid   **21.** invalid   **23.** valid
25. invalid   **27.** invalid   **29.** valid

Extension Exercises *(pages 122–124)*

1. Drew, spanakopita, Fresh Air, spearmint; Ilse, buffalo-chicken sandwich, Deltoids, cinnamon; Nash, French onion soup, Liplickers, vanilla; Uma, tuna-salad sandwich, TKO, wintergreen; Xerxes, garlic shrimp, Inti-mints, orange   **3.** 1st, Earl, Ox, fire; 2nd, Philip, Rooster, metal; 3rd, Toni, Cow, water; 4th, Lucy, Dragon, earth; 5th, Ivana, Horse, wood

5.

7	4	2	1	6	8	9	3	5
3	1	9	4	5	7	6	2	8
8	6	5	9	3	2	7	1	4
6	2	4	7	8	9	1	5	3
1	3	8	5	4	6	2	9	7
5	9	7	2	1	3	8	4	6
2	5	3	8	7	1	4	6	9
9	7	6	3	2	4	5	8	1
4	8	1	6	9	5	3	7	2

7.

8	3	9	6	5	7	2	4	1
7	1	2	9	4	3	8	5	6
4	5	6	2	1	8	3	7	9
2	6	7	1	9	4	5	3	8
3	9	1	8	2	5	4	6	7
5	4	8	7	3	6	1	9	2
1	2	3	5	6	9	7	8	4
9	8	4	3	7	2	6	1	5
6	7	5	4	8	1	9	2	3

9.

6	1	7	9	2	3	5	8	4
4	5	9	8	6	1	2	7	3
3	2	8	4	5	7	9	6	1
8	3	5	6	4	9	1	2	7
7	6	1	5	3	2	8	4	9
2	9	4	7	1	8	3	5	6
5	7	2	3	9	6	4	1	8
1	8	3	2	7	4	6	9	5
9	4	6	1	8	5	7	3	2

3.6 Exercises *(pages 130–133)*

1. valid by reasoning by transitivity   **3.** valid by modus ponens   **5.** fallacy by fallacy of the converse   **7.** valid by modus tollens   **9.** fallacy by fallacy of the inverse
11. valid by disjunctive syllogism   **13.** invalid   **15.** valid
17. invalid   **19.** valid   **21.** invalid   **23.** invalid
25. invalid
27. Every time something squeaks, I use WD-40.
   Every time I use WD-40, I go to the hardware store.
   Every time something squeaks, I go to the hardware store.

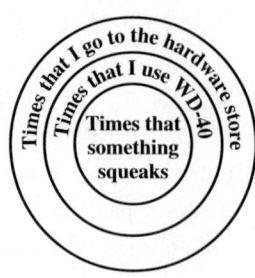

29. valid **31.** invalid **33.** invalid **35.** valid
37. valid **39.** If I tell you the time, then my life will be miserable. **41.** If it is my poultry, then it is a duck.
43. If it is a guinea pig, then it is hopelessly ignorant of music. **45.** If it is a teachable kitten, then it does not have green eyes. **47.** If I can read it, then I have not filed it. **49.** (a) $p \to \sim s$ (b) $r \to s$ (c) $q \to p$
(d) None of my poultry are officers. **51.** (a) $r \to \sim s$
(b) $u \to t$ (c) $\sim r \to p$ (d) $\sim u \to \sim q$ (e) $t \to s$
(f) All pawnbrokers are honest. **53.** (a) $r \to w$
(b) $\sim u \to \sim t$ (c) $v \to \sim s$ (d) $x \to r$ (e) $\sim q \to t$
(f) $y \to p$ (g) $w \to s$ (h) $\sim x \to \sim q$ (i) $p \to \sim u$
(j) I can't read any of Brown's letters.

Collaborative Investigation *(pages 134–135)*
1. Jan. 1, Vandyke Facility, *Penchant*, repair satellite;
Feb. 5, San Simeon Launch Center, *Falconer*, investigate radiation; Mar. 3, Cape Carnival, *Liberty*, land on moon;
Apr. 4, Willard Island, *Twilight*, test propulsion; May 2,
Eddings Air Force Base, *Bravura*, measure magnetic fields

2.

Chapter 3 Test *(pages 135–136)*
1. $6 - 3 \neq 3$ **2.** Some men are not created equal.
3. No members of the class went on the field trip.
4. That's the way you feel and I won't accept it.
5. She did not apply or did not get a student loan.
6. $\sim p \to q$ **7.** $p \to q$ **8.** $\sim q \leftrightarrow \sim p$ **9.** You won't love me and I will love you. **10.** It is not the case that you will love me or I will not love you. (Equivalently: You won't love me and I will love you.) **11.** T **12.** T
13. T **14.** F **15.** Answers will vary. **16.** (a) The antecedent must be true and the consequent must be false. (b) Both component statements must be true.
(c) Both component statements must be false.

17. TFFF **18.** TTTT (tautology) **19.** false **20.** true
Wording may vary in the answers for Exercises 21–25.
21. If the number is an integer, then it is a rational number. **22.** If a polygon is a rhombus, then it is a quadrilateral. **23.** If a number is divisible by 4, then it is divisible by 2. **24.** If she digs dinosaur bones, then she is a paleontologist. **25.** (a) If the graph helps me understand it, then a picture paints a thousand words.
(b) If a picture doesn't paint a thousand words, then the graph won't help me understand it. (c) If the graph doesn't help me understand it, then a picture doesn't paint a thousand words. **26.** (a) $(q \wedge r) \to \sim p$
(b) $p \to (\sim q \vee \sim r)$ (c) $(\sim q \vee \sim r) \to p$ **27.** valid
28. (a) A (b) F (c) C (d) D **29.** valid **30.** invalid

CHAPTER 4 NUMERATION SYSTEMS

4.1 Exercises *(pages 144–145)*
1. 13,036 **3.** 7,630,729 **5.**

7.

9. **11.**

13. **15.** 182 **17.** 14,000,000

19. MMDCCCLXI **21.** $\overline{\text{XXV}}$DCXIX **23.** 935
25. 3007 **27.** **29.** **31.** **33.**

35. 216 **37.** 53,601 **39.** 113 **41.** 7598 **43.** 1504
45. 8128 **47.** 622,500 shekels **49.** Answers will vary.
51. Answers will vary. **53.** 99,999 **55.** 3124
57. $10^d - 1$ **59.** $7^d - 1$ **61.** 9999 **63.** 666

4.2 Exercises (pages 150–151)

1. Mayan; 12   **3.** Babylonian; 32   **5.** Greek; 234
7. Mayan; 242   **9.** Babylonian; 1282   **11.** Babylonian;
2601   **13.** Mayan; 2640   **15.** Mayan; 59,954
17. Babylonian; 80,474   **19.** Greek; 15,149
21. ⟪▼   **23.** ▼▼⟪⟪⟪ ▼   **25.** ⟪▼▼▼ ▼▼ ▼   **27.** ▼⟪⟪▼▼▼⟪⟪
 ▼▼ ⟪⟪ ▼▼   ⟪⟪ ▼▼ ⟪▼▼   ▼⟪⟪▼▼▼ ⟪
29. ⟪▼▼ ▼▼▼   **31.** ÷   **33.** ⁚÷   **35.** ≡⊙   **37.** ⁝⁝⁝
  ⟪▼▼ ▼▼   ≡

39. λθ   **41.** ϙβ   **43.** ɩβ   **45.** ‚βψξθ   **47.** M̄̕ͅδψκϛ

4.3 Exercises (pages 157–158)

1. $(8 \cdot 10^1) + (4 \cdot 10^0)$
3. $(9 \cdot 10^3) + (4 \cdot 10^2) + (4 \cdot 10^1) + (6 \cdot 10^0)$

5. $(4 \cdot 10^3) + (9 \cdot 10^2) + (2 \cdot 10^1) + (4 \cdot 10^0)$
7. $(1 \cdot 10^7) + (4 \cdot 10^6) + (2 \cdot 10^5) + (0 \cdot 10^4) +$
$(6 \cdot 10^3) + (0 \cdot 10^2) + (4 \cdot 10^1) + (0 \cdot 10^0)$
9. 75   **11.** 4380   **13.** 70,401,009   **15.** 79   **17.** 53
19. 109   **21.** 733   **23.** 6   **25.** 206   **27.** 256
29. 63,259   **31.** 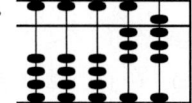   **33.**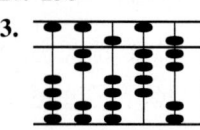

35. 1885   **37.** 38,325   **39.** 3,035,154   **41.** 496
43. 217,204   **45.** 242   **47.** 49,801   **49.** 460   **51.** 32,798

4.4 Exercises (pages 165–167)

1. 1, 2, 3, 4, 5, 6, 10, 11, 12, 13, 14, 15, 16, 20, 21, 22, 23,
24, 25, 26   **3.** 1, 2, 3, 4, 5, 6, 7, 8, 10, 11, 12, 13, 14, 15, 16,
17, 18, 20, 21, 22   **5.** 13_{five}; 20_{five} **7.** $B6E_{sixteen}$; $B70_{sixteen}$
9. 3   **11.** 11   **13.** least: $1000_{three} = 27$; greatest:
$2222_{three} = 80$ **15.** 14   **17.** 11   **19.** 956   **21.** 881
23. 28,854   **25.** 139   **27.** 5601   **29.** 321_{five} **31.** 10011_{two}
33. $93_{sixteen}$ **35.** 2131101_{five} **37.** 1001001010_{two}
39. 102112101_{three} **41.** 111134_{six} **43.** 32_{seven}
45. 1031321_{four} **47.** 11110111_{two} **49.** 467_{eight}
51. 11011100_{two} **53.** $2D_{sixteen}$ **55.** 37_{eight} **57.** 1427
59. 1000011_{two} **61.** 1101011_{two} **63.** HELP
65. $100111011001011110111_{two}$ **67.** Answers will vary.
69.   (a) The binary ones digit is 1.   **(b)** The binary twos
digit is 1.   **(c)** The binary fours digit is 1.   **(d)** The
binary eights digit is 1.   **(e)** The binary sixteens digit is 1.
71. 6   **73.** yes   **75.** yes   **77.** yes   **79.** yes

81. Answers will vary.   **83.** no   **85.** yes   **87.** Answers
will vary.   **89.** 20120011_{three} **91.** 25657_{nine} **93.** 808080
95. FF69B4

Extension Exercises (pages 173–175)

1. 11   **3.** 3   **5.** 6   **7.** 0   **9.** 1900   **11.** 0020
13. first answer: ordinary whole number arithmetic;
second answer: 12-hour clock arithmetic; third answer:
24-hour clock arithmetic   **15.** true   **17.** false   **19.** 4
21. 1   **23.** 0   **25.** 6   **27.** {3, 10, 17, 24, 31, 38, . . . }
29. {1, 2, 3, 4, 5, 6, . . . }   **31.** 100,000   **33.** 153   **35.** Chicago:
July 23 and 29; New Orleans: July 5 and August 16;
San Francisco: August 9   **37.** Sunday   **39.** Wednesday
41. Jan., April, July   **43.** June   **45.** yes   **47.** 6   **49.** no
51. 7   **53.** 3   **55.** 13

Chapter 4 Test (page 177)

1. Egyptian; 1534   **2.** Roman; 10,474   **3.** Chinese; 385
4. Babylonian; 155,540   **5.** Mayan; 50,511   **6.** Greek;
53,524   **7.** 1035   **8.** 23,862   **9.** 13,227   **10.** 73   **11.** 37
12. 48,879   **13.** 110001_{two} **14.** 43210_{five} **15.** 256_{eight}
16. $E8D_{sixteen}$ **17.** 1105   **18.** 101110101101_{two}
19. There is less repetition of symbols.
20. Place values are understood by position.
21. There are fewer symbols to learn.
22. There are fewer digits in the numerals.
23. Answers will vary.
24. $7_{nine} = 21_{three}$, $6_{nine} = 20_{three}$, and $5_{nine} = 12_{three}$. So
$765_{nine} = 212012_{three}$.

4.5 Exercises

1. 5   **3.** 6   **5.** row 2: 0, 6, 10;   row 3: 9, 0, 9;   row 4:
0, 4, 0, 8, 0;   row 5: 1, 9, 2, 7;   row 6: 6, 0, 0;   row 7: 4, 11,
6, 8, 3, 5;   row 8: 8, 4, 0, 0;   row 9: 6, 3, 9, 3, 9, 6, 3;   row
10: 6, 4, 0, 10, 8, 6, 4;   row 11: 10, 9, 8, 7, 6, 5, 4, 3, 2
7. yes   **9.** row 1: 0;   row 2: 0;   row 3: 0, 1, 2   row 4: 0,
1, 2   **11.** yes   **13.** yes (0 is its own inverse, 1 and 4 are
inverses of each other, and 2 and 3 are inverses of each other.)
15. yes   **17.** yes (1 is the identity element.)   **19.** 3
21. 4   **23.** Answers will vary.   **25.** 0700   **27.** 0000
29. false   **31.** true   **33.** 3   **35.** 3   **37.** 1
39. 10   **41.** Answers will vary.   **43.** 5   **45.** 4
47. row 1: 0;   row 2: 2, 3, 4, 5, 6, 0, 1;   row 3: 3, 4, 5, 6, 0, 1,
2;   row 4: 4, 5, 6, 0, 1, 2, 3;   row 5: 5, 6, 0, 1, 2, 3, 4;   row 6:
6, 0, 1, 2, 3, 4, 5   **49.** row 2: 1   **51.** row 2: 1, 3, 7;   row
3: 3, 0;   row 4: 3, 2, 1;   row 5: 6, 7, 4;   row 7: 3, 1, 6, 4;
row 8: 6, 5, 2   **53.** {3, 10, 17, 24, 31, 38, . . . }
55. {1, 2, 3, 4, 5, 6, . . . }   **57.** 100,000

59. (a) 365 **(b)** Friday **61.** 62 **63.** Chicago: July 23 and 29; New Orleans: July 5 and August 16; San Francisco: August 9 **65.** Sunday **67.** Wednesday **69.** June **71.** June **73.** yes **75.** 6 **77.** 2

4.6 Exercises

1. all properties; 1 is the identity element; 1 is its own inverse, as is 2. **3.** closure, commutative, associative, and identity properties; 1 is the identity element; 2, 4, and 6 have no inverses. **5.** all properties except the inverse; 1 is the identity element; 5 has no inverse. **7.** all properties; F is the identity element; A and B are inverses; F is its own inverse. **9.** all properties; t is the identity element; s and r are inverses; t and u are their own inverses. **11.** a **13.** a **15.** row b: d; row c: d, b; row d: b, c **17.** associative, commutative, identity (U), closure **19.** Answers may vary. One possibility is shown.

	a	b	c	d
a	a	b	c	d
b	b	a	d	c
c	c	d	a	b
d	d	c	b	a

21. no **23. (a)** true **(b)** true **(c)** true **(d)** true **25.** $a + b + c = 1$ or $a = 0$ **27. (a)** $a = 0$ **(b)** $a = 0$ **29.** Each side simplifies to e. **31.** Each side simplifies to d. **33.**

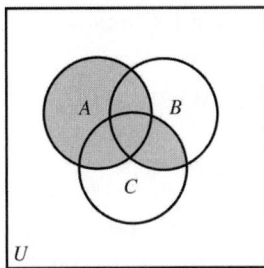

$$A \cup (B \cap C) = (A \cup B) \cap (A \cup C)$$

35. Both final columns read TTTTTFFF, when set up in the manner described in Chapter 3.

4.7 Exercises

1. No operation is specified. **3.** yes **5.** no; closure, inverse **7.** yes **9.** no; inverse **11.** no; associative, identity, inverse **13.** no; inverse **15.** yes **17.** no; closure, identity, inverse **19.** Answers will vary. **21.** S **23.** N **25.** Each side is equal to M. **27.** Each side is equal to Q. **29.** N **31.** R **33.** T **35.** no **37.** yes **39.** Answers will vary. **41.** Answers will vary. **43.** row B: D; row C: D, B; row D: C, B **45. (a)** yes **(b)** Answers will vary. **47. (a)** no **(b)** Answers will vary.

CHAPTER 5 NUMBER THEORY

5.1 Exercises (pages 184–185)

1. true **3.** true **5.** false **7.** true **9.** 1, 2, 3, 4, 6, 12 **11.** 1, 2, 4, 7, 14, 28 **13. (a)** no **(b)** yes **(c)** no **(d)** no **(e)** no **(f)** no **(g)** no **(h)** no **(i)** no **15. (a)** yes **(b)** yes **(c)** yes **(d)** yes **(e)** yes **(f)** yes **(g)** yes **(h)** yes **(i)** yes **17. (a)** Answers will vary. **(b)** 13 **(c)** square root; square root; square root **(d)** prime **19.** 2, 3; no **21.** It must be 0. **23.**

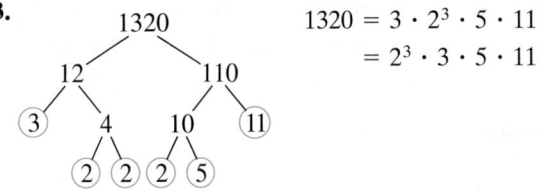

$$1320 = 3 \cdot 2^3 \cdot 5 \cdot 11$$
$$= 2^3 \cdot 3 \cdot 5 \cdot 11$$

25. $2^3 \cdot 3 \cdot 7$ **27.** $2^2 \cdot 3^2 \cdot 13$ **29.** yes **31.** no **33.** no **35.** yes **37.** The number must be divisible by both 3 and 5. That is, the sum of the digits must be divisible by 3, and the last digit must be 5 or 0. **39.** 0, 2, 4, 6, 8 **41.** 0, 4, 8 **43.** 0, 6 **45.** 8 **47.** 27 **49.** leap year **51.** not a leap year **53.** Answers will vary. **55.** Answers will vary.

5.2 Exercises (pages 189–190)

1. true **3.** false **5.** false **7.** $37 = 1^2 + 6^2; 41 = 4^2 + 5^2$ **9.** Answers will vary. **11.** $41^2 - 41 + 41 = 41^2$, and 41^2 is not a prime. **13.** B **15. (a)** 65,537 **(b)** 251 **17.** Answers will vary. **19.** Answers will vary. **21.** composite; $30,031 = 59 \cdot 509$ **23.** 63 **25.** $2^p - 1$ **27.** 3 and 31

5.3 Exercises (pages 195–197)

1. true **3.** true **5.** true **7.** false **9.** true **11.** The sum of the proper divisors is 496: $1 + 2 + 4 + 8 + 16 + 31 + 62 + 124 + 248 = 496$. **13.** 8191 is prime; 33,550,336 **15.** $1 + \frac{1}{2} + \frac{1}{3} + \frac{1}{6} = 2$ **17.** deficient **19.** abundant **21.** 12, 18, 20, 24 **23.** $1 + 3 + 5 + 7 + 9 + 15 + 21 + 27 + 35 + 45 + 63 + 105 + 135 + 189 + 315 = 975$, and $975 > 945$, so 945 is abundant. **25.** $1 + 2 + 4 + 8 + 16 + 32 + 37 + 74 + 148 + 296 + 592 = 1210$ and $1 + 2 + 5 + 10 + 11 + 22 + 55 + 110 + 121 + 242 + 605 = 1184$ **27.** $5 + 11$ **29.** $7 + 23$ **31. (a)** Let $a = 5$ and $b = 3$; $11 = 5 + 2 \cdot 3$ **(b)** $17 = 3 + 2 \cdot 7 = 7 + 2 \cdot 5 = 11 + 2 \cdot 3 = 13 + 2 \cdot 2$ **33.** 41 and 43 **35. (a)** $3^4 - 1 = 80$ is divisible by 5. **(b)** $2^6 - 1 = 63$ is divisible by 7. **37.** $5^2 + 2 = 27 = 3^3$ **39.** Answers will vary. **41.** False; For the first six, the sequence is 6, 8, 6, 8, 6, 6. **43.** one;

not happy **45.** both; happy **47.** Answers will vary.
49. B **51.** 7; yes **53.** 15; no **55.** 27; no
57. 24; 23; 25; yes; no **59.** Answers will vary. **61.** B

5.4 Exercises *(pages 203–205)*

1. true **3.** true **5.** false **7.** true **9.** true **11.** 20
13. 60 **15.** 13 **17.** 18 **19.** 10 **21.** 6 **23.** 8 **25.** 12
27. 80 **29.** Answers will vary. **31.** 270 **33.** 450
35. 840 **37.** 96 **39.** 225 **41.** 2160 **43.** 224 **45.** 216
47. 2400 **49. (a)** $p^b q^c r^c$ **(b)** $p^a q^a r^b$ **51.** 30 **53.** 15
55. 12 **57. (a)** 6 **(b)** 36 **59. (a)** 18 **(b)** 216
61. p and q are relatively prime. **63.** Answers will vary.
65. 144th **67.** 48 **69.** $600; 25 books

Extension Exercises *(page 211)*

1. 3 **3.** 4 **5.** 5 **7.** 2 **9.** 2 **11.** 13 **13.** 12 **15.** 3
17. 55; 40 **19.** 65; 48 **21.** 5 **23.** 61 **25. (a)** 27
(b) 35 **27. (a)** 11 **(b)** 23 **29.** Answers will vary.

5.5 Exercises *(pages 216–218)*

1. 2584 **3.** 28,657 **5.** $\frac{1 + \sqrt{5}}{2}$
7. $1 + 1 + 2 + 3 + 5 + 8 = 21 - 1$; Each expression is
equal to 20. **9.** $1 + 2 + 5 + 13 + 34 + 89 = 144$;
Each expression is equal to 144. **11.** $13^2 - 5^2 = 144$;
Each expression is equal to 144. **13.** $1 - 2 + 5 - 13 +$
$34 - 89 = -8^2$; Each expression is equal to -64.
15. (There are other ways to do this.) **(a)** $37 = 34 + 3$
(b) $40 = 34 + 5 + 1$ **(c)** $52 = 34 + 13 + 5$
17. (a) The greatest common factor of 10 and 4 is 2, and
the greatest common factor of $F_{10} = 55$ and $F_4 = 3$ is
$F_2 = 1$. **(b)** The greatest common factor of 12 and 6 is 6,
and the greatest common factor of $F_{12} = 144$ and $F_6 = 8$ is
$F_6 = 8$. **(c)** The greatest common factor of 14 and 6 is 2,
and the greatest common factor of $F_{14} = 377$ and $F_6 = 8$ is
$F_2 = 1$. **19. (a)** $5 \cdot 34 - 13^2 = 1$ **(b)** $13^2 - 3 \cdot 55 = 4$
(c) $2 \cdot 89 - 13^2 = 9$ **(d)** The difference will be 25,
because we are obtaining the squares of the terms of the
Fibonacci sequence. $13^2 - 1 \cdot 144 = 25 = 5^2$. **21.** 199
23. Each sum is 2 less than a Lucas number.
25. (a) $8 \cdot 18 = 144$; Each expression is equal to 144.
(b) $8 + 21 = 29$; Each expression is equal to 29.
(c) $8 + 18 = 2 \cdot 13$; Each expression is equal to 26.
(d) $18 + 47 = 5 \cdot 13$; Each expression is equal to 65.
27. 3, 4, 5 **29.** 16, 30, 34 **31.** The sums are 1, 1, 2, 3, 5,
8, 13. They are terms of the Fibonacci sequence.
33. $\frac{1 + \sqrt{5}}{2} \approx 1.618033989$ and $\frac{1 - \sqrt{5}}{2} \approx -0.618033989$.
After the decimal point, the digits are the same.
35. 377 **37.** 17,711

Chapter 5 Test *(pages 219–220)*

1. false **2.** true **3.** true **4.** true **5.** true **6.** false
7. (a) yes **(b)** no **(c)** yes **(d)** yes **(e)** no **(f)** yes
(g) no **(h)** yes **(i)** no **8. (a)** composite **(b)** prime
(c) neither **9.** $2^3 \cdot 3^2 \cdot 5 \cdot 7$ **10.** Answers will vary.
11. (a) abundant **(b)** deficient **(c)** perfect **12.** C
13. 59 and 61 **14.** 27 **15.** 450 **16.** Monday
17. 75,025 **18.** $89 - (8 + 13 + 21 + 34) = 13$;
Each expression is equal to 13. **19.** B **20.** 1, 5, 6, 11,
17, 28, 45, 73 **21.** The process will yield 19 for any term
chosen. **22.** A **23.** Answers will vary. **24.** Answers
will vary.

CHAPTER 6 THE REAL NUMBERS AND THEIR REPRESENTATIONS

6.1 Exercises *(pages 228–230)*

1. 5 **3.** 0 **5.** $\sqrt{14}$ (There are others.) **7.** true
9. true **11. (a)** 3, 7 **(b)** 0, 3, 7 **(c)** $-9, 0, 3, 7$
(d) $-9, -1\frac{1}{4}, -\frac{3}{5}, 0, 3, 5.9, 7$ **(e)** $-\sqrt{7}, \sqrt{5}$ **(f)** All are
real numbers. **13.** Answers will vary. **15.** 1046 **17.** 5436
19. $-220°$ **21.** 30; 15°; $-5°$ **23. (a)** Pacific Ocean,
Indian Ocean, Caribbean Sea, South China Sea,
Gulf of California **(b)** Point Success, Ranier,
Matlalcueyetl, Steele, McKinley **(c)** true **(d)** false

25. **27.**

29. (a) A **(b)** A **(c)** B **(d)** B **31. (a)** 2 **(b)** 2
33. (a) -6 **(b)** 6 **35. (a)** -3 **(b)** 3 **37. (a)** 0
(b) 0 **39.** $a - b$ **41.** -12 **43.** -8 **45.** 3 **47.** $|-3|$,
or 3 **49.** $-|-6|$, or -6 **51.** $|5 - 3|$, or 2 **53.** true
55. true **57.** true **59.** false **61.** true **63.** false
65. (a) Louisiana; It decreased 4.1%. **(b)** West Virginia;
It increased 0.6%. **67.** fabric mills **Answers will vary
in Exercises 69–73.** **69.** $\frac{1}{2}, \frac{5}{8}, 1\frac{3}{4}$ **71.** $-3\frac{1}{2}, -\frac{2}{3}, \frac{3}{7}$
73. $\sqrt{5}, \pi, -\sqrt{3}$

6.2 Exercises *(pages 238–242)*

1. negative **3.** $-3; 5$ **5.** Answers will vary. **7.** -20
9. -4 **11.** -11 **13.** 9 **15.** 20 **17.** 4 **19.** 24
21. -1296 **23.** 6 **25.** -6 **27.** 0 **29.** -6 **31.** 27
33. 39 **35.** -4 **37.** -2 **39.** not a real number **41.** 13
43. A, B, C **45.** commutative property of addition
47. inverse property of addition **49.** identity property of
multiplication **51.** associative property of addition

53. identity property of addition **55.** distributive property **57.** inverse property of addition **59.** closure property of multiplication **61. (a)** $-2; 2$ **(b)** commutative **(c)** Yes; choose $a = b$. For example, let $a = b = 2$. Then $2 - 2 = 2 - 2$. **63. (a)** messing up your room **(b)** spending money **(c)** decreasing the volume on your MP3 player **65.** identity **67.** No, it does not hold true. **69.** -81 **71.** 81 **73.** -81 **75.** -81 **77. (a)** 25.9 (billion dollars) **(b)** 58.2 (billion dollars) **(c)** 153.0 (billion dollars) **(d)** 237.1 (billion dollars) **79. (a)** 2000: $129 billion; 2010: $206 billion; 2020: $74 billion; 2030: $-$501 billion **(b)** The cost of Social Security will exceed revenue in 2030 by $501 billion. **81.** 16 **83.** $1045.55 **85.** 14,776 feet **87.** 45°F **89.** 112°F **91.** -60°F **93.** 27 feet **95.** 469 B.C. **97.** $15,000 **99.** $2900

6.3 Exercises *(pages 251–254)*

1. A, C, D **3.** C **5.** $\frac{1}{3}$ **7.** $-\frac{3}{7}$ **Answers will vary in Exercises 9 and 11.** **9.** $\frac{6}{16}, \frac{9}{24}, \frac{12}{32}$ **11.** $-\frac{10}{14}, -\frac{15}{21}, -\frac{20}{28}$ **13. (a)** $\frac{1}{3}$ **(b)** $\frac{1}{4}$ **(c)** $\frac{2}{5}$ **(d)** $\frac{1}{3}$ **15.** the dots in the intersection of the triangle and the rectangle as a part of the dots in the entire figure **17. (a)** O'Brien **(b)** Goldberg **(c)** Goldberg **(d)** Kelly **(e)** Taylor and Britz; $\frac{1}{2}$ **19.** $\frac{1}{2}$ **21.** $\frac{43}{48}$ **23.** $-\frac{5}{24}$ **25.** $\frac{23}{56}$ **27.** $\frac{27}{20}$ **29.** $\frac{5}{12}$ **31.** $\frac{1}{9}$ **33.** $\frac{3}{2}$ **35.** $\frac{3}{2}$ **37. (a)** $4\frac{1}{2}$ cups **(b)** $\frac{7}{8}$ cup **39.** $\frac{13}{3}$ **41.** $\frac{29}{10}$ **43.** $6\frac{3}{4}$ **45.** $6\frac{1}{8}$ **47.** $-17\frac{7}{8}$ **49.** $\frac{9}{16}$ inch **51.** 3 **53.** $\frac{3}{7}$ **55.** $-\frac{103}{89}$ **57.** $\frac{25}{9}$ **59.** $\frac{5}{8}$ **61.** $\frac{19}{30}$ **63.** $-\frac{3}{4}$ **65.** $53,221 **67.** $\frac{14}{19}$ **69.** $\frac{13}{29}$ **71.** $\frac{16}{14}$, or $\frac{8}{7}$ **73.** $\frac{5}{2}$ **75.** It gives the rational number halfway between the two integers (their average). **77.** 0.75 **79.** 0.1875 **81.** $0.\overline{27}$ **83.** $0.\overline{285714}$ **85.** $\frac{2}{5}$ **87.** $\frac{17}{20}$ **89.** $\frac{467}{500}$ **91.** repeating **93.** terminating **95.** terminating **97. (a)** $0.\overline{3}$, or $0.333\ldots$ **(b)** $0.\overline{6}$, or $0.666\ldots$ **(c)** $0.\overline{9}$, or $0.999\ldots$ **(d)** $1 = 0.\overline{9}$ **99. (a)** $\frac{4}{5}$ **(b)** $\frac{4}{5}$ **101. (a)** $\frac{33}{50}$ **(b)** $\frac{33}{50}$

6.4 Exercises *(pages 261–264)*

1. rational **3.** irrational **5.** rational **7.** rational **9.** irrational **11.** rational **13.** irrational **15. (a)** $0.\overline{8}$ **(b)** irrational; rational **17.** 6.244997998 **19.** 3.885871846 **21.** 29.73213749 **23.** 1.060660172 **25.** $5\sqrt{2}$; 7.071067812 **27.** $5\sqrt{3}$; 8.660254038 **29.** $12\sqrt{2}$; 16.97056275 **31.** $\frac{5\sqrt{6}}{6}$; 2.041241452 **33.** $\frac{\sqrt{7}}{2}$; 1.322875656 **35.** $\frac{\sqrt{21}}{3}$; 1.527525232 **37.** $3\sqrt{17}$ **39.** $4\sqrt{7}$ **41.** $10\sqrt{2}$ **43.** $3\sqrt{3}$

45.

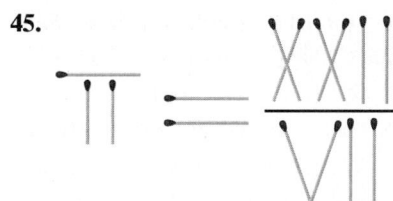

47. The result is 3.1415929, which agrees with the first seven digits in the decimal for π. **49.** 3 **51.** 4 **53.** 3.3 **55.** ϕ is positive, while its conjugate is negative. The units digit of ϕ is 1, and the units digit of its conjugate is 0. The decimal digits agree. **57.** It is just a coincidence that 1828 appears back-to-back early in the decimal. There is no repetition indefinitely, which would be indicative of a rational number. **59.** 2.5 seconds **61.** 15.3 miles **63.** 392,000 square miles **65.** The area and the perimeter are both numerically equal to 36. **67.** 5.4 feet **69. (a)** 70.5 mph **(b)** 59.8 mph **(c)** 53.9 mph **71.** 4 **73.** 7 **75.** 6 **77.** 1 **79.** 4 **81.** 8 **The number of decimal digits shown will vary among caculator models in Exercises 83–89.** **83.** 3.50339806 **85.** 5.828476683 **87.** 10.06565066 **89.** 5.578019845

6.5 Exercises *(pages 272–276)*

1. true **3.** false **5.** true **7.** true **9.** false **11.** 11.315 **13.** -4.215 **15.** 0.8224 **17.** 47.5 **19.** 31.6 **21.** $525 billion **23.** three (and you would have 0.01¢ left over) **25.** $0.06, or 6¢ **27.** 1000 **29. (a)** 0.031 **(b)** 0.035 **31.** 297 **33. (a)** 78.4 **(b)** 78.41 **35. (a)** 0.1 **(b)** 0.08 **37. (a)** 12.7 **(b)** 12.69 **39.** 42% **41.** 36.5% **43.** 0.8% **45.** 210% **47.** 20% **49.** 1% **51.** $37\frac{1}{2}$% **53.** 150% **55.** Answers will vary. **57. (a)** 5 **(b)** 24 **(c)** 8 **(d)** 0.5, or $\frac{1}{2}$ **(e)** 600 **59.** No, the price is $57.60. **61. (a)** .586 **(b)** .519 **(c)** .463 **(d)** .395 **63.** 124.8 **65.** 2.94 **67.** 150% **69.** 600 **71.** 1.4% **73.** 8% **75.** 3.8% **77.** 47.5% **79.** A **81.** C **83.** about 139% **85. (a)** $14.7 - 40 \cdot 0.13$ **(b)** 9.5 **(c)** 8.075; walking (5 mph) **87.** 892% **89.** $4.50 **91.** $0.75 **93.** $12.00 **95.** $36.00 **97.** Answers will vary.

Extension Exercises *(page 279)*

1. $12i$ **3.** $-15i$ **5.** $i\sqrt{3}$ **7.** $5i\sqrt{3}$ **9.** -5 **11.** -18 **13.** -40 **15.** $\sqrt{2}$ **17.** $3i$ **19.** 6 **21.** 1 **23.** -1 **25.** $-i$ **27.** i

Chapter 6 Test *(pages 280–282)*

1. (a) 12 **(b)** 0, 12 **(c)** $-4, 0, 12$ **(d)** $-4, -\frac{3}{2}, -0.5, 0, 4.1, 12$ **(e)** $-\sqrt{5}, \sqrt{3}$ **(f)** $-4, -\sqrt{5}, -\frac{3}{2}, -0.5, 0, \sqrt{3}, 4.1, 12$ **2. (a)** C **(b)** B **(c)** D **(d)** A

3. (a) false **(b)** true **(c)** true **(d)** false **4.** 4 **5.** 10
6. 3 **7. (a)** Minnesota; 52.74% **(b)** Maine; 10.63%
(c) false **(d)** true **8.** 5296 ft **9. (a)** $2900 **(b)** −$4000
(c) −$21,300 **(d)** −$19,100 **10. (a)** E **(b)** A **(c)** B
(d) D **(e)** F **(f)** C **11. (a)** Whitney and McElwain
(b) Moura and Dawkins **(c)** Whitney **(d)** Pritchard
and Miller; $\frac{2}{5}$ **(e)** McElwain ("J-Mac") **12.** $\frac{11}{16}$ **13.** $\frac{57}{160}$
14. $-\frac{2}{5}$ **15.** $\frac{3}{2}$ **16. (a)** 0.45 **(b)** $0.41\overline{6}$ **17. (a)** $\frac{18}{25}$
(b) $\frac{58}{99}$ **18. (a)** irrational **(b)** rational **(c)** rational
(d) rational **(e)** irrational **(f)** irrational
19. (a) 12.247448714 **(b)** $5\sqrt{6}$ **20. (a)** 4.913538149
(b) $\frac{13\sqrt{7}}{7}$ **21. (a)** −45.254834 **(b)** $-32\sqrt{2}$ **22.** Answers
will vary. **23. (a)** 13.81 **(b)** −0.315 **(c)** 38.7 **(d)** −24.3
24. (a) 9.04 **(b)** 9.045 **25. (a)** 16.65 **(b)** 101.5
26. (a) $26\frac{2}{3}\%$ **(b)** $66\frac{2}{3}\%$ **27.** D **28.** 1656; 1008; 16%;
6% **29.** 17,415,000 **30.** −13.8 (billion dollars)

CHAPTER 7 THE BASIC CONCEPTS OF ALGEBRA

7.1 Exercises (pages 290–293)

1. A and C **3.** Both sides are evaluated as 48, so 12 is
a solution. **5.** solution set **7.** B **9.** {−1} **11.** {3}
13. {−7} **15.** {0} **17.** $\left\{-\frac{5}{3}\right\}$ **19.** $\left\{-\frac{1}{2}\right\}$ **21.** {2}
23. {−2} **25.** {7} **27.** {2} **29.** $\left\{\frac{3}{2}\right\}$ **31.** {−5}
33. {3} **35.** 2 (that is, 10^2, or 100) **37.** {4} **39.** {0}
41. {0} **43.** {2000} **45.** {25} **47.** {40}
49. identity, contradiction **51.** contradiction; ∅
53. conditional; {−8} **55.** conditional; {0}
57. identity; {all real numbers} **59.** D **61.** $t = \frac{d}{r}$
63. $b = \frac{\mathscr{A}}{h}$ **65.** $a = P - b - c$ **67.** $b = \frac{2\mathscr{A}}{h}$
69. $h = \frac{S - 2\pi r^2}{2\pi r}$, or $h = \frac{S}{2\pi r} - r$ **71.** $F = \frac{9}{5}C + 32$
73. $h = \frac{3V}{\pi r^2}$ **75. (a)** $5460 **(b)** 2013
77. (a) 0.0352 **(b)** approximately 0.015, or 1.5%
(c) approximately 1 case

7.2 Exercises (pages 301–305)

1. expression **3.** equation **5.** expression **7.** yes
9. $x - 12$ **11.** $(x - 6)(x + 4)$ **13.** $\frac{25}{x}$ $(x \neq 0)$
15. Answers will vary. **17.** 3 **19.** 6 **21.** −3
23. Bon Jovi: $210.7 million; Bruce Springsteen:
$204.6 million **25.** wins: 62; losses: 20
27. Democrats: 58; Republicans: 40 **29.** shortest piece:
15 inches; middle piece: 20 inches; longest piece: 24 inches
31. gold: 51; silver: 21; bronze: 28 **33.** 70 milliliters
35. $250 **37.** $24.85 **39.** 4 liters **41.** 5 liters
43. 1 gallon **45.** $4000 at 3%; $8000 at 4%

47. $10,000 at 4.5%; $19,000 at 3% **49.** $58,000
51. 17 pennies, 17 dimes, 10 quarters **53.** 305 students,
105 nonstudents **55.** 54 seats on Row 1; 51 seats on Row 2
57. 44-cent stamps: 30; 17-cent stamps: 25
59. 328 miles **61.** No, it is not correct. The distance is
$55\left(\frac{1}{2}\right) = 27.5$ miles. **63.** $1\frac{3}{4}$ hours **65.** 11:00 A.M.
67. 8 hours **69.** 18 miles **71.** 3.326 hours
73. 1.715 hours **75.** 7.97 meters per second
77. 8.47 meters per second

7.3 Exercises (pages 313–318)

1. $\frac{5}{8}$ **3.** $\frac{1}{4}$ **5.** $\frac{2}{1}$ **7.** $\frac{3}{1}$ **9.** D **11.** Answers will vary.
13. true **15.** false **17.** true **19.** {35} **21.** {−1}
23. $\left\{-\frac{27}{4}\right\}$ **25.** $30.00 **27.** $8.75 **29.** $67.50
31. $44.55 **33.** 4 feet **35.** 2.7 inches **37.** 2.0 inches
39. $2\frac{5}{8}$ cups **41.** $428.82 **43.** 12,500 fish
45. 10-lb size; $0.429 **47.** 32-oz size; $0.093
49. 128-oz size; $0.051 **51.** 36-oz size; $0.049
53. $x = 4$ **55.** $x = 1; y = 4$
57. (a)   **(b)** 54 feet

59. $237 **61.** $272 **63.** 9 **65.** 125 **67.** $\frac{4}{9}$ **69.** $40.32
71. 20 miles per hour **73.** about 302 pounds
75. 100 pounds per square inch **77.** 20 pounds per
square foot **79.** 144 feet **81.** 1.105 liters
83. $\frac{8}{9}$ metric ton **85.** 6.2 pounds

7.4 Exercises (pages 325–327)

1. D **3.** B **5.** F **7.** Use parentheses when the symbol
is < or >. Use brackets when the symbol is ≤ or ≥.
9. $[5, \infty)$ **11.** $(7, \infty)$
13. $(-4, \infty)$ **15.** $(-\infty, -40]$
17. $(-\infty, 4]$ **19.** $\left(-\infty, -\frac{15}{2}\right)$
21. $\left[\frac{1}{2}, \infty\right)$ **23.** $(3, \infty)$
25. $(-\infty, 4)$ **27.** $\left(-\infty, \frac{23}{6}\right]$
29. $\left(-\infty, \frac{76}{11}\right)$ **31.** $(-\infty, \infty)$
33. ∅ **35.** Answers will vary.
37. $(1, 11)$ **39.** $[-14, 10]$

41. $[-5, 6]$ **43.** $\left[-\frac{14}{3}, 2\right]$

45. $\left[-\frac{1}{2}, \frac{35}{2}\right]$ **47.** $\left(-\frac{1}{3}, \frac{1}{9}\right)$

49. April, May, June, July **51.** January, February, March, August, September, October, November, December

53. PA in 2006, OH in 2005 and 2006, IA in 2005 and 2006

55. $x > y$ **57.** 2 miles **59.** at least 80 **61.** 167 miles

63. (a) 140 to 184 pounds **(b)** Answers will vary.

65. 26 DVDs

7.5 Exercises (pages 337–339)

1. A **3.** A **5.** D **7.** 625 **9.** −32 **11.** −8 **13.** −81

15. $\frac{1}{49}$ **17.** $-\frac{1}{49}$ **19.** −128 **21.** $\frac{16}{5}$ **23.** 125 **25.** $\frac{25}{16}$

27. $\frac{9}{20}$ **29.** 1 **31.** 1 **33.** 0 **35.** reciprocal; additive

inverse **37.** D **39.** x^{16} **41.** 5 **43.** $\frac{1}{27}$ **45.** $\frac{1}{81}$ **47.** $\frac{1}{t^7}$

49. $9x^2$ **51.** $\frac{1}{a^5}$ **53.** x^{11} **55.** r^6 **57.** $-\frac{56}{k^2}$ **59.** $\frac{1}{z^4}$

61. $-\frac{3}{r^7}$ **63.** $\frac{27}{a^{18}}$ **65.** $\frac{x^5}{y^2}$ **67.** D **69.** 2.3×10^2

71. 2×10^{-2} **73.** 6500 **75.** 0.0152 **77.** 6×10^5

79. 2×10^5 **81.** 2×10^5 **83.** $\$1 \times 10^9; \$1 \times 10^{12};$

$\$3.1 \times 10^{12}; 2.10385 \times 10^5$ **85.** $\$1.869 \times 10^{10}$

87. 1×10^{10} **89.** 2,000,000,000 **91. (a)** 3.041×10^8

(b) $\$1 \times 10^{12}$ **(c)** $3288 **93.** approximately

9.474×10^{-7} parsec **95.** 300 seconds

97. approximately 5.87×10^{12} miles **99.** 20,000 hours

7.6 Exercises (pages 347–348)

1. $x^2 - x + 3$ **3.** $9y^2 - 4y + 4$

5. $6m^4 - 2m^3 - 7m^2 - 4m$

7. $-2x^2 - 13x + 11$ **9.** $x^2 - 5x - 24$

11. $28r^2 + r - 2$ **13.** $12x^5 + 8x^4 - 20x^3 + 4x^2$

15. $4m^2 - 9$ **17.** $16m^2 + 16mn + 4n^2$

19. $25r^2 + 30rt + 9t^4$ **21.** $-2z^3 + 7z^2 - 11z + 4$

23. $m^2 + mn - 2n^2 - 2km + 5kn - 3k^2$

25. $a^2 - 2ab + b^2 + 4ac - 4bc + 4c^2$

27. A **29.** Answers will vary. **31.** $2m^2(4m^2 + 3m - 6)$

33. $4k^2m^3(1 + 2k^2 - 3m)$ **35.** $2(a + b)(1 + 2m)$

37. $(m - 1)(2m^2 - 7m + 7)$ **39.** $(2s + 3)(3t - 5)$

41. $(t^3 + s^2)(r - p)$ **43.** $(8a + 5b)(2a - 3b)$

45. $(5z - 2x)(4z - 9x)$ **47.** $(1 - a)(1 - b)$

49. $(x - 5)(x + 3)$ **51.** $(y + 7)(y - 5)$

53. $6(a - 10)(a + 2)$ **55.** $3m(m + 1)(m + 3)$

57. $(3k - 2p)(2k + 3p)$ **59.** $(5a + 3b)(a - 2b)$

61. $(7x + 2y)(3x - y)$ **63.** $2a^2(4a - b)(3a + 2b)$

65. $5xy^2(3xy^3 - 4x^2y + 3)$

67. $(3m - 2)^2$ **69.** $2(4a - 3b)^2$ **71.** $(2xy + 7)^2$

73. $(x + 6)(x - 6)$ **75.** $(y + w)(y - w)$

77. $(3a + 4)(3a - 4)$ **79.** $(5s^2 + 3t)(5s^2 - 3t)$

81. $(p^2 + 25)(p + 5)(p - 5)$

83. $(2 - a)(4 + 2a + a^2)$

85. $(5x - 3)(25x^2 + 15x + 9)$

87. $(3y^3 + 5z^2)(9y^6 - 15y^3z^2 + 25z^4)$

89. $(x + y)(x - 5)$ **91.** $(6m - 7n)(2m + 5n)$

93. $(2z + 7)^2$ **95.** $(10x + 7y)(100x^2 - 70xy + 49y^2)$

97. $(5m^2 - 6)(25m^4 + 30m^2 + 36)$

99. $(m - 2n)(p^4 + q)$

7.7 Exercises (pages 352–356)

1. $5; 4; -8$ **3.** Answers will vary. $\left\{\pm\frac{\sqrt{10}}{2}\right\}$

5. $\{-3, 9\}$ **7.** $\left\{\frac{7}{2}, -\frac{1}{5}\right\}$ **9.** $\{-3, 4\}$ **11.** $\{-7, -2\}$

13. $\left\{-\frac{1}{2}, \frac{1}{6}\right\}$ **15.** $\{-2, 4\}$ **17.** $\{\pm 8\}$ **19.** $\left\{\pm 2\sqrt{6}\right\}$

21. $\emptyset$ **23.** $\{1, 7\}$ **25.** $\left\{4 \pm \sqrt{3}\right\}$ **27.** $\left\{\frac{5 \pm \sqrt{13}}{2}\right\}$

29. $\left\{\frac{2 \pm \sqrt{3}}{2}\right\}$ **31.** $\left\{\frac{1 \pm \sqrt{3}}{2}\right\}$ **33.** $\left\{\frac{1 \pm \sqrt{5}}{2}\right\}$

35. $\left\{\frac{-1 \pm \sqrt{2}}{2}\right\}$ **37.** $\left\{\frac{1 \pm \sqrt{29}}{2}\right\}$ **39.** $\emptyset$

41. The presence of $2x^3$ makes it a *cubic* equation

(degree 3). **43.** 0; (c) **45.** 121; (a) **47.** 360; (b)

49. two **51.** 5.2 seconds **53.** Find s when $t = 0$.

55. (a) 1 second and 8 seconds **(b)** 9 seconds after it is

projected **57.** 8, 15, 17 **59.** 412.3 feet

61. eastbound ship: 80 miles; southbound ship: 150 miles

63. 5 centimeters, 12 centimeters, 13 centimeters

65. length: 2 centimeters; width: 1.5 centimeters

67. 1 foot **69.** length: 26 meters; width: 16 meters

71. length: 20 inches; width: 12 inches **73.** 5 or 14

75. $\{2\}$

Extension Exercises (page 357)

1. $\left\{-2i\sqrt{3}, 2i\sqrt{3}\right\}$ **3.** $\left\{1 + \frac{2}{3}i, 1 - \frac{2}{3}i\right\}$

5. $\left\{3 + i\sqrt{5}, 3 - i\sqrt{5}\right\}$ **7.** $\left\{\frac{1}{2} + \frac{\sqrt{6}}{2}i, \frac{1}{2} - \frac{\sqrt{6}}{2}i\right\}$

9. $\left\{-\frac{2}{3} + \frac{\sqrt{2}}{3}i, -\frac{2}{3} - \frac{\sqrt{2}}{3}i\right\}$

Chapter 7 Test (pages 359–360)

1. $\{2\}$ **2.** $\{4\}$ **3.** identity; {all real numbers}

4. $v = \frac{s + 16t^2}{t}$, or $v = \frac{s}{t} + 16t$ **5.** Hawaii: 4021 square

miles; Maui: 728 square miles; Kauai: 551 square miles

6. 5 liters **7.** 2.2 hours **8.** 16 slices for $4.38

9. 2300 miles **10.** 200 amps

11. $(-\infty, 4]$ **12.** $(-2, 6]$

13. C **14.** at least 82 **15.** $\frac{16}{9}$ **16.** −64 **17.** $\frac{64}{27}$ **18.** 0

19. $\frac{216}{p^4}$ **20.** $\frac{1}{m^{14}}$ **21. (a)** 693,000,000 **(b)** 0.000000125

22. 3×10^{-4} **23.** about 15,300 seconds

24. $4k^2 + 6k + 10$ **25.** $15x^2 - 14x - 8$ **26.** $16x^4 - 9$

27. $3x^3 + 20x^2 + 23x - 36$ **28.** One example is

$t^5 + 2t^4 + 3t^3 - 4t^2 + 5t + 6$. **29.** $(2p - 3q)(p - q)$

30. $(10x + 7y)(10x - 7y)$

31. $(3y - 5x)(9y^2 + 15yx + 25x^2)$

32. $(4 - m)(x + y)$ **33.** $\left\{-\frac{3}{2}, \frac{1}{3}\right\}$ **34.** $\left\{\pm\sqrt{13}\right\}$

35. $\left\{\frac{1 \pm \sqrt{29}}{2}\right\}$ **36.** 0.87 second

CHAPTER 8 GRAPHS, FUNCTIONS, AND SYSTEMS OF EQUATIONS AND INEQUALITIES

8.1 Exercises *(pages 367–370)*

1. x **3.** $(0, 0)$ **5. (a)** I   **(b)** III
(c) II   **(d)** IV   **(e)** none   **7. (a)** I or III
(b) II or IV   **(c)** II or IV   **(d)** I or III
9.–18.

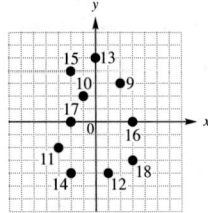

19. (a) x represents the year; y represents the revenue in billions of dollars   **(b)** about \$2400 billion
(c) $(2006, 2400)$

21. (a) $\sqrt{34}$ **(b)** $\left(\frac{1}{2}, \frac{5}{2}\right)$ **23. (a)** $\sqrt{61}$ **(b)** $\left(\frac{1}{2}, 1\right)$

25. (a) $\sqrt{146}$ **(b)** $\left(-\frac{1}{2}, \frac{3}{2}\right)$ **27.** B   **29.** D

31. $x^2 + y^2 = 36$ **33.** $(x + 1)^2 + (y - 3)^2 = 16$

35. $x^2 + (y - 4)^2 = 3$ **37.** center: $(0, 0)$; radius: r

39. $(-2, -3); 2$ **41.** $(-5, 7); 9$ **43.** $(2, 4); 4$

45.   **47.**

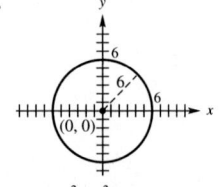   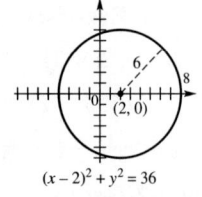

$x^2 + y^2 = 36$ $(x - 2)^2 + y^2 = 36$

49.   **51.**

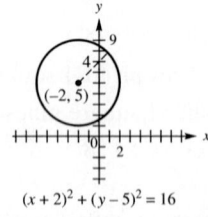   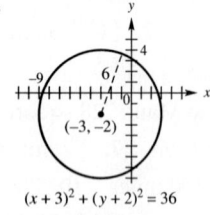

$(x + 2)^2 + (y - 5)^2 = 16$ $(x + 3)^2 + (y + 2)^2 = 36$

53. (a) $\sqrt{40} = 2\sqrt{10}$ **(b)** $(-1, 4)$ **55.** 24.15%;
This is very close to the actual figure.   **57.** \$15,481
59. Answers will vary.   **61.** Answers will vary.
63. The epicenter is $(-2, -2)$.   **65.** Answers will vary.
67. $(9, 18)$ **69.** B

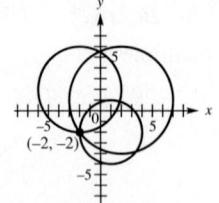

1. $(0, 5), \left(\frac{5}{2}, 0\right), (1, 3), (2, 1)$ **3.** $(0, -4), (4, 0), (2, -2),$
$(3, -1)$

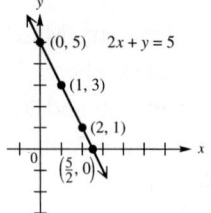   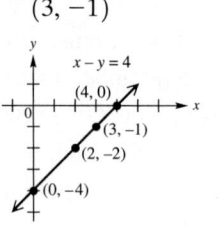

5. $(0, 4), (5, 0), \left(3, \frac{8}{5}\right), \left(\frac{5}{2}, 2\right)$

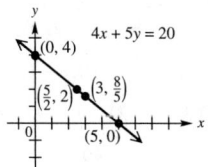

7. $(0, 4), \left(\frac{8}{3}, 0\right), (2, 1), (4, -2)$

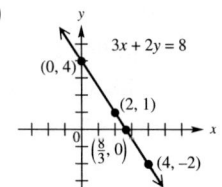

9. Answers will vary.   **11.** A
13. $(4, 0);$ $(0, 6)$

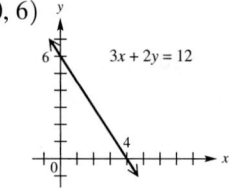

15. $(2, 0);$ $\left(0, \frac{5}{3}\right)$ **17.** $\left(\frac{5}{2}, 0\right);$ $(0, -5)$

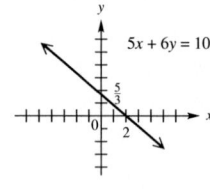   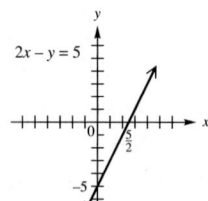

19. $(2, 0)$ $\left(0, -\frac{2}{3}\right)$ **21.** $(0, 0);$ $(0, 0)$

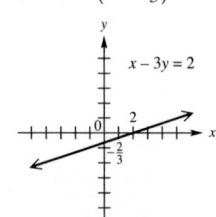   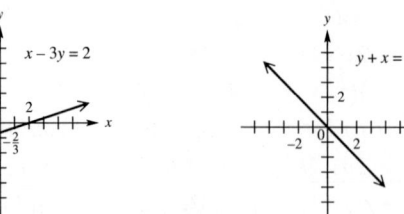

23. $(0, 0);$ $(0, 0)$ **25.** $(2, 0);$ none

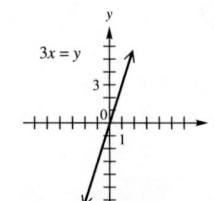   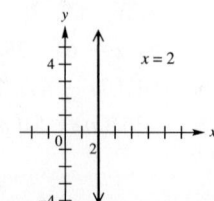

27. none; (0, 4)

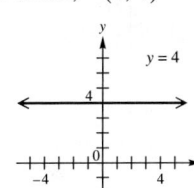

29. C **31.** A **33.** D **35.** B
37. $\frac{3}{10}$ **39.** (a) $\frac{3}{2}$ (b) $-\frac{7}{4}$ **41.** 8
43. $-\frac{5}{6}$ **45.** 0 **47.** (a) 232
(b) positive; increased
(c) 232,000 students per year
(d) -0.95 (e) negative;
decreased (f) 0.95 student per
computer per year

49.

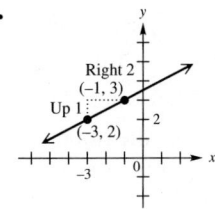

51.

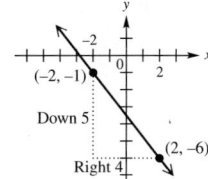

53.

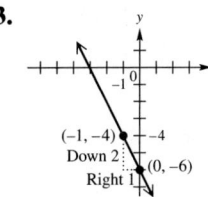

55.

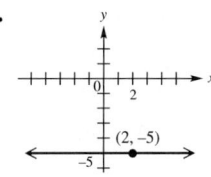

57.

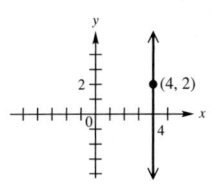

59. parallel **61.** perpendicular
63. neither parallel nor
perpendicular **65.** $\frac{7}{10}$
67. $-\$4000$ per year; The value of
the machine is decreasing by an
average of $4000 per year during
those years.

69. (a) -28.27 thousand mobile homes per year
(b) The negative slope means that the number of mobile
homes *decreased* by an average of 28.27 thousand per
year from 2000 to 2006. **71.** $1371.67 million per year;
Sales of plasma TVs *increased* by an average of $1371.67
million per year from 2003 to 2006.

8.3 Exercises *(pages 385–388)*

1. D **3.** B **5.** A **7.** C **9.** H **11.** B
13. $y = 3x - 3$ **15.** $y = -x + 3$ **17.** $y = -\frac{3}{4}x + \frac{5}{2}$
19. $y = -2x + 18$ **21.** $y = \frac{1}{2}x + \frac{13}{2}$ **23.** $y = 4x - 12$
25. $y = 5$ **27.** $x = 9$ **29.** $x = 0.5$ **31.** $y = 8$
33. $y = 2x - 2$ **35.** $y = -\frac{1}{2}x + 4$ **37.** $y = \frac{2}{13}x + \frac{6}{13}$
39. $y = 5$ **41.** $x = 7$ **43.** $y = -3$ **45.** $y = 5x + 15$
47. $y = -\frac{2}{3}x + \frac{4}{5}$ **49.** $y = \frac{2}{5}x + 5$ **51.** Answers
will vary. **53.** (a) $y = -x + 12$ (b) -1 (c) $(0, 12)$
55. (a) $y = -\frac{5}{2}x + 10$ (b) $-\frac{5}{2}$ (c) $(0, 10)$
57. (a) $y = \frac{2}{3}x - \frac{10}{3}$ (b) $\frac{2}{3}$ (c) $\left(0, -\frac{10}{3}\right)$
59. $y = 3x - 19$ **61.** $y = \frac{1}{2}x - 1$ **63.** $y = -\frac{1}{2}x + 9$
65. $y = 7$ **67.** (a) $y = 1294.7x + 3921$; Sales of digital
cameras in the United States *increased* by $1294.7 million

per year from 2003 to 2006. (b) $9099.8 million
69. (a) $y = 0.996x + 34.3$ (b) 79.1%
71. (a) $y = -790.25x + 101,430$ (b) 97,479 million;
The result using the model is a bit low.
73. (a) $y = 14.55x + 262.42$ (b) 2525 light-years
75. (a) $32°; 212°$ (b) $(0, 32); (100, 212)$ (c) $\frac{9}{5}$
(d) $F = \frac{9}{5}C + 32$ (e) $C = \frac{5}{9}(F - 32)$ (f) When
Celsius temperature is $50°$, Fahrenheit temperature is $122°$.

8.4 Exercises *(pages 397–399)*

1. Answers will vary. **3.** function; domain: {0, 1, 2, 4};
range: {0, 1, 4, 16} **5.** not a function; domain: {1, 2, 3};
range: $\{-9, -4, -1, 1, 4, 9\}$ **7.** not a function; domain:
$(0, \infty)$; range: $(-\infty, 0) \cup (0, \infty)$ **9.** function; domain:
{Hispanic, Native American, Asian American, African
American, White}; range in millions: {21.3, 1.6, 8.2, 24.6,
152.0} **11.** function; domain: $(-\infty, \infty)$; range: $(-\infty, 4]$
13. not a function; domain: $[-4, 4]$; range: $[-3, 3]$
15. function; domain: $(-\infty, \infty)$ **17.** not a function;
domain: $[0, \infty)$ **19.** not a function; domain: $(-\infty, \infty)$
21. function; domain: $[0, \infty)$ **23.** function; domain:
$(-\infty, 0) \cup (0, \infty)$ **25.** function; domain: $\left[-\frac{1}{2}, \infty\right)$
27. function; domain: $(-\infty, 2) \cup (2, \infty)$ **29.** (a) $[0, 3000]$
(b) 25 hours; 25 hours (c) 2000 gallons (d) $g(0) = 0$;
The pool is empty at time zero. **31.** Here is one
example: The cost of gasoline; number of gallons
purchased; cost; number of gallons **33.** 5 **35.** 2
37. -1 **39.** -13 **41.** 3 **43.** 0
45.

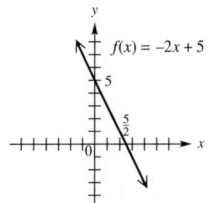

47.

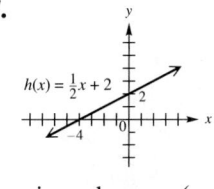

domain and range: $(-\infty, \infty)$

domain and range: $(-\infty, \infty)$

49.

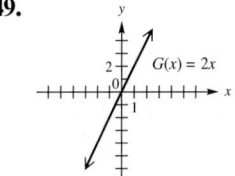

51.

domain and range: $(-\infty, \infty)$ domain: $(-\infty, \infty)$; range: {5}
53. (a) $f(x) = 3 - 2x^2$ (b) -15
55. (a) $f(x) = \frac{8 - 4x}{-3}$ (b) $\frac{4}{3}$ **57.** line; -2; $-2x + 4$;
$-2; 3; -2$ **59.** (a) $0; \$2.50; \$5.00; \$7.50$ (b) $2.50x$
(c)

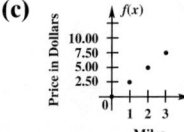

61. (a) 194.53 centimeters **(b)** 177.29 centimeters
(c) 177.41 centimeters **(d)** 163.65 centimeters
63. (a) \$160 **(b)** 70 mph **(c)** 66 mph
(d) for speeds more than 80 mph
65. (a) $C(x) = 0.02x + 200$ **(b)** $R(x) = 0.04x$
(c) 10,000 **(d)**

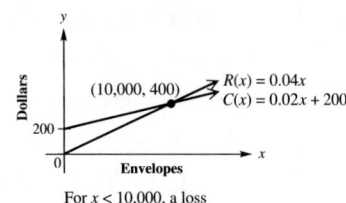

For $x < 10{,}000$, a loss
For $x > 10{,}000$, a profit

67. (a) $C(x) = 3.00x + 2300$ **(b)** $R(x) = 5.50x$
(c) 920 **(d)**

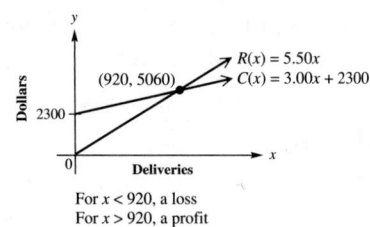

For $x < 920$, a loss
For $x > 920$, a profit

8.5 Exercises (pages 407–408)

1. F **3.** C **5.** E **7.** Answers will vary **9.** $(0, 0)$
11. $(0, 4)$ **13.** $(1, 0)$ **15.** $(-3, -4)$ **17.** Answers will
vary. **19.** downward; narrower **21.** upward; wider
23. (a) I **(b)** IV **(c)** II **(d)** III

25.

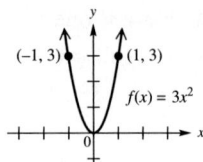

27.

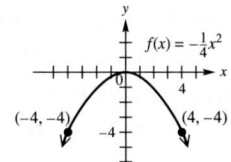

29.

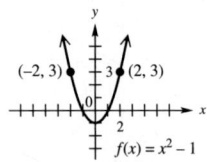

31.

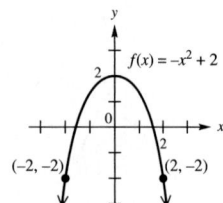

33.

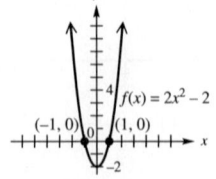

35.

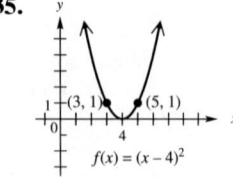

37.

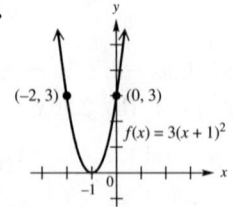

39.

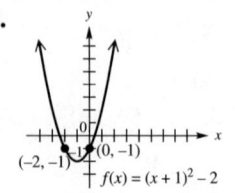

41.

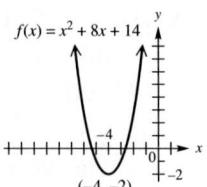

43.

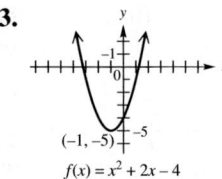

45.

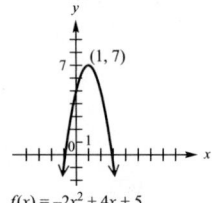

47. 25 meters **49.** 16 feet;
2 seconds **51.** 4.1 seconds;
81.6 meters **53. (a)** 19.2
hours **(b)** 84.3 ppm
55. $f(45) = 161.5$; This
means that when the speed
is 45 mph, the stopping
distance is 161.5 feet.

8.6 Exercises (pages 416–418)

1. rises; falls **3.** does not **5.** rises; falls **7.** does not
9. 2.56425419972 **11.** 1.25056505582
13. 7.41309466897 **15.** 0.0000210965628481
17.

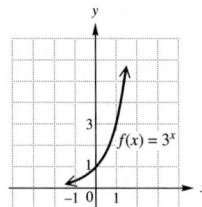

19.

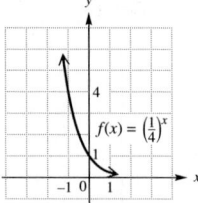

21. 20.0855369232 **23.** 0.018315638889
25. $2 = \log_4 16$ **27.** $-3 = \log_{2/3}\left(\frac{27}{8}\right)$ **29.** $2^5 = 32$
31. $3^1 = 3$ **33.** 1.38629436112 **35.** -1.0498221245
37. (a) 0.5°C **(b)** 0.35°C **39. (a)** 1.6°C **(b)** 0.5°C
41.

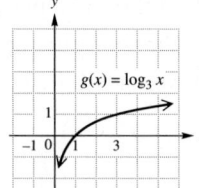

43.

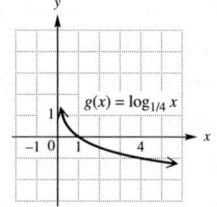

45. (a) \$22,510.18 **(b)** \$22,529.85 **47. (a)** \$31,870.48
(b) \$31,870.67 **49.** Plan A is better by \$121.81.
51. (a) 7% compounded quarterly **(b)** \$800.32
53. 27.73 years **55.** 21.97 years **57. (a)** 828 millibars
(b) 232 millibars **59. (a)** 146,250 thousand
(b) 198,403 thousand **(c)** It will have increased by
almost 36%. **61. (a)** 440 grams **(b)** 387 grams
(c) 264 grams **(d)** 21.66 years **63.** 1611.97 years
65. about 9000 years **67.** about 13,000 years

8.7 Exercises (pages 425–426)

1. 3; -6 **3.** D; The ordered pair solution must be in
quadrant IV. **5.** yes **7.** no **9.** B **11.** A

13. $\{(2, 2)\}$

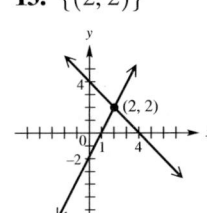

15. $\{(3, -1)\}$ **17.** $\{(2, -3)\}$

19. $\left\{\left(\frac{3}{2}, -\frac{3}{2}\right)\right\}$ **21.** $\left\{\left(\frac{6-2y}{7}, y\right)\right\}$

23. $\{(2, -4)\}$ **25.** $\emptyset$

27. $\{(1, 2)\}$ **29.** $\left\{\left(\frac{22}{9}, \frac{22}{3}\right)\right\}$ **31.** $\{(2, 3)\}$ **33.** $\{(5, 4)\}$

35. $\left\{\left(-5, -\frac{10}{3}\right)\right\}$ **37.** $\{(2, 6)\}$ **39.** Answers will vary.

41. $\{(1, 4, -3)\}$ **43.** $\{(0, 2, -5)\}$ **45.** $\left\{\left(-\frac{7}{3}, \frac{22}{3}, 7\right)\right\}$

47. $\{(4, 5, 3)\}$ **49.** $\{(2, 2, 2)\}$ **51.** $\left\{\left(\frac{8}{3}, \frac{2}{3}, 3\right)\right\}$

53. 2000, 2001, 2002, first part of 2003   **55.** approximately (3.6, 10.5) (Values may vary slightly based on the method of solution.)

8.8 Exercises *(pages 432–436)*

1. wins: 95; losses: 67   **3.** length: 94 feet; width: 50 feet
5. weekend days: 3; weekdays: 3   **7.** square: 12 cm;
triangle: 8 cm   **9.** cappucino: $1.95; house latte: $2.35
11. New York: $615; Washington: $514   **13.** New York
Yankees: $72.97; Boston Red Sox: $50.24   **15.** NHL:
$288.23; NBA: $291.93   **17. (a)** 12 ounces
(b) 30 ounces   **(c)** 48 ounces   **(d)** 60 ounces
19. $2.29x   **21.** 15% solution: $26\frac{2}{3}$ liters; 33% solution:
$13\frac{1}{3}$ liters   **23.** 3 liters   **25.** 50% juice: 150 liters; 30%
juice: 50 liters   **27.** $1.20 candy: 100 pounds; $2.40
candy: 60 pounds   **29.** 4%: $10,000; 3%: $5000
31. (a) $(10 - x)$ mph   **(b)** $(10 + x)$ mph   **33.** train:
60 mph; plane: 160 mph   **35.** boat: 21 mph; current:
3 mph   **37.** gold: 23; silver: 21; bronze: 28   **39.** 10 inches,
20 inches, 26 inches   **41.** type A: 80; type B: 160;
type C: 250   **43.** $16 tickets: 1170; $23 tickets: 985;
$40 tickets: 130   **45.** wins: 53; losses: 19;
overtime losses: 10

Extension Exercises *(page 440)*

1. $\{(2, 3)\}$ **3.** $\{(-3, 0)\}$ **5.** $\left\{\left(\frac{7}{2}, -1\right)\right\}$ **7.** $\{(1, -4)\}$
9. $\{(-1, 23, 16)\}$ **11.** $\{(2, 1, -1)\}$ **13.** $\{(3, 2, -4)\}$
15. $\{(0, 1, 0)\}$ **17.** $\{(-1, 2, 0)\}$ **19.** AT&T:
$124.0 billion; Verizon: $97.4 billion

8.9 Exercises *(pages 444–446)*

1. C   **3.** B

5.

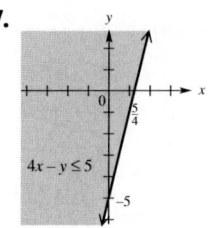

7.

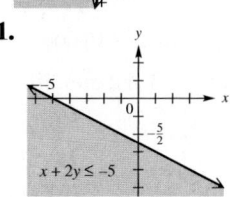

9.

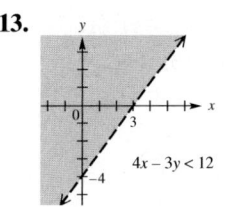

11.

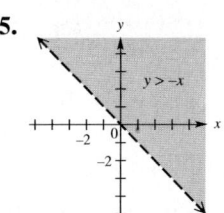

13.

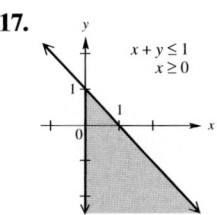

15.

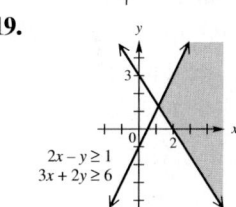

17.

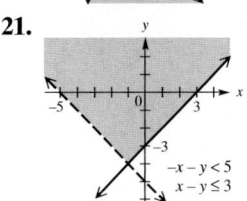

19.

21.

23. maximum of 65 at
$(5, 10)$; minimum of 8 at
$(1, 1)$ **25.** $\left(\frac{6}{5}, \frac{6}{5}\right)$; $\frac{42}{5}$
27. $\left(\frac{17}{3}, 5\right)$; $\frac{49}{3}$

29. Ship 20 to A and 80 to B, for a minimum cost of
$1040.   **31.** Take 3 red pills and 2 blue pills, for a
minimum cost of $0.70 per day.
33. Produce 6.4 million gallons of gasoline and 3.2 million
gallons of fuel oil, for a maximum revenue of $29.76 million.
35. Ship 4000 medical kits and 2000 containers of water.

Chapter 8 Test *(pages 447–448)*
1. $\sqrt{41}$ **2.** $(x + 1)^2 + (y - 2)^2 = 9$

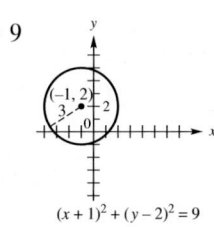

3. x-intercept: $\left(\frac{8}{3}, 0\right)$;
y-intercept: $(0, -4)$

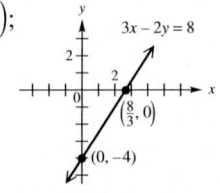

4. $\frac{2}{7}$ **5. (a)** $y = -\frac{2}{5}x + \frac{13}{5}$ **(b)** $y = -\frac{1}{2}x - \frac{3}{2}$
(c) $y = -\frac{1}{2}x + 2$ **6.** B **7. (a)** $y = 0.238x + 63.3$
(b) 80.0 **(c)** 73 (in 1978) **8.** -54.6 million CDs per year
9. $y = 0.05x + 0.50$; $(1, 0.55), (5, 0.75), (10, 1.00)$
10. $y = \frac{2}{3}x + 1$ **11. (a)** $(-\infty, \infty)$ **(b)** 22
12. (a) $(-\infty, 3) \cup (3, \infty)$ **(b)** $f(3)$ is undefined.
13. 500 units; $30,000 **14.** axis: $x = -3$;
vertex: $(-3, 4)$; domain: $(-\infty, \infty)$; range: $(-\infty, 4]$

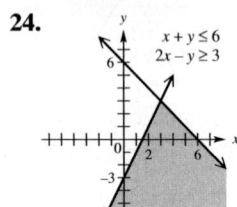

$f(x) = -(x+3)^2 + 4$

15. 80 feet by 160 feet
16. (a) 2116.31264888
(b) 0.157237166314
(c) 3.15955035878 **17. (a)** $12,740.13
(b) $12,742.04 **18. (a)** 1.62 grams
(b) 1.18 grams **(c)** 0.69 gram
(d) 2.00 grams

19. $\{(4, -2)\}$ **20.** $\{(2, 0, -1)\}$ **21.** $\{(1, 2z + 3, z)\}$
22. *Star Wars Episode IV: A New Hope:* $461 million;
Indiana Jones and the Kingdom of the Crystal Skull:
$317 million **23.** $40,000 at 10%; $100,000 at 6%;
$140,000 at 5%

24.

$x + y \le 6$
$2x - y \ge 3$

25. maximum profit: $1120;
pigs: 4; geese: 12

CHAPTER 9 GEOMETRY

9.1 Exercises *(pages 455–457)*
(The art here is not to scale with the exercise art.)
1. 90 **3.** equal **5.** true **7.** false **9.** true **11.** true
13. false **15. (a)** $\overleftrightarrow{AB}$ **(b)** A ——— B
17. (a) $\overleftrightarrow{CB}$ **(b)** A B ——— C
19. (a) $\overrightarrow{BC}$ **(b)** B C D
21. (a) $\overrightarrow{BA}$ **(b)** A ——— B
23. (a) $\overleftrightarrow{CA}$ **(b)** A B C
25. F **27.** D **29.** B **31.** E
**There may be other correct forms of the answers in
Exercises 33–39.** **33.** $\overrightarrow{MO}$ **35.** $\overrightarrow{MO}$ **37.** $\emptyset$ **39.** $\overrightarrow{OP}$
41. 62° **43.** 1° **45.** $(90 - x)°$ **47.** 48° **49.** 154°
51. $(180 - y)°$ **53.** $\angle CBD$ and $\angle ABE$; $\angle CBE$ and
$\angle DBA$ **55. (a)** 52° **(b)** 128° **57.** 107° and 73°
59. 75° and 75° **61.** 139° and 139° **63.** 65° and 115°
65. 35° and 55° **67.** 117° and 117° **69.** 141° and 141°
71. 80° **73.** 52° **75.** Measures are given in numerical

order, starting with angle 1: 55°, 65°, 60°, 65°, 60°, 120°,
60°, 60°, 55°, 55°.

9.2 Exercises *(pages 462–464)*
1. chord **3.** equilateral (or equiangular) **5.** false
7. false **9.** true **11.** Answers will vary. **13.** both
15. closed **17.** closed **19.** neither **21.** convex
23. convex **25.** not convex **27.** right, scalene
29. acute, equilateral **31.** right, scalene **33.** right,
isosceles **35.** obtuse, scalene **37.** acute, isosceles
39. An isosceles right triangle is a triangle having a 90°
angle and two perpendicular sides of equal length.
41. $A = 50°$; $B = 70°$; $C = 60°$; **43.** $A = B = C = 60°$
45. $A = B = 52°$; $C = 76°$ **47.** 165° **49.** 170°
51. (a) O **(b)** $\overrightarrow{OA}, \overrightarrow{OC}, \overrightarrow{OB}, \overrightarrow{OD}$ **(c)** $\overleftrightarrow{AC}, \overleftrightarrow{BD}$
(d) $\overleftrightarrow{AC}, \overleftrightarrow{BD}, \overleftrightarrow{BC}, \overleftrightarrow{AB}$ **(e)** $\overleftrightarrow{BC}, \overleftrightarrow{AB}$ **(f)** $\overleftrightarrow{AE}$
53. (e) The sum of the measures of the angles of a
triangle is 180° (because the pencil has gone through one-
half of a complete rotation).

Extension Exercises *(page 466)*
1. With radius of the compasses greater than one-half the
length PQ, place the point of the compasses at P and
swing arcs above and below line r. Then with the same
radius and the point of the compasses at Q, swing two
more arcs above and below line r. Locate the two points
of intersections of the arcs above and below, and call
them A and B. With a straightedge, join A and B. AB is
the perpendicular bisector of PQ.
3. With the radius of the compasses greater than the
distance from P to r, place the point of the compasses at
P and swing an arc intersecting line r in two points. Call
these points A and B. Swing arcs of equal radius to the
left of line r, with the point of the compasses at A and at
B, intersecting at point Q. With a straightedge, join P and
Q. PQ is the perpendicular from P to line r.
5. With any radius, place the point of the compasses at P
and swing arcs to the left and right, intersecting line r in
two points. Call these points A and B. With an arc of
sufficient length, place the point of the compasses first at
A and then at B, and swing arcs either both above or
both below line r, intersecting at point Q. With a
straightedge, join P and Q. PQ is perpendicular to line r
at P.
7. With any radius, place the point of the compasses at A
and swing an arc intersecting the sides of angle A at two
points. Call the point of intersection on the horizontal
side B and call the other point of intersection C. Draw a
horizontal working line, and locate any point A' on this

line. With the same radius used earlier, place the point of the compasses at A' and swing an arc intersecting the working line at B'. Return to angle A, and set the radius of the compasses equal to BC. On the working line, place the point of the compasses at B' and swing an arc intersecting the first arc at C'. Now draw line $A'C'$. Angle A' is equal to angle A.
9. Answers will vary.

9.3 Exercises *(pages 473–476)*

1.

STATEMENTS	REASONS
1. $AC = BD$	1. Given
2. $AD = BC$	2. Given
3. $AB = AB$	3. Reflexive property
4. $\triangle ABD \cong \triangle BAC$	4. SSS congruence property

3.

STATEMENTS	REASONS
1. $\overrightarrow{DB}$ is perpendicular to $\overleftrightarrow{AC}$.	1. Given
2. $AB = BC$	2. Given
3. $\angle ABD = \angle CBD$	3. Both are right angles by definition of perpendicularity.
4. $DB = DB$	4. Reflexive property
5. $\triangle ABD \cong \triangle CBD$	5. SAS congruence property

5.

STATEMENTS	REASONS
1. $\angle BAC = \angle DAC$	1. Given
2. $\angle BCA = \angle DCA$	2. Given
3. $AC = AC$	3. Reflexive property
4. $\triangle ABC \cong \triangle ADC$	4. ASA congruence property

7. $67°, 67°$ **9.** $110°$ **11.** Answers will vary.
13. $\angle A$ and $\angle P$; $\angle C$ and $\angle R$; $\angle B$ and $\angle Q$; $\overleftrightarrow{AC}$ and $\overleftrightarrow{PR}$; $\overleftrightarrow{CB}$ and $\overleftrightarrow{RQ}$; $\overleftrightarrow{AB}$ and $\overleftrightarrow{PQ}$;
15. $\angle H$ and $\angle F$; $\angle K$ and $\angle E$; $\angle HGK$ and $\angle FGE$; $\overleftrightarrow{HK}$ and $\overleftrightarrow{FE}$; $\overleftrightarrow{GK}$ and $\overleftrightarrow{GE}$; $\overleftrightarrow{HG}$ and $\overleftrightarrow{FG}$;
17. $\angle P = 78°$; $\angle M = 46°$; $\angle A = \angle N = 56°$
19. $\angle T = 74°$; $\angle Y = 28°$; $\angle Z = \angle W = 78°$
21. $\angle T = 20°$; $\angle V = 64°$; $\angle R = \angle U = 96°$
23. $a = 20$; $b = 15$ **25.** $a = 6$; $b = \frac{15}{2}$ **27.** $x = 6$
29. $x = 110$ **31.** $c = 111\frac{1}{9}$ **33.** 30 m **35.** 500 m, 700 m
37. 112.5 ft **39.** $r = \frac{108}{7}$ **41.** $c = 17$ **43.** $a = 13$
45. $c = 50$ m **47.** $a = 20$ in. **49.** The sum of the squares of the two shorter sides of a right triangle is equal to the square of the longest side.
51. $(3, 4, 5)$ **53.** $(7, 24, 25)$ **55.** $(12, 16, 20)$
57. Answers will vary. **59.** $(3, 4, 5)$ **61.** $(7, 24, 25)$
63. Answers will vary. **65.** $(4, 3, 5)$ **67.** $(8, 15, 17)$
69. Answers will vary. **71.** 24 m **73.** 16 ft **75.** 4.55 ft
77. 19 ft, 3 in. **79.** 28 ft, 10 in. **81.** (a) b (b) k

(c) cj (d) ck (e) $j + k$; $j + k$; $a^2 + b^2 = c^2$ **83.** 9
85. 16 **87.** 22.5° **89.** 15° **91.** Answers will vary.
93. Answers will vary.

9.4 Exercises *(pages 484–488)*

1. 24 **3.** 12 **5.** circumference **7.** 12 cm² **9.** 5 cm²
11. 8 in.² **13.** 4.5 cm² **15.** 418 mm² **17.** 8 cm²
19. 3.14 cm² **21.** about 1020 m² **23.** 4 m **25.** 300 ft, 400 ft, 500 ft **27.** 46 ft **29.** 23,800.10 ft² **31.** perimeter
33. 12 in., 12π in., 36π in.² **35.** 5 ft, 10π ft, 25π ft²
37. 6 cm, 12 cm, 36π cm² **39.** 10 in., 20 in., 20π in.
41. 14.5 **43.** 7 **45.** 5.1 **47.** 5 **49.** 5 **51.** 1.5
53. (a) 20 cm² (b) 80 cm² (c) 180 cm² (d) 320 cm²
(e) 4 (f) 3; 9 (g) 4; 16 (h) n^2
55. \$800 **57.** n^2 **59.** 80 **61.** 76.26 **63.** 132 ft²
65. 5376 cm² **67.** 145.34 m² **69.** 14-in. pizza
71. 14-in. pizza **73.** $\frac{1}{2}(a + b)(a + b)$
75. $\frac{1}{2}(a + b)(a + b) = \frac{1}{2}ab + \frac{1}{2}ab + \frac{1}{2}c^2$. **77.** 26 in.
79. 625 ft² **81.** 648 in.² **83.** $\frac{(4 - \pi)r^2}{4}$
85. $24 + 4\sqrt{6}$ **87.** 10 **89.** 5 in.

9.5 Exercises *(pages 493–496)*

1. true **3.** true **5.** false **7.** (a) $3\frac{3}{4}$ m³ (b) $14\frac{3}{4}$ m²
9. (a) 96 in.³ (b) 130.4 in.² **11.** (a) 267,946.67 ft³
(b) 20,096 ft² **13.** (a) 549.5 cm³ (b) 376.8 cm²
15. (a) 65.94 m³ (b) 100.00 m² **17.** 168 in.³
19. 1969.10 cm³ **21.** 427.29 cm³ **23.** 508.68 cm³
25. 2,415,766.67 m³ **27.** 0.52 m³ **29.** 12 in., 288π in.³, 144π in.² **31.** 5 ft, $\frac{500}{3}\pi$ ft³, 100π ft² **33.** 2 cm, 4 cm, 16π cm² **35.** 1 m, 2 m, $\frac{4}{3}\pi$ m³ **37.** volume **39.** $\sqrt[3]{2}x$
41. \$8100 **43.** \$37,500 **45.** 2.5 **47.** 6 **49.** 210 in.³
51. $\frac{62,500}{3}\pi$ in.³ **53.** 2 to 1 **55.** 288 **57.** 4, 4, 6, 2
59. 8, 6, 12, 2 **61.** 20, 12, 30, 2

9.6 Exercises *(pages 504–505)*

The answers are given in blue for this section.

1.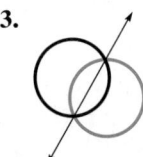

3. (figure)

5.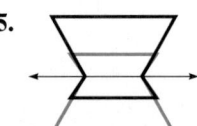

7. The figure is its own reflection image.

9.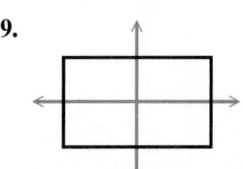

11.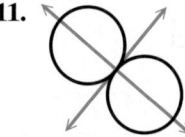

13.
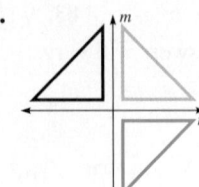

15.
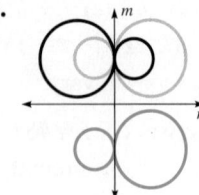

17.
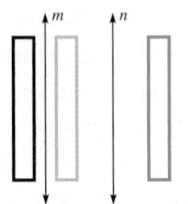

19.
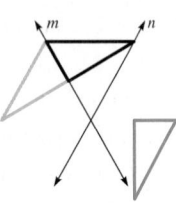

21.
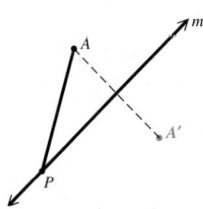

23.
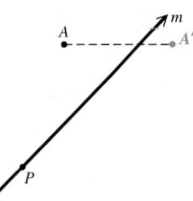

25.
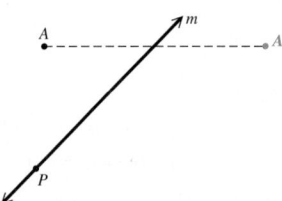

27.
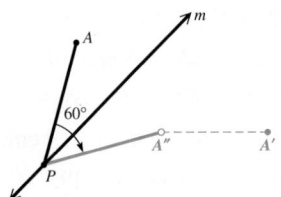

29.
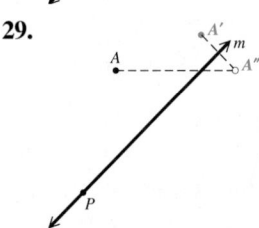

31.
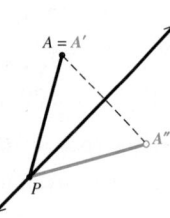

33. no **35.**
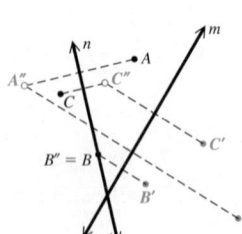

37.

39.
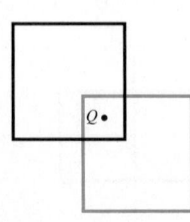

41.
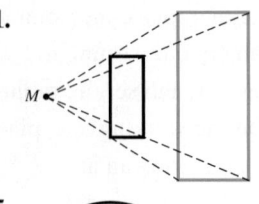

43.
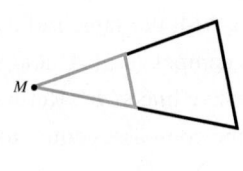

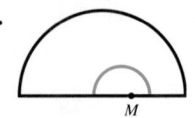

45.
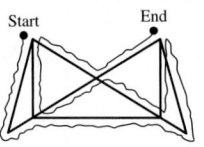

9.7 Exercises (pages 512–515)

1. Euclidean   **3.** Lobachevskian   **5.** greater than
7. Riemannian   **9.** Euclidean   **11.** no   **13.** yes **15.** C
17. A, E   **19.** A, E   **21.** none of them   **23.** 1
25. 3   **27.** 1   **29.** *A*, *C*, *D*, and *F* are even; *B* and *E* are
odd.   **31.** *A*, *B*, *C*, and *F* are odd; *D*, *E*, and *G* are even.
33. *A*, *B*, *C*, and *D* are odd; *E* is even
35. traversable
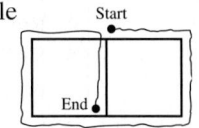
37. not traversable

39. traversable
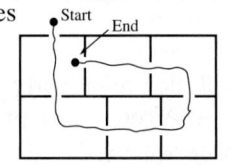

41. yes
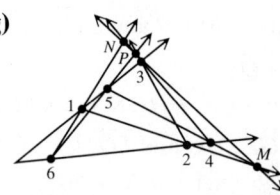
43. no

45. (a)–(g)

(h) Suppose that a hexagon is inscribed in an angle. Let
each pair of opposite sides be extended so as to intersect.
Then the three points of intersection thus obtained will
lie in a straight line.

9.8 Exercises (pages 519–520)

1. 4   **2.** 4   **3.** 2   **4.** $\frac{2}{1} = 2$ **5.** $\frac{4}{1} = 4$ **6.** $\frac{3}{1} = 3; \frac{9}{1} = 9$
7. $\frac{4}{1} = 4; \frac{16}{1} = 16$ **8.** 4, 9, 16, 25, 36, 100
9. Each ratio in the bottom row is the square of the scale
factor in the top row.   **10.** 4   **11.** 4, 9, 16, 25, 36, 100
12. Each ratio in the bottom row is again the square of
the scale factor in the top row.   **13.** Answers will vary.
Some examples are: $3^d = 9$, thus $d = 2$; $5^d = 25$, thus
$d = 2$; $4^d = 16$, thus $d = 2$.   **14.** 8   **15.** $\frac{2}{1} = 2; \frac{8}{1} = 8$

16. 8, 27, 64, 125, 216, 1000 **17.** Each ratio in the bottom row is the cube of the scale factor in the top row. **18.** Since $2^3 = 8$, the value of d in $2^d = 8$ must be 3. **19.** $\frac{3}{1} = 3$ **20.** 4 **21.** 1.262, or $\frac{\ln 4}{\ln 3}$ **22.** $\frac{2}{1} = 2$ **23.** 3 **24.** It is between 1 and 2. **25.** 1.585, or $\frac{\ln 3}{\ln 2}$ **27.** 0.842, 0.452, 0.842, 0.452, ... The two attractors are approximately 0.842 and 0.452.

Chapter 9 Test *(pages 521–523)*

1. (a) 52° **(b)** 142° **(c)** acute **2.** 40°, 140° **3.** 45°, 45° **4.** 30°, 60° **5.** 130°, 50° **6.** 117°, 117° **7.** Answers will vary. **8.** C **9.** both **10.** neither **11.** 30°, 45°, 105° **12.** 72 cm² **13.** 60 in.² **14.** 68 m² **15.** 180 m² **16.** 24π in. **17.** 1978 ft **18.** 57 cm²

19.

STATEMENTS	REASONS
1. $\angle CAB = \angle DBA$	1. Given
2. $DB = CA$	2. Given
3. $AB = AB$	3. Reflexive property
4. $\triangle ABD \cong \triangle BAC$	4. SAS congruence property

20. 20 ft **21.** 29 m **22.**

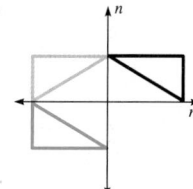

23.  **24. (a)** 904.32 in.³ **(b)** 452.16 in.²
25. (a) 864 ft³ **(b)** 552 ft²
26. (a) 1582.56 m³ **(b)** 753.60 m²

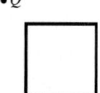

27. Answers will vary. **28. (a)** yes **(b)** no **29. (a)** yes **(b)** no

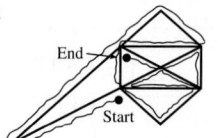

30. The only attractor is approximately 0.5238095238.

CHAPTER 10 COUNTING METHODS

10.1 Exercises *(pages 531–533)*

1. *AB, AC, AD, AE, BA, BC, BD, BE, CA, CB, CD, CE, DA, DB, DC, DE, EA, EB, EC, ED*; 20 ways **3.** *AB, AD, BA, BD, CE, DA, DB, EC*; 8 ways **5.** *ACE, AEC, BCE, BEC, DCE, DEC*; 6 ways **7.** *ABC, ABD, ABE, ACD, ACE, ADE, BCD, BCE, BDE, CDE*; 10 ways **9.** 1 **11.** 3 **13.** 5 **15.** 5

17. 3 **19.** 1 **21.** 18 **23.** 15

25.

	2	3	5	7
2	22	23	25	27
3	32	33	35	37
5	52	53	55	57
7	72	73	75	77

27. 22, 33, 55, 77 **29.** 23, 37, 53, 73 **31. (a)** tttt **(b)** hhhh, hhht, hhth, hhtt, hthh, htht, htth, thhh, thht, thth, tthh **(c)** httt, thtt, ttht, ttth, tttt **(d)** hhhh, hhht, hhth, hhtt, hthh, htht, htth, httt, thhh, thht, thth, thtt, tthh, ttht, ttth

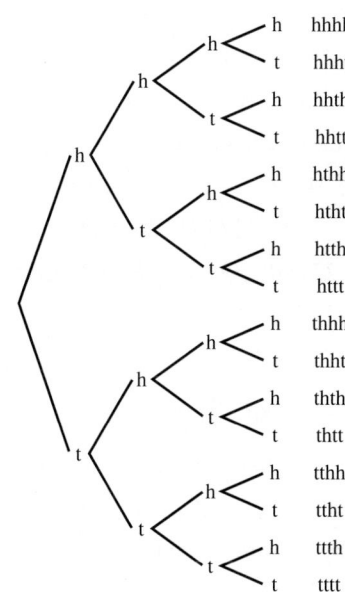

33. 16 **35.** 36 **37.** 17 **39.** 72 **41.** 12 **43.** 10 **45.** 6 **47.** 3 **49.** 9 **51.** 49 **53.** 21 **55.** 15 **57.** 16 **59.** 13 **61.** 4 **63.** 637 **65.** 3 **67.** **(a)** Find the number of ways to select an ordered pair of letters from the letters A, B, C, D, and E if repetition of letters is not allowed. **(b)** Find the number of ways to select an ordered pair of letters from the letters A, B, C, D, and E if the selection is done without replacement.

10.2 Exercises *(pages 541–543)*

1. Answers will vary. **3. (a)** no **(b)** Answers will vary. **5. (a)** no **(b)** Answers will vary. **7.** 24 **9.** 72 **11.** 20 **13.** 28 **15.** 840 **17.** 3,628,800 **19.** 3,991,680 **21.** 184,756 **23.** 980,179,200 **25.** 60 **27.** $2^3 = 8$ **29.** Answers will vary. **31.** $6^3 = 216$ **33.** $2^{10} = 1024$ **35.** $5! = 120$ **37.** $3 \cdot 2 = 6$ **39.** $3 \cdot 3 = 9$ **41.** $3 \cdot 2 \cdot 1 = 6$ **43.** $5 \cdot 2 \cdot 4 = 40$ **45.** $2^6 = 64$ **47.** $2 \cdot 3 \cdot 4 \cdot 5 = 120$ **49.** $2 \cdot 3 \cdot 4 \cdot 3 = 72$ **51.** $2 \cdot 3 \cdot 1 \cdot 3 = 18$

53. $2 \cdot 4 \cdot 6 = 48$ **55.** $5! = 120$ **57.** 800 **59. (a)** 5
(b) 2 **(c)** 4 **(d)** 3 **(e)** 2 **(f)** 1; 240 **61. (a)** 6
(b) 3 **(c)** 2 **(d)** 2 **(e)** 1 **(f)** 1; 72 **63.** Answers
will vary. **65.** 516,243 **67.** 6

10.3 Exercises *(pages 553–556)*
1. 504 **3.** 330 **5.** 116,280 **7.** 126
9. $1.805037696 \times 10^{11}$ **11.** Answers will vary.
13. Answers will vary.
15. (a) permutation **(b)** permutation
(c) combination **(d)** combination **(e)** permutation
(f) combination **(g)** permutation **(h)** permutation
17. $_8P_5 = 6720$ **19.** $_{12}P_2 = 132$
21. $_{25}P_5 = 6{,}375{,}600$ **23. (a)** $_4P_4 = 24$
(b) $_4P_4 = 24$ **25.** $_{18}C_5 = 8568$
27. (a) $_{13}C_5 = 1287$ **(b)** $_{26}C_5 = 65{,}780$
(c) 0 (impossible) **29. (a)** $_6C_3 = 20$
(b) $_6C_2 = 15$ **31.** $_9C_3 = 84$ **33. (a)** 5 **(b)** 9
35. $_{26}P_3 \cdot _{10}P_3 \cdot _{26}P_3 = 175{,}219{,}200{,}000$
37. $2 \cdot _{25}P_3 = 27{,}600$ **39.** $7 \cdot _{12}P_8 = 139{,}708{,}800$
41. (a) $7^7 = 823{,}543$ **(b)** $7! = 5040$
43. $_{15}C_1 \cdot _{14}C_2 \cdot _{12}C_3 \cdot _9C_4 \cdot _5C_5 = 37{,}837{,}800$
45. $\dfrac{_8C_3 \cdot _5C_3 \cdot _2C_2}{2!} = 280$ **47.** $_{20}C_3 = 1140$
49. (a) $_7P_2 = 42$ **(b)** $3 \cdot 6 = 18$ **(c)** $_7P_2 \cdot 5 = 210$
51. $_8P_3 = 336$ **53.** $_9C_3 \cdot _6C_3 \cdot _3C_3 \cdot 3^3 = 7560$
55. (a) $6! = 720$ **(b)** 745,896
57. (a) $6! = 720$ **(b)** $2 \cdot 4! = 48$ **(c)** $4! = 24$
59. (a) $2 \cdot 4! = 48$ **(b)** $3 \cdot 4! = 72$
61. Each equals 220.

10.4 Exercises *(pages 560–562)*
1. 6 **3.** 20 **5.** 56 **7.** 36 **9.** $_7C_1 \cdot _3C_3 = 7$
11. $_7C_3 \cdot _3C_1 = 105$ **13.** $_8C_3 = 56$ **15.** $_8C_5 = 56$
17. $_9C_4 = 126$ **19.** $1 \cdot _8C_3 = 56$ **21.** 1 **23.** 10
25. 5 **27.** 32 **29.** the even-numbered rows
31. (a) All are multiples of the row number.
(b) The same pattern holds. **(c)** The same pattern holds.
33. . . . 8, 13, 21, 34, . . . ; A number in this sequence is
the sum of the two preceding terms. This is the Fibonacci
sequence. **35.** row 8 **37.** The sum of the squares of
the entries across the top row equals the entry at the
bottom vertex. **39.** Answers will vary.
Wording may vary for Exercises 41 and 43.
41. sum $= N$; Any entry in the array equals the sum of
the two entries immediately above it and immediately to
its left. **43.** sum $= N$; Any entry in the array equals the

sum of the row of entries from the cell immediately
above it to the left boundary of the array.

Extension Exercises *(pages 564–567)*

1.

2	7	6
9	5	1
4	3	8

3.

11	10	4	23	17
18	12	6	5	24
25	19	13	7	1
2	21	20	14	8
9	3	22	16	15

5.

15	16	22	3	9
8	14	20	21	2
1	7	13	19	25
24	5	6	12	18
17	23	4	10	11

7.

24	9	12
3	15	27
18	21	6

Magic sum is 45.

9.

$\frac{17}{2}$	12	$\frac{1}{2}$	4	$\frac{15}{2}$
$\frac{23}{2}$	$\frac{5}{2}$	$\frac{7}{2}$	7	8
2	3	$\frac{13}{2}$	10	11
5	6	$\frac{19}{2}$	$\frac{21}{2}$	$\frac{3}{2}$
$\frac{11}{2}$	9	$\frac{25}{2}$	1	$\frac{9}{2}$

Magic sum is $32\frac{1}{2}$.

11. 479 **13.** 467 **15.** 269
17. (a) 73 **(b)** 70 **(c)** 74
(d) 69 **19. (a)** 7 **(b)** 22
(c) 5 **(d)** 4 **(e)** 15
(f) 19 **(g)** 6 **(h)** 23

21.

30	39	48	1	10	19	28
38	47	7	9	18	27	29
46	6	8	17	26	35	37
5	14	16	25	34	36	45
13	15	24	33	42	44	4
21	23	32	41	43	3	12
22	31	40	49	2	11	20

23. Each sum is equal to 34.
25. Each sum is equal to 68.
27. Each sum is equal to 9248.
29. Each sum is equal to 748.

31.

16	2	3	13
5	11	10	8
9	7	6	12
4	14	15	1

33.

18	20	10
8	16	24
22	12	14

The second and
third columns are
interchanged.

35.

39	48	57	10	19	28	37
47	56	16	18	27	36	38
55	15	17	26	35	44	46
14	23	25	34	43	45	54
22	24	33	42	51	53	13
30	32	41	50	52	12	21
31	40	49	58	11	20	29

Magic sum is 238.

37. 260

39. $52 + 45 + 16 + 17 + 54 + 43 + 10 + 23 = 260$

41.

5	13	21	9	17
6	19	2	15	23
12	25	8	16	4
18	1	14	22	10
24	7	20	3	11

43.

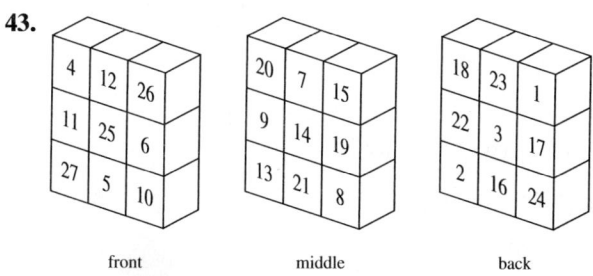

front   middle   back

10.5 Exercises *(pages 572–574)*

1. $2^4 - 1 = 15$ **3.** $2^7 - 1 = 127$ **5.** 120

7. $36 - 6 = 30$ **9.** $6 + 6 - 1 = 11$ **11.** 51

13. $90 - 9 = 81$ **15. (a)** $_{10}C_3 = 120$ **(b)** $_9C_3 = 84$

(c) $120 - 84 = 36$ **17.** $_7C_3 - _5C_3 = 25$

19. $_8P_4 - _5P_4 = 1560$ **21.** $_{10}P_3 - _7P_3 = 510$

23. $2 \cdot 26^2 + 2 \cdot 26^3 = 36,504$ **25.** $_{12}C_4 - _8C_4 = 425$

27. $13 + 4 - 1 = 16$ **29.** $25 + 22 - 18 = 29$

31. $2,598,960 - _{13}C_5 = 2,597,673$

33. $2,598,960 - _{40}C_5 = 1,940,952$

35. 56 **37.** $_{10}C_0 + _{10}C_1 + _{10}C_2 = 56$

39. $2^{10} - 56 = 968$

41. $26^2 \cdot 10^3 - _{26}P_2 \cdot _{10}P_3 = 208,000$

43. Answers will vary. **45.** $_4C_3 + _3C_3 + _5C_3 = 15$

47. $_{12}C_3 - _4C_1 \cdot _3C_1 \cdot _5C_1 = 160$ **49.** Answers will vary.

51. Answers will vary. **53.** Answers will vary.

Chapter 10 Test *(pages 575–576)*

1. $6 \cdot 7 \cdot 7 = 294$ **2.** $6 \cdot 7 \cdot 3 = 126$

3. $6 \cdot 6 \cdot 5 = 180$ **4.** $6 \cdot 5 \cdot 1 = 30$ end in 0;
$5 \cdot 5 \cdot 1 = 25$ end in 5; $30 + 25 = 55$ **5.** 13

6.

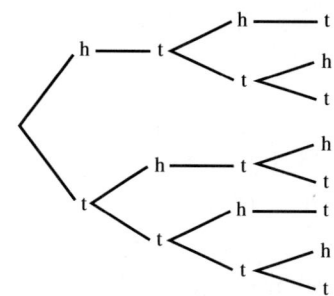

7. $4! = 24$ **8.** $3 \cdot 4! = 72$ **9.** 720

10. 56 **11.** 1320 **12.** 56 **13.** $_{26}P_5 = 7,893,600$

14. $32^5 = 33,554,432$ **15.** $_7P_2 = 42$ **16.** $5! = 120$

17. $\frac{6!}{2! \cdot 3!} = 60$ **18.** $_{10}C_4 = 210$ **19.** $\frac{_{10}C_2 \cdot _8C_2}{2!} = 630$

20. $\frac{_{10}C_5 \cdot _5C_5}{2!} = 126$ **21.** $\frac{_{10}C_4 \cdot _6C_4}{2!} = 1575$

22. $2^{10} - (_{10}C_0 + _{10}C_1 + _{10}C_2) = 968$ **23.** $2^5 = 32$

24. $2^3 = 8$ **25.** $2 \cdot 2^3 = 16$ **26.** 13 **27.** 2

28. $32 - (1 + 5) = 26$ **29.** $_6C_2 = 15$ **30.** $_5C_1 = 5$

31. $2 \cdot _5C_2 = 20$ **32.** $_5C_1 = 5$

33. $_5C_3 + _5C_2 \cdot _2C_1 = 30$ **34.** $_9C_4 = 126$

35. Answers will vary. **36.** $495 + 220 = 715$

37. the counting numbers **38.** Answers will vary.

CHAPTER 11 PROBABILITY

11.1 Exercises *(pages 585–588)*

1. (a) $\frac{1}{3}$ **(b)** $\frac{1}{3}$ **(c)** $\frac{1}{3}$ **3. (a)** $\frac{1}{2}$ **(b)** $\frac{1}{3}$ **(c)** $\frac{1}{6}$

5. (a) $\{1, 2, 3\}$ **(b)** 2 **(c)** 1 **(d)** 3 **(e)** $\frac{2}{3}$ **(f)** 2 to 1

7. (a) $\{11, 12, 13, 21, 22, 23, 31, 32, 33\}$ **(b)** $\frac{2}{3}$ **(c)** $\frac{1}{3}$

(d) $\frac{1}{3}$ **(e)** $\frac{4}{9}$ **9. (a)** 7 to 4 **(b)** 6 to 5 **(c)** 9 to 2

11. (a) $\frac{1}{50}$ **(b)** $\frac{2}{50} = \frac{1}{25}$ **(c)** $\frac{3}{50}$ **(d)** $\frac{4}{50} = \frac{2}{25}$

(e) $\frac{5}{50} = \frac{1}{10}$ **13. (a)** $\frac{1}{36}$ **(b)** $\frac{2}{36} = \frac{1}{18}$ **(c)** $\frac{3}{36} = \frac{1}{12}$

(d) $\frac{4}{36} = \frac{1}{9}$ **(e)** $\frac{5}{36}$ **(f)** $\frac{6}{36} = \frac{1}{6}$ **(g)** $\frac{5}{36}$ **(h)** $\frac{4}{36} = \frac{1}{9}$

(i) $\frac{3}{36} = \frac{1}{12}$ **(j)** $\frac{2}{36} = \frac{1}{18}$ **(k)** $\frac{1}{36}$ **15.** 0.329 **17.** $\frac{1}{9}$

19. $\frac{1}{4}$ **21.** $\frac{1}{4}$ **23. (a)** $\frac{3}{4}$ **(b)** $\frac{1}{4}$

25. $\frac{1}{250,000} = 0.000004$ **27.** $\frac{1}{4}$ **29.** $\frac{1}{4}$ **31.** $\frac{2}{4} = \frac{1}{2}$

33. $\frac{1}{500} = 0.002$ **35.** about 160 **37.** $\frac{2}{4} = \frac{1}{2}$ **39. (a)** 0

(b) no **(c)** yes **41.** Answers will vary. **43.** $\frac{12}{31}$

45. $\frac{36}{2,598,960} \approx 0.00001385$ **47.** $\frac{624}{2,598,960} \approx 0.00024010$

49. $\frac{1}{4} \cdot \frac{5108}{2,598,960} \approx 0.00049135$ **51. (a)** $\frac{5}{9}$ **(b)** $\frac{49}{144}$

(c) $\frac{5}{48}$ **53.** $3 \cdot 1 \cdot 2 \cdot 1 \cdot 1 \cdot 1 = 6$; $\frac{6}{720} = \frac{1}{120} \approx 0.0083$

55. $4 \cdot 3! \cdot 3! = 144$; $\frac{144}{720} = \frac{1}{5} = 0.2$

57. $\frac{2}{{}_7C_2} = \frac{2}{21} \approx 0.095$ **59.** $\frac{{}_5C_3}{{}_{12}C_3} = \frac{1}{22} \approx 0.045$
61. $\frac{1}{{}_{26}P_3} \approx 0.000064$ **63.** $\frac{3}{28} \approx 0.107$
65. (a) $\frac{8}{9^2} = \frac{8}{81} \approx 0.099$ **(b)** $\frac{4}{{}_9C_2} = \frac{1}{9} \approx 0.111$ **67.** 1
69. $\frac{9}{9 \cdot 10} = \frac{1}{10}$ **71.** $\frac{1}{15}$

11.2 Exercises *(pages 594–596)*

1. yes **3.** Answers will vary. **5.** $\frac{1}{2}$ **7.** $\frac{5}{6}$ **9.** $\frac{2}{3}$
11. (a) $\frac{2}{13}$ **(b)** 2 to 11 **13. (a)** $\frac{11}{26}$ **(b)** 11 to 15
15. (a) $\frac{9}{13}$ **(b)** 9 to 4 **17.** $\frac{2}{3}$ **19.** $\frac{7}{36}$
21. $P(A) + P(B) + P(C) + P(D) = 1$ **23.** 0.005365
25. 0.971285 **27.** 0.76 **29.** 0.92 **31.** 6 to 19

33.

x	$P(x)$
3	0.1
4	0.1
5	0.2
6	0.2
7	0.2
8	0.1
9	0.1

35. $n(A') = s - a$
37. $P(A) + P(A') = 1$
39. 180 **41.** $\frac{2}{3}$ **43.** 1

11.3 Exercises *(pages 603–606)*

1. independent **3.** not independent **5.** independent
7. $\frac{52}{100} = \frac{13}{25}$ **9.** $\frac{69}{100}$ **11.** $\frac{14}{31}$ **13.** $\frac{4}{7} \cdot \frac{4}{7} = \frac{16}{49}$
15. $\frac{2}{7} \cdot \frac{1}{7} = \frac{2}{49}$ **17.** $\frac{4}{7} \cdot \frac{3}{6} = \frac{2}{7}$ **19.** $\frac{1}{6}$ **21.** 0
23. $\frac{12}{51} = \frac{4}{17}$ **25.** $\frac{12}{52} \cdot \frac{11}{51} = \frac{11}{221}$ **27.** $\frac{4}{52} \cdot \frac{11}{51} = \frac{11}{663}$
29. $\frac{1}{3}$ **31.** 1 **33.** $\frac{3}{10}$ (the same)
35. $\frac{1}{2} \cdot \frac{1}{2} \cdot \frac{1}{2} \cdot \frac{1}{2} \cdot \frac{1}{2} \cdot \frac{1}{2} = \frac{1}{64}$ **37.** 0.490 **39.** 0.027
41. 0.95 **43.** 0.23 **45.** $\frac{1}{20}$ **47.** $\frac{1}{5}$ **49.** $\frac{1}{5}$ **51. (a)** $\frac{3}{4}$
(b) $\frac{1}{2}$ **(c)** $\frac{5}{16}$ **53.** 0.2704 **55.** 0.2496
57. Answers will vary. **59.** $\frac{1}{64} \approx 0.0156$ **61.** 10
63. 0.400 **65.** 0.080 **67.** $(0.90)^4 = 0.6561$
69. ${}_4C_2 \cdot (0.10) \cdot (0.20) \cdot (0.70)^2 = 0.0588$ **71.** 0.30
73. 0.49 **75.** Answers will vary.

11.4 Exercises *(pages 610–612)*

1. $\frac{1}{8}$ **3.** $\frac{3}{8}$ **5.** $\frac{3}{4}$ **7.** $\frac{1}{2}$ **9.** $\frac{3}{8}$ **11.** $x; n; n$ **13.** $\frac{7}{128}$
15. $\frac{35}{128}$ **17.** $\frac{21}{128}$ **19.** $\frac{1}{128}$ **21.** $\frac{25}{72}$ **23.** $\frac{1}{216}$ **25.** 0.041
27. 0.268 **29.** Answers will vary. **31.** Answers will vary.
33. 0.016 **35.** 0.020 **37.** 0.137 **39.** 0.572 **41.** 0.669
43. 0.975 **45.** 0.883 **47.** $6p^2(1 - p)^2$
49. $\frac{1}{1024} \approx 0.001$ **51.** $\frac{45}{1024} \approx 0.044$
53. $\frac{210}{1024} = \frac{105}{512} \approx 0.205$ **55.** $\frac{772}{1024} \approx 0.754$

11.5 Exercises *(pages 619–622)*

1. Answers will vary. **3.** $\frac{5}{2}$ **5.** \$1 **7.** \$0.50
9. no $\left(\text{expected net winnings: } -\frac{3}{4}\cancel{c}\right)$ **11.** 1.69

13. (a) −\$60 **(b)** \$36,000 **(c)** \$72,000 **15.** \$0.46
17. \$2700 **19.** 2.7 **21.** a decrease of 50 **23.** Answers
will vary. **25.** Project C **27.** \$2200 **29.** \$81,000
31. Do not purchase the insurance (because
\$86,000 > \$81,000). **33.** \$1500; \$3000; \$17,500; \$27,000
35. \$56,000 **37.** 48.7%

Extension Exercises *(page 625)*

1. Answers will vary. **3.** no **5.** $\frac{18}{50} = 0.36$ (This is quite
close to 0.375, the theoretical value.) **7.** $\frac{6}{50} = 0.12$
9. Answers will vary. **11.** Answers will vary.

Chapter 11 Test *(page 627)*

1. Answers will vary. **2.** Answers will vary. **3.** 3 to 1
4. 25 to 1 **5.** 11 to 2 **6.** row 1: CC; row 2: cC, cc
7. $\frac{1}{2}$ **8.** 1 to 3 **9.** $\frac{7}{7} \cdot \frac{6}{7} \cdot \frac{5}{7} = \frac{30}{49}$ **10.** $\frac{7}{19}$
11. $1 - \left(\frac{30}{49} + \frac{1}{49}\right) = \frac{18}{49}$ **12.** $\frac{{}_2C_2}{{}_5C_2} = \frac{1}{10}$
13. $\frac{{}_3C_2}{{}_5C_2} = \frac{3}{10}$ **14.** $\frac{6}{10} = \frac{3}{5}$ **15.** $\frac{3}{10}$
16. $\frac{3}{10}; \frac{6}{10}; \frac{1}{10}$ **17.** $\frac{9}{10}$ **18.** $\frac{18}{10} = \frac{9}{5}$ **19.** $\frac{6}{36} = \frac{1}{6}$
20. 35 to 1 **21.** 7 to 2 **22.** $\frac{4}{36} = \frac{1}{9}$ **23.** $(0.78)^3 \approx 0.475$
24. ${}_3C_2 \cdot (0.78)^2 \cdot (0.22) \approx 0.402$
25. $1 - (0.22)^3 \approx 0.989$
26. $(0.78) \cdot (0.22) \cdot (0.78) \approx 0.134$ **27.** $\frac{25}{102}$ **28.** $\frac{25}{51}$
29. $\frac{4}{51}$ **30.** $\frac{3}{26}$

CHAPTER 12 STATISTICS

12.1 Exercises *(pages 636–640)*

1. (a)

x	f	$\frac{f}{n}$
0	10	$\frac{10}{30} \approx 33\%$
1	7	$\frac{7}{30} \approx 23\%$
2	6	$\frac{6}{30} = 20\%$
3	4	$\frac{4}{30} \approx 13\%$
4	2	$\frac{2}{30} \approx 7\%$
5	1	$\frac{1}{30} \approx 3\%$

(b) **(c)**

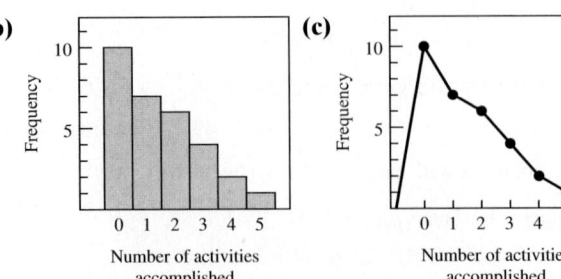

Number of activities
accomplished

Number of activities
accomplished

3. (a)

Class Limits	Tally	Frequency f	Relative Frequency $\frac{f}{n}$
45–49	III	3	$\frac{3}{54} \approx 5.6\%$
50–54	THL THL IIII	14	$\frac{14}{54} \approx 25.9\%$
55–59	THL THL THL I	16	$\frac{16}{54} \approx 29.6\%$
60–64	THL THL THL II	17	$\frac{17}{54} \approx 31.5\%$
65–69	IIII	4	$\frac{4}{54} \approx 7.4\%$

Total: $n = 54$

(b)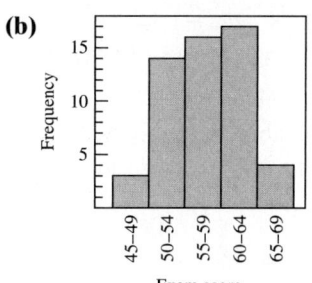

(c)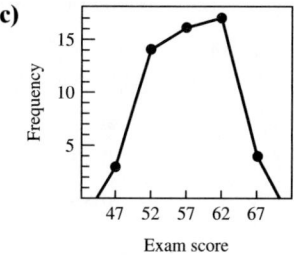

5. (a)

Class Limits	Tally	Frequency f	Relative Frequency $\frac{f}{n}$
70–74	II	2	$\frac{2}{30} \approx 6.7\%$
75–79	I	1	$\frac{1}{30} \approx 3.3\%$
80–84	III	3	$\frac{3}{30} = 10.0\%$
85–89	II	2	$\frac{2}{30} \approx 6.7\%$
90–94	THL	5	$\frac{5}{30} \approx 16.7\%$
95–99	THL	5	$\frac{5}{30} \approx 16.7\%$
100–104	THL I	6	$\frac{6}{30} = 20.0\%$
105–109	IIII	4	$\frac{4}{30} \approx 13.3\%$
110–114	II	2	$\frac{2}{30} \approx 6.7\%$

Total: $n = 30$

(b)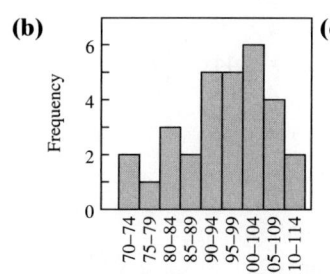

(c)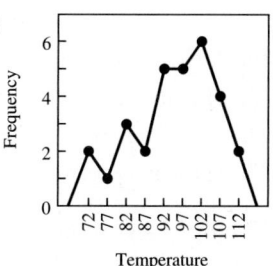

7.
```
0 | 7 9 8
1 | 1 1 2 8 9 4 3 1 0 5 0 5 5
2 | 7 0 9 6 6 2 2 5 2 3 4 4
3 | 8 1
```

9.
```
0 | 8 5 4 9 6 9 4 8
1 | 6 0 1 8 8 2 4 0 2 8 6 3
2 | 6 1 2 5 1 3
3 | 0 4 6
4 | 4
```

11. 2001 **13.** 2005, 2006, 2007, and 2011

15.
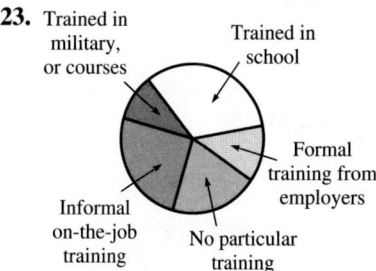

17. 3.8% in 2008 **19.** Answers will vary.

21. Medicare & Medicaid; 83°

23.
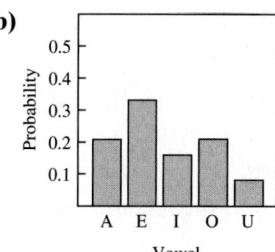

25. about 79 years **27. (a)** about 6 years **(b)** Answers will vary. **29.** Answers will vary. **31.** Answers will vary. **33.** Answers will vary.

35. (a)

Letter	Probability
A	0.208
E	0.338
I	0.169
O	0.208
U	0.078

(b)

37. Answers will vary. **39. (a)** 0.225 **(b)** 0.275 **(c)** 0.425 **(d)** 0.175

41. (a)

Sport	Probability
Sailing	0.225
Hang gliding	0.125
Snowboarding	0.175
Bicycling	0.075
Canoeing	0.300
Rafting	0.100

(b) empirical **(c)** Answers will vary.

12.2 Exercises (pages 650–653)

1. (a) 15.2 **(b)** 12 **(c)** none **3. (a)** 216.2 **(b)** 221
(c) 196 **5. (a)** 5.2 **(b)** 5.35 **(c)** 4.5 and 6.2
7. (a) 0.8 **(b)** 0.795 **(c)** none **9. (a)** 129 **(b)** 128
(c) 125 and 128 **11. (a)** 10.7 million **(b)** 10.65 million
(c) 10.6 million **13. (a)** 73.9 **(b)** 17.5 **(c)** 0
15. mean = 47.4; median and mode remain the same
17. \$59.7 billion **19.** 5.27 seconds **21.** 2.42 seconds
23. the mean **25.** mean = 77; median = 80; mode = 79
27. 92 **29. (a)** 597.4 **(b)** 600 **(c)** 615 **31.** 2.41
33. 648 million **35.** China: 372; India: 1008; United
States: 87; Indonesia: 324; Brazil: 61 **37.** 328.2 million
39. (a) 8.25 **(b)** 8 **41. (a)** 66.25 **(b)** 64.5 **43.** 6
45. (a) 19.4 **(b)** 15.5 **(c)** 11 **47. (a)** 74.8
(b) 77.5 **(c)** 78 **49.** Answers will vary.
51. (a) mean = 13.7; median = 16; mode = 18
(b) median **53. (a)** 4 **(b)** 4.25
55. (a) 6 **(b)** 9.33 **57.** 80 **59.** no
61. Answers will vary.

12.3 Exercises (pages 659–661)

1. the sample standard deviation **3. (a)** 13 **(b)** 4.24
5. (a) 19 **(b)** 6.27 **7. (a)** 40 **(b)** 11.51 **9. (a)** 1.14
(b) 0.37 **11. (a)** 12 **(b)** 3.61 **13.** $\frac{3}{4}$ **15.** $\frac{21}{25}$ **17.** 88.9%
19. 64.0% **21.** $\frac{3}{4}$ **23.** $\frac{15}{16}$ **25.** $\frac{1}{4}$ **27.** $\frac{4}{49}$
29. \$202.50 **31.** six **33.** There are at least nine.
35. (a) $s_A = 2.35$; $s_B = 2.58$ **(b)** $V_A = 46.9$; $V_B = 36.9$
(c) sample B **(d)** sample A
37. (a) $\bar{x}_A = 68.8$; $\bar{x}_B = 66.6$ **(b)** $s_A = 4.21$; $s_B = 5.27$
(c) brand A, since $\bar{x}_A > \bar{x}_B$ **(d)** brand A, since $s_A < s_B$
39. Brand A ($s_B = 3539 > 2116$) **41.** 18.71; 4.35
43. 8.71; 4.35 **45.** 56.14; 13.04 **47.** Answers will vary.
49. −3.0 **51.** 4.2 **53.** 7.55 and 23.45 **55.** no
57. Answers will vary.

12.4 Exercises (pages 665–668)

1. 58 **3.** 62 **5.** Janet (since $z = 0.48 > 0.19$)
7. Yvette (since $z = -1.44 > -1.78$)
9. −0.2 **11.** 1.0 **13.** Saudi Arabia
15. United Kingdom **17.** Canada in exports (Canada's
exports z-score was 2.4, China's imports z-score was 1.7,
and 2.4 > 1.7.) **19. (a)** The median is \$54.5 billion.
(b) The range is 261 − 12 = 249. **(c)** The middle half
of the items extend from \$29 billion to \$70 billion.
21. Answers will vary. **23.** Answers will vary.
25. Answers will vary. **27.** the overall distribution
29. Both are skewed to the right, imports about twice as
much as exports. **31. (a)** no **(b)** Answers will vary.
33. Answers will vary. **35.** Answers will vary.
37. $Q_1 = 97.6$, $Q_2 = 100.2$, $Q_3 = 104.4$

39. $P_{65} = 103.2$ **41.** 101.0
43.

45. 93.3 **47.** 10

12.5 Exercises (pages 675–676)

1. discrete **3.** continuous **5.** discrete **7.** 50
9. 68 **11.** 50% **13.** 95% **15.** 43.3% **17.** 36.0%
19. 4.5% **21.** 97.9% **23.** 1.28 **25.** −1.34
27. 5000 **29.** 640 **31.** 9970 **33.** 84.1% **35.** 37.8%
37. 15.9% **39.** 4.7% **41.** 0.994, or 99.4%
43. 189 units **45.** 0.888 **47.** about 2 eggs **49.** 24.2%
51. Answers will vary. **53.** 79 **55.** 68 **57.** 90.4
59. 40.3 **61.** Answers will vary.

Extension Exercises (pages 682–683)

1. $y' = 0.3x + 1.5$ **3.** 2.4 decimeters **5.** 48.9°
7. $y' = 3.35x - 78.4$ **9.** 156 lb

11.

13. 79 **15.** $r = 0.996$

17.

19. Answers will vary. **21.** $y' = 1.44x - 0.39$
23. The linear correlation is strong.
25. $y' = 0.5219x + 149.8$
27. The linear correlation is weak to moderate.

Chapter 12 Test (pages 684–686)

1. those who copied less than 10% **2.** those with copy
rates from 10% to 30% or greater than 50%
3. those with copy rate from 30% to 50%
4. Answers will vary. **5. (a)** 200 million barrels
(b) 334 million barrels **(c)** 138 million barrels
(d) 69 **(e)** 44 million barrels
6. (a) 281 feet **(b)** 517 inches **(c)** 1290
7. (a) 762 **(b)** 7th **(c)** 12 feet **(d)** 17 feet

8.

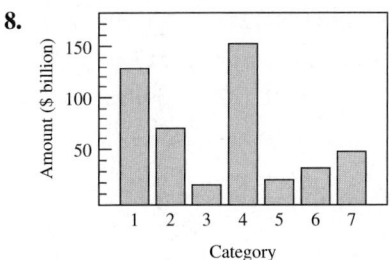

9. 19.3%   **10.** 16.8%   **11.** 44.5%

12.

Class Limits	Frequency f	Relative Frequency $\frac{f}{n}$
6–10	3	$\frac{3}{22} \approx 0.14$
11–15	6	$\frac{6}{22} \approx 0.27$
16–20	7	$\frac{7}{22} \approx 0.32$
21–25	4	$\frac{4}{22} \approx 0.18$
26–30	2	$\frac{2}{22} \approx 0.09$

13. (a)

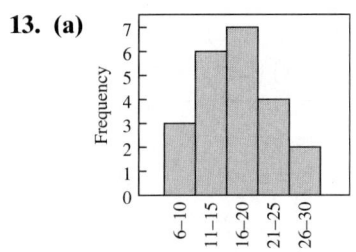

(b)

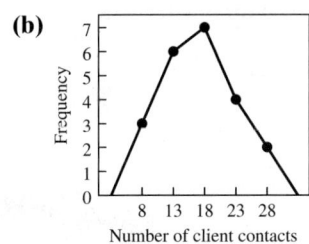

14. 8   **15.** 12.4   **16.** 12   **17.** 12   **18.** 10

19.
```
3 | 3 8
4 | 3 5 8 9
5 | 0 2 5
6 | 1 1 4 5 6 7 7 8
7 | 0 1 2 3 7 7 8 9 9
8 | 0 4 4
9 | 1
```

20. 35   **21.** 33   **22.** 37   **23.** 31   **24.** 49

25.

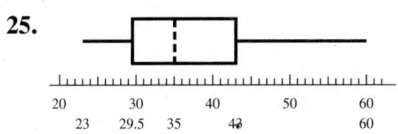

26. (a) about 95%   **(b)** about 0.3%   **(c)** about 16%
(d) about 13.5%   **27.** 0.684   **28.** 0.340   **29.** West
30. East   **31.** 84.9   **32.** Dodgers (since $z = 1.01 > 0.70$)

CHAPTER 13 PERSONAL FINANCIAL MANAGEMENT

13.1 Exercises *(pages 698–701)*
1. $48   **3.** $48.30   **5.** $488.19   **7. (a)** $826   **(b)** $835.84
9. (a) $2650   **(b)** $2653.02   **11.** $125   **13.** $13,546.67
15. $168.26   **17.** $817.17   **19.** $17,724.34; $10,224.34
21. (a) $2249.73   **(b)** $2252.32   **(c)** $2253.65
23. (a) $18,918.18   **(b)** $18,920.52   **(c)** $18,921.70
25. (a) $55.95   **(b)** $56.06   **(c)** $56.14   **(d)** $56.18
(e) $56.18   **27.** Answers will vary.   **29.** $1461.04
31. $747.26   **33.** $4499.98   **35.** $112,607.20
37. $111,576.54   **39.** 2.000%   **41.** 2.015%   **43.** 2.020%
45. 2.020%   **47.** $30,420   **49.** 17 years, 152 days
51. $r = m[(Y + 1)^{1/m} - 1]$ **53. (a)** 3.818%
(b) Bank A; $5.63   **(c)** no difference; $232.38
55. 35 years   **57.** 8 years   **59.** 10.0%   **61.** 3.2%
63. $6.51; $7.95; $9.71; $26.40
65. $20,400; $25,000; $30,500; $82,900
67. $218   **69.** $1502   **71.** $81,102,828.75

13.2 Exercises *(pages 704–706)*
1. $2950   **3.** $3422   **5.** $3922   **7.** $3645   **9.** $476.25
11. $1215; $158.75   **13.** $83.25; $46.29   **15.** $79.18; $38.39
17. $229.17   **19.** $330.75   **21.** $10,850   **23.** 6 years
25. $3.50   **27.** $5.80   **29.** $15.30   **31. (a)** $607.33
(b) $7.90   **(c)** $646.87   **33. (a)** $473.96   **(b)** $6.16
(c) $505.54   **35.** $9.27   **37. (a)** $38.18   **(b)** $38.69
(c) $39.20   **39.** 16.0%   **41.** $32.00
43–47. Answers will vary.   **49. (a)** $127.44   **(b)** $139.08

13.3 Exercises *(pages 711–713)*
1. 13.5%   **3.** 8.5%   **5.** $114.58   **7.** $92.71   **9.** 11.0%
11. 9.5%   **13. (a)** $8.93   **(b)** $511.60   **(c)** $6075.70
15. (a) $2.79   **(b)** $97.03   **(c)** $4073.57
17. (a) $206   **(b)** 9.5%   **19. (a)** $180   **(b)** 11.0%
21. (a) $41.29   **(b)** $39.70   **23. (a)** $420.68
(b) $368.47   **25. (a)** $1.80   **(b)** $14.99   **(c)** $1045.01
27. finance company APR: 12.0%; credit union APR:
11.5%; choose credit union   **29.** $32.27
31. Answers will vary.   **33.** Answers will vary.
35. 12   **37.–41.** Answers will vary.   **43.** $\frac{5}{39}$

13.4 Exercises *(pages 722–724)*
1. $675.52   **3.** $469.14   **5.** $2483.28   **7.** $1034.56
9. (a) $513.38   **(b)** $487.50   **(c)** $25.88   **(d)** $58,474.12
11. (a) $1247.43   **(b)** $775.67   **(c)** $471.76
(d) $142,728.24   **(e)** $1247.43   **(f)** $773.11   **(g)** $474.32
(h) $142,253.92   **13. (a)** $1390.93   **(b)** $776.61
(c) $614.32   **(d)** $113,035.68   **(e)** $1390.93   **(f)** $772.41

(g) $618.52 **(h)** $112,417.16 **15.** $552.18 **17.** $1127.27
19. $1168.44 **21.** 360 **23.** $247,532.80 **25. (a)** $304.01
(b) $734.73 **27. (a)** $59,032.06 **(b)** $59,875.11
29. (a) payment 176 **(b)** payment 304 **31.** $25,465.20
33. $91,030.80 **35. (a)** $674.79 **(b)** $746.36
(c) an increase of $71.57 **37. (a)** $395.83 **(b)** $466.07
39. $65.02 **41.** $140,000 **43.** $4275 **45.** $240
47. (a) $1634 **(b)** $1754 **(c)** $917 **(d)** $997
(e) $1555 **49. (a)** $2271 **(b)** $2407 **(c)** $1083
(d) $1174 **(e)** $2055 **51.–59.** Answers will vary.

13.5 Exercises *(pages 737–740)*
1. $20.93 **3.** $1.88 per share lower **5.** $16.37
7. $0.80 per share **9.** 3,327,000 shares **11.** 13.69% lower
13. 29.62 **15.** $42,768.00 **17.** $39,685.00 **19.** $863.04
21. $5479.20 **23.** $68,605.21 **25.** $98,136.00
27. $11,460.44 **29.** $35,609.44 **31.** $107,107.18
33. $20,928.47 **35.** $2050.19 net paid out
37. (a) $800 **(b)** $80 **(c)** $960 **(d)** $1040 **(e)** 130%
39. (a) $1250 **(b)** $108 **(c)** −$235 **(d)** −$127
(e) −10.16% **41.** $275.00 **43.** $177.75
45. (a) $10.49 **(b)** 334 **47. (a)** $8.27 **(b)** 3080
49. (a) $8.39 **(b)** $100.68 **(c)** 15.6%
51. (a) $57.45 **(b)** $689.40 **(c)** 27.6%
53. (a) $1203.75 **(b)** $18.06 **(c)** 19.56%
55. (a) $4179 **(b)** $76.48 **(c)** 24.31%
57. $10.00, $35.17, $29.95 **59.** $400.00, $41.80, $29.95
61. $4000.00, $91.40, $120.00 **63.** large; low
65. $129,258 **67.** $993,383 **69. (a)** $56,473.02
(b) $49,712.70 **71. (a)** $12,851.28 **(b)** $11,651.81
73. (a) $r = m\left[\left(\frac{A}{P}\right)^{1/n} - 1\right]$ **(b)** 5.4%

	Aggressive Growth	Growth	Growth & Income	Income	Cash
75.	$1400	$8600	$6200	$2800	$1000
77.	$8000	$112,000	$144,000	$116,000	$20,000

79. 3.75% **81.** 5.2% **83.–89.** Answers will vary.

Extension Exercises *(pages 745–746)*
1.
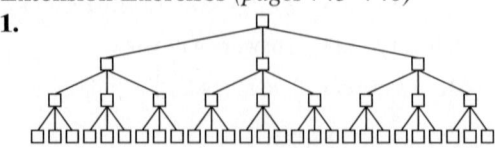

3. 3^{N-1} **5.** $26 **7.** 3^{N-1}; geometric; 1; 3; N; $\frac{3^N - 1}{2}$
9. 351 **11.** more than $\frac{26}{27}$ **13.** $0.00
15. You are in the chart only from when you pay your
entry fee until you move up three levels and get paid.

17. Answers will vary. **19.** 128 **21.** $4,400,000
23. Ponzi's $4 million would be equivalent to about $54
million in today's dollars. Madoff's $21 billion is nearly
400 times as much. **25.** Answers will vary.

Chapter 13 Test *(page 748)*
1. $130 **2.** $58.58 **3.** 3.04% **4.** 14 years **5.** $67,297.13
6. $10.88 **7.** $450 **8.** $143.75 **9.** 14.0% **10.** $34.13
11. 11.5% **12.** Answers will vary. **13.** $1162.95
14. $1528.48 **15.** $3488 **16.** Answers will vary.
17. 12.1% **18.** 15,235,100 shares **19.** $10.00
20. 0.078%; no; The given return was not for a 1-year
period. **21.** $106,728.55 **22.** Answers will vary.

CHAPTER 14 TRIGONOMETRY

14.1 Exercises *(page 754)*
1. (a) 60° **(b)** 150° **3. (a)** 45° **(b)** 135°
5. (a) 1° **(b)** 91° **7.** $(90 - x)$ degrees **9.** 83° 59′
11. 119° 27′ **13.** 38° 32′ **15.** 17° 1′ 49″ **17.** 20.900°
19. 91.598° **21.** 274.316° **23.** 31° 25′ 47″
25. 89° 54′ 1″ **27.** 178° 35′ 58″ **29.** 320° **31.** 235°
33. 179° **35.** 130° **37.** 30° + $n \cdot 360°$
39. 60° + $n \cdot 360°$

**Angles other than those given are possible in
Exercises 41–47.**

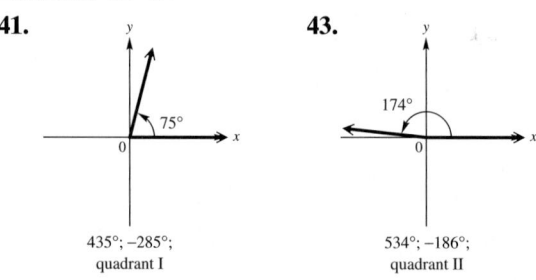

41.
435°; −285°;
quadrant I

43.
534°; −186°;
quadrant II

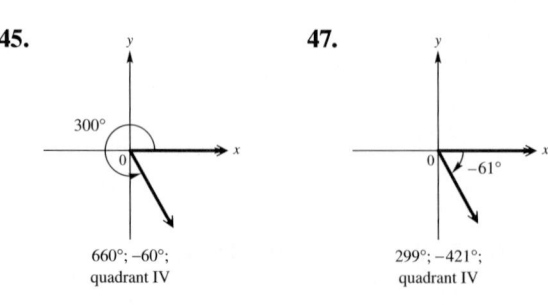

45.
660°; −60°;
quadrant IV

47.
299°; −421°;
quadrant IV

14.2 Exercises *(pages 757–758)*

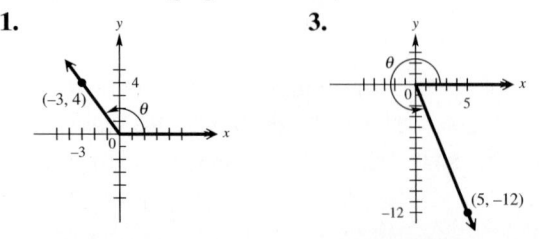

1.

3.

5. $\frac{4}{5}; -\frac{3}{5}; -\frac{4}{3}; -\frac{3}{4}; -\frac{5}{3}; \frac{5}{4}$

7. 1; 0; undefined; 0; undefined; 1

9. $\frac{\sqrt{3}}{2}; \frac{1}{2}; \sqrt{3}; \frac{\sqrt{3}}{3}; 2; \frac{2\sqrt{3}}{3}$

11. $\frac{5\sqrt{34}}{34}; \frac{3\sqrt{34}}{34}; \frac{5}{3}; \frac{3}{5}; \frac{\sqrt{34}}{3}; \frac{\sqrt{34}}{5}$

13. 0; −1; 0; undefined; −1; undefined   **15.** Answers will vary.   **17.** It is the distance from a point (x, y) on the terminal side of the angle to the origin.   **19.** positive   **21.** negative   **23.** positive   **25.** negative   **27.** 0   **29.** undefined   **31.** undefined   **33.** 0   **35.** 0   **37.** 1   **39.** 0   **41.** −1

14.3 Exercises *(pages 762–763)*

1. $-\frac{1}{3}$ **3.** $\frac{1}{3}$ **5.** −5   **7.** $2\sqrt{2}$ **9.** $-\frac{3\sqrt{5}}{5}$ **11.** $\frac{2}{3}$

13. II   **15.** I   **17.** II   **19.** II or III   **21.** III or IV

23. +; +; +   **25.** −; −; +   **27.** −; +; −   **29.** +; +; +

31. $-2\sqrt{2}$ **33.** $\frac{\sqrt{15}}{4}$ **35.** $-2\sqrt{2}$ **37.** $-\frac{\sqrt{15}}{4}$

In Exercises 39–45, we give, in order, sine, cosine, tangent, cotangent, secant, and cosecant.

39. $\frac{15}{17}; -\frac{8}{17}; -\frac{15}{8}; -\frac{8}{15}; -\frac{17}{8}; \frac{17}{15}$

41. $-\frac{4}{5}; -\frac{3}{5}; \frac{4}{3}; \frac{3}{4}; -\frac{5}{3}; -\frac{5}{4}$

43. $-\frac{\sqrt{3}}{2}; -\frac{1}{2}; \sqrt{3}; \frac{\sqrt{3}}{3}; -2; -\frac{2\sqrt{3}}{3}$

45. $\frac{\sqrt{5}}{7}; \frac{2\sqrt{11}}{7}; \frac{\sqrt{55}}{22}; \frac{2\sqrt{55}}{5}; \frac{7\sqrt{11}}{22}; \frac{7\sqrt{5}}{5}$

47. Answers will vary.

14.4 Exercises *(pages 769–770)*

In Exercises 1–5, we give, in order, sine, cosine, tangent, cotangent, secant, and cosecant.

1. $\frac{3}{5}; \frac{4}{5}; \frac{3}{4}; \frac{4}{3}; \frac{5}{4}; \frac{5}{3}$ **3.** $\frac{21}{29}; \frac{20}{29}; \frac{21}{20}; \frac{20}{21}; \frac{29}{20}; \frac{29}{21}$

5. $\frac{n}{p}; \frac{m}{p}; \frac{n}{m}; \frac{m}{n}; \frac{p}{m}; \frac{p}{n}$

In Exercises 7 and 9, we give, in order, the unknown side, sine, cosine, tangent, cotangent, secant, and cosecant.

7. $c = 13; \frac{12}{13}; \frac{5}{13}; \frac{12}{5}; \frac{5}{12}; \frac{13}{5}; \frac{13}{12}$

9. $b = \sqrt{13}; \frac{\sqrt{13}}{7}; \frac{6}{7}; \frac{\sqrt{13}}{6}; \frac{6\sqrt{13}}{13}; \frac{7}{6}; \frac{7\sqrt{13}}{13}$

11. cot 40°   **13.** sec 43°   **15.** cot 64.6°

17. sin 76° 30′   **19.** $\frac{\sqrt{3}}{3}$ **21.** $\frac{1}{2}$ **23.** $\sqrt{2}$

25. $\frac{\sqrt{2}}{2}$ **27.** $\frac{\sqrt{3}}{2}$ **29.** $\sqrt{3}$ **31.** 82°   **33.** 45°   **35.** 30°

In Exercises 37–55, we give, in order, sine, cosine, tangent, cotangent, secant, and cosecant.

37. $\frac{\sqrt{3}}{2}; -\frac{1}{2}; -\sqrt{3}; -\frac{\sqrt{3}}{3}; -2; \frac{2\sqrt{3}}{3}$

39. $\frac{1}{2}; -\frac{\sqrt{3}}{2}; -\frac{\sqrt{3}}{3}; -\sqrt{3}; -\frac{2\sqrt{3}}{3}; 2$

41. $-\frac{\sqrt{3}}{2}; -\frac{1}{2}; \sqrt{3}; \frac{\sqrt{3}}{3}; -2; -\frac{2\sqrt{3}}{3}$

43. $-\frac{\sqrt{2}}{2}; \frac{\sqrt{2}}{2}; -1; -1; \sqrt{2}; -\sqrt{2}$

45. $\frac{\sqrt{3}}{2}; \frac{1}{2}; \sqrt{3}; \frac{\sqrt{3}}{3}; 2; \frac{2\sqrt{3}}{3}$

47. $\frac{\sqrt{2}}{2}; -\frac{\sqrt{2}}{2}; -1; -1; -\sqrt{2}; \sqrt{2}$

49. $\frac{1}{2}; \frac{\sqrt{3}}{2}; \frac{\sqrt{3}}{3}; \sqrt{3}; \frac{2\sqrt{3}}{3}; 2$

51. $\frac{\sqrt{3}}{2}; \frac{1}{2}; \sqrt{3}; \frac{\sqrt{3}}{3}; 2; \frac{2\sqrt{3}}{3}$

53. $-\frac{1}{2}; \frac{\sqrt{3}}{2}; -\frac{\sqrt{3}}{3}; -\sqrt{3}; \frac{2\sqrt{3}}{3}; -2$

55. $\frac{\sqrt{3}}{2}; \frac{1}{2}; \sqrt{3}; \frac{\sqrt{3}}{3}; 2; \frac{2\sqrt{3}}{3}$

57. $\frac{\sqrt{3}}{3}, \sqrt{3}$ **59.** $\frac{\sqrt{3}}{2}, \frac{\sqrt{3}}{3}, \frac{2\sqrt{3}}{3}$ **61.** −1, −1

63. $-\frac{\sqrt{3}}{2}, -\frac{2\sqrt{3}}{3}$ **65.** 210°, 330°   **67.** 45°, 225°

69. 60°, 120°   **71.** 120°, 240°   **73.** 225°, 315°

75. 120°, 300°   **77.** 90°, 270°

14.5 Exercises *(pages 775–777)*

1. 0.5657728   **3.** 1.1342773   **5.** 1.0273488

7. 0.6383201   **9.** 1.7768146   **11.** 0.4771588

13. −5.7297416   **15.** 1.9074147   **17.** 57.997172°

19. 30.502748°   **21.** 46.173581°   **23.** 81.168073°

25. $B = 53° \, 40′; a = 571$ m; $b = 777$ m

27. $M = 38.8°; n = 154$ m; $p = 198$ m

29. $A = 47.9108°; c = 84.816$ cm; $a = 62.942$ cm

31. $B = 62.00°; a = 8.17$ ft; $b = 15.4$ ft

33. $A = 17.00°; a = 39.1$ in.; $c = 134$ in.

35. $c = 85.9$ yd; $A = 62° \, 50′; B = 27° \, 10′$

37. $b = 42.3$ cm; $A = 24° \, 10′; B = 65° \, 50′$

39. $B = 36° \, 36′; a = 310.8$ ft; $b = 230.8$ ft

41. $A = 50° \, 51′; a = 0.4832$ m; $b = 0.3934$ m

43. 9.35 meters   **45.** 88.3 meters   **47.** 26.92 inches

49. 583 feet   **51.** 28.0 meters   **53.** 469 meters

55. 146 meters   **57.** 34.0 miles

59. $a = 12, b = 12\sqrt{3}, d = 12\sqrt{3}, c = 12\sqrt{6}$

14.6 Exercises *(pages 783–785)*

1. $C = 95°, b = 13$ m, $a = 11$ m

3. $B = 37.3°, a = 38.5$ ft, $b = 51.0$ ft

5. $C = 57.36°, b = 11.13$ ft, $c = 11.55$ ft

7. $B = 18.5°, a = 239$ yd, $c = 230$ yd

9. $A = 56° \, 00′, AB = 361$ ft, $BC = 308$ ft

11. $B = 110.0°, a = 27.01$ m, $c = 21.36$ m

13. $A = 34.72°, a = 3326$ ft, $c = 5704$ ft

15. $C = 97° \, 34′, b = 283.2$ m, $c = 415.2$ m

17. 118 meters   **19.** 10.4 inches   **21.** 12   **23.** 7   **25.** 30°

27. $c = 2.83$ in., $A = 44.9°, B = 106.8°$

29. $c = 6.46$ m, $A = 53.1°, B = 81.3°$

31. $a = 156$ cm, $B = 64° \, 50′, C = 34° \, 30′$

33. $b = 9.529$ in., $A = 64.59°, C = 40.61°$

35. $a = 15.7$ m, $B = 21.6°, C = 45.6°$

37. $A = 30°, B = 56°, C = 94°$

39. $A = 82°, B = 37°, C = 61°$

41. $A = 42.0°, B = 35.9°, C = 102.1°$

43. 257 meters   **45.** 22 feet   **47.** 36° with the 45-foot cable, 26° with the 60-foot cable

Extension Exercises *(page 787)*

1. $\frac{\sqrt{3}}{2}$ **3.** $\frac{\sqrt{2}}{2}$ **5.** 46.4 m² **7.** 356 cm² **9.** 722.9 in.²
11. $24\sqrt{3}$ **13.** 78 m² **15.** 12,600 cm² **17.** 3650 ft²
19. 100 m² **21.** 33 cans

Chapter 14 Test *(pages 788–789)*

1. 74.2983° **2.** 203° **3.** $\sin \theta = -\frac{5\sqrt{29}}{29}$; $\cos \theta = \frac{2\sqrt{29}}{29}$;
$\tan \theta = -\frac{5}{2}$ **4.** III **5.** $\sin \theta = -\frac{3}{5}$; $\tan \theta = -\frac{3}{4}$;
$\cot \theta = -\frac{4}{3}$; $\sec \theta = \frac{5}{4}$; $\csc \theta = -\frac{5}{3}$ **6.** $\sin A = \frac{12}{13}$;
$\cos A = \frac{5}{13}$; $\tan A = \frac{12}{5}$; $\cot A = \frac{5}{12}$; $\sec A = \frac{13}{5}$;
$\csc A = \frac{13}{12}$

7. (a) $\frac{1}{2}$ **(b)** 1 **(c)** undefined **(d)** $-\frac{2\sqrt{3}}{3}$
(e) undefined **(f)** $-\sqrt{2}$ **8. (a)** 0.97939940
(b) 0.20834446 **(c)** 1.9362132 **(d)** 4.16529977
9. 16.16664145° **10.** 135°, 225°
11. $B = 31° 30'$, $a = 638$, $b = 391$ **12.** 15.5 ft
13. 137.5° **14.** 180 km **15.** 49.0°
16. $a = 648$ ft, $b = 456$ ft, $c = 28.0°$
17. $a = 40$ m, $B = 41°$, $C = 79°$ **18.** 2.7 miles
19. 5500 meters **20.** distance to both first and third
bases: 63.7 feet; distance to second base: 66.8 feet

CHAPTER 15 GRAPH THEORY

15.1 Exercises *(pages 803–808)*

1. 7 vertices, 7 edges **3.** 10 vertices, 9 edges
5. 6 vertices, 9 edges **7.** Two have degree 3. Three have
degree 2. Two have degree 1. Sum of degrees is 14. This is
twice the number of edges. **9.** Six have degree 1. Four
have degree 3. Sum of degrees is 18. This is twice the
number of edges. **11.** not isomorphic
13. isomorphic; Corresponding edges should be the same
color. AB should match AB, etc.

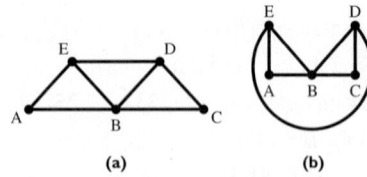

(a)   (b)

15. not isomorphic **17.** connected, 1 component
19. disconnected, 3 components **21.** disconnected,
2 components **23.** 10 **25.** 4 **27. (a)** yes **(b)** No,
because there is no edge from A to D. **(c)** No, because
there is no edge from A to E. **(d)** yes **(e)** yes **(f)** yes
29. (a) No, because it does not return to the starting vertex.
(b) yes **(c)** No, because there is no edge from C to F.
(d) No, because it does not return to starting vertex.
(e) No, because the edge from F to D is used more than

once. **31. (a)** No, because there is no edge from B to C.
(b) No, because the edge from I to G is used more than
once. **(c)** No, because there is no edge from E to I.
(d) yes **(e)** yes **(f)** No, because the edge from A to D
is used more than once. **33.** It is a walk and a path, not
a circuit. **35.** It is a walk, not a path, not a circuit.
37. It is a walk and a path, not a circuit.
39. No, because there is no edge from A to C, for example.
41. No, because there is no edge from A to F, for example.
43. yes

45. 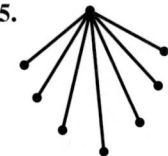 7 games **47.** 36 handshakes

49. 10 telephone conversations
51. $A \rightarrow B \rightarrow D \rightarrow A$ corresponds to tracing around the
edges of a single face. (The circuit is a triangle.)

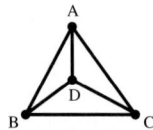

53. Answers will vary. **55.** Answers will vary.
57. Answers will vary.

59.  **61.**

63. 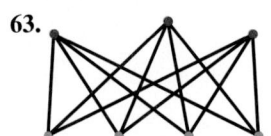 **65. (a)**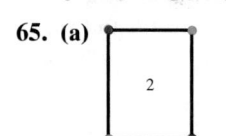

(b) 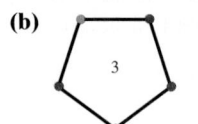 **(c)** 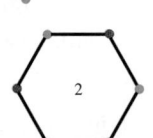 **(d)**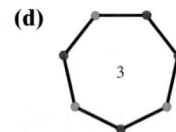

(e) A cycle with an odd number of vertices has chromatic
number 3. A cycle with an even number of vertices has
chromatic number 2.

67. 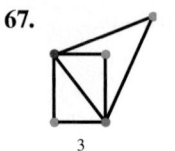 **69.**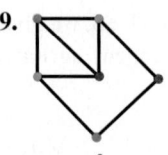

71. Three times: Choir and Forensics,
Service Club and Dance Club, and
Theater and Caribbean Club.
(There are other possible
groupings.)

73.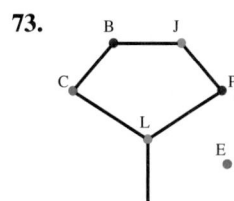

Three gatherings: Brad and Phil and Mary, Joe and Lindsay, and Caitlin and Eva. (There are other possible groupings.)

75. 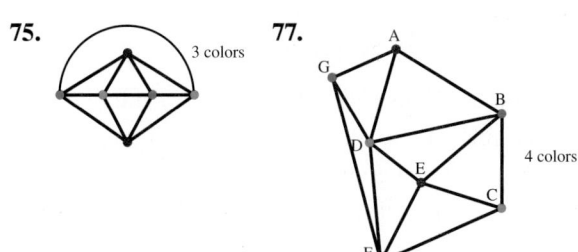 **77.**

79.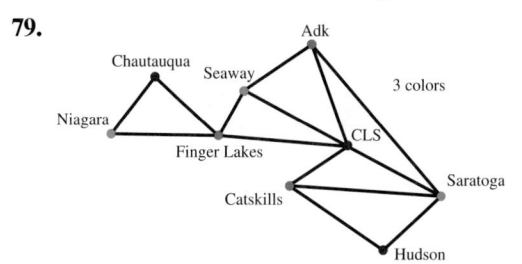

In Exercise 81, there are many different ways to draw the map.

81.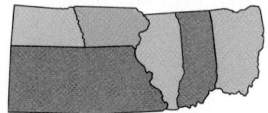

83. By the four-color theorem, this is not possible.

15.2 Exercises *(pages 816–819)*

1. (a) No, it is not a path. **(b)** yes **(c)** No, it is not a walk. **(d)** No, it is not a circuit.
3. (a) No, some edges are not used (e.g., B → F).
(b) yes **(c)** No, it is not a path. **(d)** yes
5. Yes, all vertices have even degree. **7.** No, some vertices have odd degree (e.g., G). **9.** yes
11. It has an Euler circuit. All vertices have even degree. No circuit visits each vertex exactly once.
13. It has an Euler circuit. All vertices have even degree. A → B → H → C → G → D → F → E → A visits each vertex exactly once. **15.** It has no Euler circuit. Some vertices have odd degree (e.g., B). It has no circuit that visits each vertex exactly once. **17.** No, some vertices have odd degree. **19.** Yes, all vertices have even degree.
21. none **23.** B → E or B → D **25.** B → C or B → H
27. A → C → B → F → E → D → C → F → D → A
29. Graph has an Euler circuit.
A → G → H → J → I → L → J → K → I →
H → F → G → E → F → D → E → C → D →
B → C → A → E → B → A

31. Graph does not have an Euler circuit. Some vertices have odd degree (e.g., C). **33.** There is such a route:
A → D → B → C → A → H → D → E → B →
H → G → E → F → H → J → L → C → M → A → K →
M → L → K → J → A **35.** It is not possible. Some vertices have odd degree (e.g., room at upper left).
37. no; There are more than two vertices with odd degree.
39. yes; B and G **41.** It is possible. Exactly two of the rooms have odd numbers of doors. **43.** It is not possible. All rooms have even numbers of doors.
There are other correct answers in Exercises 45–47.
45. A → B → D → C → A; There are 4 edges in any such circuit. **47.** A → B → C → D → E → F → G →
H → C → A → H → I → A; There are 12 edges in any such circuit. **49.** A complete graph has an Euler circuit if the number of vertices is an odd number greater than or equal to 3. In a complete graph with *n* vertices, the degree of each vertex is *n* − 1. "*n* − 1 is even" is equivalent to "*n* is odd."

15.3 Exercises *(pages 827–831)*

1. (a) No, because it visits E twice. **(b)** yes
(c) No, because it does not visit C. **(d)** No, because it does not visit A. **3. (a)** None, because there is no edge from B to C. **(b)** all three **(c)** none; The edge from A to D is used twice. **5.** A → B → D → E → F → C → A
7. G → H → J → I → G **9.** X → T → U → W → V → X
11. Hamilton circuit: A → B → C → D → A. The graph has no Euler circuit, because at least one of the vertices has odd degree. (In fact, all have odd degree.)

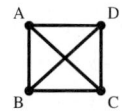

13. A → B → C → D → E → F → A is both a Hamilton and an Euler circuit.

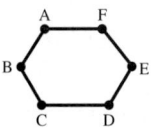

15. Hamilton circuit **17.** Euler circuit
19. Hamilton circuit **21.** 24 **23.** 362,880
25. 9! **27.** 17!
29. P → Q → R → S → P   P → Q → S → R → P
  P → R → Q → S → P   P → R → S → Q → P
  P → S → Q → R → P   P → S → R → Q → P

31. E→H→I→F→G→E   E→H→I→G→F→E

33. E→F→G→H→I→E   E→F→G→I→H→E
E→F→H→G→I→E   E→F→H→I→G→E
E→F→I→G→H→E   E→F→I→H→G→E

35. E→G→F→H→I→E   E→G→F→I→H→E
E→G→H→F→I→E   E→G→H→I→F→E
E→G→I→F→H→E   E→G→I→H→F→E

37. A→B→C→D→E→A A→A→C→B→D→E→A
A→B→C→E→D→A A→A→C→B→E→D→A
A→B→D→C→E→A A→A→C→D→B→E→A
A→B→D→E→C→A A→A→C→D→E→B→A
A→B→E→C→D→A A→A→C→E→B→D→A
A→B→E→D→C→A A→A→C→E→D→B→A
A→D→B→C→E→A A→A→E→B→C→D→A
A→D→B→E→C→A A→A→E→B→D→C→A
A→D→C→B→E→A A→A→E→C→B→D→A
A→D→C→E→B→A A→A→E→C→D→B→A
A→D→E→B→C→A A→A→E→D→B→C→A
A→D→E→C→B→A A→A→E→D→C→B→A

39. Minimum Hamilton circuit is P→Q→R→S→P;
Weight is 2200.   **41.** Minimum Hamilton circuit is
C→D→E→F→G→C; Weight is 64.

43. **(a)** A→C→E→D→B→A; Total weight is 20.
(b) C→A→B→D→E→C; Total weight is 20.
(c) D→C→A→B→E→D; Total weight is 23.
(d) E→C→A→B→D→E; Total weight is 20.

45. **(a)** A→C→D→E→B→A; Total weight is 87.
B→C→A→E→D→B; Total weight is 95.
C→A→E→D→B→C; Total weight is 95.
D→C→A→E→B→D; Total weight is 131.
E→C→A→D→B→E; Total weight is 137.
(b) A→C→D→E→B→A with total weight 87
(c) For example, A→B→C→D→E→A has total
weight 52.

47. A→B→C→D→E→F→A
A→B→C→F→E→D→A
A→B→E→D→C→F→A
A→B→E→F→C→D→A
A→D→E→F→C→B→A
A→D→E→B→C→F→A
A→D→C→B→E→F→A
A→D→C→F→E→B→A
A→F→E→B→C→D→A
A→F→E→D→C→B→A
A→F→C→D→E→B→A
A→F→C→B→E→D→A

49. A→B→C→D→E→F→A
A→B→C→E→D→F→A
A→B→C→E→F→D→A
A→B→C→F→E→D→A
A→D→E→F→C→B→A
A→D→F→E→C→B→A
A→F→D→E→C→B→A
A→F→E→D→C→B→A

51. **(a)** graphs (2) and (4)   **(b)** graphs (2) and (4)
(c) No. Graph (1) provides a counterexample.
(d) No. If $n < 3$, the graph will have no circuits at all.
(e) The degree of each vertex in a complete graph with n
vertices is $(n - 1)$. If $n \geq 3$, then $(n - 1) > \frac{n}{2}$. So we can
conclude from Dirac's theorem that the graph has a
Hamilton circuit.
53. A→F→G→R→S→T→U→Q→P→N→
M→L→K→J→I→H→B→C→D→E→A
55. Answers will vary.

15.4 Exercises *(pages 839–842)*
1. tree   **3.** No, because it is not connected.   **5.** tree
7. No, because it has a circuit.   **9.** It is not possible, since
the graph has a circuit.   **11.** tree   **13.** not necessarily a
tree · **15.** true   **17.** false

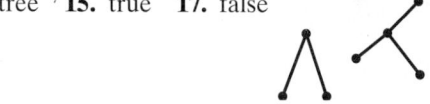

19.

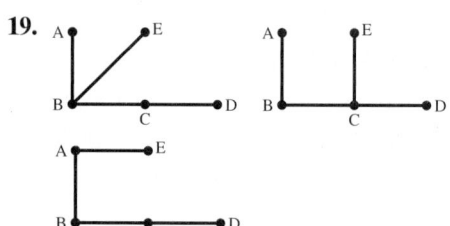

21.

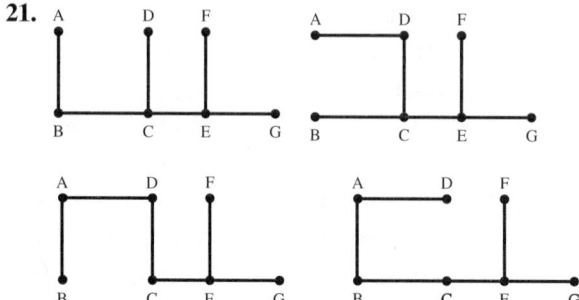

23.

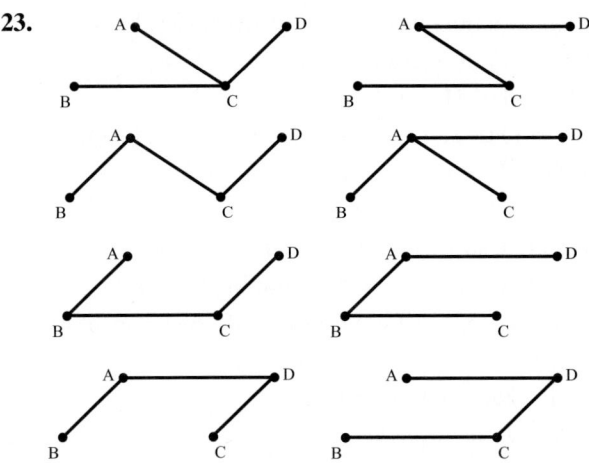

25. 20 **27.** If a connected graph has circuits, none of which have common edges, then the number of spanning trees for the graph is the product of the numbers of edges in all the circuits.

29. Total weight is 51.

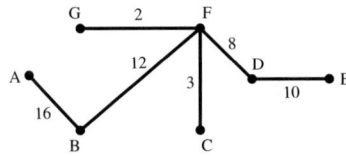

31. Total weight is 66.

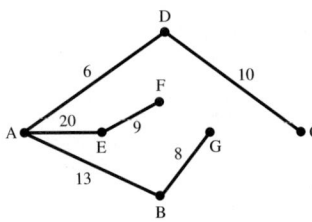

33. Total length to be covered is 140 ft.

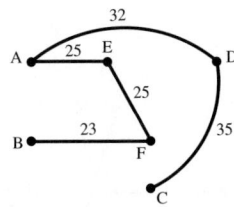

35. 33 **37.** 62 **39.** Different spanning trees must have the same number of edges. The number of vertices in the tree is the number of vertices in the original graph, and the number of edges has to be one less than this.

41. (a) 9 **(b)** 18 **(c)** 0 **(d)** 2

(e)

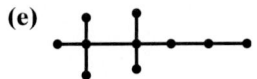

43. 22 cables **45.** This is possible. The graph must be a tree because it has one fewer edge(s) than vertices.

47. This is possible. The graph cannot be a tree, because it would have at least as many edges as vertices.

49. 3:

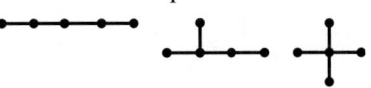

51. 125

53. 3 nonisomorphic trees:

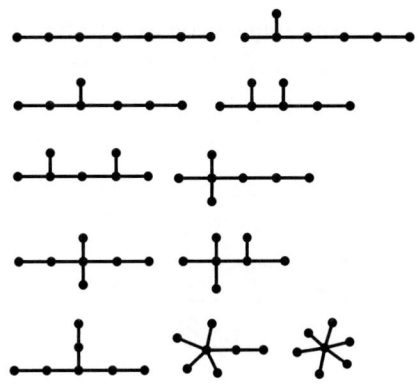

55. 11 nonisomorphic trees:

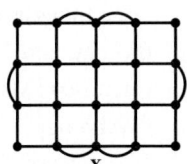

57. Answers will vary.

Extension Exercises *(page 843)*

1. In the graph shown, not all vertices have even degree. For example, the vertex marked X has degree 5. So this graph still does not have an Euler circuit.

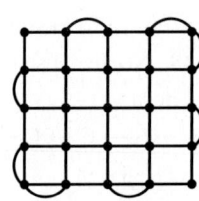

3. There are other ways of inserting the additional edges.

8 edges added

Chapter 15 Test *(pages 845–847)*

1. 7 **2.** 20 **3.** 10 **4. (a)** No, because the edge from A to B is used twice. **(b)** yes **(c)** No, because there is no edge from C to D. **5. (a)** yes **(b)** No, because for example, there is no edge from B to C. **(c)** yes

6. For example: 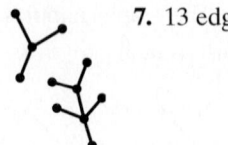 **7.** 13 edges

8. The graphs are isomorphic. Corresponding edges should be the same color. AB should match AB, etc.

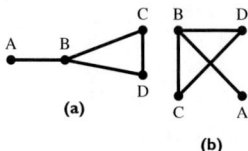

(a)

(b)

9.  The graph is connected. Tina knows the greatest number of other guests.

10. 28 games **11.** Yes, because there is an edge from each vertex to each of the remaining 6 vertices.

12. 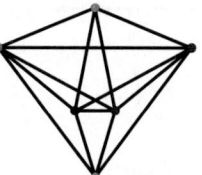 **13.**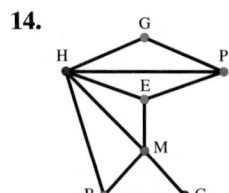

Chromatic number: 3

Chromatic number: 5

14. The Chromatic number is 3, so three separate exam times are needed. Exams could be at the same times as follows: Geography, Biology, and English; History and Chemistry; Mathematics and Psychology.

15. (a) No, because it does not use all the edges.
(b) No, because it is not a circuit (for example, there is no edge from B to C). **(c)** yes **16.** No, because some vertices have odd degree. **17.** Yes, because all vertices have even degree. **18.** No, because two of the rooms have odd numbers of doors.
19. F → B → E → D → B → C → D → K → B → A → H → G → F → A → G → J → F
20. (a) No, because it does not visit all vertices.
(b) No, because it is not a circuit (for example, there is no edge from B to C).

(c) No, because it visits some vertices twice before returning to the starting vertex.
21. F → G → H → I → E → F
F → G → H → E → I → F F → G → I → H → E → F
F → G → I → E → H → F F → G → E → H → I → F
F → G → E → I → H → F
There are 6 such Hamilton circuits.
22. P → Q → S → R → P; Total weight is 27.
23. A → E → D → C → F → B → A; Total weight is 11.85.
24. 24! **25.** Hamilton circuit
26. Any three of these:

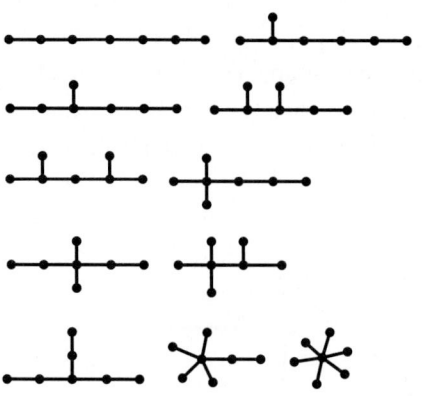

27. false **28.** true **29.** true
30. There are 4 spanning trees.

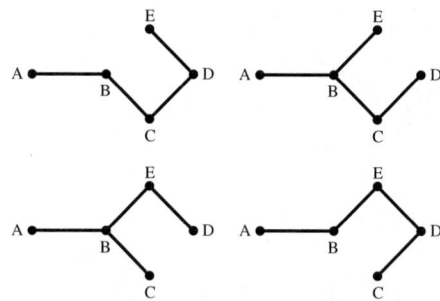

31. Weight is 24. **32.** 49

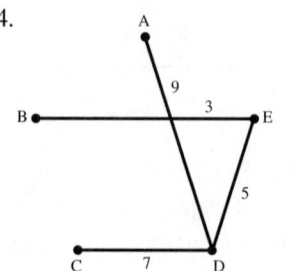

CHAPTER 16 VOTING AND APPORTIONMENT

16.1 Exercises (pages 860–862)

1. (a) $4! = 24$

(b)

Number of Voters	Ranking
3	b > c > a > d
2	a > d > c > b
1	c > d > b > a
1	d > c > b > a
1	d > a > b > c
2	c > a > d > b
1	a > c > d > b
2	a > b > c > d

(c) Australian shepherd
3. (a) c, with 3 (pairwise) points **(b)** a, with 24 (Borda) points **(c)** c **5.** $5! = 120; 7! = 5040$ **7.** For any value of $n \geq 5$ there are at least 120 possible rankings of the candidates. This means a voter must select one ranking from a huge number of possibilities. It also means the mechanics of any election method, except the plurality method, are difficult to manage. **9.** $_6C_2 = 15; {}_8C_2 = 28$
11. With 40,320 possible rankings to be examined, finding the outcomes of 28 different pairwise comparisons seems a nearly impossible task. **13. (a)** b, with 6 first-place votes **(b)** c, with 2 (pairwise) points **(c)** b, with 16 (Borda) points **(d)** c **15.** Logo a is selected by all the methods. **17. (a)** e, with 8 first-place votes **(b)** j, with 3 (pairwise) points **(c)** j, with 40 (Borda) points
(d) h **19. (a)** t, with 18 first-place votes **(b)** h, with 4 (pairwise) points **(c)** m, with 136 (Borda) points
(d) k **21.** h beats e. **23.** c beats t. **25.** In a runoff between k and c, activity k is selected. Activity k faces activity t, and k is selected. **27.** Logo a **29. (a)** 2
(b) c, with 7 pairwise points **31. (a)** 7 **(b)** e, with 7 pairwise points **33. (a)** 16 **(b)** c **35. (a)** 55 **(b)** c
37. j **39.** Answers will vary. **41.** 1; A candidate could receive a majority of first-round votes, and thus win the election. **43.** Answers will vary. One possible arrangement of the voters is 2, 4, 5, 7, 3.

16.2 Exercises (pages 871–875)

1. (a) Alternative a (6 of 11 first-place votes)
(b) b **(c)** yes **3. (a)** Alternative a (20 of 36 first-place votes) **(b)** b **(c)** yes **5. (a)** Alternative a (16 of 30 first-place votes) **(b)** b **(c)** yes **7. (a)** a **(b)** b
(c) b **(d)** a **(e)** plurality and Borda methods
9. (a) e **(b)** j **(c)** e **(d)** h **(e)** plurality and Hare

methods **11. (a)** h **(b)** t **(c)** k **(d)** m
(e) all three methods **13. (a)** m has 2 pairwise points, b and s have $1\frac{1}{2}$ pairwise points each, and c has 1 pairwise point. **(b)** b has $2\frac{1}{2}$ pairwise points, m has 2 pairwise points, s has 1 pairwise point, c has $\frac{1}{2}$ pairwise point, so b is selected. **(c)** Yes, the rearranging voters moved m, the winner of the nonbinding election, to the top of their ranking, but b wins the official selection process.
15. (a) d drops out after one round of votes; b drops out after Round two; in the third vote a is preferred to c by a margin of 11 to 6. **(b)** d drops out after one round of votes; c drops out after Round two; in the third vote b is preferred to a by a margin of 9 to 8. **(c)** Yes, the rearranging voters moved a, the winner of the nonbinding election, to the top of their ranking, but b wins the official selection process. **17. (a)** Candidate a has 75 first-place votes. **(b)** Candidate c has 80 first-place votes. **(c)** yes **19.** No; however, the second pairwise comparison results in a tie. **21. (a)** Round one eliminates b; a is preferred to c in Round two, by a margin of 22 to 12. **(b)** b **(c)** yes **23.** Answers will vary. **25.** Answers will vary. One possible voter profile is given.

Number of Voters	Ranking
10	a > b > c > d > e > f
9	b > f > e > c > d > a

Candidate a is a majority candidate and wins all of its pairwise comparisons by a margin of 10 to 9, earning 5 pairwise points. Candidate b wins all of its comparisons, except the one with a, earning 4 pairwise points.
27. Answers will vary. One possible profile is the voter profile for the animal shelter poster dog contest found in **Exercise 2(b)** of **Section 16.1**. **29. (a)** a has 2 pairwise points. **(b)** Answers will vary. The 3 voters in the bottom row all switch to the ranking $a > z > x > y$. **31.** Answers will vary. Delete Candidate c. **33.** Answers will vary. One possible profile is given.

Number of Voters	Ranking
21	g > j > e
12	j > e > g
8	j > g > e

35. Answers will vary.

16.3 Exercises *(pages 885–887)*

1. (a) 34,437 **(b)** 7 **3.** Virginia received 19 seats rather than 18. Delaware received only 1 seat rather than 2.

5. (a) 29,493; 123.40

(b)

State park	a	b	c	d	e
Number of trees	11	70	62	54	42

(c) $md = 122$

State park	a	b	c	d	e
Number of trees	11	70	62	54	42

(d) The traditionally rounded values of Q sum to 240, which is greater than the number of trees to be apportioned.

State park	a	b	c	d	e
Traditionally rounded Q	12	70	62	54	42

(e) The value of md for the Webster apportionment should be greater than $d = 123.40$, because greater divisors make lesser modified quotas with a lesser total sum.

(f) $md = 124$

State park	a	b	c	d	e
Number of trees	12	70	61	54	42

(g) The Hamilton and Jefferson apportionments are the same. The Webster apportionment is different from the other two apportionments.

7. (a) 269; 24.45

(b)

Course	Fiction	Poetry	Short Story	Multicultural
Number of sections	2	2	3	4

(c) $md = 20$

Course	Fiction	Poetry	Short Story	Multicultural
Number of sections	2	1	3	5

(d) The traditionally rounded values of Q sum to 10, which is less than the number of sections to be apportioned.

Course	Fiction	Poetry	Short Story	Multicultural
Traditionally rounded Q	2	1	3	4

(e) The value of md for the Webster apportionment should be less than $d = 24.45$ because lesser divisors make greater modified quotas with a greater total sum.

(f) $md = 23$

Course	Fiction	Poetry	Short Story	Multicultural
Number of sections	2	2	3	4

(g) The Hamilton and Webster apportionments are the same. The Jefferson apportionment is different from the other two apportionments.

(h) The Hamilton and Webster methods both apportion two sections of poetry; the Jefferson method apportions only one. If there are two sections of poetry, then the 35 enrolled students can be divided into two small sections with 17 and 18 students instead of all 35 students being forced into one large section.   **(i)** The Jefferson method apportions 5 sections of multicultural literature instead of 4. This means that the average class size will be 20 students, rather than 25 students.

9. (a)

State	Abo	Boa	Cio	Dao	Effo	Foti
Number of seats	15	22	6	19	14	55

(b) $md = 356$

State	Abo	Boa	Cio	Dao	Effo	Foti
Number of seats	15	22	6	19	13	56

(c) The Hamilton, Jefferson, and Webster apportionments all are different.

11.

State	Abo	Boa	Cio	Dao	Effo	Foti	Total
Number of seats	15	22	7	18	14	54	130

13. (a) 1721; 43.025

(b)

Hospital	A	B	C	D	E
Number of nurses	3	5	8	11	13

(c) $md = 40$

Hospital	A	B	C	D	E
Number of nurses	3	5	8	11	13

(d) The traditionally rounded values of Q sum to 41, which is greater than the number of nurses to be apportioned.

Hospital	A	B	C	D	E
Traditionally rounded Q	3	6	8	11	13

(e) The value of md for the Webster apportionment should be greater than $d = 43.025$, because greater divisors make lesser modified quotas with a lesser total sum.

(f) $md = 43.1$

Hospital	A	B	C	D	E
Number of nurses	3	5	8	11	13

(g) All three apportionments are the same.

15. Answers will vary. One possible ridership profile is given.

Bus route	a	b	c	d	e	Total
Number of riders	131	140	303	178	197	949

17. Answers will vary. One possible population profile is given.

State	a	b	c	d	e	Total
Population	50	230	280	320	120	1000

Extension Exercises (page 890)

1. Answers will vary.

3. (a) $md = 29$

Course	Fiction	Poetry	Short Story	Multicultural
Number of sections	2	2	3	4

(b) The Adams apportionment is the same as the Hamilton and Webster apportionments. It is different from the Jefferson apportionment.

5. (a) $md = 377.3$

State	Abo	Boa	Cio	Dao	Effo	Foti
Number of seats	16	22	7	18	14	54

(b) All four methods produce different apportionments of the 131 seats in Timmu's legislature.

7. $\sqrt{56 \cdot 57} = 56.498$ **9.** $\sqrt{32 \cdot 33} = 32.496$

11. If the sum is greater, then md is found by slowly increasing the value of d, because a greater divisor produces lesser modified quotas with a lesser sum.

13. (a) $md = 24$

Course	Fiction	Poetry	Short Story	Multicultural
Number of sections	2	2	3	4

(b) The Huntington-Hill apportionment is the same as the Hamilton, Webster, and Adams apportionments. It is different from the Jefferson apportionment.

15. (a) $md = 367$

State	Abo	Boa	Cio	Dao	Effo	Foti
Number of seats	15	22	7	19	14	54

(b) The Huntington-Hill apportionment is the same as the Webster apportionment. The other three apportionments differ.

16.4 Exercises (pages 900–901)

1. $md = 595$

State	a	b	c	d
Q rounded down/up	28/29	12/13	**81/82**	9/10
Number of seats	28	12	**83**	9

3. $md = 48.4$

State	a	b	c	d	e
Q rounded down/up	52/53	30/31	**164/165**	19/20	22/23
Number of seats	53	30	**166**	19	22

5.

State	a	b	c	d
Number of seats if $n = 204$	**35**	74	42	53
Number of seats if $n = 205$	**34**	75	43	53

7.

State	a	b	c	d	e
Number of seats if $n = 126$	**10**	29	34	28	25
Number of seats if $n = 127$	**9**	30	34	29	25

9.

State	a	b	c
Initial number of seats	1	4	6
Percent growth	10.91%	18.40%	13.16%
Revised number of seats	2	4	5

11.

State	a	b	c
Initial number of seats	6	5	2
Percent growth	4.84%	1.63%	1.45%
Revised number of seats	6	4	3

13. Two additional seats are added for the second apportionment.

State	Original State a	Original State b	New State c
Initial number of seats	20	55	*****
Revised number of seats	21	54	2

15. Seven additional seats are added for the second apportionment.

State	Original State a	Original State b	New State c
Initial number of seats	36	47	*****
Revised number of seats	37	46	7

17. $md = 208$

State	a	b	c	d	e
Q rounded down	8	16	33	**118**	42
Number of seats	9	17	34	**117**	43

19. The new states paradox does not occur if the new population is 531, but it does occur if the new population is 532.

21. Answers will vary.   **23.** Answers will vary.
25. Answers will vary.

Chapter 16 Test *(pages 902–904)*

1. Cancún   **2.** Aruba   **3.** the Bahamas   **4.** Aruba and Cancún each have two pairwise points and the Bahamas and Dominican Republic each have one pairwise point, so the pairwise comparison method vote results in a tie.
5. $7! = 5040$ **6.** $_{10}C_2 = 45$ **7.** Answers will vary.
8. Answers will vary.   **9.** Answers will vary.
10. Answers will vary.   **11.** Alternative a has a majority of the first-place votes, 16 of 31. The Borda method selects alternative b.   **12.** c   **13.** Alternative c is the Condorcet candidate. Plurality and Borda violate the Condorcet criterion and select b. Hare does not violate the criterion because it selects c.
14. Alternative c is selected before the five voters rearrange their ranking. Alternative s is selected after they rearrange their ranking. The rearranging voters moved alternative c, the previous pairwise selection, to the top of their ranking, but c is not selected a second time. This shows that the pairwise comparison method can violate the monotonicity criterion.
15. Alternative a is selected before the five voters rearrange their ranking. Alternative b is selected after they rearrange their ranking. The rearranging voters moved alternative a, the previous Hare selection, to the top of their ranking, but a is not selected a second time. This shows that the Hare method can violate the monotonicity criterion.
16. Alternative a is selected before losing alternative c is dropped. Alternative b is selected after c is dropped. The two outcomes show that the plurality method can violate the irrelevant alternatives criterion. A losing alternative was dropped from the selection process, but the original preferred alternative is not selected a second time.
17. Alternative b is selected before losing alternative d is dropped. Alternative a is selected after d is dropped. The two outcomes show that the Borda method can violate the irrelevant alternatives criterion. A losing alternative was dropped from the selection process, but the original preferred alternative is not selected a second time.
18. Alternative a is selected before losing alternative b is dropped. Alternative c is selected after b is dropped. The two outcomes show that the Hare method can violate the irrelevant alternatives criterion. A losing alternative was dropped from the selection process, but the original preferred alternative is not selected a second time.
19. Answers will vary.

20. standard divisor $d = 133.3692$ (That is, each seat represents 13,337 Smithapolis citizens.)

Ward	1st	2nd	3rd	4th	5th
Number of seats	11	65	57	50	12

21. $md = 131$

Ward	1st	2nd	3rd	4th	5th
Number of seats	10	65	58	50	12

22. $md = 133.7$

Ward	1st	2nd	3rd	4th	5th
Number of seats	11	65	57	50	12

23. Answers will vary.   **24.** Answers will vary.
25. Answers will vary.   **26.** Answers will vary.
27. $md = 347$

State	a	b	c	d
Q rounded down	6	12	15	**64**
Number of seats	6	12	16	**66**

28.

State	a	b	c	d	e
Number of seats if $n = 126$	**10**	29	34	28	25
Number of seats if $n = 127$	**9**	30	34	29	25

29.

State	a	b	c
Initial number of seats	1	4	6
Percent growth	14.55%	20.00%	15.79%
Revised number of seats	2	4	5

30. Fifteen additional seats are added for the second apportionment.

State	Original State a	Original State b	New State c
Initial number of seats	23	77	*****
Revised number of seats	24	76	15

APPENDIX THE METRIC SYSTEM

Appendix Exercises *(pages A-5–A-7)*
1. 8000 mm   **3.** 85 m   **5.** 689 mm   **7.** 5.98 cm
9. 5300 m   **11.** 27.5 km   **13.** 2.54 cm; 25.4 mm
15. 5 cm; 50 mm   **17.** 600 cl   **19.** 8700 ml   **21.** 9.25 L
23. 8.974 L   **25.** 8 kg   **27.** 5200 g   **29.** 4200 mg
31. 0.598 g   **33.** 30°C   **35.** −81°C   **37.** 50°F
39. −40°F   **41.** 200 nickels   **43.** 0.2 g   **45.** $40.99
47. $387.98   **49.** 1,082,400 cm³; 1.0824 m³
51. 200 bottles   **53.** 897.9 m   **55.** 201.1 km
57. 3.995 lb   **59.** 21,428.8 g   **61.** 30.22 qt   **63.** 106.7 L
65. unreasonable   **67.** reasonable   **69.** unreasonable
71. B   **73.** B   **75.** C   **77.** A   **79.** A   **81.** C
83. A   **85.** B   **87.** B   **89.** A   **91.** B   **93.** C   **95.** B

CREDITS

Text Credits

Exercises from the *Mathematics Teacher* monthly calendar appear on the following pages of the text. These are reprinted with permission from *Mathematics Teacher*, copyright © 1980–2010 by the National Council of Teachers of Mathematics. All Rights Reserved: **24–29, 41, 532, 541, 543, 554, 556, 567, 572–573, 575–576, 586, 588, 596, 604–605, 612.**

6 For Further Thought. Excerpted from Eves, Howard, *In Mathematical Circles.* Reprinted by permission of the Mathematical Association of America.   **33** "Medicare Funds" graph. From Lial/Hornsby/McGinnis, *Introductory Algebra,* 9th ed., p. 221. Copyright © 2010 Pearson Education. All Rights Reserved.   **35–36** "U.S. Milk Production" and "Average Gasoline Prices" graphs. From Lial/Hornsby/McGinnis, *Introductory Algebra,* 9th ed., p. 229. Copyright © 2010 Pearson Education. All Rights Reserved.   **42** "Unemployment Rate" graph. From Lial/Hornsby/McGinnis, *Introductory Algebra,* 9th ed., p. 295. Copyright © 2010 Pearson Education. All Rights Reserved.   **100** Exercise 83 problem. From Smullyan, Raymond, *The Lady or the Tiger and Other Logic Puzzles.* Copyright ©2009 Dover Publications. Reprinted with permission.   **100** Exercise 84 problem. Reprinted with the permission of Simon & Schuster, Inc., from *What Is the Name of This Book?* by Raymond Smullyan. Copyright © 1978, 1986 by Raymond Smullyan. All Rights Reserved.   **120–124, 134** Puzzles from *Original Logic Problems.* Penny Press, February 2010. Copyright © 2010 Penny Publications, LLC. Reprinted with permission. **121–122, 124, 135** Puzzles from *Original Sudoku.* Penny Press, March 2010. Copyright © 2010 Penny Publications, LLC. Reprinted with permission.   **130** Margin note problem. Reprinted with the permission of Simon & Schuster, Inc., from *What Is the Name of This Book?* by Raymond Smullyan. Copyright © 1978, 1986 by Raymond Smullyan. All Rights Reserved.   **227** Example 4. From Lial/Hornsby/McGinnis, *Intermediate Algebra,* 9th ed. (paperback), p.10. Copyright © 2010 Pearson Education. All Rights Reserved.   **229** Exercise 24. From Lial/Hornsby/McGinnis, *Intermediate Algebra,* 9th ed. (paperback), p. 51. Copyright © 2010 Pearson Education. All Rights Reserved.   **229** Exercise 65. From Lial/Hornsby/McGinnis, *Intermediate Algebra,* 9th ed. (paperback), p. 15. Copyright © 2010 Pearson Education. All Rights Reserved.   **262** Exercise 45. Courtesy of joyofpi.com. Reprinted by permission of David Blatner.   **269** "Spending on Kitty and Rover" graph. Adapted from Lial/Hornsby/McGinnis, *Intermediate Algebra,* 9th ed. Copyright © 2010 Pearson Education. All Rights Reserved.   **272** "2005 U.S. Government Spending" graph. Adapted from Lial/Hornsby/McGinnis, *Intermediate Algebra,* 9th ed., p.117. Copyright © 2010 Pearson Education. All Rights Reserved.   **274** Exercises 73–78. Adapted from Lial/Hornsby/McGinnis, *Introductory Algebra,* 9th ed.,

p. 221. Copyright © 2010 Pearson Education. All Rights Reserved. **282** "Composition of the U.S. Workforce in 2006" and "Medicare Funds" graphs. From Lial/Hornsby/McGinnis, *Intermediate Algebra,* 10th ed. Copyright © 2008 Pearson Education. All Rights Reserved.   **292–293** Exercises 77–78. From Lial/Hornsby/Schneider, *Beginning Algebra,* 9th ed. Copyright © 2004 Pearson Education. All Rights Reserved.   **296** Example 4. From Lial/Hornsby/McGinnis, *Study Skills Workbook for Intermediate Algebra.* Copyright © 2006 Pearson Education. All Rights Reserved.   **319** Table 4. From Lial/Hornsby/McGinnis, *Study Skills Workbook for Intermediate Algebra.* Copyright © 2006 Pearson Education. All Rights Reserved.   **320** Example 2. From Lial/Hornsby/Schneider, *Beginning Algebra,* 9th ed. Copyright © 2004 Pearson Education. All Rights Reserved.   **322** Example 3. From Lial/Hornsby/Schneider, *Beginning Algebra,* 9th ed., p. 161. Copyright © 2004 Pearson Education. All Rights Reserved. **327** "U.S. Egg Production" graph and problems. From Lial/Hornsby/McGinnis, *Introductory Algebra,* 9th ed. Copyright © 2010 Pearson Education. All Rights Reserved.   **364** Example 3. From Lial/Hornsby/Schneider, *College Algebra,* 10th ed., pp. 186–187. Copyright © 2009 Pearson Education. All Rights Reserved.   **367** For Further Thought. From Lial/Hornsby/Schneider, *College Algebra,* 10th ed., p. 198. Copyright © 2009 Pearson Education. All Rights Reserved.   **368** Exercises 19–20. Adapted from Lial/Hornsby/McGinnis, *Intermediate Algebra,* 9th ed. (paperback), p. 195. Copyright © 2010 Pearson Education. All Rights Reserved.   **369** Exercises 55–58. From Lial/Hornsby/Schneider, *College Algebra,* 10th ed., p. 192. Copyright © 2009 Pearson Education. All Rights Reserved.   **375–376** Examples 7–9. From Lial/Hornsby/McGinnis, *Intermediate Algebra,* 9th ed. (paperback), pp. 205–206. Copyright © 2010 Pearson Education. All Rights Reserved.   **378** Exercise 47 problem and graphs. From Lial/Hornsby/McGinnis, *Introductory Algebra,* 9th ed., pp. 2, 260. Copyright © 2010 Pearson Education. All Rights Reserved. **379** Exercises 67–69 problems and graphs. From Lial/Hornsby/McGinnis, *Intermediate Algebra,* 9th ed. (paperback), pp. 211–212. Copyright © 2010 Pearson Education. All Rights Reserved. **383** Example 7. From Lial/Hornsby/McGinnis, *Intermediate Algebra,* 9th ed. (paperback), p. 220. Copyright © 2010 Pearson Education. All Rights Reserved.   **387** Exercises 71–72 problems and graphs. From Lial/Hornsby/McGinnis, *Intermediate Algebra,* 9th ed. (paperback), pp. 225–226. Copyright © 2010 Pearson Education. All Rights Reserved.   **388** Exercise 74. From Lial/Hornsby/McGinnis, *Intermediate Algebra Worktext,* 7th ed., p. 201. Copyright © 2002 Pearson Education. All Rights Reserved. **408** Exercise 56. From Hornsby/Lial/Rockswold, *A Graphical Approach to College Algebra,* 5th ed., p. 404. Copyright © 2011 Pearson Education. All Rights Reserved.   **414** Example 4. From Lial/Hornsby/Schneider, *College Algebra,* 9th ed., p. 430. Copyright © 2010 Pearson Education. All Rights Reserved. **417** Exercise 58. From Lial/Hornsby/Schneider, *College Algebra,*

Photo Credits

INDEX OF APPLICATIONS

INDEX

Additional Appendices

Taken from: *Mathematical Ideas,* Eighth Edition by Charles D. Miller, Vern E. Heeren, and E. John Hornsby, Jr.

Mathematical Ideas, Sixth Edition by Charles D. Miller, Vern E. Heeren, and E. John Hornsby, Jr.

Go! Complete, Technology in Action, Fourth Edition by Alan Evans, Kendall Martin, and Mary Anne Poatsy

14

Taken from: *Mathematical Ideas*, Eighth Edition by Charles D. Miller, Vern E. Heeren, and E. John Hornsby, Jr.

Matrices and Their Applications

Although cryptography has been used by the military for centuries, only recently has the public found a need for it. Because of the large amount of electronic communication today, businesses, banks, and private individuals use cryptography to keep information secret. The process of disguising plain text into a cipher is called encryption. When a message is received, the cipher must be decoded into the original plain text using decryption.

Codes that encrypt a letter of the alphabet in the same way each time are usually easy to break. Suppose a simple code changes letters into numbers using the following technique: A = 01, B = 02, C = 03, . . . , Z = 26. After a few messages a person may be able to decipher the code because letters in the English language do not occur with equal likelihood. The most frequently used letter in the alphabet is E, which occurs approximately 13% of the time, whereas the least frequent is Z, which occurs only .1% of the time. One can quickly determine which number is associated with E and which one is associated with Z. According to one sample, the percentage P of occurrence for the most frequent letters in English text are as shown in the table.

Letter	P	Letter	P	Letter	P
E	13.0%	T	9.3%	N	7.8%
R	7.7%	O	7.4%	I	7.4%
A	7.3%	S	6.3%	D	4.4%

Matrices can be used to create sophisticated encryption methods that code blocks of letters rather than a single letter at one time. As a result, the letter E would be coded differently in the words THE and EAT. To decipher the message, the inverse of the matrix is required.

Sources: Schneier, B., *Applied Cryptography: Protocols, Algorithms, and Source Code in C,* John Wiley & Sons, Inc., 1994.

Sinkov, A., *Elementary Cryptanalysis: A Mathematical Approach,* Random House, 1968.

805

This chapter is concerned with the mathematical object called a *matrix,* which can be defined as follows.

Matrix

A **matrix** is a rectangular array of numbers. (The plural of *matrix* is *matrices.*) The numbers in the array are called the **entries,** or *elements,* of the matrix. Each horizontal line of entries is called a **row,** while each vertical line of entries is called a **column.**

Sometimes a matrix is simply a table, a convenient way of summarizing numerical data. Other times, it may reveal numerical patterns or show special relationships between two quantities. Examples already seen elsewhere in this book include magic squares, number base tables, addition and multiplication tables, probability and frequency distributions, compound interest tables, amortization schedules, and stock market listings. As you will see in this chapter, when a rectangular array is thought of as a matrix, particular symbols, notation, and manipulation techniques are utilized.

As an example, suppose you run the snack bar at the campus cinema and want to keep track of the revenue from your various snacks. For the Friday night showings of *Casablanca* with Humphrey Bogart, you list the dollar amounts as in Table 1.

TABLE 1 Friday Night Snack Bar Revenues

	Candy	Popcorn	Soft drinks
7 P.M. show	$0	$12	$10
9 P.M. show	$5	$8	$9

Following common mathematical practice, you can convey the information of this table in a matrix, enclosing the entries in brackets and denoting the matrix with an appropriate capital letter (in this case F, for Friday) as follows.

$$
F = \begin{matrix} \text{7 P.M. show} \\ \text{9 P.M. show} \end{matrix}
\begin{bmatrix} 0 & 12 & 10 \\ 5 & 8 & 9 \end{bmatrix}
$$

For example, the specific entry in row 1, column 3, namely 10, indicates that the soft drink revenue at the 7 P.M. show was $10.

Our main interest in this chapter will be to develop some algebraic operations on matrices, which make them useful in practical applications. We will see matrix F again in Section 1, where matrices will be added, subtracted, and multiplied by numbers. Section 2 involves multiplying matrices by other matrices. In Sections 3 and 4, we will discover how matrices can be used to solve systems of linear equations. Solving such systems was an important motivation for the English mathematicians who, in the 1850s, originated the development

S2

of matrix theory. These men were Arthur Cayley (1821–1895) and James Sylvester (1814–1897). (Linear systems were solved by the *elimination method* in an earlier chapter.) Section 5 of the chapter will introduce some basic ideas from *game theory,* a practical modern branch of mathematics.

Throughout the chapter we will discover various properties of matrices as a mathematical system. Some of these will probably be what you would expect, while others may surprise you.

14.1 Basic Operations on Matrices

Recall from the definition above that a matrix is a rectangular array of numbers. The number of rows and columns in a matrix determines its *size,* or its **order.** For example, we say that matrix F above is a 2×3 (read "2 by 3") matrix, or that it has order 2×3. (Notice that, when specifying the order of a matrix, we give the number of rows first and then the number of columns.)

If a matrix has the same number of rows as columns, it is called a **square matrix.** A matrix with only one row is called a **row matrix.** A matrix with only one column is called a **column matrix.** A matrix in which all entries are zero is called a **zero matrix.**

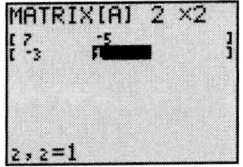

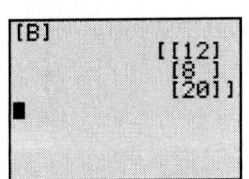

The figures above show how matrices A and B of Example 1 appear on a graphing calculator screen.

EXAMPLE 1 Give the order of each of the following matrices, and identify any that are square matrices, row matrices, column matrices, or zero matrices.

$$A = \begin{bmatrix} 7 & -5 \\ -3 & 1 \end{bmatrix} \quad B = \begin{bmatrix} 12 \\ 8 \\ 20 \end{bmatrix} \quad C = \begin{bmatrix} 1 & 4 \\ 9 & 5 \\ 6 & 2 \end{bmatrix} \quad D = \begin{bmatrix} -5 & 0 & 0 \\ 2 & 3 & 1 \\ 9 & 4 & 0 \end{bmatrix}$$

$$E = \begin{bmatrix} 10 & 50 & 30 \end{bmatrix} \quad F = \begin{bmatrix} 0 & 0 & 0 \\ 0 & 0 & 0 \end{bmatrix} \quad G = \begin{bmatrix} 6 \end{bmatrix}$$

The orders of the seven given matrices are as follows.

Matrix	A	B	C	D	E	F	G
Order	2×2	3×1	3×2	3×3	1×3	2×3	1×1

A, D, and G are square matrices. E and G are row matrices. B and G are column matrices. F is a zero matrix.

Notice that matrix G (in Example 1) is both a row matrix and a column matrix. Notice also that, even though G has only a single entry, G is a matrix and not a number. Pure numbers are commonly distinguished from matrices by referring to the numbers as *scalars.* For example, 6 is a scalar, whereas [6] is a matrix. This distinction is sometimes important, so the brackets must always be included around the entries of a matrix.

Equal Matrices

Two matrices are said to be **equal** if they have the same order and if all corresponding entries are equal.

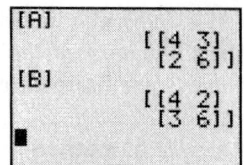

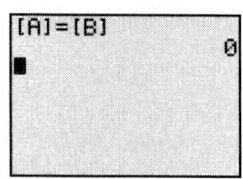

The fact that matrices A and B are not equal is illustrated by the 0 returned by the calculator in the bottom screen. Had they been equal, a 1 would have been returned.

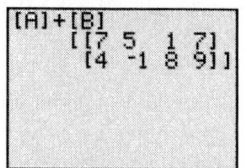

The result of Example 3 is supported in these two screens.

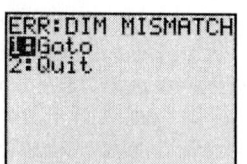

This screen, indicating a dimension (or order) mismatch, was the result of attempting to add matrices A and B as defined in Example 4.

EXAMPLE 2 In each case, determine whether matrices A and B are equal.

(a) $A = \begin{bmatrix} 4 & 3 \\ 2 & 6 \end{bmatrix}$ $\qquad B = \begin{bmatrix} 4 & 2 \\ 3 & 6 \end{bmatrix}$

Even though A and B have the same order (2×2) and include the same numbers as entries, not all *corresponding* entries are equal. For example, the row 2, column 1 entry of matrix A is 2, while the corresponding entry of matrix B is 3. Matrices A and B are not equal.

(b) $A = \begin{bmatrix} 1 & 2 & 3 \\ 6 & 5 & 1 \end{bmatrix}$ $\qquad B = \begin{bmatrix} 1 & 2 \\ 6 & 5 \end{bmatrix}$

Matrix A has order 2×3, while B has order 2×2. Since they do not have the same order, matrices A and B are not equal.

(c) $A = \begin{bmatrix} 12 & -2 & 4 \end{bmatrix}$ $\qquad B = \begin{bmatrix} 12 & -2 & 4 \end{bmatrix}$

A and B have the same order (1×3) and all corresponding entries are equal, so matrices A and B are equal. ◾

In the remainder of this section, we introduce three operations on matrices: addition, subtraction, and scalar multiplication. In each case the result is another matrix. Addition (and subtraction) can only be done when the two matrices to be added (or subtracted) have the same order. If a matrix operation can be done, we say the result is **computable.** However, if any condition (such as different orders) makes the operation impossible, we say the result is **not computable.**

Addition of Matrices

The **sum** of two matrices of the same order is found by *adding* corresponding entries. If two matrices have different orders, their sum is not computable.

EXAMPLE 3 Let $\quad A = \begin{bmatrix} 2 & -1 & 3 & 2 \\ 1 & 0 & 4 & 2 \end{bmatrix}$ and $B = \begin{bmatrix} 5 & 6 & -2 & 5 \\ 3 & -1 & 4 & 7 \end{bmatrix}$. Find $A + B$.

Add the corresponding entries.

$$
\begin{aligned}
A + B &= \begin{bmatrix} 2 & -1 & 3 & 2 \\ 1 & 0 & 4 & 2 \end{bmatrix} + \begin{bmatrix} 5 & 6 & -2 & 5 \\ 3 & -1 & 4 & 7 \end{bmatrix} \\
&= \begin{bmatrix} 2+5 & -1+6 & 3+(-2) & 2+5 \\ 1+3 & 0+(-1) & 4+4 & 2+7 \end{bmatrix} \\
&= \begin{bmatrix} 7 & 5 & 1 & 7 \\ 4 & -1 & 8 & 9 \end{bmatrix} \quad ◾
\end{aligned}
$$

EXAMPLE 4 Let $A = \begin{bmatrix} 2 & 1 \\ 3 & 4 \end{bmatrix}$ and let $B = \begin{bmatrix} 4 & -1 & 0 \\ 2 & 5 & 0 \end{bmatrix}$. Find $A + B$.

Since A is 2×2 and B is 2×3, the matrices have different orders. Their sum is not computable. ◾

EXAMPLE 5 Matrix F from the chapter introduction showed snack bar revenues for the Friday night movie showings. The corresponding Saturday night revenues are shown here.

$$S = \begin{array}{c} \text{7 P.M. show} \\ \text{9 P.M. show} \end{array} \begin{bmatrix} 4 & 15 & 11 \\ 4 & 10 & 10 \end{bmatrix}$$

Popcorn — Candy, Drinks

Derive a matrix that shows the various revenues for the weekend (Friday and Saturday combined).

The sum of matrices F and S will show the required quantities, since it adds corresponding entries in all six matrix positions.

$$W = F + S$$
$$= \begin{bmatrix} 0 & 12 & 10 \\ 5 & 8 & 9 \end{bmatrix} + \begin{bmatrix} 4 & 15 & 11 \\ 4 & 10 & 10 \end{bmatrix}$$
$$= \begin{bmatrix} 0+4 & 12+15 & 10+11 \\ 5+4 & 8+10 & 9+10 \end{bmatrix}$$

$$= \begin{array}{c} \text{7 P.M. show} \\ \text{9 P.M. show} \end{array} \begin{bmatrix} 4 & 27 & 21 \\ 9 & 18 & 19 \end{bmatrix}$$

Popcorn — Candy, Drinks

Specifically, total weekend popcorn revenues from the 9 P.M. show was $18. (Other similar amounts can also be read from matrix W.)

Subtraction of Matrices

The **difference** of two matrices of the same order is found by *subtracting* corresponding entries. If two matrices have different orders, their difference is not computable.

[A]
[[4 -3]
 [-1 5]]
[B]
[[-2 4]
 [1 5]]

[A]-[B]
[[6 -7]
 [-2 0]]

The result of Example 6 is supported in these two screens.

EXAMPLE 6 Find the indicated difference.

$$\begin{bmatrix} 4 & -3 \\ -1 & 5 \end{bmatrix} - \begin{bmatrix} -2 & 4 \\ 1 & 5 \end{bmatrix} = \begin{bmatrix} 4-(-2) & -3-4 \\ -1-1 & 5-5 \end{bmatrix}$$
$$= \begin{bmatrix} 6 & -7 \\ -2 & 0 \end{bmatrix}$$

EXAMPLE 7 Refer to the revenue matrices of Example 5. Find a matrix that shows, for each of the six revenue categories, how much more (or less) was taken in on Saturday night than on Friday night. Call this matrix E (for *Excess* revenue).

Compute the following difference.

$$E = S - F$$

$$= \begin{bmatrix} 4 & 15 & 11 \\ 4 & 10 & 10 \end{bmatrix} - \begin{bmatrix} 0 & 12 & 10 \\ 5 & 8 & 9 \end{bmatrix}$$

$$= \begin{bmatrix} 4 - 0 & 15 - 12 & 11 - 10 \\ 4 - 5 & 10 - 8 & 10 - 9 \end{bmatrix}$$

$$= \begin{matrix} \text{7 P.M. show} \\ \text{9 P.M. show} \end{matrix} \begin{bmatrix} \overset{\text{Candy}}{\downarrow} & \overset{\underset{\text{Popcorn}}{\downarrow}}{} & \overset{\text{Drinks}}{\downarrow} \\ 4 & 3 & 1 \\ -1 & 2 & 1 \end{bmatrix}$$

This result shows, for example, that candy sales at the 9 P.M. show were $1 *less* on Saturday than on Friday. (Revenues in all other categories were *greater* on Saturday.) ◢

As mentioned earlier, a real number is called a *scalar* in distinction to a matrix. Multiplication of a matrix by a scalar is defined as follows.

Scalar Multiplication of Matrices

The **product of a scalar and a matrix** is found by *multiplying each entry* of the matrix by the scalar.

[A]
      [[3 -2]
      [-4 6]]
-2[A]
      [[-6 4]
      [8 -12]]

This screen supports the result of Example 8.

EXAMPLE 8 Let $A = \begin{bmatrix} 3 & -2 \\ -4 & 6 \end{bmatrix}$ and let b represent the scalar -2, or $b = -2$. Find bA, that is, $-2A$.

Multiply each element of A by -2.

$$-2A = -2 \begin{bmatrix} 3 & -2 \\ -4 & 6 \end{bmatrix} = \begin{bmatrix} -2(3) & -2(-2) \\ -2(-4) & -2(6) \end{bmatrix} = \begin{bmatrix} -6 & 4 \\ 8 & -12 \end{bmatrix}$$ ◢

EXAMPLE 9 Refer to Example 5. Suppose the weekend revenues, shown in matrix W, are to be equally divided by two campus clubs sponsoring the sales. Find a matrix showing the amounts each club should get from each of the six revenue categories.

Since there are two clubs, the required amounts will be shown by the following product.

$$\frac{1}{2}W = \frac{1}{2}\begin{bmatrix} 4 & 27 & 21 \\ 9 & 18 & 19 \end{bmatrix} = \begin{matrix} \text{7 P.M. show} \\ \text{9 P.M. show} \end{matrix} \begin{bmatrix} \overset{\text{Candy}}{\downarrow} & \overset{\underset{\text{Popcorn}}{\downarrow}}{} & \overset{\text{Drinks}}{\downarrow} \\ 2 & 13.5 & 10.5 \\ 4.5 & 9 & 9.5 \end{bmatrix}$$

For example, each club gets $13.50 from the popcorn sales at the 7 P.M. shows. ◢

One of our objectives throughout this chapter will be to observe what we can about the way matrices behave as mathematical entities. We want to notice some properties possessed by matrices and by the operations that apply to them. For example, is addition of matrices commutative? Is it associative? What about subtraction of matrices? What about multiplication?

Problem Solving

Notice that addition, subtraction, and (scalar) multiplication *of matrices* have been defined in this section in terms of addition, subtraction, and multiplication *of real numbers*. Therefore, we should expect to be able to deduce certain properties of these operations on matrices by considering what we already know about the corresponding operations on real numbers. This idea of extending our previous knowledge to new or different situations is a key concept in mathematics (as well as other areas). As you study the following example, try to observe specific problem-solving techniques at work.

EXAMPLE 10   Consider the set of all matrices of the same order. Is addition of matrices, on this set, a *commutative* operation?

The question here pertains to all matrices of "the same order." Let us start by narrowing our attention to a particular order, say 2×3. And let us consider two particular 2×3 matrices, say

$$A = \begin{bmatrix} 1 & 3 & 5 \\ 2 & 4 & 6 \end{bmatrix} \quad \text{and} \quad B = \begin{bmatrix} 2 & 4 & 6 \\ 8 & 10 & 12 \end{bmatrix}.$$

Check to see whether $A + B = B + A$:

$$A + B = \begin{bmatrix} 1 + 2 & 3 + 4 & 5 + 6 \\ 2 + 8 & 4 + 10 & 6 + 12 \end{bmatrix} = \begin{bmatrix} 3 & 7 & 11 \\ 10 & 14 & 18 \end{bmatrix}$$

and

$$B + A = \begin{bmatrix} 2 + 1 & 4 + 3 & 6 + 5 \\ 8 + 2 & 10 + 4 & 12 + 6 \end{bmatrix} = \begin{bmatrix} 3 & 7 & 11 \\ 10 & 14 & 18 \end{bmatrix}.$$

By inspection, these two results are, indeed, equal. On the basis of this result, you may be led to conclude (inductively) that the answer to the original question is "yes." But we really have not verified the result except for the particular matrices A and B. Let us extend our attention to *all* 2×3 matrices by considering matrices

$$C = \begin{bmatrix} a & c & e \\ b & d & f \end{bmatrix} \quad \text{and} \quad D = \begin{bmatrix} g & i & k \\ h & j & l \end{bmatrix}$$

for *any* real numbers $a, b, c, \ldots, l$. Now

$$C + D = \begin{bmatrix} a + g & c + i & e + k \\ b + h & d + j & f + l \end{bmatrix}$$

and

$$D + C = \begin{bmatrix} g + a & i + c & k + e \\ h + b & j + d & l + f \end{bmatrix}.$$

We can now use our previous knowledge that addition is, in fact, commutative on the set of real numbers to conclude that $a + g = g + a, c + i = i + c$, etc., and that therefore $C + D = D + C$. This conclusion is based on *deductive* reasoning, which is totally reliable (unlike inductive reasoning).

The desired result has still only been established for 2×3 matrices (by considering C and D). Our final step is to observe that our deduction with C and D would still be valid for two equal order matrices of *any* order. (Why is this so?) Therefore, addition of matrices, on *any* set of equal order matrices, is indeed commutative. ◢

14.1 EXERCISES

Perform the indicated matrix operations. If a required result is not computable, state why not.

1. $\begin{bmatrix} 3 & 2 \\ 5 & 1 \end{bmatrix} + \begin{bmatrix} 8 & -1 \\ 4 & 3 \end{bmatrix}$

2. $\begin{bmatrix} -6 & 9 \\ 2 & 4 \end{bmatrix} + \begin{bmatrix} -2 & 5 \\ -1 & 3 \end{bmatrix}$

3. $\begin{bmatrix} 2 & 8 & -1 \\ 4 & 0 & 3 \end{bmatrix} - \begin{bmatrix} -1 & 5 & 2 \\ 0 & 4 & 3 \end{bmatrix}$

4. $\begin{bmatrix} -1 & 2 & 4 \\ -2 & 3 & 0 \end{bmatrix} - \begin{bmatrix} 2 & -1 & 4 \\ -5 & 6 & 9 \end{bmatrix}$

5. $\begin{bmatrix} -2 & 3 & 1 \\ 4 & 0 & -2 \\ 5 & -1 & 6 \end{bmatrix} + \begin{bmatrix} -1 & 1 & 1 \\ 4 & 2 & 3 \\ -1 & 4 & 7 \end{bmatrix}$

6. $\begin{bmatrix} 3 & 4 & -1 \\ 7 & -8 & 2 \\ 9 & -1 & 3 \end{bmatrix} - \begin{bmatrix} -4 & 2 & -1 \\ 3 & -1 & 8 \\ 4 & 9 & 0 \end{bmatrix}$

7. $\begin{bmatrix} -4 & 3 & 2 \\ -8 & 0 & 1 \\ 4 & 2 & 1 \end{bmatrix} - \begin{bmatrix} 3 & -4 \\ 2 & -3 \\ 8 & 9 \end{bmatrix}$

8. $\begin{bmatrix} -1 & 6 & 2 \\ 3 & 4 & 7 \\ 9 & 8 & 2 \end{bmatrix} + \begin{bmatrix} -4 & 9 & 2 & 0 \\ -3 & 1 & 4 & 0 \\ 8 & 9 & 7 & 0 \end{bmatrix}$

9. $\begin{bmatrix} 3 \\ 4 \\ 2 \end{bmatrix} + \begin{bmatrix} -1 \\ 9 \\ 8 \end{bmatrix} - \begin{bmatrix} 2 \\ 1 \\ 3 \end{bmatrix}$

10. $\begin{bmatrix} 7 \\ 8 \\ 9 \end{bmatrix} + \begin{bmatrix} 1 \\ 9 \\ 3 \end{bmatrix} - \begin{bmatrix} -4 \\ 3 \\ 8 \end{bmatrix}$

11. $\begin{bmatrix} -2 & 4 \\ 0 & 9 \end{bmatrix} + \begin{bmatrix} -8 & 1 \\ 3 & 6 \end{bmatrix} - \begin{bmatrix} 4 & 7 \\ -2 & 5 \end{bmatrix}$

12. $\begin{bmatrix} -3 & 2 \\ 4 & 8 \end{bmatrix} + \begin{bmatrix} -9 & -1 \\ 6 & 3 \end{bmatrix} + \begin{bmatrix} -2 & 5 \\ 0 & 8 \end{bmatrix}$

Let $A = \begin{bmatrix} -4 & 0 \\ 3 & -4 \end{bmatrix}$ *and let* $B = \begin{bmatrix} 2 & -1 \\ -4 & 0 \end{bmatrix}$. *Compute the following.*

13. $A + B$

14. $A - B$

15. $2A$

16. $3B$

17. $-4B$

18. $-5A$

19. $2A + 3B$

20. $-7A + 4B$

21. $(-1)A + A$

A dietician prepares a diet specifying the allowable amounts of four main food groups: group I, meats; group II, fruits and vegetables; group III, breads and starches; and group IV, milk products. Amounts are given in appropriate units (1 ounce for meat, 1/2 cup for fruits and vegetables, 1 slice for bread, and 8 ounces for milk).

22. The numbers of units for breakfast for the four food groups respectively are 2, 1, 2, and 1; for lunch, 3, 2, 2, and 1; and for dinner, 4, 3, 2, and 1. Write a 3×4 matrix to display this information.

23. The amounts of fat, carbohydrates, and protein in the food groups respectively are as follows:

    Fat: 5, 0, 0, 10   Carbohydrates: 0, 10, 15, 12   Protein: 7, 1, 2, 8.

    Display this information in a 4×3 matrix.

24. Assume there are 8 calories per unit of fat, 4 calories per unit of carbohydrate, and 5 calories per unit of protein. Show these data in a 3×1 matrix.

Don and Connie run a business (D&C Creations) in California building and selling gold rush era tables and chairs. They maintain factories in Sloughhouse (F1) and Nevada City (F2) and ship their products to warehouses in Sacramento (W1), San Francisco (W2), and Reno (W3). The table here shows shipping costs per item from each factory to each warehouse.

Route	Cost Per Item
F1 to W1	$12
F1 to W2	20
F1 to W3	25
F2 to W1	16
F2 to W2	25
F2 to W3	30

25. Construct a 2×3 matrix, C, showing the data for shipping cost per item.

26. On April 1, the freight company that *D&C* utilizes adjusted per item shipping costs as shown here. Construct a 2×3 matrix, A, showing the shipping cost adjustments.

Route	Adjustment
F1 to W1	$3
F1 to W2	-2
F1 to W3	2
F2 to W1	4
F2 to W2	2
F2 to W3	-2

27. Show an appropriate matrix operation whose result gives *D&C*'s shipping costs per item after April 1.

28. Each month, Don and Connie send to each of their warehouses 10 model-*A* tables, 12 model-*B* tables, 5 model-*C* tables, 15 model-*A* chairs, 20 model-*B* chairs, and 8 model-*C* chairs. Exhibit this information in a 2×3 matrix (with tables represented in the top row).

29. The matrix here shows stock on hand at the *D&C* Reno warehouse as of September 1.

$$R = \begin{matrix} \text{Tables} \\ \text{Chairs} \end{matrix} \begin{matrix} A & B & C \\ \begin{bmatrix} 45 & 35 & 20 \\ 65 & 40 & 35 \end{bmatrix} \end{matrix}$$

    If no stock is sent out of the warehouse during September, how much stock will be on hand October 1? Use the result of Exercise 28 and matrix methods.

30. In Exercise 29, how many model-*B* chairs were on hand October 1 at the Reno warehouse?

31. In Exercise 29, how many model-*C* tables were on hand October 1 at the Reno warehouse?

32. The number of each model held on September 1 at the Sacramento and San Francisco warehouses of *D&C* are:

$$S = \begin{bmatrix} 22 & 25 & 38 \\ 31 & 34 & 35 \end{bmatrix} \quad \text{and} \quad F = \begin{bmatrix} 30 & 32 & 28 \\ 43 & 47 & 30 \end{bmatrix}.$$

Find the total inventory in all three warehouses on September 1.

33. Suppose the Sacramento warehouse of *D&C* shipped the following numbers of items during September:

$$K = \begin{bmatrix} 5 & 10 & 8 \\ 11 & 14 & 15 \end{bmatrix}.$$

Find the stock on hand October 1, taking into account the numbers of items received and shipped during the month.

Matrix K shows the weights of four men and four women at the beginning of a diet designed to produce weight loss. Matrix M shows the weights after the diet.

$$K = \begin{matrix} \text{Men} \\ \text{Women} \end{matrix} \begin{bmatrix} 160 & 158 & 172 & 193 \\ 132 & 143 & 119 & 157 \end{bmatrix} \qquad M = \begin{matrix} \text{Men} \\ \text{Women} \end{matrix} \begin{bmatrix} 154 & 148 & 163 & 178 \\ 132 & 154 & 112 & 136 \end{bmatrix}$$

34. Show a matrix operation whose result gives the weight losses of all eight people on the diet.

35. In Exercise 34, how much weight did the third man lose?

36. In Exercise 34, what result did the second woman experience?

Find all real values of the variables that will make each of the following equalities true. In case the given equality is impossible, state why.

37. $\begin{bmatrix} x & y & z \\ 2 & 5 & 1 \end{bmatrix} = \begin{bmatrix} 7 & 2 \\ 4 & 5 \\ 2 & 1 \end{bmatrix}$

38. $\begin{bmatrix} 3 & 4 \\ z & x \end{bmatrix} = \begin{bmatrix} 3z & 4x \end{bmatrix}$

39. $\begin{bmatrix} 5 & y \\ z & 2 \end{bmatrix} = \begin{bmatrix} 5 & z \\ y & 2 \end{bmatrix}$

40. $\begin{bmatrix} x & y & z \end{bmatrix} = \begin{bmatrix} 2x & 3y & 4z \end{bmatrix}$

41. $\begin{bmatrix} 6 & y \\ k & m \end{bmatrix} = \begin{bmatrix} 6 & 3 \\ 8 & 1 \end{bmatrix}$

42. $\begin{bmatrix} 5 & 7 \\ 1 & 8 \end{bmatrix} = \begin{bmatrix} a & b \\ 1 & c \end{bmatrix}$

43. $\begin{bmatrix} x+2 & 5 & 9 \\ 1 & 3 & y \end{bmatrix} = \begin{bmatrix} 2x+1 & z-3 & 9 \\ 1 & 3 & 8 \end{bmatrix}$

44. $\begin{bmatrix} 2 & m+5 & a \\ 1 & n-3 & -1 \end{bmatrix} = \begin{bmatrix} 2 & 2m+6 & 2a \\ 1 & 4n-12 & -1 \end{bmatrix}$

45. $\begin{bmatrix} -2 & 6 \\ x & 2 \end{bmatrix} + \begin{bmatrix} x & y \\ 3 & 5 \end{bmatrix} = \begin{bmatrix} 8 & 2 \\ 7 & 7 \end{bmatrix}$

46. $\begin{bmatrix} 5 & m & 3 \\ 2 & y & 5 \end{bmatrix} - \begin{bmatrix} 3 & 4 & a \\ 1 & 6 & a \end{bmatrix} = \begin{bmatrix} 2 & 5 & 2 \\ 1 & 4 & 1 \end{bmatrix}$

The dates in the calendar display for February 1998 form a 4 × 7 matrix, as shown here.

February 1998

Sun	Mon	Tue	Wed	Thu	Fri	Sat
1	2	3	4	5	6	7
8	9	10	11	12	13	14
15	16	17	18	19	20	21
22	23	24	25	26	27	28

47. Will the month of March on a calendar ever form a matrix? Why or why not?

48. What is the next year following 1998 in which February will again form a matrix? (*Hint:* You *may* want to consider "leap years" or "perpetual calendars." You can look up these concepts in this text or elsewhere.)

Example 10 in this section established the commutative property for addition of matrices. Use similar reasoning in Exercises 49–56 to determine whether each statement is true *or* false *for matrices A, B, and C of the same order and for scalars a and b.*

49. $A - B = B - A$

50. $A + (B + C) = (A + B) + C$ (associative property for addition)

51. $A + B$ is a matrix.   (closure property)

52. If 0 is a matrix of the same order as A, containing only zero entries, then $0 + A = A$ and $A + 0 = A$.   (identity property for addition)

53. If $-A = (-1)A$, then $A + (-A) = 0$ and $-A + A = 0$.   (inverse property for addition)

54. $A - B = A + (-B)$, where $-B = (-1)B$.

55. $a(B + C) = aB + aC$

56. $(a + b)C = aC + bC$

57. Does the set of all 2×2 matrices and the operation of addition form a *mathematical system?* Explain why or why not. (*Hint:* Look up the definition of "mathematical system.")

58. Does the system of Exercise 57 form a *group?* Explain why or why not. (*Hint:* Look up the definition of a mathematical "group.")

 Multiplication of Matrices

D&C Creations is a business that manufactures and sells unfinished tables and chairs. (See Exercises 25–33 of Section 1.) Table 2 shows the units of materials required for each table, while Table 3 shows the per unit cost of materials.

TABLE 2   Materials Required for a Table

| | | Materials | |
		Wood	Hardware
Furniture	**Table**	8	5

TABLE 3   Cost of Materials

		Cost Per Unit
Materials	**Wood**	$2
	Hardware	$3

From the tabulated data we see that each table manufactured requires 8 units of wood and 5 units of hardware, and wood costs $2 per unit while hardware costs $3 per unit.

The cost of materials for each table will then be

$$8 \cdot (\$2) + 5 \cdot (\$3) = \$16 + \$15 = \$31.$$

(Make sure you understand this calculation.) To see how matrix notation can be of use here, first exhibit the material requirements for a table in the **row** matrix M:

$$M = \text{Table} \quad \begin{array}{cc} \text{Wood} & \text{Hardware} \\ [\;\; 8 & 5 \;\;] \end{array}$$

Matrix M relates the furniture item (table—on the left) to its materials (wood and hardware—at the top). Also exhibit the data on cost per unit (for materials) in the **column** matrix C:

$$C = \begin{array}{c} \\ \text{Wood} \\ \text{Hardware} \end{array} \begin{array}{c} \text{Cost per} \\ \text{unit} \\ \left[\begin{array}{c} 2 \\ 3 \end{array} \right] \end{array}$$

Matrix C relates materials (on the left) to cost (at the top).

Now define *row-column multiplication* as follows.

Row-Column Multiplication

If a row matrix and a column matrix have equal numbers of entries, then their **row-column product** is the *scalar* obtained by multiplying all of their corresponding entries (first with first, second with second, and so on) and adding the resulting products. Always position the row matrix first (on the left) and the column matrix second (on the right). If the row matrix and column matrix have different numbers of entries, their row-column product is not computable.

We can now see that the cost of materials for each table ($31 as calculated above) is the row-column product of M and C.

$$MC = \text{Table} \quad \begin{array}{cc} \text{Wood} & \text{Hardware} \\ [\;\; 8 & 5 \;\;] \end{array} \cdot \begin{array}{c} \\ \text{Wood} \\ \text{Hardware} \end{array} \begin{array}{c} \text{Cost per} \\ \text{unit} \\ \left[\begin{array}{c} 2 \\ 3 \end{array} \right] \end{array}$$

$$= 8 \cdot 2 + 5 \cdot 3$$

$$= 31.$$

Notice that matrix M relates furniture (table) to materials and matrix C relates materials to cost, so the product MC relates furniture (table) to cost. These relationships are illustrated in Figure 1.

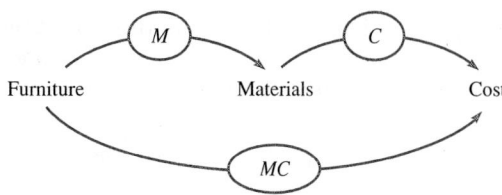

■ FIGURE 1
Quantities Related by Matrices M and C and their Row-Column Product MC

The row-column multiplication of M and C is reiterated below, without the labels, and with arrows emphasizing which entries are multiplied together.

$$MC = \begin{bmatrix} 8 & 5 \end{bmatrix} \cdot \begin{bmatrix} 2 \\ 3 \end{bmatrix} = 8 \cdot 2 + 5 \cdot 3 = 31$$

Recall that, for a row-column product to be computable, the following conditions are required.

1. The first (left) matrix must be a row matrix, and the second (right) matrix must be a column matrix.
2. The two matrices must have the same number of entries.

Row-column multiplication is important because it is the basis for defining matrix multiplication in general. To show the usefulness of general matrix multiplication, we continue our illustration with $D\&C$ Creations.

It is found that each *chair* made by $D\&C$ requires 6 units of wood and 4 units of hardware. Representing this information in the row matrix $N = \begin{bmatrix} 6 & 4 \end{bmatrix}$, we can now discover the material cost of a chair by computing another row-column product.

$$NC = \begin{bmatrix} 6 & 4 \end{bmatrix} \cdot \begin{bmatrix} 2 \\ 3 \end{bmatrix} = 6 \cdot 2 + 4 \cdot 3 = 24$$

Note that N relates a chair to its materials, and C relates those materials to their costs. Thus NC relates a chair to its cost ($24).

Now observe that the known relationships between furniture and materials (for *both tables and chairs*) can be combined into a single matrix, say R, which shows materials needed for both types of furniture.

$$R = \begin{array}{c} \text{Table} \\ \text{Chair} \end{array} \begin{bmatrix} \overset{\text{Wood}}{8} & \overset{\text{Hardware}}{5} \\ 6 & 4 \end{bmatrix}$$

We can now exhibit both row-column products MC and NC within a single matrix product, RC, as follows.

$$RC = \begin{array}{c} \text{Table} \\ \text{Chair} \end{array} \begin{bmatrix} \overset{\text{Wood}}{8} & \overset{\text{Hardware}}{5} \\ 6 & 4 \end{bmatrix} \cdot \begin{array}{c} \text{Wood} \\ \text{Hardware} \end{array} \begin{bmatrix} \overset{\text{Cost per unit}}{2} \\ 3 \end{bmatrix}$$

The computation of this matrix product involves two row-column products: row 1 of R times the column of C, and row 2 of R times the column of C. The actual calculation appears as follows.

$$RC = \begin{matrix} \text{Table} \\ \text{Chair} \end{matrix} \begin{matrix} \text{Cost} \\ \begin{bmatrix} 8 \cdot 2 + 5 \cdot 3 \\ 6 \cdot 2 + 4 \cdot 3 \end{bmatrix} \end{matrix}$$

$$= \begin{matrix} \text{Table} \\ \text{Chair} \end{matrix} \begin{matrix} \text{Cost} \\ \begin{bmatrix} 31 \\ 24 \end{bmatrix} \end{matrix}$$

This result shows that the materials (wood and hardware) cost $31 for each table and $24 for each chair.

Without labels, the above matrix product appears as follows.

$$RC = \begin{bmatrix} 8 & 5 \\ 6 & 4 \end{bmatrix} \cdot \begin{bmatrix} 2 \\ 3 \end{bmatrix} = \begin{bmatrix} 31 \\ 24 \end{bmatrix}$$

In this product, the 31 (a scalar) in row 1, column 1 is simply the row-column product of row 1 from R with column 1 from C. The 24 in row 2, column 1 is the row-column product of row 2 from R with column 1 from C. These row-column products are computable only because the rows of R have the same number of entries as the column of C. In other words, R has as many columns as C has rows (2 in both cases).

In general, the following diagram shows when the matrix product AB is computable and what the order of the product will be.

In summary, the product of two matrices can be defined as follows.

Multiplication of Two Matrices

If A is an $m \times n$ matrix and B is an $n \times p$ matrix, then the **product of the two matrices,** AB, is an $m \times p$ matrix where each particular entry, say the entry in row i, column j, is the row-column product of row i in matrix A with column j in matrix B. (If the number of columns in A is different from the number of rows in B, the product AB is not computable.)

EXAMPLE 1 Find each matrix product AB if it exists.

(a) $A = \begin{bmatrix} 2 & -1 & 3 & 1 \\ 0 & 1 & 0 & 2 \end{bmatrix}$ $\quad B = \begin{bmatrix} -1 & 2 & 3 \\ 0 & 0 & -1 \\ 1 & 2 & 0 \\ 0 & -1 & 0 \end{bmatrix}$

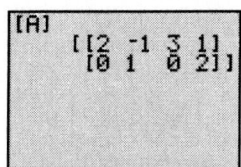

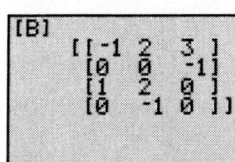

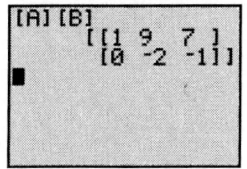

These screens illustrate how the product AB in Example 1(a) is found with a graphing calculator. Attempting to find BA would lead to an error message, however.

By the definition above, since A is of order 2×4 and B is of order 4×3, the product exists and will be of order 2×3.

$$AB = \begin{bmatrix} \square & \square & \square \\ \square & \square & \square \end{bmatrix}$$

Each entry of AB is the appropriate row-column product. For example, the row 1, column 2 entry is found as shown in Figure 2.

$$\begin{bmatrix} 2 & -1 & 3 & 1 \\ 0 & 1 & 0 & 2 \end{bmatrix} \cdot \begin{bmatrix} -1 & 2 & 3 \\ 0 & 0 & -1 \\ 1 & 2 & 0 \\ 0 & -1 & 0 \end{bmatrix} = \begin{bmatrix} \square & 9 & \square \\ \square & \square & \square \end{bmatrix}$$

Row 1   Column 2

$$2 \cdot 2 = 4$$
$$(-1) \cdot 0 = 0$$
$$3 \cdot 2 = 6$$
$$1 \cdot (-1) = -1$$
$$\text{Sum} = 9$$

■ **FIGURE 2**
Finding the Row 1, Column 2 Entry of a Matrix Product

Compute the other five entries similarly to find that

$$AB = \begin{bmatrix} 1 & 9 & 7 \\ 0 & -2 & -1 \end{bmatrix}.$$

(b) $A = \begin{bmatrix} -2 & 1 \\ 3 & 4 \end{bmatrix}$ $B = \begin{bmatrix} -1 & 2 \\ 0 & 1 \\ 4 & 0 \end{bmatrix}$

Since A is of order 2×2 and B is of order 3×2 (that is, the number of columns of A is different from the number of rows of B), the product AB is not computable. ◢

The following example establishes an important fact about matrix multiplication.

EXAMPLE 2 Decide in each case whether or not $AB = BA$.

(a) $A = \begin{bmatrix} 6 & -2 \\ 1 & 4 \\ 0 & 3 \end{bmatrix}$ $B = \begin{bmatrix} 2 & -1 & 0 & 4 \\ 1 & 3 & 2 & -2 \end{bmatrix}$

In this case, AB is computable but BA is not. (Why not?) Therefore AB and BA cannot be equal. (There is no need to compute AB.)

(b) $A = \begin{bmatrix} 4 & 2 \\ 6 & 2 \end{bmatrix}$ $B = \begin{bmatrix} 5 & 1 \\ 3 & 4 \end{bmatrix}$

Here, AB and BA are both computable.

$$AB = \begin{bmatrix} 4 & 2 \\ 6 & 2 \end{bmatrix} \cdot \begin{bmatrix} 5 & 1 \\ 3 & 4 \end{bmatrix} = \begin{bmatrix} 26 & 12 \\ 36 & 14 \end{bmatrix}$$

$$BA = \begin{bmatrix} 5 & 1 \\ 3 & 4 \end{bmatrix} \cdot \begin{bmatrix} 4 & 2 \\ 6 & 2 \end{bmatrix} = \begin{bmatrix} 26 & 12 \\ 36 & 14 \end{bmatrix}$$

In this case, AB and BA are equal.

(c) $A = \begin{bmatrix} -2 & 3 \\ 2 & -1 \end{bmatrix}$ $B = \begin{bmatrix} -1 & -3 \\ -2 & 2 \end{bmatrix}$

Again, AB and BA are both computable.

$$AB = \begin{bmatrix} -2 & 3 \\ 2 & -1 \end{bmatrix} \cdot \begin{bmatrix} -1 & -3 \\ -2 & 2 \end{bmatrix} = \begin{bmatrix} -4 & 12 \\ 0 & -8 \end{bmatrix}$$

$$BA = \begin{bmatrix} -1 & -3 \\ -2 & 2 \end{bmatrix} \cdot \begin{bmatrix} -2 & 3 \\ 2 & -1 \end{bmatrix} = \begin{bmatrix} -4 & 0 \\ 8 & -8 \end{bmatrix}$$

In this case, AB and BA are *not* equal!

Suppose we had asked the following question: Given two matrices A and B such that AB and BA are both computable, are AB and BA *sometimes* equal, *always* equal, or *never* equal? In light of parts (b) and (c) of Example 2, AB and BA are *sometimes* equal. Generally, the condition "sometimes" is established by exhibiting one case where the statement is true and another case where it is false. The conditions "always" and "never" take more than examples for their proofs. (See Example 5.)

Part (c) of Example 2 shows that AB and BA are not always equal. Therefore *matrix multiplication is not commutative.* This fact delayed the acceptance of matrix theory during its early development since mathematicians tended to doubt the usefulness of a non-commutative multiplication operation. The significance of this result is emphasized in the following statement.

Matrix Multiplication Is *Not* Commutative

Given two matrices A and B, even when the products AB and BA are both computable, AB does not always equal BA. (In fact, AB and BA are equal only in rare cases.)

EXAMPLE 3 Recall that *D&C* Creations makes unfinished tables and chairs. The matrices

$$R = \begin{array}{c} \\ \text{Table} \\ \text{Chair} \end{array} \begin{array}{c} \text{Wood} \quad \text{Hardware} \\ \begin{bmatrix} 8 & 5 \\ 6 & 4 \end{bmatrix} \end{array} \quad \text{and} \quad C = \begin{array}{c} \\ \text{Wood} \\ \text{Hardware} \end{array} \begin{array}{c} \text{Cost per unit} \\ \begin{bmatrix} 2 \\ 3 \end{bmatrix} \end{array}$$

relate furniture to materials and materials to cost, respectively.

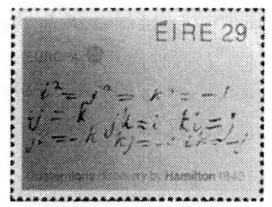
Don and Connie have observed that most potential customers prefer to buy furniture that is already finished, so they have begun to finish their tables and chairs. They find that each table requires 3 units of paint, each chair requires 2 units of paint, and paint costs $1 per unit.

(a) Expand the original matrices R and C to reflect this new information.
The expanded matrices are as follows.

$$R = \begin{array}{c} \text{Table} \\ \text{Chair} \end{array} \begin{bmatrix} 8 & 5 & 3 \\ 6 & 4 & 2 \end{bmatrix} \quad \text{and} \quad C = \begin{array}{c} \text{Wood} \\ \text{Hardware} \\ \text{Paint} \end{array} \begin{bmatrix} 2 \\ 3 \\ 1 \end{bmatrix}$$

(with R columns labeled Wood, Hardware, Paint and C labeled Cost per unit)

Notice that, in their new versions, R still relates furniture (on the left) to materials (at the top) and C still relates materials (at the left) to cost (at the top).

(b) Compute the new product RC, if possible, and explain its meaning.
The new product RC is still computable. A 2×3 matrix times a 3×1 matrix will produce a 2×1 matrix.

$$RC = \begin{array}{c} \text{Table} \\ \text{Chair} \end{array} \begin{bmatrix} 8 & 5 & 3 \\ 6 & 4 & 2 \end{bmatrix} \cdot \begin{array}{c} \text{Wood} \\ \text{Hardware} \\ \text{Paint} \end{array} \begin{bmatrix} 2 \\ 3 \\ 1 \end{bmatrix} = \begin{array}{c} \text{Table} \\ \text{Chair} \end{array} \begin{bmatrix} 34 \\ 26 \end{bmatrix}$$

The result shows that (including paint) the materials will now cost $34 for each table and $26 for each chair.

EXAMPLE 4 Let $M = \begin{bmatrix} -8 & 6 \\ 2 & 1 \end{bmatrix}$ and $I = \begin{bmatrix} 1 & 0 \\ 0 & 1 \end{bmatrix}$. Find MI and IM.

Use the definition of matrix multiplication to find MI.

$$MI = \begin{bmatrix} -8 & 6 \\ 2 & 1 \end{bmatrix} \cdot \begin{bmatrix} 1 & 0 \\ 0 & 1 \end{bmatrix}$$

$$= \begin{bmatrix} -8 \cdot 1 + 6 \cdot 0 & -8 \cdot 0 + 6 \cdot 1 \\ 2 \cdot 1 + 1 \cdot 0 & 2 \cdot 0 + 1 \cdot 1 \end{bmatrix} = \begin{bmatrix} -8 & 6 \\ 2 & 1 \end{bmatrix} = M$$

Here $MI = M$. Multiplying in the same way will show that $IM = M$.

Matrix I of Example 4 preserves the identity of matrix M for multiplication and is called the **identity matrix.**

Identity matrices of any square order can be found. For example, the 3×3 identity matrix is displayed here.

$$\begin{bmatrix} 1 & 0 & 0 \\ 0 & 1 & 0 \\ 0 & 0 & 1 \end{bmatrix} \quad \text{3 × 3 identity matrix}$$

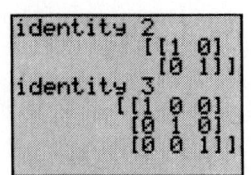

The identity matrices of orders 2 and 3 are shown in this screen.

Notice the similarity between I, the identity for matrix multiplication, and 1, the identity for multiplication of real numbers. Just as $a \cdot 1 = a$ and $1 \cdot a = a$ for every real number a, it is also true that $MI = M$ and $IM = M$ for any square matrix M and identity matrix I of the same order.

EXAMPLE 5 Prove that the equalities $MI = M$ and $IM = M$ are both *always* true for 2×2 matrices M.

Let $M = \begin{bmatrix} a & c \\ b & d \end{bmatrix}$ for any real numbers a, b, c, and d. Then

$$MI = \begin{bmatrix} a & c \\ b & d \end{bmatrix} \cdot \begin{bmatrix} 1 & 0 \\ 0 & 1 \end{bmatrix} = \begin{bmatrix} a \cdot 1 + c \cdot 0 & a \cdot 0 + c \cdot 1 \\ b \cdot 1 + d \cdot 0 & b \cdot 0 + d \cdot 1 \end{bmatrix} = \begin{bmatrix} a & c \\ b & d \end{bmatrix} = M$$

and

$$IM = \begin{bmatrix} 1 & 0 \\ 0 & 1 \end{bmatrix} \cdot \begin{bmatrix} a & c \\ b & d \end{bmatrix} = \begin{bmatrix} 1 \cdot a + 0 \cdot b & 1 \cdot c + 0 \cdot d \\ 0 \cdot a + 1 \cdot b & 0 \cdot c + 1 \cdot d \end{bmatrix} = \begin{bmatrix} a & c \\ b & d \end{bmatrix} = M.$$

We complete this section with an application of matrices to communication networks. The ideas apply to a great variety of situations, including computer networks, telephone systems, genetic evolution, spread of rumors or diseases, and many other kinds of communication among countries, individuals, businesses, or other social and economic groups.

Suppose four computers in a small office are connected as shown in Figure 3. Computer A is connected directly to computers B and C, C is connected to A, B, and D, and so on. All direct connections can be shown in the **communication matrix** M, where an entry of 1 indicates a direct connection while a 0 indicates no direct connection. (The main diagonal of the matrix, from upper left to lower right, contains all 0s since a computer is not considered to be directly connected to itself.)

$$M = \begin{array}{c@{}c} & \begin{array}{cccc} A & B & C & D \end{array} \\ \begin{array}{c} A \\ B \\ C \\ D \end{array} & \begin{bmatrix} 0 & 1 & 1 & 0 \\ 1 & 0 & 1 & 0 \\ 1 & 1 & 0 & 1 \\ 0 & 0 & 1 & 0 \end{bmatrix} \end{array}$$

Define the column matrix K (of all 1s) as follows.

$$K = \begin{bmatrix} 1 \\ 1 \\ 1 \\ 1 \end{bmatrix}$$

Then compute the product MK.

$$MK = \begin{bmatrix} 0 & 1 & 1 & 0 \\ 1 & 0 & 1 & 0 \\ 1 & 1 & 0 & 1 \\ 0 & 0 & 1 & 0 \end{bmatrix} \cdot \begin{bmatrix} 1 \\ 1 \\ 1 \\ 1 \end{bmatrix} = \begin{bmatrix} 2 \\ 2 \\ 3 \\ 1 \end{bmatrix}$$

■ FIGURE 3
A Small Computer Network

Verify, by comparing Figure 3, that MK gives, for each computer in the network, the number of other computers with which it has a direct connection.

Notice that A and D are not directly connected. To communicate with D, A must go through one or more intermediaries. For example, A could send data to D through the single intermediary C or by way of the two intermediaries B and C.

The following example utilizes the matrix M^2. (Exponents on matrices work just as on real numbers.)

EXAMPLE 6   For matrix M above, find M^2 and explain its meaning.

$$M^2 = MM = \begin{bmatrix} 0 & 1 & 1 & 0 \\ 1 & 0 & 1 & 0 \\ 1 & 1 & 0 & 1 \\ 0 & 0 & 1 & 0 \end{bmatrix} \cdot \begin{bmatrix} 0 & 1 & 1 & 0 \\ 1 & 0 & 1 & 0 \\ 1 & 1 & 0 & 1 \\ 0 & 0 & 1 & 0 \end{bmatrix} = \begin{bmatrix} 2 & 1 & 1 & 1 \\ 1 & 2 & 1 & 1 \\ 1 & 1 & 3 & 0 \\ 1 & 1 & 0 & 1 \end{bmatrix}$$

Each entry in M^2 indicates the number of different ways one computer can send data to another through a single intermediary. For example, the 1 in row 3, column 2 shows that C can get to B through a single intermediary in just 1 way. (Figure 3 shows that the one way is through A.)   ◆

Practical applications of matrices often involve orders much greater than what we have illustrated here, and can require tremendous amounts of calculation. (A 30×20 matrix times a 20×40 matrix requires 24,000 individual products of entries, plus 1,200 sums of 20 terms each. And the original entries may involve several decimal places.)

Fortunately, modern computers, and even handheld calculators, can do matrix operations directly.

EXAMPLE 7   Compute the following matrix product.

$$\begin{bmatrix} 2.8 & 8.1 & 7.7 \\ 3.6 & 4.6 & 6.4 \\ 4.7 & 8.2 & 5.5 \\ 1.9 & 9.3 & 8.9 \\ 7.3 & 4.6 & 7.8 \\ 3.5 & 2.5 & 4.2 \end{bmatrix} \cdot \begin{bmatrix} 3.2 & 8.2 & 6.4 & 8.6 & 2.9 \\ 2.7 & 3.7 & 6.1 & 4.8 & 8.6 \\ 9.3 & 3.4 & 1.8 & 2.5 & 4.7 \end{bmatrix}$$

The 90 required products (2.8 times 3.2, and so on) could be done individually, but with a calculator we just enter the two matrices A and B and then enter matrix A times matrix B. (Most of the work is in keying in the entries.) The resulting product is

$$\begin{bmatrix} 102.44 & 79.11 & 81.19 & 82.21 & 113.97 \\ 83.46 & 68.30 & 62.62 & 69.04 & 80.08 \\ 88.33 & 87.58 & 90.00 & 93.53 & 110.00 \\ 113.96 & 80.25 & 84.91 & 83.23 & 127.32 \\ 108.32 & 103.40 & 88.82 & 104.36 & 97.39 \\ 57.01 & 52.23 & 45.21 & 52.60 & 51.39 \end{bmatrix} \cdot$$ ◆

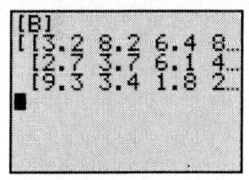

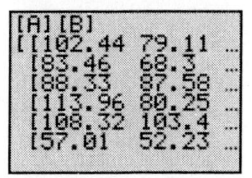

The computation in Example 7 is easily accomplished with a graphing calculator having matrix capability. Notice that the second and third screens are incomplete. The user must scroll to the right in order to read the hidden entries (indicated by the ellipsis . . .).

The ability to accomplish all the tedious calculations on a machine helps make matrix theory of practical use. For example, if *D&C* Creations expanded to a product line of, say, 30 items utilizing 20 materials (rather than 2 or 3 of each), the matrices *R* and *C* (relating products to materials and materials to cost) would become quite large, but the relationship between products and material costs would still be exhibited in the single matrix product *RC*.

14.2 EXERCISES

Compute each of the following products, if possible. If a product is not computable, state why not.

1. $\begin{bmatrix} -3 & 2 \\ 4 & 1 \end{bmatrix} \cdot \begin{bmatrix} -2 & 0 \\ 1 & 3 \end{bmatrix}$

2. $\begin{bmatrix} -5 & 2 \\ 1 & 4 \end{bmatrix} \cdot \begin{bmatrix} -1 & 4 \\ 3 & 0 \end{bmatrix}$

3. $\begin{bmatrix} 0 & -2 \\ 5 & 1 \end{bmatrix} \cdot \begin{bmatrix} -3 & 6 \\ 1 & 4 \end{bmatrix}$

4. $\begin{bmatrix} -3 & 5 \\ 1 & 0 \end{bmatrix} \cdot \begin{bmatrix} 8 & -2 \\ 1 & 7 \end{bmatrix}$

5. $\begin{bmatrix} 1 & 3 \\ 4 & 1 \end{bmatrix} \cdot \begin{bmatrix} 2 & 1 & 0 \\ 5 & 2 & 3 \end{bmatrix}$

6. $\begin{bmatrix} -5 & 6 \\ 3 & 4 \end{bmatrix} \cdot \begin{bmatrix} -3 & 5 & 0 \\ 0 & 1 & 5 \end{bmatrix}$

7. $\begin{bmatrix} 3 & 2 \\ 5 & 1 \\ 0 & 4 \end{bmatrix} \cdot \begin{bmatrix} 2 & -1 \\ 1 & 3 \end{bmatrix}$

8. $\begin{bmatrix} -1 & 0 \\ 4 & 1 \\ 2 & 0 \end{bmatrix} \cdot \begin{bmatrix} -5 & 0 \\ 4 & 2 \end{bmatrix}$

9. $\begin{bmatrix} -5 & 1 \\ 6 & 2 \end{bmatrix} \cdot \begin{bmatrix} -3 & 2 \\ 4 & 1 \\ 5 & 8 \end{bmatrix}$

10. $\begin{bmatrix} -7 & 3 \\ 9 & 2 \end{bmatrix} \cdot \begin{bmatrix} 4 & -1 \\ 2 & -5 \\ 3 & 6 \end{bmatrix}$

11. $\begin{bmatrix} -5 & 1 & 3 \\ 2 & 0 & 4 \\ 3 & 0 & 2 \end{bmatrix} \cdot \begin{bmatrix} -2 & 0 & 0 \\ 4 & 1 & 0 \\ 0 & 1 & 0 \end{bmatrix}$

12. $\begin{bmatrix} -3 & 4 & 0 \\ 2 & -1 & 5 \\ 0 & 4 & 1 \end{bmatrix} \cdot \begin{bmatrix} 0 & 4 & 0 \\ 2 & 0 & 3 \\ 0 & 5 & 1 \end{bmatrix}$

13. Harry's Donuts, a small neighborhood bakery, sells four main items: sweet rolls, bread, cakes, and pies. Matrix *A* below shows the number of units of the main ingredients needed for these items.

$$A = \begin{array}{c} \\ \text{Sweet rolls} \\ \text{Bread} \\ \text{Cakes} \\ \text{Pies} \end{array} \begin{array}{c} \text{Eggs} \quad \text{Flour} \quad \text{Sugar} \quad \text{Shortening} \quad \text{Milk} \\ \begin{bmatrix} 1 & 4 & 1/4 & 1/4 & 1 \\ 0 & 3 & 0 & 1/4 & 0 \\ 4 & 3 & 2 & 1 & 1 \\ 0 & 1 & 0 & 1/3 & 0 \end{bmatrix} \end{array}$$

The cost, in cents per egg or per cup, of each ingredient when purchased in large lots or in small lots is given by matrix *B*.

$$B = \begin{array}{c} \\ \text{Eggs} \\ \text{Flour} \\ \text{Sugar} \\ \text{Shortening} \\ \text{Milk} \end{array} \begin{array}{c} \text{PURCHASE OPTION} \\ \text{Large lot} \quad \text{Small lot} \\ \begin{bmatrix} 5 & 5 \\ 8 & 10 \\ 10 & 12 \\ 12 & 15 \\ 5 & 6 \end{bmatrix} \end{array}$$

Use matrix multiplication to find a matrix representing the comparative costs per item for the two purchase options (buying in large lots or in small lots).

Suppose a day's orders at Harry's (see Exercise 13) consist of 20 dozen sweet rolls, 200 loaves of bread, 50 cakes, and 60 pies.

14. Write this day's orders as a 1 × 4 matrix *D*, and use matrix multiplication to write as a matrix the amount of each ingredient needed to fill the day's orders.

15. Use matrix multiplication to find a matrix representing the costs to fill the day's orders under the two purchase options.

Refer to the expanded matrices of Example 3, part (a). Assume that Don and Connie have now expanded their product line to include desks, each requiring 10 units of wood, 7 units of hardware, and 4 units of paint.

16. Set up a matrix R relating furniture to materials for the complete line of *D&C* Creations.

17. Set up and compute an appropriate matrix product that will relate furniture to cost of materials.

18. Don and Connie have found that the *labor* required for assembling and finishing is four hours per table, two hours per chair, and five hours per desk, and that their labor cost is $9 per hour. Write a column matrix relating furniture to labor cost.

19. Combine your answers from Exercises 17 and 18 to obtain a 3×2 matrix relating furniture (table, chair, desk) to cost of resources (materials, labor).

20. Write a column matrix relating furniture to selling price. Assume the selling price of each furniture item must cover its own material and labor costs, plus $10 in overhead expenses, plus a profit ($20 per table, $10 per chair, and $25 per desk).

In Ohio, high school football teams are ranked by the Harbin Football Team Rating System. A team is granted one level 1 point for each team it defeats, and is also granted one level 2 point for each time that a team it defeats beats another team. Teams A, B, C, and D all played one another. The results are shown in matrix H, where an entry of 1 indicates a win. For example, A beat C only, B beat both A and D, and so on.

$$H = \begin{array}{c} \\ A \\ B \\ C \\ D \end{array} \begin{array}{cccc} A & B & C & D \\ \left[\begin{array}{cccc} 0 & 0 & 1 & 0 \\ 1 & 0 & 0 & 1 \\ 0 & 1 & 0 & 1 \\ 1 & 0 & 0 & 0 \end{array}\right] \end{array}$$

21. Complete the table below for these four teams.

Team	Level 1 Points	Level 2 Points	Total Points
A	____	____	____
B	____	____	____
C	____	____	____
D	____	____	____

22. Let K be a 4×1 matrix with every entry a 1.
  (a) Compute the product HK.
  (b) What does HK represent?

23. (a) Compute H^2K.
  (b) What does H^2K represent?

24. (a) Compute $HK + H^2K$.
  (b) What does $HK + H^2K$ represent?

25. Is it true that $(H + H^2)K = HK + H^2K$? If so, verify it by direct computation.

26. Is it true that $(I + H)HK = HK + H^2K$? If so, verify it by direct computation. (In this case, I is the 4×4 identity matrix.)

Consider the matrices $A = \begin{bmatrix} 1 & 2 \\ 3 & 2 \end{bmatrix}$, $B = \begin{bmatrix} -1 & -3 \\ 2 & 2 \end{bmatrix}$, $C = \begin{bmatrix} 1 & 2 \\ -1 & -3 \end{bmatrix}$, *and* $I = \begin{bmatrix} 1 & 0 \\ 0 & 1 \end{bmatrix}$.

The following statements illustrate (but do not prove) several algebraic properties of the system of 2×2 matrices. In each case, verify the given statement by direct computation.

27. AB is computable and is of order 2×2. (closure property)

28. $AI = IA = A$. (identity property)

29. $(AB)C = A(BC)$. (associative property)

30. $(A + B)C = AC + BC$. (the right distributive property for addition)

31. $(A - B)C = AC - BC$. (the right distributive property for subtraction)

32. Explain why the verifications in Exercises 27–31 do not actually prove the corresponding properties for the system of 2×2 matrices.

In Exercises 33–36, determine whether $AB = BA$.

33. $A = \begin{bmatrix} 8 & 6 \\ 3 & 5 \end{bmatrix}$ $B = \begin{bmatrix} 10 & 14 \\ 7 & 3 \end{bmatrix}$

34. $A = \begin{bmatrix} -5/3 & -2/3 \\ -2 & -1 \end{bmatrix}$ $B = \begin{bmatrix} -3 & 2 \\ 6 & -5 \end{bmatrix}$

35. $A = \begin{bmatrix} 2 & 7 \\ -3 & 4 \end{bmatrix}$ $B = \begin{bmatrix} 6 & -4 \\ 1 & 2 \end{bmatrix}$

36. $A = \begin{bmatrix} 1 & 0 \\ 1 & 1 \end{bmatrix}$ $B = \begin{bmatrix} 1 & 1 \\ 0 & 1 \end{bmatrix}$

37. Find an original example of 2×2 matrices A and B such that $AB = BA$.

38. Let $M = \begin{bmatrix} 1 & 1 \\ 1 & 1 \end{bmatrix}$.
  (a) Compute M^2.
  (b) Compute M^3.
  (c) Compute M^4.
  (d) Without actually computing it, what is M^{10}?

39. (a) Prove that $SI = S$ for every 3×3 matrix S.

(b) Does part (a) establish that $I = \begin{bmatrix} 1 & 0 & 0 \\ 0 & 1 & 0 \\ 0 & 0 & 1 \end{bmatrix}$ is the identity for multiplication of 3×3 matrices? Explain why or why not.

40. In Example 6, how do you interpret the entry 3 in row 3, column 3 of the matrix M^2?

41. Refer to Example 6. Compute the matrix M^3 and interpret the meaning of its entries.

Assume that a fifth computer is introduced into the network referred to in Example 6. It is connected as shown here.

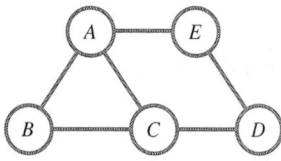

42. Write the communication matrix M for this new network.

43. Compute M^2.

44. According to M^2, how many ways can computer E send data to C through a single intermediary?

45. Without computing M^3, how many channels of communication would it show from B to E? What are those channels?

46. How many channels of communication from B to E would be shown in the matrix M^4?

The real numbers 2/5 and 5/2 are "multiplicative inverses" of each other because $(2/5) \cdot (5/2) = 1$, which is the identity for multiplication of real numbers. Similarly, two matrices A and B are multiplicative inverses of each other if $AB = I$ and $BA = I$, where I is the identity (of the same order in both cases) for multiplication of matrices. (In Section 4, we will address matrix inverses in more detail.)

47. In verifying that A and B are inverses, is it really necessary to compute both AB and BA? Why or why not?

48. What can you say about the orders of A and B if they are to be multiplicative inverses of each other?

Use the definition of matrix inverses (preceding Exercise 47) to determine whether each of the following pairs are inverses of each other.

49. $\begin{bmatrix} 1 & 0 \\ 0 & -1 \end{bmatrix}$ and $\begin{bmatrix} 1 & 0 \\ 0 & -1 \end{bmatrix}$

50. $\begin{bmatrix} 0 & 1 \\ 1 & 0 \end{bmatrix}$ and $\begin{bmatrix} 0 & 1 \\ 1 & 0 \end{bmatrix}$

51. $\begin{bmatrix} 2 & 1 \\ 4 & 3 \end{bmatrix}$ and $\begin{bmatrix} 3/2 & -1/2 \\ -2 & 1 \end{bmatrix}$

52. $\begin{bmatrix} -3 & 2 \\ 6 & -5 \end{bmatrix}$ and $\begin{bmatrix} -5/3 & -2/3 \\ -2 & -1 \end{bmatrix}$

53. $\begin{bmatrix} 3 & 1 & 4 \\ 1 & 0 & 1 \end{bmatrix}$ and $\begin{bmatrix} -1 & 1 \\ 0 & 1 \\ 1 & -1 \end{bmatrix}$

54. $\begin{bmatrix} -2 & 1/3 & 1 \\ 1/4 & 3 & 2 \end{bmatrix}$ and $\begin{bmatrix} 1 & 3 \\ 1/2 & 3/2 \end{bmatrix}$

55. $\begin{bmatrix} 5 & 6 \\ -10 & -13 \end{bmatrix}$ and $\begin{bmatrix} 13/5 & 6/5 \\ -2 & 1 \end{bmatrix}$

56. $\begin{bmatrix} 1 & 1 \\ 1 & -1 \end{bmatrix}$ and $\begin{bmatrix} 1/2 & 1/2 \\ 1/2 & 1/2 \end{bmatrix}$

57. $\begin{bmatrix} 1 & 3 & 3 \\ 1 & 4 & 3 \\ 1 & 3 & 4 \end{bmatrix}$ and $\begin{bmatrix} 7 & -3 & -3 \\ -1 & 1 & 0 \\ -1 & 0 & 1 \end{bmatrix}$

58. $\begin{bmatrix} -1 & 0 & 2 \\ 3 & 1 & 0 \\ 0 & 2 & -3 \end{bmatrix}$ and $\begin{bmatrix} -1/5 & 4/15 & -2/15 \\ 3/5 & 1/5 & 2/5 \\ 2/5 & 2/15 & -1/15 \end{bmatrix}$

59. Explain in your own words what a *row-column product* is, and how it is related to multiplication of matrices in general.

60. Explain why, in Example 7, the matrix product involves 90 products of entries.

Use a calculator to compute the following matrix products.

61. $\begin{bmatrix} 23.8 & 10.6 & 12.8 & 21.9 \\ 15.8 & 24.5 & 11.6 & 14.8 \\ 13.8 & 10.6 & 13.3 & 14.7 \\ 16.4 & 12.8 & 11.1 & 15.9 \\ 21.3 & 12.3 & 13.2 & 32.1 \end{bmatrix} \cdot \begin{bmatrix} 8.23 & 7.45 & 8.25 & 6.27 & 9.91 & 7.29 \\ 2.29 & 6.52 & 3.35 & 5.94 & 6.37 & 6.73 \\ 2.58 & 9.88 & 1.28 & 7.53 & 1.23 & 3.28 \\ 8.45 & 5.27 & 6.37 & 4.38 & 4.39 & 3.46 \end{bmatrix}$

62.
$$\begin{bmatrix} 4.56 & 9.87 & 2.91 \\ 6.37 & 2.81 & 6.81 \\ 5.28 & 4.79 & 4.21 \\ 5.28 & 6.97 & 1.38 \\ 3.84 & 5.28 & 3.91 \\ 4.68 & 2.38 & 1.54 \\ 4.44 & 5.55 & 6.66 \\ 9.63 & 8.52 & 7.41 \end{bmatrix} \cdot \begin{bmatrix} 8.23 & 4.19 & 2.28 & 9.28 & 8.27 \\ 1.32 & 6.58 & 7.17 & 8.23 & 9.82 \\ 3.37 & 8.26 & 1.49 & 6.54 & 9.87 \end{bmatrix}$$

Matrix Row Operations and Systems of Equations

Linear systems of equations were solved in an earlier chapter by the elimination method. That method can be streamlined into a systematic procedure based on matrices. Matrix methods are particularly suitable for computer solutions of large systems of equations having many unknowns.

To begin, consider a system of three equations and three unknowns such as

$$a_1 x + b_1 y + c_1 z = d_1$$
$$a_2 x + b_2 y + c_2 z = d_2$$
$$a_3 x + b_3 y + c_3 z = d_3.$$

This system can be written in an abbreviated form as the following 3×4 matrix.

$$\begin{bmatrix} a_1 & b_1 & c_1 & d_1 \\ a_2 & b_2 & c_2 & d_2 \\ a_3 & b_3 & c_3 & d_3 \end{bmatrix}$$

(Recall that each number in a matrix is called an *element,* or *entry.*) The last column of this matrix consists of the constants from the right in the original system of equations. By using a vertical line to set that column apart from the others (which consist of the coefficients of the variables), we obtain the following **augmented matrix.** (The square coefficient matrix is "augmented" with the column of constants.)

$$\left[\begin{array}{ccc|c} a_1 & b_1 & c_1 & d_1 \\ a_2 & b_2 & c_2 & d_2 \\ a_3 & b_3 & c_3 & d_3 \end{array}\right]$$

Each row of this augmented matrix represents one of the equations in the original system. By making a series of legitimate transformations in the matrix, we can eventually obtain a matrix that will produce an equivalent simpler system, one whose solution will be apparent. (Two systems of equations are *equivalent* if they have identical solutions.)

The trick is to use only matrix transformations such that the system corresponding to each successive matrix is equivalent to the previous system. The allowed transformations are the same as those used in the elimination method. In matrix language, they are called **matrix row operations.** They are listed here.

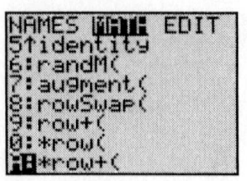

Options 8, 9, 0, and A in this menu allow the user to perform the matrix row operations described in the text.

Matrix Row Operations

For any nonzero real number k and any augmented matrix of a system of linear equations, the following **matrix row operations** will produce the matrix of an equivalent system:

1. **interchanging any two rows of a matrix,**
2. **multiplying the elements of any row of a matrix by the same nonzero number k, and**
3. **adding a common multiple of the elements of one row to the corresponding elements of another row.**

Our objective is to use row operations to transform the augmented matrix above into the form

$$\begin{bmatrix} 1 & 0 & 0 & | & a \\ 0 & 1 & 0 & | & b \\ 0 & 0 & 1 & | & c \end{bmatrix}$$

since the corresponding system will then be

$$\begin{cases} 1 \cdot x + 0 \cdot y + 0 \cdot z = a \\ 0 \cdot x + 1 \cdot y + 0 \cdot z = b \quad \text{or} \quad \begin{cases} x = a \\ y = b. \\ z = c \end{cases} \\ 0 \cdot x + 0 \cdot y + 1 \cdot z = c \end{cases}$$

The solution set is then $\{(a, b, c)\}$.

In effect, we use row operations to produce the elements of the identity

$$\begin{matrix} 1 & 0 & 0 \\ 0 & 1 & 0 \\ 0 & 0 & 1 \end{matrix}$$

to the left of the vertical line, and then read the solution (the variable values) from the right side of the vertical line. Any number of variables may occur in the system to be solved. For example, if we were solving a system of two equations with two unknowns, we would want to obtain a matrix of the form

$$\begin{bmatrix} 1 & 0 & | & a \\ 0 & 1 & | & b \end{bmatrix}.$$

This procedure is called the **Gauss-Jordan method.** It is illustrated in the following examples.

EXAMPLE 1 Solve the linear system

$$3x - 4y = 1$$
$$5x + 2y = 19.$$

The equations should all be in the same form, with the variable terms in the same order on the left, and the constant term on the right. Begin by writing the augmented matrix.

$$\begin{bmatrix} 3 & -4 & | & 1 \\ 5 & 2 & | & 19 \end{bmatrix}$$

The goal is to transform this augmented matrix into the form

$$\begin{bmatrix} 1 & 0 & | & k \\ 0 & 1 & | & j \end{bmatrix}$$

for real numbers k and j. Once the augmented matrix is in this form, the matrix can be rewritten as a linear system to get

$$x = k$$
$$y = j.$$

The necessary transformations are performed as follows. It is best to work in columns beginning in each column with the element that is to become a 1. In the augmented matrix

$$\begin{bmatrix} 3 & -4 & | & 1 \\ 5 & 2 & | & 19 \end{bmatrix}$$

there is a 3 in the first row, first column position. Use row operation 2, multiplying each entry in the first row by $1/3$ to get a 1 in this position. (This step is abbreviated as $(1/3)$R1.)

$$\begin{bmatrix} 1 & -4/3 & | & 1/3 \\ 5 & 2 & | & 19 \end{bmatrix} \quad \frac{1}{3}R1$$

Get a 0 in the second row, first column by multiplying each element of the first row by -5 and adding the result to the corresponding element in the second row, using row operation 3.

$$\begin{bmatrix} 1 & -4/3 & | & 1/3 \\ 0 & 26/3 & | & 52/3 \end{bmatrix} \quad -5R1 + R2$$

Get a 1 in the second row, second column by multiplying each element of the second row by $3/26$, using row operation 2.

$$\begin{bmatrix} 1 & -4/3 & | & 1/3 \\ 0 & 1 & | & 2 \end{bmatrix} \quad \frac{3}{26}R2$$

Finally, get a 0 in the first row, second column by multiplying each element of the second row by $4/3$ and adding the result to the corresponding element in the first row, using row operation 3.

$$\begin{bmatrix} 1 & 0 & | & 3 \\ 0 & 1 & | & 2 \end{bmatrix} \quad \frac{4}{3}R2 + R1$$

This last matrix corresponds to the system

$$x = 3$$
$$y = 2,$$

which has the solution set $\{(3, 2)\}$. This solution could have been read directly from the third column of the final matrix.

The **determinant** of the 2×2 matrix $\begin{bmatrix} a & c \\ b & d \end{bmatrix}$ is symbolized with vertical "fences" rather than brackets:

$$\begin{vmatrix} a & c \\ b & d \end{vmatrix}.$$

This determinant stands for a real number: by definition, the product of the two numbers on the diagonal from NW to SE minus the product of the two numbers on the diagonal from SW to NE. (See Exercises 33–36 in the next section.) For example,

$$\begin{vmatrix} 4 & 1 \\ 6 & -2 \end{vmatrix} = 4(-2) - 6(1) = -14.$$

In 1750, Gabriel Cramer (1704–1752) published the theory of determinants. It provided a way of solving linear systems which predated more general matrix methods by a century. Cramer's rule is still used today. The system

$$3x + y = 5$$
$$2x - y = 10$$

is solved by first forming three determinants as follows.

$D = \begin{vmatrix} 3 & 1 \\ 2 & -1 \end{vmatrix}$ (the determinant of the coefficient matrix)

$D_x = \begin{vmatrix} 5 & 1 \\ 10 & -1 \end{vmatrix}$ (the same as D but with the x-coefficients replaced by the constants)

$D_y = \begin{vmatrix} 3 & 5 \\ 2 & 10 \end{vmatrix}$ (the same as D but with the y-coefficients replaced by the constants)

Now $D = 3(-1) - 2(1) = -5$, $D_x = 5(-1) - 10(1) = -15$, and $D_y = 3(10) - 2(5) = 20$. The solution values are then

$$x = \frac{D_x}{D} = \frac{-15}{-5} = 3 \quad \text{and} \quad y = \frac{D_y}{D} = \frac{20}{-5} = -4.$$

In other words, the solution set of the system of equations is $\{(3, -4)\}$.

For Group Discussion
1. Apply Cramer's rule to the following system.

$$2x - 4y = 14$$
$$5x + 3y = -30$$

2. Apply Cramer's rule to the following system.

$$3x - 4y = 6$$
$$-12x + 16y = 10$$

3. Why do you think Cramer's rule failed to produce a solution for the system in problem 2 above? Could another method be used to solve the system?

EXAMPLE 2 At the Evergreen Ranch, 6 goats and 5 sheep sell for $305, while 2 goats and 9 sheep cost $285. Find the cost of a goat and the cost of a sheep.

To solve this problem, first write a system of equations. Then use the Gauss-Jordan method to solve the system. Begin by identifying the variables.

$$x = \text{cost of a goat} \quad \text{and} \quad y = \text{cost of a sheep}$$

From the given information, 6 goats and 5 sheep cost a total of $305, so that

$$6x + 5y = 305.$$

Also, 2 goats and 9 sheep cost a total of $285, so that

$$2x + 9y = 285.$$

We must now find the common solution for these two equations, that is, the solution of the linear system

$$6x + 5y = 305$$
$$2x + 9y = 285.$$

Write the augmented matrix and then apply the appropriate row operations.

$$\begin{bmatrix} 6 & 5 & | & 305 \\ 2 & 9 & | & 285 \end{bmatrix}$$

$$\begin{bmatrix} 1 & 5/6 & | & 305/6 \\ 2 & 9 & | & 285 \end{bmatrix} \quad \frac{1}{6}R1$$

$$\begin{bmatrix} 1 & 5/6 & | & 305/6 \\ 0 & 22/3 & | & 550/3 \end{bmatrix} \quad -2R1 + R2$$

$$\begin{bmatrix} 1 & 5/6 & | & 305/6 \\ 0 & 1 & | & 25 \end{bmatrix} \quad \frac{3}{22}R2$$

$$\begin{bmatrix} 1 & 0 & | & 30 \\ 0 & 1 & | & 25 \end{bmatrix} \quad -\frac{5}{6}R2 + R1$$

From the rightmost column, read $x = 30$, $y = 25$. Each goat costs $30, while each sheep costs $25.

EXAMPLE 3 Use the Gauss-Jordan method to solve the system

$$x - y + 5z = -6$$
$$3x + 3y - z = 10$$
$$x + 3y + 2z = 5.$$

Since the system is in proper form, begin by writing the augmented matrix of the linear system.

$$\begin{bmatrix} 1 & -1 & 5 & | & -6 \\ 3 & 3 & -1 & | & 10 \\ 1 & 3 & 2 & | & 5 \end{bmatrix}$$

The final matrix is to be of the form

$$\begin{bmatrix} 1 & 0 & 0 & | & m \\ 0 & 1 & 0 & | & n \\ 0 & 0 & 1 & | & p \end{bmatrix},$$

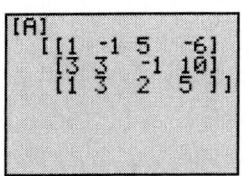

This is the augmented matrix for the original system in Example 3.

where m, n, and p are real numbers. This final form of the matrix gives the system $x = m$, $y = n$, and $z = p$, so the solution set is $\{(m, n, p)\}$.

The original augmented matrix already has a 1 in the first row, first column. Get a 0 in the second row, first column by multiplying each element in the first row by -3 and adding the result to the corresponding element in the second row, using row operation 3.

$$\begin{bmatrix} 1 & -1 & 5 & -6 \\ 0 & 6 & -16 & 28 \\ 1 & 3 & 2 & 5 \end{bmatrix} \quad -3R1 + R2$$

Now, to change the last element in the first column to a 0, use row operation 3 and multiply each element of the first row by -1, and add the result to the corresponding element of the third row.

$$\begin{bmatrix} 1 & -1 & 5 & -6 \\ 0 & 6 & -16 & 28 \\ 0 & 4 & -3 & 11 \end{bmatrix} \quad -1R1 + R3$$

The same procedure is used to transform the second and third columns. For both of these columns perform the additional step of getting a 1 in the appropriate position of each column. Do this by multiplying the elements of the row by the reciprocal of the number in that position. (As row operations are performed, any fractions appearing in various positions can be reduced to lowest terms.)

$$\begin{bmatrix} 1 & -1 & 5 & -6 \\ 0 & 1 & -8/3 & 14/3 \\ 0 & 4 & -3 & 11 \end{bmatrix} \quad \frac{1}{6}R2$$

$$\begin{bmatrix} 1 & 0 & 7/3 & -4/3 \\ 0 & 1 & -8/3 & 14/3 \\ 0 & 4 & -3 & 11 \end{bmatrix} \quad R2 + R1$$

$$\begin{bmatrix} 1 & 0 & 7/3 & -4/3 \\ 0 & 1 & -8/3 & 14/3 \\ 0 & 0 & 23/3 & -23/3 \end{bmatrix} \quad -4R2 + R3$$

$$\begin{bmatrix} 1 & 0 & 7/3 & -4/3 \\ 0 & 1 & -8/3 & 14/3 \\ 0 & 0 & 1 & -1 \end{bmatrix} \quad \frac{3}{23}R3$$

$$\begin{bmatrix} 1 & 0 & 0 & 1 \\ 0 & 1 & -8/3 & 14/3 \\ 0 & 0 & 1 & -1 \end{bmatrix} \quad -\frac{7}{3}R3 + R1$$

$$\begin{bmatrix} 1 & 0 & 0 & 1 \\ 0 & 1 & 0 & 2 \\ 0 & 0 & 1 & -1 \end{bmatrix} \quad \frac{8}{3}R3 + R2$$

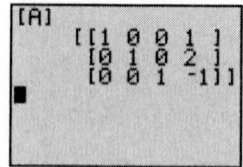

This is the augmented matrix for the final system in Example 3.

The linear system associated with this final matrix is

$$x = 1$$
$$y = 2$$
$$z = -1,$$

and the solution set is $\{(1, 2, -1)\}$. ◼

14.3 EXERCISES

Let $A = \begin{bmatrix} -4 & 0 & 1 \\ 3 & -4 & 2 \\ -1 & 2 & 1 \end{bmatrix}$ and $B = \begin{bmatrix} 2 & -1 & 3 \\ -4 & 0 & 1 \\ 1 & 3 & -3 \end{bmatrix}$.

Apply the row operations indicated in each case, and write out the resulting matrix. (We work here with a square matrix rather than an augmented matrix just to practice row operations.)

1. Interchange rows 1 and 3 of A.

2. Interchange rows 2 and 3 of B.

3. Multiply each element of row 2 of A by -3.

4. Double each element in row 1 of A.

5. Multiply each element of row 2 of B by -4, and add the results to row 1.

6. Multiply each element of row 3 of A by 5, and add the results to row 2.

7. Multiply each element of row 1 of A by 3, and add the results to row 3.

8. Multiply each element of row 3 of B by -1, and add the results to row 2.

9. Form matrix $A + B$. Multiply each element of row 2 of $A + B$ by -3, and add the results to row 1.

10. Form matrix $B - A$. Multiply each element of row 1 of $B - A$ by 5, and add the results to row 3.

State which row operation must be applied to matrix A or B from above to get the following matrices.

11. to A; $\begin{bmatrix} 3 & -4 & 2 \\ -4 & 0 & 1 \\ -1 & 2 & 1 \end{bmatrix}$

12. to B; $\begin{bmatrix} 3 & 2 & 0 \\ -4 & 0 & 1 \\ 1 & 3 & -3 \end{bmatrix}$

13. to A; $\begin{bmatrix} -4 & 0 & 1 \\ 6 & -8 & 4 \\ -1 & 2 & 1 \end{bmatrix}$

14. to A; $\begin{bmatrix} -4 & 0 & 1 \\ 3 & -4 & 2 \\ 1/2 & -1 & -1/2 \end{bmatrix}$

15. to B; $\begin{bmatrix} 2 & -1 & 3 \\ 0 & -2 & 7 \\ 1 & 3 & -3 \end{bmatrix}$

16. to B; $\begin{bmatrix} -1 & -10 & 12 \\ -4 & 0 & 1 \\ 1 & 3 & -3 \end{bmatrix}$

Find the sequence of row operations that will change each of the following matrices into the identity matrix, if possible.

17. $\begin{bmatrix} 1 & 2 \\ 0 & -1 \end{bmatrix}$

18. $\begin{bmatrix} 2 & 1 \\ 1 & -1 \end{bmatrix}$

19. $\begin{bmatrix} -2 & 2 \\ 4 & 1 \end{bmatrix}$

20. $\begin{bmatrix} 0 & -1 \\ -2 & 0 \end{bmatrix}$

21. $\begin{bmatrix} 6 & 3 & 0 \\ 0 & 4 & 0 \\ 0 & 0 & 2 \end{bmatrix}$

22. $\begin{bmatrix} -2 & 2 & 0 \\ 0 & 1 & 0 \\ 1 & 1 & 1 \end{bmatrix}$

Write the augmented matrix for each system. Do not try to solve.

23. $2x + 3y = 11$
$x + 2y = 8$

24. $3x + 5y = -13$
$2x + 3y = -9$

25. $x + 5y = 6$
$3x - 4y = 1$

26. $2x + 7y = 1$
$5x + y = -15$

27. $2x + y + z = 3$
$3x - 4y + 2z = -7$
$x + y + z = 2$

28. $4x - 2y + 3z = 4$
$3x + 5y + z = 7$
$5x - y + 4z = 7$

29. $x + y = 6$
$2y + z = 2$
$z = 2$

30. $x = 6$
$y + 2z = 2$
$x - 3z = 2$

Use matrix row operations to solve the following systems of equations.

31. $x + y = 5$
$x - y = -1$

32. $x + 2y = 5$
$2x + y = -2$

33. $x + y = -3$
$2x - 5y = -6$

34. $3x - 2y = 4$
$3x + y = -2$

35. $2x - 3y = 10$
$2x + 2y = 5$

36. $6x + y = 5$
$5x + y = 3$

37. $2x - 5y = 10$
$3x + y = 15$

38. $4x - y = 3$
$-2x + 3y = 1$

39. $2x - 3y = 2$
$4x - 6y = 1$

40. $x + 2y = 1$
$2x + 4y = 3$

41. $x + y = -1$
$y + z = 4$
$x + z = 1$

42. $x - z = -3$
$y + z = 9$
$x + z = 7$

43. $x + y - z = 6$
$2x - y + z = -9$
$x - 2y + 3z = 1$

44. $x + 3y - 6z = 7$
$2x - y + z = 1$
$x + 2y + 2z = -1$

45. $-x + y = -1$
$y - z = 6$
$x + z = -1$

46. $x + y = 1$
$2x - z = 0$
$y + 2z = -2$

47. $3x + 2y - w = 0$
$2x + z + 2w = 5$
$x + 2y - z = -2$
$2x - y + z + w = 2$

48. $x + 3y - 2z - w = 9$
$4x + y + z + 2w = 2$
$-3x - y + z - w = -5$
$x - y - 3z - 2w = 2$

Use the Gauss-Jordan method to solve each problem.

49. Linda Ramirez is a building contractor. If she hires 7 day laborers and 2 concrete finishers, her payroll for the day is $692, while 1 day laborer and 5 concrete finishers cost $476. Find the daily wage charge for each type of worker.

50. A biologist wants to grow two types of algae, types *A* and *B*. She has available 15 gal of nutrient I and 26 gal of nutrient II. A vat of algae *A* needs 2 gal of nutrient I and 3 gal of nutrient II, while a vat of algae *B* needs 1 gal of I and 2 gal of II. How many vats of each type of algae should the biologist grow in order to use all the nutrients?

51. To make his portrait bust of Millard Fillmore, Harry bought 2 lb of dark clay and 3 lb of light clay, paying $13 for the clay. He later needed one more pound of dark clay and 2 lb of light clay, costing $7 altogether. How much did he pay per pound for each type of clay?

52. The perimeter of a triangle is 21 cm. If two sides are of equal length, and the third side is 3 cm longer than one of the equal sides, find the lengths of the sides.

53. The secretary of the local consumer group bought some decals at 8¢ each and some bumper stickers at 10¢ each to give to the members. He spent a total of $15.52. If he bought a total of 170 items, how many of each kind did he buy?

54. The Matrix and the Patrix, a local musical group, is coming to play at a school festival. The reporter for the school newspaper doesn't know how many guitarists and how many members of the rhythm section there are in the group. Janet, one of the guitarists, says that, not counting herself, there are three times as many members of the rhythm group as guitarists. Steve, a member of the rhythm section, says that, not counting himself, the number of members of the rhythm section is one less than twice the number of guitarists. How many of each are there in the group?

14.4 **Matrix Inverses; Input-Output Models**

Two matrices A and B are said to be **inverses** of each other if $AB = I$ and $BA = I$, where I is the appropriate identity matrix (the same one in both cases). For example, the matrices

$$\begin{bmatrix} 3 & 5 \\ 1 & 2 \end{bmatrix} \quad \text{and} \quad \begin{bmatrix} 2 & -5 \\ -1 & 3 \end{bmatrix}$$

are inverses of each other, since

$$\begin{bmatrix} 3 & 5 \\ 1 & 2 \end{bmatrix} \cdot \begin{bmatrix} 2 & -5 \\ -1 & 3 \end{bmatrix} = \begin{bmatrix} 1 & 0 \\ 0 & 1 \end{bmatrix}$$

and

$$\begin{bmatrix} 2 & -5 \\ -1 & 3 \end{bmatrix} \cdot \begin{bmatrix} 3 & 5 \\ 1 & 2 \end{bmatrix} = \begin{bmatrix} 1 & 0 \\ 0 & 1 \end{bmatrix}.$$

The inverse of matrix A is written A^{-1} (read "A inverse").

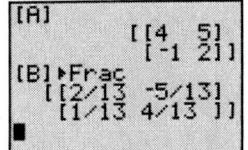

Matrix Inverses

Matrices A and A^{-1} are inverses of each other if

$$AA^{-1} = I \qquad \text{and} \qquad A^{-1}A = I.$$

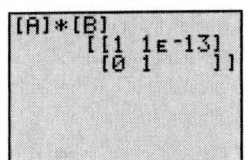

These screens support the result of Example 1. Notice that the entry in row 1, column 2 of the product is 1×10^{-13}, which is as close as the calculator can get to 0 for this computation. *One must always be aware of the limitations of technology!*

EXAMPLE 1 Determine whether or not

$$\begin{bmatrix} 4 & 5 \\ -1 & 2 \end{bmatrix} \quad \text{and} \quad \begin{bmatrix} 2/13 & -5/13 \\ 1/13 & 4/13 \end{bmatrix}$$

are inverses of each other.

Find the two products.

$$\begin{bmatrix} 4 & 5 \\ -1 & 2 \end{bmatrix} \cdot \begin{bmatrix} 2/13 & -5/13 \\ 1/13 & 4/13 \end{bmatrix} = \begin{bmatrix} 8/13 + 5/13 & -20/13 + 20/13 \\ -2/13 + 2/13 & 5/13 + 8/13 \end{bmatrix}$$
$$= \begin{bmatrix} 1 & 0 \\ 0 & 1 \end{bmatrix}$$

and

$$\begin{bmatrix} 2/13 & -5/13 \\ 1/13 & 4/13 \end{bmatrix} \cdot \begin{bmatrix} 4 & 5 \\ -1 & 2 \end{bmatrix} = \begin{bmatrix} 8/13 + 5/13 & 10/13 - 10/13 \\ 4/13 - 4/13 & 5/13 + 8/13 \end{bmatrix}$$
$$= \begin{bmatrix} 1 & 0 \\ 0 & 1 \end{bmatrix}.$$

Since both products are equal to I (the 2×2 identity matrix in this case), the two given matrices *are* inverses of each other. ◢

Only square matrices can possibly have inverses. (Why is this so?) Furthermore, not all square matrices have inverses. (See Example 4.) As we develop a way to find inverses, we will at first consider only square matrices of order 2×2.

First, by the definition of matrix inverse, if A is a 2×2 matrix and A^{-1} is its inverse, then $A^{-1}A = I$. Therefore if we can find the matrix multiplier that changes A into I, then we have found A^{-1}.

To begin our search for such a multiplier, we observe that applying any of the three row operations of the previous section to a 2×2 matrix has the same effect as multiplying that matrix by another (appropriate) 2×2 matrix. For example, let $M = \begin{bmatrix} 2 & 4 \\ 3 & 5 \end{bmatrix}$ and multiply M by the 2×2 multiplier $\begin{bmatrix} 0 & 1 \\ 1 & 0 \end{bmatrix}$:

$$\begin{bmatrix} 0 & 1 \\ 1 & 0 \end{bmatrix} \cdot \begin{bmatrix} 2 & 4 \\ 3 & 5 \end{bmatrix} = \begin{bmatrix} 0 \cdot 2 + 1 \cdot 3 & 0 \cdot 4 + 1 \cdot 5 \\ 1 \cdot 2 + 0 \cdot 3 & 1 \cdot 4 + 0 \cdot 5 \end{bmatrix} = \begin{bmatrix} 3 & 5 \\ 2 & 4 \end{bmatrix}.$$

This particular multiplier has the same effect as row operation 1 (interchanging the two rows). In Exercises 27–30, you will see that the other two row operations are also equivalent to multiplying by (appropriate) matrix multipliers.

Since a product of two (or more) 2×2 matrices is another 2×2 matrix, a sequence of row operations, applied in succession, has the net effect of multiplying by some single matrix. Now we know that

$$A^{-1}A = I \qquad \text{and also} \qquad A^{-1}I = A^{-1},$$

so that the multiplier, A^{-1}, that changes A to I will also change I to A^{-1}. This means that any sequence of row operations that changes A to I will also change I to A^{-1}. This fact enables us to use row operations to find A^{-1}. Form a new augmented matrix of the form $[A\,|\,I]$ and apply row operations to change A (on the left) to I. The I (on the right) will automatically become A^{-1}, as illustrated here.

James Joseph Sylvester
(1814–1897) was working as an actuary in the early 1850s in London when Cayley (see facing page) was practicing law there. They met, and while not collaborators as such, they worked side-by-side on the algebra of invariants. Sylvester thought up "matrix" and a number of other terms such as "invariant" and "syzygy" (look that up!). Sylvester's early career was hampered by English law, which required a religious test (Sylvester was Jewish). Thus he did not get his degree from Cambridge until 1872. Sylvester, in contrast to Cayley, taught at several institutions, including a brief stay at the University of Virginia (1841). He was at Johns Hopkins from 1877 to 1883, where his influence helped to establish mathematical research at the university level. He founded the *American Journal of Mathematics*.

Sylvester was also a poet, and he published his *Laws of Verse* in 1870, applying principles of "phonetic syzygy."

$$[A\,|\,I]$$

Apply row operations to obtain

$$[I\,|\,A^{-1}]$$

EXAMPLE 2 Find the inverse of the matrix $A = \begin{bmatrix} 2 & -5 \\ -1 & 3 \end{bmatrix}$.

Form the augmented matrix $[A\,|\,I]$ and then change A to I on the left, using row operations as in Section 3.

$$[A\,|\,I]$$

$$\begin{bmatrix} 2 & -5 & | & 1 & 0 \\ -1 & 3 & | & 0 & 1 \end{bmatrix}$$

First obtain a 1 in row 1, column 1:

$$\left[\begin{array}{cc|cc} 1 & -5/2 & 1/2 & 0 \\ -1 & 3 & 0 & 1 \end{array}\right] \quad \tfrac{1}{2}\,\text{R1}$$

Next obtain a 0 in row 2, column 1:

$$\left[\begin{array}{cc|cc} 1 & -5/2 & 1/2 & 0 \\ 0 & 1/2 & 1/2 & 1 \end{array}\right] \quad \text{R1} + \text{R2}$$

Next obtain a 1 in row 2, column 2:

$$\left[\begin{array}{cc|cc} 1 & -5/2 & 1/2 & 0 \\ 0 & 1 & 1 & 2 \end{array}\right] \quad 2\text{R2}$$

Finally obtain a 0 in row 1, column 2:

$$\left[\begin{array}{cc|cc} 1 & 0 & 3 & 5 \\ 0 & 1 & 1 & 2 \end{array}\right] \quad \tfrac{5}{2}\,\text{R2} + \text{R1}$$
$$[\,I\,|\,A^{-1}\,]$$

This result shows that $A^{-1} = \begin{bmatrix} 3 & 5 \\ 1 & 2 \end{bmatrix}$. You can verify this by computing AA^{-1} and $A^{-1}A$. Both of these products should equal I, the 2×2 identity matrix.

The procedure above generalizes to a square matrix of any order (3×3, 4×4, and so on), as summarized here.

Finding the Inverse of a Matrix

Given any square matrix A, its inverse A^{-1} (if there is an inverse) is found by performing the following steps:

1. Form the augmented matrix $[A\,|\,I]$.
2. Use row operations to obtain a 1 in row 1, column 1.
3. Obtain 0s in all other column 1 positions.
4. Obtain a 1 in row 2, column 2.
5. Obtain 0s in all other column 2 positions.
6. Continue until A is changed into I.
7. The right half of the final result is now A^{-1}.

If any one of these steps is impossible, then matrix A has no inverse.

EXAMPLE 3 Find the inverse of $B = \begin{bmatrix} 1 & 3 & 3 \\ 1 & 4 & 3 \\ 1 & 3 & 4 \end{bmatrix}$.

Perform the steps listed above.

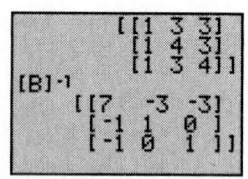

Matrix *B* of Example 3 is defined at the top of this screen. Its inverse, B^{-1}, is displayed at the bottom.

Step 1:

$$\left[\begin{array}{ccc|ccc} 1 & 3 & 3 & 1 & 0 & 0 \\ 1 & 4 & 3 & 0 & 1 & 0 \\ 1 & 3 & 4 & 0 & 0 & 1 \end{array}\right]$$

Step 2: There is already a 1 in row 1, column 1.

Step 3:

$$\left[\begin{array}{ccc|ccc} 1 & 3 & 3 & 1 & 0 & 0 \\ 0 & 1 & 0 & -1 & 1 & 0 \\ 0 & 0 & 1 & -1 & 0 & 1 \end{array}\right] \begin{array}{l} -R1 + R2 \\ -R1 + R3 \end{array}$$

Step 4: There is already a 1 in row 2, column 2.

Step 5:

$$\left[\begin{array}{ccc|ccc} 1 & 0 & 3 & 4 & -3 & 0 \\ 0 & 1 & 0 & -1 & 1 & 0 \\ 0 & 0 & 1 & -1 & 0 & 1 \end{array}\right] \begin{array}{l} -3R2 + R1 \end{array}$$

Step 6:

$$\left[\begin{array}{ccc|ccc} 1 & 0 & 0 & 7 & -3 & -3 \\ 0 & 1 & 0 & -1 & 1 & 0 \\ 0 & 0 & 1 & -1 & 0 & 1 \end{array}\right] \begin{array}{l} -3R3 + R1 \end{array}$$

Step 7:

$$B^{-1} = \left[\begin{array}{ccc} 7 & -3 & -3 \\ -1 & 1 & 0 \\ -1 & 0 & 1 \end{array}\right]$$

To check, show that $BB^{-1} = I$ and $B^{-1}B = I$. ◢

EXAMPLE 4 Let $C = \begin{bmatrix} 2 & 1 \\ 6 & 3 \end{bmatrix}$. Find C^{-1}.

Proceed as before.

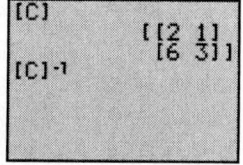

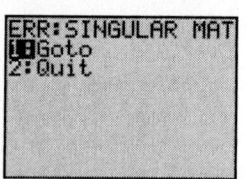

Matrix *C*, as defined in Example 4, has no inverse. Such a matrix is called a *singular matrix*, as seen on the bottom screen.

$$\left[\begin{array}{cc|cc} 2 & 1 & 1 & 0 \\ 6 & 3 & 0 & 1 \end{array}\right]$$

$$\left[\begin{array}{cc|cc} 1 & 1/2 & 1/2 & 0 \\ 6 & 3 & 0 & 1 \end{array}\right] \begin{array}{l} \frac{1}{2} R1 \end{array}$$

$$\left[\begin{array}{cc|cc} 1 & 1/2 & 1/2 & 0 \\ 0 & 0 & -3 & 1 \end{array}\right] \begin{array}{l} -6R1 + R2 \end{array}$$

We cannot go further. There is no way to obtain a 1 in row 2, column 2 without losing the 0 just obtained in row 2, column 1. Thus, matrix *C* has no inverse. ◢

The matrix operations introduced in this chapter (addition, subtraction, multiplication by a scalar, and multiplication of two matrices) form the basis of *matrix algebra,* which is similar (but not identical) to real number algebra. Matrix algebra has many applications.

The ability to perform algebraic operations on matrices enables us to formulate the matrix solution of systems of equations in a simpler way. For example, in Example 1 of Section 3, the system

$$3x - 4y = 1$$
$$5x + 2y = 19$$

was solved using row operations. Notice now that if we arrange the x and y coefficients, the variables of the system, and the constants of the system into the three separate matrices

$$A = \begin{bmatrix} 3 & -4 \\ 5 & 2 \end{bmatrix}, \qquad X = \begin{bmatrix} x \\ y \end{bmatrix}, \qquad \text{and} \qquad B = \begin{bmatrix} 1 \\ 19 \end{bmatrix},$$

the system can be written as the single matrix equation

$$AX = B.$$

Verify that the statement

$$\begin{bmatrix} 3 & -4 \\ 5 & 2 \end{bmatrix} \cdot \begin{bmatrix} x \\ y \end{bmatrix} = \begin{bmatrix} 1 \\ 19 \end{bmatrix}$$

is equivalent to the original system of equations.

Now we solve the matrix equation $AX = B$ using matrix algebra as follows.

$$AX = B$$
$$A^{-1}(AX) = A^{-1}B \qquad \text{Multiply both sides by } A^{-1}.$$
$$(A^{-1}A)X = A^{-1}B \qquad \text{Use the associative property on the left.}$$
$$IX = A^{-1}B \qquad A^{-1}A = I \text{ by the definition of inverse.}$$
$$X = A^{-1}B \qquad IX = X \text{ by the definition of identity.}$$

When multiplying both sides of a matrix equation by another matrix (as was done above), be sure to multiply in the same order on both sides of the equation, since matrix multiplication is not commutative.

The matrix X, which now contains the variable values, that is, the solution of the system, is simply the product $A^{-1}B$. We summarize this result as follows.

Solving a Linear System Using Matrix Algebra

A system of linear equations represented by the matrix equation

$$AX = B$$

can be solved by finding A^{-1} and computing the product $A^{-1}B$. If A^{-1} does not exist, the system does not have a unique solution.

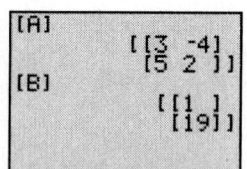

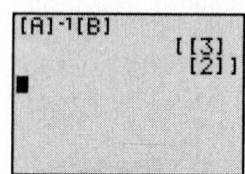

A graphing calculator with matrix capability can easily accomplish the system-solving procedure described in Example 5.

EXAMPLE 5   Solve the system

$$3x - 4y = 1$$
$$5x + 2y = 19$$

using matrix algebra.

First find A^{-1} as outlined in this section.

$$\left[\begin{array}{cc|cc} 3 & -4 & 1 & 0 \\ 5 & 2 & 0 & 1 \end{array}\right]$$

$$\left[\begin{array}{cc|cc} 1 & -4/3 & 1/3 & 0 \\ 5 & 2 & 0 & 1 \end{array}\right] \qquad \frac{1}{3}\,R1$$

$$\left[\begin{array}{cc|cc} 1 & -4/3 & 1/3 & 0 \\ 0 & 26/3 & -5/3 & 1 \end{array}\right] \qquad -5R1 + R2$$

$$\left[\begin{array}{cc|cc} 1 & -4/3 & 1/3 & 0 \\ 0 & 1 & -5/26 & 3/26 \end{array}\right] \qquad \frac{3}{26}\,R2$$

$$\left[\begin{array}{cc|cc} 1 & 0 & 1/13 & 2/13 \\ 0 & 1 & -5/26 & 3/26 \end{array}\right] \qquad \frac{4}{3}\,R2 + R1$$

Now

$$X = A^{-1}B = \begin{bmatrix} 1/13 & 2/13 \\ -5/26 & 3/26 \end{bmatrix} \cdot \begin{bmatrix} 1 \\ 19 \end{bmatrix} = \begin{bmatrix} 3 \\ 2 \end{bmatrix}$$

so the solution set of the system is $\{(3, 2)\}$.

It may have occurred to you that this matrix algebra method of solving a linear system is really no better than the row operation method of the last section. In fact, finding A^{-1} here required the same sequence of row operations that we used before. In addition, we then had to compute the product $A^{-1}B$.

The real advantage of this last method is that modern calculators (and computers) can easily compute matrix inverses as well as products. So when using a calculator, finding $A^{-1}B$ simply requires entering matrices A and B from the system of equations and then calculating an inverse and a product on the machine. (And these calculations are no more work for large systems than for small ones—except that there are more numbers to enter.)

EXAMPLE 6   Use matrix algebra to solve this system.

$$3x - 5y + 2z = 8$$
$$x + 3y - z = 5$$
$$x - 11y + 4z = -2$$

Start with the coefficient matrix

$$A = \begin{bmatrix} 3 & -5 & 2 \\ 1 & 3 & -1 \\ 1 & -11 & 4 \end{bmatrix}.$$

When we try to calculate A^{-1}, we find that A does not have an inverse. (Verify this.) Therefore the given system does not have a unique solution.

Input-Output Models

The economist W. W. Leontief, winner of a Nobel Prize in 1973, developed a method for analyzing an economy which involves matrices. The method is generally known as a **Leontief model,** or an **input-output model.** Suppose that an economy produces n commodities. The production of each uses some (perhaps all) of the other commodities in the economy. Thus, the production of oil requires oil, as well as steel, electricity, and so on. The amounts of all commodities used in the production of one unit of each commodity can be written as an $n \times n$ matrix, called the *input-output matrix*, or the **technological matrix** of the system. Denote the technological matrix A.

Let each of the following be an $n \times 1$ matrix showing the appropriate amounts of all commodities in the economy.

P = Gross Production (total of all commodities produced)

U = Internal Use (amounts of commodities used up in the production process itself)

D = Demand for net production (amounts of commodities needed above and beyond internal use)

The gross production must be sufficient to supply internal use plus the demand for net production:

$$P = U + D.$$

Consider an economy with only two basic products, wheat and oil. Assume that the production of 1 metric ton of wheat requires 1/4 metric ton of wheat and 1/3 metric ton of oil. The production of 1 metric ton of oil requires 1/12 metric ton of wheat and 1/9 metric ton of oil. This leads to the following technological matrix.

$$A = \text{INPUT} \quad \begin{matrix} \text{Wheat} \\ \text{Oil} \end{matrix} \overset{\begin{matrix} \text{OUTPUT} \\ \text{Wheat} \quad \text{Oil} \end{matrix}}{\begin{bmatrix} 1/4 & 1/12 \\ 1/3 & 1/9 \end{bmatrix}}, \quad \text{or simply} \quad A = \begin{bmatrix} 1/4 & 1/12 \\ 1/3 & 1/9 \end{bmatrix}$$

(Notice that input appears on the left of the matrix and output on the top.)

We now claim that the internal use matrix is given by

$$U = AP.$$

To illustrate, suppose the gross production was

$$P = \begin{matrix} \text{Wheat} \\ \text{Oil} \end{matrix} \overset{\begin{matrix} \text{Gross} \\ \text{production} \end{matrix}}{\begin{bmatrix} 864 \\ 4,320 \end{bmatrix}}.$$

Then

$$\begin{pmatrix} \text{Wheat used} \\ \text{internally} \end{pmatrix} = \begin{pmatrix} \text{Wheat} \\ \text{used} \\ \text{per unit} \\ \text{of wheat} \\ \text{produced} \end{pmatrix} \cdot \begin{pmatrix} \text{Units of} \\ \text{wheat} \\ \text{produced} \end{pmatrix} + \begin{pmatrix} \text{Wheat} \\ \text{used} \\ \text{per unit} \\ \text{of oil} \\ \text{produced} \end{pmatrix} \cdot \begin{pmatrix} \text{Units} \\ \text{of oil} \\ \text{produced} \end{pmatrix}$$

$$= \frac{1}{4} \cdot 864 + \frac{1}{12} \cdot 4{,}320$$

$$= 576$$

and

$$\begin{pmatrix} \text{Oil used} \\ \text{internally} \end{pmatrix} = \begin{pmatrix} \text{Oil used} \\ \text{per unit} \\ \text{of wheat} \\ \text{produced} \end{pmatrix} \cdot \begin{pmatrix} \text{Units of} \\ \text{wheat} \\ \text{produced} \end{pmatrix} + \begin{pmatrix} \text{Oil used} \\ \text{per unit} \\ \text{of oil} \\ \text{produced} \end{pmatrix} \cdot \begin{pmatrix} \text{Units} \\ \text{of oil} \\ \text{produced} \end{pmatrix}$$

$$= \frac{1}{3} \cdot 864 + \frac{1}{9} \cdot 4{,}320$$

$$= 768$$

so
$$U = \begin{matrix} \\ \text{Wheat} \\ \text{Oil} \end{matrix} \overset{\begin{matrix}\text{Internal}\\\text{use}\end{matrix}}{\begin{bmatrix} 576 \\ 768 \end{bmatrix}}.$$

But this is just what we obtain from the product AP:

$$AP = \begin{bmatrix} 1/4 & 1/12 \\ 1/3 & 1/9 \end{bmatrix} \cdot \begin{bmatrix} 864 \\ 4{,}320 \end{bmatrix} = \begin{bmatrix} 576 \\ 768 \end{bmatrix}.$$

Since $U = AP$, the equation

$$P = U + D$$

now becomes

$$P = AP + D \qquad \text{or} \qquad P - AP = D.$$

This equation, however, gives D in terms of P. The usual situation is that D is known and we need to find P. So we use matrix algebra to solve for P.

$$P - AP = D$$
$$IP - AP = D \qquad \text{Replace } P \text{ with } IP, \text{ where } I \text{ is the identity matrix with the same order as } A.$$
$$(I - A)P = D \qquad \text{Distributive property}$$
$$(I - A)^{-1}(I - A)P = (I - A)^{-1}D \qquad \text{Multiply both sides by } (I - A)^{-1}.$$
$$IP = (I - A)^{-1}D \qquad \text{Replace } (I - A)^{-1}(I - A) \text{ with } I.$$
$$P = (I - A)^{-1}D \qquad \text{Replace } IP \text{ with } P.$$

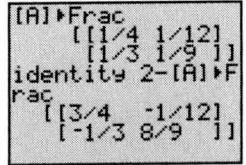

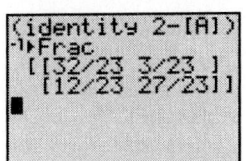

As you read through Example 7, follow these screens from top to bottom to see how a graphing calculator accomplishes the computation.

We now have a method of finding the gross production, P, required to meet a demand for net production, D.

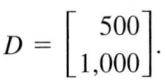 **EXAMPLE 7** Find the gross production required in the wheat/oil economy above if the demand for net production is

$$D = \begin{bmatrix} 500 \\ 1{,}000 \end{bmatrix}.$$

First compute $I - A$:

$$I - A = \begin{bmatrix} 1 & 0 \\ 0 & 1 \end{bmatrix} - \begin{bmatrix} 1/4 & 1/12 \\ 1/3 & 1/9 \end{bmatrix} = \begin{bmatrix} 3/4 & -1/12 \\ -1/3 & 8/9 \end{bmatrix}.$$

Obtain the inverse of $I - A$ (using the procedure described earlier, or a calculator).

$$(I - A)^{-1} = \begin{bmatrix} 32/23 & 3/23 \\ 12/23 & 27/23 \end{bmatrix}$$

Now

$$P = (I - A)^{-1} \cdot D = \begin{bmatrix} 32/23 & 3/23 \\ 12/23 & 27/23 \end{bmatrix} \cdot \begin{bmatrix} 500 \\ 1{,}000 \end{bmatrix} = \begin{bmatrix} 826 \\ 1{,}435 \end{bmatrix}.$$

(Final amounts have been rounded to whole numbers.) A demand for net production of 500 metric tons of wheat and 1,000 metric tons of oil requires a gross production of 826 metric tons of wheat and 1,435 metric tons of oil.

 EXERCISES

Find the inverse of each matrix that has an inverse.

1. $\begin{bmatrix} 1 & 0 \\ 0 & -1 \end{bmatrix}$
2. $\begin{bmatrix} 0 & 1 \\ 1 & 0 \end{bmatrix}$
3. $\begin{bmatrix} 2 & 1 \\ 4 & 3 \end{bmatrix}$
4. $\begin{bmatrix} -3 & 2 \\ 6 & -5 \end{bmatrix}$

5. $\begin{bmatrix} 1 & 1 \\ 1 & 1 \end{bmatrix}$
6. $\begin{bmatrix} -1 & -1 \\ 1 & 1 \end{bmatrix}$
7. $\begin{bmatrix} 1 & 2 & 0 \\ 0 & 1 & 0 \\ 1 & -1 & 1 \end{bmatrix}$
8. $\begin{bmatrix} 0 & 1 & 0 \\ 0 & 0 & -2 \\ 1 & -1 & 0 \end{bmatrix}$

9. $\begin{bmatrix} 4 & 3 & 3 \\ -1 & 0 & -1 \\ -4 & -4 & -3 \end{bmatrix}$
10. $\begin{bmatrix} 1 & 0 & 2 \\ -1 & 0 & -2 \\ 1 & 1 & 1 \end{bmatrix}$

Use matrix algebra to find the unique solution of each system. If the system has no unique solution, state why.

11. $4x + y = 5$
$2x + y = 3$

12. $3x - 7y = 31$
$2x - 4y = 18$

13. $5x - y = 6$
$-10x + 2y = 15$

14. $5x - y = 14$
$x + 8y = 11$

15. $x + y - z = 6$
$2x - y + z = -9$
$x - 2y + 3z = 1$

16. $4x + 2y - 3z = 6$
$x - 4y + z = -4$
$-x + 2z = 2$

17. $2x - y + 3z = 0$
$x + 2y - z = 5$
$2y + z = 1$

18. $x + y = 1$
$2x - z = 0$
$y + 2z = -2$

19. $2x - 3y + z = 4$
$x + y - z = 1$
$ -5y + 3z = 2$

20. $x + 3y = 7$
$2x - y - 5z = 12$
$7y + 5z = 2$

In each of Exercises 1 and 2, the given matrix was its own inverse. In each of the following cases, find the missing elements to make the given matrix its own inverse.

21. $\begin{bmatrix} 3 & \square \\ 2 & \square \end{bmatrix}$
22. $\begin{bmatrix} \square & 8 \\ \square & 5 \end{bmatrix}$
23. $\begin{bmatrix} 2 & \square \\ \square & -2 \end{bmatrix}$
24. $\begin{bmatrix} \square & 5 \\ -7 & \square \end{bmatrix}$

Assuming that a and b are real numbers, determine whether each of the following statements is sometimes true, always true, *or* never true. *If sometimes true, give the conditions under which it is true.*

25. $\begin{bmatrix} a & 0 \\ 0 & a \end{bmatrix}$ and $\begin{bmatrix} b & 0 \\ 0 & b \end{bmatrix}$ are inverses of each other.

26. $\begin{bmatrix} 0 & a \\ a & 0 \end{bmatrix}$ and $\begin{bmatrix} 0 & b \\ b & 0 \end{bmatrix}$ are inverses of each other.

27. Recall that "row operation 2" is to multiply a given row by some nonzero constant. Show that the following product has the effect (on the second matrix) of multiplying its first row by k.

$$\begin{bmatrix} k & 0 \\ 0 & 1 \end{bmatrix} \cdot \begin{bmatrix} 2 & 4 \\ 3 & 5 \end{bmatrix}$$

28. What 2×2 multiplier, on the left, will change

$$\begin{bmatrix} 2 & 4 \\ 3 & 5 \end{bmatrix} \quad \text{to} \quad \begin{bmatrix} 2 & 4 \\ 3k & 5k \end{bmatrix}$$

(that is, multiply the second row by the constant k)?

29. "Row operation 3" is to add some multiple of one row to another row. Show that the following product has the effect (on the second matrix) of adding twice its first row elements to its corresponding second row elements.

$$\begin{bmatrix} 1 & 0 \\ 2 & 1 \end{bmatrix} \cdot \begin{bmatrix} 2 & 4 \\ 3 & 5 \end{bmatrix}$$

30. What 2×2 multiplier, on the left, will change

$$\begin{bmatrix} 2 & 4 \\ 3 & 5 \end{bmatrix} \quad \text{to} \quad \begin{bmatrix} 11 & 19 \\ 3 & 5 \end{bmatrix}$$

(that is, add three times the second row to the first row)?

The matrix in Example 4 had no inverse. Here are several other 2×2 matrices that do not have inverses:

$$\begin{bmatrix} 5 & 1 \\ 10 & 2 \end{bmatrix}, \quad \begin{bmatrix} 6 & -3 \\ -8 & 4 \end{bmatrix}, \quad \begin{bmatrix} 17 & 22 \\ 34 & 44 \end{bmatrix}.$$

31. Describe the characteristic shared by the above matrices that causes them to not have inverses.

32. Find two additional 2×2 matrices, neither of which has an inverse.

The **determinant** *of a 2×2 matrix is denoted by vertical bars (similar to absolute value signs), so that, for example, the determinant of* $\begin{bmatrix} 2 & 6 \\ 5 & 8 \end{bmatrix}$ *is denoted* $\begin{vmatrix} 2 & 6 \\ 5 & 8 \end{vmatrix}$. *The numerical* **value** *of a determinant is defined as follows:*

$$\begin{vmatrix} a & c \\ b & d \end{vmatrix} = ad - bc.$$

Evaluate each determinant.

33. $\begin{vmatrix} 7 & 4 \\ 5 & 3 \end{vmatrix}$
   34. $\begin{vmatrix} 2 & 8 \\ -3 & -6 \end{vmatrix}$
   35. $\begin{vmatrix} -4 & 8 \\ 5 & -10 \end{vmatrix}$
   36. $\begin{vmatrix} 3 & -2 \\ 6 & -4 \end{vmatrix}$

37. Extend the concept of a determinant to 3×3 matrices, and show how to evaluate a 3×3 determinant. (You may want to consult an algebra book.)

38. Give an example of a 3×3 determinant with the value 0.

*A matrix is called **singular** if its determinant has the value 0.*

39. Explain why a system of linear equations has no unique solution if its coefficient matrix is singular.

40. If A is a singular square matrix, what can you say about A^{-1}?

Use a calculator to find the inverse of each matrix. Give all elements to three decimal places.

41. $\begin{bmatrix} 1.2 & 3.7 \\ -4.8 & 5.5 \end{bmatrix}$
       42. $\begin{bmatrix} 7/6 & 2/11 \\ 5/13 & 1/9 \end{bmatrix}$

43. $\begin{bmatrix} 14.8 & 18.1 & 11.6 \\ 8.2 & 12.6 & 9.5 \\ 15.1 & 13.8 & 7.4 \end{bmatrix}$
   44. $\begin{bmatrix} 125 & 391 & 416 \\ 277 & 143 & 209 \\ 610 & 157 & 504 \end{bmatrix}$

45. In the real number system, how many numbers do not have multiplicative inverses? What are they?

46. In the system of 2×2 matrices, how many matrices do not have multiplicative inverses? What are they?

47. Assume the same basic wheat/oil economy described in the text. Find the gross production required for a net production of 750 metric tons of wheat and 1,000 metric tons of oil. Round final amounts to whole numbers.

48. Find the gross production required in Exercise 47 if production of 1 metric ton of wheat consumes 1/3 metric ton of oil (and no wheat), while the production of 1 metric ton of oil consumes 1/5 metric ton of wheat (and no oil). Round final amounts to whole numbers.

49. Consider an economy depending on three basic commodities: agriculture, manufacturing, and transportation. Suppose 1/4 unit of manufacturing and 1/2 unit of transportation are required to produce 1 unit of agriculture, 1/2 unit of agriculture and 1/4 unit of transportation are required to produce 1 unit of manufacturing, and 1/4 unit of agriculture and 1/4 unit of manufacturing are required to produce 1 unit of transportation. How many units of each commodity should be produced to satisfy a demand for 1,000 units of each commodity? Round final amounts to whole numbers.

50. A simple economy depends on three commodities: oil, corn, and coffee. Production of one unit of oil requires .1 unit of oil, .2 unit of corn, and no units of coffee. To produce one unit of corn requires .2 unit of oil, .1 unit of corn, and .05 unit of coffee. To produce one unit of coffee requires .1 unit of oil, .05 unit of corn, and .1 unit of coffee. Find the gross production required to give a net production of 1,000 units each of oil, corn, and coffee. Round final amounts to whole numbers.

Cryptography

Cryptography, or **code theory,** is one of the areas being continually affected by advancing mathematical theory. "Secret codes," of various forms, have been used throughout history, for purposes that range from international intrigue to childhood pastimes. Today, with more and more information being stored and exchanged within computerized networks, businesses and other interests depend upon advanced cryptographic systems for protection of their data.

A common type of code is constructed by replacing each letter of the alphabet with another letter or symbol, such as

$$A = 3 \quad C = \# \quad E = +$$
$$B = \$ \quad D = 9 \quad F = *$$

and so on. A code like this is very easy for an expert to break. This is because mere substitution of one symbol for another does not change the relative frequency of occurrence of the symbols. Thus, in the substitution of symbols for letters in the English language, + would occur most frequently in any reasonably long message simply because + represents E, and E is the most common letter used in English. (We say "reasonably long message" since in some short messages, such as "summer sessions seldom stimulate", the letter E might not be the most common.) Code breakers have spent a lot of time deciding on the frequency of occurrence of letters. The sample referred to on the opening page of this chapter yields the following percentages for all letters of the alphabet.

Letter	Percent	Letter	Percent	Letter	Percent
E	13.0	D	4.4	G, W	1.6
T	9.3	H, L	3.5	V	1.3
N	7.8	C	3.0	B	.9
R	7.7	F	2.8	X	.5
I, O	7.4	P, U	2.7	K, Q	.3
A	7.3	M	2.5	J	.2
S	6.3	Y	1.9	Z	.1

Governments and computer users need to develop more sophisticated methods of coding and decoding messages. Several of the methods depend on matrix theory. To see how, assign numbers to letters of the alphabet. For simplicity, let A correspond to 1, B to 2, C to 3, and so on. Ignore punctuation and let 27 correspond to a blank space.

A = 1	G = 7	M = 13	S = 19	Y = 25
B = 2	H = 8	N = 14	T = 20	Z = 26
C = 3	I = 9	O = 15	U = 21	space = 27
D = 4	J = 10	P = 16	V = 22	
E = 5	K = 11	Q = 17	W = 23	
F = 6	L = 12	R = 18	X = 24	

Break the message into groups of three letters (and spaces) each. For example, the message SOME CODES ARE EASILY BROKEN becomes

SOM E__C ODE S__A RE__ EAS ILY __BR OKE N____

where ___ represents a blank. Each group of letters is then converted to a 3×1 matrix. For example, the letters S, O, and M convert to 19, 15, and 13, respectively, so that

$$\begin{bmatrix} S \\ O \\ M \end{bmatrix} \quad \text{corresponds to} \quad \begin{bmatrix} 19 \\ 15 \\ 13 \end{bmatrix}.$$

Our message corresponds to the following sequence of matrices.

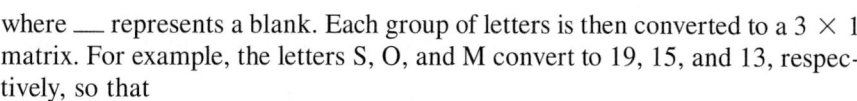

$$\begin{bmatrix} 19 \\ 15 \\ 13 \end{bmatrix} \begin{bmatrix} 5 \\ 27 \\ 3 \end{bmatrix} \begin{bmatrix} 15 \\ 4 \\ 5 \end{bmatrix} \begin{bmatrix} 19 \\ 27 \\ 1 \end{bmatrix} \begin{bmatrix} 18 \\ 5 \\ 27 \end{bmatrix} \begin{bmatrix} 5 \\ 1 \\ 19 \end{bmatrix} \begin{bmatrix} 9 \\ 12 \\ 25 \end{bmatrix} \begin{bmatrix} 27 \\ 2 \\ 18 \end{bmatrix} \begin{bmatrix} 15 \\ 11 \\ 5 \end{bmatrix} \begin{bmatrix} 14 \\ 27 \\ 27 \end{bmatrix}$$

Now choose any 3×3 "multiplier" matrix that has an inverse. Let us choose matrix M as follows.

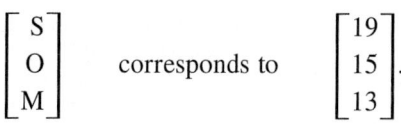

$$M = \begin{bmatrix} 1 & 3 & 3 \\ 1 & 4 & 3 \\ 1 & 3 & 4 \end{bmatrix}$$

Finding the product of M and each of the preceding matrices gives

$$\begin{bmatrix} 103 \\ 118 \\ 116 \end{bmatrix} \begin{bmatrix} 95 \\ 122 \\ 98 \end{bmatrix} \begin{bmatrix} 42 \\ 46 \\ 47 \end{bmatrix}$$

and so on. (See Exercise 5.) The process of translating the message into this series of matrices is called "encoding." In effect, it disguises the original sequence of matrices. The entries of these product matrices can then be transmitted as the message. The recipient of the message divides the numbers into groups of 3 and converts each group of 3 into a matrix. After multiplying these matrices by the matrix M^{-1}, the message can be read.

A code of this type is simple to use but hard to decode for anyone not knowing the multiplication matrix M. For further information on codes, see *The Codebreakers* by David Kahn. Further information on the substitution of symbols for letters is given in the Sherlock Holmes story "The Dancing Men" and in Edgar Allan Poe's "The Gold Bug" (see the marginal note at the left).

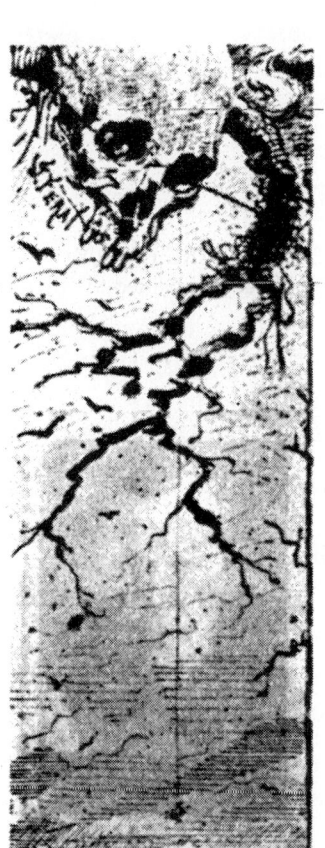

"Shoot from the left eye of the death's head. . . ." In Poe's tale *The Gold-Bug* (1843), the image of a skull on an old piece of parchment starts Legrand, the central character, on a treasure hunt. In the course of it he must decode a message by comparing the frequency of its given symbols with the frequency of letters in the English language. The illustration shows the gold bug (instead of a bullet) dropped from the left eye socket of the skull.

Extension Exercises

1. The message

THE THREE TENORS

is to be encoded by using the matrix method described in the text. The message is broken into groups of two letters (and spaces). Find the sequence of matrices derived from the given message.

2. Use the multiplier matrix $M = \begin{bmatrix} -1 & 2 \\ 2 & -5 \end{bmatrix}$ to encode the sequence of matrices of Exercise 1, and list the resulting sequence of 2×1 matrices.

3. A message that was encoded with the multiplier matrix of Exercise 2 was received as the following sequence of numbers.

$$39, -98, -19, 34, -7, 10, 3, -11, 36,$$
$$-99, 21, -62, 7, -18, 33, -87, 41, -109$$

What multiplier matrix should be used for decoding this message?

4. Find the original message (of Exercise 3).

5. Finish encoding the message SOME CODES ARE EASILY BROKEN given in the text.

6. The person receiving the message of Exercise 5 (SOME CODES ARE EASILY BROKEN) also received the following encoded message (already converted to matrix form).

$$\begin{bmatrix} 99 \\ 119 \\ 107 \end{bmatrix} \begin{bmatrix} 116 \\ 134 \\ 135 \end{bmatrix} \begin{bmatrix} 84 \\ 85 \\ 102 \end{bmatrix} \begin{bmatrix} 98 \\ 125 \\ 102 \end{bmatrix} \begin{bmatrix} 45 \\ 51 \\ 51 \end{bmatrix} \begin{bmatrix} 81 \\ 84 \\ 102 \end{bmatrix} \begin{bmatrix} 153 \\ 173 \\ 180 \end{bmatrix}$$

Decode this second message, assuming it was encoded using the multiplier matrix given in the text.

7. Suppose you are a special agent. The encoding multiplier matrix for today is $M = \begin{bmatrix} 2 & 1 & 2 \\ 3 & 4 & 3 \\ 3 & 1 & 2 \end{bmatrix}$. You need to send the message

DESTROY FILES IMMEDIATELY

to another agent. What sequence of numbers would you transmit?

8. After your transmission of Exercise 7, you receive the response

45, 90, 51, 83, 172, 88, 51, 89, 55, 88, 177, 108, 63, 107, 88.

What is the message?

9. Could the encoding matrix (the multiplier) used in the type of cryptography discussed here be of order 4×4? Explain why or why not.

10. What are the restrictions (if any) on the type of matrix used as the encoding multiplier?

11. Explain why the matrix type code discussed here would be difficult to break.

12. The following message is written in a code in which the frequency of the symbols is the main key to the solution.

)?--8))6*+8506*3×6;4?*7*&×*-6.48()6)985)?(8+2:;48)81&?(;46*3)6*;
48&(+8(*598+.8()8=8(5*-8-5(81?098;4&+)&15*50:)6*;?6;6&*0?-7

Find the frequency of each symbol. By comparing high frequency symbols with the high frequency letters in English (see the text above), try to decipher the message. (*Hint:* look for repeated two-symbol combinations and double letters for added clues. Try to identify vowels first.)

14.5

Matrices and Game Theory*

In this section, we discuss a large and still growing branch of mathematics called **game theory.** While the name may suggest something frivolous, the applications certainly are not. Game theory was developed in the 1940s as a means of analyzing competitive situations in business, warfare, and social settings.

A **two-player game,** the most common case, involves two opponents. These opponents can be two persons, two teams of persons, two countries, and so on. One player may even be a nonpersonal entity. For example, imagine that you are a California citrus farmer in the winter playing a strategic game against nature. You can protect your crop against freezing by burning smudge pots at night at a cost of $1,000. If you burn smudge pots, you will be able to sell your crop for a net profit of $14,000, provided that the freeze does develop. If you do nothing, you will either lose $3,000 in planting costs if the freeze comes, or will gain $8,000 profit if no freeze occurs.

To analyze this situation we set up a **payoff matrix,** which shows the farmer's possible actions, or **strategies,** on the left and nature's strategies (the "States of Nature") on the top. The entries of the matrix are the amounts of profit (or loss) for the various combinations of strategy choices.

STATES OF NATURE

		Freeze	No freeze
FARMER'S	Use smudge pots	$14,000	$7,000
STRATEGIES:	Don't use them	−$3,000	$8,000

Several criteria may be used in the decision making. If you are an optimist, you might choose the **maximax** criterion, which selects the action that *maximizes* the *maximum* gain. In our example, if you use smudge pots, your maximum gain would be $14,000, while if you do not use smudge pots, your maximum gain would be $8,000. Using the maximax criterion, you would choose the action that gives the larger of the two maximums and use smudge pots.

On the other hand, you might be a pessimist. In that case, the **maximin** criterion, which *maximizes* the *minimum* payoff, would suit you just fine. The minimum payoffs under the two actions are $7,000, with smudge pots, and −$3,000 if nothing is done. The larger of these occurs if smudge pots are used, so that this is the appropriate action for this criterion, too.

If you are neither an optimist nor a pessimist, and if you can assign some probability p to the "freeze" state of nature, then you can compromise by choosing the action with the greatest expected payoff. Suppose you believe (the weather forecaster has convinced you) that the probability of a freeze is .4. The probability of no freeze would then be .6, with the expected payoffs as follows.

If smudge pots are used: $14,000(.4) + 7,000(.6) = \$9,800$

If no pots are used: $-3,000(.4) + 8,000(.6) = \$3,600$

Economic Behavior   In 1944 a new direction in economics was set by the *Theory of Games and Economic Behavior,* containing the famous minimax theorem. It was written by mathematician John von Neumann (see page 853) and economist Oskar Morgenstern. The book's impact relates to the question about which mathematics is proper to economics. Beginning with Antoine Cournot in the 1830s, economists looked to physics for analogies in thermodynamics or mechanics since physics had been so successfully "mathematized." The game-theoretic approach was a break with the past, showing how mathematics other than the calculus could give models of economic behavior.

---

* The material in this section depends somewhat on the ideas of probability and expected value, which were discussed in an earlier chapter.

Con(traption) Game This stamp from Hungary pictures Turk, an automaton built in 1769 that ostensibly played chess—it was actually operated from within by a concealed chess player. Turk was exhibited in the U.S. in the 1830s by Johann Maelzel, inventor of the metronome (and a friend of Beethoven). Edgar Allan Poe's essay on Turk deduces the person inside. Poe observed *Schlumberger,* a European chess player, just before and after Turk's chess game, but never during. Schlumberger is psyched out by Thomas Gavin in his novel *King-kill* (Random House, 1977): Schlumberger hides within Turk to avoid the ordeal of playing chess as his own man. (The title refers to the origin of "checkmate" in the Arabic *shah mat*—"the king is left unable to escape.")

Turk eventually wound up in the Chinese Museum, Philadelphia. It was wrecked by a fire there in 1854. Fire also destroyed Ajeeb, another chess automaton, this time at Coney Island in 1929. The U.S. Chess Master Harry Nelson Pillsbury operated Ajeeb at the turn of the century.

This criterion, choosing the maximum of the expected payoffs, also indicates that smudge pots should be used. Note that, as your subjective beliefs about the probability of a freeze change, so would the expected payoffs. To assign probabilities to such unique events requires a subjective or personal assessment of the event. It works out here that pots should be used as long as you feel the probability of a freeze is greater than 1/18.

In the example discussed here, all three criteria led to the same action. However, if the cost of using the smudge pots were much larger, or the profit when they were used in the event of a freeze were much smaller, the situation would look very different. Also, for the payoff matrix to be helpful the effect of all important factors must somehow be included. At the least, the use of a payoff matrix does clarify the problem and permit an orderly approach to considering the alternatives.

Notice that in a two-player game player A's strategies (1, 2, and so on) are shown at the left of the payoff matrix, and player B's strategies (I, II, and so on) are shown at the top of the payoff matrix. Each row of the game matrix (the payoff matrix) represents one of A's possible strategies, while each column represents one of B's possible strategies. Each entry in the matrix is the payoff that results for that particular choice of strategies. We assume that if the payoff is a positive number, A receives that amount from B; if it is negative, A pays B. Under this assumption, one player must lose whatever the other wins. This condition defines a **zero-sum game.** Not all games are zero-sum games. The stock market, for example, is *not.* Stocks can go up or down according to outside forces. (In effect, money enters this system from sources other than investors.) Therefore, it is possible that all investors can make money or that they can all lose.

The remainder of this section will be restricted. We discuss two-player, zero-sum games only.

EXAMPLE 1 Assume the payoffs here are dollar amounts. What are the results of each possible combination of strategy choices?

$$
\begin{array}{c}
 & & B \\
 & & \begin{array}{cc} \text{I} & \text{II} \end{array} \\
A & \begin{array}{c} 1 \\ 2 \end{array} & \begin{bmatrix} 2 & -1 \\ -3 & 4 \end{bmatrix}
\end{array}
$$

From the payoff matrix, we observe the following.

If A applies strategy 1 and B applies strategy I, then A receives \$2 from B.

If A applies strategy 1 and B applies strategy II, then A pays B \$1.

If A applies strategy 2 and B applies strategy I, then A pays B \$3.

If A applies strategy 2 and B applies strategy II, then A receives \$4 from B.

An $m \times n$ (matrix) game is one in which player A has m possible strategies (rows) and player B has n strategies (columns). For example, a 3×3 game is shown here.

$$
\begin{array}{c}
 & & B \\
 & & \begin{array}{ccc} \text{I} & \text{II} & \text{III} \end{array} \\
A \begin{array}{c} 1 \\ 2 \\ 3 \end{array} & \left[\begin{array}{ccc} -3 & -6 & 10 \\ 3 & 0 & 1 \\ 5 & -4 & -8 \end{array} \right]
\end{array}
$$

From B's viewpoint, strategy II is better than strategy I no matter which strategy A selects, since a gain of \$6 is better than a gain of \$3; breaking even is better than paying \$3 to A; and a gain of \$4 is better than a loss of \$5. Therefore, B should never select strategy I. In a situation like this, strategy II is said to *dominate* strategy I (or strategy I is *dominated* by II). Column II dominates column I since *every* column II payoff is *less than* the corresponding column I payoff.

From A's viewpoint, no strategy (row) in the original matrix above dominates another, since for a row to dominate another, its payoffs must all be greater than the corresponding payoffs in the other row. (Verify that this condition does not occur in the payoff matrix above.)

It is sometimes possible to reduce the order of an $m \times n$ game by eliminating dominated strategies. (No player would ever choose to employ a dominated strategy anyway.)

EXAMPLE 2 Reduce the 3×3 game matrix above by eliminating any dominated strategies.

As observed above, A sees no dominant strategies initially but B would eliminate strategy I, so we arrive at the following reduced matrix.

$$
\begin{array}{c}
 & & B \\
 & & \begin{array}{cc} \text{II} & \text{III} \end{array} \\
A \begin{array}{c} 1 \\ 2 \\ 3 \end{array} & \left[\begin{array}{cc} -6 & 10 \\ 0 & 1 \\ -4 & -8 \end{array} \right]
\end{array}
$$

But now that strategy I for B has been removed, it turns out that strategy 2 for A dominates strategy 3. Therefore, we can finally reduce the game to a 2×2 matrix as follows.

$$
\begin{array}{c}
 & & B \\
 & & \begin{array}{cc} \text{II} & \text{III} \end{array} \\
A \begin{array}{c} 1 \\ 2 \end{array} & \left[\begin{array}{cc} -6 & 10 \\ 0 & 1 \end{array} \right]
\end{array}
$$

Which strategies should be chosen by A and B? The goal of game theory is to find *optimum* strategies, those which are most profitable (or least costly) for a player. The resulting payoff, assuming both players select their respective optimum strategies, is called the *value* of the game. We usually find optimum strategies using the **minimax** criterion, in which we *minimize* the *maximum* possible loss. For example, a game for players A and B is shown here.

$$
\begin{array}{cc}
 & B \\
 & \begin{array}{ccc} \text{I} & \text{II} & \text{III} \end{array} \\
A \quad \begin{array}{c} 1 \\ 2 \\ 3 \end{array} & \begin{bmatrix} -7 & 8 & -1 \\ 4 & 7 & 0 \\ -9 & 3 & -6 \end{bmatrix}
\end{array}
$$

In this game, player A's greatest possible losses for his or her strategy choices are \$7, \$0, and \$9, respectively. To minimize the maximum possible loss, player A should select strategy 2. In the same way, B's greatest possible losses are \$4, \$8, and \$0, so that B can minimize possible losses by choosing strategy III. Thus, the payoff will be \$0 (strategy 2 for A and III for B), which is the value of the game. A game whose value is \$0 is called a **fair game.**

The pair of strategies (2, III) determined by the minimax criterion is called the **saddle point** of the game. The saddle point is the pair of strategies for which the entry in the payoff matrix is both the *minimum* in its row and *maximum* in its column. This fact makes the saddle point easy to determine, if it exists. For example, in the matrix below, by the definition above, the saddle point is (4, I) and the value of the game is \$3. (Whenever there are two or more saddle points, they must all yield equal values.)

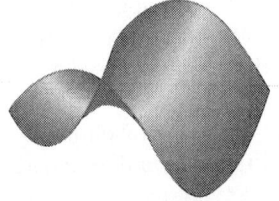

The name **saddle point** comes from a saddle. The seat of the saddle is the maximum from one direction and the minimum from another direction.

$$
\begin{array}{cc}
 & B \\
 & \begin{array}{cc} \text{I} & \text{II} \end{array} \\
A \quad \begin{array}{c} 1 \\ 2 \\ 3 \\ 4 \end{array} & \begin{bmatrix} 2 & 2 \\ 0 & 4 \\ 1 & 6 \\ 3 & 7 \end{bmatrix}
\end{array}
$$

Unfortunately, not every $m \times n$ game has a saddle point. When there is no saddle point, another approach must be used. Both players will have to *mix* their strategies. If this mixing were to be done in some systematic fashion, the competitor would soon guess it and play accordingly. For this reason, it is best to mix strategies according to previously determined probabilities. For example, if a player has only two strategies and has decided to select them with equal probability, the random choice can be made by tossing a coin. Heads could represent one strategy; tails the other. Although this would result in the two strategies being used about equally over the long run, on a particular play no player could predetermine which strategy would be used. Some other device, such as a spinner, a die, or random numbers, is necessary for more than two strategies, or when the predetermined probability is different from 1/2.

To see how to decide on the probability with which a particular strategy is selected, return to the example about the smudge pots. Suppose you must decide several times each season whether or not to use smudge pots, and you don't really know the probability of a freeze. We need to find the fraction of the time (the probability) that you should use smudge pots. There is no saddle point for this game. Thus, let x represent the probability that you will choose strategy 1, with $1 - x$ the probability that you will choose strategy 2.

$$\text{NATURE}$$

$$\begin{array}{c} \\ \text{YOU} \end{array} \begin{array}{c} \\ 1 \\ 2 \end{array} \begin{array}{cc} \text{I} & \text{II} \\ \left[\begin{array}{cc} \$14{,}000 & \$7{,}000 \\ -\$3{,}000 & \$8{,}000 \end{array} \right] \end{array}$$

For Nature's strategy I (a freeze) your expected profit is

$$E_{\text{I}} = 14{,}000x - 3{,}000(1 - x).$$

For Nature's strategy II (no freeze) your expected profit is

$$E_{\text{II}} = 7{,}000x + 8{,}000(1 - x).$$

You will maximize your profit in the long run if you choose a value of x for which $E_{\text{I}} = E_{\text{II}}$. (This fact was proved in 1928 by John von Neumann. We will use it here without proof.) To make $E_{\text{I}} = E_{\text{II}}$, solve as follows.

$$E_{\text{I}} = E_{\text{II}}$$
$$14{,}000x - 3{,}000(1 - x) = 7{,}000x + 8{,}000(1 - x)$$
$$17{,}000x - 3{,}000 = -1{,}000x + 8{,}000$$
$$18{,}000x = 11{,}000$$
$$x = \frac{11}{18}$$

Thus, the optimum strategy here is to use strategy 1 (use smudge pots) $11/18$ of the time, and strategy 2 (don't use them) a total of

$$1 - x = 1 - \frac{11}{18} = \frac{7}{18}$$

of the time.

John von Neumann
(1903–1957) achieved much in a life cut short by cancer. Stories told about him made him a living legend. In 1933 he joined the Institute for Advanced Study, newly founded, and was one of its original six mathematicians. By then he had already written important papers on set theory, quantum mechanics, and the minimax theorem. After 1940 he turned to the applications of mathematics, working with Stanislaw Ulam during World War II and extending game theory with Morgenstern. Von Neumann was intensely interested in the theory and use of computers and automata. His interest in artificial intelligence is expressed in his lecture notes published as *The Computer and the Brain* (Yale paperback).

EXAMPLE 3 Find the farmer's expected gain from the smudge pot strategy outlined above.

We can substitute $11/18$ for x in either E_{I} or E_{II}. Using E_{I} gives

$$14{,}000\left(\frac{11}{18}\right) - 3{,}000\left(\frac{7}{18}\right) = \frac{133{,}000}{18} = \$7{,}388.89.$$

This result, $\$7,388.89$, is the value of the game. The value comes out the same no matter which player's optimum strategy and expected gain are considered.

14.5 **EXERCISES**

In the following games, assume that player A chooses rows and player B chooses columns. Eliminate all dominated strategies from each of the following games.

1. $\begin{bmatrix} 1 & 4 \\ 4 & -1 \\ 3 & 5 \\ -4 & 0 \end{bmatrix}$

2. $\begin{bmatrix} 2 & 3 & 1 & -5 \\ -1 & 5 & 4 & 1 \\ 1 & 0 & 2 & -3 \end{bmatrix}$

3. $\begin{bmatrix} 8 & 12 & -7 \\ -2 & 1 & 4 \end{bmatrix}$

4. $\begin{bmatrix} 6 & 2 \\ -1 & 10 \\ 3 & 5 \end{bmatrix}$

Where it exists, find the saddle point and the value of the game for each of the following.

5. $\begin{bmatrix} -6 & 2 \\ -1 & -10 \\ 3 & 5 \end{bmatrix}$

6. $\begin{bmatrix} 7 & 8 \\ -2 & 15 \end{bmatrix}$

7. $\begin{bmatrix} 3 & -4 & 1 \\ 5 & 3 & 2 \end{bmatrix}$

8. $\begin{bmatrix} 2 & 3 & 1 \\ -1 & 4 & -7 \\ 5 & 2 & 0 \\ 8 & -4 & -1 \end{bmatrix}$

9. $\begin{bmatrix} 1 & 4 & -3 & 1 & -1 \\ 2 & 5 & 0 & 4 & 10 \\ 1 & -3 & -2 & 5 & 2 \end{bmatrix}$

10. $\begin{bmatrix} -4 & 2 & -3 & -7 \\ 4 & 3 & 5 & 9 \end{bmatrix}$

Solve each of the following problems.

11. Hillsdale College has sold out all tickets for a jazz concert to be held in the stadium. If it rains, the show will have to be moved into the gym, which has a much smaller seating capacity. The dean must decide in advance whether to set up the seats and the stage in the gym or in the stadium, or both, just in case. The matrix below shows the net profit in each case.

		NATURE	
		Rain	No rain
	Set up stadium	−$1,550	$1,500
ACTIONS	Set up gym	$1,000	$1,000
	Set up both	$750	$1,400

(a) What action should the dean take if he is an optimist?

(b) If he is a pessimist?

(c) If the weather forecaster predicts rain with a probability of .6, what action should the dean take to maximize expected profit?

12. A community is considering an anti-smoking campaign. The city manager has been asked to recommend one of three possible actions: a campaign for everyone in the community over age 10, a campaign for youths only, or no campaign at all. The two states of nature are a true cause-effect relationship between smoking and cancer or no such relationship. The cost to the community (including loss of life and productivity) in each case is shown below.*

	Cause-effect relationship	No such relationship
Campaign for all	$100,000	$800,000
Campaign for youth	$2,820,000	$20,000
No campaign	$3,100,100	$0

*This problem is based on an article by B. G. Greenburg in the September 1969 issue of the *Journal of the American Statistical Association*.

(a) What action should the manager recommend if she is an optimist?

(b) If she is a pessimist?

(c) If the Director of Public Health estimates that the probability of a true cause-effect relationship is .8, which action should be recommended to minimize expected costs?

13. The research department of Allied Manufacturing has developed a new process that they feel will result in an improved product. Management must decide whether or not to market the new product. The new product may be better than the old, or it may not be better. If the new product is better, and the company decides to market it, sales should increase by $50,000. If it is not better and they replace the old product with the new product on the market, they will lose $25,000 to competitors. If they decide not to market the new product, they will lose $40,000 if it is better and research costs of $10,000 if it is not.

(a) Prepare a payoff matrix.

(b) If management believes that the probability is .4 that the new product is better, find the expected profits under each possible course of action, and find the best action.

14. Suppose Allied Manufacturing (of Exercise 13) decides to put their new product on the market with a big advertising campaign. At the same time, they find out that their major competitor, Bates Manufacturing, has also decided on a big advertising campaign for its version of the product. The payoff matrix below shows the increased sales in millions for Allied, which also represent decreases for Bates.

$$
\begin{array}{c}
\text{BATES} \\
\begin{array}{cc}
\text{TV} & \text{Radio}
\end{array} \\
\text{ALLIED} \begin{array}{c} \text{TV} \\ \text{Radio} \end{array}
\begin{bmatrix}
1.0 & -.7 \\
-.5 & .5
\end{bmatrix}
\end{array}
$$

Find the optimum strategy for Allied, and find the value of the game.

In each of the following games, find the optimum strategy for each player, and find the value of the game. Identify any fair games.

15. $\begin{bmatrix} 5 & 1 \\ 3 & 4 \end{bmatrix}$

16. $\begin{bmatrix} -4 & 5 \\ 3 & -4 \end{bmatrix}$

17. $\begin{bmatrix} -2 & 4 \\ 0 & 5 \end{bmatrix}$

18. $\begin{bmatrix} 0 & -4 \\ 4 & 0 \end{bmatrix}$

19. In the game of matching coins, two players each flip a coin. If both coins match (both show heads or both show tails), player A wins $1. If there is no match, player B wins $1, as in the matrix below. Find the optimum strategies for each player, and find the value of the game.

$$
\begin{bmatrix}
1 & -1 \\
-1 & 1
\end{bmatrix}
$$

20. Explain the meaning of a "zero-sum" game. Give an example of a zero-sum game and an example of a non–zero-sum game.

21. Explain these terms: *maximax criterion, maximin criterion,* and *minimax criterion.*

22. Explain why, in a game matrix, a dominant row has entries that are *greater* than those of the dominated row, whereas a dominant column has entries that are *less* than those of the dominated column.

23. Explain what is meant by a "mixed" strategy.

Refer to the original payoff matrix in the text for the citrus farmer. Assume the farmer is neither an optimist nor a pessimist. Each of Exercises 24–26 gives a probability of having a freeze. In each case find **(a)** *the expected payoff for strategy 1 (use smudge pots) and* **(b)** *the expected payoff for strategy 2 (don't use them).*

24. $1/17$ **25.** $1/18$ **26.** $1/19$

27. Discuss how your answers to Exercises 24–26 relate to the claim in the text that "pots should be used as long as you feel the probability of a freeze is greater than $1/18$."

28. Refer to Example 3 in the text. Use E_{II} to find the farmer's expected gain for Nature's strategy II. Is the value the same as was obtained in the example using E_{I}?

In Example 3 it was stated that the value of a game (with no saddle point) comes out the same no matter which player's optimum strategy and expected gain are considered. Work the following exercises to consider the smudge pot question from Nature's viewpoint. Assume the original payoff matrix and suppose that Nature will randomly impose a freeze a certain fraction of the time, given by x.

29. Derive an expression for E_1, the expected payoff in case the farmer chooses to use smudge pots.

30. Derive an expression for E_2, the expected payoff in case the farmer chooses not to use smudge pots.

31. Equate E_1 and E_2 from Exercises 29 and 30 to find Nature's optimum strategy.

32. Find the value (expected payoff) of the game when Nature employs the strategy of Exercise 31. Is the value the same as that arrived at in Example 3?

Another citrus farmer facing the smudge pot decision has calculated the following payoff matrix. Refer to it for Exercises 33–37.

$$\begin{array}{c} \\ \text{Use smudge pots} \\ \text{Don't use them} \end{array} \begin{array}{cc} \text{Freeze} & \text{No freeze} \\ \left[\begin{array}{cc} \$8{,}000 & \$7{,}000 \\ -\$5{,}000 & \$10{,}000 \end{array} \right] \end{array}$$

33. Which strategy would an optimist choose?

34. Which strategy would a pessimist choose?

35. If the farmer is neither an optimist nor a pessimist but is able to reasonably assess the probability of a freeze, how large must that probability be for the farmer's preferred strategy to be to use smudge pots?

36. The payoff matrix above still has no saddle point, so the farmer's best plan is probably to use a mixed strategy. Use the procedure described just before Example 3 to decide what fraction of the time the farmer should use smudge pots.

37. By using smudge pots the fraction of the time computed in Exercise 36, what expected gain does the farmer have? (Compare with Example 3.)

38. For the citrus farmer problem, devise a new 2×2 payoff matrix for which an optimist and a pessimist would both choose not to use smudge pots. Describe conditions that might give rise to the payoffs in your matrix.

In this activity, the algebraic structure of the system of 2 × 2 matrices will be compared with that of the system of real numbers.

1. First, as an entire class, review the following description of the real number system to clarify the meanings of the various properties.

   The set of real numbers R, along with the operations of addition ($+$) and multiplication ($\cdot$) and the relation of equality ($=$), is a **mathematical system.** Specifically, R is an **abelian (commutative) group** under the operation $+$ because the following five properties are satisfied. For all a, b, and c in R:

   (1) $a + b$ is in R. (closure property of $+$)
   (2) $a + b = b + a$. (commutative property of $+$)
   (3) $(a + b) + c = a + (b + c)$. (associative property of $+$)
   (4) there is an element 0 in R such that $a + 0 = a$. (identity property of $+$)
   (5) there exists an element $-a$ in R such that $a + (-a) = 0$. (inverse property of $+$)

   Furthermore, the system R is an **associative ring** because the following three additional properties are satisfied. For all a, b, and c in R:

   (6) $a \cdot b$ is in R. (closure property of $\cdot$)
   (7) $a \cdot (b \cdot c) = (a \cdot b) \cdot c$. (associative property of $\cdot$)
   (8) $a \cdot (b + c) = a \cdot b + a \cdot c$ and $(b + c) \cdot a = b \cdot a + c \cdot a$. (the left and right distributive properties)

   In addition, R is a **commutative ring with unit element** because of the following two properties. For all a and b in R:

   (9) $a \cdot b = b \cdot a$. (commutative property of $\cdot$)
   (10) there is an element 1 in R such that $a \cdot 1 = 1 \cdot a = a$. (identity property of $\cdot$)

   Finally, R is a **field** because of one more property. For all a in R (other than 0):

   (11) there exists an element a^{-1} in R such that $a \cdot a^{-1} = 1$. (inverse property of $\cdot$)

   In summary, the real numbers comprise a field because

   A. all real numbers are an abelian group under $+$, and
   B. all nonzero real numbers are an abelian group under $\cdot$.

2. Next, divide into groups of three or four students each. Each small group is to consider the system of all 2 × 2 matrices with real number entries, together with the operations of $+$ and $\cdot$ and the relation of $=$. Investigate the eleven properties listed above, in turn, for this new system. In each case, try examples, or make use of corresponding properties of the real numbers to prove the results, or use results established in this chapter (including appropriate exercises). Decide, within your group, on answers to the following questions.

   (1) Do the 2 × 2 matrices form a mathematical field? If not, which ones of the eleven properties fail to hold?
   (2) If the system of matrices is not a field, is it at least a commutative ring with unit element?
   (3) If not, is it at least an associative ring?
   (4) If not, is it at least a commutative group under addition?

3. Once the individual groups have decided on their opinions, come back together and share your reasoning. Try to come up with a firm conclusion as a class.

Chapter 14 Test

Let $A = \begin{bmatrix} 2 & -1 & 3 \\ 2 & 0 & 1 \\ 4 & 1 & 3 \end{bmatrix}$ and $B = \begin{bmatrix} -3 & 0 & 1 \\ 0 & 2 & -1 \\ -1 & 0 & 3 \end{bmatrix}$. *Perform the indicated matrix operations.*

1. $A + B$ **2.** $A - B$ **3.** AB **4.** BA **5.** $2A$ **6.** $-3B + A$

Apply the following row operations to matrix A from above.

7. Interchange rows 2 and 3.

8. Multiply each element of row 2 of A by -3, and add the results to row 1.

Find each of the following products, when possible. If not possible, state why not.

9. $\begin{bmatrix} -2 & 1 \\ 3 & 4 \end{bmatrix} \cdot \begin{bmatrix} 2 \\ 1 \end{bmatrix}$

10. $\begin{bmatrix} 3 & 4 & 1 \\ 2 & 0 & 8 \end{bmatrix} \cdot \begin{bmatrix} 1 & 0 & 2 \\ 0 & 0 & 1 \\ 3 & 0 & 2 \end{bmatrix}$

11. $\begin{bmatrix} 1 & 6 & 1 \end{bmatrix} \cdot \begin{bmatrix} 3 \\ 2 \\ 1 \end{bmatrix}$

12. $\begin{bmatrix} 8 & 9 & 7 \\ 2 & 1 & 3 \end{bmatrix} \cdot \begin{bmatrix} 2 & 3 \\ 4 & 2 \end{bmatrix}$

Find the inverse of each of the following matrices, where possible.

13. $\begin{bmatrix} 2 & 1 \\ 5 & 3 \end{bmatrix}$

14. $\begin{bmatrix} 1 & 0 & 1 \\ 2 & 3 & 1 \\ 1 & 3 & 2 \end{bmatrix}$

Set up the augmented matrix for each of the following systems of equations. Do not solve the systems.

15. $9x - 4y = 20$
$\quad\ \ 5x + 10y = 12$

16. $2x + y - 6z = 6$
$\quad\ \ 5x + 12z = 15$
$\quad\ \ 6y + 3z = 8$

Solve each system of equations by the Gauss-Jordan method (Exercises 17 and 18).

17. $5x + 6y = 15$
$\quad\ \ 3x + 7y = 9$

18. $3x + 4y + \ z = 10$
$\quad\ \ x - 3y - 5z = -3$
$\quad\ \ 2x + 7y = 1$

19. If the system of equations

$$x + y = 1$$
$$2x - y = -7$$

is written as $AX = B$, what exactly is represented by each of the following?
(a) A **(b)** X **(c)** B

20. Given the matrix equation $AX = B$, express X in terms of A and B.

21. Use matrix algebra to solve the system of equations of Exercise 19.

22. Explain the conditions under which the matrix product AB is computable.

The economy of a small country involves bananas and coal. Production of 1 unit of bananas consumes .3 unit of bananas and .1 unit of coal. Production of 1 unit of coal consumes .2 unit of bananas and .4 unit of coal.

23. Set up the technological matrix for this economy.

24. Find the gross production required to meet a demand for net production of 400 units of bananas and 300 units of coal.

25. Remove any dominated strategies from the following game.

$$\begin{bmatrix} 6 & 8 & -3 & 4 \\ 2 & 0 & 2 & -1 \end{bmatrix}$$

26. Identify any saddle points in the following game.

$$\begin{bmatrix} -3 & 1 & 4 & 2 \\ 8 & 9 & 6 & 4 \\ 9 & 10 & 15 & 19 \end{bmatrix}$$

27. Find the optimum strategy for player A and the value of the following game.

$$
\begin{array}{cc}
 & B \\
 & \begin{array}{cc} \text{I} & \text{II} \end{array} \\
A \begin{array}{c} 1 \\ 2 \end{array} & \begin{bmatrix} -3 & -4 \\ -4 & 5 \end{bmatrix}
\end{array}
$$

28. Find two different pairs of values for the missing entries in the matrix

$$A = \begin{bmatrix} \square & -3 \\ 5 & \square \end{bmatrix}$$

that will cause A to be its own inverse.

Arturo Hogan makes silver jewelry inlaid with turquoise. Each ring requires 1.6 units of silver and .7 unit of turquoise, each bracelet requires 5.8 units of silver and 7.5 units of turquoise, and each necklace requires 26.3 units of silver and 18.8 units of turquoise. Arturo pays \$5.50 per unit for silver and \$2.10 per unit for turquoise.

29. Set up a matrix M relating jewelry items (ring, bracelet, necklace) to materials (silver, turquoise), and another matrix C relating materials to cost (per unit).

30. Perform an appropriate matrix operation to obtain a matrix relating jewelry items to cost (per item) for materials.

14.1 Exercises   (Page 812)

1. $\begin{bmatrix} 11 & 1 \\ 9 & 4 \end{bmatrix}$ **3.** $\begin{bmatrix} 3 & 3 & -3 \\ 4 & -4 & 0 \end{bmatrix}$ **5.** $\begin{bmatrix} -3 & 4 & 2 \\ 8 & 2 & 1 \\ 4 & 3 & 13 \end{bmatrix}$

7. It is not computable because the matrices do not have the same order.   **9.** $\begin{bmatrix} 0 \\ 12 \\ 7 \end{bmatrix}$ **11.** $\begin{bmatrix} -14 & -2 \\ 5 & 10 \end{bmatrix}$

13. $A + B = \begin{bmatrix} -2 & -1 \\ -1 & -4 \end{bmatrix}$ **15.** $2A = \begin{bmatrix} -8 & 0 \\ 6 & -8 \end{bmatrix}$ **17.** $-4B = \begin{bmatrix} -8 & 4 \\ 16 & 0 \end{bmatrix}$

19. $2A + 3B = \begin{bmatrix} -2 & -3 \\ -6 & -8 \end{bmatrix}$ **21.** $(-1)A + A = \begin{bmatrix} 0 & 0 \\ 0 & 0 \end{bmatrix}$

23.

	Fat	Carbohydrates	Protein
I	5	0	7
II	0	10	1
III	0	15	2
IV	10	12	8

25. $C = \begin{array}{c} \\ F1 \\ F2 \end{array} \begin{array}{ccc} W1 & W2 & W3 \end{array} \begin{bmatrix} 12 & 20 & 25 \\ 16 & 25 & 30 \end{bmatrix}$

27. $C + A = \begin{bmatrix} 15 & 18 & 27 \\ 20 & 27 & 28 \end{bmatrix}$ **29.** $\begin{bmatrix} 45 & 35 & 20 \\ 65 & 40 & 35 \end{bmatrix} + \begin{bmatrix} 10 & 12 & 5 \\ 15 & 20 & 8 \end{bmatrix} = \begin{bmatrix} 55 & 47 & 25 \\ 80 & 60 & 43 \end{bmatrix}$

31. 25 model-C tables   **33.** $\begin{bmatrix} 22 & 25 & 38 \\ 31 & 34 & 35 \end{bmatrix} + \begin{bmatrix} 10 & 12 & 5 \\ 15 & 20 & 8 \end{bmatrix} - \begin{bmatrix} 5 & 10 & 8 \\ 11 & 14 & 15 \end{bmatrix} = \begin{bmatrix} 27 & 27 & 35 \\ 35 & 40 & 28 \end{bmatrix}$

35. 9 pounds   **37.** The given equality is impossible because the two matrices have different orders.
39. $\{(y, z) \mid y = z\}$ **41.** $k = 8, m = 1, y = 3$ **43.** $x = 1, y = 8, z = 8$

45. The given equality is impossible. In the first row, first column of the matrix $\begin{bmatrix} x & y \\ 3 & 5 \end{bmatrix}$, x must be equal to 10.

But in the second row, first column of the matrix $\begin{bmatrix} -2 & 6 \\ x & 2 \end{bmatrix}$, x must be equal to 4.

47. No. On a calendar, there are seven columns. In order for the days of a given month to form a matrix, the number of days in that month must be divisible by 7. March has 31 days, which is not divisible by 7; therefore the month of March on a calendar will never form a matrix.   **49.** false   **51.** true   **53.** true   **55.** true

14.2 Exercises   (Page 824)

1. $\begin{bmatrix} 8 & 6 \\ -7 & 3 \end{bmatrix}$ **3.** $\begin{bmatrix} -2 & -8 \\ -14 & 34 \end{bmatrix}$ **5.** $\begin{bmatrix} 17 & 7 & 9 \\ 13 & 6 & 3 \end{bmatrix}$ **7.** $\begin{bmatrix} 8 & 3 \\ 11 & -2 \\ 4 & 12 \end{bmatrix}$ **9.** It is not computable because the

number of columns in the first matrix is not equal to the number of rows in the second matrix.

11. $\begin{bmatrix} 14 & 4 & 0 \\ -4 & 4 & 0 \\ -6 & 2 & 0 \end{bmatrix}$

13. $AB = $

	PURCHASE OPTION	
	Large lot	Small lot
Sweet rolls	47.5	57.75
Bread	27	33.75
Cakes	81	95
Pies	12	15

15. $(DA)B = $ Day's orders $\quad [\;$ Cost (large lot) 11,120 $\quad$ Cost (small lot) 13,555 $\;]$

17. $RC = $

	Cost per unit
Table	34
Chair	26
Desk	45

19.

	Materials	Labor
Table	34	36
Chair	26	18
Desk	45	45

21.

Team	Level 1 pts	Level 2 pts	Total pts
A	1	2	3
B	2	2	4
C	2	3	5
D	1	1	2

23. (a) $H^2K = \begin{bmatrix} 2 \\ 2 \\ 3 \\ 1 \end{bmatrix}$ (b) H^2K represents the number of Level 2 points earned by each team.

25. $(H + H^2)K = \begin{bmatrix} 3 \\ 4 \\ 5 \\ 2 \end{bmatrix}$; Yes, $(H + H^2)K = HK + H^2K$. **27.** $AB = \begin{bmatrix} 3 & 1 \\ 1 & -5 \end{bmatrix}$ **29.** $(AB)C = \begin{bmatrix} 2 & 3 \\ 6 & 17 \end{bmatrix}$;

$A(BC) = \begin{bmatrix} 2 & 3 \\ 6 & 17 \end{bmatrix}$ **31.** $(A - B)C = \begin{bmatrix} -3 & -11 \\ 1 & 2 \end{bmatrix}$; $AC - BC = \begin{bmatrix} -3 & -11 \\ 1 & 2 \end{bmatrix}$

33. $AB = \begin{bmatrix} 122 & 130 \\ 65 & 57 \end{bmatrix}$; $BA = \begin{bmatrix} 122 & 130 \\ 65 & 57 \end{bmatrix}$; Yes, $AB = BA$.

35. $AB = \begin{bmatrix} 19 & 6 \\ -14 & 20 \end{bmatrix}$; $BA = \begin{bmatrix} 24 & 26 \\ -4 & 15 \end{bmatrix}$; No, AB is not equal to BA.

39. (a) Let $S = \begin{bmatrix} a & b & c \\ d & e & f \\ g & h & j \end{bmatrix}$; $I = \begin{bmatrix} 1 & 0 & 0 \\ 0 & 1 & 0 \\ 0 & 0 & 1 \end{bmatrix}$.

Then $SI = \begin{bmatrix} a \cdot 1 + b \cdot 0 + c \cdot 0 & a \cdot 0 + b \cdot 1 + c \cdot 0 & a \cdot 0 + b \cdot 0 + c \cdot 1 \\ d \cdot 1 + e \cdot 0 + f \cdot 0 & d \cdot 0 + e \cdot 1 + f \cdot 0 & d \cdot 0 + e \cdot 0 + f \cdot 1 \\ g \cdot 1 + h \cdot 0 + j \cdot 0 & g \cdot 0 + h \cdot 1 + j \cdot 0 & g \cdot 0 + h \cdot 0 + j \cdot 1 \end{bmatrix} = \begin{bmatrix} a & b & c \\ d & e & f \\ g & h & j \end{bmatrix} = S.$

43. $M^2 = \begin{bmatrix} 3 & 1 & 1 & 2 & 0 \\ 1 & 2 & 1 & 1 & 1 \\ 1 & 1 & 3 & 0 & 2 \\ 2 & 1 & 0 & 2 & 0 \\ 0 & 1 & 2 & 0 & 2 \end{bmatrix}$ **45.** 2 ways: B to C to A to E and B to C to D to E

49. $\begin{bmatrix} 1 & 0 \\ 0 & -1 \end{bmatrix} \cdot \begin{bmatrix} 1 & 0 \\ 0 & -1 \end{bmatrix} = \begin{bmatrix} 1 & 0 \\ 0 & 1 \end{bmatrix}$;   Yes, they are inverses.

51. $\begin{bmatrix} 2 & 1 \\ 4 & 3 \end{bmatrix} \cdot \begin{bmatrix} 3/2 & -1/2 \\ -2 & 1 \end{bmatrix} = \begin{bmatrix} 1 & 0 \\ 0 & 1 \end{bmatrix}$; $\begin{bmatrix} 3/2 & -1/2 \\ -2 & 1 \end{bmatrix} \cdot \begin{bmatrix} 2 & 1 \\ 4 & 3 \end{bmatrix} = \begin{bmatrix} 1 & 0 \\ 0 & 1 \end{bmatrix}$;   Yes, they are inverses.

53. No, they are not inverses.   **55.** $\begin{bmatrix} 5 & 6 \\ -10 & -13 \end{bmatrix} \cdot \begin{bmatrix} 13/5 & 6/5 \\ -2 & 1 \end{bmatrix} = \begin{bmatrix} 1 & 12 \\ 0 & -25 \end{bmatrix}$;   No, they are not inverses.

57. $\begin{bmatrix} 1 & 3 & 3 \\ 1 & 4 & 3 \\ 1 & 3 & 4 \end{bmatrix} \cdot \begin{bmatrix} 7 & -3 & -3 \\ -1 & 1 & 0 \\ -1 & 0 & 1 \end{bmatrix} = \begin{bmatrix} 1 & 0 & 0 \\ 0 & 1 & 0 \\ 0 & 0 & 1 \end{bmatrix}$; $\begin{bmatrix} 7 & -3 & -3 \\ -1 & 1 & 0 \\ -1 & 0 & 1 \end{bmatrix} \cdot \begin{bmatrix} 1 & 3 & 3 \\ 1 & 4 & 3 \\ 1 & 3 & 4 \end{bmatrix} = \begin{bmatrix} 1 & 0 & 0 \\ 0 & 1 & 0 \\ 0 & 0 & 1 \end{bmatrix}$;
Yes, they are inverses.

61. Product $= \begin{bmatrix} 438.227 & 488.299 & 387.747 & 404.496 & 415.265 & 362.598 \\ 341.127 & 470.054 & 321.549 & 396.768 & 391.883 & 369.323 \\ 296.377 & 380.795 & 260.023 & 314.025 & 285.172 & 266.426 \\ 327.277 & 399.097 & 293.671 & 332.085 & 327.514 & 297.122 \\ 508.767 & 538.464 & 438.303 & 446.607 & 446.589 & 392.418 \end{bmatrix}$

14.3 Exercises   (Page 833)

1. $\begin{bmatrix} -1 & 2 & 1 \\ 3 & -4 & 2 \\ -4 & 0 & 1 \end{bmatrix}$ **3.** $\begin{bmatrix} -4 & 0 & 1 \\ -9 & 12 & -6 \\ -1 & 2 & 1 \end{bmatrix}$ **5.** $\begin{bmatrix} 18 & -1 & -1 \\ -4 & 0 & 1 \\ 1 & 3 & -3 \end{bmatrix}$ **7.** $\begin{bmatrix} -4 & 0 & 1 \\ 3 & -4 & 2 \\ -13 & 2 & 4 \end{bmatrix}$

9. $\begin{bmatrix} 1 & 11 & -5 \\ -1 & -4 & 3 \\ 0 & 5 & -2 \end{bmatrix}$ **11.** Interchange rows 1 and 2.   **13.** Double each element of row 2.   **15.** Multiply
each element of row 1 by 2, and add the results to row 2.   **17.** Multiply row 2 by -1. Multiply row 2 by -2
and add to row 1.   **19.** Multiply row 1 by $-1/2$. Multiply row 1 by -4 and add to row 2. Multiply row 2 by
$1/5$. Multiply row 2 by 1 and add to row 1.   **21.** Multiply row 1 by $1/6$. Multiply row 2 by $1/4$. Multiply row 2
by $-1/2$ and add to row 1. Multiply row 3 by $1/2$.   **23.** $\left[\begin{array}{cc|c} 2 & 3 & 11 \\ 1 & 2 & 8 \end{array}\right]$ **25.** $\left[\begin{array}{cc|c} 1 & 5 & 6 \\ 3 & -4 & 1 \end{array}\right]$

27. $\left[\begin{array}{ccc|c} 2 & 1 & 1 & 3 \\ 3 & -4 & 2 & -7 \\ 1 & 1 & 1 & 2 \end{array}\right]$ **29.** $\left[\begin{array}{ccc|c} 1 & 1 & 0 & 6 \\ 0 & 2 & 1 & 2 \\ 0 & 0 & 1 & 2 \end{array}\right]$ **31.** $\{(2, 3)\}$ **33.** $\{(-3, 0)\}$ **35.** $\{(7/2, -1)\}$
37. $\{(5, 0)\}$ **39.** $\emptyset$ **41.** $\{(-2, 1, 3)\}$ **43.** $\{(-1, 23, 16)\}$ **45.** $\{(3, 2, -4)\}$ **47.** $\{(-1, 2, 5, 1)\}$
49. A laborer charges \$76 per day and a concrete finisher charges \$80 per day.   **51.** Dark clay costs \$5 per lb,
light clay costs \$1 per lb.   **53.** 74 decals and 96 bumper stickers were purchased.

14.4 Exercises   (Page 843)

1. $\begin{bmatrix} 1 & 0 \\ 0 & -1 \end{bmatrix}$ **3.** $\begin{bmatrix} 3/2 & -1/2 \\ -2 & 1 \end{bmatrix}$ **5.** no inverse   **7.** $\begin{bmatrix} 1 & -2 & 0 \\ 0 & 1 & 0 \\ -1 & 3 & 1 \end{bmatrix}$ **9.** $\begin{bmatrix} 4 & 3 & 3 \\ -1 & 0 & -1 \\ -4 & -4 & -3 \end{bmatrix}$

11. $(1, 1)$ **13.** There is no unique solution because the coefficient matrix has no inverse.   **15.** $(-1, 23, 16)$

17. $(2, 1, -1)$ **19.** There is no unique solution because the coefficient matrix has no inverse.   **21.** $\begin{bmatrix} 3 & -4 \\ 2 & -3 \end{bmatrix}$

23. The missing elements can be any two numbers with a product of -3.   **25.** sometimes true (true whenever
the numbers a and b are reciprocals of each other)

27. $\begin{bmatrix} k & 0 \\ 0 & 1 \end{bmatrix} \cdot \begin{bmatrix} 2 & 4 \\ 3 & 5 \end{bmatrix} = \begin{bmatrix} 2k + 0{\cdot}3 & 4k + 0{\cdot}5 \\ 0{\cdot}2 + 1{\cdot}3 & 0{\cdot}4 + 1{\cdot}5 \end{bmatrix} = \begin{bmatrix} 2k & 4k \\ 3 & 5 \end{bmatrix}$ (The first row is multiplied by k.)

29. $\begin{bmatrix} 1 & 0 \\ 2 & 1 \end{bmatrix} \cdot \begin{bmatrix} 2 & 4 \\ 3 & 5 \end{bmatrix} = \begin{bmatrix} 1{\cdot}2 + 0{\cdot}3 & 1{\cdot}4 + 0{\cdot}5 \\ 2{\cdot}2 + 1{\cdot}3 & 2{\cdot}4 + 1{\cdot}5 \end{bmatrix} = \begin{bmatrix} 2 & 4 \\ 2{\cdot}2 + 3 & 2{\cdot}4 + 5 \end{bmatrix}$ **33.** 1   **35.** 0

41. $\begin{bmatrix} .226 & -.152 \\ .197 & .049 \end{bmatrix}$ **43.** $\begin{bmatrix} -.871 & .602 & .594 \\ 1.905 & -1.511 & -1.047 \\ -1.774 & 1.590 & .876 \end{bmatrix}$ **45.** one; 0   **47.** 1,174 metric tons of wheat

and 1,565 metric tons of oil   **49.** 3,077 units of agriculture;   2,564 units of manufacturing;   3,179 units of transportation

Extension Exercises   (Page 847)

1. $\begin{bmatrix} 20 \\ 8 \end{bmatrix}\begin{bmatrix} 5 \\ 27 \end{bmatrix}\begin{bmatrix} 20 \\ 8 \end{bmatrix}\begin{bmatrix} 18 \\ 5 \end{bmatrix}\begin{bmatrix} 5 \\ 27 \end{bmatrix}\begin{bmatrix} 20 \\ 5 \end{bmatrix}\begin{bmatrix} 14 \\ 15 \end{bmatrix}\begin{bmatrix} 18 \\ 19 \end{bmatrix}$ **3.** $\begin{bmatrix} -5 & -2 \\ -2 & -1 \end{bmatrix}$

5. $\begin{bmatrix} 103 \\ 118 \\ 116 \end{bmatrix}\begin{bmatrix} 95 \\ 122 \\ 98 \end{bmatrix}\begin{bmatrix} 42 \\ 46 \\ 47 \end{bmatrix}\begin{bmatrix} 103 \\ 130 \\ 104 \end{bmatrix}\begin{bmatrix} 114 \\ 119 \\ 141 \end{bmatrix}\begin{bmatrix} 65 \\ 66 \\ 84 \end{bmatrix}\begin{bmatrix} 120 \\ 132 \\ 145 \end{bmatrix}\begin{bmatrix} 87 \\ 89 \\ 105 \end{bmatrix}\begin{bmatrix} 63 \\ 74 \\ 68 \end{bmatrix}\begin{bmatrix} 176 \\ 203 \\ 203 \end{bmatrix}$

7. 51, 89, 55, 88, 177, 108, 89, 201, 114, 40, 90, 49, 83, 192, 102, 49, 106, 62, 19, 51, 23, 69, 116, 89, 131, 264, 156

14.5 Exercises   (Page 854)

1. $\begin{bmatrix} 4 & -1 \\ 3 & 5 \end{bmatrix}$ **3.** $\begin{bmatrix} 8 & -7 \\ -2 & 4 \end{bmatrix}$ **5.** (3, I); 3   **7.** (2, III); 2   **9.** (2, III); 0   **11. (a)** Set up stadium **(b)** Set up gym   **(c)** Set up both   **13. (a)**

	Better	**Not**
Market New	50,000	−25,000
Don't	−40,000	−10,000

(b) \$5,000 and −\$22,000;   Market new   **15.** 1: 1/5; 2: 4/5; I: 3/5; II: 2/5; value = 17/5
17. The saddle point gives a value of 0. The game is fair. The first player should select strategy (row) 2, while the second player should select strategy (column) I.   **19.** Both A and B should choose either strategy with a probability of 1/2. The value of the game is 0, a fair game.   **25. (a)** \$7,388.89 **(b)** \$7,388.89
29. $7,000x + 7,000$ **31.** Nature should impose a freeze 1/18 of the time.   **33.** strategy 2   **35.** greater than 3/16   **37.** \$7,187.50

Chapter 14 Test   (Page 858)

1. $\begin{bmatrix} -1 & -1 & 4 \\ 2 & 2 & 0 \\ 3 & 1 & 6 \end{bmatrix}$ **2.** $\begin{bmatrix} 5 & -1 & 2 \\ 2 & -2 & 2 \\ 5 & 1 & 0 \end{bmatrix}$ **3.** $\begin{bmatrix} -9 & -2 & 12 \\ -7 & 0 & 5 \\ -15 & 2 & 12 \end{bmatrix}$ **4.** $\begin{bmatrix} -2 & 4 & -6 \\ 0 & -1 & -1 \\ 10 & 4 & 6 \end{bmatrix}$ **5.** $\begin{bmatrix} 4 & -2 & 6 \\ 4 & 0 & 2 \\ 8 & 2 & 6 \end{bmatrix}$

6. $\begin{bmatrix} 11 & -1 & 0 \\ 2 & -6 & 4 \\ 7 & 1 & -6 \end{bmatrix}$ **7.** $\begin{bmatrix} 2 & -1 & 3 \\ 4 & 1 & 3 \\ 2 & 0 & 1 \end{bmatrix}$ **8.** $\begin{bmatrix} -4 & -1 & 0 \\ 2 & 0 & 1 \\ 4 & 1 & 3 \end{bmatrix}$ **9.** $\begin{bmatrix} -3 \\ 10 \end{bmatrix}$ **10.** $\begin{bmatrix} 6 & 0 & 12 \\ 26 & 0 & 20 \end{bmatrix}$

11. [16]   **12.** There is no product, since the first matrix has a different number of columns than the second has

rows.   **13.** $\begin{bmatrix} 3 & -1 \\ -5 & 2 \end{bmatrix}$ **14.** $\begin{bmatrix} 1/2 & 1/2 & -1/2 \\ -1/2 & 1/6 & 1/6 \\ 1/2 & -1/2 & 1/2 \end{bmatrix}$ **15.** $\begin{bmatrix} 9 & -4 & | & 20 \\ 5 & 10 & | & 12 \end{bmatrix}$ **16.** $\begin{bmatrix} 2 & 1 & -6 & | & 6 \\ 5 & 0 & 12 & | & 15 \\ 0 & 6 & 3 & | & 8 \end{bmatrix}$

17. $\{(3, 0)\}$ **18.** $\{(4, -1, 2)\}$ **19. (a)** $\begin{bmatrix} 1 & 1 \\ 2 & -1 \end{bmatrix}$ **(b)** $\begin{bmatrix} x \\ y \end{bmatrix}$ **(c)** $\begin{bmatrix} 1 \\ -7 \end{bmatrix}$ **20.** $X = A^{-1}B$ **21.** $\{(-2, 3)\}$

23. $A = \begin{array}{c} \\ \text{Bananas} \\ \text{Coal} \end{array} \begin{array}{c} \text{Bananas} \quad \text{Coal} \\ \begin{bmatrix} .3 & .2 \\ .1 & .4 \end{bmatrix} \end{array}$ **24.** 750 units of bananas, 625 units of coal   **25.** $\begin{bmatrix} 8 & -3 \\ 0 & 2 \end{bmatrix}$

26. 9   **27.** Select strategy one 9/10 of the time and strategy two 1/10 of the time;   value is $-31/10$.

28. 4 and -4, or -4 and 4

29. $M = \begin{array}{c} \\ \text{Ring} \\ \text{Bracelet} \\ \text{Necklace} \end{array} \begin{array}{c} \text{Silver} \quad \text{Turquoise} \\ \begin{bmatrix} 1.6 & .7 \\ 5.8 & 7.5 \\ 26.3 & 18.8 \end{bmatrix} \end{array}$; $C = \begin{array}{c} \\ \text{Silver} \\ \text{Turquoise} \end{array} \begin{array}{c} \text{Cost} \\ \text{per unit} \\ \begin{bmatrix} 5.50 \\ 2.10 \end{bmatrix} \end{array}$

30. $MC = \begin{bmatrix} 1.6 & .7 \\ 5.8 & 7.5 \\ 26.3 & 18.8 \end{bmatrix} \cdot \begin{bmatrix} 5.50 \\ 2.10 \end{bmatrix} = \begin{array}{c} \\ \text{Ring} \\ \text{Bracelet} \\ \text{Necklace} \end{array} \begin{array}{c} \text{Cost} \\ \text{per item} \\ \begin{bmatrix} 10.27 \\ 47.65 \\ 184.13 \end{bmatrix} \end{array}$

3.5 Arithmetic in Other Bases

Table 3.16

+	0	1	2	3	4
0	0	1	2	3	4
1	1	2	3	4	10
2	2	3	4	10	11
3	3	4	10	11	12
4	4	10	11	12	13

Addition in any positional system depends on face values, place values, and the ability to add any two single digits. When a sum has two digits we "carry" the left digit to the next position. See Section 3.3. In the decimal system, for example, we need only memorize sums as high as $9 + 9$ (though most of us learn them beyond that).

In a different base, say five, the process is the same. We simply must remember that the place values are now the powers of five rather than ten, and the face values go only as high as 4 rather than 9. Table 3.16 is a base five addition table, though you should be able to quickly find all these sums without the aid of a table. For example, $3 + 4$ is not 7 in this system (since the symbol 7 is not available in base five). "Seven" must be expressed as one 5 and two 1s, so

$$3_{\text{five}} + 4_{\text{five}} = 12_{\text{five}}.$$

Example 1   Add 324_{five} and 223_{five}.

First arrange the numbers just as for ordinary decimal (base ten) addition. Then add in columns, beginning on the right.

Step 1

$$\begin{array}{r} {}^{1} \\ 3\ 2\ 4 \\ +\ 2\ 2\ 3 \\ \hline 2 \end{array}$$

$4 + 3 = 7_{\text{ten}} = 12_{\text{five}}$

Write 2, carry 1

Step 2

$$\begin{array}{r} {}^{1}\ {}^{1} \\ 3\ 2\ 4 \\ +\ 2\ 2\ 3 \\ \hline 0\ 2 \end{array}$$

$1 + 2 + 2 = 5_{\text{ten}} = 10_{\text{five}}$

Write 0, carry 1

Step 3

$$\begin{array}{r} {}^{1}\ {}^{1} \\ 3\ 2\ 4 \\ +\ 2\ 2\ 3 \\ \hline 1\ 1\ 0\ 2 \end{array}$$

$1 + 3 + 2 = 6_{\text{ten}} = 11_{\text{five}}$

Write 11

Finally, $324_{\text{five}} + 223_{\text{five}} = 1102_{\text{five}}$.

Expanded notation shows why this process works. (Notice that the symbol 10 denotes the number five here.)

$$\begin{array}{rl} 324_{\text{five}} = & (3 \times 10^2) + (2 \times 10^1) + (4 \times 10^0) \\ +\ 223_{\text{five}} = & (2 \times 10^2) + (2 \times 10^1) + (3 \times 10^0) \\ \hline \text{Sum:} & (10 \times 10^2) + (4 \times 10^1) + (12 \times 10^0) \end{array}$$

Now modify the expansion (carry) just as with base ten expansions in Section 3.3.

$$= (10 \times 10^2) + (4 \times 10^1) + (12 \times 10^0)$$

Distributive property

$$= (10 \times 10^2) + (4 \times 10^1) + \overbrace{(10 \times 10^0) + (2 \times 10^0)}$$
$$= (10 \times 10^2) + \underbrace{(4 \times 10^1) + (1 \times 10^1)} + (2 \times 10^0)$$

Distributive property

$$= (10 \times 10^2) + (10 \times 10^1) + (2 \times 10^0)$$
$$= (1 \times 10^3) + (1 \times 10^2) + (2 \times 10^0)$$
$$= 1102_{\text{five}}. \ \blacksquare$$

Example 2 Add 443_{five}, 1220_{five}, and 4344_{five}.

Work as follows.

Step 1	*Step 2*	*Step 3*	*Step 4*
1	$2\ 1$	$2\ 2\ 1$	$2\ 2\ 1$
$4\ 4\ 3$	$4\ 4\ 3$	$4\ 4\ 3$	$4\ 4\ 3$
$1\ 2\ 2\ 0$	$1\ 2\ 2\ 0$	$1\ 2\ 2\ 0$	$1\ 2\ 2\ 0$
$+\ 4\ 3\ 4\ 4$	$+\ 4\ 3\ 4\ 4$	$+\ 4\ 3\ 4\ 4$	$+\ 4\ 3\ 4\ 4$
2	$1\ 2$	$1\ 1\ 2$	$1\ 2\ 1\ 1\ 2$
$3 + 0 + 4$ $= 12_{\text{five}}$	$1 + 4 + 2$ $+ 4 =$ 21_{five}	$2 + 4 + 2$ $+ 3 =$ 21_{five}	$2 + 1 + 4$ $= 12_{\text{five}}$

The answer, 12112_{five}, can be checked by converting the original numbers to decimal (base ten) form, adding in that familiar system, and converting back to base five:

$$443_{\text{five}} = (4 \times 25) + (4 \times 5) + (3 \times 1) = 100 + 20 + 3 = 123$$
$$1220_{\text{five}} = (1 \times 125) + (2 \times 25) + (2 \times 5) = 125 + 50 + 10 = 185$$
$$4344_{\text{five}} = (4 \times 125) + (3 \times 25) + (4 \times 5) + (4 \times 1)$$
$$= 500 + 75 + 20 + 4 = 599.$$

$$
\begin{array}{r}
123 \\
185 \\
+599 \\
\hline
907
\end{array}
\longrightarrow
\begin{array}{ll}
5\,\lfloor\ 907 \\
5\,\lfloor 181 & 2 \\
5\,\lfloor 36 & 1 \\
5\,\lfloor 7 & 1 \\
5\,\lfloor 1 & 2 \\
0 & 1
\end{array}
\longrightarrow
\text{Answer: } 12112_{\text{five}} \ \blacksquare
$$

Add in base ten   Convert to base five

Subtraction also is basically the same in any positional system, regardless of the base. Sometimes "borrowing" is required. Again, see Section 3.3.

Work each base five subtraction problem.

(a)

$$\begin{array}{r} 343 \\ -212 \\ \hline 131 \end{array}$$

Check by adding 131_{five} and 212_{five}.

(b)

$$\begin{array}{r} 432 \\ -134 \end{array}$$

Begin by borrowing 1 five from the 3 fives in the top number (since 4 cannot be taken from 2).

$$\begin{array}{r} 2 \\ 4\ \cancel{3}\ ^12 \\ -\ 1\ 3\ 4 \\ \hline 3 \end{array} \qquad 12_{\text{five}} - 4_{\text{five}} = 3_{\text{five}}$$

Now borrow from the 4 in the top number.

$$\begin{array}{r} 3 \quad 12 \\ \cancel{4}\ \cancel{3}\ ^12 \\ -\ 1\ 3\ 4 \\ \hline 2\ 4\ 3 \end{array} \qquad \begin{array}{l} 12_{\text{five}} - 3_{\text{five}} = 4_{\text{five}} \\[4pt] \text{and } 3_{\text{five}} - 1_{\text{five}} = 2_{\text{five}} \end{array}$$

Check by adding 243_{five} and 134_{five}. ▨

Multiplication (and division) in base five requires a knowledge of products at least up to 4×4. For example, $3 \times 4 = 12_{\text{ten}} = 22_{\text{five}}$. (Twelve consists of two 5s and two 1s.) Table 3.17 gives all base five products of two single digits. Again, the table is a handy reference but we should be able to obtain any of its entries quickly without referring to it. For those of us accustomed to base ten work, a good rule of thumb for working in other bases is: *Reason the steps of a calculation in base ten, but write down the results in the other base.* Whenever a partial result is *written down,* be sure it is written in the other base.

Table 3.17

×	0	1	2	3	4
0	0	0	0	0	0
1	0	1	2	3	4
2	0	2	4	11	13
3	0	3	11	14	22
4	0	4	13	22	31

Example 4 Multiply 24_{five} times 43_{five}.

Step 1

$$\begin{array}{r} 2 \\ 4\ 3 \\ \times\ 2\ 4 \\ \hline 2 \end{array} \qquad \begin{array}{l} 4 \times 3 = 12_{\text{ten}} = 22_{\text{five}} \\[6pt] \text{Write 2, carry 2} \end{array}$$

Step 2

$$\begin{array}{r} 2 \\ 4\ 3 \\ \times\ 2\ 4 \\ \hline 3\ 3\ 2 \end{array} \qquad \begin{array}{l} 4 \times 4 = 16_{\text{ten}} \\ 16_{\text{ten}} + 2_{\text{ten}} = 18_{\text{ten}} = 33_{\text{five}} \\ \text{Write 33} \end{array}$$

Step 3
$$\overset{1}{}$$
$$\begin{array}{r} 4\ 3 \\ \times\ 2\ 4 \\ \hline 3\ 3\ 2 \\ 1 \end{array}$$
$2 \times 3 = 6_{ten} = 11_{five}$

Write 1, carry 1

Step 4
$$\overset{1}{}$$
$$\begin{array}{r} 4\ 3 \\ \times\ 2\ 4 \\ \hline 3\ 3\ 2 \\ 1\ 4\ 1 \end{array}$$
$2 \times 4 = 8_{ten}$

$8_{ten} + 1_{ten} = 9_{ten} = 14_{five}$
Write 14

Step 5
$$\begin{array}{r} 4\ 3 \\ \times\ 2\ 4 \\ \hline 3\ 3\ 2 \\ 1\ 4\ 1 \\ \hline 2\ 2\ 4\ 2 \end{array}$$
Add 332_{five} and 1410_{five}

Answer: 2242_{five} ▰

To divide in base five, reason the steps in base ten, but write results in base five.

Example 5   Divide 4232_{five} by 3_{five}.

The divisor is $3_{five} = 3_{ten}$. Work as follows.

Step 1
$$\begin{array}{r} 1 \\ 3\overline{)4232} \\ 3 \\ \hline 1 \end{array}$$
3 goes into 4 once
Multiply and subtract

Step 2
$$\begin{array}{r} 12 \\ 3\overline{)4232} \\ 3 \\ \hline 12 \\ 11 \\ \hline 1 \end{array}$$
Bring down 2
$12_{five} = 7_{ten}$
3 goes into 7 twice
Multiply and subtract

Step 3
$$\begin{array}{r} 122 \\ 3\overline{)4232} \\ 3 \\ \hline 12 \\ 11 \\ \hline 13 \\ 11 \\ \hline 2 \end{array}$$
Bring down 3
$13_{five} = 8_{ten}$
3 goes into 8 twice
Multiply and subtract

Step 4

$$
\begin{array}{r}
1224 \\
3\overline{)4232} \\
\underline{3} \\
12 \\
\underline{11} \\
13 \\
\underline{11} \\
22 \\
\underline{22} \\
0
\end{array}
$$

Bring down 2
$22_{\text{five}} = 12_{\text{ten}}$
3 goes into 12 four times
Multiply and subtract

The remainder is 0, so $4232_{\text{five}} \div 3_{\text{five}} = 1224_{\text{five}}$. ▨

The final example of this section illustrates arithmetic procedures in several other bases.

Example 6   Work each arithmetic problem in the indicated base.

(a) $523_{\text{eight}} + 705_{\text{eight}}$

$$
\begin{array}{r}
1 \\
5\ 2\ 3 \\
+7\ 0\ 5 \\
\hline
1\ 4\ 3\ 0
\end{array}
$$

(b) $T7_{\text{twelve}} \times 8E_{\text{twelve}}$

$$
\begin{array}{r}
8\ E \\
\times T\ 7 \\
\hline
5\ 2\ 5 \\
7\ 5\ 2 \\
\hline
7\ T\ 4\ 5
\end{array}
$$

(c) $9CA3_{\text{sixteen}} - ABC_{\text{sixteen}}$

(Recall that ten, eleven, twelve, thirteen, fourteen, and fifteen are denoted A, B, C, D, E, and F.)

$$
\begin{array}{r}
\text{B}\ \ 19 \\
9\ \not{C}\ \not{A}\ {}^{1}3 \\
-\ \ \ A\ B\ C \\
\hline
9\ 1\ E\ 7
\end{array}
$$

(d) $100110010_{\text{two}} \div 110_{\text{two}}$

$$
\begin{array}{r}
110011 \\
110\overline{)100110010} \\
110 \\
\hline
111 \\
110 \\
\hline
1001 \\
110 \\
\hline
110 \\
110 \\
\hline
0
\end{array}
$$

3.5 Exercises

Work the following problems in base five.

1. 31
  + 12

2. 22
  + 13

3. 142
  + 303

4. 114
  + 34

5. 121
  32
  + 404

6. 101
  20
  + 324

7. 424
  − 13

8. 122
  − 41

9. 1302
  − 433

10. 1222
  − 333

11. 241
  × 3

12. 403
  × 2

13. 24
  × 32

14. 12
  × 43

15. 413
  × 23

16. 2334
  × 42

17. 31^2

18. 204^2

19. 12^3

20. 42^3

21. $2\overline{)132}$

22. $3\overline{)212}$

23. $4\overline{)3023}$

24. $3\overline{)1333332}$

25. Complete the base seven addition table.

+	0	1	2	3	4	5	6
0	0	1	2	3	4	5	6
1	1	2	3	4	5	6	10
2	2	3	4	5	6		
3	3	4	5	6		11	
4	4	5	6		11		13
5	5	6		11		13	14
6							

26. Complete the base seven multiplication table.

×	0	1	2	3	4	5	6
0	0	0	0	0	0	0	0
1	0	1	2	3	4	5	6
2	0	2	4	6	11	13	15
3	0	3	6			21	
4	0	4	11		22		33
5	0	5		21		34	42
6	0	6					51

Work the following base seven problems. (You may want to make use of the tables in Exercises 25 and 26.)

27. 36
       +41

28. 44
       +62

29. 365
         242
        +216

30. 245
         345
        +466

31. 253
        − 46

32. 412
        −105

33. 4651
       − 266

34. 3654
       − 666

35. 43
        × 6

36. 25
        × 6

37. 325
        × 42

38. 416
        × 55

Work the following problems in the indicated bases.

39. $202_{three} + 121_{three}$

40. $82_{nine} + 148_{nine}$

41. $241_{six} - 155_{six}$

42. $222_{four} - 133_{four}$

43. $TE_{twelve} \times 34_{twelve}$

44. $183_{eleven} \times 2T_{eleven}$

45. $1110_{four} \div 32_{four}$

46. $11732_{eight} \div 25_{eight}$

47. 52
         23
        +14
     (base seven)

48. 301
         223
        +320
     (base four)

49. E92
        − 4E
     (base twelve)

50. CBA
        −ABC
     (base sixteen)

51. 2021
        × 212
     (base three)

52. 6012
        × 343
     (base eight)

53. 26)13750
     (base nine)

54. 53)3211120
     (base six)

55. 32^2
     (base four)

56. 4)TOT
     (base eleven)

57. ET^2
     (base twelve)

58. D^2
     (base sixteen)

59. What is the rule for telling when a base ten numeral represents a number that is divisible by ten?

Use the results of Exercise 59 to help you decide the answers to the following questions.

60. Which of the following base five numerals represent numbers that are divisible by five?

3402, 400, 230, 1002, 4030

61. Which of the following base seven numerals represent numbers that are divisible by seven?

$$50, 63, 105, 240, 5230$$

62. Which of the following base twelve numerals represent numbers that are divisible by twelve?

$$48, 60, 108, 240, 250, 1224, 1970$$

63. Complete the binary addition table below.

+	0	1
0		
1		10

Work these binary addition and subtraction problems.

64.
```
  10
+ 10
```

65.
```
  1010
+ 1101
```

66.
```
  100111
+  11101
```

67.
```
  1001011
+ 1011010
```

68.
```
   10
    1
+  11
```

69.
```
   11
   10
+  11
```

70.
```
  100
  111
+ 101
```

71.
```
  1001
   101
+ 1101
```

72.
```
  1101
   101
+ 1100
```

73.
```
  10110
−  1011
```

74.
```
  1101110
−  110101
```

75.
```
  101101010
−   1011011
```

76. Complete the binary multiplication table below.

×	0	1
0		
1		1

Find each of the following products in binary.

77.
```
  10
× 10
```

78.
```
  10
× 11
```

79.
```
  101
×  10
```

80.
```
  111
×  10
```

81.
```
  10001
×   101
```

82.
```
  1110
×  110
```

*83.
```
  110110
×   1011
```

*84.
```
  110111
×    111
```

Find each binary quotient.

85. $11\overline{)11011}$

86. $11\overline{)100111}$

87. $101\overline{)1111000}$

88. $111\overline{)11000100}$

Chapter 3   Summary

Important types of numeration systems

Simple grouping
Multiplicative grouping
Positional

Some numeration systems of history

Egyptian (simple grouping, base 10)

1	10	100	1000	10,000	100,000	1,000,000
I	∩	૭	⌐	⌐	⌐	⌐

Roman (modified simple grouping, base 10)

1	5	10	50	100	500	1000
I	V	X	L	C	D	M

Chinese (modified multiplicative grouping, base 10)

1	2	3	4	5	6	7	8	9	10	100	1000	0
一	二	三	四	五	六	七	八	九	十	百	千	零

Babylonian (combination of base 10 simple grouping within base 60 positional)

1	10
▼	‹

Hindu-Arabic (positional, base 10)

| 0 | 1 | 2 | 3 | 4 | 5 | 6 | 7 | 8 | 9 |

Basics of a positional numeral

Each digit conveys

1. face value: the inherent value of the digit symbol
2. place value: the power of the base associated with the digit's position

Some decimal equivalents in the common computer-oriented bases

Base ten (Decimal)	Base sixteen (Hexadecimal)	Base eight (Octal)	Base two (Binary)
0	0	00	0000
1	1	01	0001
2	2	02	0010
3	3	03	0011
4	4	04	0100
5	5	05	0101
6	6	06	0110
7	7	07	0111
8	8	10	1000
9	9	11	1001
10	A	12	1010
11	B	13	1011
12	C	14	1100
13	D	15	1101
14	E	16	1110
15	F	17	1111

Chapter 3   Test

Identify each of the following base five numerals as simple grouping, multiplicative grouping, or positional. Convert to our system.

1. ΛΛΛ| |

2. ⊙Ν ⊙Λ⊙|

3. ⊙⊙⊙⊙⊙

Identify the numeration system for each of the following. Then convert to our system.

4. ₤ ₤ ₤ ⁹⁹⁹∩∩∩ ⁹⁹ ∩∩ | | | | |

5. LXVII

6. ⟨⟨▼

7. ⟨▼ ⟨▼▼ ⟨▼▼▼

Write each of the following in expanded notation.

8. 28

9. 4690

10. Simplify: $(6 \times 10^3) + (5 \times 10^2) + (7 \times 10^1) + (4 \times 10^0)$.

Convert each of the following to base ten.

11. 475_{eight}

12. 216_{seven}

13. $34T_{\text{twelve}}$

14. 110111_{two}

Convert from base ten as indicated.

15. 98 to base four

16. 2914 to base eight

17. 2481 to base twelve

18. 683 to base nine

19. 242 to base two

Perform the following calculations. Use the addition and multiplication tables in the text as needed.

20.   725
      + 37

(base eight)

21.   5365
      − 2717

(base eight)

22.   37
      × 56

(base eight)

23.   1101
      + 101

(base two)

24.   5T4
      × 6E

(base twelve)

25. 11)¯100111¯

(base two)

Section 3.5 *(page 165)*

1. 43_{five} **3.** 1000_{five} **5.** 1112_{five} **7.** 411_{five} **9.** 314_{five} **11.** 1323_{five} **13.** 1423_{five} **15.** 21104_{five} **17.** 2011_{five}
19. 2333_{five} **21.** 41_{five} **23.** 342_{five} **25.** Row 2: 10, 11; row 3: 10, 12; row 4: 10, 12; row 5: 10, 12; row 6: 6, 10, 11, 12,
13, 14, 15 **27.** 110_{seven} **29.** 1156_{seven} **31.** 204_{seven} **33.** 4352_{seven} **35.** 354_{seven} **37.** 20343_{seven} **39.** 1100_{three} **41.** 42_{six}
43. 3048_{twelve} **45.** 12_{four} **47.** 122_{seven} **49.** $E43_{\text{twelve}}$ **51.** 1220222_{three} **53.** 473_{nine} **55.** 3010_{four} **57.** $E804_{\text{twelve}}$
59. The numeral must end in 0. **61.** 50; 240; 5230

63.

	0	1
0	0	1
1	1	10

65. 10111_{two} **67.** 10100101_{two} **69.** 1000_{two} **71.** 11011_{two} **73.** 1011_{two} **75.** 100001111_{two} **77.** 100_{two} **79.** 1010_{two}
81. 1010101_{two} **83.** 1001010010_{two} **85.** 1001_{two} **87.** 11000_{two}

Chapter 3 Test *(page 169)*

1. Simple grouping; 17 **2.** Multiplicative grouping; 119 **3.** Positional; 1391 **4.** Egyptian; 3555 **5.** Roman; 67
6. Babylonian; 21 **7.** Babylonian; 40,333 **8.** $(2 \times 10^1) + (8 \times 10^0)$ **9.** $(4 \times 10^3) + (6 \times 10^2) + (9 \times 10^1) + (0 \times 10^0)$
10. 6574 **11.** 317 **12.** 111 **13.** 490 **14.** 55 **15.** 1202_{four} **16.** 5542_{eight} **17.** 1529_{twelve} **18.** 838_{nine}
19. 11110010_{two} **20.** 764_{eight} **21.** 2446_{eight} **22.** 2622_{eight} **23.** 10010_{two} **24.** 34658_{twelve} **25.** 1101_{two}

*4.4 Number Sequences

In Section 2.5 we examined number sequences in conjunction with inductive reasoning. In this section we shall look at two special types of sequences. Recall that a list of numbers having a first number, a second number, a third number, and so on, is called a **sequence**. The numbers in a sequence are called **terms** of the sequence.

Example 1 Examples of sequences:

(a) Even positive integers: 2, 4, 6, 8, 10, . . .

(b) Positive multiples of 5: 5, 10, 15, 20, 25, . . .

(c) Powers of 2: 2, 4, 8, 16, 32, 64, . . .

(d) Divisions on a ruler: $1, \dfrac{1}{2}, \dfrac{1}{4}, \dfrac{1}{8}, \dfrac{1}{16}, \dfrac{1}{32}$

(e) Periodic withdrawals of $10 from a bank account of $500 generate the sequence

$$500, 490, 480, 470, 460, \ldots , 20, 10, 0.$$

This sequence would stop when $0 is reached.

In this section we shall study *arithmetic* and *geometric* sequences. To do so, you should be familiar with the rules for the arithmetic operations with positive and negative numbers. While these rules are covered in detail in Chapter 5, we summarize them (with examples) below.

In adding two numbers with *like* signs, the sum will have the same sign, and the numeral of the sum is obtained by adding the numerals of the addends.

$$5 + 7 = 12 \qquad (-15) + (-4) = -19$$

In adding two numbers with *unlike* signs, the sign of the sum corresponds to the sign of the addend with the larger numeral part. The numeral of the sum is obtained by subtracting the smaller addend numeral from the larger.

$$(-5) + 7 = 2 \qquad (-15) + 4 = -11$$

To subtract $a - b$, rewrite as the sum of a and the opposite of b; that is,

$$a - b = a + (-b)$$

$$4 - 7 = 4 + (-7) = -3 \qquad -3 - (-8) = -3 + 8 = 5$$
$$-6 - 5 = -6 + (-5) = -11$$

When multiplying or dividing signed numbers, the answer is positive if the two numbers have the same sign, while the answer is negative if they have different signs.

$$3 \cdot 8 = 24 \qquad (-3)(8) = -24 \qquad 3(-8) = -24 \qquad (-3)(-8) = 24$$

$$\frac{24}{8} = 3 \qquad \frac{-24}{8} = -3 \qquad \frac{-24}{-8} = 3 \qquad \frac{24}{-3} = -8$$

A negative number raised to an even power gives a positive number, while a negative number raised to an odd power gives a negative number.

$$(-4)^2 = 16 \qquad (-4)^3 = -64 \qquad \left(-\frac{1}{2}\right)^5 = -\frac{1}{32}$$

The sequences in parts **(a)** and **(b)** of Example 1 are examples of *arithmetic sequences*. In an **arithmetic sequence,** each term after the first is found by adding the same number to the preceding term. For example,

$$9, 17, 25, 33, 41, \ldots$$

is an arithmetic sequence. Each term after the first is found by adding 8 to the preceding term. The number 8 is called the *common difference*. To find the **common difference** for an arithmetic sequence, choose any term except the first and subtract the preceding term.

Example 2 Find the common difference in each arithmetic sequence.

(a) 11, 14, 17, 20, 23, 26, 29, . . .

Choose any term except the first and subtract the term coming just before it. Choosing 14 and 17 gives

$$\text{Common difference} = 17 - 14 = 3.$$

(b) 13, 7, 1, -5, -11, -17, . . .

Let us choose 7 and 1.

$$\text{Common difference} = 1 - 7 = -6 \ \blacksquare$$

If the first term and common difference of an arithmetic sequence are known, it is possible to write as many terms in the sequence as desired. For example, suppose the first term of the sequence is 3. The first term of a sequence is often named a_1 (read "a sub one"), so $a_1 = 3$. If the common difference is 5, then the second term of the sequence, a_2, is

$$a_2 = a_1 + 5 = 3 + 5 = 8.$$

Find further terms as follows:

$$a_3 = a_2 + 5 = (a_1 + 5) + 5 = a_1 + 2 \cdot 5 = 3 + 10 = 13$$
$$a_4 = a_3 + 5 = (a_2 + 5) + 5 = (a_1 + 5) + 5 + 5$$
$$= a_1 + 3 \cdot 5 = 3 + 15 = 18$$
$$a_5 = a_4 + 5 = a_1 + 4 \cdot 5 = 3 + 20 = 23, \text{ and so on.}$$

In summary, starting with a_1 gives the pattern shown at the side. Each shaded number is one less than the corresponding "sub" number. Use this pattern to find additional terms of the sequence: for example,

$$a_{12} = a_1 + 11 \cdot 5 \qquad 11 = 12 - 1$$
$$a_{20} = a_1 + 19 \cdot 5 \qquad 19 = 20 - 1.$$

This result can be generalized:

$a_2 = a_1 + 1 \cdot 5$

$a_3 = a_1 + 2 \cdot 5$

$a_4 = a_1 + 3 \cdot 5$

$a_5 = a_1 + 4 \cdot 5$

and so on.

> If a_1 is the first term of an arithmetic sequence, and if d is the common difference for the sequence, then the **general term,** or **nth term,** of the sequence is given by a_n, where
>
> $$a_n = a_1 + (n - 1)d.$$

Example 3 Find the indicated term for each arithmetic sequence.

(a) 7, 12, 17, 22, 27, ... Find the fifteenth term.

The first term of this sequence is $a_1 = 7$, and the common difference is $d = 5$. (Find 5 by subtracting any two adjacent terms.) To find the fifteenth term, a_{15}, replace n with 15 in the formula for a_n.

$$a_n = a_1 + (n - 1)d \qquad \text{Formula}$$
$$a_{15} = 7 + (15 - 1)5 \qquad \text{Let } n = 15, d = 5, a_1 = 7$$
$$= 7 + (14)5$$
$$= 7 + 70$$
$$a_{15} = 77. \qquad\qquad\qquad \text{Fifteenth term}$$

(b) $23, 16, 9, 2, -5, -12, \ldots$. Find a_{19}.

For this sequence, $a_1 = 23$ and $d = -7$.

$$a_{19} = a_1 + (19 - 1)d \qquad \text{Let } n = 19$$
$$= 23 + (18)(-7) \qquad \text{Let } a_1 = 23, d = -7$$
$$= 23 + (-126)$$
$$a_{19} = -103 \qquad\qquad \text{Nineteenth term} \quad \blacksquare$$

We can also find a formula for the *sum of the first n terms* of an arithmetic sequence. This formula can be developed by a method used by the mathematician K. F. Gauss (1777–1855) when he was a child.

According to an old story,* one of Gauss' teachers was a small-time tyrant. One day he asked the students to find the sum of the first hundred counting numbers, or the sum

$$1 + 2 + 3 + 4 + 5 + 6 + \ldots + 100.$$

The other students in the class began by adding two numbers at a time, but Gauss found a quicker way. He first wrote the sum twice:

$$1 + 2 + 3 + 4 + \ldots + 99 + 100$$
$$100 + 99 + 98 + 97 + \ldots + 2 + 1.$$

He then noticed that by adding vertically, each pair of numbers adds up to 101.

$$\begin{array}{ccccccccc} 1 + & 2 + & 3 + & 4 + & \ldots + & 99 + & 100 \\ 100 + & 99 + & 98 + & 97 + & \ldots + & 2 + & 1 \\ \hline 101 + & 101 + & 101 + & 101 + & \ldots + & 101 + & 101 \end{array}$$

There are 100 of these sums of 101, for a total of $100 \cdot 101$, or 10,100. However, in finding the total, the numbers 1 through 100 were added twice. So the final result should actually be half of 10,100 or

$$1 + 2 + 3 + 4 + \ldots + 99 + 100 = \frac{10,100}{2} = 5050.$$

Using a method very similar to this would give the following formula for the sum of the first n terms of an arithmetic sequence.

Doubling "cubes" Doubling in backgammon is a vital aspect of the modern game. A player who is ahead offers to double the stakes; the opponent must agree or concede the game immediately. In return, only the player who accepted the double may redouble later in the game.

The photo shows "super-cubes" from the Chicago Chess and Backgammon Shop. Two of them were shot together to show what either of them looks like on all the sides. (The shape is technically an 8-sided prism.) Numbers on the sides are in geometric sequence, beginning with 2 and doubling. (It is also a sequence of powers of 2 from 2^1 to 2^8.)

---

*Another version of this story appears in the Exercises of Section 2.5.

Let S_n represent the **sum of the first n terms** of an arithmetic sequence with first term a_1 and common difference d. Then

$$S_n = \frac{n}{2}(a_1 + a_n).$$

Use this result to check the Gauss example: $n = 100$, $a_1 = 1$, and $a_{100} = 100$, so that

$$S_{100} = \frac{100}{2}(1 + 100) = 50 \cdot 101 = 5050.$$

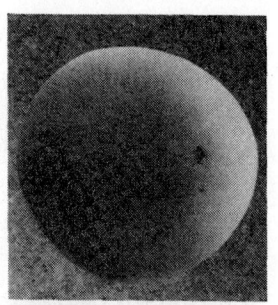

Example 4 Find the sum of the indicated number of terms in each of the following arithmetic sequences.

(a) Find S_9 in 12, 19, 26, 33, 40, . . .

To find S_9, the sum of the first nine terms of this arithmetic sequence, start with the formula for S_n given above. This formula requires a_1, a_9, and n. To find a_9, use the formula $a_n = a_1 + (n - 1)d$, with $n = 9$, $d = 7$, and $a_1 = 12$. Verify that $a_9 = 68$. Now

$$S_n = \frac{n}{2}(a_1 + a_n)$$
$$S_9 = \frac{9}{2}(12 + 68)$$
$$= \frac{9}{2}(80)$$
$$S_9 = 360.$$

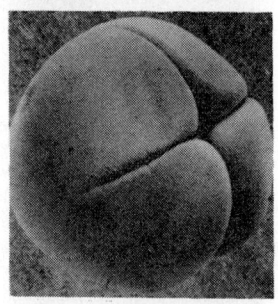

(b) Find S_{20} in 5, 13, 21, 29, 37, ...

Finding S_{20} by the formula requires a_{20}. To find a_{20}, use $a_1 = 5$ and $d = 8$. We find that $a_{20} = 5 + (20 - 1)8 = 5 + 152 = 157$. Then

$$S_{20} = \frac{20}{2}(5 + 157) = 10(162) = 1620. \ \blacksquare$$

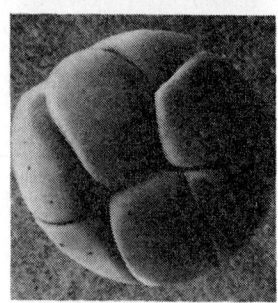

Geometric sequences occur in nature when a fertilized egg divides into 2 cells, then 4, 8, and so on. The enlargements here show cell division of a frog egg.

In an arithmetic sequence, each term after the first is found by *adding* the same number to the previous term. In a **geometric sequence**, each term after the first is found by *multiplying* the previous term by a fixed number. For example,

$$1, 2, 4, 8, 16, 32, 64, \ldots$$

is a geometric sequence, with each term after the first found by multiplying the previous term by 2. The number 2 is called the *common ratio*. The **common ratio** can be found in a geometric sequence by choosing any term

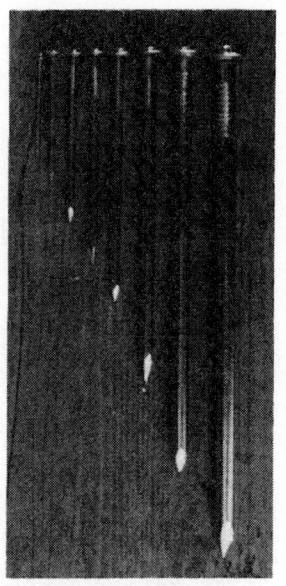

A geometric sequence is formed by the lengths of these nails. Its common ratio is about 1.3.

except the first and then dividing it by the preceding term. In the sequence above, the common ratio could be found by choosing the term 16, for example, and dividing it by the preceding term: 16/8 = 2.

Example 5   Identify any of the following sequences that are geometric. If a sequence is geometric, find the common ratio.

(a)   6, 24, 96, 384, . . .

Each term after the first is found by multiplying the preceding term by 4, so the sequence is geometric, and the common ratio is 4. The common ratio could also have been found by dividing: 96/24 = 4, for example.

(b)   8, −16, 32, −64, 128, . . .

Since each term is found by multiplying the preceding term by −2, the sequence is geometric with common ratio −2.

(c)   100, 90, 81, 73, 66, 60, . . .

This sequence is not geometric. (Is it an arithmetic sequence?)

Working in a manner similar to that for arithmetic sequences would give the following results for geometric sequences. (See a standard college algebra text for details.)

Let a geometric sequence have first term a_1 and common ratio r. Then the **nth term, a_n,** is given by

$$a_n = a_1 \cdot r^{n-1}$$

and the **sum of the first n terms, S_n,** is

$$S_n = \frac{a_1(r^n - 1)}{r - 1}, \qquad r \neq 1.$$

Example 6   A geometric sequence has $a_1 = 243$ and $r = -2/3$. Find each of the following.

(a) a_6

The sixth term is found with the formula for a_n given above.

$$a_n = a_1 r^{n-1}$$

Let $n = 6$, $a_1 = 243$, and $r = -2/3$.

$$a_6 = 243 \cdot \left(-\frac{2}{3}\right)^{6-1} = 243\left(-\frac{2}{3}\right)^5 = 243\left(-\frac{32}{243}\right) = -32$$

(b) S_6

The sum of the first six terms of this sequence is

$$S_n = \frac{a_1(r^n - 1)}{r - 1}$$

$$S_6 = \frac{243\left[\left(-\dfrac{2}{3}\right)^6 - 1\right]}{-\dfrac{2}{3} - 1}$$

$$= \frac{243\left[\dfrac{64}{729} - 1\right]}{-\dfrac{5}{3}}$$

$$= 243\left(\frac{-665}{729}\right)\left(-\frac{3}{5}\right)$$

$$S_6 = 133.$$

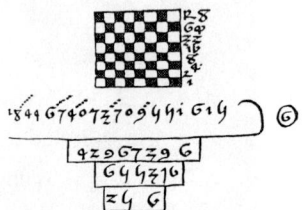

Chessboard problem The drawing here is from the early 1400s, but the problem is much older. One medieval Arabic version says that after Sissah ibn Dahir invented chess, his king was happy enough to give him any reward he wanted. Sissah asked for 1 wheat grain on the first square of the board, 2 grains on the second, 4 grains on the third, and so on. Again we get a geometric (and doubling) sequence. The grains total $2^{64} - 1$, or 18,446,744,073,709,551,615.

4.4 Exercises

In each of Exercises 1–16, a formula for the general term of a sequence is given. Use the given formula to find the first five terms of the sequence. Do this by replacing n, in turn, with 1, 2, 3, 4, and 5. Then identify each sequence as arithmetic, geometric, or neither.

1. $a_n = 6n + 5$

2. $a_n = 12n - 3$

3. $a_n = 3n - 7$

4. $a_n = 5n - 12$

5. $a_n = -6n + 4$

6. $a_n = -11n + 10$

7. $a_n = 2^n$

8. $a_n = 3^n$

9. $a_n = (-2)^n$

10. $a_n = (-3)^n$

11. $a_n = 3 \cdot 2^n$

12. $a_n = -4 \cdot 2^n$

13. $a_n = \dfrac{n + 1}{n + 2}$

14. $a_n = \dfrac{2n}{n + 1}$

15. $a_n = \dfrac{1}{n + 1}$

16. $a_n = \dfrac{1}{n + 8}$

Identify each sequence as arithmetic, geometric, or neither. For an arithmetic sequence, give the common difference. For a geometric sequence, give the common ratio.

17. 6, 14, 22, 30, 38, 46, . . .

18. 40, 46, 52, 58, 64, . . .

19. 5, 8, 11, 14, 17, 20, 23, . . .

20. 23, 34, 45, 56, 67, 78, . . .

21. 4, 12, 36, 108, . . .

22. 7, 14, 28, 56, 112, . . .

23. 2, 5, 9, 14, 20, 27, . . .

24. 1, 4, 9, 16, 25, 36, . . .

25. 12, 9, 6, 3, 0, −3, −6, . . .

26. 37, 31, 25, 19, 13, 7, . . .

27. $-18, -15, -12, -9, -6, \ldots$ **28.** $-21, -17, -13, -9, -5, \ldots$

29. $3, -6, 12, -24, 48, -96, \ldots$ **30.** $-5, 10, -20, 40, -80, \ldots$

31. $-5, 6, -7, 8, -9, 10, -11, \ldots$ **32.** $-12, 9, -6, 3, \ldots$

Find the indicated term for each arithmetic sequence.

33. $a_1 = 10, d = 5$; find a_{13} **34.** $a_1 = 6, d = 9$; find a_8

35. $a_1 = 8, d = 3$; find a_{20} **36.** $a_1 = 13, d = 7$; find a_{11}

37. $a_1 = 28, d = -3$; find a_8 **38.** $a_1 = 47, d = -5$; find a_7

39. $a_1 = 12, d = -7$; find a_{12} **40.** $a_1 = 18, d = -9$; find a_{13}

41. $6, 9, 12, 15, 18, \ldots$; find a_{25} **42.** $14, 17, 20, 23, 26, 29, \ldots$; find a_{13}

*43. $-9, -13, -17, -21, -25, \ldots$; find a_{15} ***44.** $-4, -11, -18, -25, -32, \ldots$; find a_{18}

Find the sum of the first twelve terms in each arithmetic sequence.

45. $3, 6, 9, 12, 15, 18, \ldots$ **46.** $11, 13, 15, 17, 19, 21, \ldots$

47. $9, 17, 25, 33, 41, 49, \ldots$ **48.** $28, 32, 36, 40, 44, 48, \ldots$

49. $88, 98, 108, 118, 128, 138, \ldots$ **50.** $92, 95, 98, 101, 104, 107, \ldots$

51. $a_1 = 8, d = 9$ **52.** $a_1 = 12, d = 6$ **53.** $a_1 = 7, d = -2$

54. $a_1 = 13, d = -5$ **55.** $a_1 = -8, d = -7$ **56.** $a_1 = -15, d = -2$

*57. Find the sum of the first 1000 counting numbers.

*58. Find the sum of the first 10,000 counting numbers.

Find a_6 and S_6 for each geometric sequence.

59. $6, 18, 54, \ldots$ **60.** $7, 14, 28, \ldots$ **61.** $64, 32, 16, \ldots$

62. $729, 243, 81, \ldots$ **63.** $12, -24, 48, -96, \ldots$ **64.** $3125, -625, 125, -25, \ldots$

65. $18, -12, 8, -16/3, \ldots$ **66.** $8, -12, 18, -27, \ldots$ **67.** $a_1 = 6, r = -3/4$

68. $a_1 = -5, r = -2/5$ **69.** $a_1 = -3/8, r = -2/3$ **70.** $a_1 = 15/16, r = -1/2$

71. Fifteen balls are used in the game of pool. The balls are numbered from 1 through 15. In the game of "rotation," when a player "sinks" a ball in a pocket of the table, the player receives as many points as the number on the ball. Answer the following questions about this game. For some of them you can use the formula for the sum of the terms of an arithmetic sequence.

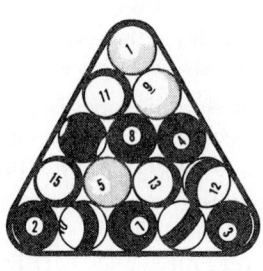

   (a) How many points would a player score if he or she sank all fifteen balls?
   (b) Suppose player A sank balls 1 through 10 in the pockets, and player B sank balls 11 through 15. Find the total score for player A.
   (c) Find the total score for player B.
   (d) Who sank more balls into the pockets? Who won the game?
   (e) Suppose now that player A sank all the even-numbered balls, and player B sank all the odd-numbered balls. What was each player's score? Who won?

72. Suppose you save the given amounts of money over a five-week period.

Week	1st	2nd	3rd	4th	5th
Money	28¢	45¢	62¢	79¢	96¢

(a) Find the value of a_1.
(b) Find d.
(c) Find the amount that you would save in the 52nd week.
*(d) Find the total amount that you would save in 52 weeks.

73. A man is offered a $10,000 starting salary, with an annual raise of $800.

    (a) List his annual salaries for the first five years. Start with $10,000.
    (b) Find d.
    (c) Find his salary in year 10.

74. A water lily has an area of 8 square inches. These lilies reproduce so fast that the area they cover will double every week.

    (a) If two lilies are introduced into a pond, what area will be covered in eight weeks?
    (b) in ten weeks?   **(c)** in twelve weeks?   **(d)** in fifteen weeks?

75. A vacuum pump removes 1/4 of the air in a cylinder with each stroke of a piston. (Thus, 3/4 of the air remains.)

    (a) What fraction of the air will still be in the cylinder after 6 strokes?
    (b) after 8 strokes?

76. In a chain letter you receive a list with six names on it. You are to send one dollar to the name at the top of the list, cross off that name, add your name at the bottom, and mail the list to six people, each of whom repeats all these steps. The first person sends six letters, and each of the six recipients sends six letters.

    (a) How many letters will be sent in the second mailing?
    (b) Each of the 36 recipients then sends 6 letters, producing how many letters in the third mailing?

77. In Exercise 76, how many letters will be sent in each of the following mailings?

    (a) Fourth   **(b)** Sixth   **(c)** Eighth   **(d)** Eleventh

    The population of the United States is about 230,000,000; by the eleventh mailing more letters will have been sent than there are residents of the country, and the people who started the chain will have made a tidy sum. Chain letters are illegal, however, and postal inspectors go after the originators with a zeal not always shown by mail handlers.

78. A sheet of paper is 1/512 inch thick. If you fold the sheet in half, the total thickness of the two sheets will be 1/256 inch. A second fold produces a stack 1/128 inch thick. How thick would the stack be after the following numbers of folds?

    (a) Four folds   **(b)** Six folds   **(c)** Eight folds   **(d)** Ten folds
    (e) Fifteen folds   **(f)** Twenty folds   **(g)** Thirty folds
    (h) Take a double sheet of newspaper and see how many times you can fold it in half.

79. Suppose that you are offered a job for the month of January. The boss gives you a choice of how you will be paid. You can be paid a flat salary of $10,000 for the month's work, or you can be paid 1 cent on Jan. 1, 2 cents on Jan. 2, 4 cents on Jan. 3, and so on, doubling the previous day's salary each time. What choice would you make, and why? (*Hint:* $2^{31} = 2,147,483,648$)

80. An **equilateral triangle** is a triangle whose sides all measure the same length. The **perimeter** of an equilateral triangle is the sum of all the lengths of its sides, or equivalently, if a side measures *x*, the perimeter is 3*x*. A sequence of equilateral triangles is to be constructed, with each successive triangle being formed by joining the midpoints of the previous triangle.

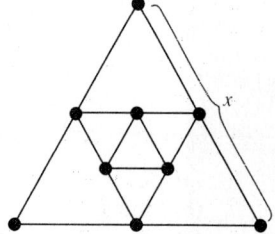

(a) What is the perimeter of the fifth such triangle?
(b) What is the sum of the perimeters of the first five triangles?

Section 4.4   *(page 195)*

1. 11, 17, 23, 29, 35; arithmetic   **3.** −4, −1, 2, 5, 8; arithmetic   **5.** −2, −8, −14, −20, −26; arithmetic   **7.** 2, 4, 8, 16, 32; geometric   **9.** −2, 4, −8, 16, −32; geometric   **11.** 6, 12, 24, 48, 96; geometric   **13.** 2/3, 3/4, 4/5, 5/6, 6/7; neither **15.** 1/2, 1/3, 1/4, 1/5, 1/6; neither   **17.** Arithmetic; 8   **19.** Arithmetic; 3   **21.** Geometric; 3   **23.** Neither **25.** Arithmetic; −3   **27.** Arithmetic; 3   **29.** Geometric; −2   **31.** Neither   **33.** 70   **35.** 65   **37.** 7   **39.** −65   **41.** 78 **43.** −65   **45.** 234   **47.** 636   **49.** 1716   **51.** 690   **53.** −48   **55.** −558   **57.** 500,500   **59.** 1458; 2184   **61.** 2; 126 **63.** −384; −252   **65.** −64/27; 266/27   **67.** −729/512; 1443/512   **69.** 4/81; −133/648   **71.** (a) 120   (b) 55   (c) 65 (d) A; B   (e) 56; 64; B   **73.** (a) $10,000, $10,800, $11,600, $12,400, $13,200   (b) $800   (c) $17,200   **75.** (a) 729/4096 or about 18%   (b) 6561/65,536 or about 10%   **77.** (a) 1296   (b) 46,656   (c) 1,679,616   (d) 362,797,056   **79.** Choose the doubling method. The total wages earned for the month using this method would be $21,474,836.47.

Taken from: *Go! Complete, Technology in Action,* Fourth Edition by Alan Evans,
Kendall Martin, and Mary Anne Poatsy

Making the PC Possible: Early Computers

Since the first Altair was introduced in the 1970s, more than a billion personal computers have been distributed around the globe. Because of the declining prices of computers and the growth of the Internet, it's estimated that a billion more computers will be sold within the next decade. But what made all this possible? The computer is a compilation of parts, all of which are the result of individual inventions. From the earliest days of humankind, we have been looking for a more systematic way to count and calculate. Thus, the evolution of counting machines has led to the development of the computer we know today.

The Pascalene Calculator and the Jacquard Loom

The **Pascalene** was the first accurate mechanical calculator. This machine, created by the French mathematician **Blaise Pascal** in 1642, used revolutions of gears to count by tens, similar to odometers in cars. The Pascalene could be used to add, subtract, multiply, and divide. The basic design of the Pascalene was so sound that it lived on in mechanical calculators for more than 300 years.

Nearly 200 years later, **Joseph Jacquard** revolutionized the fabric industry by creating a machine that automated the weaving of complex patterns. Although not a counting or calculating machine, the **Jacquard Loom** (shown in Figure 16) was significant because it relied on stiff cards with punched holes to automate the process. Much later this process would be adopted as a means to record and read data by using punch cards in computers.

Babbage's Engines

Decades later, in 1834, **Charles Babbage** designed the first automatic calculator, called the **Analytical Engine** (see Figure 17). The machine was actually based on another

FIGURE 16

The Jacquard Loom used holes punched in stiff cards to make complex designs. This technique would later be used in the form of punch cards to control the input and output of data in computers.

machine called the **Difference Engine**, which was a huge steam-powered mechanical calculator Babbage designed to print astronomical tables. Babbage stopped working on the Difference Engine to build the Analytical Engine. Although it was never developed, Babbage's detailed drawings and descriptions of the machine include components similar to those found in today's computers, including the store (RAM) and the mill (central processing unit), as well as input and output devices. This invention gave Charles Babbage the title of the "father of computing."

Meanwhile, Ada Lovelace, the daughter of poet Lord Byron and a student of mathematics (which was unusual for women of that time), was fascinated with Babbage's Engine. She translated an Italian paper on Babbage's machine, and at the request of Babbage added her own extensive notes. Her efforts are thought of as the best description of Babbage's Engines.

The Hollerith Tabulating Machine

In 1890, **Herman Hollerith**, while working for the U.S. Census Bureau, was the first to take Jacquard's punch card concept and apply it to computing. Hollerith developed a machine called the **Hollerith Tabulating Machine** that used punch cards to tabulate census data. Up until that time, census data had been tabulated in a long, laborious process. Hollerith's tabulating machine automatically read data that had been punched onto small punch cards, speeding up the tabulation process. Hollerith's machine became so successful that he left the Census Bureau in 1896 to start the Tabulating Machine Company. His company later changed its name to International Business Machines, or IBM.

The Z1 and Atanasoff-Berry Computer

German inventor **Konrad Zuse** is credited with a number of computing inventions. His first, in 1936, was a mechanical calculator called the **Z1**. The Z1 is thought to be the first computer to include features that are integral to today's systems, including a control unit and separate memory functions, noted as important breakthroughs for future computer design.

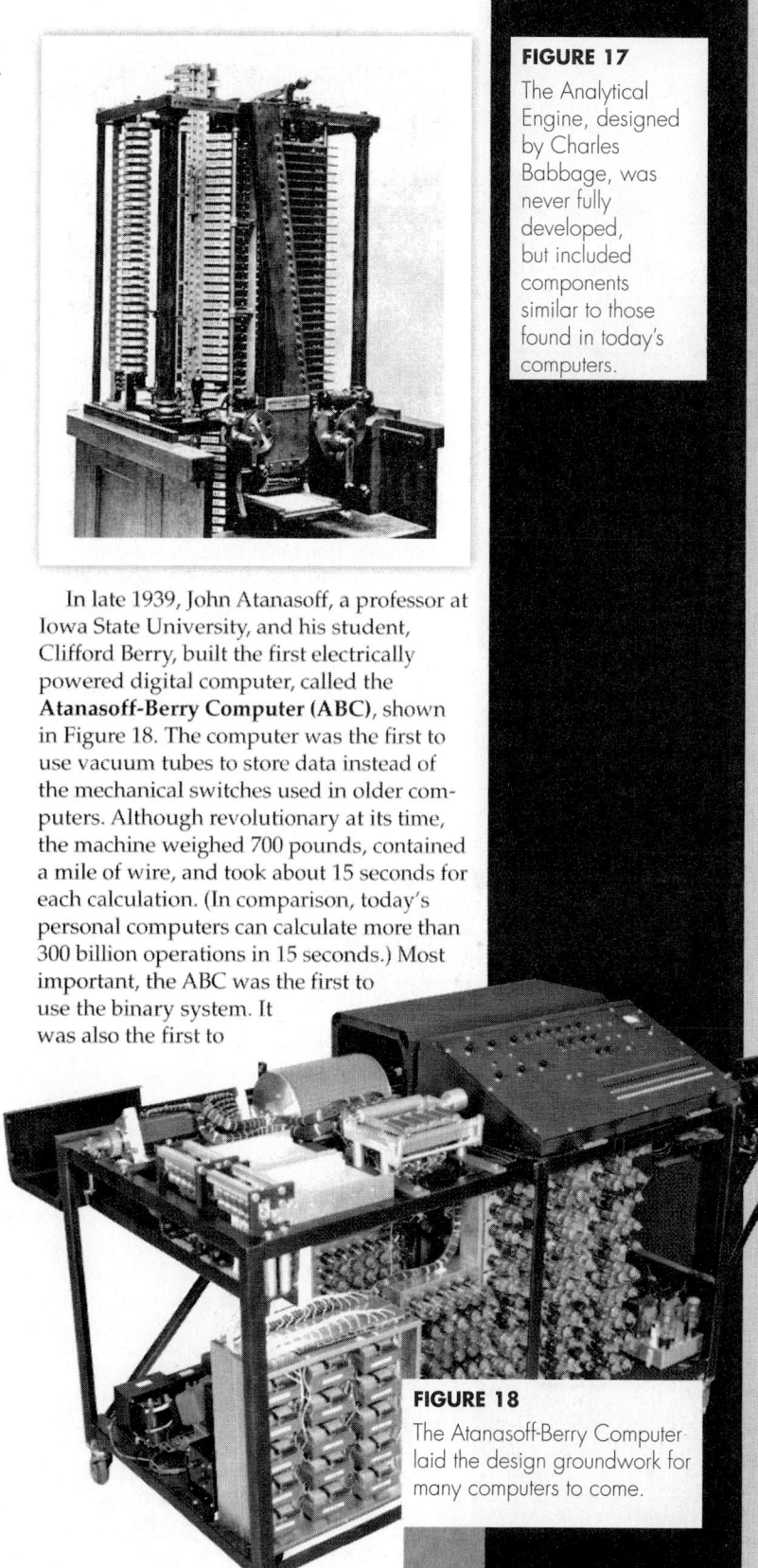

FIGURE 17
The Analytical Engine, designed by Charles Babbage, was never fully developed, but included components similar to those found in today's computers.

In late 1939, John Atanasoff, a professor at Iowa State University, and his student, Clifford Berry, built the first electrically powered digital computer, called the **Atanasoff-Berry Computer (ABC)**, shown in Figure 18. The computer was the first to use vacuum tubes to store data instead of the mechanical switches used in older computers. Although revolutionary at its time, the machine weighed 700 pounds, contained a mile of wire, and took about 15 seconds for each calculation. (In comparison, today's personal computers can calculate more than 300 billion operations in 15 seconds.) Most important, the ABC was the first to use the binary system. It was also the first to

FIGURE 18
The Atanasoff-Berry Computer laid the design groundwork for many computers to come.

have memory that repowered itself upon booting. The design of the ABC would end up being central to that of future computers.

The Harvard Mark I

From the late 1930s to the early 1950s, **Howard Aiken** and **Grace Hopper** designed the Mark series of computers at Harvard University. The U.S. Navy used these computers for ballistic and gunnery calculations. Aiken, an electrical engineer and physicist, designed the computer, while Hopper did the programming. The **Harvard Mark I**, finished in 1944, could perform all four arithmetic operations (addition, subtraction, multiplication, and division).

However, many believe Hopper's greatest contribution to computing was the invention of the **compiler**, a program that translates English language instructions into computer language. The team was also responsible for a common computer-related expression. Hopper was the first to "debug" a computer when she removed a moth that had flown into the Harvard Mark I. The moth caused the computer to break down. After that, problems that caused the computer to not run were called "bugs."

The Turing Machine

Meanwhile, in 1936, the British mathematician **Alan Turing** created an abstract computer model that could perform logical operations. The **Turing Machine** was not a real machine but rather a hypothetical model that mathematically defined a mechanical procedure (or algorithm). Additionally, Turing's concept described a process by which the machine could read, write, or erase symbols written on squares of an infinite paper tape. This concept of an infinite tape that could be read, written to, and erased was the precursor to today's RAM.

The ENIAC

The **Electronic Numerical Integrator and Computer (ENIAC)**, shown in Figure 20, was another U.S. government-sponsored machine developed to calculate the settings used for weapons. Created by **John W. Mauchly** and **J. Presper Eckert** at the University of Pennsylvania, it was placed in operation in June 1944. Although the ENIAC is generally thought of as the first successful high-speed electronic digital computer, it was big and clumsy. The ENIAC used nearly 18,000 vacuum tubes and filled approximately 1,800 square feet of floor space. Although inconvenient, the ENIAC served its purpose and remained in use until 1955.

FIGURE 19

Grace Hopper coined the term *computer bug*, referring to a moth that had flown into the Harvard Mark I, causing it to break down.

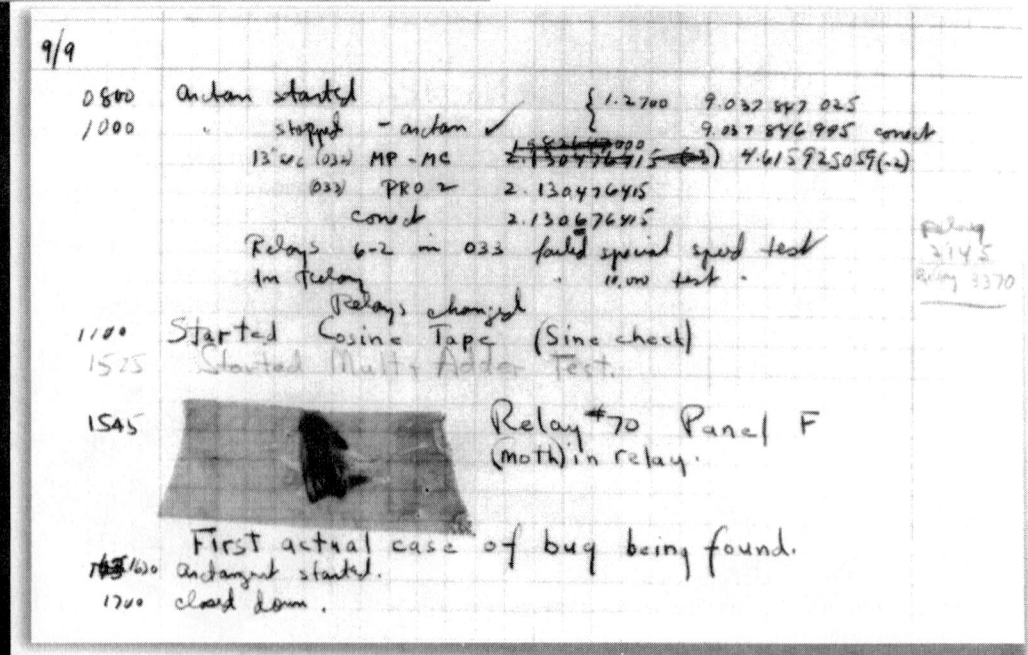

The UNIVAC

The **Universal Automatic Computer**, or **UNIVAC**, was the first commercially successful electronic digital computer. Completed in June 1951 and owned by the company Remington Rand, the UNIVAC operated on magnetic tape (as opposed to its competitors, which ran on punch cards). The UNIVAC gained notoriety when, in a 1951 publicity stunt, it was used to predict the outcome of the Stevenson-Eisenhower presidential race. By analyzing only 5 percent of the popular vote, the UNIVAC correctly identified Dwight D. Eisenhower as the victor. After that, the UNIVAC soon became a household name. The UNIVAC and computers like it were considered **first-generation computers** and were the last to use vacuum tubes to store data.

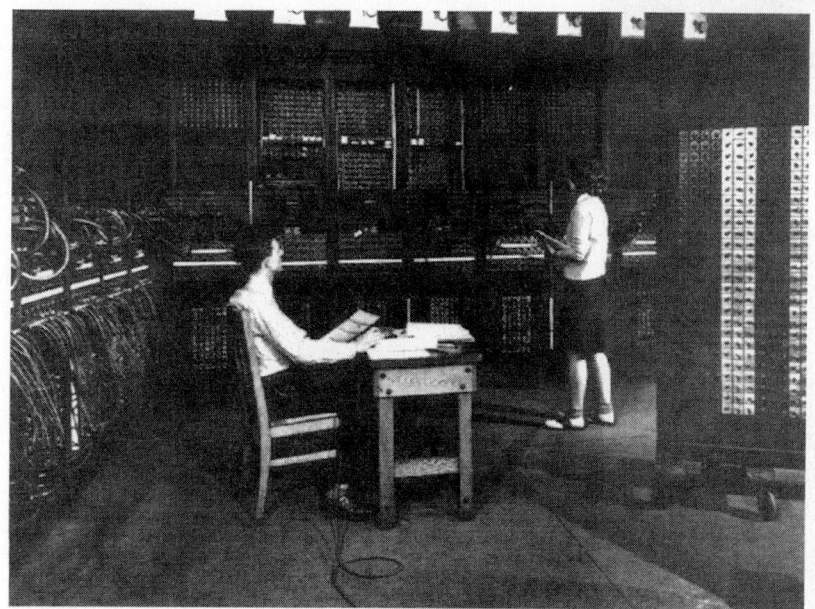

FIGURE 20

The ENIAC took up an entire room and required several people to manipulate it.

Transistors and Beyond

Only a year after the ENIAC was completed, scientists at the Bell Telephone Laboratories in New Jersey invented the **transistor** as a means to store data. The transistor replaced the bulky vacuum tubes of earlier computers and was smaller and more powerful. It was used in almost everything, from radios to phones. Computers that used transistors were referred to as **second-generation computers**. Still, transistors were limited as to how small they could be made.

A few years later, in 1958, **Jack Kilby**, while working at Texas Instruments, invented the world's first **integrated circuit**, a small chip capable of containing thousands of transistors. This consolidation in design enabled computers to become smaller and lighter. The computers in this early integrated circuit generation were considered **third-generation computers**.

Other innovations in the computer industry further refined the computer's speed, accuracy, and efficiency. However, none were as significant as the 1971 introduction by the Intel Corporation of the **microprocessor chip**, a small chip containing millions of transistors. The microprocessor functions as the central processing unit (CPU), or brains, of the computer. Computers that used a microprocessor chip were called **fourth-generation computers**. Over time, Intel and Motorola became the leading manufacturers of microprocessors. Today, the Intel Itanium 2 chip, shown in Figure 21, is one of Intel's most powerful processors.

As you can see, personal computers have come a long way since the Altair and have a number of inventions and people to thank for their amazing popularity. What will the future bring? If current trends continue, computers will be smaller, lighter, and more powerful. The advancement of wireless technology will also certainly play a big role in the development of the personal computer.

FIGURE 21

The Intel Itanium 2 is one of Intel's most powerful processors.